WORDSWORTH CLASSICS
OF WORLD LITERATURE

General Editor: Tom Griffith

JEWISH ANTIQUITIES

Jewish Antiquities

❖

FLAVIUS JOSEPHUS

Translated by William Whiston,
with an Introduction
by Brian McGing

WORDSWORTH CLASSICS
OF WORLD LITERATURE

In loving memory of
MICHAEL TRAYLER
the founder of Wordsworth Editions

For customers interested in other titles from
Wordsworth Editions visit our website at
www.wordsworth-editions.com

For our latest list and a full mail-order service contact
Bibliophile Books, 5 Thomas Road, London E14 7BN

Tel: +44 0207 515 9222   Fax: +44 0207 538 4115
e-mail: orders@bibliophilebooks.com

This edition published 2006 by Wordsworth Editions Limited
8B East Street, Ware, Hertfordshire SG12 9HJ

ISBN 978-1-84022-132-9

This edition © Wordsworth Editions Limited 2006
Introduction © Brian McGing 2006

Wordsworth® is a registered trademark of
Wordsworth Editions Limited

All rights reserved. This publication may not be reproduced, stored
in a retrieval system or transmitted in any form or by
any means, electronic, mechanical, photocopying, recording
or otherwise, without the prior permission of the publishers.

3

Typeset in Great Britain by Antony Gray
Printed by Clays Ltd, St Ives plc

CONTENTS

INTRODUCTION

1 Josephus' life

Joseph son of Matthias, better known to us as Flavius Josephus, was, and remains to this day, one of the most famous and important recorders of their history that the Jewish people has ever produced. The fame of his voluminous writings has not always been accompanied by an equal measure of favour, as his life fell into two distinct phases, in the second of which many Jews felt, and perhaps still feel, he betrayed his people, his country and his God. Judgments of him may differ, but noone can deny the variety, drama and excitement of his life and of the times in which he lived.

Josephus was born in Jerusalem in AD 37 during Caligula's first year as emperor of Rome. By this stage there had been a Roman presence in the Near East for a hundred years: in 63 BC the great general Pompey had made Judaea tributary to Rome as part of his reorganisation of the eastern empire. This first visitation by a leading Roman proved an unhappy start to the relationship between Rome and the Jews. Pompey had found the two Maccabean princes, Aristoboulos and Hyrcanus, feuding for control of the Jewish state, and ended up besieging Aristoboulos' supporters in the Temple in Jerusalem: he stormed the Temple, killing thousands, and then committed the grave offence of entering the 'Holy of Holies', an act forbidden to all but the High Priest. Although subsequently Julius Caesar was a great friend of the Jews, the relationship with Rome was never likely to be friendly: the Roman empire was a more intrusive force than the Jews had recently experienced; indeed for the previous half century or more Judaea had been in effect an independent state. Since the great days of the Jewish kingdom under David and Solomon, the Jews had been subjected to various imperial powers – Assyrians, Babylonians, Persians, Ptolemies and most recently the Seleucids (like the Ptolemies, one of the lines of successor kings to Alexander the Great). Neither the Persians nor the Ptolemies or Seleucids imposed a very close system of imperial rule: the Jews were mostly allowed to run their own affairs (the 'abomination of desolation', the religious persecution carried out by Antiochus IV in the 160s BC, was an uncharacteristic and short-lived exception). In the course of the 2nd century BC the Seleucids began to slip into terminal decline, and by the end of the century the Maccabean leaders, capitalising on Seleucid weakness and now proclaiming themselves kings, had more or less restored Jewish independence.

No sooner had they achieved this than Rome arrived on the doorstep. Pompey's intervention and subsequent Roman interference (in 53 BC, for instance, Crassus brazenly robbed the Temple Treasury on his way to defeat by the Parthians), must have been a bitter pill for the Jews to swallow. To a certain extent the Roman profile in Judaea was lowered when Herod the Great became king in 37 BC. It would be unfair to call him a puppet king, as he was a strong, capable and in many ways remarkable monarch, but he ruled only with the consent and backing of Rome. On Herod's death in 4 BC the emperor Augustus persevered with the policy of backing a Jewish king, but Herod's son Archelaus proved unequal to the task, and in AD 6 Rome declared Judaea a province (or more probably attached it to the existing province of Syria). There were immediate disturbances, brutally suppressed. Things appear to have settled down (or at least we do not hear of any further problems) until in AD 26 Pontius Pilate became prefect (i.e. Rome's representative on the spot). Pilate remained in office for some ten years, during which time he antagonised his subjects on a number of occasions; although probably not, it should be noted, when he ordered the execution of a Jewish man named Jesus: this was scarcely controversial at the time and barely, if at all, makes it into Josephus' account (AJ 18.63–4, the so-called Testimonium Flavianum, which may be in part, or in whole, a later Christian interpolation).

The posting in Judaea was not a plum job, and, like Pilate, most of the succeeding prefects, later called procurators, were relatively low-ranking officials of no great distinction or ability: the Roman administration was characterised by a sort of careless insensitivity and ready brutality that sorely tested the patience of, what seemed to the Romans, their distinctly cantankerous and uncooperative Jewish subjects. This, then, was the political atmosphere into which Josephus was born. Within a short time things got worse: Caligula decided to set up a statue of himself in the Temple in Jerusalem – another 'abomination', of course, in Jewish eyes. The Jews opposed the plan with fury, and as Petronius, the able and perceptive governor of Syria to whom the task had been entrusted, soon realised, the Jews would rise up in revolt if the plan was carried out. Petronius courageously dragged his feet until Caligula was conveniently assassinated, and the threat of disaster was averted. But not for long. As Josephus saw the situation, a combination of Jewish extremism and Roman corruption and incompetence combined to send Judaea into a spiral of ever-worsening crises, leading to the disintegration of ordered government: eventually in AD 66 the province erupted in revolt against Rome. This was almost the mid-point of Josephus' life, and it was certainly its great deciding moment.

His family was a prominent one, with priestly ancestors stretching far back in time, and with a connection to the famous Maccabean rulers of Judaea. Such a priestly and royal background automatically placed him in elite Jewish circles. He received a traditional, and probably Pharisaic education, at which, he says himself in his autobiography, he excelled: at the age of 14 he was recognised for his learning and was consulted on matters of law by High Priests and other leading Jews (Vita 9). This calls to mind the young Jesus (Luke 2.41–52) and, along with other literary commonplaces and a clear apologetic tone in parts of the work, warns us to treat Josephus' account of his own life with care. When he was sixteen he set out on a sort of spiritual odyssey to learn more about the teachings of the three Jewish sects, Sadducees, Pharisees and Essenes, so that he might choose the best. Having also spent time in the desert eating very little and taking frequent cold showers as the disciple of an ascetic guru named Bannus, Josephus returned to the mainstream of Jewish life and began to conduct himself as a Pharisee.

The next important event in his career occurred at the age of twenty six, when he set out on a diplomatic mission to Rome to rescue some Jewish priests sent there by the procurator Felix (Vita 13–16). On the way he was shipwrecked but rescued (suspiciously like St. Paul and other famous people). At Rome he met a popular Jewish actor named Aliturus, favourite of the emperor Nero, who introduced him to Nero's mistress Poppaea. With the help of Poppaea, who seems to have been a Jewish sympathiser, he secured the release of the priests and returned home, satisfied, no doubt, at a job well done. His life was about to become a great deal more complicated.

Back in Judaea he was appalled to find his countrymen on the brink of revolt against Rome. Such a course of action he regarded as madness: the Jews, he argued, could not begin to match the power of Rome and the only possible outcome was defeat. But he and other moderate Jewish leaders failed to cool the war fever and in the course of AD 66 Judaea slipped from unrest into open war: the Roman garrison at Masada was slaughtered and the fortress occupied, the same in Jerusalem, and the daily sacrifice on behalf of the emperor ceased. Cestius Gallus, the governor of Syria, briefly confronted the rebels in Jerusalem, but unexpectedly and inexplicably withdrew and was heavily defeated as he retired. Judaea for the moment was in the hands of the Jews. At a special assembly held in Jerusalem generals were chosen to organise the resistance to Rome, and Josephus found himself placed in command of Galilee and the city of Gamala. This may seem surprising in view of his hostility to the revolt, but he had not deserted the ship like other pro-Roman aristocrats, and we might surmise that he shared the view he attributes to the High Priest Ananus (BJ 4.320), that although the cause was hopeless, once the war had started they must do their best.

Command in Galilee was not simply a matter of organising its defence against Rome. Comfortable notions of a unified national resistance to the foreign oppressors would be sadly misplaced: the years of the 'Great Revolt' are characterised as much by the ferocity of the internal struggles among the Jews themselves as by the military challenge to Rome. In Galilee Josephus had to deal with a complicated tangle of conflicting interests, rivalries and competitors. It is no small tribute to his abilities that he does seem to have established control of the area. But that was the extent of his success: as he had foreseen, he was unable to withstand the Romans. The man Nero entrusted with the job of crushing the Jewish revolt was the future emperor Vespasian. In the spring of AD 67 Vespasian began, without much difficulty, to subdue Galilee. The first major check to his advance came at the town of Jotapata to which he laid siege. Josephus organised its defence and held out for June and much of July, but eventually the town was taken. In the confusion of its capture Josephus escaped with forty others to a cave. His behaviour there, which he decribes himself with disarming honesty (BJ 3.340–391), was far from heroic. The Romans discovered the fugitives after two days and tried to persuade Josephus to surrender. At first he refused, but then pondering on his special position as a prophet of God, he decided he was too valuable to die and resolved to surrender. This was easier to decide than to achieve as his fellow escapees now vowed to kill themselves and offered Josephus the choice of dying honourably by his own hand or being killed by them as a traitor. Keeping his wits about him, he suggested they all draw lots to kill each other, the last one to kill himself. He somehow engineered it that he was one of the last two left alive, and he persuaded the other to surrender with him.

This moment marked the beginning of a new, Roman, phase in Josephus' life. On being granted the opportunity to speak directly with Vespasian, he prophesied that both Vespasian and his son Titus would become emperor. This may have been an inspired hunch, or, more probably, represents a pre-dating of the prediction for Josephus' own purposes or even for Vespasian's. At any rate, of course, in AD 69 it came true: after the suicide of Nero in 68 and the short-lived reigns of Galba, Otho and Vitellius (the 'year of the four emperors'), Vespasian's troops proclaimed him emperor. Up till that time Josephus had remained a prisoner of war. When it had become known that he had not died at Jotapata, but had given himself up and was being well treated by the Romans, the Jewish rebels denounced him as a coward and deserter, thus beginning a long tradition of Jewish hostility towards Josephus. Apart from this and marriage (his second) to a Jewish prisoner, ordered by Vespasian, Josephus has nothing to say about his period in captivity. Vespasian, on his proclamation as emperor, remembered Josephus' prophecy and immediately freed him; and Josephus became a trusted member of the imperial retinue. He went with Vespasian and Titus to Alexandria, where he married for a third time, and then returned with Titus to Judaea, to act as a go-between with the Jewish rebels. At the siege of Jerusalem in AD 70 Josephus tried hard on a number of occasions to persuade them to surrender, thus cementing his reputation as a traitor. When the city fell, his stature in the Roman camp enabled him to win freedom for over two hundred Jewish captives, but although Titus, and later Vespasian, gave him grants of land in Judaea, his loyalty was irretrievably compromised in the eyes of his countrymen, and he left with Titus for Rome, never, as far as we know, to return to his homeland.

After the adventures of his life to this point Josephus' remaining years were relatively uneventful – although for a devout Jew born and bred in Jerusalem, rebel leader in a revolt against Rome, surely highly unusual. Vespasian gave him Roman citizenship, a salary and a residence and he continued to enjoy the imperial patronage of the Flavian family in the principates of Titus (AD 79–81) and Domitian (AD 81–96). He married for a fourth time and settled down to a comfortable and productive literary career. The only shadow cast on these sunny last decades came from the constant criticism and sniping he received from the hands of some of his fellow Jews. Although he reports this without rancour (Vita 425, 428–9) and never seems to have regretted the political views he held and decisions he made, he felt the barbs and felt the need to explain himself: although the *Life* may not only be apologetic, it, and indeed all his other works, contain elements of self-justification. The *Jewish Antiqities* was published in AD 93–4 and the *Against Apion* some time after that. This is the last secure date we have for Josephus. At this stage he was not yet sixty years old, so it is theoretically possible that he lived on into the reigns of Nerva (AD 96–8) and Trajan (AD 98–117). On the other hand, at the end of the *Antiquities* (AJ 20.267–8) he does announce further publication plans – another work of history summarising the war with Rome and investigating what happened to the Jews in the subsequent decades; and three books about Jewish theology and law – but we have no record that he ever wrote them, and it seems likely that as the 1st century waned, so too his extraordinary life came to an end.

2   The works and importance of Josephus

Josephus' life and career affected everything he wrote. It is difficult to imagine how it could be otherwise. Central to all his works is a great passion for Judaism, to defend, praise, promote and explain it: however much some of his fellow Jews despised him, he remained a determined, eloquent and powerful spokesman for Judaism. Complicating this simple message, of course, was his regard for the oppressors of his own people, the Romans. At one level this was a matter of pragmatism: he understood the power of Rome and recognised that it could not be resisted. Any Jews who failed to appreciate this reality were dangerous and could only damage Jewish national interests: and indeed precisely this failure was, in his opinion, one of the main ingredients in the mixture that resulted in revolt. At another level Josephus clearly admired the Romans and their institutions, to such an extent that he accepted generous imperial patronage and lived the second half of his life in Rome. Joseph son of Matthias became Flavius Josephus.

This transformation and Josephus' own involvement in the affairs he relates have given grounds down the ages for many to question his veracity and reliability. These factors certainly have to be taken into account when assessing his value as a historian, but of his two great works, they relate much more obviously to the *Jewish War* than to the *Jewish Antiquities*: the main controversies about Josephus have nearly always been to do with his life and the parts of his works on which it directly impinged. In spite of these doubts, Josephus was exceptionally well qualified to write history: background, education and practical political experience at the highest level, both in peace and war, marked him out as what the famous 2nd century BC Greek historian Polybius would have regarded as an ideal person to write his nation's history. Although at the beginning and end of the *Antiquities* Josephus claims a degree of unease writing in the Greek language (AJ 1.7; 20.263), it is abundantly clear that he was both well read in the literature of the Greeks and comfortable composing in the Greco-Roman tradition of historiography.

The fact that we have no other substantial account of the Jewish revolt against Rome, and very few parallel sources for much of the material in the later books of the *Antiquities*, makes Josephus a historian of exceptional importance for the period from about 150 BC to AD 74. But it also means that we have very little evidence against which to 'check' what he tells us about this period; that is, to assess his historical reliability. Occasionally archaeology helps: modern excavations at Caesarea, for instance, or Masada, have demonstrated a high degree of accuracy in Josephus' accounts of both sites (Caesarea – AJ 15.331–341; Masada – BJ 7.252–406), although that may just mean he was good at recording such physical details: it does not necessarily tell us anything more general about his reliability. Beyond such occasional assistance, we have to scrutinise Josephus' account for inherent plausibility and consistency, identifying biases and self-interests; we must examine his rhetorical and artistic strategies; and we can extrapolate from his treatment of the Biblical sources he used for the first dozen books of the Antiquities. On the whole, the results of such analysis have tended to identify Josephus as a reasonably careful and accurate historian of good faith, who strove – most of the time – to write the truth, as he claimed.

The Jewish War

Within a decade of moving to Rome Josephus had completed his first major work, the *Jewish War*, an account in seven books of the recent revolt of the Jewish people against Rome. He wrote a version first in Aramaic, which does not survive: what we have is the Greek translation, or more probably, expanded version, which he decided to make for subjects of the Roman empire. Internal references indicate a publication date between AD 75 and 79. Having himself been a leading participant in the revolt, and having just witnessed the tragedy of the Temple's destruction, it is not surprising that he turned to this cataclysmic event for his first historical venture. He says at the start (BJ 1–3) that he is going to tell the truth, to correct the false stories about the war that others have made up, but the work is not just an account of what happened: it is also an explanation. The climax is undoubtedly the narrative of the siege and fall of Jerusalem in books 5 and 6, a tragedy of huge dimensions for the Jewish people, but it is most interesting to observe where Josephus starts in his search for the origins of the crisis: he goes right back to the persecution of the Jews by Antiochus IV in the 160s BC, and spends all of book 1 and a large part of book 2 bringing the story up, in summary fashion, to the outbreak of the revolt. Twenty years later he was to go over the same ground in much more detail in the *Jewish Antiquities*. Once he gets under way, in the latter part of book 2, with the events of the revolt proper, Josephus' account of the war with Rome is extremely detailed. We have no other major source of information on the Jewish revolt, and indeed the *Jewish War* is the most sustained analysis we have of the causes, nature and structure of insurrection anywhere within the Roman empire. For these reasons it is a work of unusual importance.

The Life

Although treated as a separate work, it is clear from the final chapters of the *Jewish Antiquities* (20.266) that what has come down to us as the *Life* was in fact a sort of autobiographical appendix attached to the end of the *Antiquities*. It is by no means a full account of Josephus' life: out of 430 chapters he devotes 383 to the period of little over half a year when he was commander of the Jewish forces in Galilee in AD 66–7. This is preceded by a short account of his earlier years and followed by an equally short account of his life after his capture at Jotapata. His brief military career has clearly been under attack, particularly from his chief opponent, Justus of Tiberias, and it is difficult to avoid the feeling that he is primarily interested in defending his reputation. It may be the case that by parading his priestly background and demonstrating his leading role in Jewish affairs at the beginning of the revolt he is also establishing his qualifications to write the history of the Jewish people, but most scholars have seen the *Life* as a work of polemic.

Against Apion

The manuscript title of this, Josephus' last publication, is unlikely to be its original title, as it is only in the second of the two books that there is any response to the attacks made on Judaism by Apion, an Alexandrian Greek and older contemporary of Josephus. The impetus for writing the *Apion* seems to be the hostile response that Josephus' *Jewish Antiquities* had received in some quarters. Critics' launched their attacks in two main directions: first, there was a refusal to believe that the Jews were an ancient people, on the grounds that Greek authors wrote nothing about them; and second, malicious calumnies of various sorts were laid against the Jews. In a spirited counter-attack, organised according to the best principles of Greco-Roman rhetorical theory (and, incidentally, preserving extensive and valuable quotations from authors whose work is otherwise completely unknown to us), Josephus skilfully rebuts the accusations, and in the latter part of book 2 takes the offensive with a moving description of the law and constitution of the Jews. Was Josephus merely trying to defend his people and their culture from anti-semitic assault, or did he also have an aggressive missionary purpose? It is difficult to say, but one way or another, the *Against Apion* represents a fascinating defence of the antiquity, wisdom and character of Judaism in the ancient world.

The Jewish Antiquities

The scope and size of Josephus' largest work, published in AD 93–4, are by modern standards breathtakingly ambitious: nothing less than a history of the Jews from the Creation to the outbreak of the Great Revolt in AD 66. It comprises twenty books, and if not quite the size of Livy's massive one hundred and forty two volume history of Rome from its beginnings, is still a major undertaking conceived on the grandest of scales. No parallel study by another single author survives from antiquity: after the Old Testament it is quite simply the most important account of Jewish ancient history we have.

Although structurally it seems to divide into two neat halves – books 1–10 the history of the first Temple period, books 11–20 the history of the second Temple period – a more significant division might be where Josephus finally runs out of Biblical source material in about 140 BC (at 13.217). Up to this point we know the history of the Jews; or at least, we have the narrative books of the Old Testament from which we can, with a certain amount of difficulty, extract a story. Josephus extracts that story for us in a remarkable 'rendering' of the Bible into a coherent, Greco-Roman historical narrative. It is not a series of Biblical 'highlights' loosely stitched together, but rather an entire adaptation of the Biblical story. It is all composed in his own Greek style and with his own hellenised slant on things. Particular attention, for instance, has been paid to his treatment of the famous figures of the Old Testament, such as Abraham, Moses, David, Solomon: they tend to be presented in a Greek mould as the sort of wise men, lawgivers, soldiers, philosophers that a hellenised audience would recognise and appreciate.

This part of the *Antiquities* represents no mean intellectual achievement, but the excitement of Josephus' history increases greatly when he moves from the Maccabean resistance to Seleucid persecution into the second half of the 2nd century BC and begins to tell us a story we did not already know. The events of the persecution itself are familiar to us from the first two books of Maccabees, but it is at about this point that Josephus begins to develop one of the main analytical themes that informs his account of the two hundred years leading up to the revolt against Rome: how internal dissension among the Jews themselves contributed to their own troubles. Feuding among the Jewish elite in the 170s BC, and radically different approaches to the question of how hellenised the Jews should become, were at least partly responsible for bringing the Seleucid persecution down on their own heads. Conversely, for most of the rest of the 2nd century the unification of the Jewish people under Maccabean leadership, combined with internal Seleucid problems, brought the Jews success and political independence.

Towards the end of the century another source of dispute arose: social, political and religious disagreements began to express themselves in a split between Sadducees and Pharisees. This, combined with family feuding, led to a further outbreak of internecine strife on the death of Queen Alexandra in 67 BC, and again caused disastrous foreign intervention, in the person of Pompey. The continuing struggle between Hyrcanus and Aristoboulos fed at least some of the disorder of the middle decades of the 1st century BC. This unsettled period was replaced by the relative stability of Herod the Great's reign (37–4 BC), but in many ways the stability was more apparent than real, and served to mask the intensification of internal Jewish tensions that Herod's rule brought about. This became obvious on Herod's death when there was upheaval all over Judaea, making the development from indirect to direct Roman rule in AD 6 almost inevitable. Josephus is not afraid to castigate corrupt and incapable Roman governors – and his account of the disintegration of law and order in Judaea under what he presents as an increasingly malevolent administration in the years AD 44–66 (AJ 20) is a damning indictment of Rome's imperial rule – but he also has bitter words for the multitude of competing Jewish political and religious agitators that arises – bandits, false prophets, magicians, pretenders, terrorists – who are equally to blame for what happened. It is the misguided reaction of Jewish extremists to worsening Roman government that drags an otherwise right-thinking and reluctant Jewish majority into revolt. This is Josephus' message, or one of his messages, to his Roman audience.

It is worth emphasising just how big the gaps in our knowledge would be without the *Antiquities* (or the early overlapping sections of the *Jewish War*). We would have very little idea of Rome's treatment of, and impact on, Judaea and the Jews in the 1st centuries BC and AD; and equally little notion of the history of the later members of the Maccabean dynasty. There would be serious gaps in our knowledge of the careers of several leading Romans: Pompey, Gabinius, Crassus, Mark Antony, Julius Caesar, Augustus, Agrippa, Varus, Petronius and more. We would know virtually nothing about Herod's father Antipater and little more about Herod himself. Josephus' account of Herod's reign covers four books (14–17) and is easily the most detailed treatment of a Roman 'client' king we have. Although there are times when the minutiae of Herod's family affairs become tiresome, it is one of the great highlights of the *Antiquities*. Herod's children and grandhildren would be almost unknown to us, in particular Julius Agrippa, Herod's grandson, who ruled Judaea from AD 41–44 (books 18–19). Apart from his name we would know nothing about Judas the Galilean and the movement he started (Josephus calls it the Fourth Philosophy – AJ 18. 23–5), which inspired armed resistance to Rome. We would scarcely know the names of the Roman prefects and procurators of Judaea. Pontius Pilate would be familiar from the Gospels (and from one incident recorded by the Jewish philosopher Philo of Alexandria), but Josephus provides crucial further evidence on his actions and character (AJ 18.55–89). The whole story of Judaea's slide into revolt would be very largely a mystery to us.

But Josephus' importance is not just that he tells us things we would not otherwise know. He also provides an indispensable background to the transformation of Judaism in directions that helped to shape the modern world – into the dynamic force of Rabbinic Judaism on the one hand, and into the equally dynamic offshoot that became Christianity on the other. A less successful, but still very important strand of Judaism at this time was the sect whose texts are preserved in the Dead Sea Scrolls. With the help of Josephus (and other sources) we can identify this group as members of the Essene movement. They proved unable to survive the Roman conquest, but were still a vital part of the world out of which Christianity and Rabbinic Judaism developed. It is Josephus, particularly in his *Jewish Antiquities*, who supplies a crucial framework for understanding this world.

3   Whiston's translation of Josephus

William Whiston, astronomer, philosopher, mathematician, theologian, believed, among other unwise notions, that a new millennium would begin in 1766, when there would be no more gaming tables in Tunbridge Wells or infidels in Christendom. Not surprisingly the Dictionary of National Biography (vol xxi, p.13) describes him as belonging 'to a familiar type, as a man of acute but ill-balanced intellect'. He was born in 1667, the son of a country rector. In 1686 he began undergraduate studies at Cambridge, where he attended some of Isaac Newton's lectures. After qualifying (B.A. 1690, M.A. 1693) he was ordained, but was far more interested in matters intellectual than ecclesiastical. In 1701 he was appointed deputy to Newton, and in 1703 succeeded Newton as Lucasian Professor of Mathematics at Cambridge. Unsound theological views, however, saw him removed from his chair and banished from the university in 1710. Newton had liked him, but had fallen out with him over differing interpretations of Biblical chronology, and did nothing to help him. Indeed, in 1720 when Whiston was proposed for membership of the Royal Society, Newton prevented his election. Although he wrote at length on a large variety of subjects, and engaged in many ventures (including characteristically unsuccessful attempts to establish longitude), Whiston's only enterprise of lasting fame and success was his translation of the works of Josephus in 1737. He died in 1752. Whiston's Josephus remained the canonical English version for two hundred years, until forced from its position of primacy by the appearance in the 20th century of the Loeb Classical Library translation in ten volumes (Harvard University Press 1926–1981). Contributing to Whiston's demise was the abandoning by scholars of the older chapter divisions he used in favour of a new reference system devised by the German scholar Niese, which made it very difficult to track down particular passages in Whiston. The present volume adds the new, and now standard, divisions, and thus, it is hoped, will restore the usefulness of Whiston's translation of Josephus' major historical work.

BRIAN MCGING
Trinity College, Dublin

FURTHER READING

Bilde, P., *Flavius Josephus between Jerusalem and Rome*, Sheffield 1988

Cohen, S .J. D., *Josephus in Galilee and Rome: His* Vita *and Development as a Historian*, Leiden 1979

Feldman, L., *Jew and Gentile in the Ancient World: Attitudes and Interactions from Alexander to Justinian*, Princeton 1993

Rajak, T., *Josephus: The Historian and his Society*, London 1983

Richardson, P., *Herod: King of the Jews and Friend of the Romans*, Columbia SC, 1996

Schürer, E., *The History of the Jewish People in the Age of Jesus Christ*, revised and edited by G. Vermes. F. Millar *et al.*, 3 vols, Edinburgh 1973–1987

Schwartz, S., *Josephus and Judaean Politics*, Leiden 1990

Shutt, R. J. H., *Studies in Josephus*, London 1961

Williamson, G. A., *The World of Josephus*, Boston 1964

ABBREVIATIONS

Jewish War = BJ
Jewish Antiquities = AJ
Life = Vita
Against Apion = Ap.

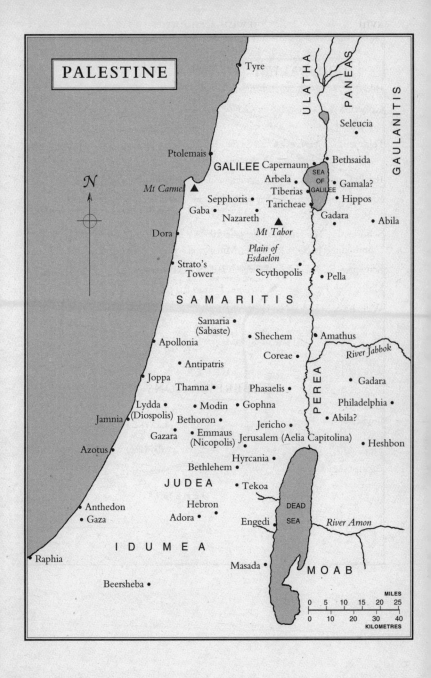

PALESTINE

Tyre

ULATHA

PANEAS

GAULANITIS

Seleucia

Ptolemais

GALILEE   Capernaum   Bethsaida

SEA OF GALILEE

Mt Carmel ▲   Arbela   Gamala?

Sepphoris   Tiberias   Hippos

Gaba   Taricheae

Nazareth   Gadara   Abila

Mt Tabor ▲

Dora

Plain of Esdaelon

Strato's Tower   Scythopolis   Pella

SAMARITIS

Samaria (Sabaste)   Shechem   Amathus

Apollonia   Coreae   *River Jabbok*

Antipatris   PEREA

Joppa   Phasaelis   Gadara

Thamna

Lydda (Diospolis)   Modin   Gophna   Philadelphia

Jamnia   Bethoron   Jericho   Abila?

Gazara   Emmaus (Nicopolis)   Jerusalem (Aelia Capitolina)   Heshbon

Azotus

Hyrcania

Bethlehem

JUDEA   Tekoa

Anthedon   Hebron   DEAD SEA

Gaza   Adora   Engedi   *River Arnon*

Raphia

IDUMEA

Masada   MOAB

Beersheba

MILES
0 5 10 15 20 25
0 10 20 30 40
KILOMETRES

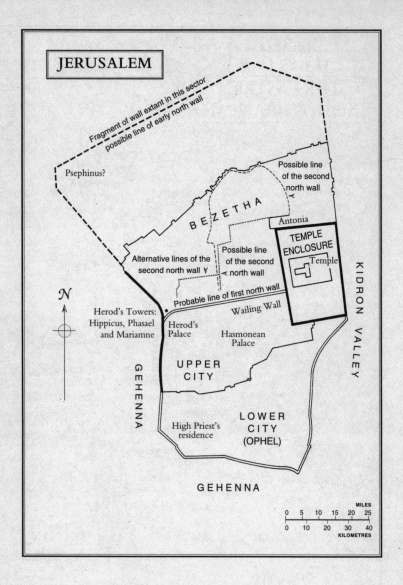

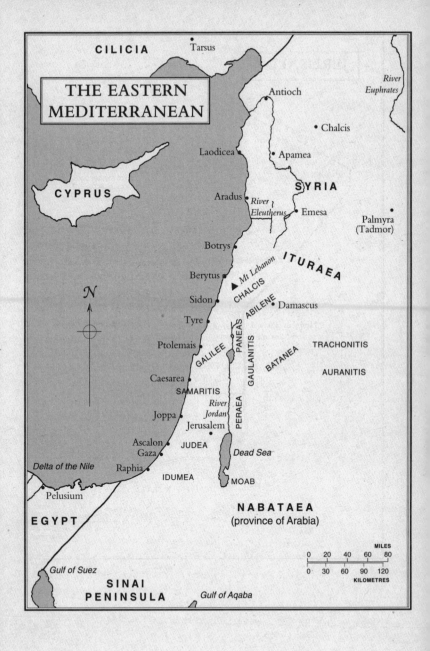

THE EASTERN
MEDITERRANEAN

CILICIA
Tarsus

River
Euphrates

Antioch

Chalcis

Laodicea

Apamea

CYPRUS

SYRIA

Aradus   *River
Eleutherus*   Emesa

Palmyra
(Tadmor)

Botrys

N

Berytus   ▲*Mt Lebanon*   ITURAEA
CHALCIS

Sidon   CHALCIS

Tyre   ABILENE   Damascus

PANEAS

Ptolemais   GALILEE

GAULANITIS   BATANEA   TRACHONITIS

Caesarea   AURANITIS

SAMARITIS

*River
Jordan*

Joppa   PERAEA

Jerusalem

Ascalon   JUDEA
Gaza

Dead Sea

Delta of the Nile   Raphia

IDUMEA   MOAB

Pelusium

NABATAEA
(province of Arabia)

EGYPT

MILES
0   20   40   60   80

0   30   60   90   120
KILOMETRES

Gulf of Suez

SINAI
PENINSULA   *Gulf of Aqaba*

JEWISH ANTIQUITIES

PREFACE

(1) Those who undertake to write histories do not, I perceive, take that trouble on one and the same account, but for many reasons, and those such as are very different one from another; (2) for some of them apply themselves to this part of learning to show their skill in composition, and that they may therein acquire a reputation for speaking finely; others of them there are who write histories, in order to gratify those that happened to be concerned in them, and on that account have spared no pains, but rather go beyond their own abilities in the performance; (3) but others there are who, of necessity and by force, are driven to write history because they are concerned in the facts, and so cannot excuse themselves from committing them to writing, for the advantage of posterity; nay, there are not a few who are induced to draw their historical facts out of darkness into light, and to produce them for the benefit of the public on account of the great importance of the facts themselves with which they have been concerned. (4) Now of these several reasons for writing history, I must profess the two last were my own reasons also; for since I was myself interested in that war which we Jews had with the Romans, and knew myself its particular actions, and what conclusion it had, I was forced to give the history of it, because I saw that others perverted the truth of those actions in their writings.

(5) Now I have undertaken the present work, as thinking it will appear to all the Greeks worthy of their study; for it will contain all our antiquities, and the constitution of our government, as interpreted out of the Hebrew Scriptures; (6) and indeed I did formerly intend, when I wrote of the war, to explain who the Jews originally were – what fortunes they had been subjected to – and by what legislator they had been instructed in piety and the exercise of other virtues, what wars also they had made in remote ages, till they were unwillingly engaged in this last with the Romans; (7) but because this work would take up a great compass, I separated it into a set treatise by itself, with a beginning of its own, and its own conclusion; but in process of time, as usually happens to such as undertake great things, I grew weary, and went on slowly, it being a large subject, and a difficult thing to translate our history into a foreign, and to us unaccustomed, language. (8) However, some persons there were who desired to know our history, and so exhorted me to go on with it; and, above all the rest, Epaphroditus, a man who is a lover of all kind of learning, but is principally delighted with the knowledge of history; and this on

account of his having been himself concerned in great affairs, and many turns
of fortune, and having shown a wonderful vigour of an excellent nature, and
an immovable virtuous resolution in them all. (9) I yielded to this man's
persuasions, who always excites such as have abilities in what is useful and
acceptable, to join their endeavours with his. I was also ashamed myself to
permit any laziness of disposition to have a greater influence upon me than the
delight of taking pains in such studies as were very useful: I thereupon stirred
up myself, and went on with my work more cheerfully. Besides the foregoing
motives, I had others which I greatly reflected on; and these were, that our
forefathers were willing to communicate such things to others; and that some
of the Greeks took considerable pains to know the affairs of our nation.

(10) I found, therefore, that the second of the Ptolemies was a king who was
extraordinarily diligent in what concerned learning and the collection of
books; that he was also peculiarly ambitious to procure a translation of our law,
and of the constitution of our government therein contained, into the Greek
tongue. (11) Now Eleazar, the high priest, one not inferior to any other of that
dignity among us, did not envy the forenamed king the participation of that
advantage, which otherwise he would for certain have denied him, but that he
knew the custom of our nation was, to hinder nothing of what we esteemed
ourselves from being communicated to others. (12) Accordingly, I thought it
became me both to imitate the generosity of our high priest, and to suppose
there might even now be many lovers of learning like the king; for he did not
obtain all our writings at that time; but those who were sent to Alexandria as
interpreters, gave him only the books of the law, (13) while there were a vast
number of other matters in our sacred books. They indeed contain in them the
history of five thousand years; in which time happened many strange accidents,
many chances of war, and great actions of the commanders, and mutations of
the form of our government. (14) Upon the whole, a man that will peruse this
history, may principally learn from it, that all events succeed well, even to an
incredible degree, and the reward of felicity is proposed by God; but then it is
to those that follow his will, and do not venture to break his excellent laws –
and that so far as men any way apostatise from the accurate observation of
them, what was practicable before becomes impracticable; and whatsoever
they set about as a good thing is converted into an incurable calamity; (15) and
now I exhort all those that peruse these books to apply their minds to God, and
to examine the mind of our legislator, whether he hath not understood his
nature in a manner worthy of him; and hath not ever ascribed to him such
operations as become his power, and hath not preserved his writings from
those indecent fables which others have framed, (16) although, by the great
distance of time when he lived, he might have securely forged such lies; for
he lived two thousand years ago, at which vast distance of ages the poets

themselves have not been so hardy as to fix even the generations of their gods, much less the actions of their men, or their own laws. (17) As I proceed, therefore, I shall accurately describe what is contained in our records, in the order of time that belongs to them; for I have already promised so to do throughout this undertaking, and this without adding anything to what is therein contained, or taking away anything therefrom.

(18) But because almost all our constitution depends on the wisdom of Moses, our legislator, I cannot avoid saying somewhat concerning him beforehand, though I shall do it briefly; I mean, because otherwise those that read my book may wonder how it comes to pass that my discourse, which promises an account of laws and historical facts, contains so much of philosophy. (19) The reader is therefore to know, that Moses deemed it exceeding necessary that he who would conduct his own life well, and give laws to others, in the first place should consider the divine nature, and upon the contemplation of God's operations, should thereby imitate the best of all patterns, so far as it is possible for human nature to do, and to endeavour to follow after it, (20) neither could the legislator himself have a right mind without such a contemplation; nor would anything he should write tend to the promotion of virtue in his readers; I mean, unless they be taught first of all that God is the father and Lord of all things, and sees all things, and that thence he bestows a happy life upon those that follow him; but plunges such as do not walk in the paths of virtue into inevitable miseries. (21) Now when Moses was desirous to teach this lesson to his countrymen, he did not begin the establishment of his laws after the same manner that other legislators did; I mean, upon contracts and other rites between one man and another, but by raising their minds upwards to regard God, and his creation of the world; and by persuading them, that we men are the most excellent of the creatures of God upon earth. Now when once he had brought them to submit to religion, he easily persuaded them to submit in all other things; (22) for, as to other legislators, they followed fables, and, by their discourses, transferred the most reproachful of human vices unto the gods, and so afforded wicked men the most plausible excuses for their crimes; (23) but, as for our legislator, when he had once demonstrated that God was possessed of perfect virtue, he supposed that man also ought to strive after the participation of it; and on those who did not so think and so believe he inflicted the severest punishments. (24) I exhort, therefore, my readers to examine this whole undertaking in that view; for thereby it will appear to them that there is nothing therein disagreeable either to the majesty of God, or to his love to mankind; for all things have here a reference to the nature of the universe; while our legislator speaks some things wisely but enigmatically, and others under a decent allegory, but still explains such things as required a direct explication plainly and expressly. (25) However, those that have a mind to

know the reason of everything, may find here a very curious philosophical theory, which I now indeed shall waive the explication of; but if God afford me time for it, I will set about writing it after I have finished the present work. (26) I shall now betake myself to the history before me, after I have first mentioned what Moses says of the creation of the world, which I find described in the sacred books after the manner following.

BOOK ONE

CHAPTER I

(27) In the beginning God created the heaven and the earth; but when the earth did not come into sight, but was covered with thick darkness, and a wind moved upon its surface, God commanded that there should be light; (28) and when that was made, he considered the whole mass, and separated the light and the darkness; and the name he gave to one was *Night*, and the other he called *Day*; and he named the beginning of light, and the time of rest, *the Evening* and *the Morning*; (29) and this was indeed the first day: but Moses said it was one day, – the cause of which I am able to give even now; but because I have promised to give such reasons for all things in a treatise by itself, I shall put off its exposition till that time. (30) After this, on the second day, he placed the heaven over the whole world, and separated it from the other parts; and he determined it should stand by itself. He also placed a crystalline [firmament] round it, and put it together in a manner agreeable to the earth, and fitted it for giving moisture and rain, and for affording the advantage of dews. (31) On the third day he appointed the dry land to appear, with the sea itself round about it; and on the very same day he made the plants and the seeds to spring out of the earth. On the fourth day he adorned the heaven with the sun, the moon, and the other stars; and appointed them their motions and courses, that the vicissitudes of the seasons might be clearly signified. (32) And on the fifth day he produced the living creatures, both those that swim and those that fly; the former in the sea, the latter in the air: he also sorted them as to society and mixture, for procreation, and that their kinds might increase and multiply. On the sixth day he created the four-footed beasts, and made them male and female: on the same day he also formed man. (33) Accordingly Moses says, that in just six days the world and all that is therein was made; and that the seventh day was a rest, and a release from the labour of such operations – whence it is that we celebrate a rest from our labours on that day, and call it the Sabbath; which word denotes *rest* in the Hebrew tongue.

(34) Moreover, Moses, after the seventh day was over, begins to talk philosophically; and concerning the formation of man, says thus: that God took dust from the ground, and formed man, and inserted in him a spirit and a soul. This man was called Adam, which in the Hebrew tongue signifies *one that is red*, because he was formed out of red earth, compounded together; for of that kind is virgin and true earth. (35) God also presented the living creatures,

when he had made them, according to their kinds, both male and female, to Adam, who gave them those names by which they are still called. But when he saw that Adam had no female companion, no society, for there was no such created, and that he wondered at the other animals which were male and female, he laid him asleep, and took away one of his ribs, and out of it formed the woman; (36) whereupon Adam knew her when she was brought to him, and acknowledged that she was made out of himself. Now a woman is called in the Hebrew tongue *Issa*; but the name of this woman was Eve, which signifies *the mother of all living*.

(37) Moses says further, that God planted a paradise in the east, flourishing with all sorts of trees; and that among them was the tree of life, and another of knowledge, whereby was to be known what was good and evil; (38) and that when he brought Adam and his wife into this garden, he commanded them to take care of the plants. Now the garden was watered by one river, which ran round about the whole earth, and was parted into four parts. And Phison, which denotes a multitude, running into India, makes its exit into the sea, and is by the Greeks called Ganges. (39) Euphrates also, as well as Tigris, goes down into the Red Sea. Now the name Euphrates, or Phrath, denotes either a dispersion, or a flower: by Tigris, or Diglath, is signified what is swift, with narrowness; and Geon runs through Egypt, and denotes what arises from the east, which the Greeks call Nile.

(40) God therefore commanded that Adam and his wife should eat of all the rest of the plants, but to abstain from the tree of knowledge; and foretold to them that, if they touched it, it would prove their destruction. (41) But while all the living creatures had one language, at that time the serpent, which then lived together with Adam and his wife, showed an envious disposition at his supposal of their living happily, and in obedience to the commands of God; (42) and imagining, that when they disobeyed them, they would fall into calamities, he persuaded the woman, out of a malicious intention, to taste of the tree of knowledge, telling them, that in that tree was the knowledge of good and evil; which knowledge when they should obtain, they would lead a happy life, nay, a life not inferior to that of a god: (43) by which means he overcame the woman, and persuaded her to despise the command of God. Now when she had tasted of that tree, and was pleased with its fruit, she persuaded Adam to make use of it also. (44) Upon this they perceived that they were become naked to one another; and being ashamed thus to appear abroad, they invented somewhat to cover them; for the tree sharpened their under-standing; and they covered themselves with fig leaves; and tying these before them, out of modesty, they thought they were happier than they were before, as they had discovered what they were in want of. (45) But when God came into the garden, Adam, who was wont before to come and converse with him,

being conscious of his wicked behaviour, went out of the way. This behaviour surprised God; and he asked what was the cause of this his procedure, and why he, that before delighted in that conversation, did now fly from it and avoid it. (46) When he made no reply, as conscious to himself that he had transgressed the command of God, God said, 'I had before determined about you both, how you might lead a happy life, without any affliction, and care, and vexation of soul; and that all things which might contribute to your enjoyment and pleasure should grow up by my providence, of their own accord, without your own labour and painstaking; which state of labour and painstaking would soon bring on old age; and death would not be at any remote distance; (47) but now thou hast abused this my good will, and hast disobeyed my commands; for thy silence is not the sign of thy virtue, but of thy evil conscience.' (48) However, Adam excused his sin, and entreated God not to be angry at him, and laid the blame of what was done upon his wife; and said that he was deceived by her, and thence became an offender; while she again accused the serpent. (49) But God allotted him punishment, because he weakly submitted to the counsel of his wife; and said, the ground should not henceforth yield its fruits of its own accord, but that when it should be harassed by their labour, it should bring forth some of its fruits, and refuse to bring forth others. He also made Eve liable to the inconveniency of breeding, and the sharp pains of bringing forth children, and this because she persuaded Adam with the same arguments wherewith the serpent had persuaded her, and had thereby brought him into a calamitous condition. (50) He also deprived the serpent of speech, out of indignation at his malicious disposition towards Adam. Besides this, he inserted poison under his tongue, and made him an enemy to man; and suggested to them that they should direct their strokes against his head, that being the place wherein lay his mischievous designs towards men, and it being easiest to take vengeance on him that way: and when he had deprived him of the use of his feet, he made him go rolling all along, and dragging himself upon the ground. (51) And when God had appointed these penalties for them, he removed Adam and Eve out of the garden into another place.

CHAPTER 2

(52) Adam and Eve had two sons; the elder of them was named Cain; which name, when it is interpreted, signifies *a possession*. The younger was Abel, which signifies *sorrow*. They had also daughters. (53) Now, the two brethren were pleased with different courses of life, for Abel, the younger, was a lover of righteousness, and, believing that God was present at all his actions, he excelled in virtue; and his employment was that of a shepherd. But Cain was not only very wicked in other respects, but was wholly intent upon getting; and he

first contrived to plough the ground. He slew his brother on the occasion following: (54) they had resolved to sacrifice to God. Now Cain brought the fruits of the earth, and of his husbandry; but Abel brought milk, and the first fruits of his flocks; but God was more delighted with the latter oblation, when he was honoured with what grew naturally of its own accord, than he was with what was the invention of a covetous man, and gotten by forcing the ground; (55) whence it was that Cain was very angry that Abel was preferred by God before him; and he slew his brother, and hid his dead body, thinking to escape discovery. But God, knowing what had been done, came to Cain, and asked him what was become of his brother, because he had not seen him of many days, whereas he used to observe them conversing together at other times. (56) But Cain was in doubt with himself, and knew not what answer to give to God. At first he said that he was himself at a loss about his brother's disappearing; but when he was provoked by God, who pressed him vehemently, as resolving to know what the matter was, he replied, he was not his brother's guardian or keeper, nor was he an observer of what he did. (57) But in return, God convicted Cain, as having been the murderer of his brother; and said, 'I wonder at thee, that thou knowest not what is become of a man whom thou thyself hast destroyed.' (58) God therefore did not inflict the punishment [of death] upon him, on account of his offering sacrifice, and thereby making supplication to him not to be extreme in his wrath to him; but he made him accursed, and threatened his posterity in the seventh generation. He also cast him, together with his wife, out of that land. (59) And when he was afraid, that in wandering about he should fall among wild beasts, and by that means perish, God bid him not to entertain such a melancholy suspicion, and to go over all the earth without fear of what mischief he might suffer from wild beasts; and setting a mark upon him that he might be known, he commanded him to depart.

(60) And when Cain had travelled over many countries, he, with his wife, built a city, named Nod, which is a place so called, and there he settled his abode; where also he had children. However, he did not accept of his punishment, in order to amendment, but to increase his wickedness; for he only aimed to procure everything that was for his own bodily pleasure, though it obliged him to be injurious to his neighbours. (61) He augmented his household substance with much wealth, by rapine and violence; he excited his acquaintance to procure pleasures and spoils by robbery, and became a great leader of men into wicked courses. He also introduced a change in that way of simplicity wherein men lived before; and was the author of measures and weights. And whereas they lived innocently and generously while they knew nothing of such arts, he changed the world into cunning craftiness. (62) He first of all set boundaries about lands; he built a city, and fortified it with walls, and

he compelled his family to come together to it; and called that city Enoch, after the name of his eldest son Enoch. (63) Now Jared was the son of Enoch; whose son was Malaliel; whose son was Mathusala; whose son was Lamech, who had seventy-seven children by two wives, Silla and Ada. (64) Of those children by Ada, one was Jabal; he erected tents, and loved the life of a shepherd. But Jubal, who was born of the same mother with him, exercised himself in music, and invented the psaltery and the harp. But Tubal, one of his children by the other wife, exceeded all men in strength, and was very expert and famous in martial performances. He procured what tended to the pleasures of the body by that method, and first of all invented the art of making brass. (65) Lamech was also the father of a daughter, whose name was Naamah; and because he was so skilful in matters of divine revelation, that he knew he was to be punished for Cain's murder of his brother, he made that known to his wives. (66) Nay, even while Adam was alive, it came to pass that the posterity of Cain became exceeding wicked, every one successively dying one after another more wicked than the former. They were intolerable in war, and vehement in robberies; and if anyone were slow to murder people, yet was he bold in his profligate behaviour, in acting unjustly and doing injuries for gain.

(67) Now Adam, who was the first man, and made out of the earth (for our discourse must now be about him) after Abel was slain, and Cain fled away on account of his murder, was solicitous for posterity, and had a vehement desire of children, he being two hundred and thirty years old; after which time he lived other seven hundred, and then died. (68) He had indeed many other children, but Seth in particular. As for the rest, it would be tedious to name them; I will therefore only endeavour to give an account of those that proceeded from Seth. Now this Seth, when he was brought up, and came to those years in which he could discern what was good, became a virtuous man; and as he was himself of an excellent character, so did he leave children behind him who imitated his virtues. (69) All these proved to be of good dispositions. They also inhabited the same country without dissensions, and in a happy condition, without any misfortunes falling upon them till they died. They also were the inventors of that peculiar sort of wisdom which is concerned with the heavenly bodies, and their order. (70) And that their inventions might not be lost before they were sufficiently known, upon Adam's prediction that the world was to be destroyed at one time by the force of fire, and at another time by the violence and quantity of water, they made two pillars; the one of brick, the other of stone: they inscribed their discoveries on them both, (71) that in case the pillar of brick should be destroyed by the flood, the pillar of stone might remain, and exhibit those discoveries to mankind; and also inform them that there was another pillar of brick erected by them. Now this remains in the land of Siriad to this day.

CHAPTER 3

(72) Now this posterity of Seth continued to esteem God as the Lord of the universe, and to have an entire regard to virtue, for seven generations; but in process of time they were perverted, and forsook the practices of their forefathers, and did neither pay those honours to God which were appointed them, nor had they any concern to do justice towards men. But for what degree of zeal they had formerly shown for virtue, they now showed by their actions a double degree of wickedness; whereby they made God to be their enemy, (73) for many angels of God accompanied with women, and begat sons that proved unjust, and despisers of all that was good, on account of the confidence they had in their own strength; for the tradition is, that these men did what resembled the acts of those whom the Grecians call giants. (74) But Noah was very uneasy at what they did; and, being displeased at their conduct, persuaded them to change their dispositions and their acts for the better; but, seeing they did not yield to him, but were slaves to their wicked pleasures, he was afraid they would kill him, together with his wife and children, and those they had married; so he departed out of that land.

(75) Now God loved this man for his righteousness; yet he not only condemned those other men for their wickedness, but determined to destroy the whole race of mankind, and to make another race that should be pure from wickedness; and, cutting short their lives, and making their years not so many as they formerly lived, but one hundred and twenty only, he turned the dry land into sea; (76) and thus were all these men destroyed: but Noah alone was saved, for God suggested to him the following contrivance and way of escape: (77) that he should make an ark of four stories high, three hundred cubits long, fifty cubits broad, and thirty cubits high. Accordingly he entered into that ark, and his wife and sons, and their wives; and put into it not only other provisions, to support their wants there, but also sent in with the rest all sorts of living creatures, the male and his female, for the preservation of their kinds; and others of them by sevens. (78) Now this ark had firm walls, and a roof, and was braced with cross beams, so that it could not be any way drowned or overborne by the violence of the water; and thus was Noah, with his family, preserved. (79) Now he was the tenth from Adam, as being the son of Lamech, whose father was Mathusala. He was the son of Enoch, the son of Jared; and Jared was the son of Malaleel, who, with many of his sisters, were the children of Cainan, the son of Enos. Now Enos was the son of Seth, the son of Adam.

(80) This calamity happened in the six hundredth year of Noah's government [age], in the second month, called by the Macedonians *Dius*, but by the Hebrews, *Marchesuan*; for so did they order their year in Egypt; (81) but Moses

appointed that *Nisan*, which is the same with Xanthicus, should be the first month for their festivals, because he brought them out of Egypt in that month; so that this month began the year as to all the solemnities they observed to the honour of God, although he preserved the original order of the months as to selling and buying, and other ordinary affairs. Now he says that this flood began on the twenty-seventh [seventeenth] day of the forementioned month; (82) and this was two thousand six hundred and fifty-six [one thousand six hundred and fifty-six] years from Adam, the first man; and the time is written down in our sacred books, those who then lived having noted down, with great accuracy, both the births and deaths of illustrious men.

(83) For indeed Seth was born when Adam was in his two hundred and thirtieth year, who lived nine hundred and thirty years. Seth begat Enos in his two hundred and fifth year; who, when he had lived nine hundred and twelve years, delivered the government to Cainan his son, whom he had in his hundred and ninetieth year; he lived nine hundred and five years. (84) Cainan, when he had lived nine hundred and ten years, had his son Malaleel, who was born in his hundred and seventieth year. This Malaleel, having lived eight hundred and ninety-five years, died, leaving his son Jared, whom he begat when he was in his hundred and sixty-fifth year. (85) He lived nine hundred and sixty-two years, and then his son Enoch succeeded him, who was born when his father was one hundred and sixty-two years old. Now he, when he had lived three hundred and sixty-five years, departed, and went to God; whence it is that they have not written down his death. (86) Now Mathusala, the son of Enoch, who was born to him when he was one hundred and sixty-five years old, had Lamech for his son when he was one hundred and eighty-seven years of age; to whom he delivered the government, when he had retained it nine hundred and sixty-nine years. (87) Now Lamech, when he had governed seven hundred and seventy-seven years, appointed Noah, his son, to be ruler of the people, who was born to Lamech when he was one hundred and eighty-two years old, and retained the government nine hundred and fifty years. (88) These years, collected together, make up the sum before set down; but let no one inquire into the deaths of these men, for they extended their lives along together with their children and grandchildren; but let him have regard to their births only.

(89) When God gave the signal, and it began to rain, the water poured down forty entire days, till it became fifteen cubits higher than the earth; which was the reason why there was no greater number preserved, since they had no place to fly to. (90) When the rain ceased, the water did but just begin to abate, after one hundred and fifty days (that is, on the seventeenth day of the seventh month) it then ceasing to subside for a little while. After this the ark rested on the top of a certain mountain in Armenia; which, when Noah understood, he opened it; and seeing a small piece of land about it, he continued quiet, and

conceived some cheerful hopes of deliverance; (91) but a few days afterwards, when the water was decreased to a greater degree, he sent out a raven, as desirous to learn, whether any other part of the earth were left dry by the water, and whether he might go out of the ark with safety; but the raven, finding all the land still overflowed, returned to Noah again. And after seven days he sent out a dove, to know the state of the ground; (92) which came back to him covered with mud, and bringing an olive branch. Hereby Noah learned that the earth was become clear of the flood. So after he had stayed seven more days, he sent the living creatures out of the ark; and both he and his family went out, when he also sacrificed to God, and feasted with his companions. However, the Armenians call this place (*Apobatērion*) *The Place of Descent;* for the ark being saved in that place, its remains are shown there by the inhabitants to this day.

(93) Now all the writers of barbarian histories make mention of this flood and of this ark; among whom is Berosus the Chaldean; for when he is describing the circumstances of the flood, he goes on thus: 'It is said there is still some part of this ship in Armenia, at the mountain of the Cordyaeans; and that some people carry off pieces of the bitumen, which they take away, and use chiefly as amulets for the averting of mischiefs.' (94) Hieronymus the Egyptian, also, who wrote the *Phoenician Antiquities*, and Mnaseas, and a great many more, make mention of the same. Nay, Nicolaus of Damascus, in his ninety-sixth book, hath a particular relation about them, where he speaks thus: (95) 'There is a great mountain in Armenia, over Minyas, called Baris, upon which it is reported that many who fled at the time of the Deluge were saved; and that one who was carried in an ark came on shore upon the top of it; and that the remains of the timber were a great while preserved. This might be the man about whom Moses, the legislator of the Jews, wrote.'

(96) But as for Noah, he was afraid, since God had determined to destroy mankind, lest he should drown the earth every year; so he offered burnt offerings, and besought God that Nature might hereafter go on in its former orderly course, and that he would not bring on so great a judgment any more, by which the whole race of creatures might be in danger of destruction; but that, having now punished the wicked, he would of his goodness spare the remainder, and such as he had hitherto judged fit to be delivered from so severe a calamity; (97) for that otherwise these last must be more miserable than the first, and that they must be condemned to a worse condition than the others, unless they be suffered to escape entirely; that is, if they be reserved for another deluge, while they must be afflicted with the terror and sight of the first deluge, and must also be destroyed by a second. (98) He also entreated God to accept of his sacrifice, and to grant that the earth might never again undergo the like effects of his wrath; that men might be permitted to go on

cheerfully in cultivating the same – to build cities, and live happily in them; and that they might not be deprived of any of those good things which they enjoyed before the Flood; but might attain to the like length of days and old age which the ancient people had arrived at before.

(99) When Noah had made these supplications, God, who loved the man for his righteousness, granted entire success to his prayers, and said, that it was not he who brought the destruction on a polluted world, but that they underwent that vengeance on account of their own wickedness; and that he had not brought men into the world if he had himself determined to destroy them, (100) it being an instance of greater wisdom not to have granted them life at all, than, after it was granted, to procure their destruction; 'but the injuries,' said he, 'they offered to my holiness and virtue, forced me to bring this punishment upon them; (101) but I will leave off for the time to come to require such punishments, the effects of so great wrath, for their future wicked actions, and especially on account of thy prayers; but if I shall at any time send tempests of rain in an extraordinary manner, be not affrighted at the largeness of the showers, for the waters shall no more overspread the earth. (102) However, I require you to abstain from shedding the blood of men, and to keep yourselves pure from murder, and to punish those that commit any such thing. I permit you to make use of all the other living creatures at your pleasure, and as your appetites lead you; for I have made you lords of them all, both of those that walk on the land, and those that swim in the waters, and of those that fly in the regions of the air on high – excepting their blood, for therein is the life: (103) but I will give you a sign that I have left off my anger, by my bow' [whereby is meant the rainbow, for they determined that the rainbow was the bow of God]; and when God had said and promised thus, he went away.

(104) Now when Noah had lived three hundred and fifty years after the Flood, and that all that time happily, he died, having lived the number of nine hundred and fifty years: (105) but let no one, upon comparing the lives of the ancients with our lives, and with the few years which we now live, think that what we have said of them is false, or make the shortness of our lives at present an argument that neither did they attain to so long a duration of life; (106) for those ancients were beloved of God and [lately] made by God himself; and because their food was then fitter for the prolongation of life, might well live so great a number of years; and besides, God afforded them a longer time of life on account of their virtue and the good use they made of it in astronomical and geometrical discoveries, which would not have afforded the time of foretelling [the periods of the stars] unless they had lived six hundred years; for the Great Year is completed in that interval. (107) Now I have for witnesses to what I have said, all those that have written Antiquities, both among the Greeks and barbarians; for even Manetho, who wrote the *Egyptian History*,

and Berosus, who collected the *Chaldean Monuments*, and Mochus and
Hestiaeus, and besides these, Hieronymus the Egyptian, and those who
composed the *Phoenician History*, agree to what I here say: (108) Hesiod also,
and Hecataeus, Hellanicus, and Acusilaus; and besides these, Ephorus and
Nicolaus relate that the ancients lived a thousand years; but as to these matters
let everyone look upon them as he thinks fit.

CHAPTER 4

(109) Now the sons of Noah were three – Shem, Japhet, and Ham, born one
hundred years before the Deluge. These first of all descended from the
mountains into the plains and fixed their habitations there, and persuaded
others who were greatly afraid of the lower grounds on account of the floods
and so were very loth to come down from the higher place, to venture to
follow their examples. (110) Now the plain in which they first dwelt was
called Shinar. God also commanded them to send colonies abroad, for the
thorough peopling of the earth, that they might not raise seditions among
themselves, but might cultivate a great part of the earth, and enjoy its fruits
after a plentiful manner: but they were so ill instructed, that they did not obey
God; for which reason they fell into calamities, and were made sensible by
experience, of what sin they had been guilty; (111) for when they flourished
with a numerous youth, God admonished them again to send out colonies;
but they, imagining the prosperity they enjoyed was not derived from the
favour of God, but supposing that their own power was the proper cause of
the plentiful condition they were in, did not obey him. (112) Nay, they added
to this their disobedience to the divine will, the suspicion that they were
therefore ordered to send out separate colonies, that, being divided asunder,
they might the more easily be oppressed.

(113) Now it was Nimrod who excited them to such an affront and
contempt of God. He was the grandson of Ham, the son of Noah – a bold
man, and of great strength of hand. He persuaded them not to ascribe it to God
as if it was through his means they were happy, but to believe that it was their
own courage which procured that happiness. (114) He also gradually changed
the government into tyranny, seeing no other way of turning men from the
fear of God, but to bring them into a constant dependence upon his power. He
also said he would be revenged on God, if he should have a mind to drown the
world again; for that he would build a tower too high for the waters to be able
to reach, and that he would avenge himself on God for destroying their
forefathers!

(115) Now the multitude were very ready to follow the determination of
Nimrod, and to esteem it a piece of cowardice to submit to God: and they

built a tower, neither sparing any pains nor being in any degree negligent about the work: and by reason of the multitude of hands employed in it, it grew very high sooner than anyone could expect; (116) but the thickness of it was so great, and it was so strongly built, that thereby its great height seemed, upon the view, to be less than it really was. It was built of burnt brick cemented together with mortar made of bitumen, that it might not be liable to admit water. When God saw that they acted so madly he did not resolve to destroy them utterly, since they were not growing wiser by the destruction of the former sinners (117) but he caused a tumult among them, by producing in them divers languages: and causing that, through the multitude of those languages, they should not be able to understand one another. The place wherein they built the tower is now called *Babylon*, because of the confusion of that language which they readily understood before; for the Hebrews mean by the word *Babel*, Confusion. (118) The Sibyl also makes mention of this tower, and of the confusion of the language, when she says thus: 'When all men were of one language, some of them built a high tower, as if they would thereby ascend up to heaven; but the gods sent storms of wind and overthrew the tower, and gave everyone his peculiar language; and for this reason it was that the city was called *Babylon*.' (119) But as to the plain of Shinar, in the country of Babylonia, Hestiaeus mentions it when he says thus: 'Such of the priests as were saved took the sacred vessels of Jupiter Enyalius, and came to Shinar of Babylonia.'

CHAPTER 5

(120) After this they were dispersed abroad, on account of their languages, and went out by colonies everywhere; and each colony took possession of that land which they light upon and unto which God led them; so that the whole continent was filled with them, both the inland and maritime countries. There were some also who passed over the sea in ships, and inhabited the islands: (121) and some of those nations do still retain the denominations which were given them by their first founders; but some have lost them also; and some have only admitted certain changes in them, that they might be the more intelligible to the inhabitants; and they were the Greeks who became the authors of such mutations; for when, in after-ages, they grew potent, they claimed to themselves the glory of antiquity – giving names to the nations that sounded well (in Greek) that they might be better understood among themselves, and setting agreeable forms of government over them, as if they were a people derived from themselves.

CHAPTER 6

(122) Now they were the grandchildren of Noah, in honour of whom names were imposed on the nations by those that first seized upon them. Japhet, the son of Noah, had seven sons: they inhabited so, that, beginning at the mountain Taurus and Amanus, they proceeded along Asia as far as the river Tanais, and along Europe to Cadiz; and setting themselves on the lands which they light upon, which none had inhabited before, they called the nations by their own names; (123) for Gomer founded those whom the Greeks now call Galatians [Galls], but were then called Gomerites. Magog founded those that from him were named Magogites, but who are by the Greeks called Scythians. (124) Now as to Javan and Madai, the sons of Japhet; from Madai came the Madeans, who are called Medes by the Greeks; but from Javan, Ionia and all the Grecians are derived. Thobel founded the Thobelites, who are now called Iberes; (125) and the Mosocheni were founded by Mosoch; now they are Cappadocians. There is also a mark of their ancient denomination still to be shown; for there is even now among them a city called Mazaca, which may inform those that are able to understand, that so was the entire nation once called. Thiras also called those whom he ruled over, Thirasians; but the Greeks changed the name into Thracians. (126) And so many were the countries that had the children of Japhet for their inhabitants. Of the three sons of Gomer, Aschanax founded the Aschanaxians, who are now called by the Greeks Rheginians. So did Riphath found the Ripheans, now called Paphlagonians; and Thrugramma the Thrugrammeans, who, as the Greeks resolved, were named Phrygians. (127) Of the three sons of Javan also, the son of Japhet, Elisa gave name to the Eliseans, who were his subjects; they are now the Aeolians. Tharsus to the Tharsians; for so was Cilicia of old called; the sign of which is this, that the noblest city they have, and a metropolis also, is Tarsus, the *tau* being by change put for the *theta*. (128) Cethimus possessed the island Cethima; it is now called Cyprus: and from that it is that all islands, and the greatest part of the seacoasts, are named Cethim by the Hebrews; and one city there is in Cyprus that has been able to preserve its denomination; it is called Citius by those who use the language of the Greeks, and has not, by the use of that dialect, escaped the name of Cethim. And so many nations have the children and grandchildren of Japhet possessed. (129) Now when I have premised somewhat, which perhaps the Greeks do not know, I will return and explain what I have omitted; for such names are pronounced here after the manner of the Greeks, to please my readers; for our own country language does not so pronounce them, but the names in all cases are of one and the same ending; for the name we here pronounce Noeas, is there Noah, and in every case retains the same termination.

(130) The children of Ham possessed the land from Syria and Amanus, and the mountains of Libanus, seizing upon all that was on its seacoasts and as far as the ocean, and keeping it as their own. Some indeed of its names are utterly vanished away; others of them being changed, and another sound given them, are hardly to be discovered; yet a few there are which have kept their denominations entire; (131) for of the four sons of Ham, time has not at all hurt the name of Chus; for the Ethiopians, over whom he reigned, are even at this day, both by themselves and by all men in Asia, called Chusites. (132) The memory also of the Mesraites is preserved in their name; for all we who inhabit this country [of Judea] call Egypt Mestre, and the Egyptians Mestreans. Phut also was the founder of Libya, and called the inhabitants Phutites, from himself: (133) there is also a river in the country of the Moors which bears that name; whence it is that we may see the greatest part of the Grecian historiographers mention that river and the adjoining country by the appellation of Phut: but the name it has now, has been by change given it from one of the sons of Mesraim, who was called Lybyos. We will inform you presently what has been the occasion why it has been called Africa also. (134) Canaan, the fourth son of Ham, inhabited the country now called Judea, and called it from his own name Canaan. The children of these [four] were these: Sabas, who founded the Sabeans; Evilas, who founded the Evileans, who are called Getuli; Sabathes founded the Sabathens; they are now called by the Greeks, Astaborans; (135) Sabactas settled the Sabactens; and Ragmus the Ragmeans; and he had two sons, the one of whom, Judadas, settled the Judadeans, a nation of the western Ethiopians, and left them his name; as did Sabas to the Sabeans. But Nimrod, the son of Chus, stayed and tyrannised at Babylon, as we have already informed you. (136) Now all the children of Mesraim, being eight in number, possessed the country from Gaza to Egypt, though it retained the name of one only, the Philistim; for the Greeks call part of that country Palestine. (137) As for the rest, Ludicim, and Enemim, and Labim, who alone inhabited in Libya, and called the country from himself, Nedim, and Phethrosim, and Chesloim, and Cephthorim, we know nothing of them besides their names; for the Ethiopic war, which we shall describe hereafter, was the cause that those cities were overthrown. (138) The sons of Canaan were these: Sidonius, who also built a city of the same name; it is called by the Greeks, Sidon; Amathus inhabited in Amathine, which is even now called Amathe by the inhabitants, although the Macedonians named it Epiphania, from one of his posterity: Arudeus possessed the island Aradus: Arucas possessed Arce, which is in Libanus; (139) but for the seven others, [Eueus], Chetteus, Jebuseus, Amorreus, Gergesus, Eudeus, Sineus, Samareus, we have nothing in the sacred books but their names, for the Hebrews overthrew their cities; and their calamities came upon them on the occasion following:

(140) Noah, when, after the Deluge, the earth was resettled in its former condition, set about its cultivation; and when he had planted it with vines, and when the fruit was ripe, and he had gathered the grapes in their season, and the wine was ready for use, he offered sacrifice, and feasted, (141) and being drunk, he fell asleep; and lay naked in an unseemly manner. When his youngest son saw this, he came laughing, and showed him to his brethren; but they covered their father's nakedness. (142) And when Noah was made sensible of what had been done, he prayed for prosperity to his other sons; but for Ham, he did not curse him, by reason of his nearness in blood, but cursed his posterity. And when the rest of them escaped that curse, God inflicted it on the children of Canaan. But as to these matters, we shall speak more hereafter.

(143) Shem, the third son of Noah, had five sons, who inhabited the land that began at Euphrates, and reached to the Indian Ocean; for Elam left behind him the Elamites, the ancestors of the Persians. Ashur lived at the city Nieve, and named his subjects Assyrians, who became the most fortunate nation, beyond others. (144) Arphaxad named the Arphaxadites, who are now called Chaldeans. Aram had the Aramites, which the Greeks call Syrians; as Laud founded the Laudites, which are now called Lydians. (145) Of the four sons of Aram, Uz founded Trachonitis and Damascus; this country lies between Palestine and Celesyria. Ul founded Armenia; and Gather the Bactrians; and Mesa the Mesaneans; it is now called Charax Spasini. (146) Sala was the son of Arphaxad; and his son was Heber, from whom they originally called the Jews Hebrews. Heber begat Joctan and Phaleg; he was called Phaleg, because he was born at the dispersion of the nations to their several countries; for Phaleg, among the Hebrews, signifies *division*. (147) Now Joctan, one of the sons of Heber, had these sons: Elmodad, Saleph, Asermoth, Jera, Adoram, Aizel, Decla, Ebal, Abimael, Sabeus, Ophir, Euilat and Jobab. These inhabited from Cophen, an Indian river, and in part of Asia adjoining to it. And this shall suffice concerning the sons of Shem.

(148) I will now treat of the Hebrews. The son of Phaleg, whose father was Heber, was Ragau; whose son was Serug, to whom was born Nahor; his son was Terah, who was the father of Abraham, who accordingly was the tenth from Noah, and was born in the two hundred and ninety-second year after the Deluge; (149) for Terah begat Abram in his seventieth year; Nahor begat Haran when he was one hundred and twenty years old; Nahor was born to Serug in his hundred and thirty-second year; Ragau had Serug at one hundred and thirty; at the same age also Phaleg had Ragau; (150) Heber begat Phaleg in his hundred and thirty-fourth year; he himself being begotten by Sala when he was an hundred and thirty years old, whom Arphaxad had for his son at the hundred and thirty-fifth year of his age. Arphaxad was the son of Shem, and born twelve years after the Deluge. (151) Now Abraham had two brethren,

Nahor and Haran; of these Haran left a son, Lot, as also Sarai and Milcha his daughters, and died among the Chaldeans, in a city of the Chaldeans called Ur; and his monument is shown to this day. These married their nieces. Nahor married Milcha, and Abram married Sarai. (152) Now Terah hating Chaldea, on account of his mourning for Haran, they all removed to Haran of Mesopotamia, where Terah died and was buried, when he had lived to be two hundred and five years old; for the life of man was already by degrees diminished, and became shorter than before, till the birth of Moses; after whom the term of human life was one hundred and twenty years, God determining it to the length that Moses happened to live. (153) Now Nahor had eight sons by Milcha; Uz and Buz, Kemuel, Chesed, Azau, Pheldas, Jadelph, and Bethuel. These were all the genuine sons of Nahor; for Teba, and Gaam, and Tachas, and Maaca, were born of Reuma his concubine; but Bethuel had a daughter, Rebecca, and a son, Laban.

CHAPTER 7

(154) Now Abram having no son of his own, adopted Lot, his brother Haran's son, and his wife Sarai's brother; and he left the land of Chaldea when he was seventy-five years old, and at the command of God went into Canaan, and therein he dwelt himself, and left it to his posterity. He was a person of great sagacity, both for understanding all things and persuading his hearers, and not mistaken in his opinions; (155) for which reason he began to have higher notions of virtue than others had, and he determined to renew and to change the opinion all men happened then to have concerning God; for he was the first that ventured to publish this notion, that there was but one God, the Creator of the universe; and that, as to other [gods], if they contributed anything to the happiness of men, that each of them afforded it only according to his appointment, and not by their own power. (156) This his opinion was derived from the irregular phenomena that were visible both at land and sea, as well as those that happen to the sun and moon, and all the heavenly bodies, thus: 'If [said he] these bodies had power of their own, they would certainly take care of their own regular motions; but since they do not preserve such regularity, they make it plain that in so far as they cooperate to our advantage, they do it not of their own abilities, but as they are subservient to him that commands them; to whom alone we ought justly to offer our honour and thanksgiving.' (157) For which doctrines, when the Chaldeans and other people of Mesopotamia raised a tumult against him, he thought fit to leave that country; and at the command and by the assistance of God, he came and lived in the land of Canaan. And when he was there settled, he built an altar, and performed a sacrifice to God.

(158) Berosus mentions our father Abram without naming him, when he says thus: 'In the tenth generation after the Flood, there was among the Chaldeans a man righteous and great, and skilful in the celestial science.' (159) But Hecataeus does more than barely mention him; for he composed and left behind him a book concerning him. And Nicolaus of Damascus, in the fourth book of his history, says thus: 'Abram reigned at Damascus, being a foreigner, who came with an army out of the land above Babylon, called the land of the Chaldeans. (160) But after a long time he got him up, and removed from that country also with his people, and went into the land then called the land of Canaan, but now the land of Judea, and this when his posterity were become a multitude; as to which posterity of his, we relate their history in another work. Now the name of Abram is even still famous in the country of Damascus; and there is shown a village named from him, *The Habitation of Abram*.

CHAPTER 8

(161) Now, after this, when a famine had invaded the land of Canaan, and Abram had discovered that the Egyptians were in a flourishing condition, he was disposed to go down to them, both to partake of the plenty they enjoyed, and to become an auditor of their priests, and to know what they said concerning the gods; designing either to follow them if they had better notions than he, or to convert them into a better way, if his own notions proved the truest. (162) Now, seeing he was to take Sarai with him, and was afraid of the madness of the Egyptians with regard to women, lest the king should kill him on occasion of his wife's great beauty, he contrived this device: he pretended to be her brother, and directed her in a dissembling way to pretend the same, for he said it would be for their benefit. (163) Now, as soon as he came into Egypt, it happened to Abram as he supposed it would; for the fame of his wife's beauty was greatly talked of, for which reason Pharaoh the king of Egypt would not be satisfied with what was reported of her, but would needs see her himself, and was preparing to enjoy her; (164) but God put a stop to his unjust inclinations, by sending upon him a distemper, and a sedition against his government. And when he inquired of the priests, how he might be freed from these calamities, they told him that this his miserable condition was derived from the wrath of God, upon account of his inclination to abuse the stranger's wife. (165) He then out of fear asked Sarai who she was, and who it was that she brought along with her. And when he had found out the truth he excused himself to Abram, that supposing the woman to be his sister, and not his wife, he set his affections on her, as desiring an affinity with him by marrying her, but not as incited by lust to abuse her. He also made him a large present in money, and gave him leave to enter into conversation with the most

learned among the Egyptians; from which conversation, his virtue and his reputation became more conspicuous than they had been before.

(166) For whereas the Egyptians were formerly addicted to different customs, and despised one another's sacred and accustomed rites, and were very angry one with another on that account, Abram conferred with each of them, and, confuting the reasonings they made use of, every one for their own practices, demonstrated that such reasonings were vain and void of truth; (167) whereupon he was admired by them in those conferences as a very wise man, and one of great sagacity, when he discoursed on any subject he undertook; and this not only in understanding it, but in persuading other men also to assent to him. He communicated to them arithmetic, and delivered to them the science of astronomy; (168) for, before Abram came into Egypt, they were unacquainted with those parts of learning; for that science came from the Chaldeans into Egypt, and from thence to the Greeks also.

(169) As soon as Abram was come back into Canaan, he parted the land between him and Lot, upon account of the tumultuous behaviour of their shepherds, concerning the pastures wherein they should feed their flocks. However, he gave Lot his option, or leave, to choose which lands he would take; (170) and he took himself what the other left, which were the lower grounds at the foot of the mountains; and he himself dwelt in Hebron, which is a city seven years more ancient than Tanis of Egypt. But Lot possessed the land of the plain, and the river Jordan, not far from the city of Sodom, which was then a fine city, but is now destroyed by the will and wrath of God – the cause of which I shall show in its proper place hereafter.

CHAPTER 9

(171) At this time, when the Assyrians had the dominion over Asia, the people of Sodom were in a flourishing condition, both as to riches and the number of their youth. There were five kings that managed the affairs of this country: Ballas, Barsas, Senabar, and Sumobor, with the king of Bela; and each king led on his own troops; (172) and the Assyrians made war upon them; and, dividing their army into four parts, fought against them. Now every part of the army had its own commander; and when the battle was joined, the Assyrians were conquerors, and imposed a tribute on the kings of the Sodomites, (173) who submitted to this slavery twelve years; and so long they continued to pay their tribute: but on the thirteenth year they rebelled, and then the army of the Assyrians came upon them, under their commanders Amraphel, Arioch, Chodorlaomer, and Tidal. (174) These kings had laid waste all Syria, and overthrown the offspring of the giants; and when they were come over against Sodom, they pitched their camp at the vale called the Slime Pits, for at that

time there were pits in that place; but now, upon the destruction of the city of Sodom, that vale became the Lake Asphaltitis, as it is called. (175) However, concerning this lake we shall speak more presently. Now when the Sodomites joined battle with the Assyrians, and the fight was very obstinate, many of them were killed, and the rest were carried captive; among which captives was Lot, who had come to assist the Sodomites.

CHAPTER 10

(176) When Abram heard of their calamity, he was at once afraid for Lot his kinsman, and pitied the Sodomites, his friends and neighbours; (177) and thinking it proper to afford them assistance, he did not delay it, but marched hastily, and the fifth night fell upon the Assyrians, near Dan, for that is the name of the other spring of Jordan; and before they could arm themselves, he slew some as they were in their beds, before they could suspect any harm; and others, who were not yet gone to sleep, but were so drunk they could not fight, ran away. (178) Abram pursued after them, till on the second day he drove them in a body unto Hoba, a place belonging to Damascus; and thereby demonstrated that victory does not depend on multitude and the number of hands, but the alacrity and courage of soldiers overcome the most numerous bodies of men, while he got the victory over so great an army with no more than three hundred and eighteen of his servants and three of his friends: but all those that fled returned home ingloriously.

(179) So Abram, when he had saved the captive Sodomites who had been taken by the Assyrians, and Lot also, his kinsman, returned home in peace. Now the king of Sodom met him at a certain place, which they called The King's Dale, (180) where Melchizedek, king of the city Salem, received him. That name signifies *the righteous king*; and such he was without dispute, insomuch that, on this account, he was made the priest of God: however, they afterward called Salem *Jerusalem*. (181) Now this Melchizedek supplied Abram's army in an hospitable manner, and gave them provisions in abundance; and as they were feasting he began to praise him, and to bless God for subduing his enemies under him. And when Abram gave him the tenth part of his prey, he accepted of the gift: (182) but the king of Sodom desired Abram to take the prey, but entreated that he might have those men restored to him whom Abram had saved from the Assyrians because they belonged to him; but Abram would not do so; nor would make any other advantage of that prey than what his servants had eaten, but still insisted that he should afford a part to his friends that had assisted him in the battle. The first of them was called Eschol, and then Enner, and Mambre.

(183) And God commended his virtue, and said, Thou shalt not, however,

lose the rewards thou hast deserved to receive by such thy glorious actions. He answered, And what advantage will it be to me to have such rewards, when I have none to enjoy them after me? – for he was hitherto childless. And God promised that he should have a son, and that his posterity should be very numerous, insomuch that their number should be like the stars. (184) When he heard that, he offered a sacrifice to God, as he commanded him. The manner of the sacrifice was this: he took an heifer of three years old, and a she-goat of three years old, and a ram in like manner of three years old, and a turtledove and a pigeon; and, as he was enjoined, he divided the three former, but the birds he did not divide. (185) After which, before he built his altar, where the birds of prey flew about, as desirous of blood, a divine voice came to him, declaring that their neighbours would be grievous to his posterity when they should be in Egypt, for four hundred years, during which time they should be afflicted; but afterwards should overcome their enemies, should conquer the Canaanites in war, and possess themselves of their land and of their cities.

(186) Now Abram dwelt near the oak called Ogyges – the place belongs to Canaan, not far from the city of Hebron: but being uneasy at his wife's barrenness, he entreated God to grant that he might have male issue; (187) and God required of him to be of good courage, and said, that he would add to all the rest of the benefits that he had bestowed on him ever since he led him out of Mesopotamia, the gift of children. Accordingly Sarai, at God's command, brought to his bed one of her handmaidens, a woman of Egyptian descent, in order to obtain children by her; (188) and when this handmaid was with child, she triumphed, and ventured to affront Sarai, as if the dominion were to come to a son to be born of her; but when Abram resigned her into the hand of Sarai to punish her, she contrived to fly away, as not able to bear the instances of Sarai's severity to her; and she entreated God to have compassion on her. (189) Now a divine angel met her, as she was going forward in the wilderness, and bid her return to her master and mistress; for, if she would submit to that wise advice, she would live better hereafter; for that the reason of her being in such a miserable case was this, that she had been ungrateful and arrogant towards her mistress. (190) He also told her, that if she disobeyed God, and went on still in her way, she should perish; but if she would return back, she should become the mother of a son who should reign over that country. These admonitions she obeyed, and returned to her master and mistress, and obtained forgiveness. A little while afterwards, she bare Ismael, which may be interpreted *Heard of God*, because God had heard his mother's prayer.

(191) The forementioned son was born to Abram when he was eighty-six years old: but when he was ninety-nine, God appeared to him, and promised him that he should have a son by Sarai, and commanded that his name should be Isaac; and showed him, that from this son should spring great nations and

kings, and that they should obtain all the land of Canaan by war, from Sidon to Egypt. (192) But he charged him, in order to keep his posterity unmixed with others, that they should be circumcised in the flesh of their foreskin, and that this should be done on the eighth day after they were born: the reason of which circumcision I will explain in another place. (193) And Abram inquiring also concerning Ismael, whether he should live or not, God signified to him that he should live to be very old, and should be the father of great nations. Abram, therefore, gave thanks to God for these blessings; and then he, and all his family, and his son Ismael, were circumcised immediately, the son being that day thirteen years of age, and he ninety-nine.

CHAPTER II

(194) About this time the Sodomites grew proud, on account of their riches and great wealth: they became unjust towards men, and impious towards God, insomuch that they did not call to mind the advantages they received from him: they hated strangers, and abused themselves with Sodomitical practices. (195) God was therefore much displeased at them, and determined to punish them for their pride, and to overthrow their city, and to lay waste their country, until there should neither plant nor fruit grow out of it.

(196) When God had thus resolved concerning the Sodomites, Abraham, as he sat by the oak of Mambre, at the door of his tent, saw three angels; and, thinking them to be strangers, he rose up and saluted them, and desired they would accept of an entertainment, and abide with him; (197) to which when they agreed, he ordered cakes of meal to be made presently: and when he had slain a calf, he roasted it, and brought it to them, as they sat under the oak. Now they made a show of eating; and besides, they asked him about his wife Sarah, where she was; and when he said she was within, they said they would come again hereafter, and find her become a mother. (198) Upon which the woman laughed, and said that it was impossible she should bear children, since she was ninety years of age, and her husband was a hundred. Then they concealed themselves no longer, but declared that they were angels of God; and that one of them was sent to inform them about the child, and two of the overthrow of Sodom.

(199) When Abraham heard this, he was grieved for the Sodomites; and he rose up, and besought God for them, and entreated him that he would not destroy the righteous with the wicked. (200) And when God had replied that there was no good man among the Sodomites; for if there were but ten such men among them, he would not punish any of them for their sins, Abraham held his peace. And the angels came to the city of the Sodomites, and Lot entreated them to accept of a lodging with him; for he was a very generous and

hospitable man, and one that had learned to imitate the goodness of Abraham.
Now when the Sodomites saw the young men to be of beautiful countenances,
and this to an extraordinary degree, and that they took up their lodgings with
Lot, they resolved themselves to enjoy these beautiful boys by force and
violence; (201) and when Lot exhorted them to sobriety, and not to offer
anything immodest to the strangers, but to have regard to their lodging in his
house; and promised, that if their inclinations could not be governed, he would
expose his daughters to their lust, instead of these strangers – neither thus were
they made ashamed.

(202) But God was much displeased at their impudent behaviour, so that he
both smote those men with blindness, and condemned the Sodomites to
universal destruction. But Lot, upon God's informing him of the future
destruction of the Sodomites, went away, taking with him his wife and
daughters, who were two, and still virgins: for those that were betrothed to
them were above the thoughts of going, and deemed that Lot's words were
trifling. (203) God then cast a thunderbolt upon the city, and set it on fire, with
its inhabitants; and laid waste the country with the like burning, as I formerly
said when I wrote the *Jewish War*. But Lot's wife continually turning back to
view the city as she went from it, and being too nicely inquisitive what would
become of it, although God had forbidden her so to do, was changed into a
pillar of salt; for I have seen it, and it remains at this day. (204) Now he and his
daughters fled to a certain small place, encompassed with the fire, and settled in
it. It is to this day called *Zoar*, for that is the word which the Hebrews use for
a small thing. There it was that he lived a miserable life, on account of his
having no company, and his want of provisions.

(205) But his daughters, thinking that all mankind were destroyed,
approached to their father, though taking care not to be perceived. This they
did, that humankind might not utterly fail. And they bare sons; the son of the
elder was named Moab, which denotes one derived from his father. The
younger bare Ammon, which name denotes one derived from a kinsman.
(206) The former of whom was the father of the Moabites, which is even still
a great nation; the latter was the father of the Ammonites; and both of them are
inhabitants of Celesyria. And such was the departure of Lot from among the
Sodomites.

CHAPTER 12

(207) Abraham now removed to Gerar of Palestine, leading Sarah along with
him, under the notion of his sister, using the like dissimulation that he had used
before, and this out of fear; for he was afraid of Abimelech, the king of that
country, who did also himself fall in love with Sarah, and was disposed to

corrupt her; (208) but he was restrained from satisfying his lust, by a dangerous distemper, which befell him from God. Now when his physicians despaired of curing him, he fell asleep, and saw a dream, warning him not to abuse the stranger's wife; and when he recovered he told his friends that God had inflicted that disease upon him by way of punishment, for his injury to the stranger, and in order to preserve the chastity of his wife; for that she did not accompany him as his sister, but as his legitimate wife; and that God had promised to be gracious to him for the time to come, if this person be once secure of his wife's chastity. (209) When he had said this, by the advice of his friends, he sent for Abraham, and bid him not be concerned about his wife, or fear the corruption of her chastity; for that God took care of him, and that it was by His providence that he received his wife again, without her suffering any abuse; and he appealed to God, and to his wife's conscience, and said that he had not any inclination at first to enjoy her, if he had known she was his wife; but since, said he, thou ledst her about as thy sister, I was guilty of no offence. (210) He also entreated him to be at peace with him, and to make God propitious to him; and that if he thought fit to continue with him he should have what he wanted in abundance; but that if he designed to go away, he should be honourably conducted, and have whatsoever supply he wanted when he came thither. (211) Upon his saying this, Abraham told him that his pretence of kindred to his wife was no lie, because she was his brother's daughter; and that he did not think himself safe in his travels abroad, without this sort of dissimulation; and that he was not the cause of his distemper, but was only solicitous for his own safety. He said also, that he was ready to stay with him. (212) Whereupon Abimelech assigned him land and money; and they covenanted to live together without guile, and took an oath at a certain well called Beersheba, which may be interpreted *The Well of the Oath*. And so it is named by the people of the country unto this day.

(213) Now in a little time Abraham had a son by Sarah, as God had foretold to him, whom he named Isaac, which signifies *Laughter*; and indeed they so called him, because Sarah laughed when God said that she should bear a son, she not expecting such a thing, as being past the age of child bearing; for she was ninety years old, and Abraham an hundred; (214) so that this son was born to them both in the last year of each of those decimal numbers. And they circumcised him upon the eighth day. And from that time the Jews continue the custom of circumcising their sons within that number of days. But as for the Arabians, they circumcise after the thirteenth year, because Ismael, the founder of their nation, who was born to Abraham of the concubine, was circumcised at that age; concerning whom I will presently give a particular account, with great exactness.

(215) As for Sarah, she at first loved Ismael, who was born of her own

handmaid Hagar, with an affection not inferior to that of her own son, for he was brought up, in order to succeed in the government; but when she herself had borne Isaac, she was not willing that Ismael should be brought up with him, as being too old for him, and able to do him injuries when their father should be dead; (216) she therefore persuaded Abraham to send him and his mother to some distant country. Now, at the first he did not agree to what Sarah was so zealous for, and thought it an instance of the greatest barbarity to send away a young child and a woman unprovided of necessaries; (217) but at length he agreed to it; because God was pleased with what Sarah had determined; so he delivered Ismael to his mother, as not yet able to go by himself; and commanded her to take a bottle of water, and a loaf of bread, and so to depart, and to take Necessity for her guide. (218) But as soon as her necessary provisions failed, she found herself in an evil case; and when the water was almost spent, she laid the young child, who was ready to expire, under a fig tree, and went on further, that so he might die while she was absent. (219) But a divine angel came to her, and told her of a fountain hard by, and bid her take care and bring up the child, because she should be very happy by the preservation of Ismael. She then took courage upon the prospect of what was promised her, and, meeting with some shepherds, by their care she got clear of the distresses she had been in.

(220) When the lad was grown up, he married a wife, by birth an Egyptian, from whence the mother was herself derived originally. Of this wife were born to Ismael twelve sons; Nabaioth, Kedar, Abdeel, Mabsam, Idumas, Masmaos, Masoss, Chodad, Theman, Jetur, Naphesus, Cadmas. (221) These inhabited all the country from Euphrates to the Red Sea, and called it Nabatene. They are an Arabian nation and name their tribes from these, both because of their own virtue and because of the dignity of Abraham their father.

CHAPTER 13

(222) Now Abraham greatly loved Isaac, as being his only begotten, and given to him at the borders of old age, by the favour of God. The child also endeared himself to his parents still more by the exercise of every virtue, and adhering to his duty to his parents, and being zealous in the worship of God. (223) Abraham also placed his own happiness in this prospect, that, when he should die, he should leave this his son in a safe and secure condition; which accordingly he obtained by the will of God; who, being desirous to make an experiment of Abraham's religious disposition towards himself, appeared to him, and enumerated all the blessings he had bestowed on him; (224) how he had made him superior to his enemies; and that his son Isaac who was the principal part of his present happiness, was derived from him; and he said that

he required this son of his as a sacrifice and holy oblation. Accordingly he commanded him to carry him to the mountain Moriah, and to build an altar, and offer him for a burnt offering upon it; for that this would best manifest his religious disposition towards him, if he preferred what was pleasing to God before the preservation of his own son.

(225) Now Abraham thought that it was not right to disobey God in anything, but that he was obliged to serve him in every circumstance of life, since all creatures that live enjoy their life by his providence, and the kindness he bestows on them. Accordingly he concealed this command of God, and his own intentions about the slaughter of his son, from his wife, as also from every one of his servants, otherwise he should have been hindered from his obedience to God; and he took Isaac, together with two of his servants, and laying what things were necessary for a sacrifice upon an ass, he went away to the mountain. (226) Now the two servants went along with him two days; but on the third day, as soon as he saw the mountain, he left those servants that were with him till then in the plain, and, having his son alone with him, he came to the mountain. It was that mountain upon which king David afterwards built the temple. (227) Now they had brought with them everything necessary for a sacrifice excepting the animal that was to be offered only. Now Isaac was twenty-five years old. And as he was building the altar he asked his father what he was about to offer, since there was no animal there for an oblation: to which it was answered, 'That God would provide himself an oblation, he being able to make a plentiful provision for men out of what they have not, and to deprive others of what they already have, when they put too much trust therein; that therefore, if God pleased to be present and propitious at this sacrifice, he would provide himself an oblation.'

(228) As soon as the altar was prepared, and Abraham had laid on the wood, and all things were entirely ready, he said to his son, 'O son! I poured out a vast number of prayers that I might have thee for my son; when thou wast come into the world, there was nothing that could contribute to thy support for which I was not greatly solicitous, nor anything wherein I thought myself happier than to see thee grown up to man's estate, and that I might leave thee at my death the successor to my dominion; (229) but since it was by God's will that I became thy father, and it is now his will that I relinquish thee, bear this consecration to God with a generous mind; for I resign thee up to God, who has thought fit now to require this testimony of honour to himself, on account of the favours he hath conferred on me, in being to me a supporter and defender. (230) Accordingly thou, my son, wilt now die, not in any common way of going out of the world, but sent to God, the Father of all men, beforehand, by thy own father, in the nature of a sacrifice. I suppose he thinks thee worthy to get clear of this world neither by disease, neither by

war, nor by any other severe way, by which death usually comes upon men, (231) but so that he will receive thy soul with prayers and holy offices of religion, and will place thee near to himself, and thou wilt there be to me a succourer and supporter in my old age; on which account I principally brought thee up, and thou wilt thereby procure me God for my Comforter instead of thyself.'

(232) Now Isaac was of such a generous disposition as became the son of such a father, and was pleased with this discourse; and said 'That he was not worthy to be born at first, if he should reject the determination of God and of his father, and should not resign himself up readily to both their pleasures; since it would have been unjust if he had not obeyed, even if his father alone had so resolved.' So he went immediately to the altar to be sacrificed. (233) And the deed had been done if God had not opposed it; for he called loudly to Abraham by his name, and forbade him to slay his son; and said, 'It was not out of a desire of human blood that he was commanded to slay his son, nor was he willing that he should be taken away from him whom he had made his father, but to try the temper of his mind, whether he would be obedient to such a command. (234) Since, therefore, he now was satisfied as to that his alacrity, and the surprising readiness he showed in this his piety, he was delighted in having bestowed such blessings upon him; and that he would not be wanting in all sort of concern about him, and in bestowing other children upon him; and that his son should live to a very great age; that he should live a happy life, and bequeath a large principality to his children, who should be good and legitimate.' (235) He foretold also, that his family should increase into many nations; and that those patriarchs should leave behind them an everlasting name; that they should obtain the possession of the land of Canaan, and be envied by all men. When God had said this, he produced to them a ram, which did not appear before, for the sacrifice. (236) So Abraham and Isaac receiving each other unexpectedly, and having obtained the promises of such great blessings, embraced one another; and when they had sacrificed, they returned to Sarah, and lived happily together, God affording them his assistance in all things they desired.

CHAPTER 14

(237) Now Sarah died a little while after, having lived one hundred and twenty-seven years. They buried her in Hebron, the Canaanites publicly allowing them a burying place: which piece of ground Abraham bought, for four hundred shekels, of Ephron, an inhabitant of Hebron; and both Abraham and his descendants built themselves sepulchres in that place.

CHAPTER 15

(238) Abraham after this married Keturah, by whom six sons were born to him, men of courage and of sagacious minds: Zambran, and Jazar, and Madan, and Madian, and Josabak, and Sous. Now the sons of Sous were Sabathan and Dadan; the sons of Dadan were Latusim, and Assur, and Luom; the sons of Madian were Ephas, and Ophren, and Anoch, and Ebidas, and Eldas. (239) Now, for all these sons and grandsons, Abraham contrived to settle them in colonies; and they took possession of Troglodytis, and the country of Arabia the Happy, as far as it reaches to the Red Sea. It is related of this Ophren, that he made war against Libya, and took it; and that his grandchildren when they inhabited it, called it (from his name) Africa; (240) and indeed Alexander Polyhistor gives his attestation to what I here say; who speaks thus: 'Cleodemus the prophet, who was also called Malchus, who wrote a history of the Jews, in agreement with the History of Moses, their legislator, relates that there were many sons born to Abraham by Keturah; (241) nay, he names three of them, Apher, and Surim, and Japhran: that from Surim was the land of Assyria denominated; and that from the other two (Apher and Japhran) the country of Africa took its name; because these men were auxiliaries to Hercules, when he fought against Libya and Antaeus; and that Hercules married Aphra's daughter, and of her he begat a son, Diodorus; and that Sophon was his son, from whom that barbarous people called Sophacians were denominated.'

CHAPTER 16

(242) Now when Abraham, the father of Isaac, had resolved to take Rebeka, who was granddaughter to his brother Nahor, for a wife to his son Isaac, who was then about forty years old, he sent the ancientest of his servants to betroth her, after he had obliged him to give him the strongest assurance of his fidelity; (243) which assurances were given after the manner following: they put each other's hands under each other's thighs; then they called upon God as the witness of what was to be done. He also sent such presents to those that were there as were in esteem, on account that they either rarely or never were seen in that country. The servant got thither not under a considerable time; (244) for it requires much time to pass through Mesopotamia, in which it is tedious travelling, both in the winter, for the depth of the clay – and in summer for want of water; and, besides this, for the robberies there committed, which are not to be avoided by travellers but by caution beforehand. However, the servant came to Haran; and when he was in the suburbs, he met a considerable number of maidens going to the water; (245) he therefore prayed to God that

Rebeka might be found among them, or her whom Abraham sent him as his servant to espouse to his son, in case his will were that this marriage should be consummated; and that she might be made known to him by the sign, that while others denied him water to drink, she might give it him.

(246) With this intention he went to the well, and desired the maidens to give him some water to drink; but while the others refused, on pretence that they wanted it all at home, and could spare none for him, one only of the company rebuked them for their peevish behaviour towards the stranger; and said, What is there that you will ever communicate to anybody, who have not so much as given the man some water? She then offered him water in an obliging manner; (247) and now he began to hope that his grand affair would succeed; but desiring still to know the truth, he commended her for her generosity and good nature, that she did not scruple to afford a sufficiency of water to those that wanted it, though it cost her some pains to draw it; and asked who were her parents, and wished them joy of such a daughter. 'And mayest thou be espoused,' said he, 'to their satisfaction, into the family of an agreeable husband, and bring him legitimate children!' (248) Nor did she disdain to satisfy his enquiries, but told him her family. 'They,' says she, 'call me Rebeka; my father was Bethuel, but he is dead; and Laban is my brother and, together with my mother, takes care of all our family affairs, and is the guardian of my virginity.' (249) When the servant heard this he was very glad at what had happened, and at what was told him, as perceiving that God had thus plainly directed his journey: and producing his bracelets, and some other ornaments which it was esteemed decent for virgins to wear, he gave them to the damsel, by way of acknowledgment, and as a reward for her kindness in giving him water to drink; saying, it was but just that she should have them, because she was so much more obliging than any of the rest. (250) She desired also that he would come and lodge with them, since the approach of the night gave him not time to proceed further; and producing his precious ornaments for women, he said he desired to trust them to none more safely than to such as she had shown herself to be; and that he believed he might guess at the humanity of her mother and brother, that they would not be displeased, from the virtue he found in her; for he would not be burdensome, but would pay the hire for his entertainment, and spend his own money. (251) To which she replied, that he guessed right as to the humanity of her parents; but complained that he should think them so parsimonious as to take money, for that he should have all on free cost; but she said she would first inform her brother Laban, and, if he gave her leave, she would conduct him in.

(252) As soon then as this was over, she introduced the stranger; and for the camels, the servants of Laban brought them in, and took care of them; and he was himself brought into supper by Laban. And, after supper, he says to him,

and to the mother of the damsel, addressing himself to her, 'Abraham is the son of Terah, and a kinsman of yours; for Nahor, the grandfather of these children, was the brother of Abraham, by both father and mother; (253) upon which account he hath sent me to you, being desirous to take this damsel for his son to wife. He is his legitimate son, and is brought up as his only heir. He could indeed have had the most happy of all the women in that country for him, but he would not have his son marry any of them; but, out of regard to his own relations, he desired him to match here, (254) whose affection and inclination I would not have you despise; for it was by the good pleasure of God that other accidents fell out in my journey, and that thereby I lighted upon your daughter and your house; for when I was near to the city, I saw a great many maidens coming to a well, and I prayed that I might meet with this damsel, which has come to pass accordingly. (255) Do you, therefore, confirm that marriage, whose espousals have been already made by a divine appearance; and show the respect you have for Abraham, who hath sent me with so much solicitude, in giving your consent to the marriage of this damsel.' Upon this they understood it to be the will of God, and greatly approved of the offer, and sent their daughter as was desired. Accordingly Isaac married her, the inheritance being now come to him; for the children of Keturah were gone to their own remote habitations.

CHAPTER 17

(256) A little while after this Abraham died. He was a man of incomparable virtue, and honoured by God in a manner agreeable to his piety towards him. The whole time of his life was one hundred seventy and five years; and he was buried in Hebron, with his wife Sarah, by their sons Isaac and Ismael.

CHAPTER 18

(257) Now Isaac's wife proved with child, after the death of Abraham; and when her belly was greatly burdened, Isaac was very anxious, and inquired of God; who answered that Rebeka should bear twin, and that two nations should take the names of those sons, and that he who appeared the second should excel the elder. (258) Accordingly she, in a little time, as God had foretold, bare twins; the elder of whom, from his head to his feet, was very rough and hairy; but the younger took hold of his heel as they were in the birth. Now the father loved the elder, who was called Esau, a name agreeable to his roughness, for the Hebrews call such an hairy roughness [Esau, or] Seir; but Jacob the younger was best beloved by his mother.

(259) When there was a famine in the land, Isaac resolved to go into Egypt,

the land there being good; but he went to Gerar, as God commanded him. Here Abimelech the king received him, because Abraham had formerly lived with him, and had been his friend; and as in the beginning he treated him exceeding kindly, so he was hindered from continuing in the same disposition to the end, by his envy at him; (260) for when he saw that God was with Isaac, and took such great care of him, he drove him away from him. But Isaac, when he saw how envy had changed the temper of Abimelech, retired to a place called the Valley, not far from Gerar; and as he was digging a well, the shepherds fell upon him, and began to fight, in order to hinder the work; and because he did not desire to contend, the shepherds seemed to get the better of him; (261) so he still retired, and dug another well; and when certain other shepherds of Abimelech's began to offer him violence, he left that also, and still retired, thus purchasing security to himself by a rational and prudent conduct. (262) At length the king gave him leave to dig a well without disturbance. He named this well Rehoboth, which denotes *a large space*; but of the former wells, one was called Escon, which denotes *strife*; the other Sitenna, which name signifies *enmity*.

(263) It was now that Isaac's affairs increased, and his power was in a flourishing condition; and this from his great riches. But Abimelech, thinking Isaac throve in opposition to him, while their living together made them suspicious of each other, and Isaac's retiring showing a secret enmity also, he was afraid that his former friendship with Isaac would not secure him, if Isaac should endeavour to revenge the injuries he had formerly offered him; he therefore renewed his friendship with him, and brought with him Philoc, one of his generals. (264) And when he had obtained everything he desired, by reason of Isaac's good nature, who preferred the earlier friendship Abimelech had shown to himself and his father to his later wrath against him, he returned home.

(265) Now when Esau, one of the sons of Isaac, whom the father principally loved, was now come to the age of forty years, he married Adah, the daughter of Helon, and Aholibamah, the daughter of Esebeon, which Helon and Esebeon were great lords among the Canaanites, thereby taking upon himself the authority, and pretending to have dominion over his own marriages, without so much as asking the advice of his father; (266) for had Isaac been the arbitrator, he had not given him leave to marry thus, for he was not pleased with contracting any alliance with the people of that country; but not caring to be uneasy to his son, by commanding him to put away these wives, he resolved to be silent.

(267) But when he was old and could not see at all, he called Esau to him, and told him, that besides his blindness and the disorder of his eyes, his very old age hindered him from his worship of God [by sacrifice]; (268) he bid him therefore to go out a-hunting, and when he had caught as much venison as he

could, to prepare him a supper, that after this he might make supplication to God, to be to him a supporter and an assister during the whole time of his life; saying, that it was uncertain when he should die, and that he was desirous, by prayers for him, to procure, beforehand, God to be merciful to him.

(269) Accordingly Esau went out a-hunting; but Rebeka thinking it proper to have the supplication made for obtaining the favour of God to Jacob and that without the consent of Isaac, bid him kill kids of the goats, and prepare a supper. So Jacob obeyed his mother, according to all her instructions. (270) Now when the supper was got ready, he took a goat's skin, and put it about his arm, that by reason of its hairy roughness, he might by his father be believed to be Esau; for they being twins, and in all things else alike, differed only in this thing. This was done out of his fear, that before his father had made his supplications, he should be caught in his evil practice; and lest he should, on the contrary, provoke his father to curse him. So he brought in the supper to his father. (271) Isaac perceiving, by the peculiarity of his voice, who he was, called his son to him, who gave him his hand, which was covered with the goat's skin. When Isaac felt that, he said, 'Thy voice is like the voice of Jacob, yet, because of the thickness of thy hair, thou seemest to be Esau.' (272) So suspecting no deceit, he ate the supper, and betook himself to his prayers and intercessions with God; and said, 'O Lord of all ages, and Creator of all substance; for it was thou that didst propose to my father great plenty of good things, and hast vouchsafed to bestow on me what I have; and hast promised to my posterity to be their kind supporter, and to bestow on them still greater blessings – (273) do thou, therefore, confirm these thy promises, and do not overlook me, because of my present weak condition, on account of which I most earnestly pray to thee. Be gracious to this my son, and preserve him, and keep him from everything that is evil. Give him a happy life and the possession of as many good things as thy power is able to bestow. Make him terrible to his enemies, and honourable and beloved among his friends!'

(274) Thus did Isaac pray to God, thinking his prayers had been made for Esau. He had but just finished them, when Esau came in from hunting; and when Isaac perceived his mistake, he was silent; but Esau required that he might be made partaker of the like blessing from his father that his brother had partook of; (275) but his father refused it because all his prayers had been spent upon Jacob; so Esau lamented the mistake. However, his father being grieved at his weeping said, that 'he should excel in hunting and strength of body, in arms, and all such sorts of work; and should obtain glory forever on those accounts, he and his posterity after him; but still should serve his brother.'

(276) Now the mother delivered Jacob, when she was afraid that his brother would inflict some punishment upon him, because of the mistake about the prayers of Isaac; for she persuaded her husband to take a wife for

Jacob out of Mesopotamia, of her own kindred, (277) Esau having married already Basemmath, the daughter of Ismael, without his father's consent; for Isaac did not like the Canaanites, so that he disapproved of Esau's former marriages, which made him take Basemmath to wife, in order to please him and indeed he had a great affection for her.

CHAPTER 19

(278) Now Jacob was sent by his mother to Mesopotamia, in order to marry Laban her brother's daughter (which marriage was permitted by Isaac, on account of his obsequiousness to the desires of his wife); and he accordingly journeyed through the land of Canaan; and because he hated the people of that country, he would not lodge with any of them, (279) but took up his lodging in the open air, and laid his head on a heap of stones that he had gathered together. At which time he saw in his sleep such a vision standing by him: heaven, and persons descending upon the ladder that seemed more excellent than human; and at last God himself stood above it, and was plainly visible to him; who, calling him by his name, spake to him in these words:

(280) 'O Jacob, it is not fit for thee, who art the son of a good father, and grandson of one who had obtained a great reputation for his eminent virtue, to be dejected at thy present circumstances, but to hope for better times, (281) for thou shalt have great abundance of all good things by my assistance; for I brought Abraham hither out of Mesopotamia, when he was driven away by his kinsmen, and I made thy father a happy man; nor will I bestow a lesser degree of happiness on thyself; (282) be of good courage, therefore, and under my conduct proceed on this thy journey, for the marriage thou goest so zealously about shall be consummated; and thou shalt have children of good characters, but their multitude shall be innumerable; and they shall leave what they have to a still more numerous posterity, to whom, and to whose posterity, I give the dominion of all the land, and their posterity shall fill the entire earth and sea, so far as the sun beholds them; (283) but do not thou fear any danger, nor be afraid of the many labours thou must undergo, for by my providence I will direct thee what thou art to do in the time present, and still much more in the time to come.'

(284) Such were the predictions which God made to Jacob; whereupon he became very joyful at what he had seen and heard: and he poured oil on the stones, because on them the prediction of such great benefits was made. He also vowed a vow, that he would offer sacrifices upon them, if he lived and returned safe; and if he came again in such a condition, he would give the tithe of what he had gotten to God. He also judged the place to be honourable, and gave it the name of Bethel, which, in the Greek, is interpreted, *The House of God*.

(285) So he proceeded on his journey to Mesopotamia, and at length came to Haran; and meeting with shepherds in the suburbs, with boys grown up, and maidens sitting about a certain well, he stayed with them, as wanting water to drink; and beginning to discourse with them, he asked them whether they knew such a one as Laban, and whether he was still alive. (286) Now they all said they knew him, for he was not so inconsiderable a person as to be unknown to any of them; and that his daughter fed her father's flock together with them; and that indeed they wondered that she was not yet come, for by her means thou mightest learn more exactly whatever thou desirest to know about that family. While they were saying this the damsel came, and the other shepherds that came down along with her. (287) Then they showed her Jacob, and told her that he was a stranger, who came to inquire about her father's affairs. But she, as pleased, after the custom of children, with Jacob's coming, asked him who he was, and whence he came to them, and what it was he lacked, that he came thither. She also wished it might he in their power to supply the wants he came about.

(288) But Jacob was quite overcome, not so much by their kindred, nor by that affection which might arise thence, as by his love to the damsel, and his surprise at her beauty, which was so flourishing, as few of the women of that age could vie with. He said then, 'There is a relation between thee and me, elder than either thy or my birth, if thou be the daughter of Laban; (289) for Abraham was the son of Terah, as well as Haran and Nahor. Of the last of whom (Nahor) Bethuel thy grandfather was the son. Isaac my father was the son of Abraham and of Sarah, who was the daughter of Haran. But there is a nearer and later cement of mutual kindred which we bear to one another, (290) for my mother Rebeka was sister to Laban thy father, both by the same father and mother; I therefore and thou are cousin-germans; and I am now come to salute you, and to renew that affinity which is proper between us.' (291) Upon this the damsel, at the mention of Rebeka, as usually happens to young persons, wept, and that out of the kindness she had for her father, and embraced Jacob, she having learned an account of Rebeka from her father, and knew that her parents loved to hear her name; (292) and when she had saluted him, she said that 'he brought the most desirable and greatest pleasures to her father, with all their family, who was always mentioning his mother, and always thinking of her, and her alone; and that this will make thee equal in his eyes to any advantageous circumstances whatsoever.' Then she bid him go to her father, and follow her while she conducted him to him; and not to deprive him of such a pleasure, by staying any longer away from him.

(293) When she had said thus, she brought him to Laban; and being owned by his uncle, he was secure himself, as being among his friends; and he brought a great deal of pleasure to them by his unexpected coming. (294) But a little

while afterward, Laban told him that he could not express in words the joy he had at his coming; but still he inquired of him the occasion of his coming, and why he left his aged mother and father, when they wanted to be taken care of by him; and that he would afford him all the assistance he wanted. (295) Then Jacob gave him an account of the whole occasion of his journey, and told him, 'that Isaac had two sons that were twins, himself and Esau; who, because he failed of his father's prayers, which by his mother's wisdom were put up for him, sought to kill him, as deprived of the kingdom which was to be given him of God, and of the blessings for which their father prayed; (296) and that this was the occasion of his coming hither, as his mother had commanded him to do; for we are all (says he) brethren one to another; but our mother esteems an alliance with your family more than she does one with the families of the country; so I look upon yourself and God to be the supporters of my travels, and think myself safe in my present circumstances.'

(297) Now Laban promised to treat him with great humanity, both on account of his ancestors, and particularly for the sake of his mother, towards whom, he said, he would show his kindness, even though she were absent, by taking care of him; for he assured him he would make him the head shepherd of his flock, and give him authority sufficient for that purpose; and when he should have a mind to return to his parents, he would send him back with presents, and this in as honourable a manner as the nearness of their relation should require. (298) This Jacob heard gladly; and said he would willingly, and with pleasure, undergo any sort of pains while he tarried with him, but desired Rachel to wife, as the reward of those pains, who was not only on other accounts esteemed by him, but also because she was the means of his coming to him; for he said he was forced by the love of the damsel to make this proposal. (299) Laban was well pleased with this agreement, and consented to give the damsel to him, as not desirous to meet with any better son-in-law; and said he would do this, if he would stay with him some time, for he was not willing to send his daughter to be among the Canaanites, for he repented of the alliance he had made already by marrying his sister there. (300) And when Jacob had given his consent to this, he agreed to stay seven years; for so many years he had resolved to serve his father-in-law, that, having given a specimen of his virtue, it might be better known what sort of a man he was: and Jacob accepting of his terms, after the time was over he made the wedding feast; (301) and when it was night, without Jacob's perceiving it, he put his other daughter into bed to him, who was both elder than Rachel, and of no comely countenance: Jacob lay with her that night, as being both in drink and in the dark. However, when it was day he knew what had been done to him; and he reproached Laban for his unfair proceeding with him; (302) who asked pardon for that necessity which forced him to do what he did; for he did not give him Lea out of any ill design,

but as overcome by another greater necessity; that, notwithstanding this, nothing should hinder him from marrying Rachel; but that when he had served another seven years he would give him her whom he loved. Jacob submitted to this condition, for his love to the damsel did not permit him to do otherwise; and when another seven years were gone, he took Rachel to wife.

(303) Now each of these had handmaids, by their father's donation. Zilpha was handmaid to Lea, and Bilha to Rachel; by no means slaves, but however subject to their mistresses. Now Lea was sorely troubled at her husband's love to her sister; and she expected she should be better esteemed if she bare him children; so she entreated God perpetually; (304) and when she had borne a son, and her husband was on that account better reconciled to her, she named her son Reubel, because *God had had mercy upon her, in giving her a son*; for that is the signification of this name. After some time she bare three more sons: Simeon, which name signifies *that God had hearkened to her prayer*. Then she bare Levi, *the confirmer of their friendship*. After him was born Judah, which denotes *thanksgiving*. (305) But Rachel, fearing lest the fruitfulness of her sister should make herself enjoy a lesser share of Jacob's affections, put to bed to him her handmaid Bilha; by whom Jacob had Dan; one may interpret that name into the Greek tongue, *divine judgment*. And after him Nepthalim, as it were, *unconquerable in stratagems*, since Rachel tried to conquer the fruitfulness of her sister by this stratagem. (306) Accordingly, Lea took the same method, and used a counter-stratagem to that of her sister; for she put to bed to him her own handmaid. Jacob therefore had by Zilpha a son, whose name was Gad, which may be interpreted *fortune;* and after him Asher, which may be called *a happy man*, because he added glory to Lea. (307) Now Reubel, the eldest son of Lea, brought apples of mandrakes to his mother. When Rachel saw them, she desired that she would give her the apples, for she longed to eat them; but when she refused, and bid her be content that she had deprived her of the benevolence she ought to have had from her husband, Rachel, in order to mitigate her sister's anger said she would yield her husband to her; and he should lie with her that evening. (308) She accepted of the favour; and Jacob slept with Lea, by the favour of Rachel. She bare then these sons: Issachar, denoting *one born by hire*; and Zabulon, *one born as a pledge of benevolence towards her;* and a daughter, Dina. After some time Rachel had a son, named Joseph, which signified *there should be another added to him*.

(309) Now Jacob fed the flocks of Laban, his father-in-law, all this time, being twenty years; after which he desired leave of his father-in-law to take his wives and go home; but when his father-in-law would not give him leave, he contrived to do it secretly. (310) He made trial, therefore, of the disposition of his wives, what they thought of this journey; when they appeared glad, and approved of it. Rachel took along with her the images of the gods which,

according to their laws, they used to worship in their own country, and ran away together with her sister. The children also of them both, and the handmaids, and what possessions they had, went along with them. (311) Jacob also drove away half the cattle, without letting Laban know of it beforehand; but the reason why Rachel took the images of the gods, although Jacob had taught her to despise such worship of those gods, was this, that in case they were pursued, and taken by her father, she might have recourse to these images, in order obtain his pardon.

(312) But Laban, after one day's time, being acquainted with Jacob's and his daughters' departure, was much troubled, and pursued after them, leading a band of men with him; and on the seventh day overtook them, and found them resting on a certain hill; (313) and then indeed he did not meddle with them, for it was eventide; but God stood by him in a dream, and warned him to receive his son-in-law and his daughters in a peaceable manner, and not to venture upon anything rashly, or in wrath to them, but to make a league with Jacob; and he told him, that if he despised their small number, and attacked them in a hostile manner, he would assist them. (314) When Laban had been thus forewarned by God, he called Jacob to him the next day, in order to treat with him, and showed him what dream he had; in dependence whereupon he came confidently to him, and began to accuse him, alleging that he had entertained him when he was poor, and in want of all things, and had given him plenty of all things which he had. 'For,' said he, 'I have joined my daughters to thee in marriage, and supposed that thy kindness to me would be greater than before; (315) but thou hast had no regard to either thy mother's relation to me, nor to the affinity now newly contracted between us; nor to those wives whom thou hast married; nor to those children, of whom I am the grandfather. Thou hast treated me as an enemy, by driving away my cattle, and by persuading my daughters to run away from their father, (316) and by carrying home those sacred paternal images which were worshipped by my forefathers, and have been honoured with the like worship which they paid them, by myself. In short, thou hast done this whilst thou art my kinsman, and my sister's son, and the husband of my daughters, and wast hospitably treated by me, and didst eat at my table.' (317) When Laban had said this, Jacob made his defence: that he was not the only person in whom God had implanted the love of his native country, but that he had made it natural to all men; and that therefore it was but reasonable that, after so long time, he should go back to it. (318) 'But as to the prey, of whose driving away thou accusest me, if any other person were the arbitrator, thou wouldst be found in the wrong; for, instead of those thanks I ought to have had from thee, for both keeping thy cattle and increasing them, how is it that thou art unjustly angry at me because I have taken, and have with me a small portion of them? But then, as to thy

daughters, take notice, that it is not through any evil practices of mine that they follow me in my return home, but from that just affection which wives naturally have to their husbands. They follow, therefore, not so properly myself as their own children.' (319) And thus far of his apology was made, in order to clear himself of having acted unjustly. To which he added his own complaint and accusation of Laban, saying, While I was thy sister's son, and thou hadst given me thy daughters in marriage thou hast worn me out with thy harsh commands, and detained me twenty years under them. That, indeed, which was required in order to my marrying thy daughters, hard as it was, I own to have been tolerable; but as to those that were put upon me after those marriages, they were worse, and such indeed as an enemy would have avoided.' (320) For certainly Laban had used Jacob very ill; for when he saw that God was assisting to Jacob in all that he desired, he promised him, that of the young cattle which should be born, he should have sometimes what was of a white colour, and sometimes what should be of a black colour; (321) but when those that came to Jacob's share proved numerous, he did not keep his faith with him, but said he would give them to him the next year, because of his envying him the multitude of his possessions. He promised him as before, because he thought such an increase was not to be expected; but when it appeared to be fact, he deceived him.

(322) But then, as to the sacred images, he bid him search for them; and when Laban accepted of the offer, Rachel, being informed of it, put those images into that camel's saddle on which she rode, and sat upon it; and said, that her natural purgation hindered her rising up: (323) so Laban left off searching any further, not supposing that his daughter in such circumstances would approach to those images. So he made a league with Jacob, and bound it by oaths, that he would not bear him any malice on account of what had happened; and Jacob made the like league, and promised to love Laban's daughters. (324) And these leagues they confirmed with oaths also, which they made upon certain mountains, whereon they erected a pillar, in the form of an altar; whence that hill is called Gilead; and from thence they call that land the Land of Gilead at this day. Now when they had feasted, after the making of the league, Laban returned home.

CHAPTER 20

(325) Now as Jacob was proceeding on his journey to the land of Canaan, angels appeared to him, and suggested to him good hope of his future condition; and that place he named the Camp of God. And being desirous of knowing what his brother's intentions were to him, he sent messengers, to give him an exact account of everything, as being afraid, on account of the enmities between them. (326) He charged those that were sent, to say to Esau, 'Jacob had thought it wrong to live together with him, while he was in anger against him, and so had gone out of the country; and that he now, thinking the length of time of his absence must have made up their differences, was returning; that he brought with him his wives and his children, with what possessions he had gotten; and delivered himself, with what was most dear to him, into his hands; and should think it his greatest happiness to partake together with his brother of what God had bestowed upon him.' (327) So these messengers told him this message. Upon which Esau was very glad, and met his brother with four hundred men. And Jacob, when he heard that he was coming to meet him with such a number of men, was greatly afraid; however, he committed his hope of deliverance to God; and considered how, in his present circumstances, he might preserve himself and those that were with him, and overcome his enemies if they attacked him injuriously. (328) He therefore distributed his company into parts; some he sent before the rest, and the others he ordered to come close behind, that so, if the first were overpowered when his brother attacked them, they might have those that followed as a refuge to fly unto. (329) And when he had put his company in this order, he sent some of them to carry presents to his brother. The presents were made up of cattle, and a great number of four-footed beasts, of many kinds, such as would be very acceptable to those that received them, on account of their rarity. (330) Those who were sent went at certain intervals of space asunder, that, by following thick one after another, they might appear to be more numerous; that Esau might remit of his anger on account of these presents, if he were still in a passion. Instructions were also given to those that were sent to speak gently to him.

(331) When Jacob had made these appointments all the day, and night came on, he moved on with his company; and, as they were gone over a certain river called Jabboc, Jacob was left behind; and meeting with an angel he wrestled with him, the angel beginning the struggle; but he prevailed over the angel, (332) who used a voice, and spake to him in words, exhorting him to be pleased with what had happened to him, and not to suppose that his victory was a small one, but that he had overcome a divine angel, and to esteem the

victory as a sign of great blessings that should come to him; and that his offspring should never fail; and that no man should be too hard for his power. (333) He also commanded him to be called Israel, which in the Hebrew tongue signifies *one that struggled with the divine angel*. These promises were made at the prayer of Jacob; for when he perceived him to be the angel of God, he desired he would signify to him what should befall him hereafter. And when the angel had said what is before related, he disappeared; (334) but Jacob was pleased with these things, and named the place Phanuel, which signifies, *the face of God*. Now when he felt pain, by this struggling, upon his broad sinew, he abstained from eating that sinew himself afterward; and for his sake it is still not eaten by us.

(335) When Jacob understood that his brother was near, he ordered his wives to go before, each by herself, with the handmaids, that they might see the actions of the men as they were fighting, if Esau were so disposed. He then went up to his brother Esau, and bowed down to him, who had no evil design upon him, (336) but saluted him; and asked him about the company of the children and of the women; and desired, when he had understood all he wanted to know about them, that he would go along with him to their father; but Jacob pretending that the cattle were weary, Esau returned to Seir, for there was his place of habitation; he having named the place Roughness, from his own hairy roughness.

CHAPTER 21

(337) Hereupon Jacob came to the place, till this day called Tents (Succoth); from whence he went to Shechem, which is a city of the Canaanites. Now as the Shechemites were keeping a festival, Dina, who was the only daughter of Jacob, went into the city to see the finery of the women of that country. But when Shechem, the son of Hamor the king, saw her, he defiled her by violence; and, being greatly in love with her, desired of his father that he would procure the damsel to him for a wife: (338) to which desire he condescended, and came to Jacob, desiring him to give leave that his son Shechem might, according to law, marry Dina. But Jacob not knowing how to deny the desire of one of such great dignity, and yet not thinking it lawful to marry his daughter to a stranger, entreated him to give him leave to have a consultation about what he desired him to do. (339) So the king went away, in hopes that Jacob would grant him this marriage. But Jacob informed his sons of the defilement of their sister, and of the address of Hamor; and desired them to give their advice what they should do. Upon this the greatest part said nothing, not knowing what advice to give. But Simeon and Levi, the brethren of the damsel by the same mother, agreed between themselves upon the action

following: (340) it being now the time of a festival, when the Shechemites were employed in ease and feasting, they fell upon the watch when they were asleep, and, coming into the city, slew all the males, as also the king and his son with them, but spared the women; and when they had done this without their father's consent, they brought away their sister.

(341) Now while Jacob was astonished at the greatness of this act, and was severely blaming his sons for it, God stood by him, and bid him be of good courage; but to purify his tents, and to offer those sacrifices which he had vowed to offer when he went first into Mesopotamia, and saw his vision. (342) As he was therefore purifying his followers, he lighted upon the gods of Laban (for he did not before know they were stolen by Rachel); and he hid them in the earth, under an oak, in Shechem; and departing thence, he offered sacrifice at Bethel, the place where he saw his dream, when he went first into Mesopotamia.

(343) And when he was gone thence, and was come over against Ephrata, he there buried Rachel, who died in childbed; she was the only one of Jacob's kindred that had not the honour of burial at Hebron; and when he had mourned for her a great while, he called the son that was born of her Benjamin, because of the sorrow the mother had with him. (344) These are all the children of Jacob, twelve males and one female – of them eight were legitimate, viz., six of Lea, and two of Rachel; and four were of the handmaids, two of each; all whose names have been set down already.

CHAPTER 22

(345) From thence Jacob came to Hebron, a city situate among the Canaanites; and there it was that Isaac lived; and so they lived together for a little while; for as to Rebeka, Jacob did not find her alive. Isaac also died not long after the coming of his son; and was buried by his sons, with his wife, in Hebron, where they had a monument belonging to them from their forefathers. (346) Now Isaac was a man who was beloved of God, and was vouchsafed great instances of providence by God, after Abraham his father, and lived to be exceeding old; for when he had lived virtuously one hundred and eighty-five years, he then died.

BOOK TWO

CHAPTER 1

(1) After the death of Isaac, his sons divided their habitations respectively; nor did they retain what they had before; but Esau departed from the city of Hebron, and left it to his brother, and dwelt in Seir, and ruled over Idumea. He called the country by that name from himself, for he was named Adom; which appellation he got on the following occasion: (2) one day returning from the toil of hunting very hungry (it was when he was a child in age), he lighted on his brother when he was getting ready lentil pottage for his dinner, which was of a very red colour; on which account he the more earnestly longed for it, and desired him to give him some of it to eat: (3) but he made advantage of his brother's hunger, and forced him to resign up to him his birthright; and he, being pinched with famine, resigned it up to him, under an oath. Whence it came that, on account of the redness of this pottage, he was, in way of jest, by his contemporaries, called *Adom*, for the Hebrews call what is red *Adom*; and this was the name given to this country: but the Greeks gave it a more agreeable pronunciation, and named it *Idumea*.

(4) He became the father of five sons; of whom Jaus and Jalomus and Coreus were by one wife, whose name was Alibama; but of the rest, Aliphaz was born to him by Ada, and Raguel by Basemmath: (5) and these were the sons of Esau. Aliphaz had five legitimate sons: Theman, Omer, Saphus, Gotham, and Kanaz; for Amalek was not legitimate, but by a concubine, whose name was Thamna. (6) These dwelt in that part of Idumea which is called Gebalitis, and that denominated from Amalek, Amalekitis; for Idumea was a large country, and did then preserve the name of the whole, while in its several parts it kept the name of its peculiar inhabitants.

CHAPTER 2

(7) It happened that Jacob came to so great happiness as rarely any other person had arrived at. He was richer than the rest of the inhabitants of that country; and was at once envied and admired for such virtuous sons, for they were deficient in nothing, but were of great souls, both for labouring with their hands and enduring of toil, and shrewd also in understanding; (8) and God exercised such a providence over him, and such a care of his happiness, as to bring him the greatest blessings, even out of what appeared to be the most

sorrowful condition; and to make him the cause of our forefathers' departure out of Egypt, him and his posterity. The occasion was this: (9) when Jacob had his son Joseph born to him by Rachel, his father loved him above the rest of his sons, both because of the beauty of his body and the virtues of his mind; for he excelled the rest in prudence. (10) This affection of his father excited the envy and the hatred of his brethren; as did also his dreams which he saw, and related to his father and to them, which foretold his future happiness, it being usual with mankind to envy their very nearest relations such their prosperity. Now the visions which Joseph saw in his sleep were these:

(11) When they were in the middle of harvest, and Joseph was sent by his father, with his brethren, to gather the fruits of the earth, he saw a vision in a dream, but greatly exceeding the accustomary appearances that come when we are asleep; which, when he was got up, he told his brethren, that they might judge what it portended. He said he saw the last night, that his wheat sheaf stood still in the place where he set it, but that their sheaves ran to bow down to it, as servants bow down to their masters; (12) but as soon as they perceived the vision foretold that he should obtain power and great wealth, and that his power should be in opposition to them, they gave no interpretation of it to Joseph, as if the dream were not by them understood: but they prayed that no part of what they suspected to be its meaning might come to pass; and they bare a still greater hatred to him on that account.

(13) But God, in opposition to their envy, sent a second vision to Joseph, which was much more wonderful than the former; for it seemed to him that the sun took with him the moon and the rest of the stars, and came down to the earth, and bowed down to him. (14) He told the vision to his father, and that as suspecting nothing of ill will from his brethren, when they were there also, and desired him to interpret what it should signify. (15) Now Jacob was pleased with the dream; for, considering the prediction in his mind, and shrewdly and wisely guessing at its meaning, he rejoiced at the great things thereby signified, because it declared the future happiness of his son; and that, by the blessing of God, the time would come when he should be honoured, and thought worthy of worship by his parents and brethren, (16) as guessing that the moon and sun were like his mother and father; the former, as she that gave increase and nourishment to all things, and the latter, he that gave form and other powers to them; and that the stars were like his brethren, since they were eleven in number, as were the stars that receive their power from the sun and moon.

(17) And thus did Jacob make a judgment of this vision, and that a shrewd one also; but these interpretations caused very great grief to Joseph's brethren; and they were affected to him hereupon as if he were a certain stranger that was to have those good things which were signified by the dreams, and not as one

that was a brother, with whom it was probable they should be joint partakers; and as they had been partners in the same parentage, so should they be of the same happiness. (18) They also resolved to kill the lad; and having fully ratified that intention of theirs, as soon as their collection of the fruits was over, they went to Shechem, which is a country good for feeding of cattle and for pasturage; there they fed their flocks, without acquainting their father with their removal thither; (19) whereupon he had melancholy suspicions about them, as being ignorant of his sons' condition, and receiving no messenger from the flocks that could inform him of the true state they were in; so, because he was in great fear about them, he sent Joseph to the flocks, to learn the circumstances his brethren were in, and to bring him word how they did.

CHAPTER 3

(20) Now these brethren rejoiced as soon as they saw their brother coming to them, not indeed as at the presence of a near relation, or as at the presence of one sent by their father, but as at the presence of an enemy, and one that by divine providence was delivered into their hands, and they already resolved to kill him, and not let slip the opportunity that lay before them; (21) but when Reubel, the eldest of them, saw them thus disposed, and that they had agreed together to execute their purpose, he tried to restrain them, showing them the heinous enterprise they were going about, and the horrid nature of it; (22) that this action would appear wicked in the sight of God, and impious before men, even though they should kill one not related to them, but much more flagitious and detestable to appear to have slain their own brother; by which act the father must be treated unjustly in the son's slaughter, and the mother also be in perplexity while she laments that her son is taken away from her, and this not in a natural way neither. (23) So he entreated them to have a regard to their own consciences, and wisely to consider what mischief would betide them upon the death of so good a child, and their youngest brother; that they would also fear God, who was already both a spectator and a witness of the designs they had against their brother; that he would love them if they abstained from this act, and yielded to repentance and amendment; (24) but in case they proceeded to do the fact, all sorts of punishments would overtake them from God for this murder of their brother, since they polluted his providence, which was everywhere present, and which did not overlook what was done, either in deserts or in cities; for wheresoever a man is, there ought he to suppose that God is also. (25) He told them further, that their consciences would be their enemies, if they attempted to go through so wicked an enterprise, which they can never avoid, whether it be a good conscience, or whether it be such an one as they will have within them when once they have

killed their brother. (26) He also added this besides to what he had before said, that it was not a righteous thing to kill a brother, though he had injured them; that it is a good thing to forget the actions of such near friends, even in things wherein they might seem to have offended; but that they were going to kill Joseph, who had been guilty of nothing that was ill towards them, in whose case the infirmity of his small age should rather procure him mercy, and move them to unite together in the care of his preservation; (27) that the cause of killing him made the act itself much worse, while they determined to take him off out of envy at his future prosperity, an equal share of which they would naturally partake while he enjoyed it, since they were to him not strangers, but the nearest relations, (28) for they might reckon upon what God bestowed upon Joseph as their own; and that it was fit for them to believe that the anger of God would for this cause be more severe upon them, if they slew him who was judged by God to be worthy of that prosperity which was to be hoped for; and while, by murdering him, they made it impossible for God to bestow it upon him.

(29) Reubel said these and many other things, and used entreaties to them, and thereby endeavoured to divert them from the murder of their brother; but when he saw that his discourse had not mollified them at all, and that they made haste to do the fact, he advised them to alleviate the wickedness they were going about, in the manner of taking Joseph off; (30) for as he had exhorted them first, when they were going to revenge themselves, to be dissuaded from doing it, so, since the sentence for killing their brother had prevailed, he said that they would not, however, be so grossly guilty, if they would be persuaded to follow his present advice, which would include what they were so eager about, but was not so very bad, but, in the distress they were in, of a lighter nature. (31) He begged of them, therefore, not to kill their brother with their own hands, but to cast him into the pit that was hard by, and so to let him die; by which they would gain so much, that they would not defile their own hands with his blood. To this the young men readily agreed; so Reubel took the lad and tied him to a cord, and let him down gently into the pit, for it had no water at all in it; who, when he had done this, went his way to seek for such pasturage as was fit for feeding his flocks.

(32) But Judas, being one of Jacob's sons also, seeing some Arabians, of the posterity of Ismael, carrying spices and Syrian wares out of the land of Gilead to the Egyptians, after Reubel was gone, advised his brethren to draw Joseph out of the pit, and sell him to the Arabians; (33) for if he should die among strangers a great way off, they should be freed from this barbarous action. This, therefore, was resolved on; so they drew Joseph up out of the pit, and sold him to the merchants for twenty pounds. He was now seventeen years old; (34) but Reubel, coming in the night-time to the pit, resolved to save Joseph, without

the privity of his brethren; and when, upon his calling to him, he made no answer, he was afraid that they had destroyed him after he was gone; of which he complained to his brethren; but when they had told him what they had done, Reubel left off his mourning.

(35) When Joseph's brethren had done thus to him, they considered what they should do to escape the suspicions of their father. Now they had taken away from Joseph the coat which he had on when he came to them at the time they let him down into the pit; so they thought proper to tear that coat to pieces, and to dip it into goat's blood, and then to carry it and show it to their father, that he might believe he was destroyed by wild beasts; (36) and when they had so done, they came to the old man, but this not till what had happened to his son had already come to his knowledge. Then they said that they had not seen Joseph, nor knew what mishap had befallen him; but that they had found his coat bloody and torn to pieces, whence they had a suspicion that he had fallen among wild beasts, and so perished, if that was the coat he had on when he came from home. (37) Now Jacob had before some better hopes that his son was only made a captive; but now he laid aside that notion, and supposed that this coat was an evident argument that he was dead, for he well remembered that this was the coat he had on when he sent him to his brethren; so he hereafter lamented the lad as now dead, (38) and as if he had been the father of no more than one, without taking any comfort in the rest; and so he was also affected with his misfortune before he met with Joseph's brethren, when he also conjectured that Joseph was destroyed by wild beasts. He sat down also clothed in sackcloth and in heavy affliction, insomuch that he found no ease when his sons comforted him, neither did his pains remit by length of time.

CHAPTER 4

(39) Now Potiphar, an Egyptian, who was chief cook to king Pharaoh, bought Joseph of the merchants, who sold him to him. He had him in the greatest honour, and taught him the learning that became a free man, and gave him leave to make use of a diet better than was allotted to slaves. He entrusted also the care of his house to him. (40) So he enjoyed these advantages, yet did not he leave that virtue which he had before, upon such a change of his condition; but he demonstrated that wisdom was able to govern the uneasy passions of life, in such as have it in reality, and do not only put it on for a show, under a present state of prosperity.

(41) For when his master's wife was fallen in love with him, both on account of his beauty of body and his dexterous management of affairs; and supposed, that if she should make it known to him, she could easily persuade him to

come and lie with her, and that he would look upon it as a piece of happy fortune that his mistress should entreat him, (42) as regarding that state of slavery he was in, and not his moral character, which continued after his condition was changed; so she made known her naughty inclinations, and spake to him about lying with her. However, he rejected her entreaties, not thinking it agreeable to religion to yield so far to her, as to do what would tend to the affront and injury of him that purchased him, and had vouchsafed him so great honours. (43) He on the contrary exhorted her to govern that passion; and laid before her the impossibility of her obtaining her desires, which he thought might be conquered, if she had no hope of succeeding; and he said that as to himself, he would endure anything whatever before he would be persuaded to it; for although it was fit for a slave, as he was, to do nothing contrary to his mistress, he might well be excused in a case where the contradiction was to such sort of commands only. (44) But this opposition of Joseph, when she did not expect it, made her still more violent in her love to him; and as she was sorely beset with this naughty passion, so she resolved to compass her design by a second attempt.

(45) When, therefore, there was a public festival coming on, in which it was the custom for women to come to the public solemnity, she pretended to her husband that she was sick, as contriving an opportunity for solitude and leisure, that she might entreat Joseph again; which opportunity being obtained, she used more kind words to him than before, (46) and said that it had been good for him to have yielded to her first solicitation, and to have given her no repulse, both because of the reverence he ought to bear to her dignity who solicited him, and because of the vehemence of her passion; by which she was forced, though she were his mistress, to condescend beneath her dignity; but that he may now, by taking more prudent advice, wipe off the imputation of his former folly; (47) for, whether it were that he expected the repetition of her solicitations she had now made, and that with greater earnestness than before, for that she had pretended sickness on this very account, and had preferred this conversation before the festival and its solemnity; or whether he opposed her former discourses, as not believing she could be in earnest, she now gave him sufficient security, by thus repeating her application, that she meant not in the least by fraud to impose upon him; (48) and assured him, that if he complied with her affections, he might expect the enjoyment of the advantages he already had; and if he were submissive to her, he should have still greater advantages; but that he must look for revenge and hatred from her, in case he rejected her desires, and preferred the reputation of chastity before his mistress; (49) for that he would gain nothing by such procedure, because she would then become his accuser, and would falsely pretend to her husband that he had attempted her chastity; and that

Potiphar would hearken to her words rather than to his, let his be ever so agreeable to the truth.

(50) When the woman had said thus, and even with tears in her eyes, neither did pity dissuade Joseph from his chastity, nor did fear compel him to a compliance with her; but he opposed her solicitations, and did not yield to her threatenings, and was afraid to do an ill thing, and chose to undergo the sharpest punishment rather than to enjoy his present advantages, by doing what his own conscience knew would justly deserve that he should die for it. (51) He also put her in mind that she was a married woman, and that she ought to cohabit with her husband only; and desired her to suffer these considerations to have more weight with her than the short pleasure of lustful dalliance, which would bring her to repentance afterwards, would cause trouble to her, and yet would not amend what had been done amiss. He also suggested to her the fear she would be in lest they should be caught; and that the advantage of concealment was uncertain, and that only while the wickedness was not known [would there be any quiet for them]; (52) but that she might have the enjoyment of her husband's company without any danger; and he told her, that in the company of her husband she might have great boldness from a good conscience, both before God and before men; nay, that she would act better like his mistress, and make use of her authority over him better while she persisted in her chastity, than when they were both ashamed for what wickedness they had been guilty of; and that it is much better to depend on a good life, well acted, and known to have been so, than upon the hopes of the concealment of evil practices.

(53) Joseph, by saying this, and more, tried to restrain the violent passion of the woman, and to reduce her affections within the rules of reason; but she grew more ungovernable and earnest in the matter; and since she despaired of persuading him, she laid her hands upon him, and had a mind to force him. (54) But as soon as Joseph had got away from her anger, leaving also his garment with her, for he left that to her and leaped out of her chamber, she was greatly afraid lest he should discover her lewdness to her husband, and greatly troubled at the affront he had offered her; so she resolved to be beforehand with him, and to accuse Joseph falsely to Potiphar, and by that means to revenge herself on him for his pride and contempt of her; and she thought it a wise thing in itself, and also becoming a woman, thus to prevent his accusation. (55) Accordingly she sat sorrowful and in confusion, framing herself so hypocritically and angrily, that the sorrow, which was really for her being disappointed of her lust, might appear to be for the attempt upon her chastity; so that when her husband came home, and was disturbed at the sight of her, and inquired what was the cause of the disorder she was in, she began to accuse Joseph: and, 'O, husband,' said she, 'mayest thou not live a day longer if thou dost not punish the wicked slave who has desired to defile thy bed; (56) who

has neither minded who he was when he came to our house, so as to behave himself with modesty; nor has he been mindful of what favours he had received from thy bounty (as he must be an ungrateful man indeed, unless he, in every respect, carry himself in a manner agreeable to us): this man, I say, laid a private design to abuse thy wife, and this at the time of a festival, observing when thou wouldst be absent. So that it now is clear that his modesty, as it appeared to be formerly, was only because of the restraint he was in out of fear of thee, but that he was not really of a good disposition. (57) This has been occasioned by his being advanced to honour beyond what he deserved and what he hoped for; insomuch that he concluded, that he who was deemed fit to be trusted with thy estate and the government of thy family, and was preferred above thy eldest servants, might be allowed to touch thy wife also.' (58) Thus when she had ended her discourse, she showed him his garment, as if he then left it with her when he attempted to force her. But Potiphar not being able to disbelieve what his wife's tears showed, and what his wife said, and what he saw himself, and being seduced by his love to his wife, did not set himself about the examination of the truth, (59) but taking it for granted that his wife was a modest woman, and condemning Joseph as a wicked man, he threw him into the malefactors' prison; and had a still higher opinion of his wife, and bare her witness that she was a woman of a becoming modesty and chastity.

CHAPTER 5

(60) Now Joseph, commending all his affairs to God, did not betake himself to make his defence, nor to give an account of the exact circumstances of the fact, but silently underwent the bonds and the distress he was in, firmly believing that God, who knew the cause of his affliction and the truth of the fact, would be more powerful than those that inflicted the punishments upon him: a proof of whose providence he quickly received; (61) for the keeper of the prison taking notice of his care and fidelity in the affairs he had set him about, and the dignity of his countenance, relaxed his bonds, and thereby made his heavy calamity lighter and more supportable to him: he also permitted him to make use of a diet better than that of the rest of the prisoners. (62) Now, as his fellow prisoners, when their hard labours were over, fell to discoursing once among another, as is usual in such as are equal sufferers, and to inquire one of another, what were the occasions of their being condemned to a prison, (63) among them the king's cupbearer, and one that had been respected by him, was put in bonds, on the king's anger at him. This man was under the same bonds with Joseph, and grew more familiar with him; and upon his observing that Joseph had a better understanding than the rest had, he told him of a dream he had,

and desired he would interpret its meaning, complaining that, besides the afflictions he underwent from the king, God did also add to him trouble from his dreams.

(64) He therefore said, that in his sleep he saw three clusters of grapes hanging upon three branches of a vine, large already, and ripe for gathering; and that he squeezed them into a cup which the king held in his hand; and when he had strained the wine, he gave it to the king to drink, and that he received it from him with a pleasant countenance. (65) This, he said, was what he saw; and he desired Joseph, that if he had any portion of understanding in such matters, he would tell him what this vision foretold: who bid him be of good cheer, and expect to be loosed from his bonds in three days' time, because the king desired his service, and was about to restore him to it again; (66) for he let him know that God bestows the fruit of the vine upon men for good; which wine is poured out to him, and is the pledge of fidelity and mutual confidence among men; and puts an end to their quarrels, takes away passion and grief out of the minds of them that use it, and makes them cheerful. (67) 'Thou sayest that thou didst squeeze this wine from three clusters of grapes with thine hands, and that the king received it: know, therefore, that this vision is for thy good, and foretells a release from thy present distress within the same number of days as the branches had whence thou gatheredst thy grapes in thy sleep. (68) However, remember what prosperity I have foretold thee when thou hast found it true by experience; and when thou art in authority, do not overlook us in this prison, wherein thou wilt leave us when thou art gone to the place we have foretold; for we are not in prison for any crime, (69) but for the sake of our virtue and sobriety are we condemned to suffer the penalty of malefactors, and because we are not willing to injure him that has thus distressed us, though it were for our own pleasure.' The cupbearer, therefore, as was natural to do, rejoiced to hear such an interpretation of his dream, and waited the completion of what had been thus shown him beforehand.

(70) But another servant there was of the king, who had been chief baker, and was now bound in prison with the cupbearer; he also was in good hope, upon Joseph's interpretation of the other's vision, for he had seen a dream also: so he desired that Joseph would tell him what the visions he had seen the night before might mean. (71) They were these that follow: 'Methought,' says he, 'I carried three baskets upon my head; two were full of loaves, and the third full of sweetmeats and other eatables, such as are prepared for kings; but that the fowls came flying, and eat them all up, and had no regard to my attempt to drive them away;' – (72) and he expected a prediction like to that of the cupbearer. But Joseph, considering and reasoning about the dream, said to him, that he would willingly be an interpreter of good events to him, and not of such as his dream denounced to him; but he told him that he had only three

days in all to live, for that the [three] baskets signify, (73) that on the third day he should be crucified, and devoured by fowls, while he was not able to help himself. Now both these dreams had the same several events that Joseph foretold they should have, and this to both the parties; for on the third day before mentioned, when the king solemnised his birthday, he crucified the chief baker, but set the butler free from his bonds, and restored him to his former ministration.

(74) But God freed Joseph from his confinement, after he had endured his bonds two years, and had received no assistance from the cupbearer, who did not remember what he had said to him formerly; and God contrived this method of deliverance for him. (75) Pharaoh the king had seen in his sleep the same evening two visions, and after them had the interpretations of them both given him. He had forgotten the latter, but retained the dreams themselves. Being therefore troubled at what he had seen, for it seemed to him to be all of a melancholy nature, the next day he called together the wisest men among the Egyptians, desiring to learn from them the interpretation of his dreams. (76) But when they hesitated about them, the king was so much the more disturbed. And now it was that the memory of Joseph, and his skill in dreams, came into the mind of the king's cupbearer, when he saw the confusion that Pharaoh was in; (77) so he came and mentioned Joseph to him, as also the vision he had seen in prison, and how the event proved as he had said; as also that the chief baker was crucified on the very same day, and that this also happened to him according to the interpretation of Joseph. (78) That Joseph himself was laid on bonds by Potiphar, who was his head cook, as a slave; but, he said, he was one of the noblest of the stock of the Hebrews; and said, further, his father lived in great splendour. 'If, therefore, thou wilt send for him, and not despise him on the score of his misfortunes, thou wilt learn what thy dreams signify.' (79) So the king commanded that they should bring Joseph into his presence; and those who received the command came and brought him with them, having taken care of his habit, that it might be decent, as the king had enjoined them to do.

(80) But the king took him by the hand; and, 'O young man,' says he, 'for my servant bears witness that thou art at present the best and most skilful person I can consult with, vouchsafe me the same favours which thou bestowedst on this servant of mine, and tell me what events they are which the visions of my dreams foreshow; and I desire thee to suppress nothing out of fear, nor to flatter me with lying words, or with what may please me, although the truth should be of a melancholy nature. (81) For it seemed to me that, as I walked by the river, I saw kine fat and very large, seven in number, going from the river to the marshes; and other kine of the same number like them, met them out of the marshes, exceeding lean and ill-favoured, which

ate up the fat and the large kine, and yet were no better than before, and not less miserably pinched with famine. (82) After I had seen this vision, I awaked out of my sleep; and being in disorder, and considering with myself what this appearance should be, I fell asleep again, and saw another dream, much more wonderful than the foregoing, which did still more affright and disturb me: (83) I saw seven ears of corn growing out of one root, having their heads borne down by the weight of the grains, and bending down with the fruit, which was now ripe and fit for reaping; and near these I saw seven other ears of corn, meagre and weak, for want of rain, which fell to eating and consuming those that were fit for reaping, and put me into great astonishment.'

(84) To which Joseph replied: 'This dream,' said he, 'O king, although seen under two forms, signifies one and the same event of things; for when thou sawest the fat kine, which is an animal made for the plough and for labour, devoured by the worser kine, (85) and the ears of corn eaten up by the smaller ears, they foretell a famine, and want of the fruits of the earth for the same number of years, and equal with those when Egypt was in a happy state; and this so far, that the plenty of these years will be spent in the same number of years of scarcity, and that scarcity of necessary provisions will be very difficult to be corrected; (86) as a sign whereof, the ill-favoured kine, when they had devoured the better sort, could not be satisfied. But still God foreshows what is to come upon men, not to grieve them, but that, when they know it beforehand, they may by prudence make the actual experience of what is foretold the more tolerable. If thou, therefore, carefully dispose of the plentiful crops which will come in the former years, thou wilt procure that the future calamity will not be felt by the Egyptians.'

(87) Hereupon the king wondered at the discretion and wisdom of Joseph; and asked him by what means he might so dispense the foregoing plentiful crops, in the happy years, as to make the miserable crops more tolerable. (88) Joseph then added this his advice: To spare the good crops, and not permit the Egyptians to spend them luxuriously; but to reserve what they would have spent in luxury beyond their necessity, against the time of want. He also exhorted him to take the corn of the husbandmen, and give them only so much as will be sufficient for their food. (89) Accordingly Pharaoh being surprised at Joseph, not only for his interpretation of the dream, but for the counsel he had given him, entrusted him with dispensing the corn, with power to do what he thought would be for the benefit of the people of Egypt, and for the benefit of the king, as believing that he who first discovered this method of acting, would prove the best overseer of it. (90) But Joseph having this power given him by the king, with leave to make use of his seal and to wear purple, drove in his chariot through all the land of

Egypt, and took the corn of the husbandmen, allotting as much to everyone as would be sufficient for seed and for food, but without discovering to anyone the reason why he did so.

<h2>CHAPTER 6</h2>

(91) Joseph was now grown up to thirty years of age, and enjoyed great honours from the king, who called him Psothom Phanech, out of regard to his prodigious degree of wisdom; for that name denotes *the revealer of secrets*. He also married a wife of very high quality; for he married the daughter of Petephres, one of the priests of Heliopolis; she was a virgin, and her name was Asenath. (92) By her he had children before the scarcity came on; Manasseh, the elder, which signifies *forgetful*, because his present happiness made him forget his former misfortunes; and Ephraim, the younger, which signifies *restored*, because he was restored to the freedom of his forefathers. (93) Now after Egypt had happily passed over seven years, according to Joseph's interpretation of the dreams, the famine came upon them in the eighth year; and because this misfortune fell upon them when they had no sense of it beforehand, they were all sorely afflicted by it, and came running to the king's gates; (94) and he called upon Joseph, who sold the corn to them, being become confessedly a saviour to the whole multitude of the Egyptians. Nor did he open this market of corn for the people of that country only, but strangers had liberty to buy also, Joseph being willing that all men, who are naturally akin to one another, should have assistance from those that lived in happiness.

(95) Now Jacob also, when he understood that foreigners might come, sent all his sons into Egypt to buy corn; for the land of Canaan was grievously afflicted with the famine and this great misery touched the whole continent. He only retained Benjamin, who was born to him by Rachel, and was of the same mother with Joseph. (96) These sons of Jacob then came into Egypt, and applied themselves to Joseph, wanting to buy corn; for nothing of this kind was done without his approbation, since even then only was the honour that was paid the king himself advantageous to the persons that paid it, when they took care to honour Joseph also. (97) Now when he well knew his brethren, they thought nothing of him; for he was but a youth when he left them, and was now come to an age so much greater, that the lineaments of his face were changed, and he was not known by them; besides this, the greatness of the dignity wherein he appeared, suffered them not so much as to suspect it was he. He now made trial what sentiments they had about affairs of the greatest consequence; (98) for he refused to sell them corn, and said they were come as spies of the king's affairs; and that they came from several countries, and joined

themselves together, and pretended that they were of kin, it not being possible that a private man should breed up so many sons, and those of so great beauty of countenance as they were, such an education of so many children being not easily obtained by kings themselves. (99) Now this he did in order to discover what concerned his father, and what happened to him after his own departure from him, and as desiring to know what was become of Benjamin his brother; for he was afraid that they had ventured on the like wicked enterprise against him that they had done to himself, and had taken him off also.

(100) Now these brethren of his were under distraction and terror, and thought that very great danger hung over them; yet not at all reflecting upon their brother Joseph, and standing firm under the accusations laid against them, they made their defence by Reubel, the eldest of them, who now became their spokesman: (101) 'We come not hither,' said he, 'with any unjust design, nor in order to bring any harm to the king's affairs; we only want to be preserved, as supposing your humanity might be a refuge for us from the miseries which our country labours under, we having heard that you proposed to sell corn not only to your own countrymen, but to strangers also, and that you determined to allow that corn, in order to preserve all that want it; (102) but that we are brethren, and of the same common blood, the peculiar lineaments of our faces, and those not so much different from one another, plainly show. Our father's name is Jacob, an Hebrew man, who had twelve of us for his sons by four wives; which twelve of us, while we were all alive, were a happy family; (103) but when one of our brethren, whose name was Joseph, died, our affairs changed for the worse; for our father could not forbear to make a long lamentation for him; and we are in affliction, both by the calamity of the death of our brother, and the miserable state of our aged father. (104) We are now, therefore, come to buy corn, having entrusted the care of our father, and the provision for our family, to Benjamin, our youngest brother; and if thou sendest to our house thou mayest learn whether we are guilty of the least falsehood in what we say.'

(105) And thus did Reubel endeavour to persuade Joseph to have a better opinion of them. But when he had learned from them that Jacob was alive, and that his brother was not destroyed by them, he for the present put them in prison, as intending to examine more into their affairs when he should be at leisure. But on the third day he brought them out, and said to them, (106) 'Since you constantly affirm that you are not come to do any harm to the king's affairs; that you are brethren, and the sons of the father whom you named, you will satisfy me of the truth of what you say, if you leave one of your company with me, who shall suffer no injury here; and if, when ye have carried corn to your father, you will come to me again, and bring your brother, whom you say you left there, along with you, for this shall be by me esteemed an assurance of

the truth of what you have told me.' (107) Hereupon they were in greater grief than before; they wept, and perpetually deplored one among another the calamity of Joseph; and said, they were fallen into this misery as a punishment inflicted by God for what evil contrivances they had against him. And Reubel was large in his reproaches of them for their too late repentance, whence no profit arose to Joseph; and earnestly exhorted them to bear with patience whatever they suffered, since it was done by God in way of punishment, on his account. (108) Thus they spake to one another, not imagining that Joseph understood their language. A general sadness also seized on them at Reubel's words, and a repentance for what they had done; and they condemned the wickedness they had perpetrated, for which they judged they were justly punished by God. (109) Now when Joseph saw that they were in this distress, he was so affected at it that he fell into tears, and, not being willing that they should take notice of him, he retired; and after a while came to them again, (110) and taking Symeon, in order to his being a pledge for his brethren's return, he bid them take the corn they had bought, and go their way. He also commanded his steward privily to put the money which they had brought with them for the purchase of corn into their sacks, and to dismiss them therewith; who did what he was commanded to do.

(111) Now when Jacob's sons were come into the land of Canaan, they told their father what had happened to them in Egypt, and that they were taken to have come thither as spies upon the king; and how they said they were brethren, and had left their eleventh brother with their father, but were not believed; and how they had left Symeon with the governor, until Benjamin should go thither, and be a testimonial of the truth of what they had said: (112) and they begged of their father to fear nothing, but to send the lad along with them. But Jacob was not pleased with anything his sons had done; and he took the detention of Symeon heinously, and thence thought it a foolish thing to give up Benjamin also. (113) Neither did he yield to Reubel's persuasion, though he begged it of him, and gave leave that the grandfather might, in way of requital, kill his own sons, in case any harm came to Benjamin in the journey. So they were distressed, and knew not what to do: nay, there was another accident that still disturbed them more – the money that was found hidden in their sacks of corn. (114) Yet when the corn they had brought failed them, and when the famine still afflicted them, and necessity forced them, Jacob did [not] still resolve to send Benjamin with his brethren, (115) although there was no returning into Egypt unless they came with what they had promised. Now the misery growing every day worse, and his sons begging it of him, he had no other course to take in his present circumstances. (116) And Judas, who was of a bold temper on other occasions, spake his mind very freely to him: 'That it did not become him to be afraid on account of his son,

nor to suspect the worst, as he did; for nothing could be done to his son but by the appointment of God, which must also for certain come to pass, though he were at home with him; (117) that he ought not to condemn them to such manifest destruction, nor deprive them of that plenty of food they might have from Pharaoh, by his unreasonable fear about his son Benjamin, but ought to take care of the preservation of Symeon, lest, by attempting to hinder Benjamin's journey, Symeon should perish. He exhorted him to trust God for him, and said he would either bring his son back to him safe, or together with his, lose his own life.' (118) So that Jacob was at length persuaded, and delivered Benjamin to them, with the price of the corn doubled; he also sent presents to Joseph of the fruits of the land of Canaan: balsam and rosin, as also turpentine and honey. Now their father shed many tears at the departure of his sons, as well as themselves. (119) His concern was that he might receive them back again safe after their journey; and their concern was that they might find their father well, and no way afflicted with grief for them. And this lamentation lasted a whole day; so that the old man was at last tired with grief, and stayed behind; but they went on their way for Egypt, endeavouring to mitigate their grief for their present misfortunes, with the hopes of better success hereafter.

(120) As soon as they came into Egypt, they were brought down to Joseph; but here no small fear disturbed them; lest they should be accused about the price of the corn, as if they had cheated Joseph. They then made a long apology to Joseph's steward, and told him, that when they came home they found the money in their sacks, and that they had now brought it along with them. (121) He said he did not know what they meant: so they were delivered from that fear. And when he had loosed Symeon, and put him into a handsome habit, he suffered him to be with his brethren; at which time Joseph came from his attendance on the king. So they offered him their presents; and upon his putting the question to them about their father, they answered, that they found him well. (122) He also upon his discovery that Benjamin was alive, asked whether this was their younger brother; for he had seen him. Whereupon they said he was: he replied, that the God over all was his protector. (123) But when his affection to him made him shed tears, he retired, desiring he might not be seen in that plight by his brethren. Then Joseph took them to supper, and they were set down in the same order as they used to sit at their father's table. And although Joseph treated them all kindly, yet did he send a mess to Benjamin that was double to what the rest of the guests had for their shares.

(124) Now when after supper they had composed themselves to sleep, Joseph commanded his steward both to give them their measures of corn, and to hide its price again in their sacks; and that withal they should put into

Benjamin's sack the golden cup, out of which he loved himself to drink: (125) which things he did, in order to make trial of his brethren, whether they would stand by Benjamin when he should be accused of having stolen the cup, and should appear to be in danger; or whether they would leave him, and, depending on their own innocency, go to their father without him. (126) When the servant had done as he was bidden, the sons of Jacob, knowing nothing of all this, went their way, and took Symeon along with them, and had a double cause of joy, both because they had received him again, and because they took back Benjamin to their father, as they had promised. (127) But presently a troop of horsemen encompassed them, and brought with them Joseph's servant, who had put the cup into Benjamin's sack. Upon which unexpected attack of the horsemen they were much disturbed, and asked what the reason was that they came thus upon men (128) who a little before had been by their lord thought worthy of an honourable and hospitable reception! They replied, by calling them wicked wretches, who had forgot that very hospitable and kind treatment which Joseph had given them, and did not scruple to be injurious to him, and to carry off that cup out of which he had in so friendly a manner drank to them, and not regarding their friendship with Joseph no more than the danger they should be in if they were taken, in comparison of the unjust gain. (129) Hereupon he threatened that they should be punished; for though they had escaped the knowledge of him who was but a servant, yet had they not escaped the knowledge of God, nor had gone off with what they had stolen; and after all, asked why we come upon them, as if they knew nothing of the matter; and he told them that they should immediately know it by their punishment. This and more of the same nature, did the servant say, in way of reproach to them; (130) but they being wholly ignorant of anything here that concerned them, laughed at what he said; and wondered at the abusive language which the servant gave them, when he was so hardy as to accuse those who did not before so much as retain the price of their corn, which was found in their sacks, but brought it again, though nobody else knew of any such thing – so far were they from offering any injury to Joseph voluntarily. (131) But still, supposing that a search would be a more sure justification of themselves than their own denial of the fact, they bid him search them, and that if any of them had been guilty of the theft to punish them all; for being no way conscious to themselves of any crime, they spake with assurance, and as they thought, without any danger to themselves also. The servants desired there might be a search made; but they said the punishment should extend to him alone who should be found guilty of the theft. (132) So they made the search; and, having searched all the rest, they came last of all to Benjamin, as knowing it was Benjamin's sack in which they had hidden the cup, they having indeed searched the rest only for a show of accuracy; (133) so the rest were out of fear for themselves, and were now only concerned about Benjamin, but still were well assured that he would also be found innocent; and they reproached those that came after them for their hindering them, while they might, in the meanwhile, have gotten a good way on their journey. (134) But as soon as they had searched Benjamin's sack, they found the cup, and took it from him; and all was changed into mourning and lamentation. They rent their garments, and wept for the punishment which their brother was to undergo for his theft, and for the delusion they had put on their father, when they promised they would bring Benjamin safe to him. (135) What added to their misery was, that this melancholy accident came unfortunately at a time when they thought they had been gotten off clear; but they confessed that this misfortune of their brother, as well as the grief of their father for him, was owing to themselves, since it was they that forced their father to send him with them, when he was averse to it.

(136) The horsemen therefore took Benjamin and brought him to Joseph, his brethren also following him: who, when he saw him in custody, and them in the habit of mourners, said, 'How came you, vile wretches as you are, to have such a strange notion of my kindness to you, and of God's providence, as impudently to do thus to your benefactor, who in such an hospitable manner had entertained you?' – Whereupon they gave up themselves to be punished, in order to save Benjamin; and called to mind what a wicked enterprise they had been guilty of against Joseph. They also pronounced him more happy than themselves, if he were dead, in being freed from the miseries of this life; and if he were alive, that he enjoyed the pleasure of seeing God's vengeance upon them. They said further, that they were the plague of their father, since they should now add to his former affliction for Joseph, this other affliction for Benjamin. Reubel also was large in cutting them upon this occasion. (138) But Joseph dismissed them; for he said they had been guilty of no offence, and that he would content himself with the lad's punishment: for he said it was not a fit thing to let him go free, for the sake of those who had not offended; nor was it a fit thing to punish them together with him who had been guilty of stealing. And when he promised to give them leave to go away in safety, (139) the rest of them were under great consternation, and were able to say nothing on this sad occasion. But Judas, who had persuaded their father to send the lad from him, being otherwise also a very bold and active man, determined to hazard himself for the preservation of his brother. (140) 'It is true,' said he, 'O governor, that we have been very wicked with regard to thee, and on that account deserve punishment; even all of us may justly be punished, although the theft were not committed by all, but only by one of us, and he the youngest also: but yet there remains some hope for us, who otherwise must be under despair on his account, and this from thy goodness, which promises us a

deliverance out of our present danger. (141) And now I beg thou wilt not look at us, or at that great crime we have been guilty of, but at thy own excellent nature, and take advice of thine own virtue, instead of that wrath thou hast against us; which passion those that otherwise are of lower character indulge, as they do their strength, and that not only on great, but also on very trifling occasions. Overcome, Sir, that passion, and be not subdued by it, nor suffer it to slay those that do not otherwise presume upon their own safety, but are desirous to accept of it from thee; (142) for this is not the first time that thou wilt bestow it on us, but before, when we came to buy corn, thou affordedst us great plenty of food, and gavest us leave to carry so much home to our family as has preserved them from perishing by famine. (143) Nor is there any difference between not overlooking men that were perishing for want of necessaries, and not punishing those that seem to be offenders, and have been so unfortunate as to lose the advantage of that glorious benefaction which they received from thee. This will be an instance of equal favour, though bestowed after a different manner; (144) for thou wilt save those this way whom thou didst feed the other; and thou wilt hereby preserve alive, by thy own bounty, those souls which thou didst not suffer to be distressed by famine, it being indeed at once a wonderful and a great thing to sustain our lives by corn, and to bestow on us that pardon whereby, now we are distressed, we may continue those lives. (145) And I am ready to suppose, that God is willing to afford thee this opportunity of showing thy virtuous disposition, by bringing us into this calamity, that it may appear thou canst forgive the injuries that are done to thyself and mayst be esteemed kind to others, besides those who, on other accounts, stand in need of thy assistance; (146) since it is indeed a right thing to do well to those who are in distress for want of food, but still a more glorious thing to save those who deserve to be punished, when it is on account of heinous offences against thyself; for if it be a thing deserving commendation to forgive such as have been guilty of small offences, that tend to a person's loss, and this be praiseworthy in him that overlooks such offences, to restrain a man's passion as to crimes which are capital to the guilty, is to be like the most excellent nature of God himself: (147) and truly, as for myself, had it not been that we had a father, who had discovered, on occasion of the death of Joseph, how miserably he is always afflicted at the loss of his sons, I had not made any words on account of the saving of our own lives; I mean, any further than as that would be an excellent character for thyself, to preserve even those that would have nobody to lament them when they were dead, but we would have yielded ourselves up to suffer whatsoever thou pleasedst; (148) but now, (for we do not plead for mercy to ourselves, though indeed, if we die, it will be while we are young, and before we have had the enjoyment of life) have regard to our father, and take pity of his old age, on whose account it is that we make these supplications to thee. We beg thou wilt give us those lives which this wickedness of ours has rendered obnoxious to thy punishment; (149) and this for his sake who is not himself wicked, nor does his being our father make us wicked. He is a good man, and not worthy to have such trials of his patience; and now we are absent, he is afflicted with care for us: but if he hear of our deaths, and what was the cause of it, he wilt on that account die an immature death; (150) and the reproachful manner of our ruin will hasten his end, and will directly kill him, nay, will bring him to a miserable death, while he will make haste to rid himself out of the world, and bring himself to a state of insensibility, before the sad story of our end come abroad into the rest of the world. (151) Consider these things in this manner, although our wickedness does now provoke thee with a just desire of punishing that wickedness, and forgive it for our father's sake; and let thy commiseration of him weigh more with thee than our wickedness. Have regard to the old age of our father, who, if we perish, will be very lonely while he lives, and will soon die himself also. Grant this boon to the name of fathers, (152) for thereby thou wilt honour him that begat thee, and will grant it to thyself also, who enjoyest already that denomination; thou wilt then, by that denomination be preserved of God, the Father of all – by showing a pious regard to which, in the case of our father, thou wilt appear to honour him who is styled by the same name; I mean, if thou wilt have this pity on our father, upon this consideration, how miserable he will be if he be deprived of his sons! (153) It is their part therefore to bestow on us what God has given us, when it is in thy power to take it away, and so to resemble him entirely in charity; for it is good to use that power, which can either give or take away on the merciful side; and when it is in thy power to destroy, to forget that thou ever hadst that power, and to look on thyself as only allowed power for preservation; and that the more anyone extends this power, the greater reputation does he gain to himself. (154) Now, by forgiving our brother what he has unhappily committed, thou wilt preserve us all; for we cannot think of living if he be put to death, since we dare not show ourselves alive to our father without our brother, but here must we partake of one and the same catastrophe of his life; (155) and so far we beg of thee, O governor, that if thou condemnest our brother to die, thou wilt punish us together with him, as partners of his crime – for we shall not think it reasonable to be reserved to kill ourselves for grief of our brother's death, but so to die rather as equally guilty with him of this crime! (156) I will only leave with thee this one consideration, and then will say no more, viz., that our brother committed his fault when he was young, and not yet of confirmed wisdom in his conduct; and that men naturally forgive such young persons. I end here, without adding what more I have to say, that in case thou condemnest us, that omission may be supposed to have hurt us, and permitted thee to take the severer side; (157)

but in case thou settest us free, that this may be ascribed to thy own goodness, of which thou art inwardly conscious, that thou freest us from condemnation; and that not by barely preserving us, but by granting us such a favour as will make us appear more righteous than we really are, and by representing to thyself more motives for our deliverance than we are able to produce ourselves. (158) If, therefore, thou resolvest to slay him, I desire thou wilt slay me in his stead, and send him back to his father; or if thou pleasest to retain him with thee as a slave, I am fitter to labour for thy advantage in that capacity, and, as thou seest, am better prepared for either of those sufferings.' (159) So Judas, being very willing to undergo anything whatever for the deliverance of his brother, cast himself down at Joseph's feet, and earnestly laboured to assuage and pacify his anger. All his brethren also fell down before him, weeping and delivering themselves up to destruction for the preservation of the life of Benjamin.

(160) But Joseph, as overcome now with his affections, and no longer able to personate an angry man, commanded all that were present to depart, that he might make himself known to his brethren when they were alone; and when the rest were gone out, he made himself known to his brethren; and said: (161) 'I commend you for your virtue, and your kindness to our brother: I find you better men than I could have expected from what you contrived about me. Indeed, I did all this to try your love to your brother; so I believe you were not wicked by nature in what you did in my case, but that all has happened according to God's will, who has hereby procured our enjoyment of what good things we have; and, if he continue in a favourable disposition, of what we hope for hereafter. (162) Since, therefore, I know that our father is safe and well, beyond expectation, and I see you so well disposed to your brother, I will no longer remember what guilt you seem to have had about me, but will leave off to hate you for that your wickedness; and do rather return you my thanks, that you have concurred with the intentions of God to bring things to their present state. (163) I would have you also rather to forget the same, since that imprudence of yours is come to such a happy conclusion, than to be uneasy and blush at those your offences. Do not, therefore, let your evil intentions, when you condemned me, and that bitter remorse which might follow, be a grief to you now, because those intentions were frustrated. (164) Go, therefore, your way, rejoicing in what has happened by the Divine Providence, and inform your father of it, lest he should be spent with cares for you, and deprive me of the most agreeable part of my felicity; I mean, lest he should die before he comes into my sight, and enjoys the good things that we now have. (165) Bring, therefore, with you, our father, and your wives and children, and all your kindred, and remove your habitations hither; for it is not proper that the persons dearest to me should live remote from me, now

my affairs are so prosperous, especially when they must endure five more years of famine.' (166) When Joseph had said this, he embraced his brethren, who were in tears and sorrow; but the generous kindness of their brother seemed to leave among them no room for fear, lest they should be punished on account of what they had consulted and acted against him; and they were then feasting. (167) Now the king, as soon as he heard that Joseph's brethren were come to him, was exceeding glad of it, as if it had been a part of his own good fortune; and gave them wagons full of corn, and gold and silver, to be conveyed to his father. Now when they had received more of their brother, part to be carried to their father, and part as free gifts to every one of themselves, Benjamin having still more than the rest, they departed.

CHAPTER 7

(168) As soon as Jacob came to know, by his sons returning home, in what state Joseph was; that he had not only escaped death, for which yet he lived all along in mourning, but that he lived in splendour and happiness, and ruled over Egypt, jointly with the king, and had entrusted to his care almost all his affairs, (169) he did not think any thing he was told to be incredible, considering the greatness of the works of God, and his kindness to him, although that kindness had, for some late times, been intermitted; so he immediately and zealously set out upon his journey to him.

(170) When he came to the Well of the Oath (Beersheba), he offered sacrifice to God; and being afraid that the happiness there was in Egypt might tempt his posterity to fall in love with it and settle in it, and no more think of removing into the land of Canaan, and possessing it, as God had promised them; (171) as also being afraid, lest, if this descent into Egypt were made without the will of God, his family might be destroyed there; out of fear withal, lest he should depart this life before he came to the sight of Joseph, he fell asleep, revolving these doubts in his mind.

(172) But God stood by him, and called to him twice by his name; and when he asked who he was, God said, 'No, sure, it is not just that thou, Jacob, shouldst be unacquainted with that God who has been ever a protector and a helper to thy forefathers, and after them to thyself; (173) for when thy father would have deprived thee of the dominion, I gave it thee; and by my kindness it was that, when thou wast sent into Mesopotamia all alone, thou obtainedst good wives, and returnedst with many children and much wealth. (174) Thy whole family also has been preserved by my providence; and it was I who conducted Joseph, thy son, whom thou gavest up for lost, to the enjoyment of great prosperity. I also made him lord of Egypt, so that he differs but little from a king. (175) Accordingly, I come now as a guide to thee in this journey; and

foretell to thee, that thou shalt die in the arms of Joseph: and I inform thee, that thy posterity shall be many ages in authority and glory, and that I will settle them in the land which I have promised them.'

(176) Jacob, encouraged by this dream, went on more cheerfully for Egypt with his sons, and all belonging to them. Now they were in all seventy. I once, indeed, thought it best not to set down the names of this family, especially because of their difficult pronunciation [by the Greeks]; (177) but, upon the whole, I think it necessary to mention those names, that I may disprove such as believe that we came not originally from Mesopotamia, but are Egyptians. Now Jacob had twelve sons; of these Joseph was come thither before. We will therefore set down the names of Jacob's children and grandchildren. (178) Reuben had four sons – Anoch, Phallu, Assaron, Charmi; Simeon had six – Jamuel, Jamin, Avod, Jachin, Soar, Saul; Levi had three sons – Gersom, Caath, Merari; Judas had three sons – Sala, Phares, Zerah; and by Phares two grandchildren – Esrom and Amar; Issachar had four sons – Thola, Phua, Jasob, Samaron; (179) Zabulon had with him three sons – Sarad, Helon, Jalel. So far is the posterity of Lea; with whom went her daughter Dinah. These are thirty-three. (180) Rachel had two sons, the one of whom, Joseph, had two sons also, Manasses and Ephraim. The other, Benjamin, had ten sons – Bolau, Bacchar, Asabel, Geras, Naaman, Jes, Ros, Momphis, Opphis, Arad. These fourteen added to the thirty-three before enumerated, amount to the number forty-seven; (181) and this was the legitimate posterity of Jacob. He had besides, by Bilhah, the handmaid of Rachel, Dan and Nephthali; which last had four sons that followed him – Jesel, Guni, Issari, and Sellim. Dan had an only begotten son, Usi. (182) If these be added to those before mentioned, they complete the number fifty-four. Gad and Asher were the sons of Zilpha, who was the handmaid of Lea. These had with them, Gad seven – Saphoniah, Augis, Sunis, Azabon, Aerin, Eroed, Ariel. (183) Asher had a daughter, Sarah, and six male children, whose names were Jomne, Isus, Isoui, Baris, Abar and Melchiel. If we add these, which are sixteen, to the fifty-four, the forementioned number [70] is completed, Jacob not being himself included in that number.

(184) When Joseph understood that his father was coming, for Judas his brother was come before him, and informed him of his approach, he went out to meet him; and they met together at Heliopolis. But Jacob almost fainted away at this unexpected and great joy; however, Joseph revived him, being yet not himself able to contain from being affected in the same manner, at the pleasure he now had; yet was he not wholly overcome with his passion, as his father was. (185) After this he desired Jacob to travel on slowly; but he himself took five of his brethren with him, and made haste to the king, to tell him that Jacob and his family were come; which was a joyful hearing to him. He also bid Joseph tell him what sort of life his brethren loved to lead, that he might

give them leave to follow the same; (186) who told him they were good shepherds, and had been used to follow no other employment but this alone. Whereby he provided for them, that they should not be separated, but live in the same place, and take care of their father; as also hereby he provided, that they might be acceptable to the Egyptians, by doing nothing that would be common to them with the Egyptians; for the Egyptians are prohibited to meddle with feeding of sheep.

(187) When Jacob was come to the king, and saluted him, and wished all prosperity to his government, Pharaoh asked him how old he now was: (188) upon whose answer, that he was a hundred and thirty years old, he admired Jacob on account of the length of his life. And when he had added, that still he had not lived so long as his forefathers, he gave him leave to live with his children in Heliopolis; for in that city the king's shepherds had their pasturage.

(189) However, the famine increased among the Egyptians; and this heavy judgment grew more oppressive to them, because neither did the river overflow the ground, for it did not rise to its former height, nor did God send rain upon it; nor did they indeed make the least provision for themselves, so ignorant were they what was to be done; but Joseph sold them corn for their money. But when their money failed them, they bought corn with their cattle and their slaves; (190) and if any of them had a small piece of land, they gave up that to purchase them food, by which means the king became the owner of all their substance; and they were removed, some to one place and some to another, that so the possession of their country might be firmly assured to the king, excepting the lands of the priests; for their country continued still in their own possession. (191) And indeed this sore famine made their minds as well as their bodies slaves, and at length compelled them to procure a sufficiency of food by such dishonourable means. But when this misery ceased, and the river overflowed the ground, and the ground brought forth its fruits plentifully, (192) Joseph came to every city, and gathered the people thereto belonging together, and gave them back entirely the land which, by their own consent, the king might have possessed alone, and alone enjoyed the fruits of it. He also exhorted them to look on it as everyone's own possession, and to fall to their husbandry with cheerfulness; and to pay, as a tribute to the king, the fifth part of the fruits for the land which the king, when it was his own, restored to them. (193) These men rejoiced upon their becoming unexpectedly owners of their lands, and diligently observed what was enjoined them; and by this means Joseph procured to himself a greater authority among the Egyptians, and greater love to the king from them. Now this law, that they should pay the fifth part of their fruits as tribute, continued until their later kings.

CHAPTER 8

(194) Now when Jacob had lived seventeen years in Egypt, he fell into a disease, and died in the presence of his sons; but not till he made his prayers for their enjoying prosperity, and till he had foretold to them prophetically how every one of them was to dwell in the land of Canaan. But this happened many years afterward. (195) He also enlarged upon the praises of Joseph; how he had not remembered the evil doings of his brethren to their disadvantage; nay, on the contrary, was kind to them, bestowing upon them so many benefits, as seldom are bestowed on men's own benefactors. He then commanded his own sons that they should admit Joseph's sons, Ephraim and Manasses, into their number, and divide the land of Canaan in common with them; concerning whom we shall treat hereafter. (196) However, he made it his request that he might be buried at Hebron. So he died, when he had lived full a hundred and fifty years, three only abated, having not been behind any of his ancestors in piety towards God, and having such a recompense for it, as it was fit those should have who were so good as these were. But Joseph, by the king's permission, carried his father's dead body to Hebron, and there buried it, at a great expense. (197) Now his brethren were at first unwilling to return back with him, because they were afraid lest, now their father was dead, he should punish them for their secret practices against him; since he was now gone, for whose sake he had been so gracious to them. But he persuaded them to fear no harm, and to entertain no suspicions of him: so he brought them along with him, and gave them great possessions, and never left off his particular concern for them.

(198) Joseph also died when he had lived a hundred and ten years, having been a man of admirable virtue, and conducting all his affairs by the rules of reason, and used his authority with moderation, which was the cause of his so great felicity among the Egyptians, even when he came from another country, and that in such ill circumstances also, as we have already described. (199) At length his brethren died, after they had lived happily in Egypt. Now the posterity and sons of these men, after some time, carried their bodies, and buried them at Hebron; (200) but as to the bones of Joseph, they carried them into the land of Canaan afterward, when the Hebrews went out of Egypt, for so had Joseph made them promise him upon oath; but what became of every one of these men, and by what toils they got the possession of the land of Canaan, shall be shown hereafter, when I have first explained upon what account it was that they left Egypt.

CHAPTER 9

(201) Now it happened that the Egyptians grew delicate and lazy, as to painstaking; and gave themselves up to other pleasures, and in particular to the love of gain. They also became very ill affected towards the Hebrews, as touched with envy at their prosperity; (202) for when they saw how the nation of the Israelites flourished, and were become eminent already in plenty of wealth, which they had acquired by their virtue and natural love of labour, they thought their increase was to their own detriment; and having, in length of time, forgotten the benefits they had received from Joseph, particularly the crown being now come into another family, they became very abusive to the Israelites, and contrived many ways of afflicting them; (203) for they enjoined them to cut a great number of channels for the river, and to build walls for their cities and ramparts, that they might restrain the river, and hinder its waters from stagnating, upon its running over its own banks: they set them also to build pyramids, and by all this wore them out and forced them to learn all sorts of mechanical arts, and to accustom themselves to hard labour. (204) And four hundred years did they spend under these afflictions; for they strove one against the other which should get the mastery, the Egyptians desiring to destroy the Israelites by these labours, and the Israelites desiring to hold out to the end under them.

(205) While the affairs of the Hebrews were in this condition, there was this occasion offered itself to the Egyptians, which made them more solicitous for the extinction of our nation. One of those sacred scribes, who are very sagacious in foretelling future events truly, told the king, that about this time there would a child be born to the Israelites, who, if he were reared, would bring the Egyptian dominion low, and would raise the Israelites; that he would excel all men in virtue, and obtain a glory that would be remembered through all ages. (206) Which thing was so feared by the king, that, according to this man's opinion, he commanded that they should cast every male child which was born to the Israelites into the river, and destroy it; that besides this, the Egyptian midwives should watch the labours of the Hebrew women, and observe what is born, (207) for those were the women who were enjoined to do the office of midwives to them; and by reason of their relation to the king, would not transgress his commands. He enjoined also, that if any parents should disobey him, and venture to save their male children alive, they and their families should be destroyed. (208) This was a severe affliction indeed to those that suffered it, not only as they were deprived of their sons, and while they were the parents themselves, they were obliged to be subservient to the destruction of their own children, but as it was to be supposed to tend to the

extirpation of their nation, while upon the destruction of their children, and their own gradual dissolution, the calamity would become very hard and inconsolable to them; (209) and this was the ill state they were in. But no one can be too hard for the purpose of God, though he contrive ten thousand subtle devices for that end; for this child, whom the sacred scribe foretold, was brought up and concealed from the observers appointed by the king; and he that foretold him did not mistake in the consequences of his preservation, which were brought to pass after the manner following:

(210) A man, whose name was Amram, one of the nobler sort of the Hebrews, was afraid for his whole nation, lest it should fail, by the want of young men to be brought up hereafter, and was very uneasy at it, his wife being then with child, and he knew not what to do. (211) Hereupon he betook himself to prayer to God; and entreated him to have compassion on those men who had nowise transgressed the laws of his worship, and to afford them deliverance from the miseries they at that time endured, and to render abortive their enemies' hopes of the destruction of their nation. (212) Accordingly God had mercy on him, and was moved by his supplication. He stood by him in his sleep, and exhorted him not to despair of his future favours. He said further, that he did not forget their piety towards him, and would always reward them for it, as he had formerly granted his favour to their forefathers, and made them increase from a few to so great a multitude. (213) He put him in mind that when Abraham was come alone out of Mesopotamia into Canaan, he had been made happy, not only in other respects, but that when his wife was at first barren, she was afterwards by him enabled to conceive seed, and bear him sons. That he left to Ismael and to his posterity the country of Arabia; as also to his sons by Ketura, Troglodytis; and to Isaac, Canaan. (214) That by my assistance, said he, he did great exploits in war, which, unless you be yourselves impious, you must still remember. As for Jacob, he became well known to strangers also, by the greatness of that prosperity in which he lived, and left to his sons, who came into Egypt with no more than seventy souls, while you are now become above six hundred thousand. (215) Know, therefore, that I shall provide for you all in common what is for your good, and particularly for thyself what shall make thee famous; for that child, out of dread of whose nativity the Egyptians have doomed the Israelite children to destruction, shall be this child of thine, and shall be concealed from those who watch to destroy him: (216) and when he is brought up in a surprising way, he shall deliver the Hebrew nation from the distress they are under from the Egyptians. His memory shall be famous while the world lasts; and this not only among the Hebrews, but foreigners also: all which shall be the effect of my favour to thee, and to thy posterity. He shall also have such a brother, that he shall himself obtain my priesthood, and his posterity shall have it after him to the end of the world.

(217) When the vision had informed him of these things, Amram awaked and told it to Jochebed, who was his wife. And now the fear increased upon them on account of the prediction in Amram's dream; for they were under concern, not only for the child, but on account of the great happiness that was to come to him also. (218) However, the mother's labour was such as afforded a confirmation to what was foretold by God; for it was not known to those that watched her, by the easiness of her pains, and because the throes of her delivery did not fall upon her with violence. And now they nourished the child at home privately for three months; (219) but after that time Amram, fearing he should be discovered, and by falling under the king's displeasure, both he and his child should perish, and so he should make the promise of God of none effect, he determined rather to entrust the safety and care of the child to God, than to depend on his own concealment of him, which he looked upon as a thing uncertain, and whereby both the child, so privately to be nourished, and himself, should be in imminent danger; (220) but he believed that God would some way for certain procure the safety of the child, in order to secure the truth of his own predictions. When they had thus determined, they made an ark of bulrushes, after the manner of a cradle, and of a bigness sufficient for an infant to be laid in, without being too straitened: they then daubed it over with slime, (221) which would naturally keep out the water from entering between the bulrushes, and put the infant into it, and setting it afloat upon the river, they left its preservation to God; so the river received the child, and carried him along. But Miriam, the child's sister, passed along upon the bank over against him, as her mother had bid her, to see whither the ark would be carried; (222) where God demonstrated that human wisdom was nothing, but that the Supreme Being is able to do whatsoever he pleases: that those who, in order to their own security, condemn others to destruction, and use great endeavours about it, fail of their purpose, (223) but that others are in a surprising manner preserved, and obtain a prosperous condition almost from the very midst of their calamities; those, I mean, whose dangers arise by the appointment of God. And, indeed, such a providence was exercised in the case of this child, as showed the power of God.

(224) Thermuthis was the king's daughter. She was now diverting herself by the banks of the river; and seeing a cradle borne along by the current, she sent some that could swim, and bid them bring the cradle to her. When those that were sent on this errand came to her with the cradle, and she saw the little child, she was greatly in love with it, on account of its largeness and beauty; (225) for God had taken such great care in the formation of Moses, that he caused him to be thought worthy of bringing up, and providing for, by all those that had taken the most fatal resolutions, on account of the dread of his nativity, for the destruction of the rest of the Hebrew nation. Thermuthis bid

them bring her a woman that might afford her breast to the child; (226) yet would not the child admit of her breast, but turned away from it, and did the like to many other women. Now Miriam was by when this happened, not to appear to be there on purpose, but only as staying to see the child; and she said, 'It is in vain that thou, O queen, callest for these women for the nourishing of the child, who are no way of kin to it; but still, if thou wilt order one of the Hebrew women to be brought, perhaps it may admit the breast of one of its own nation.' (227) Now since she seemed to speak well, Thermuthis bid her procure such a one, and to bring one of those Hebrew women that gave suck. So when she had such authority given her, she came back and brought the mother, who was known to nobody there. And now the child gladly admitted the breast, and seemed to stick close to it; and so it was, that, at the queen's desire, the nursing of the child was entirely entrusted to the mother.

(228) Hereupon it was that Thermuthis imposed this name *Mouses* upon him from what had happened when he was put into the river; for the Egyptians call water by the name of *Mo*, and such as are saved out of it, by the name of *Uses*; so by putting these two words together, they imposed this name upon him; (229) and he was, by the confession of all, according to God's prediction, as well for his greatness of mind, as for his contempt of difficulties, the best of all the Hebrews; for Abraham was his ancestor of the seventh generation. For Moses was the son of Amram, who was the son of Caath, whose father, Levi, was the son of Jacob, who was the son of Isaac, who was the son of Abraham. (230) Now Moses's understanding became superior to his age, nay, far beyond that standard; and when he was taught, he discovered greater quickness of apprehension than was usual at his age; and his actions at that time promised greater, when he should come to the age of a man. God did also give him that tallness, when he was but three years old, as was wonderful; (231) and as for his beauty, there was nobody so unpolite as, when they saw Moses, they were not greatly surprised at the beauty of his countenance; nay, it happened frequently, that those that met him as he was carried along the road, were obliged to turn again upon seeing the child; that they left what they were about, and stood still a great while to look on him; for the beauty of the child was so remarkable and natural to him on many accounts that it detained the spectators, and made them stay longer to look upon him.

(232) Thermuthis, therefore, perceiving him to be so remarkable a child, adopted him for her son, having no child of her own. And when one time she had carried Moses to her father, she showed him to him, and said she thought to make him her father's successor, if it should please God she should have no legitimate child of her own; and to him, 'I have brought up a child who is of a divine form, and of a generous mind; and as I have received him from the bounty of the river, in a wonderful manner, I thought proper to adopt him for

my son and the heir of thy kingdom.' (233) And when she had said this, she put the infant into her father's hands; so he took him, and hugged him close to his breast; and on his daughter's account, in a pleasant way, put his diadem upon his head; but Moses threw it down to the ground, and, in a puerile mood he wreathed it round, and trod upon it with his feet; (234) which seemed to bring along with evil presage concerning the kingdom of Egypt. But when the sacred scribe saw this (he was the same person who foretold that his nativity would bring the dominion of that kingdom low), he made a violent attempt to kill him; and crying out in a frightful manner, he said, (235) 'This, O king! this child is he of whom God foretold, that if we kill him we shall be in no danger; he himself affords an attestation to the prediction of the same thing, by his trampling upon thy government, and treading upon thy diadem. Take him, therefore, out of the way, and deliver the Egyptians from the fear they are in about him; and deprive the Hebrews of the hope they have of being encouraged by him.' (236) But Thermuthis prevented him, and snatched the child away. And the king was not hasty to slay him, God himself, whose providence protected Moses, inclining the king to spare him. He was, therefore, educated with great care. So the Hebrews depended on him, and were of good hopes that great things would be done by him; (237) but the Egyptians were suspicious of what would follow such his education. Yet because, if Moses had been slain, there was no one, either akin or adopted, that had any oracle on his side, for pretending to the crown of Egypt, and likely to be of greater advantage to them, they abstained from killing him.

CHAPTER 10

(238) Moses, therefore, when he was born, and brought up in the foregoing manner, and came to the age of maturity, made his virtue manifest to the Egyptians; and showed that he was born for the bringing them down, and raising the Israelites; and the occasion he laid hold of was this: (239) the Ethiopians, who are next neighbours to the Egyptians, made an inroad into their country, which they seized upon, and carried off the effects of the Egyptians, who, in their rage, fought against them, and revenged the affronts they had received from them; but, being overcome in battle, some of them were slain, and the rest ran away in a shameful manner, and by that means saved themselves; (240) whereupon the Ethiopians followed after them in the pursuit, and thinking that it would be a mark of cowardice if they did not subdue all Egypt, they went on to subdue the rest with greater vehemence; and when they had tasted the sweets of the country, they never left off the prosecution of the war; and as the nearest parts had not courage enough at first to fight with them, they proceeded as far as Memphis and the sea itself; while

not one of the cities was able to oppose them. (241) The Egyptians under this sad oppression, betook themselves to their oracles and prophecies, and when God had given them this counsel, to make use of Moses the Hebrew, and take his assistance, the king commanded his daughter to produce him, that he might be the general of their army. (242) Upon which, when she had made him swear that he would do him no harm, she delivered him to the king, and supposed his assistance would be of great advantage to them. She withal reproached the priest, who, when they had before admonished the Egyptians to kill him, was not ashamed now to own their want of his help.

(243) So Moses, at the persuasion both of Thermuthis and the king himself, cheerfully undertook the business; and the sacred scribes of both nations were glad; those of the Egyptians that they should at once overcome their enemies by his valour, and that by the same piece of management Moses would be slain; but those of the Hebrews, that they should escape from the Egyptians, because Moses was to be their general; (244) but Moses prevented the enemies, and took and led his army before those enemies were apprised of his attacking them; for he did not march by the river, but by land, where he gave a wonderful demonstration of his sagacity; (245) for when the ground was difficult to be passed over, because of the multitude of serpents (which it produces in vast numbers, and indeed is singular in some of those productions, which other countries do not breed, and yet such as are worse than others in power and mischief, and an unusual fierceness of sight, some of which ascend out of the ground unseen, and also fly in the air, and do come upon men at unawares, and do them a mischief). Moses invented a wonderful stratagem to preserve the army safe, and without hurt; (246) for he made baskets like unto arks, of sedge, and filled them with ibes, and carried them along with them; which animal is the greatest enemy to serpents imaginable, for they fly from them when they come near them; and as they fly they are caught and devoured by them, as if it were done by the harts; (247) but the ibes are tame creatures, and only enemies to the serpentine kind; but about these ibes I say no more at present, since the Greeks themselves are not unacquainted with this sort of bird. As soon, therefore as Moses was come to the land which was the breeder of these serpents, he let loose the ibes, and by their means repelled the serpentine kind, and used them for his assistants before the army came upon that ground. When he had therefore proceeded thus on his journey, he came upon the Ethiopians before they had expected him; (248) and joining battle with them he beat them, and deprived them of the hopes they had of success against the Egyptians, and went on in overthrowing their cities, and indeed made a great slaughter of these Ethiopians. Now when the Egyptian army had once tasted of this prosperous success, by the means of Moses, they did not slacken their diligence, insomuch that the Ethiopians were in danger of being

reduced to slavery, and all sorts of destruction; (249) and at length they retired to Saba, which was a royal city of Ethiopia, which Cambyses afterwards named Meroë after the name of his own sister. The place was to be besieged with very great difficulty, since it was both encompassed by the Nile, quite round, and the other rivers, Astapus and Astaboras, made it a very difficult thing for such as attempted to pass over them; (250) for the city was situate in a retired place, and was inhabited after the manner of an island, being encompassed with a strong wall, and having the rivers to guard them from their enemies, and having great ramparts between the wall and the rivers, insomuch that when the waters come with the greatest violence it can never be drowned; which ramparts make it next to impossible for even such as are gotten over the rivers to take the city. (251) However, while Moses was uneasy at the army's lying idle (for the enemies durst not come to a battle), this accident happened: (252) Tharbis was the daughter of the king of the Ethiopians: she happened to see Moses as he led the army near the walls and fought with great courage; and admiring the subtlety of his undertakings, and believing him to be the author of the Egyptians' success, when they had before despaired of recovering their liberty, and to be the occasion of the great danger the Ethiopians were in, when they had before boasted of their great achievements, she fell deeply in love with him; and upon the prevalency of that passion, sent to him the most faithful of all her servants to discourse with him about their marriage. (253) He thereupon accepted the offer, on condition she would procure the delivering up of the city; and gave her the assurance of an oath to take her to his wife; and that when he had once taken possession of the city, he would not break his oath to her. No sooner was the agreement made, but it took effect immediately; and when Moses had cut off the Ethiopians, he gave thanks to God, and consummated his marriage, and led the Egyptians back to their own land.

CHAPTER II

(254) Now the Egyptians, after they had been preserved by Moses, entertained a hatred to him, and were very eager in compassing their designs against him, as suspecting that he would take occasion, from his good success, to raise a sedition, and bring innovations into Egypt; and told the king he ought to be slain. (255) The king had also some intentions of himself to the same purpose, and this as well out of envy at his glorious expedition at the head of his army, as out of fear of being brought low by him; and being instigated by the sacred scribes, he was ready to undertake to kill Moses; (256) but when he had learned beforehand what plots there were against him, he went away privately, and because the public roads were watched, he took his flight through the deserts, and where his enemies could not suspect he would travel; and, though he was

destitute of food, he went on, and despised that difficulty courageously; (257) and when he came to the city Midian, which lay upon the Red Sea, and was so denominated from one of Abraham's sons by Keturah, he sat upon a certain well, and rested himself there after his laborious journey, and the affliction he had been in. It was not far from the city, and the time of the day was noon, where he had an occasion offered him by the custom of the country of doing what recommended his virtue, and afforded him an opportunity of bettering his circumstances.

(258) For that country having but little water, the shepherds used to seize on the wells before others came, lest their flocks should want water and lest it should be spent by others before they came. There were now come, therefore, to this well seven sisters that were virgins, the daughters of Raguel, a priest, and one thought worthy by the people of the country of great honour. (259) These virgins, who took care of their father's flocks, which sort of work it was customary and very familiar for women to do in the country of the Troglodytes, they came first of all, and drew water out of the well in a quantity sufficient for their flocks, into troughs which were made for the reception of that water; (260) but when the shepherds came upon the maidens, and drove them away, that they might have the command of the water themselves, Moses, thinking it would be a terrible reproach upon him if he overlooked the young women under unjust oppression, and should suffer the violence of the men to prevail over the right of the maidens, he drove away the men, who had a mind to more than their share, and afforded a proper assistance to the women; (261) who, when they had received such a benefit from him, came to their father, and told him how they had been affronted by the shepherds, and assisted by a stranger, and entreated that he would not let this generous action be done in vain, nor go without a reward. Now the father took it well from his daughters that they were so desirous to reward their benefactor; and bid them bring Moses into his presence, that he might be rewarded as he deserved; (262) and when Moses came, he told him what testimony his daughters bare to him, that he had assisted them; and that, as he admired him for his virtue, he said that Moses had bestowed such his assistance on persons not insensible of benefits, but where they were both able and willing to return the kindness, and even to exceed the measure of his generosity. (263) So he made him his son, and gave him one of his daughters in marriage, and appointed him to be the guardian and superintendent over his cattle; for of old all the wealth of the barbarians was in those cattle.

CHAPTER 12

(264) Now Moses, when he had obtained the favour of Jethro, for that was one of the names of Raguel, stayed there and fed his flock; but some time afterward, taking his station at the mountain called Sinai, he drove his flocks thither to feed them. (265) Now this is the highest of all the mountains thereabout, and the best for pasturage, the herbage being there good; and it had not been before fed upon, because of the opinion men had that God dwelt there, the shepherds not daring to ascend up to it; and here it was that a wonderful prodigy happened to Moses; (266) for a fire fed upon a thornbush, yet did the green leaves and the flowers continue untouched, and the fire did not at all consume the fruit branches, although the flame was great and fierce. (267) Moses was affrighted at this strange sight, as it was to him, but he was still more astonished when the fire uttered a voice, and called to him by name, and spake words to him, by which it signified how bold he had been in venturing to come into a place whither no man had ever come before, because the place was divine; and advised him to remove a great way off from the flame, and to be contented with what he had seen; and though he were himself a good man, and the offspring of great men, yet that he should not pry any further; (268) and he foretold to him, that he should have glory and honour among men, by the blessing of God upon him. He also commanded him to go away thence with confidence to Egypt, in order to his being the commander and conductor of the body of the Hebrews and to his delivering his own people from the injuries they suffered there. (269) 'For,' said God, 'they shall inhabit this happy land which your forefather Abraham inhabited, and shall have the enjoyment of all sorts of good things; and thou, by thy prudence, shalt guide them to those good things.' But still he enjoined him, when he had brought the Hebrews out of the land of Egypt, to come to that place, and to offer sacrifices of thanksgiving there. Such were the divine oracles which were delivered out of the fire.

(270) But Moses was astonished at what he saw, and much more at what he heard; and he said, 'I think it would be an instance of too great madness, O Lord, for one of that regard I bear to thee, to distrust thy power, since I myself adore it, and know that it has been made manifest to my progenitors; (271) but I am still in doubt how I, who am a private man, and one of no abilities, should either persuade my countrymen to leave the country they now inhabit, and to follow me to a land whither I lead them; or, if they should be persuaded, how can I force Pharaoh to permit them to depart, since they augment their own wealth and prosperity by the labours and works they put upon them?'

(272) But God persuaded him to be courageous on all occasions, and

promised to be with him, and to assist him in his words, when he was to persuade men; and in his deeds, when he was to perform wonders. He bid him also to take a signal of the truth of what he said, by throwing his rod upon the ground; which when he had done, it crept along, and was become a serpent, and rolled itself round in its folds, and erected its head, as ready to revenge itself on such as should assault it: after which it became a rod again as it was before. (273) After this God bid Moses to put his right hand into his bosom: he obeyed, and when he took it out it was white, and in colour like to chalk, but afterward it returned to its wonted colour again. He also, upon God's command, took some of the water that was near him, and poured it upon the ground, and saw the colour was that of blood. (274) Upon the wonder that Moses showed at these signs, God exhorted him to be of good courage, and to be assured that he would be the greatest support to him; and bid him make use of those signs, in order to obtain belief among all men, that 'thou art sent by me, and dost all things according to my commands. Accordingly I enjoin thee to make no more delays, but to make haste to Egypt, and to travel night and day, and not to draw out the time, and so make the slavery of the Hebrews and their sufferings to last the longer.'

(275) Moses having now seen and heard these wonders that assured him of the truth of these promises of God, had no room left him to disbelieve them; he entreated him to grant him that power when he should be in Egypt, and besought him to vouchsafe him the knowledge of his own name; and, since he had heard and seen him, that he would also tell him his name, that when he offered sacrifice he might invoke him by such his name in his oblations. (276) Whereupon God declared to him his holy name, which had never been discovered to men before; concerning which it is not lawful for me to say any more. Now these signs accompanied Moses, not then only, but always when he prayed for them; of all which signs he attributed the firmest assent to the fire in the bush; and believing that God would be a gracious supporter to him, he hoped he should be able to deliver his own nation, and bring calamities on the Egyptians.

CHAPTER 13

(277) So Moses, when he understood that the Pharaoh in whose reign he fled away, was dead, asked leave of Raguel to go to Egypt, for the benefit of his own people; and he took with him Zipporah, the daughter of Raguel, whom he had married, and the children he had by her, Gersom and Eleazer, and made haste into Egypt. (278) Now the former of those names, Gersom, in the Hebrew tongue signifies *that he was in a strange land*; and Eleazer that, *by the assistance of the God of his fathers, he had escaped from the Egyptians.* (279) Now

when they were near the borders, Aaron his brother, by the command of God, met him, to whom he declared what had befallen him at the mountain, and the commands that God had given him. But as they were going forward, the chief men among the Hebrews, having learned that they were coming, met them; (280) to whom Moses declared the signs he had seen; and while they could not believe them, he made them see them. So they took courage at these surprising and unexpected sights, and hoped well of their entire deliverance, as believing now that God took care of their preservation.

(281) Since then Moses found that the Hebrews would be obedient to whatsoever he should direct, as they promised to be, and were in love with liberty, he came to the king, who had indeed but lately received the government, (282) and told him how much he had done for the good of the Egyptians, when they were despised by the Ethiopians, and their country laid waste by them; and how he had been the commander of their forces, and had laboured for them as if they had been his own people: and he informed him in what danger he had been during that expedition, without having any proper returns made him as he had deserved. (283) He also informed him distinctly what things happened to him at Mount Sinai, and what God said to him; and the signs that were done by God, in order to assure him of the authority of those commands which he had given him. He also exhorted him not to disbelieve what he told him, nor to oppose the will of God.

(284) But when the king derided Moses, he made him in earnest see the signs that were done at Mount Sinai. Yet was the king very angry with him, and called him an ill man, who had formerly run away from his Egyptian slavery, and came now back with deceitful tricks and wonders and magical arts, to astonish him. (285) And when he had said this, he commanded the priests to let him see the same wonderful sights, as knowing that the Egyptians were skilful in this kind of learning, and that he was not the only person who knew them, and pretended them to be divine; as also he told him, that when he brought such wonderful sights before him, he would only be believed by the unlearned. Now when the priests threw down their rods, they became serpents. (286) But Moses was not daunted at it; and said, 'O king, I do not myself despise the wisdom of the Egyptians, but I say that what I do is so much superior to what these do by magic arts and tricks, as divine power exceeds the power of man: but I will demonstrate that what I do is not done by craft, or counterfeiting what is not really true, but that they appear by the providence and power of God.' (287) And when he had said this, he cast his rod down upon the ground, and commanded it to turn itself into a serpent. It obeyed him, and went all round, and devoured the rods of the Egyptians, which seemed to be dragons, until it had consumed them all. It then returned to its own form, and Moses took it into his hand again.

(288) However, the king was no more moved when this was done than before; and being very angry, he said that he should gain nothing by this his cunning and shrewdness against the Egyptians; and he commanded him that was the chief taskmaster over the Hebrews, to give them no relaxation from their labours, but to compel them to submit to greater oppressions than before; (289) and though he allowed them chaff before for making their bricks, he would allow it them no longer, but he made them to work hard at brick-making in the daytime and to gather chaff in the night. Now when their labour was thus doubled upon them, they laid the blame upon Moses, because their labour and their misery were on his account become more severe to them; (290) but Moses did not let his courage sink for the king's threatenings, nor did he abate of his zeal on account of the Hebrews' complaints; but he supported himself and set his soul resolutely against them both, and used his own utmost diligence to procure liberty to his countrymen. (291) So he went to the king, and persuaded him to let the Hebrews to Mount Sinai, and there to sacrifice to God, because God had enjoined them so to do. He persuaded him also not to counterwork the designs of God, but to esteem his favour above all things, and to permit them to depart, lest, before he be aware, he lay an obstruction in the way of the divine commands, and so occasion his own suffering such punishments as it was probable anyone that counterworked the divine commands should undergo, (292) since the severest afflictions arise from every object to those that provoke the divine wrath against them; for such as these have neither the earth nor the air for their friends; nor are the fruits of the womb according to nature, but everything is unfriendly and adverse towards them. He said further, that the Egyptians should know this by sad experience; and that besides, the Hebrew people should go out of their country without their consent.

CHAPTER 14

(293) But when the king despised the words of Moses, and had no regard at all to them, grievous plagues seized the Egyptians; every one of which I will describe, both because no such plagues did ever happen to any other nation as the Egyptians now felt, and because I would demonstrate that Moses did not fail in any one thing that he foretold them; and because it is for the good of mankind, that they may learn this caution: not to do anything that may displease God, lest he be provoked to wrath, and avenge their iniquities upon them. (294) For the Egyptian river ran with bloody water at the command of God, insomuch that it could not be drunk, and they had no other spring of water neither; for the water was not only of the colour of blood, but it brought upon those that ventured to drink of it, great pains and bitter

torment. (295) Such was the river to the Egyptians; but it was sweet and fit for drinking to the Hebrews, and no way different from what it naturally used to be. As the king therefore knew not what to do in these surprising circumstances, and was in fear for the Egyptians, he gave the Hebrews leave to go away; but when the plague ceased, he changed his mind again, and would not suffer them to go.

(296) But when God saw that he was ungrateful, and upon the ceasing of this calamity would not grow wiser, he sent another plague upon the Egyptians: an innumerable multitude of frogs consumed the fruit of the ground; the river was also full of them, insomuch that those who drew water had it spoiled by the blood of these animals, as they died in, and were destroyed by, the water; (297) and the country was full of filthy slime, as they were born and as they died: they also spoiled their vessels in their houses, which they used, and were found among what they eat and what they drank, and came in great numbers upon their beds. There was also an ungrateful smell, and a stink arose from them, as they were born, and as they died therein. (298) Now, when the Egyptians were under the oppression of these miseries, the king ordered Moses to take the Hebrews with him, and be gone. Upon which the whole multitude of the frogs vanished away, and both the land and the river returned to their former natures. (299) But as soon as Pharaoh saw the land freed from this plague, he forgot the cause of it, and retained the Hebrews; and, as though he had a mind to try the nature of more such judgments, he would not yet suffer Moses and his people to depart, having granted that liberty rather out of fear than out of any good consideration.

(300) Accordingly God punished his falseness with another plague, added to the former; for there arose out of the bodies of the Egyptians an innumerable quantity of lice, by which, wicked as they were, they miserably perished, as not able to destroy this sort of vermin either with washes or with ointments. (301) At which terrible judgment the king of Egypt was in disorder, upon the fear into which he reasoned himself, lest his people should be destroyed, and that the manner of this death was also reproachful, so that he was forced in part to recover himself from his wicked temper to a sounder mind, (302) for he gave leave for the Hebrews themselves to depart. But when the plague thereupon ceased, he thought it proper to require that they should leave their children and wives behind them, as pledges of their return; whereby he provoked God to be more vehemently angry at him, as if he thought to impose on his providence, and as if it were only Moses, and not God, who punished the Egyptians for the sake of the Hebrews; (303) for he filled that country full of various sorts of pestilential creatures, with their various properties, such indeed as had never come into the sight of men before, by whose means the men perished themselves, and the land was destitute of

husbandmen for its cultivation; but if anything escaped destruction from them, it was killed by a distemper which the men underwent also.

(304) But when Pharaoh did not even then yield to the will of God, but, while he gave leave to the husbands to take their wives with them, yet insisted that the children should be left behind, God presently resolved to punish his wickedness with several sorts of calamities, and those worse than the foregoing, which yet had so generally afflicted them; for their bodies had terrible boils, breaking forth with blains, while they were already inwardly consumed; and a great part of the Egyptians perished in this manner. (305) But when the king was not brought to reason by this plague, hail was sent down from heaven; and such hail it was, as the climate of Egypt had never suffered before, nor was it like to that which falls in other climates in wintertime, but was larger than that which falls in the middle of spring to those that dwell in the northern and northwestern regions. This hail broke down their boughs laden with fruit. (306) After this a tribe of locusts consumed the seed which was not hurt by the hail; so that to the Egyptians all hopes of the future fruits of the ground were entirely lost.

(307) One would think the forementioned calamities might have been sufficient for one that was only foolish, without wickedness, to make him wise, and to make him sensible what was for his advantage. But Pharaoh, led not so much by his folly as by his wickedness, even when he saw the cause of his miseries, he still contested with God, and willfully deserted the cause of virtue; so he bid Moses take the Hebrews away, with their wives and children, but to leave their cattle behind, since their own cattle were destroyed. (308) But when Moses said that what he desired was unjust, since they were obliged to offer sacrifices to God of those cattle; and the time being prolonged on this account, a thick darkness, without the least light, spread itself over the Egyptians, whereby their sight being obstructed, and their breathing hindered by the thickness of the air, they died miserably, and under a terror lest they should be swallowed up by the dark cloud. (309) Besides this, when the darkness, after three days and as many nights, was dissipated, and when Pharaoh did not still repent and let the Hebrews go, Moses came to him and said, 'How long wilt thou be disobedient to the command of God? For he enjoins thee to let the Hebrews go; nor is there any other way of being freed from the calamities you are under, unless you do so.' (310) But the king was angry at what he said, and threatened to cut off his head if he came any more to trouble him about these matters. Hereupon Moses said he would not speak to him any more about them, for that he himself, together with the principal men among the Egyptians, should desire the Hebrews to go away. So when Moses had said this, he went his way.

(311) But when God had signified, that with one more plague he would

compel the Egyptians to let the Hebrews go, he commanded Moses to tell the people that they should have a sacrifice ready, and that they should prepare themselves on the tenth day of the month Xanthicus, against the fourteenth (which month is called by the Egyptians Pharmuth, and Nisan by the Hebrews; but the Macedonians call it Xanthicus) and that he should carry away the Hebrews with all they had. (312) Accordingly, he having got the Hebrews ready for their departure, and having sorted the people into tribes, he kept them together in one place; but when the fourteenth day was come, and all were ready to depart, they offered the sacrifice, and purified their houses with the blood, using bunches of hyssop for that purpose; and when they had supped, they burnt the remainder of the flesh, as just ready to depart. (313) Whence it is that we do still offer this sacrifice in like manner to this day, and call this festival *Pascha*, which signifies *the feast of the passover*, because on that day God passed us over, and sent the plague upon the Egyptians; for the destruction of the first-born came upon the Egyptians that night, so that many of the Egyptians who lived near the king's palace, persuaded Pharaoh to let the Hebrews go. (314) Accordingly he called for Moses, and bid them begone; as supposing, that if once the Hebrews were gone out of the country, Egypt should be freed from its miseries. They also honoured the Hebrews with gifts; some, in order to get them to depart quickly, and others on account of their neighbourhood, and the friendship they had with them.

CHAPTER 15

(315) So the Hebrews went out of Egypt, while the Egyptians wept, and repented that they had treated them so hardly. Now they took their journey by Letopolis, a place at that time deserted, but where Babylon was built afterwards, when Cambyses laid Egypt waste: but as they went away hastily, on the third day they came to a place called Baalzephon, on the Red Sea; (316) and when they had no food out of the land, because it was a desert, they eat of loaves kneaded of flour only, warmed by a gentle heat; and this food they made use of for thirty days; for what they brought with them out of Egypt would not suffice them any longer time; and this only while they dispensed it to each person, to use so much only as would serve for necessity, but not for satiety. (317) Whence it is that, in memory of the want we were then in, we keep a feast for eight days, which is called *the feast of unleavened bread*. Now the entire multitude of those that went out, including the women and children, was not easy to be numbered; but those that were of an age fit for war, were six hundred thousand.

(318) They left Egypt in the month of Xanthicus, on the fifteenth day of the lunar month, four hundred and thirty years after our forefather Abraham came

into Canaan, but two hundred and fifteen years only after Jacob removed into Egypt. (319) It was the eightieth year of the age of Moses, and of that of Aaron three more. They also carried out the bones of Joseph with them, as he had charged his sons to do.

(320) But the Egyptians soon repented that the Hebrews were gone; and the king also was mightily concerned that this had been procured by the magic arts of Moses; so they resolved to go after them. Accordingly they took their weapons and other warlike furniture, and pursued after them, in order to bring them back, if once they overtook them, because they would now have no pretence to pray to God against them, since they had already been permitted to go out; (321) and they thought they should easily overcome them, as they had no armour, and would be weary with their journey; so they made haste in their pursuit, and asked of everyone they met which way they were gone. And indeed that land was difficult to be travelled over, not only by armies, but by single persons. (322) Now Moses led the Hebrews this way, that in case the Egyptians should repent and be desirous to pursue after them, they might undergo the punishment of their wickedness, and of the breach of those promises they had made to them. As also he led them this way on account of the Philistines, who had quarrelled with them, and hated them of old, that by all means they might not know of their departure, for their country is near to that of Egypt; (323) and thence it was that Moses led them not along the road that tended to the land of the Philistines, but he was desirous that they should go through the desert, that so after a long journey, and after many afflictions, they might enter upon the land of Canaan. Another reason of this was, that God commanded him to bring the people to Mount Sinai, that there they might offer him sacrifices. (324) Now when the Egyptians had overtaken the Hebrews, they prepared to fight them, and by their multitude they drove them into a narrow place; for the number that pursued after them was six hundred chariots, with fifty thousand horsemen, and two hundred thousand footmen, all armed. They also seized on the passages by which they imagined the Hebrews might fly, shutting them up between inaccessible precipices and the sea; (325) for there was [on each side] a [ridge of] mountains that terminated at the sea, which were impassable by reason of their roughness, and obstructed their flight; wherefore they were pressed upon the Hebrews with their army, where [the ridges of] the mountains were closed with the sea; which army they placed at the chops of the mountains, that so they might deprive them of any passage into the plain.

(326) When the Hebrews, therefore, were neither able to bear up, being thus, as it were, besieged, because they wanted provisions, nor saw any possible way of escaping; and if they should have thought of fighting, they had no weapons, they expected a universal destruction, unless they delivered themselves up to the

Egyptians. (327) So they laid the blame on Moses, and forgot all the signs that had been wrought by God for the recovery of their freedom; and this so far, that their incredulity prompted them to throw stones at the prophet, while he encouraged them and promised them deliverance; and they resolved that they would deliver themselves up to the Egyptians. (328) So there was sorrow and lamentation among the women and children, who had nothing but destruction before their eyes, while they were encompassed with mountains, the sea, and their enemies, and discerned no way of flying from them.

(329) But Moses, though the multitude looked fiercely at him, did not, however, give over the care of them, but despised all dangers, out of his trust in God, who, as he had afforded them the several steps already taken for the recovery of their liberty, which he had foretold them, would not now suffer them to be subdued by their enemies, to be either made slaves or be slain by them; (330) and standing in the midst of them, he said, 'It is not just of us to distrust even men, when they have hitherto well managed our affairs, as if they would not be the same men hereafter; but it is no better than madness, at this time, to despair of the providence of God, by whose power all those things have been performed which he promised, when you expected no such things: (331) I mean all that I have been concerned in for your deliverance and escape from slavery. Nay, when we are in the utmost distress, as you see we are, we ought rather to hope that God will succour us, by whose operation it is that we are now encompassed within this narrow place, (332) that he may deliver us out of such difficulties as are otherwise insurmountable, and out of which neither you nor your enemies expect you can be delivered, and may at once demonstrate his own power and his providence over us. Nor does God use to give his help in small difficulties to those whom he favours, but in such cases where no one can see how any hope in man can better their condition. (333) Depend, therefore, upon such a protector as is able to make small things great, and to show that this mighty force against you is nothing but weakness, and be not affrighted at the Egyptian army, nor do you despair of being preserved, because the sea before, and the mountains behind, afford you no opportunity for flying; for even these mountains, if God so please, may be made plain ground for you, and the sea become dry land.'

CHAPTER 16

(334) When Moses had said this, he led them to the sea, while the Egyptians looked on, for they were within sight. Now these were so distressed by the toil of their pursuit, that they thought proper to put off fighting till the next day. But when Moses was come to the seashore, he took his rod, and made supplication to God, and called upon him to be their helper and assistant; and

said, (335) 'Thou art not ignorant, O Lord, that it is beyond human strength and human contrivance to avoid the difficulties we are now under; but it must be by thy work altogether to procure deliverance to this army, which has left Egypt at thy appointment. (336) We despair of any other assistance or contrivance, and have recourse only to that hope we have in thee; and if there by any method that can promise us an escape by thy providence, we look up to thee for it. And let it come quickly, and manifest thy power to us; and do thou raise up this people unto good courage and hope of deliverance, who are deeply sunk into a disconsolate state of mind. (337) We are in a helpless place, but still it is a place that thou possesseth; still the sea is thine, the mountains also that enclose us are thine; so that these mountains will open themselves if thou commandest them, and the sea also, if thou commandest it, will become dry land. Nay, we might escape by a flight through the air, if thou shouldst determine we should have that way of salvation.'

(338) When Moses had thus addressed himself to God, he smote the sea with his rod, which parted asunder at the stroke, and receiving those waters into itself, left the ground dry, as a road and a place of flight for the Hebrews. (339) Now when Moses saw this appearance of God, and that the sea went out of its own place, and left dry land, he went first of all into it, and bid the Hebrews to follow him along that divine road, and to rejoice at the danger their enemies that followed them were in; and gave thanks to God for this so surprising a deliverance which appeared from him.

(340) Now, while these Hebrews made no stay, but went on earnestly, led by God's presence with them, the Egyptians supposed at first that they were distracted, and were going rashly upon manifest destruction. But when they saw that they were going a great way without any harm, and that no obstacle or difficulty fell in their journey, they made haste to pursue them, hoping that the sea would be calm for them also. They put their horse foremost, and went down themselves into the sea. (341) Now the Hebrews, while these were putting on their armour, and therein spending their time, were beforehand with them, and escaped them, and got first over to the land on the other side without any hurt. Whence the others were encouraged, and more courageously pursued them, as hoping no harm would come to them neither; (342) but the Egyptians were not aware that they went into a road made for the Hebrews, and not for others; that this road was made for the deliverance of those in danger, but not for those that were earnest to make use of it for the others' destruction. (343) As soon, therefore, as ever the whole Egyptian army was within it, the sea flowed to its own place, and came down with a torrent raised by storms of wind, and encompassed the Egyptians. Showers of rain also came down from the sky, and dreadful thunders and lightning, with flashes of fire. Thunderbolts also were darted upon them,

(344) nor was there anything which used to be sent by God upon men, as indications of his wrath, which did not happen at this time; for a dark and dismal night oppressed them. And thus did all these men perish, so that there was not one man left to be a messenger of this calamity to the rest of the Egyptians.

(345) But the Hebrews were not able to contain themselves for joy at their wonderful deliverance, and destruction of their enemies. Now indeed, supposing themselves firmly delivered, when those that would have forced them into slavery were destroyed, and when they found they had God so evidently for their protector; (346) and now these Hebrews having escaped the danger they were in, after this manner, and besides that, seeing their enemies punished in such a way as is never recorded of any other men whomsoever, were all the night employed in singing of hymns, and in mirth. Moses also composed a song unto God, containing his praises, and a thanksgiving for his kindness, in hexameter verse.

(347) As for myself, I have delivered every part of this history as I found it in the sacred books; nor let anyone wonder at the strangeness of the narration, if a way were discovered to those men of old time, who were free from the wickedness of the modern ages, whether it happened by the will of God, or whether it happened of its own accord – (348) while, for the sake of those that accompanied Alexander, king of Macedonia, who yet lived, comparatively, but a little while ago, the Pamphylian Sea retired and afforded them a passage through itself, when they had no other way to go; I mean, when it was the will of God to destroy the monarchy of the Persians: and this is confessed to be true by all that have written about the actions of Alexander, but as to these events, let every one determine as he pleases.

(349) On the next day Moses gathered together the weapons of the Egyptians, which were brought to the camp of the Hebrews by the current of the sea, and the force of the winds assisting it; and he conjectured that this also happened by Divine Providence, that so they might not be destitute of weapons. So when he had ordered the Hebrews to arm themselves with them, he led them to Mount Sinai, in order to offer sacrifice to God, and to render oblations for the salvation of the multitude, as he was charged to do beforehand.

BOOK THREE

CHAPTER I

(1) When the Hebrews had obtained such a wonderful deliverance, the country was a great trouble to them, for it was entirely a desert, and without all sustenance for them; and also had exceeding little water, so that it not only was not at all sufficient for the men, but not enough to feed any of the cattle; for it was parched up, and had no moisture that might afford nutriment to the vegetables; so they were forced to travel over this country, as having no other country but this to travel in. (2) They had indeed carried water along with them, from the land over which they had travelled before, as their conductor had bidden them; but when that was spent, they were obliged to draw water out of wells, with pain, by reason of the hardness of the soil. Moreover, what water they found was bitter, and not fit for drinking, and this in small quantities also; (3) and as they thus travelled, they came late in the evening to a place called Marah, which had that name from the badness of its water, for *Mar* denotes *bitterness*. Thither they came afflicted both by the tediousness of their journey, and by their want of food, for it entirely failed them at that time. (4) Now here was a well, which made them choose to stay in the place, which, although it were not sufficient to satisfy so great an army, did yet afford them some comfort, as found in such desert places; for they heard from those who had been to search, that there was nothing to be found, if they travelled on further. Yet was this water bitter, and not fit for men to drink; and, not only so, but it was intolerable even to the cattle themselves.

(5) When Moses saw how much the people were cast down, and that the occasion of it could not be contradicted, for the people were not in the nature of a complete army of men, who might oppose a manly fortitude to the necessity that distressed them; the multitude of the children, and of the women also, being of too weak capacities to be persuaded by reason, blunted the courage of the men themselves – he was therefore in great difficulties, and made everybody's calamity his own; (6) for they ran all of them to him, and begged of him; the women begged for their infants, and the men for the women, that he would not overlook them, but procure some way or other for their deliverance. He therefore betook himself to prayer to God, that he would change the water from its present badness and make it fit for drinking. (7) And when God had granted him that favour, he took the top of a stick that lay down at his feet, and divided it in the middle, and made the section

lengthways. He then let it down into the well, and persuaded the Hebrews that God had hearkened to his prayers, and had promised to render the water such as they desired it to be, in case they would be subservient to him in what he should enjoin them to do, and this not after a remiss or negligent manner. (8) And when they asked what they were to do in order to have the water changed for the better, he bid the strongest men among them that stood there, to draw up water; and told them, that when the greatest part was drawn up, the remainder would be fit to drink; so they laboured at it till the water was so agitated and purged as to be fit to drink.

(9) And now removing from thence they came to Elim; which place looked well at a distance, for there was a grove of palm trees; but when they came near to it, it appeared to be a bad place, for the palm trees were no more than seventy; and they were ill grown and creeping trees, by the want of water, for the country about was all parched, and no moisture sufficient to water them, and make them hopeful and useful, (10) was derived to them from the fountains, which were in number twelve: they were rather a few moist places than springs, which not breaking out of the ground, nor running over, could not sufficiently water the trees. And when they dug into the sand, they met with no water; and if they took a few drops of it into their hands, they found it to be useless, on account of its mud. (11) The trees also were too weak to bear fruit, for want of being sufficiently cherished and enlivened by the water. So they laid the blame on their conductor, and made heavy complaints against him; and said that this their miserable state, and the experience they had of adversity, were owing to him; for that they had then journeyed an entire thirty days, and had spent all the provisions they had brought with them; and meeting with no relief, they were in a very desponding condition. (12) And by fixing their attention upon nothing but their present misfortunes, they were hindered from remembering what deliverances they had received from God, and those by the virtue and wisdom of Moses also; so they were very angry at their conductor, and were zealous in their attempt to stone him, as the direct occasion of their present miseries.

(13) But as for Moses himself, while the multitude were irritated and bitterly set against him, he cheerfully relied upon God, and upon his consciousness of the care he had taken of these his own people: and he came into the midst of them, even while they clamoured against him, and had stones in their hands in order to dispatch him. Now he was of an agreeable presence, and very able to persuade the people by his speeches; (14) accordingly he began to mitigate their anger, and exhorted them not to be over-mindful of their present adversities, lest they should thereby suffer the benefits that had formerly been bestowed on them to slip out of their memories; and he desired them by no means, on account of their present uneasiness, to cast those great and wonderful favours

and gifts, which they had obtained of God, out of their minds, but to expect deliverance out of those their present troubles which they could not free themselves from, (15) and this by the means of that Divine Providence which watched over them; seeing it is probable that God tries their virtue, and exercises their patience by these adversities, that it may appear what fortitude they have, and what memory they retain of his former wonderful works in their favour, and whether they will not think of them upon occasion of the miseries they now feel. (16) He told them, it appeared they were not really good men, either in patience or in remembering what had been successfully done for them, sometimes by condemning God and his commands, when by those commands they left the land of Egypt; and sometimes by behaving themselves ill towards him who was the servant of God, and this when he had never deceived them, either in what he said or had ordered them to do by God's command. (17) He also put them in mind of all that had passed: how the Egyptians were destroyed when they attempted to detain them contrary to the command of God; and after what manner the very same river was to the others bloody, and not fit for drinking, but was to them sweet and fit for drinking; (18) and how they went a new road through the sea, which fled a long way from them, by which very means they were themselves preserved, but saw their enemies destroyed; and that when they were in want of weapons, God gave them plenty of them: and so he recounted all the particular instances, how when they were, in appearance, just going to be destroyed, God had saved them in a surprising manner; that he had still the same power; (19) and that they ought not even now to despair of his providence over them; and accordingly he exhorted them to continue quiet, and to consider that help would not come too late, though it come not immediately, if it be present with them before they suffer any great misfortune; that they ought to reason thus: that God delays to assist them, not because he has no regard to them, but because he will first try their fortitude, and the pleasure they take in their freedom, (20) that he may learn whether you have souls great enough to bear want of food, and scarcity of water, on its account; or whether you rather love to be slaves, as cattle are slaves to such as own them and feed them liberally, but only in order to make them more useful in their service. (21) That as for himself, he shall not be so much concerned for his own preservation; for if he die unjustly, he shall not reckon it any affliction; but that he is concerned for them, lest, by casting stones at him, they should be thought to condemn God himself.

(22) By this means Moses pacified the people, and restrained them from stoning him, and brought them to repent of what they were going to do; and because he thought the necessity they were under made their passion less unjustifiable, he thought he ought to apply himself to God by prayer and supplication; and going up to an eminence, he requested of God for some

succour for the people, (23) and some way of deliverance from the want they were in, because in him, and in him alone, was their hope of salvation: and he desired that he would forgive what necessity had forced the people to do, since such was the nature of mankind, hard to please, and very complaining under adversities. Accordingly God promised he would take care of them and afford them the succour they were desirous of. (24) Now when Moses had heard this from God, he came down to the multitude: but as soon as they saw him joyful at the promises he had received from God, they changed their sad countenances into gladness. So he placed himself in the midst of them, and told them he came to bring them from God a deliverance from their present distresses. (25) Accordingly a little after came a vast number of quails, which is a bird more plentiful in this Arabian Gulf than anywhere else, flying over the sea, and hovered over them, till wearied with their laborious flight, and, indeed, as usual, flying very near to the earth, they fell down upon the Hebrews, who caught them and satisfied their hunger with them, and supposed that this was the method whereby God meant to supply them with food. Upon which Moses returned thanks to God for affording them his assistance so suddenly, and sooner than he had promised them.

(26) But presently after this first supply of food, he sent them a second; for as Moses was lifting up his hands in prayer, a dew fell down; and Moses, when he found it stick to his hands, supposed this was also come for food from God to them: he tasted it, (27) and perceiving that the people knew not what it was, and thought it snowed, and that it was what usually fell at that time of the year, he informed them that this dew did not fall from heaven after the manner they imagined, but came for their preservation and sustenance. So he tasted it, and gave them some of it, that they might be satisfied about what he told them. (28) They also imitated their conductor, and were pleased with the food, for it was like honey in sweetness and pleasant taste, but like in its body to bdellium, one of the sweet spices, and in bigness equal to coriander seed. And very earnest they were in gathering it; (29) but they were enjoined to gather it equally, the measure of an omer for each one every day, because this food should not come in too small a quantity, lest the weaker might not be able to get their share, by reason of the overbearing of the strong in collecting it. (30) However, these strong men when they had gathered more than the measure appointed for them, had no more than others, but only tired themselves more in gathering it, for they found no more than an omer apiece; and the advantage they got by what was superfluous was none at all, it corrupting, both by the worms breeding in it, and by its bitterness. So divine and wonderful a food was this! (31) It also supplied the want of other sorts of food to those that fed on it; and even now, in all that place, this manna comes down in rain, according to what Moses then obtained of God, to send it to the people for their sustenance.

(32) Now the Hebrews call this food *manna;* for the particle *man*, in our language, is the asking of a question. *What is this*? So the Hebrews were very joyful at what was sent them from heaven. Now they made use of this food for forty years, or as long as they were in the wilderness.

(33) As soon as they were removed thence, they came to Rephidim, being distressed to the last degree by thirst; and while in the foregoing days they had lit on a few small fountains, but now found the earth entirely destitute of water, they were in an evil case. They again turned their anger against Moses; (34) but he at first avoided the fury of the multitude, and then betook himself to prayer to God, beseeching him, that as he had given them food when they were in the greatest want of it, so he would give them drink, since the favour of giving them food was of no value to them while they had nothing to drink: (35) and God did not long delay to give it them, but promised Moses that he would procure them a fountain, and plenty of water from a place they did not expect any; so he commanded him to smite the rock which they saw lying there, with his rod, and out of it to receive plenty of what they wanted: for he had taken care that drink should come to them without any labour or painstaking. (36) When Moses had receive this command from God, he came to the people, who waited for him and looked upon him; for they saw already that he was coming apace from his eminence. As soon as he was come, he told them that God would deliver them from their present distress, and had granted them an unexpected favour; and informed them, that a river should run for their sakes out of the rock; (37) but they were amazed at that hearing, supposing they were of necessity to cut the rock in pieces, now they were distressed by their thirst and by their journey – while Moses, only smiting the rock with his rod, opened a passage, and out of it burst water, and that in great abundance, and very clear; (38) but they were astonished at this wonderful effect, and, as it were, quenched their thirst by the very sight of it. So they drank this pleasant, this sweet water; and such it seemed to be, as might well be expected where God was the donor. They were also in admiration how Moses was honoured by God; and they made grateful returns of sacrifices to God for his providence towards them. Now that Scripture which is laid up in the temple, informs us, how God foretold to Moses that water should in this manner be derived out of the rock.

CHAPTER 2

(39) The name of the Hebrews began already to be everywhere renowned, and rumours about them ran abroad. This made the inhabitants of those countries to be in no small fear. Accordingly they sent ambassadors to one another, and exhorted one another to defend themselves, and to endeavour to destroy these men. (40) Those that induced the rest to do so, were such as inhabited Gobolitis

and Petra. They were called *Amalekites*, and were the most warlike of the nations that lived thereabout; and whose kings exhorted one another and their neighbours to go to this war against the Hebrews, telling them that an army of strangers, and such a one as had run away from slavery under the Egyptians, lay in wait to ruin them; (41) which army they were not, in common prudence and regard to their own safety, to overlook, but to crush them before they gather strength and come to be in prosperity; and perhaps attack them first in a hostile manner, as presuming upon our indolence in not attacking them before; and that we ought to avenge ourselves of them for what they have done in the wilderness, but that this cannot be so well done when they have once laid their hands on our cities and our goods: (42) that those who endeavour to crush a power in its first rise are wiser than those that endeavour to put a stop to its progress when it is become formidable; for these last seem to be angry only at the flourishing of others, but the former do not leave any room for their enemies to become troublesome to them. After they had sent such ambassages to the neighbouring nations, and among one another, they resolved to attack the Hebrews in battle.

(43) These proceedings of the people of those countries occasioned perplexity and trouble to Moses, who expected no such warlike preparations; and when these nations were ready to fight, and the multitude of the Hebrews were obliged to try the fortune of war, they were in a mighty disorder, and in want of all necessaries, and yet were to make war with men who were thoroughly well prepared for it. (44) Then, therefore, it was that Moses began to encourage them, and to exhort them to have a good heart and rely on God's assistance, by which they had been advanced into a state of freedom, and to hope for victory over those who were ready to fight with them, in order to deprive them of that blessing: (45) that they were to suppose their own army to be numerous, wanting nothing, neither weapons, nor money, nor provisions, nor such other conveniences as, when men are in possession of, they fight undauntedly; and that they are to judge themselves to have all these advantages in the divine assistance. They are also to suppose the enemy's army to be small, unarmed, weak, and such as want those conveniences which they know must be wanted, when it is God's will that they shall be beaten; (46) and how valuable God's assistance is, they had experienced in abundance of trials, and those such as were more terrible than war, for that is only against men; but these were against famine and thirst, things indeed that are in their own nature insuperable; as also against mountains, and that sea which afforded them no way for escaping; yet had all these difficulties been conquered by God's gracious kindness to them. So he exhorted them to be courageous at this time, and to look upon their entire prosperity to depend on the present conquest of their enemies.

(47) And with these words did Moses encourage the multitude, who then called together the princes of their tribes and their chief men both separately and conjointly. The young men he charged to obey their elders, and the elders to hearken to their leader. (48) So the people were elevated in their minds, and ready to try their fortune in battle, and hoped to be thereby at length delivered from all their miseries: nay, they desired that Moses would immediately lead them against their enemies without the least delay, that no backwardness might be a hindrance to their present resolution. (49) So Moses sorted all that were fit for war into different troops, and set Joshua, the son of Nun, of the tribe of Ephraim, over them; one that was of great courage, and patient to undergo labours; of great abilities to understand, and to speak what was proper; and very serious in the worship of God; and indeed made, like another Moses, a teacher of piety towards God. (50) He also appointed a small party of the armed men to be near the water, and to take care of the children and the women, and of the entire camp. So that whole night they prepared themselves for the battle; they took their weapons, if any of them had such as were well made, and attended to their commanders as ready to rush forth to the battle as soon as Moses should give the word of command. Moses also kept awake, teaching Joshua after what manner he should order his camp. (51) But when the day began, Moses called for Joshua again, and exhorted him to approve himself in deeds such a one as a his reputation made men expect from him; and to gain glory by the present expedition, in the opinion of those under him, for his exploits in this battle. He also gave a particular exhortation to the principal men of the Hebrews, and encouraged the whole army as it stood armed before him. (52) And when he had thus animated the army, both by his words and works, and prepared everything, he retired to a mountain, and committed the army to God and to Joshua.

(53) So the armies joined battle; and it came to a close fight, hand to hand, both sides showing great alacrity, and encouraging one another. And indeed while Moses stretched out his hand towards heaven, the Hebrews were too hard for the Amalekites: but Moses not being able to sustain his hands thus stretched out (for as often as he let down his hands, so often were his own people worsted), (54) he bade his brother Aaron, and Hur their sister Miriam's husband, to stand on each side of him, and take hold of his hands, and not permit his weariness to prevent it, but to assist him in the extension of his hands. When this was done, the Hebrews conquered the Amalekites by main force; and indeed they had all perished, unless the approach of the night had obliged the Hebrews to desist from killing any more. (55) So our forefathers obtained a most signal and most seasonable victory; for they not only overcame those that fought against them, but terrified also the neighbouring nations, and got great and splendid advantages, which they obtained of their enemies by

their hard pains in this battle: for when they had taken the enemy's camp, they got ready booty for the public, and for their own private families, whereas till then they had not any sort of plenty, even of necessary food. (56) The forementioned battle, when they had once got it, was also the occasion of their prosperity, not only for the present, but for the future ages also; for they not only made slaves of the bodies of their enemies, but subdued their minds also, and after this battle, became terrible to all that dwelt round about them. Moreover, they acquired a vast quantity of riches; (57) for a great deal of silver and gold was left in the enemy's camp, as also brazen vessels, which they made common use of in their families; many utensils also that were embroidered, there were of both sorts, that is of what were weaved, and what were the ornaments of their armour, and other things that served for use in the family, and for the furniture of their rooms; they got also the prey of their cattle, and of whatsoever uses to follow camps, when they remove from one place to another. (58) So the Hebrews now valued themselves upon their courage, and claimed great merit for their valour; and they perpetually inured themselves to take pains, by which they deemed every difficulty might be surmounted. Such were the consequences of this battle.

(59) On the next day, Moses stripped the dead bodies of their enemies, and gathered together the armour of those that were fled, and gave rewards to such as had signalised themselves in the action; and highly commended Joshua, their general, who was attested to by all the army, on account of the great actions he had done. Nor was any one of the Hebrews slain; but the slain of the enemy's army were too many to be enumerated. (60) So Moses offered sacrifices of thanksgiving to God, and built an altar, which he named *The Lord the Conqueror*. He also foretold that the Amalekites should utterly be destroyed; and that hereafter none of them should remain, because they fought against the Hebrews, and this when they were in the wilderness, and in their distress also. Moreover, he refreshed the army with feasting. (61) And thus did they fight this first battle with those that ventured to oppose them, after they were gone out of Egypt. But when Moses had celebrated this festival for the victory, he permitted the Hebrews to rest for a few days, and then he brought them out after the fight, in order of battle: (62) for they had now many soldiers in light armour. And going gradually on, he came to Mount Sinai, in three months' time after they were removed out of Egypt; at which mountain, as we have before related, the vision of the Bush, and the other wonderful appearances, had happened.

CHAPTER 3

(63) Now when Raguel, Moses's father-in-law, understood in what a prosperous condition his affairs were, he willingly came to meet him. And Moses took Zipporah, his wife, and his children, and pleased himself with his coming. And when he had offered sacrifice, he made a feast for the multitude, near the Bush he had formerly seen; (64) which multitude, every one, according to their families, partook of the feast. But Aaron and his family took Raguel, and sung hymns to God, as to him who had been the author and procurer of their deliverance and their freedom. (65) They also praised their conductor, as him by whose virtue it was that all things had succeeded so well with them. Raguel also, in his eucharistical oration to Moses, made great encomiums upon the whole multitude: and he could not but admire Moses for his fortitude, and that humanity he had shown in the delivery of his friends.

CHAPTER 4

(66) The next day, as Raguel saw Moses in the midst of a crowd of business (for he determined the differences of those that referred them to him, every one still going to him, and supposing that they should then only obtain justice, if he were the arbitrator; (67) and those that lost their causes thought it no harm while they thought they lost them justly, and not by partiality); Raguel, however, said nothing to him at that time, as not desirous to be any hindrance to such as had a mind to make use of the virtue of their conductor. But afterward he took him to himself, and when he had him alone, he instructed him in what he ought to do, (68) and advised him to leave the trouble of lesser causes to others, but himself to take care of the greater, and of the people's safety; for that certain others of the Hebrews might be found that were fit to determine causes, but that nobody but a Moses could take care of the safety of so many ten thousands. (69) 'Be not, therefore,' says he, 'insensible of thine own virtue, and what thou hast done by ministering under God to the people's preservation. Permit, therefore, the determination of common causes to be done by others, but do thou reserve thyself to the attendance on God only, and look out for methods of preserving the multitude from their present distress. (70) Make use of the method I suggest to you, as to human affairs; and take a review of the army, and appoint chosen rulers over tens of thousands, and then over thousands; then divide them into five hundreds, and again into hundreds, and into fifties; (71) and set rulers over each of them, who may distinguish them into thirties, and keep them in order; and at last number them by twenties and by tens: and let there be one commander over each number, to

be denominated from the number of those over whom they are rulers, but such as the whole multitude have tried, and do approve of, as being good and righteous men; (72) and let those rulers decide the controversies they have one with another. But if any great cause arise, let them bring the cognisance of it before the rulers of a higher dignity; but if any great difficulty arise that is too hard for even their determination, let them send it to thee. By these means two advantages will be gained; the Hebrews will have justice done them, and thou wilt be able to attend constantly on God, and procure him to be more favourable to the people.'

(73) This was the admonition of Raguel; and Moses received his advice very kindly, and acted according to his suggestion. Nor did he conceal the invention of this method, nor pretend to it himself, but informed the multitude who it was that invented it: (74) nay, he has named Raguel in the books he wrote, as the person who invented this ordering of the people, as thinking it right to give a true testimony to worthy persons, although he might have gotten reputation by ascribing to himself the inventions of other men; whence we may learn the virtuous disposition of Moses: but of such his disposition, we shall have proper occasion to speak in other places of these books.

CHAPTER 5

(75) Now Moses called the multitude together, and told them that he was going from them unto mount Sinai to converse with God; to receive from him, and to bring back with him, a certain oracle; but he enjoined them to pitch their tents near the mountain, and prefer the habitation that was nearest to God, before one more remote. (76) When he had said this, he ascended up to Mount Sinai, which is the highest of all the mountains that are in that country, and is not only very difficult to be ascended by men, on account of its vast altitude, but because of the sharpness of its precipices also; nay, indeed, it cannot be looked at without pain of the eyes; and besides this, it was terrible and inaccessible, on account of the rumour that passed about, that God dwelt there. (77) But the Hebrews removed their tents as Moses had bidden them, and took possession of the lowest parts of the mountain; and were elevated in their minds, in expectation that Moses would return from God with promises of the good things he had proposed to them. (78) So they feasted and waited for their conductor, and kept themselves pure as in other respects, and not accompanying with their wives for three days, as he had before ordered them to do. And they prayed to God that he would favourably receive Moses in his conversing with them, and bestow some such gift upon them by which they might live well. They also lived more plentifully as to their diet; and put on

their wives and children more ornamental and decent clothing than they usually wore.

(79) So they passed two days in this way of feasting; but on the third day before the sun was up, a cloud spread itself over the whole camp of the Hebrews, such a one as none had before seen, and encompassed the place where they had pitched their tents; (80) and while all the rest of the air was clear, there came strong winds, that raised up large showers of rain, which became a mighty tempest. There was also such lightning as was terrible to those that saw it, and thunder, with its thunderbolts, were sent down, and declared God to be there present in a gracious way to such as Moses desired he should be gracious. (81) Now, as to these matters, every one of my readers may think as he pleases; but I am under a necessity of relating this history as it is described in the sacred books. This sight, and the amazing sound that came to their ears, disturbed the Hebrews to a prodigious degree, (82) for they were not such as they were accustomed to; and then the rumour that was spread abroad, how God frequented that mountain, greatly astonished their minds, so they sorrowfully contained themselves within their tents, as both supposing Moses to be destroyed by the divine wrath, and expecting the like destruction for themselves.

(83) When they were under these apprehensions, Moses appeared as joyful and greatly exalted. When they saw him, they were freed from their fear, and admitted of more comfortable hopes as to what was to come. The air also was become clear and pure of its former disorders, upon the appearance of Moses; (84) whereupon he called together the people to a congregation, in order to their hearing what God would say to them; and when they were gathered together, he stood on an eminence whence they might all hear him, and said, 'God has received me graciously, O Hebrews, as he has formerly done; and has suggested a happy method of living for you, and an order of political government, and is now present in the camp; (85) I therefore charge you, for his sake and the sake of his works, and what we have done by his means, that you do not put a low value on what I am going to say, because the commands have been given by me that now deliver them to you, nor because it is the tongue of a man that delivers them to you; but if you have a due regard to the great importance of the things themselves, you will understand the greatness of him whose institutions they are, and who has not disdained to communicate them to me for our common advantage; (86) for it is not to be supposed that the author of these institutions is barely Moses, the son of Amram and Jochebed, but he who obliged the Nile to run bloody for your sakes, and tamed the haughtiness of the Egyptians by various sorts of judgments; he who provided a way through the sea for us; he who contrived a method of sending us food from Heaven, when we were distressed for want of it; he who made

the water to issue out of a rock, when we had very little of it before; (87) he by whose means Adam was made to partake of the fruits both of the land and of the sea; he by whose means Noah escaped the deluge; he by whose means our forefather Abraham, of a wandering pilgrim, was made the heir of the land of Canaan; he by whose means Isaac was born of parents that were very old; he by whose means Jacob was adorned with twelve virtuous sons; he by whose means Joseph became a potent lord over the Egyptians; he it is who conveys these instructions to you by me as his interpreter. (88) And let them be to you venerable, and contended for more earnestly by you than your own children and your own wives; for if you will follow them, you will lead a happy life, you will enjoy the land fruitful, the sea calm, and the fruit of the womb born complete, as nature requires; you will be also terrible to your enemies; for I have been admitted into the presence of God, and been made a hearer of his incorruptible voice; so great is his concern for your nation and its duration.'

(89) When he had said this, he brought the people, with their wives and children, so near the mountain, that they might hear God himself speaking to them about the precepts which they were to practice; that the energy of what should be spoken might not be hurt by its utterance by that tongue of a man, which could but imperfectly deliver it to their understanding. (90) And they all heard a voice that came to all of them from above, insomuch that no one of these words escaped them, which Moses wrote on two tables; which it is not lawful for us to set down directly, but their import we will declare.

(91) The first commandment teaches us: that there is but one God, and that we ought to worship him only; the second commands us not to make the image of any living creature to worship it; the third, that we must not swear by God in a false matter; the fourth, that we must keep the seventh day, by resting from all sorts of work; (92) the fifth, that we must honour our parents; the sixth, that we must abstain from murder; the seventh, that we must not commit adultery; the eighth, that we must not be guilty of theft; the ninth, that we must not bear false witness; the tenth, that we must not admit of the desire of anything that is another's.

(93) Now when the multitude had heard God himself giving those precepts which Moses had discoursed of, they rejoiced at what was said, and the congregation was dissolved; but on the following days they came to his tent, and desired him to bring them, besides, other laws from God. (94) Accordingly he appointed such laws, and afterwards informed them in what manner they should act in all cases; which laws I shall make mention of in their proper time; but I shall reserve most of those laws for another work, and make there a distinct explication of them.

(95) When matters were brought to this state, Moses went up again to Mount Sinai, of which he had told them beforehand. He made his ascent in

their sight; and while he stayed there so long a time (for he was absent from them forty days), fear seized upon the Hebrews, lest Moses should have come to any harm; nor was there anything else so sad, and that so much troubled them, as this supposal that Moses was perished. (96) Now there was a variety in their sentiments about it, some saying that he was fallen among wild beasts, and those that were of this opinion were chiefly such as were ill-disposed to him, but others said that he was departed, and gone to God; (97) but the wiser sort were led by their reason to embrace neither of those opinions with any satisfaction, thinking that as it was a thing that sometimes happens to men to fall among wild beasts, and perish that way, so it was probably enough that he might depart and go to God, on account of his virtue; they therefore were quiet, and expected the event; (98) yet were they exceeding sorry upon the supposal that they were deprived of a governor and a protector, such a one indeed as they could never recover again; nor would this suspicion give them leave to expect any comfortable event about this man, nor could they prevent their trouble and melancholy upon this occasion. However, the camp durst not remove all this while, because Moses had bidden them afore to stay there.

(99) But when the forty days, and as many nights, were over, Moses came down, having tasted nothing of food usually appointed for the nourishment of men. His appearance filled the army with gladness, and he declared to them what care God had of them, and by what manner of conduct of their lives they might live happily, telling them that during these days of his absence (100) he had suggested to him also that he would have a tabernacle built for him, into which he would descend when he came to them; and how we should carry it about with us when we remove from this place; and that there would be no longer any occasion for going up to Mount Sinai, but that he would himself come and pitch his tabernacle amongst us, and be present at our prayers; (101) as also, that the tabernacle should be of such measures and construction as he had shown him; and that you are to fall to the work, and prosecute it diligently. When he had said this, he showed them the two tables, with the ten commandments engraven upon them, five upon each table; and the writing was by the hand of God.

CHAPTER 6

(102) Hereupon the Israelites rejoiced at what they had seen and heard of their conductor, and were not wanting in diligence according to their ability; for they brought silver and gold and brass, and of the best sorts of wood, and such as would not at all decay by putrefaction; camels' hair also, and sheepskins, some of them dyed of a blue colour, and some of a scarlet; some brought the flower for the purple colour, and others for white, (103) with wool dyed by the flowers

aforementioned; and fine linen and precious stones, which those that use costly ornaments set in buckles of gold; they brought also a great quantity of spices; for of these materials did Moses build the tabernacle, which did not at all differ from a movable and ambulatory temple. (104) Now when these things were brought together with great diligence (for everyone was ambitious to further the work even beyond their ability), he set architects over the works, and this by the command of God; and indeed the very same which the people themselves would have chosen, had the election been allowed to them. (105) Now their names are set down in writing in the sacred books; and they were these: Besaleel the son of Uri, of the tribe of Judah, the grandson of Miriam, the sister of their conductor; and Aholiab, the son of Ahisamach, of the tribe of Dan. (106) Now the people went on with what they had undertaken with so great alacrity, that Moses was obliged to restrain them, by making proclamation that what had been brought was sufficient, as the artificers had informed him; so they fell to work upon the building of the tabernacle. (107) Moses also informed them, according to the direction of God, both what the measures were to be, and its largeness; and how many vessels it ought to contain for the use of the sacrifices. The women also were ambitious to do their parts, about the garments of the priests, and about other things that would be wanted in this work, both for ornament and for the divine service itself.

(108) Now when all things were prepared, the gold and the silver and the brass, and what was woven, Moses, when he had appointed beforehand that there should be a festival, and that sacrifices should be offered according to everyone's ability, reared up the tabernacle; and when he had measured the open court, fifty cubits broad and a hundred long, (109) he set up brazen pillars, five cubits high, twenty on each of the longer sides, and ten pillars for the breadth behind; every one of the pillars also had a ring. Their chapiters were of silver, but their bases were of brass; they resembled the sharp ends of spears, and were of brass, fixed into the ground. (110) Cords were also put through the rings, and were tied at their further ends to brass nails of a cubit long, which, at every pillar, were driven into the floor, and would keep the tabernacle from being shaken by the violence of winds; but a curtain of fine soft linen went round all the pillars, and hung down in a flowing and loose manner from their chapiters, and enclosed the whole space, and seemed not at all unlike to a wall about it. (111) And this was the structure of three of the sides of this enclosure; but as for the fourth side, which was fifty cubits in extent, and was the front of the whole, twenty cubits of it were for the opening of the gates, wherein stood two pillars on each side, after the resemblance of open gates. (112) These were made wholly of silver, and polished, and that all over, excepting the bases, which were of brass. Now on each side of the gates there stood three pillars, which were inserted into the concave bases of the gates, and were suited to

them; and round them was drawn a curtain of fine linen; (113) but to the gates themselves, which were twenty cubits in extent, and five in height, the curtain was composed of purple and scarlet and blue, and fine linen, and embroidered with many and divers sorts of figures, excepting the figures of animals. (114) Within these gates was the brazen laver for purification, having a basin beneath of the like matter, whence the priests might wash their hands and sprinkle their feet; and this was the ornamental construction of the enclosure about the court of the tabernacle, which was exposed to the open air.

(115) As to the tabernacle itself, Moses placed it in the middle of that court, with its front to the east, that when the sun arose it might send its first rays upon it. Its length when it was set up, was thirty cubits, and its breadth was twelve [ten] cubits. The one of its walls was on the south, and the other was exposed to the north, and on the back part of it remained the west. (116) It was necessary that its height should be equal to its breadth [ten cubits]. There were also pillars made of wood, twenty on each side; they were wrought into a quadrangular figure, in breadth a cubit and a half, but the thickness was four fingers; (117) they had thin plates of gold affixed to them on both sides, inwardly and outwardly: they had each of them two tenons belonging to them, inserted into their bases, and these were of silver, in each of which bases there was a socket to receive the tenon; (118) but the pillars on the west wall were six. Now all these tenons and sockets accurately fitted one another, insomuch that the joints were invisible, and both seemed to be one entire and united wall. It was also covered with gold, both within and without. The number of pillars was equal on the opposite sides, (119) and there were on each part twenty, and every one of them had the third part of a span in thickness; so that the number of thirty cubits were fully made up between them; but as to the wall behind, where the six pillars made up together only nine cubits, they made two other pillars, and cut them out of one cubit, which they placed in the corners, and made them equally fine with the other. (120) Now every one of the pillars had rings of gold affixed to their fronts outward, as if they had taken root in the pillars, and stood one row over against another round about, through which were inserted bars gilt over with gold, each of them five cubits long, and these bound together the pillars, the head of one bar running into another, after the nature of one tenon inserted into another; (121) but for the wall behind, there was but one row of bars that went through all the pillars, into which row ran the ends of the bars on each side of the longer walls, the male with its female being so fastened in their joints, that they held the whole firmly together; and for this reason was all this joined so fast together, that the tabernacle might not be shaken, either by the winds or by any other means, but that it might preserve itself quiet and immovable continually.

(122) As for the inside, Moses parted its length into three partitions. At the

distance of ten cubits from the most secret end, Moses placed four pillars, the workmanship of which was the very same with that of the rest; and they stood upon the like bases with them, each a small matter distant from his fellow. Now the room within those pillars was the most holy place; but the rest of the room was the tabernacle, which was open for the priests. (123) However, this proportion of the measures of the tabernacle proved to be an imitation of the system of the world: for that third part thereof which was within the four pillars, to which the priests were not admitted, is, as it were, a Heaven peculiar to God; but the space of the twenty cubits, is, as it were, sea and land, on which men live, and so this part is peculiar to the priests only: (124) but at the front, where the entrance was made, they placed pillars of gold that stood on bases of brass, in number seven; but then they spread over the tabernacle veils of fine linen and purple and blue and scarlet colours, embroidered. (125) The first veil was ten cubits every way, and this they spread over the pillars which parted the temple, and kept the most holy place concealed within; and this veil was that which made this part not visible to any. Now the whole temple was called *The Holy Place*; but that part which was within the four pillars, and to which none were admitted, was called *The Holy of Holies*. (126) This veil was very ornamental, and embroidered with all sorts of flowers which the earth produces; and there were interwoven into it all sorts of variety that might be an ornament, excepting the forms of animals. (127) Another veil there was which covered the five pillars that were at the entrance. It was like the former in its magnitude and texture and colour; and at the corner of every pillar a ring retained it from the top downwards half the depth of the pillars, the other half affording an entrance for the priests, who crept under it. (128) Over this there was a veil of linen, of the same largeness with the former: it was to be drawn this way or that way by cords, the rings of which, fixed to the texture of the veil and to the cords also, were subservient to the drawing and undrawing of the veil, and to the fastening it at the corner, that then it might be no hindrance to the view of the sanctuary, especially on solemn days; (129) but that on other days, and especially when the weather was inclined to snow, it might be expanded, and afford a covering to the veil of divers colours; whence that custom of ours is derived, of having a fine linen veil, after the temple has been built, to be drawn over the entrances; (130) but the ten other curtains were four cubits in breadth, and twenty-eight in length; and had golden clasps, in order to join the one curtain to the other, which was done so exactly that they seemed to be one entire curtain. These were spread over the temple, and covered all the top and parts of the walls, on the sides and behind, so far as within one cubit of the ground. (131) There were other curtains of the same breadth with these, but one more in number, and longer, for they were thirty cubits long; but these were woven of hair, with the like subtlety as those of wool were made, and were extended loosely down to the ground, appearing like a triangular front and elevation at the gates, the eleventh curtain being used for this very purpose. (132) There were also other curtains made of skins above these, which afforded covering and protection to those that were woven, both in hot weather and when it rained; and great was the surprise of those who viewed these curtains at a distance, for they seemed not at all to differ from the colour of the sky; (133) but those that were made of hair and of skins, reached down in the same manner as did the veil at the gates, and kept off the heat of the sun, and what injury the rains might do, and after this manner was the tabernacle reared.

(134) There was also an ark made, sacred to God, of wood that was naturally strong, and could not be corrupted. This was called *Eron*, in our own language. (135) Its construction was thus: its length was five spans, but its breadth and height was each of them three spans; it was covered all over with gold, both within and without, so that the wooden part was not seen. It had also a cover united to it, by golden hinges, after a wonderful manner; which cover was every way evenly fitted to it, and had no eminences to hinder its exact conjunction. (136) There were also two golden rings belonging to each of the longer boards, and passing through the entire wood, and through them gilt bars passed along each board, that it might thereby be moved and carried about, as occasion should require; for it was not drawn in a cart by beasts of burden, but borne on the shoulders of the priests. (137) Upon this its cover were two images, which the Hebrews call *Cherubims*; they are flying creatures, but their form is not like to that of any of the creatures which men have seen, though Moses said he had seen such beings near the throne of God. (138) In this ark he put the two tables whereon the ten commandments were written, five upon each table, and two and a half upon each side of them: and this ark he placed in the most holy place.

(139) But in the holy place he placed a table, like those at Delphi: its length was two cubits, and its breadth one cubit, and its height three spans. It had feet also, the lower half of which were complete feet, resembling those which the Dorians put to their bedsteads; but the upper parts towards the table were wrought into a square form. (140) The table had a hollow towards every side, having a ledge of four fingers' depth, that went round about like a spiral, both on the upper and lower part of the body of the work. Upon every one of the feet was there also inserted a ring, not far from the cover, through which went bars of wood beneath, but gilded, to be taken out upon occasion, (141) there being a cavity where it was joined to the rings; for they were not entire rings, but before they came quite round they ended in acute points, the one of which was inserted into the prominent part of the table, and the other into the foot; and by these it was carried when they journeyed. (142) Upon this table, which was placed on the north side of the temple, not far from the most holy place,

were laid twelve unleavened loaves of bread, six upon each heap, one above another: they were made of two tenth-deals of the purest flour, which tenth-deal [an omer] is a measure of the Hebrews, containing seven Athenian *cotylae;* (143) and above those loaves were put two vials full of frankincense. Now after seven days other loaves were brought in their stead, on the day which is by us called the *Sabbath;* for we call the seventh day the *Sabbath.* But for the occasion of this invention of placing loaves here, we will speak of it in another place.

(144) Over against this table, near the southern wall, was set a candlestick of cast gold, hollow within, being of the weight of one hundred pounds, which the Hebrews call *Chinchares;* if it be turned into the Greek language, it denotes a *talent.* (145) It was made with its knops, and lilies, and pomegranates, and bowls (which ornaments amounted to seventy in all); by which means the shaft elevated itself on high from a single base, and spread itself into as many branches as there are planets, including the sun among them. (146) It terminated in seven heads, in one row, all standing parallel to one another; and these branches carried seven lamps, one by one, in imitation of the number of the planets. These lamps looked to the east and to the south, the candlestick being situate obliquely.

(147) Now between this candlestick and the table, which, as we said, were within the sanctuary, was the altar of incense, made of wood indeed, but of the same wood of which the foregoing vessels were made, such as was not liable to corruption; it was entirely crusted over with a golden plate. Its breadth on each side was a cubit, but the altitude double. (148) Upon it was a grate of gold, that was extant above the altar, which had a golden crown encompassing it round about, whereto belonged rings and bars, by which the priests carried it when they journeyed. (149) Before this tabernacle there was reared a brazen altar, but it was within made of wood, five cubits by measure on each side, but its height was but three, in like manner adorned with brass plates as bright as gold. It had also a brazen hearth of network; for the ground underneath received the fire from the hearth, because it had no basis to receive it. (150) Hard by this altar lay the basins, and the vials, and the censers, and the caldrons, made of gold; but the other vessels, made for the use of the sacrifices, were all of brass. And such was the construction of the tabernacle; and these were the vessels thereto belonging.

CHAPTER 7

(151) There were peculiar garments appointed for the priests, and for all the rest, which they call *Cahanaeae* [priestly] garments, as also for the high priests, which they call *Cahanaeae Rabbae*, and denote the high priest's garments. Such was therefore the habit of the rest; (152) but when the priest approaches the

sacrifices, he purifies himself with the purification which the law prescribes; and, in the first place, he puts on that which is called *Machanase*, which means somewhat that is fast tied. It is a girdle, composed of fine twined linen, and is put about the privy parts, the feet being to be inserted into them, in the nature of breeches; but above half of it is cut off, and it ends at the thighs and is there tied fast.

(153) Over this he wore a linen vestment, made of fine flax doubled: it is called *Chethone*, and denotes *linen*, for we call linen by the name of *Chethone*. This vestment reaches down to the feet, and sits close to the body, and has sleeves that are tied fast to the arms: (154) it is girded to the breast a little above the elbows, by a girdle often going round, four fingers broad, but so loosely woven, that you would think it were the skin of a serpent. It is embroidered with flowers of scarlet and purple and blue, and fine twined linen; but the warp was nothing but fine linen. (155) The beginning of its circumvolution is at the breast; and when it has gone often round, it is there tied, and hangs loosely there down to the ankles: I mean this, all the time the priest is not about any laborious service, for in this position it appears in the most agreeable manner to the spectators; but when he is obliged to assist at the offering sacrifices, and to do the appointed service, that he may not be hindered in his operations by its motion, he throws it to the left, and bears it on his shoulder. (156) Moses indeed calls this belt *Abaneth*; but we have learned from the Babylonians to call it *Emia*, for so it is by them called. This vestment has no loose or hollow parts anywhere in it, but only a narrow aperture about the neck; and it is tied with certain strings hanging down from the edge over the breast and back, and is fastened above each shoulder: it is called *Massabazanes*.

(157) Upon his head he wears a cap, not brought to a conic form nor encircling the whole head, but still covering more than the half of it, which is called *Masnaemphthes*: and its make is such that it seems to be a crown, being made of thick swathes, but the contexture is of linen, and it is doubled round many times, and sewed together: (158) besides which, a piece of fine linen covers the whole cap from the upper part, and reaches down to the forehead, and hides the seams of the swathes, which would otherwise appear indecently: this adheres closely upon the solid part of the head, and is thereto so firmly fixed that it may not fall off during the sacred service about the sacrifices. So we have now shown you what is the habit of the generality of the priests.

(159) The high priest is indeed adorned with the same garments that we have described, without abating one; only over these he puts on a vestment of a blue colour. This also is a long robe, reaching to his feet [in our language it is called *Meeir*], and is tied round with a girdle, embroidered with the same colours and flowers as the former, with a mixture of gold interwoven. (160) To the bottom of which garment are hung fringes, in colour like pomegranates,

with golden bells, by a curious and beautiful contrivance, so that between two bells hangs a pomegranate, and between two pomegranates a bell. (161) Now this vesture was not composed of two pieces, nor was it sewed together upon the shoulders and the sides, but it was one long vestment so woven as to have an aperture for the neck; not an oblique one, but parted all along the breast and the back. A border also was sewed to it, lest the aperture should look too indecently: it was also parted where the hands were to come out.

(162) Besides these, the high priest put on a third garment, which is called the *Ephod*, which resembles the Epomis of the Greeks. Its make was after this manner: it was woven to the depth of a cubit, of several colours, with gold intermixed, and embroidered, but it left the middle of the breast uncovered: it was made with sleeves also; nor did it appear to be at all differently made from a short coat. (163) But in the void place of this garment there was inserted a piece of the bigness of a span, embroidered with gold and the other colours of the ephod, and was called *Essen* [the breastplate], which in the Greek language signifies the *Oracle*. (164) This piece exactly filled up the void space in the ephod. It was united to it by golden rings at every corner, the like rings being annexed to the ephod, and a blue ribbon was made use of to tie them together by those rings; (165) and that the space between the rings might not appear empty, they contrived to fill it up with stitches of blue ribbons. There were also two sardonyxes upon the ephod, at the shoulders, to fasten it in the nature of buttons, having each end running to the sardonyxes of gold, that they might be buttoned by them. (166) On these were engraven the names of the sons of Jacob, in our own country letters, and in our own tongue, six on each of the stones, on either side; and the elder sons' names were on the right shoulder. Twelve stones also there were upon the breastplate, extraordinary in largeness and beauty; and they were an ornament not to be purchased by men, because of their immense value. (167) These stones, however, stood in three rows, by four in a row, and were inserted into the breastplate itself, and they were set in buckles of gold, that were themselves inserted in the breastplate and were so made that they might not fall out. (168) Now the first three stones were a sardonyx, a topaz, and an emerald. The second row contained a carbuncle, a jasper, and a sapphire. The first of the third row was a ligure, then an amethyst, and the third an agate, being the ninth of the whole number. The first of the fourth row was a chrysolite, the next was an onyx, and then a beryl, which was the last of all. (169) Now the names of all those sons of Jacob were engraven in these stones, whom we esteem the heads of our tribes, each stone having the honour of a name, in the order according to which they were born. (170) And whereas the rings were too weak of themselves to bear the weight of the stones, they made two other rings of a larger size, at the edge of that part of the breastplate which reached to the neck, and inserted into the very texture of the

breastplate, to receive chains finely wrought, which connected them with golden bands to the tops of the shoulders, whose extremity turned backwards, and went into the ring on the prominent back part of the ephod; (171) and this was for the security of the breastplate, that it might not fall out of its place. There was also a girdle sewed to the breastplate, which was of the fore-mentioned colours, with gold intermixed, which when it had gone once round was tied again upon the seam, and hung down. There were also golden loops that admitted its fringes at each extremity of the girdle, and included them entirely.

(172) The high priest's mitre was the same that we described before, and was wrought like that of all the other priests; above which there was another, with swathes of blue embroidered, and round it was a golden crown polished, of three rows, one above another, out of which arose a cup of gold, which resembled the herb which we call *Saccharus*: but those Greeks that are skilful in botany call it *Hyoscyamus*. (173) Now, lest anyone that has seen this herb, but has not been taught its name, and is unacquainted with its nature, or, having known its name, knows not the herb when he sees it, I shall give such as these are a description of it. (174) This herb is oftentimes in tallness above three spans, but its root is like that of a turnip (for he that should compare it thereto would not be mistaken); but its leaves are like the leaves of mint. Out of its branches it sends out a calyx, cleaving to the branch; and a coat encompasses it, which it naturally puts off when it is changing, in order to produce its fruit. This calyx is of the bigness of the bone of the little finger, but in the compass of its aperture is like a cup. This I will further describe, for the use of those that are unacquainted with it. (175) Suppose a sphere be divided into two parts, round at the bottom, but having another segment that grows up to a circumference from that bottom; suppose it become narrower by degrees, and that the cavity of that part grow decently smaller, and then gradually grow wider again at the brim, such as we see in the navel of a pomegranate, with its notches. (176) And indeed such a coat grows over this plant as renders it an hemisphere, and that, as one may say, turned accurately in a lathe, and having its notches extant above it, which, as I said, grow like a pomegranate, only that they are sharp, and end in nothing but prickles. (177) Now the fruit is preserved by this coat of the calyx, which fruit is like the seed of the herb Sideritis: it sends out a flower that may seem to resemble that of poppy. (178) Of this was a crown made, as far as from the hinder part of the head to each of the temples; but this *Ephielis*, for so this calyx may be called, did not cover the forehead, but it was covered with a golden plate, which had inscribed upon it the name of God in sacred characters. And such were the ornaments of the high priest.

(179) Now here one may wonder at the ill will which men bear to us, and

which they profess to bear on account of our despising that deity which they pretend to honour; (180) for if anyone do but consider the fabric of the tabernacle, and take a view of the garments of the high priest, and of those vessels which we make use of in our sacred ministration, he will find that our legislator was a divine man, and that we are unjustly reproached by others: for if anyone do without prejudice, and with judgment, look upon these things, he will find they were every one made in way of imitation and representation of the universe. (181) When Moses distinguished the tabernacle into three parts, and allowed two of them to the priests, as a place accessible and common, he denoted the land and the sea, these being of general access to all; but he set apart the third division for God, because heaven is inaccessible to men. (182) And when he ordered twelve loaves to be set on the table, he denoted the year, as distinguished into so many months. By branching out the candlestick into seventy parts, he secretly intimated the *Decani*, or seventy divisions of the planets; and as to the seven lamps upon the candlesticks, they referred to the course of the planets, of which that is the number. (183) The vails, too, which were composed of four things, they declared the four elements; for the fine linen was proper to signify the earth, because the flax grows out of the earth; the purple signified the sea, because that colour is dyed by the blood of a sea shellfish; the blue is fit to signify the air; and the scarlet will naturally be an indication of fire. (184) Now the vestment of the high priest being made of linen, signified the earth; the blue denoted the sky, being like lightning in its pomegranates, and in the noise of the bells resembling thunder. And for the ephod, it showed that God had made the universe of four [elements]; and as for the gold interwoven, I suppose it related to the splendour by which all things are enlightened. (185) He also appointed the breastplate to be placed in the middle of the ephod, to resemble the earth, for that has the very middle place of the world. And the girdle which encompassed the high priest round, signified the ocean, for that goes round about and includes the universe. Each of the sardonyxes declare to us the sun and the moon; those, I mean, that were in the nature of buttons on the high priest's shoulders. (186) And for the twelve stones, whether we understand by them the months, or whether we understand the like number of the signs of that circle which the Greeks call the *Zodiac*, we shall not be mistaken in their meaning. And for the mitre, which was of a blue colour, it seems to me to mean heaven; (187) for how otherwise could the name of God be inscribed upon it? That it was also illustrated with a crown, and that of gold also, is because of that splendour with which God is pleased. Let this explication suffice at present, since the course of my narration will often, and on many occasions, afford me the opportunity of enlarging upon the virtue of our legislator.

CHAPTER 8

(188) When what has been described was brought to a conclusion, gifts not being yet presented, God appeared to Moses and enjoined him to bestow the high priesthood upon Aaron his brother, as upon him that best of them all deserved to obtain that honour, on account of his virtue. And when he had gathered the multitude together, he gave them an account of Aaron's virtue, and of his good will to them, and of the dangers he had undergone for their sakes. (189) Upon which, when they had given testimony to him in all respects, and showed their readiness to receive him, Moses said to them, 'O you Israelites, this work is already brought to a conclusion, in a manner most acceptable to God, and according to our abilities. And now since you see that he is received into this tabernacle, we shall first of all stand in need of one that may officiate for us, and may minister to the sacrifices and to the prayers that are to be put up for us; (190) and indeed had the inquiry after such a person been left to me, I should have thought myself worthy of this honour, both because all men are naturally fond of themselves, and because I am conscious to myself that I have taken a great deal of pains for your deliverance; but now God himself has determined that Aaron is worthy of this honour, and has chosen him for his priest, as knowing him to be the most righteous person among you. (191) So that he is to put on the vestments which are consecrated to God; he is to have the care of the altars, and to make provision for the sacrifices; and he it is that must put up prayers for you to God, who will readily hear them, not only because he is himself solicitous for your nation, but also because he will receive them as offered by one that he hath himself chosen to this office.' (192) The Hebrews were pleased with what was said, and they gave their approbation to him whom God had ordained, for Aaron was, of them all, the most deserving of this honour, on account of his own stock and gift of prophecy, and his brother's virtue. He had at that time four sons: Nadab, Abihu, Eleazar, and Ithamar.

(193) Now Moses commanded them to make use of all the utensils which were more than were necessary to the structure of the tabernacle, for covering the tabernacle itself, the candlestick, and altar of incense, and the other vessels, that they might not be at all hurt when they journeyed, either by the rain or by the rising of the dust. (194) And when he had gathered the multitude together again, he ordained that they should offer half a shekel for every man, as an oblation to God; (195) which shekel is a piece among Hebrews, and is equal to four Athenian drachmae. (196) Whereupon they readily obeyed what Moses had commanded; and the number of the offerers was six hundred and five thousand five hundred and fifty. Now this money that was brought by the men

that were free, was given by such as were above twenty years old, but under fifty; and what was collected was spent in the uses of the tabernacle.

(197) Moses now purified the tabernacle and the priests; which purification was performed after the following manner: he commanded them to take five hundred shekels of choice myrrh, an equal quantity of cassia, and half the foregoing weight of cinnamon and calamus (this last is a sort of sweet spice); to beat them small, and wet them with an hin of oil of olives (an *hin* is our own country measure, and contains two Athenian *choas*, or *congiuses*); then mix them together, and boil them, and prepare them after the art of the apothecary, and make them into a very sweet ointment; (198) and afterward to take it to anoint and to purify the priests themselves, and all the tabernacle, as also the sacrifices. There were also many, and those of various kinds, of sweet spices, that belonged to the tabernacle, and such as were of very great price, and were brought to the golden altar of incense, the nature of which I do not now describe, lest it should be troublesome to my readers; (199) but incense was to be offered twice a day, both before sunrising and at sunsetting. They were also to keep oil already purified for the lamps; three of which were to give light all day long, upon the sacred candlestick, before God, and the rest were to be lighted at the evening.

(200) Now all was finished. Besaleel and Aholiab appeared to be the most skilful of the workmen; for they invented finer works than what others had done before them, and were of great abilities to gain notions of what they were formerly ignorant of; and of these, Besaleel was judged to be the best. (201) Now the whole time they were about this work was the interval of seven months; and after this it was that was ended the first year since their departure out of Egypt. But at the beginning of the second year, on the month *Xanthicus*, as the Macedonians call it, but on the month *Nisan*, as the Hebrews call it, on the new moon, they consecrated the tabernacle and all its vessels, which I have already described.

(202) Now God showed himself pleased with the work of the Hebrews, and did not permit their labours to be in vain; nor did he disdain to make use of what they had made, but he came and sojourned with them, and pitched his tabernacle in the holy house. And in the following manner did he come to it: (203) the sky was clear, but there was a mist over the tabernacle only, encompassing it, but not with such a very deep and thick cloud as is seen in the winter season, nor yet in so thin a one as men might be able to discern anything through it; but from it there dropped a sweet dew, and such a one as showed the presence of God to those that desired and believed it.

(204) Now when Moses had bestowed such honorary presents on the workmen, as it was fit they should receive, who had wrought so well, he offered sacrifices in the open court of the tabernacle, as God commanded him:

a bull, a ram, and a kid of the goats, for a sin offering. (205) Now I shall speak of what we do in our sacred offices in my discourse about sacrifices; and therein shall inform men in what cases Moses bid us offer a whole burnt offering, and in what case the law permits us to partake of them as of food. And when Moses had sprinkled Aaron's vestments, himself and his sons, with the blood of the beasts that were slain, and had purified them with spring waters and ointment, they became God's priests. (206) After this manner did he consecrate them and their garments for seven days together. The same he did to the tabernacle, and the vessels thereto belonging, both with oil first incensed, as I said, and with the blood of bulls and of rams, slain day by day, one according to its kind. But on the eighth day he appointed a feast for the people, and commanded them to offer sacrifice according to their ability. (207) Accordingly they contended one with another and were ambitious to exceed each other in the sacrifices which they brought, and so fulfilled Moses's injunctions. But as the sacrifices lay upon the altar, a sudden fire was kindled from among them of its own accord, and appeared to the sight like fire from a flash of lightning, and consumed whatsoever was upon the altar.

(208) Hereupon an affliction befell Aaron, considered as a man and a father, but was undergone by him with true fortitude; for he had indeed a firmness of soul in such accidents, and he thought this calamity came upon him according to God's will: (209) for whereas he had four sons, as I said before, the two elder of them, Nadab and Abihu, did not bring those sacrifices which Moses bade them bring, but which they used to offer formerly, and were burnt to death. Now when the fire rushed upon them, and began to burn them, nobody could quench it. (210) Accordingly they died in this manner. And Moses bid their father and their brethren to take up their bodies, to carry them out of the camp, and to bury them magnificently. Now the multitude lamented them, and were deeply affected at this their death, which so unexpectedly befell them. (211) But Moses entreated their brethren and their father not to be troubled for them, and to prefer the honour of God before their grief about them; for Aaron had already put on his sacred garments.

(212) But Moses refused all that honour which he saw the multitude ready to bestow upon him, and attended to nothing else but the service of God. He went no more up to Mount Sinai; but he went into the tabernacle, and brought back answers from God for what he prayed for. His habit was also that of a private man; and in all other circumstances he behaved himself like one of the common people, and was desirous to appear without distinguishing himself from the multitude, but would have it known that he did nothing else but take care of them. (213) He also set down in writing the form of their government, and those laws, by obedience whereto they would lead their lives so as to please God, and so as to have no quarrels one among another.

However, the laws he ordained were such as God suggested to him; so I shall now discourse concerning that form of government, and those laws.

(214) I will now treat of what I before omitted, the garment of the high priest: for he [Moses] left no room for the evil practices of [false] prophets; but if some of that sort should attempt to abuse the divine authority, he left it to God to be present at his sacrifices when he pleased, and when he pleased to be absent. And he was willing this should be known, not to the Hebrews only, but to those foreigners also who were there. (215) For as to those stones, which we told you before the high priest bare on his shoulders, which were sardonyxes (and I think it needless to describe their nature, they being known to everybody), the one of them shined out when God was present at their sacrifices; I mean that which was in the nature of a button on his right shoulder, bright rays darting out thence, and being seen even by those that were most remote; which splendour yet was not before natural to the stone. (216) This has appeared a wonderful thing to such as have not so far indulged themselves in philosophy as to despise Divine Revelation. Yet will I mention what is still more wonderful than this: for God declared beforehand, by those twelve stones which the high priest bare on his breast, and which were inserted into his breastplate, when they should be victorious in battle; (217) for so great a splendour shone forth from them before the army began to march, that all the people were sensible of God's being present for their assistance. Whence it came to pass that those Greeks, who had a veneration for our laws, because they could not possibly contradict this, called that breastplate *the Oracle*. (218) Now this breastplate and this sardonyx left off shining two hundred years before I composed this book, God having been displeased at the transgressions of his laws. Of which things we shall further discourse on a fitter opportunity; but I will now go on with my proposed narration.

(219) The tabernacle being now consecrated, and a regular order being settled for the priests, the multitude judged that God now dwelt among them, and betook themselves to sacrifices and praises to God, as being now delivered from all expectation of evils, and as entertaining a hopeful prospect of better times hereafter. They offered also gifts to God, some as common to the whole nation, and others as peculiar to themselves, and these tribe by tribe; (220) for the heads of the tribes combined together, two by two, and brought a wagon and a yoke of oxen. These amounted to six, and they carried the tabernacle when they journeyed. Besides which, each head of a tribe brought a bowl, and a charger a spoon, of ten darics, full of incense. (221) Now the charger and the bowl were of silver, and together they weighed two hundred shekels, but the bowl cost no more than seventy shekels; and these were full of fine flour mingled with oil, such as they used on the altar about the sacrifices. They brought also a young bullock, and a

ram, with a lamb of a year old, for a whole burnt offering, as also a goat for the forgiveness of sins. (222) Every one of the heads of the tribes brought also other sacrifices, called *peace offerings*: for every day two bulls, and five rams, with lambs of a year old, and kids of the goats. These heads of tribes were twelve days in sacrificing, one sacrificing every day. Now Moses went no longer up to Mount Sinai, but went into the tabernacle, and learned of God what they were to do, and what laws should be made; (223) which laws were preferable to what have been devised by human understanding, and proved to be firmly observed for all time to come, as being believed to be the gift of God, insomuch that the Hebrews did not transgress any of those laws, either as tempted in times of peace by luxury, or in times of war by distress of affairs. But I say no more here concerning them, because I have resolved to compose another work concerning our laws.

CHAPTER 9

(224) I will now, however, make mention of a few of our laws which belong to purifications and the like sacred offices, since I am accidentally come to this matter of sacrifices. These sacrifices were of two sorts; of those sorts one was offered for private persons, and the other for the people in general; and they are done in two different ways; (225) in the one case, what is slain is burnt, as a whole burnt offering, whence that name is given to it; but the other is a thank offering, and is designed for feasting those that sacrifice. I will speak of the former. (226) Suppose a private man offer a burnt offering, he must slay either a bull, a lamb, or a kid of the goats, and the two latter of the first year, though of bulls he is permitted to sacrifice those of a greater age; but all burnt offerings are to be of males. When they are slain, the priests sprinkle the blood round about the altar: (227) they then cleanse the bodies, and divide them into parts, and salt them with salt, and lay them upon the altar, while the pieces of wood are piled one upon another, and the fire is burning; they next cleanse the feet of the sacrifices and the innards in an accurate manner, and so lay them to the rest to be purged by the fire, while the priests received the hides. This is the way of offering a burnt offering.

(228) But those that offer thank offerings do indeed sacrifice the same creatures, but such as are unblemished and above a year old; however, they may take either males or females. They also sprinkle the altar with their blood; but they lay upon the altar the kidneys and the caul, and all the fat, and the lobe of the liver, together with the rump of the lamb; (229) then, giving the breast and the right shoulder to the priests, the offerers feast upon the remainder of the flesh for two days; and what remains they burn.

(230) The sacrifices for sins are offered in the same manner as is the thank

offering. But those who are unable to purchase complete sacrifices, offer two pigeons or turtle doves; the one of which is made a burnt offering to God, the other they give as food to the priests. But we shall treat more accurately about the oblation of these creatures in our discourse concerning sacrifices. (231) But if a person fall into sin by ignorance, he offers an ewe lamb, or a female kid of the goats, of the same age; and the priests sprinkle the blood at the altar, not after the former manner, but at the corners of it. They also bring the kidneys and the rest of the fat, together with the lobe of the liver, to the altar, while the priests bear away the hides and the flesh, and spend it in the holy place, on the same day; for the law does not permit them to leave of it until the morning. (232) But if anyone sin, and is conscious of it himself, but hath nobody that can prove it upon him, he offers a ram, the law enjoining him so to do; the flesh of which the priests eat, as before, in the holy place, on the same day. And if the rulers offer sacrifices for their sins, they bring the same oblations that private men do; only they so far differ, that they are to bring for sacrifices a bull or a kid of the goats, both males.

(233) Now the law requires, both in private and public sacrifices, that the finest flour be also brought; for a lamb the measure of one tenth deal, for a ram two, and for a bull three. This they consecrate upon the altar, when it is mingled with oil; (234) for oil is also brought by those that sacrifice; for a bull the half of an hin, and for a ram the third part of the same measure, and one quarter of it for a lamb. This hin is an ancient Hebrew measure, and is equivalent to two Athenian choas (or congiuses). They bring the same quantity of oil which they do of wine, and they pour the wine about the altar; (235) but if anyone does not offer a complete sacrifice of animals, but brings fine flour only for a vow, he throws a handful upon the altar as its first fruits, while the priests take the rest for their food, either boiled or mingled with oil, but made into cakes of bread. But whatsoever it be that a priest himself offers, it must of necessity be all burnt. (236) Now the law forbids us to sacrifice any animal at the same time with its dam: and, in other cases, not till the eighth day after its birth. Other sacrifices there are also appointed for escaping distempers, or for other occasions, in which meat offerings are consumed, together with the animals that are sacrificed; of which it is not lawful to leave any part till the next day, only the priests are to take their own share.

CHAPTER 10

(237) The law requires, that out of the public expenses a lamb of the first year be killed every day, at the beginning and at the ending of the day; but on the seventh day, which is called the *Sabbath*, they kill two, and sacrifice them in the same manner. (238) At the new moon, they both perform the daily sacrifices,

and slay two bulls, with seven lambs of the first year, and a kid of the goats also, for the expiation of sins; that is, if they have sinned through ignorance.

(239) But on the seventh month, which the Macedonians call *Hyperberetaeus*, they make an addition to those already mentioned, and sacrifice a bull, a ram, and seven lambs, and a kid of the goats, for sins.

(240) On the tenth day of the same lunar month, they fast till the evening; and this day they sacrifice a bull, and two rams, and seven lambs, and a kid of the goats, for sins. (241) And, besides these, they bring two kids of the goats; the one of which is sent alive out of the limits of the camp into the wilderness for the scapegoat, and to be an expiation for the sins of the whole multitude; but the other is brought into a place of great cleanness within the limits of the camp, and is there burnt, with its skin, without any sort of cleansing. (242) With this goat was burnt a bull, not brought by the people, but by the high priest, at his own charges; which, when it was slain, he brought of the blood into the holy place, together with the blood of the kid of the goats, and sprinkled the ceiling with his finger seven times, (243) as also its pavement, and again as often toward the most holy place, and about the golden altar: he also at last brings it into the open court, and sprinkles it about the great altar. Besides this, they set the extremities, and the kidneys, and the fat, with the lobe of the liver upon the altar. The high priest likewise presents a ram to God as a burnt offering.

(244) Upon the fifteenth day of the same month, when the season of the year is changing for winter, the law enjoins us to pitch tabernacles in every one of our houses, so that we preserve ourselves from the cold of that time of the year; (245) as also that when we should arrive at our own country, and come to that city which we should have then for our metropolis, because of the temple therein to be built, and keep a festival for eight days, and offer burnt offerings, and sacrifice thank offerings, that we should then carry in our hands a branch of myrtle, and willow, and a bough of the palm tree, with the addition of the pomecitron. (246) That the burnt offering on the first of those days was to be a sacrifice of thirteen bulls and fourteen lambs and fifteen rams, with the addition of a kid of the goats, as an expiation for sins: and on the following days the same number of lambs, and of rams, with the kids of the goats, but abating one of the bulls every day till they amounted to seven only. (247) On the eighth day all work was laid aside, and then, as we said before, they sacrificed to God a bullock, a ram, and seven lambs, with a kid of the goats, for an expiation of sins. And this is the accustomed solemnity of the Hebrews, when they pitch their tabernacles.

(248) In the month of Xanthicus, which is by us called *Nisan*, and is the beginning of our year, on the fourteenth day of the lunar month, when the sun is in Aries (for in this month it was that we were delivered from bondage under the Egyptians, and law ordained that we should every year slay that sacrifice

which I before told you we slew when we came out of Egypt, and which was called the *Passover*; and so we do celebrate this passover in companies, leaving nothing of what we sacrifice till the day following. (249) The feast of unleavened bread succeeds that of the passover, and falls on the fifteenth day of the month, and continues seven days, wherein they feed on unleavened bread; on every one of which days two bulls are killed, and one ram, and seven lambs. Now these lambs are entirely burnt, besides the kid of the goats which is added to all the rest, for sins; for it is intended as a feast for the priest on every one of those days. (250) But on the second day of unleavened bread, which is the sixteenth day of the month, they first partake of the fruits of the earth, for before that day they do not touch them. And while they suppose it proper to honour God, from whom they obtain this plentiful provision, in the first place, they offer the first fruits of their barley, and that in the manner following: (251) They take a handful of the ears, and dry them, then beat them small, and purge the barley from the bran; they then bring one tenth deal to the altar, to God; and, casting one handful of it upon the fire, they leave the rest for the use of the priest; and after this it is that they may publicly or privately reap their harvest. They also at this participation of the first fruits of the earth, sacrifice a lamb, as a burnt offering to God.

(252) When a week of weeks has passed over after this sacrifice (which weeks contain forty and nine days), on the fiftieth day, which is Pentecost, but is called by the Hebrews *Asartha*, which signifies *Pentecost*, they bring to God a loaf made of wheat flour, of two tenth deals, with leaven; and for sacrifices they bring two lambs; (253) and when they have only presented them to God, they are made ready for supper for the priests; nor is it permitted to leave anything of them till the day following. They also slay three bullocks for a burnt offering and two rams; and fourteen lambs, with two kids of the goats, for sins; (254) nor is there any one of the festivals but in it they offer burnt offerings; they also allow themselves to rest on every one of them. Accordingly, the law prescribes in them all what kinds they are to sacrifice, and how they are to rest entirely, and must slay sacrifices, in order to feast upon them.

(255) However, out of the common charges, baked bread was set on the table of shewbread, without leaven, of twenty-four tenth deals of flour, for so much is spent upon this bread; two heaps of these were baked; they were baked the day before the sabbath, but were brought into the holy place on the morning of the sabbath, and set upon the holy table, six on a heap, one loaf still standing over against another; (256) where two golden cups full of frank-incense were also set upon them, and there they remained till another Sabbath, and then other loaves were brought in their stead, while the loaves were given to the priests for their food, and the frankincense was burnt in that sacred fire wherein all their offerings were burnt also; and so other frankincense was set upon the loaves instead of what was there before. (257) The [high] priest also,

of his own charges, offered a sacrifice, and that twice every day. It was made of flour mingled with oil, and gently baked by the fire; and quantity was one tenth deal of flour; he brought the half of it to the fire in the morning, and the other half at night. The account of these sacrifices I shall give more accurately hereafter; but I think I have premised what for the present may be sufficient concerning them.

CHAPTER II

(258) Moses took out the tribe of Levi from communicating with the rest of the people, and set them apart to be a holy tribe: and purified them by water taken from perpetual springs, and with such sacrifices as were usually offered to God on the like occasions. He delivered to them also the tabernacle and the sacred vessels, and the other curtains which were made for covering the tabernacle, that they might minister under the conduct of the priests, who had been already consecrated to God.

(259) He also determined concerning animals, which of them might be used for food, and which they were obliged to abstain from; which matters, when this work shall give me occasion, shall be further explained; and the causes shall be added, by which he was moved to allot some of them to be our food, and enjoined us to abstain from others. (260) However, he entirely forbade us the use of blood for food, and esteemed it to contain the soul and spirit. He also forbade us to eat the flesh of an animal that died of itself, as also the caul, and the fat of goats and sheep and bulls.

(261) He also ordered that those whose bodies were afflicted with leprosy, and who had a gonorrhea, should not come into the city; nay, he removed the women, when they had their natural purgations, till the seventh day; after which he looked on them as pure, and permitted them to come in again. (262) The law permits those also who have taken care of funerals to come in after the same manner, when this number of days is over; but if any continued longer than that number of days in a state of pollution, the law appointed the offering two lambs for a sacrifice; the one of which they are to purge by fire, and for the other, the priests take it for themselves. (263) In the same manner do those sacrifice who have had the gonorrhea. But he that sheds his seed in his sleep, if he go down into cold water, has the same privilege with those that have lawfully accompanied with their wives. (264) And for the lepers, he suffered them not to come into the city at all, nor to live with any others, as if they were in effect dead persons; but if anyone had obtained by prayer to God, the recovery from that distemper and had gained a healthful complexion again, such a one returned thanks to God with several sorts of sacrifices; concerning which we will speak hereafter.

(265) Whence one cannot but smile at those who say that Moses was himself afflicted with the leprosy when he fled out of Egypt, and that he became the conductor of those who on that account left that country, and led them into the land of Canaan; (266) for had this been true, Moses would not have made these laws to his own dishonour, which indeed it was more likely he would have opposed, if others had endeavoured to introduce them; and this the rather, because there are lepers in many nations, who yet are in honour, and not only free from reproach and avoidance, but who have been great captains of armies, and been entrusted with high offices in the commonwealth, and have had the privilege of entering into holy places and temples; (267) so that nothing hindered, but if either Moses himself, or the multitude that was with him, had been liable to such a misfortune in the colour of his skin, he might have made laws about them for their credit and advantage, and have laid no manner of difficulty upon them. (268) Accordingly, it is a plain case, that it is out of violent prejudice only that they report these things about us; but Moses was pure from any such distemper, and lived with countrymen who were pure of it also, and thence made the laws which concerned others that had the distemper. He did this for the honour of God; but as to these matters, let everyone consider them after what manner he pleases.

(269) As to the women when they have borne a child, Moses forbade them to come into the temple or touch the sacrifices before forty days were over, supposing it to be a boy; but if she has borne a girl, the law is that she cannot be admitted before twice that number of days be over; and when after the before-mentioned time appointed for them, they perform their sacrifices, the priests distribute them before God.

(270) But if anyone suspect that his wife has been guilty of adultery, he was to bring a tenth deal of barley flour; they then cast one handful to God, and gave the rest of it to the priests for food. One of the priests set the woman at the gates that are turned towards the temple, and took the veil from her head, and wrote the name of GOD on parchment, (271) and enjoined her to swear that she had not at all injured her husband; and to wish that, if she had violated her chastity, her right thigh might be put out of joint; that her belly might swell, and that she might die thus; but that if her husband, by the violence of his affection, and of the jealousy which arose from it, had been rashly moved to this suspicion, that she might bear a male child in the tenth month. (272) Now when these oaths were over, the priest wiped the name of GOD out of the parchment, and wrung the water into a vial. He also took some dust out of the temple (if any happened to be there, and put a little of it into the vial, and gave it her to drink; whereupon the woman, if she were unjustly accused, conceived with child, and brought it to perfection in her womb; (273) but if she had broken her faith of wedlock to her husband, and had sworn falsely

before God, she died in a reproachful manner; her thigh fell off from her, and her belly swelled with a dropsy. And these are the ceremonies about sacrifices, and about the purifications thereto belonging, which Moses provided for his countrymen. He also prescribed the following laws to them:

CHAPTER 12

(274) As for adultery, Moses forbade it entirely, as esteeming it a happy thing that men should be wise in the affairs of wedlock; and that it was profitable both to cities and families that children should be known to be genuine. He also abhorred men's lying with their mothers, as one of the greatest crimes; and the like for lying with the father's wife, and with aunts, and sisters, and sons' wives, as all instances of abominable wickedness. (275) He also forbade a man to lie with his wife when she was defiled by her natural purgation; and not to come near brute beasts, nor to approve of the lying with a male, which was to hunt after unlawful pleasures on account of beauty. To those who were guilty of such insolent behaviour, he ordained death for their punishment.

(276) As for the priests, he prescribed to them a double degree of purity: for he restrained them in the instances above, and moreover forbade them to marry harlots. He also forbade them to marry a slave or a captive, and such as got their living by cheating trades, and by keeping inns: as also a woman parted from her husband, on any account whatsoever. (277) Nay, he did not think it proper for the high priest to marry even the widow of one that was dead, though he allowed that to the priests; but he permitted him only to marry a virgin, and to retain her. Whence it is that the high priest is not to come near to one that is dead, although the rest are not prohibited from coming near to their brethren or parents or children, when they are dead; (278) but they are to be unblemished in all respects. He ordered that the priest who had any blemish, should have his portion indeed among the priests; but he forbade him to ascend the altar, or to enter into the holy house. He also enjoined them, not only to observe purity in their sacred ministrations, but in their daily conversation, that it might be unblamable also; (279) and on this account it is that those who wear the sacerdotal garments are without spot, and eminent for their purity and sobriety: nor are they permitted to drink wine so long as they wear those garments. Moreover, they offer sacrifices that are entire, and have no defect whatsoever.

(280) And truly Moses gave them all these precepts, being such as were observed during his own lifetime; but though he lived now in the wilderness, yet did he make provision how they might observe the same laws when they should have taken the land of Canaan. (281) He gave them rest to the land from ploughing and planting every seventh year, as he had prescribed to them

to rest from working every seventh day; and ordered, that then what grew of its own accord out of the earth, should in common belong to all that pleased to use it, making no distinction in that respect between their own countrymen and foreigners: and he ordained, that they should do the same after seven times seven years, (282) which in all are fifty years; and that fiftieth year is called by the Hebrews *The Jubilee*, wherein debtors are freed from their debts, and slaves are set at liberty; which slaves became such, though they were of the same stock, by transgressing some of those laws the punishment of which was not capital, but they were punished by this method of slavery. (283) This year also restores the land to its former possessors in the manner following: when the Jubilee is come, which name denotes *liberty*, he that sold the land, and he that bought it, meet together, and make an estimate, on one hand, of the fruits gathered; and, on the other hand, of the expenses laid out upon it. If the fruits gathered come to more than the expenses laid out, he that sold it takes the land again; (284) but if the expenses prove more than the fruits, the present possessor receives of the former owner the difference that was wanting, and leaves the land to him; and if the fruits received, and the expenses laid out, prove equal to one another, the present possessor relinquishes it to the former owners. (285) Moses would have the same law obtain as to those houses also which were sold in villages; but he made a different law for such as were sold in a city, for if he that sold it tendered the purchaser his money again within a year, he was forced to restore it; but in case a whole year had intervened, the purchaser was to enjoy what he had bought. (286) This was the constitution of the laws which Moses learned of God when the camp lay under Mount Sinai; and this he delivered in writing to the Hebrews.

(287) Now when this settlement of laws seemed to be well over, Moses thought fit at length to take a review of the host, as thinking it proper to settle the affairs of war. So he charged the heads of the tribes, excepting the tribe of Levi, to take an exact account of the number of those that were able to go to war; for as to the Levites they were holy, and free from all such burdens. (288) Now when the people had been numbered, there were found six hundred thousand that were able to go to war, from twenty to fifty years of age, besides three thousand six hundred and fifty. Instead of Levi, Moses took Manasseh, the son of Joseph, among the heads of tribes; and Ephraim instead of Joseph. It was indeed the desire of Jacob himself to Joseph, that he would give him his sons to be his own by adoption, as I have before related.

(289) When they set up the tabernacle, they received it into the midst of their camp, three of the tribes pitching their tents on each side of it; and roads were cut through the midst of these tents. It was like a well appointed market; and everything was there ready for sale in due order; and all sorts of artificers were in the shops; and it resembled nothing so much as a city that sometimes

was movable, and sometimes fixed. (290) The priests had the first places about the tabernacle; then the Levites, who, because their whole multitude was reckoned from thirty days old, were twenty-three thousand eight hundred and eighty males; and during the time that the cloud stood over the tabernacle, they thought proper to stay in the same place, as supposing that God there inhabited among them; but when that removed, they journeyed also.

(291) Moreover, Moses was the inventor of the form of their trumpet, which was made of silver. Its description is this: in length it was little less than a cubit. It was composed of a narrow tube, somewhat thicker than a flute, but with so much breadth as was sufficient for admission of the breath of a man's mouth: it ended in the form of a bell, like common trumpets. Its sound was called in the Hebrew tongue *Asosra*. (292) Two of these being made, one of them was sounded when they required the multitude to come together to congregations. When the first of them gave a signal, the heads of the tribes were to assemble, and consult about the affairs to them properly belonging; but when they gave the signal by both of them, they called the multitude together. (293) Whenever the tabernacle was removed, it was done in this solemn order: at the first alarm of the trumpet, those whose tents were on the east quarter prepared to remove; when the second signal was given, those that were on the south quarter did the like; in the next place, the tabernacle was taken to pieces, and was carried in the midst of six tribes that went before, and of six that followed, all the Levites assisting about the tabernacle; (294) when the third signal was given, that part which had their tents towards the west put themselves in motion; and at the fourth signal those on the north did so likewise. They also made use of these trumpets in their sacred ministrations, when they were bringing their sacrifices to the altar, as well on the Sabbaths as on the rest of the [festival] days; and now it was that Moses offered that sacrifice which was called the *Passover in the Wilderness*, as the first he had offered after the departure out of Egypt.

CHAPTER 13

(295) A little while afterwards he rose up, and went from Mount Sinai; and having passed through several mansions, of which we will speak anon, he came to a place called *Hazeroth*, where the multitude began again to be mutinous, and to blame Moses for the misfortunes they had suffered in their travels; (296) and that when he had persuaded them to leave a good land, they at once had lost land, and instead of that happy state he had promised them, they were still wandering in their miserable condition, being already in want of water; and if the manna should happen to fail, they must then utterly perish. (297) Yet while they generally spake many and sore things against the man, there was one of

them who exhorted them not to be unmindful of Moses, and of what great pains he had been at about their common safety; and not to despair of assistance from God. The multitude thereupon became still more unruly, and more mutinous against Moses than before. (298) Hereupon Moses, although he was so basely abused by them, encouraged them in their despairing condition, and promised that he would procure them a great quantity of flesh-meat, and that not for a few days only, but for many days. This they were not willing to believe; and when one of them asked whence he could obtain such vast plenty of what he promised, he replied, 'Neither God nor I, although we hear such opprobrious language from you, will leave off our labours for you; and this shall soon appear also.' (299) As soon as ever he had this, the whole camp was filled with quails, and they stood round about them, and gathered them in great numbers. However, it was not long ere God punished the Hebrews for their insolence, and those reproaches they had used towards him, for no small number of them died; and still to this day the place retains the memory of this destruction, and is named *Kibroth-hattaavah*, which is, *The Graves of Lust*.

CHAPTER 14

(300) When Moses had led the Hebrews away from thence to a place called *Paran*, which was near to the borders of the Canaanites, and a place difficult to be continued in, he gathered the multitude together in a congregation; and standing in the midst of them, he said, 'Of the two things that God determined to bestow upon us, Liberty, and the Possession of a Happy Country, the one of them ye already are partakers of, by the gift of God, and the other you will quickly obtain; (301) for we now have our abode near the borders of the Canaanites, and nothing can hinder the acquisition of it, when we now at last are fallen upon it: I say, not only no king nor city, but neither the whole race of mankind, if they were all gathered together, could do it. Let us therefore prepare ourselves for the work, for the Canaanites will not resign up their land to us without fighting, but it must be wrested from them by great struggles in war. (302) Let us then send spies, who may take a view of the goodness of the land, and what strength it is of; but, above all things, let us be of one mind, and let us honour God, who above all is our helper and assister.'

(303) When Moses had said thus, the multitude requited him with marks of respect; and chose twelve spies, of the most eminent men, one out of each tribe, who, passing over all the land of Canaan from the borders of Egypt, came to the city Hamath, and to Mount Lebanon; and having learned the nature of the land and of its inhabitants, they came home, having spent forty days in the whole work. (304) They also brought with them of the fruits which the land

bare; they also showed them the excellency of those fruits, and gave an account of the great quantity of the good things that land afforded, which were motives to the multitude to go to war. But then they terrified them again with the great difficulty there was in obtaining it; that the rivers were so large and deep that they could not be passed over; and that the hills were so high that they could not travel along for them; that the cities were strong with walls and their firm fortifications round about them. (305) They told them also, that they found at Hebron the posterity of the giants. Accordingly these spies, who had seen the land of Canaan, when they perceived that all these difficulties were greater there than they had met with since they came out of Egypt, they were affrighted at them themselves and endeavoured to affright the multitude also.

(306) So they supposed, from what they had heard, that it was impossible to get the possession of the country. And when the congregation was dissolved they, their wives and children, continued their lamentation, as if God would not indeed assist them, but only promised them fair. (307) They also again blamed Moses, and made a clamour against him and his brother Aaron, the high priest. Accordingly they passed that night very ill, and with contumelious language against them; but in the morning they ran to a congregation, intending to stone Moses and Aaron, and so to return back into Egypt.

(308) But of the spies, there were Joshua, the son of Nun, of the tribe of Ephraim, and Caleb, of the tribe of Judah, that were afraid of the consequence, and came into the midst of them and stilled the multitude, and desired them to be of good courage; and neither to condemn God as having told them lies, nor to hearken to those who had affrighted them by telling them what was not true concerning the Canaanites, but to those that encouraged them to hope for good success; and that they should gain possession of the happiness promised them, (309) because neither the height of mountains nor the depth of rivers could hinder men of true courage from attempting them, especially while God would take care of them beforehand, and be assistant to them. 'Let us then go,' said they, 'against our enemies, and have no suspicion of ill success, trusting in God to conduct us, and following those that are to be our leaders.' (310) Thus did these two exhort them, and endeavour to pacify the rage they were in. But Moses and Aaron fell on the ground, and besought God, not for their own deliverance, but that he would put a stop to what the people were unwarily doing, and would bring their minds to a quiet temper, which were now disordered by their present passion. The cloud also did now appear, and stood over the tabernacle, and declared to them the presence of God to be there.

CHAPTER 15

(311) Moses came now boldly to the multitude, and informed them that God was moved at their abuse of him, and would inflict punishment upon them, not indeed such as they deserved for their sins, but such as parents inflict on their children, in order to their correction; (312) For, he said, that when he was in the tabernacle, and was bewailing with tears that destruction which was coming upon them God put him in mind what things he had done for them, and what benefits they had received from him, and yet how ungrateful they had been to him, that just now they had been induced, through the timorousness of the spies, to think that their words were truer than his own promise to them; (313) and that on this account, though he would not indeed destroy them all, nor utterly exterminate their nation which he had honoured more than any other part of mankind, yet he would not permit them to take possession of the land of Canaan, nor enjoy its happiness; (314) but would make them wander in the wilderness, and live without a fixed habitation and without a city, for forty years together, as a punishment for this their transgression; but that he hath promised to give that land to our children, and that he would make them the possessors of those good things which, by your ungoverned passions, you have deprived yourselves of.

(315) When Moses had discoursed thus to them, according to the direction of God, the multitude grieved, and were in affliction; and entreated Moses to procure their reconciliation to God, and to permit them no longer to wander in the wilderness, but to bestow cities upon them; but he replied that God would not admit of any such trial, for that God was not moved to this determination from any human levity or anger, but that he had judicially condemned them to that punishment. (316) Now we are not to disbelieve that Moses, who was but a single person, pacified so many ten thousands when they were in anger, and converted them to a mildness of temper; for God was with him, and prepared way to his persuasions of the multitude; and as they had often been disobedient, they were now sensible that such disobedience was disadvantageous to them, and that they had still thereby fallen into calamities.

(317) But this man was admirable for his virtue, and powerful in making men give credit to what he delivered, not only during the time of his natural life, but even there is still no one of the Hebrews who does not act even now as if Moses were present, and ready to punish him if he should do anything that is indecent; nay, there is no one but is obedient to what laws he ordained, although they might be concealed in their transgressions. (318) There are also many other demonstrations that his power was more than human, for still some there have

been, who have come from the parts beyond Euphrates, a journey of four months, through many dangers and at great expenses, in honour of our temple; and yet, when they had offered their oblations, could not partake of their own sacrifices, because Moses had forbidden it, by somewhat in the law that did not permit them, or somewhat that had befallen them, which our ancient customs made inconsistent therewith; (319) some of these did not sacrifice at all, and others left their sacrifices in an imperfect condition; nay, many were not able, even at first, so much as to enter into the temple, but went their ways in this state, as preferring a submission to the laws of Moses before the fulfilling of their own inclinations, even when they had no fear upon them that anybody could convict them, but only out of a reverence to their own conscience. (320) Thus this legislation, which appeared to be divine, made this man to be esteemed as one superior to his own nature. Nay, further, a little before the beginning of this war, when Claudius was emperor of the Romans, and Ismael was our high priest, and when so great a famine was come upon us, that one-tenth deal [of wheat] was sold for four drachmae, (321) and when no less than seventy cori of flour were brought into the temple, at the feast of unleavened bread (these cori are thirty-one Sicilian, but forty-one Athenian medimni), not one of the priests was so hardy as to eat one crumb of it, even while so great a distress was upon the land; and this out of a dread of the law, and of that wrath which God retains against acts of wickedness, even when no one can accuse the actors. (322) Whence, we are not to wonder at what was then done, while to this very day, the writings left by Moses have so great a force, that even those that hate us, do confess, that he who established this settlement was God, and that it was by the means of Moses, and of his virtue; but as to these matters, let everyone take them as he thinks fit.

BOOK FOUR

CHAPTER I

(1) Now this life of the Hebrews in the wilderness was so disagreeable and troublesome to them, and they were so uneasy at it, that although God had forbidden them to meddle with the Canaanites, yet could they not be persuaded to be obedient to the words of Moses, and to be quiet; but supposing they should be able to beat their enemies, even without his approbation, they accused him and suspected that he made it his business to keep them in a distressed condition, that they might always stand in need of his assistance. (2) Accordingly they resolved to fight with the Canaanites, and said that God gave them his assistance – not out of regard to Moses's intercessions, but because he took care of their entire nation on account of their forefathers, whose affairs he took under his own conduct; as also that it was on account of their own virtue that he had formally procured them their liberty, and would be assisting to them, now they were willing to take pains for it. (3) They also said that they were possessed of abilities sufficient for the conquest of their enemies, although Moses should have a mind to alienate God from them; that, however, it was to their advantage to be their own masters, and not so far to rejoice in their deliverance from the indignities they endured under the Egyptians, as to bear the tyranny of Moses over them, and to suffer themselves to be deluded, and live according to his pleasure, (4) as though God did only foretell what concerns us out of his kindness to him, as if they were not all the posterity of Abraham; that God made him alone the author of all the knowledge we have, and we must still learn it from him; (5) that it would be a piece of prudence to oppose his arrogant pretences, and to put their confidence in God, and to resolve to take possession of that land which he had promised them, and not to give ear to him, who, on this account, and under the pretence of divine authority, forbade them so to do. (6) Considering, therefore, the distressed state they were in at present, and that in those desert places they were still to expect things would be worse with them, they resolved to fight with the Canaanites, as submitting only to God, their supreme commander, and not waiting for any assistance from their legislator.

(7) When, therefore, they had come to this resolution, as being best for them, they went against their enemies; but those enemies were not dismayed either at the attack itself, or at the great multitude that made it, and received them with great courage. Many of the Hebrews were slain; and the remainder

of the army, upon the disorder of their troops, were pursued, and fled, after a shameful manner, to their camp. (8) Whereupon this unexpected misfortune made them quite despond; and they hoped for nothing that was good; as gathering from it, that this affliction came from the wrath of God, because they rashly went out to war without his approbation.

(9) But when Moses saw how deeply they were affected with this defeat, and being afraid lest the enemies should grow insolent upon this victory, and should be desirous of gaining still greater glory, and should attack them, he resolved that it was proper to withdraw the army into the wilderness to a further distance from the Canaanites; (10) so the multitude gave themselves up again to his conduct; for they were sensible that, without his care for them, their affairs could not be in a good condition; and he caused the host to remove, and he went further into the wilderness, as intending there to let them rest, and not to permit them to fight the Canaanites before God should afford them a more favourable opportunity.

CHAPTER 2

(11) That which is usually the case of great armies, and especially upon ill success, to be hard to be pleased, and governed with difficulty, did now befall the Jews; for they being in number six hundred thousand, and, by reason of their great multitude, not readily subject to their governors, even in prosperity, they at this time were more than usually angry, both against one another and against their leader, because of the distress they were in, and the calamities they then endured. (12) Such a sedition overtook them, as we have not the like example either among the Greeks or the Barbarians, by which they were in danger of being all destroyed, but were notwithstanding saved by Moses, who would not remember that he had been almost stoned to death by them. (13) Nor did God neglect to prevent their ruin; but, notwithstanding the indignities they had offered their legislator and the laws, and their disobedience to the commandments which he had sent them by Moses, he delivered them from those terrible calamities, which, without his providential care, had been brought upon them by this sedition. So I will first explain the cause whence this sedition arose, and then will give an account of the sedition itself; as also of what settlements Moses made for their government, after it was over.

(14) Corah, a Hebrew of principal account both by his family and by his wealth, one that was also able to speak well, and one that could easily persuade the people by his speeches, saw that Moses was in an exceeding great dignity, and was uneasy at it, and envied him on that account (he was of the same tribe with Moses, and of kin to him); he was particularly grieved, because he thought he better deserved that honourable post on account of his great riches, and not

inferior to him in his birth. (15) So he raised a clamour against him among the Levites, who were of the same tribe, and especially among his kindred, saying, 'That it was a very sad thing that they should overlook Moses, while he hunted after, and paved the way to glory for himself, and by ill arts should obtain it, under the pretence of God's command, while, contrary to the laws, he had given the priesthood to Aaron, not by the common suffrage of the multitude, but by his own vote, (16) as bestowing dignities in a tyrannical way on whom he pleased.' He added, 'That this concealed way of imposing on them was harder to be borne than if it had been done by an open force upon them, because he did not not only take away their power without their consent, but even while they were unapprised of his contrivances against them; (17) for whosoever is conscious to himself that he deserves any dignity, aims to get it by persuasion, and not by an arrogant method of violence; but those that believe it impossible to obtain honours justly, make a show of goodness, and do not introduce force, but by cunning tricks grow wickedly powerful: (18) that it was proper for the multitude to punish such men, even while they think themselves concealed in their designs, and not suffer them to gain strength till they have them for their open enemies. For what account,' added he, 'is Moses able to give, why he has bestowed the priesthood on Aaron and his sons? (19) for if God had determined to bestow that honour on one of the tribe of Levi, I am more worthy of it than he is; I myself being equal to Moses by my family, and superior to him both in riches and in age; but if God had determined to bestow it on the eldest tribe, that of Reuben might have it most justly; and then Dathan, and Abiram, and [On, the son of] Peleth, would have it; for these are the oldest men of that tribe, and potent on account of their great wealth also.'

(20) Now Corah, when he said this, had a mind to appear to take care of the public welfare; but in reality he was endeavouring to procure to have that dignity transferred by the multitude to himself. Thus did he, out of a malignant design, but with plausible words, discourse to those of his own tribe; (21) and when these words did gradually spread to more of the people, and when the hearers still added to what tended to the scandals that were cast upon Aaron, the whole army was full of them. Now of those that conspired with Corah, there were two hundred and fifty, and those of the principal men also, who were eager to have the priesthood taken away from Moses's brother, and to bring him into disgrace: (22) nay, the multitude themselves were provoked to be seditious, and attempted to stone Moses, and gathered themselves together after an indecent manner, with confusion and disorder. And now they all were, in a tumultuous manner, raising a clamour before the tabernacle of God, to prosecute the tyrant, and to relieve the multitude from their slavery under him who, under colour of the divine commands, laid violent injunctions upon them; (23) for that had it been God who chose one that was to perform the

office of a priest, he would have raised a worthy person to that dignity, and would not have produced such a one as was inferior to many others, nor have given him that office; and that in case he had judged it fit to bestow it on Aaron, he would have permitted it to the multitude to bestow it, and not have left it to be bestowed by his own brother.

(24) Now although Moses had a great while ago foreseen this calumny of Corah, and had seen the people were irritated, yet was he not affrighted at it: but being of good courage, because he had given them right advice about their affairs, and knowing that his brother had been made partaker of the priesthood at the command of God, and not by his own favour to him, he came to the assembly; (25) and, as for the multitude, he said not a word to them, but spake as loud to Corah as he could; and being very skilful in making speeches, and having this natural talent, among others, that he could greatly move the multitude with his discourses, he said, 'O Corah, both thou and all these with thee (pointing to the two hundred and fifty men) seem to be worthy of this honour; nor do I pretend but that this whole company may be worthy of the like dignity, although they may not be so rich or so great as you are: (26) nor have I taken and given this office to my brother, because he excelled others in riches, for thou exceedest us both in the greatness of thy wealth; nor indeed because he was of an eminent family, for God, by giving us the same common ancestor, has made our families equal: nay, nor was it out of brotherly affection, which another might yet have justly done; (27) for certainly, unless I had bestowed this honour out of regard to God and to his laws, I had not passed by myself, and given it to another, as being nearer of kin to myself than to my brother, and having a closer intimacy with myself than I have with him; for surely it would not be a wise thing for me to expose myself to the dangers of offending, and to bestow the happy employment on this account upon another. (28) But I am above such base practices; nor would God have overlooked this matter, and seen himself thus despised; nor would he have suffered you to be ignorant of what you were to do in order to please him; but he hath himself chosen one that is to perform that sacred office to him, and thereby freed us from that care. (29) So that it was not a thing that I pretend to give, but only according to the determination of God; I therefore propose it still to be contended for by such as please to put in for it, only desiring, that he who has been already preferred, and has already obtained it, may be allowed now also to offer himself for a candidate. (30) He prefers your peace, and your living without sedition, to this honourable employment, although in truth it was with your approbation that he obtained it; for though God were the donor, yet do we not offend when we think fit to accept it with your good will; (31) yet would it have been an instance of impiety not to have taken that honourable employment when he offered it; nay, it had been exceedingly

unreasonable, when God had thought fit anyone should have it for all time to come and had made it secure and firm to him, to have refused it. However, he himself will judge again who it shall be whom he would have to offer sacrifices to him, and to have the direction of matters of religion; (32) for it is absurd that Corah, who is ambitious of this honour, should deprive God of the power of giving it to whom he pleases. Put an end, therefore, to your sedition and disturbance on this account; and tomorrow morning do every one of you that desire the priesthood bring a censer from home, and come hither with incense and fire: (33) and do thou, O Corah, leave the judgment to God, and await to see on which side he will give his determination upon this occasion, but do not thou make thyself greater than God. Do thou also come, that this contest about this honourable employment may receive determination. And I suppose we may admit Aaron without offence, to offer himself to this scrutiny, since he is of the same lineage with thyself, and has done nothing in his priesthood that can be liable to exception. (34) Come ye therefore together, and offer your incense in public before all the people; and when you offer it, he whose sacrifice God shall accept shall be ordained to the priesthood, and shall be clear of the present calumny on Aaron, as if I had granted him that favour because he was my brother.

CHAPTER 3

(35) When Moses had said this, the multitude left off the turbulent behaviour they had indulged, and the suspicion they had of Moses, and commended what he had said; for those proposals were good, and were so esteemed of the people. At that time therefore they dissolved the assembly; but on the next day they came to the congregation, in order to be present at the sacrifice, and at the determination that was to be made between the candidates for the priesthood. (36) Now this congregation proved a turbulent one, and the multitude were in great suspense in expectation of what was to be done; for some of them would have been pleased if Moses had been convicted of evil practices, but the wiser sort desired that they might be delivered from the present disorder and disturbance: for they were afraid that if this sedition went on the good order of their settlement would rather be destroyed; (37) but the whole body of the people do naturally delight in clamours against their governors, and, by changing their opinions upon the harangues of every speaker, disturb the public tranquillity. And now Moses sent messengers for Abiram and Dathan, and ordered them to come to the assembly, and wait there for the holy offices that were to be performed. (38) But they answered the messenger, that they would not obey his summons; nay, would not overlook Moses's behaviour, who was growing too great for them by evil practices. Now when Moses

heard of this their answer, he desired the heads of the people to follow him, and he went to the faction of Dathan, not thinking it any frightful thing at all to go to these insolent people; so they made no opposition, but went along with him. (39) But Dathan and his associates, when they understood that Moses and the principal of the people were coming to them, came out, with their wives and children, and stood before their tents, and looked to see what Moses would do. They had also their servants about them to defend themselves, in case Moses should use force against them.

(40) But he came near, and lifted up his hands to heaven, and cried out with a loud voice, in order to be heard by the whole multitude and said, 'O Lord of the creatures that are in the heaven, in the earth, and in the sea; for thou art the most authentic witness to what I have done, that it has all been done by thy appointment, and that it was thou that afforded us assistance when we attempted anything, and showedst mercy on the Hebrews in all their distresses, do thou come now, and hear all that I say, (41) for no action or thought escapes thy knowledge; so that thou wilt not disdain to speak what is true, for my vindication without any regard to the ungrateful imputations of these men. As for what was done before I was born, thou knowest best, as not learning them by report, but seeing them, and being present with them when they were done: but for what has been done of late, and which these men, although they know them well enough, unjustly pretend to suspect, be thou my witness. (42) When I lived a private quiet life, I left those good things, which by my own diligence, and by thy counsel, I enjoyed with Raguel my father-in-law; and I gave myself up to this people, and underwent many miseries on their account. I also bore great labours at first, in order to obtain liberty for them, and now in order to their preservation; and have always showed myself ready to assist them in every distress of theirs. (43) Now, therefore, since I am suspected by those very men whose being is owing to my labours, come thou, as it is reasonable to hope thou wilt; thou, I say, who showedst me that fire at Mount Sinai, and madest me to hear its voice, and to see the several wonders which that place afforded me; thou who commandedst me to go to Egypt, and declare thy will to this people; (44) thou who disturbedst the happy estate of the Egyptians, and gavest us the opportunity of flying away from our slavery under them, and madest the dominion of Pharaoh inferior to my dominion; thou who didst make the sea dry land for us, when we knew not whither to go, and didst overwhelm the Egyptians with those destructive waves which had been divided for us; thou who didst bestow upon us the security of weapons when we were naked; (45) thou who didst make the fountains that were corrupted to flow, so as to be fit for drinking, and didst furnish us with water that came out of the rocks, when we were in the greatest want of it; thou who didst

preserve our lives with [quails, which was] food from the sea, when the fruits of the ground failed us; thou who didst send us such food from heaven as had never been seen before; thou who didst suggest to us the knowledge of thy laws, and appoint to us a form of government – (46) come thou, I say, O Lord of the whole world, and that as such a Judge and a Witness to me as cannot be bribed, and show how I never admitted of any gift against justice from any of the Hebrews, and have never condemned a poor man that ought to have been acquitted, on account of one that was rich; and have never attempted to hurt this commonwealth. I am now here present, and am suspected of a thing the remotest from my intentions, as if I had given the preisthood to Aaron, not at thy command, but out of my own favour to him; (47) do thou at this time demonstrate that all things are administered by thy providence, and that nothing happens by chance, but is governed by thy will, and thereby attains its end; as also demonstrate that thou takest care of those that have done good to the Hebrews; demonstrate this, I say, by the punishment of Abiram and Dathan, who condemn thee as an insensible being, and one overcome by my contrivances. (48) This wilt thou do by inflicting such an open punishment on these men who so madly fly in the face of thy glory, as will take them out of the world, not in an ordinary manner, but so that it may appear they do die after the manner of other men: let that ground which they tread upon open about them and consume them, with their families and goods. (49) This will be a demonstration of thy power to all men: and this method of their sufferings will be an instruction of wisdom for those that entertain profane sentiments of thee. By this means I shall be found a good servant, in the precepts thou hast given by me. (50) But if the calumnies they have raised against me be true, mayest thou preserve these men from every evil accident, and bring all that destruction on me which I have imprecated upon them. And when thou hast inflicted punishment on those that have endeavoured to deal unjustly with this people, bestow upon them concord and peace. Save this multitude that follow thy commandments, and preserve them free from harm, and let them not partake of the punishment of those that have sinned; for thou knowest thyself it is not just, that for the wickedness of those men the whole body of the Israelites should suffer punishment.'

(51) When Moses had said this, with tears in his eyes, the ground was moved on a sudden: and the agitation that set it in motion was like that which the wind produces in waves of the sea. The people were all affrighted; and the ground that was about their tents sunk down at the great noise, with a terrible sound, and carried whatsoever was dear to the seditious into itself, (52) who so entirely perished that there was not the least appearance that any man had ever been seen there, the earth that had opened itself about them, closing again, and

becoming entire as it was before, insomuch that such as saw it, afterward did not perceive that any such accident had happened to it. Thus did these men perish, and become a demonstration of the power of God. (53) And truly, anyone would lament them, not only on account of this calamity that befell them, which yet deserves our commiseration, but also because their kindred were pleased with their sufferings; for they forgot the relation they bare to them, and at the sight of this sad accident approved of the judgment given against them; and because they looked upon the people about Dathan as pestilent men, they thought they perished as such, and did not grieve for them.

(54) And now Moses called for those that contended about the priesthood, that trial might be made who should be priest, and that he whose sacrifice God was best pleased with might be ordained to that function. There attended two hundred and fifty men, who indeed were honoured by the people, not only on account of the power of their ancestors, but also on account of their own, in which they excelled the others: Aaron also and Corah came forth, and they all offered incense, in those censers of theirs which they brought with them, before the tabernacle. (55) Hereupon so great a fire shone out as no one ever saw in any that is made by the hand of man, neither in those eruptions out of the earth that are caused by subterraneous burnings, nor in such fires as arise of their own accord in the woods, when the agitation is caused by the trees rubbing one against another: but this fire was very bright, and had a terrible flame, such as is kindled at the command of God; (56) by whose irruption on them, all the company and Corah himself, were destroyed, and this so entirely, that their very bodies left no remains behind them. Aaron alone was preserved, and not at all hurt by the fire, because it was God that sent the fire to burn those only who ought to be burned. (57) Hereupon Moses, after these men were destroyed, was desirous that the memory of this judgment might be delivered down to posterity, and that future ages might be acquainted with it; and so he commanded Eleazar, the son of Aaron, to put their censers near the brazen altar, (58) that they might be a memorial to posterity of what these men suffered for supposing that the power of God might be eluded. And thus Aaron was now no longer esteemed to have the priesthood by the favour of Moses, but by the public judgment of God; and thus he and his children peaceably enjoyed that honour afterwards.

CHAPTER 4

(59) However, this sedition was so far from ceasing upon this destruction, that it grew much stronger, and became more intolerable. And the occasion of its growing worse was of that nature, as made it likely the calamity would never cease, but last for a long time; (60) for the men, believing already that nothing

is done without the providence of God, would have it that these things came thus to pass, not without God's favour to Moses; they therefore laid the blame upon him, that God was so angry, and that this happened, not so much because of the wickedness of those that were punished, as because Moses procured the punishment; (61) and that these men had been destroyed without any sin of theirs, only because they were zealous about the divine worship; as also, that he who had been the cause of this diminution of the people, by destroying so many men, and those the most excellent of them all, besides his escaping any punishment himself, had now given the priesthood to his brother so firmly, (62) that nobody could any longer dispute it with him; for no one else, to be sure, could now put in for it, since he must have seen those that first did so to have miserably perished. Nay, besides this, the kindred of those that were destroyed made great entreaties to the multitude to abate the arrogance of Moses, because it would be safest for them so to do.

(63) Now Moses, upon his hearing for a good while that the people were tumultuous, was afraid that they would attempt some other innovation, and that some great and sad calamity would be the consequence. He called the multitude to a congregation, and patiently heard what apology they had to make for themselves, without opposing them, and this lest he should embitter the multitude: he only desired the heads of the tribes to bring their rods, with the names of their tribes inscribed upon them, (64) and that he should receive the priesthood in whose rod God should give a sign. This was agreed to. So the rest brought their rods, as did Aaron also, who had written the tribe of Levi on his rod. These rods Moses laid up in the tabernacle of God. On the next day he brought out the rods, which were known from one another by those who brought them, they having distinctly noted them, as had the multitude also; (65) and as to the rest, in the same form Moses had received them, in that they saw them still; but they also saw buds and branches grown out of Aaron's rod, with ripe fruits upon them: they were almonds, the rod having been cut out of that tree. (66) The people were so amazed at this strange sight, that though Moses and Aaron were before under some degree of hatred, they now laid that hatred aside, and began to admire the judgment of God concerning them; so that hereafter they applauded what God had decreed, and permitted Aaron to enjoy the priesthood peaceably. And thus God ordained him priest three several times, and he retained that honour without further disturbance. And hereby this sedition of the Hebrews, which had been a great one, and had lasted a great while, was at last composed.

(67) And now Moses, because the tribe of Levi was made free from war and warlike expeditions, and was set apart for the divine worship, lest they should want and seek after the necessaries of life, and so neglect the temple, commanded the Hebrews, according to the will of God, that when they

should gain the possession of the land of Canaan, they should assign forty-eight good and fair cities to the Levites; and permit them to enjoy their suburbs, as far as the limit of two thousand cubits would extend from the walls of the city. (68) And besides this, he appointed that the people should pay the tithe of their annual fruits of the earth, both to the Levites and to the priests. And this is what that tribe receives of the multitude; but I think it necessary to set down what is paid by all, peculiarly to the priests.

(69) Accordingly he commanded the Levites to yield up to the priests thirteen of their forty-eight cities, and to set apart for them the tenth part of the tithes which they every year receive of the people; (70) as also, that it was but just to offer to God the first fruits of the entire product of the ground; and that they should offer the first-born of those four-footed beasts that are appointed for sacrifices, if it be a male, to the priests, to be slain, that they and their entire families may eat them in the holy city; (71) but that the owners of those first born which are not appointed for sacrifices in the laws of our country, should bring a shekel and a half in their stead: but for the first-born of a man, five shekels: that they should also have the first fruits out of the shearing of the sheep; and that when any baked bread-corn, and made loaves of it, they should give somewhat of what they had baked to them. (72) Moreover, when any have made a sacred vow, I mean those that are called *Nazirites*, that suffer their hair to grow long, and use no wine, when they consecrate their hair, and offer it for a sacrifice, they are to allot that hair for the priests [to be thrown into the fire]. (73) Such also as dedicate themselves to God, as a corban, which denotes what the Greeks call a *gift*, when they are desirous of being freed from that ministration, are to lay down money for the priests; thirty shekels if it be a woman, and fifty if it be a man; but if any be too poor to pay the appointed sum, it shall be lawful for the priests to determine that sum as they think fit. (74) And if any slay beasts at home for a private festival, but not for a religious one, they are obliged to bring the maw and the cheek [or breast], and the right shoulder of the sacrifice to the priests. With these Moses contrived that the priests should be plentifully maintained, besides what they had out of those offerings for sins, which the people gave them, as I have set it down in the foregoing book. (75) He also ordered, that out of everything allotted for the priests, their servants [their sons], their daughters, and their wives, should partake, as well as themselves, excepting what came to them out of the sacrifices that were offered for sins; for of those none but the males of the family of the priests might eat, and this in the temple also, and that the same day they were offered.

(76) When Moses had made these constitutions, after the sedition was over, he removed, together with the whole army, and came to the borders of Idumea. He then sent ambassadors to the king of the Idumeans, and desired him to give him a passage through his country; and agreed to send him what

hostages he should desire, to secure him from an injury. He desired him also, that he would allow his army liberty to buy provisions; and, if he insisted upon it, he would pay down a price for the very water they should drink. (77) But the king was not pleased with this embassage from Moses: nor did he allow a passage for the army, but brought his people armed to meet Moses, and to hinder them, in case they should endeavour to force their passage. Upon which Moses consulted God by the oracle, who would not have him begin the war first; and so he withdrew his forces, and travelled round about through the wilderness.

(78) Then it was that Miriam, the sister of Moses, came to her end, having completed her fortieth year since she left Egypt, on the first day of the lunar month Xanthicus. They then made a public funeral for her, at a great expense. She was buried upon a certain mountain, which they call *Sin;* and when they had mourned for her thirty days, Moses purified the people after this manner: (79) He brought a heifer that had never been used to the plough or to husbandry, that was complete in all its parts, and entirely of a red colour, at a little distance from the camp, into a place perfectly clean. This heifer was slain by the high priest, and her blood sprinkled with his finger seven times before the tabernacle of God; (80) after this, the entire heifer was burnt in that state, together with its skin and entrails; and they threw cedar wood, and hyssop, and scarlet wool, into the midst of the fire; then a clean man gathered all her ashes together, and laid them in a place perfectly clean. (81) When therefore any persons were defiled by a dead body, they put a little of these ashes into spring water, with hyssop, and, dipping part of these ashes in it, they sprinkled them with it, both on the third day and on the seventh, and after that they were clean. This he enjoined them to do also when the tribes should come into their own land.

(82) Now when this purification, which their leader made upon the mourning for his sister, as it has been now described, was over, he caused the army to remove and to march through the wilderness and through Arabia; and when he came to a place which the Arabians esteem their metropolis, which was formerly called *Arce*, but has now the name of *Petra*, (83) at this place, which was encompassed with high mountains, Aaron went up one of them in the sight of the whole army, Moses having before told him that he was to die, for this place was over against them. He put off his pontifical garments, and delivered them to Eleazar his son, to whom the high priesthood belonged, because he was the elder brother; and died while the multitude looked upon him. (84) He died in the same year wherein he lost his sister, having lived in all a hundred and twenty-three years. He died on the first day of that lunar month which is called by the Athenians *Hecatombaeon*, by the Macedonians *Lous*, but by the Hebrews *Abba*.

CHAPTER 5

(85) The people mourned for Aaron thirty days, and when this mourning was over, Moses removed the army from that place, and came to the river Arnon, which, issuing out of the mountains of Arabia, and running through all that wilderness, falls into the lake Asphaltitis, and becomes the limit between the land of the Moabites and the land of the Amorites. This land is fruitful, and sufficient to maintain a great number of men with the good things it produces. (86) Moses therefore sent messengers to Sihon, the king of this country, desiring that he would grant his army a passage, upon what security he should please to require; he promised that he should be no way injured, neither as to that country which Sihon governed, nor as to its inhabitants; and that he would buy his provisions at such a price as should be to their advantage, even though he should desire to sell them their very water. But Sihon refused his offer, and put his army into battle array, and was preparing everything in order to hinder their passing over Arnon.

(87) When Moses saw that the Amorite king was disposed to enter upon hostilities with them, he thought he ought not to bear that insult; and, determining to wean the Hebrews from their indolent temper, and prevent the disorders which arose thence, which had been the occasion of their former sedition (nor indeed were they now thoroughly easy in their minds), he inquired of God, whether he would give him leave to fight? (88) Which when he had done, and God also promised him the victory, he was himself very courageous, and ready to proceed to fighting. Accordingly he encouraged the soldiers; and he desired of them that they would take the pleasure of fighting, now God gave them leave so to do. They then, upon the receipt of this permission, which they so much longed for, put on their whole armour, and set about the work without delay. (89) But the Amorite king was not now like to himself when the Hebrews were ready to attack him; but both he himself was affrighted at the Hebrews, and his army, which before had showed themselves to be of good courage, were then found to be timorous; so they could not sustain the first onset, nor bear up against the Hebrews, but fled away, as thinking this would afford them a more likely way for their escape than fighting; (90) for they depended upon their cities, which were strong, from which yet they reaped no advantage when they were forced to fly to them; for as soon as the Hebrews saw them giving ground, they immediately pursued them close; and when they had broken their ranks, they greatly terrified them, (91) and some of them broke off from the rest, and ran away to the cities. Now the Hebrews pursued them briskly, and obstinately persevered in the labours they had already undergone; and being very skilful in slinging,

and very dexterous in throwing of darts, or anything else of that kind; and also having nothing but light armour, which made them quick in the pursuit, they overtook their enemies; and for those that were most remote, and could not be overtaken, they reached them by their slings and their bows, (92) so that many were slain; and those that escaped the slaughter were sorely wounded, and these were more distressed with thirst than with any of those that fought against them, for it was the summer season; and when the greatest number of them were brought down to the river out of a desire to drink, as also when others fled away by troops, the Hebrews came round them, and shot at them; so that, what with darts and what with arrows, they made a slaughter of them all. (93) Sihon their king was also slain. So the Hebrews spoiled the dead bodies, and took their prey. The land also which they took was full of abundance of fruits, (94) and the army went all over it without fear, and fed their cattle upon it; and they took the enemies prisoners, for they could no way put a stop to them, since all the fighting men were destroyed. Such was the destruction which overtook the Amorites, who were neither sagacious in counsel, nor courageous in action. Hereupon the Hebrews took possession of their land, (95) which is a country situate between three rivers, and naturally resembling an island; the river Arnon being its southern limit; the river Jabbok determining its northern side, which, running into Jordan, loses its own name, and takes the other; while Jordan itself runs along by it, on its western coast.

(96) When matters were come to this state, Og, the king of Gilead and Gaulanitis, fell upon the Israelites. He brought an army with him, and came in haste to the assistance of his friend Sihon; but though he found him already slain, yet did he resolve still to come and fight the Hebrews, supposing he should be too hard for them, and being desirous to try their valour; (97) but failing of his hope, he was both himself slain in the battle, and all his army was destroyed. So Moses passed over the river Jabbok, and overran the kingdom of Og. He overthrew their cities, and slew all their inhabitants, who yet exceeded in riches all the men in that part of the continent, on account of the goodness of the soil, and the great quantity of their wealth. (98) Now Og had very few equals, either in the largeness of his body or handsomeness of his appearance. He was also a man of great activity in the use of his hands, so that his actions were not unequal to the vast largeness and handsome appearance of his body; and men could easily guess at his strength and magnitude when they took his bed at Rabbath, the royal city of the Ammonites; its structure was of iron, its breadth four cubits, and its length a cubit more than double thereto. (99) However, his fall did not only improve the circumstances of the Hebrews for the present, but by his death he was the occasion of further good success to them; for they presently took those sixty cities which were encompassed with excellent walls, and had been subject to him; and all got both in general and in particular a great prey.

CHAPTER 6

(100) Now Moses, when he had brought his army to Jordan, pitched his camp in the great plain over against Jericho. This city is a very happy situation, and very fit for producing palm trees and balsam; and now the Israelites began to be very proud of themselves, and were very eager for fighting. (101) Moses then, after he had offered for a few days sacrifices of thanksgiving to God, and feasted the people, sent a party of armed men to lay waste the country of the Midianites, and to take their cities. Now the occasion which he took for making wars upon them was this that follows:

(102) When Balak, the king of the Moabites, who had from his ancestors a friendship and league with the Midianites, saw how great the Israelites were grown, he was much affrighted on account of his own and his kingdom's danger; for he was not acquainted with this, that the Hebrews would not meddle with any other country, but were to be contented with the possession of the land of Canaan, God having forbidden them to go any farther. So he, with more haste than wisdom, resolved to make an attempt upon them by words; (103) but he did not judge it prudent to fight against them, after they had such prosperous successes, and even became out of ill successes more happy than before; but he thought to hinder them if he could from growing greater, and so he resolved to send ambassadors to the Midianites about them. (104) Now these Midianites knowing there was one Balaam, who lived by Euphrates, and was the greatest of the prophets at that time, and one that was in friendship with them, sent some of their honourable princes along with the ambassadors of Balak, to entreat the prophet to come to them, that he might imprecate curses to the destruction of the Israelites. (105) So Balaam received the ambassadors, and treated them very kindly; and when he had supped, he inquired what was God's will, and what this matter was for which the Midianites entreated him to come to them. But when God opposed his going, he came to the ambassadors, and told them that he was himself very willing and desirous to comply with their request, but informed them that God was opposite to his intentions, even that God who had raised him to great reputation on account of the truth of his predictions; (106) for that this army, which they entreated him to come and curse, was in the favour of God; on which account he advised them to go home again, and not to persist in their enmity against the Israelites; and when he had given them that answer, he dismissed the ambassadors.

(107) Now the Midianites, at the earnest request and fervent entreaties of Balak, sent other ambassadors to Balaam, who, desiring to gratify the men, inquired again of God; but he was displeased at this [second] trial, and bid him

by no means to contradict the ambassadors. Now Balaam did not imagine that God gave this injunction in order to deceive him, so he went along with the ambassadors; (108) but when the divine angel met him in the way, when he was in a narrow passage, and hedged in with a wall on both sides, the ass on which Balaam rode understood that it was a divine spirit that met him, and thrust Balaam to one of the walls, without regard to the stripes which Balaam, when he was hurt by the wall, gave her; (109) but when the ass, upon the angel's continuing to distress her, and upon the stripes which were given her, fell down, by the will of God, she made use of the voice of a man, and complained of Balaam as acting unjustly to her; that whereas he had no fault to find with her in her former service to him, he now inflicted stripes upon her, as not understanding that she was hindered from serving him in what he was now going about, by the providence of God. (110) And when he was disturbed by reason of the voice of the ass, which was that of a man, the angel plainly appeared to him, and blamed him for the stripes he had given his ass; and informed him that the brute creature was not in fault, but that he was himself come to obstruct his journey, as being contrary to the will of God. (111) Upon which Balaam was afraid, and was preparing to return back again; yet did God excite him to go on his intended journey, but added this injunction, that he should declare nothing but what he himself should suggest to his mind.

(112) When God had given him this charge, he came to Balak; and when the king had entertained him in a magnificent manner, he desired him to go to one of the mountains to take a view of the state of the camp of the Hebrews. Balak himself also came to the mountain, and brought the prophet along with him, with a royal attendance. This mountain lay over their heads, and was distant sixty furlongs from the camp. (113) Now when he saw them, he desired the king to build him seven altars, and to bring him as many bulls and rams; to which desire the king did presently conform. He then slew the sacrifices, and offered them as burnt offerings, that he might observe some signal of the flight of the Hebrews. (114) Then said he, 'Happy is this people, on whom God bestows the possession of innumerable good things, and grants them his own providence to be their assistant and their guide; so that there is not any nation among mankind but you will be esteemed superior to them in virtue, and in the earnest prosecution of the best rules of life, and of such as are pure from wickedness, and will leave those rules to your excellent children, and this out of the regard that God bears to you, and the provision of such things for you as may render you happier than any other people under the sun. (115) You shall retain that land to which he hath sent you, and it shall ever be under the command of your children; and both all the earth, as well as the sea, shall be filled with your glory: and you shall be sufficiently numerous to supply the world in general, and every region of it in particular, with

inhabitants out of your stock. (116) However, O blessed army, wonder that you are become so many from one father: and truly, the land of Canaan can now hold you, as being yet comparatively few; but know ye that the whole world is proposed to be your place of habitation forever. The multitude of your posterity also shall live as well in the islands as on the continent, and that more in number than are the stars of heaven. And when you are become so many, God will not relinquish the care of you, but will afford you an abundance of all good things in times of peace, with victory and dominion in times of war. (117) May the children of your enemies have an inclination to fight against you, and may they be so hardy as to come to arms, and to assault you in battle, for they will not return with victory, nor will their return be agreeable to their children and wives. To so great a degree of valour will you be raised by the providence of God, who is able to diminish the affluence of some, and to supply the wants of others.'

(118) Thus did Balaam speak by inspiration, as not being in his own power, but moved to say what he did by the divine spirit. But then Balak was displeased, and said he had broken the contract he had made, whereby he was to come, as he and his confederates had invited him, by the promise of great presents: for whereas he came to curse their enemies, he had made an encomium upon them, and had declared that they were the happiest of men. (119) To which Balaam replied, 'O Balak, if thou rightly considerest this whole matter, canst thou suppose that it is in our power to be silent, or to say anything, when the Spirit of God seizes upon us? For he puts such words as he pleases in our mouths, and such discourses as we are not ourselves conscious of. (120) I well remember by what entreaties both you and the Midianites so joyfully brought me hither and on that account I took this journey. It was my prayer, that I might not put any affront upon you, as to what you desired of me; (121) but God is more powerful than the purposes I had made to serve you; for those that take upon them to foretell the affairs of mankind, as from their own abilities, are entirely unable to do it, or to forbear to utter what God suggests to them, or to offer violence to his will; for when he prevents us and enters into us, nothing that we say is our own. (122) I then did not intend to praise this army, nor to go over the several good things which God intended to do to their race; but since he was so favourable to them, and so ready to bestow upon them a happy life and eternal glory, he suggested the declaration of those things to me: (123) but now, because it is my desire to oblige thee thyself, as well as the Midianites whose entreaties it is not decent for me to reject, go to, let us again rear other altars, and offer the like sacrifices that we did before, that I may see whether I can persuade God to permit me to bind these men with curses. (124) Which, when Balak had agreed to, God would not, even upon second sacrifices, consent to his

cursing the Israelites. (125) Then fell Balaam upon his face, and foretold what calamities would befall the several kings of the nations, and the most eminent cities, some of which of old were not so much as inhabited; which events have come to pass among the several people concerned, both in the foregoing ages, and in this, till my own memory, both by sea and by land. From which completion of all these predictions that he made, one may easily guess that the rest will have their completion in time to come.

(126) But Balak being very angry that the Israelites were not cursed, sent away Balaam without thinking him worthy of any honour. Whereupon, when he was just upon his journey, in order to pass the Euphrates, he sent for Balak, and for the princes of the Midianites, (127) and spake thus to them: 'O Balak, and you Midianites that are here present (for I am obliged even without the will of God to gratify you), it is true no entire destruction can seize upon the nation of the Hebrews, neither by war, nor by plague, nor by scarcity of the fruits of the earth, nor can any other unexpected accident be their entire ruin; (128) for the providence of God is concerned to preserve them from such a misfortune; nor will it permit any such calamity to come upon them whereby they may all perish; but some small misfortunes, and those for a short time, whereby they may appear to be brought low, may still befall them; but after that they will flourish again, to the terror of those that brought those mischiefs upon them. (129) So that if you have a mind to gain a victory over them for a short space of time you will obtain it by following my directions: do you therefore set out the handsomest of such of your daughters as are most eminent for beauty, and proper to force and conquer the modesty of those that behold them, and these decked and trimmed to the highest degree you are able. Then do you send them to be near the Israelites' camp and give them in charge, that when the young men of the Hebrews desire their company, they allow it them; (130) and when they see that they are enamoured of them, let them take their leaves; and if they entreat them to stay, let them not give their consent till they have persuaded them to leave off their obedience to their own laws and the worship of that God who established them, and to worship the gods of the Midianites and Moabites; for by this means God will be angry at them.' Accordingly, when Balaam had suggested this counsel to them, he went his way.

(131) So when the Midianites had sent their daughters, as Balaam had exhorted them, the Hebrew young men were allured by their beauty, and came to discourse with them, and besought them not to grudge them the enjoyment of their beauty, nor to deny them their conversation. These daughters of the Midianites received their words gladly, and consented to it and stayed with them; (132) but when they had brought them to be enamoured of them, and their inclinations to them were grown to ripeness,

they began to think of departing from them: then it was that these men became greatly disconsolate at the women's departure, and they were urgent with them not to leave them, but begged they would continue there, and become their wives; and they promised them they should be owned as mistresses of all they had. (133) This they said with an oath, and called God for the arbitrator of what they promised; and this with tears in their eyes, and all other such marks of concern as might show how miserable they thought themselves without them, and so might move their compassion for them. So the women, as soon as they perceived they had made them their slaves, and had caught them with their conservation, began to speak thus to them:

(134) 'O you illustrious young men, we have houses of our own at home and great plenty of good things there, together with the natural affectionate love of our parents and friends; nor is it out of our want of any such things that we came to discourse with you: nor did we admit of your invitation with design to prostitute the beauty of our bodies for gain; but taking you for brave and worthy men, we agreed to your request, that we might treat you with such honours as hospitality required: (135) and now seeing you say that you have a great affection for us, and are troubled when you think we are departing, we are not averse to your entreaties; and if we may receive such assurance of your good will as we think can be alone sufficient, we will be glad to lead our lives with you as your wives; (136) but we are afraid that you will in time be weary of our company, and will then abuse us, and send us back to our parents, after an ignominious manner.' And so they desired that they would excuse them in their guarding against that danger. But the young men professed they would give them any assurance they should desire; nor did they at all contradict what they requested, so great was the passion they had for them. (137) 'If then,' said they, 'this be your resolution; since you make use of such customs and conduct of life as are entirely different from all other men, insomuch that your kinds of food are peculiar to yourselves, and your kinds of drink not common to others, it will be absolutely necessary if you would have us for your wives, that you do withal worship our gods; nor can there be any other demonstration of the kindness which you say you already have, and promised to have hereafter to us, than this, that you worship the same gods that we do. (138) For has anyone reason to complain, that now you are come into this country, you should worship the proper gods of the same country? Especially while our gods are common to all men, and yours such as belong to nobody else but yourselves.' So they said they must either come into such methods of divine worship as all others came into, or else they must look out for another world, wherein they may live by themselves, according to their own laws.

(139) Now the young men were induced by the fondness they had for these women, to think they spake very well; so they gave themselves up to what they

persuaded them, and transgressed their own laws; and supposing there were many gods, and resolving that they would sacrifice to them according to the laws of that country which ordained them, they both were delighted with their strange food, and went on to do everything that the women would have them do, though in contradiction to their own laws; (140) so far, indeed, that this transgression was already gone through the whole army of the young men, and they fell into a sedition that was much worse than the former, and into danger of the entire abolition of their own institutions; for when once the youth had tasted of these strange customs, they went with insatiable inclinations into them; and even where some of the principal men were illustrious on account of the virtues of their fathers, they also were corrupted together with the rest.

(141) Even Zimri, the head of the tribe of Simeon, accompanied with Cozbi, a Midianitish woman, who was the daughter of Sur, a man of authority in that country; and being desired by his wife to disregard the laws of Moses, and to follow those she was used to, he complied with her; and this both by sacrificing after a manner different from his own, and by taking a stranger to wife. (142) When things were thus, Moses was afraid that matters should grow worse, and called the people to a congregation, but then accused nobody by name, as unwilling to drive those into despair who, by lying concealed, might come to repentance; (143) but he said that they did not do what was either worthy of themselves or of their fathers, by preferring pleasure to God, and to the living according to his will; that it was fit they should change their courses while their affairs were still in a good state; and think that to be true fortitude which offers not violence to their laws, but that which resists their lusts. (144) And besides that, he said it was not a reasonable thing, when they had lived soberly in the wilderness, to act madly now when they were in prosperity; and that they ought not to lose, now they have abundance, what they had gained when they had little: and so did he endeavour by saying this to correct the young men, and to bring them to repentance for what they had done.

(145) But Zimri arose up after him, and said, 'Yes, indeed, Moses, thou art at liberty to make use of such laws as thou art so fond of, and hast, by accustoming thyself to them, made them firm; otherwise, if things had not been thus, thou hadst often been punished before now, and hadst known that the Hebrews are not easily put upon; (146) but thou shalt not have me one of thy followers in thy tyrannical commands, for thou dost nothing else hitherto but, under pretence of laws and of God, wickedly impose on us slavery, and gain dominion to thyself, while thou deprivest us of the sweetness of life, which consists in acting according to our own wills, and is the right of free men, and of those that have no lord over them. (147) Nay, indeed, this man is harder upon the Hebrews then were the Egyptians themselves, as pretending to punish, according to his laws, everyone's acting what is most agreeable to

himself; but thou thyself better deservest to suffer punishment, who presumest to abolish what everyone acknowledges to be what is good for him, and aimest to make thy single opinion to have more force than that of all the rest: (148) and what I now do, and think to be right, I shall not hereafter deny to be according to my own sentiments. I have married, as thou sayest rightly, a strange woman, and thou hearest what I do from myself as from one that is free; for truly I did not intend to conceal myself. (149) I also own that I sacrificed to those gods to whom you do not think it fit to sacrifice; and I think it right to come at truth by inquiring of many people, and not like one that lives under tyranny, to suffer the whole hope of my life to depend upon one man; nor shall anyone find cause to rejoice who declares himself to have more authority over my actions than myself.'

(150) Now when Zimri had said these things about what he and some others had wickedly done the people held their peace, both out of fear of what might come upon them, and because they saw that their legislator was not willing to bring his insolence before the public any further, or openly to contend with him; (151) for he avoided that, lest many should imitate the impudence of his language, and thereby disturb the multitude. Upon this the assembly was dissolved. However, the mischievous attempt had proceeded further, if Zimri had not been first slain, which came to pass on the following occasion: (152) Phineas, a man in other respects better than the rest of the young men, and also one that surpassed his contemporaries in the dignity of his father (for he was the son of Eleazar the high priest, and the grandson of [Aaron] Moses' brother), who was greatly troubled at what was done by Zimri, he resolved in earnest to inflict punishment on him, before his unworthy behaviour should grow stronger by impunity, and in order to prevent this transgression from proceeding further, which would happen if the ringleaders were not punished. (153) He was of so great magnanimity, both in strength of mind and body, that when he undertook any very dangerous attempt, he did not leave it off till he overcame it, and got an entire victory. So he came into Zimri's tent, and slew him with his javelin, and with it he slew Cozbi also. (154) Upon which all those young men that had a regard to virtue, and aimed to do a glorious action, imitated Phineas' boldness, and slew those that were found to be guilty of the same crime with Zimri. Accordingly, many of those that had transgressed perished by the magnanimous valour of these young men, (155) and the rest all perished by a plague, which distemper God himself inflicted upon them. So that all those their kindred, who, instead of hindering them from such wicked actions, as they ought to have done, had persuaded them to go on, were esteemed by God as partners in their wickedness, and died. Accordingly there perished out of the army no fewer than fourteen [twenty-four] thousand at this time.

(156) This was the cause why Moses was provoked to send an army to

destroy the Midianites, concerning which expedition we shall speak presently, when we have first related what we have omitted; for it is but just not to pass over our legislator's due encomium, on account of his conduct here, (157) because, although this Balaam, who was sent for by the Midianites to curse the Hebrews, and when he was hindered from doing it by divine providence, did still suggest that advice to them, by making use of which our enemies had well nigh corrupted the whole multitude of the Hebrews with their wiles, till some of them were deeply infected with their opinions; yet did he do him great honour, by setting down his prophecies in writing. (158) And while it was in his power to claim this glory to himself, and make men believe they were his own predictions, here being no one that could be a witness against him, and accuse him for so doing, he still gave his attestation to him, and did him the honour to make mention of him on this account. But let everyone think of these matters as he pleases.

CHAPTER 7

(159) Now Moses sent an army against the land of Midian, for the causes forementioned, in all twelve thousand, taking an equal number out of every tribe, and appointed Phineas for their commander; of which Phineas we made mention a little before, as he that had guarded the laws of the Hebrews, and had inflicted punishment on Zimri when he had transgressed them. (160) Now the Midianites perceived beforehand how the Hebrews were coming, and would suddenly be upon them: so they assembled their army together, and fortified the entrances into their country, and there awaited the enemy's coming. (161) When they were come, and they had joined battle with them, an immense multitude of the Midianites fell; nor could they be numbered, they were so very many; and among them fell all their kings, five in number, viz., Evi, Zur, Reba, Hur, and Rekem, who was of the same name with a city, the chief and capital of all Arabia, which is still now so called by the whole Arabian nation, *Arecem*, from the name of the king that built it; but is by the Greeks called *Petra*. (162) Now when the enemies were discomfited, the Hebrews spoiled their country, and took a great prey, and destroyed the men that were its inhabitants, together with the women; only they let the virgins alone, as Moses had commanded Phineas to do, (163) who indeed came back, bringing with him an army that had received no harm, and a great deal of prey; fifty-two thousand beeves, seventy-five thousand six hundred sheep, sixty thousand asses, with an immense quantity of gold and silver furniture, which the Midianites made use in their houses; for they were so wealthy, that they were very luxurious. There were also led captive about thirty-two thousand virgins. (164) So Moses parted the prey into parts, and gave one fiftieth part to

Eleazar and the two priests, and another fiftieth part to the Levites; and distributed the rest of the prey among the people. After which they lived happily, as having obtained an abundance of good things by their valour, and there being no misfortune that attended them, or hindered their enjoyment of that happiness.

(165) But Moses was now grown old, and appointed Joshua for his successor, both to receive directions from God as a prophet, and for a commander of the army, if they should at any time stand in need of such a one; and this was done by the command of God, that to him the care of the public should be committed. Now Joshua had been instructed in all those kinds of learning which concerned the laws and God himself, and Moses had been his instructor.

(166) At this time it was that the two tribes of Gad and Reuben, and the half tribe of Manasseh, abounded in a multitude of cattle, as well as in all other kinds of prosperity; whence they had a meeting, and in a body came and besought Moses to give them, as their peculiar portion, that land of the Amorites which they had taken by right of war, because it was fruitful, and good for feeding of cattle; (167) but Moses, supposing that they were afraid of fighting with the Canaanites, and invented this provision for their cattle as a handsome excuse for avoiding that war, he called them *arrant cowards*, and said they had only contrived a decent excuse for that cowardice; and that they had a mind to live in luxury and ease, while all the rest were labouring with great pains to obtain the land they were desirous to have; (168) and that they were not willing to march along, and undergo the remaining hard service, whereby they were, under the divine promise, to pass over Jordan, and overcome those our enemies which God had shown them, and so obtain their land. (169) But these tribes, when they saw that Moses was angry with them, and when they could not deny but he had a just cause to be displeased at their petition, made an apology for themselves; and said that it was not on account of their fear of dangers, nor on account of their laziness, that they made this request to him, (170) but that they might leave the prey they had gotten in places of safety, and thereby might be more expedite, and ready to undergo difficulties, and to fight battles. They added this also, that when they had built cities, wherein they might preserve their children and wives and possessions, if he would bestow them upon them, they would go along with the rest of the army. (171) Hereupon Moses was pleased with what they said; so he called for Eleazar the high priest, and Joshua, and the chief of the tribes, and permitted these tribes to possess the land of the Amorites; but upon this condition, that they should join with their kinsmen in the war until all things were settled. Upon which condition they took possession of the country, and built them strong cities, and put into them their children and their wives and whatsoever else they had that might be an impediment to the labours of their future marches.

(172) Moses also now built those ten cities which were to be of the number of the forty-eight [for the Levites]; three of which he allotted to those that slew any person involuntarily and fled to them; and he assigned the same time for their banishment with that of the life of that high priest under whom the slaughter and flight happened; after which death of the high priest he permitted the slayer to return home. During the time of his exile, the relations of him that was slain may, by this law, kill the man-slayer, if they caught him without the bounds of the city to which he fled, though this permission was not granted to any other person. (173) Now the cities which were set apart for this flight were these: Bezer, at the borders of Arabia; Ramoth, in the land of Gilead; and Golan, in the land of Bashan. There were to be also, by Moses' command, three other cities allotted for the habitations of these fugitives out of the cities of the Levites, but not till after they should be in possession of the land of Canaan.

(174) At this time the chief men of the tribe of Manasseh came to Moses, and informed him that there was an eminent man of their tribe dead, whose name was Zelophehad, who left no male children, but left daughters; and asked him whether these daughters might inherit his land or not. He made this answer: (175) That if they shall marry into their own tribe, they shall carry their estate along with them, but if they dispose of themselves in marriage to men of another tribe they shall leave their inheritance in their father's tribe. And then it was that Moses ordained, that everyone's inheritance should continue in his own tribe.

CHAPTER 8

(176) When forty years were completed, within thirty days Moses gathered the congregation together near Jordan, where the city Abila now stands, a place full of palm trees; and all the people being come together, he spake thus to them:

(177) 'O you Israelites and fellow soldiers, who have been partners with me in this long and uneasy journey; since it is now the will of God, and the course of old age, at a hundred and twenty, requires it that I should depart out of this life; and since God has forbidden me to be a patron or an assistant to you in what remains to be done beyond Jordan, (178) I thought it reasonable not to leave off my endeavours even now for your happiness, but to do my utmost to procure for you the eternal enjoyment of good things, and a memorial for myself, when you shall be in the fruition of great plenty and prosperity: (179) come, therefore, let me suggest to you by what means you may be happy, and may leave an eternal prosperous possession thereof to your children after you, and then let me thus go out of the world; and I cannot but deserve to be

believed by you, both on account of the great things I have already done for you, and because when souls are about to leave the body, they speak with the sincerest freedom. (180) O children of Israel! there is but one source of happiness for all mankind, the favour of God; for he alone is able to give good things to those that deserve them, and to deprive those of them that sin against him; towards whom, if you behave yourselves according to his will, and according to what I, who well understand his mind, do exhort you to, you will both be esteemed blessed, and will be admired by all men; and will never come into misfortunes, nor cease to be happy: you will then preserve the possession of the good things you already have, and will quickly obtain those that you are at present in want of – (181) only do you be obedient to those whom God would have you to follow: nor do you prefer any other constitution of the government before the laws now given you; neither do you disregard that way of divine worship which you now have, nor change it for any other form: and if you do this, you will be the most courageous of all men in undergoing the fatigues of war, and will not be easily conquered by any of your enemies; (182) for while God is present with you to assist you, it is to be expected that you will be able to despise the opposition of all mankind: and great rewards of virtue are proposed for you, if you preserve that virtue through your whole lives. Virtue itself is indeed the principal and the first reward, and after that it bestows abundance of others; (183) so that your exercise of virtue towards other men will make your own lives happy, and render you more glorious than foreigners can be, and procure you an undisputed reputation with posterity. These blessings you will be able to obtain, in case you hearken to and observe those laws which, by divine revelation, I have ordained for you; that is, in case you withal meditate upon the wisdom that is in them. (184) I am going from you myself, rejoicing in the good things you enjoy; and I recommend you to the wise conduct of your law, to the becoming order of your polity, and to the virtues of your commanders, who will take care of what is for your advantage; (185) and that God, who has been till now your leader, and by whose good will I have myself been useful to you, will not put a period now to his providence over you, but, as long as you desire to have him your Protector in your pursuits after virtue, so long will you enjoy his care over you. (186) Your high priest also Eleazar, as well as Joshua, with the senate, and chief of your tribes, will go before you, and suggest the best advices to you; by following which advices you will continue to be happy: to whom do you give ear without reluctance, as sensible that all such as know well how to be governed will also know how to govern, if they be promoted to that authority themselves; (187) and do not you esteem liberty to consist in opposing such directions as your governors think fit to give you for your practice – as at present indeed you place your liberty in nothing else but abusing your benefactors; which error if you can avoid for the time to come, your affairs will be in a better condition than they have hitherto been; (188) nor do you ever indulge such a degree of passion in these matters as you have oftentimes done when you have been very angry at me; for you know that I have been oftener in danger of death from you than from our enemies. (189) What I now put you in mind of, is not done in order to reproach you; for I do not think it proper, now I am going out of the world, to bring this to your remembrance in order to leave you offended at me, since, at the time when I underwent those hardships from you, I was not angry at you; but I do it in order to make you wiser hereafter, and to teach you that this will be for your security; I mean, that you never be injurious to those that preside over you, even when you are become rich, as you will be to a great degree when you have passed over Jordan, and are in possession of the land of Canaan. (190) Since, when you shall have once proceeded so far by your wealth, as to a contempt and disregard of virtue, you will also forfeit the favour of God; and when you have made him your enemy, you will be beaten in war, and will have the land which you possess taken away again from you by your enemies, and this with great reproaches upon your conduct. You will be scattered over the whole world, and will, as slaves, entirely fill both sea and land; (191) and when once you have had the experience of what I now say, you will repent and remember the laws you have broken when it is too late. Whence I would advise you, if you intend to preserve these laws, to leave none of your enemies alive when you have conquered them, but to look upon it as for your advantage to destroy them all, lest, if you permit them to live, you taste of their manners, and thereby corrupt your own proper institutions. (192) I also do further exhort you, to overthrow their altars and their groves, and whichsoever temples they have among them, and to burn all such, their nation, and their very memory with fire; for by this means alone the safety of your own happy constitution can be firmly secured to you. (193) And in order to prevent your ignorance of virtue, and the degeneracy of your nature into vice, I have also ordained your laws by divine suggestion, and a form of government, which are so good that, if you regularly observe them, you will be esteemed of all men the most happy.'

(194) When he had spoken thus, he gave them the laws and the constitution of government written in a book. Upon which the people fell into tears, and appeared already touched with the sense that they should have a great want of their conductor, because they remembered what a number of dangers he had passed through, and what care he had taken of their preservation: they desponded about what would come upon them after he was dead, and thought they should never have another governor like him; and feared that God would then take less care of them when Moses was gone, who used to intercede for them. (195) They also repented of what they had said to him in the wilderness

when they were angry; and were in grief on those accounts, insomuch that the whole body of the people fell into tears with such bitterness, that it was past the power of words to comfort them in their affliction. However, Moses gave them some consolation; and by calling them off the thought, how worthy he was of their weeping for him, he exhorted them to keep to that form of government he had given them; and then the congregation was dissolved at that time.

(196) Accordingly, I shall now first describe this form of government which was agreeable to the dignity and virtue of Moses; and shall thereby inform those that read these Antiquities, what our original settlements were, and shall then proceed to the remaining histories. Now those settlements are all still in writing, as he left them; and we shall add nothing by way of ornament, nor anything besides what Moses left us; (197) only we shall so far innovate, as to digest the several kinds of laws into a regular system; for they were by him left in writing as they were accidentally scattered in their delivery, and as he upon inquiry had learned them of God. On which account I have thought it necessary to premise this observation beforehand, lest any of my own countrymen should blame me, as having been guilty of an offence herein. (198) Now part of our constitution will include the laws that belong to our political state. As for those laws which Moses left concerning our common conversation and intercourse one with another, I have reserved that for a discourse concerning our manner of life, and the occasions of those laws; which I propose to myself, with God's assistance, to write, after I have finished the work I am now upon.

(199) When you have possessed yourselves of the land of Canaan, and have leisure to enjoy the good things of it, and when you have afterward determined to build cities, if you will do what is pleasing to God, you will have a secure state of happiness. (200) Let there be then one city of the land of Canaan, and this situate in the most agreeable place for its goodness, and very eminent in itself, and let it be that which God shall choose for himself by prophetic revelation. Let there also be one temple therein, and one altar, not reared of hewn stones, but of such as you gather together at random; which stones, when they are whited over with mortar, will have a handsome appearance, and be beautiful to the sight. (201) Let the ascent to it be not by steps, but by an acclivity of raised earth. And let there be neither an altar nor a temple in any other city; for God is but one, and the nation of the Hebrews is but one.

(202) He that blasphemeth God, let him be stoned, and let him hang upon a tree all that day, and then let him be buried in an ignominious and obscure manner.

(203) Let those that live as remote as the bounds of the land which the Hebrews shall possess, come to that city where the temple shall be, and this three times in a year, that they may give thanks to God for his former benefits,

and may entreat him for those they shall want hereafter; and let them, by this means, maintain a friendly correspondence with one another by such meetings and feastings together, (204) for it is a good thing for those that are of the same stock, and under the same institution of laws, not to be unacquainted with each other; which acquaintance will be maintained by thus conversing together, and by seeing and talking with one another, and so renewing the memorials of this union; for if they do not thus converse together continually, they will appear like mere strangers to one another.

(205) Let there be taken out of your fruits a tenth, besides that which you have allotted to give to the priests and Levites. This you may indeed sell in the country, but it is to be used in those feasts and sacrifices that are to be celebrated in the holy city; for it is fit that you should enjoy those fruits of the earth which God gives you to possess, so as may be to the honour of the donor.

(206) You are not to offer sacrifices out of the hire of a woman who is a harlot, for the Deity is not pleased with anything that arises from such abuses of nature; of which sort none can be worse than this prostitution of the body. In like manner no one may take the price of the covering of a bitch, either of one that is used in hunting, or in keeping of sheep, and thence sacrifice to God.

(207) Let no one blaspheme those gods which other cities esteem such; nor may anyone steal what belongs to strange temples; nor take away the gifts that are dedicated to any god.

(208) Let not any one of you wear a garment made of wool and linen, for that is appointed to be for the priests alone.

(209) When the multitude are assembled together unto the holy city for sacrificing every seventh year, at the Feast of Tabernacles, let the high priest stand upon a high desk, whence he may be heard, and let him read the laws to all the people; and let neither the women nor the children be hindered from hearing, no, nor the servants neither; (210) for it is a good thing that those laws should be engraven in their souls, and preserved in their memories, that so it may not be possible to blot them out; for by this means they will not be guilty of sin, when they cannot plead ignorance of what the laws have enjoined them. The laws also will have a greater authority among them as foretelling what they will suffer if they break them, and imprinting in their souls by this hearing what they command them to do, (211) that so there may always be within their minds that intention of the laws which they have despised and broken, and have thereby been the causes of their own mischief. Let the children also learn the laws, as the first thing they are taught, which will be the best thing they can be taught, and will be the cause of their future felicity.

(212) Let everyone commemorate before God the benefits which he bestowed upon them at their deliverance out of the land of Egypt, and this twice every day, both when the day begins and when the hour of sleep comes

on, gratitude being in its own nature a just thing, and serving not only by way of return for past, but also by way of invitation of future favours. (213) They are also to inscribe the principal blessings they have received from God upon their doors, and show the same remembrance of them upon their arms; as also they are to bear on their forehead and their arm those wonders which declare the power of God, and his good will towards them, that God's readiness to bless them may appear everywhere conspicuous about them.

(214) Let there be seven men to judge in every city, and these such as have been before most zealous in the exercise of virtue and righteousness. Let every judge have two officers, allotted him out of the tribe of Levi. (215) Let those that are chosen to judge in the several cities be had in great honour, and let none be permitted to revile any others when these are present, nor to carry themselves in an insolent manner to them; it being natural that reverence towards those in high offices among men should procure men's fear and reverence towards God. (216) Let those that judge be permitted to determine according as they think to be right, unless anyone can show that they have taken bribes, to the perversion of justice, or can allege any other accusation against them, whereby it may appear that they have passed an unjust sentence; for it is not fit that causes should be openly determined out of regard to gain, or to the dignity of the suitors, but that the judges should esteem what is right before all other things, (217) otherwise God will by that means be despised, and esteemed inferior to those, the dread of whose power has occasioned the unjust sentence; for justice is the power of God. He therefore that gratifies those in great dignity, supposes them more potent than God himself. (218) But if these judges be unable to give a just sentence about the causes that come before them (which case is not unfrequent in human affairs), let them send the cause undetermined to the holy city, and there let the high priest, the prophet, and the sanhedrin, determine as it shall seem good to them.

(219) But let not a single witness be credited; but three, or two at the least, and those such whose testimony is confirmed by their good lives. But let not the testimony of women be admitted, on account of the levity and boldness of their sex, nor let servants be admitted to give testimony on account of the ignobility of their soul; since it is probable that they may not speak truth, either out of hope of gain or fear of punishment. But if anyone be believed to have borne false witness, let him, when he is convicted, suffer all the very same punishments which he against whom he bore witness was to have suffered.

(220) If a murder be committed in any place, and he that did it be not found, nor is there any suspicion upon one as if he had hated the man, and so had killed him, let there be a very diligent inquiry made after the man, and rewards proposed to anyone who will discover him; but if still no information can be procured, let the magistrates and senate of those cities that lie near the place

in which the murder was committed, assemble together, and measure the distance from the place where the dead body lies; (221) then let the magistrates of the nearest city thereto purchase a heifer, and bring it to a valley, and to a place therein where there is no land ploughed or trees planted, and let them cut the sinews of the heifer; (222) then the priests and Levites, and the senate of that city, shall take water and wash their hands over the head of the heifer; and they shall openly declare that their hands are innocent of this murder, and that they have neither done it themselves, nor been assisting to any that did it. They shall also beseech God to be merciful to them, that no such horrid act may any more be done in that land.

(223) Aristocracy, and the way of living under it, is the best constitution; and may you never have any inclination to any other form of government; and may you always love that form, and have the laws for your governors, and govern all your actions according to them; for you need no supreme governor but God. But if you shall desire a king, let him be one of your own nation; let him be always careful of justice and other virtues perpetually; (224) let him submit to the laws, and esteem God's commands to be his highest wisdom; but let him do nothing without the high priest and the votes of the senators; let him not have a great number of wives, nor pursue after abundance of riches, nor a multitude of horses, whereby he may grow too proud to submit to the laws. And if he affect any such things, let him be restrained, lest he become so potent that his state be inconsistent with your welfare.

(225) Let it not be esteemed lawful to remove boundaries, neither our own, nor of those with whom we are at peace. Have a care you do not take those landmarks away which are, as it were, a divine and unshaken limitation of rights made by God himself, to last forever; since this going beyond limits and gaining ground upon others, is the occasion of wars and seditions; for those that remove boundaries are not far off an attempt to subvert the laws.

(226) He that plants a piece of land, the trees of which produce fruits before the fourth year, is not to bring thence any first fruits to God, nor is he to make use of that fruit himself, for it is not produced in its proper season; for when Nature has a force put upon her at an unseasonable time, the fruit is not proper for God, nor for the master's use; (227) but let the owner gather all that is grown on the fourth year, for then it is in its proper season; and let him that has gathered it carry it to the holy city, and spend that, together with the tithe of his other fruits, in feasting with his friends, with the orphans and the widows. But on the fifth year the fruit is his own, and he may use it as he pleases.

(228) You are not to sow with seed a piece of land which is planted with vines; for it is enough that it supply nourishment to that plant, and be not harassed by ploughing also. You are to plough your land with oxen, and not to oblige other animals to come under the same yoke with them, but to till your

land with those beasts that are of the same kind with each other. The seeds are also to be pure, and without mixture, and not to be compounded of two or three sorts, since Nature does not rejoice in the union of things that are not in their own nature alike; (229) nor are you to permit beasts of different kinds to gender together, for there is reason to fear that this unnatural abuse may extend from beasts of different kinds to men, though it takes its first rise from evil practices about such smaller things. (230) Nor is anything to be allowed, by imitation whereof any degree of subversion may creep into the constitution; nor do the laws neglect small matters, but provide that even those may be managed after an unblamable manner.

(231) Let not those that reap and gather in the corn that is reaped, gather in the gleanings also, but let them rather leave some handfuls for those that are in want of the necessaries of life, that it may be a support and a supply to them, in order to their subsistence. In like manner when they gather their grapes, let them leave some smaller bunches for the poor, and let them pass over some of the fruits of the olive trees, when they gather them, and leave them to be partaken of by those that have none of their own; (232) for the advantage arising from the exact collection of all, will not be so considerable to the owners as will arise from the gratitude of the poor; and God will provide that the land shall more willingly produce what shall be for the nourishment of its fruits, in case you do not merely take care of your own advantage, but have regard to the support of others also; (233) nor are you to muzzle the mouths of the oxen when they tread the ears of corn in the thrashing floor; for it is not just to restrain our fellow-labouring animals, and those that work in order to its production, of this fruit of their labours; (234) nor are you to prohibit those that pass by at the time when your fruits are ripe to touch them, but to give them leave to fill themselves full of what you have; and this whether they be of your own country or strangers – as being glad of the opportunity of giving them some part of your fruits when they are ripe; but let it not be esteemed lawful for them to carry any away; (235) nor let those that gather the grapes, and carry them to the wine presses, restrain those whom they meet from eating of them; for it is unjust, out of envy, to hinder those that desire it, to partake of the good things that come into the world according to God's will, and this while the season is at the height, and is hastening away as it pleases God. (236) Nay, if some, out of bashfulness, are unwilling to touch these fruits, let them be encouraged to take of them (I mean those that are Israelites) as if they were themselves the owners and lords, on account of the kindred there is between them; nay, let them desire men that come from other countries, to partake of these tokens of friendship which God has given in their proper season; (237) for that is not to be deemed as idly spent, which anyone out of kindness communicates to another, since God bestows plenty of good things on men,

not only for themselves to reap the advantage, but also to give to others in a way of generosity; and he is desirous, by this means, to make known to others his peculiar kindness to the people of Israel, and how freely he communicates happiness to them, while they abundantly communicate out of their great superfluities to even these foreigners also. (238) But for him that acts contrary to this law, let him be beaten with forty stripes, save one, by the public executioner; let him undergo this punishment, which is a most ignominious one for a free man, and this because he was such a slave to gain as to lay a blot upon his dignity; (239) for it is proper for you who have had the experience of the afflictions in Egypt, and of those in the wilderness, to make provision for those that are in the like circumstances; and while you have now obtained plenty yourselves, through the mercy and providence of God, to distribute of the same plenty, by the like sympathy, to such as stand in need of it.

(240) Besides those two tithes, which I have already said you are to pay every year, the one for the Levites, the other for the festivals, you are to bring every third year a third tithe to be distributed to those that want; to women also that are widows, and to children that are orphans. (241) But as to the ripe fruits, let them carry that which is ripe first of all into the temple; and when they have blessed God for that land which bare them, and which he had given them for a possession, when they have also offered those sacrifices which the law has commanded them to bring, let them give the first fruits to the priests. (242) But when anyone hath done this, and hath brought the tithe of all that he has, together with those first fruits that are for the Levites, and for the festivals, and when he is about to go home, let him stand before the holy house, and return thanks to God, that he hath delivered them from the injurious treatment they had in Egypt, and hath given them a good land, and a large, and lets them enjoy the fruits thereof; and when he hath openly testified that he hath fully paid the tithes [and other dues] according to the laws of Moses, (243) let him entreat God that he will be ever merciful and gracious to him, and continue so to be to all the Hebrews, both by preserving the good things which he hath already given them, and by adding what it is still in his power to bestow upon them.

(244) Let the Hebrews marry, at the age fit for it, virgins that are free, and born of good parents. And he that does not marry a virgin, let him not corrupt another man's wife, and marry her, nor grieve her former husband; nor let free men marry slaves, although their affections should strongly bias any of them so to do; for it is decent, and for the dignity of the persons themselves, to govern those their affections. (245) And further, no one ought to marry a harlot, whose matrimonial oblations, arising from the prostitution of her body, God will not receive; for by these means the dispositions of the children will be liberal and virtuous; I mean, when they are not born of base parents, and of the

lustful conjunction of such as marry women that are not free. (246) If anyone has been espoused to a woman as to a virgin, and does not afterwards find her so to be, let him bring his action, and accuse her, and let him make use of such indications to prove his accusation as he is furnished withal; and let the father or the brother of the damsel, or someone that is after them nearest of kin to her, defend her. (247) If the damsel obtain a sentence in her favour, that she had not been guilty, let her live with her husband that accused her; and let him not have any further power at all to put her away, unless she give him very great occasions of suspicion, and such as can be no way contradicted; (248) but for him that brings an accusation and calumny against his wife in an impudent and rash manner, let him be punished by receiving forty stripes save one, and let him pay fifty shekels to her father: but if the damsel be convicted, as having been corrupted, and is one of the common people, let her be stoned, because she did not preserve her virginity till she were lawfully married; but if she were the daughter of a priest, let her be burnt alive. (249) If anyone has two wives, and if he greatly respect and be kind to one of them, either out of his affection to her, or for her beauty, or for some other reason, while the other is of less esteem with him; and if the son of her that is beloved be the younger by birth than another born of the other wife, but endeavours to obtain the right of primogeniture from his father's kindness to his mother, and would thereby obtain a double portion of his father's substance, for that double portion is what I have allotted him in the laws – let not this be permitted: (250) for it is unjust that he who is the elder by birth should be deprived of what is due to him, on the father's disposition of his estate, because his mother was not equally regarded by him. (251) He that hath corrupted a damsel espoused to another man, in case he had her consent, let both him and her be put to death, for they are both equally guilty; the man because he persuaded the woman willingly to submit to a most impure action, and to prefer it to lawful wedlock: the woman because she was persuaded to yield herself to be corrupted, either for pleasure or for gain. (252) However, if a man light on a woman when she is alone, and forces her, where nobody was present to come to her assistance, let him only be put to death. Let him that hath corrupted a virgin not yet espoused, marry her; but if the father of the damsel be not willing that she should be his wife, let him pay fifty shekels as the price of her prostitution. (253) He that desires to be divorced from his wife for any cause whatsoever (and many such causes happen among men), let him in writing give assurance that he will never use her as his wife any more; for by this means she may be at liberty to marry another husband, although before this bill of divorce be given, she is not to be permitted so to do: but if she be misused by him also, or if, when he is dead, her first husband would marry her again, it shall not be lawful for her to return to him. (254) If a woman's husband die, and leave her without children, let his brother marry her; and let him call the son that is born to him by his brother's name, and educate him as the heir of his inheritance; for this procedure will be for the benefit of the public, because thereby families will not fail, and the estate will continue among the kindred; and this will be for the solace of wives under their affliction, that they are to be married to the next relation of their former husbands; (255) but if the brother will not marry her, let the woman come before the senate, and protest openly that this brother will not admit her for his wife, but will injure the memory of his deceased brother, while she is willing to continue in the family and to bear him children; and when the senate have inquired of him for what reason it is that he is averse to this marriage, whether he gives a bad or a good reason, the matter must come to this issue: (256) that the woman shall loose the sandals of the brother, and shall spit in his face and say, He deserves this reproachful treatment from her, as having injured the memory of the deceased – and then let him go away out of the senate, and bear this reproach upon him all his life long; and let her marry to whom she pleases, of such as seek her in marriage. (257) But now, if any man take captive either a virgin or one that hath been married, and has a mind to marry her, let him not be allowed to bring her to bed to him, or to live with her as his wife, before she hath her head shaven, and hath put on her mourning habit, and lamented her relations and friends that were slain in the battle, (258) that by this means she may give vent to her sorrow for them, and after that may betake herself to feasting and matrimony; for it is good for him that takes a woman in order to have children by her, to be complaisant to her inclinations, and not merely to pursue his own pleasure, while he hath no regard to what is agreeable to her; (259) but when thirty days are past, as the time of mourning, for so many are sufficient to prudent persons for lamenting the dearest friends, then let them proceed to the marriage; but in case, when he hath satisfied his lust, he be too proud to retain her for his wife, let him not have it in his power to make her a slave, but let her go away whither she pleases, and have that privilege of a free woman.

(260) As to those young men that despise their parents, and do not pay them honour, but offer them affronts, either because they are ashamed of them, or think themselves wiser than they – in the first place let their parents admonish them in words (for they are by nature of authority sufficient for becoming their judges), (261) and let them say thus to them: that they cohabited together, not for the sake of pleasure, nor for the augmentation of their riches, by joining both their stocks together, but that they might have children to take care of them in their old age, and might by them have what they then should want: and say further to him, 'That when thou wast born, we took thee up with gladness, and gave God the greatest thanks for thee, and brought thee up with great care, and spared for nothing that appeared useful for thy preservation, and

for thy instruction in what was most excellent; (262) and now, since it is reasonable to forgive the sins of those that are young, let it suffice thee to have given so many indications of thy contempt of us – reform thyself, and act more wisely for the time to come; considering that God is displeased with those that are insolent towards their parents, because he is himself the Father of the whole race of mankind, and seems to bear part of that dishonour which falls upon those that have the same name, when they do not meet with due returns from their children; and on such the law inflicts inexorable punishment, of which punishment mayst thou never have the experience!' (263) Now if the insolence of young men be thus cured, let them escape the reproach which their former errors deserved; for by this means the lawgiver will appear to be good, and parents happy, while they never behold either a son or a daughter brought to punishment; (264) but if it happen that these words and instructions conveyed by them in order to reclaim the man, appear to be useless, then the offender renders the laws implacable enemies to the insolence he has offered his parents; let him therefore be brought forth by these very parents out of the city with a multitude following him, and there let him be stoned; and when he has continued there for one whole day, that all the people may see him, let him be buried in the night; (265) and thus it is that we bury all whom the laws condemn to die, upon any account whatsoever. Let our enemies that fall in battle be also buried, nor let any one dead body lie above the ground, or suffer a punishment beyond what justice requires.

(266) Let no one lend to anyone of the Hebrews upon usury, neither usury of what is eaten or what is drunken; for it is not just to make advantage of the misfortunes of one of thy own countrymen: but when thou hast been assisted to his necessities, think it thy gain if thou obtainest their gratitude to thee and withal that reward which will come to thee from God for thy humanity towards him.

(267) Those who have borrowed either silver or any sort of fruits, whether dry or wet (I mean this, when the Jewish affairs shall, by the blessing of God, be to their own mind), let the borrowers bring them again, and restore them with pleasure to those who lent them; laying them up, as it were, in their own treasuries, and justly expecting to receive them thence, if they shall want them again: (268) but if they be without shame, and do not restore it, let not the lender go to the borrower's house, and take a pledge himself, before judgment be given concerning it; but let him require the pledge, and let the debtor bring it of himself, without the least opposition to him that comes upon him under the protection of the law; (269) and if he that gave the pledge be rich, let the creditor retain it till what he lent be paid him again; but if he be poor, let him that takes it return it before the going down of the sun, especially if the pledge be a garment, that the debtor may have it for a covering in his sleep, God

himself naturally showing mercy to the poor. (270) It is also not lawful to take a millstone, nor any utensil thereto belonging, for a pledge, that the debtors may not be deprived of instruments to get their food withal, and lest they be undone by their necessity.

(271) Let death be the punishment for stealing a man; but he that hath purloined gold or silver, let him pay double. If anyone kill a man that is stealing something out of his house, let him be esteemed guiltless, although the man were only breaking in at the wall. (272) Let him that hath stolen cattle pay fourfold what is lost, excepting the case of an ox, for which let the thief pay fivefold. Let him that is so poor that he cannot pay what mulct is laid upon him, be his servant to whom he was adjudged to pay it.

(273) If anyone be sold to one of his own nation, let him serve him six years, and on the seventh let him go free. But if he have a son by a woman-servant in his purchaser's house, and if, on account of his good will to his master and his natural affection to his wife and children, he will be his servant still, let him be set free only at the coming of the year of jubilee, which is the fiftieth year, and let him then take away with him his children and wife, and let them be free also.

(274) If anyone find gold or silver on the road, let him inquire after him that lost it, and make proclamation of the place where he found it, and then restore it to him again, as not thinking it right to make his own profit by the loss of another. And the same rule is to be observed in cattle found to have wandered away into a lonely place. If the owner be not presently discovered, let him that is the finder keep it with himself, and appeal to God that he has not purloined what belongs to another.

(275) It is not lawful to pass by any beast that is in distress, when in a storm it is fallen down in the mire, but to endeavour to preserve it, as having a sympathy with it in its pain.

(276) It is also a duty to show the roads to those who do not know them, and not to esteem it a matter for sport, when we hinder others' advantages by setting them in a wrong way.

In like manner, let no one revile a person blind or dumb.

(277) If men strive together, and there be no instrument of iron, let him that is smitten be avenged immediately, by inflicting the same punishment on him that smote him: but if when he is carried home he lie sick many days, and then die, let him that smote him escape punishment; but if he that is smitten escape death, and yet be at great expense for his cure, the smiter shall pay for all that has been expended during the time of his sickness, and for all that he has paid the physician. (278) He that kicks a woman with child, so that the woman miscarry, let him pay a fine in money, as the judges shall determine, as having diminished the multitude by the destruction of what was in her womb; and let money also be given the woman's husband by him that kicked her; but if she

die of the stroke, let him also be put to death, the law judging it equitable that life should go for life.

(279) Let no one of the Israelites keep any poison that may cause death, or any other harm; but if he be caught with it, let him be put to death, and suffer the very same mischief that he would have brought upon them for whom the poison was prepared.

(280) He that maimeth anyone, let him undergo the like himself, and be deprived of the same member of which he hath deprived the other, unless he that is maimed will accept of money instead of it; for the law makes the sufferer the judge of the value of what he hath suffered, and permits him to estimate it, unless he will be more severe.

(281) Let him that is the owner of an ox which pusheth with his horn, kill him: but if he pushes and gores anyone in the thrashing floor, let him be put to death by stoning, and let him not be thought fit for food: but if his owner be convicted as having known what his nature was, and hath not kept him up, let him also be put to death, as being the occasion of the ox's having killed a man. (282) But if the ox have killed a manservant or a maidservant, let him be stoned; and let the owner of the ox pay thirty shekels to the master of him that was slain; but if it be an ox that is thus smitten and killed, let both the oxen, that which smote the other and that which was killed, be sold, and let the owners of them divide their price between them.

(283) Let those that dig a well or a pit, be careful to lay planks over them, and so keep them shut up, not in order to hinder any persons from drawing water, but that there may be no danger of falling into them: (284) but if anyone's beast fall into such a well or pit thus digged and not shut up, and perish, let the owner pay its price to the owner of the beast. Let there be a battlement round the tops of your houses instead of a wall, that may prevent any persons from rolling down and perishing.

(285) Let him that has received anything in trust for another, take care to keep it as a sacred and divine thing; and let no one invent any contrivance, whereby to deprive him that hath entrusted it with him of the same, and this whether he be a man or a woman; no, not although he or she were to gain an immense sum of gold, and this where he cannot be convicted of it by anybody; (286) for it is fit that a man's own conscience, which knows what he hath, should, in all cases, oblige him to do well. Let this conscience be his witness, and make him always act so as may procure him commendation from others; but let him chiefly have regard to God, from whom no wicked man can lie concealed; (287) but if he in whom the trust was reposed, without any deceit of his own, lose what he was entrusted withal, let him come before the seven judges, and swear by God that nothing hath been lost willingly, or with a wicked intention, and that he hath not made use of any part thereof, and so let

him depart without blame; but if he hath made use of the least part of what was committed to him, and it be lost, let him be condemned to repay all that he had received. (288) After the same manner as in these trusts, it is to be, if anyone defraud those that undergo bodily labour for him. And let it be always remembered, that we are not to defraud a poor man of his wages, as being sensible that God has allotted these wages to him instead of land and other possessions; nay, this payment is not at all to be delayed, but to be made that very day, since God is not willing to deprive the labourer of the immediate use of what he hath laboured for.

(289) You are not to punish children for the faults of their parents, but on account of their own virtue rather to vouchsafe them commiseration, because they were born of wicked parents, than hatred, because they were born of bad ones: nor indeed ought we to impute the sin of children to their fathers, while young persons indulge themselves in many practices different from what they have been instructed in, and this by their proud refusal of such instruction.

(290) Let those that have made themselves eunuchs be had in detestation; and do you avoid any conversation with them who have deprived themselves of their manhood, and of that fruit of generation which God has given to men for the increase of their kind; let such be driven away, as if they had killed their children, since they beforehand have lost what should procure them; (291) for evident it is, that while their soul is become effeminate, they have withal transfused that effeminacy to their body also. In like manner do you treat all that is of a monstrous nature when it is looked on; nor is it lawful to geld man or any other animals.

(292) Let this be the constitution of your political laws in time of peace, and God will be so merciful as to preserve this excellent settlement free from disturbance: and may that time never come which may innovate anything, and change it for the contrary. (293) But since it must needs happen that mankind fall into troubles and dangers, either undesignedly or intentionally, come let us make a few constitutions concerning them, that so being apprised beforehand what ought to be done, you may have salutary counsels ready when you want them, and may not then be obliged to go to seek what is to be done, and so be unprovided, and fall into dangerous circumstances. (294) May you be a laborious people, and exercise your souls in virtuous actions, and thereby possess and inherit the land without wars, while neither any foreigners make war upon it, and so afflict you, nor any internal sedition seize upon it, (295) whereby you may do things that are contrary to your fathers, and so lose the laws which they have established: and may you continue in the observation of those laws which God hath approved of, and hath delivered to you. Let all sort of warlike operations, whether they befall you now in your own time, or hereafter in the times of your posterity, be done out of your own borders, (296)

but when you are about to go to war, send ambassages and heralds to those who are your voluntary enemies, for it is a right thing to make use of words to them before you come to your weapons of war; and assure them thereby, that although you have a numerous army, with horses and weapons, and, above these, a God merciful to you, and ready to assist you, you do however desire them not to compel you to fight against them, nor to take from them what they have, which will indeed be our gain, but what they will have no reason to wish we should take to ourselves; (297) and if they hearken to you, it will be proper for you to keep peace with them; but if they trust in their own strength as superior to yours, and will not do you justice, lead your army against them, making use of God as your supreme commander, but ordaining for a lieutenant under him, one that is of the greatest courage among you; for these different commanders, besides their being an obstacle to actions that are to be done on the sudden, are a disadvantage to those that make use of them. (298) Lead an army pure, and of chosen men, composed of all such as have extraordinary strength of body and hardiness of soul; but do you send away the timorous part, lest they run away in the time of action, and so afford an advantage to your enemies. Do you also give leave to those that have lately built them houses, and have not yet lived in them a year's time; and to those that have planted them vineyards, and have not yet been partakers of their fruits, to continue in their own country; as well as those also who have betrothed, or lately married them wives, lest they have such an affection for these things that they be too sparing of their lives, and, by reserving themselves for these enjoyments, they become voluntary cowards, on account of their wives.

(299) When you have pitched your camp, take care that you do nothing that is cruel; and when you are engaged in a siege, and want timber for the making of warlike engines, do not you render the land naked by cutting down trees that bear fruit, but spare them, as considering that they were made for the benefit of men; and that if they could speak, they would have a just plea against you, because, though they are not occasions of the war, they are unjustly treated, and suffer in it; and would, if they were able, remove themselves into another land. (300) When you have beaten your enemies in battle, slay those that have fought against you, but preserve the others alive, that they may pay you tribute, excepting the nation of the Canaanites; for as to that people, you must entirely destroy them.

(301) Take care, especially in your battles, that no woman use the habit of a man, nor man the garment of a woman.

(302) This was the form of political government which was left us by Moses. Moreover, he had already delivered laws in writing, in the fortieth year [after they came out of Egypt], concerning which we will discourse in another book. But now on the following days (for he called them to assemble continually)

he delivered blessings to them, and curses upon those that should not live according to the laws, but should transgress the duties that were determined for them to observe. (303) After this, he read to them a poetic song, which was composed in hexameter verse; and left it to them in the holy book; it contained a prediction of what was to come to pass afterward; agreeably whereto all things have happened all along, and do still happen to us; and wherein he has not at all deviated from the truth. (304) Accordingly, he delivered these books to the priests, with the ark; into which he also put the Ten Commandments, written on two tables. He delivered to them the tabernacle also; and exhorted the people, that when they had conquered the land, and were settled in it, they should not forget the injuries of the Amalekites, but make war against them, and inflict punishment upon them for what mischief they did them when they were in the wilderness; (305) and that, when they had destroyed the whole multitude of its inhabitants, as they ought to do, they should erect an altar that should face the rising sun, not far from the city of Shechem, between the two mountains, that of Gerizzim, situate on the right hand, and that called Ebal, on the left; and that the army should be so divided that six tribes should stand upon each of the two mountains, and with them the Levites and the priests. (306) And that first, those that were upon Mount Gerizzim should pray for the best blessings upon those who were diligent about the worship of God, and the observation of his laws, and who did not reject what Moses had said to them, while the other wished them all manner of happiness also; and when these last put up the like prayers, the former praised them. (307) After this, curses were denounced upon those that should transgress those laws, they answering one another alternately, by way of confirmation of what had been said. Moses also wrote their blessings and their curses, that they might learn them so thoroughly, that they might never be forgotten by length of time. (308) And when he was ready to die, he wrote these blessings and curses upon the altar, on each side of it; where he says also the people stood, and then sacrificed and offered burnt offerings; though after that day they never offered upon it any other sacrifice, for it was not lawful so to do. These are the constitutions of Moses; and the Hebrew nation still live according to them.

(309) On the next day, Moses called the people together, with the women and children, to a congregation, so as the very slaves were present also, that they might engage themselves to the observation of these laws by oath; and that, duly considering the meaning of God in them, they might not either for favour of their kindred, or out of fear of anyone or indeed for any motive whatsoever, think anything ought to be preferred to these laws, and so might transgress them; (310) that in case anyone of their own blood, or any city, should attempt to confound or dissolve their constitution of government, they should take vengeance upon them, both all in general and each person in

particular; and when they had conquered them, should overturn their city to the very foundations, and, if possible, should not leave the least footsteps of such madness: but that if they were not able to take such vengeance, they should still demonstrate that what was done was contrary to their wills. So the multitude bound themselves by oath so to do.

(311) Moses taught them also by what means their sacrifices might be the most acceptable to God; and how they should go forth to war, making use of the stones (in the high priest's breastplate) for their direction, as I have before signified. Joshua also prophesied while Moses was present. (312) And when Moses had recapitulated whatsoever he had done for the preservation of the people, both in their wars and in peace, and had composed them a body of laws, and procured them an excellent form of government, he foretold, as God had declared to him, 'That if they transgressed that institution for the worship of God, they should experience the following miseries. (313) Their land should be full of weapons of war from their enemies, and their cities should be overthrown, and their temple should be burnt; that they should be sold for slaves to such men as would have no pity on them in their afflictions; that they would then repent, when that repentance would no way profit them under their sufferings. (314) Yet,' said he, 'will that God who founded your nation, restore your cities to your citizens, with their temple also; and you shall lose these advantages, not once only, but often.'

(315) Now when Moses had encouraged Joshua to lead out the army against the Canaanites, by telling him that God would assist him in all his undertakings, and had blessed the whole multitude, he said, 'Since I am going to my forefathers, and God has determined that this should be the day of my departure to them, I return him thanks while I am still alive and present with you, (316) for that providence he hath exercised over you, which hath not only delivered us from the miseries we lay under, but hath bestowed a state of prosperity upon us; as also, that he hath assisted me in the pains I took, and in all the contrivances I had in my care about you, in order to better your condition, and hath on all occasions showed himself favourable to us; (317) or rather he it was who first conducted our affairs, and brought them to a happy conclusion, by making use of me as a vicarious general under him, and as a minister in those matters wherein he was willing to do you good: (318) on which account I think it proper to bless that Divine Power which will take care of you for the time to come, and this in order to repay that debt which I owe him, and to leave behind me a memorial that we are obliged to worship and honour him, and to keep those laws which are the most excellent gift of all those he hath already bestowed upon us, or which, if he continue favourable to us, he will bestow upon us hereafter. (319) Certainly a human legislator is a terrible enemy when his laws are affronted, and are made to no purpose. And

may you never experience that displeasure of God which will be the consequence of the neglect of these his laws, which he who is your Creator hath given you!'

(320) When Moses had spoken thus at the end of his life, and had foretold what would befall to every one of their tribes afterward, with the addition of a blessing to them, the multitude fell into tears, insomuch that even the women, by beating their breasts, made manifest the deep concern they had when he was about to die. The children also lamented still more, as not able to contain their grief; and thereby declared, that even at their age they were sensible of his virtue and mighty deeds; (321) and truly there seemed to be a strife betwixt the young and the old, who should most grieve for him. The old grieved, because they knew what a careful protector they were to be deprived of, and so lamented their future state; but the young grieved not only for that, but also because it so happened that they were to be left by him before they had well tasted of his virtue. (322) Now one may make a guess at the excess of this sorrow and lamentation of the multitude, from what happened to the legislator himself; for although he was always persuaded that he ought not to be cast down at the approach of death, since the undergoing it was agreeable to the will of God and the law of nature, yet what the people did so overbore him, that he wept himself. (323) Now as he went thence to the place where he was to vanish out of their sight, they all followed after him weeping; but Moses beckoned with his hand to those that were remote from him, and bade them stay behind in quiet, while he exhorted those that were near to him that they would not render his departure so lamentable. (324) Whereupon they thought they ought to grant him that favour, to let him depart according as he himself desired: so they restrained themselves, though weeping still towards one another. All those who accompanied him were the senate, and Eleazar the high priest, and Joshua their commander. (325) Now as soon as they were come to the mountain called *Abarim* (which is a very high mountain, situated over against Jericho and one that affords, to such as are upon it, a prospect of the greatest part of the excellent land of Canaan), he dismissed the senate; (326) and as he was going to embrace Eleazar and Joshua, and was still discoursing with them, a cloud stood over him on the sudden, and he disappeared in a certain valley, although he wrote in the holy books that he died, which was done out of fear, lest they should venture to say that, because of his extraordinary virtue, he went to God.

(327) Now Moses lived in all one hundred and twenty years; a third part of which time, abating one month, he was the people's ruler; and he died on the last month of the year, which is called by the Macedonians *Dystrus*, but by us *Adar* on the first day of the month. (328) He was one that exceeded all men that ever were in understanding, and made the best use of what that

understanding suggested to him. He had a very graceful way of speaking and addressing himself to the multitude; and as to his other qualifications, he had such a full command of his passions, (329) as if he hardly had any such in his soul, and only knew them by their names, as rather perceiving them in other men than in himself. He was also such a general of an army as is seldom seen, as well as such a prophet as was never known, and this to such a degree, that whatsoever he pronounced, you would think you heard the voice of God himself. (330) So the people mourned for him thirty days; nor did ever any grief so deeply affect the Hebrews as did this upon the death of Moses; (331) nor were those that had experienced his conduct the only persons that desired him, but those also that perused the laws he left behind him had a strong desire after him, and by them gathered the extraordinary virtues he was master of. And this shall suffice for the declaration of the manner of the death of Moses.

BOOK FIVE

CHAPTER I

(1) When Moses was taken away from among men, in the manner already described, and when all the solemnities belonging to the mourning for him were finished, and the sorrow for him was over, Joshua commanded the multitude to get themselves ready for an expedition. (2) He also sent spies to Jericho, to discover what forces they had, and what were their intentions; but he put his camp in order, as intending soon to pass over Jordan at a proper season. (3) And calling to him the rulers of the tribe of Reuben, and the governors of the tribe of Gad, and [the half tribe of] Manasseh, for half of this tribe had been permitted to have their habitation in the country of the Amorites, which was the seventh part of the land of Canaan, (4) he put them in mind what they had promised Moses; and he exhorted them that, for the sake of the care that Moses had taken of them, who had never been weary of taking pains for them, no, not when he was dying, and for the sake of the public welfare, they would prepare themselves, and readily perform what they had promised; so he took fifty thousand of them who followed him, and he marched from Abila to Jordan, sixty furlongs.

(5) Now when he had pitched his camp, the spies came to him immediately, well acquainted with the whole state of the Canaanites; for at first, before they were at all discovered, they took a full view of the city of Jericho without disturbance, and saw which parts of the walls were strong, and which parts were otherwise, and indeed insecure, and which of the gates were so weak as might afford an entrance to their army. (6) Now those that met them took no notice of them when they saw them, and supposed they were only strangers, who used to be very curious in observing everything in the city, and did not take them for enemies; (7) but at even they retired to a certain inn that was near to the wall, whither they went to eat their supper; (8) which supper when they had done, and were considering how to get away, information was given to the king as he was at supper, that there were some persons come from the Hebrews' camp to view the city as spies, and that they were in the inn kept by Rahab, and were very solicitous that they might not be discovered. So he sent immediately some to them, and commanded to catch them, and bring them to him, that he might examine them by torture, and learn what their business was there. (9) As soon as Rahab understood that these messengers were coming, she hid the spies under stalks of flax, which were laid to dry on the top of her

house; and said to the messengers that were sent by the king, that certain unknown strangers had supped with her a little before sunsetting, and were gone away, who might easily be taken, if they were any terror to the city, or likely to bring any danger to the king. (10) So these messengers being thus deluded by the woman, and suspecting no imposition, went their ways, without so much as searching the inn; but they immediately pursued them along those roads which they most probably supposed them to have gone, and those particularly which led to the river, but could hear no tidings of them; so they left off the pains of any further pursuit. (11) But when the tumult was over, Rahab brought the men down, and desired them as soon as they should have obtained possession of the land of Canaan, when it would be in their power to make her amends for her preservation of them, to remember what danger she had undergone for their sakes; for that if she had been caught concealing them, she could not have escaped a terrible destruction, she and all her family with her, and so bid them go home; (12) and desired them to swear to her to preserve her and her family when they should take the city and destroy all its inhabitants, as they had decreed to do; for so far she said she had been assured by those divine miracles of which she had been informed. (13) So these spies acknowledged that they owed her thanks for what she had done already, and withal swore to requite her kindness, not only in words, but in deeds; but they gave her this advice, that when she should perceive that the city was about to be taken, she should put her goods and all her family, by way of security, in her inn, and to hang out scarlet threads before her doors [or windows], that the commander of the Hebrews might know her house, and take care to do her no harm; (14) for, said they, we will inform him of this matter, because of the concern thou hast had to preserve us; but if any one of thy family fall in the battle, do not thou blame us; and we beseech that God, by whom we have sworn, not then to be displeased with us, as though we had broken our oaths. (15) So these men, when they had made this agreement, went away, letting themselves down by a rope from the wall, and escaped, and came and told their own people whatsoever they had done in their journey to this city. Joshua also told Eleazar the high priest, and the senate, what the spies had sworn to Rahab; and they confirmed what had been sworn.

(16) Now while Joshua, the commander, was in fear about their passing over Jordan, for the river ran with a strong current, and could not be passed over with bridges, for there never had been bridges laid over it hitherto; and while he suspected, that if he should attempt to make a bridge, that their enemies would not afford him time to perfect it, and for ferry boats they had none – God promised so to dispose of the river, that they might pass over it, and that by taking away the main part of its waters. (17) So Joshua, after two days, caused the army and the whole multitude to pass over in the manner

following: the priests went first of all, having the ark with them; then went the Levites bearing the tabernacle and the vessels which belonged to the sacrifices; after which the entire multitude followed, according to their tribes, having their children and their wives in the midst of them, as being afraid for them, lest they should be borne away by the stream. (18) But as soon as the priests had entered the river first, it appeared fordable, the depth of the water being restrained, and the sand appearing at the bottom, because the current was neither so strong nor so swift as to carry it away by its force; so they all passed over the river without fear, finding it to be in the very same state as God had foretold he would put it in; (19) but the priests stood still in the midst of the river till the multitude should be passed over, and should get to the shore in safety; and when all were gone over, the priests came out also, and permitted the current to run freely as it used to do before. Accordingly the river, as soon as the Hebrews were come out of it, arose again presently, and came to its own proper magnitude as before.

(20) So the Hebrews went on further fifty furlongs, and pitched their camp at the distance of ten furlongs from Jericho; but Joshua built an altar of those stones which all the heads of the tribes, at the command of the prophet, had taken out of the deep, to be afterwards a memorial of the division of the stream of this river, and upon it offered sacrifice to God; and in that place celebrated the passover, (21) and had great plenty of all the things which they wanted hitherto; for they reaped the corn of the Canaanites, which was now ripe, and took other things as prey; for then it was that their former food, which was manna, and of which they had eaten forty years, failed them.

(22) Now while the Israelites did this, and the Canaanites did not attack them, but kept themselves quiet within their own walls, Joshua resolved to besiege them; so on the first day of the feast [of the passover], the priests carried the ark round about, with some part of the armed men to be a guard to it. (23) These priests went forward, blowing with their seven trumpets; and exhorted the army to be of good courage, and went round about the city, with the senate following them; and when the priests had only blown with the trumpets, for they did nothing more at all, they returned to the camp; (24) and when they had done this for six days, on the seventh Joshua gathered the armed men and all the people together, and told them these good tidings, that the city should now be taken, since God would on that day give it them, by the falling down of the walls, and this of their own accord, and without their labour. (25) However, he charged them to kill everyone they should take, and not to abstain from the slaughter of their enemies, either for weariness or for pity, and not to fall on the spoil, and be thereby diverted from pursuing their enemies as they ran away; (26) but to destroy all the animals, and to take nothing for their own peculiar advantage. He commanded them also to bring

together all the silver and gold, that it might be set apart as first fruits unto God out of this glorious exploit, as having gotten them from the city they first took; only that they should save Rahab and her kindred alive, because of the oath which the spies had sworn to her.

(27) When he had said this, and had set his army in order, be brought it against the city; so they went round the city again, the ark going before them, and the priests encouraging the people to be zealous in the work; and when they had gone round it seven times, and had stood still a little, the wall fell down, while no instruments of war, nor any other force, was applied to it by the Hebrews.

(28) So they entered into Jericho, and slew all the men that were therein, while they were affrighted at the surprising overthrow of the walls, and their courage was become useless, and they were not able to defend themselves: so they were slain, and their throats cut, some in the ways, and others as caught in their houses – (29) nothing afforded them assistance, but they all perished, even to the women and the children: and the city was filled with dead bodies, and not one person escaped. They also burnt the whole city, and the country about it: (30) but they saved alive Rahab, with her family, who had fled to her inn, and when she was brought to him, Joshua owned to her that they owed her thanks for her preservation of the spies; so he said he would not appear to be behind her in his benefaction to her; whereupon he gave her certain lands immediately, and had her in great esteem ever afterwards.

(31) And if any part of the city escaped the fire, he overthrew it from the foundation; and he denounced a curse against its inhabitants, if any should desire to rebuild it; how, upon his laying the foundation of the walls, he should be deprived of his eldest son; and upon finishing it, he should lose his youngest son. But what happened hereupon, we shall speak of hereafter.

(32) Now there was an immense quantity of silver and gold, and besides those of brass also, that was heaped together out of the city when it was taken, no one transgressing the decree, nor purloining for their own peculiar advantage; which spoils Joshua delivered to the priests, to be laid up among their treasures. And thus did Jericho perish.

(33) But there was one Achar, the son [of Charmi, the son] of Zebedias, of the tribe of Judah, who, finding a royal garment woven entirely of gold, and a piece of gold that weighted two hundred shekels; and thinking it a very hard case, that what spoils he, by running some hazard, had found, he must give away, and offer it to God, who stood in no need of it, while he that wanted it must go without it – made a deep ditch in his own tent, and laid them up therein, as supposing he should not only be concealed from his fellow soldiers, but from God himself also.

(34) Now the place where Joshua pitched his camp was called Gilgal, which

denotes *liberty;* for since now they had passed over Jordan, they looked on themselves as freed from the miseries which they had undergone from the Egyptians, and in the wilderness.

(35) Now, a few days after the calamity that befell Jericho, Joshua sent three thousand armed men to take Ai, a city situate above Jericho; but, upon the sight of the people of Ai, with them they were driven back, and lost thirty-six of their men. (36) When this was told the Israelites, it made them very sad, and exceeding disconsolate, not so much because of the relation the men that were destroyed bare to them, though those that were destroyed were all good men, and deserved their esteem, as by the despair it occasioned; (37) for while they believed that they were already, in effect, in possession of the land, and should bring back the army out of the battles without loss, as God had promised beforehand, they now saw unexpectedly their enemies bold with success; so they put sackcloth over their garments, and continued in tears and lamentation all the day, without the least inquiry after food, but laid what had happened greatly to heart.

(38) When Joshua saw the army so much afflicted, and possessed with forebodings of evil as to their whole expedition, he used freedom with God, (39) and said, 'We are not come thus far out of any rashness of our own, as though we thought ourselves able to subdue this land with our own weapons, but at the instigation of Moses thy servant for this purpose, because thou hast promised us, by many signs, that thou wouldst give us this land for a possession, and that thou wouldst make our army always superior in war to our enemies, (40) and accordingly some success has already attended upon us agreeably to thy promises; but because we have now unexpectedly been foiled, and have lost some men out of our army, we are grieved at it, as fearing what thou hast promised us, and what Moses foretold us, cannot be depended on by us; and our future expectation troubles us the more, because we have met with such a disaster in this our first attempt; (41) but do thou, O Lord, free us from these suspicions, for thou art able to find a cure for these disorders, by giving us victory, which will both take away the grief we are in at present, and prevent our distrust as to what is to come.'

(42) These intercessions Joshua put up to God, as he lay prostrate on his face; whereupon God answered him, that he should rise up, and purify his host from the pollution that had got into it; that 'things consecrated to me have been imprudently stolen from me,' and that 'this has been the occasion why this defeat had happened to them; and that when they should search out and punish the offender, he would ever take care they should have the victory over their enemies. This Joshua told the people; (43) and calling for Eleazar the high priest and the men in authority, he cast lots, tribe by tribe; and when the lot showed that this wicked action was done by one of the tribe of Judah, he then

again proposed the lot to the several families thereto belonging; so the truth of this wicked action was found to belong to the family of Zachar; (44) and when the inquiry was made, man by man, they took Achar, who, upon God's reducing him to a terrible extremity, could not deny the fact; so he confessed the theft, and produced what he had taken in the midst of them, whereupon he was immediately put to death; and attained no more than to be buried in the night in a disgraceful manner, and such as was suitable to a condemned malefactor.

(45) When Joshua had thus purified the host, he led them against Ai: and having by night laid an ambush round about the city, he attacked the enemies as soon as it was day; but as they advanced boldly against the Israelites, because of their former victory, he made them believe he retired, and by that means drew them a great way from the city, they still supposing that they were pursuing their enemies, and despised them, as though the case had been the same with that in the former battle; (46) after which Joshua ordered his forces to turn about, and placed them against their front: he then made the signals agreed upon to those that lay in ambush, and so excited them to fight; so they ran suddenly into the city, the inhabitants being upon the walls, nay, others of them being in perplexity, and coming to see those that were without the gates. (47) Accordingly, these men took the city, and slew all that they met with; but Joshua forced those that came against him to come to a close fight, and discomfited them, and made them run away: and when they were driven towards the city, and thought it had not been touched, as soon as they saw it was taken, and perceived it was burnt, with their wives and children, they wandered about in the fields in a scattered condition, and were no way able to defend themselves, because they had none to support them. (48) Now when this calamity was come upon the men of Ai, there were a great number of children and women and servants, and an immense quantity of other furniture. The Hebrews also took herds of cattle, and a great deal of money, for this was a rich country. So when Joshua came to Gilgal, he divided all these spoils among the soldiers.

(49) But the Gibeonites, who inhabited very near to Jerusalem, when they saw what miseries had happened to the inhabitants of Jericho, and to those of Ai, and suspected that the like sore calamity would come as far as themselves, they did not think fit to ask for mercy of Joshua; for they supposed they should find little mercy from him, who made war that he might entirely destroy the nation of the Canaanites; (50) but they invited the people of Cephirah and Kiriath-jearim, who were their neighbours, to join in league with them; and told them, that neither could they themselves avoid the danger they were all in, if the Israelites should prevent them, and seize upon them; so when they had persuaded them, they resolved to endeavour to

escape the forces of the Israelites. (51) Accordingly, upon their agreement to what they proposed, they sent ambassadors to Joshua to make a league of friendship with him, and those such of the citizens as were best approved of, and most capable of doing what was most advantageous to the multitude. (52) Now these ambassadors thought it dangerous to confess themselves to be Canaanites, but thought they might, by this contrivance, avoid the danger, namely, by saying that they bare no relation to the Canaanites at all, but dwelt at a very great distance from them; and they said further, that they came a long way, on account of the reputation he had gained for his virtue; and as a mark of the truth of what they said, they showed him the habit they were in, (53) for that their clothes were new when they came out, but were greatly worn by the length of time they had been on their journey; for indeed they took torn garments, on purpose that they might make him believe so. (54) So they stood in the midst of the people, and said that they were sent by the people of Gibeon, and of the circumjacent cities, which were very remote from the land where they now were, to make such a league of friendship with them, and this on such conditions as were customary among their forefathers; for when they understood that, by the favour of God and his gift to them, they were to have the possession of the land of Canaan bestowed upon them, they said that they were very glad to hear it, and desired to be admitted into the number of their citizens. (55) Thus did these ambassadors speak; and showing them the marks of their long journey, they entreated the Hebrews to make a league of friendship with them. Accordingly Joshua, believing what they said, that they were not of the nation of the Canaanites, entered into friendship with them: and Eleazar the high priest, with the senate, swore to them that they would esteem them their friends and associates, and would attempt nothing that should be unfair against them, the multitude also assenting to the oaths that were made to them. (56) So these men having obtained what they desired, by deceiving the Israelites, went home: but when Joshua led his army to the country at the bottom of the mountains of this part of Canaan, he understood that the Gibeonites dwelt not far from Jerusalem, and that they were of the stock of the Canaanites; so he sent for their governors, and reproached them with the cheat they had put upon him; (57) but they alleged, on their own behalf, that they had no other way to save themselves but that, and were therefore forced to have recourse to it. So he called for Eleazar the high priest, and for the senate, who thought it right to make them public servants, that they might not break the oath they had made to them; and they ordained them to be so: and this was the method by which these men found safety and security under the calamity that was ready to overtake them.

(58) But the king of Jerusalem took it to heart that the Gibeonites had gone

over to Joshua; so he called upon the kings of the neighbouring nations to join together, and make war against them. Now when the Gibeonites saw these kings, which were four, besides the king of Jerusalem, and perceived that they had pitched their camp at a certain fountain not far from their city, and were getting ready for the siege of it, they called upon Joshua to assist them; (59) for such was their case, as to expect to be destroyed by these Canaanites, but to suppose they should be saved by those that came for the destruction of the Canaanites, because of the league of friendship that was between them. (60) Accordingly, Joshua made haste with his whole army to assist them, and marching day and night, in the morning he fell upon the enemies as they were going up to the siege; and when he had discomfited them he followed them, and pursued them down the descent of the hills. The place is called Beth-horon; where he also understood that God assisted him, which he declared by thunder and thunderbolts, as also by the falling of hail larger than usual. (61) Moreover, it happened that the day was lengthened, that the night might not come on too soon, and be an obstruction to the zeal of the Hebrews in pursuing their enemies; insomuch that Joshua took the kings, who were hidden in a certain cave at Makkedah, and put them to death. Now, that the day was lengthened at this time, and was longer than ordinary, is expressed in the books laid up in the temple.

(62) These kings which made war with, and were ready to fight, the Gibeonites, being thus overthrown, Joshua returned again to the mountainous parts of Canaan; and when he had made a great slaughter of the people there, and took their prey, he came to the camp at Gilgal. (63) And now there went a great fame abroad among the neighbouring people, of the courage of the Hebrews: and those that heard what a number of men were destroyed, were greatly affrighted at it; so the kings that lived about Mount Libanus, who were Canaanites, and those Canaanites that dwelt in the plain country, with auxiliaries out of the land of the Philistines, pitched their camp at Beroth, a city of the Upper Galilee, not far from Cadesh, which is itself also a place in Galilee. (64) Now the number of the whole army was three hundred thousand armed footmen, and ten thousand horsemen, and twenty thousand chariots; so that the multitude of the enemies affrighted both Joshua himself and the Israelites; and they, instead of being full of hopes of good success, were superstitiously timorous, with the great terror with which they were stricken. (65) Where-upon God upbraided them with the fear they were in, and asked them, whether they desired a greater help than he could afford them; and promised them that they should overcome their enemies; and withal charged them to make their enemies' horses useless, and to burn their chariots. So Joshua became full of courage upon these promises of God, and went out suddenly against the enemies; (66) and after five days' march he came upon them, and

joined battle with them, and there was a terrible fight, and such a number were slain as could not be believed by those that heard it. He also went on in the pursuit a great way, and destroyed the entire army of the enemies, few only excepted, and all the kings fell in the battle; (67) insomuch that when there wanted men to be killed, Joshua slew their horses, and burnt their chariots, and passed all over their country without opposition, no one daring to meet him in battle; but he still went on, taking their cities by siege, and again killing whatever he took.

(68) The fifth year was not past, and there was not one of the Canaanites remained any longer, excepting some that had retired to places of great strength. So Joshua removed his camp to the mountainous country, and placed the tabernacle in the city of Shiloh, for that seemed a fit place for it, because of the beauty of its situation, until such time as their affairs would permit them to build a temple; (69) and from thence he went to Shechem, together with all the people, and raised an altar where Moses had beforehand directed; then did he divide the army, and place one half of them on Mount Gerizzim, and the other half on Mount Ebal, on which mountain the altar was; he also placed there the tribe of Levi, and the priests. (70) And when they had sacrificed, and denounced the [blessings and the] curses, and had left them engraven upon the altar, they returned to Shiloh.

(71) And now Joshua was old, and saw that the cities of the Canaanites were not easily to be taken, not only because they were situate in such strong places, but because of the strength of the walls themselves, which being built round about, the natural strength of the places on which the cities stood seemed capable of repelling their enemies from besieging them, and of making those enemies despair of taking them; (72) for when the Canaanites had learned that the Israelites came out of Egypt in order to destroy them, they were busy all that time in making their cities strong. So he gathered the people together to a congregation at Shiloh; (73) and when they, with great zeal and haste, were come thither, he observed to them what prosperous successes they had already had, and what glorious things had been done, and those such as were worthy of that God who enabled them to do those things, and worthy of the virtue of those laws which they followed. He took notice also, that thirty-one of those kings that ventured to give them battle were overcome, and every army, how great soever it were, that confided in their own power, and fought with them, was utterly destroyed; so that not so much as any of their posterity remained; (74) and as for the cities, since some of them were taken, but the others must be taken in length of time, by long sieges, both on account of the strength of their walls, and of the confidence the inhabitants had in them thereby, he thought it reasonable that those tribes that came along with them from beyond Jordan, and had partaken of the dangers they had undergone, being their own kindred,

should now be dismissed and sent home, and should have thanks for the pains they had taken together with them. (75) As also, he thought it reasonable that they should send one man out of every tribe, and he such as had the testimony of extraordinary virtue, who should measure the land faithfully, and without any fallacy or deceit should inform them of its real magnitude.

(76) Now Joshua, when he had thus spoken to them, found that the multitude approved of his proposal. So he sent men to measure their country, and sent with them some geometricians, who could not easily fail of knowing the truth, on account of their skill in that art. He also gave them a charge to estimate the measure of that part of the land that was most fruitful, and what was not so good; (77) for such is the nature of the land of Canaan, that one may see large plains, and such as are exceeding fit to produce fruit, which yet if they were compared to other parts of the country, might be reckoned exceedingly fruitful; yet if it be compared with the fields about Jericho, and to those that belong to Jerusalem, will appear to be of no account at all; (78) and although it so falls out that these people have but a very little of this sort of land, and that it is, for the main, mountainous also, yet does it not come behind other parts, on account of its exceeding goodness and beauty; for which reason Joshua thought the land for the tribes should be divided by estimation of its goodness, rather than the largeness of its measure, it often happening, that one acre of some sort of land was equivalent to a thousand other acres. (79) Now the men that were sent, which were in number ten, travelled all about, and made an estimation of the land, and in the seventh month came to him to the city of Shiloh, where they had set up the tabernacle.

(80) So Joshua took both Eleazar and the senate, and with them the heads of the tribes, and distributed the land to the nine tribes, and to the half tribe of Manasseh, appointing the dimensions to be according to the largeness of each tribe. (81) So when he had cast lots, Judah had assigned him by lot the upper part of Judea reaching as far as Jerusalem, and its breadth extended to the Lake of Sodom. Now in the lot of this tribe there were the cities of Askelon and Gaza. (82) The lot of Simeon, which was the second, included that part of Idumea which bordered upon Egypt and Arabia. As to the Benjamites, their lot fell so, that its length reached from the river Jordan to the sea, but in breadth it was bounded by Jerusalem and Bethel; and this lot was the narrowest of all, by reason of the goodness of the land; for it included Jericho and the city of Jerusalem. (83) The tribe of Ephraim had by lot the land that extended in length from the river Jordan to Gezer, but in breadth as far as from Bethel till it ended at the Great Plain. The half tribe of Manasseh had the land from Jordan to the city Dora, (84) but its breadth was at Bethshan, which is now called Scythopolis; and after these was Issachar, which had its limits in length, Mount Carmel and the river, but its limit in breadth was Mount Tabor. The tribe of

Zebulon's lot included the land which lay as far as the Lake of Genesareth, and that which belonged to Carmel and the sea. (85) The tribe of Asher had that part which was called the *Valley*, for such it was, and all that part which lay over against Sidon. The city Arce belonged to their share, which is also named Actipus. (86) The Naphthalites received the eastern parts, as far as the city of Damascus and the Upper Galilee, unto Mount Libanus, and the Fountains of Jordan, which rise out of that mountain; that is, out of that part of it whose limits belong to the neighbouring city of Arce. (87) The Danites' lot included all that part of the valley which respects the sunsetting, and were bounded by Azotus and Dora; as also they had all Jamnia and Gath, from Ekron to that mountain where the tribe of Judah begins.

(88) After this manner did Joshua divide the six nations that bear the name of the sons of Canaan, with their land, to be possessed by the nine tribes and a half; (89) for Moses had prevented him, and had already distributed the land of the Amorites, which itself was so called also from one of the sons of Canaan, to the two tribes and a half, as we have shown already. But the parts about Sidon, as also those that belong to the Arkites and the Amathites and the Aradians, were not yet regularly disposed of.

(90) But now was Joshua hindered by his age from executing what he intended to do (as did those that succeeded him in the government take little care of what was for the advantage of the public); so he gave it in charge to every tribe to leave no remainder of the race of the Canaanites in the land that had been divided to them by lot; that Moses had assured them beforehand, and they might rest fully satisfied about it, that their own security and their observation of their own laws depended wholly upon it. (91) Moreover, he enjoined them to give thirty-eight cities to the Levites, for they had already received ten in the country of the Amorites; and three of these he assigned to those that fled from the man-slayers, who were to inhabit there; for he was very solicitous that nothing should be neglected which Moses had ordained. These cities were: of the tribe of Judah, Hebron; of that of Ephraim, Shechem; and of the tribe of Naphthali, Cadesh, which is a place of the Upper Galilee. (92) He also distributed among them the rest of the prey not yet distributed, which was very great; whereby they had an affluence of great riches, both all in general, and everyone in particular; and this of gold and of vestments, and of other furniture, besides a multitude of cattle, whose number could not be told.

(93) After this was over, he gathered the army together to a congregation, and spake thus to those tribes that had their settlement in the land of the Amorites, beyond Jordan – for fifty thousand of them had armed themselves, and had gone to the war along with them: 'Since that God, who is the Father and Lord of the Hebrew nation, has now given us this land for a possession, and promised to preserve us in the enjoyment of it as our own forever; (94) and

since you have with alacrity offered yourselves to assist us when we wanted that assistance on all occasions, according to his command, it is but just, now all our difficulties are over, that you should be permitted to enjoy rest, and that we should trespass on your alacrity to help us no longer; that so, if we should again stand in need of it, we may readily have it on any future emergency, and not tire you out so much now as may make you slower in assisting us another time. (95) We, therefore, return you our thanks for the dangers you have undergone with us, and we do it not at this time only, but we shall always be thus disposed, and be so good as to remember our friends, and to preserve in mind what advantages we have had from them; and how you have put off the enjoyments of your own happiness for our sakes, and have laboured for what we have now by the good will of God obtained, and resolved not to enjoy your own prosperity till you had afforded us that assistance. (96) However, you have, by joining your labour with ours, gotten great plenty of riches, and will carry home with you much prey, with gold and silver, and, what is more than all these, our good will towards you, and a mind willingly disposed to make a requital of your kindness to us, in what case soever you shall desire it, for you have not omitted anything which Moses beforehand required of you, nor have you despised him because he was dead and gone from you, so that there is nothing to diminish that gratitude which we owe to you. (97) We therefore dismiss you joyful to your own inheritances; and we entreat you to suppose, that there is no limit to be set to the intimate relation that is between us; and that you will not imagine, because this river is interposed between us, that you are of a different race from us, and not Hebrews; for we are all the posterity of Abraham, both we that inhabit here, and you that inhabit there; and it is the same God that brought our forefathers and yours into the world, (98) whose worship and form of government we are to take care of, which he has ordained, and are most carefully to observe; because, while you continue in those laws God will also show himself merciful and assisting to you; but if you imitate the other nations, and forsake those laws, he will reject your nation.' (99) When Joshua had spoken thus, and saluted them all, both those in authority one by one, and the whole multitude in common, he himself stayed where he was; but the people conducted those tribes on their journey, and that not without tears in their eyes and indeed they hardly knew how to part one from the other.

(100) Now when the tribe of Reuben, and that of Gad, and as many of the Manassites as followed them, were passed over the river, they built an altar on the banks of Jordan, as a monument to posterity, and a sign of their relation to those that should inhabit on the other side. (101) But when those on the other side heard that those who had been dismissed had built an altar, but did not hear with what intention they built it but supposed it to be by way of

innovation, and for the introduction of strange gods, they did not incline to disbelieve it; but thinking this defamatory report, as if it were built for divine worship, was credible, they appeared in arms, as though they would avenge themselves on those that built the altar; and they were about to pass over the river, and to punish them for their subversion of the laws of their country; (102) for they did not think it fit to regard them on account of their kindred, or the dignity of those that had given the occasion, but to regard the will of God, and the manner wherein he desired to be worshipped; (103) so these men put themselves in array for war. But Joshua, and Eleazar the high priest, and the senate, restrained them; and persuaded them first to make trial by words of their intention, and afterwards, if they found that their intention was evil, then only to proceed to make war upon them. (104) Accordingly, they sent as ambassadors to them Phineas the son of Eleazar, and ten more persons that were in esteem among the Hebrews, to learn of them what was in their mind when, upon passing over the river, they had built an altar upon its banks; (105) and as soon as these ambassadors were passed over, and were come to them, and a congregation was assembled, Phineas stood up and said: that the offence they had been guilty of was of too heinous a nature to be punished by words alone, or by them only to be amended for the future, yet that they did not so look at the heinousness of their transgression as to have recourse to arms, and to a battle for their punishment immediately; but that, on account of their kindred, and the probability there was that they might be reclaimed, they took this method of sending an ambassage to them: (106) 'That when we have learned the true reasons by which you have been moved to build this altar, we may neither seem to have been too rash in assaulting you by our weapons of war, if it prove that you made the altar for justifiable reasons, and may then justly punish you if the accusation prove true; (107) for we can hardly suppose that you who have been acquainted with the will of God, and have been hearers of those laws which he himself hath given us, now you are separated from us, and gone to that patrimony of yours which you, through the grace of God and that providence which he exercises over you, have obtained by lot, can forget him, and can leave that ark and that altar which is peculiar to us, and can introduce strange gods and imitate the wicked practices of the Canaanites. (108) Now this will appear to have been a small crime if you repent now, and proceed no further in your madness, but pay a due reverence to, and keep in mind the laws of your country; but if you persist in your sins, we will not grudge our pains to preserve our laws; but we will pass over Jordan and defend them, and defend God also, and shall esteem of you as of men no way differing from the Canaanites, but shall destroy you in the like manner as we destroy them; (109) for do not you imagine that, because you are got over the river, you are got out of the reach of God's power; you are everywhere in places that belong to him, and impossible it is to overrun his power, and the punishment he will bring on men thereby; but if you think that your settlement here will be any obstruction to your conversion to what is good, nothing need hinder us from dividing the land anew, and leaving this old land to be for the feeding of sheep; (110) but you will do well to return to your duty, and to leave off these new crimes, and we beseech you, by your children and wives, not to force us to punish you. Take therefore such measures in this assembly, as supposing that your own safety, and the safety of those that are dearest to you, is therein concerned, and believe that it is better for you to be conquered by words than to continue in your purpose, and to experience deeds and war therefore.'

(111) When Phineas had discoursed thus, the governors of the assembly, and the whole multitude, began to make an apology for themselves, concerning what they were accused of; and they said, that they neither would depart from the relation they bare to them, nor had they built the altar by way of innovation; (112) that they owned one and the same common God with all the Hebrews, and that brazen altar which was before the tabernacle, on which they would offer their sacrifices; that as to the altar they had raised, on account of which they were thus suspected, it was not built for worship, 'but that it might be a sign and a monument of our relation to you forever, and a necessary caution to us to act wisely, and to continue in the laws of our country, but not a handle for transgressing them, as you suspect; (113) and let God be our authentic witness, that this was the occasion of our building this altar; whence we beg you will have a better opinion of us, and do not impute such a thing to us as would render any of the posterity of Abraham well worthy of perdition, in case they attempt to bring in new rites, and such as are different from our usual practices.'

(114) When they had made this answer, and Phineas had commended them for it, he came to Joshua and explained before the people what answer they had received. Now Joshua was glad that he was under no necessity of setting them in array or of leading them to shed blood, and make war against men of their own kindred; and accordingly he offered sacrifices of thanksgiving to God for the same. (115) So Joshua after that dissolved this great assembly of the people and sent them to their own inheritances, while he himself lived in Shechem. But in the twentieth year after this, being very old, he sent for those of the greatest dignity in the several cities, with those in authority and the senate, and as many of the common people as could be present; and when they were come he put them in mind of all the benefits God had bestowed on them, which could not but be a great many, since from a low estate they were advanced to so great a degree of glory and plenty; (116) and exhorted them to take notice of the intentions of God, which had been so gracious towards them; and told them that the Deity would continue their friend by nothing

else but their piety; and that it was proper for him, now that he was about to depart out of this life, to leave such an admonition to them; and he desired that they would keep in memory this his exhortation to them.

(117) So Joshua when he had thus discoursed to them, died, having lived a hundred and ten years; forty of which he lived with Moses, in order to learn what might be for his advantage afterwards. He also became their commander after his death for twenty-five years. (118) He was a man that wanted not wisdom nor eloquence to declare his intentions to the people, but very eminent on both accounts. He was of great courage and magnanimity in action and in dangers, and very sagacious in procuring the peace of the people, and of great virtue at all proper seasons. (119) He was buried in the city of Timnah, of the tribe of Ephraim. About the same time died Eleazar the high priest, leaving the high priesthood to his son Phineas. His monument also and sepulchre are in the city of Gabatha.

CHAPTER 2

(120) After the death of Joshua and Eleazar, Phineas prophesied, that according to God's will they should commit the government to the tribe of Judah, and that this tribe should destroy the race of the Canaanites; for then the people were concerned to learn what was the will of God. They also took to their assistance the tribe of Simeon; but upon this condition, that when those that had been tributary to the tribe of Judah should be slain, they should do the like for the tribe of Simeon.

(121) But the affairs of the Canaanites were at this time in a flourishing condition, and they expected the Israelites with a great army at the city Bezek, having put the government into the hands of Adonibezek, which name denotes the *Lord of Bezek*, for *Adoni* in the Hebrew tongue signifies *Lord*. Now they hoped to have been too hard for the Israelites, because Joshua was dead; (122) but when the Israelites had joined battle with them, I mean the two tribes before mentioned, they fought gloriously, and slew above ten thousand of them, and put the rest to flight; and in the pursuit they took Adonibezek, who, when his fingers and toes were cut off by them, said, (123) 'Nay, indeed, I was not always to lie concealed from God, as I find by what I now endure, while I have not been ashamed to do the same to seventy-two kings.' (124) So they carried him alive as far as Jerusalem; and when he was dead, they buried him in the earth, and went on still in taking the cities; and when they had taken the greatest part of them, they besieged Jerusalem; and when they had taken the lower city, which was not under a considerable time, they slew all the inhabitants; but the upper city was not to be taken without great difficulty, through the strength of its walls, and the nature of the place.

(125) For which reason they removed their camp to Hebron; and when they had taken it, they slew all the inhabitants. There were till then left the race of giants, who had bodies so large, and countenances so entirely different from other men, that they were surprising to the sight, and terrible to the hearing. The bones of these men are still shown to this very day, unlike to any creditable relations of other men. (126) Now they gave this city to the Levites as an extraordinary reward, with the suburbs of two thousand cities: but the land thereto belonging they gave as a free gift to Caleb, according to the injunctions of Moses. This Caleb was one of the spies which Moses sent into the land of Canaan. (127) They also gave land for habitation to the posterity of Jethro, the Midianite, who was the father-in-law to Moses; for they had left their own country, and followed them, and accompanied them in the wilderness.

(128) Now the tribes of Judah and Simeon took the cities which were in the mountainous part of Canaan, as also Askelon and Ashdod, of those that lay near the sea: but Gaza and Ekron escaped them, for they, lying in a flat country, and having a great number of chariots, sorely galled those that attacked them; so these tribes, when they were grown very rich by this war, retired to their own cities, and laid aside their weapons of war.

(129) But the Benjamites, to whom belonged Jerusalem, permitted its inhabitants to pay tribute. So they all left off, the one to kill, and the other to expose themselves to danger, and had time to cultivate the ground. The rest of the tribes imitated that of Benjamin, and did the same; and, contenting themselves with the tributes that were paid them, permitted the Canaanites to live in peace.

(130) However, the tribe of Ephraim, when they besieged Bethel, made no advance, nor performed anything worthy of the time they spent and of the pains they took about that siege; yet did they persist in it, still sitting down before the city, though they endured great trouble thereby; (131) but after some time, they caught one of the citizens that came to them to get necessaries, and they gave him some assurances that, if he would deliver up the city to them, they would preserve him and his kindred; so he sware that, upon those terms, he would put the city into their hands. Accordingly, he that thus betrayed the city was preserved with his family; and the Israelites slew all the inhabitants, and retained the city for themselves.

(132) After this, the Israelites grew effeminate as to fighting any more against their enemies, but applied themselves to the cultivation of the land, which producing them great plenty and riches, they neglected the regular disposition of their settlement, and indulged themselves in luxury and pleasures; nor were they any longer careful to hear the laws that belonged to their political government; (133) whereupon God was provoked to anger, and put them in mind, first how, contrary to his directions, they had spared the Canaanites;

and, after that, how those Canaanites, as opportunity served, used them very barbarously. (134) But the Israelites, though they were in heaviness at these admonitions from God, yet were they very unwilling to go to war; and since they got large tributes from the Canaanites, and were indisposed for taking pains by their luxury, (135) they suffered their aristocracy to be corrupted also, and did not ordain themselves a senate, nor any other such magistrates as their laws had formerly required, but they were very much given to cultivating their fields, in order to get wealth; which great indolence of theirs brought a terrible sedition upon them, and they proceeded so far as to fight one against another, from the following occasion:

(136) There was a Levite, a man of a vulgar family, that belonged to the tribe of Ephraim, and dwelt therein; this man married a wife from Bethlehem, which is a place belonging to the tribe of Judah. Now he was very fond of his wife and overcome with her beauty; but he was unhappy in this, that he did not meet with the like return of affection from her, (137) for she was averse to him, which did more inflame his passion for her, so that they quarrelled one with another perpetually; and at last the woman was so disgusted at these quarrels, that she left her husband, and went to her parents in the fourth month. The husband being very uneasy at this her departure, and that out of his fondness for her, came to his father and mother-in-law, and made up their quarrels, and was reconciled to her, (138) and lived with them there four days as being kindly treated by her parents. On the fifth day he resolved to go home, and went away in the evening; for his wife's parents were loth to part with their daughter, and delayed the time till the day was gone. Now they had one servant that followed them, and an ass on which the woman rode; (139) and when they were near Jerusalem, having gone already thirty furlongs, the servant advised them to take up their lodgings somewhere, lest some misfortune should befall them if they travelled in the night, especially since they were not far off enemies, that season often giving reason for suspicion of dangers from even such as are friends; (140) but the husband was not pleased with this advice, nor was he willing to take up his lodging among strangers, for the city belonged to the Canaanites, but desired rather to go twenty furlongs further, and so to take their lodgings in some Israelite city. Accordingly, he obtained his purpose, and came to Gibeah, a city of the tribe of Benjamin, when it was just dark; (141) and while no one that lived in the market place invited him to lodge with him, there came an old man out of the field, one that was indeed of the tribe of Ephraim, but resided in Gibeah, and met him, and asked him who he was, and for what reason he came thither so late, and why he was looking out for provisions for supper when it was dark? (142) To which he replied, that he was a Levite, and was bringing his wife from her parents, and was going home: but he told him his habitation was in the tribe of Ephraim;

so the old man, as well because of their kindred as because they lived in the same tribe, and also because they had thus accidentally met together, took him in to lodge with him. (143) Now certain young men of the inhabitants of Gibeah, having seen the woman in the market place, and admiring her beauty, when they understood that she lodged with the old man, came to the doors as condemning the weakness and fewness of the old man's family; and when the old man desired them to go away, and not to offer any violence or abuse there, they desired him to yield them up the strange woman, and then he should have no harm done to him: (144) and when the old man alleged that the Levite was of his kindred, and that they would be guilty of horrid wickedness if they suffered themselves to be overcome by their pleasures, and so offend against their laws, they despised his righteous admonition, and laughed him to scorn. They also threatened to kill him if he became an obstacle to their inclinations; (145) whereupon when he found himself in great distress, and yet was not willing to overlook his guests, and see them abused, he produced his own daughter to them; and told them that it was a smaller breach of the law to satisfy their lust upon her, than to abuse his guests, supposing that he himself should by this means prevent any injury to be done to those guests. (146) When they no way abated of their earnestness for the strange woman, but insisted absolutely on their desire to have her, he entreated them not to perpetrate any such act of injustice; but they proceeded to take her away by force, and indulging still more the violence of their inclinations, they took the woman away to their house, and when they had satisfied their lust upon her the whole night, they let her go about daybreak. (147) So she came to the place where she had been entertained, under great affliction at what had happened; and was very sorrowful upon occasion of what she had suffered, and durst not look her husband in the face for shame, for she concluded that he would never forgive her for what she had done; so she fell down, and gave up the ghost: (148) but her husband supposed that his wife was only fast asleep, and, thinking nothing of a more melancholy nature had happened, endeavoured to raise her up, resolving to speak comfortably to her, since she did not voluntarily expose herself to these men's lust, but was forced away to their house; (149) but as soon as he perceived she was dead, he acted as prudently as the greatness of his misfortunes would admit, and laid his dead wife upon the beast, and carried her home; and cutting her, limb by limb, into twelve pieces, he sent them to every tribe, and gave it in charge to those that carried them, to inform the tribes of those that were the causes of his wife's death and of the violence they had offered to her.

(150) Upon this the people were greatly disturbed at what they saw, and at what they heard, as never having had the experience of such a thing before; so they gathered themselves to Shiloh, out of a prodigious and a just anger, and assembling in a great congregation before the tabernacle, they immediately

resolved to take arms, and to treat the inhabitants of Gibeah as enemies; (151) but the senate restrained them from doing so, and persuaded them, that they ought not so hastily to make war upon people of the same nation with them, before they discoursed them by words concerning the accusation laid against them; it being part of their law, that they should not bring an army against foreigners themselves, when they appear to have been injurious, without sending an ambassage first and trying thereby whether they will repent or not; (152) and accordingly they exhorted them to do what they ought to do in obedience to their laws, that is, to send to the inhabitants of Gibeah, to know whether they would deliver up the offenders to them, and, if they delivered them up to rest satisfied with the punishment of those offenders; but if they despised the message that was sent them, to punish them, by taking up arms against them. (153) Accordingly they sent to the inhabitants of Gibeah, and accused the young men of the crimes committed in the affair of the Levite's wife, and required of them those that had done what was contrary to the law, that they might be punished, as having justly deserved to die for what they had done: (154) but the inhabitants of Gibeah would not deliver up the young men, and thought it too reproachful to them, out of fear of war, to submit to other men's demands upon them; vaunting themselves to be no way inferior to any in war, neither in their number nor in courage. The rest of their tribe were also making great preparation for war, for they were so insolently mad as also to resolve to repel force by force.

(155) When it was related to the Israelites what the inhabitants of Gibeah had resolved upon, they took their oath that no one of them would give his daughter in marriage to a Benjamite, but make war with greater fury against them than we have learned our forefathers made war against the Canaanites; (156) and sent out presently an army of four hundred thousand against them, while the Benjamites' army was twenty-five thousand and six hundred; five hundred of whom were excellent at slinging stones with their left hands, (157) insomuch that when the battle was joined at Gibeah the Benjamites beat the Israelites, and of them there fell two thousand men; and probably more had been destroyed had not the night came on and prevented it, and broken off the fight: (158) so the Benjamites returned to the city with joy, and the Israelites returned to their camp in a great fright at what had happened. On the next day, when they fought again, the Benjamites beat them; and eighteen thousand of the Israelites were slain, and the rest deserted their camp out of fear of a greater slaughter. (159) So they came to Bethel, a city that was near their camp, and fasted on the next day; and besought God, by Phineas the high priest, that his wrath against them might cease, and that he would be satisfied with these two defeats, and give them the victory and power over their enemies. Accordingly God promised them so to do, by the prophesying of Phineas.

(160) When therefore they had divided the army into two parts, they laid the one half of them in ambush about the city Gibeah, by night, while the other half attacked the Benjamites; who retiring upon the assault, the Benjamites pursued them, while the Hebrews retired by slow degrees, as very desirous to draw them entirely from the city; and the other followed them as they retired, (161) till both the old men and the young men that were left in the city, as too weak to fight, came running out together with them, as willing to bring their enemies under. However, when they were a great way from the city, the Hebrews ran away no longer, but turned back to fight them, and lifted up the signal they had agreed on to those that lay in ambush, (162) who rose up, and with a great noise fell upon the enemy. Now, as soon as ever they perceived themselves to be deceived, they knew not what to do; and when they were driven into a certain hollow place which was in a valley, they were shot at by those that encompassed them, till they were all destroyed, excepting six hundred, (163) which formed themselves into a close body of men, and forced their passage through the midst of their enemies, and fled to the neighbouring mountains, and, seizing upon them, remained there; but the rest of them, being about twenty-five thousand, were slain. (164) Then did the Israelites burn Gibeah, and slew the women and the males that were under age; and did the same also to the other cities of the Benjamites – and indeed, they were enraged to that degree, that they sent twelve thousand men out of the army, and gave them orders to destroy Jabesh Gilead, because it did not join with them in fighting against the Benjamites. (165) Accordingly, those that were sent slew the men of war, with their children and wives, excepting four hundred virgins. To such a degree had they proceeded in their anger, because they not only had the suffering of the Levite's wife to avenge but the slaughter of their own soldiers.

(166) However, they afterward were sorry for the calamity they had brought upon the Benjamites, and appointed a fast on that account, although they supposed those men had suffered justly for their offence against the laws; so they recalled by their ambassadors those six hundred which had escaped. These had seated themselves on a certain rock called *Rimmon*, which was in the wilderness. (167) So the ambassadors lamented not only the disaster that had befallen the Benjamites, but themselves also, by this destruction of their kindred; and persuaded them to take it patiently, and to come and unite with them, and not, so far as in them lay, to give their suffrage to the utter destruction of the tribe of Benjamin; and said to them, 'We give you leave to take the whole land of Benjamin to yourselves, and as much prey as you are able to carry away with you.' (168) So these men with sorrow confessed, that what had been done was according to the decree of God, and had happened for their own wickedness; and assented to those that invited them, and came down to their own tribe. The Israelites also gave them the four hundred virgins of Jabesh Gilead for wives; but

as to the remaining two hundred, they deliberated about it how they might compass wives enough for them, and that they might have children by them; (169) and whereas they had, before the war began, taken an oath, that no one would give his daughter to wife to a Benjamite, some advised them to have no regard to what they had sworn, because the oath had not been taken advisedly and judiciously, but in a passion, and thought that they should do nothing against God, if they were able to save a whole tribe which was in danger of perishing; and that perjury was then a sad and dangerous thing, not when it is done out of necessity, but when it is done with a wicked intention. (170) But when the senate were affrighted at the very name of perjury, a certain person told them that he could show them a way whereby they might procure the Benjamites wives enough, and yet keep their oath. They asked him what his proposal was. He said, 'that three times in a year, when we meet in Shiloh, our wives and our daughters accompany us: (171) let then the Benjamites be allowed to steal away, and marry such women as they can catch, while we will neither incite them nor forbid them; and when their parents take it ill, and desire us to inflict punishment upon them, we will tell them, that they were themselves the cause of what had happened, by neglecting to guard their daughters, and that they ought not to be over-angry at the Benjamites, since that anger was permitted to rise too high already.' (172) So the Israelites were persuaded to follow this advice, and decreed, that the Benjamites should be allowed thus to steal themselves wives. So when the festival was coming on, these two hundred Benjamites lay in ambush before the city, by two and three together, and waited for the coming of the virgins, in the vineyards and other places where they could lie concealed. (173) Accordingly the virgins came along playing, and suspected nothing of what was coming upon them, and walked after an unguarded manner, so those that laid scattered in the road rose up, and caught hold of them: by this means these Benjamites got them wives, and fell to agriculture, and took good care to recover their former happy state. (174) And thus was this tribe of the Benjamites, after they had been in danger of entirely perishing, saved in the manner forementioned, by the wisdom of the Israelites: and accordingly it presently flourished, and soon increased to be a multitude, and came to enjoy all other degrees of happiness. And such was the conclusion of this war.

CHAPTER 3

(175) Now it happened that the tribe of Dan suffered in like manner with the tribe of Benjamin; and it came to do so on the occasion following: (176) when the Israelites had already left off the exercise of their arms for war, and were intent upon their husbandry, the Canaanites despised them, and brought

together an army, not because they expected to suffer by them, but because they had a mind to have a sure prospect of treating the Hebrews ill when they pleased, and might thereby for the time to come dwell in their own cities the more securely; (177) they prepared therefore their chariots, and gathered their soldiery together, their cities also combined together, and drew over to them Askelon and Ekron, which were within the tribe of Judah, and many more of those that lay in the plain. They also forced the Danites to fly into the mountainous country, and left them not the least portion of the plain country to set their foot on. (178) Since then these Danites were not able to fight them, and had not land enough to sustain them, they sent five of their men into the midland country to seek for a land to which they might remove their habitation. So these men went as far as the neighbourhood of Mount Libanus, and the fountains of the Lesser Jordan, at the great plain of Sidon, a day's journey from the city; and when they had taken a view of the land, and found it to be good and exceeding fruitful, they acquainted their tribe with it, whereupon they made an expedition with the army, and built there the city Dan, of the same name with the son of Jacob, and of the same name with their own tribe.

(179) The Israelites grew so indolent, and unready of taking pains, that misfortunes came heavier upon them, which also proceeded in part from their contempt of the divine worship: for when they had once fallen off from the regularity of their political government, they indulged themselves further in living according to their own pleasure, and according to their own will, till they were full of the evil doings that were common among the Canaanites. (180) God therefore was angry with them, and they lost that their happy state which they had obtained by innumerable labours, by their luxury; for when Chushan, king of the Assyrians, had made war against them, they lost many of their soldiers in the battle, and when they were besieged, they were taken by force; (181) nay, there were some who, out of fear, voluntarily submitted to him, and though the tribute laid upon them was more than they could bear, yet did they pay it, and underwent all sort of oppression for eight years; after which time they were freed from them in the following manner:

(182) There was one whose name was Othniel, the son of Kenaz, of the tribe of Judah, an active man and of great courage. He had an admonition from God, not to overlook the Israelites in such a distress as they were now in, but to endeavour boldly to gain them their liberty; so when he had procured some to assist him in this dangerous undertaking (and few they were who, either out of shame at their present circumstances, or out of a desire of changing them, could be prevailed on to assist him), (183) he first of all destroyed that garrison which Chushan had set over them; but when it was perceived that he had not failed in his first attempt, more of the people came to his assistance; so they joined battle with the Assyrians, and drove them entirely before them, and

compelled them to pass over Euphrates. (184) Hereupon Othniel, who had given such proofs of his valour, received from the multitude authority to judge the people: and when he had ruled over them forty years, he died.

CHAPTER 4

(185) When Othniel was dead, the affairs of the Israelites fell again into disorder: and while they neither paid to God the honour due to him, nor were obedient to the laws, their afflictions increased, (186) till Eglon, king of the Moabites, did so greatly despise them on account of the disorders of their political government, that he made war upon them, and overcame them in several battles, and made the most courageous to submit, and entirely subdued their army, and ordered them to pay him tribute. (187) And when he had built him a royal palace at Jericho, he omitted no method whereby he might distress them; and indeed he reduced them to poverty for eighteen years. But when God had once taken pity of the Israelites on account of their afflictions, and was moved to compassion by their supplications put up to him, he freed them from the hard usage they had met with under the Moabites. This liberty he procured for them in the following manner:

(188) There was a young man of the tribe of Benjamin, whose name was Ehud, the son of Gera, a man of very great courage in bold undertakings, and of a very strong body, fit for hard labour, but best skilled in using his left hand, in which was his whole strength; and he also dwelt at Jericho. (189) Now this man became familiar with Eglon, and that by means of presents, with which he obtained his favour, and insinuated himself into his good opinion; whereby he was also beloved of those that were about the king. (190) Now, when on a time he was bringing presents to the king, and had two servants with him, he put a dagger on his right side secretly, and went in to him; it was then summer time, and the middle of the day, when the guards were not strictly on the watch, both because of the heat and because they were gone to dinner. (191) So the young man, when he had offered his presents to the king, who then resided in a small parlour that stood conveniently to avoid the heat, fell into discourse with him, for they were now alone, the king having bid his servants that attended him to go their ways, because he had a mind to talk with Ehud. (192) He was now sitting on his throne; and fear seized upon Ehud lest he should miss his stroke, and not give him a deadly wound; (193) so he raised himself up, and said he had a dream to impart to him by the command of God; upon which the king leaped out of his throne for joy of the dream; so Ehud smote him to the heart, and, leaving his dagger in his body, he went out and shut the door after him. Now the king's servants were very still, as supposing that the king had composed himself to sleep.

(194) Hereupon Ehud informed the people of Jericho privately of what he had done, and exhorted them to recover their liberty; who heard him gladly, and went to their arms, and sent messengers over the country, that should sound trumpets of rams' horns; for it was our custom to call the people together by them. (195) Now the attendants of Eglon were ignorant of what misfortune had befallen him for a great while; but, towards the evening, fearing some uncommon accident had happened, they entered into his parlour, and when they found him dead, they were in great disorder, and knew not what to do; and before the guards could be got together, the multitude of the Israelites came upon them, (196) so that some of them were slain immediately, and some were put to flight, and ran away toward the country of Moab, in order to save themselves. Their number was above ten thousand. The Israelites seized upon the ford of Jordan, and pursued them, and slew them, and many of them they killed at the ford, nor did one of them escape out of their hands; (197) and by this means it was that the Hebrews freed themselves from slavery under the Moabites. Ehud also was on this account dignified with the government over all the multitude, and died after he had held the government eighty years. He was a man worthy of commendation, even besides what he deserved for the forementioned act of his. After him Shamgar, the son of Anath, was elected for their governor, but died in the first year of his government.

CHAPTER 5

(198) And now it was that the Israelites, taking no warning by their former misfortunes to amend their manners, and neither worshipping God nor submitting to the laws, were brought under slavery by Jabin the king of the Canaanites, and that before they had a short breathing time after the slavery under the Moabites; (199) for this Jabin came out of Hazor, a city that was situate over the lake Semechonitis, and had in pay three hundred thousand footmen and ten thousand horsemen, with no fewer than three thousand chariots. Sisera was the commander of all his army, and was the principal person in the king's favour. He so sorely beat the Israelites when they fought with him, that he ordered them to pay tribute.

(200) So they continued to undergo that hardship for twenty years, as not good enough of themselves to grow wise by their misfortunes. God was willing also hereby the more to subdue their obstinacy and ingratitude towards himself: so when at length they were become penitent, and were so wise as to learn that their calamities arose from their contempt of the laws, they besought Deborah, a certain prophetess among them (which name in the Hebrew tongue signifies a *Bee*), (201) to pray to God to take pity on them, and not to overlook them, now they were ruined by the Canaanites. So God granted

them deliverance, and chose them a general, Barak, one that was of the tribe of Naphtali. Now Barak, in the Hebrew tongue, signifies *Lightning*.

(202) So Deborah sent for Barak, and bade him choose out ten thousand young men to go against the enemy because God had said that that number was sufficient, and promised them victory. (203) But when Barak said that he would not be the general unless she would also go as a general with him, she had indignation at what he said, and replied, 'Thou, O Barak, deliverest up meanly that authority which God hath given thee into the hand of a woman, and I do not reject it!' So they collected ten thousand men, and pitched their camp at Mount Tabor (204) where, at the king's command, Sisera met them, and pitched his camp not far from the enemy; whereupon the Israelites, and Barak himself, were so affrighted at the multitude of those enemies, that they were resolved to march off, had not Deborah retained them, and commanded them to fight the enemy that very day for that they should conquer them, and God would be their assistance.

(205) So the battle began; and when they were come to a close fight, there came down from heaven a great storm, with a vast quantity of rain and hail, and the wind blew the rain in the face of the Canaanites, and so darkened their eyes, that their arrows and slings were of no advantage to them, nor would the coldness of the air permit the soldiers to make use of their swords; (206) while this storm did not so much incommode the Israelites, because it came in their backs. They also took such courage, upon the apprehension that God was assisting them, that they fell upon the very midst of their enemies, and slew a great number of them; so that some of them fell by the Israelites, some fell by their own horses, which were put into disorder, and not a few were killed by their own chariots. (207) At last Sisera, as soon as he saw himself beaten, fled away, and came to a woman whose name was Jael, a Kenite, who received him, when he desired to be concealed; and when he asked for somewhat to drink, she gave him sour milk, (208) of which he drank so unmeasurably that he fell asleep; but when he was asleep, Jael took an iron nail, and with a hammer drove it through his temples into the floor; and when Barak came a little afterward, she showed Sisera nailed to the ground; (209) and thus was this victory gained by a woman, as Deborah had foretold. Barak also fought with Jabin at Hazor; and when he met with him, he slew him; and when the general was fallen, Barak overthrew the city to the foundation, and was the commander of the Israelites for forty years.

CHAPTER 6

(210) Now when Barak and Deborah were dead, whose deaths happened about the same time, afterwards the Midianites called the Amalekites and Arabians to their assistance, and made war against the Israelites, and were too hard for those that fought against them; and when they had burnt the fruits of the earth, they carried off the prey. (211) Now when they had done this for three years, the multitude of the Israelites retired to the mountains, and forsook the plain country. They also made themselves hollows under ground, and caverns, and preserved therein whatsoever had escaped their enemies; (212) for the Midianites made expeditions in harvest time, but permitted them to plough the land in winter, that so, when the others had taken the pains, they might have fruits for them to carry away. Indeed, there ensued a famine and a scarcity of food; upon which they betook themselves to their supplications to God, and besought him to save them.

(213) Gideon also, the son of Joash, one of the principal persons of the tribe of Manasseh, brought his sheaves of corn privately, and thrashed them at the wine press; for he was too fearful of their enemies to thrash them openly in the thrashing floor. At this time somewhat appeared to him in the shape of a young man, and told him that he was a happy man, and beloved of God. To which he immediately replied. 'A mighty indication of God's favour to me, that I am forced to use this wine press instead of a thrashing floor!' (214) But the appearance exhorted him to be of good courage, and to make an attempt for the recovery of their liberty. He answered, that it was impossible for him to recover it, because the tribe to which he belonged was by no means numerous, and because he was but young himself, and too inconsiderable to think of such great actions; but the other promised him, that God would supply what he was defective in, and would afford the Israelites victory under his conduct.

(215) Now, therefore, as Gideon was relating this to some young men, they believed him, and immediately there was an army of ten thousand men got ready for fighting. But God stood by Gideon in his sleep, and told him that mankind were too fond of themselves, and were enemies to such as excelled in virtue. Now that they might not pass God over, but ascribe the victory to him, and might not fancy it obtained by their own power, because they were a great army and able of themselves to fight their enemies, (216) but might confess that it was owing to his assistance, he advised him to bring his army about noon, in the violence of the heat, to the river, and to esteem those that bent down on their knees and so drank, to be men of courage; but for all those that drank tumultuously that he should esteem them to do it out of fear, and as in dread of their enemies. (217) And when Gideon had done as God had suggested to him,

there were found three hundred men that took water with their hands tumultuously; so God bid him take these men, and attack the enemy. Accordingly they pitched their camp at the river Jordan, as ready the next day to pass over it.

(218) But Gideon was in great fear, for God had told him beforehand that he should set upon his enemies in the night-time; but God, being willing to free him from his fear, bid him take one of his soldiers, and go near to the Midianites' tents, for that he should from that very place have his courage raised, and grow bold. (219) So he obeyed, and went and took his servant Phurah with him; and as he came near to one of the tents, he discovered that those that were in it were awake, and that one of them was telling to his fellow soldiers a dream of his own, and that so plainly, that Gideon could hear him. The dream was this: he thought he saw a barley cake, such a one as could hardly be eaten by men, it was so vile, rolling through the camp, and overthrowing the royal tent, and the tents of all the soldiers. (220) Now the other soldier explained this vision to mean the destruction of the army; and told him what his reason was which made him so conjecture, viz., that the seed called *barley* was all of it allowed to be of the vilest sort of seed, and that the Israelites were known to be the vilest of all the people of Asia, agreeably to the seed of barley, (221) and that what seemed to look big among the Israelites was this Gideon and the army that was with him; 'and since thou sayest thou didst see the cake overturning our tents, I am afraid lest God hath granted the victory over us to Gideon.'

(222) When Gideon had heard this dream, good hope and courage came upon him; and he commanded his soldiers to arm themselves, and told them of this vision of their enemies. They also took courage at what was told them, and were ready to perform what he should enjoin them; (223) so Gideon divided his army into three parts, and brought it out about the fourth watch of the night, each part containing a hundred men: they all bare empty pitchers and lighted lamps in their hands, that their onset might not be discovered by their enemies. They had also each of them a ram's horn in his right hand, which he used instead of a trumpet. (224) The enemy's camp took up a large space of ground, for it happened that they had a great many camels; and as they were divided into different nations, so they were all contained in one circle. (225) Now when the Hebrews did as they were ordered beforehand, upon their approach to their enemies, and, on the signal given, sounded with their rams' horns, and brake their pitchers, and set upon their enemies with their lamps, and a great shout, and cried, 'Victory to Gideon, by God's assistance,' (226) a disorder and a fright seized upon the other men while they were half asleep, for it was night-time, as God would have it; so that a few of them were slain by their enemies, but the greatest part by their own soldiers, on account of the

diversity of their language; and when they were once put into disorder, they killed all that they met with, as thinking them to be enemies also. Thus there was a great slaughter made; (227) and as the report of Gideon's victory came to the Israelites, they took their weapons and pursued their enemies, and overtook them in a certain valley encompassed with torrents, a place which these could not get over; so they encompassed them, and slew them all, with their kings, Oreb and Zeeb; (228) but the remaining captains led those soldiers that were left, which were about eighteen thousand, and pitched their camp a great way off the Israelites. However, Gideon did not grudge his pains, but pursued them with all his army, and joining battle with them, cut off the whole enemies' army, and took the other leaders, Zebah and Zalmuna, and made them captives. (229) Now there were slain in this battle of the Midianites, and of their auxiliaries the Arabians, about a hundred and twenty thousand; and the Hebrews took a great prey, gold, and silver, and garments, and camels, and asses; and when Gideon was come to his own country of Ophrah, he slew the kings of the Midianites.

(230) However, the tribe of Ephraim was so displeased at the good success of Gideon, that they resolved to make war against him, accusing him because he did not tell them of his expedition against their enemies: but Gideon, as a man of temper, and that excelled in every virtue, pleaded, that it was not the result of his own authority or reasoning, that made him attack the enemy without them, but that it was the command of God, and still the victory belonged to them as well as those in the army – (231) and by this method of cooling their passions, he brought more advantage to the Hebrews, than by the success he had against these enemies, for he thereby delivered them from a sedition which was arising among them; yet did this tribe afterwards suffer the punishment of this their injurious treatment of Gideon, of which we will give an account in due time.

(232) Hereupon Gideon would have laid down the government, but was over-persuaded to take it, which he enjoyed forty years, and distributed justice to them, as the people came to him in their differences; and what he determined was esteemed valid by all; and when he died, he was buried in his own country of Ophrah.

CHAPTER 7

(233) Now Gideon had seventy sons that were legitimate, for he had many wives; but he had also one that was spurious, by his concubine Drumah, whose name was Abimelech, who, after his father's death, retired to Shechem to his mother's relations, for they were of that place; (234) and when he had got money of such of them as were eminent for many instances of injustice, he

came with them to his father's house, and slew all his brethren, except Jotham, for he had the good fortune to escape and be preserved; but Abimelech made the government tyrannical, and constituted himself a lord, to do what he pleased, instead of obeying the laws; and he acted most rigidly against those that were the patrons of justice.

(235) Now when, on a certain time, there was a public festival at Shechem, and all the multitude was there gathered together, Jotham his brother, whose escape we before related, went up to Mount Gerizzim, which hangs over the city Shechem, and cried out so as to be heard by the multitude, who were attentive to him. He desired they would consider what he was going to say to them; (236) so when silence was made, he said, that when the trees had a human voice, and there was an assembly of them gathered together, they desired that the fig tree would rule over them; but when that tree refused so to do, because it was contented to enjoy that honour which belonged peculiarly to the fruit it bare, and not that which should be derived to it from abroad, the trees did not leave off their intentions to have a ruler, so they thought proper to make the offer of that honour to the vine; (237) but when the vine was chosen, it made use of the same words which the fig tree had used before, and excused itself from accepting the government; and when the olive tree had done the same, the brier, whom the trees had desired to take the kingdom (238) (it is a sort of wood good for firing), it promised to take the government, and to be zealous in the exercise of it; but that then they must sit down under its shadow, and if they should plot against it to destroy it, the principle of fire that was in it should destroy them. (239) He told them, that what he had said was no laughing matter; for that when they had experienced many blessings from Gideon, they overlooked Abimelech, when he over-ruled all, and had joined with him in slaying his brethren; and that he was no better than a fire himself. So when he had said this, he went away, and lived privately in the mountains for three years, out of fear of Abimelech.

(240) A little while after this festival, the Shechemites, who had now repented themselves of having slain the sons of Gideon, drove Abimelech away both from their city and their tribe; whereupon he contrived how he might distress their city. (241) Now at the season of vintage, the people were afraid to go out and gather their fruits, for fear Abimelech should do them some mischief. Now it happened that there had come to them a man of authority, one Gaal, that sojourned with them, having his armed men and his kinsmen with him; so the Shechemites desired that he would allow them a guard during their vintage; whereupon he accepted of their desires, and so the people went out, and Gaal with them at the head of his soldiery; (242) so they gathered their fruit with safety; and when they were at supper in several companies, they then ventured to curse Abimelech openly; and the magistrates

laid ambushes in places about the city, and caught many of Abimelech's followers, and destroyed them.

(243) Now there was one Zebul, a magistrate of the Shechemites, that had entertained Abimelech. He sent messengers, and informed him how much Gaal had irritated the people against him, and excited him to lay ambushes before the city, for that he would persuade Gaal to go out against him, which would leave it in his power to be revenged on him; and when that was once done, he would bring him to be reconciled to the city. (244) So Abimelech laid ambushes and himself lay with them. Now Gaal abode in the suburbs, taking little care of himself; and Zebul was with him. Now as Gaal saw the armed men coming on, he said to Zebul, that some armed men were coming; (245) but the other replied, they were only shadows of huge stones: and when they were come nearer, Gaal perceived what was the reality, and said, they were not shadows but men lying in ambush. Then said Zebul, 'Didst not thou reproach Abimelech for cowardice? Why dost thou not then show how very courageous thou art thyself, and go and fight him?' (246) So Gaal, being in disorder, joined battle with Abimelech, and some of his men fell; whereupon he fled into the city, and took his men with him. But Zebul managed his matters so in the city, that he procured them to expel Gaal out of the city, and this by accusing him of cowardice in this action with the soldiers of Abimelech. (247) But Abimelech, when he had learned that the Shechemites were again coming out to gather their grapes, placed ambushes before the city, and when they were coming out, the third part of his army took possession of the gates, to hinder the citizens from returning in again, while the rest pursued those that were scattered abroad, and so there was slaughter everywhere; (248) and when he had overthrown the city to the very foundations, for it was not able to bear a siege, and had sown its ruins with salt, he proceeded on with his army till all the Shechemites were slain. As for those that were scattered about the country, and so escaped the danger, they were gathered together unto a certain strong rock, and settled themselves upon it, and prepared to build a wall about it: (249) and when Abimelech knew their intentions he prevented them, and came upon them with his forces and laid faggots of dry wood round the place, he himself bringing some of them, and by his example encouraging the soldiers to do the same. And when the rock was encompassed round about with these faggots, they set them on fire, and threw in whatsoever by nature caught fire the most easily: so a mighty flame was raised, (250) and nobody could fly away from the rock, but every man perished, with their wives and children, in all about fifteen hundred men, and the rest were a great number also. And such was the calamity which fell upon the Shechemites; and men's grief on their account had been greater than it was, had they not brought so much mischief on a person who had so well

deserved of them, and had they not themselves esteemed this as a punishment for the same.

(251) Now Abimelech, when he had affrighted the Israelites with the miseries he had brought upon the Shechemites, seemed openly to affect greater authority than he now had, and appeared to set no bounds to his violence, unless it were with the destruction of all. Accordingly he marched to Thebes, and took the city on the sudden; and there being a great tower therein, whereunto the whole multitude fled, he made preparation to besiege it. (252) Now as he was rushing with violence near the gates, a woman threw a piece of a millstone upon his head, upon which Abimelech fell down, and desired his armour bearer to kill him, lest his death should be thought to be the work of a woman; who did what he was bid to do. (253) So he underwent this death as a punishment for the wickedness he had perpetrated against his brethren, and his insolent barbarity to the Shechemites. Now the calamity that happened to those Shechemites was according to the prediction of Jotham. However, the army that was with Abimelech, upon his fall, was scattered abroad, and went to their own homes.

(254) Now it was that Jair the Gileadite, of the tribe of Manasseh, took the government. He was a man happy in other respects also, but particularly in his children, who were of a good character. They were thirty in number and very skilful in riding on horses, and were entrusted with the government of the cities of Gilead. He kept the government twenty-two years, and died an old man, and he was buried in Camon, a city of Gilead.

(255) And now all the affairs of the Hebrews were managed uncertainly, and tended to disorder, and to the contempt of God and of the laws. So the Ammonites and Philistines had them in contempt, and laid waste the country with a great army; and when they had taken all Perea, they were so insolent as to attempt to gain the possession of all the rest; (256) but the Hebrews being now amended by the calamities they had undergone, betook themselves to supplications to God; and brought sacrifices to him, beseeching him not to be too severe upon them, but to be moved by their prayers to leave off his anger against them. So God became more merciful to them, and was ready to assist them.

(257) When the Ammonites had made an expedition into the land of Gilead, the inhabitants of the country met them at a certain mountain, but wanted a commander. Now there was one whose name was Jephtha, who, both on account of his father's virtue, and on account of that army which he maintained at his own expenses, was a potent man; (258) the Israelites therefore sent to him, and entreated him to come to their assistance, and promised him to dominion over them all his lifetime. But he did not admit of their entreaty; and accused them that they did not come to his assistance when he was unjustly treated, and

this in an open manner by his brethren; (259) for they cast him off as not having the same mother with the rest, but born of a strange mother that was introduced among them by his father's fondness; and this they did out of a contempt of his inability [to vindicate himself]. (260) So he dwelt in the country of Gilead, as it is called, and received all that came to him, let them come from what place soever, and paid them wages. However, when they pressed him to accept the dominion, and swore they would grant him the government over them all his life, he led them to the war.

(261) And when Jephtha had taken immediate care of their affairs he placed his army at the city Miseph, and sent a message to the Ammonite [king], complaining of his unjust possession of their land. But that king sent a contrary message, and complained of the exodus of the Israelites out of Egypt, and desired him to go out of the land of the Amorites, and yield it up to him, as at first his paternal inheritance. (262) But Jephtha returned this answer: that he did not justly complain of his ancestors about the land of the Amorites, and ought rather to thank them that they left the land of the Ammonites to them, since Moses could have taken it also; and that neither would he recede from that land of their own which God had obtained for them, and they had now inhabited [above] three hundred years, but would fight with them about it.

(263) And when he had given them this answer, he sent the ambassadors away. And when he had prayed for victory and had vowed to perform sacred offices, and if he came home in safety, to offer in sacrifice what living creature soever should first meet him, he joined battle with the enemy and gained a great victory, and in his pursuit slew the enemies all along as far as the city Minnith. He then passed over to the land of the Ammonites, and overthrew many of their cities, and took their prey, and freed his own people from that slavery which they had undergone for eighteen years. (264) But as he came back, he fell into a calamity no way correspondent to the great actions he had done; for it was his daughter that came to meet him; she was also an only child and a virgin: upon this Jephtha heavily lamented the greatness of his affliction, and blamed his daughter for being so forward in meeting him, for he had vowed to sacrifice her to God. (265) However, this action that was to befall her was not ungrateful to her, since she should die upon the occasion of her father's victory, and the liberty of her fellow citizens: she only desired her father to give her leave, for two months, to bewail her youth with her fellow citizens; and then she agreed, that at the forementioned time he might do with her according to his vow. (266) Accordingly, when that time was over, he sacrificed his daughter as a burnt offering, offering such an oblation as was neither conformable to the law nor acceptable to God, not weighing with himself what opinion the hearers would have of such a practice.

(267) Now the tribe of Ephraim fought against him, because he did not take

them along with him in his expedition against the Ammonites, but because he alone had the prey and the glory of what was done to himself. As to which he said, first, that they were not ignorant how his kindred had fought against him, and that when they were invited, they did not come to his assistance, whereas they ought to have come quickly, even before they were invited. (268) And in the next place, that they were going to act unjustly; for while they had not courage enough to fight their enemies, they came hastily against their own kindred: and he threatened them, that; with God's assistance, he would inflict a punishment upon them, unless they would grow wiser. (269) But when he could not persuade them, he fought with them with those forces which he sent for out of Gilead, and he made a great slaughter among them; and when they were beaten, he pursued them, and seized on the passages of Jordan by a part of his army which he had sent before, and slew about forty-two thousand of them.

(270) So when Jephtha had ruled six years, he died, and was buried in his own country, Sebee, which is a place in the land of Gilead.

(271) Now, when Jephtha was dead, Ibzan took the government, being of the tribe of Judah, and of the city of Bethlehem. He had sixty children, thirty of them sons and the rest daughters: all whom he left alive behind him, giving the daughters in marriage to husbands, and taking wives for his sons. He did nothing in the seven years of his administration that was worth recording, or deserved a memorial. So he died an old man, and was buried in his own country.

(272) When Ibzan was dead after this manner, neither did Helon, who succeeded him in the government, and kept it ten years, do anything remarkable; he was of the tribe of Zebulon.

(273) Abdon also, the son of Hilel, of the tribe of Ephraim, and born at the city Pyrathon, was ordained their supreme governor after Helon. He is only recorded to have been happy in his children; for the public affairs were then so peaceable, and in such security, that neither did he perform any glorious action. (274) He had forty sons, and by them left thirty grandchildren; and he marched in state with these seventy; who were all very skilful in riding horses: and he left them all alive after him. He died an old man, and obtained a magnificent burial in Pyrathon.

CHAPTER 8

(275) After Abdon was dead, the Philistines overcame the Israelites, and received tribute of them for forty years; from which distress they were delivered after this manner:

(276) There was one Manoah, a person of such great virtue, that he had few men his equals, and without dispute the principal person of his country. He

had a wife celebrated for her beauty, and excelling her contemporaries. He had no children; and being uneasy at his want of posterity, he entreated God to give them seed of their own bodies to succeed them; and with that intent he came constantly into the suburbs, together with his wife; which suburbs were in the Great Plain. (277) Now, he was fond of his wife to a degree of madness, and on that account was unmeasurably jealous of her. Now when his wife was once alone, an apparition was seen by her: it was an angel of God, and resembled a young man, beautiful and tall, and brought her the good news, that she should have a son, born by God's providence, that should be a goodly child, of great strength; by whom, when he was grown up to man's estate, the Philistines should be afflicted. (278) He exhorted her also not to poll his hair, and that he should avoid all other kinds of drink (for so had God commanded), and be entirely contented with water. So the angel, when he had delivered that message, went his way, his coming having been by the will of God.

(279) Now the wife informed her husband when he came home of what the angel had said, who showed so great an admiration of the beauty and tallness of the young man that had appeared to her, that her husband was astonished, and out of himself for jealousy, and such suspicions as are excited by that passion; (280) but she was desirous of having her husband's unreasonable sorrow taken away; accordingly she entreated God to send the angel again, that he might be seen by her husband. So the angel came again by the favour of God, while they were in the suburbs, and appeared to her when she was alone, without her husband. She desired the angel to stay so long till she might bring her husband; and that request being granted, she goes to call Manoah. (281) When he saw the angel he was not yet free from suspicion, and he desired him to inform him of all that he had told his wife; but when he said it was sufficient that she alone knew what he had said, he then requested him to tell who he was, that when the child was born, they might return him thanks and give him a present. (282) He replied that he did not want any present, for that he did not bring them the good news of the birth of a son out of the want of anything; and when Manoah had entreated him to stay and partake of his hospitality, he did not give his consent. However he was persuaded at the earnest request of Manoah, to stay so long as while he brought him one mark of his hospitality; (283) so he slew a kid of the goats, and bid his wife boil it. When all was ready the angel enjoined him to set the loaves and the flesh, but without the vessels, upon the rock; (284) which when they had done, he touched the flesh with the rod which he had in his hand, which, upon the breaking out of a flame, was consumed, together with the loaves; and the angel ascended openly in their sight up to heaven, by means of the smoke as by a vehicle. Now Manoah was afraid that some danger would come to them from this sight of God; but his wife bade him be of good courage, for that God appeared to them for their benefit.

(285) So the woman proved with child, and was careful to observe the injunctions that were given her; and they called the child when he was born, Samson, which name signifies one that is *strong*. So the child grew apace; and it appeared evidently that he would be a prophet, both by the moderation of his diet, and the permission of his hair to grow.

(286) Now when he once came with his parents to Timnath, a city of the Philistines, where there was a great festival, he fell in love with a maid of that country, and he desired of his parents that they would procure him the damsel for his wife; but they refused so to do, because she was not of the stock of Israel; yet because this marriage was of God, who intended to convert it to the benefit of the Hebrews, he over-persuaded them to procure her to be espoused to him; (287) and as he was continually coming to her parents, he met a lion, and though he was naked, he received his onset, and strangled him with his hands, and cast the wild beast into a woody piece of ground on the inside of the road.

(288) And when he was going another time to the damsel, he lit upon a swarm of bees making their combs in the breast of that lion; and taking three honeycombs away, he gave them together with the rest of his presents, to the damsel. (289) Now the people of Timnath, out of a dread of the young man's strength, gave him during the time of the wedding feast (for he then feasted them all) thirty of the most stout of their youth, in pretence to be his companions, but in reality to be a guard upon him, that he might not attempt to give them any disturbance. Now as they were drinking merrily and playing, Samson said, as was usual at such times, (290) 'Come, if I propose you a riddle, and you can expound it in these seven days' time, I will give you every one a linen shirt and a garment, as the reward of your wisdom.' So they being very ambitious to obtain the glory of wisdom, together with the gains, desired him to propose his riddle: he said, 'That a devourer produced sweet food out of itself, though itself were very disagreeable': (291) and when they were not able in three days' time to find out the meaning of the riddle, they desired the damsel to discover it by the means of her husband, and tell it them; and they threatened to burn her if she did not tell it them. So when the damsel entreated Samson to tell it her, he at first refused to do it; (292) but when she lay hard at him, and fell into tears, and made his refusal to tell it a sign of his unkindness to her, he informed her of his slaughter of a lion, and how he found bees in his breast, and carried away three honeycombs, and brought them to her. (293) Thus he, suspecting nothing of deceit, informed her of all, and she revealed it to those that desired to know it. Then on the seventh day, whereon they were to expound the riddle proposed to them, they met together before sunsetting, and said, 'Nothing is more disagreeable than a lion to those that light on it; and nothing is sweeter than honey to those that make use of it.' (294) To which Samson made this rejoinder: 'Nothing is more deceitful than a woman, for

such was the person that discovered my interpretation to you.' Accordingly he gave them the presents he had promised them, making such Askelonites as met him upon the road his prey, who were themselves Philistines also. But he divorced this his wife; and the girl despised his anger, and was married to his companion who made the former match between them.

(295) At this injurious treatment Samson was so provoked that he resolved to punish all the Philistines, as well as her; so it being then summer time, and the fruits of the land being almost ripe enough for reaping, he caught three hundred foxes, and joining lighted torches to their tails, he sent them into the fields of the Philistines, by which means the fruits of the fields perished. (296) Now when the Philistines knew that this was Samson's doing, and knew also for what cause he did it, they sent their rulers to Timnah, and burnt his former wife, and her relations, who had been the occasion of their misfortunes.

(297) Now when Samson had slain many of the Philistines in the plain country, he dwelt at Etam, which is a strong rock of the tribe of Judah; for the Philistines at that time made an expedition against that tribe: but the people of Judah said that they did not act justly with them, in inflicting punishments upon them while they paid their tribute, and this only on account of Samson's offences. They answered, that in case they would not be blamed themselves, they must deliver up Samson, and put him into their power. (298) So they being desirous not to be blamed themselves, came to the rock with three thousand armed men, and complained to Samson of the bold insults he had made upon the Philistines, who were men able to bring calamity upon the whole nation of the Hebrews: and they told him they were come to take him and to deliver him up to them, and put him into their power; so they desired him to bear this willingly. (299) Accordingly, when he had received assurance from them upon oath, that they would do him no other harm than only to deliver him into his enemies' hands, he came down from the rock, and put himself into the power of his countrymen. Then did they bind him with two cords and lead him on, in order to deliver him to the Philistines; (300) and when they came to a certain place, which is now called *the Jawbone*, on account of the great action there performed by Samson, though of old it had no particular name at all, the Philistines, who had pitched their camp not far off, came to meet them with joy and shouting, as having done a great thing, and gained what they desired; but Samson broke his bonds asunder, and catching up the jawbone of an ass that lay down at his feet, fell upon his enemies, and smiting them with his jawbone, slew a thousand of them, and put the rest to flight and into great disorder.

(301) Upon this slaughter Samson was too proud of what he had performed, and said that this did not come to pass by the assistance of God, but that his success was to be ascribed to his own courage, and vaunted himself, that it was

out of a dread of him that some of his enemies fell, and the rest ran away upon his use of the jawbone; (302) but when a great thirst came upon him, he considered that human courage is nothing, and bare his testimony that all is to be ascribed to God, and besought him that he would not be angry at anything he had said, nor give him up into the hands of his enemies, but afford him help under his affliction, and deliver him from the misfortune he was under. (303) Accordingly God was moved with his entreaties, and raised him up a plentiful fountain of sweet water at a certain rock; whence it was that Samson called the place *The Jawbone*, and so it is called to this day.

(304) After this fight Samson held the Philistines in contempt, and came to Gaza, and took up his lodgings in a certain inn. When the rulers of Gaza were informed of his coming thither, they seized upon the gates, and placed men in ambush about them, that he might not escape without being perceived; (305) but Samson, who was acquainted with their contrivances against him, arose about midnight, and ran by force upon the gates, with their posts and beams, and the rest of their wooden furniture, and carried them away on his shoulders, and bare them to the mountain that is over Hebron, and there laid them down.

(306) However he at length transgressed the laws of his country, and altered his own regular way of living, and imitated the strange customs of foreigners, which thing was the beginning of his miseries; for he fell in love with a woman that was a harlot among the Philistines: her name was Delilah, and he lived with her. (307) So those that administered the public affairs of the Philistines came to her, and with promises, induced her to get out of Samson what was the cause of that his strength, by which he became unconquerable to his enemies. Accordingly when they were drinking, and had the like conversation together, she pretended to admire the actions he had done, and contrived to get out of him by subtlety, by what means he so much excelled others in strength. (308) Samson, in order to delude Delilah, for he had not yet lost his senses, replied, that if he were bound with seven such green withs of a vine as might still be wreathed, he should be weaker than any other man. (309) The woman said no more then, but told this to the rulers of the Philistines, and hid certain of the soldiers in ambush within the house; and when he was disordered in drink and asleep, she bound him as fast as possible with the withs; (310) and then upon her awakening him, she told him some of the people were upon him; but he broke the withs, and endeavoured to defend himself, as though some of the people were upon him. Now this woman, in the constant conversation Samson had with her, pretended that she took it very ill that he had such little confidence in her affections to him, that he would not tell her what she desired, as if she would not conceal what she knew it was for his interest to have concealed. (311) However, he deluded her again, and told her, that if they bound him with seven cords, he should lose his strength. And

when upon doing this, she gained nothing, he told her the third time, that his hair should be woven into a web; (312) but when, upon doing this, the truth was not yet discovered, at length Samson, upon Delilah's prayer (for he was doomed to fall into some affliction), was desirous to please her, and told her that God took care of him, and that he was born by his providence, and that, 'thence it is that I suffer my hair to grow, God having charged me never to poll my head, and thence my strength is according to the increase and continuance of my hair.' (313) When she had learned thus much, and had deprived him of his hair, she delivered him up to his enemies, when he was not strong enough to defend himself from their attempts upon him; so they put out his eyes, and bound him, and had him led about among them.

(314) But in process of time Samson's hair grew again. And there was a public festival among the Philistines, when the rulers and those of the most eminent character were feasting together (now the room wherein they were had its roof supported by two pillars); so they sent for Samson, and he was brought to their feast, that they might insult him in their cups. (315) Hereupon he, thinking it one of the greatest misfortunes, if he should not be able to revenge himself when he was thus insulted, persuaded the boy that led him by the hand, that he was weary and wanted to rest himself, and desired he would bring him near the pillars; (316) and as soon as he came to them, he rushed with force against them, and overthrew the house by overthrowing its pillars, with three thousand men in it who were all slain, and Samson with them. And such was the end of this man, when he had ruled over the Israelites twenty years. (317) And indeed this man deserves to be admired for his courage and strength, and magnanimity at his death, and that his wrath against his enemies went so far as to die himself with them. But as for his being ensnared by a woman, that is to be ascribed to human nature, which is too weak to resist the temptations to that sin; but we ought to bear him witness, that in all other respects he was one of extraordinary virtue. But his kindred took away his body, and buried it in Sarasat, his own country, with the rest of his family.

CHAPTER 9

(318) Now after the death of Samson, Eli the high priest was governor of the Israelites. Under him, when the country was afflicted with a famine, Elimelech of Bethlehem, which is a city of the tribe of Judah, being not able to support his family under so sore a distress, took with him Naomi his wife, and the children that were born to him by her, Chilion and Mahlon, and removed his habitation into the land of Moab; (319) and upon the happy prosperity of his affairs there, he took for his sons wives of the Moabites, Orpah for Chilion, and Ruth for Mahlon. But in the compass of ten years

both Elimelech, and, a little while after him, the sons died; (320) and Naomi being very uneasy at these accidents, and not being able to bear her lonesome condition, now those that were dearest to her were dead, on whose account it was that she had gone away from her own country, she returned to it again, for she had been informed it was now in a flourishing condition. (321) However, her daughters-in-law were not able to think of parting with her; and when they had a mind to go out of the country with her, she could not dissuade them from it; but when they insisted upon it, she wished them a more happy wedlock than they had with her sons, and that they might have prosperity in other respects also; (322) and seeing her own affairs were so low, she exhorted them to stay where they were, and not to think of leaving their own country, and partaking with her of that uncertainty under which she must return. Accordingly Orpah stayed behind; but she took Ruth along with her, as not to be persuaded to stay behind her, but would take her fortune with her, whatsoever it should prove.

(323) When Ruth was come with her mother-in-law to Bethlehem, Boaz, who was near of kin to Elimelech, entertained her; and when Naomi was so called by her fellow citizens, according to her true name, she said, 'You might more truly call me *Mara*. Now Naomi signifies in the Hebrew tongue *happiness*, and Mara, *sorrow*. (324) It was now reaping time; and Ruth, by the leave of her mother-in-law, went out to glean, that they might get a stock of corn for their food. Now it happened that she came into Boaz's field; and after some time Boaz came thither, and when he saw the damsel he inquired of his servant that was set over the reapers, concerning the girl. The servant had a little before inquired about all her circumstances, and told them to his master, (325) who kindly embraced her, both on account of her affection to her mother-in-law, and her remembrance of that son of hers to whom she had been married, and wished that she might experience a prosperous condition; so he desired her not to glean, but to reap what she was able, and gave her leave to carry it home. He also gave it in charge to that servant who was over the reapers, not to hinder her when she took it away, and bade him give her her dinner, and make her drink when he did the like to the reapers. (326) Now what corn Ruth received of him, she kept for her mother-in-law, and came to her in the evening, and brought the ears of corn with her; and Naomi had kept for her a part of such food as her neighbours had plentifully bestowed upon her. Ruth also told her mother-in-law what Boaz had said to her; (327) and when the other had informed her that he was near of kin to them, and perhaps was so pious a man as to make some provision for them, she went out again on the days following, to gather the gleanings with Boaz's maidservants.

(328) It was not many days before Boaz, after the barley was winnowed, slept in his thrashing floor. When Naomi was informed of this circumstance,

she contrived it so that Ruth should lie down by him, for she thought it might be for their advantage that he should discourse with the girl. Accordingly she sent the damsel to sleep at his feet; (329) who went as she bade her, for she did not think it consistent with her duty to contradict any command of her mother-in-law. And at first she lay concealed from Boaz, as he was fast asleep; but when he awaked about midnight, and perceived a woman lying by him he asked who she was; (330) and when she told him her name, and desired that he whom she owned for her lord, would excuse her, he then said no more; but in the morning, before the servants began to set about their work, he awaked her, and bid her take as much barley as she was able to carry, and go to her mother-in-law before anybody there should see that she had lain down by him, because it was but prudent to avoid any reproach that might arise on that account, especially when there had been nothing done that was ill. (331) But as to the main point she aimed at, the matter should rest here – 'He that is nearer of kin than I am, shall be asked whether he wants to take thee to wife: if he says he does, thou shalt follow him; but if he refuse it, I will marry thee, according to the law.'

(332) When she had informed her mother-in-law of this, they were very glad of it, out of the hope they had that Boaz would make provision for them. Now about noon Boaz went down into the city, and gathered the senate together, and when he had sent for Ruth, he called for her kinsman also; (333) and when he was come, he said, 'Dost not thou retain the inheritance of Elimelech and his sons?' He confessed that he did retain it, and that he did as he was permitted to do by the laws, because he was their nearest kinsman. Then said Boaz, 'Thou must not remember the laws by halves, but do everything according to them; for the wife of Mahlon is come hither, whom thou must marry according to the law, in case thou wilt retain their fields.' (334) So the man yielded up both the field and the wife to Boaz, who was himself of kin to those that were dead, as alleging that he had a wife already and children also; (335) so Boaz called the senate to witness, and bid the woman to loose his shoe and spit in his face, according to the law; and when this was done Boaz married Ruth, and they had a son within a year's time. (336) Naomi was herself a nurse to this child; and by the advice of the women, called him *Obed*, as being to be brought up in order to be subservient to her in her old age, for Obed in the Hebrew dialect signifies a *servant*. The son of Obed was Jesse, and David was his son, who was king, and left his dominions to his sons for one-and-twenty generations. (337) I was therefore obliged to relate this history of Ruth, because I had a mind to demonstrate the power of God, who, without difficulty, can raise those that are of ordinary parentage to dignity and splendour, to which he advanced David, though he were born of such mean parents.

CHAPTER 10

(338) And now upon the ill state of the affairs of the Hebrews, they made war again upon the Philistines. The occasion was this: Eli, the high priest, had two sons, Hophni and Phineas. (339) These sons of Eli were guilty of injustice towards men, and of impiety towards God, and abstained from no sort of wickedness. Some of their gifts they carried off, as belonging to the honourable employment they had; others of them they took away by violence. They also were guilty of impurity with the women that came to worship God [at the tabernacle], obliging some to submit to their lust by force, and enticing others by bribes; nay, the whole course of their lives was no better than tyranny. (340) Their father therefore was angry at them for such their wickedness, and expected that God would suddenly inflict his punishments upon them for what they had done. The multitude took it heinously also: and as soon as God had foretold what calamity would befall Eli's sons, which he did both to Eli himself and to Samuel the prophet, who was yet but a child, he openly showed his sorrow for his sons' destruction.

(341) I will first dispatch what I have to say about the prophet Samuel, and after that will proceed to speak of the sons of Eli, and the miseries they brought on the whole people of the Hebrews. (342) Elcanah, a Levite, one of a middle condition among his fellow citizens, and one that dwelt at Ramathaim, a city of the tribe of Ephraim, married two wives, Hannah and Peninnah. He had children by the latter; but he loved the other best, although she was barren. (343) Now Elcanah came with his wives to the city Shiloh to sacrifice, for there it was that the tabernacle of God was fixed, as we have formerly said. Now when, after he had sacrificed, he distributed at that festival portions of the flesh to his wives and children, and when Hannah saw the other wife's children sitting round about their mother, she fell into tears, and lamented herself on account of her barrenness and lonesomeness; (344) and suffering her grief to prevail over her husband's consolations to her, she went to the tabernacle to beseech God to give her seed, and to make her a mother; and to vow to consecrate the first son she should bear to the service of God, and this in such a way, that his manner of living should not be like that of ordinary men. (345) And as she continued at her prayers a long time, Eli, the high priest, for he sat there before the tabernacle, bid her go away, thinking she had been disordered with wine; but when she said she had drank water, but was in sorrow for want of children, and was beseeching God for them, he bid her be of good cheer, and told her that God would send her children.

(346) So she came to her husband full of hope, and ate her meal with gladness. And when they had returned to their own country she found herself

with child, and they had a son born to them, to whom they gave the name of Samuel, which may be styled one that was *asked of God*. They therefore came to the tabernacle to offer sacrifice for the birth of the child, and brought their tithes with them; (347) but the woman remembered the vow she had made concerning her son, and delivered him to Eli, dedicating him to God, that he might become a prophet. Accordingly his hair was suffered to grow long, and his drink was water. So Samuel dwelt and was brought up in the temple. But Elcanah had other sons by Hannah, and three daughters.

(348) Now when Samuel was twelve years old, he began to prophesy: and once when he was asleep, God called to him by his name; and he, supposing he had been called by the high priest, came to him: but when the high priest said he did not call him, God did so thrice. (349) Eli was then so far illuminated, that he said to him, 'Indeed, Samuel, I was silent now as well as before: it is God that calls thee; do thou therefore signify it to him, and say I am here ready.' So when he heard God speak again, he desired him to speak, and to deliver what oracles he pleased to him, for he would not fail to perform any ministration whatsoever he should make use of him in; (350) to which God replied, 'since thou art here ready, learn what miseries are coming upon the Israelites – such indeed as words cannot declare, nor faith believe; for the sons of Eli shall die on one day, and the priesthood shall be transferred into the family of Eleazar; for Eli hath loved his sons more than he hath loved my worship, and to such a degree, as is not for their advantage.' (351) Which message Eli obliged the prophet by oath to tell him, for otherwise he had no inclination to afflict him by telling it. And now Eli had a far more sure expectation of the perdition of his sons; but the glory of Samuel increased more and more, it being found by experience that whatsoever he prophesied came to pass accordingly.

CHAPTER 11

(352) About this time it was that the Philistines made war against the Israelites, and pitched their camp at the city Aphek. Now when the Israelites had expected them a little while, the very next day they joined battle, and the Philistines were conquerors, and slew above four thousand of the Hebrews, and pursued the rest of their multitude to their camp.

(353) So the Hebrews being afraid of the worst, sent to the senate and to the high priest, and desired that they would bring the ark of God, that by putting themselves in array, when it was present with them, they might be too hard for their enemies, as not reflecting that he who had condemned them to endure these calamities was greater than the ark, and for whose sake it was that this ark came to be honoured. (354) So the ark came, and the sons of the high priest

with it, having received a charge from their father, that if they pretended to survive the taking of the ark, they should come no more into his presence; for Phineas officiated already as high priest, his father having resigned his office to him, by reason of his great age. (355) So the Hebrews were full of courage, as supposing that, by the coming of the ark, they should be too hard for their enemies; their enemies also were greatly concerned, and were afraid of the ark's coming to the Israelites; however, the upshot did not prove agreeable to the expectation of both sides, but when the battle was joined, (356) that victory which the Hebrews expected was gained by the Philistines, and that defeat the Philistines were afraid of, fell to the lot of the Israelites, and thereby they found that they had put their trust in the ark in vain, for they were presently beaten as soon as they came to a close fight with their enemies, and lost about thirty thousand men, among whom were the sons of the high priest; but the ark was carried away by the enemies.

(357) When the news of this defeat came to Shiloh, with that of the captivity of the ark (for a certain young man, a Benjamite, who was in the action, came as a messenger thither), the whole city was full of lamentations. (358) And Eli, the high priest, who sat upon a high throne at one of the gates, heard their mournful cries, and supposed that some strange thing had befallen his family. So he sent for the young man; and when he understood what had happened in the battle, he was not much uneasy as to his sons, or what was told him withal about the army, as having beforehand known by divine revelation that those things would happen, and having himself declared them beforehand – for what sad things come unexpectedly they distress men the most; (359) but as soon as [he heard] the ark was carried captive by their enemies, he was very much grieved at it, because it fell out quite differently from what he expected; so he fell down from his throne and died, having in all lived ninety-eight years, and of them retained the government forty.

(360) On the same day his son Phineas's wife died also, as not able to survive the misfortune of her husband; for they told her of her husband's death as she was in labour. However, she bare a son at seven months, who lived, and to whom they gave the name of Icabod, which name signified *disgrace* – and this because the army received a disgrace at this time.

(361) Now Eli was the first of the family of Ithamar, the other son of Aaron, that had the government; for the family of Eleazar officiated as high priest at first, the son still receiving that honour from the father which Eleazar bequeathed to his son Phineas; (362) after whom Abiezer his son took the honour, and delivered it to his son, whose name was Bukki, from whom his son Ozi received it; after whom Eli, of whom we have been speaking, had the priesthood, and so he and his posterity until the time of Solomon's reign; but then the posterity of Eleazar resumed it.

BOOK SIX

CHAPTER I

(1) When the Philistines had taken the ark of the Hebrews captive, as I said a little before, they carried it to the city of Ashdod, and put it by their own god, who was called Dagon, as one of their spoils; (2) but when they went into his temple the next morning to worship their god, they found him paying the same worship to the ark, for he lay along, as having fallen down from the basis whereon he had stood; so they took him up and set him on his basis again and were much troubled at what had happened; and as they frequently came to Dagon and found him still lying along, in a posture of adoration to the ark, they were in very great distress and confusion. (3) At length God sent a very destructive disease upon the city and country of Ashdod, for they died of the dysentery or flux, a sore distemper, that brought death upon them very suddenly; for before the soul could, as usual in easy deaths, be well loosed from the body, they brought up their entrails, and vomited up what they had eaten, and what was entirely corrupted by the disease. And as to the fruits of their country, a great multitude of mice arose out of the earth and hurt them, and spared neither the plants nor the fruits. (4) Now while the people of Ashdod were under these misfortunes, and were not able to support themselves under their calamities, they perceived that they suffered thus because of the ark, and that the victory they had gotten, and their having taken the ark captive, had not happened for their good; they therefore sent to the people of Askelon, and desired that they would receive the ark among them. (5) This desire of the people of Ashdod was not disagreeable to those of Askelon, so they granted them that favour. But when they had gotten the ark, they were in the same miserable condition; for the ark carried along with it the disasters that the people of Ashdod had suffered, to those who received it from them. Those of Askelon also sent it away from themselves to others; (6) nor did it stay among those others neither; for since they were pursued by the same disasters, they still sent it to the neighbouring cities; so that the ark went round, after this manner, to the five cities of the Philistines, as though it exacted these disasters as a tribute to be paid it for its coming among them.

(7) When those that had experienced these miseries were tired out with them, and when those that heard of them were taught thereby not to admit the ark among them since they paid so dear a tribute for it, at length they sought for some contrivance and method how they might get free from it: (8) so the

governors of the five cities, Gath, and Ekron, and Askelon, as also of Gaza and Ashdod, met together, and considered what was fit to be done; and at first they thought proper to send the ark back to its own people, as allowing that God had avenged its cause; that the miseries they had undergone came along with it, and that these were sent on their cities upon its account, and together with it. (9) However, there were those that said, they should not do so, nor suffer themselves to be deluded, as ascribing the cause of their miseries to it, because it could not have such power and force upon them; for, had God had such a regard to it, it would not have been delivered into the hands of men: so they exhorted them to be quiet, and to take patiently what had befallen them, and to suppose there was no other cause of it but nature, which, at certain revolutions of time, produces such mutations in the bodies of men, in the earth, in plants, and in all things that grow out on the earth. (10) But the counsel that prevailed over those already described was that of certain men, who were believed to have distinguished themselves in former times for their understanding and prudence, and who, in their present circumstances, seemed above all the rest to speak properly. These men said, it was not right either to send the ark away, or to retain it, but to dedicate five golden images, one for every city, as a thank offering to God, on account of his having taken care of their preservation, and having kept them alive when their lives were likely to be taken away by such distempers as they were not able to bear up against. They also would have them make five golden mice like to those that devoured and destroyed their country, (11) to put them in a bag, and lay them upon the ark; to make them a new cart also for it, and to yoke milch kine to it; but to shut up their calves, and keep them from them, lest, by following after them, they should prove a hindrance to their dams, and that the dams might return the faster out of a desire of those calves; then to drive these milch kin that carried the ark, and leave it at a place where three ways met, and to leave it to the kine to go along which of those ways they pleased; (12) that in case they went the way to the Hebrews, and ascended to their country, they should suppose that the ark was the cause of their misfortunes; but if they turned into another road, they said, 'We will pursue after it, and conclude that it has no such force in it.'

(13) So they determined that these men spake well; and they immediately confirmed their opinion by doing accordingly. And when they had done as has been already described, they brought the cart to a place where three ways met, and left it there, and went their ways; but the kine went the right way, as if some persons had driven them, while the rulers of the Philistines followed after them, as desirous to know where they would stand still, and to whom they would go. (14) Now there was a certain village of the tribe of Judah, the name of which was Bethshemesh, and to that village did the kine go; and though

there was a great and good plain before them to proceed in, they went no farther, but stopped the cart there. This was a sight to those of that village, and they were very glad; for it being then summertime, and all the inhabitants being then in the fields gathering in their fruits, they left off their labours of their hands for joy, as soon as they saw the ark, and ran to the cart; (15) and taking the ark down, and the vessel that had the images in it and the mice, they set them upon a certain rock which was in the plain; and when they had offered a splendid sacrifice to God, and feasted, they offered the cart and the kine as a burnt offering: and when the lords of the Philistines saw this, they returned back.

(16) But now it was that the wrath of God overtook them, and struck seventy persons of the village of Bethshemesh dead, who, not being priests, and so not worthy to touch the ark, had approached to it. Those of that village wept for these that had thus suffered, and made such a lamentation as was naturally to be expected on so great a misfortune that was sent from God; and everyone mourned for his relation. (17) And since they acknowledged themselves unworthy of the ark's abode with them, they sent to the public senate of the Israelites, and informed them that the ark was restored by the Philistines; which when they knew, they brought it away to Kirjath-jearim, a city in the neighbourhood of Bethshemesh. (18) In this city lived one Abinadab, by birth a Levite, and who was greatly commended for his righteous and religious course of life; so they brought the ark to his house, as to a place fit for God himself to abide in, since therein did inhabit a righteous man. His sons also ministered to the divine service at the ark, and were the principal curators of it for twenty years; for so many years it continued in Kirjath-jearim, having been but four months with the Philistines.

CHAPTER 2

(19) Now while the city of Kirjath-jearim had the ark with them, the whole body of the people betook themselves all that time to offer prayers and sacrifices to God, and appeared greatly concerned and zealous about his worship. So Samuel the prophet, seeing how ready they were to do their duty, thought this a proper time to speak to them, while they were in this good disposition, about the recovery of their liberty, and of the blessings that accompanied the same. Accordingly he used such words to them as he thought were most likely to excite that inclination, and to persuade them to attempt it: (20) 'O you Israelites,' said he, 'to whom the Philistines are still grievous enemies, but to whom God begins to be gracious, it behooves you not only to be desirous of liberty, but to take the proper methods to obtain it. Nor are you to be contented with an inclination to get clear of your lords and masters,

while you still do what will procure your continuance under them. (21) Be righteous then, and cast wickedness out of your souls, and by your worship supplicate the Divine Majesty with all your hearts, and persevere in the honour you pay to him; for if you act thus, you will enjoy prosperity; you will be freed from your slavery, and will get the victory over your enemies: which blessings it is not possible you should attain either by weapons of war, or by the strength of your bodies, or by the multitude of your assistants: for God has not promised to grant these blessings by those means, but by being good and righteous men; and if you will be such, I will be security to you for the performance of God's promises.' (22) When Samuel had said thus, the multitude applauded his discourse, and were pleased with his exhortation to them, and gave their consent to resign themselves up to do what was pleasing to God. So Samuel gathered them together to a certain city called Mizpah, which, in the Hebrew tongue, signifies a *watchtower*; there they drew water, and poured it out to God, and fasted all day, and betook themselves to their prayers.

(23) This their assembly did not escape the notice of the Philistines: so when they had learned that so large a company had met together, they fell upon the Hebrews with a great army and mighty forces, as hoping to assault them when they did not expect it, nor were prepared for it. (24) This thing affrighted the Hebrews, and put them into disorder and terror; so they came running to Samuel, and said that their souls were sunk by their fears, and by the former defeat they had received, and 'that thence it was that we lay still, lest we should excite the power of our enemies against us. Now while thou has brought us hither to offer up our prayers and sacrifices, and take oaths [to be obedient], our enemies are making an expedition against us, while we are naked and unarmed; wherefore we have no other hope of deliverance but that by thy means, and by the assistance God shall afford us upon thy prayers to him, we shall obtain deliverance from the Philistines.' (25) Hereupon Samuel bade them be of good cheer, and promised them that God would assist them; and taking a sucking lamb, he sacrificed it for the multitude, and besought God to hold his protecting hand over them when they should fight with the Philistines, and not to overlook them, nor suffer them to come under a second misfortune. Accordingly God hearkened to his prayers, and accepting their sacrifice with a gracious intention, and such as was disposed to assist them, he granted them victory and power over their enemies. (26) Now while the altar had the sacrifice of God upon it, and had not yet consumed it wholly by its sacred fire, the enemy's army marched out of their camp, and was put in order of battle, and this in hope that they should be conquerors, since the Jews were caught in distressed circumstances, as neither having their weapons with them nor being assembled there in order to fight. But things so fell out, that they would hardly have been credited though they

had been foretold by anybody; (27) for, in the first place, God disturbed their enemies with an earthquake, and moved the ground under them to such a degree, that he caused it to tremble, and made them to shake, insomuch that by its trembling he made some unable to keep their feet, and made them fall down, and, by opening its chasms, he caused that others should be hurried down into them; after which he caused such a noise of thunder to come among them, and made fiery lightning shine so terribly round about them, that it was ready to burn their faces; and he so suddenly shook their weapons out of their hands, that he made them fly and return home naked. (28) So Samuel with the multitude pursued them to Bethcar, a place so called; and there he set up a stone as a boundary of their victory and their enemies' flight, and called it the *Stone of Power*, as a signal of that power God had given them against their enemies.

(29) So the Philistines, after this stroke, made no more expeditions against the Israelites, but lay still out of fear, and out of remembrance of what had befallen them, and what courage the Philistines had formerly against the Hebrews. (30) Samuel also made an expedition against the Philistines, and slew many of them, and entirely humbled their proud hearts, and took from them that country which, when they were formerly conquerors in battle, they had cut off from the Jews, which was the country that extended from the borders of Gath to the city of Ekron: but the remains of the Canaanites were at this time in friendship with the Israelites.

CHAPTER 3

(31) But Samuel the prophet, when he had ordered the affairs of the people after a convenient manner, and had appointed a city for every district of them, he commanded them to come to such cities, to have the controversies that they had one with another determined in them, he himself going over those cities twice in a year, and doing them justice; and by that means he kept them in very good order for a long time.

(32) But afterwards he found himself oppressed with old age, and not able to do what he used to do, so he committed the government and the care of the multitude to his sons – the elder of whom was called Joel, and the name of the younger was Abiah. He also enjoined them to reside and judge the people, the one at the city of Bethel and the other at Beersheba, and divided the people into districts that should be under the jurisdiction of each of them. (33) Now these men afford us an evident example and demonstration how some children are not of the like dispositions with their parents; (34) but sometimes perhaps good and moderate, though born of wicked parents; and sometimes showing themselves to be wicked, though born of good parents; for these men turning

aside from their father's good courses, and taking a course that was contrary to them, perverted justice for the filthy lucre of gifts and bribes, and made their determinations not according to truth, but according to bribery, and turned aside to luxury, and a costly way of living; so that as, in the first place, they practised what was contrary to the will of God, so did they, in the second place, what was contrary to the will of the prophet their father, who had taken a great deal of care, and made a very careful provision that the multitude should be righteous.

(35) But the people, upon these injuries offered to their former constitution and government by the prophet's sons, were very uneasy at their actions, and came running to the prophet who then lived at the city Ramah, and informed him of the transgressions of his sons; and said that, as he was himself old already, and too infirm by that age of his to oversee their affairs in the manner he used to do, (36) so they begged of him and entreated him, to appoint some person to be king over them, who might rule over the nation, and avenge them of the Philistines, who ought to be punished for their former oppressions. These words greatly afflicted Samuel, on account of his innate love of justice, and his hatred to kingly government, for he was very fond of an aristocracy, as what made the men that used it of a divine and happy disposition; (37) nor could he either think of eating or sleeping, out of his concern and torment of mind at what they had said, but all the night long did he continue awake and revolved these notions in his mind.

(38) While he was thus disposed, God appeared to him, and comforted him, saying, that he ought not to be uneasy at what the multitude desired, because it was not he, but himself whom they so insolently despised, and would not have to be alone their king; that they had been contriving these things from the very day that they came out of Egypt; that however in no long time they would sorely repent of what they did, which repentance yet could not undo what was thus done for futurity: that they would be sufficiently rebuked for their contempt, and the ungrateful conduct they have used towards me, and towards thy prophetic office. (39) 'So I command thee to ordain them such a one as I shall name beforehand to be their king, when thou hast first described what mischiefs kingly government will bring upon them, and openly testified before them into what a great change of affairs they are hasting.'

(40) When Samuel had heard this, he called the Jews early in the morning, and confessed to them that he was to ordain them a king; but he said that he was first to describe to them what would follow, what treatment they would receive from their kings, and with how many mischiefs they must struggle. 'For know ye,' said he, 'that, in the first place, they will take your sons away from you, and they will command some of them to be drivers of their chariots, and some to be their horsemen, and the guards of their body, and others of

them to be runners before them, and captains of thousands, and captains of hundreds; they will also make them their artificers, makers of armour, and of chariots and of instruments; they will make them their husbandmen also and the curators of their own fields, and the diggers of their own vineyards; (41) nor will there be anything which they will not do at their commands, as if they were slaves bought with money. They will also appoint your daughters to be confectioners and cooks and bakers; and these will be obliged to do all sorts of work which women slaves that are in fear of stripes and torments submit to. They will, besides this, take away your possessions, and bestow them upon their eunuchs and the guards of their bodies, and will give the herds of your cattle to their own servants; (42) and to say briefly all at once, you, and all that is yours, will be servants to your king, and will become no way superior to his slaves, and when you suffer thus, you will thereby be put in mind of what I now say; and when you repent of what you have done, you will beseech God to have mercy upon you, and to grant you a quick deliverance from your kings; but he will not accept your prayers, but will neglect you, and permit you to suffer the punishment your evil conduct has deserved.'

(43) But the multitude was still so foolish as to be deaf to these predictions of what would befall them; and too peevish to suffer a determination which they had injudiciously once made, to be taken out of their mind; for they could not be turned from their purpose, nor did they regard the words of Samuel, but peremptorily insisted on their resolution, and desired him to ordain them a king immediately, and not to trouble himself with fears of what would happen hereafter, (44) for that it was necessary they should have with them one to fight their battles, and to avenge them of their enemies, and that it was no way absurd, when their neighbours were under kingly government, that they should have the same form of government also. So when Samuel saw that what he had said had not diverted them from their purpose, but that they continued resolute, he said, 'Go you every one home for the present; when it is fit I will send for you, as soon as I shall have learned from God who it is that he will give you for your king.'

CHAPTER 4

(45) There was one of the tribe of Benjamin, a man of a good family, and of a virtuous disposition: his name was Kish. He had a son, a young man of a comely countenance, and of a tall body, but his understanding and his mind were preferable to what was visible in him: (46) they called him Saul. Now this Kish had some fine she-asses that were wandered out of the pasture wherein they fed, for he was more delighted with these than with any other cattle he had, so he sent out his son, and one servant with him, to search for the beasts;

(47) but when he had gone over his own tribe in search after the asses, he went to other tribes; and when he found them not there neither, he determined to go his way home, lest he should occasion any concern to his father about himself; but when his servant that followed him told him as they were near the city of Ramah, that there was a true prophet in that city, and advised him to go to him, for that by him they should know the upshot of the affair of their asses, he replied, that if they should go to him, they had nothing to give him as a reward for his prophecy, for their subsistence money was spent. (48) The servant answered, that he had still the fourth part of a shekel, and he would present him with that; for they were mistaken out of ignorance, as not knowing that the prophet received no such reward. So they went to him; and when they were before the gates, they lit upon certain maidens that were going to fetch water, and they asked them which was the prophet's house. They showed them which it was, and bid them make haste before he sat down to supper, for he had invited many guests to a feast, and that he used to sit down before those that were invited. (49) Now Samuel had then gathered many together to feast with him on this very account; for while he every day prayed to God to tell him beforehand whom he would make king, he had informed him of this man the day before, for that he would send him a certain young man out of the tribe of Benjamin about this hour of the day; and he sat on the top of the house in expectation of that time's being come. And when the time was completed, he came down and went to supper; (50) so he met with Saul, and God discovered to him that this was he who should rule over them. Then Saul went up to Samuel and saluted him, and desired him to inform him which was the prophet's house; for he said he was a stranger and did not know it. (51) When Samuel had told him that he himself was the person, he led him in to supper, and assured him that the asses were found which he had been to seek, and that the greatest of good things were assured to him: he replied, 'I am too inconsiderable to hope for any such thing, and of a tribe too small to have kings made out of it, and of a family smaller than several other families; but thou tellest me this in jest, and makest me an object of laughter, when thou discoursest with me of greater matters than what I stand in need of.' (52) However, the prophet led him in to the feast, and made him sit down, him and his servant that followed him, above the other guests that were invited, which were seventy in number; and he gave orders to the servants to set the royal portion before Saul. And when the time of going to bed was come, the rest rose up, and every one of them went home; but Saul stayed with the prophet, he and his servant, and slept with him.

(53) Now as soon as it was day, Samuel raised up Saul out of his bed, and conducted him homeward; and when he was out of the city, he desired him to cause his servant to go before, but to stay behind himself, for that he had

somewhat to say to him, when nobody else was present. (54) Accordingly, Saul sent away his servant that followed him; then did the prophet take a vessel of oil and poured it upon the head of the young man, and kissed him, and said, 'be thou a king by the ordination of God, against the Philistines, and for avenging the Hebrews for what they have suffered by them; of this thou shalt have a sign, which I would have thee take notice of: (55) as soon as thou art departed hence, thou wilt find three men upon the road, going to worship God at Bethel; the first of whom thou wilt see carrying three loaves of bread, the second carrying a kid of the goats, and the third will follow them carrying a bottle of wine. These three men will salute thee, and speak kindly to thee, and will give thee two of their loaves, which thou shalt accept of. (56) And thence thou shalt come to a place called *Rachel's Monument*, where thou shalt meet with those that will tell thee thy asses are found; after this, when thou comest to Gabatha, thou shalt overtake a company of prophets, and thou shalt be seized with the divine spirit, and prophesy along with them, till everyone that sees thee shall be astonished, and wonder, and say, Whence is it that the son of Kish has arrived at this degree of happiness? (57) And when these signs have happened to thee, know that God is with thee; then do thou salute thy father and thy kindred. Thou shalt also come when I send for thee to Gilgal, that we may offer thank offerings to God for these blessings.' When Samuel had said this, and foretold these things, he sent the young man away. Now all things fell out to Saul according to the prophecy of Samuel.

(58) But as soon as Saul came into the house of his kinsman Abner, whom indeed he loved better than the rest of his relations, he was asked by him concerning his journey, and what accidents happened to him therein; and he concealed none of the other things from him, no, not his coming to Samuel the prophet, nor how he told him the asses were found; but he said nothing to him about the kingdom, and what belonged thereto, (59) which he thought would procure him envy, and when such things are heard, they are not easily believed; nor did he think it prudent to tell those things to him, although he appeared very friendly to him, and one whom he loved above the rest of his relations, considering, I suppose, what human nature really is, that no one is a firm friend neither among our intimates nor our kindred; nor do they preserve that kind disposition when God advances men to great prosperity, but they are still ill-natured and envious at those that are in eminent stations.

(60) Then Samuel called the people together to the city Mizpah, and spake to them in the words following, which he said he was to speak by the command of God: that when he had granted them a state of liberty and brought their enemies into subjection, they were become unmindful of his benefits, and rejected God that he should not be their king, as not considering that it would be most for their advantage to be presided over by the best of

beings; (61) for God is the best of beings, and they chose to have a man for their king, while kings will use their subjects as beasts, according to the violence of their own wills and inclinations, and other passions, as wholly carried away with the lust of power, but will not endeavour so to preserve the race of mankind as his own workmanship and creation, which, for that very reason, God would take care of. 'But since you have come to a fixed resolution, and this injurious treatment of God has quite prevailed over you, dispose yourselves by your tribes and sceptres, and cast lots.'

(62) When the Hebrews had so done, the lot fell upon the tribe of Benjamin; and when the lot was cast for the families of this tribe, that which was called *Matri* was taken; and when the lot was cast for the single persons of that family, Saul, the son of Kish, was taken for their king. (63) When the young man knew this he prevented [their sending for him] and immediately went away and hid himself. I suppose that it was because he would not have it thought that he willingly took the government upon him; nay, he showed such a degree of command over himself, and of modesty, that while the greatest part are not able to contain their joy, even in the gaining of small advantages, but presently show themselves publicly to all men, this man did not only show nothing of that nature, when he was appointed to be the lord of so many and so great tribes, but crept away and concealed himself out of the sight of those he was to reign over, and made them seek him, and that with a good deal of trouble. (64) So when the people were at a loss, and solicitous, because Saul disappeared, the prophet besought God to show where the young man was, and to produce him before them. (65) So when they had learned of God the place where Saul was hidden, they sent men to bring him; and when he was come, they set him in the midst of the multitude. Now he was taller than any of them, and his stature was very majestic.

(66) Then said the prophet, 'God gives you this man to be your king: see how he is higher than any of the people, and worthy of this dominion.' So as soon as the people had made acclamation, *God save the King*, the prophet wrote down what would come to pass in a book, and read it in the hearing of the king, and laid up the book in the tabernacle of God, to be a witness to future generations of what he had foretold. (67) So when Samuel had finished this matter, he dismissed the multitude, and came himself to the city Ramah, for it was his own country. Saul also went away to Gibeah, where he was born; and many good men there were who paid him the respect that was due to him; but the greater part were ill men, who despised him and derided the others, who neither did bring him presents, nor did they in affection, or even in words, regard to please him.

CHAPTER 5

(68) After one month, the war which Saul had with Nahash, the king of the Ammonites, obtained him respect from all the people; for this Nahash had done a great deal of mischief to the Jews that lived beyond Jordan by the expedition he had made against them with a great and warlike army. (69) He also reduced their cities into slavery, and that not only by subduing them for the present, which he did by force and violence, but by weakening them by subtlety and cunning that they might not be able afterward to get clear of the slavery they were under to him: for he put out the right eyes of those that either delivered themselves to him upon terms, or were taken by him in war; (70) and this he did, that when their left eyes were covered by their shields, they might be wholly useless in war. (71) Now when the king of the Ammonites had served those beyond Jordan in this manner, he led his army against those that were called *Gileadites*; and having pitched his camp at the metropolis of his enemies, which was the city of Jabesh, he sent ambassadors to them, commanding them either to deliver themselves up, on condition to have their right eyes plucked out, or to undergo a siege, and to have their cities overthrown. He gave them their choice, whether they would cut off a small member of their body, or universally perish. (72) However, the Gileadites were so affrighted at these offers, that they had not courage to say anything to either of them, neither that they would deliver themselves up, nor that they would fight him; but they desired that he would give them seven days respite, that they might send ambassadors to their countrymen, and entreat their assistance; and if they came to assist them they would fight, but if that assistance were impossible to be obtained from them, they said they would deliver themselves up to suffer whatever he pleased to inflict upon them.

(73) So Nahash, condemning the multitude of the Gileadites and the answer they gave, allowed them a respite, and gave them leave to send to whomsoever they pleased for assistance. So they immediately sent to the Israelites, city by city, and informed them what Nahash had threatened to do to them, and what great distress they were in. (74) Now the people fell into tears and grief at the hearing of what the ambassadors from Jabesh said; and the terror they were in permitted them to do nothing more; but when the messengers were come to the city of King Saul, and declared the dangers in which the inhabitants of Jabesh were, the people were in the same affliction as those in the other cities, for they lamented the calamity of those related to them; (75) and when Saul was returned from his husbandry into the city, he found his fellow citizens weeping; and when, upon inquiry, he had learned the cause of the confusion and sadness they were in, he was seized with a divine fury, (76) and sent away

the ambassadors from the inhabitants of Jabesh, and promised them to come to their assistance on the third day, and to beat their enemies before sunrising, that the sun upon its rising might see that they had already conquered, and were freed from the fears they were under; but he bid some of them stay to conduct them the right way to Jabesh.

(77) So being desirous to turn the people to this war against the Ammonites by fear of the losses they should otherwise undergo, and that they might the more suddenly be gathered together, he cut the sinews of his oxen, and threatened to do the same to all such as did not come with their armour to Jordan the next day, and follow him and Samuel the prophet whithersoever they should lead them. (78) So they came together, out of fear of the losses they were threatened with, at the appointed time; and the multitude were numbered at the city Bezek; and he found the number of those that were gathered together, besides that of the tribe of Judah, to be seven hundred thousand, while those of that tribe were seventy thousand. (79) So he passed over Jordan and proceeded in marching all that night, thirty furlongs, and came to Jabesh before sunrising. So he divided the army into three companies; and fell upon their enemies on every side on the sudden, and when they expected no such thing; and joining battle with them, they slew a great many of the Ammonites, as also their king Nahash. (80) This glorious action was done by Saul, and was related with great commendation of him to all the Hebrews; and he thence gained a wonderful reputation for his valour; for although there were some of them that condemned him before, they now changed their minds, and honoured him, and esteemed him as the best of men; for he did not content himself with having saved the inhabitants of Jabesh only, but he made an expedition into the country of the Ammonites, and laid it all waste, and took a large prey, and so returned to his own country most gloriously; (81) so the people were greatly pleased at these excellent performances of Saul, and rejoiced that they had constituted him their king. They also made a clamour against those that pretended he would be of no advantage to their affairs; and they said, Where now are these men? Let them be brought to punishment, with all the like things that multitudes usually say when they are elevated with prosperity against those that lately had despised the authors of it; (82) but Saul, although he took the good will and the affection of these men very kindly, yet did he swear that he would not see any of his countrymen slain that day, since it was absurd to mix this victory, which God had given them, with the blood and slaughter of those that were of the same lineage with themselves; and that it was more agreeable to be men of a friendly disposition, and so to betake themselves to feasting.

(83) And when Samuel had told them that he ought to confirm the kingdom to Saul by a second ordination of him, they all came together to the city of

Gilgal, for thither did he command them to come. So the prophet anointed Saul with the holy oil in the sight of the multitude, and declared him to be king the second time; and so the government of the Hebrews was changed into a regal government; (84) for in the days of Moses and his disciple Joshua, who was their general, they continued under an aristocracy; but after the death of Joshua, for eighteen years in all, the multitude had no settled form of government, but were in an anarchy, (85) after which they returned to their former government; they then permitted themselves to be judged by him who appeared to be the best warrior and most courageous, whence it was that they called this interval of their government the *Judges*.

(86) Then did Samuel the prophet call another assembly also, and said to them, 'I solemnly adjure you, by God Almighty, who brought those excellent brethren, I mean Moses and Aaron, into the world, and delivered our fathers from the Egyptians, and from the slavery they endured under them, that you will not speak what you say to gratify me, nor suppress anything out of fear of me, nor be overborne by any other passion, but say, what have I ever done that was cruel or unjust? Or what have I done out of lucre or covetousness, or to gratify others? (87) Bear witness against me, if I have taken an ox or a sheep, or any such thing, which yet when they are taken to support men, it is esteemed blameless; or have I taken an ass for mine own use of anyone to his grief? Lay someone such crime to my charge, now we are in your king's presence.' But they cried out, that no such thing had been done by him, but that he had presided over the nation after a holy and righteous manner.

(88) Hereupon Samuel, when such a testimony had been given him by them all, said, 'Since you grant that you are not able to lay any ill thing to my charge hitherto, come on now, and do you hearken while I speak with great freedom to you. You have been guilty of great impiety against God, in asking you a king. (89) It behooves you to remember, that our grandfather Jacob came down into Egypt, by reason of a famine, with seventy souls only of our family, and that their posterity multiplied there to many ten thousands, whom the Egyptians brought into slavery and hard oppression; that God himself, upon the prayers of our fathers, sent Moses and Aaron, who were brethren, and gave them power to deliver the multitude out of their distress, and this without a king. These brought us into this very land which you now possess; (90) and when you enjoyed these advantages from God, you betrayed his worship and religion; nay, moreover, when you were brought under the hands of your enemies, he delivered you first by rendering you superior to the Assyrians and their forces; he then made you to overcome the Ammonites and the Moabites, and last of all the Philistines; and these things have been achieved under the conduct of Jephtha and Gideon. (91) What madness therefore possessed you to fly from God, and to desire to be under a king? Yet have I ordained him for

king whom he chose for you. However, that I may make it plain to you that God is angry and displeased at your choice of kingly government, I will so dispose him that he shall declare this very plainly to you by strange signals; for what none of you ever saw here before, I mean a winter storm in the midst of harvest, I will entreat of God, and will make it visible to you.' (92) Now, as soon as he had said this, God gave such great signals by thunder and lightning, and the descent of hail, as attested the truth of all that the prophet had said, insomuch that they were amazed and terrified, and confessed they had sinned, and had fallen into that sin through ignorance; and besought the prophet, as one that was a tender and gentle father to them, to render God so merciful as to forgive this their sin, which they had added to those other offences whereby they had affronted him and transgressed against him. (93) So he promised them that he would beseech God, and persuade him to forgive them these their sins. However, he advised them to be righteous and to be good, and ever to remember the miseries that had befallen them on account of their departure from virtue; as also to remember the strange signs God had shown them, and the body of laws that Moses had given them, if they had any desire of being preserved and made happy with their king: (94) but he said, that if they should grow careless of these things, great judgment would come from God upon them, and upon their king; And when Samuel had thus prophesied to the Hebrews, he dismissed them to their own homes, having confirmed the kingdom to Saul the second time.

CHAPTER 6

(95) Now Saul chose out of the multitude about three thousand men, and he took two thousand of them to be the guards of his own body, and abode in the city Bethel, but he gave the rest of them to Jonathan his son, to be the guards of his body; and sent him to Gibeah, where he besieged and took a certain garrison of the Philistines, not far from Gilgal; (96) for the Philistines of Gibeah had beaten the Jews, and taken their weapons away, and had put garrisons into the strongest places of the country, and had forbidden them to carry any instrument of iron, or at all to make use of any iron in any case whatsoever; and on account of this prohibition it was that the husbandmen, if they had occasion to sharpen any of their tools, whether it were the coulter or the spade, or any instrument of husbandry, they came to the Philistines to do it. (97) Now as soon as the Philistines heard of this slaughter of their garrison, they were in a rage about it, and, looking on this contempt as a terrible affront offered them, they made war against the Jews, with three hundred thousand footmen, and thirty thousand chariots, and six thousand horses; (98) and they pitched their camp at the city Michmash. When Saul, the king of the Hebrews, was

informed of this, he went down to the city Gilgal, and made proclamation over all the country, that they should try to regain their liberty; and called them to the war against the Philistines, diminishing their forces, and despising them as not very considerable, and as not so great but they might hazard a battle with them. (99) But when the people about Saul observed how numerous the Philistines were, they were under a great consternation; and some of them hid themselves in caves, and in dens underground, but the greater part fled into the land beyond Jordan, which belonged to Gad and Reuben.

(100) But Saul sent to the prophet, and called him to consult with him about the war and the public affairs; so he commanded him to stay there for him, and to prepare sacrifices, for he would come to him within seven days, that they might offer sacrifices on the seventh day, and might then join battle with their enemies. (101) So he waited, as the prophet sent to him to do; yet did not he, however, observe the command that was given him, but when he saw that the prophet tarried longer than he expected, and that he was deserted by the soldiers, he took the sacrifices and offered them; and when he heard that Samuel was come, he went out to meet him. (102) But the prophet said he had not done well in disobeying the injunctions he had sent to him, and had not stayed till his coming, which being appointed according to the will of God, he had prevented him in offering up those prayers and those sacrifices that he should have made for the multitude, and that he therefore had performed divine offices in an ill manner, and had been rash in performing them. (103) Hereupon Saul made an apology for himself, and said that he had waited as many days as Samuel had appointed him: that he had been so quick in offering his sacrifices, upon account of the necessity he was in, and because his soldiers were departing from him, out of their fear of the enemy's camp at Michmash, the report being gone abroad that they were coming down upon him to Gilgal. To which Samuel replied, (104) 'Nay, certainly, if thou hadst been a righteous man, and hadst not disobeyed me, nor slighted the commands which God suggested to me concerning the present state of affairs, and hadst not acted more hastily than the present circumstances required, thou wouldst have been permitted to reign a long time, and thy posterity after thee.' (105) So Samuel, being grieved at what happened, returned home; but Saul came to the city Gibeah, with his son Jonathan, having only six hundred men with him; and of these the greater part had no weapons, because of the scarcity of iron in that country, as well as of those that could make such weapons; for, as we showed a little before, the Philistines had not suffered them to have such iron or such workmen. (106) Now the Philistines divided their army into three companies, and took as many roads, and laid waste the country of the Hebrews, while King Saul and his son Jonathan saw what was done, but were not able to defend the land, having no more than six hundred men with them; (107) but as

he, and his son, and Abiah the high priest, who was of the posterity of Eli the high priest, were sitting upon a pretty high hill, and seeing the land laid waste, they were mightily disturbed at it. Now Saul's son agreed with his armour bearer, that they would go privately to the enemy's camp, and make a tumult and a disturbance among them; (108) and when the armour bearer had readily promised to follow him whithersoever he should lead him, though he should be obliged to die in the attempt, Jonathan made use of the young man's assistance, and descended from the hill, and went to their enemies. Now the enemies' camp was upon a precipice which had three tops, that ended in a small but sharp and long extremity, while there was a rock that surrounded them, like lines made to prevent the attacks of an enemy. (109) There it so happened, that the out-guards of the camp were neglected, because of the security that here arose from the situation of the place, and because they thought it altogether impossible, not only to ascend up to the camp on that quarter, but so much as to come near it. (110) As soon, therefore, as they came to the camp, Jonathan encouraged his armour bearer, and said to him. 'Let us attack our enemies: and if, when they see us, they bid us come up to them, take that for a signal of victory; but if they say nothing as not intending to invite us to come up, let us return back again.' (111) So when they were approaching to the enemy's camp, just after break of day, and the Philistines saw them, they said one to another, 'the Hebrews come out of their dens and caves'; and they said to Jonathan and to his armour bearer, 'Come on, ascend up to us, that we may inflict a just punishment upon you, for your rash attempt upon us.' (112) So Saul's son accepted of that invitation, as what signified to him victory, and he immediately came out of the place whence they were seen by their enemies; so he changed his place, and came to the rock which had none to guard it, because of its own strength; (113) from thence they crept up with great labour and difficulty and so far overcame by force the nature of the place till they were able to fight with their enemies. So they fell upon as they were asleep, and slew about twenty of them, and thereby filled them with disorder and surprise, insomuch that some of them threw away their entire armour and fled; (114) but the greatest part, not knowing one another, because they were of different nations, suspected one another to be enemies (for they did not imagine there were only two of the Hebrews that came up), and so they fought one against another; and some of them died in the battle, and some, as they were flying away, were thrown down from the rock headlong.

(115) Now Saul's watchmen told the king that the camp of the Philistines was in confusion: then he inquired whether anybody was gone away from the army; and when he heard that his son, and with him his armour bearer, were absent, he bade the high priest take the garments of his high priesthood, and prophesy to him what success they should have; who said that they should

get the victory, and prevail against their enemies. So he went out after the Philistines, and set upon them as they were slaying one another. (116) Those also who had fled to dens and caves, upon hearing that Saul was gaining a victory, came running to him. When, therefore, the number of the Hebrews that came to Saul amounted to about ten thousand, he pursued the enemy, who were scattered all over the country; but then he fell into an action, which was a very unhappy one, and liable to be very much blamed; for whether out of ignorance, or whether out of joy for a victory gained so strangely (for it frequently happens that persons so fortunate are not then able to use their reason consistently), (117) as he was desirous to avenge himself, and to exact a due punishment of the Philistines, he denounced a curse upon the Hebrews, that if anyone put a stop to his slaughter of the enemy, and fell on eating, and left off the slaughter or the pursuit before the night came on and obliged them so to do, he should be accursed. (118) Now after Saul had denounced this curse, since they were now in a wood belonging to the tribe of Ephraim, which was thick and full of bees, Saul's son, who did not hear his father denounce that curse, nor hear of the approbation the multitude gave to it, broke off a piece of a honeycomb, and ate part of it. (119) But, in the meantime, he was informed with what a curse his father had forbidden them to taste anything before sunsetting: so he left off eating, and said his father had not done well in this prohibition, because, had they taken some food, they had pursued the enemy with greater vigour and alacrity, and had both taken and slain many more of their enemies.

(120) When, therefore, they had slain many ten thousands of the Philistines, they fell upon spoiling the camp of the Philistines, but not till late in the evening. They also took a great deal of prey and cattle, and killed them, and ate them with their blood. This was told to the king by the scribes, that the multitude were sinning against God as they sacrificed, and were eating before the blood was well washed away, and the flesh was made clean. (121) Then did Saul give order that a great stone should be rolled into the midst of them, and he made proclamation that they should kill their sacrifices upon it, and not feed upon the flesh with the blood, for that was not acceptable to God. And when all the people did as the king commanded them, Saul erected an altar there and offered burnt offerings upon it to God. This was the first altar that Saul built.

(122) So when Saul was desirous of leading his men to the enemy's camp before it was day, in order to plunder it, and when the soldiers were not unwilling to follow him, but indeed showed great readiness to do as he commanded them, the king called Ahitub the high priest, and enjoined him to know of God whether he would grant them the favour and permission to go against the enemy's camp, in order to destroy those that were in it; (123) and when the priest said that God did not give any answer, Saul replied, 'And not

without some cause does God refuse to answer what we inquire of him, while yet a little while ago he declared to us all that we desired beforehand, and even prevented us in his answer. To be sure, there is some sin against him that is concealed from us, which is the occasion of his silence. (124) Now I swear by him himself, that though he hath committed this sin should prove to be my own son Jonathan, I will slay him, and by that means will appease the anger of God against us, and that in the very same manner as if I were to punish a stranger, and one not at all related to me, for the same offence.' (125) So when the multitude cried out to him so to do, he presently set all the rest on one side, and he and his son stood on the other side, and he sought to discover the offender by lot. Now the lot appeared to fall upon Jonathan himself. (126) So when he was asked by his father what sin he had been guilty of, and what he was conscious of in the course of his life that might be esteemed instances of guilt or profaneness, his answer was this: 'O father, I have done nothing more than that yesterday, without knowing of the curse and oath thou hadst denounced, while I was in pursuit of the enemy, I tasted of a honeycomb.' But Saul sware that he would slay him, and prefer the observation of his oath before all the ties of birth and of nature; (127) and Jonathan was not dismayed at this threatening of death, but, offering himself to it generously, and undauntedly, he said, 'Nor do I desire you, father, to spare me: death will be to me very acceptable, when it proceed from thy piety, and after a glorious victory; for it is the greatest consolation to me that I leave the Hebrews victorious over the Philistines.' (128) Hereupon all the people were very sorry, and greatly afflicted for Jonathan; and they sware that they would not overlook Jonathan, and see him die, who was the author of their victory. By which means they snatched him out of the danger he was in from his father's curse, while they made their prayers to God also for the young man, that he would remit his sin.

(129) So Saul, having slain about sixty thousand of the enemy, returned home to his own city, and reigned happily: and he also fought against the neighbouring nations, and subdued the Ammonites, and Moabites, and Philistines, and Edomites, and Amalekites, as also the king of Zobah. He had three male children, Jonathan and Isui and Melchishua; with Merab and Michal, his daughters. He had also Abner, his uncle's son, for the captain of his host: (130) that uncle's name was Ner. Now Ner, and Kish the father of Saul, were brothers. Saul had also a great many chariots and horsemen, and against whomsoever he made war he returned conqueror, and advanced the affairs of the Hebrews to a great degree of success and prosperity, and made them superior to other nations; and he made such of the young men as were remarkable for tallness and comeliness the guards of his body.

CHAPTER 7

(131) Now Samuel came unto Saul, and said to him, that he was sent by God to put him in mind that God had preferred him before all others, and ordained him king; that he therefore ought to be obedient to him, and to submit to his authority, as considering, that though he had the dominion over the other tribes, yet that God had the dominion over him, and over all things; (132) that accordingly God said to him, that 'because the Amalekites did the Hebrews a great deal of mischief while they were in the wilderness, and when, upon their coming out of Egypt, they were making their way to that country which is now their own, I enjoin thee to punish the Amalekites, by making war upon them; and when thou hast subdued them, to leave none of them alive, (133) but to pursue them through every age, and to slay them, beginning with the women and the infants, and to require this as a punishment to be inflicted upon them for the mischief they did to our forefathers: to spare nothing, neither asses nor other beasts; nor to reserve any of them for your own advantage and possession, but to devote them universally to God, and, in obedience to the commands of Moses, to blot out the name of Amalek entirely.'

(134) So Saul promised to do what he was commanded; and supposing that his obedience to God would be shown, not only in making war against the Amalekites, but more fully in the readiness and quickness of his proceedings, he made no delay, but immediately gathered together all his forces; and when he had numbered them in Gilgal, he found them to be about four hundred thousand of the Israelites, besides the tribe of Judah, for that tribe contained by itself thirty thousand. (135) Accordingly Saul made an irruption into the country of the Amalekites, and set many men in several parties in ambush at the river, that so he might not only do them a mischief, by open fighting, but might fall upon them unexpectedly in the ways, and might thereby compass them round about and kill them. (136) And when he had joined battle with the enemy, he beat them; and pursuing them as they fled, he destroyed them all. And when that undertaking had succeeded, according as God had foretold, he set upon the cities of the Amalekites; he besieged them, and took them by force, partly by warlike machines, partly by mines dug under ground, and partly by building walls on the outsides. Some they starved out with famine, and some they gained by other methods; and after all, he betook himself to slay the women and the children, and thought he did not act therein either barbarously or inhumanly; first, because they were enemies whom he thus treated, and, in the next place, because it was done by the command of God, whom it was dangerous not to obey. (137) He also took Agag, the enemies' king, captive – the beauty and tallness of whose body he admired so much, that

he thought him worthy of preservation; yet was not this done however according to the will of God, but by giving way to human passions, and suffering himself to be moved with an unseasonable commiseration, in a point where it was not safe for him to indulge it; (138) for God hated the nation of the Amalekites to such a degree, that he commanded Saul to have no pity on even those infants which we by nature chiefly compassionate; but Saul preserved their king and governor from the miseries which the Hebrews brought on the people, as if he preferred the fine appearance of the enemy to the memory of what God had sent him about. (139) The multitude were also guilty, together with Saul; for they spared the herds and the flocks, and took them for a prey, when God had commanded they should not spare them. They also carried off with them the rest of their wealth and riches; but if there were anything that was not worthy of regard, that they destroyed.

(140) But when Saul had conquered all these Amalekites that reached from Pelusium of Egypt to the Red Sea, he laid waste all the rest of the enemy's country; but for the nation of the Shechemites, he did not touch them, although they dwelt in the very middle of the country of Midian; for before the battle, Saul had sent to them, and charged them to depart thence, lest they should be partakers of the miseries of the Amalekites; for he had a just occasion for saving them, since they were of the kindred of Raguel, Moses' father-in-law.

(141) Hereupon Saul returned home with joy, for the glorious things he had done, and for the conquest of his enemies, as though he had not neglected anything which the prophet had enjoined him to do when he was going to make war with the Amalekites, and as though he had exactly observed all that he ought to have done. (142) But God was grieved that the king of the Amalekites was preserved alive, and that the multitude had seized on the cattle for a prey, because these things were done without his permission; for he thought it an intolerable thing that they should conquer and overcome their enemies by that power which he gave them, and then that he himself should be so grossly despised and disobeyed by them, that a mere man that was a king would not bear it. (143) He therefore told Samuel the prophet, that he repented that he had made Saul king, while he did nothing that he had commanded him, but indulged his own inclinations. When Samuel heard that, he was in confusion; and began to beseech God all that night to be reconciled to Saul, and not to be angry with him; (144) but he did not grant that forgiveness to Saul which the prophet asked for, as not deeming it a fit thing to grant forgiveness of [such] sins at his entreaties, since injuries do not otherwise grow so great as by the easy tempers of those that are injured; for while they hunt after the glory of being thought gentle and good-natured, before they are aware, they produce other sins. (145) As soon therefore as God had rejected the intercession of the prophet, and it plainly appeared he would not change

his mind, at break of day Samuel came to Saul at Gilgal. When the king saw him, he ran to him, and embraced him, and said, 'I return thanks to God, who hath given me the victory, for I have performed everything that he hath commanded me.' (146) To which Samuel replied, 'How is it then that I hear the bleating of the sheep and the lowing of the greater cattle in the camp?' Saul made answer, that the people had reserved them for sacrifices; but that, as to the nation of the Amalekites, it was entirely destroyed, as he had received it in command to see done, and that no one man was left; but that he had saved alive the king alone, and brought him to him, concerning whom, he said they would advise together what should be done with him. (147) But the prophet said, 'God is not delighted with sacrifices, but with good and with righteous men, who are such as follow his will and his laws, and never think that anything is well done by them but when they do it as God had commanded them; that he then looks upon himself as affronted, not when anyone does not sacrifice, but when anyone appears to be disobedient to him. (148) But that from those who do not obey him, nor pay him that duty which is the alone true and acceptable worship, he will not kindly accept their oblations, be those they offer ever so many and so fat, and be the presents they make him ever so ornamental, nay, though they were made of gold and silver themselves, but he will reject them, and esteem them instances of wickedness, and not of piety. (149) And that he is delighted with those that still bear in mind this one thing, and this only, how to do that, whatsoever it be, which God pronounces or commands for them to do, and to choose rather to die than to transgress any of those commands; nor does he require so much as a sacrifice from them. And when these do sacrifice, though it be a mean oblation, he better accepts of it as the honour of poverty than such oblations as come from the richest men that offer them to him. (150) Wherefore take notice, that thou art under the wrath of God, for thou hast despised and neglected what he commanded thee. How dost thou then suppose that he will respect a sacrifice out of such things as he hath doomed to destruction, unless perhaps thou dost imagine that it is almost all one to offer it in sacrifice to God as to destroy it? Do thou therefore expect that thy kingdom will be taken from thee, and that authority which thou hast abused by such insolent behaviour, as to neglect that God who bestowed it upon thee.' (151) Then did Saul confess that he had acted unjustly, and did not deny that he had sinned, because he had transgressed the injunctions of the prophet; but he said that it was out of a dread and fear of the soldiers, that he did not prohibit and restrain them when they seized on the prey. 'But forgive me,' said he, 'and be merciful to me, for I will be cautious how I offend for the time to come.' He also entreated the prophet to go back with him, that he might offer his thank offerings to God; but Samuel went home, because he saw that God would not be reconciled to him.

(152) But then Saul was so desirous to retain Samuel, that he took hold of his cloak, and because the vehemence of Samuel's departure made the motion to be violent, the cloak was rent. (153) Upon which the prophet said, that after the same manner should the kingdom be rent from him, and that a good and a just man should take it; that God persevered in what he had decreed about him: that to be mutable and changeable in what is determined, is agreeable to human passions only, but is not agreeable to the Divine Power. (154) Hereupon Saul said that he had been wicked; but that what was done could not be undone; he therefore desired him to honour him so far, that the multitude might see that he would accompany him in worshipping God. So Samuel granted him that favour, and went with him and worshipped God. (155) Agag also, the king of the Amalekites, was brought to him; and when the king asked, How bitter death was? Samuel said, 'As thou hast made many of the Hebrew mothers to lament and bewail the loss of their children, so shalt thou, by thy death, cause thy mother to lament thee also.' Accordingly he gave order to slay him immediately at Gilgal, and then went away to the city Ramah.

CHAPTER 8

(156) Now Saul being sensible of the miserable condition he had brought himself into, and that he had made God to be his enemy, he went up to his royal palace at Gibeah, which name denotes a *hill*, and after that day he came no more into the presence of the prophet. (157) And when Samuel mourned for him, God bid him leave off his concern for him, and to take the holy oil, and go to Bethlehem, to Jesse the son of Obed, and to anoint such of his sons as he should show him for their future king. But Samuel said, he was afraid lest Saul, when he came to know of it, should kill him, either by some private method or even openly. But upon God's suggesting to him a safe way of going thither, he came to the forementioned city; (158) and when they all saluted him, and asked what was the occasion of his coming, he told them he came to sacrifice to God. When, therefore, he had gotten the sacrifice ready, he called Jesse and his sons to partake of those sacrifices; and when he saw his eldest son to be a tall and handsome man, he guessed by his comeliness that he was the person who was to be their future king. (159) But he was mistaken in judging about God's providence; for when Samuel inquired of God whether he should anoint this youth, whom he so admired, and esteemed worthy of the kingdom, God said, 'Men do not see as God seeth. (160) Thou indeed hast respect to the fine appearance of this youth, and thence esteemest him worthy of the kingdom, while I propose the kingdom as a reward, not of the beauty of bodies, but of the virtue of souls, and I inquire after one that is perfectly comely in that respect; I mean one who is beautiful in piety and righteousness, and fortitude and

obedience; for in them consists the comeliness of the soul.' (161) When God had said this, Samuel bade Jesse to show him all his sons. So he made five others of his sons to come to him; of all of whom Eliab was the eldest, Aminadab the second, Shammah the third, Nathaniel the fourth, Rael the fifth, and Asam the sixth. (162) And when the prophet saw that these were no way inferior to the eldest in their countenances, he inquired of God which of them it was whom he chose for their king; and when God said it was none of them, he asked Jesse whether he had not some other sons besides these; (163) and when he said that he had one more, named David, but that he was a shepherd, and took care of the flocks, Samuel bade them call him immediately, for that till he was come they could not possibly sit down to the feast. (164) Now, as soon as his father had sent for David, and he was come, he appeared to be of a yellow complexion, of a sharp sight, and a comely person in other respects also. This is he, said Samuel privately to himself, whom it pleases God to make our king. So he sat down to the feast, and placed the youth under him, and Jesse also, with his other sons; (165) after which he took oil in the presence of David, and anointed him, and whispered him in the ear, and acquainted him that God chose him to be their king; and exhorted him to be righteous, and obedient to his commands, for that by this means his kingdom would continue for a long time, and that his house should be of great splendour, and celebrated in the world; that he should overthrow the Philistines, and that against what nations soever he should make war, he should be the conqueror, and survive the fight; and that while he lived he should enjoy a glorious name and leave such a name to his posterity also.

(166) So Samuel, when he had given him these admonitions, went away. But the Divine Power departed from Saul, and removed to David, who upon this removal of the Divine Spirit to him, began to prophesy; but as for Saul, some strange and demoniacal disorders came upon him, and brought upon him such suffocations as were ready to choke him; for which the physicians could find no other remedy but this, that if any person could charm those passions by singing, and playing upon the harp, they advised them to inquire for such a one, and to observe when these demons came upon him and disturbed him, and to take care that such a person might stand over him, and play upon the harp, and recite hymns to him. (167) Accordingly Saul did not delay, but commanded them to seek out such a man; and when a certain stander-by said that he had seen in the city of Bethlehem a son of Jesse, who was yet no more than a child in age, but comely and beautiful, and in other respects one that was deserving of great regard, who was skilful in playing on the harp, and in singing of hymns [and an excellent soldier in war], he sent to Jesse, and desired him to take David away from the flocks, and send him to him, for he had a mind to see him, as having heard an advantageous character of his comeliness and his valour. (168) So Jesse sent his son, and gave him

presents to carry to Saul; and when he was come, Saul was pleased with him, and made him his armour bearer, and had him in very great esteem; for he charmed his passion, and was the only physician against the trouble he had from the demons, whensoever it was that it came upon him, and this by reciting of hymns, and playing upon the harp, and bringing Saul to his right mind again. (169) However, he sent to Jesse, the father of the child, and desired him to permit David to stay with him, for that he was delighted with his sight and company; which stay, that he might not contradict Saul, he granted.

CHAPTER 9

(170) Now the Philistines gathered themselves together again, no very long time afterward; and having gotten together a great army, they made war against the Israelites; and having seized a place between Shochoh and Azekah, they there pitched their camp. Saul also drew out his army to oppose them; and by pitching his own camp upon a certain hill, he forced the Philistines to leave their former camp, and to encamp themselves upon such another hill, over against that on which Saul's army lay, (171) so that a valley, which was between the two hills on which they lay, divided their camps asunder. Now there came down a man out of the camp of the Philistines, whose name was Goliath, of the city of Gath, a man of vast bulk, for he was of four cubits and a span in tallness, and had about him weapons suitable to the largeness of his body, for he had a breastplate on that weighed five thousand shekels: he had also a helmet and greaves of brass, as large as you would naturally suppose might cover the limbs of so vast a body. His spear was also such as was not carried like a light thing in his right hand, but he carried it as lying on his shoulders. He had also a lance of six hundred shekels; and many followed him to carry his armour. (172) Wherefore this Goliath stood between the two armies, as they were in battle array, and sent out a loud voice, and said to Saul and the Hebrews, 'I will free you from fighting and from dangers; for what necessity is there that your army should fall and be afflicted? (173) Give me a man of you that will fight with me, and he that conquers shall have the reward of the conqueror, and determine the war; for these shall serve those others to whom the conqueror shall belong; and certainly it is much better and more prudent to gain what you desire by the hazard of one man than of all.' (174) When he had said this, he retired to his own camp; but the next day he came again, and used the same words, and did not leave off for forty days together, to challenge the enemy in the same words, till Saul and his army were therewith terrified, while they put themselves in array as if they would fight, but did not come to a close battle.

(175) Now while this war between the Hebrews and the Philistines was

going on, Saul sent away David to his father Jesse, and contented himself with those three sons of his whom he had sent to his assistance, and to be partners in the dangers of the war; (176) and at first David returned to feed his sheep and his flocks; but after no long time he came to the camp of the Hebrews, as sent by his father, to carry provisions to his brethren, and to know what they were doing, (177) while Goliath came again, and challenged them and reproached them, that they had no man of valour among them that durst come down to fight him; and as David was talking with his brethren about the business for which his father had sent him, he heard the Philistines reproaching and abusing the army, and had indignation at it, and said to his brethren, 'I am ready to fight a single combat with this adversary.' (178) Whereupon Eliab, his eldest brother, reproved him, and said that he spake too rashly and improperly for one of his age, and bid him go to his flocks, and to his father. So he was abashed at his brother's words, and went away, but still he spake to some of the soldiers that he was willing to fight with him that challenged them. (179) And when they had informed Saul what was the resolution of the young man, the king sent for him to come to him; and when the king asked what he had to say, he replied, 'O king, be not cast down, nor afraid, for I will depress the insolence of this adversary, and will go down and fight with him, and will bring him under me, as tall and as great as he is, till he shall be sufficiently laughed at, (180) and thy army shall get great glory when he shall be slain by one that is not yet of man's estate, neither fit for fighting, nor capable of being entrusted with the marshalling an army, or ordering a battle, but by one that looks like a child, and is really no elder in age than a child.'

(181) Now Saul wondered at the boldness and alacrity of David, but durst not presume on his ability, by reason of his age; but said, he must on that account be too weak to fight with one that was skilled in the art of war. 'I undertake this enterprise,' said David, 'in dependence on God's being with me, for I have had experience already of his assistance; (182) for I once pursued after and caught a lion that assaulted my flocks and took away a lamb from them, and I snatched the lamb out of the wild beast's mouth, and when he leaped upon me with violence, I took him by the tail, and dashed him against the ground. (183) In the same manner did I avenge myself on a bear also; and let this adversary of ours be esteemed like one of these wild beasts, since he has a long while reproached our army and blasphemed our God, who yet will reduce him under my power.'

(184) However, Saul prayed that the end might be, by God's assistance, not disagreeable to the alacrity and boldness of the child; and said, 'Go thy way to the fight.' So he put about him his breastplate, and girded on his sword, and fitted the helmet to his head, and sent him away. (185) But David was burdened with his armour, for he had not been exercised to it, nor had he

learned to walk with it; so he said, 'Let this armour be thine, O king, who art able to bear it; but give me leave to fight as thy servant, and as I myself desire.' Accordingly he laid by the armour, and taking his staff with him, and putting five stones out of the brook into a shepherd's bag, and having a sling in his right hand, he went toward Goliath. (186) But the adversary seeing him come in such a manner, disdained him, and jested upon him, as if he had not such weapons with him as are usual when one man fights against another, but such as are used in driving away and avoiding of dogs; and said, 'Dost thou take me not for a man, but a dog?' To which he replied, 'No, not for a dog, but for a creature worse than a dog.' This provoked Goliath to anger, who thereupon cursed him by the name of God, and threatened to give his flesh to the beasts of the earth, and to the fowls of the air, to be torn in pieces by them. (187) To whom David answered, 'Thou comest to me with a sword, and with a spear, and with a breastplate; but I have God for my armour in coming against thee, who will destroy thee and all thy army by my hands; for I will this day cut off thy head and cast the other parts of thy body to the dogs; and all men shall learn that God is the protector of the Hebrews, and that our armour and our strength is in his providence; and that without God's assistance all other warlike preparations and power are useless.' (188) So the Philistine being retarded by the weight of his armour, when he attempted to meet David in haste, came on but slowly, as despising him, and depending upon it that he should slay him who was both unarmed and a child also, without any trouble at all.

(189) But the youth met his antagonist being accompanied with an invisible assistant, who was not other than God himself. And taking one of the stones that he had out of the brook, and had put into his shepherd's bag, and fitting it to his sling, he slang it against the Philistine. This stone fell upon his forehead, and sank into his brain, insomuch that Goliath was stunned, and fell upon his face. (190) So David ran, and stood upon his adversary as he lay down, and cut off his head with his own sword; for he had no sword himself. (191) And upon the fall of Goliath, the Philistines were beaten, and fled; for when they saw their champion prostrate on the ground, they were afraid of the entire issue of their affairs, and resolved not to stay any longer, but committed themselves to an ignominious and indecent flight, and thereby endeavoured to save themselves from the dangers they were in. But Saul and the entire army of the Hebrews made a shout and rushed upon them, and slew a great number of them, and pursued the rest to the borders of Gath, and to the gates of Ekron; (192) so that there were slain of the Philistines thirty thousand and twice as many wounded. But Saul returned to their camp and pulled their fortifications to pieces, and burnt it; but David carried the head of Goliath into his own tent, but dedicated his sword to God [at the tabernacle].

CHAPTER 10

(193) Now the women were an occasion of Saul's envy and hatred to David; for they came to meet their victorious army with cymbals and drums, and all demonstrations of joy, and sang thus: the wives said, that 'Saul had slain his many thousands of the Philistines:' the virgins replied, that 'David had slain his ten thousands.' (194) Now, when the king heard them singing thus, and that he had himself the smallest share in their commendations, and the greater number, the ten thousands, were ascribed to the young man; and when he considered with himself that there was nothing more wanting to David, after such a mighty applause, but the kingdom, he began to be afraid and suspicious of David. (195) Accordingly he removed him from the station he was in before, for he was his armour bearer, which out of fear seemed to him much too near a station for him; and so he made him captain over a thousand, and bestowed on him a post better indeed in itself, but, as he thought, more for his own security; for he had a mind to send him against the enemy, and into battles, as hoping he would be slain in such dangerous conflicts.

(196) But David had God going along with him whithersoever he went, and accordingly he greatly prospered in his undertakings, and it was visible that he had mighty success, insomuch that Saul's daughter, who was still a virgin, fell in love with him; and her affection so far prevailed over her, that it could not be concealed, and her father became acquainted with it. (197) Now Saul heard this gladly, as intending to make use of it for a snare against David, and he hoped that it would prove the cause of destruction and of hazard to him; so he told those that informed him of his daughter's affection, that he would willingly give David the virgin in marriage, and said, 'I engage myself to marry my daughter to him if he will bring me six hundred heads of my enemies, (198) supposing that when a reward so ample was proposed to him, and when he should aim to get him great glory, by undertaking a thing so dangerous and incredible, he would immediately set about it, and so perish by the Philistines; and my designs about him will succeed finely to my mind for I shall be freed from him, and get him slain, not by myself, but by another man.' (199) So he gave order to his servants to try how David would relish this proposal of marrying the damsel. Accordingly, they began to speak thus to him: that King Saul loved him, as well as did all the people, and that he was desirous of his affinity by the marriage of this damsel. (200) To which he gave this answer: 'Seemeth it to you a light thing to be made the king's son-in-law? It does not seem so to me, especially when I am one of a family that is low, and without any glory or honour.' Now when Saul was informed by his servants what answer David had made, he said, 'Tell him, that I do not want any money nor

dowry from him, which would be rather to set my daughter to sale than to give her in marriage; but I desire only such a son-in-law as hath in him fortitude, and all other kinds of virtue,' of which he saw David was possessed, (201) and that his desire was to receive of him, on account of his marrying his daughter, neither gold nor silver, nor that he should bring such wealth out of his father's house, but only some revenge on the Philistines, and indeed six hundred of their heads, (202) than which a more desirable or a more glorious present could not be brought him; and that he had much rather obtain this than any of the accustomed dowries for his daughter, viz., that she should be married to a man of that character, and to one who had a testimony as having conquered his enemies.

(203) When these words of Saul were brought to David, he was pleased with them, and supposed that Saul was really desirous of this affinity with him; so that without bearing to deliberate any longer, or casting about in his mind whether what was proposed was possible, or was difficult or not, he and his companions immediately set upon the enemy, and went about doing what was proposed as the condition of the marriage. Accordingly, because it was God who made all things easy and possible to David, he slew many [of the Philistines], and cut off the heads of six hundred of them, and came to the king, and by showing him these heads of the Philistines, required that he might have his daughter in marriage. (204) Accordingly Saul, having no way of getting off his engagements, as thinking it a base thing either to seem a liar when he promised him this marriage, or to appear to have acted treacherously by him in putting him upon what was in a manner impossible, in order to have him slain, he gave him his daughter in marriage: her name was Michal.

CHAPTER 11

(205) However, Saul was not disposed to persevere long in the state wherein he was; for when he saw that David was in great esteem both with God and with the multitude, he was afraid; and being not able to conceal his fear as concerning great things, his kingdom and his life, to be deprived of either of which was a very great calamity, he resolved to have David slain; and commanded his son Jonathan and his most faithful servants to kill him: (206) but Jonathan wondered at his father's change with relation to David, that it should be made to so great a degree, from showing him no small good will to contrive how to have him killed. Now, because he loved the young man, and reverenced him for his virtue, he informed him of the secret charge his father had given, and what his intentions were concerning him. (207) However, he advised him to take care and be absent the next day, for that he would salute his father, and, if he met with a favourable opportunity, he would discourse

with him about him, and learn the cause of his disgust, and show how little
ground there was for it, (208) and that for it he ought not to kill a man that had
done so many good things to the multitude, and had been a benefactor to
himself, on account of which he ought in reason to obtain pardon, had he
been guilty of the greatest crimes: and 'I will then inform thee of my father's
resolution.' Accordingly David complied with such an advantageous advice,
and kept himself then out of the king's sight.

(209) On the next day Jonathan came to Saul, as soon as he saw him in a
cheerful and joyful disposition, and began to introduce a discourse about
David: 'What unjust action, O father, either little or great, hast thou found so
exceptionable in David, as to induce thee to order us to slay a man who hath
been of great advantage to thy own preservation, and of still greater to the
punishment of the Philistines? (210) A man who hath delivered the people of
the Hebrews from reproach and derision, which they underwent for forty days
together, when he alone had courage enough to sustain the challenge of the
adversary, and after that brought as many heads of our enemies as he was
appointed to bring, and had, as a reward for the same, my sister in marriage;
insomuch that his death would be very sorrowful to us, not only on account of
his virtue, but on account of the nearness of our relation; for thy daughter must
be injured at the same time that he is slain, and must be obliged to experience
widowhood before she can come to enjoy any advantage from their mutual
conversation. (211) Consider these things, and change your mind to a more
merciful temper, and do no mischief to a man who, in the first place, hath done
us the greatest kindness of preserving thee; for when an evil spirit and demons
had seized upon thee, he cast them out, and procured rest to thy soul from
their incursions; and, in the second place, hath avenged us of our enemies; for
it is a base thing to forget such benefits.' (212) So Saul was pacified with these
words; and sware to his son that he would do David no harm, for righteous
discourse proved too hard for the king's anger and fear; so Jonathan sent for
David, and brought him good news from his father, that he was to be
preserved. He also brought him to his father; and David continued with the
king as formerly.

(213) About this time it was that, upon the Philistines making a new
expedition against the Hebrews, Saul sent David with an army to fight with
them; and joining battle with them he slew many of them, and after his victory
he returned to the king. But his reception by Saul was not as he expected upon
such success, for he was grieved at his prosperity, because he thought he would
be more dangerous to him by having acted so gloriously; (214) but when the
demoniacal spirit came upon him, and put him into disorder, and disturbed
him, he called for David into his bed chamber wherein he lay, and having a
spear in his hand, he ordered him to charm him with playing on his harp, and

with singing hymns; which when David did at his command, he with great force threw the spear at him; but David was aware of it before it came, and avoided it, and fled to his own house, and abode there all that day.

(215) But at night the king sent officers, and commanded that he should be watched till the morning, lest he should get quite away, that he might come into the judgment hall, and so might be delivered up, and condemned and slain. But when Michal, David's wife, the king's daughter, understood what her father designed, she came to her husband, as having small hopes of his deliverance, and as greatly concerned about her own life also, for she could not bear to live in case she were deprived of him; and she said, (216) 'Let not the sun find thee here when it rises, for if it do, that will be the last time it will see thee: fly away then while the night may afford thee opportunity, and may God lengthen it for thy sake! For know this, that if my father find thee, thou art a dead man.' (217) So she let him down by a cord out of the window, and saved him: and after she had done so, she fitted up a bed for him as if he were sick, and put under the bed clothes a goat's liver; and when her father, as soon as it was day, sent to seize David, she said to those that were there, that he had not been well that night, and showed them the bed covered, and made them believe, by the leaping of the liver, which caused the bed clothes to move also, that David breathed like one that was asthmatic. (218) So when those that were sent told Saul that David had not been well in the night, he ordered him to be brought in that condition, for he intended to kill him. Now when they came, and uncovered the bed, and found out the woman's contrivance, they told it to the king; (219) and when her father complained of her that she had saved his enemy, and had put a trick upon himself, she invented this plausible defence for herself, and said, that when he threatened to kill her, she lent him her assistance for his preservation, out of fear; for which her assistance she ought to be forgiven, because it was not done of her own free choice, but out of necessity: 'For,' said she, 'I do not suppose that thou wast so zealous to kill thy enemy, as thou wast that I should be saved.' Accordingly Saul forgave the damsel; (220) but David, when he had escaped this danger, came to the prophet Samuel to Ramah, and told him what snares the king had laid for him, and how he was very near to death by Saul's throwing a spear at him, although he had been no way guilty with relation to him, nor had he been cowardly in his battles with his enemies, but had succeeded well in them all, by God's assistance; which thing was indeed the cause of Saul's hatred to David.

(221) When the prophet was made acquainted with the unjust proceedings of the king, he left the city Ramah, and took David with him, to a certain place called Naioth, and there he abode with him. But when it was told Saul that David was with the prophet, he sent soldiers to him, and ordered them to take him, and bring him to him; (222) and when they came to Samuel, and found

there a congregation of prophets, they became partakers of the Divine Spirit, and began to prophesy; which when Saul heard of, he sent others to David, who prophesying in like manner as did the first, he again sent others; which third sort prophesying also, at last he was angry, and went thither in great haste himself; (223) and when he was just by the place, Samuel, before he saw him, made him prophesy also. And when Saul came to him, he was disordered in mind, and under the vehement agitation of a spirit; and, putting off his garments, he fell down, and lay on the ground all that day and night, in the presence of Samuel and David.

(224) And David went thence, and came to Jonathan, the son of Saul, and lamented to him what snares were laid for him by his father; and said, that though he had been guilty of no evil, nor had offended against him, yet he was very zealous to get him killed. Hereupon Jonathan exhorted him not to give credit to such his own suspicions, nor to the calumnies of those that raised those reports, if there were any that did so, but to depend on him, and take courage; for that his father had no such intentions, since he would have acquainted him with that matter, and have taken his advice, had it been so, as he used to consult with him in common when he acted in other affairs. (225) But David sware to him that so it was; and he desired him rather to believe him, and to provide for his safety, than to despise what he, with great sincerity, told him: that he would believe what he said, when he should either see him killed himself, or learn it upon inquiry from others: and that the reason why his father did not tell him of these things, was this, that he knew of the friendship and affection that he bore towards him.

(226) Hereupon, when Jonathan found that this intention of Saul was so well attested, he asked him what he would have him do for him? To which David replied, 'I am sensible that thou art willing to gratify me in everything, and procure me what I desire. Now, tomorrow is the new moon, and I was accustomed to sit down then with the king at supper: (227) now, if it seem good to thee, I will go out of the city, and conceal myself privately there; and if Saul inquire why I am absent, tell him that I am gone to my own city Bethlehem, to keep a festival with my own tribe; and add this also, that thou gavest me leave so to do. And if he say, as is usually said in the case of friends that are gone abroad, It is well that he went, then assure thyself that no latent mischief or enmity may be feared at his hand; but if he answers otherwise, that will be a sure sign that he hath some designs against me. (228) Accordingly thou shalt inform me of thy father's inclinations; and that, out of pity to my case and out of thy friendship for me, as instances of which friendship thou hast vouchsafed to accept of the assurances of my love to thee, and to give the like assurances to me, that is, those of a master to his servant; but if thou discoverest any wickedness in me, do thou prevent thy father, and kill me thyself.'

(229) But Jonathan heard these last words with indignation, and promised to do what he desired of him, and to inform him if his father's answers implied anything of a melancholy nature, and any enmity against him. And that he might the more firmly depend upon him, he took him out into the open field, into the pure air, and sware that he would neglect nothing that might tend to the preservation of David; (230) and he said, 'I appeal to that God, who, as thou seest, is diffused everywhere, and knoweth this intention of mine, before I explain it in words, as the witness of this my covenant with thee, that I will not leave off to make frequent trials of the purpose of my father till I learn whether there be any lurking distemper in the most secret parts of his soul; (231) and when I have learnt it, I will not conceal it from thee, but will discover it to thee, whether he be gently or peevishly disposed; for this God himself knows, that I pray he may always be with thee, for he is with thee now, and will not forsake thee, and will make thee superior to thine enemies, whether my father be one of them, or whether I myself be such. (232) Do thou only remember what we now do; and if it fall out that I die, preserve my children alive, and requite what kindness thou hast now received, to them.' When he had thus sworn, he dismissed David, bidding him go to a certain place of that plain wherein he used to perform his exercises; for that, as soon as he knew the mind of his father, he would come thither to him, with one servant only; (233) 'and if,' says he, 'I shoot three darts at the mark, and then bid my servant to carry these three darts away for they are before him, know thou that there is no mischief to be feared from my father; but if thou hearest me say the contrary, expect the contrary from the king. (234) However, thou shalt gain security by my means, and shalt by no means suffer any harm; but see thou dost not forget what I have desired of thee in the time of thy prosperity, and be serviceable to my children.' Now David, when he had received these assurances from Jonathan, went his way to the place appointed.

(235) But on the next day, which was the new moon, the king, when he had purified himself, as the custom was, came to supper; and when there sat by him his son Jonathan on his right hand, and Abner, the captain of his host, on the other hand, he saw David's seat was empty, but said nothing, supposing that he had not purified himself since he had accompanied with his wife, and so could not be present; (236) but when he saw that he was not there the second day of the month neither, he inquired of his son Jonathan why the son of Jesse did not come to the supper and the feast, neither the day before nor that day. So Jonathan said that he was gone, according to the agreement between them, to his own city, where his tribe kept a festival, and that by his permission; that he also invited him to come to their sacrifice; 'and,' says Jonathan, 'if thou wilt give me leave, I will go thither, for thou knowest the good will that I bear him;' (237) and then it was that Jonathan understood his father's hatred to

David, and plainly saw his entire disposition; for Saul could not restrain his anger, but reproached Jonathan, and called him the son of a runagate, and an enemy; and said he was a partner with David, and his assistant, and that by his behaviour he showed he had no regard to himself or to his mother, and would not be persuaded of this, that while David is alive, their kingdom was not secure to them; yet did he bid him send for him, that he might be punished; (238) and when Jonathan said, in answer, 'what hath he done that thou wilt punish him?' Saul no longer contented himself to express his anger in bare words, but snatched up his spear, and leaped upon him, and was desirous to kill him. He did not indeed do what he intended, because he was hindered by his friends; but it appeared plainly to his son that he hated David, and greatly desired to despatch him, insomuch that he had almost slain his son with his own hands on his account.

(239) And then it was that the king's son rose hastily from supper; and being unable to admit anything into his mouth for grief, he wept all night, both because he had himself been near destruction, and because the death of David was determined; but as soon as it was day, he went out into the plain that was before the city, as going to perform his exercises, but in reality to inform his friend what disposition his father was in towards him, as he had agreed with him to do; (240) and when Jonathan had done what had been thus agreed, he dismissed his servant that followed him, to return to the city; but he himself went into the desert, and came into his presence, and communed with him. So David appeared and fell at Jonathan's feet, and bowed down to him, and called him the preserver of his soul; (241) but he lifted him up from the earth, and they mutually embraced one another, and made a long greeting, and that not without tears. They also lamented their age, and that familiarity which envy would deprive them of, and that separation which must now be expected, which seemed to them no better than death itself. So recollecting themselves at length from their lamentation, and exhorting one another to be mindful of the oaths they had sworn to each other, they parted asunder.

CHAPTER I2

(242) But David fled from the king, and that death he was in danger of by him, and came to the city Nob, to Ahimelech the priest, who, when he saw him coming all alone, and neither a friend nor a servant with him, he wondered at it, and desired to learn of him the cause why there was nobody with him. (243) To which David answered, that the king had commanded him to do a certain thing that was to be kept secret, to which, if he had a mind to know so much, he had no occasion for anyone to accompany him; 'however, I have ordered my servants to meet me at such and such a place.' So he desired him to let him

have somewhat to eat; and that in case he would supply him, be would act the part of a friend, and be assisting to the business he was now about; (244) and when he had obtained what he desired, he also asked him whether he had any weapons with him, either sword or spear. Now there was at Nob a servant of Saul, by birth a Syrian, whose name was Doeg, one that kept the king's mules. The high priest said that he had no such weapons; but, he added, 'Here is the sword of Goliath, which, when thou hadst slain the Philistine, thou didst dedicate to God.'

(245) When David had received the sword, he fled out of the country of the Hebrews into that of the Philistines, over which Achish reigned; and when the king's servants knew him, and he was made known to the king himself, the servants informing him that he was that David who had killed many ten thousands of the Philistines, David was afraid lest the king should put him to death, and that he should experience that danger from him which he had escaped from Saul; so he pretended to be distracted and mad, so that his spittle ran out of his mouth; and he did other the like actions before the king of Gath, which might make him believe that they proceeded from such a distemper. (246) Accordingly the king was very angry at his servants that they had brought him a madman, and he gave orders that they should eject David immediately [out of the city].

(247) So when David had escaped in this manner out of Gath, he came to the tribe of Judah, and abode in a cave by the city of Adullam. Then it was that he sent to his brethren, and informed them where he was, who then came to him with all their kindred, and as many others as were either in want or in fear of King Saul, came and made a body together, and told him they were ready to obey his orders; they were in all about four hundred. (248) Whereupon he took courage, now such a force and assistance was come to him; so he removed thence, and came to the king of the Moabites, and desired him to entertain his parents in his country while the issue of his affairs were in such an uncertain condition. The king granted him this favour, and paid great respect to David's parents all the time they were with him.

(249) As for himself, upon the prophet's commanding him to leave the desert, and to go into the portion of the tribe of Judah, and abide there, he complied therewith; and coming to the city Hareth, which was in that tribe, he remained there. (250) Now when Saul heard that David had been seen with a multitude about him, he fell into no small disturbance and trouble; but as he knew that David was a bold and courageous man, he suspected that somewhat extraordinary would appear from him, and that openly also, which would make him weep and put him into distress; (251) so he called together to him his friends and his commanders, and the tribe from which he was himself derived, to the hill where his palace was; and sitting upon a place called Aroura, his

courtiers that were in dignities, and the guards of his body, being with him, he spake thus to them: 'You that are men of my own tribe, I conclude that you remember the benefits that I have bestowed upon you, and that I have made some of you owners of land, and made you commanders, and bestowed posts of honour upon you, and set some of you over the common people, and others over the soldiers; (252) I ask you, therefore, whether you expect greater and more donations from the son of Jesse? for I know that you are all inclinable to him (even my own son Jonathan himself is of that opinion, and persuades you to be of the same); (253) for I am not unacquainted with the oaths and the covenants that are between him and David, and that Jonathan is a counsellor, and an assistant to those that conspire against me, and none of you are concerned about these things, but you keep silence and watch, to see what will be the upshot of these things.' (254) When the king had made this speech, not one of the rest of those that were present made any answer; but Doeg the Syrian, who fed his mules, said that he saw David when he came to the city Nob to Ahimelech the high priest, and that he learned future events by his prophesying; that he received food from him, and the sword of Goliath, and was conducted by him with security to such as he desired to go to.

(255) Saul, therefore, sent for the high priest, and for all his kindred, and said to them, 'What terrible or ungrateful thing hast thou suffered from me, that thou hast received the son of Jesse, and hast bestowed on him both food and weapons, when he was contriving to get the kingdom? And farther, why didst thou deliver oracles to him concerning futurities? For thou couldst not be unacquainted that he was fled away from me, and that he hated my family.' (256) But the high priest did not betake himself to deny what he had done, but confessed boldly that he had supplied him with these things not to gratify David, but Saul himself: and he said, 'I did not know that he was thy adversary, but a servant of thine, who was very faithful to thee, and a captain over a thousand of thy soldiers, and, what is more than these, thy son-in-law and kinsman. (257) Men do not choose to confer such favours on their adversaries, but on those who are esteemed to bear the highest good will and respect to them. Nor is this the first time that I prophesied for him, but I have done it often, and at other times, as well as now. And when he told me that he was sent by thee in great haste to do somewhat, if I had furnished him with nothing that he desired, I should have thought that it was rather in contradiction to thee than to him; (258) wherefore do not thou entertain any ill opinion of me, nor do thou have a suspicion of what I then thought an act of humanity, from what is now told thee of David's attempts against thee, for I did then to him as to thy friend and son-in-law, and captain of a thousand, and not as to thine adversary.'

(259) When the high priest had spoken thus, he did not persuade Saul, his fear was so prevalent, that he could not give credit to an apology that was very

just. So he commanded his armed men that stood about him to kill him, and all his kindred; but as they durst not touch the high priest, but were more afraid of disobeying God than the king, he ordered Doeg the Syrian to kill them. (260) Accordingly, he took to his assistance such wicked men as were like himself, and slew Ahimelech and all his family, who were in all three hundred and eighty-five. Saul also sent to Nob, the city of the priests, and slew all that were there, without sparing either women or children, or any other age, and burnt it; (261) only there was one son of Ahimelech, whose name was Abiathar, who escaped. However, these things came to pass as God had foretold to Eli the high priest, when he said that his posterity should be destroyed, on account of the transgression of his two sons.

(262) Now this king Saul, by perpetrating so barbarous a crime, and murdering the whole family of the high priestly dignity, by having no pity of the infants, nor reverence for the aged, and by overthrowing the city which God had chosen for the property and for the support of the priests and prophets which were there, and had ordained as the only city allotted for the education of such men, gives all to understand and consider the disposition of men, (263) that while they are private persons and in a low condition, because it is not in their power to indulge nature, nor to venture upon what they wish for, they are equitable and moderate, and pursue nothing but what is just, and bend their whole minds and labours that way; then it is that they have this belief about God, that he is present to all the actions of their lives, and that he does not only see the actions that are done, but clearly knows those their thoughts also, whence those actions do arise: (264) but when once they are advanced into power and authority, then they put off all such notions, and, as if they were no others than actors upon a theatre, their disguised parts and manners, and take up boldness, insolence, and a contempt of both human and divine laws, (265) and this at a time when they especially stand in need of piety and righteousness, because they are then most of all exposed to envy, and all they think and all they say are in the view of all men; then it is that they become so insolent in their actions, as though God saw them no longer, or were afraid of them because of their power; (266) and whatsoever it is that they either are afraid of by the rumours they hear, or they hate by inclination, or they love without reason, these seem to them to be authentic, and firm, and true, and pleasing both to men and to God; but as to what will come hereafter, they have not the least regard to it. (267) They raise those to honour indeed who have been at a great deal of pains for them, and after that honour they envy them; and when they have brought them into high dignity, they do not only deprive them of what they have obtained, but also on that very account of their lives also, and that on wicked accusations, and such as on account of their extravagant nature are incredible. They also

punish men for their actions, not such as deserve condemnation, but from
calumnies and accusations without examination; and this extends not only to
such as deserve to be punished, but to as many as they are able to kill. (268)
This reflection is openly confirmed to us from the example of Saul, the
son of Kish, who was the first king who reigned after our aristocracy and
government under the judges were over; and that by his slaughter of three
hundred priests and prophets, on occasion of his suspicion about Ahimelech,
and by the additional wickedness of the overthrow of their city, and this as if
he were endeavouring in some sort to render the temple destitute both of
priests and prophets; which endeavour he showed by slaying so many of
them, and not suffering the very city belonging to them to remain, that so
others might succeed them.

(269) But Abiathar, the son of Ahimelech, who alone could be saved out of
the family of priests slain by Saul, fled to David, and informed him of the
calamity that had befallen their family, and of the slaughter of his father: (270)
who hereupon said, he was not unapprised of what would follow with relation
to them when he saw Doeg there; for he had then a suspicion that the high
priest would be falsely accused by him to the king; and he blamed himself as
having been the cause of this misfortune. But he desired him to stay there, and
abide with him, as in a place where he might be better concealed than
anywhere else.

CHAPTER 13

(271) About this time it was that David heard how the Philistines had made an
inroad into the country of Keilah, and robbed it; so he offered himself to fight
against them, if God, when he should be consulted by the prophet, would
grant him the victory. And when the prophet said that God gave a signal of
victory, he made a sudden onset upon the Philistines with his companions, and
he shed a great deal of their blood, and carried off their prey, (272) and stayed
with the inhabitants of Keilah till they had securely gathered in their corn and
their fruits. However, it was told Saul the king that David was with the men of
Keilah; for what had been done, and the great success that had attended him,
were not confined among the people where the things were done, but the
fame of it went all abroad, and came to the hearing of others, and both the fact
as it stood and the author of the fact, were carried to the king's ears. (273) Then
was Saul glad when he heard David was in Keilah: and he said, 'God hath now
put him into my hands, since he hath obliged him to come into a city that hath
walls, and gates, and bars;' so he commanded all the people suddenly, and,
when they had besieged and taken it, to kill David. (274) But when David
perceived this, and learned of God that if he stayed there the men of Keilah

would deliver him up to Saul, he took his four hundred men and retired into a desert that was over against a city called Engedi. So that when the king heard he was fled away from the men of Keilah, he left off his expedition against him.

(275) Then David removed thence, and came to a certain place called the New Place, belonging to Ziph; where Jonathan, the son of Saul, came to him, and saluted him, and exhorted him to be of good courage, and to hope well as to his condition hereafter, and not to despond at his present circumstances, for that he should be king, and have all the forces of the Hebrews under him: he told him that such happiness uses to come with great labour and pains: (276) they also took oaths, that they would, all their lives long, continue in good will and fidelity one to another; and he called God to witness as to what execrations he had made upon himself if he should transgress his covenant, and should change to a contrary behaviour. So Jonathan left him there, having rendered his cares and fears somewhat lighter, and returned home. (277) Now the men of Ziph, to gratify Saul, informed him that David abode with them, and [assured him] that if he would come to them, they would deliver him up, for that if the king would seize on the straits of Ziph, David would not escape to any other people. (278) So the king commended them, and confessed that he had reason to thank them, because they had given him information of his enemy; and he promised them, that it should not be long ere he would requite their kindness. He also sent men to seek for David, and to search the wilderness wherein he was; and he promised that he himself would follow them. (279) Accordingly they went before the king, to hunt for and to catch David, and used endeavours not only to show their good will to Saul, by informing him where his enemy was, but to evidence the same more plainly by delivering him up into his power. But these men failed of those their unjust and wicked desires, who, while they underwent no hazard by not discovering such an ambition of revealing this to Saul, (280) yet did they falsely accuse and promise to deliver up a man beloved of God, and one that was unjustly sought after to be put to death, and one that might otherwise have lain concealed, and this out of flattery, and expectation of gain from the king; for when David was apprised of the malignant intentions of the men of Ziph, and the approach of Saul, he left the Straits of that country, and fled to the great rock that was in the wilderness of Maon.

(281) Hereupon Saul made haste to pursue him thither; for, as he was marching, he learned that David was gone away from the Straits of Ziph, and Saul removed to the other side of the rock. But the report that the Philistines had again made an incursion into the country of the Hebrews, called Saul another way from the pursuit of David, when he was ready to be caught; for he returned back again to oppose those Philistines, who were naturally their enemies, as judging it more necessary to avenge himself of them than to take a

great deal of pains to catch an enemy of his own, and to overlook the ravage that was made in the land.

(282) And by this means David unexpectedly escaped out of the danger he was in, and came to the Straits of Engedi; and when Saul had driven the Philistines out of the land, there came some messengers, who told him that David abode within the bounds of Engedi; (283) so he took three thousand chosen men that were armed, and made haste to him; and when he was not far from those places, he saw a deep and hollow cave by the wayside; it was open to a great length and breadth, and there it was that David with his four hundred men were concealed. When therefore he had occasion to ease nature, he entered into it by himself alone; and being seen by one of David's companions, (284) and he that saw him saying to him that he had now, by God's providence, an opportunity of avenging himself of his adversary; and advising him to cut off his head, and so deliver himself out of that tedious wandering condition, and the distress he was in, he rose up, and only cut off the skirt of that garment which Saul had on; but he soon repented of what he had done; and said it was not right to kill him that was his master, and one whom God had thought worthy of the kingdom: 'for that although he were wickedly disposed towards us, yet does it not behoove me to be so disposed towards him.' (285) But when Saul had left the cave, David came near and cried out aloud, and desired Saul to hear him; whereupon the king turned his face back, and David according to custom, fell down on his face before the king, and bowed to him; and said 'O king, thou oughtest not to hearken to wicked men, nor to such as forge calumnies, nor to gratify them so far as to believe what they say, nor to entertain suspicions of such as are your best friends, but to judge of the dispositions of all men by their actions; (286) for calumny deludes men, but men's own actions are a clear demonstration of their kindness. Words indeed, in their own nature, may be either true or false, but men's actions expose their intentions nakedly to our view. (287) By these, therefore, it will be well for thee to believe me, as to my regard to thee and to thy house, and not to believe those that frame such accusations against me as never came into my mind, nor are possible to be executed, and do this further by pursuing after my life, and have no concern either day or night, but how to compass my life and to murder me, which thing I think thou dost unjustly prosecute; (288) for how comes it about that thou hast embraced this false opinion about me, as if I had a desire to kill thee? Or how canst thou escape the crime of impiety towards God, when thou wishest thou couldst kill, and deemest thine adversary, a man who had it in his power this day to avenge himself, and to punish thee, but would not do it? Nor make use of such an opportunity, which, if it had fallen out to thee against me, thou hadst not let it slip; (289) for when I cut off the skirt of thy garment, I could have done the same to thy head.' So he showed him the piece of his garment,

and thereby made him agree to what he said to be true; and added, 'I, for certain, have abstained from taking a just revenge upon thee, yet art thou not ashamed to prosecute me with unjust hatred. May God do justice and determine about each of our dispositions!' (290) But Saul was amazed at the strange delivery he had received; and, being greatly affected with the moderation and the disposition of the young man, he groaned; and when David had done the same, the king answered that he had the justest occasion to groan, 'for thou hast been the author of good to me, as I have been the author of calamity to thee; and thou hast demonstrated this day, that thou possessest the righteousness of the ancients, who determined that men ought to save their enemies, though they caught them in a desert place. (291) I am now persuaded that God reserves the kingdom for thee, and that thou wilt obtain the dominion over all the Hebrews. Give me then assurances upon oath, that thou wilt not root out my family, nor, out of remembrance of what evil I have done thee, destroy my posterity, but save and preserve my house.' So David sware as he desired, and sent back Saul to his own kingdom; but he, and those that were with him, went up the Straits of Mastheroth.

(292) About this time Samuel the prophet died. He was a man whom the Hebrews honoured in an extraordinary degree; for that lamentation which the people made for him, and this during a long time, manifested his virtue, and the affection which the people bore for him; as also did the solemnity and concern that appeared about his funeral, and about the complete observation of all his funeral rites. (293) They buried him in his own city of Ramah, and wept for him a very great number of days, not looking on it as a sorrow for the death of another man, but as that in which they were every one themselves concerned. (294) He was a righteous man, and gentle in his nature; and on that account he was very dear to God. Now he governed and presided over the people alone, after the death of Eli the high priest, twelve years, and eighteen years together with Saul the king. And thus we have finished the history of Samuel.

(295) There was a man that was a Ziphite, of the city of Maon, who was rich, and had a vast number of cattle; for he fed a flock of three thousand sheep and another flock of a thousand goats. Now David had charged his associates to keep these flocks without hurt and without damage, and to do them no mischief, neither out of covetousness, nor because they were in want, nor because they were in the wilderness, and so could not easily be discovered, but to esteem freedom from injustice above all other motives, and to look upon the touching of what belonged to another man as a horrible crime, and contrary to the will of God. (296) These were the instructions he gave, thinking that the favours he granted this man were granted to a good man, and one that deserved to have such care taken of his affairs. This man was Nabal,

for that was his name – a harsh man, and of a very wicked life, being like a cynic in the course of his behaviour, but still had obtained for his wife a woman of a good character, wise and handsome. (297) To this Nabal, therefore, David sent ten men of his attendants at the time when he sheared his sheep, and by them saluted him, and also wished he might do what he now did for many years to come, but desired him to make him a present of what he was able to give him, since he had, to be sure, learned from his shepherds that we had done them no injury, but had been their guardians a long time together, while we continued in the wilderness; and he assured him he should never repent of giving anything to David. (298) When the messengers had carried this message to Nabal, he accosted them after an inhuman and rough manner; for he asked them who David was? And when he heard that he was the son of Jesse, he said, 'Now is the time that fugitives grow insolent, and make a figure, and leave their masters.' (299) When they told David this, he was wroth, and commanded four hundred armed men to follow him, and left two hundred to take care of the stuff (for he had already six hundred), and went against Nabal: he also swore that he would that night utterly destroy the whole house and possessions of Nabal, for that he was grieved, not only that he had proved ungrateful to them, without making any return for the humanity they had shown him, but that he had also reproached them, and used ill language to them, when he had received no cause of disgust from them.

(300) Hereupon one of those that kept the flocks of Nabal, said to his mistress, Nabal's wife, that when David sent to her husband he had received no civil answer at all from him, but that her husband had moreover added very reproachful language, while yet David had taken extraordinary care to keep his flocks from harm, and that what had passed would prove very pernicious to his master. (301) When the servant had said this, Abigail, for that was his wife's name, saddled her asses, and loaded them with all sorts of presents; and, without telling her husband anything of what she was about (for he was not sensible on account of his drunkenness), she went to David. She was then met by David as she was descending a hill, who was coming against Nabal with four hundred men. (302) When the woman saw David, she leaped down from her ass, and fell on her face, and bowed down to the ground; and entreated him not to bear in mind the words of Nabal, since he knew that he resembled his name. Now Nabal, in the Hebrew tongue, signifies *folly*. So she made her apology, that she did not see the messengers whom he sent. (303) 'Forgive me, therefore,' said she, 'and thank God, who hath hindered thee from shedding human blood; for so long as thou keepest thyself innocent, he will avenge thee of wicked men, for what miseries await Nabal, they will fall upon the heads of thine enemies. (304) Be thou gracious to me, and think me so far worthy as to accept of these presents from me; and, out of regard to me, remit that wrath

and that anger which thou hast against my husband and his house, for mildness and humanity become thee, especially as thou art to be our king.' (305) Accordingly David accepted her presents, and said, 'Nay, but, O woman, it was no other than God's mercy which brought thee to us today; for, otherwise, thou hadst never seen another day, I having sworn to destroy Nabal's house this very night, and to leave alive not one of you who belonged to a man that was wicked and ungrateful to me and my companions; but now hast thou prevented me, and seasonably mollified my anger, as being thyself under the care of God's providence: but as for Nabal, although for thy sake he now escape punishment, he will not always avoid justice; for his evil conduct, on some other occasion, will be his ruin.'

(306) When David had said this, he dismissed the woman. But when she came home and found her husband feasting with a great company, and oppressed with wine, she said nothing to him then about what had happened; but on the next day, when he was sober, she told him all the particulars, and made his whole body to appear like that of a dead man by her words, and by that grief which arose from them; so Nabal survived ten days, and no more, and then died. (307) And when David heard of his death, he said that God had justly avenged him of this man, for that Nabal had died by his own wickedness, and had suffered punishment on his account, while he had kept his own hands clean. At which time he understood that the wicked are prosecuted by God; that he does not overlook any man, but bestows on the good what is suitable to them, and inflicts a deserved punishment on the wicked. (308) So he sent to Nabal's wife, and invited her to come to him, to live with him, and to be his wife. Whereupon she replied to those that came, that she was not worthy to touch his feet: however, she came, with all her servants, and became his wife, having received that honour on account of her wise and righteous course of life. She also obtained the same honour partly on account of her beauty. (309) Now David had a wife before, whom he married from the city Abesar; for as to Michal, the daughter of king Saul, who had been David's wife, her father had given her in marriage to Phalti, the son of Laish, who was of the city of Gallim.

(310) After this came certain of the Ziphites, and told Saul that David was come again into their country, and, if he would afford them his assistance, they could catch him. So he came to them with three thousand armed men; and upon the approach of night, he pitched his camp at a certain place called Hachilah. (311) But when David heard that Saul was coming against him, he sent spies, and bid them let him know to what place of the country Saul was already come; and when they told him that he was at Hachilah, he concealed his going away from his companions, and came to Saul's camp, having taken with him Abishai, his sister Zeruiah's son, and Ahimelech the Hittite. (312) Now Saul

was asleep, and the armed men, with Abner their commander, lay round about him in a circle. Hereupon David entered into the king's tent; but he did neither kill Saul, though he knew where he lay, by the spear that was stuck down by him, nor did he give leave to Abishai, who would have killed him, and was earnestly bent upon it so to do; for he said it was a horrid crime to kill one that was ordained king by God, although he was a wicked man; for that he who gave him the dominion would in time inflict punishment upon him. So he restrained his eagerness: (313) but that it might appear to have been in his power to have killed him when he refrained from it, he took his spear, and the cruse of water which stood by Saul as he lay asleep, without being perceived by any in the camp, who were all asleep, and went securely away, having performed everything among the king's attendants that the opportunity afforded, and his boldness encouraged him to do. (314) So when he had passed over a brook, and was gotten up to the top of a hill, whence he might be sufficiently heard, he cried aloud to Saul's soldiers, and to Abner their commander, and awaked them out of their sleep, and called both to him and to the people. Hereupon the commander heard him, and asked who it was that called him. To whom David replied, (315) 'It is I, the son of Jesse, whom you make a vagabond. But what is the matter? Dost thou, that art a man of so great dignity, and of the first rank in the king's court, take so little care of thy master's body? And is sleep of more consequence to thee than his preservation and thy care of him? This negligence of yours deserves death, and punishment to be inflicted on you, who never perceived when, a little while ago, some of us entered into your camp, nay, as far as to the king himself, and to all the rest of you. If thou look for the king's spear and his cruse of water, thou wilt learn what a mighty misfortune was ready to overtake you in your very camp without your knowing it.' (316) Now when Saul knew David's voice, and understood that when he had him in his power while he was asleep, and his guards took no care of him, yet did not he kill him, but spared him, when he might justly have cut him off, he said that he owed him thanks for his preservation; and exhorted him to be of good courage, and not be afraid of suffering any mischief from him any more, and to return to his own home, (317) for he was now persuaded that he did not love himself so well as he was loved by him: that he had driven away him that could guard him and had given many demonstrations of his good will to him: that he had forced him to live so long in a state of banishment, and in great fears of his life, destitute of his friends and his kindred, while still he was often saved by him, and frequently received his life again when it was evidently in danger of perishing. (318) So David bade them send for the spear and the cruse of water, and take them back; adding this withal, that God would be the judge of both their dispositions, and of the actions that flowed from the same, 'who knows that when it was this day in my power to have killed thee, I abstained from it.'

(319) Thus Saul having escaped the hands of David twice, he went his way to his royal palace, and his own city: but David was afraid, that if he stayed there he should be caught by Saul; so he thought it better to go up into the land of the Philistines and abide there. Accordingly he came with the six hundred men that were with him to Achish, the king of Gath, which was one of their five cities. (320) Now the king received both him and his men, and gave them a place to inhabit in. He had with him also his two wives, Ahinoam and Abigail, and he dwelt in Gath. But when Saul heard this, he took no farther care about sending to him, or going after him, because he had been twice in a manner caught by him, while he was himself endeavouring to catch him. (321) However, David had no mind to continue in the city of Gath, but desired the king, that since he had received him with such humanity, that he would grant him another favour, and bestow upon him some place of that country for his habitation, for he was ashamed, by living in this city, to be grievous and burdensome to him. (322) So Achish gave him a certain village called Ziklag; which place David and his sons were fond of when he was king, and reckoned it to be their peculiar inheritance. But about those matters we shall give the reader further information elsewhere. Now the time that David dwelt in Ziklag, in the land of the Philistines, was four months and twenty days. (323) And now he privately attacked those Geshurites and Amalekites that were neighbours to the Philistines, and laid waste their country, and took much prey of their beasts and camels, and then returned home; but David abstained from the men, as fearing they should discover him to king Achish; yet did he send part of the prey to him as a free gift. (324) And when the king inquired whom they had attacked when they brought away the prey, he said, those that lay to the south of the Jews, and inhabited in the plain; whereby he persuaded Achish to approve of what he had done, for he hoped that David had fought against his own nation, and that now he should have him for his servant all his life long, and that he would stay in his country.

CHAPTER 14

(325) About the same time the Philistines resolved to make war against the Israelites, and sent to all their confederates that they would go along with them to the war to Reggan, [near the city Shunem], whence they might gather themselves together and suddenly attack the Hebrews. Then did Achish, the king of Gath, desire David to assist them with his armed men against the Hebrews. (326) This he readily promised; and said that the time was now come wherein he might requite him for his kindness and hospitality; so the king promised to make him the keeper of his body after the victory, supposing that the battle with the enemy succeeded to their mind; which promise of honour

and confidence he made on purpose to increase his zeal for his service.

(327) Now Saul, the king of the Hebrews, had cast out of the country the fortune tellers and the necromancers, and all such as exercised the like arts, excepting the prophets; but when he heard that the Philistines were already come, and had pitched their camp near the city Shunem, situate in the plain, he made haste to oppose them with his forces; (328) and when he was come to a certain mountain called Gilboa, he pitched his camp over against the enemy; but when he saw the enemy's army he was greatly troubled, because it appeared to him to be numerous, and superior to his own; and he inquired of God by the prophets concerning the battle, that he might know beforehand what would be the event of it; (329) and when God did not answer him, Saul was under a still greater dread, and his courage fell, foreseeing, as was but reasonable to suppose, that mischief would befall him, now God was not there to assist him; yet did he bid his servants to inquire out for him some woman that was a necromancer, and called up the souls of the dead, that so he might know whether his affairs would succeed up his mind; (330) for this sort of necromantic women that bring up the souls of the dead, do by them foretell future events to such as desire them. And one of his servants told him that there was such a woman in the city Endor, but was known to nobody in the camp; hereupon Saul put off his royal apparel, and took two of those his servants with him, whom he knew to be most faithful to him, and came to Endor to the woman, and entreated her to act the part of a fortune teller, and to bring up such a soul to him as he should name to her. (331) But when the woman opposed his motion, and said, she did not despise the king, who had banished this sort of fortune tellers, and that he did not do well himself, when she had done him no harm, to endeavour to lay a snare for her, and to discover that she exercised a forbidden art, in order to procure her to be punished, he sware that nobody should know what she did, and that he would not tell anyone else what she foretold, but that she should incur no danger. (332) As soon as he had induced her by this oath to fear no harm, he bade her bring up to him the soul of Samuel. She not knowing who Samuel was, called him out of Hades. When he appeared, and the woman saw one that was venerable, and of a divine form, she was in disorder, and, being astonished at the sight, she said, 'Art not thou King Saul?' for Samuel had informed her who he was. (333) When he had owned that to be true, and had asked her whence her disorder arose, she said, that she saw a certain person ascend, who in his form was like to a god. And when he bid her tell him what he resembled, in what habit he appeared, and of what age he was, she told him he was an old man already, and of a glorious personage, and had on a sacerdotal mantle. (334) So the king discovered by these signs that he was Samuel; and he fell down upon the ground and saluted, and worshipped him. And when the soul of Samuel asked him why he had

disturbed him, and caused him to be brought up, he lamented the necessity he was under; for he said that his enemies pressed heavily upon him; that he was in distress what to do in his present circumstances; that he was forsaken of God, and could obtain no prediction of what was coming, neither by prophets nor by dreams; and that 'these were the reasons why I have recourse to thee, who always tookest care of me.' (335) But Samuel, seeing that the end of Saul's life was come, said, 'It is in vain for thee to desire to learn of me anything future, when God hath forsaken thee: however, hear what I say, that David is to be king, and to finish this war with good success; (336) and thou art to lose thy dominion and thy life, because thou didst not obey God in the war with the Amalekites, and hast not kept his commandments, as I foretold thee while I was alive. Know, therefore, that the people shall be made subject to their enemies, and that thou, with thy sons, shall fall in the battle tomorrow, and thou shalt then be with me [in Hades].'

(337) When Saul heard this, he could not speak for grief, and fell down on the floor, whether it were from the sorrow that arose upon what Samuel had said, or from his emptiness, for he had taken no food the foregoing day nor night, he easily fell quite down; (338) and when with difficulty he had recovered himself, the woman would force him to eat, begging this of him as a favour on account of her concern in that dangerous instance of fortune telling, which it was not lawful for her to have done, because of the fear she was under of the king, while she knew not who he was, yet did she undertake it, and go through with it: on which account she entreated him to admit that a table and food might be set before him, that he might recover his strength, and so get safe to his own camp. And when he opposed her motion, and entirely rejected it, by reason of his anxiety, she forced him, and at last persuaded him to it. (339) Now she had one calf that she was very fond of, and one that she took a great deal of care of, and fed it herself, for she was a woman that got her living by the labour of her own hands, and had not other possession but that one calf; this she killed, and made ready its flesh, and set it before his servants and himself. So Saul came to the camp while it was yet night.

(340) Now it is but just to recommend the generosity of this woman, because when the king had forbidden her to use that art whence her circumstances were bettered and improved, and when she had never seen the king before, she still did not remember to his disadvantage that he had condemned her sort of learning, and did not refuse him as a stranger, and one that she had had no acquaintance with; (341) but she had compassion upon him, and comforted him, and exhorted him to do what he was greatly averse to, and offered him the only creature she had, as a poor woman, and that earnestly, and with great humanity, while she had no requital made her for her kindness, nor hunted after any future favours from him, for she knew he

was to die; whereas men are naturally either ambitious to please those that bestow benefits upon them, or are very ready to serve those from whom they may receive some advantage. (342) It would be well therefore to imitate the example of this woman, and to do kindnesses to all such as are in want; and to think that nothing is better, nor more becoming mankind, than such a general beneficence, nor what will sooner render God favourable, and ready to bestow good things upon us. And so far may suffice to have spoken concerning this woman. (343) But I shall speak further upon another subject, which will afford me all opportunity of discoursing on what is for the advantage of cities, and people, and nations, and suited to the taste of good men, and will encourage them all in the prosecution of virtue, and is capable of showing them the method of acquiring glory, and an everlasting fame; and of imprinting in the kings of nations, and the rulers of cities, great inclination and diligence of doing well; as also of encouraging them to undergo dangers, and to die for their countries, and of instructing them how to despise all the most terrible adversities; (344) and I have a fair occasion offered me to enter on such a discourse by Saul the king of the Hebrews; for although he knew what was coming upon him, and that he was to die immediately by the prediction of the prophet, he did not resolve to fly from death, nor so far to indulge in the love of life as to betray his own people to the enemy, or to bring a disgrace on his royal dignity; (345) but, exposing himself as well as all his family and children to dangers, he thought it a brave thing to fall together with them, as he was fighting for his subjects, and that it was better his sons should die thus, showing their courage, than to leave them to their uncertain conduct afterward, while, instead of succession and posterity, they gained commendation and a lasting name. (346) Such a one alone seems to me to be a just, a courageous, and a prudent man; and when anyone has at these dispositions, or shall hereafter arrive at them, he is the man that ought to be by all honoured with the testimony of a virtuous or courageous man; for as to those that go out to war with hopes of success, and that they shall return safe, supposing they should have performed some glorious action, I think those do not do well who call those valiant men, as so many historians, and other writers who treat of them are wont to do, (347) although I confess those do justly deserve some commendation also; but those only may be styled courageous and bold in great undertakings, and despisers of adversities, who imitate Saul; for as for those that do not know what the event of war will be as to themselves, and though they do not faint in it, but deliver themselves up to uncertain futurity, and are tossed this way and that way, this is not so very eminent an instance of a generous mind, although they happen to perform many great exploits: (348) but when men's minds expect no good event, but they know beforehand they must die, and that they must undergo that death in the battle also, after this, neither to be affrighted nor to be astonished at the terrible fate that is coming, but to go directly upon it when they know it beforehand – this it is that I esteem the character of a man truly courageous. (349) Accordingly this Saul did, and thereby demonstrated, that all men who desire fame after they are dead, are so to act as they may obtain the same; this especially concerns kings who ought not to think it enough in their high stations that they are not wicked in the government of their subjects, but to be no more than moderately good to them. (350) I could say more than this about Saul and his courage, the subject affording matter sufficient; but that I may not appear to run out improperly in his commendation, I return again to that history from which I made this digression.

(351) Now when the Philistines, as I said before, had pitched their camp, and had taken an account of their forces, according to their nations and kingdoms and governments, king Achish came last of all with his own army; after whom came David with his six hundred armed men. (352) And when the commanders of the Philistines saw him, they asked the king whence these Hebrews came, and at whose invitation. He answered, that it was David, who was fled away from his master Saul, and that he had entertained him when he came to him, and that now he was willing to make him this requital for his favours, and to avenge himself upon Saul, and so was become his confederate. (353) The commanders complained of this, that he had taken him for a confederate who was an enemy; and gave him counsel to send him away, lest he should unawares do his friends a great deal of mischief, by entertaining him, for that he afforded him an opportunity of being reconciled to his master, by doing a mischief to our army. (354) They thereupon desired him, out of a prudent foresight of this, to send him away with his six hundred armed men, to the place he had given him for his habitation; for that this was that David whom the virgins celebrated in their hymns, as having destroyed many ten thousands of the Philistines. When the king of Gath heard this, he thought they spake well; so he called David, and said to him, 'As for myself, (355) I can bear witness that thou hast shown great diligence and kindness about me, and on that account it was that I took thee for my confederate; however, what I have done does not please the commanders of the Philistines; go therefore within a day's time to the place I have given thee, without suspecting any harm, and there keep my country, lest any of our enemies should make an incursion upon it, which will be one part of that assistance which I expect from thee.' (356) So David came to Ziklag, as the king of Gath bade him; but it happened, that while he was gone to the assistance of the Philistines, the Amalekites had made an incursion, and taken Ziklag before, and had burnt it; and when they had taken a great deal of other prey out of that place, and out of the other parts of the Philistines' country, they departed.

(357) Now when David found that Ziklag was laid waste, and that it was all spoiled, and that as well his own wives, who were two, as the wives of his companions, with their children, were made captives, he presently rent his clothes, (358) weeping and lamenting, together with his friends; and indeed he was so cast down with these misfortunes, that at length tears themselves failed him. He was also in danger of being stoned to death by his companions, who were greatly afflicted at the captivity of their wives and children, for they laid the blame upon him of what had happened; (359) but when he had recovered himself out of his grief, and had raised up his mind to God, he desired the high priest Abiathar to put on his sacerdotal garments, and to inquire of God, and to prophesy to him, whether God would grant, that if he pursued after the Amalekites, he should overtake them, and save their wives and their children, and avenge himself on the enemies – (360) and when the high priest bade him to pursue after them, he marched apace, with his four hundred men, after the enemy; and when he was come to a certain brook called Besor, and had lighted upon one that was wandering about, an Egyptian by birth, who was almost dead with want and famine (for he had continued wandering about without food in the wilderness three days), he first of all gave him sustenance, both meat and drink, and thereby refreshed him. He then asked him to whom he belonged, and whence he came. (361) Whereupon the man told him he was an Egyptian by birth, and was left behind by his master, because he was so sick and weak that he could not follow him. He also informed him that he was one of those who had burnt and plundered, not only other parts of Judea, but Ziklag itself also. (362) So David made use of him as a guide to find out the Amalekites; and when he had overtaken them, as they lay scattered about on the ground, some at dinner, some disordered, and entirely drunk with wine, and in the fruition of their spoils and their prey, he fell upon them on the sudden, and made a great slaughter among them, for they were naked and expected no such thing, but had betaken themselves to drinking and feasting, and so they were all easily destroyed. (363) Now some of them that were overtaken as they lay at the table, were slain in that posture; and their blood brought up with it their meat and their drink. They slew others of them as they were drinking to one another in their cups; and some of them when their full bellies had made them fall asleep; and for so many as had time to put on their armour, they slew them with the sword, with no less ease than they did those that were naked; (364) and for the partisans of David, they continued also the slaughter from the first hour of the day to the evening, so that there were not above four hundred of the Amalekites left; and they only escaped by getting upon their dromedaries and camels. Accordingly David recovered not only all the other spoils which the enemy had carried away, but his wives also, and the wives of his companions; (365) but when they were come to the place where

they had left the two hundred men, which were not able to follow them, but were left to take care of the stuff, the four hundred men did not think fit to divide among them any other parts of what they had gotten, or of the prey, since they did not accompany them, but pretended to be feeble, and did not follow them in pursuit of the enemy, but said they should be contented to have safely recovered their wives; (366) yet did David pronounce that this opinion of theirs was evil and unjust, and that when God had granted them such a favour, that they had avenged themselves on their enemies, and had recovered all that belonged to themselves, they should make an equal distribution of what they had gotten to all, because the rest had tarried behind to guard their stuff; (367) and from that time this law obtained among them, that those who guarded the stuff should receive an equal share with those that had fought in the battle. Now when David was come to Ziklag, he sent portions of the spoils to all that had been familiar with him, and to his friends in the tribe of Judah; and thus ended the affairs of the plundering of Ziklag, and of the slaughter of the Amalekites.

(368) Now upon the Philistines joining battle, there followed a sharp engagement, and the Philistines became the conquerors, and slew a great number of their enemies, but Saul the king of Israel, and his sons, fought courageously, and with the utmost alacrity, as knowing that their entire glory lay in nothing else but dying honourably, and exposing themselves to the utmost danger from the enemy (for they had nothing else to hope for); (369) so they brought upon themselves the whole power of the enemy, till they were encompassed round and slain, but not before they had killed many of the Philistines. Now the sons of Saul were Jonathan, and Abinadab, and Malchisua; and when these were slain the multitude of the Hebrews were put to flight, and all was disorder and confusion and slaughter, upon the Philistines pressing in upon them. (370) But Saul himself fled, having a strong body of soldiers about him; and upon the Philistines sending after him those that threw javelins and shot arrows, he lost all his company except a few. As for himself he fought with great bravery; and when he had received so many wounds that he was not able to bear up, nor to oppose any longer, and yet was not able to kill himself, he bid his armour bearer draw his sword and run him through, before the enemy should take him alive. (371) But his armour bearer not daring to kill his master, he drew his own sword, and placing himself over against its point, he threw himself upon it; and when he could neither run it through him, nor, by leaning against it, make the sword pass through him, he turned him round, and asked a certain young man that stood by, who he was; and when he understood that he was an Amalekite, he desired him to force the sword through him, because he was not able to do it with his own hands, and thereby to procure him such a death as he desired.

(372) This the young man did accordingly; and he took the golden bracelet that was on Saul's arm, and his royal crown that was on his head, and ran away. And when Saul's armour bearer saw that he was slain, he killed himself; nor did any of the king's guards escape, but they all fell upon the mountain called Gilboa. (373) But when those Hebrews that dwelt in the valley beyond Jordan, and those who had their cities in the plain, heard that Saul and his sons were fallen, and that the multitude about them were destroyed, they left their own cities, and fled to such as were the best fortified and fenced; and the Philistines finding those cities deserted, came and dwelt in them.

(374) On the next day, when the Philistines came to strip their enemies that were slain, they got the bodies of Saul and of his sons, and stripped them, and cut off their heads. And they sent messengers all about their country, to acquaint them that their enemies were fallen; and they dedicated their armour in the temple of Astarte, but hung their bodies on crosses at the walls of the city Bethshan, which is now called Scythopolis. (375) But when the inhabitants of Jabesh-Gilead heard that they had dismembered the dead bodies of Saul and of his sons, they deemed it so horrid a thing to overlook this barbarity, and to suffer them to be without funeral rites, that the most courageous and hardy among them (and indeed that city had in it men that were very stout, both in body and mind) journeyed all night, and came to Bethshan, (376) and approached to the enemy's wall, and taking down the bodies of Saul and of his sons, they carried them to Jabesh, while the enemy were not able enough, nor bold enough, to hinder them, because of their great courage; (377) so the people of Jabesh wept all in general, and buried their bodies in the best place of their country, which was called Aroura; and they observed a public mourning for them seven days, with their wives and children, beating their breasts, and lamenting the king and his sons, without tasting either meat or drink [till the evening.]

(378) To this his sad end did Saul come, according to the prophecy of Samuel, because he disobeyed the commands of God about the Amalekites, and on the account of his destroying the family of Ahimelech, the high priest, with Ahimelech himself, and the city of the high priests. Now Saul, when he had reigned eighteen years while Samuel was alive, and after his death two [and twenty], ended his life in this manner.

BOOK SEVEN

CHAPTER I

(1) This fight proved to be on the same day whereon David was come back to Ziklag, after he had overcome the Amalekites. Now when he had been already two days at Ziklag, there came to him the man who slew Saul, which was the third day after the fight. He had escaped out of the battle which the Israelites had with the Philistines, and had his clothes rent, and ashes upon his head. (2) And when he made his obeisance to David, he inquired of him whence he came. He replied, from the battle of the Israelites: and he informed him that the end of it was unfortunate, many ten thousands of the Israelites having been cut off, and Saul, together with his sons, slain. (3) He also said that he could well give him this information, because he was present at the victory gained over the Hebrews, and was with the king when he fled. Nor did he deny that he had himself slain the king, when he was ready to be taken by the enemy, and he himself exhorted him to do it, because, when he was fallen on his sword, his great wounds had made him so weak that he was not able to kill himself. (4) He also produced demonstrations that the king was slain, which were the golden bracelets that had been on the king's arms, and his crown, which he had taken away from Saul's dead body, and had brought them to him. So David having no longer room to call in question the truth of what he said, but seeing most evident marks that Saul was dead, he rent his garments, and continued all that day, with his companions, in weeping and lamentation. (5) This grief was augmented by the consideration of Jonathan, the son of Saul, who had been his most faithful friend, and the occasion of his own deliverance. He also demonstrated himself to have such great virtue, and such great kindness for Saul, as not only to take his death to heart, though he had been frequently in danger of losing his life by his means, but to punish him that slew him: (6) for when David had said to him, that he was become his own accuser, as the very man who had slain the king, and when he understood that he was the son of an Amalekite, he commanded him to be slain. He also committed to writing some lamentations and funeral commendations of Saul and Jonathan, which have continued to my own age.

(7) Now when David had paid these honours to the king, he left off his mourning, and inquired of God, by the prophet, which of the cities of the tribe of Judah he would bestow upon him to dwell in; who answered that he bestowed upon him Hebron. So he left Ziklag, and came to Hebron, and took

with him his wives, who were in number two, and his armed men; (8) whereupon all the people of the forementioned tribe came to him, and ordained him their king. But when he heard that the inhabitants of Jabesh-Gilead had buried Saul and his sons [honourably], he sent to them and commended them, and took what they had done kindly, and promised to make them amends for their care of those that were dead; and at the same time he informed them that the tribe of Judah had chosen him for their king.

(9) But as soon as Abner, the son of Ner, who was general of Saul's army, and a very active man, and good-natured, knew that the king and Jonathan, and his two other sons, were fallen in the battle, he made haste into the camp; and, taking away with him the remaining son of Saul, whose name was Ishbosheth, he passed over to the land beyond Jordan, and ordained him the king of the whole multitude, excepting the tribe of Judah; (10) and made his royal seat in a place called in our language *Mahanaim*, but in the language of the Grecians, *The Camps;* from whence Abner made haste with a select body of soldiers, to fight with such of the tribe of Judah as were disposed to it, for he was angry that this tribe had set up David for their king; (11) but Joab, whose father was Suri, and his mother Zeruiah, David's sister, who was general of David's army, met him, according to David's appointment. He had with him his brethren, Abishai and Asahel, as also all David's armed men. Now when he met Abner at a certain fountain, in the city of Gibeon, he prepared to fight; (12) and when Abner said to him that he had a mind to know which of them had the more valiant soldiers, it was agreed between them that twelve soldiers of each side should fight together. So those that were chosen out by both the generals for this fight, came between the two armies, and throwing their lances one against the other, they drew their swords, and catching one another by the head, they held one another fast, and ran each other's swords into their sides and groins, until they all, as it were by mutual agreement, perished together. (13) When these were fallen down dead, the rest of the army came to a sore battle, and Abner's men were beaten; and when they were beaten, Joab did not leave off pursuing them, but he pressed upon them, and excited the soldiers to follow them close, and not to grow weary of killing them. (14) His brethren also pursued them with great alacrity, especially the younger Asahel, who was the most eminent of them. He was very famous for his swiftness of foot, for he could not only be too hard for men, but is reported to have overrun a horse, when they had a race together. This Asahel ran violently after Abner, and would not turn in the least out of the straight way, either to the one side or to the other. (15) Hereupon Abner turned back, and attempted artfully to avoid his violence. Sometimes he bade him leave off the pursuit, and take the armour of one of his soldiers; and sometimes, when he could not persuade him so to do, he exhorted him to restrain himself, and not to pursue him any longer, lest

he should force him to kill him, and he should then not be able to look his brother in the face: but when Asahel would not admit of any persuasions, but still continued to pursue him, Abner smote him with his spear, as he held it in his flight, and that by a back stroke, and gave him a deadly wound, so that he died immediately; (16) but those that were with him pursuing Abner, when they came to the place where Asahel lay, they stood round about the dead body, and left off the pursuit of the enemy. However, both Joab himself, and his brother Abishai, ran past the dead corpse, and making their anger at the death of Asahel an occasion of greater zeal against Abner, they went on with incredible haste and alacrity, and pursued Abner to a certain place called Ammah: it was about sunset. (17) Then did Joab ascend a certain hill, as he stood at that place, having the tribe of Benjamin with him, whence he took a view of them, and of Abner also. Hereupon Abner cried aloud, and said that it was not fit that they should irritate men of the same nation to fight so bitterly one against another; that as for Asahel his brother, he was himself in the wrong, when he would not be advised by him not to pursue him any further, which was the occasion of his wounding and death. So Joab consented to what he said, and accepted these words as an excuse [about Asahel] and called the soldiers back with the sound of the trumpet, as a signal for their retreat, and thereby put a stop to any further pursuit. (18) After which Joab pitched his camp there that night. But Abner marched all that night, and passed over the river Jordan, and came to Ishbosheth, Saul's son, to Mahanaim. On the next day Joab counted the dead men, and took care of all their funerals. (19) Now there were slain of Abner's soldiers about three hundred and sixty; but of those of David nineteen, and Asahel, whose body Joab and Abishai carried to Bethlehem; and when they had buried him in the sepulchre of their fathers, they came to David to Hebron. (20) From this time, therefore, they began an intestine war, which lasted a great while, in which the followers of David grew stronger in the dangers they underwent; and the servants and subjects of Saul's sons did almost every day become weaker.

(21) About this time David was become the father of six sons, born of as many mothers. The eldest was by Ahinoam, and he was called Ammon; the second was Daniel, by his wife Abigail; the name of the third was Absalom, by Maacah, the daughter of Talmai, king of Geshur; the fourth he named Adonijah, by his wife Haggith; the fifth was Shephatiah, by Abitail; the sixth he called Ithream, by Eglah. (22) Now while this intestine war went on, and the subjects of the two kings came frequently to action and to fighting, it was Abner, the general of the host of Saul's son, who, by his prudence and the great interest he had among the multitude, made them all continue with Ishbosheth; and indeed it was a considerable time that they continued of his party; (23) but afterwards Abner was blamed, and an accusation was laid against him, that he

went in unto Saul's concubine: her name was Rispah, the daughter of Aiah. So when he was complained of by Ishbosheth, he was very uneasy and angry at it, because he had not justice done him by Ishbosheth, to whom he had shown the greatest kindness; whereupon he threatened to transfer the kingdom to David, and demonstrate that he did not rule over the people beyond Jordan by his own abilities and wisdom, but by his warlike conduct and fidelity in leading his army. (24) So he sent ambassadors to Hebron to David, and desired that he would give him security upon oath that he would esteem his companion and his friend, upon condition that he should persuade the people to leave Saul's son, and choose him king of the whole country; (25) and when David had made that league with Abner, for he was pleased with his message to him, he desired that he would give this as the first mark of performance of the present league, that he might have his wife Michal restored to him, as her whom he had purchased with great hazards, and with those six hundred heads of the Philistines which he had brought to Saul her father. (26) So Abner took Michal from Phaltiel, who was then her husband, and sent her to David, Ishbosheth himself affording him his assistance; for David had written to him that of right he ought to have this his wife restored to him. Abner also called together the elders of the multitude, the commanders and captains of thousands, and spake thus to them: (27) that he had formerly dissuaded them from their own resolution, when they were ready to forsake Ishbosheth, and to join themselves to David; that, however, he now gave them leave so to do, if they had a mind to it, for they knew that God had appointed David to be king of all the Hebrews, by Samuel the prophet, and had foretold that he should punish the Philistines, and overcome them, and bring them under. (28) Now when the elders and rulers heard this, and understood that Abner was come over to those sentiments about the public affairs which they were of before, they changed their measures, and came in to David. (29) When these men had agreed to Abner's proposal, he called together the tribe of Benjamin, for all of that tribe were the guards of Ishbosheth's body, and he spake to them to the same purpose; and when he saw that they did not in the least oppose what he said, but resigned themselves up to his opinion, he took about twenty of his friends and came to David, in order to receive himself security upon oath from him; for we may justly esteem those things to be firmer which every one of us do by ourselves, than those which we do by another. He also gave him an account of what he had said to the rulers, and to the whole tribe of Benjamin; (30) and when David had received him in a courteous manner, and had treated him with great hospitality for many days, Abner, when he was dismissed, desired him to permit him to bring the multitude with him, that he might deliver up the government to him when David himself was present, and a spectator of what was done.

(31) When David had sent Abner away, Joab, the general of his army, came immediately to Hebron; and when he had understood that Abner had been with David, and had parted with him a little before under leagues and agreements that the government should be delivered up to David, he feared lest David should place Abner, who had assisted him to gain the kingdom, in the first rank of dignity, especially since he was a shrewd man in other respects, in understanding affairs, and in managing them artfully, as proper season should require, and that he should himself be put lower, and deprived of the command of the army; so he took a knavish and a wicked course. (32) In the first place, he endeavoured to calumniate Abner to the king, exhorting him to have a care of him, and not to give attention to what he had engaged to do for him, because all he did tended to confirm the government to Saul's son; that he came to him deceitfully, and with guile, and was gone away in hopes of gaining his purpose by this management: (33) but when he could not thus persuade David, nor saw him at all exasperated, he betook himself to a project bolder than the former: he determined to kill Abner; and in order thereto, he sent some messengers after him, to whom he gave in charge, that when they should overtake him they should recall him in David's name, and tell him that he had somewhat to say to him about his affairs, which he had not remembered to speak of when he was with him. (34) Now when Abner heard what the messengers said (for they overtook him in a certain place called *Besira*, which was distant from Hebron twenty furlongs), he suspected none of the mischief which was befalling him, and came back. Hereupon Joab met him in the gate, and received him in the kindest manner, as if he were Abner's most benevolent acquaintance and friend; for such as undertake the vilest actions, in order to prevent the suspicion of any private mischief intended, do frequently make the greatest pretences to what really good men sincerely do. (35) So he took him aside from his own followers, as if he would speak with him in private, and brought him into a void place of the gate, having himself nobody with him but his brother Abishai; then he drew his sword, and smote him in the groin; (36) upon which Abner died by this treachery of Joab, which, as he said himself, was in the way of punishment for his brother Asahel, whom Abner smote and slew as he was pursuing after him in the battle of Hebron, but as the truth was, out of his fear of losing his command of the army and his dignity with the king, and lest he should be deprived of those advantages, and Abner should obtain the first rank in David's court. (37) By these examples anyone may learn how many and how great instances of wickedness men will venture upon for the sake of getting money and authority, and that they may not fail of either of them; for as when they are desirous of obtaining the same, they acquire them by ten thousand evil practices, so when they are afraid of losing them, they get them confirmed to

them by practices much worse than the former, (38) as if [no] other calamity so terrible could befall them as the failure of acquiring so exalted an authority; and when they have acquired it, and by long custom found the sweetness of it, the losing it again: and since this last would be the heaviest of all afflictions, they all of them contrive and venture upon the most difficult actions, out of the fear of losing the same. But let it suffice, that I have made these short reflections upon that subject.

(39) When David heard that Abner was slain, it grieved his soul; and he called all men to witness, with stretching out his hands to God and crying out, that he was not a partaker in the murder of Abner, and that his death was not procured by his command or approbation. He also wished the heaviest curses might light upon him that slew him, and upon his whole house; and he devoted those that had assisted him in this murder to the same penalties on its account; (40) for he took care not to appear to have had any hand in this murder, contrary to the assurances he had given and the oaths he had taken to Abner. However, he commanded all the people to weep and lament this man, and to honour his dead body with the usual solemnities; that is, by rending their garments, and putting on sackcloth, and that this should be the habit in which they should go before the bier; (41) after which he followed it himself, with the elders and those that were rulers, lamenting Abner and by his tears demonstrating his good will towards him while he was alive, and his sorrow for him now he was dead, and that he was not taken off with his consent. (42) So he buried him at Hebron in a magnificent manner, and indited funeral elegies for him; he also stood first over the monument weeping, and caused others to do the same; nay, so deeply did the death of Abner disorder him, that his companions could by no means force him to take any food, for he affirmed with an oath that he would taste nothing till the sun was set. (43) This procedure gained him the good will of the multitude; for such as had an affection for Abner were mightly satisfied with the respect he paid him when he was dead, and the observation of that faith he had plighted to him, which was shown in his vouchsafing him all the usual ceremonies, as if he had been his kinsman and his friend, and not suffering him to be neglected and injured with a dishonourable burial, as if he had been his enemy; insomuch that the entire nation rejoiced at the king's gentleness and mildness of disposition, everyone being ready to suppose that the king would have taken the same care of them in the like circumstances, which they saw he showed in the burial of the dead body of Abner. (44) And indeed David principally intended to gain a good reputation, and therefore he took care to do what was proper in this case, whence none had any suspicion that he was the author of Abner's death. He also said this to the multitude, that he was greatly troubled at the death of so good a man, and that the affairs of the Hebrews had suffered great detriment by

being deprived of him, who was of so great abilities to preserve them by his excellent advice, and by the strength of his hands in war. (45) But he added, that 'God, who hath a regard to all men's actions, will not suffer this man [Joab] to go off unrevenged; but know ye, that I am not able to do anything to these sons of Zeruiah, Joab, and Abishai, who have more power than I have; but God will requite their insolent attempts upon their own heads.' And this was the fatal conclusion of the life of Abner.

CHAPTER 2

(46) When Ishbosheth, the son of Saul, had heard of the death of Abner, he took it to heart to be deprived of a man that was of his kindred, and had indeed given him the kingdom, and was greatly afflicted, and Abner's death very much troubled him; nor did he himself outlive any long time, but was treacherously set upon by the sons of Rimmon (Baanah and Rechab were their names), and was slain by them; (47) for these being of a family of the Benjamites, and of the first rank among them, thought that if they should slay Ishbosheth, they should obtain large presents from David, and be made commanders by him, or, however, should have some other trust committed to them. (48) So when they once found him alone, and asleep at noon, in an upper room, when none of his guards were there, and when the woman that kept the door was not watching, but was fallen asleep also, partly on account of the labour she had undergone, and partly on account of the heat of the day, these men went into the room in which Ishbosheth, Saul's son, lay asleep, and slew him; (49) they also cut off his head, and took their journey all that night and the next day, as supposing themselves flying away from those they had injured to one that would accept of this action as a favour, and would afford them security. So they came to Hebron, and showed David the head of Ishbosheth, and presented themselves to him as his well-wishers, and such as had killed one that was his enemy and antagonist. (50) Yet David did not relish what they had done as they expected, but said to them, 'You vile wretches, you shall immediately receive the punishment you deserve. Did not you know what vengeance I executed on him that murdered Saul, and brought me his crown of gold, and this while he who made this slaughter did it as a favour to him, that he might not be caught by his enemies? (51) Or do you imagine that I am altered in my disposition, and suppose that I am not the same man I then was, but am pleased with men that are wicked doers, and esteem your vile actions, when you are become murderers of your master, as grateful to me, when you have slain a righteous man upon his bed, who never did evil to anybody, and treated you with great good will and respect? (52) Wherefore you shall suffer the punishment due on his account, and the vengeance I ought

to inflict upon you for killing Ishbosheth, and for supposing that I should take his death kindly at your hands: for you could not lay a greater blot on my honour than by making such a supposal.' When David had said this, he tormented them with all sorts of torments, and then put them to death; and he bestowed all accustomed rites on the burial of the head of Ishbosheth, and laid it in the grave of Abner.

(53) When these things were brought to this conclusion, all the principal men of the Hebrew people came to David to Hebron, with the heads of thousands, and other rulers, and delivered themselves up to him, putting him in mind of the good will they had borne to him in Saul's lifetime, and the respect they then had not ceased to pay him when he was captain of a thousand, as also that he was chosen of God by Samuel the prophet, he and his sons; and declaring besides, how God had given him power to save the land of the Hebrews, and overcome the Philistines. (54) Whereupon he received kindly this their alacrity on his account, and exhorted them to continue in it, for that they should have no reason to repent of being thus disposed to him. So when he had feasted them, and treated them kindly, he sent them out to bring all the people to him; (55) upon which there came to him about six thousand and eight hundred armed men of the tribe of Judah, who bore shields and spears for their weapons, for these had [till now] continued with Saul's son, when the rest of the tribe of Judah had ordained David for their king. (56) There came also seven thousand and one hundred out of the tribe of Simeon. Out of the tribe of Levi came four thousand and seven hundred, having Jehoiada for their leader. After these came Zadok the high priest, with twenty-two captains of his kindred. Out of the tribe of Benjamin the armed men were four thousand; but the rest of the tribe continued, still expecting that someone of the house of Saul should reign over them. (57) Those of the tribe of Ephraim were twenty thousand and eight hundred; and these mighty men of valour, and eminent for their strength. Out of the half-tribe of Manasseh came eighteen thousand of the most potent men. Out of the tribe of Issachar came two hundred, who foreknew what was to come hereafter, but of armed men twenty thousand. (58) Of the tribe of Zebulon fifty thousand chosen men. This was the only tribe that came universally in to David; and all these had the same weapons with the tribe of Gad. Out of the tribe of Naphthali the eminent men and rulers were one thousand, whose weapons were shields and spears; and the tribe itself followed after, being (in a manner) innumerable [thirty-seven thousand]. (59) Out of the tribe of Dan there were of chosen men twenty-seven thousand and six hundred. Out of the tribe of Asher were forty thousand. Out of the two tribes that were beyond Jordan, and the rest of the tribe of Manasseh, such as used shields and spears and headpieces and swords, were an hundred and twenty thousand. The rest of the tribes also made use of

swords. (60) This multitude came together to Hebron to David, with a great quantity of corn and wine, and all other sorts of food, and established David in his kingdom with one consent; and when the people had rejoiced for three days in Hebron, David and all the people removed and came to Jerusalem.

CHAPTER 3

(61) Now the Jebusites, who were the inhabitants of Jerusalem, and were by extraction Canaanites, shut their gates, and placed the blind and the lame, and all their maimed persons, upon the wall, in way of derision of the king; and said that the very lame themselves would hinder his entrance into it. This they did out of contempt of his power, and as depending on the strength of their walls. David was hereby enraged, and began the siege of Jerusalem, and employed his utmost diligence and alacrity therein, (62) as intending, by the taking of this place, to demonstrate his power, and to intimidate all others that might be of the like [evil disposition towards him]: so he took the lower city by force, (63) but the citadel held out still; whence it was that the king, knowing that the proposal of dignities and rewards would encourage the soldiers to greater actions, promised that he who should first go over the ditches that were beneath the citadel, and should ascend to the citadel itself and take it, should have the command of the entire people conferred upon him. (64) So they all were ambitious to ascend, and thought no pains too great in order to ascend thither, out of their desire of the chief command. However, Joab, the son of Zeruiah, prevented the rest; and as soon as he was got up to the citadel, cried out to the king, and claimed the chief command.

(65) When David had cast the Jebusites out of the citadel, he also rebuilt Jerusalem, and named it, *The City of David*, and abode there all the time of his reign; but for the time that he reigned over the tribe of Judah only in Hebron, it was seven years and six months. Now when he had chosen Jerusalem to be his royal city, his affairs did more and more prosper, by the providence of God, who took care that they should improve and be augmented. (66) Hiram also, the king of the Tyrians, sent ambassadors to him, and made a league of mutual friendship and assistance with him. He also sent him presents, cedar trees and mechanics, and men skilful in building and architecture, that they might build him a royal palace at Jerusalem. Now David made buildings round about the lower city; he also joined the citadel to it, and made it one body; and when he had encompassed all with walls, he appointed Joab to take care of them. (67) It was David, therefore who first cast the Jebusites out of Jerusalem, and called it by his own name, *The City of David;* for under our forefather Abraham it was called (Salem or) Solyma; but after that time, some say that Homer mentions it by that name of Solyma, [for he named the temple

Solyma, according to the Hebrew language, which denotes *security*]. (68) Now the whole time from the warfare under Joshua our general against the Canaanites, and from that war in which he overcame them, and distributed the land among the Hebrews (nor could the Israelites ever cast the Canaanites out of Jerusalem until this time, when David took it by siege) – this whole time was five hundred and fifteen years.

(69) I shall now make mention of Araunah, who was a wealthy man among the Jebusites, but was not slain by David in the siege of Jerusalem, because of the good will he bore to the Hebrews, and a particular benignity and affection which he had to the king himself; which I shall take a more seasonable opportunity to speak of a little afterwards. (70) Now David married other wives over and above those which he had before; he had also concubines. The sons whom he had were in number eleven, whose names were Ammon, Emnos, Eban, Nathan, Solomon, Jeban, Elien, Phalna, Ennaphen, Jenae, Eliphale; and a daughter, Tamar. Nine of these were born of legitimate wives, but the two last named of concubines; and Tamar had the same mother with Absalom.

CHAPTER 4

(71) When the Philistines understood that David was made king of the Hebrews, they made war against him at Jerusalem; and when they had seized upon that valley which is called *The Valley of the Giants*, and is a place not far from the city, they pitched their camp therein: (72) but the king of the Jews, who never permitted himself to do anything without prophecy and the command of God, and without depending on him as a security for the time to come, bade the high priest to foretell to him what was the will of God, and what would be the event of this battle. (73) And when he foretold that he should gain the victory and the dominion, he led out his army against the Philistines; and when the battle was joined, he came himself behind, and fell upon the enemy on the sudden, and slew some of them, and put the rest to flight. (74) And let no one suppose that it was a small army of the Philistines that came against the Hebrews, as guessing so from the suddenness of their defeat, and from their having performed no great action, or that was worth recording, from the slowness of their march and want of courage; but let him know that all Syria and Phoenicia, with many other nations besides them, and those warlike nations also, came to their assistance and had a share in this war: (75) which thing was the only cause why, when they had been so often conquered, and had lost so many ten thousands of their men, they still came upon the Hebrews with greater armies; nay, indeed, when they had so often failed of their purpose in these battles, they came upon David with an army three times as numerous as before, and pitched their camp on the same spot of

ground as before. (76) The king of Israel therefore inquired of God again concerning the event of the battle; and the high priest prophesied to him, that he should keep his army in the groves called the *Groves of Weeping* which were not far from the enemy's camp, and that he should not move, nor begin to fight, till the trees of the grove should be in motion without the wind's blowing; (77) but as soon as these trees moved, and the time foretold to him by God was come, he should, without delay, go out to gain what was an already prepared and evident victory; for the several ranks of the enemy's army did not sustain him, but retreated at the first onset, whom he closely followed, and slew them as he went along, and pursued them to the city of Gaza (which is the limit of their country): after this he spoiled their camp, in which he found great riches; and he destroyed their gods.

(78) When this had proved the event of the battle, David thought it proper, upon a consultation with the elders and rulers, and captains of thousands, to send for those that were in the flower of their age out of all his countrymen, and out of the whole land, and withal for the priests and the Levites, in order to their going to Kirjath-jearim, to bring up the ark of God out of that city, and to carry it to Jerusalem, and there to keep it, and offer before it those sacrifices and those other honours with which God used to be well pleased; (79) for had they done thus in the reign of Saul, they had not undergone any great misfortunes at all. So when the whole body of the people were come together, as they had resolved to do, the king came to the ark, which the priests brought out of the house of Aminadab, and laid it upon a new cart, and permitted their brethren and their children to draw it, together with the oxen. (80) Before it went the king, and the whole multitude of the people with him, singing hymns to God, and making use of all sorts of songs usual among them, with variety of the sounds of musical instruments, and with dancing and singing of psalms, as also with the sounds of trumpets and of cymbals, and so brought the ark to Jerusalem. (81) But as they were come to the threshing floor of Chidon, a place so called, Uzzah was slain by the anger of God; for as the oxen shook the ark, he stretched out his hand, and would needs take hold of it. Now because he was not a priest, and yet touched the ark, God struck him dead. (82) Hereupon both the king and the people were displeased at the death of Uzzah; and the place where he died is still called the *Breach of Uzzah* unto this day. So David was afraid, and supposing that if he received the ark to himself into the city, he might suffer in the like manner as Uzzah had suffered, who, upon his bare putting out his hand to the ark, died in the manner already mentioned, (83) he did not receive it to himself into the city, but he took it aside unto a certain place belonging to a righteous man, whose name was Obededom, who was by his family a Levite, and deposited the ark with him; and it remained there three entire months. This augmented the house of Obededom, and

conferred many blessings upon it; (84) and when the king heard what had befallen Obededom, how he was become, of a poor man in a low estate, exceedingly happy, and the object of envy to all those that saw or inquired after his house, he took courage, and hoping that he should meet with no misfortune thereby, he transferred the ark to his own house, (85) the priests carrying it, while seven companies of singers, who were set in that order by the king, went before it, and while he himself played upon the harp, and joined in the music, insomuch that when his wife Michal, the daughter of Saul, who was our first king, saw him so doing, she laughed at him; (86) but when they had brought in the ark, they placed it under the tabernacle which David had pitched for it, and he offered costly sacrifices and peace offerings, and treated the whole multitude, and dealt both to the women and the men and the infants, a loaf of bread and a cake, and another cake baked in a pan, with a portion of the sacrifice. So when he had thus feasted the people, he sent them away, and he himself returned to his own house.

(87) But when Michal his wife, the daughter of Saul, came and stood by him, she wished him all other happiness, and entreated that whatsoever he should further desire, to the utmost possibility, might be given him by God, and that he might be favourable to him; yet did she blame him, that so great a king as he was should dance after an unseemly manner, and in his dancing uncover himself among the servants and handmaidens; (88) but he replied, that he was not ashamed to do what was acceptable to God, who had preferred him before her father and before all others; that he would play frequently, and dance, without any regard to what the handmaidens and she herself thought of it. (89) So this Michal had no children; however, when she was afterward married to him to whom Saul her father had given her (for at this time David had taken her away from him, and had her himself), she bare five children. But concerning those matters I shall discourse in a proper place.

(90) Now when the king saw that his affairs grew better almost every day, by the will of God, he thought he should offend him if, while he himself continued in houses made of cedar, such as were of a great height, and had the most curious works of architecture in them, he should overlook the ark while it was laid in a tabernacle, (91) and was desirous to build a temple to God, as Moses had predicted such a temple should be built. And when he had discoursed with Nathan the prophet about these things, and had been encouraged by him to do whatsoever he had a mind to do, as having God with him and his helper in all things, he was thereupon the more ready to set about that building. (92) But God appeared to Nathan that very night, and commanded him to say to David, that he took his purpose and his desires kindly, since nobody had before now taken it into their head to build him a temple, although upon his having such a notion he would not permit him to build him that temple, because he had

made many wars, and was defiled with the slaughter of his enemies; (93) that, however, after his death in his old age, and when he had lived a long life, there should be a temple built by a son of his, who should take the kingdom after him, and should be called Solomon, whom he promised to provide for as a father provides for his son, by preserving the kingdom for his son's posterity, and delivering it to them; but that he would still punish him if he sinned, with diseases and barrenness of land. (94) When David understood this from the prophet, and was overjoyful at this knowledge of the sure continuance of the dominion to his posterity, and that his house should be splendid and very famous, he came to the ark, (95) and fell down on his face, and began to adore God, and to return thanks to him for all his benefits, as well for those that he had already bestowed upon him, in raising him from a low state, and from the employment of a shepherd, to so great dignity of dominion and glory, as for those also which he had promised to his posterity; and besides, for that providence which he had exercised over the Hebrews, in procuring them the liberty they enjoyed. And when he had said thus, and had sung an hymn of praise to God, he went his way.

CHAPTER 5

(96) A little while after this he considered that he ought to make war against the Philistines, and not to see any idleness or laziness permitted in his management, that so it might prove, as God had foretold to him, that when he had overthrown his enemies, he should leave his posterity to reign in peace afterward; (97) so he called together his army again, and when he had charged them to be ready and prepared for war, and when he thought that all things in his army were in a good state, he removed from Jerusalem, and came against the Philistines; (98) and when he had overcome them in battle, and had cut off a great part of their country and adjoined it to the country of the Hebrews, he transferred the war to the Moabites; and when he had overcome two parts of their army in battle, he took the remaining part captive and imposed tribute upon them, to be paid annually. (99) He then made war against Hadadezer, the son of Rehob, king of Sophene; and when he had joined battle with him at the river Euphrates, he destroyed twenty thousand of his footmen and about seven thousand of his horsemen; he also took a thousand of his chariots, and destroyed the greatest part of them, and ordered that no more than one hundred should be kept.

(100) Now when Hadad, king of Damascus and of Syria, heard that David fought against Hadadezer, who was his friend, he came to his assistance with a powerful army, in hopes to rescue him; and when he had joined battle with David at the river Euphrates, he failed of his purpose, and lost in the battle a

great number of his soldiers; for there were slain of the army of Hadad twenty thousand, and all the rest fled. (101) Nicolaus [of Damascus] also makes mention of this king in the fourth book of his histories, where he speaks thus: 'A great while after these things had happened, there was one of that country whose name was Hadad, who was become very potent; he reigned over Damascus and the other parts of Syria, excepting Phoenicia. He made war against David, the king of Judea, and tried his fortune in many battles, and particularly in the last battle at Euphrates, wherein he was beaten. He seemed to have been the most excellent of all their kings in strength and manhood.' (102) Nay, besides this, he says of his posterity, that 'They succeeded one another in his kingdom, and in his name;' where he thus speaks: 'When Hadad was dead, his posterity reigned for ten generations, each of his successors receiving from his father *that* his dominion, and *this* his name, as did the Ptolemies in Egypt. (103) But the third was the most powerful of them all, and was willing to avenge the defeat his forefather had received; so he made an expedition against the Jews, and laid waste the city which is now called Samaria.' Nor did he err from the truth; for this is that Hadad who made the expedition against Samaria, in the reign of Ahab, king of Israel; concerning whom we shall speak in due place hereafter.

(104) Now when David had made an expedition against Damascus and the other parts of Syria, and had brought it all into subjection, and had placed garrisons in the country, and appointed that they should pay tribute, he returned home. He also dedicated to God at Jerusalem the golden quivers, the entire armour which the guards of Hadad used to wear; (105) which Shishak, the king of Egypt, took away when he fought with David's grandson, Rehoboam, with a great deal of other wealth which he carried out of Jerusalem. However, these things will come to be explained in their proper places hereafter. Now as for the king of the Hebrews, he was assisted by God, who gave him great success in his wars; and he made all expedition against the best cities of Hadadezer, Betah and Machon; so he took them by force, and laid them waste. (106) Therein was found a very great quantity of gold and silver, besides that sort of brass which is said to be more valuable than gold; of which brass Solomon made that large vessel which was called *The [Brazen] Sea*, and those most curious lavers, when he built the temple for God.

(107) But when the king of Hamath was informed of the ill success of Hadadezer, and had heard of the ruin of his army, he was afraid on his own account, and resolved to make a league of friendship and fidelity with David, before he should come against him; so he sent to him his son Joram, and professed that he owed him thanks for fighting against Hadadezer, who was his enemy, and made a league with him of mutual assistance and friendship. (108) He also sent him presents, vessels of ancient workmanship, both of gold, of

silver, and of brass. So when David had made this league of mutual assistance with Toi (for that was the name of the king of Hamath), and had received the presents he sent him, he dismissed his son with that respect which was due on both sides; but then David brought those presents that were sent by him, as also the rest of the gold and silver which he had taken of the cities whom he had conquered, and dedicated them to God. (109) Nor did God give victory and success to him only when he went to the battle himself, and led his own army, but he gave victory to Abishai, the brother of Joab, general of his forces, over the Idumeans, and by him to David, when he sent him with an army into Idumea; for Abishai destroyed eighteen thousand of them in the battle; whereupon the king [of Israel] placed garrisons through all Idumea, and received the tribute of the country, and of every head among them. (110) Now David was in his nature just, and made his determination with regard to truth. He had for the general of his whole army Joab; and he made Jehoshaphat, the son of Ahilud, recorder; he also appointed Zadok, of the family of Phineas, to be high priest, together with Abiathar, for he was his friend; he also made Seisan the scribe; and committed the command over the guards of his body to Benaiah, the son of Jehoiada. His elder sons were near his body, and had the care of it also.

(111) He also called to mind the covenants and the oaths he had made with Jonathan, the son of Saul, and the friendship and affection Jonathan had for him; for besides all the rest of his excellent qualities with which he was endowed, he was also exceeding mindful of such as had at other times bestowed benefits upon him. (112) He therefore gave order that inquiry should be made, whether any of Jonathan's lineage were living, to whom he might make return of that familiar acquaintance which Jonathan had had with him, and for which he was still debtor. And when one of Saul's freedmen was brought to him, who was acquainted with those of his family that were still living, he asked him whether he could tell him of anyone belonging to Jonathan that was now alive, and capable of a requital of the benefits which he had received from Jonathan. (113) And when he said that a son of his was remaining, whose name was Mephibosheth, but that he was lame of his feet, for that when his nurse heard that the father and grandfather of the child were fallen in the battle, she snatched him up, and fled away, and let him fall from her shoulders, and his feet were lamed – when he had learned where and by whom he was brought up, he sent messengers to Machir, to the city of Lodebar, for with him was the son of Jonathan brought up, and sent for him to come to him. (114) So when Mephibosheth came to the king, he fell on his face and worshipped him, but David encouraged him, and bade him be of good cheer, and expect better times. So he gave him his father's house, and all the estate which his grandfather Saul was in possession of, and bade him come and diet with him at his own table, and never to be absent one day from that

table. (115) And when the youth had worshipped him, on account of his words and gifts given to him, he called for Ziba, and told him that he had given the youth his father's house, and all Saul's estate. He also ordered that Ziba should cultivate his land and take care of it, and bring him the profits of all to Jerusalem. Accordingly David brought him to his table every day, and bestowed upon the youth, Ziba and his sons, who were in number fifteen, and his servants, who were in number twenty. (116) When the king had made these appointments, and Ziba had worshipped him, and promised to do all that he had bidden him, he went his way; so that this son of Jonathan dwelt at Jerusalem, and dieted at the king's table, and had the same care that a son could claim taken of him. He also had himself a son, whom he named Micha.

CHAPTER 6

(117) These were the honours that such as were left of Saul's and Jonathan's lineage received from David. About this time died Nahash, the king of the Ammonites, who was a friend of David's; and when his son had succeeded his father in the kingdom, David sent ambassadors to him to comfort him, and exhorted him to take his father's death patiently, and to expect that he would continue the same kindness to himself which he had shown to his father. (118) But the princes of the Ammonites took this message in evil part, and not as David's kind dispositions gave reason to take it; and they excited the king to resent it, and said that David had sent men to spy out the country and what strength it had, under the pretence of humanity and kindness. They further advised him to have a care, and not to give heed to David's words, lest he should be deluded by him, and so fall into an inconsolable calamity. (119) Accordingly Nahash's [son], the king of the Ammonites, thought these princes spake what was more probable than the truth would admit, and so abused the ambassadors after a very harsh manner; for he shaved the one half of their beards, and cut off one half of their garments, and sent his answer not in words but in deeds. (120) When the king of Israel saw this, he had indignation at it, and showed openly that he would not overlook this injurious and contumelious treatment, but would make war with the Ammonites, and would avenge this wicked treatment of his ambassadors on their king. (121) So that the king's intimate friends and commanders, understanding that they had violated their league, and were liable to be punished for the same, made preparations for war; they also sent a thousand talents to the Syrian king of Mesopotamia, and endeavoured to prevail with him to assist them for that pay, and Shobach. Now these kings had twenty thousand footmen. They also hired the king of the country called Maacah, and a fourth king, by name Ishtob; which last had twelve thousand armed men.

(122) But David was under no consternation at this confederacy, nor at the forces of the Ammonites; and putting his trust in God, because he was going to war in a just cause, on account of the injurious treatment he had met with, he immediately sent Joab, the captain of his host, against them, and gave him the flower of his army; (123) who pitched his camp by Rabbath, the metropolis of the Ammonites; whereupon the enemy came out, and set themselves in array, not all of them together, but in two bodies; for the auxiliaries were set in array in the plain by themselves, but the army of the Ammonites at the gates over against the Hebrews. (124) When Joab saw this, he opposed one stratagem against another, and chose out the most hardy part of his men, and set them in opposition to the king of Syria and the kings that were with him, and gave the other part to his brother Abishai, and bid him set them in opposition to the Ammonites; and said to him, that in case he should see that the Syrians distressed him, and were too hard for him, he should order his troops to turn about, and assist him: and he said, that he himself would do the same to him, if he saw him in the like distress from the Ammonites. (125) So he sent his brother before, and encouraged him to do everything courageously and with alacrity, which would teach them to be afraid of disgrace, and to fight manfully; and so he dismissed him to fight with the Ammonites, while he fell upon the Syrians. (126) And though they made a strong opposition for a while, Joab slew many of them, but compelled the rest to betake themselves to flight; which, when the Ammonites saw, and were withal afraid of Abishai and his army, they stayed no longer, but imitated their auxiliaries, and fled to the city. So Joab, when he had thus overcome the enemy, returned with great joy to Jerusalem to the king.

(127) This defeat did not still induce the Ammonites to be quiet, nor to own those that were superior to them to be so, and be still, but they sent to Chalaman, the king of the Syrians, beyond Euphrates, and hired [him] for an auxiliary. He had Shobach for the captain of his host, with eighty thousand footmen and ten thousand horsemen. (128) Now when the king of the Hebrews understood that the Ammonites had again gathered so great an army together, he determined to make war with them no longer by his generals, but he passed over the river Jordan himself with all his army; and when he met them he joined battle with them, and overcame them, and slew forty thousand of their footmen and seven thousand of their horsemen. He also wounded Shobach, the general of Chalaman's forces, who died of that stroke; (129) but the people of Mesopotamia, upon such a conclusion of the battle, delivered themselves up to David, and sent him presents, who at wintertime returned to Jerusalem. But at the beginning of the spring he sent Joab, the captain of his host, to fight against the Ammonites; who overran all their country and laid it waste, and shut them up in their metropolis Rabbah, and besieged them therein.

CHAPTER 7

(130) But David fell now into a very grievous sin, though he were otherwise naturally a righteous and a religious man, and one that firmly observed the laws of our fathers; for when late in an evening he took a view round him from the roof of his royal palace, where he used to walk at that hour, he saw a woman washing herself in her own house: she was one of extraordinary beauty, and therein surpassed all other women; her name was Bathsheba. So he was overcome by that woman's beauty, and was not able to restrain his desires, but sent for her, and lay with her. (131) Hereupon she conceived with child, and sent to the king, that he should contrive some way for concealing her sin (for according to the laws of their fathers, she who had been guilty of adultery ought to be put to death). So the king sent for Joab's armour bearer from the siege, who was the woman's husband; and his name was Uriah: and when he was come, the king inquired of him about the army, and about the siege; (132) and when he had made answer that all their affairs went according to their wishes, the king took some portions of meat from his supper and gave them to him, and bade him go home to his wife, and take his rest with her. Uriah did not do so, but slept near the king with the rest of his armour bearers. (133) When the king was informed of this, he asked him why he did not go home to his house and to his wife, after so long an absence; which is the natural custom of all men, when they come from a long journey. He replied, that it was not right, while his fellow soldiers, and the general of the army, slept upon the ground, in the camp, and in an enemy's country, that he should go and take his rest, and solace himself with his wife. (134) So when he had thus replied, the king ordered him to stay there that night, that he might dismiss him the next day to the general. So the king invited Uriah to supper, and after a cunning and dextrous manner plied him with drink at supper till he was thereby disordered; yet did he nevertheless sleep at the king's gates, without any inclination to go to his wife. (135) Upon this the king was very angry at him, and wrote to Joab, and commanded him to punish Uriah, for he told him that he had offended him; and he suggested to him the manner in which he would have him punished, that it might not be discovered that he was himself the author of this his punishment; (136) for he charged him to set him over against that part of the enemy's army where the attack would be most hazardous, and where he might be deserted, and be in the greatest jeopardy; for he bade him order his fellow soldiers to retire out of the fight. When he had written thus to him, and sealed the letter with his own seal, he gave it to Uriah to carry to Joab. (137) When Joab had received it, and upon reading it understood the king's purpose, he set Uriah in that place where he

knew the enemy would be most troublesome to them, and gave him for his partners some of the best soldiers in the army, and said that he would also come to their assistance with the whole army, that if possible they might break down some part of the wall, and enter the city. (138) And he desired him to be glad of the opportunity of exposing himself to such great pains, and not to be displeased at it, since he was a valiant soldier, and had a great reputation for his valour, both with the king and with his countrymen. And when Uriah undertook the work he was set upon with alacrity, he gave private orders to those who were to be his companions, that when they saw the enemy make a sally, they should leave him. (139) When, therefore, the Hebrews made an attack upon the city, the Ammonites were afraid that the enemy might prevent them, and get up into the city, and this at the very place whither Uriah was ordered; so they exposed their best soldiers to be in the forefront, and opened their gates suddenly, and fell upon the enemy with great vehemence, and ran violently upon them. (140) When those that were with Uriah saw this, they all retreated backward, as Joab had directed them beforehand; but Uriah, as ashamed to run away and leave his post, sustained the enemy, and receiving the violence of their onset, he slew many of them; but being encompassed round, and caught in the midst of them, he was slain, and some other of his companions were slain with him.

(141) When this was done, Joab sent messengers to the king, and ordered them to tell him that he did what he could to take the city soon; but that as they made an assault on the wall, they had been forced to retire with great loss; and bade them, if they saw the king was angry at it, to add this, that Uriah was slain also. (142) When the king had heard this of the messengers, he took it heinously, and said that they did wrong when they assaulted the wall, whereas they ought, by undermining and other stratagems of war, to endeavour the taking of the city, especially when they had before their eyes the example of Abimelech, the son of Gideon, who would need take the tower in Thebes by force, and was killed by a large stone thrown at him by an old woman; and although he was a man of great prowess, he died ignominiously by the dangerous manner of his assault. (143) That they should remember this accident, and not come near the enemy's wall, for that the best method of making war with success was to call to mind the accidents of former wars, and what good or bad success had attended them in the like dangerous cases, that so they might imitate the one, and avoid the other. (144) But when the king was in this disposition, the messenger told him that Uriah was slain also; whereupon he was pacified. So he bade the messenger go back to Joab and tell him, that this misfortune is no other than what is common among mankind; and that such is the nature, and such the accidents of war, insomuch that sometimes the enemy will have success therein, and sometimes others; (145) but that he ordered him to go on still in his care

about the siege, that no ill accidents might befall him in it hereafter: that they should raise bulwarks and use machines in besieging the city; and when they have gotten it, to overturn its very foundations, and to destroy all those that are in it. Accordingly the messenger carried the king's message with which he was charged, and made haste to Joab. (146) But Bathsheba, the wife of Uriah, when she was informed of the death of her husband, mourned for his death many days; and when her mourning was over, and the tears which she shed for Uriah were dried up, the king took her to wife presently, and a son was born to him by her.

(147) With this marriage God was not well pleased, but was thereupon angry at David; and he appeared to Nathan the prophet in his sleep, and complained of the king. Now Nathan was a fair and prudent man; and considering that kings, when they fall into a passion, are guided more by that passion than they are by justice, he resolved to conceal the threatenings that proceeded from God, and made a good-natured discourse to him, and this after the manner following: (148) he desired that the king would give him his opinion in the following case: 'There were,' said he, 'two men inhabiting the same city; the one of them was rich and [the other poor.] The rich man had a great many flocks of cattle, of sheep, and of kine; but the poor man had but one ewe lamb. (149) This he brought up with his children, and let her eat her food with them, and he had the same natural affection for her which anyone might have for a daughter. Now upon the coming of a stranger to the rich man, he would not vouchsafe to kill any of his own flocks, and thence feast his friend; but he sent for the poor man's lamb, and took her away from him, and made her ready for food, and thence feasted the stranger.' (150) This discourse troubled the king exceedingly; and he denounced to Nathan, that 'this man was a wicked man, who could dare to do such a thing; and that it was but just that he should restore the lamb fourfold, and be punished with death for it also.' Upon this, Nathan immediately said, that he was himself the man who ought to suffer those punishments, and that by his own sentence; and that it was he who had perpetrated this great and horrid crime. (151) He also revealed to him, and laid before him, the anger of God against him, who had made him king over the army of the Hebrews, and lord of all the nations, and those many and great nations round about him; who had formerly delivered him out of the hands of Saul, and had given him such wives as he had justly and legally married; and now this God was despised by him, and affronted by his impiety, when he had married, and now had another man's wife; and by exposing her husband to the enemy, had really slain him; (152) that God would inflict punishments upon him on account of those instances of wickedness; that his own wives should be forced by one of his sons, and that he should be treacherously supplanted by the same son; and that although he had perpetrated his wickedness secretly, yet should that punishment which he was to undergo be inflicted publicly upon

him; 'that, moreover,' said he, 'the child who was born to thee of her, shall soon die.' (153) When the king was troubled at these messages, and sufficiently confounded, and said, with tears and sorrow, that he had sinned (for he was without controversy a pious man, and guilty of no sin at all in his whole life, excepting those in the matter of Uriah), God had compassion on him, and was reconciled to him, and promised that he would preserve to him both his life and his kingdom; for he said, that seeing he repented of the things he had done, he was no longer displeased with him. So Nathan, when he had delivered this prophecy to the king, returned home.

(154) However, God sent a dangerous distemper upon the child that was born to David of the wife of Uriah; at which the king was troubled, and did not take any food for seven days, although his servants almost forced him to take it; but he clothed himself in a black garment, and fell down, and lay upon the ground in sackcloth, entreating God for the recovery of the child, for he vehemently loved the child's mother; (155) but when, on the seventh day, the child was dead, the king's servants durst not tell him of it, as supposing that when he knew it, he would still less admit of food and other care of himself, by reason of his grief at the death of his son, since when the child was only sick, he so greatly afflicted himself, and grieved for him; (156) but when the king perceived that his servants were in disorder, and seemed to be affected as those are who are very desirous to conceal something, he understood that the child was dead; and when he had called one of his servants to him, and discovered that so it was, he arose up and washed himself, and took a white garment, and came into the tabernacle of God. (157) He also commanded them to set supper before him, and thereby greatly surprised his kindred and servants, while he did nothing of this when the child was sick, but did it all when he was dead. Whereupon, having first begged leave to ask him a question, they besought him to tell them the reason of this his conduct; he then called them unskilful people, (158) and instructed them how he had hopes of the recovery of the child while it was alive, and accordingly did all that was proper for him to do, as thinking by such means to render God propitious to him; but that when the child was dead, there was no longer any occasion for grief, which was then to no purpose. When he had said this, they commended the king's wisdom and understanding. He then went in unto Bathsheba his wife, and she conceived and bare a son; and, by the command of Nathan the prophet, called his name Solomon.

(159) But Joab sorely distressed the Ammonites in the siege, by cutting off their waters, and depriving them of other means of subsistence, till they were in the greatest want of meat and drink, for they depended only on one small well of water, and this they durst not drink of too freely, lest the fountain should entirely fail them. (160) So he wrote to the king, and informed him thereof; and persuaded him to come himself to take the city, that he might

have the honour of the victory. Upon this letter of Joab's, the king accepted of his good will and fidelity, and took with him his army, and came to the destruction of Rabbah; and when he had taken it by force, he gave it to his soldiers to plunder it; (161) but he himself took the king of the Ammonites' crown, the weight of which was a talent of gold; and it had in its middle a precious stone called a sardonyx; which crown David ever after wore on his own head. He also found many other vessels in the city, and those both splendid and of great price; but as for the men, he tormented them, and then destroyed them: and when he had taken the other cities of the Ammonites by force, he treated them after the same manner.

CHAPTER 8

(162) When the king was returned to Jerusalem, a sad misfortune befell his house, on the occasion following: He had a daughter, who was yet a virgin, and very handsome, insomuch that she surpassed all the most beautiful women; her name was Tamar; she had the same mother with Absalom. (163) Now Amnon, David's eldest son, fell in love with her, and being not able to obtain his desires on account of her virginity, and the custody she was under, was so much out of order, nay, his grief so eat up his body, that he grew lean, and his colour was changed. (164) Now there was one Jenadab, a kinsman and friend of his, who discovered this his passion, for he was an extraordinary wise man, and of great sagacity of mind. When, therefore, he saw that every morning Amnon was not in body as he ought to be, he came to him, and desired him to tell him what was the cause of it: however, he said that he guessed that it arose from the passion of love. (165) Amnon confessed his passion, that he was in love with a sister of his, who had the same father with himself. So Jonadab suggested to him by what method and contrivance he might obtain his desires; for he persuaded him to pretend sickness, and bade him when his father should come to him, to beg of him that his sister might come and minister to him; for if that were done, he should be better, and should quickly recover from his distemper. (166) So Amnon lay down on his bed, and pretended to be sick, as Jonadab had suggested. When his father came and inquired how he did, he begged of him to send his sister to him. Accordingly, he presently ordered her to be brought to him; and when she was come, Amnon bade her make cakes for him, and fry them in a pan, (167) and do it all with her own hands, because he should take them better from her hand [than from anyone's else]. So she kneaded the flour in the sight of her brother, and made him cakes, and baked them in a pan, and brought them to him; but at that time he would not taste them, but gave order to the servants to send all that were there out of his chamber, because he had a mind to repose

himself, free from tumult and disturbance. (168) As soon as what he had commanded was done, he desired his sister to bring his supper to him into the inner parlour; which when the damsel had done, he took hold of her, and endeavoured to persuade her to lie with him. Whereupon the damsel cried out, and said, 'Nay, brother, do not force me, nor be so wicked as to transgress the laws, and bring upon thyself the utmost confusion. Curb this thy unrighteous and impure lust, from which our house will get nothing but reproach and disgrace.' (169) She also advised him to speak to his father about this affair; for he would permit him [to marry her]. This she said, as desirous to avoid her brother's violent passion at present. But he would not yield to her, but, inflamed with love and blinded with the vehemency of his passion, he forced his sister: (170) but as soon as Amnon had satisfied his lust, he hated her immediately, and giving her reproachful words, bade her rise up and be gone. And when she said that this was a more injurious treatment than the former if, now he had forced her, he would not let her stay with him till the evening, but bid her go away in the daytime, and while it was light, that she might meet with people that would be witness of her shame, he commanded his servant to turn her out of his house. (171) Whereupon she was sorely grieved at the injury and violence that had been offered to her, and rent her loose coat (for the virgins of old time wore such loose coats tied at the hands, and let down to the ankles, that the inner coats might not be seen), and sprinkled ashes on her head; and went up the middle of the city, crying out and lamenting for the violence that had been offered her. (172) Now Absalom, her brother, happened to meet her, and asked her what sad thing had befallen her, that she was in that plight; and when she had told him what injury had been offered her, he comforted her, and desired her to be quiet, and take all patiently, and not to esteem her being corrupted by her brother as an injury. So she yielded to his advice, and left off her crying out, and discovering the force offered her to the multitude; and she continued as a widow with her brother Absalom a long time.

(173) When David his father knew this, he was grieved at the actions of Amnon; but because he had an extraordinary affection for him, for he was his eldest son, he was compelled not to afflict him; but Absalom watched for a fit opportunity of revenging this crime upon him, for he thoroughly hated him. (174) Now the second year after this wicked affair about his sister was over, and Absalom was about to go to shear his own sheep at Baalhazor, which is a city in the portion of Ephraim, he besought his father, as well as his brethren, to come and feast with him: (175) but when David excused himself, as not being willing to be burdensome to him, Absalom desired he would however send his brethren; whom he did send accordingly. Then Absalom charged his own servants, that when they should see Amnon disordered and drowsy with wine, and he should give them a signal, they should fear nobody, but kill him.

(176) When they had done as they were commanded, the rest of his brethren were astonished and disturbed, and were afraid for themselves, so they immediately got on horseback, and rode away to their father: but somebody there was who prevented them, and told their father they were all slain by Absalom; (177) whereupon he was overcome with sorrow, as for so many of his sons that were destroyed at once, and that by their brother also; and by this consideration, that it was their brother that appeared to have slain them, he aggravated his sorrow for them. So he neither inquired what was the cause of this slaughter, nor stayed to hear anything else, which yet it was but reasonable to have done, when so very great, and by that greatness so incredible, a misfortune was related to him; he rent his clothes, and threw himself upon the ground, and there lay lamenting the loss of all his sons, both those who, as he was informed, were slain, and of him who slew them. (178) But Jonadab, the son of his brother Shemeah, entreated him not to indulge his sorrow so far, for as to the rest of his sons he did not believe that they were slain, for he found no cause for such a suspicion; but he said it might deserve inquiry as to Amnon, for it was not unlikely that Absalom might venture to kill him on account of the injury he had offered to Tamar. (179) In the meantime, a great noise of horses, and a tumult of some people that were coming, turned their attention to them; they were the king's sons, who were fled away from the feast. So their father met them as they were in their grief, and he himself grieved with them; but it was more than he expected to see those his sons again, whom he had a little before heard to have perished. (180) However, there were tears on both sides, they lamenting their brother who was killed, and the king lamenting his son, who was killed also; but Absalom fled to Geshur, to his grandfather by his mother's side, who was king of that country, and he remained with him three whole years.

(181) Now David had a design to send to Absalom not that he should come to be punished, but that he might be with him, for the effects of his anger were abated by length of time. It was Joab, the captain of his host, that chiefly persuaded him so to do; (182) for he suborned an ordinary woman, that was stricken in age, to go to the king in mourning apparel, who said thus to him — that two of her sons, in a coarse way, had some difference between them, and that in the progress of that difference they came to an open quarrel, and that one was smitten by the other, and was dead; (183) and she desired him to interpose in this case, and to do her the favour to save this her son from her kindred, who were very zealous to have him that had slain his brother put to death, that so she might not be further deprived of the hopes she had of being taken care of in her old age by him; and that if he would hinder this slaughter of her son by those that wished for it, he would do her a great favour, because the kindred would not be restrained from their purpose by anything else than

by the fear of him: (184) and when the king had given his consent to what the woman had begged of him, she made this reply to him: 'I owe thee thanks for thy benignity to me in pitying my old age, and preventing the loss of my only remaining child; but in order to assure me of this thy kindness, be first reconciled to thine own son, and cease to be angry with him; (185) for how shall I persuade myself that thou hast really bestowed this favour upon me, while thou thyself continuest after the like manner in thy wrath to thine own son? For it is a foolish thing to add wilfully another to thy dead son, while the death of the other was brought about without thy consent.' (186) And now the king perceived that this pretended story was a subornation derived from Joab, and was of his contrivance; and when, upon inquiry of the old woman, he understood it to be so in reality, he called for Joab, and told him he had obtained what he requested according to his own mind; and he bid him bring Absalom back, for he was not now displeased, but had already ceased to be angry with him. (187) So Joab bowed himself down to the king, and took his words kindly, and went immediately to Geshur, and took Absalom with him, and came to Jerusalem.

(188) However, the king sent a message to his son beforehand, as he was coming, and commanded him to retire to his own house, for he was not yet in such a disposition as to think fit at present to see him. Accordingly, upon the father's command, he avoided coming into his presence, and contented himself with the respects paid him by his own family only. (189) Now his beauty was not impaired, either by the grief he had been under, or by the want of such care as was proper to be taken of a king's son, for he still surpassed and excelled all men in the tallness of his body, and was more eminent [in a fine appearance] than those that dieted the most luxuriously; and indeed such was the thickness of the hair of his head, that it was with difficulty he was polled every eighth day; and his hair weighed two hundred shekels, which are five pounds. (190) However, he dwelt in Jerusalem two years, and became the father of three sons and one daughter; which daughter was of very great beauty, and which Rehoboam, the son of Solomon, took to wife afterward, and had by her a son named Abijah; (191) but Absalom sent to Joab, and desired him to pacify his father entirely towards him, and to beseech him to give him leave to come to him to see him, and speak with him; but when Joab neglected so to do, he sent some of his own servants, and set fire to the field adjoining to him; which, when Joab understood, he came to Absalom, and accused him of what he had done; and asked him the reason why he did so? (192) To which Absalom replied, that 'I have found out this stratagem that might bring thee to us, while thou hast taken no care to perform the injunction I laid upon thee, which was this, to reconcile my father to me; and I really beg it of thee, now thou art here, to pacify my father as to me, since I esteem my

coming hither to be more grievous than my banishment, while my father's wrath against me continues.' (193) Hereby Joab was persuaded, and pitied the distress that Absalom was in, and became an intercessor with the king for him; and when he had discoursed with his father, he soon brought him to that amicable disposition towards Absalom that he presently sent for him to come to him; and when he had cast himself down upon the ground, and had begged for the forgiveness of his offences, the king raised him up, and promised him to forget what he had formerly done.

CHAPTER 9

(194) Now Absalom, upon this his success with the king, procured to himself a great many horses, and many chariots, and that in a little time also. He had moreover fifty armour bearers that were about him, (195) and he came early every day to the king's palace, and spake what was agreeable to such as came for justice and lost their causes, as if that happened for want of good counsellors about the king, or perhaps because the judges mistook in that unjust sentence they gave; whereby he gained the good will of them all. He told them, that had he but such authority committed to him, he would distribute justice to them in a most equitable manner. (196) When he had made himself so popular among the multitude, he thought he had already the good will of the people secured to him; but when four years had passed since his father's reconciliation to him, he came to him, and besought him to give him leave to go to Hebron, and pay a sacrifice to God, because he vowed it to him when he fled out of the country. So when David had granted his request, he went thither, and great multitudes came running together to him, for he had sent to a great number so to do.

(197) Among them came Ahithophel the Gilonite, a counsellor of David's, and two hundred men out of Jerusalem itself, who knew not his intentions, but were sent for as to a sacrifice. So he was appointed king by all of them, which he obtained by this stratagem. (198) As soon as this news was brought to David, and he was informed of what he did not expect from his son, he was affrighted at this his impious and bold undertaking, and wondered that he was so far from remembering how his offence had been so lately forgiven him, that he undertook much worse and more wicked enterprises; first, to deprive him of that kingdom which was given him of God; and, secondly, to take away his own father's life. He therefore resolved to fly to the parts beyond Jordan; (199) so he called his most intimate friends together, and communicated to them all that he had heard of his son's madness. He committed himself to God, to judge between them about all their actions, and left the care of his royal palace to his ten concubines, and went away from Jerusalem, being willingly accompanied

by the rest of the multitude, who went hastily away with him, and particularly by those six hundred armed men, who had been with him from his first flight in the days of Saul. (200) But he persuaded Abiathar and Zadok, the high priests, who had determined to go away with him, as also all the Levites, who were with the ark, to stay behind, as hoping that God would deliver him without its removal; (201) but he charged them to let him know privately how all things went on; and he had their sons, Ahimaaz the son of Zadok, and Jonathan the son of Abiathar, for faithful ministers in all things; but Ittai the Gittite went out with him whether David would let him or not, for he would have persuaded him to stay, and on that account he appeared the more friendly to him; (202) but as he was ascending the Mount of Olives barefooted, and all his company were in tears, it was told him that Ahithophel was with Absalom, and was of his side. This hearing augmented his grief, and he besought God earnestly to alienate the mind of Absalom from Ahithophel, for he was afraid that he should persuade him to follow his pernicious counsel, for he was a prudent man, and very sharp in seeing what was advantageous. (203) When David was gotten upon the top of the mountain, he took a view of the city, and prayed to God with abundance of tears, as having already lost his kingdom; and here it was that a faithful friend of his, whose name was Hushai, met him. (204) When David saw him with his clothes rent, and having ashes all over his head, and in lamentation for the great change of affairs, he comforted him, and exhorted him to leave off grieving; nay, at length he besought him to go back to Absalom, and appear as one of his party, and to fish out the secretest counsels of his mind, and to contradict the counsels of Ahithophel, for that he could not do him so much good by being with him as he might by being with Absalom. So he was prevailed on by David, and left him, and came to Jerusalem, whither Absalom himself came also a little while afterward.

(205) When David was gone a little further, there met him Ziba, the servant of Mephibosheth (whom he had sent to take care of the possessions which had been given him, as the son of Jonathan, the son of Saul) with a couple of asses, laden with provisions, and desired him to take as much of them as he and his followers stood in need of. (206) And when the king asked him where he had left Mephibosheth, he said he had left him in Jerusalem, expecting to be chosen king in the present confusions, in remembrance of the benefits Saul had conferred upon them. At this the king had great indignation, and gave to Ziba all that he had formally bestowed on Mephibosheth, for he determined that it was much fitter that he should have them than the other; at which Ziba greatly rejoiced.

(207) When David was at Bahurim, a place so called, there came out a kinsman of Saul's whose name was Shimei, and threw stones at him, and gave him reproachful words; and as his friends stood about the king and protected

him, he persevered still more in his reproaches, and called him a bloody man, and the author of all sorts of mischief. (208) He bade him also go out of the land as an impure and accursed wretch; and he thanked God for depriving him of his kingdom, and causing him to be punished for what injuries he had done to his master [Saul], and this by the means of his own son. Now when they all were provoked against him, and angry at him, and particularly Abishai, who had a mind to kill Shimei, David restrained his anger. (209) 'Let us not,' said he, 'bring upon ourselves another fresh misfortune to those we have already, for truly I have not the least regard nor concern for this dog that raves at me: I submit myself to God, by whose permission this man treats me in such a wild manner; nor is it any wonder that I am obliged to undergo these abuses from him, while I experience the like from an impious son of my own; but perhaps God will have some commiseration upon us, if it be his will we shall overcome them.' (210) So he went on his way without troubling himself with Shimei, who ran along the other side of the mountain, and threw out his abusive language plentifully. But when David was come to Jordan, he allowed those that were with him to refresh themselves, for they were weary.

(211) But when Absalom, and Ahithophel his counsellor, were come to Jerusalem, with all the people, David's friend Hushai came to them; and when he had worshipped Absalom, he withal wished that his kingdom might last a long time, and continue for all ages. But when Absalom said to him, 'How comes this, that he who was so intimate a friend of my father's, and appeared faithful to him in all things, is not with him now, but hath left him, and is come over to me?' Hushai's answer was very pertinent and prudent; (212) for he said, 'We ought to follow God and the multitude of the people; while these, therefore, my lord and master, are with thee, it is fit that I should follow them, for thou hast received the kingdom from God. I will therefore, if thou believest me to be thy friend, show the same fidelity and kindness to thee, which thou knowest I have shown to thy father; nor is there any reason to be in the least dissatisfied with the present state of affairs, for the kingdom is not transferred into another, but remains still in the same family, by the son's receiving it after his father.' (213) This speech persuaded Absalom, who before suspected Hushai. And now he called Ahithophel, and consulted with him what he ought to do; he persuaded him to go in unto his father's concubines; for he said, that 'by this action the people would believe that thy difference with thy father is irreconcilable, and will thence fight with great alacrity against thy father, for hitherto they are afraid of taking up open enmity against him, out of an expectation that you will be reconciled again.' (214) Accordingly Absalom was prevailed on by this advice, and commanded his servants to pitch him a tent upon the top of the royal palace, in the sight of the multitude; and he went in and lay with his father's concubines. Now this came to pass

according to the prediction of Nathan, when he prophesied and signified to him that his son would rise up in rebellion against him.

(215) And when Absalom had done what he was advised to by Ahithophel, he desired his advice, in the second place, about the war against his father. Now Ahithophel only asked him to let him have ten thousand chosen men, and he promised he would slay his father, and bring the soldiers back again in safety; and he said that then the kingdom would be firm to him when David was dead [but not otherwise]. (216) Absalom was pleased with this advice, and called for Hushai, David's friend (for so did he style him), and informed him of the opinion of Ahithophel; he asked, further, what was his opinion concerning that matter. Now he was sensible that if Ahithophel's counsel were followed, David would be in danger of being seized on, and slain; so he attempted to introduce a contrary opinion, and said, (217) 'Thou art not unacquainted, O king, with the valour of thy father, and of those that are now with him; that he hath made many wars, and hath always come off with victory, though probably he now abides in the camp, for he is very skilful in stratagems, and in foreseeing the deceitful tricks of his enemies; (218) yet will he leave his own soldiers in the evening, and will either hide himself in some valley, or will place an ambush at some rock; so that, when our army joins battle with him, his soldiers will retire for a little while, but will come upon us again, as encouraged by the king's being near them; and in the meantime your father will show himself suddenly in the time of the battle, and will infuse courage into his own people when they are in danger, but bring consternation to thine. (219) Consider, therefore, my advice, and reason upon it, and if thou canst not but acknowledge it to be the best, reject the opinion of Ahithophel. Send to the entire country of the Hebrews, and order them to come and fight with thy father; and do thou thyself take the army, and be thine own general in this war, and do not trust its management to another; (220) then expect to conquer him with ease, when thou overtakest him openly with his few partisans, but hast thyself many ten thousands, who will be desirous to demonstrate to thee their diligence and alacrity. And if thy father shall shut himself up in some city, and bear a siege, we will overthrow that city with machines of war, and by undermining it.' (221) When Hushai had said this, he obtained his point against Ahithophel, for his opinion was preferred by Absalom before the other's; however, it was no other than God who made the counsel of Hushai appear best to the mind of Absalom.

(222) So Hushai made haste to the high priests, Zadok and Abiathar, and told them the opinion of Ahithophel, and his own, and that the resolution was taken to follow this latter advice. He therefore bade them send to David, and tell him of it, and to inform him of the counsels that had been taken; and to desire him further to pass quickly over Jordan, lest his son should change his

mind, and make haste to pursue him, and so prevent him, and seize upon him before he be in safety. (223) Now the high priests had their sons concealed in a proper place out of the city, that they might carry news to David of what was transacted. Accordingly, they sent a maidservant whom they could trust, to them, to carry the news of Absalom's counsels, and ordered them to signify the same to David with all speed. (224) So they made no excuse nor delay, but taking along with them their father's injunctions, because pious and faithful ministers, and judging that quickness and suddenness was the best mark of faithful service, they made haste to meet with David. (225) But certain horsemen saw them when they were two furlongs from the city, and informed Absalom of them, who immediately sent some to take them; but when the sons of the high priests perceived this, they went out of the road, and betook themselves to a certain village (that village was called Bahurim); there they desired a certain woman to hide them, and afford them security. (226) Accordingly she let the young men down by a rope into a well, and laid fleeces of wool over them; and when those that pursued them came to her, and asked her whether she saw them, she did not deny that she had seen them, for that they had stayed with her some time, but she said they then went their ways, and she foretold that, however, if they would follow them directly, they would catch them; but when, after a long pursuit, they could not catch them, they came back again; (227) and when the woman saw those men were returned, and that there was no longer any fear of the young men's being caught by them, she drew them up by the rope, and bade them go on their journey. Accordingly they used great diligence in the prosecution of that journey, and came to David and informed him accurately of all the counsels of Absalom. So he commanded those that were with him to pass over Jordan while it was night, and not to delay at all on that account.

(228) But Ahithophel, on rejection of his advice, got upon his ass and rode away to his own country, Gilon; and, calling his family together, he told them distinctly what advice he had given Absalom; and since he had not been persuaded by it, he said he would evidently perish, and this in no long time, and that David would overcome him, and return to his kingdom again; (229) so he said it was better that he should take his own life away with freedom and magnanimity, than expose himself to be punished by David, in opposition to whom he had acted entirely for Absalom. When he had discoursed thus to them, he went into the inmost room of his house, and hanged himself; and thus was the death of Ahithophel, who was self-condemned; and when his relations had taken him down from the halter, they took care of his funeral. (230) Now, as for David, he passed over Jordan, as we have said already, and came to Mahanaim, a very fine and very strong city; and all the chief men of the country received him with great pleasure, both out of the shame they had that he should

be forced to flee away from Jerusalem, and out of the respect they bare him while he was in his former prosperity. These were Barzillai the Gileadite, and Siphar the ruler among the Ammonites, and Machir the principal man of Gilead; (231) and these furnished him with plentiful provisions for himself and his followers, insomuch that they wanted no beds nor blankets for them, nor loaves of bread, nor wine; nay, they brought them a great many cattle for slaughter, and afforded them what furniture they wanted for their refreshment when they were weary, and for food, with plenty of other necessaries.

CHAPTER 10

(232) And this was the state of David and his followers; but Absalom got together a vast army of the Hebrews to oppose his father, and passed therewith over the river Jordan, and sat down not far from Mahanaim, in the country of Gilead. He appointed Amasa to be captain of all his host, instead of Joab his kinsman; his father was Ithra, and his mother Abigail; now she and Zeruiah, the mother of Joab, were David's sisters; (233) but when David had numbered his followers, and found them to be about four thousand, he resolved not to tarry till Absalom attacked him, but set over his men captains of thousands, and captains of hundreds, and divided his army into three parts; the one part he committed to Joab, the next to Abishai, Joab's brother, and the third to Ittai, David's companion and friend, but one that came from the city Gath; (234) and when he was desirous of fighting himself among them, his friends would not let him; and this refusal of theirs was founded upon very wise reasons: 'For,' said they, 'if we be conquered when he is with us, we have lost all good hopes of recovering ourselves; but if we should be beaten in one part of our army, the other parts may retire to him, and may thereby prepare a greater force, while the enemy will naturally suppose that he hath another army with him.' (235) So David was pleased with this their advice, and resolved himself to tarry at Mahanaim; and as he sent his friends and commanders to the battle, he desired them to show all possible alacrity and fidelity, and to bear in mind what advantages they had received from him, which, though they had not been very great, yet had they not been quite inconsiderable; and he begged of them to spare the young man Absalom, lest some mischief should befall himself, if he should be killed; and thus did he send out his army to the battle, and wished them victory therein.

(236) Then did Joab put his army in battle array over against the enemy in the Great Plain, where he had a wood behind him. Absalom also brought his army into the field to oppose him. Upon the joining of the battle, both sides showed great actions with their hands and their boldness; the one side exposing themselves to the greatest hazards, and using their utmost alacrity, that David

might recover his kingdom; and the other being no way deficient, either in doing or suffering, that Absalom might not be deprived of that kingdom, and be brought to punishment by his father, for his impudent attempt against him. (237) Those also that were the most numerous were solicitous that they might not be conquered by those few that were with Joab and with the other commanders, because that would be the greatest disgrace to them; while David's soldiers strove greatly to overcome so many ten thousands as the enemy had with them. Now David's men were conquerors, as superior in strength and skill in war; (238) so they followed the others as they fled away through the forests and valleys; some they took prisoners, and many they slew, and more in the flight than in the battle, for there fell about twenty thousand that day. But all David's men ran violently upon Absalom, for he was easily known by his beauty and tallness. (239) He was himself also afraid lest his enemies should seize on him, so he got upon the king's mule and fled; but as he was carried with violence and noise, and a great motion, as being himself light, he entangled his hair greatly in the large boughs of a knotty tree that spread a great way, and there he hung, after a surprising manner; and as for the beast it went on farther, and that swiftly, as if his master had been still upon his back; but he hanging in the air upon the boughs, was taken by his enemies. (240) Now when one of David's soldiers saw this, he informed Joab of it; and when the general said, that if he had shot at and killed Absalom, he would have given him fifty shekels, he replied, 'I would not have killed my master's son if thou wouldst have given me a thousand shekels, especially when he desired that the young man might be spared, in the hearing of us all.' (241) But Joab bade him show him where it was he saw Absalom hang; whereupon he shot him to the heart, and slew him, and Joab's armour bearers stood round the tree, and pulled down his dead body, (242) and cast it into a great chasm that was out of sight, and laid a heap of stones upon him, till the cavity was filled up, and had both the appearance and the bigness of a grave. Then Joab sounded a retreat, and recalled his own soldiers from pursuing the enemy's army, in order to spare their countrymen.

(243) Now Absalom had erected for himself a marble pillar in the king's dale, two furlongs distant from Jerusalem, which he named Absalom's Hand, saying that if his children were killed, his name would remain by that pillar; for he had three sons and one daughter named Tamar, as we said before, (244) who, when she was married to David's grandson, Rehoboam, bore a son, Abijah by name, who succeeded his father in the kingdom; but of these we shall speak in a part of our history which will be more proper. After the death of Absalom, they returned every one to their own home respectively.

(245) But now Ahimaaz, the son of Zadok the high priest, went to Joab, and desired he would permit him to go and tell David of this victory, and to bring

him the good news that God had afforded his assistance and his providence to him. (246) However, he did not grant his request, but said to him, 'Wilt thou, who hast always been the messenger of good news, now go and acquaint the king that his son is dead?' So he desired him to desist. He then called Cushi, and committed the business to him, that he should tell the king what he had seen. (247) But when Ahimaaz again desired him to let him go as a messenger, and assured him that he would only relate what concerned the victory, but not concerning the death of Absalom, he gave him leave to go to David. Now he took a nearer road than the former did, for nobody knew it but himself, and he came before Cushi. (248) Now as David was sitting between the gates, and waiting to see when somebody would come to him from the battle, and tell him how it went, one of the watchmen saw Ahimaaz running, and before be could discern who he was, he told David that he saw somebody coming to him, (249) who said he was a good messenger. A little while after, he informed him, that another messenger followed him; whereupon the king said that he also was a good messenger; but when the watchman saw Ahimaaz, and that he was already very near, he gave the king notice, that it was the son of Zadok the high priest, who came running. So David was very glad, and said he was a messenger of good tidings, and brought him some such news from the battle as be desired to hear.

(250) While the king was saying thus, Ahimaaz appeared, and worshipped the king. And when the king inquired of him about the battle, he said he brought him the good news of victory and dominion. And when he inquired what he had to say concerning his son, he said that he came away on the sudden as soon as the enemy was defeated, but that he heard a great noise of those that pursued Absalom, and that he could learn no more, because of the haste he made when Joab sent him to inform him of the victory. (251) But when Cushi was come, and had worshipped him, and informed him of the victory, he asked him about his son, who replied, 'May the like misfortune befall thine enemies as hath befallen Absalom.' (252) That word did not permit either himself or his soldiers to rejoice at the victory, though it was a very great one; but David went up to the highest part of the city, and wept for his son, and beat his breast, tearing [the hair of] his head, tormenting himself all manner of ways, and crying out, 'O, my son! I wish that I had died myself, and ended my days with thee!' for he was of a tender natural affection, and had extraordinary compassion for this son in particular. (253) But when the army of Joab heard that the king mourned for his son, they were ashamed to enter the city in the habit of conquerors, but they all came in as cast down, and in tears, as if they had been beaten. (254) Now while the king covered himself, and grievously lamented his son, Joab went in to him, and said, 'O my lord the king, thou art not aware that thou layest a blot on thyself by what thou now doest; for thou now seemest to

hate those that love thee and undergo dangers for thee; nay to hate thyself and thy family, and to love those that are thy bitter enemies, and do desire the company of those that are no more, and who have been justly slain; (255) for had Absalom gotten the victory, and firmly settled himself in the kingdom, there had been none of us left alive, but all of us, beginning with thyself and thy children, had miserably perished, while our enemies had not wept for his, but rejoiced over us, and punished even those that pitied us in our misfortunes; and thou art not ashamed to do this in the case of one that has been thy bitter enemy, who, while he was thine own son, hath proved so wicked to thee. (256) Leave off, therefore, thy unreasonable grief, and come abroad and be seen by thy soldiers, and return them thanks for the alacrity they showed in the fight; for I myself will this day persuade the people to leave thee, and to give the kingdom to another, if thou continuest to do thus; and then I shall make thee to grieve bitterly and in earnest.' (257) Upon Joab's speaking thus to him, he made the king leave off his sorrow, and brought him to the consideration of his affairs. So David changed his habit, and exposed himself in a manner fit to be seen by the multitude, and sat in the gates: whereupon all the people heard of it, and ran together to him, and saluted him. And this was the present state of David's affairs.

CHAPTER II

(258) Now those Hebrews that had been with Absalom, and had retired out of the battle, when they were all returned home, sent messengers to every city to put them in mind of what benefits David had bestowed upon them, and of that liberty which he had procured them, by delivering them from many and great wars. (259) But they complained, that whereas they had ejected him out of his kingdom, and committed it to another governor, which other governor, whom they had set up, was already dead, they did not now beseech David to leave off his anger at them and to become friends with them, and as he used to do, to resume the care of their affairs, and take the kingdom again. (260) This was often told to David. And, this notwithstanding, David sent to Zadok and Abiathar the high priests, that they should speak to the rulers of the tribe of Judah after the manner following: that it would be a reproach upon them to permit the other tribes to choose David for their king, before their tribe, and this, said he, while you are akin to him, and of the same common blood. (261) He commanded them also to say the same to Amasa the captain of their forces, that whereas he was his sister's son, he had not persuaded the multitude to restore the kingdom to David: that he might expect from him not only a reconciliation, for that was already granted, but that supreme command of the army also which Absalom had bestowed upon him. (262) Accordingly the

high priests, when they had discoursed with the rulers of the tribe, and said what the king had ordered them, persuaded Amasa to undertake the care of his affairs. So he persuaded that tribe to send immediately ambassadors to him, to beseech him to return to his own kingdom. The same did all the Israelites, at the like persuasion of Amasa.

(263) When the ambassadors came to him, he came to Jerusalem; and the tribe of Judah was the first that came to meet the king at the river Jordan; and Shimei, the son of Gera, came with a thousand men, which he brought with him out of the tribe of Benjamin; and Ziba, the freedman of Saul, with his sons, fifteen in number, and with his twenty servants. (264) All these, as well as the tribe of Judah, laid a bridge [of boats] over the river, that the king and those that were with him might with ease pass over it. Now as soon as he was come to Jordan, the tribe of Judah saluted him. Shimei also came upon the bridge, took hold of his feet, and prayed him to forgive him what he had offended, and not to be too bitter against him, nor to think fit to make him the first example of severity under his new authority; but to consider that he had repented of his failure of duty, and had taken care to come first of all to him. (265) While he was thus entreating the king, and moving him to compassion, Abishai, Joab's brother, said, And shall not this man die for this, that he hath cursed that king whom God hath appointed to reign over us? But David turned himself to him, and said, 'Will you never leave off, ye sons of Zeruiah? Do not you, I pray, raise new troubles and seditions among us, now the former are over; (266) for I would not have you ignorant, that I this day begin my reign, and therefore swear to remit to all offenders their punishments, and not to animadvert on anyone that has sinned. Be thou, therefore,' said he, 'O Shimei, of good courage, and do not at all fear being put to death.' So he worshipped him, and went on before him.

(267) Mephibosheth also, Saul's grandson, met David, clothed in a sordid garment, and having his hair thick and neglected: for after David was fled away, he was in such grief that he had not polled his head, nor had he washed his clothes, as dooming himself to undergo such hardships upon occasion of the change of the king's affairs. Now he had been unjustly calumniated to the king by Ziba, his steward. (268) When he had saluted the king, and worshipped him, the king began to ask him why he did not go out of Jerusalem with him, and accompany him during his flight? He replied, that this piece of injustice was owing to Ziba; because, when he was ordered to get things ready for his going out with him, he took no care of it, but regarded him no more than if he had been a slave; (269) 'and, indeed, had I had my feet sound and strong, I had not deserted thee, for I could then have made use of them in my flight; but this is not all the injury that Ziba has done me as to my duty to thee, my lord and master, but he hath calumniated me besides, and told lies about me of his own

invention; but I know thy mind will not admit of such calumnies, but is righteously disposed and a lover of truth, (270) which it is also the will of God should prevail. For when thou wast in the greatest danger of suffering by my grandfather, and when, on that account, our whole family might justly have been destroyed, thou wast moderate and merciful, and didst then especially forget all those injuries, when, if thou hadst remembered them, thou hadst the power of punishing us for them; but thou hast judged me to be thy friend, and hast set me every day at thine own table; nor have I wanted anything which one of thine own kinsmen, of greatest esteem with thee, could have expected.' (271) When he had said this, David resolved neither to punish Mephibosheth, nor to condemn Ziba, as having belied his master; but said to him, that as he had [before] granted all his estate to Ziba, because he did not come along with him, so he [now] promised to forgive him, and ordered that the one half of his estate should be restored to him. Whereupon Mephibosheth said, 'Nay, let Ziba take all; it suffices me that thou hast recovered thy kingdom.'

(272) But David desired Barzillai the Gileadite, that great and good man, and one that had made a plentiful provision for him at Mahanaim, and had conducted him as far as Jordan, to accompany him to Jerusalem, for he promised to treat him in his old age with all manner of respect – to take care of him, and provide for him. (273) But Barzillai was so desirous to live at home, that he entreated him to excuse him from attendance on him; and said, that his age was too great to enjoy the pleasures [of a court], since he was fourscore years old, and was therefore making provision for his death and burial; so he desired him to gratify him in this request, and dismiss him; (274) for he had no relish of his meat or his drink, by reason of his age; and that his ears were too much shut up to hear the sound of pipes, or the melody of other musical instruments, such as all those that live with kings delight in. When he entreated for this so earnestly, the king said, 'I dismiss thee; but thou shalt grant me thy son Chimham, and upon him I will bestow all sorts of good things.' (275) So Barzillai left his son with him, and worshipped the king, and wished him a prosperous conclusion of all his affairs according to his own mind, and then returned home: but David came to Gilgal, having about him half the people [of Israel] and the [whole] tribe of Judah.

(276) Now the principal men of the country came to Gilgal to him with a great multitude, and complained of the tribe of Judah, that they had come to him in a private manner, whereas they ought all conjointly, and with one and the same intention, to have given him the meeting. But the rulers of the tribe of Judah desired them not to be displeased if they had been prevented by them: for, said they, 'We are David's kinsmen, and on that account we the rather took care of him, and loved him, and so came first to him;' yet had they not, by their early coming, received any gifts from him, which might give them who

came last any uneasiness. (277) When the rulers of the tribe of Judah had said this, the rulers of the other tribe were not quiet, but said further, 'O brethren, we cannot but wonder at you when you call the king your kinsman alone, whereas he that hath received from God the power over all of us in common, ought to be esteemed a kinsman to us all; for which reason the whole people have eleven parts in him, and you but one part: we are also elder than you; wherefore you have not done justly in coming to the king in this private and concealed manner.'

(278) While these rulers were thus disputing one with another, a certain wicked man, who took a pleasure in seditious practices (his name was Sheba, the son of Bichri, of the tribe of Benjamin) stood up in the midst of the multitude, and cried aloud, and spake thus to them: 'We have no part in David, nor inheritance in the son of Jesse.' (279) And when he had used those words, he blew with a trumpet, and declared war against the king; and they all left David, and followed him; the tribe of Judah alone stayed with him, and settled him at his royal palace at Jerusalem. But as for his concubines, with whom Absalom his son had accompanied, truly he removed them to another house, and ordered those that had the care of them to make a plentiful provision for them; but he came not near them any more. (280) He also appointed Amasa for the captain of his forces, and gave him the same high office which Joab before had; and he commanded him to gather together, out of the tribe of Judah, as great an army as he could, and come to him within three days, that he might deliver to him his entire army, and might send him to fight against [Sheba] the son of Bichri. (281) Now while Amasa was gone out, and made some delay in gathering the army together, and so was not yet returned, on the third day the king said to Joab, 'It is not fit we should make any delay in this affair of Sheba, lest he get a numerous army about him, and be the occasion of greater mischief, and hurt our affairs more than did Absalom himself; (282) do not thou therefore wait any longer, but take such forces as thou hast at hand, and that [old] body of six hundred men and thy brother Abishai with thee, and pursue after our enemy, and endeavour to fight him wheresoever thou canst overtake him. Make haste to prevent him, lest he seize upon some fenced cities, and cause us great labour and pains before we take him.'

(283) So Joab resolved to make no delay, but taking with him his brother and those six hundred men, and giving orders that the rest of the army which was at Jerusalem should follow him, he marched with great speed against Sheba; and when he was come to Gibeon, which is a village forty furlongs distant from Jerusalem, Amasa brought a great army with him, and met Joab. Now Joab was girded with a sword, and his breastplate on; (284) and when Amasa came near him to salute him, he took particular care that his sword

should fall out, as it were of its own accord; so he took it up from the ground, and while he approached Amasa, who was then near him, as though he would kiss him, he took hold of Amasa's beard with his other hand, and he smote him in his belly when he did not foresee it, and slew him. This impious and altogether profane action, Joab did to a young man, and his kinsman, and one that had done him no injury, and this out of jealousy that he would obtain the chief command of the army, and be in equal dignity with himself about the king: (285) and for the same cause it was that he killed Abner; but as to that former wicked action, the death of his brother Asahel, which he seemed to revenge, afforded him a decent pretence, and made that crime a pardonable one; but in this murder of Amasa there was no such covering for it. (286) Now when Joab had killed this general, he pursued after Sheba, having left a man with the dead body, who was ordered to proclaim aloud to the army that Amasa was justly slain, and deservedly punished. 'But,' said he, 'if you be for the king, follow Joab his general, and Abishai, Joab's brother:' (287) but because the body lay on the road, and all the multitude came running to it, and, as is usual with the multitude, stood wondering a great while at it, he that guarded it removed it thence, and carried it to a certain place that was very remote from the road, and there laid it, and covered it with his garment. When this was done, all the people followed Joab. (288) Now as he pursued Sheba through all the country of Israel, one told him that he was in a strong city, called Abel–beth–maachah. Hereupon Joab went thither, and set about it with his army, and cast up a bank round it, and ordered his soldiers to undermine the walls, and to overthrow them; and since the people in the city did not admit him, he was greatly displeased at them.

(289) Now there was a woman of small account, and yet both wise and intelligent, who seeing her native city lying at the last extremity, ascended upon the wall, and, by means of the armed men, called for Joab; and when he came to her, she began to say, that 'God ordained kings and generals of armies, that they might cut off the enemies of the Hebrews, and introduce a universal peace among them; but thou art endeavouring to overthrow and depopulate a metropolis of the Israelites, which hath been guilty of no offence.' (290) But he replied, 'God continue to be merciful unto me: I am disposed to avoid killing anyone of the people, much less would I destroy such a city as this; and if they will deliver me up Sheba, the son of Bichri, who hath rebelled against the king, I will leave off the siege, and withdraw the army from the place.' (291) Now as soon as the woman heard what Joab said, she desired him to intermit the siege for a little while, for that he should have the head of his enemy thrown out to him presently. So she went down to the citizens, and said to them, 'Will you be so wicked as to perish miserably, with your children and wives, for the sake of a vile fellow, and one whom nobody knows who he is? And will you have

him for your king instead of David, who hath been so great a benefactor to you, and oppose your city alone to such a mighty and strong army?' (292) So she prevailed with them, and they cut off the head of Sheba, and threw it into Joab's army. When this was done, the king's general sounded a retreat, and raised the siege. And when he was come to Jerusalem, he was again appointed to be general of all the people. (293) The king also constituted Benaiah captain of the guards, and of the six hundred men. He also set Adoram over the tribute, and Sabathes and Achilaus over the records. He made Sheva the scribe, and appointed Zadok and Abiathar the high priests.

CHAPTER 12

(294) After this, when the country was greatly afflicted with a famine, David besought God to have mercy on the people, and to discover to him what was the cause of it, and how a remedy might be found for that distemper. And when the prophets answered, that God would have the Gibeonites avenged, whom Saul the king was so wicked as to betray to slaughter, and had not observed the oath which Joshua the general and the senate had sworn to them. (295) If, therefore, said God, the king would permit such vengeance to be taken for those that were slain as the Gibeonites should desire, he promised that he would be reconciled to them, and free the multitude from their miseries. (296) As soon therefore as the king understood that this it was which God sought, he sent for the Gibeonites, and asked them what it was they would have; and when they desired to have seven sons of Saul delivered to them to be punished, he delivered them up, but spared Mephibosheth the son of Jonathan. (297) So when the Gibeonites had received the men, they punished them as they pleased; upon which God began to send rain, and to recover the earth to bring forth its fruits as usual, and to free it from the foregoing drought, so that the country of the Hebrews flourished again. (298) A little afterward the king made war against the Philistines; and when he had joined battle with them, and put them to flight, he was left alone, as he was in pursuit of them; (299) and when he was quite tired down, he was seen by one of the enemy, his name was Achmon, the son of Araph; he was one of the sons of the giants. He had a spear, the handle of which weighed three hundred shekels, and a breastplate of chain-work, and a sword. He turned back, and ran violently to slay [David] their enemy's king, for he was quite tired out with labour; but Abishai, Joab's brother, appeared on the sudden, and protected the king with his shield, as he lay down, and slew the enemy. (300) Now the multitude were very uneasy at these dangers of the king, and that he was very near to be slain: and the rulers made him swear that he would no more go out with them to battle, lest he should come to some great misfortune by his

courage and boldness, and thereby deprive the people of the benefits they now enjoyed by his means, and of those that they might hereafter enjoy by his living a long time among them.

(301) When the king heard that the Philistines were gathered together at the city Gazara, he sent an army against them, when Sibbechai the Hittite, one of David's most courageous men, behaved himself so as to deserve great commendation, for he slew many of those that bragged they were the posterity of the giants, and vaunted themselves highly on that account, and thereby was the occasion of victory to the Hebrews. (302) After which defeat, the Philistines made war again; and when David had sent an army against them, Nephan his kinsman fought in a single combat with the stoutest of all the Philistines, and slew him, and put the rest to flight. Many of them also were slain in the fight. (303) Now a little while after this, the Philistines pitched their camp at a city which lay not far off the bounds of the country of the Hebrews. They had a man who was six cubits tall, and had on each of his feet and hands one more toe and finger than men naturally have. (304) Now the person who was sent against them by David out of his army was Jonathan, the son of Shimea, who fought this man in a single combat, and slew him; and as he was the person who gave the turn to the battle, he gained the greatest reputation for courage therein. This man also vaunted himself to be of the sons of the giants. But after this fight, the Philistines made war no more against the Israelites.

(305) And now David being freed from wars and dangers, and enjoying for the future a profound peace, composed songs and hymns to God, of several sorts of meter; some of those which he made were *trimeters*, and some were *pentameters*. He also made instruments of music, and taught the Levites to sing hymns to God, both on that called the sabbath day, and on other festivals. (306) Now the construction of the instruments was thus: the viol was an instrument of ten strings, it was played upon with a bow; the psaltery had twelve musical notes, and was played upon by the fingers; the cymbals were broad and large instruments, and were made of brass. And so much shall suffice to be spoken by us about these instruments, that the readers may not be wholly unacquainted with their nature.

(307) Now all the men that were about David, were men of courage. Those that were most illustrious and famous of them for their actions were thirty-eight; of five of whom I will only relate the performances, for these will suffice to make manifest the virtues of the others also; for these were powerful enough to subdue countries, and conquer great nations. (308) First, therefore, was Jessai, the son of Achimaas, who frequently leaped upon the troops of the enemy, and did not leave off fighting till he overthrew nine hundred of them. After him was Eleazar, the son of Dodo, who was with the king at Arasam.

(309) This man, when once the Israelites were under a consternation at the multitude of the Philistines, and were running away, stood alone, and fell upon the enemy, and slew many of them, till his sword clung to his hand by the blood he had shed, and till the Israelites, seeing the Philistines retire by his means, came down from the mountains and pursued them, and at that time won a surprising and a famous victory, while Eleazar slew the men, and the multitude followed and spoiled their dead bodies. The third was Sheba, the son of Ilus. (310) Now this man, when, in the wars against the Philistines, they pitched their camp at a place called Lehi, and when the Hebrews were again afraid of their army, and did not stay, he stood still alone, as an army and a body of men; and some of them he overthrew, and some who were not able to abide his strength and force, he pursued. (311) These are the works of the hands, and of fighting, which these three performed. Now at the time when the king was once at Jerusalem, and the army of the Philistines came upon him to fight him, David went up to the top of the citadel, as we have already said, to inquire of God concerning the battle, (312) while the enemy's camp lay in the valley that extends to the city Bethlehem, which is twenty furlongs distant from Jerusalem. Now David said to his companions, 'We have excellent water in my own city, especially that which is in the pit near the gate,' wondering if anyone would bring him some of it to drink; but he said that he would rather have it than a great deal of money. (313) When these three men heard what he said, they ran away immediately, and burst through the midst of their enemy's camp, and came to Bethlehem; and when they had drawn the water, they returned again through the enemy's camp to the king, insomuch that the Philistines were so surprised at their boldness and alacrity, that they were quiet, and did nothing against them as if they despised their small number. (314) But when the water was brought to the king, he would not drink it, saying, that it was brought by the danger and the blood of men, and that it was not proper on that account to drink it. But he poured it out to God, and gave him thanks for the salvation of the men. (315) Next to these was Abishai, Joab's brother; for he in one day slew six hundred. The fifth of these was Benaiah, by lineage a priest; for being challenged by (two) eminent men in the country of Joab, he overcame them by his valour. Moreover, there was a man, by nation an Egyptian, who was of a vast bulk, and challenged him, yet did he, when he was unarmed, kill him with his own spear, which he threw at him, for he caught him by force, and took away his weapons while he was alive and fighting, and slew him with his own weapons. (316) One may also add this to the forementioned actions of the same man, either as the principal of them in alacrity, or as resembling the rest. When God sent a snow, there was a lion who slipped and fell into a certain pit, and because the pit's mouth was narrow, it was evident he would perish, being enclosed with the

snow; so when he saw no way to get out and save himself, he roared. (317) When Benaiah heard the wild beast, he went towards him, and coming at the noise he made, he went down into the mouth of the pit and smote him, as he struggled, with a stake that lay there, and immediately slew him. The other thirty-three were like these in valour also.

CHAPTER 13

(318) Now king David was desirous to know how many ten thousands there were of the people, but forgot the commands of Moses, who told them beforehand, that if the multitude were numbered, they should pay half a shekel to God for every head. Accordingly the king commanded Joab, the captain of his host, to go and number the whole multitude; (319) but when he said there was no necessity for such a numeration, he was not persuaded [to countermand it], but he enjoined him to make no delay, but to go about the numbering of the Hebrews immediately. So Joab took with him the heads of the tribes, and the scribes, and went over the country of the Israelites, and took notice how numerous the multitude were, and returned to Jerusalem to the king, after nine months and twenty days; and he gave in to the king the number of the people, without the tribe of Benjamin, for he had not yet numbered that tribe, (320) no more than the tribe of Levi, for the king repented of his having sinned against God. Now the number of the rest of the Israelites was nine hundred thousand men who were able to bear arms and go to war: but the tribe of Judah, by itself, was four hundred thousand men.

(321) Now when the prophets had signified to David that God was angry at him, he began to entreat him, and to desire he would be merciful to him, and forgive him his sin. But God sent Nathan the prophet to him to propose to him the election of three things, that he might choose which he liked best: whether he would have a famine come upon the country for seven years, or would have a war, and be subdued three months by his enemies? Or whether God should send a pestilence and a distemper upon the Hebrews for three days? (322) But as he was fallen to a fatal choice of great miseries, he was in trouble, and sorely confounded; and when the prophet had said that he must of necessity make his choice, and had ordered him to answer quickly, that he might declare what he had chosen to God, the king reasoned with himself, that in case he should ask for famine, he would appear to do it for others, and without danger to himself, since he had a great deal of corn hoarded up, but to the harm of others; (323) that in case he should choose to be overcome [by his enemies] for three months, he would appear to have chosen war, because he had valiant men about him, and strongholds, and that therefore he feared nothing therefrom: so he chose that affliction which is common to kings and

to their subjects, and in which the fear was equal on all sides; and said this beforehand, that it was much better to fall into the hands of God, than into those of his enemies.

(324) When the prophet had heard this, he declared it to God; who thereupon sent a pestilence and a mortality upon the Hebrews; nor did they die after one and the same manner, nor so that it was easy to know what the distemper was. Now, the miserable disease was one indeed, but it carried them off by ten thousand causes and occasions, which those that were afflicted could not understand; (325) for one died upon the neck of another, and the terrible malady seized them before they were aware, and brought them to their end suddenly, some giving up the ghost immediately with very great pains and bitter grief; and some were worn away by their distempers, and had nothing remaining to be buried, but as soon as ever they fell were entirely macerated; (326) some were choked, and greatly lamented their case, as being also stricken with a sudden darkness; some there were who, as they were burying a relation, fell down dead, without finishing the rites of the funeral. Now there perished of this disease, which began with the morning, and lasted till the hour of dinner, seventy thousand. (327) Nay, the angel stretched out his hand over Jerusalem, as sending this terrible judgment upon it; but David had put on sackcloth, and lay upon the ground, entreating God, and begging that the distemper might now cease, and that he would be satisfied with those that had already perished; and when the king looked up into the air, and saw the angel carried along thereby into Jerusalem, with his sword drawn, (328) he said to God, that he might justly be punished, who was their shepherd; but that the sheep ought to be preserved, as not having sinned at all; and he implored God that he would send his wrath upon him, and upon all his family, but spare the people.

(329) When God heard his supplication, he caused the pestilence to cease, and sent Gad the prophet to him, and commanded him to go up immediately to the thrashing floor of Araunah the Jebusite, and build an altar there to God, and offer sacrifices. When David heard that, he did not neglect his duty, but made haste to the place appointed him. (330) Now Araunah was thrashing wheat; and when he saw the king and all his servants coming to him, he ran before, and came to him, and worshipped him: he was by his lineage a Jebusite, but a particular friend of David's; and for that cause it was that, when he overthrew the city, he did him no harm, as we informed the reader a little before. (331) Now Araunah inquired, wherefore is my lord come to his servant? He answered, to buy of him the thrashing floor, that he might therein build an altar to God, and offer a sacrifice. He replied, that he freely gave him both the thrashing floor, and the ploughs and the oxen for a burnt offering; and he besought God graciously to accept his sacrifice. (332) But the king made

answer, that he took his generosity and magnanimity kindly, and accepted his good will, but he desired him to take the price of them all, for that it was not just to offer a sacrifice that cost nothing. And when Araunah said he would do as he pleased, he bought the thrashing floor of him for fifty shekels; (333) and when he had built an altar, he performed divine service, and brought a burnt offering, and offered peace offerings also. With these God was pacified, and became gracious to them again. Now it happened that Abraham came and offered his son Isaac for a burnt offering at that very place; and when the youth was ready to have his throat cut, a ram appeared on a sudden, standing by the altar, which Abraham sacrificed in the stead of his son, as we have before related. (334) Now when King David saw that God had heard his prayer, and had graciously accepted of his sacrifice, he resolved to call that entire place, *The Altar of all the People*, and to build a temple to God there; which words he uttered very appositely to what was to be done afterward; for God sent the prophet to him, and told him that there should his son build him an altar – that son who was to take the kingdom after him.

CHAPTER 14

(335) After the delivery of this prophecy, the king commanded the strangers to be numbered, and they were found to be one hundred and eighty thousand; of these he appointed fourscore thousand to be hewers of stone, and the rest of the multitude to carry the stones, and of them he set over the workmen three thousand and five hundred. He also prepared a great quantity of iron and brass for the work, with many (and those exceeding large) cedar trees, the Tyrians and Sidonians sending them to him, for he had sent to them for a supply of those trees; (336) and he told his friends that these things were now prepared, that he might leave materials ready for the building of the temple to his son, who was to reign after him, and that he might not have them to seek then, when he was very young and, by reason of his age, unskilful in such matters, but might have them lying by him, and so might the more readily complete the work.

(337) So David called his son Solomon, and charged him, when he had received the kingdom, to build a temple to God; and said, 'I was willing to build God a temple myself, but he prohibited me, because I was polluted with blood and wars; but he hath foretold that Solomon, my youngest son, should build him a temple, and should be called by that name; over whom he hath promised to take the like care as a father takes over his son; and that he would make the country of the Hebrews happy under him, and that not only in other respects, but by giving it peace, and freedom from wars and from internal seditions, which are the greatest of all blessings. (338) Since therefore,' says he, 'thou wast

ordained king by God himself before thou wast born, endeavour to render thyself worthy of this his providence, as in other instances, so particularly in being religious, and righteous, and courageous. Keep thou also his commands and his laws, which he hath given us by Moses, and do not permit others to break them. (339) Be zealous also to dedicate to God a temple, which he hath chosen to be built under thy reign; nor be thou affrighted by the vastness of the work, nor set about it timorously, for I will make all things ready before I die: (340) and take notice, that there are already ten thousand talents of gold and a hundred thousand talents of silver collected together. I have also laid together brass and iron without number, and an immense quantity of timber and of stones. Moreover, thou hast many ten thousand stonecutters and carpenters; and if thou shalt want anything farther, do thou add somewhat of thine own. Wherefore, if thou performest this work, thou wilt be acceptable to God, and have him for thy patron.' (341) David also further exhorted the rulers of the people to assist his son in this building, and to attend to the divine service, when they should be free from all their misfortunes, for that they by this means should enjoy, instead of them, peace and a happy settlement; with which blessings God rewards such men as are religious and righteous. (342) He also gave orders that when the temple should be once built, they should put the ark therein, with the holy vessels; and he assured them that they ought to have had a temple long ago, if their fathers had not been negligent of God's commands, who had given it in charge, that when they had got the possession of this land they should build him a temple. Thus did David discourse to the governors, and to his son.

(343) David was now in years, and his body, by length of time, was become cold and benumbed, insomuch that he could get no heat by covering himself with many clothes; and when the physicians came together, they agreed to this advice, that a beautiful virgin, chosen out of the whole country, should sleep by the king's side, and that this damsel would communicate heat to him, and be a remedy against his numbness. (344) Now there was found in the city one woman, of a superior beauty to all other women (her name was Abishag), who, sleeping with the king, did no more than communicate warmth to him, for he was so old that he could not know her as a husband knows his wife; but of this woman we shall speak more presently.

(345) Now the fourth son of David was a beautiful young man, and tall, born to him of Haggith his wife. He was named Adonijah, and was in his disposition like to Absalom; and exalted himself as hoping to be king, and told his friends that he ought to take the government upon him. He also prepared many chariots and horses, and fifty men to run before him. (346) When his father saw this, he did not reprove him, nor restrain him from his purpose, nor did he go so far as to ask wherefore he did so. Now Adonijah had for his assistants Joab, the captain of the army, and Abiathar the high priest; and the

only persons that opposed him were Zadok the high priest, and the prophet Nathan, and Benaiah, who was captain of the guards, and Shimei, David's friend, with all the other most mighty men. (347) Now Adonijah had prepared a supper out of the city, near the fountain that was in the king's paradise, and had invited all his brethren except Solomon and had taken with him Joab, the captain of the army, and Abiathar, and the rulers of the tribe of Judah, but had not invited to this feast either Zadok the high priest, or Nathan the prophet, or Benaiah, the captain of the guards, nor any of those of the contrary party. (348) This matter was told by Nathan the prophet to Bathsheba, Solomon's mother, that Adonijah was king, and that David knew nothing of it; and he advised her to save herself and her son Solomon, and to go by herself to David, and say to him, that he had indeed sworn that Solomon should reign after him; but that, in the meantime, Adonijah had already taken the kingdom. (349) He said that he, the prophet himself, would come after her, and when she had spoken thus to the king, would confirm what she had said. Accordingly Bathsheba agreed with Nathan, and went in to the king and worshipped him; and when she had desired leave to speak with him, (350) she told him all things in the manner that Nathan had suggested to her, and related what a supper Adonijah had made, and who they were whom he had invited: Abiathar the high priest, and Joab the general, and David's sons, excepting Solomon and his intimate friends. She also said, that all the people had their eyes upon him, to know whom he would choose for their king. She desired him also to consider how, after his departure, Adonijah, if he were king would slay her and her son Solomon.

(351) Now, as Bathsheba was speaking, the keeper of the king's chambers told him that Nathan desired to see him; and when the king had commanded that he should be admitted, he came in, and asked him whether he had ordained Adonijah to be king, and delivered the government to him, or not; (352) for that he had made a splendid supper and invited all his sons, except Solomon; as also that he had invited Joab, the captain of his host [and Abiathar the high priest], who are feasting with applauses, and many joyful sounds of instruments, and wish that his kingdom may last forever; but he hath not invited me, nor Zadok the high priest, nor Benaiah the captain of the guards; and it is but fit that all should know whether this be done by thy approbation or not. (353) When Nathan had said thus, the king commanded that they should call Bathsheba to him, for she had gone out of the room when the prophet came; and when Bathsheba was come, David said, 'I swear by Almighty God, that my son Solomon shall certainly be king, as I formerly swore; and that he shall sit upon my throne, and that this very day also.' (354) So Bathsheba worshipped him, and wished him a long life; and the king sent for Zadok the high priest, and Benaiah the captain of the guards; and when they were come, he ordered them to take with them Nathan the prophet, and

all the armed men about the palace, (355) and to set his son Solomon upon the king's mule, and to carry him out of the city to the fountain called Gihon, and to anoint him there with the holy oil, and to make him king. This he charged Zadok the high priest, and Nathan the prophet, to do; (356) and commanded them to follow Solomon through the midst of the city, and to sound the trumpets, and to wish aloud that Solomon the king may sit upon the royal throne forever, that so all the people may know that he is ordained king by his father. He also gave Solomon a charge concerning his government, to rule the whole nation of the Hebrews, and particularly the tribe of Judah, religiously and righteously. (357) And when Benaiah had prayed to God to be favourable to Solomon, without any delay they set Solomon upon the mule, and brought him out of the city to the fountain, and anointed him with oil, and brought him into the city again, with acclamations and wishes that his kingdom might continue a long time: (358) and when they had introduced him into the king's house, they set him upon the throne: whereupon all the people betook themselves to make merry, and to celebrate a festival, dancing and delighting themselves with musical pipes, till both the earth and the air echoed with the multitude of the instruments of music.

(359) Now when Adonijah and his guests perceived this noise, they were in disorder; and Joab the captain of the host said he was not pleased with these echoes, and the sound of these trumpets. And when supper was set before them, nobody tasted of it, but they were all very thoughtful what would be the matter. Then Jonathan, the son of Abiathar the high priest, came running to them; (360) and when Adonijah saw the young man gladly, and said to him that he was a good messenger, he declared to them the whole matter about Solomon, and the determination of king David; hereupon both Adonijah and all his guests rose hastily from the feast, and everyone fled to their own homes. (361) Adonijah also, as afraid of the king for what he had done, became a supplicant to God, and took hold of the horns of the altar, which were prominent. It was also told Solomon that he had so done, and that he desired to receive assurances from him that he would not remember the injury he had done, and not to inflict any severe punishment for it. (362) Solomon answered very mildly and prudently, that he forgave him this his offence; but said withal, that if he were found out in any attempt for new innovations, that he would be the author of his own punishment. So he sent to him, and raised him up from the place of his supplication. And when he was come to the king, and had worshipped him, the king bid him go away to his own house, and have no suspicion of any harm; and desired him to show himself a worthy man, as what would tend to his own advantage.

(363) But David being desirous of ordaining his son king of all the people, called together their rulers to Jerusalem, with the priests and the Levites, and

having first numbered the Levites, he found them to be thirty-eight thousand, from thirty years old to fifty; (364) out of which he appointed twenty-three thousand to take care of the building of the temple, and out of the same, six thousand to be judges of the people and scribes; four thousand for porters to the house of God, and as many for singers, to sing to the instruments which David had prepared, as we have said already. (365) He divided them also into courses: and when he had separated the priests from them, he found of these priests twenty-four courses, sixteen of the house of Eleazar, and eight of that of Ithamar; and he ordained that one course should minister to God eight days, from Sabbath to Sabbath. (366) And thus were the courses distributed by lot, in the presence of David and Zadok and Abiathar, the high priest, and of all the rulers: and that course which came up first was written down as the first, and accordingly the second, and so on to the twenty-fourth; and this partition hath remained to this day. (367) He also made twenty-four parts of the tribe of Levi; and when they cast lots, they came up in the same manner for their courses of eight days: he also honoured the posterity of Moses, and made them the keepers of the treasures of God, and of the donations which the king dedicated: he also ordained that all the tribe of Levi, as well as the priests, should serve God night and day as Moses had enjoined them.

(368) After this he parted the entire army into twelve parts, with their leaders [and captains of hundreds], and commanders. Now every part had twenty-four thousand, which were ordered to wait on Solomon, by thirty days at a time, from the first day to the last, with the captains of thousands and captains of hundreds: (369) he also set rulers over every part, such as he knew to be good and righteous men; he set others also to take charge of the treasures, and of the villages, and of the fields, and of the beasts, whose names I do not think it necessary to mention. (370) When David had ordered all these offices after the manner before mentioned, he called the rulers of the Hebrews, and their heads of tribes, and the officers over the several divisions, and those that were appointed over every work and every possession; and standing upon a high pulpit, he said to the multitude as follows: (371) 'My brethren and my people, I would have you know that I intended to build a house for God, and prepared a large quantity of gold, and a hundred thousand talents of silver; but God prohibited me by the prophet Nathan, because of the wars I had on your account, and because my right hand was polluted with the slaughter of our enemies; but he commanded that my son, who was to succeed me in the kingdom, should build a temple for him. (372) Now therefore, since you know that of the twelve sons whom Jacob our forefather had, Judah was appointed to be king, and that I was preferred before my six brethren, and received the government from God, and that none of them were uneasy at it, so do I also desire that my sons be not seditious one against another, now

Solomon has received the kingdom, but to bear him cheerfully for their lord, as knowing that God hath chosen him; (373) for it is not a grievous thing to obey even a foreigner as a ruler if it be God's will, but it is fit to rejoice when a brother hath obtained that dignity, since the rest partake of it with him. (374) And I pray that the promises of God may be fulfilled, and that this happiness which he hath promised to bestow upon king Solomon, over all the country, may continue therein for all time to come. And these promises, O son, will be firm, and come to a happy end, if thou showest thyself to be a religious and a righteous man, and an observer of the laws of thy country; but if not, expect adversity upon thy disobedience to them.'

(375) Now when the king had said this, he left off, but gave the description and pattern of the building of the temple in sight of them all, to Solomon; of the foundations and of the chambers, inferior and superior; how many there were to be, and how large in height and in breadth; as also he determined the weight of the golden and silver vessels; (376) moreover, he earnestly excited them with his words, to use the utmost alacrity about the work: he exhorted the rulers also, and particularly the tribe of Levi, to assist him, both because of his youth, and because God had chosen him to take care of the building of the temple, and of the government of the kingdom. (377) He also declared to them that the work would be easy, and not very laborious to them, because he had prepared for it many talents of gold, and more of silver, with timber and a great many carpenters and stonecutters, and a large quantity of emeralds and all sorts of precious stones: (378) and he said, that even now he would give of the proper goods of his own dominion two hundred talents, and three hundred other talents of pure gold, for the most holy place; and for the chariot of God, the cherubim, which are to stand over the ark. Now, when David had done speaking, there appeared great alacrity among the rulers and the priests and the Levites, who now contributed and made great and splendid promises for a future contribution; (379) for they undertook to bring of gold five thousand talents, and ten thousand drachmas, and of silver ten thousand talents, and many ten thousand talents of iron: and if anyone had a precious stone he brought it, and bequeathed it to be put among the treasures; of which Jachiel, one of the posterity of Moses, had the care.

(380) Upon this occasion all the people rejoiced, as in particular did David, when he saw the zeal and forward ambition of the rulers and the priests, and of all the rest; and he began to bless God with a loud voice, calling him the Father and Parent of the universe, and the Author of human and divine things, with which he had adorned Solomon, the patron and guardian of the Hebrew nation, and of its happiness, and of that kingdom which he hath given his Son. (381) Besides this, he prayed for happiness to all the people; and to Solomon his son a sound and a righteous mind, and confirmed in all sorts of virtue; and then

he commanded the multitude to bless God. Upon which they all fell down upon the ground and worshipped him. They also gave thanks to David, on account of all the blessing which they had received ever since he had taken the kingdom. (382) On the next day he presented sacrifices to God, a thousand bullocks and as many lambs, which they offered for burnt offerings. They also offered peace offerings, and slew many ten thousand sacrifices; and the king feasted all day, together with all the people; and they anointed Solomon a second time with the oil, and appointed him to be king, and Zadok to be the high priest of the whole multitude. And when they had brought Solomon to the royal palace, and had set him upon his father's throne, they were obedient to him from that day.

CHAPTER 15

(383) A little afterward, David also fell into a distemper, by reason of his age; and perceiving that he was near to death, he called his son Solomon, and discoursed to him thus: 'I am now, O my son, going to my grave, and to my fathers, which is the common way which all men that now are, or shall be hereafter, must go; from which way it is no longer possible to return, and to know anything that is done in this world. (384) On which account I exhort thee, while I am still alive, though already very near to death, in the same manner as I have formerly said in my advice to thee, to be righteous towards thy subjects, and religious towards God, that hath given thee thy kingdom; to observe his commands and his laws, which he hath sent us by Moses; and neither do thou, out of favour nor flattery, allow any lust or other passion to weigh with thee to disregard them; (385) for if thou transgressest his laws, thou wilt lose the favour of God, and thou wilt turn away his providence from thee in all things; but if thou behave thyself so as it behooves thee, and as I exhort thee, thou wilt preserve our kingdom to our family, and no other house will bear rule over the Hebrews, but we ourselves for all ages. (386) Be thou also mindful of the transgressions of Joab the captain of the host, who hath slain two generals out of envy, and those righteous and good men, Abner the son of Ner, and Amasa the son of Jether; whose death do thou avenge as shall seem good to thee, since Joab hath been too hard for me, and more potent than myself, and so hath escaped punishment hitherto. (387) I also commit to thee the son of Barzillai, the Gileadite, whom, in order to gratify me, thou shalt have in great honour, and take great care of; for we have not done good to him first, but we only repay that debt which we owe to his father, for what he did to me in my flight. (388) There is also Shimei, the son of Gera, of the tribe of Benjamin, who, after he had cast many reproaches upon me when, in my flight, I was going to Mahanaim, met me at Jordan, and received assurances

that he should then suffer nothing. Do thou now seek out for some just occasion, and punish him.'

(389) When David had given these admonitions to his son about public affairs, and about his friends, and about those whom he knew to deserve punishment, he died, having lived seventy years, and reigned seven years and six months in Hebron, over the tribe of Judah, and thirty-three in Jerusalem, over all the country. (390) This man was of an excellent character, and was endowed with all virtues that were desirable in a king, and in one that had the preservation of so many tribes committed to him; for he was a man of valour in a very extraordinary degree, and went readily and first of all into dangers, when he was to fight for his subjects, as exciting the soldiers to action by his own labours, and fighting for them, and not by commanding them in a despotic way. (391) He was also of very great abilities in understanding, and apprehension of present and future circumstances, when he was to manage any affairs. He was prudent and moderate, and kind to such as were under any calamities; he was righteous and humane, which are good qualities peculiarly fit for kings; nor was he guilty of any offence in the exercise of so great an authority, but in the business of the wife of Uriah. He also left behind him greater wealth than any other king, either of the Hebrews or of other nations, ever did.

(392) He was buried by his son Solomon, in Jerusalem, with great magnificence, and with all the other funeral pomp which kings use to be buried with; moreover, he had great and immense wealth buried with him, the vastness of which may be easily conjectured at by what I shall now say: (393) for a thousand and three hundred years afterwards, Hyrcanus the high priest, when he was besieged by Antiochus, that was called the Pious, the son of Demetrius, and was desirous of giving him money to get him to raise the siege and draw off his army; and having no other method of compassing the money, opened one room of David's sepulchre, and took out three thousand talents, and gave part of that sum to Antiochus, and by this means caused the siege to be raised, as we have informed the reader elsewhere. (394) Nay, after him, and that many years, Herod the king opened another room, and took away a great deal of money, and yet neither of them came at the coffins of the kings themselves, for their bodies were buried under the earth so artfully, that they did not appear even to those that entered into their monuments – but so much shall suffice us to have said concerning these matters.

BOOK EIGHT

CHAPTER I

(1) We have already treated of David and his virtue, and of the benefits he was the author of to his countrymen; of his wars also and battles, which he managed with success, and then died an old man, in the foregoing book. (2) And when Solomon his son, who was but a youth in age, had taken the kingdom, and whom David had declared, while he was alive, the lord of that people, according to God's will; when he sat upon the throne, the whole body of the people made joyful acclamations to him, as is usual at the beginning of a reign; and wished that all his affairs might come to a blessed conclusion and that he might arrive at a great age, and at the most happy state of affairs possible.

(3) But Adonijah, who while his father was living attempted to gain possession of the government, came to the king's mother Bathsheba, and saluted her with great civility; and when she asked him, whether he came to her as desiring her assistance in anything or not, and bade him tell her if that were the case, (4) for that she would cheerfully afford it him, he began to say, that she knew herself that the kingdom was his, both on account of his elder age, and of the disposition of the multitude; and that yet it was transferred to Solomon her son, according to the will of God. He also said that he was contented to be a servant under him, and was pleased with the present settlement; (5) but he desired her to be a means of obtaining a favour from his brother to him, and to persuade him to bestow on him in marriage Abishag, who had indeed slept by his father, but, because his father was too old, he did not lie with her, and she was still a virgin. (6) So Bathsheba promised him to afford him her assistance very earnestly, and to bring this marriage about, because the king would be willing to gratify him in such a thing, and because she would press it to him very earnestly. Accordingly he went away, in hopes of succeeding in this match. So Solomon's mother went presently to her son, to speak to him about what she had promised, upon Adonijah's supplication to her. (7) And when her son came forward to meet her, and embraced her, and when he had brought her into the house where his royal throne was set, he sat thereon, and bid them set another throne on the right hand, for his mother. When Bathsheba was sat down, she said, 'O my son, grant me one request that I desire of thee, and do not anything to me that is disagreeable or ungrateful, which thou wilt do if thou deniest me.' (8) And when Solomon bid her to lay her commands upon him, because it was agreeable to his duty to grant her

everything she should ask, and complained that she did not begin her discourse with a firm expectation of obtaining what she desired, but had some suspicion of a denial, she entreated him to grant that his brother Adonijah might marry Abishag.

(9) But the king was greatly offended at these words, and sent away his mother, and said that Adonijah aimed at great things; and that he wondered that she did not desire him to yield up the kingdom to him, as to his elder brother, since she desired that he might marry Abishag; and that he had potent friends, Joab the captain of the host, and Abiathar the priest. So he called for Benaiah, the captain of the guards, and ordered him to slay his brother Adonijah; (10) he also called for Abiathar, the priest, and said to him, 'I will not put thee to death, because of those other hardships which thou hast endured with my father, and because of the ark which thou hast borne along with him; but I inflict this following punishment upon thee, because thou wast among Adonijah's followers, and wast of his party. Do not thou continue here, nor come any more into my sight, but go to thine own town, and live on thy own fields, and there abide all thy life; for thou hast offended so greatly, that it is not just that thou shouldest retain thy dignity any longer.' (11) For the fore-mentioned cause, therefore, it was that the house of Ithamar was deprived of the sacerdotal dignity, as God had foretold to Eli the grandfather of Abiathar. So it was transferred to the family of Phineas, to Zadok. (12) Now those that were of the family of Phineas, but lived privately during the time that the high priesthood was transferred to the house of Ithamar (of which family Eli was the first that received it) were these that follow: Bukki, the son of Abishua the high priest; his son was Joatham; Joatham's son was Meraioth; Meraioth's son was Arophaeus; Arophaeus's son was Ahitub; and Ahitub's son was Zadok, who was first made high priest in the reign of David.

(13) Now when Joab the captain of the host heard of the slaughter of Adonijah, he was greatly afraid, for he was a greater friend to him than to Solomon; and suspecting, not without reason, that he was in danger, on account of his favour to Adonijah, he fled to the altar, and supposed he might procure safety thereby to himself, because of the king's piety towards God. (14) But when some told the king what Joab's supposal was, he sent Benaiah, and commanded him to raise him up from the altar, and bring to the judgment seat, in order to make his defence. However, Joab said he would not leave the altar, but would die there rather than in another place. (15) And when Benaiah had reported his answer to the king, Solomon commanded him to cut off his head there, and let him take that as a punishment for those two captains of the host whom he had wickedly slain, and to bury his body, that his sins might never leave his family, but that himself and his father, by Joab's death, might be guiltless; (16) and when Benaiah had done what he was commanded to do, he

was himself appointed to be captain of the whole army. The king also made Zadok to be alone the high priest, in the room of Abiathar, whom he had removed.

(17) But as to Shimei, Solomon commanded that he should build him a house, and stay at Jerusalem, and attend upon him, and should not have authority to go over the brook Cedron; and that if he disobeyed that command, death should be his punishment. He also threatened him so terribly, that he compelled him to take an oath that he would obey. (18) Accordingly Shimei said that he had reason to thank Solomon for giving him such an injunction, and added an oath, that he would do as he bade him; and leaving his own country, he made his abode in Jerusalem; but three years afterwards, when he heard that two of his servants were run away from him, and were in Gath, he went for his servants in haste; (19) and when he was come back with them, the king perceived it, and was much displeased that he had condemned his commands, and, what was more, had no regard to the oaths he had sworn to God; so he called him, and said to him, 'Didst not thou swear never to leave me, nor to go out of this city to another? (20) Thou shalt not therefore escape punishment for thy perjury; but I will punish thee, thou wicked wretch, both for this crime and for those wherewith thou didst abuse my father when he was in his flight, that thou mayst know that wicked men gain nothing at last although they be not punished immediately upon their unjust practices; but that in all the time wherein they think themselves secure, because they have yet suffered nothing, their punishment increases, and is heavier upon them, and that to a greater degree than if they had been punished immediately upon the commission of their crimes.' So Benaiah, on the king's command, slew Shimei.

CHAPTER 2

(21) Solomon having already settled himself firmly in his kingdom, and having brought his enemies to punishment, he married the daughter of Pharaoh, king of Egypt, and built the walls of Jerusalem much larger and stronger than those that had been before, and thenceforward he managed public affairs very peaceably, nor was his youth any hindrance in the exercise of justice, or in the observation of the laws, or in the remembrance of what charges his father had given him at his death; but he discharged every duty with great accuracy, that might have been expected from such as are aged and of the greatest prudence. (22) He now resolved to go to Hebron, and sacrifice to God upon the brazen altar that was built by Moses. Accordingly he offered there burnt offerings, in number a thousand; and when he had done this, he thought he had paid great honour to God; for, as he was asleep that very night, God appeared to him, and commanded him to ask of him some gifts which he was ready to give him

as a reward for his piety. (23) So Solomon asked of God what was most excellent, and of the greatest worth in itself, what God would bestow with the greatest joy, and what it was most profitable for man to receive; for he did not desire to have bestowed upon him either gold or silver or any other riches, as a man and a youth might naturally have done, for these are the things that generally are esteemed by most men, as alone of the greatest worth, and the best gifts of God; but, said he, 'Give me, O Lord, a sound mind and a good understanding, whereby I may speak and judge the people according to truth and righteousness.' (24) With these petitions God was well pleased; and promised to give him all those things that he had not mentioned in his option, riches, glory, victory over his enemies; and, in the first place, understanding and wisdom, and this in such a degree as no other mortal man, neither kings nor ordinary persons, ever had. He also promised to preserve the kingdom to his posterity for a very long time, if he continued righteous and obedient to him, and imitated his father in those things wherein he excelled. (25) When Solomon heard this from God, he presently leaped out of his bed; and when he had worshipped him, he returned to Jerusalem; and after he had offered great sacrifices before the tabernacle, he feasted all his own family.

(26) In these days a hard cause came before him in judgment, which it was very difficult to find any end of; and I think it necessary to explain the fact about which the contest was, that such as light upon my writings may know what a difficult cause Solomon was to determine; and those that are concerned in such matters may take this sagacity of the king for a pattern, that they may the more easily give sentence about such questions. (27) There were two women, who were harlots in the course of their lives, that came to him, of whom she that seemed to be injured began to speak first, and said, 'O king, I and this other woman dwell together in one room. Now it came to pass that we both bore a son at the same hour of the same day; (28) and on the third day this woman overlaid her son, and killed it, and then took my son out of my bosom, and removed him to herself; and as I was asleep she laid her dead son in my arms. (29) Now, when in the morning I was desirous to give the breast to the child, I did not find my own, but saw the woman's dead child lying by me; for I considered it exactly, and found it so to be. Hence it was that I demanded my son, and when I could not obtain him, I have recourse, my lord, to thy assistance; for since we were alone, and there was nobody there that could convict her, she cares for nothing, but perseveres in the stout denial of the fact.' (30) When this woman had told this her story, the king asked the other woman what she had to say in contradiction to that story. But when she denied that she had done what was charged upon her, and said that it was her child that was living, and that it was her antagonist's child that was dead, and when no one could devise what judgment could be given, and the whole court were blind in

their understanding, and could not tell how to find out this riddle, the king alone invented the following way how to discover it. (31) He bade them bring in both the dead child and the living child; and sent one of his guards, and commanded him to fetch a sword, and draw it, and to cut both the children into two pieces, that each of the women might have half the living and half the dead child. (32) Hereupon all the people privately laughed at the king, as no more than a youth. But, in the meantime, she that was the real mother of the living child cried out, that he should not do so, but deliver that child to the other woman as her own, for she would be satisfied with the life of the child and with the sight of it, although it were esteemed the other's child; but the other woman was ready to see the child divided, and was desirous, moreover, that the first woman should be tormented. (33) When the king understood that both their words proceeded from the truth of their passions, he adjudged the child to her that cried out to save it, for that she was the real mother of it; and he condemned the other as a wicked woman, who had not only killed her own child, but was endeavouring to see her friend's child destroyed also. (34) Now the multitude looked on this determination as a great sign and demonstration of the king's sagacity and wisdom; and, after that day, attended to him as to one that had a divine mind.

(35) Now the captains of his armies, and officers appointed over the whole country were these: over the lot of Ephraim was Ures; over the toparchy of Bethlehem was Dioclerus; Abinadab, who married Solomon's daughter, had the region of Dora and the seacoast under him; (36) the Great Plain was under Benaiah, the son of Achilus; he also governed all the country as far as Jordan; Gabaris ruled over Gilead and Gaulantis, and had under him the sixty great and fenced cities [of Og]; Achinadab managed the affairs of all Galilee, as far as Sidon, and had himself also married a daughter of Solomon's, whose name was Basima; (37) Banacates had the seacoast about Arce; as had Shaphot Mount Tabor, and Carmel, and [the Lower] Galilee as far as the river Jordan; one man was appointed over all this country; Shimei was entrusted with the lot of Benjamin; and Gabares had the country beyond Jordan, over whom there was again one governor appointed. (38) Now the people of the Hebrews, and particularly the tribe of Judah, received a wonderful increase when they betook themselves to husbandry and the cultivation of their grounds: for as they enjoyed peace, and were not distracted with wars and troubles, and having besides an abundant fruition of the most desirable liberty, everyone was busy in augmenting the product of their own lands, and making them worth more than they had formerly been.

(39) The king had also other rulers, who were over the land of Syria, and of the Philistines, which reached from the river Euphrates to Egypt, and these collected his tributes of the nations. (40) Now these contributed to the king's

table, and to his supper every day, thirty cori of fine flour, and sixty of meal; as also ten fat oxen, and twenty oxen out of the pastures, and a hundred fat lambs; all these were besides what were taken by hunting harts and buffaloes, and birds and fishes which were brought to the king by foreigners day by day. (41) Solomon had also so great a number of chariots, that the stalls of his horses for those chariots were forty thousand; and besides these, he had twelve thousand horsemen, the one half of whom waited upon the king in Jerusalem, and the rest were dispersed abroad, and dwelt in the royal villages; but the same officer who provided for the king's expenses, supplied also the fodder for the horses, and still carried it to the place where the king abode at that time.

(42) Now the sagacity and wisdom which God had bestowed on Solomon was so great, that he exceeded the ancients, insomuch that he was no way inferior to the Egyptians, who are said to have been beyond all men in understanding; nay, indeed, it is evident that their sagacity was very much inferior to that of the king's. (43) He also excelled and distinguished himself in wisdom above those who were most eminent among the Hebrews at that time for shrewdness: those I mean were Ethan, and Heman, and Chalcol, and Darda, the sons of Mahol. (44) He also composed books of odes and songs, a thousand and five; of parables and similitudes, three thousand; for he spake a parable upon every sort of tree, from the hyssop to the cedar; and in like manner also about beasts, about all sorts of living creatures, whether upon the earth, or in the seas, or in the air; for he was not unacquainted with any of their natures, nor omitted inquiries about them, but described them all like a philosopher, and demonstrated his exquisite knowledge of their several properties. (45) God also enabled him to learn that skill which expels demons, which is a science useful and sanative to men. He composed such incantations also by which distempers are alleviated. And he left behind him the manner of using exorcisms, by which they drive away demons so that they never return, (46) and this method of cure is of great force unto this day; for I have seen a certain man of my own country whose name was Eleazar, releasing people that were demoniacal in the presence of Vespasian, and his sons and his captains, and the whole multitude of his soldiers. The manner of the cure was this: (47) he put a ring that had a root of one of those sorts mentioned by Solomon to the nostrils of the demoniac, after which he drew out the demon through his nostrils; and when the man fell down immediately, he abjured him to return into him no more, making still mention of Solomon, and reciting the incantations which he composed. (48) And when Eleazar would persuade and demonstrate to the spectators that he had such a power, he set a little way off a cup or basin full of water, and commanded the demon, as he went out of the man, to overturn it, and thereby to let the spectators know that he had left the man; (49) and when this was done, the skill and wisdom of

Solomon was shown very manifestly; for which reason it is, that all men may know the vastness of Solomon's abilities, and how he was beloved of God, and that the extraordinary virtues of every kind with which this king was endowed may not be unknown to any people under the sun; for this reason, I say, it is that we have proceeded to speak so largely of these matters.

(50) Moreover Hiram, king of Tyre, when he had heard that Solomon succeeded to his father's kingdom, was very glad of it, for he was a friend of David's. So he sent ambassadors to him, and saluted him, and congratulated him on the present happy state of his affairs. Upon which Solomon sent him an epistle, the contents of which here follow:

SOLOMON TO KING HIRAM

(51) 'Know thou that my father would have built a temple to God, but was hindered by wars, and continual expeditions: for he did not leave off to overthrow his enemies till he made them all subject to tribute. (52) But I give thanks to God for the peace I at present enjoy, and on that account I am at leisure, and design to build a house to God, for God foretold to my father that such a house should he built by me; wherefore I desire thee to send some of thy subjects with mine to Mount Lebanon, to cut down timber; for the Sidonians are more skilful than our people in cutting of wood. As for wages to the hewers of wood, I will pay whatsoever price thou shalt determine.'

(53) When Hiram had read this epistle, he was pleased with it, and wrote back this answer to Solomon:

HIRAM TO KING SOLOMON

'It is fit to bless God, that he hath committed thy father's government to thee, who art a wise man, and endowed with all virtues. As for myself, I rejoice at the condition thou art in, and will be subservient to thee in all that thou sendest to me about; (54) for when by my subjects I have cut down many and large trees of cedar and cypress wood, I will send them to sea, and will order my subjects to make floats of them, and to sail to what place soever of thy country thou shalt desire, and leave them there, after which thy subjects may carry them to Jerusalem: but do thou take care to procure us corn for this timber, which we stand in need of, because we inhabit in an island.'

(55) The copies of these epistles remain at this day, and are preserved not only in our books, but among the Tyrians also; insomuch that if anyone would know the certainty about them, he may desire of the keepers of the public records of Tyre to show him them, and he will find what is there set down to agree with what we have said. (56) I have said so much out of a desire that my readers may know that we speak nothing but the truth, and do not compose a history out of some plausible relations, which deceive men and please them at

the same time, nor attempt to avoid examination, nor desire men to believe us immediately; nor are we at liberty to depart from speaking truth, which is the proper commendation of an historian, and yet to be blameless. But we insist upon no admission of what we say, unless we be able to manifest its truth by demonstration and the strongest vouchers.

(57) Now King Solomon, as soon as this epistle of the king of Tyre was brought him, commended the readiness and goodwill he declared therein, and repaid him in what he desired, and sent him yearly twenty thousand cori of wheat, and as many baths of oil; now the bath is able to contain seventy-two sextaries. He also sent him the same measure of wine. (58) So the friendship between Hiram and Solomon hereby increased more and more; and they swore to continue it forever. And the king appointed a tribute to be laid on all the people, of thirty thousand labourers, whose work he rendered easy to them, by prudently dividing it among them; for he made ten thousand cut timber in Mount Lebanon for one month, and then to come home and rest two months, until the time when the other twenty thousand had finished their task at the appointed time; (59) and so afterward it came to pass, that the first ten thousand returned to their work every fourth month; and it was Adoram who was over this tribute. There were also of the strangers who were left by David, who were to carry the stones and other materials, seventy thousand; and of those that cut the stones, eighty thousand. Of these three thousand and three hundred were rulers over the rest. (60) He also enjoined them to cut out large stones for the foundations of the temple, and that they should fit them and unite them together in the mountain, and so bring them to the city. This was done not only by our own country workmen, but by those workmen whom Hiram sent also.

CHAPTER 3

(61) Solomon began to build the temple in the fourth year of his reign, on the second month, which the Macedonians call *Artemisius*, and the Hebrews *Jur*, five hundred and ninety-two years after the exodus out of Egypt, but one thousand and twenty years from Abraham's coming out of Mesopotamia into Canaan; and after the Deluge one thousand four hundred and forty years; (62) and from Adam, the first man who was created, until Solomon built the temple, there had passed in all three thousand one hundred and two years. Now that year on which the temple began to be built, was already the eleventh year of the reign of Hiram; but from the building of Tyre to the building of the temple, there had passed two hundred and forty years.

(63) Now, therefore, the king laid the foundations of the temple very deep in the ground, and the materials were strong stones, and such as would resist

the force of time; these were to unite themselves with the earth, and become a basis and a sure foundation for that superstructure which was to be erected over it; they were to be so strong, in order to sustain with ease those vast superstructures and precious ornaments, whose own weight was to be not less than the weight of those other high and heavy buildings which the king designed to be very ornamental and magnificent. (64) They erected its entire body, quite up to the roof, of white stone; its height was sixty cubits, and its length was the same, and its breadth twenty. There was another building erected over it, equal to it in its measures; so that the entire altitude of the temple was a hundred and twenty cubits. Its front was to the east. (65) As to the porch, they built it before the temple; its length was twenty cubits, and it was so ordered that it might agree with the breadth of the house; and it had twelve cubits in latitude, and its height was raised as high as a hundred and twenty cubits. He also built round about the temple thirty small rooms, which might include the whole temple, by their closeness one to another, and by their number, and outward position round it. He also made passages through them, that they might come into one through another. (66) Every one of these rooms had five cubits in breadth, and the same in length, but in height twenty. Above these were other rooms, and others above them, equal both in their measures and number; so that these reached to a height equal to the lower part of the house; for the upper part had no buildings about it. (67) The roof that was over the house was of cedar; and truly every one of these rooms had a roof of their own, that was not connected with the other rooms; but for the other parts, there was a covered roof common to them all, and built with very long beams, that passed through the rest and through the whole building, that so the middle walls, being strengthened by the same beams of timber, might be thereby made firmer; (68) but as for that part of the roof that was under the beams, it was made of the same materials, and was all made smooth, and had ornaments proper for roofs, and plates of gold nailed upon them; and as he enclosed the walls with boards of cedar, so he fixed on them plates of gold, which had sculptures upon them: so that the whole temple shined, and dazzled the eyes of such as entered, by the splendour of the gold that was on every side of them. (69) Now the whole structure of the temple was made, with great skill, of polished stones, and those laid together so very harmoniously and smoothly, that there appeared to the spectators no sign of any hammer, or other instrument of architecture, but as if, without any use of them, the entire materials had naturally united themselves together, that the agreement of one part with another seemed rather to have been natural than to have arisen from the force of tools upon them. (70) The king also had a fine contrivance for an ascent to the upper room over the temple, and that was by steps in the thickness of its wall; for it had no large door on the east end, as the lower house had, but the entrances were by the sides, through very small doors. He also overlaid the temple, both within and without, with boards of cedar, that were kept close together by thick chains, so that this contrivance was in the nature of a support and a strength to the building.

(71) Now when the king had divided the temple into two parts, he made the inner house of twenty cubits [every way] to be the most secret chamber, but he appointed that of forty cubits to be the sanctuary; and when he had cut a door-place out of the wall, he put therein doors of cedar, and overlaid them with a great deal of gold, that had sculptures upon it. (72) He also had veils of blue and purple and scarlet, and the brightest and softest linen, with the most curious flowers wrought upon them, which were to be drawn before those doors. He also dedicated for the most secret place, whose breadth was twenty cubits, and length the same, two cherubims of solid gold; the height of each of them was five cubits; they had each of them two wings stretched out as far as five cubits; (73) wherefore Solomon set them up not far from each other, that with one wing they might touch the southern wall of the secret place, and with another the northern; their other wings, which joined to each other, were a covering to the ark, which was set between them: but nobody can tell, or even conjecture, what was the shape of these cherubims. (74) He also laid the floor of the temple with plates of gold; and he added doors to the gate of the temple, agreeable to the measure of the height of the wall, but in breadth twenty cubits, and on them he glued gold plates; (75) and, to say all in one word, he left no part of the temple, neither internal nor external, but what was covered with gold. He also had curtains drawn over these doors in like manner as they were drawn over the inner doors of the most holy place; but the porch of the temple had nothing of that sort.

(76) Now Solomon sent for an artificer out of Tyre, whose name was Hiram: he was by birth of the tribe of Naphtali, on the mother's side (for she was of that tribe); but his father was Ur, of the stock of the Israelites. This man was skilful in all sorts of work, but his chief skill lay in working in gold, in silver, and brass; by whom were made all the mechanical works about the temple, according to the will of Solomon. (77) Moreover, this Hiram made two [hollow] pillars, whose outsides were of brass; and the thickness of the brass was four fingers' breadth, and the height of the pillars was eighteen cubits, and their circumference twelve cubits; but there was cast with each of their chapiters lily work, that stood upon the pillar, and it was elevated five cubits, round about which there was network interwoven with small palms, made of brass, and covered the lily work. (78) To this also were hung two hundred pomegranates, in two rows. The one of these pillars he set at the entrance of the porch on the right hand and called it *Jachin;* and the other at the left hand, and called it *Boaz.*

(79) Solomon also cast a brazen sea, whose figure of which was that of an hemisphere. This brazen vessel was called *a sea* for its largeness, for the laver was ten feet in diameter, and cast of the thickness of a palm; its middle part rested on a short pillar, that had ten spirals round it, and that pillar was ten cubits in diameter. (80) There stood round about it twelve oxen, that looked to the four winds of heaven, three to each wind, having their hinder parts depressed, that so the hemispherical vessel might rest upon them, which itself was also depressed round about inwardly. Now this sea contained three thousand baths.

(81) He also made ten brazen bases for so many quadrangular lavers: the length of every one of these bases was five cubits, and the breadth four cubits, and the height six cubits. This vessel was partly turned, and was thus contrived: There were four small quadrangular pillars, that stood one at each corner; these had the sides of the base fitted to them on each quarter; they were parted into three parts; (82) every interval had a border fitted to support [the laver]; upon which was engraven, in one place a lion, and in another place a bull and an eagle. The small pillars had the same animals engraven that were engraven on the sides. (83) The whole work was elevated, and stood upon four wheels, which were also cast, which had also naves and felloes, and were a foot and a half in diameter. Anyone who saw the spokes of the wheels, how exactly they were turned, and united to the sides of the bases, and with what harmony they agreed to the felloes, would wonder at them. However, their structure was this: (84) Certain shoulders of hands stretched out held the corners above, upon which rested a short spiral pillar, that lay under the hollow part of the laver, resting upon the fore part of the eagle and the lion, which were adapted to them, insomuch that those who viewed them would think they were of one piece: between these were engravings of palm trees. This was the construction of the ten bases: (85) he also made ten large round brass vessels, which were the lavers themselves, each of which contained forty baths; for it had its height four cubits, and its edges were as much distant from each other: he also placed these lavers upon the ten bases that were called Mechonoth: (86) and he set five of the lavers on the left side of the temple, which was that side towards the north wind, and as many on the right side, towards the south, but looking towards the east; the same [eastern] way he also set the sea. (87) Now, he appointed the sea to be for washing the hands and the feet of the priests when they entered into the temple and were to ascend the altar; but the lavers to cleanse the entrails of the beasts that were to be burnt offerings, with their feet also.

(88) He also made a brazen altar, whose length was twenty cubits, and its breadth the same, and its height ten, for the burnt offerings: he also made all its vessels of brass: the pots and the shovels and the basins; and besides these, the snuffers and the tongs, and all its other vessels he made of brass, and such brass

as was in splendour and beauty like gold. (89) The king also dedicated a great number of tables, but one that was large and made of gold, upon which they set the loaves of God; and he made ten thousand more that resembled them, but were done after another manner, upon which lay the vials and the cups; those of gold were twenty thousand, those of silver were forty thousand. (90) He also made ten thousand candlesticks, according to the command of Moses, one of which he dedicated for the temple, that it might burn in the daytime, according to the law; and one table with loaves upon it, on the north side of the temple, over against the candlestick; for this he set on the south side, but the golden altar stood between them. All these vessels were contained in that part of the holy house which was forty cubits long, and were before the vail of that most secret place wherein the ark was to be set.

(91) The king also made pouring vessels, in number eighty thousand, and a hundred thousand golden vials, and twice as many silver vials: of golden dishes, in order therein to offer kneaded fine flour at the altar, there were eighty thousand, and twice as many of silver. Of large basins also, wherein they mixed fine flour with oil, sixty thousand of gold, and twice as many of silver. (92) Of the measures like those which Moses called the *Hin* and the *Assaron* (a tenth deal), there were twenty thousand of gold, and twice as many of silver. The golden censers, in which they carried the incense to the altar, were twenty thousand: the other censers, in which they carried fire from the great altar to the little altar, within the temple, were fifty thousand. (93) The sacerdotal garments which belong to the high priest, with the long robes and the oracle and the precious stones, were a thousand; but the crown upon which Moses wrote [the name of God], was only one, and hath remained to this very day. He also made ten thousand sacerdotal garments of fine linen, with purple girdles, for every priest; (94) and two hundred thousand trumpets, according to the command of Moses; also two hundred thousand garments of fine linen for the singers that were Levites; and he made musical instruments, and such as were invented for singing of hymns, called *Nablae* and *Cinyrae* [psalteries and harps], which were made of electrum [the finest brass], forty thousand.

(95) Solomon made all these things for the honour of God, with great variety and magnificence, sparing no cost, but using all possible liberality in adorning the temple; and these things he dedicated to the treasures of God. He also placed a partition round about the temple, which in our tongue we call *Gison*, but it is called *Thrinkos* by the Greeks, and he raised it up to the height of three cubits; and it was for the exclusion of the multitude from coming into the temple, and showing that it was a place that was free and open only for the priests. (96) He also built beyond this court a temple, the figure of which was that of a quadrangle, and erected for it great and broad cloisters; this was entered into by very high gates, each of which had its front

exposed to one of the [four] winds, and were shut by golden doors. Into this temple all the people entered that were distinguished from the rest by being pure, and observant of the laws; (97) but he made that temple which was beyond this a wonderful one indeed, and such as exceeds all description in words; nay, if I may so say, it is hardly believed upon sight; for when he had filled up great valleys with earth, which on account of their immense depth could not be looked on when you bended down to see them, without pain, and had elevated the ground four hundred cubits, he made it to be on a level with the top of the mountain on which the temple was built, and by this means the utmost temple, which was exposed to the air, was even with the temple itself. (98) He encompassed this also with a building of a double row of cloisters, which stood on high, upon pillars of native stone, while the roofs were of cedar, and were polished in a manner proper for such high roofs; but he made all the doors of this temple of silver.

<h2 style="text-align:center">CHAPTER 4</h2>

(99) When King Solomon had finished these works, these large and beautiful buildings, and had laid up his donations in the temple, and all this in the interval of seven years, and had given a demonstration of his riches and alacrity therein, insomuch that anyone who saw it would have thought that it must have been an immense time ere it could have been finished, and [would be surprised] that so much should be finished in so short a time – short, I mean, if compared with the greatness of the work: he also wrote to the rulers and elders of the Hebrews, and ordered all the people to gather themselves together to Jerusalem, both to see the temple which he had built, and to remove the ark of God into it; (100) and when this invitation of the whole body of the people to come to Jerusalem was everywhere carried abroad, it was the seventh month before they came together; which month is, by our countrymen, called *Thisri*, but by the Macedonians *Hyperberetaeus*. The Feast of Tabernacles happened to fall at the same time, which was kept by the Hebrews as a most holy and most eminent feast. (101) So they carried the ark and the tabernacle which Moses had pitched, and all the vessels that were for ministration to the sacrifices of God, and removed them to the temple. The king himself, and all the people and the Levites, went before, rendering the ground moist with sacrifices and drink offerings, and the blood of a great number of oblations, and burning an immense quantity of incense; (102) and this till the very air itself everywhere round about was so full of these odours, that it met, in a most agreeable manner, persons at a great distance, and was an indication of God's presence, and, as men's opinion was, of his habitation with them in this newly built and consecrated place, for they did not grow weary either of singing hymns, or of

dancing, until they came to the temple; (103) and in this manner did they carry the ark; but when they should transfer it into the most secret place, the rest of the multitude went away, and only those priests that carried it set it between the two cherubims, which embracing it with their wings (for so they were framed by the artificer), they covered it, as under a tent or a cupola. (104) Now the ark contained nothing else but those two tables of stone that preserved the ten commandments, which God spake to Moses in Mount Sinai, and which were engraved upon them; but they set the candlestick and the table and the golden altar, in the temple, before the most secret place, in the very same places wherein they stood till that time in the tabernacle. So they offered up the daily sacrifices; (105) but for the brazen altar, Solomon set it before the temple, over against the door, that when the door was opened, it might be exposed to sight, and the sacred solemnities, and the richness of the sacrifices, might be thence seen; and all the rest of the vessels they gathered together, and put them within the temple.

(106) Now, as soon as the priests had put all things in order about the ark, and were gone out, there came down a thick cloud, and stood there; and spread itself, after a gentle manner, into the temple: such a cloud it was as was diffused and temperate − not such a rough one as we see full of rain in the winter season. This cloud so darkened the place, that one priest could not discern another; but it afforded to the minds of all a visible image and glorious appearance of God's having descended into this temple, and of his having gladly pitched his tabernacle therein. (107) So these men were intent upon this thought; but Solomon rose up (for he had been sitting before), and used such words to God as he thought agreeable to the divine nature to receive, and fit for him to give; for he said, 'Thou hast an eternal house, O Lord, and such a one as thou hast created for thyself out of thine own works; we know it to be the heaven, and the air, and the earth, and the sea, which thou pervadest, nor art thou contained within their limits. (108) I have indeed built this temple to thee and thy name, that from thence, when we sacrifice and perform sacred operations, we may send our prayers up into the air, and may constantly believe that thou art present, and art not remote from what is thine own; for neither when thou seest all things, and hearest all things, nor now, when it pleases thee to dwell here, dost thou leave off the care of all men, but rather thou art very near to them all, but especially thou art present to those that address themselves to thee, whether by night or by day.' (109) When he had thus solemnly addressed himself to God, he converted his discourse to the multitude, and strongly represented the power and providence of God to them − how he had shown all things that were come to pass to David his father, as many of those things had already come to pass, and the rest would certainly come to pass hereafter; (110) and how he had given him his name,

and told to David what he should be called before he was born and foretold that, when he should be king, after his father's death he should build him a temple, which, since they saw accomplished according to his prediction, he required them to bless God, and by believing him, from the sight of what they had seen accomplished, never to despair of any thing that he had promised for the future, in order to their happiness, or suspect that it would not come to pass.

(111) When the king had thus discoursed to the multitude, he looked again towards the temple, and lifting up his right hand to the multitude, he said, 'It is not possible by what men can do to return sufficient thanks to God for his benefits bestowed upon them, for the Deity stands in need of nothing, and is above any such requital; but so far as we have been made superior, O Lord, to other animals by thee, it becomes us to bless thy Majesty, and it is necessary for us to return thee thanks for what thou hast bestowed upon our house, and upon the Hebrew people; (112) for with what other instrument can we better appease thee, when thou art angry at us, or more properly preserve thy favour, than with our voice; which, as we have it from the air, so do we know that by the air it ascends upwards [towards thee]. I therefore ought myself to return thee thanks thereby, in the first place concerning my father, whom thou hast raised from obscurity unto so great joy; (113) and in the next place, concerning myself, since thou hast performed all that thou hast promised unto this very day; and I beseech thee for the time to come, to afford us whatsoever thou, O God, hast power to bestow on such as thou dost esteem; and to augment our house for all ages, as thou hast promised to David my father to do, both in his lifetime and at his death, that our kingdom shall continue, and that his posterity should successively receive it to ten thousand generations. Do not thou therefore fail to give us these blessings, and to bestow on my children that virtue in which thou delightest; (114) and besides all this, I humbly beseech thee, that thou wilt let some portion of thy Spirit come down and inhabit in this temple, that thou mayest appear to be with us upon earth. As to thyself, the entire heavens, and the immensity of the things that are therein, are but a small habitation for thee, much more is this poor temple so; but I entreat thee to keep it as thine own house, from being destroyed by our enemies forever, and to take care of it as thine own possession; (115) but if this people be found to have sinned, and be thereupon afflicted by thee with any plague, because of their sin, as with dearth, or pestilence, or any other affliction which thou usest to inflict on those that transgress any of thy holy laws, and if they fly all of them to this temple beseeching thee, and begging of thee to deliver them, then do thou hear their prayers, as being within thine house, and have mercy upon them, and deliver them from their afflictions! (116) Nay, moreover, this help is what I implore of thee, not for the Hebrews only, when they are in distress,

but when they shall come hither from any ends of the world whatsoever, and shall return from their sins and implore thy pardon, do thou then pardon them, and hear their prayers! (117) For hereby all shall learn that thou thyself wast pleased with the building of this house for thee; and that we are not ourselves of an unsociable nature, nor behave ourselves like enemies to such as are not of our own people, but are willing that thy assistance should be communicated by thee to all men in common, and that they may have the enjoyment of thy benefits bestowed upon them.'

(118) When Solomon had said this and had cast himself upon the ground, and worshipped a long time, he rose up and brought sacrifices to the altar; and when he had filled it with unblemished victims, he most evidently discovered that God had with pleasure accepted of all that he had sacrificed to him, for there came a fire running out of the air, and rushed with violence upon the altar, in the sight of all, and caught hold of and consumed the sacrifices. (119) Now, when this divine appearance was seen, the people supposed it to be a demonstration of God's abode in the temple, and were pleased with it, and fell down upon the ground and worshipped. Upon which the king began to bless God, and exhorted the multitude to do the same, as now having sufficient indications of God's favourable disposition to them; (120) and to pray that they might always have the like indications from him, and that he would preserve in them a mind pure from all wickedness in righteousness and religious worship, and that they might continue in the observation of those precepts which God had given them by Moses, because by that means the Hebrew nation would be happy, and indeed the most blessed of all nations among all mankind. (121) He exhorted them also to be mindful that by what methods they had attained their present good things, by the same they must preserve them sure to themselves, and make them greater, and more than they were at present; for that it was not sufficient for them to suppose that they had received them on account of their piety and righteousness, but that they had no other way of preserving them for the time to come; for that it is not so great a thing for men to acquire somewhat which they want, as to preserve what they have acquired, and to be guilty of no sin, whereby it may be hurt.

(122) So when the king had spoken thus to the multitude, he dissolved the congregation, but not till he had completed his oblations, both for himself and for the Hebrews, insomuch that he sacrificed twenty and two thousand oxen, and a hundred and twenty thousand sheep; (123) for then it was that the temple did first of all taste of the victims; and all the Hebrews, with their wives and children, feasted therein: nay, besides this, the king then observed splendidly and magnificently the feast which is called the *Feast of Tabernacles*, before the temple for twice seven days, and he then feasted together with all the people.

(124) When all these solemnities were abundantly satisfied, and nothing was

omitted that concerned the divine worship, the king dismissed them; and everyone went to their own homes, giving thanks to the king for the care he had taken of them, and the works he had done for them, and praying to God to preserve Solomon to be their king for a long time. They also took their journey home with rejoicing and making merry, and singing hymns to God: and indeed the pleasure they enjoyed took away the sense of the pains they all underwent in their journey home. (125) So when they had brought the ark into the temple, and had seen its greatness, and how fine it was, and had been partakers of the many sacrifices that had been offered, and of the festivals that had been solemnised, they every one returned to their own cities. But a dream that appeared to the king in his sleep, informed him that God had heard his prayers, (126) and that he would not only preserve the temple, but would always abide in it; that is, in case his posterity and the whole multitude would be righteous. And for himself, it said, that if he continued according to the admonitions of his father, he would advance him to an immense degree of dignity and happiness, and that then his posterity should be kings of that country, of the tribe of Judah, forever; (127) but that still, if he should be found a betrayer of the ordinances of the law, and forget them, and turn away to the worship of strange gods, he would cut them off by the roots, and would neither suffer any remainder of his family to continue, nor would overlook the people of Israel, or preserve them any longer from afflictions, but would utterly destroy them with ten thousand wars and misfortunes; would cast them out of the land which he had given their fathers, and make them sojourners in strange lands; (128) and deliver that temple which was now built, to be burnt and spoiled by their enemies; and that city to be utterly overthrown by the hands of their enemies; and make their miseries deserve to be a proverb, and such as should very hardly be credited for their stupendous magnitude, (129) till their neighbours, when they should hear of them, should wonder at their calamities, and very earnestly inquire for the occasion, why the Hebrews who had been so far advanced by God to such glory and wealth, should be then so hated by him? And that the answer that should be made by the remainder of the people should be, by confessing their sins, and their transgression of the laws of their country. Accordingly, we have it transmitted to us in writing, that thus did God speak to Solomon in his sleep.

CHAPTER 5

(130) After the building of the temple, which, as we have before said, was finished in seven years, the king laid the foundation of his palace, which he did not finish under thirteen years; for he was not equally zealous in the building of this palace as he had been about the temple; for as to that, though it was a

great work, and required wonderful and surprising application, yet God, for whom it was made, so far cooperated therewith, that it was finished in the forementioned number of years; (131) but the palace, which was a building much inferior in dignity to the temple, both on account that its materials had not been so long beforehand gotten ready, nor had been so zealously prepared, and on account that this was only a habitation for kings, and not for God, it was longer in finishing. (132) However, this building was raised so magnificently, as suited the happy state of the Hebrews, and of the king thereof: but it is necessary that I describe the entire structure and disposition of the parts, that so those that light upon this book may thereby make a conjecture, and, as it were, have a prospect of its magnitude.

(133) This house was a large and curious building, and was supported by many pillars, which Solomon built to contain a multitude for hearing causes and taking a cognisance of suits. It was sufficiently capacious to contain a great body of men who would come together to have their causes determined. It was a hundred cubits long, and fifty broad, and thirty high, supported by quadrangular pillars, which were all of cedar; but its roof was according to the Corinthian order, with folding doors, and their adjoining pillars of equal magnitude, each fluted with three cavities: which building was at once firm and very ornamental. (134) There was also another house so ordered, that its entire breadth was placed in the middle: it was quadrangular, and its breadth was thirty cubits, having a temple over against it, raised upon massy pillars; in which temple there was a large and very glorious room, wherein the king sat in judgment. To this was joined another house, that was built for his queen. There were other smaller edifices for diet, and for sleep, after public matters were over; and these were all floored with boards of cedar. (135) Some of these Solomon built with stones of ten cubits, and wainscoted the walls with other stones that were sawed, and were of great value, such as are dug out of the earth for the ornaments of temples, and to make fine prospects in royal palaces, and which make the mines whence they are dug famous. (136) Now the contexture of the curious workmanship of these stones was in three rows, but the fourth row would make one admire its sculptures, whereby were represented trees, and all sorts of plants, with the shades that arose from their branches, and leaves that hung down from them. Those trees and plants covered the stone that was beneath them, and their leaves were wrought so prodigious thin and subtle, that you would think they were in motion, (137) but the other part, up to the roof, was plastered over, and, as it were, embroidered with colours and pictures. He, moreover, built other edifices for pleasure; as also very long cloisters, and those situate in an agreeable place of the palace; and among them a most glorious dining room, for feastings and compotations, and full of gold, and such other furniture as so fine a room

ought to have for the conveniency of the guests, and where all the vessels were made of gold. (138) Now it is very hard to reckon up the magnitude and the variety of the royal apartments; how many rooms there were of the largest sort, how many of a bigness inferior to those, and how many that were subterraneous and invisible; the curiosity of those that enjoyed the fresh air and the groves for the most delightful prospect, for the avoiding the heat, and covering of their bodies. (139) And to say all in brief, Solomon made the whole building entirely of white stone and cedar wood, and gold and silver. He also adorned the roofs and walls with stones set in gold, and beautified them thereby in the same manner as he had beautified the temple of God with the like stones. (140) He also made himself a throne of prodigious bigness, of ivory, constructed as a seat of justice, and having six steps to it; on every one of which stood, on each end of the step, two lions, two other lions standing above also; but at the sitting place of the throne, hands came out, and received the king; and when he sat backward, he rested on half a bullock, that looked towards his back; but still all was fastened together with gold.

(141) When Solomon had completed all this in twenty years' time, because Hiram king of Tyre had contributed a great deal of gold and more silver to these buildings, as also cedar wood and pine wood, he also rewarded Hiram with rich presents: corn he sent him also year by year, and wine and oil, which were the principal things that he stood in need of, because he inhabited an island, as we have already said. (142) And besides these, he granted him certain cities of Galilee, twenty in number, that lay not far from Tyre; which when Hiram went to, and viewed, and did not like the gift, he sent word to Solomon that he did not want such cities as they were; and after that time those cities were called the land of Cabul; which name, if it be interpreted according to the language of the Phoenicians, denotes *what does not please*. (143) Moreover, the king of Tyre sent sophisms and enigmatical sayings to Solomon, and desired he would solve them, and free them from the ambiguity that was in them. Now so sagacious and understanding was Solomon, that none of these problems were too hard for him; but he conquered them all by his reasonings, and discovered their hidden meaning, and brought it to light. (144) Menander also, one who translated the Tyrian archives out of the dialect of the Phoenicians into the Greek language, makes mention of these two kings, where he says thus: 'When Abibalus was dead, his son Hiram received the kingdom from him, who, when he had lived fifty-three years, reigned thirty-four. (145) He raised a bank in the large place, and dedicated the golden pillar which is in Jupiter's temple. He also went and cut down materials of timber out of the mountain called Libanus, for the roof of temples; (146) and when he had pulled down the ancient temples, he both built the temple of Hercules and that of Astarte; and he first set up the temple of Hercules in the month Peritius; he also

made an expedition against the Euchii [or Titii], who did not pay their tribute; and when he had subdued them to himself he returned. Under this king there was Abdemon, a very youth in age, who always conquered the difficult problems which Solomon, king of Jerusalem, commanded him to explain. Dius also makes mention of him, where he says thus: (147) 'When Abibalus was dead, his son Hiram reigned. He raised the eastern parts of the city higher, and made the city itself larger. He also joined the temple of Jupiter, which before stood by itself, to the city, by raising a bank in the middle between them; and he adorned it with donations of gold. Moreover, he sent up to Mount Libanus, and cut down materials of wood for the building of the temples.' (148) He says also, that 'Solomon, who was then king of Jerusalem, sent riddles to Hiram, and desired to receive the like from him; but that he who could not solve them should pay money to them that did solve them; (149) and that Hiram accepted the conditions, and when he was not able to solve the riddles [proposed by Solomon], he paid a great deal of money for his fine; but that he afterwards did solve the proposed riddles by means of Abdemon, a man of Tyre; and that Hiram proposed other riddles, which, when Solomon could not solve, he paid back a great deal of money to Hiram.' This it is which Dius wrote.

CHAPTER 6

(150) Now when the king saw that the walls of Jerusalem stood in need of being better secured, and made stronger (for he thought the walls that encompassed Jerusalem ought to correspond to the dignity of the city) he both repaired them and made them higher, with great towers upon them; (151) he also built cities which might be counted among the strongest, Hazor and Megiddo, and the third Gezer, which had indeed belonged to the Philistines; but Pharaoh, the king of Egypt, had made an expedition against it, and besieged it, and taken it by force; and when he had slain all its inhabitants, he utterly overthrew it, and gave it as a present to his daughter, who had been married to Solomon: (152) for which reason the king rebuilt it, as a city that was naturally strong, and might be useful in wars and the mutations of affairs that sometimes happen. Moreover, he built two other cities not far from it; Beth-horon was the name of one of them, and Balaath of the other. (153) He also built other cities that lay conveniently for these in order to the enjoyment of pleasures and delicacies in them, such as were naturally of a good temperature of the air, and agreeable for fruits ripe in their proper seasons, and well watered with springs. Nay, Solomon went as far as the desert above Syria, and possessed himself of it, and built there a very great city, which was distant two days' journey from Upper Syria, and one day's journey from Euphrates, and six

long days' journey from Babylon the Great. (154) Now the reason why this city lay so remote from the parts of Syria that are inhabited, is this: that below there is no water to be had, and that it is in that place only that there are springs and pits of water. When he had therefore built this city, and encompassed it with very strong walls, he gave it the name of Tadmor; and that is the name it is still called by at this day among the Syrians; but the Greeks name it Palmyra.

(155) Now Solomon the king was at this time engaged in building these cities. But if any inquire why all the kings of Egypt from Menes, who built Memphis, and was many years earlier than our forefather Abraham, until Solomon, where the interval was more than one thousand three hundred years, were called Pharaohs, and took it from one Pharaoh that lived after the kings of that interval, I think it necessary to inform them of it, and this in order to cure their ignorance, and to make the occasion of that name manifest. Pharaoh, in the Egyptian tongue, signifies a *king*, (156) but I suppose they made use of other names from their childhood; but when they were made kings, they changed them into the name which, in their own tongue, denoted their authority; for thus it was also that the kings of Alexandria, who were called formerly by other names, when they took the kingdom, were named Ptolemies, from their first king. (157) The Roman emperors also were, from their nativity, called by other names, but are styled Caesars, their empire and their dignity imposing that name upon them, and not suffering them to continue in those names which their fathers gave them. I suppose also that Herodotus of Halicarnassus, when he said there were three hundred and thirty kings of Egypt after Menes, who built Memphis, did therefore not tell us their names, because they were in common called Pharaohs; (158) for when after their death there was a queen reigned, he calls her by her name Nicaule, as thereby declaring, that while the kings were of the male line, and so admitted of the same name, while a woman did not admit the same, he did therefore set down that her name, which she could not naturally have. (159) As for myself, I have discovered from our own books, that after Pharaoh, the father-in-law of Solomon, no other king of Egypt did any longer use that name; and that it was after that time when the forenamed queen of Egypt and Ethiopia came to Solomon, concerning whom we shall inform the reader presently; but I have now made mention of these things, that I may prove that our books and those of the Egyptians agree together in many things.

(160) But King Solomon subdued to himself the remnant of the Canaanites that had not before submitted to him – those I mean that dwelt in Mount Lebanon, and as far as the city Hamath; and ordered them to pay tribute. He also chose out of them every year such as were to serve him in the meanest offices, and to do his domestic works, and to follow husbandry; (161) for none of the Hebrews were servants [in such low employments]; nor was it

reasonable that, when God had brought so many nations under their power, they should depress their own people to such mean offices of life, rather than those nations; but all the Israelites were concerned in warlike affairs, and were in armour, and were set over the chariots and the horses rather than leading the life of slaves. (162) He appointed also five hundred and fifty rulers over those Canaanites who were reduced to such domestic slavery, who received the entire care of them from the king, and instructed them in those labours and operations wherein he wanted their assistance.

(163) Moreover, the king built many ships in the Egyptian Bay of the Red Sea, in a certain place called Ezion-geber: it is now called Berenice, and is not far from the city Eloth. This country belonged formerly to the Jews, and became useful for shipping, from the donation of Hiram, king of Tyre; (164) for he sent a sufficient number of men thither for pilots, and such as were skilful in navigation; to whom Solomon gave this command: that they should go along with his own stewards to the land that was of old called Ophir, but now the Aurea Chersonesus, which belongs to India, to fetch him gold. And when they had gathered four hundred talents together, they returned to the king again.

(165) There was then a woman, queen of Egypt and Ethiopia; she was inquisitive into philosophy, and one that on other accounts also was to be admired. When this queen heard of the virtue and prudence of Solomon, she had a great mind to see him; and the reports that went every day abroad induced her to come to him, (166) she being desirous to be satisfied by her own experience, and not by a bare hearing (for reports thus heard, are likely enough to comply with a false opinion, while they wholly depend on the credit of the relators); so she resolved to come to him, and that especially, in order to have a trial of his wisdom, while she proposed questions of very great difficulty, and entreated that he would solve their hidden meaning. Accordingly she came to Jerusalem with great splendour and rich furniture; (167) for she brought with her camels laden with gold, with several sorts of sweet spices, and with precious stones. Now, upon the king's kind reception of her, he both showed a great desire to please her, and easily comprehending in his mind the meaning of the curious questions she propounded to him, he resolved them sooner than anybody could have expected. (168) So she was amazed at the wisdom of Solomon, and discovered that it was more excellent upon trial than what she had heard by report beforehand; and especially she was surprised at the fineness and largeness of his royal palace, and not less so at the good order of the apartments, for she observed that the king had therein shown great wisdom; (169) but she was beyond measure astonished at the house which was called the *Forest of Lebanon*, as also at the magnificence of his daily table, and the circumstances of its preparation and ministration, with the apparel of his servants that waited, and the skilful and decent management of their attendance:

nor was she less affected with those daily sacrifices which were offered to God, and the careful management which the priests and Levites used about them. (170) When she saw this done every day, she was in the greatest admiration imaginable, insomuch that she was not able to contain the surprise she was in, but openly confessed how wonderfully she was affected; for she proceeded to discourse with the king, and thereby owned that she was overcome with admiration at the things before related; and said, (171) 'All things, indeed, O king, that came to our knowledge by report, came with uncertainty as to our belief of them; but as to those good things that to thee appertain, both such as thou thyself possessest, I mean wisdom and prudence, and the happiness thou hast from thy kingdom, certainly the same that came to us was no falsity; it was not only a true report, but it related thy happiness after a much lower manner than I now see it to be before my eyes. (172) For as for the report, it only attempted to persuade our hearing, but did not so make known the dignity of the things themselves as does the sight of them, and being present among them. I, indeed, who did not believe what was reported, by reason of the multitude and grandeur of the things I inquired about, do see them to be much more numerous than they were reported to be. (173) Accordingly, I esteem the Hebrew people, as well as thy servants and friends, to be happy, who enjoy thy presence and hear thy wisdom every day continually. One would therefore bless God, who hath so loved this country and those that inhabit therein, as to make thee king over them.'

(174) Now when the queen had thus demonstrated in words how deeply the king had affected her, her disposition was known by certain presents, for she gave him twenty talents of gold, and an immense quantity of spices and precious stones. (They say also that we possess the root of that balsam which our country still bears by this woman's gift). (175) Solomon also repaid her with many good things, and principally by bestowing upon her what she chose of her own inclination, for there was nothing that she desired which he denied her: and as he was very generous and liberal in his own temper, so did he show the greatness of his soul in bestowing on her what she herself desired of him. So when this queen of Ethiopia had obtained what we have already given an account of, and had again communicated to the king what she brought with her, she returned to her own kingdom.

CHAPTER 7

(176) About the same time there were brought to the king from the Aurea Chersonesus, a country so called, precious stones and pine trees, and these trees he made use of for supporting the temple and the palace, as also for the materials of musical instruments, the harps and the psalteries, that the Levites

might make use of them in their hymns to God. The wood which was brought to him at this time was larger and finer than any that had ever been brought before; (177) but let no one imagine that these pine trees were like those which are now so named, and which take that their denomination from the merchants, who so called them, that they may procure them to be admired by those that purchase them; for those we speak of were to the sight like the wood of the fig tree, but were whiter and more shining. (178) Now we have said thus much, that nobody may be ignorant of the difference between these sorts of wood, nor unacquainted with the nature of the genuine pine tree; and we thought it both a seasonable and humane thing when we mentioned it, and the uses the king made of it, to explain this difference so far as we have done.

(179) Now the weight of gold that was brought him was six hundred and sixty-six talents, not including in that sum what was brought by the merchants, nor what the toparchs and king of Arabia gave him in presents. He also cast two hundred targets of gold, each of them weighing six hundred shekels; (180) he also made three hundred shields, every one weighing three pounds of gold, and he had them carried and put into that house which was called *The Forest of Lebanon*. He also made cups of gold and of [precious] stones, for the entertainment of his guests, and had them adorned in the most artificial manner; and he contrived that all his other furniture of vessels should be of gold, (181) for there was nothing then to be sold or bought for silver; for the king had many ships which lay upon the sea of Tarsus, these he commanded to carry out all sorts of merchandise into the remotest nations, by the sale of which silver and gold were brought to the king, and a great quantity of ivory, and Ethiopians, and apes; and they finished their voyage, going and returning, in three years' time.

(182) Accordingly there went a great fame all around the neighbouring countries, which proclaimed the virtue and wisdom of Solomon, insomuch that all the kings everywhere were desirous to see him, as not giving credit to what was reported, on account of its being almost incredible; they also demonstrated the regard they had for him by the presents they made him; (183) for they sent him vessels of gold and silver, and purple garments, and many sorts of spices, and horses and chariots, and as many mules for his carriages as they could find proper to please the king's eyes by their strength and beauty. This addition then he made to those chariots and horses which he had before from those that were sent him, augmented the number of his chariots by above four hundred, for he had a thousand before, and augmented the number of his horses by two thousand, for he had twenty thousand before. (184) These horses also were so much exercised, in order to their making a fine appearance, and running swiftly, that no others could, upon the comparison,

appear either finer or swifter; but they were at once the most beautiful of all others, and their swiftness was incomparable also. (185) Their riders also were a further ornament to them, being, in the first place, young men in the most delightful flower of their age, and being eminent for their largeness, and far taller than other men. They had also very long heads of hair hanging down, and were clothed in garments of Tyrian purple. They had also dust of gold every day sprinkled on their hair, so that their heads sparkled with the reflection of the sunbeams from the gold. (186) The king himself rode upon a chariot in the midst of these men, who were still in armour, and had their bows fitted to them. He had on a white garment, and used to take his progress out of the city in the morning. There was a certain place, about fifty furlongs distant from Jerusalem, which is called Etham, very pleasant it is in fine gardens, and abounding in rivulets of water; thither did he use to go out in the morning, sitting on high [in his chariot].

(187) Now Solomon had a divine sagacity in all things, and was very diligent and studious to have things done after an elegant manner; so he did not neglect the care of the ways, but he laid a causeway of black stone along the roads that led to Jerusalem, which was the royal city, both to render them easy for travellers, and to manifest the grandeur of his riches and government. (188) He also parted his chariots, and set them in a regular order, that a certain number of them should be in every city, still keeping a few about him; and those cities he called the *cities of his chariots;* and the king made silver as plentiful in Jerusalem as the stones on the street; and so multiplied cedar trees in the plains of Judea, which did not grow there before, that they were like the multitude of common sycamore trees. (189) He also ordained the Egyptian merchants that brought him their merchandise, to sell him a chariot, with a pair of horses, for six hundred drachmae of silver, and he sent them to the kings of Syria, and to those kings that were beyond Euphrates.

(190) But although Solomon was become the most glorious of kings, and the best beloved by God, and had exceeded in wisdom and riches those that had been rulers of the Hebrews before him, yet did not he persevere in this happy state till he died. Nay, he forsook the observation of the laws of his father, and came to an end no way suitable to our foregoing history of him. (191) He grew mad in his love of women, and laid no restraint on himself in his lusts; nor was he satisfied with the women of his country alone, but he married many wives out of foreign nations: Sidonians and Tyrians and Ammonites and Edomites; and he transgressed the laws of Moses, which forbade Jews to marry any but those that were of their own people. (192) He also began to worship their gods, which he did in order to the gratification of his wives, and out of his affection for them. This very thing our legislator suspected, and so admonished us beforehand, that we should not marry women of other countries, lest we

should be entangled with foreign customs, and apostatise from our own; lest we should leave off to honour our own God, and should worship their gods. (193) But Solomon was fallen headlong into unreasonable pleasures, and regarded not those admonitions; for when he had married seven hundred wives, the daughters of princes and of eminent persons, and three hundred concubines, and these besides the king of Egypt's daughter, he soon was governed by them, till he came to imitate their practices. He was forced to give them this demonstration of his kindness and affection to them, to live according to the laws of their countries. (194) And as he grew into years, and his reason became weaker by length of time, it was not sufficient to recall to his mind the institutions of his own country; so he still more and more condemned his own God, and continued to regard the gods that his marriages had introduced; (195) nay, before this happened, he sinned, and fell into an error about the observation of the laws, when he made the images of brazen oxen that supported the brazen sea, and the images of lions about his own throne; for these he made, although it was not agreeable to piety so to do; (196) and this he did, notwithstanding that he had his father as a most excellent and domestic pattern of virtue, and knew what a glorious character he had left behind him, because of his piety towards God; nor did he imitate David, although God had twice appeared to him, in his sleep, and exhorted him to imitate his father; so he died ingloriously. (197) There came therefore a prophet to him, who was sent by God, and told him that his wicked actions were not concealed from God, and threatened him that he should not long rejoice in what he had done; that indeed the kingdom should not be taken from him while he was alive, because God had promised to his father David that he would make him his successor, (198) but that he would take care that this should befall his son when he was dead; not that he would withdraw all the people from him, but that he would give ten tribes to a servant of his, and leave only two tribes to David's grandson for his sake, because he loved God, and for the sake of the city of Jerusalem, wherein he should have a temple.

(199) When Solomon heard that, he was grieved, and greatly confounded upon this change of almost all that happiness which had made him to be admired, into so bad a state; nor had there much time passed after the prophet had foretold what was coming, before God raised up an enemy against him, whose name was Ader, who took the following occasion of his enmity to him: (200) he was a child of the stock of the Edomites, and of the blood royal; and when Joab, the captain of David's host, laid waste the land of Edom, and destroyed all that were men grown, and able to bear arms, for six months time this Hadad fled away, and came to Pharaoh, the king of Egypt, (201) who received him kindly, and assigned him a house to dwell in, and a country to supply him with food; and when he was grown up he loved him exceedingly,

insomuch that he gave him his wife's sister, whose name was Tahpenes, to wife, by whom he had a son, who was brought up with the king's children. (202) When Hadad heard in Egypt that both David and Joab were dead, he came to Pharaoh, and desired that he would permit him to go to his own country; upon which the king asked what it was that he wanted, and what hardship he had met with, that he was so desirous to leave him; and when he was often troublesome to him, and entreated him to dismiss him, he did not then do it. (203) But at the time when Solomon's affairs began to grow worse, on account of his forementioned transgressions, and God's anger against him for the same, Hadad, by Pharaoh's permission, came to Edom; and when he was not able to make the people forsake Solomon, for it was kept under by many garrisons, and an innovation was not to be made with safety, he removed thence, and came into Syria; (204) there he lighted upon one Rezon, who had run away from Hadadezer, king of Zobah, his master, and was become a robber in that country, and joined friendship with him, who had already a band of robbers about him. So he went up and seized upon that part of Syria, and was made king thereof. He also made incursions into the land of Israel, and did no small mischief, and spoiled it, and that in the lifetime of Solomon. And this was the calamity which the Hebrews suffered by Hadad.

(205) There was also one of Solomon's own nation that made an attempt against him, Jeroboam the son of Nebat, who had an expectation of rising, from a prophecy that had been made to him long before. He was left a child by his father and brought up by his mother; and when Solomon saw that he was of an active and bold disposition, he made him the curator of the walls which he built round about Jerusalem; (206) and he took such care of those works, that the king approved of his behaviour, and gave him, as a reward for the same, the charge of the tribe of Joseph. And when about that time Jeroboam was once going out of Jerusalem, a prophet of the city Shilo, whose name was Ahijah, met him and saluted him; and when he had taken him a little aside, to a place out of the way, where there was not one other person present, (207) he rent the garment he had on into twelve pieces, and bid Jeroboam take ten of them; and told him beforehand, that 'this is the will of God; he will part the dominion of Solomon, and give one tribe, with that which is next it, to his son, because of the promise made to David for his succession, and will give ten tribes to thee, because Solomon hath sinned against him and delivered up himself to women, and to their gods. (208) Seeing therefore that thou knowest the cause for which God hath changed his mind, and is alienated from Solomon, be thou righteous and keep the laws, because he hath proposed to thee the greatest of all rewards for thy piety, and the honour thou shalt pay to God, namely, to be as greatly exalted as thou knowest David to have been.'

(209) So Jeroboam was elevated by these words of the prophet; and being a

young man of a warm temper, and ambitious of greatness, he could not be quiet; and when he had so great a charge in the government, and called to mind what had been revealed to him by Ahijah, he endeavoured to persuade the people to forsake Solomon, to make a disturbance, and to bring the government over to himself; (210) but when Solomon understood his intention and treachery, he sought to catch him and kill him; but Jeroboam was informed of it beforehand, and fled to Shishak, the king of Egypt, and there abode till the death of Solomon, by which means he gained these two advantages – to suffer no harm from Solomon, and to be preserved for the kingdom. (211) So Solomon died when he was already an old man, having reigned eighty years, and lived ninety-four. He was buried in Jerusalem, having been superior to all other kings in happiness and riches and wisdom, excepting that when he was growing into years he was deluded by women, and transgressed the law; concerning which transgressions, and the miseries which befell the Hebrews thereby, I think proper to discourse at another opportunity.

CHAPTER 8

(212) Now when Solomon was dead, and his son Rehoboam (who was born of an Ammonite wife, whose name was Naamah) had succeeded him in the kingdom, the rulers of the multitude sent immediately into Egypt, and called back Jeroboam; and when he was come to them, to the city Shechem, Rehoboam came to it also, for he had resolved to declare himself king to the Israelites, while they were there gathered together. (213) So the rulers of the people, as well as Jeroboam, came to him, and besought him, and said that he ought to relax, and to be gentler than his father, in the servitude he had imposed on them, because they had borne a heavy yoke, and that then they should be better affected to him, and be well contented to serve him under his moderate government, and should do it more out of love than fear; (214) but Rehoboam told them they should come to him again in three days' time when he would give an answer to their request. This delay gave occasion to a present suspicion, since he had not given them a favourable answer to their mind immediately, for they thought that he should have given them a humane answer offhand, especially since he was but young. However, they thought that this consultation about it, and that he did not presently give them a denial, afforded them some good hope of success.

(215) Rehoboam now called his father's friends and advised with them what sort of answer he ought to give to the multitude; upon which they gave him the advice which became friends, and those that knew the temper of such a multitude. They advised him to speak in a way more popular than suited the grandeur of a king, because he would thereby oblige them to submit to him

with good will, it being most agreeable to subjects that their king should be almost upon the level with them; (216) but Rehoboam rejected this so good, and in general so profitable, advice (it was such at least at that time when he was to be made king), God himself, I suppose, causing what was most advantageous to be condemned by him. So he called for the young men who were brought up with him, and told them what advice the elders had given him, and bade them speak what they thought he ought to do. (217) They advised him to give the following answer to the people (for neither their youth nor God himself suffered them to discern what was best): that his little finger should be thicker than his father's loins; and if they had met with hard usage from his father, they should experience much rougher treatment from him; and if his father had chastised them with whips, that they must expect that he would do it with scorpions. (218) The king was pleased with this advice and thought it agreeable to the dignity of his government to give them such an answer. Accordingly when the multitude came together to hear his answer on the third day, all the people were in great expectation, and very intent to hear what the king would say to them, and supposed they should hear somewhat of a kind nature; but he passed by his friends, and answered as the young men had given him counsel. Now this was done according to the will of God, that what Ahijah had foretold might come to pass.

(219) By these words the people were struck, as it were by an iron hammer, and were so grieved at the words, as if they had already felt the effects of them; and they had great indignation at the king, and all cried out aloud, and said, 'we will have no longer any relation to David or his posterity after this day'; and they said farther, 'We only leave to Rehoboam the temple which his father built;' and they threatened to forsake him. (220) Nay, they were so bitter, and retained their wrath so long, that when he sent Adoram which was over the tribute, that he might pacify them and render them milder, and persuade them to forgive him, if he had said anything that was rash or grievous to them in his youth, they would not hear it, but threw stones at him and killed him. (221) When Rehoboam saw this, he thought himself aimed at by those stones with which they had killed his servant, and feared lest he should undergo the last of punishments in earnest; so he got immediately into his chariot, and fled to Jerusalem, where the tribe of Judah and that of Benjamin ordained him king; but the rest of the multitude forsook the sons of David from that day, and appointed Jeroboam to be the ruler of their public affairs. (222) Upon this Rehoboam Solomon's son, assembled a great congregation of those two tribes that submitted to him, and was ready to take a hundred and eighty thousand chosen men out of the army, to make an expedition against Jeroboam and his people, that he might force them by war to be his servants; (223) but he was forbidden of God by the prophet [Shemaiah] to go to war; for that it was not

just that brethren of the same country should fight one against another. He also said, that this defection of the multitude was according to the purpose of God. So he did not proceed in this expedition: (224) and now I will relate first the actions of Jeroboam, the king of Israel, after which we will relate what are therewith connected, the actions of Rehoboam, the king of the two tribes; by this means we shall preserve the good order of the history entire.

(225) When therefore Jeroboam had built him a palace in the city Shechem, he dwelt there. He also built him another at Penuel, a city so called; and now the Feast of Tabernacles was approaching in a little time, Jeroboam considered, if he should permit the multitude to go to worship God at Jerusalem, and there to celebrate the festival, they would probably repent of what they had done, and be enticed by the temple and by the worship of God there performed, and would leave him, and return to their first king; and so he should run the risk of losing his own life; so he invented this contrivance: (226) he made two golden heifers, and built two little temples for them, the one in the city Bethel, and the other in Dan, which last was at the fountains of the Lesser Jordan, and he put the heifers into both the little temples, in the forementioned cities. And when he had called those ten tribes together, over whom he ruled, he made a speech to the people in these words: (227) 'I suppose, my countrymen, that you know this, that every place hath God in it; nor is there any one determinate place in which he is, but he everywhere hears and sees those that worship him; on which account I do not think it right for you to go so long a journey to Jerusalem, which is an enemy's city, to worship him. (228) It was a man that built the temple: I have also made two golden heifers, dedicated to the same God; and one of them I have consecrated in the city Bethel, and the other in Dan, to the end that those of you that dwell nearest those cities, may go to them, and worship God there: and I will ordain for you certain priests and Levites from among yourselves, that you may have no want of the tribe of Levi, or of the sons of Aaron; but let him that is desirous among you of being a priest, bring to God a bullock and a ram, which they say Aaron the first priest brought also.' (229) When Jeroboam had said this, he deluded the people, and made them to revolt from the worship of their forefathers, and to transgress their laws. This was the beginning of miseries to the Hebrews, and the cause why they were overcome in war by foreigners and so fell into captivity. But we shall relate those things in their proper places hereafter.

(230) When the Feast [of Tabernacles] was just approaching, Jeroboam was desirous to celebrate it himself in Bethel, as did the two tribes celebrate it in Jerusalem. Accordingly he built an altar before the heifer, and undertook to be high priest himself. So he went up to the altar, with his own priests about him, (231) but when he was going to offer the sacrifices, and the burnt offerings in the sight of all the people, a prophet, whose name was Jadon, was sent by God,

and came to him from Jerusalem, who stood in the midst of the multitude, and in the hearing of the king, and directing his discourse to the altar, said thus: (232) 'God foretells that there shall be a certain man of the family of David, Josiah by name, who shall slay upon thee those false priests that shall live at that time, and upon thee shall burn the bones of those deceivers of the people, those impostors and wicked wretches. However, that this people may believe that these things shall come to pass, I foretell a sign to them that shall also come to pass: this altar shall be broken to pieces immediately, and all the fat of the sacrifices that is upon it shall be poured upon the ground.' (233) When the prophet had said this, Jeroboam fell into a passion, and stretched out his hand, and bid them lay hold of him: but the hand which he stretched out was enfeebled, and he was not able to pull it in again to him, for it was become withered, and hung down as if it were a dead hand. The altar also was broken to pieces, and all that was upon it was poured out, as the prophet had foretold should come to pass. (234) So the king understood that he was a man of veracity, and had a divine foreknowledge; and entreated him to pray to God that he would restore his right hand. Accordingly the prophet did pray to God to grant him that request. So the king having his hand recovered to its natural state, rejoiced at it, and invited the prophet to sup with him; (235) but Jadon said, that he could not endure to come into his house, nor to taste of bread or water in this city, for that was a thing God had forbidden him to do; as also to go back by the same way which he came; but he said he was to return by another way. So the king wondered at the abstinence of the man; but was himself in fear, as suspecting a change of his affairs for the worse, from what had been said to him.

CHAPTER 9

(236) Now there was a certain wicked man in that city, who was a false prophet, whom Jeroboam had in great esteem, but was deceived by him and his flattering words. This man was bedrid, by reason of the infirmities of old age; however, he was informed by his sons concerning the prophet that was come from Jerusalem, and concerning the signs done by him; (237) and how, when Jeroboam's right hand had been enfeebled, at the prophet's prayer he had it revived again. Whereupon he was afraid that this stranger and prophet should be in better esteem with the king than himself, and obtain greater honour from him; and he gave order to his sons to saddle his ass presently, and make all ready that he might go out. (238) Accordingly they made haste to do what they were commanded, and he got upon the ass, and followed after the prophet; and when he had overtaken him, as he was resting himself under a very large oak tree that was thick and shady, he at first saluted him, but

presently he complained of him, because he had not come into his house, and partaken of his hospitality. (239) And when the other said, that God had forbidden him to taste of anyone's provision in that city, he replied, that 'For certain God had not forbidden that I should set food before thee, for I am a prophet as thou art, and worship God in the same manner that thou dost; and I am now come as sent by him, in order to bring thee into my house, and make thee my guest.' (240) Now Jadon gave credit to this lying prophet, and returned back with him. But when they were at dinner, and merry together, God appeared to Jadon, and said, that he should suffer punishment for transgressing his commands – and he told him what that punishment should be: for he said that he should meet with a lion as he was going on his way, by which lion he should be torn in pieces, and be deprived of burial in the sepulchres of his fathers: (241) which things came to pass, as I suppose, according to the will of God, that so Jeroboam might not give heed to the words of Jadon, as of one that had been convicted of lying. However, as Jadon was again going to Jerusalem a lion assaulted him, and pulled him off the beast he rode on, and slew him; yet did he not at all hurt the ass, but sat by him, and kept him, as also the prophet's body. This continued till some travellers that saw it came and told it in the city to the false prophet, (242) who sent his sons and brought the body into the city, and made a funeral for him at great expense. He also charged his sons to bury himself with him; and said, that all which he had foretold against that city, and the altar, and priests, and false prophets, would prove true; and that if he were buried with him, he should receive no injurious treatment after his death, the bones not being then to be distinguished asunder. (243) But now, when he had performed those funeral rites to the prophet, and had given that charge to his sons, as he was a wicked and an impious man, he goes to Jeroboam, and says to him, 'And wherefore is it now that thou art disturbed at the words of this silly fellow?' And when the king had related to him what had happened about the altar, and about his own hand, and gave him the names of *divine man*, and *an excellent prophet*, he endeavoured, by a wicked trick, to weaken that his opinion; and by using plausible words concerning what had happened, he aimed to injure the truth that was in them; (244) for he attempted to persuade him, that his hand was enfeebled by the labour it had undergone in supporting the sacrifices, and that upon its resting a while it returned to its former nature again; and that as to the altar, it was but new, and had borne abundance of sacrifices, and those large ones too, and was accordingly broken to pieces, and fallen down by the weight of what had been laid upon it. He also informed him of the death of him that had foretold those things, and how he perished; [whence he concluded that] he had not anything in him of a prophet, nor spake anything like one. (245) When he had thus spoken, he persuaded the king, and entirely alienated his mind from God, and from doing works that were righteous and holy, and encouraged him to go on in his impious practices; and accordingly, he was to that degree injurious to God, and so great a transgressor, that he sought for nothing else every day but how he might be guilty of some new instances of wickedness, and such as should be more detestable than what he had been so insolent as to do before. And so much shall at present suffice to have said concerning Jeroboam.

CHAPTER 10

(246) Now Rehoboam, the son of Solomon, who, as we said before, was king of the two tribes, built strong and large cities, Bethlehem, and Etam, and Tekoa, and Bethzur, and Shoco, and Adullam, and Ipan, and Maresha, and Ziph, and Adoriam, and Lachish, and Azekah, and Zorah, and Aijalon, and Hebron; (247) these he built first of all in the tribe of Judah. He also built other large cities in the tribe of Benjamin, and walled them about, and put garrisons in them all, and captains, and a great deal of corn and wine and oil; and he furnished every one of them plentifully with other provisions that were necessary for sustenance: moreover, he put therein shields and spears for many ten thousand men. (248) The priests also that were in all Israel, and the Levites, and if there were any of the multitude that were good and righteous men, they gathered themselves together to him, having left their own cities, that they might worship God in Jerusalem; for they were not willing to be forced to worship the heifers which Jeroboam had made; and they augmented the kingdom of Rehoboam for three years. (249) And after he had married a woman of his own kindred, and had by her three children born to him, he married also another of his own kindred, who was daughter of Absalom by Tamar whose name was Maachah; and by her he had a son, whom he named Abijah. He had moreover many other children by other wives, but he loved Maachah above them all. (250) Now he had eighteen legitimate wives, and thirty concubines, and he had born to him twenty-eight sons and threescore daughters; but he appointed Abijah, whom he had by Maachah, to be his successor in the kingdom, and entrusted him already with the treasures and the strongest cities.

(251) Now I cannot but think that the greatness of a kingdom and its change into prosperity, often become the occasion of mischief and of transgression to men; for when Rehoboam saw that his kingdom was so much increased, he went out of the right way, unto unrighteous and irreligious practices, and he despised the worship of God, till the people themselves imitated his wicked actions; (252) for so it usually happens, that the manners of subjects are corrupted at the same time with those of their governors; which subjects then

lay aside their own sober way of living, as a reproof of their governors' intemperate courses, and follow their wickedness as if it were virtue; for it is not possible to show that men approve of the actions of their kings unless they do the same actions with them. (253) Agreeable whereto it now happened to the subjects of Rehoboam; for when he was grown impious, and a transgressor himself, they endeavoured not to offend him by resolving still to be righteous; but God sent Shishak, king of Egypt, to punish them for their unjust behaviour towards him; concerning whom Herodotus was mistaken, and applied his actions to Sesostris; (254) for this Shishak, in the fifth year of the reign of Rehoboam, made an expedition [into Judea] with many ten thousand men; for he had one thousand two hundred chariots in number that followed him, and threescore thousand horsemen, and four hundred thousand footmen. These he brought with him, and they were the greatest part of them Libyans and Ethiopians. (255) Now, therefore, when he fell upon the country of the Hebrews, he took the strongest cities of Rehoboam's kingdom without fighting; and when he had put garrisons in them, he came last of all to Jerusalem.

Now when Rehoboam, and the multitude with him, were shut up in Jerusalem by the means of the army of Shishak, and when they besought God to give them victory and deliverance, they could not persuade God to be on their side; (256) but Shemaiah the prophet told them, that God threatened to forsake them as they had forsaken his worship. When they heard this, they were immediately in a consternation of mind, and seeing no way of deliverance, they all earnestly set themselves to confess that God might justly overlook them since they had been guilty of impiety towards him, and had let his laws lie in confusion. (257) So when God saw them in that disposition, and that they acknowledged their sins, he told the prophet that he should not destroy them, but that he would, however, make them servants to the Egyptians, that they may learn whether they will suffer less by serving men or God. (258) So when Shishak had taken the city without fighting, because Rehoboam was afraid, and received him into it, yet did not Shishak stand to the covenants he had made, but he spoiled the temple, and emptied the treasures of God and those of the king, and carried off innumerable ten thousands of gold and silver, and left nothing at all behind him. (259) He also took away the bucklers of gold, and the shields, which Solomon the king had made; nay, he did not leave the golden quivers which David had taken from the king of Zobah, and had dedicated to God; and when he had thus done, he returned to his own kingdom. (260) Now Herodotus of Halicarnassus mentions this expedition, having only mistaken the king's name; and [in saying that] he made war upon many other nations also, and brought Syria of Palestine into subjection, and took the men that were therein prisoners without fighting. (261) Now it is manifest that he intended to declare that our nation was subdued by him; for he saith, that he left behind him pillars in the land of those that delivered themselves up to him without fighting, and engraved upon them the secret parts of women. Now our king Rehoboam delivered up our city without fighting. (262) He says withal, that the Ethiopians learned to circumcise their privy parts from the Egyptians; with this addition, that the Phoenicians and Syrians that live in Palestine confess that they learned it of the Egyptians; yet it is evident that no other of the Syrians that live in Palestine, besides us alone, are circumcised. But as to such matters, let everyone speak what is agreeable to his own opinion.

(263) When Shishak was gone away, king Rehoboam made bucklers and shields of brass, instead of those of gold, and delivered the same number of them to the keepers of the king's palace; so, instead of warlike expeditions, and that glory which results from those public actions, he reigned in great quietness, though not without fear, as being always an enemy to Jeroboam; (264) and he died when he had lived fifty-seven years, and reigned seventeen. He was in his disposition a proud and a foolish man, and lost [part of his] dominions by not hearkening to his father's friends. He was buried in Jerusalem, in the sepulchres of the kings; and his son Abijah succeeded him in the kingdom, and this, in the eighteenth year of Jeroboam's reign over the ten tribes; (265) and this was the conclusion of these affairs. It must be now our business to relate the affairs of Jeroboam, and how he ended his life; for he ceased not, nor rested to be injurious to God, but every day raised up altars upon high mountains and went on making priests out of the multitude.

CHAPTER 11

(266) However, God was in no long time ready to return Jeroboam's wicked actions, and the punishment they deserved, upon his own head, and upon the heads of all his house; and whereas a son of his lay sick at that time, who was called Abijah, he enjoined his wife to lay aside her robes, and to take the garments belonging to a private person, and to go to Ahijah the prophet, (267) for that he was a wonderful man in foretelling futurities, it having been he who told me that I should be king. He also enjoined her when she came to him, to inquire concerning the child, as if she were a stranger, whether he should escape this distemper. So she did as her husband bade her, and changed her habit, and came to the city Shiloh, for there did Ahijah live: (268) and as she was going into his house, his eyes being then dim with age, God appeared to him, and informed him of two things; that the wife of Jeroboam was come to him, and what answer he should make to her inquiry. (269) Accordingly, as the woman was coming into the house like a private person and a stranger, he cried out, Come in, O thou wife of Jeroboam! Why concealest thou thyself? Thou art not concealed from God, who hath appeared to me, and informed

me that thou wast coming, and hath given me in command what I shall say to thee.' So he said that she should go away to her husband, and speak to him thus: (270) 'Since I made thee a great man when thou wast little, or rather wast nothing, and rent the kingdom from the house of David, and gave it to thee, and thou hast been unmindful of these benefits, hast left off my worship, hast made thee molten gods, and honoured them, I will in like manner cast thee down again, and destroy all thy house, and make them food for the dogs and the fowls; (271) for a certain king is rising up, by appointment, over all this people, who shall leave none of the family of Jeroboam remaining. The multitude also shall themselves partake of the same punishment, and shall be cast out of this good land, and shall be scattered into the places beyond Euphrates, because they have followed the wicked practices of their king, and have worshipped the gods that he made, and forsaken my sacrifices. (272) But do thou, O woman, make haste back to thy husband, and tell him this message; but thou shalt then find thy son dead, for as thou enterest the city he shall depart this life; yet shall he be buried with the lamentation of all the multitude, and honoured with a general mourning, for he is the only person of goodness of Jeroboam's family.' (273) When the prophet had foretold these events, the woman went hastily away with a disordered mind and greatly grieved at the death of the forenamed child: so she was in lamentation as she went along the road, and mourned for the death of her son, that was just at hand. She was indeed in a miserable condition, at the unavoidable misery of his death, and went apace, but in circumstances very unfortunate, because of her son; for the greater haste she made, she would the sooner see her son dead, yet was she forced to make such haste, on account of her husband. Accordingly, when she was come back, she found that the child had given up the ghost, as the prophet had said; and she related all the circumstances to the king.

(274) Yet did not Jeroboam lay any of these things to heart, but he brought together a very numerous army, and made a warlike expedition against Abijah, the son of Rehoboam, who had succeeded his father in the kingdom of the two tribes; for he despised him because of his age. But when he heard of the expedition of Jeroboam, he was not affrighted at it, but proved of a courageous temper of mind, superior both to his youth and to the hopes of his enemy; so he chose him an army out of the two tribes, and met Jeroboam at a place called Mount Zemaraim, and pitched his camp near the other, and prepared everything necessary for the fight. (275) His army consisted of four hundred thousand, but the army of Jeroboam was double to it. Now, as the armies stood in array, ready for action and dangers, and were just going to fight, Abijah stood upon an elevated place, and beckoning with his hand, he desired the multitude and Jeroboam himself to hear first with silence what he had to say. (276) And when silence was made, he began to speak, and told them –

'God had consented that David and his posterity should be their rulers for all time to come, and this you yourselves are not unacquainted with; but I cannot but wonder how you should forsake my father, and join yourselves to his servant Jeroboam, and are now here with him to fight against those who, by God's own determination, are to reign, and to deprive them of that dominion which they have still retained; for as to the greater part of it, Jeroboam is unjustly in possession of it. (277) However, I do not suppose he will enjoy it any longer; but when he hath suffered that punishment which God thinks due to him for what is past, he will leave off the transgressions he hath been guilty of, and the injuries he hath offered to him, and which he hath still continued to offer, and hath persuaded you to do the same; yet when you were not any farther unjustly treated by my father, than that he did not speak to you so as to please you, and this only in compliance with the advice of wicked men, you in anger forsook him, as you pretended, but, in reality, you withdrew yourselves from God, and from his laws, (278) although it had been right for you to have forgiven a man that was young in age, and not used to govern people, not only some disagreeable words, but if his youth and his unskilfulness in affairs had led him into some unfortunate actions, and that for the sake of his father Solomon and the benefits you received from him; for men ought to excuse the sins of posterity on account of the benefactions of parents; (279) but you considered nothing of all this then, neither do you consider it now, but come with so great an army against us. And what is it you depend upon for victory? Is it upon these golden heifers and the altars that you have on high places, which are demonstrations of your impiety, and not of religious worship? Or is it the exceeding multitude of your army which gives you such good hopes? (280) Yet certainly there is no strength at all in an army of many ten thousands, when the war is unjust; for we ought to place our surest hopes of success against our enemies in righteousness alone, and in piety towards God; which hope we justly have, since we have kept the laws from the beginning, and have worshipped our own God, who was not made by hands out of corruptible matter, nor was he formed by a wicked king, in order to deceive the multitude; but who is his own workmanship, and the beginning and end of all things. (281) I therefore give you counsel even now to repent, and to take better advice, and to leave off the prosecution of the war; to call to mind the laws of your country, and to reflect what it hath been that hath advanced you to so happy a state as you are now in.'

(282) This was the speech which Abijah made to the multitude. But, while he was still speaking, Jeroboam sent some of his soldiers privately to encompass Abijah round about, on certain parts of the camp that were not taken notice of; and when he was thus within the compass of the enemy, his army was affrighted, and their courage failed them. But Abijah encouraged

them, and exhorted them to place their hopes on God, for that he was not encompassed by the enemy. (283) So they all at once implored the divine assistance, while the priests sounded with the trumpets and they made a shout, and fell upon their enemies;(284) and God brake the courage, and cast down the force of their enemies, and made Abijah's army superior to them, for God vouchsafed to grant them a wonderful and very famous victory; and such a slaughter was now made of Jeroboam's army as is never recorded to have happened in any other war, whether it were of the Greeks or of the barbarians, for they overthrew [and slew] five hundred thousand of their enemies, and they took their strongest cities by force, and spoiled them; and besides those, they did the same to Bethel and her towns, and Jeshanah and her towns. (285) And after this defeat, Jeroboam never recovered himself during the life of Abijah, who yet did not long survive, for he reigned but three years, and was buried in Jerusalem in the sepulchres of his forefathers. He left behind him twenty-two sons and sixteen daughters, and he had also those children by fourteen wives; (286) and Asa his son succeeded in the kingdom; and the young man's mother was Michaiah. Under his reign the country of the Israelites enjoyed peace for ten years.

(287) And so far concerning Abijah, the son of Rehoboam, the son of Solomon, as his history hath come down to us; but Jeroboam, the king of the ten tribes, died when he had governed them two-and-twenty years; whose son Nadab succeeded him, in the second year of the reign of Asa. Now Jeroboam's son governed two years, and resembled his father in impiety and wickedness. (288) In these two years he made an expedition against Gibbethon, a city of the Philistines, and continued the siege in order to take it; but he was conspired against while he was there, by a friend of his, whose name was Baasha, the son of Ahijah, and was slain; which Baasha took the kingdom after the other's death, and destroyed the whole house of Jeroboam. (289) It also came to pass, according as God had foretold, that some of Jeroboam's kindred that died in the city were torn to pieces and devoured by dogs: and that others of them that died in the fields, were torn and devoured by the fowls. So the house of Jeroboam suffered the just punishment of his impiety and of his wicked actions.

CHAPTER 12

(290) Now Asa, the king of Jerusalem, was of an excellent character, and had a regard to God, and neither did nor designed anything but what had relation to the observation of the laws. He made a reformation of his kingdom, and cut off whatsoever was wicked therein, and purified it from every impurity. (291) Now he had an army of chosen men, that were armed with targets and spears: out of the tribe of Judah three hundred thousand; and out of the tribe of

Benjamin, that bore shields and drew bows, two hundred and fifty thousand; (292) but when he had already reigned ten years, Zerah, king of Ethiopia, made an expedition against him, with a great army of nine hundred thousand footmen, and one hundred thousand horsemen, and three hundred chariots, and came as far as Mareshah, a city that belonged to the tribe of Judah. Now when Zerah had passed so far with his own army, Asa met him, (293) and put his army in array over against him, in a valley called Zephathah, not far from the city; and when he saw the multitude of the Ethiopians, he cried out, and besought God to give him the victory, and that he might kill many ten thousands of the enemy: 'For,' said he, 'I depend on nothing else but that assistance which I expect from thee, which is able to make the fewer superior to the more numerous, and the weaker to the stronger; and thence it is alone that I venture to meet Zerah and fight him.'

(294) While Asa was saying this, God gave him a signal of victory, and joining battle cheerfully on account of what God had foretold about it, he slew a great many of the Ethiopians; and when he had put them to flight, he pursued them to the country of Gerar; and when they left off killing their enemies, they betook themselves to spoiling them (for the city Gerar was already taken), and to spoiling their camp, so that they carried off much gold, and much silver, and a great deal of [other] prey, and camels, and great cattle, and flocks of sheep. (295) Accordingly, when Asa and his army had obtained such a victory, and such wealth from God, they returned to Jerusalem. Now, as they were coming, a prophet, whose name was Azariah, met them on the road, and bade them stop their journey a little, and began to say to them thus: that the reason why they had obtained this victory from God was this, that they had showed themselves righteous and religious men, and had done everything according to the will of God; (296) that therefore, he said, if they persevered therein, God would grant that they should always overcome their enemies, and live happily; but that if they left off his worship, all things shall fall out on the contrary; and a time should come, wherein no true prophet shall be left in your whole multitude, nor a priest who shall deliver you a true answer from the oracle; (297) but your cities shall be overthrown, and your nation scattered over the whole earth, and live the life of strangers and wanderers. So he advised them, while they had time, to be good, and not to deprive themselves of the favour of God. When the king and the people heard this, they rejoiced; and all in common, and everyone in particular, took great care to behave themselves righteously. The king also sent some to take care that those in the country should observe the laws also.

(298) And this was the state of Asa, king of the two tribes. I now return to Baasha, the king of the multitude of the Israelites who slew Nadab, the son of Jeroboam, and retained the government. (299) He dwelt in the city Tirzah,

having made that his habitation, and reigned twenty-four years. He became more wicked and impious than Jeroboam or his son. He did a great deal of mischief to the multitude, and was injurious to God, who sent the prophet Jehu, and told him beforehand that his whole family should be destroyed, and that he would bring the same miseries on his house which had brought that of Jeroboam to ruin; (300) because when he had been made king by him, he had not requited his kindness, by governing the multitude righteously and religiously; which things, in the first place, tended to their own happiness; and, in the next place, were pleasing to God: that he had imitated this very wicked king Jeroboam; and although that man's soul had perished, yet did he express to the life his wickedness; and he said that he should therefore justly experience the like calamity with him, since he had been guilty of the like wickedness. (301) But Baasha, though he heard beforehand what miseries would befall him and his whole family for their insolent behaviour, yet did not he leave off his wicked practices for the time to come, nor did he care to appear to be other than worse and worse till he died; nor did he then repent of his past actions, nor endeavour to obtain pardon of God for them, (302) but did as those do who have rewards proposed to them; when they have once in earnest set about their work, they do not leave off their labours; for thus did Baasha, when the prophet foretold to him what would come to pass, grow worse, as if what were threatened, the perdition of his family and the destruction of his house (which are really among the greatest of evils), were good things; and, as if he were a combatant for wickedness, he every day took more and more pains for it; (303) and at last he took his army, and assaulted a certain considerable city called Ramah, which was forty furlongs distance from Jerusalem; and when he had taken it, he fortified it, having determined beforehand to leave a garrison in it, that they might thence make excursions, and do mischief to the kingdom of Asa.

(304) Whereupon Asa was afraid of the attempts the enemy might make upon him; and considering with himself what mischiefs this army that was left in Ramah might do to the country over which he reigned, he sent ambassadors to the king of the Damascens, with gold and silver, desiring his assistance, and putting him in mind that we have had a friendship together from the times of our forefathers. (305) So he gladly received that sum of money, and made a league with him, and broke the friendship he had with Baasha, and sent the commanders of his own forces into the cities that were under Baasha's dominion, and ordered them to do them mischief. So they went and burnt some of them, and spoiled others: Ijon, and Dan, and Abelmain, and many others. (306) Now when the king of Israel heard this, he left off building and fortifying Ramah, and returned presently to assist his own people under the distresses they were in; but Asa made use of the materials that were prepared

for building that city, for building in the same place two strong cities, the one of which was called Geba, and the other Mizpah; (307) so that after this, Baasha had no leisure to make expeditions against Asa, for he was prevented by death, and was buried in the city Tirzah; and Elah, his son, took the kingdom, who, when he had reigned two years, died, being treacherously slain by Zimri, the captain of half his army; (308) for when he was at Arza, his steward's house, he persuaded some of the horsemen that were under him to assault Elah, and by that means he slew him when he was without his armed men and his captains, for they were all busied in the siege of Gibbethon, a city of the Philistines.

(309) When Zimri, the captain of the army, had killed Elah, he took the kingdom himself, and, according to Jehu's prophecy, slew all the house of Baasha; for it came to pass that Baasha's house utterly perished, on account of his impiety, in the same manner as we have already described the destruction of the house of Jeroboam; (310) but the army that was besieging Gibbethon, when they heard what had befallen the king, and that when Zimri had killed him he had gained the kingdom, they made Omri their general king, who drew off his army from Gibbethon and came to Tirzah, where the royal palace was, and assaulted the city, and took it by force. (311) But when Zimri saw that the city had none to defend it, he fled into the inmost part of the palace, and set it on fire, and burnt himself with it, when he had reigned only seven days. Upon which the people of Israel were presently divided, and part of them would have Tibni to be king, and part Omri; but when those that were for Omri's ruling had beaten Tibni, Omri reigned over all the multitude. (312) Now it was in the thirtieth year of the reign of Asa that Omri reigned for twelve years; six of these years he reigned in the city Tirzah, and the rest in the city called Semareon, but named by the Greeks Samaria; but he himself called it Semareon, from Semer, who sold him the mountain whereon he built it. (313) Now Omri was no way different from those kings that reigned before him, but that he grew worse than they, for they all sought how they might turn the people away from God, by their daily wicked practices; and on that account it was that God made one of them to be slain by another, and that no one person of their families should remain. This Omri also died in Samaria, and Ahab his son succeeded him.

(314) Now by these events we may learn what concern God hath for the affairs of mankind, and how he loves good men, and hates the wicked and destroys them root and branch: for many of these kings of Israel, they and their families, were miserably destroyed and taken away one by another in a short time for their transgression and wickedness; but Asa, who was king of Jerusalem, and of the two tribes, attained, by God's blessing, a long and a blessed old age, for his piety and righteousness, and died happily, when he had reigned forty and one years; (315) and when he was dead, his son Jehoshaphat

succeeded him in the government. He was born of Asa's wife Azubah. And all men allowed that he followed the works of David his forefather, and this both in courage and piety; but we are not obliged now to speak any more of the affairs of this king.

CHAPTER 13

(316) Now Ahab, the king of Israel, dwelt in Samaria, and held the government for twenty-two years; and made no alteration in the conduct of the kings that were his predecessors, but only in such things as were of his own invention for the worse, and in his most gross wickedness. He imitated them in their wicked courses, and in their injurious behaviour towards God; and more especially he imitated the transgression of Jeroboam; (317) for he worshipped the heifers that he had made; and he contrived other absurd objects of worship besides those heifers; he also took to wife the daughter of Ethbaal, king of the Tyrians and Sidonians, whose name was Jezebel, of whom he learned to worship her own gods. (318) This woman was active and bold, and fell into so great a degree of impurity and wickedness, that she built a temple to the god of the Tyrians, which they called Belus, and planted a grove of all sorts of trees; she also appointed priests and false prophets to this god. The king also himself had many such about him; and so exceeded in madness and wickedness all [the kings] that went before him.

(319) There was now a prophet of God Almighty, of Thesbon, a country in Gilead, that came to Ahab, and said to him, that God foretold he would not send rain nor dew in those years upon the country but when he should appear. And when he had confirmed this by an oath, he departed into the southern parts, and made his abode by a brook, out of which he had water to drink; for as for his food, ravens brought it to him every day; (320) but when that river was dried up for want of rain, he came to Zarephath, a city not far from Sidon and Tyre, for it lay between them, and this at the command of God, for [God told him] that he should there find a woman, who was a widow, that should give him sustenance: (321) so when he was not far off the city, he saw a woman that laboured with her own hands, gathering of sticks: so God informed him that this was the woman who was to give him sustenance; so he came and saluted her, and desired her to bring him some water to drink; but as she was going so to do, he called to her, and would have her to bring him a loaf of bread also; (322) whereupon she affirmed upon oath, that she had at home nothing more than one handful of meal and a little oil, and that she was going to gather some sticks, that she might knead it, and make bread for herself and her son; after which, she said, they must perish, and be consumed by the famine, for they had nothing for themselves any longer. Hereupon he said, 'Go

on with good courage, and hope for better things; and first of all make me a little cake, and bring it to me, for I foretell to thee that this vessel of meal and this cruse of oil shall not fail until God send rain.' (323) When the prophet had said this, she came to him and made him the before-named cake: of which she had part for herself, and gave the rest to her son, and to the prophet also; nor did anything of this fail until the drought ceased. (324) Now Menander mentions this drought in his account of the acts of Ethbaal, king of the Tyrians; where he says thus: 'Under him, there was a want of rain from the month Hyperberetaeus till the month Hyperberetaeus of the year following; but when he made supplications, there came great thunders. This Ethbaal built the city Botrys in Phoenicia, and the city Auza in Libya.' By these words he designed the want of rain that was in the days of Ahab; for at that time it was that Ethbaal also reigned over the Tyrians, as Menander informs us.

(325) Now this woman of whom we spake before, that sustained the prophet, when her son was fallen into a distemper till he gave up the ghost and appeared to be dead, came to the prophet weeping, and beating her breasts with her hands, and sending out such expressions as her passions dictated to her, and complained to him that he had come to her to reproach her for her sins, and that on this account it was that her son was dead. (326) But he bid her be of good cheer, and deliver her son to him, for that he would deliver him again to her alive. So when she had delivered her son up to him, he carried him into an upper room, where he himself lodged, and laid him down upon the bed, and cried unto God, and said, that God had not done well in rewarding the woman who had entertained him and sustained him, by taking away her son; and he prayed that he would send again the soul of the child into him, and bring him to life again. (327) Accordingly God took pity on the mother, and was willing to gratify the prophet, that he might not seem to have come to do her a mischief; and the child, beyond all expectation, came to life again. So the mother returned the prophet thanks, and said she was then clearly satisfied that God did converse with him.

(328) After a little while Elijah came to king Ahab, according to God's will, to inform him that rain was coming. Now the famine had seized upon the whole country, and there was a great want of what was necessary for sustenance, insomuch that it was not only men that wanted it, but the earth itself also, which did not produce enough for the horses and the other beasts, of what was useful for them to feed on, by reason of the drought. (329) So the king called for Obadiah, who was steward over his cattle, and said to him, that he would have him go to the fountains of water, and to the brooks, that if any herbs could be found for them, they might mow it down, and reserve it for the beasts. And when he had sent persons all over the habitable earth, to discover the prophet Elijah, and they could not find him, he bade Obadiah accompany him: (330) so

it was resolved they should make a progress, and divide the ways between them: and Obadiah took one road, and the king another. Now it happened, that the same time when queen Jezebel slew the prophets, this Obadiah had hidden a hundred prophets, and had fed them with nothing but bread and water. (331) But when Obadiah was alone, and absent from the king, the prophet Elijah met him; and Obadiah asked him who he was; and when he had learned it from him, he worshipped him. Elijah then bid him go to the king, and tell him that I am here ready to wait on him. (332) But Obadiah replied, 'What evil have I done to thee, that thou sendest me to one who seeketh to kill thee, and hath sought over all the earth for thee?' Or was he so ignorant as not to know that the king had left no place untouched unto which he had not sent persons to bring him back, in order, if they could take him, to have him put to death? (333) For he told him he was afraid lest God should appear to him again, and he should go away into another place; and that when the king should send him for Elijah, and he should miss of him, and not be able to find him anywhere upon earth, he should be put to death. (334) He desired him therefore to take care of his preservation; and told him how diligently he had provided for those of his own profession, and had saved a hundred prophets, when Jezebel slew the rest of them, and had kept them concealed, and that they had been sustained by him. But Elijah bade him fear nothing, but go to the king; and he assured him upon oath, that he would certainly show himself to Ahab that very day.

(335) So when Obadiah had informed the king that Elijah was there, Ahab met him, and asked him in anger, if he were the man that afflicted the people of the Hebrews, and was the occasion of the drought they lay under? But Elijah, without any flattery, said that he was himself the man; he and his house, which brought such afflictions upon them; and that by introducing strange gods into their country, and worshipping them, and by leaving their own, who was the only true God, and having no manner of regard to him. (336) However, he bade him go his way, and gather together all the people to him, to Mount Carmel, with his own prophets and those of his wife, telling him how many there were of them, as also the prophets of the groves, about four hundred in number. (337) And as all the men whom Ahab sent for ran away to the forenamed mountain, the prophet Elijah stood in the midst of them, and said, 'How long will you live thus in uncertainty of mind and opinion?' He also exhorted them, that in case they esteemed their own country god to be the true and the only God, they would follow him and his commandments; but in case they esteemed him to be nothing, but had an opinion of the strange gods, and that they ought to worship them, his counsel was, that they should follow them. (338) And when the multitude made no answer to what he said, Elijah desired that, for a trial of the power of the strange gods and of their own God, he who was his only prophet, while they had four hundred, might take a heifer

and kill it as a sacrifice, and lay it upon pieces of wood, and not kindle any fire, and that they should do the same things, and call upon their own gods to set the wood on fire, for if that were done, they would thence learn the nature of the true God. (339) This proposal pleased the people. So Elijah bade the prophets to choose out a heifer first, and kill it, and to call on their gods; but when there appeared no effect of the prayer or invocation of the prophets upon their sacrifice, Elijah derided them, for they might either be on a journey or asleep; (340) and when these prophets had done so from morning till noon, and cut themselves with swords and lances, according to the customs of their country, and he was about to offer his sacrifice, he bid [the prophets] go away; but bade [the people] come near and observe what he did, lest he should privately hide fire among the pieces of wood. (341) So, upon the approach of the multitude, he took twelve stones, one for each tribe of the people of the Hebrews, and built an altar with them, and dug a very deep trench; and when he had laid the pieces of wood upon the altar, and upon them had laid the pieces of the sacrifices, he ordered them to fill four barrels with the water of the fountain, and to pour it upon the altar, till it ran over it, and till the trench was filled with the water poured into it. (342) When he had done this, he began to pray to God, and to invocate him to make manifest his power to a people that had already been in an error a long time; upon which words a fire came on a sudden from heaven, in the sight of the multitude, and fell upon the altar, and consumed the sacrifice, till the very water was set on fire, and the place was become dry.

(343) Now when the Israelites saw this, they fell down upon the ground, and worshipped one God, and called him *The great and the only true God;* but they called the others mere names, framed by the evil and wild opinions of men. So they caught their prophets, and, at the command of Elijah, slew them. Elijah also said to the king, that he should go to dinner without any further concern, for that in a little time he would see God send them rain. (344) Accordingly, Ahab went his way; but Elijah went up to the highest top of Mount Carmel, and sat down upon the ground, and leaned his head upon his knees, and bade his servant go up to a certain elevated place, and look towards the sea, and when he should see a cloud rising anywhere, he should give him notice of it, for till that time the air had been clear. (345) When the servant had gone up, and had said many times that he saw nothing, at the seventh time of his going up, he said that he saw a small black thing in the sky, not larger than a man's foot. When Elijah heard that, he sent to Ahab, and desired him to go away to the city before the rain came down. (346) So he came to the city Jezreel; and in a little time the air was all obscured, and covered with clouds, and a vehement storm of wind came upon the earth, and with it a great deal of rain; and the prophet was under a divine fury, and ran along with the king's chariot unto Jezreel, a city of Izar [Isachar].

(347) When Jezebel, the wife of Ahab, understood what signs Elijah had wrought, and how he had slain her prophets, she was angry, and sent messengers to him, and by them threatened to kill him, as he had destroyed her prophets. (348) At this Elijah was affrighted, and fled to the city called Beersheba, which is situate at the utmost limits of the country belonging to the tribe of Judah, towards the land of Edom; and there he left his servant, and went away into the desert. He prayed also that he might die, for that he was not better than his fathers, (349) nor need he be very desirous to live, when they were dead; and he lay and slept under a certain tree; and when somebody awakened him, and he was risen up, he found food set by him and water; so when he had eaten, and recovered his strength by that his food, he came to that mountain which is called Sinai, where it is related that Moses received his laws from God; (350) and finding there a certain hollow cave, he entered into it, and continued to make his abode in it. But when a certain voice came to him, but from whence he knew not, and asked him, why he was come thither, and had left the city, he said that because he had slain the prophets of the foreign gods, and had persuaded the people that he alone whom they had worshipped from the beginning was God, he was sought for by the king's wife to be punished for so doing. (351) And when he had heard another voice, telling him that he should come out the next day into the open air, and should thereby know what he was to do, he came out of the cave the next day accordingly, when he both heard an earthquake, and saw the bright splendour of a fire; (352) and after a silence made, a divine voice exhorted him not to be disturbed with the circumstances he was in, for that none of his enemies should have power over him. The voice also commanded him to return home, and to ordain Jehu, the son of Nimshi, to be king over their own multitude; and Hazael, of Damascus, to be over the Syrians; and Elisha, of the city Abel, to be a prophet in his stead: and that of the impious multitude, some should be slain by Hazael, and others by Jehu. (353) So Elijah, upon hearing this charge, returned into the land of the Hebrews. And when he found Elisha, the son of Shaphat, ploughing, and certain others with him, driving twelve yoke of oxen, he came to him, and cast his own garment upon him; (354) upon which Elisha began to prophesy presently, and leaving his oxen, he followed Elijah. And when he desired leave to salute his parents, Elijah gave him leave so to do: and when he had taken his leave of them, he followed him, and became the disciple and the servant of Elijah all the days of his life. And thus have I dispatched the affairs in which this prophet was concerned.

(355) Now there was one Naboth, of the city Izar [Jezreel], who had a field adjoining to that of the king: the king would have persuaded him to sell him that his field, which lay so near to his own lands, at what price he pleased, that

he might join them together, and make them one farm; and if he would not accept of money for it, he gave him leave to choose any of his other fields in its stead. But Naboth said he would not do so, but would keep the possession of that land of his own, which he had by inheritance from his father. (356) Upon this the king was grieved, as if he had received an injury, when he could not get another man's possession, and he would neither wash himself, nor take any food: and when Jezebel asked him what it was that troubled him, and why he would neither wash himself, nor eat either dinner or supper, he related to her the perverseness of Naboth; and how when he had made use of gentle words to him, and such as were beneath the royal authority, he had been affronted, and had not obtained what he desired. (357) However, she persuaded him not to be cast down at this accident, but to leave off his grief, and return to the usual care of his body, for that she would take care to have Naboth punished: (358) and she immediately sent letters to the rulers of the Israelites [Jezreelites] in Ahab's name, and commanded them to fast, and to assemble a congregation, and to set Naboth at the head of them, because he was of an illustrious family, and to have three bold men ready to bear witness that he had blasphemed God and the king, and then to stone him, and slay him in that manner. (359) Accordingly, when Naboth had been thus testified against, as the queen had written to them, that he had blasphemed against God and Ahab the king, she desired him to take possession of Naboth's vineyard on free cost. (360) So Ahab was glad at what had been done, and rose up immediately from the bed wherein he lay, to go to see Naboth's vineyard; but God had great indignation at it, and sent Elijah the prophet to the field of Naboth, to speak to Ahab, and to say to him, that he had slain the true owner of that field unjustly. (361) And as soon as he came to him, and the king had said that he might do with him what he pleased (for he thought it a reproach to him to be thus caught in his sin), Elijah said, that in that very place in which the dead body of Naboth was eaten by dogs, both his own blood and that of his wife's should be shed; and that all his family should perish, because he had been so insolently wicked, and had slain a citizen unjustly and contrary to the laws of his country. (362) Hereupon Ahab began to be sorry for the things he had done, and to repent of them; and he put on sackcloth, and went barefoot, and would not touch any food; he also confessed his sins, and endeavoured thus to appease God. But God said to the prophet, that while Ahab was living he would put off the punishment of his family, because he repented of those insolent crimes he had been guilty of, but that still he would fulfill his threatening under Ahab's son. Which message the prophet delivered to the king.

CHAPTER 14

(363) When the affairs of Ahab were thus, at that very time the son of Hadad [Benhadad], who was king of the Syrians and of Damascus, got together an army out of all his country, and procured thirty-two kings beyond Euphrates, to be his auxiliaries: so he made an expedition against Ahab; (364) but because Ahab's army was not like that of Benhadad, he did not set it in array to fight him, but having shut up everything that was in the country in the strongest cities he had, he abode in Samaria himself, for the walls about it were very strong, and it appeared to be not easily to be taken in other respects also. So the king of Syria took his army with him, and came to Samaria, and placed his army round about the city, and besieged it. (365) He also sent a herald to Ahab, and desired he would admit the ambassadors he would send him, by whom he would let him know his pleasure. So upon the king of Israel's permission for him to send, those ambassadors came, and by their king's command spake thus: that Ahab's riches, and his children, and his wives, were Benhadad's, and if he would make an agreement, and give him leave to take as much of what he had as he pleased, he would withdraw his army, and leave off the siege. (366) Upon this Ahab bade the ambassadors to go back, and tell their king that both he himself, and all that he hath, were his possessions. (367) And when these ambassadors had told this to Benhadad, he sent to him again, and desired, since he confessed that all he had was his, that he would admit those servants of his which he should send the next day; and he commanded him to deliver to those whom he should send, whatsoever, upon their searching his palace and the houses of his friends and kindred, they should find to be excellent in its kind; but that what did not please them they should leave to him. (368) At this second embassage of the king of Syria, Ahab was surprised, and gathered together the multitude to a congregation, and told them, that for himself, he was ready, for their safety and peace, to give up his own wives and children to the enemy, and to yield to him all his own possessions, for that was what the Syrian king required at his first embassage; (369) but that now he desires to send his servants to search all their houses, and in them to leave nothing that is excellent in its kind, seeking an occasion of fighting against him, 'as knowing that I would not spare what is mine own for your sakes, but taking a handle from the disagreeable terms he offers concerning you to bring a war upon us: however, I will do what you shall resolve is fit to be done.' (370) But the multitude advised him to hearken to none of his proposals, but to despise him, and be in readiness to fight him. Accordingly, when he had given the ambassadors this answer to be reported, that he still continued in the mind to comply with what terms he at first desired, for the safety of the

citizens; but as for his second desires, he cannot submit to them – he dismissed them.

(371) Now when Benhadad heard this, he had indignation, and sent ambassadors to Ahab the third time, and threatened that his army would raise a bank higher than those walls, in confidence of whose strength he despised him, and that by only each man of his army taking a handful of earth; hereby making a show of the great number of his army, and aiming to affright him. (372) Ahab answered, that he ought not to vaunt himself when he had only put on his armour, but when he should have conquered his enemies in the battle. So the ambassadors came back, and found the king at supper with his thirty-two kings, and informed him of Ahab's answer; who then immediately gave order for proceeding thus: to make lines round the city, and raise a bulwark, and to prosecute the siege all manner of ways. (373) Now, as this was doing, Ahab was in a great agony, and all his people with him; but he took courage, and was freed from his fears, upon a certain prophet coming to him, and saying to him, that God had promised to subdue so many ten thousands of his enemies under him; (374) and, when he inquired by whose means the victory was to be obtained, be said, 'By the sons of the princes, but under thy conduct as their leader, by reason of their unskilfulness [in war].' Upon which he called for the sons of the princes; and found them to be two hundred and thirty-two persons. So when he was informed that the king of Syria had betaken himself to feasting and repose, he opened the gates, and sent out the princes' sons. (375) Now when the sentinels told Benhadad of it, he sent some to meet them, and commanded them, that if these men were come out for fighting, they should bind them, and bring them to him; and that if they came out peaceably they should do the same. (376) Now Ahab had another army ready within the walls, but the sons of the princes fell upon the out-guard, and slew many of them, and pursued the rest of them to the camp; and when the king of Israel saw that these had the upper hand, he sent out all the rest of his army, which, (377) falling suddenly upon the Syrians, beat them, for they did not think they would have come out; on which account it was that they assaulted them when they were naked and drunk, insomuch that they left all their armour behind them when they fled out of the camp, and the king himself escaped with difficulty, by flying away on horseback. (378) But Ahab went a great way in pursuit of the Syrians; and when he had spoiled their camp, which contained a great deal of wealth, and moreover a large quantity of gold and silver, he took Benhadad's chariots and horses, and returned to the city; but as the prophet told him he ought to have his army ready, because the Syrian king would make another expedition against him the next year, Ahab was busy in making provision for it accordingly.

(379) Now, Benhadad, when he had saved himself, and as much of his army

as he could, out of the battle, he consulted with his friends how he might make another expedition against the Israelites. Now those friends advised him not to fight with them on the hills, because their God was potent in such places, and thence it had come to pass that they had very lately been beaten; but they said, that if they joined battle with them in the plain they should beat them. (380) They also gave him this further advice, to send home those kings whom he had brought as his auxiliaries, but to retain their army, and to set captains over it instead of the kings, and to raise an army out of their country, and let them be in the place of the former who perished in the battle, together with horses and chariots. So he judged their counsel to be good, and acted according to it in the management of the army.

(381) At the beginning of the spring, Benhadad took his army with him, and led it against the Hebrews; and when he was come to a certain city which was called Aphek, he pitched his camp in the Great Plain. Ahab also went to meet him with his army, and pitched his camp over against him, although his army was a very small one, if it were compared with the enemy's; (382) but the prophet came again to him, and told him, that God would give him the victory, that he might demonstrate his own power to be not only on the mountains, but on the plains also; which it seems was contrary to the opinion of the Syrians. So they lay quiet in their camp seven days; but on the last of those days, when the enemies came out of their camp, and put themselves in array in order to fight, Ahab also brought out his own army; (383) and when the battle was joined, and they fought valiantly, he put the enemy to flight, and pursued them, and pressed upon them and slew them; nay, they were destroyed by their own chariots, and by one another; nor could any more than a few of them escape to their own city Aphek, (384) who were also killed by the walls falling upon them, being in number twenty-seven thousand. Now there were slain in this battle a hundred thousand more; but Benhadad, the king of the Syrians, fled away with certain others of his most faithful servants, and hid himself in a cellar under ground; (385) and when these told him that the kings of Israel were humane and merciful men, and that they might make use of the usual manner of supplication, and obtain deliverance from Ahab, in case he would give them leave to go to him; he gave them leave accordingly. So they came to Ahab, clothed in sackcloth, with ropes about their heads (for this was the ancient manner of supplication among the Syrians), and said, that Benhadad desired he would save him; and that he would ever be a servant to him for that favour. (386) Ahab replied he was glad that he was alive, and not hurt in the battle; and he further promised him the same honour and kindness that a man would show to his brother. So they received assurances upon oath from him, that when he came to him he should receive no harm from him, and then went and brought him out of the cellar wherein he was hid, and

brought him to Ahab as he sat in his chariot. So Benhadad worshipped him; (387) and Ahab gave him his hand, and made him come up to him into his chariot, and kissed him, and bid him be of good cheer, and not to expect that any mischief should be done to him. So Benhadad returned him thanks, and professed that he would remember his kindness to him all the days of his life, and promised he would restore those cities of the Israelites which the former kings had taken from them, and grant that he should have leave to come to Damascus, as his forefathers had to come to Samaria. (388) So they confirmed their covenant by oaths; and Ahab made him many presents, and sent him back to his own kingdom. And this was the conclusion of the war that Benhadad made against Ahab and the Israelites.

(389) But a certain prophet, whose name was Micaiah, came to one of the Israelites, and bade him smite him on the head, for by so doing he would please God; but when he would not do so, he foretold to him, that since he disobeyed the commands of God, he should meet with a lion and be destroyed by him. When this sad accident had befallen the man, the prophet came again to another, and gave him the same injunction; (390) so he smote him, and wounded his skull: upon which he bound up his head and came to the king, and told him that he had been a soldier of his, and had the custody of one of the prisoners committed to him by an officer, and that the prisoner being run away, he was in danger of losing his own life by the means of that officer, who had threatened him, that if the prisoner escaped he would kill him; (391) and when Ahab had said that he would justly die, he took off the binding that was about his head, and was known by the king to be Micaiah the prophet, who made use of this artifice as a prelude to the following words; (392) for he said that God would punish him who had suffered Benhadad, a blasphemer against him, to escape punishment; and that he would so bring it about, that he should die by the other's means, and his people by the other's army. Upon which Ahab was very angry at the prophet, and gave commandment that he should be put in prison, and there kept; but for himself, he was in confusion at the words of Micaiah, and returned to his own house.

CHAPTER 15

(393) And these were the circumstances in which Ahab was. But I now return to Jehoshaphat, the king of Jerusalem, who, when he had augmented his kingdom, and had set garrisons in the cities of the countries belonging to his subjects, and had put such garrisons no less into those cities which were taken out of the tribe of Ephraim by his grandfather Abijah, when Jeroboam reigned over the ten tribes [than he did into the other]. (394) But then he had God favourable and assisting to him, as being both righteous and religious, and

seeking to do somewhat every day that should be agreeable and acceptable to God. The kings also that were round about him honoured him with the presents they made him, till the riches that he had acquired were immensely great, and the glory he had gained was of a most exalted nature.

(395) Now, in the third year of this reign, he called together the rulers of the country and the priests, and commanded them to go round the land, and teach all the people that were under him, city by city, the laws of Moses, and to keep them, and to be diligent in the worship of God. With this the whole multitude was so pleased, that they were not so eagerly set upon or affected with anything so much as the observation of the laws. (396) The neighbouring nations also continued to love Jehoshaphat, and to be at peace with him. The Philistines paid their appointed tribute, and the Arabians supplied him every year with three hundred and sixty lambs, and as many kids of the goats. He also fortified the great cities, which were many in number, and of great consequence. He prepared also a mighty army of soldiers and weapons against their enemies. (397) Now the army of men that wore their armour was three hundred thousand of the tribe of Judah, of whom Adnah was the chief; but John was chief of two hundred thousand. The same man was chief of the tribe of Benjamin, and had two hundred thousand archers under him. There was another chief, whose name was Jehozabad, who had a hundred and fourscore thousand armed men. This multitude was distributed to be ready for the king's service, besides those whom he sent to the best fortified cities.

(398) Jehoshaphat took for his son Jehoram to wife, the daughter of Ahab, the king of the ten tribes, whose name was Athaliah. And when, after some time, he went to Samaria, Ahab received him courteously, and treated the army that followed him in a splendid manner, with great plenty of corn and wine, and of slain beasts; and desired that he would join with him in his war against the king of Syria, that he might recover from him the city Ramoth, in Gilead; (399) for though it had belonged to his father, yet had the king of Syria's father taken it away from him; and upon Jehoshaphat's promise to afford him his assistance (for indeed his army was not inferior to the other), and his sending for his army from Jerusalem to Samaria, the two kings went out of the city, and each of them sat on his own throne, and each gave their orders to their several armies. (400) Now Jehoshaphat bade them call some of the prophets, if there were any there, and inquire of them concerning this expedition against the king of Syria, whether they would give them counsel to make that expedition at this time, for there was peace at that time between Ahab and the king of Syria, which had lasted three years, from the time he had taken him captive till that day.

(401) So Ahab called his own prophets, being in number about four hundred, and bade them inquire of God whether he would grant him the

victory, if he made an expedition against Benhadad, and enable him to
overthrow that city, for whose sake it was that he was going to war. (402) Now
these prophets gave their counsel for making this expedition; and said, that he
would beat the king of Syria, and, as formerly, would reduce him under his
power. But Jehoshaphat, understanding by their words that they were false
prophets, asked Ahab whether there were not some other prophet, and he
belonging to the true God, that we may have sure information concerning
futurities. (403) Hereupon Ahab said, there was indeed such a one, but that he
hated him, as having prophesied evil to him, and having foretold that he
should be overcome and slain by the king of Syria, and that for this cause he
had him now in prison, and that his name was Micaiah, the son of Imlah. But
upon Jehoshaphat's desire that he might be produced, Ahab sent a eunuch,
who brought Micaiah to him. (404) Now the eunuch had informed him by
the way, that all the other prophets had foretold that the king should gain the
victory; but he said, that it was not lawful for him to lie against God; but that he
must speak what he should say to him about the king, whatsoever it were.
When he came to Ahab, and he had adjured him upon oath to speak the truth
to him, he said that God had shown to him the Israelites running away, and
pursued by the Syrians, and dispersed upon the mountains by them, as flocks of
sheep are dispersed when their shepherd is slain. (405) He said further, that
God signified to him that those Israelites should return in peace to their
own home, and that he only should fall in the battle. When Micaiah had thus
spoken, Ahab said to Jehoshaphat, 'I told thee a little while ago the disposition
of the man with regard to me, and that he uses to prophesy evil to me.' (406)
Upon which Micaiah replied, that he ought to hear all, whatsoever it be, that
God foretells; and that in particular, they were false prophets that encouraged
him to make this war in hope of victory, whereas he must fight and be killed.
Whereupon the king was in suspense with himself: But Zedekiah, one of those
false prophets, came near, and exhorted him not to hearken to Micaiah, for he
did not at all speak truth; (407) as a demonstration of which, he instanced in
what Elijah had said, who was a better prophet in foretelling futurities than
Micaiah; for he foretold that the dogs should lick his blood in the city of
Jezreel, in the field of Naboth, as they licked the blood of Naboth, who by his
means was there stoned to death by the multitude; (408) that therefore it was
plain that this Micaiah was a liar, as contradicting a greater prophet than
himself, and saying that he should be slain at three days' journey distance: 'and
[said he] you shall soon know whether he be a true prophet, and hath the
power of the Divine Spirit; for I will smite him, and let him then hurt my
hand, as Jadon caused the hand of Jeroboam the king to wither when he would
have caught him; for I suppose thou hast certainly heard of that accident.' (409)
So when, upon his smiting Micaiah, no harm happened to him, Ahab took

courage, and readily led his army against the king of Syria; for, as I suppose, fate was too hard for him, and made him believe that the false prophets spake truer than the true one, that it might take an occasion of bringing him to his end. However, Zedekiah made horns of iron, and said to Ahab, that God made those horns signals, that by them he should overthrow all Syria. (410) But Micaiah replied, that Zedekiah, in a few days, should go from one secret chamber to another, to hide himself, that he might escape the punishment of his lying. Then did the king give orders that they should take Micaiah away, and guard him to Amon, the governor of the city, and to give him nothing but bread and water.

(411) Then did Ahab, and Jehoshaphat the king of Jerusalem, take their forces, and marched to Ramoth, a city of Gilead; and when the king of Syria heard of this expedition, he brought out his army to oppose them, and pitched his camp not far from Ramoth. (412) Now Ahab and Jehoshaphat had agreed that Ahab should lay aside his royal robes, but that the king of Jerusalem should put on his [Ahab's] proper habit, and stand before the army, in order to disprove, by this artifice, what Micaiah had foretold. But Ahab's fate found him out without his robes; (413) for Benhadad the king of Assyria had charged his army, by means of their commanders, to kill nobody else but only the king of Israel. So when the Syrians, upon their joining battle with the Israelites, saw Jehoshaphat stand before the army, and conjectured that he was Ahab, they fell violently upon him, (414) and encompassed him round: but when they were near, and knew that it was not he, they all returned back; and while the fight lasted from the morning light till late in the evening, and the Syrians were conquerors, they killed nobody, as their king had commanded them; and when they sought to kill Ahab alone, but could not find him, there was a young nobleman belonging to king Benhadad, whose name was Naaman; he drew his bow against the enemy, and wounded the king through his breast-plate, in his lungs. (415) Upon this Ahab resolved not to make his mischance known to his army, lest they should run away; but he bid the driver of his chariot to turn it back, and carry him out of the battle, because he was sorely and mortally wounded. However, he sat in his chariot and endured the pain till sunset, and then he fainted away and died.

(416) And now the Syrian army, upon the coming on of the night, retired to their camp; and when the herald belonging to the camp gave notice that Ahab was dead, they returned home; and they took the dead body of Ahab to Samaria, and buried it there; (417) but when they had washed his chariot in the fountain of Jezreel, which was bloody with the dead body of the king, they acknowledged that the prophecy of Elijah was true, for the dogs licked his blood, and the harlots continued afterwards to wash themselves in that fountain; but still he died at Ramoth, as Micaiah had foretold. (418) And as

what things were foretold should happen to Ahab by the two prophets came to pass, we ought thence to have high notions of God, and everywhere to honour and worship him, and never to suppose that what is pleasant and agreeable is worthy of belief before what is true; and to esteem nothing more advantageous than the gift of prophecy, and that foreknowledge of future events which is derived from it, since God shows men thereby what we ought to avoid. (419) We may also guess, from what happened to this king and have reason to consider the power of fate, that there is no way of avoiding it, even when we know it. It creeps upon human souls, and flutters them with pleasing hopes, till it leads them about to the place where it will be too hard for them. (420) Accordingly Ahab appears to have been deceived thereby, till he disbelieved those that foretold his defeat; but by giving credit to such as foretold what was grateful to him, was slain; and his son Ahaziah succeeded him.

BOOK NINE

(1) When Jehoshaphat the king was come to Jerusalem, from the assistance he had afforded Ahab, the king of Israel, when he fought with Benhadad, king of Syria, the prophet Jehu met him, and accused him for assisting Ahab, a man both impious and wicked; and said to him, that God was displeased with him for so doing, but that he delivered him from the enemy, notwithstanding he had sinned, because of his own proper disposition, which was good. (2) Whereupon the king betook himself to thanksgivings and sacrifices to God; after which he presently went over all that country which he ruled round about, and taught the people, as well the laws which God gave them by Moses, as that religious worship that was due to him. (3) He also constituted judges in every one of the cities of his kingdom, and charged them to have regard to nothing so much in judging the multitude as to do justice, and not to be moved by bribes, nor by the dignity of men eminent for either their riches or their high birth, but to distribute justice equally to all, as knowing that God is conscious of every secret action of theirs. (4) When he had himself instructed them thus, and gone over every city of the two tribes, he returned to Jerusalem. He there also constituted judges out of the priests and the Levites and principal persons of the multitude, and admonished them to pass all their sentences with care and justice. (5) And that if any of the people of his country had differences of great consequence, they should send them out of the other cities to these judges, who would be obliged to give righteous sentences concerning such causes; and this with the greater care, because it is proper that the sentences which are given in that city wherein the temple of God is, and wherein the king dwells, be given with great care and the utmost justice. (6) Now he set over them Amariah the priest and Zebadiah, [both] of the tribe of Judah: and after this manner it was that the king ordered these affairs.

(7) About the same time the Moabites and Ammonites made an expedition against Jehoshaphat, and took with them a great body of Arabians, and pitched their camp at Engedi, a city that is situate at the lake Asphaltitis, and distant three hundred furlongs from Jerusalem. In that place grows the best kind of palm trees, and the opobalsamum. (8) Now Jehoshaphat heard that the enemies had passed over the lake, and had made an irruption into that country which belonged to his kingdom; at which news he was affrighted, and called the people of Jerusalem to a congregation in the temple, and standing over

against the temple itself, he called upon God to afford power and strength, so as to inflict punishment on those that made this expedition against them (9) (for that those who built this his temple had prayed that he would protect that city, and take vengeance on those that were so bold as to come against it); for they are come to take from us that land which thou hast given us for a possession. When he had prayed thus, he fell into tears; and the whole multitude, together with their wives and children, made their supplications also: (10) upon which a certain prophet, Jahaziel by name, came into the midst of the assembly, and cried out, and spake both to the multitude and to the king, that God heard their prayers, and promised to fight against their enemies. He also gave order that the king should draw his forces out the next day, (11) for that he should find them between Jerusalem and the ascent of Engedi, at a place called *The Eminence*, and that he should not fight against them, but only stand still, and see how God would fight against them. When the prophet had said this, both the king and the multitude fell on their faces, and gave thanks to God, and worshipped him: and the Levites continued singing hymns to God with their instruments of music.

(12) As soon as it was day, and the king was come into that wilderness which is under the city of Tekoa, he said to the multitude, 'that they ought to give credit to what the prophet had said, and not to set themselves in array for fighting; (13) but to set the priests with their trumpets, and the Levites with the singers of hymns, to give thanks to God, as having already delivered our country from our enemies.' This opinion of the king pleased [the people], and they did what he advised them to do. So God caused a terror and a commotion to arise among the Ammonites, who thought one another to be enemies, and slew one another, insomuch that not one man out of so great an army escaped; (14) and when Jehoshaphat looked upon that valley wherein their enemies had been encamped, and saw it full of dead men, he rejoiced at so surprising an event as was this assistance of God, while he himself by his own power, and without their labour, had given them the victory. He also gave his army leave to take the prey of the enemy's camp, and to spoil their dead bodies; (15) and indeed so they did for three days together, till they were weary, so great was the number of the slain; and on the fourth day, all the people were gathered together, unto a certain hollow place or valley, and blessed God for his power and assistance; from which the place had this name given it, the *Valley of* [*Berachah*, or] *Blessing*.

(16) And when the king had brought his army back to Jerusalem, he betook himself to celebrate festivals, and offer sacrifices, and this for many days; and indeed, after this destruction of their enemies, and when it came to the ears of the foreign nations, they were all greatly affrighted, as supposing that God would openly fight for him hereafter. So Jehoshaphat from that time lived in

great glory and splendour, on account of his righteousness and his piety towards God. (17) He was also in friendship with Ahab's son, who was king of Israel; and he joined with him in the building of ships that were to sail to Pontus and the traffic cities of Thrace; but he failed of his gains, for the ships were destroyed by being so great [and unwieldy]; on which account he was no longer concerned about shipping. And this is the history of Jehoshaphat, the king of Jerusalem.

CHAPTER 2

(18) And now Ahaziah, the son of Ahab, reigned over Israel, and made his abode in Samaria. He was a wicked man, and in all respects like to both his parents, and to Jeroboam, who first of all transgressed and began to deceive the people. (19) In the second year of his reign, the king of Moab fell off from his obedience, and left off paying those tributes which he before paid to his father Ahab. Now it happened that Ahaziah, as he was coming down from the top of his house, fell down from it, and in his sickness sent to the Fly which was the god of Ekron, for that was this god's name, to inquire about his recovery: (20) but the God of the Hebrews appeared to Elijah the prophet, and commanded him to go and meet the messengers that were sent and to ask them, whether the people of Israel had not a God of their own, that the king sent to a foreign god to inquire about his recovery? And to bid them return and tell the king that he would not escape this disease. (21) And when Elijah had performed what God had commanded him, and the messengers had heard what he said, they returned to the king immediately; and when the king wondered how they could return so soon, and asked them the reason of it, they said, that a certain man met them, and forbade them to go on any further; but to return and tell thee, from the command of the God of Israel, that this disease will have a bad end. (22) And when the king bade them describe the man that said this to them, they replied, that he was a hairy man, and was girt about with a girdle of leather. So the king understood by this that the man who was described by the messengers was Elijah; whereupon he sent a captain to him, with fifty soldiers, and commanded them to bring Elijah (23) to him; and when the captain that was sent found Elijah sitting upon the top of a hill, he commanded him to come down, and to come to the king, for so had he enjoined; but that in case he refused, they would carry him by force. Elijah said to him, that you may have a trial whether I be a true prophet, I will pray that fire may fall from heaven, and destroy both the soldiers and yourself.' So he prayed, and a whirlwind of fire fell [from heaven], and destroyed the captain and those that were with him. (24) And when the king was informed of the destruction of these men, he was very angry, and sent another captain with the like number

of armed men that were sent before. And when this captain also threatened the prophet, that unless he came down of his own accord, he would take him and carry him away, upon his prayer against him, the fire [from heaven] slew this captain as well as the other. (25) And when, upon inquiry, the king was informed of what happened to him, he sent out a third captain. But when this captain, who was a wise man, and of a mild disposition, came to the place where Elijah happened to be, and spake civilly to him, and said, that he knew that it was without his own consent, and only in submission to the king's command that he came to him; and that those that came before did not come willingly, but on the same account – he therefore desired him to have pity on those armed men that were with him; and that he would come down and follow him to the king. (26) So Elijah accepted of his discreet words and courteous behaviour, and came down and followed him. And when he came to the king, he prophesied to him, and told him that God said, 'Since thou hast despised him as not being God, and so unable to foretell the truth about thy distemper, but hast sent to the god of Ekron to inquire of him what will be the end of this thy distemper, know this, that thou shalt die.'

(27) Accordingly the king in a very little time died, as Elijah had foretold; but Jehoram his brother succeeded him in the kingdom, for he died without children; but for this Jehoram, he was like his father Ahab in wickedness, and reigned twelve years, indulging himself in all sorts of wickedness and impiety towards God, for, leaving off his worship, he worshipped foreign gods; but in other respects he was an active man. (28) Now at this time it was that Elijah disappeared from among men, and no one knows of his death to this very day; but he left behind him his disciple Elisha, as we have formerly declared. And indeed, as to Elijah, and as to Enoch, who was before the Deluge, it is written in the sacred books that they disappeared; but so that nobody knew that they died.

CHAPTER 3

(29) When Joram had taken upon him the kingdom, he determined to make an expedition against the king of Moab, whose name was Mesha; for, as we told you before, he was departed from his obedience to his brother [Ahaziah], while he paid to his father Ahab two hundred thousand sheep, with their fleeces of wool. (30) When therefore he had gathered his own army together, he sent also to Jehoshaphat, and entreated him, that since he had from the beginning been a friend to his father, he would assist him in the war that he was entering into against the Moabites, who had departed from their obedience, who not only himself promised to assist him, but would also oblige the king of Edom, who was under his authority, to make the same expedition also. (31) When Joram had received these assurances of assistance from Jehoshaphat, he

took his army with him, and came to Jerusalem; and when he had been sumptuously entertained by the king of Jerusalem, it was resolved upon by them to take their march against their enemies through the wilderness of Edom: (32) and when they had taken a compass of seven days' journey, they were in distress for want of water for the cattle and for the army, from the mistake of their roads by the guides that conducted them, insomuch that they were all in an agony, especially Joram; and cried to God, by reason of their sorrow, and [desired to know] what wickedness had been committed by them that induced him to deliver three kings together, without fighting, unto the king of Moab. (33) But Jehoshaphat, who was a righteous man, encouraged him, and bade him send to the camp and know whether any prophet of God was come along with them, that we might by him learn from God what we should do. And when one of the servants of Joram said that he had seen there Elisha, the son of Shaphat, the disciple of Elijah, the three kings went to him at the entreaty of Jehoshaphat; (34) and when they were come at the prophet's tent, which tent was pitched out of the camp, they asked him, what would become of the army? And Joram was particularly very pressing with him about it. And when he replied to him, that he should not trouble him, but go to his father's and his mother's prophets, for they (to be sure) were true prophets – he still desired him to prophesy, and to save them. (35) So he sware by God that he would not answer him, unless it were on account of Jehoshaphat, who was a holy and righteous man: and when, at his desire, they brought him a man that could play on the psaltery, the divine spirit came upon him as the music played, and he commanded them to dig many trenches in the valley; (36) for, said he, 'though there appear neither cloud, nor wind, nor storm of rain, ye shall see this river full of water, till the army and the cattle be saved for you by drinking of it; nor will this be all the favour that you shall receive from God, but you shall also overcome your enemies, and take the best and strongest cities of the Moabites, and you shall cut down their fruit trees, and lay waste their country, and stop up their fountains and rivers.'

(37) When the prophet had said this, the next day, before the sunrising, a great torrent ran strongly; for God had caused it to rain very plentifully at the distance of three days' journey into Edom, so that the army and the cattle found water to drink in abundance. (38) But when the Moabites heard that the three kings were coming upon them, and made their approach through the wilderness, the king of Moab gathered his army together presently, and commanded them to pitch their camp upon the mountains, that when the enemy should attempt to enter their country, they might not be concealed from them. (39) But when, at the rising of the sun, they saw the water in the torrent, for it was not far from the land of Moab, and that it was of the colour of blood, for at such a time the water especially looks red, by the shining of the

sun upon it, they formed a false notion of the state of their enemies, as if they had slain one another for thirst, and that the river ran with their blood. (40) However, supposing that this was the case, they desired their king would send them out to spoil their enemies; whereupon they all went in haste, as to an advantage already gained, and came to the enemy's camp, as supposing them destroyed already; but their hope deceived them, for as their enemies stood round about them, some of them were cut to pieces, and others of them were dispersed, and fled to their own country; (41) and when the kings fell into the land of Moab, they overthrew the cities that were in it, and spoiled their fields, and marred them filling them with stones out of the brooks, and cut down the best of their trees, and stopped up their fountains of water, and overthrew their walls to their foundations; (42) but the king of Moab, when he was pursued, endured a siege, and seeing his city in danger of being overthrown by force, made a sally, and went out with seven hundred men, in order to break through the enemy's camp with his horsemen, on that side where the watch seemed to be kept most negligently; and when, upon trial, he could not get away, for he lighted upon a place that was carefully watched, he returned into the city, and did a thing that showed despair, and the utmost distress; (43) for he took his eldest son, who was to reign after him, and lifting him up upon the wall, that he might be visible to all the enemies, he offered him as a whole burnt offering to God, whom, when the kings saw, they commiserated the distress that was the occasion of it, and were so affected, in way of humanity and pity, that they raised the siege, and everyone returned to his own house. (44) So Jehoshaphat came to Jerusalem, and continued in peace there, and outlived this expedition but a little time, and then died, having lived in all sixty years, and of them reigned twenty-five. He was buried in a magnificent manner in Jerusalem, for he had imitated the actions of David.

CHAPTER 4

(45) Jehoshaphat had a good number of children; but he appointed his eldest son, Jehoram, to be his successor, who had the same name with his mother's brother, that was king of Israel and the son of Ahab. (46) Now when the king of Israel was come out of the land of Moab to Samaria, he had with him Elisha the prophet, whose acts I have a mind to go over particularly, for they were illustrious and worthy to be related, as we have them set down in the sacred books.

(47) For they say that the widow of Obadiah, Ahab's steward, came to him, and said, that he was not ignorant how her husband had preserved the prophets that were to be slain by Jezebel, the wife of Ahab; for she said that he hid a hundred of them, and had borrowed money for their maintenance, and that,

after her husband's death, she and her children were carried away to be made slaves by the creditors; and she desired of him to have mercy upon her on account of what her husband did, and afford her some assistance. (48) And when he asked her what she had in the house, she said, 'Nothing but a very small quantity of oil in a cruse.' So the prophet bid her go away, and borrow a great many empty vessels of her neighbours, and when she had shut her chamber door, to pour the oil into them all; for that God would fill them full. (49) And when the woman had done what she was commanded to do, and bade her children bring every one of the vessels, and all were filled, and not one left empty, she came to the prophet, and told him that they were all full; (50) upon which he advised her to go away and sell the oil, and pay the creditors what was owing to them, for that there would be some surplus of the price of the oil, which she might make use of for the maintenance of her children: and thus did Elisha discharge the woman's debts, and free her from the vexation of her creditors.

(51) Elisha also sent a hasty message to Joram, and exhorted him to take care of that place, for that therein were some Syrians lying in ambush to kill him. So the king did as the prophet exhorted him, and avoided his going a-hunting; (52) and when Benhadad missed of the success of his lying in ambush, he was wroth with his own servants, as if they had betrayed his ambushment to Joram; and he sent for them, and said they were the betrayers of his secret counsels; and he threatened that he would put them to death, since such their practice was evident, because he had entrusted this secret to none but them, and yet it was made known to his enemy; (53) and when one that was present said that he should not mistake himself, nor suspect that they had discovered to his enemy his sending men to kill him, but that he ought to know that it was Elisha the prophet who discovered all to him, and laid open all his counsels. So he gave order that they should send some to learn in what city Elisha dwelt. (54) Accordingly, those that were sent brought word that he was in Dothan; wherefore Benhadad sent to that city a great army, with horses and chariots, to take Elisha; so they encompassed the city round about by night, and kept him therein confined: but when the prophet's servant in the morning perceived this, and that his enemies sought to take Elisha, he came running, and crying out after a disordered manner to him, and told him of it; (55) but he encouraged him, and bade him not be afraid, and to despise the enemy, and trust in the assistance of God, and was himself without fear; and he besought God to make manifest to his servant his power and presence, so far as was possible, in order to the inspiring him with hope and courage. Accordingly God heard the prayer of the prophet, and made the servant see a multitude of chariots and horses encompassing Elisha, till he laid aside his fear, and his courage revived at the sight of what he supposed was come to their assistance.

(56) After this Elisha did farther entreat God, that he would dim the eyes of their enemies, and cast a mist before them, whereby they might not discern him. When this was done, he went into the midst of his enemies, and asked them who it was they came to seek; and when they replied, 'The prophet Elisha', he promised he would deliver him to them, if they would follow him to the city where he was. (57) So these men were so darkened by God in their sight and in their mind, that they followed him very diligently; and when Elisha had brought them to Samaria, he ordered Joram the king to shut the gates, and to place his own army round about them; and prayed to God to clear the eyes of these their enemies, and take the mist from before them. Accordingly, when they were freed from the obscurity they had been in, they saw themselves in the midst of their enemies; (58) and as the Syrians were strangely amazed and distressed, as was but reasonable, at an action so divine and surprising; and as king Joram asked the prophet if he would give him leave to shoot at them, Elisha forbade him so to do; and said, that 'it is just to kill those that are taken in battle; but that these men had done the country no harm, but, without knowing it, were come thither by the Divine Power' – (59) so that his counsel was to treat them in a hospitable manner at his table, and then send them away without hurting them. Wherefore Joram obeyed the prophet; and when he had feasted the Syrians in a splendid and magnificent manner, he let them go to Benhadad, their king.

(60) Now when these men were come back, and had showed Benhadad how strange an accident had befallen them, and what an appearance and power they had experienced of the God of Israel he wondered at it, as also at that prophet with whom God was so evidently present; so he determined to make no more secret attempts upon the king of Israel, out of fear of Elisha, but resolved to make open war with them, as supposing he could be too hard for his enemies by the multitude of his army and power. (61) So he made an expedition with a great army against Joram, who, not thinking himself a match for him, shut himself up in Samaria, and depended on the strength of its walls; but Benhadad supposed he should take the city, if not by his engines of war, yet that he should overcome the Samaritans by famine, and the want of necessaries, and brought his army upon them, and besieged the city; (62) and the plenty of necessaries was brought so low with Joram, that from the extremity of want, an ass's head was sold in Samaria for fourscore pieces of silver; and the Hebrews bought a sextary of dove's dung, instead of salt, for five pieces of silver. (63) Now Joram was in fear least somebody should betray the city to the enemy, by reason of the famine, and went every day round the walls and the guards, to see whether any such were concealed among them: and by being thus seen, and taking such care, he deprived them of the opportunity of contriving any such thing; and if they had a mind to do it, he by this means

prevented them; (64) but upon a certain woman's crying out, 'Have pity on me, my Lord,' while he thought that she was about to ask for somewhat to eat, he imprecated God's curse upon her, and said he had neither thrashing flour, nor winepress, whence he might give her anything at her petition. (65) Upon which she said, she did not desire his aid in any such thing, nor trouble him about food, but desired that he would do her justice as to another woman; and when he bade her say on, and let him know what she desired, she said, she had made an agreement with the other woman, who was her neighbour and her friend, that because the famine and the want was intolerable, they should kill their children, each of them having a son of their own, 'and we will live upon them ourselves for two days – the one day upon one son, and the other day upon the other; and,' said she, (66) 'I have killed my son the first day, and we lived upon my son yesterday; but this other woman will not do the same thing, but hath broken her agreement, and hath hid her son.' (67) This story mightily grieved Joram when he heard it; so he rent his garment, and cried out with a loud voice, and conceived great wrath against Elisha the prophet, and set himself eagerly to have him slain, because he did not pray to God to provide them some exit and way of escape out of the miseries with which they were surrounded; and sent one away immediately to cut off his head, (68) who made haste to kill the prophet; but Elisha was not unacquainted with the wrath of the king against him; for as he sat in his house by himself, with none but his disciples about him, he told them that Joram, who was the son of a murderer, had sent one to take away his head; (69) 'but,' said he, 'when he that is commanded to do this comes, take care that you do not let him come in, but press the door against him, and hold him fast there, for the king himself will follow him, and come to me, having altered his mind.' Accordingly, they did as they were bidden, when he that was sent by the king to kill Elisha came: (70) but Joram repented of his wrath against the prophet; and for fear he that was commanded to kill him should have done it before he came he made haste to hinder the slaughter, and to save the prophet; and when he came to him he accused him that he did not pray to God for their deliverance from the miseries they now lay under, but saw them so sadly destroyed by them. (71) Hereupon Elisha promised that the very next day, at the very same hour in which the king came to him, they should have great plenty of food, and that two seahs of barley should be sold in the market for a shekel, and a seah of fine flour should be sold for a shekel. (72) This prediction made Joram, and those that were present, very joyful, for they did not scruple believing what the prophet said, on account of the experience they had of the truth of his former predictions; and the expectation of plenty made the want they were in that day with the uneasiness that accompanied it, appear a light thing to them; (73) but the captain of the third band, who was a friend of the king, and on whose hand the king leaned said, 'Thou talkest of incredible things, O prophet! For as it is impossible for God to pour down torrents of barley, or fine flour, out of Heaven, so it is impossible that what thou sayest should come to pass.' To which the prophet made this reply: 'Thou shalt see these things come to pass, but thou shalt not be in the least a partaker of them.'

(74) Now what Elisha had thus foretold came to pass in the manner following: there was a law at Samaria, that those that had the leprosy, and whose bodies were not cleansed from it, should abide without the city. And there were four men that on this account abode before the gates, while nobody gave them any food, by reason of the extremity of the famine; (75) and as they were prohibited from entering into the city by the law, and they considered that if they were permitted to enter, they would miserably perish by the famine; as also, that if they stayed where they were, they should suffer in the same manner – they resolved to deliver themselves up to the enemy, that in case they should spare them, they should live; but if they should be killed, that would be an easy death. (76) So when they had confirmed this their resolution, they came by night to the enemy's camp. Now God had begun to affright and disturb the Syrians, and to bring the noise of chariots and armours to their ears, as though an army were coming upon them, and had made them suspect that it was coming nearer and nearer to them. (77) In short, they were in such a dread of this army, that they left their tents, and ran together to Benhadad, and said, that Joram, the king of Israel, had hired for auxiliaries both the king of Egypt and the king of the Islands, and led them against them; for they heard the noise of them as they were coming; (78) and Benhadad believed what they said (for there came the same noise to his ears as well as it did to theirs); so they fell into a mighty disorder and tumult, and left their horses and beasts in their camp, with immense riches also, and betook themselves to flight. (79) And those lepers who had departed from Samaria, and were gone to the camp of the Syrians, of whom we made mention a little before, when they were in the camp, saw nothing but great quietness and silence; accordingly they entered into it, and went hastily into one of their tents; and when they saw nobody there, they eat and drank, and carried garments, and a great quantity of gold, and hid it out of the camp; (80) after which they went into another tent, and carried off what was in it, as they did at the former, and this did they for several times, without the least interruption from anybody; so they gathered thereby that the enemies were departed; whereupon they reproached themselves that they did not inform Joram and the citizens of it. (81) So they came to the walls of Samaria, and called aloud to the watchmen, and told them in what state the enemies were, as did these tell the king's guards, by whose means Joram came to know of it; who then sent for his friends, and the captains of his host, (82) and said to them, that he suspected that this departure of the king of Syria was

by way of ambush and treachery; 'and that out of despair of ruining you by famine, when you imagine them to be fled away, you may come out of the city to spoil their camp, and he may then fall upon you on a sudden, and may both kill you, and take the city without fighting; whence it is that I exhort you to guard the city carefully, and by no means to go out of it, or proudly to despise your enemies, as though they were really gone away.' (83) And when a certain person said, that he did very well and wisely to admit such a suspicion, but that he still advised him to send a couple of horsemen to search all the country as far as Jordan, that 'if they were seized by an ambush of the enemy, they might be a security to your army, that they may not go out as if they suspected nothing, nor undergo the like misfortune; and,' said he, 'those horsemen may be numbered among those that have died by the famine, supposing they be caught and destroyed by the enemy.' (84) So the king was pleased with this opinion, and sent such as might search out the truth, who performed their journey over a road that was without any enemies; but found it full of provisions and of weapons, that they had therefore thrown away and left behind them, in order to their being light and expeditious in their flight. When the king heard this, he sent out the multitude to take the spoils of the camp; (85) which gains of theirs were not of things of small value; but they took a great quantity of silver, and flocks of all kinds of cattle. They also possessed themselves of [so many] ten thousand measures of wheat and barley, as they never in the least dreamed of; and were not only freed from their former miseries, but had such plenty, that two seahs of barley were bought for a shekel, and a seah of fine flour for a shekel, according to the prophecy of Elisha. Now a seah is equal to an Italian modius and a half. (86) The captain of the third band was the only man that received no benefit by this plenty; for as he was appointed by the king to oversee the gate, that he might prevent the too great crowd of the multitude, and they might not endanger one another to perish, by treading on one another in the press, he suffered himself in that very way, and died in that very manner, as Elisha had foretold this his death, when he alone of them all disbelieved what he said concerning that plenty of provisions which they should soon have.

(87) Hereupon, when Benhadad, the king of Syria, had escaped to Damascus, and understood that it was God himself that cast all his army into this fear and disorder, and that it did not arise from the invasion of enemies, he was mightily cast down at his having God so greatly for his enemy, and fell into a distemper. (88) Now it happened that Elisha the prophet, at that time, was gone out of his own country to Damascus, of which Benhadad was informed: he sent Hazael, the most faithful of his servants, to meet him, and to carry him presents; and bade him inquire of him about his distemper, and whether he should escape the danger that it threatened. (89) So Hazael came to Elisha with forty camels, that

carried the best and most precious fruits that the country of Damascus afforded, as well as those which the king's palace supplied. He saluted him kindly, and said, that he was sent to him by king Benhadad, and brought presents to him, in order to inquire concerning his distemper, whether he should recover from it or not. (90) Whereupon the prophet bade him tell the king no melancholy news; but still he said he would die. So the king's servant was troubled to hear it; and Elisha wept also, and his tears ran down plenteously at his foresight of what miseries his people would undergo after the death of Benhadad; (91) and when Hazael asked him what was the occasion of this confusion he was in, he said, that he wept out of his commiseration for the multitude of the Israelites, and what terrible miseries they will suffer by thee; 'for thou wilt slay the strongest of them, and wilt burn their strongest cities, and wilt destroy their children, and dash them against the stones, and wilt rip up their women with child.' (92) And when Hazael said, 'How can it be that I should have power enough to do such things?' the prophet replied, that God had informed him that he should be king of Syria. So when Hazael was come to Benhadad, he told him good news concerning his distemper; but on the next day he spread a wet cloth, in the nature of a net, over him, and strangled him, and took his dominion. (93) He was an active man, and had the good will of the Syrians, and of the people of Damascus, to a great degree; by whom both Benhadad himself, and Hazael, who ruled after him, are honoured to this day as gods, by reason of their benefactions, and their building them temples, by which they adorned the city of the Damascens. (94) They also every day do with great pomp pay their worship to these kings, and value themselves upon their antiquity; nor do they know that these kings are much later then they imagine, and that they are not yet eleven hundred years old. Now when Joram, the king of Israel, heard that Benhadad was dead, he recovered out of the terror and dread he had been in on his account, and was very glad to live in peace.

CHAPTER 5

(95) Now Jehoram, the king of Jerusalem, for we have said before that he had the same name with the king of Israel, as soon as he had taken the government upon him, betook himself to the slaughter of his brethren, and his father's friends, who were governors under him, and thence made a beginning and a demonstration of his wickedness; nor was he at all better than those kings of Israel who at first transgressed against the laws of their country, and of the Hebrews, and against God's worship: (96) and it was Athalia, the daughter of Ahab, whom he had married, who taught him to be a bad man in other respects, and also to worship foreign gods. Now God would not quite root out this family, because of the promise he had made to David. However, Jehoram

did not leave off the introduction of new sorts of customs to the propagation of impiety, and to the ruin of the customs of his own country. (97) And when the Edomites about that time had revolted from him, and slain their former king, who was in subjection to his father, and had set up one of their own choosing, Jehoram fell upon the land of Edom, with the horsemen that were about him, and the chariots, by night, and destroyed those that lay near to his own kingdom; but did not proceed further. (98) However, this expedition did him no service, for they all revolted from him, with those that dwelt in the country of Libnah. He was indeed so mad as to compel the people to go up to the high places of the mountains, and worship foreign gods.

(99) As he was doing this, and had entirely cast his own country laws out of his mind, there was brought him an epistle from Elijah the prophet, which declared, that God would execute great judgments upon him, because he had not imitated his own fathers, but had followed the wicked courses of the kings of Israel; and had compelled the tribe of Judah and the citizens of Jerusalem to leave the holy worship of their own God, and to worship idols, as Ahab had compelled the Israelites to do, (100) and because he had slain his brethren, and the men that were good and righteous. And the prophet gave him notice in this epistle what punishment he should undergo for these crimes, namely, the destruction of his people, with the corruption of the king's own wives and children; (101) and that he should himself die of a distemper in his bowels, with long torments, those his bowels falling out by the violence of the inward rottenness of the parts, insomuch that, though he see his own misery, he shall not be able at all to help himself, but shall die in that manner. This it was which Elijah denounced to him in that epistle.

(102) It was not long after this that an army of those Arabians that lived near to Ethiopia, and of the Philistines, fell upon the kingdom of Jehoram, and spoiled the country and the king's house; moreover, they slew his sons and his wives; one only of his sons was left him, who escaped the enemy; his name was Ahaziah; (103) after which calamity, he himself fell into that disease which was foretold by the prophet, and lasted a great while (for God inflicted this punishment upon him in his belly, out of his wrath against him), and so he died miserably, and saw his own bowels fall out. The people also abused his dead body; (104) I suppose it was because they thought that such his death came upon him by the wrath of God, and that therefore he was not worthy to partake of such a funeral as became kings. Accordingly, they neither buried him in the sepulchres of his fathers, nor vouchsafed him any honours, but buried him like a private man, and this when he had lived forty years, and reigned eight; and the people of Jerusalem delivered the government to his son Ahaziah.

CHAPTER 6

(105) Now Joram, the king of Israel, after the death of Benhadad, hoped that he might now take Ramoth, a city of Gilead, from the Syrians. Accordingly he made an expedition against it, with a great army; but as he was besieging it, an arrow was shot at him by one of the Syrians, but the wound was not mortal; so he returned to have his wound healed in Jezreel, but left his whole army in Ramoth – and Jehu, the son of Nimshi, for their general; for he had already taken the city by force; (106) and he proposed, after he was healed, to make war with the Syrians; but Elisha the prophet sent one of his disciples to Ramoth, and gave him holy oil to anoint Jehu, and to tell him that God had chosen him to be their king. He also sent him to say other things to him, and bade him to take his journey as if he fled, that when he came away he might escape the knowledge of all men. (107) So when he was come to the city, he found Jehu sitting in the midst of the captains of the army, as Elisha had foretold he should find him. So he came up to him, and said that he desired to speak with him about certain matters; (108) and when he was arisen, and had followed him into an inward chamber, the young man took the oil, and poured it on his head, and said that God ordained him to be king, in order to his destroying the house of Ahab, and that he might revenge the blood of the prophets that were unjustly slain by Jezebel, (109) that so their house might utterly perish, as those of Jeroboam the son of Nebat and of Baasha had perished for their wickedness, and no seed might remain of Ahab's family. So when he had said this, he went away hastily out of the chamber, and endeavoured not to be seen by any of the army.

(110) But Jehu came out, and went to the place where he before sat with the captains; and when they asked him, and desired him to tell them wherefore it was that this young man came to him, and added withal that he was mad, he replied, 'You guess right; for the words he spake were the words of a madman:' (111) and when they were eager about the matter, and desired he would tell them, he answered, that God had said he had chosen him to be king over the multitude. When he had said this, every one of them put off his garment, and strewed it under him, and blew with trumpets, and gave notice that Jehu was king. (112) So when he had gotten the army together, he was preparing to set out immediately against Joram, at the city Jezreel, in which city, as we said before, he was healing of the wound which he had received in the siege of Ramoth. It happened also that Ahaziah, king of Jerusalem, was now come to Joram, for he was his sister's son, as we have said already, to see how he did after his wound, and this upon account of their kindred: (113) but as Jehu was desirous to fall upon Joram and those with him on the sudden, he desired that none of the soldiers might run away and tell to Joram what had

happened, for that this would be an evident demonstration of their kindness to him, and would show that their real inclinations were to make him king.

(114) So they were pleased with what he did, and guarded the roads, lest somebody should privately tell the thing to those that were at Jezreel. Now Jehu took his choice horsemen, and sat upon his chariot, and went on for Jezreel; and when he was come near, the watchman whom Joram had set there to spy out such as came to the city, saw Jehu marching on, and told Joram that he saw a troop of horsemen marching on. (115) Upon which he immediately gave orders, that one of his horsemen should be sent out to meet them, and to know who it was that was coming. So when the horseman came up to Jehu, he asked him in what condition the army was, for that the king wanted to know it; but Jehu bade him not at all to meddle with such matters, but to follow him. (116) When the watchman saw this, he told Joram that the horseman had mingled himself among the company, and came along with them. And when the king had sent a second messenger, Jehu commanded him to do as the former did: (117) and as soon as the watchman told this also to Joram, he at last got upon his chariot himself, together with Ahaziah, the king of Jerusalem; for, as we said before, he was there to see how Joram did, after he had been wounded, as being his relation. So he went out to meet Jehu, who marched slowly, and in good order; (118) and when Joram met him in the field of Naboth, he asked him if all things were well in the camp; but Jehu reproached him bitterly, and ventured to call his mother a witch and a harlot. Upon this the king fearing what he intended, and suspecting he had no good meaning, turned his chariot about as soon as he could, and said to Ahaziah, 'We are fought against by deceit and treachery.' But Jehu drew his bow, and smote him, the arrow going through his heart: (119) so Joram fell down immediately on his knee, and gave up the ghost. Jehu also gave orders to Bidkar, the captain of the third part of his army, to cast the dead body of Joram into the field of Naboth, putting him in mind of the prophecy which Elijah prophesied to Ahab his father, when he had slain Naboth, that both he and his family should perish in that place; for (120) that as they sat behind Ahab's chariot, they heard the prophet say so, and that it was now come to pass according to his prophecy. Upon the fall of Joram, Ahaziah was afraid of his own life, and turned his chariot into another road, supposing he should not be seen by Jehu; (121) but he followed after him, and overtook him at a certain acclivity, and drew his bow, and wounded him; so he left his chariot, and got upon his horse, and fled from Jehu to Megiddo; and though he was under care, in a little time he died from that wound, and was carried to Jerusalem, and buried there, after he had reigned one year, and had proved a wicked man, and worse than his father.

(122) Now when Jehu was come to Jezreel, Jezebel adorned herself and

stood upon a tower, and said, he was a fine servant that had killed his master! And when he looked up to her, he asked who she was, and commanded her to come down to him. At last he ordered the eunuchs to throw her down from the tower; (123) and being thrown down, she besprinkled the wall with her blood, and was trodden upon by the horses, and so died. When this was done, Jehu came to the palace with his friends, and took some refreshment after his journey, both with other things, and by eating a meal. He also bade his servants to take up Jezebel and bury her, because of the nobility of her blood, for she was descended from kings; (124) but those that were appointed to bury her found nothing else remaining but the extreme parts of her body, for all the rest were eaten by dogs. When Jehu heard this, he admired the prophecy of Elijah, for he foretold that she should perish in this manner at Jezreel.

(125) Now Ahab had seventy sons brought up in Samaria. So Jehu sent two epistles, the one to them that brought up the children, the other to the rulers of Samaria, which said, that they should set up the most valiant of Ahab's sons for king, for that they had abundance of chariots, and horses, and armour, and a great army, and fenced cities, and that by so doing they might avenge the murder of Ahab. (126) This he wrote to try the intentions of those of Samaria. Now when the rulers, and those that had brought up the children, had read the letter, they were afraid; and considering that they were not at all able to oppose him, who had already subdued two very great kings, they returned him this answer: that they owned him for their lord, and would do whatsoever he bade them. (127) So he wrote back to them such a reply as enjoined them to obey what he gave order for, and to cut off the heads of Ahab's sons, and send them to him. Accordingly the rulers sent for those that brought up the sons of Ahab, and commanded them to slay them, to cut off their heads, and send them to Jehu. So they did whatsoever they were commanded, without omitting anything at all, and put them up in wicker baskets, and sent them to Jezreel. (128) And when Jehu, as he was at supper with his friends, was informed that the heads of Ahab's sons were brought, he ordered them to make two heaps of them, one before each of the gates; (129) and in the morning he went out to take a view of them, and when he saw them, he began to say to the people that were present, that he did himself make an expedition against his master [Joram], and slew him; but that it was not he that slew all these: and he desired them to take notice, that as to Ahab's family, all things had come to pass according to God's prophecy, and his house was perished, according as Elijah had foretold. (130) And when he had further destroyed all the kindred of Ahab that were found in Jezreel, he went to Samaria; and as he was upon the road, he met the relations of Ahaziah, king of Jerusalem, and asked them, whither they were going? (131) They replied, that they came to salute Joram, and their own king Ahaziah, for they knew not that he had slain them both. So Jehu gave

orders that they should catch these, and kill them, being in number forty-two persons.

(132) After these, there met him a good and a righteous man, whose name was Jehonadab, and who had been his friend of old. He saluted Jehu, and began to commend him, because he had done everything according to the will of God, in extirpating the house of Ahab. (133) So Jehu desired him to come up into his chariot, and make his entry with him into Samaria; and told him that he would not spare one wicked man, but would punish the false prophets and false priests, and those that deceived the multitude, and persuaded them to leave the worship of God Almighty, and to worship foreign gods; and that it was a most excellent and a most pleasing sight to a good and righteous man to see the wicked punished. (134) So Jehonadab was persuaded by these arguments, and came up into Jehu's chariot, and came to Samaria. And Jehu sought out for all Ahab's kindred, and slew them. And being desirous that none of the false prophets, nor the priests of Ahab's god, might escape punishment, he caught them deceitfully by this wile: (135) for he gathered all the people together, and said, that he would worship twice as many gods as Ahab worshipped, and desired that his priests and prophets and servants, might be present, because he would offer costly and great sacrifices to Ahab's god; and that if any of his priests were wanting they should be punished with death. Now Ahab's god was called Baal: (136) and when he had appointed a day on which he would offer these sacrifices, he sent messengers through all the country of the Israelites, that they might bring the priests of Baal to him. So Jehu commanded to give all the priests vestments; and when they had received them, he went into the house [of Baal], with his friend Jehonadab, and gave orders to make search whether there were not any foreigner or stranger among them, for he would have no one of a different religion to mix among their sacred offices. (137) And when they said that there was no stranger there, and they were beginning their sacrifices, he set fourscore men without, they being such of his soldiers as he knew to be most faithful to him, and bade them slay the prophets, and now vindicate the laws of their country, which had been a long time in disesteem. He also threatened, that if any one of them escaped, their own lives should go for them. So (138) they slew them all with the sword; and burnt the house of Baal, and by that means purged Samaria of foreign customs [idolatrous worship]. Now this Baal was the god of the Tyrians; and Ahab, in order to gratify his father-in-law Ethbaal, who was the king of Tyre and Sidon, built a temple for him in Samaria, and appointed him prophets, and worshipped him with all sorts of worship, (139) although, when this god was demolished, Jehu permitted the Israelites to worship the golden heifers. However, because he had done thus, and taken care to punish the wicked, God foretold by his prophet, that his sons should reign over Israel for four generations: and in this condition was Jehu at this time.

CHAPTER 7

(140) Now when Athaliah, the daughter of Ahab, heard of the death of her brother Joram, and of her son Ahaziah, and of the royal family, she endeavoured that none of the house of David might be left alive, but that the whole family might be exterminated, that no king might arise out of it afterward; (141) and, as she thought, she had actually done it; but one of Ahaziah's sons was preserved, who escaped death after the manner following: Ahaziah had a sister by the same father, whose name was Jehosheba, and she was married to the high priest Jehoiada. (142) She went into the king's palace, and found Jehoash, for that was the little child's name, who was not above a year old, among those that were slain, but concealed with his nurse; so she took him with her into a secret bed chamber, and shut him up there; and she and her husband Jehoiada brought him up privately in the temple six years, during which time Athaliah reigned over Jerusalem and the two tribes.

(143) Now, on the seventh year, Jehoiada communicated the matter to certain of the captains of hundreds, five in number, and persuaded them to be assisting to what attempts he was making against Athaliah, and to join with him in asserting the kingdom to the child. He also received such oaths from them as are proper to secure those that assist one another from the fear of discovery; and he was then of good hope that they should depose Athaliah. (144) Now those men whom Jehoiada the priest had taken to be his partners, went into all the country, and gathered together the priests and the Levites, and heads of the tribes out of it, and came and brought them to Jerusalem, to the high priest. (145) So he demanded the security of an oath of them, to keep private whatsoever he should discover to them, which required both their silence and their assistance. So when they had taken the oath, and had thereby made it safe for him to speak, he produced the child that he had brought up, of the family of David, and said to them, 'This is your king, of that house which you know God hath foretold should reign over you for all time to come: (146) I exhort you, therefore, that one-third part of you guard him in the temple, and that a fourth part keep watch at all the gates of the temple, and that the next part of you keep guard at the gate which opens and leads to the king's palace, and let the rest of the multitude be unarmed in the temple, and let no armed person go into the temple, but the priest only.' (147) He also gave them this order besides, 'That a part of the priests and the Levites should be about the king himself, and be a guard to him, with their drawn swords, and to kill that man immediately, whoever he be, that should be so bold as to enter armed into the temple; and bade them be afraid of nobody, but persevere in guarding the king.' (148) So these men obeyed what the high priest advised them to, and

declared the reality of their resolution by their actions. Jehoiada also opened that armoury which David had made in the temple, and distributed to the captains of hundreds, as also to the priests and Levites, all the spears and quivers, and what kind of weapons soever it contained and set them armed in a circle round about the temple, so as to touch one another's hands, and by that means excluding those from entering that ought not to enter. (149) So they brought the child into the midst of them, and put on him the royal crown, and Jehoiada anointed him with the oil, and made him king; and the multitude rejoiced, and made a noise, and cried, 'God save the king!'

(150) When Athaliah unexpectedly heard the tumult and the acclamations, she was greatly disturbed in her mind, and suddenly issued out of the royal palace with her own army; and when she was come to the temple, the priests received her, but as for those that stood round about the temple, as they were ordered by the high priest to do, they hindered the armed men that followed her from going in. (151) But when Athaliah saw the child standing upon a pillar, with the royal crown upon his head, she rent her clothes, and cried out vehemently, and commanded [her guards] to kill him that had laid snares for her and endeavoured to deprive her of the government; but Jehoiada called for the captains of hundreds, and commanded them to bring Athaliah to the valley of Cedron, and slay her there, (152) for he would not have the temple defiled with the punishments of this pernicious woman; and he gave order, that if anyone came near to help her, he should be slain also; wherefore those that had the charge of her slaughter took hold of her, and led her to the gate of the king's mules, and slew her there.

(153) Now as soon as what concerned Athaliah was, by this stratagem, after this manner, dispatched, Jehoiada called together the people and the armed men into the temple, and made them take an oath that they would be obedient to the king, and take care of his safety, and of the safety of his government; after which he obliged the king to give security [upon oath] that he would worship God, and not transgress the laws of Moses. (154) They then ran to the house of Baal, which Athaliah and her husband Jehoram had built, to the dishonour of the God of their fathers, and to the honour of Ahab, and demolished it, and slew Mattan, that had his priesthood. (155) But Jehoiada entrusted the care and custody of the temple to the priests and Levites, according to the appointment of King David, and enjoined them to bring their regular burnt offerings twice a day, and to offer incense according to the law. He also ordained some of the Levites, with the porters, to be a guard to the temple, that no one that was defiled might come there.

(156) And when Jehoiada had set these things in order, he, with the captains of hundreds, and the rulers, and all the people, took Jehoash out of the temple into the king's palace, and when he had set him upon the king's throne, the

people shouted for joy, and betook themselves to feasting, and kept a festival for many days; but the city was quiet upon the death of Athaliah. (157) Now Jehoash was seven years old when he took the kingdom: his mother's name was Zibiah, of the city Beersheba. And all the time that Jehoiada lived, Jehoash was careful that the law should be kept, and very zealous in the worship of God; (158) and when he was of age, he married two wives, who were given to him by the high priest, by whom were born to him both sons and daughters. And thus much shall suffice to have related concerning King Jehoash, how he escaped the treachery of Athaliah, and how he received the kingdom.

CHAPTER 8

(159) Now Hazael, king of Syria, fought against the Israelites and their king Jehu, and spoiled the eastern parts of the country beyond Jordan, which belonged to the Reubenites and Gadites, and to [the half tribe of] Manassites; as also Gilead and Bashan, burning and spoiling and offering violence to all that he laid his hands on, (160) and this without impeachment of Jehu, who made no haste to defend the country when it was under this distress; nay, he was become a condemner of religion, and a despiser of holiness and of the laws, and died when he had reigned over the Israelites twenty-seven years. He was buried in Samaria, and left Jehoahaz his son his successor in the government.

(161) Now Jehoash, king of Jerusalem, had an inclination to repair the temple of God; so he called Jehoiada, and bade him send the Levites and priests through all the country, to require half a shekel of silver for every head, towards the rebuilding and repairing of the temple, which was brought to decay by Jehoram, and Athaliah and her sons. (162) But the high priests did not do this, as concluding that no one would willingly pay that money; but in the twenty-third year of Jehoash's reign, when the king sent for him and the Levites, and complained that they had not obeyed what he enjoined them, and still commanded them to take care of the rebuilding the temple, he used this stratagem for collecting the money, with which the multitude was pleased. (163) He made a wooden chest, and closed it up fast on all sides, but opened one hole in it; he then set it in the temple beside the altar, and desired everyone to cast into it through the hole, what he pleased, for the repair of the temple. This contrivance was acceptable to the people; and they strove one with another, and brought in jointly large quantities of silver and gold, (164) and when the scribe and the priest that were over the treasuries had emptied the chest, and counted the money in the king's presence, they then set it in its former place, and thus did they every day. But when the multitude appeared to have cast in as much as was wanted, the high priest Jehoiada, and King Joash sent to hire masons and carpenters, and to buy large pieces of timber, and of the

most curious sort; (165) and when they had repaired the temple, they made use of the remaining gold and silver, which was not a little, for bowls and basins and cups, and other vessels, and they went on to make the altar every day fat with sacrifices of great value. And these things were taken suitable care of as long as Jehoiada lived.

(166) But as soon as he was dead (which was when he had lived one hundred and thirty years, having been a righteous, and in every respect a very good man, and was buried in the king's sepulchres at Jerusalem, because he had recovered the kingdom to the family of David), King Jehoash betrayed his [want of] care about God. (167) The principal men of the people were corrupted also together with him, and offended against their duty, and what their constitution determined to be most for their good. Hereupon God was displeased with the change that was made on the king, and on the rest of the people, and sent prophets to testify to them what their actions were, and to bring them to leave off their wickedness: (168) but they had gotten such a strong affection, and so violent an inclination to it, that neither could the examples of those that had offered affronts to the laws, and had been so severely punished, they and their entire families; nor could the fear of what the prophets now foretold bring them to repentance, and turn them back from their course of transgression to their former duty. But the king commanded that Zechariah, the son of the high priest Jehoiada, should be stoned to death in the temple, and forgot the kindnesses he had received from his father; (169) for when God had appointed him to prophesy, he stood in the midst of the multitude, and give this counsel to them and to the king: that they should act righteously; and foretold to them, that if they would not hearken to his admonitions, they should suffer a heavy punishment: but as Zechariah was ready to die, he appealed to God as a witness of what he suffered for the good counsel he had given them, and how he perished, after a most severe and violent manner, for the good deeds his father had done to Jehoash.

(170) However, it was not long before the king suffered punishment for his transgression, for when Hazael, king of Syria, made an irruption into his country, and when he had overthrown Gath, and spoiled it, he made an expedition against Jerusalem; upon which Jehoash was afraid, and emptied all the treasures of God, and of the kings [before him], and took down the gifts that had been dedicated [in the temple], and sent them to the king of Syria, (171) and procured so much by them, that he was not besieged, nor his kingdom quite endangered; but Hazael was induced, by the greatness of the sum of money, not to bring his army against Jerusalem; yet Jehoash fell into a severe distemper, and was set upon by his friends, in order to revenge the death of Zechariah, the son of Jehoiada. These laid snares for the king, and slew him. (172) He was indeed buried in Jerusalem, but not in the royal sepulchres of his

forefathers, because of his impiety. He lived forty-seven years; and Amaziah his son succeeded him in the kingdom.

(173) In the one-and-twentieth year of the reign of Jehoash, Jehoahaz, the son of Jehu, took the government of the Israelites in Samaria, and held it seventeen years. He did not [properly] imitate his father, but was guilty of as wicked practices as those that first had God in contempt. (174) But the king of Syria brought him low, and, by expeditions against him, did so greatly reduce his forces, that there remained no more of so great an army than ten thousand armed men, and fifty horsemen. He also took away from him his great cities, and many of them also, and destroyed his army. (175) And these were the things that the people of Israel suffered, according to the prophecy of Elisha, when he foretold that Hazael should kill his master, and reign over the Syrians and Damascens. But when Jehoahaz was under such unavoidable miseries, he had recourse to prayer and supplication to God, and besought him to deliver him out of the hands of Hazael, and not overlook him, and give him up into his hands. (176) Accordingly, God accepted of his repentance instead of virtue; and, being desirous rather to admonish those that might repent, and not to determine that they should be utterly destroyed, he granted him deliverance from war and dangers. So the country having obtained peace, returned again to its former condition, and flourished as before.

(177) Now after the death of Jehoahaz, his son Joash took the kingdom, in the thirty-seventh year of Jehoash, the king of the tribe of Judah. This Joash then took the kingdom of Israel in Samaria, for he had the same name with the king of Jerusalem, and he retained the kingdom sixteen years. (178) He was a good man, and in his disposition was not at all like his father. Now at this time it was that when Elisha the prophet, who was already very old, and was now fallen into a disease, the king of Israel came to visit him; (179) and when he found him very near death, he began to weep in his sight, and lament to call him his father, and his weapons, because it was by his means that he never made use of his weapons against his enemies, but that he overcame his own adversaries by his prophecies, without fighting; and that he was now departing this life, and leaving him to the Syrians, that were already armed, and to other enemies of his that were under their power; (180) so he said it was not safe for him to live any longer, but that it would be well for him to hasten to his end, and depart out of this life with him. As the king was thus bemoaning himself, Elisha comforted him, and bade the king bend a bow that was brought him; and when the king had fitted the bow for shooting, Elisha took hold of his hands and bade him shoot; (181) and when he had shot three arrows, and then left off, Elisha said, 'If though hadst shot more arrows, thou hadst cut the kingdom of Syria up by the roots; but since thou hast been satisfied with shooting three times only, thou shalt fight and beat the Syrians no more times than three, that

thou mayest recover that country which they cut off from thy kingdom in the reign of thy father.' So when the king had heard that, he departed; (182) and a little while after, the prophet died. He was a man celebrated for righteousness, and in eminent favour with God. He also performed wonderful and surprising works by prophecy, and such as were gloriously preserved in memory by the Hebrews. He also obtained a magnificent funeral, such a one indeed as it was fit a person so beloved of God should have. (183) It also happened, that at that time certain robbers cast a man, whom they had slain, into Elisha's grave, and upon his dead body coming close to Elisha's body, it revived again. And thus far have we enlarged about the actions of Elisha the prophet, both such as he did while he was alive, and how he had divine power after his death also.

(184) Now upon the death of Hazael, the king of Syria, that kingdom came to Adad, his son, with whom Joash, king of Israel, made war; and when he had beaten him in three battles, he took from him all that country, and all those cities and villages, which his father Hazael had taken from the kingdom of Israel, (185) which came to pass, however, according to the prophecy of Elisha. But when Joash happened to die, he was buried in Samaria; and the government devolved on his son Jeroboam.

CHAPTER 9

(186) Now, in the second year of the reign of Joash over Israel, Amaziah reigned over the tribe of Judah in Jerusalem. His mother's name was Jehoaddan, who was born at Jerusalem. He was exceeding careful of doing what was right, and this when he was very young; but when he came to the management of affairs, and to the government, he resolved that he ought first of all to avenge his father Jehoash and to punish those his friends that had laid violent hands upon him; (187) so he seized upon them all, and put them to death; yet did he execute no severity on their children, but acted therein according to the laws of Moses, who did not think it just to punish children for the sins of their fathers. (188) After this he chose him an army out of the tribes of Judah and Benjamin, of such as were in the flower of their age, and about twenty years old; and when he had collected about three hundred thousand of them together, he set captains of hundreds over them. He also sent to the king of Israel, and hired a hundred thousand of his soldiers for a hundred talents of silver, for he had resolved to make an expedition against the nations of the Amalekites, and Edomites, and Gebalites; (189) but as he was preparing for his expedition, and ready to go out to the war, a prophet gave him counsel to dismiss the army of the Israelites, because they were bad men, and because God foretold that he should be beaten, if he made use of them as auxiliaries; but that he should overcome his enemies, though he had but a few soldiers, when it so pleased

God. (190) And when the king grudged at his having already paid the hire of the Israelites, the prophet exhorted him to do what God would have him, because he should thereby obtain much wealth from God. So he dismissed them, and said, that he still freely gave them their pay, and went himself with his own army, and made war with the nations before mentioned; (191) and when he had beaten them in battle, he slew of them ten thousand, and took as many prisoners alive, whom he brought to the great rock in Arabia, and threw them down from it headlong. He also brought away a great deal of prey and vast riches from those nations; (192) but while Amaziah was engaged in this expedition, those Israelites whom he had hired and then dismissed, were very uneasy at it, and taking their dismissal for an affront (as supposing that this would not have been done to them but out of contempt), they fell upon his kingdom, and proceeded to spoil the country as far as Beth-horon, and took much cattle, and slew three thousand men.

(193) Now upon the victory which Amaziah had gotten, and the great acts he had done, he was puffed up, and began to overlook God, who had given him the victory, and proceeded to worship the gods he had brought out of the country of the Amalekites. (194) So a prophet came to him, and said, that he wondered how he could esteem these to be gods, who had been of no advantage to their own people who paid them honours, nor had delivered them from his hands, but had overlooked the destruction of many of them, and had suffered themselves to be carried captive, for that they had been carried to Jerusalem in the same manner as anyone might have taken some of the enemy alive, and led them thither. (195) This reproof provoked the king to anger, and he commanded the prophet to hold his peace, and threatened to punish him if he meddled with his conduct. So he replied, that he should indeed hold his peace; but foretold withal, that God would not overlook his attempts for innovation; (196) but Amaziah was not able to contain himself under that prosperity which God had given him, although he had affronted God thereupon; but in a vein of insolence he wrote to Joash, the king of Israel, and commanded that he and all his people should be obedient to him, as they had formerly been obedient to his progenitors, David and Solomon; and he let him know, that if he would not be so wise as to do what he commanded him, he must fight for his dominion. (197) To which message Joash returned this answer in writing: 'King Joash to King Amaziah. There was a vastly tall cypress tree in Mount Lebanon, as also a thistle; this thistle sent to the cypress tree to give the cypress tree's daughter in marriage to the thistle's son; but as the thistle was saying this, there came a wild beast, and trod down the thistle; (198) and this may be a lesson to thee, not to be so ambitious, and to have a care, lest upon thy good success in the fight against the Amalekites, thou growest so proud, as to bring dangers upon thyself and upon thy kingdom.'

(199) When Amaziah had read this letter, he was more eager upon this expedition; which, I suppose, was by the impulse of God, that he might be punished for his offence against him. But as soon as he let out his army against Joash, and they were going to join battle with him, there came such a fear and consternation upon the army of Amaziah, as God, when he is displeased, sends upon men, and discomfited them, even before they came to a close fight. (200) Now it happened, that as they were scattered about by the terror that was upon them, Amaziah was left alone, and was taken prisoner by the enemy; whereupon Joash threatened to kill him, unless he would persuade the people of Jerusalem to open their gates to him, and receive him and his army into the city. (201) Accordingly Amaziah was so distressed, and in such fear of his life, that he made his enemy to be received into the city. So Joash overthrew a part of the wall, of the length of four hundred cubits, and drove his chariot through the breach into Jerusalem, and led Amaziah captive along with him; (202) by which means he became master of Jerusalem, and took away the treasures of God, and carried off all the gold and silver that was in the king's palace, and then freed the king from captivity, and returned to Samaria. (203) Now these things happened to the people of Jerusalem in the fourteenth year of the reign of Amaziah, who after this had a conspiracy made against him by his friends, and fled to the city Lachish, and was there slain by the conspirators, who sent men thither to kill him. So they took up his dead body, and carried it to Jerusalem, and made a royal funeral for him. (204) This was the end of the life of Amaziah, because of his innovations in religion, and his contempt of God, when he had lived fifty-four years, and had reigned twenty-nine. He was succeeded by his son, whose name was Uzziah.

CHAPTER 10

(205) In the fifteenth year of the reign of Amaziah, Jeroboam the son of Joash reigned over Israel in Samaria forty years. This king was guilty of contumely against God, and became very wicked in worshipping of idols, and in many undertakings that were absurd and foreign. He was also the cause of ten thousand misfortunes to the people of Israel. (206) Now one Jonah, a prophet, foretold to him that he should make war with the Syrians, and conquer their army, and enlarge the bounds of his kingdom on the northern parts, to the city Hamath, and on the southern to the lake Asphaltitis; (207) for the bounds of the Canaanites originally were these, as Joshua their general had determined them. So Jeroboam made an expedition against the Syrians, and overran all their country, as Jonah had foretold.

(208) Now I cannot but think it necessary for me, who have promised to give an accurate account of our affairs, to describe the actions of this prophet,

so far as I have found them written down in the Hebrew books. Jonah had been commanded by God to go to the kingdom of Nineveh; and, when he was there, to publish it in that city, how it should lose the dominion it had over the nations. But he went not, out of fear; nay, he ran away from God to the city of Joppa, and finding a ship there, he went into it, and sailed to Tarsus, to Cilicia, (209) and upon the rise of a most terrible storm, which was so great that the ship was in danger of sinking, the mariners, the master, and the pilot himself made prayers and vows, in case they escaped the sea. But Jonah lay still and covered [in the ship], without imitating anything that the others did; (210) but as the waves grew greater, and the sea became more violent by the winds, they suspected, as is usual in such cases, that some one of the persons that sailed with them was the occasion of this storm, and agreed to discover by lot which of them it was. (211) When they had cast lots, the lot fell upon the prophet; and when they asked him whence he came, and what he had done? he replied, that he was a Hebrew by nation, and a prophet of Almighty God; and he persuaded them to cast him into the sea, if they would escape the danger they were in, for that he was the occasion of the storm which was upon them. (212) Now at the first they durst not do so, as esteeming it a wicked thing to cast a man, who was a stranger, and who had committed his life to them, into such manifest perdition; but at last, when their misfortunes overbore them, and the ship was just going to be drowned, and when they were animated to do it by the prophet himself, and by the fear concerning their own safety, they cast him into the sea; (213) upon which the sea became calm. It is also related that Jonah was swallowed down by a whale, and that when he had been there three days, and as many nights, he was vomited out upon the Euxine Sea, and this alive, and without any hurt upon his body; (214) and there, on his prayer to God, he obtained pardon for his sins, and went to the city Nineveh, where he stood so as to be heard; and preached, that in a very little time they should lose the dominion of Asia; and when he had published this, he returned. Now, I have given this account about him, as I found it written [in our books].

(215) When Jeroboam the king had passed his life in great happiness, and had ruled forty years, he died, and was buried in Samaria, and his son Zechariah took the kingdom. (216) After the same manner did Uzziah, the son of Amaziah, begin to reign over the two tribes in Jerusalem, in the fourteenth year of the reign of Jeroboam. He was born of Jecoliah, his mother, who was a citizen of Jerusalem. He was a good man, and by nature righteous and magnanimous, and very laborious in taking care of the affairs of his kingdom. (217) He made an expedition also against the Philistines, and overcame them in battle, and took the cities of Gath and Jabneh, and brake down their walls; after which expedition, he assaulted those Arabs that adjoined to Egypt. He also built a city upon the Red Sea, and put a garrison into it. (218) He after this

overthrew the Ammonites, and appointed that they should pay tribute. He also overcame all the countries as far as the bounds of Egypt, and then began to take care of Jerusalem itself for the rest of his life; for he rebuilt and repaired all those parts of the wall which had either fallen down by length of time, or by the carelessness of the kings his predecessors, as well as all that part which had been thrown down by the king of Israel, when he took his father Amaziah prisoner, and entered with him into the city. (219) Moreover, he built a great many towers, of one hundred and fifty cubits high, and built walled towns in desert places, and put garrisons into them, and dug many channels for conveyance of water. He had also many beasts for labour, and an immense number of cattle; for his country was fit for pasturage. (220) He was also given to husbandry, and took care to cultivate the ground, and planted it with all sorts of plants, and sowed it with all sorts of seeds. He had also about him an army composed of chosen men, in number three hundred and seventy thousand, who were governed by general officers and captains of thousands, who were men of valour and of unconquerable strength, in number two thousand. (221) He also divided his whole army into bands, and armed them, giving everyone a sword, with brazen bucklers and breastplates, with bows and slings; and besides these, he made for them many engines of war for besieging of cities, such as cast stones and darts, with grapplers and other instruments of that sort.

(222) While Uzziah was in this state, and making preparations [for futurity], he was corrupted in his mind by pride, and became insolent, and this on account of that abundance which he had of things that will soon perish, and despised that power which is of eternal duration (which consisted in piety towards God, and in the observation of his laws); (223) so he fell by occasion of the good success of his affairs, and was carried headlong into those sins of his father, which the splendour of that prosperity he enjoyed, and the glorious actions he had done, led him into, while he was not able to govern himself well about them. Accordingly, when a remarkable day was come, and a general festival was to be celebrated, he put on the holy garment, and went into the temple to offer incense to God upon the golden altar, (224) which he was prohibited to do by Azariah the high priest, who had fourscore priests with him, and who told him that it was not lawful for him to offer sacrifice, and that 'none besides the posterity of Aaron were permitted so to do.' And when they cried out, that he must go out of the temple, and not transgress against God, he was wroth at them, and threatened to kill them, unless they would hold their peace. (225) In the meantime, a great earthquake shook the ground, and a rent was made in the temple, and the bright rays of the sun shone through it, and fell upon the king's face, insomuch that the leprosy seized upon him immediately; and before the city, at a place called Eroge, half

the mountain broke off from the rest on the west, and rolled itself four furlongs, and stood still at the east mountain, till the roads, as well as the king's gardens, were spoiled by the obstruction. (226) Now, as soon as the priest saw that the king's face was infected with the leprosy, they told him of the calamity he was under, and commanded that he should go out of the city as a polluted person. Hereupon he was so confounded at the sad distemper, and sensible that he was not at liberty to contradict, that he did as he was commanded, and underwent this miserable and terrible punishment for an intention beyond what befitted a man to have, and for that impiety against God which was implied therein. (227) So he abode out of the city for some time, and lived a private life, while his son Jotham took the government; after which he died with grief and anxiety at what had happened to him, when he had lived sixty-eight years, and reigned of them fifty-two; and was buried by himself in his own gardens.

CHAPTER I I

(228) Now when Zechariah, the son of Jeroboam, had reigned six months over Israel, he was slain by the treachery of a certain friend of his, whose name was Shallum, the son of Jabesh, who took the kingdom afterward, but kept it no longer than thirty days; for (229) Menahem, the general of his army, who was at that time in the city Tirzah, and heard of what had befallen Zechariah, removed thereupon with all his forces to Samaria, and joining battle with Shallum, slew him; and when he had made himself king, he went thence, and came to the city Tiphsah; (230) but the citizens that were in it shut their gates, and barred them against the king, and would not admit him; but in order to be avenged on them, he burnt the country round about it, and took the city by force, upon a siege; (231) and being very much displeased at what the inhabitants of Tiphsah had done, he slew them all, and spared not so much as the infants, without omitting the utmost instances of cruelty and barbarity; for he used such severity upon his own countrymen, as would not be pardonable with regard to strangers who had been conquered by him. (232) And after this manner it was that this Menahem continued to reign with cruelty and barbarity for ten years: but when Pul, king of Assyria, had made an expedition against him, he did not think meet to fight or engage in battle with the Assyrians, but he persuaded him to accept of a thousand talents of silver, and to go away, and so put an end to the war. (233) This sum the multitude collected for Menahem, by exacting fifty drachmae as poll money for every head; after which he died, and was buried in Samaria, and left his son Pekahiah his successor in the kingdom, who followed the barbarity of his father, and so ruled but two years only, (234) after which he was slain with his friends at a

feast, by the treachery of one Pekah, the general of his horse, and the son of Remaliah, who had laid snares for him. Now this Pekah held the government twenty years, and proved a wicked man and a transgressor. (235) But the king of Assyria, whose name was Tiglath-Pileser, when he had made an expedition against the Israelites, and had overrun all the land of Gilead, and the region beyond Jordan, and the adjoining country, which is called Galilee, and Kadesh, and Hazor, he made the inhabitants prisoners, and transplanted them into his own kingdom. And so much shall suffice to have related here concerning the king of Assyria.

(236) Now Jotham, the son of Uzziah, reigned over the tribe of Judah in Jerusalem, being a citizen thereof by his mother, whose name was Jerusha. This king was not defective in any virtue, but was religious towards God, and righteous towards men, and careful of the good of the city (237) (for what part soever wanted to be repaired or adorned, he magnificently repaired and adorned them). He also took care of the foundations of the cloisters in the temple, and repaired the walls that were fallen down, and built very great towers, and such as were almost impregnable; and if anything else in his kingdom had been neglected, he took great care of it. (238) He also made an expedition against the Ammonites, and overcame them in battle, and ordered them to pay tribute, a hundred talents, and ten thousand cori of wheat, and as many of barley, every year, and so augmented his kingdom that his enemies could not despise it; and his own people lived happily.

(239) Now there was at that time a prophet, whose name was Nahum, who spake after this manner concerning the overthrow of the Assyrians and Nineveh: 'Nineveh shall be a pool of water in motion; so shall all her people be troubled and tossed, and go away by flight, while they say one to another, Stand, stand still, seize their gold and silver, (240) for there shall be no one to wish them well, for they will rather save their lives than their money; for a terrible contention shall possess them one with another, and lamentation, and loosing of the members, and their countenances shall be perfectly black with fear. (241) And there will be the den of the lions, and the mother of the young lions! God says to thee, Nineveh, that they shall deface thee, and the lion shall no longer go out from thee to give laws to the world.' (242) And indeed this prophet prophesied many other things besides these concerning Nineveh, which I do not think necessary to repeat, and I here omit them, that I may not appear troublesome to my readers; all which things happened about Nineveh a hundred and fifteen years afterward: so this may suffice to have spoken of these matters.

CHAPTER 12

(243) Now Jotham died when he had lived forty-one years, and of them reigned sixteen, and was buried in the sepulchres of the kings; and the kingdom came to his son Ahaz, who proved most impious toward God, and a transgressor of the laws of his country. He imitated the kings of Israel, and reared altars in Jerusalem, and offered sacrifices upon them to idols; to which also he offered his own son as a burnt offering, according to the practices of the Canaanites. His other actions were also of the same sort. (244) Now as he was going on in this mad course, Rezin, the king of Syria and Damascus, and Pekah, the king of Israel, who were now at amity one with another, made war with him; and when they had driven them into Jerusalem, they besieged that city a long while, making but a small progress on account of the strength of its walls; (245) and when the king of Syria had taken the city Elath, upon the Red Sea, and had slain the inhabitants, he peopled it with Syrians; and when he had slain those in the other garrisons, and the Jews in their neighbourhood, and had driven away much prey, he returned with his army back to Damascus. (246) Now when the king of Jerusalem knew that the Syrians were returned home, he, supposing himself a match for the king of Israel, drew out his army against him, and joining battle with him was beaten; and this happened because God was angry with him on account of his many and great enormities. (247) Accordingly, there were slain by the Israelites one hundred and twenty thousand of his men that day, whose general, Amaziah by name, slew Zechariah the king's son in his conflict with Ahaz, as well as the governor of the kingdom, whose name was Azricam. He also carried Elkanah, the general of the troops of the tribe of Judah, into captivity. They also carried the women and children of the tribe of Benjamin captives; and when they had gotten a great deal of prey, they returned to Samaria.

(248) Now there was one Obed, who was a prophet at that time in Samaria; he met the army before the city walls, and with a loud voice told them that they had gotten the victory not by their own strength, but by reason of the anger God had against King Ahaz. (249) And he complained that they were not satisfied with the good success they had had against him, but were so bold as to make captives out of their kinsmen, the tribes of Judah and Benjamin. He also gave them counsel to let them go home without doing them any harm, for that if they did not obey God herein they should be punished. (250) So the people of Israel came together to their assembly, and considered of these matters, when a man whose name was Berechiah, and who was one of chief reputation in the government, stood up, and three others with him, and said, 'We will not suffer the citizens to bring these prisoners into the city, lest we be

all destroyed by God: we have sins enough of our own that we have committed against him, as the prophets assure us; nor ought we therefore to introduce the practice of new crimes.' (251) When the soldiers heard that, they permitted them to do what they thought best. So the forenamed men took the captives and let them go, and took care of them, and gave them provisions, and sent them to their own country, without doing them any harm. However, these four went along with them, and conducted them as far as Jericho, which is not far from Jerusalem, and returned to Samaria.

(252) Hereupon King Ahaz, having been so thoroughly beaten by the Israelites, sent to Tiglath-Pileser, king of the Assyrians, and sued for assistance from him in his war against the Israelites and Syrians and Damascens, with a promise to send him much money; he sent him also great presents at the same time. (253) Now this king, upon the reception of those ambassadors, came to assist Ahaz, and made war upon the Syrians, and laid their country waste, and took Damascus by force, and slew Rezin their king, and transplanted the people of Damascus into the Upper Media, and brought a colony of Assyrians, and planted them in Damascus. (254) He also afflicted the land of Israel, and took many captives out of it. While he was doing thus with the Syrians, King Ahaz took all the gold that was in the king's treasures, and the silver, and what was in the temple of God, and what precious gifts were there, and he carried them with him, and came to Damascus, and give it to the king of Assyria, according to his agreement. So he confessed that he owed him thanks for all that he had done for him, and returned to Jerusalem. (255) Now this king was so sottish and thoughtless of what was for his own good, that he would not leave off worshipping the Syrian gods when he was beaten by them, but he went on in worshipping them, as though they would procure him the victory; (256) and when he was beaten again he began to honour the gods of the Assyrians; and he seemed more desirous to honour any other gods than his own paternal and true God, whose anger was the cause of his defeat: (257) nay, he proceeded to such a degree of despite and contempt [of God's worship], that he shut up the temple entirely, and forbade them to bring in the appointed sacrifices, and took away the gifts that had been given to it. And when he had offered these indignities to God, he died, having lived thirty-six years, and out of them reigned sixteen; and he left his son Hezekiah for his successor.

CHAPTER 13

(258) About the same time Pekah the king of Israel died, by the treachery of a friend of his, whose name was Hoshea, who retained the kingdom nine years' time; but was a wicked man, and a despiser of the divine worship: (259) and Shalmaneser, the king of Assyria, made an expedition against him, and

overcame him (which must have been because he had not God favourable nor assistant to him), and brought him to submission, and ordered him to pay an appointed tribute. (260) Now in the fourth year of the reign of Hoshea, Hezekiah, the son of Ahaz, began to reign in Jerusalem; and his mother's name was Abijah, a citizen of Jerusalem. His nature was good, and righteous, and religious; for when he came to the kingdom, he thought that nothing was prior, or more necessary, or more advantageous, to himself and to his subjects, than to worship God. Accordingly he called the people together, and the priests and the Levites, and made a speech to them, and said, (261) 'You are not ignorant how, by the sins of my father, who transgressed that sacred honour which was due to God, you have had experience of many and great miseries, while you were corrupted in your mind by him, and were induced to worship those which he supposed to be gods: (262) I exhort you, therefore, who have learned by sad experience how dangerous a thing impiety is, to put that immediately out of your memory, and to purify yourselves from your former pollutions, and to open the temple to these priests and Levites who are here convened, and to cleanse it with the accustomed sacrifices, and to recover all to the ancient honour which our fathers paid to it; for by this means we may render God favourable, and he will remit the anger he hath had to us.'

(263) When the king had said this, the priests opened the temple; and when they had set in order the vessels of God, and cast out what was impure, they laid the accustomed sacrifices upon the altar. The king also sent to the country that was under him, and called the people to Jerusalem to celebrate the feast of unleavened bread, for it had been intermitted a long time, on account of the wickedness of the forementioned kings. (264) He also sent to the Israelites, and exhorted them to leave off their present way of living, and return to their ancient practices, and to worship God, for that he gave them leave to come to Jerusalem, and to celebrate, all in one body, the feast of unleavened bread; and this he said was by way of invitation only, and to be one of their own good will, and for their own advantage, and not out of obedience to him, because it would make them happy. (265) But the Israelites, upon the coming of the ambassadors, and upon their laying before them what they had in charge from their own king, were so far from complying therewith, that they laughed the ambassadors to scorn, and mocked them as fools: as also they affronted the prophets who gave them the same exhortations, and foretold what they would suffer if they did not return to the worship of God, insomuch that at length they caught them, and slew them; (266) nor did this degree of transgressing suffice them, but they had more wicked contrivances than what have been described: nor did they leave off, before God, as a punishment for their impiety, brought them under their enemies: but of that more hereafter. (267)

However, many there were of the tribe of Manasseh, and of Zebulon, and of Issachar, who were obedient to what the prophets exhorted them to do, and returned to the worship of God. Now all these came running to Jerusalem, to Hezekiah, that they might worship God [there].

(268) When these men were come, King Hezekiah went up into the temple, with the rulers and all the people, and offered for himself seven bulls, and as many rams, with seven lambs, and as many kids of the goats. The king also himself, and the rulers, laid their hands on the heads of the sacrifices, and permitted the priests to complete the sacred offices about them. (269) So they both slew the sacrifices and burnt the burnt offerings while the Levites stood round about them with their musical instruments, and sang hymns to God, and played on their psalteries, as they were instructed by David to do, and this while the rest of the priests returned the music, and sounded the trumpets which they had in their hands: and when this was done, the king and the multitude threw themselves down upon their faces, and worshipped God. (270) He also sacrificed seventy bulls, one hundred rams, and two hundred lambs. He also granted the multitude sacrifices to feast upon, six hundred oxen, and three thousand other cattle; and the priests performed all things according to the law. Now the king was so pleased herewith, that he feasted with the people, and returned thanks to God; (271) but as the feast of unleavened bread was now come, when they had offered that sacrifice which is called the Passover, they after that offered other sacrifices for seven days. When the king had bestowed on the multitude, besides what they sanctified of themselves, two thousand bulls, and seven thousand other cattle, the same thing was done by the rulers; for they gave them a thousand bulls, and a thousand and forty other cattle. (272) Nor had this festival been so well observed from the days of King Solomon, as it was now first observed with great splendour and magnificence; and when the festival was ended, they went out into the country, and purged it; (273) and cleansed the city of all the pollution of the idols. The king also gave order that the daily sacrifices should be offered, at his own charges, and according to the law; and appointed that the tithes and the first fruits should be given by the multitude to the priests and Levites, and that they might constantly attend upon divine service, and never be taken off from the worship of God. (274) Accordingly, the multitude brought together all sorts of their fruits to the priests and the Levites. The king also made garners and receptacles for these fruits, and distributed them to every one of the priests and Levites, and to their children and wives; and thus did they return to their old form of divine worship. (275) Now when the king had settled these matters after the manner already described, he made war upon the Philistines, and beat them, and possessed himself of all the enemy's cities, from Gaza to Gath; but the king of Assyria sent to him, and threatened to overturn all his

dominions, unless he would pay him the tribute which his father paid him formerly; (276) but king Hezekiah was not concerned at his threatenings, but depended on his piety towards God, and upon Isaiah the prophet, by whom he inquired, and accurately knew all future events: and thus much shall suffice for the present concerning this king Hezekiah.

CHAPTER 14

(277) When Shalmaneser, the king of Assyria, had it told him, that [Hoshea] the king of Israel had sent privately to So, the king of Egypt, desiring his assistance against him, he was very angry, and made an expedition against Samaria, in the seventh year of the reign of Hoshea; (278) but when he was not admitted [into the city] by the king, he besieged Samaria three years, and took it by force in the ninth year of the reign of Hoshea, and in the seventh year of Hezekiah, king of Jerusalem, and quite demolished the government of the Israelites, and transplanted all the people into Media and Persia, among whom he took King Hoshea alive; (279) and when he had removed these people out of this their land, he transplanted other nations out of Cuthah, a place so called (for there is [still] a river of that name in Persia), into Samaria, and into the country of the Israelites. (280) So the ten tribes of the Israelites were removed out of Judea, nine hundred and forty-seven years after their forefathers were come out of the land of Egypt and possessed themselves of this country, but eight hundred years after Joshua had been their leader, and, as I have already observed, two hundred and forty years, seven months, and seven days, after they had revolted from Rehoboam, the grandson of David, and had given the kingdom to Jeroboam. (281) And such a conclusion overtook the Israelites, when they had transgressed the laws, and would not hearken to the prophets, who foretold that this calamity would come upon them, if they would not leave off their evil doings. (282) What gave birth to these evil doings, was that sedition which they raised against Rehoboam, the grandson of David, when they set up Jeroboam, his servant, to be their king, who, by sinning against God, and bringing them to imitate his bad example, made God to be their enemy, while Jeroboam underwent that punishment which he justly deserved.

(283) And now the king of Assyria invaded all Syria and Phoenicia in a hostile manner. The name of this king is also set down in the archives of Tyre, for he made an expedition against Tyre in the reign of Eluleus; and Menander attests to it, who, when he wrote his Chronology, and translated the archives of Tyre into the Greek language, gives us the following history: (284) 'One whose name was Eluleus, reigned thirty-six years: this king, upon the revolt of the Citteans, sailed to them, and reduced them again to a submission. Against these did the king of Assyria send an army, and in a hostile manner overrun all

Phoenicia, but soon made peace with them all, and returned back; (285) but Sidon, and Ace, and Palaetyrus, revolted; and many other cities there were which delivered themselves up to the king of Assyria. Accordingly, when the Tyrians would not submit to him, the king returned, and fell upon them again, while the Phoenicians had furnished him with threescore ships, and eight hundred men to row them; (286) and when the Tyrians had come upon them in twelve ships, and the enemy's ships were dispersed, they took five hundred men prisoners and the reputation of all the citizens of Tyre was thereby increased; (287) but the king of Assyria returned, and placed guards at their rivers and aqueducts, who should hinder the Tyrians from drawing water. This continued for five years; and still the Tyrians bore the siege, and drank of the water they had out of the wells they dug.' And this is what is written in the Tyrian archives concerning Shalmaneser, the king of Assyria.

(288) But now the Cutheans, who removed into Samaria (for that is the name they have been called by to this time, because they were brought out of the country called Cuthah, which is a country of Persia, and there is a river of the same name in it), each of them, according to their nations, which were in number five, brought their own gods into Samaria, and by worshipping them, as was the custom of their own countries, they provoked Almighty God to be angry and displeased at them, (289) for a plague seized upon them, by which they were destroyed; and when they found no cure for their miseries, they learned by the oracle that they ought to worship Almighty God, as the method for their deliverance. So they sent ambassadors to the king of Assyria, and desired him to send them some of those priests of the Israelites whom he had taken captive. (290) And when he thereupon sent them, and the people were by them taught the laws and the holy worship of God, they worshipped him in a respectful manner, and the plague ceased immediately; and indeed they continue to make use of the very same customs to this very time, and are called in the Hebrew tongue *Cutheans;* but in the Greek *Samaritans.* (291) And when they see the Jews in prosperity, they pretend that they are changed, and allied to them, and call them kinsmen, as though they were derived from Joseph, and had by that means an original alliance with them: but when they see them falling into a low condition, they say they are no way related to them, and that the Jews have no right to expect any kindness or marks of kindred from them, but they declare that they are sojourners, that come from other countries. But of these we shall have a more seasonable opportunity to discourse hereafter.

BOOK TEN

(1) It was now the fourteenth year of the government of Hezekiah, king of the two tribes, when the king of Assyria, whose name was Sennacherib, made an expedition against him with a great army, and took all the cities of the tribes of Judah and Benjamin by force; (2) and when he was ready to bring his army against Jerusalem, Hezekiah sent ambassadors to him beforehand, and promised to submit, and pay what tribute he should appoint. Hereupon Sennacherib, when he heard of what offers the ambassadors made, resolved not to proceed in the war, but to accept of the proposals that were made him: and if he might receive three hundred talents of silver, and thirty talents of gold, he promised that he would depart in a friendly manner; and he gave security upon oath to the ambassadors that he would then do him no harm, but go away as he came. (3) So Hezekiah submitted, and emptied his treasures, and sent the money, as supposing he should be freed from his enemy, and from any farther distress about his kingdom. (4) Accordingly, the Assyrian king took it, and yet had no regard to what he had promised; but while he himself went to the war against the Egyptians and Ethiopians, he left his general Rabshakeh, and two other of his principal commanders, with great forces, to destroy Jerusalem. The names of the two other commanders were Tartan and Rabsaris.

(5) Now as soon as they were come before the walls, they pitched their camp, and sent messengers to Hezekiah, and desired that they might speak with him; but he did not himself come out to them for fear, but he sent three of his most intimate friends; the name of the one was Eliakim, who was over the kingdom, and Shebna, and Joab the recorder. (6) So these men came out, and stood over against the commanders of the Assyrian army; and when Rabshakeh saw them, he bade them go and speak to Hezekiah in the manner following: that Sennacherib, the great king, desires to know of him, on whom it is that he relies and depends, in flying from his lord, and will not hear him, nor admit his army into the city? Is it on account of the Egyptians, and in hopes that his army would be beaten by them? (7) Whereupon he lets him know, that if this be what he expects, he is a foolish man, and like one who leans on a broken reed; while such a one will not only fall down, but will have his hand pierced and hurt by it. That he ought to know he makes this expedition against him by the will of God, who hath granted this favour to him, that he shall overthrow the kingdom of Israel, and that in the very manner he shall destroy

those that are his subjects also. (8) When Rabshakeh had made this speech in the Hebrew tongue, for he was skilful in that language, Eliakim was afraid lest the multitude that heard him should be disturbed; so he desired him to speak in the Syrian tongue. But the general understanding what he meant, and perceiving the fear that he was in, he made his answer with a greater and louder voice, but in the Hebrew tongue; and said, that 'since they all heard what were the king's commands, they would consult their own advantage in delivering up themselves to us; (9) for it is plain that both you and your king dissuade the people from submitting by vain hopes, and so induce them to resist; but if you be courageous, and think to drive our forces away, I am ready to deliver to you two thousand of these horses that are with me for your use, if you can set as many horsemen on their back, and show your strength; but what you have not, you cannot produce. (10) Why, therefore, do you delay to deliver up yourselves to a superior force, who can take you without your consent – although it will be safer for you to deliver yourselves up voluntarily, while a forcible capture, when you are beaten, must appear more dangerous, and will bring further calamities upon you?'

(11) When the people, as well as the ambassadors, heard what the Assyrian commander said, they related it to Hezekiah, who thereupon put off his royal apparel, and clothed himself with sackcloth, and took the habit of a mourner, and, after the manner of his country, he fell upon his face, and besought God, and entreated him to assist them, now they had no other hope of relief. (12) He also sent some of his friends, and some of the priests, to the prophet Isaiah, and desired that he would pray to God, and offer sacrifices for their common deliverance, and so put up supplications to him, that he would have indignation at the expectations of their enemies, and have mercy upon his people. (13) And when the prophet had done accordingly, an oracle came from God to him, and encouraged the king and his friends that were about him; and foretold, that their enemies should be beaten without fighting, and should go away in an ignominious manner, and not with that insolence which they now show, (14) for that God would take care that they should be destroyed. He also foretold that Sennacherib, the king of Assyria, should fail of his purpose against Egypt, and that when he came home, he should perish by the sword.

(15) About the same time also the king of Assyria wrote an epistle to Hezekiah, in which he said he was a foolish man in supposing that he should escape from being his servant, since he had already brought under many and great nations; and he threatened, that, when he took him, he would utterly destroy him, unless he now opened the gates, and willingly received his army into Jerusalem. (16) When he had read this epistle, he despised it, on account of the trust that he had in God; but he rolled up the epistle, and laid it up within the temple; and as he made his farther prayers to God for the city, and for the

preservation of all the people, the prophet Isaiah said, that God had heard his prayer, and that he should not at this time be besieged by the king of Assyria; that, for the future, he might be secure of not being at all disturbed by him; and that the people might go on peaceably and without fear, with their husbandry and other affairs; (17) but after a little while, the king of Assyria, when he had failed of his treacherous designs against the Egyptians, returned home without success on the following occasion: he spent a long time in the siege of Pelusium; and when the banks that he had raised over against the walls were of a great height, and when he was ready to make an immediate assault upon them, but heard that Trihaka, king of the Ethiopians, was coming, and bringing great forces to aid the Egyptians, and was resolved to march through the desert, and so to fall directly upon the Assyrians, (18) this king Sennacherib was disturbed at the news; and, as I said before, left Pelusium, and returned back without success. Now concerning this Sennacherib, Herodotus also says, in the second book of his histories, how 'this king came against the Egyptian king, who was the priest of Vulcan; and that as he was besieging Pelusium, he broke up the siege on the following occasion: this Egyptian priest prayed to God, and God heard his prayer, and sent a judgment upon the Arabian king. (19) But in this Herodotus was mistaken when he called this king not king of the Assyrians, but of the Arabians; for he saith, that 'a multitude of mice gnawed to pieces in one night both the bows and the rest of the armour of the Assyrians; and that it was on that account that the king, when he had no bows left, drew his army from Pelusium.' (20) And Herodotus does indeed give us this history; nay, and Berosus, who wrote of the affairs of Chaldea, makes mention of this king Sennacherib, and that he ruled over the Assyrians, and that he made an expedition against all Asia and Egypt; and says thus:

(21) 'Now when Sennacherib was returning from his Egyptian war to Jerusalem, he found his army under Rabshakeh his general in danger [by a plague], for God had sent a pestilential distemper upon his army; and on the very first night of the siege, a hundred fourscore and five thousand, with their captains and generals, were destroyed. (22) So the king was in a great dread, and in a terrible agony at this calamity; and being in great fear for his whole army, he fled with the rest of his forces to his own kingdom, and to his city Nineveh; (23) and when he had abode there a little while, he was treacherously assaulted, and died by the hands of his elder sons, Adrammelech and Seraser, and was slain in his own temple, which was called Araske. Now these sons of his were driven away, on account of the murder of their father, by the citizens, and went into Armenia, while Assarachoddas took the kingdom of Sennacherib.' And this proved to be the conclusion of this Assyrian expedition against the people of Jerusalem.

CHAPTER 2

(24) Now Hezekiah being thus delivered, after a surprising manner, from the dread he was in, offered thank-offerings to God, with all his people because nothing else had destroyed some of their enemies, and made the rest so fearful of undergoing the same fate that they departed from Jerusalem, but that divine assistance; (25) yet, while he was very zealous and diligent about the worship of God, did he soon afterwards fall into a severe distemper, insomuch that the physicians despaired of him, and expected no good issue of his sickness, as neither did his friends; and besides the distemper itself, there was a very melancholy circumstance that disordered the king, which was the consideration that he was childless, and was going to die, and leave his house and his government without a successor of his own body; (26) so he was troubled at the thoughts of this his condition, and lamented himself, and entreated of God that he would prolong his life for a little while till he had some children, and not suffer him to depart this life before he was become a father. (27) Hereupon God had mercy upon him, and accepted of his supplication, because the trouble he was under at his supposed death was not because he was soon to leave the advantages he enjoyed in the kingdom; nor did he on that account pray that he might have a longer life afforded him, but in order to have sons that might receive the government after him. And God sent Isaiah the prophet, and commanded him to inform Hezekiah, that within three days' time he should get clear of his distemper, and should survive it fifteen years, and that he should have children also. (28) Now upon the prophet's saying this as God had commanded him, he could hardly believe it, both on account of the distemper he was under, which was very sore, and by reason of the surprising nature of what was told him; so he desired that Isaiah would give him some sign or wonder, that he might believe him in what he had said, and be sensible that he came from God: for things that are beyond expectation, and greater than our hopes, are made credible by actions of the like nature. (29) And when Isaiah had asked him what sign he desired to be exhibited, he desired that he would make the shadow of the sun, which he had already made to go down ten steps [or degrees] in his house, to return again to the same place, and to make it as it was before. And when the prophet prayed to God to exhibit this sign to the king, he saw what he desired to see, and was freed from his distemper, and went up to the temple, where he worshipped God and made vows to him.

(30) At this time it was that the dominion of the Assyrians was overthrown by the Medes; but of these things I shall treat elsewhere. But the king of Babylon, whose name was Baladan, sent ambassadors to Hezekiah with presents, and desired he would be his ally and his friend. (31) So he received the ambassadors

gladly, and made them a feast, and showed them his treasures and his armoury, and the other wealth he was possessed of, in precious stones and in gold, and gave them presents to be carried to Baladan, and sent them back to him. (32) Upon which the prophet Isaiah came to him, and inquired of him whence those ambassadors came: to which he replied, that they came from Babylon, from the king; and that he had showed them all he had, that by the shift of his riches and forces he might thereby guess at [the plenty he was in], and be able to inform the king of it. (33) But the prophet rejoined and said – 'Know thou, that after a little while, these riches of thine shall be carried away to Babylon, and thy posterity shall be made eunuchs there, and lose their manhood, and be servants to the king of Babylon; for that God foretold such things would come to pass.' (34) Upon which words Hezekiah was troubled, and said, that he was himself unwilling that his nation should fall into such calamities; yet since it is not possible to alter what God had determined, he prayed that there might be peace while he lived. Berosus also makes mention of this Baladan, king of Babylon. (35) Now as to this prophet [Isaiah], he was by the confession of all, a divine and wonderful man in speaking truth; and out of the assurance that he had never written what was false, he wrote down all his prophecies, and left them behind him in books, that their accomplishment might be judged of from the events by posterity. Nor did this prophet do so alone, but the others, which were twelve in number, did the same. And whatsoever is done among us, whether it be good or whether it be bad, comes to pass according to their prophecies; but of every one of these we shall speak hereafter.

CHAPTER 3

(36) When king Hezekiah had survived the interval of time already mentioned, and had dwelt all that time in peace, he died, having completed fifty-four years of his life, and reigned twenty-nine. (37) But when his son Manasseh, whose mother's name was Hephzibah, of Jerusalem, had taken the kingdom, he departed from the conduct of his father, and fell into a course of life quite contrary thereto, and showed himself in his manners most wicked in all respects, and omitted no sort of impiety, but imitated those transgressions of the Israelites, by the commission of which against God, they had been destroyed; for he was so hardy as to defile the temple of God, and the city, and the whole country; (38) for, by setting out from a contempt of God, he barbarously slew all the righteous men that were among the Hebrews; nor would he spare the prophets, for he every day slew some of them, till Jerusalem was overflown with blood. (39) So God was angry at these proceedings, and sent prophets to the king, and to the multitude, by whom he threatened the very same calamities to them which their brethren the Israelites, upon the like affronts

offered to God, were now under. But these men would not believe their words, by which belief they might have reaped the advantage of escaping all those miseries; yet did they in earnest learn that what the prophets had told them was true.

(40) And when they persevered in the same course of life, God raised up war against them from the king of Babylon and Chaldea, who sent an army against Judea, and laid waste the country; and caught king Manasseh by treachery, and ordered him to be brought to him, and had him under his power to inflict what punishment he pleased upon him. (41) But then it was that Manasseh perceived what a miserable condition he was in, and esteeming himself the cause of all, he besought God to render his enemy human and merciful to him. Accordingly, God heard his prayer, and granted him what he prayed for. So Manasseh was released by the king of Babylon, and escaped the danger he was in; (42) and when he was come to Jerusalem, he endeavoured, if it were possible, to cast out of his memory those his former sins against God, of which he now repented, and to apply himself to a very religious life. He sanctified the temple, and purged the city, and for the remainder of his days he was intent on nothing but to return his thanks to God for his deliverance, and to preserve him propitious to him all his life long. (43) He also instructed the multitude to do the same, as having very nearly experienced what a calamity he was fallen into by a contrary conduct. He also rebuilt the altar, and offered the legal sacrifices, as Moses commanded; (44) and when he had re-established what concerned the divine worship, as it ought to be, he took care of the security of Jerusalem: he did not only repair the old walls with great diligence, but added another wall to the former. He also built very lofty towers, and the garrisoned places before the city he strengthened, not only in other respects, but with provisions of all sorts that they wanted: (45) and indeed, when he had changed his former course, he so led his life for the time to come, that from the time of his return to piety towards God, he was deemed a happy man, and a pattern for imitation. (46) When therefore he had lived sixty-seven years, he departed this life, having reigned fifty-five years, and was buried in his own garden; and the kingdom came to his son Amon, whose mother's name was Meshulemeth, of the city of Jotbath.

CHAPTER 4

(47) This Amon imitated those works of his father which he insolently did when he was young: so he had a conspiracy made against him by his own servants, and was slain in his own house, when he had lived twenty-four years, and of them had reigned two; (48) but the multitude punished those that slew Amon, and buried him with his father, and gave the kingdom to his son Josiah,

who was eight years old. His mother was of the city of Boscath, and her name was Jedidah. (49) He was of a most excellent disposition, and naturally virtuous, and followed the actions of King David, as a pattern and a rule to him in the whole conduct of his life; (50) and when he was twelve years old he gave demonstrations of his religious and righteous behaviour; for he brought the people to a sober way of living, and exhorted them to leave off the opinion they had of their idols, because they were not gods, but to worship their own God; and by reflecting on the actions of his progenitors, he prudently corrected what they did wrong, like a very elderly man, and like one abundantly able to understand what was fit to be done, and what he found they had well done, he observed all the country over, and imitated the same; (51) and thus he acted in following the wisdom and sagacity of his own nature, and in compliance with the advice and instruction of the elders; for by following the laws it was that he succeeded so well in the order of his government, and in piety with regard to the divine worship: and this happened because the transgressions of the former kings were seen no more, but quite vanished away; (52) for the king went about the city and the whole country, and cut down the groves, which were devoted to strange gods, and overthrew their altars; and if there were any gifts dedicated to them by his forefathers, he made them ignominious, and plucked them down; (53) and by this means he brought the people back from their opinion about them to the worship of God. He also offered his accustomed sacrifices and burnt offerings upon the altar. Moreover, he ordained certain judges and overseers, that they might order the matters to them severally belonging, and have regard to justice above all things, and distribute it with the same concern they would have about their own soul. (54) He also sent over all the country, and desired such as pleased to bring gold and silver for the repairs of the temple according to everyone's inclinations and abilities; (55) and when the money was brought in, he made one Maaseiah the governor of the city, and Shaphan the scribe, and Joah the recorder, and Eliakim the high priest, curators of the temple, and of the charges contributed thereto; (56) who made no delay, nor put the work off at all, but prepared architects, and whatsoever was proper for those repairs, and set closely about the work. So the temple was repaired by this means, and became a public demonstration of the king's piety.

(57) But when he was now in the eighteenth year of his reign, he sent to Eliakim the high priest, and gave order, that out of what money was overplus, he should cast cups and dishes and vials, for ministration [in the temple]; and besides, that they should bring all the gold or silver which was among the treasures, and expend that also in making cups and like vessels; (58) but as the high priest was bringing out the gold, he lighted upon the holy books of Moses that were laid up in the temple; and when he had brought them out, he gave them to Shaphan the scribe, who, when he had read them, came to the king

and informed him that all was finished which he had ordered to be done. He also read over the books to him, (59) who, when he had heard them read, rent his garment, and called for Eliakim the high priest, and for [Shaphan] the scribe, and for certain [other] of his most particular friends, and sent them to Huldah the prophetess, the wife of Shallum (which Shallum was a man of dignity, and of an eminent family), and bade them go to her and say that [he desired] she would appease God, and endeavour to render him propitious to them, for that there was cause to fear lest, upon the transgression of the laws of Moses by their forefathers, they should be in peril of going into captivity, and of being cast out of their own country; lest they should be in want of all things, and so end their days miserably. (60) When the prophetess had heard this from the messengers that were sent to her by the king, she bade them go back to the king, and say that God had already given sentence against them, to destroy the people, and cast them out of their country, and deprive them of all the happiness they enjoyed; which sentence none could set aside by any prayers of theirs, since it was passed on account of their transgressions of the laws, and of their not having repented in so long a time, while the prophets had exhorted them to amend, and had foretold the punishments that would ensue on their impious practices; which (61) threatening God would certainly execute upon them, that they might be persuaded that he is God, and had not deceived them in any respect as to what he had denounced by his prophets; that yet because Josiah was a righteous man, he would at present delay those calamities, but that, after his death, he would send on the multitude what miseries he had determined for them.

(62) So these messengers, upon this prophecy of the woman, came and told it to the king; whereupon he sent to the people everywhere, and ordered that the priests and the Levites should come together to Jerusalem; and commanded that those of every age should be present also; (63) and when they were gathered together, he first read to them the holy books; after which he stood upon the pulpit, in the midst of the multitude, and obliged them to make a covenant with an oath, that they would worship God and keep the law of Moses. (64) Accordingly, they gave their assent willingly, and undertook to do what the king had recommended to them. (65) So they immediately offered sacrifices, and that after an acceptable manner, and besought God to be gracious and merciful to them. He also enjoined the high priest, that if there remained in the temple any vessel that was dedicated to idols, or to foreign gods, they should cast it out; so when a great number of such vessels were got together, he burnt them, and scattered their ashes abroad, and slew the priests of the idols that were not of the family of Aaron.

(66) And when he had done thus in Jerusalem, he came into the country, and utterly destroyed what buildings had been made therein by King Jeroboam,

in honour of strange gods; and he burnt the bones of the false prophets upon that altar which Jeroboam first built; (67) and, as the prophet [Jadon], who came to Jeroboam when he was offering sacrifice, and when all the people heard him, foretold what would come to pass, viz., that a certain man of the house of David, Josiah by name, should do what is here mentioned. And it happened that those predictions took effect after three hundred and sixty-one years.

(68) After these things Josiah went also to such other Israelites as had escaped captivity and slavery under the Assyrians, and persuaded them to desist from their impious practices, and to leave off the honours they paid to strange gods, but to worship rightly their own Almighty God, and adhere to him. (69) He also searched the houses and the villages and the cities, out of a suspicion that somebody might have one idol or other in private; nay, indeed, he took away the chariots [of the sun] that were set up in his royal palace, which his predecessors had framed, and what thing soever there was besides which they worshipped as a god. (70) And when he had thus purged all the country, he called the people to Jerusalem, and there celebrated the feast of unleavened bread, and that called the Passover. He also gave the people for paschal sacrifices, young kids of the goats, and lambs, thirty thousand, and three thousand oxen for burnt offerings. (71) The principal of the priests also gave to the priests against the passover two thousand and six hundred lambs; the principal of the Levites also gave to the Levites five thousand lambs and five hundred oxen, (72) by which means there was great plenty of sacrifices; and they offered those sacrifices according to the laws of Moses, while every priest explained the matter, and ministered to the multitude. And indeed there had been no other festival thus celebrated by the Hebrews from the time of Samuel the prophet; and the plenty of sacrifices now was the occasion that all things were performed according to the laws, and according to the custom of their forefathers. (73) So when Josiah had after this lived in peace, nay, in riches and reputation also, among all men, he ended his life in the manner following.

CHAPTER 5

(74) Now Neco, king of Egypt, raised an army, and marched to the river Euphrates, in order to fight with the Medes and Babylonians, who had overthrown the dominion of the Assyrians, for he had a desire to reign over Asia. (75) Now when he was come to the city Mendes, which belonged to the kingdom of Josiah, he brought an army to hinder him from passing through his own country, in his expedition against the Medes. Now Neco sent a herald to Josiah, and told him, that he had not made this expedition against him, but was making haste to Euphrates; and desired that he would not provoke him to fight against him, because he obstructed his march to the place whither he had

resolved to go. (76) But Josiah did not admit of this advice of Neco, but put himself into a posture to hinder him from his intended march. I suppose it was fate that pushed him on this conduct, that it might take an occasion against him; (77) for as he was setting his army in array, and rode about in his chariot, from one wing of his army to another, one of the Egyptians shot an arrow at him, and put an end to his eagerness of fighting; for, being sorely wounded, he commanded a retreat to be sounded for his army, and returned to Jerusalem, and died of that wound; and was magnificently buried in the sepulchre of his fathers, when he had lived thirty-nine years, and of them had reigned thirty-one. (78) But all the people mourned greatly for him, lamenting and grieving on his account many days; and Jeremiah the prophet composed an elegy to lament him, which is extant till this time also. (79) Moreover, this prophet denounced beforehand the sad calamities that were coming upon the city. He also left behind him in writing a description of that destruction of our nation which has lately happened in our days, and the taking of Babylon; nor was he the only prophet who delivered such predictions beforehand to the multitude; but so did Ezekiel also, who was the first person that wrote, and left behind him in writing two books concerning these events. (80) Now these two prophets were priests by birth, but of them Jeremiah dwelt in Jerusalem, from the thirteenth year of the reign of Josiah until the city and temple were utterly destroyed. However as to what befell this prophet, we will relate it in its proper place.

(81) Upon the death of Josiah, which we have already mentioned, his son Jehoahaz by name, took the kingdom, being about twenty-three years old. He reigned in Jerusalem; and his mother was Hamutal, of the city Libnah. He was an impious man, and impure in his course of life; (82) but as the king of Egypt returned from the battle, he sent for Jehoahaz to come to him, to the city called Hamath, which belongs to Syria; and when he was come, he put him in bands, and delivered the kingdom to a brother of his by the father's side, whose name was Eliakim, and changed his name to Jehoiakim, and laid a tribute upon the land of a hundred talents of silver, and a talent of gold; (83) and this sum of money Jehoiakim paid by way of tribute; but Neco carried away Jehoahaz into Egypt, where he died, when he had reigned three months and ten days. Now Jehoiakim's mother was called Zebudah, of the city Rumah. He was of a wicked disposition, and ready to do mischief; nor was he either religions towards God or good-natured towards men.

CHAPTER 6

(84) Now in the fourth year of the reign of Jehoiakim, one whose name was Nebuchadnezzar took the government over the Babylonians, who at the same time went up with a great army to the city Carchemish, which was at Euphrates, upon a resolution he had taken to fight with Neco, king of Egypt, under whom all Syria then was. (85) And when Neco understood the intention of the king of Babylon, and that this expedition was made against him, he did not despise his attempt, but made haste with a great band of men to Euphrates to defend himself from Nebuchadnezzar; (86) and when they had joined battle, he was beaten, and lost many ten thousands [of his soldiers] in the battle. So the king of Babylon passed over Euphrates, and took all Syria, as far as Pelusium, excepting Judea. (87) But when Nebuchadnezzar had already reigned four years, which was the eighth of Jehoiakim's government over the Hebrews, the king of Babylon made an expedition with mighty forces against the Jews, and required tribute of Jehoiakim, and threatened on his refusal, to make war against him. He was affrighted at his threatening, and bought his peace with money, and brought the tribute he was ordered to bring for three years.

(88) But on the third year, upon hearing that the king of the Babylonians made an expedition against the Egyptians, he did not pay his tribute; yet was he disappointed of his hope, for the Egyptians durst not fight at this time. (89) And indeed the prophet Jeremiah foretold every day, how vainly they relied on their hopes from Egypt, and how the city would be overthrown by the king of Babylon, and Jehoiakim the king would be subdued by him. (90) But what he thus spake proved to be of no advantage to them, because there were none that should escape; for both the multitude, and the rulers, when they heard him, had no concern about what they heard; but being displeased at what was said, as if the prophet were a diviner against the king, they accused Jeremiah, and bringing him before the court, they required that a sentence and a punishment might be given against him. (91) Now all the rest gave their votes for his condemnation, but the elders refused, who prudently sent away the prophet from the court [of the prison], and persuaded the rest to do Jeremiah no harm; (92) for they said that he was not the only person who foretold what would come to the city, but that Micah signified the same before him, as well as many others, none of whom suffered anything of the kings that then reigned, but were honoured as the prophets of God. (93) So they mollified the multitude with these words, and delivered Jeremiah from the punishment to which he was condemned. Now when this prophet had written all his prophecies, and the people were fasting, and assembled at the temple, on the ninth month of

the fifth year of Jehoiakim, he read the book he had composed of his predictions of what was to befall the city and the temple and the multitude; (94) and when the rulers heard of it, they took the book from him, and bade him and Baruch the scribe to go their ways, lest they should be discovered by one or other; but they carried the book, and gave it to the king; so he gave order, in the presence of his friends, that his scribe should take it and read it. (95) When the king heard what it contained, he was angry, and tore it, and cast it into the fire, where it was consumed. He also commanded that they should seek for Jeremiah and Baruch the scribe, and bring them to him, that they might be punished. However, they escaped his anger.

(96) Now a little time afterwards, the king of Babylon made an expedition against Jehoiakim, whom he received [into the city], and this out of fear of the foregoing predictions of this prophet, as supposing he should suffer nothing that was terrible, because he neither shut the gates, nor fought against him; (97) yet when he was come into the city, he did not observe the covenants he had made; but he slew such as were in the flower of their age, and such as were of the greatest dignity, together with their king Jehoiakim, whom he commanded to be thrown before the walls, without any burial; and made his son Jehoiachin king of the country and of the city: (98) he also took the principal persons in dignity for captives, three thousand in number, and led them away to Babylon; among whom was the prophet Ezekiel, who was then but young. And this was the end of king Jehoiakim, when he had lived thirty-six years, and of them reigned eleven. But Jehoiachin succeeded him in the kingdom, whose mother's name was Nehushta; she was a citizen of Jerusalem. He reigned three months and ten days.

CHAPTER 7

(99) But a terror seized on the king of Babylon, who had given the kingdom to Jehoiachin, and that immediately; he was afraid that he should bear him a grudge, because of his killing his father, and thereupon should make the country revolt from him; wherefore he sent an army, and besieged Jehoiachin in Jerusalem; (100) but because he was of a gentle and just disposition, he did not desire to see the city endangered on his account, but he took his mother and kindred, and delivered them to the commanders sent by the king of Babylon, and accepted of their oaths, that neither should they suffer any harm, nor the city; (101) which agreement they did not observe for a single year, for the king of Babylon did not keep it, but gave orders to his generals to take all that were in the city captives, both the youth and the handicraftsmen, and bring them bound to him; their number was ten thousand eight hundred and thirty-two; as also Jehoiachin, and his mother and friends; (102) and when these were

brought to him, he kept them in custody, and appointed Jehoiachin's uncle, Zedekiah, to be king; and made him take an oath, that he would certainly keep the kingdom for him, and make no innovation, nor have any league of friendship with the Egyptians.

(103) Now Zedekiah was twenty-and-one years old when he took the government; and had the same mother with his brother Jehoiachin, but was a despiser of justice and of his duty, for truly those of the same age with him were wicked about him, and the whole multitude did what unjust and insolent things they pleased; (104) for which reason the prophet Jeremiah came often to him, and protested to him, and insisted, that he must leave off his impieties and transgressions, and take care of what was right, and neither give ear to the rulers (among whom were wicked men) nor give credit to their false prophets who deluded them, as if the king of Babylon would make no more war against him, and as if the Egyptians would make war against him, and conquer him, since what they said was not true; and the events would not prove such [as they expected]. (105) Now as to Zedekiah himself, while he heard the prophet speak, he believed him, and agreed to everything as true, and supposed it was for his advantage; but then his friends perverted him, and dissuaded him from what the prophet advised, and obliged him to do what they pleased. (106) Ezekiel also foretold in Babylon what calamities were coming upon the people, which when he heard, he sent accounts of them unto Jerusalem; but Zedekiah did not believe their prophecies, for the reason following: it happened that the two prophets agreed with one another in what they said as in all other things, that the city should be taken, and Zedekiah himself should be taken captive; but Ezekiel disagreed with him, and said, that Zedekiah should not see Babylon; while Jeremiah said to him, that the king of Babylon should carry him away thither in bonds; (107) and because they did not both say the same thing as to this circumstance, he disbelieved what they both appeared to agree in, and condemned them as not speaking truth therein, although all the things foretold him did come to pass according to their prophecies, as we shall show upon a fitter opportunity.

(108) Now when Zedekiah had preserved the league of mutual assistance he had made with the Babylonians for eight years, he brake it, and revolted to the Egyptians, in hopes, by their assistance, of overcoming the Babylonians. (109) When the king of Babylon knew this, he made war against him: he laid his country waste, and took his fortified towns, and came to the city Jerusalem itself to besiege it: (110) but when the king of Egypt heard what circumstances Zedekiah his ally was in, he took a great army with him, and came into Judea, as if he would raise the siege; upon which the king of Babylon departed from Jerusalem, and met the Egyptians, and joined battle with them, and beat them; and when he had put them to flight, he pursued them, and drove them out of

all Syria. (111) Now as soon as the king of Babylon was departed from Jerusalem, the false prophets deceived Zedekiah, and said, that the king of Babylon would not any more make war against him or his people, nor remove them out of their own country into Babylon; and that those then in captivity would return, with all those vessels of the temple, of which the king of Babylon had despoiled that temple. (112) But Jeremiah came among them, and prophesied what contradicted those predictions, and what proved to be true, that they did ill, and deluded the king; that the Egyptians would be of no advantage to them, but that the king of Babylon would renew the war against Jerusalem, and besiege it again, and would destroy the people by famine, and carry away those that remained into captivity, and would take away what they had as spoils, and would carry off those riches that were in the temple; nay, that besides this, he would burn it, and utterly overthrow the city, and that they should serve him and his posterity seventy years, (113) that then the Persians and the Medes should put an end to their servitude, and overthrow the Babylonians; 'and that we shall be dismissed, and return to this land, and rebuild the temple, and restore Jerusalem.' (14) When Jeremiah said this, the greater part believed him; but the rulers, and those that were wicked, despised him, as one disordered in his senses. Now he had resolved to go elsewhere, to his own country, which was called Anathoth, and was twenty furlongs distant from Jerusalem; and as he was going, one of the rulers met him, and seized upon him, and accused him falsely, as though he were going as a deserter to the Babylonians; (115) but Jeremiah said that he accused him falsely, and added, that he was only going to his own country; but the other would not believe him, but seized upon him, and led him away to the rulers, and laid an accusation against him, under whom he endured all sorts of torments and tortures, and was reserved to be punished; and this was the condition he was in for some time, while he suffered what I have already described unjustly.

(116) Now in the ninth year of the reign of Zedekiah, on the tenth day of the tenth month, the king of Babylon made a second expedition against Jerusalem, and lay before it eighteen months, and besieged it with the utmost application. There came upon them also two of the greatest calamities, at the same time that Jerusalem was besieged, a famine and a pestilential distemper, and made great havoc of them: (117) and though the prophet Jeremiah was in prison, he did not rest, but cried out and proclaimed aloud, and exhorted the multitude to open their gates, and admit the king of Babylon, for that, if they did so, they should be preserved, and their whole families; but if they did not so, they should be destroyed; (118) and he foretold, that if anyone stayed in the city, he should certainly perish by one of these ways – either be consumed by the famine, or slain by the enemy's sword; but that if he would fly to the enemy he should escape death: (119) yet did not these rulers who heard believe

him, even when they were in the midst of their sore calamities; but they came to the king, and in their anger informed him what Jeremiah said, and accused him, and complained of the prophet as of a madman, and one that disheartened their minds, and, by the denunciation of miseries, weakened the alacrity of the multitude, who were otherwise ready to expose themselves to dangers for him, and for their country, while he, in a way of threatening, warned them to flee to the enemy, and told them that the city should certainly be taken, and be utterly destroyed.

(120) But for the king himself, he was not at all irritated against Jeremiah, such was his gentle and righteous disposition; yet, that he might not be engaged in a quarrel with those rulers at such a time, by opposing what they intended, he let them do with the prophet whatsoever they would: (121) whereupon, when the king had granted them such a permission, they presently came into the prison and took him, and let him down with a cord into a pit full of mire, that he might be suffocated, and die of himself. So he stood up to the neck in the mire, which was all about him, and so continued: (122) but there was one of the king's servants, who was in esteem with him, an Ethiopian by descent, who told the king what a state the prophet was in, and said, that his friends and his rulers had done evil in putting the prophet into the mire, and by this means contriving against him that he should suffer a death more bitter than that by his bonds only. (123) When the king heard this, he repented of his having delivered up the prophet to the rulers, and bade the Ethiopian take thirty men of the king's guards, and cords with them, and whatsoever else they understood to be necessary for the prophet's preservation, and to draw him up immediately. So the Ethiopian took the men that he was ordered to take, and drew up the prophet out of the mire, and left him at liberty in the prison.

(124) But when the king had sent to call him privately, and inquired what he could say to him from God, which might be suitable to his present circumstances, and desired him to inform him of it, Jeremiah replied, that he had somewhat to say; but he said withal, he should not be believed, nor, if he admonished them, should be hearkened to; 'for,' said he, 'thy friends have determined to destroy me, as though I had been guilty of some wickedness: and where are now those men who deceived us, and said that the king of Babylon would not come and fight against us any more? But I am afraid now to speak the truth, lest thou shouldest condemn me to die.' (125) And when the king had assured him upon oath that he would neither himself put him to death, nor deliver him up to the rulers, he became bold upon that assurance that was given him, and gave him this advice: that he should deliver the city up to the Babylonians; (126) and he said that it was God who prophesied this by him, that [he must do so], if he would be preserved, and escape out of the

danger he was in, and that then neither should the city fall to the ground, nor should the temple be burned; but that [if he disobeyed] he would be the cause of these miseries coming upon the citizens, and of the calamity that would befall his whole house. (127) When the king heard this, he said that he would willingly do what he persuaded him to, and what he declared would be to his advantage, but that he was afraid of those of his own country that had fallen away to the Babylonians; lest he should be accused by them to the king of Babylon, and be punished. (128) But the prophet encouraged him, and said he had no cause to fear such punishment, for that he should not have the experience of any misfortune, if he would deliver all up to the Babylonians, neither himself nor his children nor his wives, and that the temple should then continue unhurt. (129) So when Jeremiah had said this, the king let him go, and charged him to betray what they had resolved on to none of the citizens, nor to tell any of these matters to any of the rulers, if they should have learned that he had been sent for, and should inquire of him what it was that he was sent for, and what he had said to him; but to pretend to them that he besought him that he might not be kept in bonds and in prison. (130) And indeed he said so to them, for they came to the prophet, and asked him what advice it was that he came to give the king relating to them: and thus I have finished what concerns this matter.

CHAPTER 8

(131) Now the king of Babylon was very intent and earnest upon the siege of Jerusalem; and he erected towers upon great banks of earth and from them repelled those that stood upon the walls: he also made a great number of such banks round about the whole city, the height of which was equal to those walls. (132) However, those that were within bore the siege with courage and alacrity, for they were not discouraged either by the famine or by the pestilential distemper, but were of cheerful minds in the prosecution of the war, although those miseries within oppressed them also; and they did not suffer themselves to be terrified, either by the contrivances of the enemy or by their engines of war, but contrived still different engines to oppose all the other withal, (133) till indeed there seemed to be an entire struggle between the Babylonians and the people of Jerusalem, who had the greater sagacity and skill; the former party supposing they should be thereby too hard for the other, for the destruction of the city; the latter placing their hopes of deliverance in nothing else but in persevering in such inventions, in opposition to the other, as might demonstrate the enemy's engines were useless to them; (134) and this siege they endured for eighteen months, until they were destroyed by the famine, and by the darts which the enemy threw at them from the towers.

(135) Now the city was taken on the ninth day of the fourth month, in the eleventh year of the reign of Zedekiah. They were indeed only generals of the king of Babylon, to whom Nebuchadnezzar committed the care of the siege, for he abode himself in the city of Riblah. The names of these generals who ravaged and subdued Jerusalem, if anyone desire to know them, were these: Nergal Sharezer, Sangar Nebo, Rabsaris, Sarsechim, and Rabmag; (136) and when the city was taken about midnight, and the enemy's generals were entered into the temple, and when Zedekiah was sensible of it, he took his wives and his children, and his captains and friends, and with them fled out of the city through the fortified ditch, and through the desert; (137) and when certain of the deserters had informed the Babylonians of this, at break of day, they made haste to pursue after Zedekiah, and overtook him not far from Jericho, and encompassed him about. But for those friends and captains of Zedekiah who had fled out of the city with him, when they saw their enemies near them, they left him and dispersed themselves, some one way and some another, and every one resolved to save himself; (138) so the enemy took Zedekiah alive, when he was deserted by all but a few, with his children and his wives, and brought him to the king. When he was come, Nebuchadnezzar began to call him a wicked wretch, and covenant-breaker, and one that had forgotten his former words, when he promised to keep the country for him. (139) He also reproached him for his ingratitude, that when he had received the kingdom from him, who had taken it from Jehoiachin, and given it him, he had made use of the power he gave him against him that gave it: 'but,' said he, 'God is great, who hateth that conduct of thine, and hath brought thee under us.' (140) And when he had used these words to Zedekiah, he commanded his sons and his friends to be slain, while Zedekiah and the rest of the captains looked on; after which he put out the eyes of Zedekiah, and bound him, and carried him to Babylon. (141) And these things happened to him, as Jeremiah and Ezekiel had foretold to him, that he should be caught, and brought before the king of Babylon, and should speak to him face to face, and should see his eyes with his own eyes; and thus far did Jeremiah prophesy. But he was also made blind, and brought to Babylon but did not see it, according to the prediction of Ezekiel.

(142) We have said thus much because it was sufficient to show the nature of God to such as are ignorant of it that it is various, and acts many different ways, and that all events happen after a regular manner, in their proper season, and that it foretells what must come to pass. It is also sufficient to show the ignorance and incredulity of men, whereby they are not permitted to foresee anything that is future, and are, without any guard, exposed to calamities, so that it is impossible for them to avoid the experience of those calamities.

(143) And after this manner have the kings of David's race ended their lives,

being in number twenty-one until the last king, who all together reigned five hundred and fourteen years, and six months, and ten days: of whom Saul, who was their first king, retained the government twenty years, though he was not of the same tribe with the rest.

(144) And now it was that the king of Babylon sent Nebuzaradan, the general of his army, to Jerusalem, to pillage the temple; who had it also in command to burn it and the royal palace, and to lay the city even with the ground, and to transplant the people into Babylon. (145) Accordingly, he came to Jerusalem, in the eleventh year of king Zedekiah, and pillaged the temple, and carried out the vessels of God, both gold and silver, and particularly that large laver which Solomon dedicated, as also the pillars of brass, and their chapiters, with the golden tablets and the candlesticks: (146) and when he had carried these off, he set fire to the temple in the fifth month, the first day of the month, in the eleventh year of the reign of Zedekiah, and in the eighteenth year of Nebuchadnezzar; he also burnt the palace, and overthrew the city. (147) Now the temple was burnt four hundred and seventy years, six months, and ten days, after it was built. It was then one thousand and sixty-two years, six months, and ten days, from the departure out of Egypt; and from the Deluge to the destruction of the temple, the whole interval was one thousand nine hundred and fifty-seven years, six months, and ten days; (148) but from the generation of Adam until this befell the temple, there were three thousand five hundred and thirteen years, six months, and ten days; so great was the number of years hereto belonging; and what actions were done during these years, we have particularly related. (149) But the general of the Babylonian king now overthrew the city to the very foundations, and removed all the people, and took for prisoners the high priest Seraiah, and Zephaniah, the priest that was next to him and the rulers that guarded the temple, who were three in number, and the eunuch who was over the armed men, and seven friends of Zedekiah, and his scribe, and sixty other rulers; all whom, together with the vessels they had pillaged, he carried to the king of Babylon to Riblah, a city of Syria. (150) So the king commanded the heads of the high priest and of the rulers to be cut off there; but he himself led all the captives and Zedekiah to Babylon. He also led Josedek the high priest, away bound. He was the son of Seraiah, the high priest, whom the king of Babylon had slain in Riblah, a city of Syria, as we just now related.

(151) And now, because we have enumerated the succession of the kings, and who they were, and how long they reigned, I think it necessary to set down the names of the high priests, and who they were that succeeded one another in the high priesthood under the kings. (152) The first high priest then at the temple which Solomon built was Zadok; after him his son Achimas received that dignity; after Achimas was Azarias; his son was Joram,

and Joram's son was Isus; after him was Axioramus; (153) his son was Phideas, and Phideas' son was Sudeas, and Sudeas' son was Juelus, and Juelus' son was Jotham, and Jotham's son was Urias, and Urias' son was Nerias, and Nerias' son was Odeas, and his son was Sallumus, and Sallumus' son was Elcias, and his son [was Azarias, and his son] was Sareas, and his son was Josedec, who was carried captive to Babylon. All these received the high priesthood by succession, the sons from their father.

(154) When the king was come to Babylon, he kept Zedekiah in prison until he died, and buried him magnificently, and dedicated the vessels he had pillaged out of the temple of Jerusalem to his own gods, and planted the people in the country of Babylon, but freed the high priest from his bonds.

CHAPTER 9

(155) Now the general of the army, Nebuzaradan, when he had carried the people of the Jews into captivity, left the poor, and those that had deserted, in the country; and made one, whose name was Gedaliah, the son of Ahikam, a person of a noble family, their governor; which Gedaliah was of a gentle and righteous disposition. (156) He also commanded them that they should cultivate the ground, and pay an appointed tribute to the king. He also took Jeremiah the prophet out of prison, and would have persuaded him to go along with him to Babylon, for that he had been enjoined by the king to supply him with whatsoever he wanted; and if he did not like to do so, he desired him to inform him where he resolved to dwell, that he might signify the same to the king. (157) But the prophet had no mind to follow him, nor to dwell anywhere else, but would gladly live in the ruins of his country, and in the miserable remains of it. When the general understood what his purpose was, he enjoined Gedaliah whom he left behind, to take all possible care of him, and to supply him with whatsoever he wanted; so when he had given him rich presents, he dismissed him. (158) Accordingly, Jeremiah abode in a city of that country, which was called Mispah; and desired of Nebuzaradan that he would set at liberty his disciple Baruch, the son of Neriah, one of a very eminent family, and exceeding skilful in the language of his country.

(159) When Nebuzaradan had done thus, he made haste to Babylon; but as to those that fled away during the siege of Jerusalem, and had been scattered over the country, when they heard that the Babylonians were gone away, and had left a remnant in the land of Jerusalem, and those such as were to cultivate the same, they came together from all parts to Gedaliah to Mispah. (160) Now the rulers that were over them were Johanan, the son of Kareah, and Jezaniah, and Seraiah, and others beside them. Now there was of the royal family one Ishmael, a wicked man and very crafty, who during the siege of Jerusalem, fled

to Baalis, king of the Ammonites, and abode with him during that time; (161) and Gedaliah persuaded them, now they were there, to stay with him, and to have no fear of the Babylonians, for that if they would cultivate the country, they should suffer no harm. This he assured them of by oath; and said that they should have him for their patron, and if any disturbance should arise, they should find him ready to defend them. (162) He also advised them to dwell in any city, as every one of them pleased; and that they would send men along with his own servants, and rebuild their houses upon the old foundations, and dwell there; and he admonished them beforehand, that they should make preparation, while the season lasted, of corn and wine and oil, that they might have whereon to feed during the winter. When he had thus discoursed to them, he dismissed them, that everyone might dwell in what part of the country he pleased.

(163) Now when this report was spread abroad as far as the nations that bordered on Judea, that Gedaliah kindly entertained those that came to him, after they had fled away, upon this [only] condition, that they should pay tribute to the king of Babylon, they also came readily to Gedaliah, and inhabited the country. (164) And when Johanan, and the rulers that were with him, observed the country, and the humanity of Gedaliah, they were exceedingly in love with him, and told him that Baalis, the king of the Ammonites, had sent Ishmael to kill him by treachery, and secretly, that he might have the dominion over the Israelites, as being of the royal family; (165) and they said that he might deliver himself from this treacherous design, if he would give them leave to slay Ishmael, and nobody should know it; for they told him they were afraid that when he was killed by the other, the entire ruin of the remaining strength of the Israelites would ensue. (166) But he professed that he did not believe what they said, when they told him of such a treacherous design in a man that had been well treated by him; because it was not probable that one who, under such a want of all things, had failed of nothing that was necessary for him, should be found so wicked and ungrateful towards his benefactor, that when it would be an instance of wickedness in him not to save him had he been treacherously assaulted by others, to endeavour, and that earnestly, to kill him with his own hand: (167) that, however, if he ought to suppose this information to be true, it was better for himself to be slain by the other, than destroy a man who fled to him for refuge, and entrusted his own safety to him, and committed himself to his disposal.

(168) So Johanan, and the rulers that were with him, not being able to persuade Gedaliah, went away; but after the interval of thirty days was over, Ishmael came again to Gedaliah, to the city Mispah, and ten men with him: and when he had feasted Ishmael, and those that were with him, in a splendid manner at his table, and had given them presents, he became disordered in

drink, while he endeavoured to be very merry with them: (169) and when Ishmael saw him in that case, and that he was drowned in his cups to the degree of insensibility, and fallen asleep, he rose up on a sudden, with his ten friends, and slew Gedaliah and those that were with him at the feast; and when he had slain them, he went out by night, and slew all the Jews that were in the city, and those soldiers also which were left therein by the Babylonians; (170) but the next day fourscore men came out of the country with presents to Gedaliah, none of them knowing what had befallen him; when Ishmael saw them, he invited them in to Gedaliah, and when they were come in, he shut up the court and slew them, and cast their dead bodies down into a certain deep pit, that they might not be seen; (171) but of these fourscore men Ishmael spared those that entreated him not to kill them, till they had delivered up to him what riches they had concealed in the fields, consisting of their furniture and garments and corn; (172) but he took captive the people that were in Mispah, with their wives and children; among whom were the daughters of king Zedekiah, whom Nebuzaradan, the general of the army of Babylon, had left with Gedaliah; and when he had done this, he came to the king of the Ammonites.

(173) But when Johanan and the rulers with him heard of what was done at Mispah by Ishmael, and of the death of Gedaliah, they had indignation at it, and every one of them took his own armed men, and came suddenly to fight with Ishmael, and overtook him at the fountain in Hebron; (174) and when those that were carried away captives by Ishmael, saw Johanan and the rulers, they were very glad, and looked upon them as coming to their assistance; so they left him that had carried them captives, and came over to Johanan; then Ishmael, with eight men, fled to the king of the Ammonites; (175) but Johanan took those whom he had rescued out of the hands of Ishmael, and the eunuchs, and their wives and children, and came to a certain place called Mandara, and there they abode that day, for they had determined to remove from thence and go into Egypt, out of fear, lest the Babylonians should slay them, in case they continued in the country, and that out of anger at the slaughter of Gedaliah, who had been by them set over it for governor.

(176) Now while they were under this deliberation, Johanan, the son of Kareah, and the rulers that were with him, came to Jeremiah the prophet, and desired that he would pray to God, that because they were at an utter loss about what they ought to do, he would discover it to them, and they swore that they would do whatsoever Jeremiah should say to them: (177) and when the prophet said he would be their intercessor with God, it came to pass, that after ten days God appeared to him, and said, that he should inform Johanan and the other rulers and all the people, that he would be with them while they continued in that country, and take care of them, and keep them from being

hurt by the Babylonians, of whom they were afraid; but that he would desert
them if they went into Egypt; and, out of this wrath against them, would inflict
the same punishments upon them which they knew their brethren had already
endured. (178) So when the prophet had informed Johanan and the people
that God had foretold these things, he was not believed when he said that God
commanded them to continue in the country; but they imagined that he said
so to gratify Baruch, his own disciple, and belied God, and that he persuaded
them to stay there, that they might be destroyed by the Babylonians. (179)
Accordingly, both the people and Johanan disobeyed the counsel of God,
which he gave them by the prophet, and removed into Egypt, and carried
Jeremiah and Baruch along with them.

(180) And when they were there, God signified to the prophet that the
king of Babylon was about making an expedition against the Egyptians, and
commanded him to foretell to the people that Egypt should be taken, and the
king of Babylon should slay some of them, and should take others captive, and
bring them to Babylon; (181) which things came to pass accordingly; for on
the fifth year after the destruction of Jerusalem, which was the twenty-third of
the reign of Nebuchadnezzar, he made an expedition against Celesyria; and
when he had possessed himself of it, he made war against the Ammonites and
Moabites; (182) and when he had brought all those nations under subjection,
he fell upon Egypt, in order to overthrow it; and he slew the king that then
reigned, and set up another; and he took those Jews that were there captives,
and led them away to Babylon; (183) and such was the end of the nation of the
Hebrews, as it hath been delivered down to us, it having twice gone beyond
Euphrates; for the people of the ten tribes were carried out of Samaria by the
Assyrians in the days of king Hoshea; after which the people of the two tribes
that remained after Jerusalem was taken [were carried away] by Nebuchadnezzar, the king of Babylon and Chaldea. (184) Now as to Shalmanezer, he
removed the Israelites out of their country, and placed therein the nation of the
Cutheans, who had formerly belonged to the inner parts of Persia and Media,
but were then called *Samaritans*, by taking the name of the country to which
they were removed: but the king of Babylon, who brought out the two tribes,
placed no other nation in their country, by which means all Judea and
Jerusalem, and the temple, continued to be a desert for seventy years; (185) but
the entire interval of time which passed from the captivity of the Israelites to
the carrying away of the two tribes proved to be a hundred and thirty years, six
months, and ten days.

CHAPTER 10

(186) But now Nebuchadnezzar, king of Babylon, took some of the most noble of the Jews that were children, and the kinsmen of Zedekiah their king, such as were remarkable for their beauty of their bodies and comeliness of their countenances, and delivered them into the hands of tutors, and to the improvement to be made by them. He also made some of them to be eunuchs; (187) which course he took also with those of other nations whom he had taken in the flower of their age and afforded them their diet from his own table, and had them instructed in the institutes of the country, and taught the learning of the Chaldeans; and they had now exercised themselves sufficiently in that wisdom which he had ordered they should apply themselves to. (188) Now among these there were four of the family of Zedekiah, of most excellent dispositions, the one of whom was called Daniel, another was called Ananias, another Misael, and the fourth Azarias: and the king of Babylon changed their names, and commanded that they should make use of other names. (189) Daniel he called Baltasar; Ananias, Shadrach; Misael, Meshach; and Azarias, Abednego. These the king had in esteem, and continued to love, because of the very excellent temper they were of, and because of their application to learning, and the progress they had made in wisdom.

(190) Now Daniel and his kinsmen had resolved to use a severe diet, and to abstain from those kinds of food which came from the king's table, and entirely to forbear to eat of all living creatures; so he came to Ashpenaz, who was that eunuch to whom the care of them was committed, and desired him to take and spend what was brought for them from the king; but to give them pulse and dates for their food, and anything else besides the flesh of living creatures, that he pleased, for that their inclinations were to that sort of food, and that they despised the other. (191) He replied, that he was ready to serve them in what they desired, but he suspected that they would be discovered by the king, from the meagre bodies and the alteration of their countenances; because it could not be avoided but their bodies and colours must be changed with their diet, especially while they would be clearly discovered by the finer appearance of the other children, who would fare better, and thus they should bring him into danger, and occasion him to be punished; (192) yet did they persuade Arioch, who was thus fearful to give them what food they desired, for ten days by way of trial; and in case the habit of their bodies were not altered, to go on in the same way, as expecting that they should not be hurt thereby afterwards; but if he saw them look meagre, and worse than the rest, he should reduce them to their former diet. (193) Now when it appeared that they were so far from becoming worse by the use of this food, that they grew plumper and fuller in

body than the rest, insomuch that he thought those who fed on what came from the king's table seemed less plump and full, while those that were with Daniel looked as if they had lived in plenty, and in all sorts of luxury, Arioch, from that time, securely took himself what the king sent every day from his supper, according to custom, to the children, but gave them the forementioned diet, (194) while they had their souls in some measure more pure, and less burdened, and so fitter for learning, and had their bodies in better trim for hard labour; for they neither had the former oppressed and heavy with variety of meats, nor were the other effeminate on the same account: so they readily understood all the learning that was among the Hebrews and among the Chaldeans, as especially did Daniel, who being already sufficiently skilled in wisdom, was very busy about the interpretation of dreams: and God manifested Himself to him.

(195) Now two years after the destruction of Egypt, King Nebuchadnezzar saw a wonderful dream, the accomplishment of which God showed him in his sleep; but when he arose out of his bed, he forgot the accomplishment: so he sent for the Chaldeans and magicians, and the prophets, and told them that he had seen a dream and informed them that he had forgot the accomplishment of what he had seen, and he enjoined them to tell him both what the dream was, and what was its signification; (196) and they said that this was a thing impossible to be discovered by men; but they promised him, that if he would explain to them what dream he had seen, they would tell him its signification. Whereupon he threatened to put them to death, unless they told him his dream: and he gave command to have them all put to death, since they confessed they could not do what they were commanded to do. (197) Now when Daniel heard that the king had given a command that all the wise men should be put to death, and that among them himself and his three kinsmen were in danger, he went to Arioch, who was captain of the king's guards, (198) and desired to know of him what was the reason why the king had given command that all the wise men and Chaldeans and magicians, should be slain. So when he had learned that the king had had a dream, and had forgotten it, and that when they were enjoined to inform the king of it, they had said they could not do it, and had thereby provoked him to anger, he desired of Arioch that he would go in to the king, and desire respite for the magicians for one night, and to put off their slaughter so long, for that he hoped within that time to obtain, by prayer to God, the knowledge of the dream. (199) Accordingly Arioch informed the king of what Daniel desired; so the king bid them delay the slaughter of the magicians till he knew what Daniel's promise would come to; but the young man retired to his own house, with his kinsmen, and besought God that whole night to discover the dream, and thereby deliver the magicians and Chaldeans, with whom they were themselves to perish, from

the king's anger, by enabling him to declare his vision, and to make manifest what the king had seen the night before in his sleep, but had forgotten it. (200) Accordingly, God, out of pity to those that were in danger, and out of regard to the wisdom of Daniel, made known to him the dream and its interpretation, that so the king might understand by him its signification also. (201) When Daniel had obtained this knowledge from God, he arose very joyful, and told it his brethren, and made them glad, and to hope well that they should now preserve their lives, of which they despaired before, and had their minds full of nothing but the thoughts of dying. (202) So when he had with them returned thanks to God, who had commiserated their youth, when it was day he came to Arioch, and desired him to bring him to the king, because he would discover to him that dream which he had seen the night before.

(203) When Daniel was come in to the king, he excused himself first, that he did not pretend to be wiser than the other Chaldeans and magicians, when, upon their entire inability to discover his dream, he was undertaking to inform him of it; for this was not by his own skill, or on account of his having better cultivated his understanding than the rest; but he said, 'God hath pity upon us, when we were in danger of death, and when I prayed for the life of myself and of those of my own nation, hath made manifest to me both the dream and the interpretation thereof; (204) for I was not less concerned for thy glory than for the sorrow that we were by thee condemned to die, while thou didst so unjustly command men, both good and excellent in themselves, to be put to death, when thou enjoinedst them to do what was entirely above the reach of human wisdom, and requiredst of them what was only the work of God. (205) Wherefore, as thou in thy sleep wast solicitous concerning those that should succeed the government of the whole world, God was desirous to show thee all those that should reign after thee, and to that end exhibited to thee the following dream: (206) thou seemedst to see a great image standing before thee, the head of which proved to be of gold, the shoulders and arms of silver, and the belly and the thighs of brass, but the legs and feet of iron; (207) after which thou sawest a stone broken off from a mountain, which fell upon the image and threw it down, and brake it to pieces, and did not permit any part of it to remain whole; but the gold, the silver, the brass and the iron, became smaller than meal, which, upon the blast of a violent wind, was by force carried away and scattered abroad; but the stone did increase to such a degree that the whole earth beneath it seemed to be filled therewith. (208) This is the dream which thou sawest, and its interpretation is as follows: the head of gold denotes thee, and the kings of Babylon that have been before thee; but the two hands and arms signify this, that your government shall be dissolved by two kings; (209) but another king that shall come from the west, armed with brass, shall destroy that government; and another government, that shall be like unto iron,

shall put an end to the power of the former, and shall have dominion over all the earth, on account of the nature of iron, which is stronger than that of gold, of silver, and of brass.' (210) Daniel did also declare the meaning of the stone to the king; but I do not think proper to relate it, since I have only undertaken to describe things past or things present, but not things that are future: yet if anyone be so very desirous of knowing truth, as not to waive such points of curiosity, and cannot curb his inclination for understanding the uncertainties of futurity, and whether they will happen or not, let him be diligent in reading the book of Daniel, which he will find among the sacred writings.

(211) When Nebuchadnezzar heard this, and recollected his dream, he was astonished at the nature of Daniel, and fell upon his face, and saluted Daniel in the manner that men worship God, (212) and gave command that he should be sacrificed to as a god. And this was not all, for he also imposed the name of his own god upon him [Baltasar], and made him and his kinsmen rulers of his whole kingdom; which kinsmen of his happened to fall into great danger by the envy of malice [of their enemies]; for they offended the king upon the occasion following: (213) he made an image of gold, the height of which was sixty cubits, and its breadth six cubits, and set it in the great plain of Babylon; and when he was going to dedicate the image, he invited the principal men out of all the earth that was under his dominions, and commanded them, in the first place, that when they should hear the sound of the trumpet, they should then fall down and worship the image; and he threatened, that those who did not do so should be cast into a fiery furnace. (214) When, therefore, all the rest, upon the hearing of the sound of the trumpet, worshipped the image, they relate that Daniel's kinsmen did not do it, because they would not transgress the laws of their country: so these men were convicted, and cast immediately into the fire, but were saved by Divine Providence, and after a surprising manner escaped death; (215) for the fire did not touch them, and I suppose that it touched them not, as if it reasoned with itself that they were cast into it without any fault of theirs, and that therefore, it was too weak to burn the young men when they were in it. This was done by the power of God, who made their bodies so far superior to the fire, that it could not consume them. This it was which recommended them to the king as righteous men, and men beloved of God; on which account they continued in great esteem with him.

(216) A little after this the king saw in his sleep again another vision; how he should fall from his dominion, and feed among the wild beasts; and that, when he had lived in this manner in the desert for seven years, he should recover his dominion again. When he had seen this dream, he called the magicians together again, and inquired of them about it, and desired them to tell him what it signified; (217) but when none of them could find out the meaning of the dream, nor discover it to the king, Daniel was the only person that

explained it; and as he foretold, so it came to pass; for after he had continued in the wilderness the forementioned interval of time, while no one durst attempt to seize his kingdom during those seven years, he prayed to God that he might recover his kingdom, and he returned to it. (218) But let no one blame me for writing down everything of this nature, as I find it in our ancient books; for as to that matter, I have plainly assured those that think me defective in any such point, or complain of my management, and have told them, in the beginning of this history, that I intended to do no more than translate the Hebrew books into the Greek language, and promised them to explain those facts, without adding anything to them of my own, or taking anything away from there.

CHAPTER II

(219) Now when King Nebuchadnezzar had reigned forty-three years, he ended his life. He was an active man, and more fortunate than the kings that were before him. Now Berosus makes mention of his actions in the third book of his Chaldaic History, where he says thus: (220) 'When his father Nebuchodonosor [Nabopollassar] heard that the governor whom he had set over Egypt, and the places about Celesyria and Phoenicia, had revolted from him, while he was not himself able any longer to undergo the hardships [of war], he committed to his son Nebuchadnezzar, who was still but a youth, some parts of his army, and sent them against him. (221) So when Nebuchadnezzar had given battle, and fought with the rebel, he beat him, and reduced the country from under his subjection, and made it a branch of his own kingdom; but about that time it happened that his father Nebuchodonosor [Nabopollassar] fell ill, and ended his life in the city of Babylon, when he had reigned twenty-one years; (222) and when he was made sensible, as he was in a little time, that his father Nebuchodonosor [Nabopollassar] was dead, and having settled the affairs of Egypt and the other countries, as also those that concerned the captive Jews and Phoenicians and Syrians, and those of the Egyptian nations, and having committed the conveyance of them to Babylon to certain of his friends, together with the gross of his army, and the rest of their ammunition and provisions, he went himself hastily, accompanied with a few others, over the desert, and came to Babylon. (223) So he took upon him the management of public affairs, and of the kingdom which had been kept for him by one that was the principal of the Chaldeans, and he received the entire dominions of his father, and appointed, that when the captives came, they should be placed as colonies in the most proper places of Babylonia; (224) but then he adorned the temple of Belus, and the rest of the temples, in a magnificent manner, with the spoils he had taken in the war. He also added another city to that which was there of old, and rebuilt it, that such as would besiege it hereafter might no

more turn the course of the river, and thereby attack the city itself: he therefore built three walls round the inner city, and three others about that which was the outer, and this he did with burnt brick. (225) And after he had, after a becoming manner walled the city, and adorned its gates gloriously, he built another palace before his father's palace, but so that they joined to it; to describe the vast height and immense riches of which it would perhaps be too much for me to attempt; yet, as large and lofty as they were, they were completed in fifteen days. (226) He also erected elevated places for walking, of stone, and made it resemble mountains, and built it so that it might be planted with all sorts of trees. He also erected what was called a pensile paradise, because his wife was desirous to have things like her own country, she having been bred up in the palaces of Media. (227) Megasthenes also, in his fourth book of his *Accounts of India*, makes mention of these things, and thereby endeavours to show that this king [Nebuchadnezzar] exceeded Hercules in fortitude, and in the greatness of his actions; for he saith, that he conquered a great part of Libya and Iberia. (228) Diocles also, in the second book of his *Accounts of Persia*, mentions this king; as does Philostratus in his *Accounts* both of India and of Phoenicia, say, that this king besieged Tyre thirteen years, while at the same time Ethbaal reigned at Tyre. These are all the histories that I have met with concerning this king.

(229) But now, after the death of Nebuchadnezzar, Evil-merodach his son succeeded in the kingdom, who immediately set Jeconiah at liberty, and esteemed him amongst his most intimate friends. He also gave him many presents, and made him honourable above the rest of the kings that were in Babylon; (230) for his father had not kept his faith with Jeconiah, when he voluntarily delivered up himself to him, with his wives and children, and his whole kindred, for the sake of his country, that it might not be taken by siege, and utterly destroyed, as we said before. (231) When Evil-merodach was dead, after a reign of eighteen years, Neglissar his son took the government, and retained it forty years, and then ended his life; and after him the succession in the kingdom came to his son Labosordacus, who continued in it in all but nine months; and when he was dead, it came to Baltasar, who by the Babylonians was called Naboandelus: (232) against him did Cyrus, the king of Persia, and Darius, the king of Media, make war; and when he was besieged in Babylon, there happened a wonderful and prodigious vision. He was sat down at supper in a large room, and there were a great many vessels of silver, such as were made for royal entertainments, and he had with him his concubines and his friends; (233) whereupon he came to a resolution, and commanded that those vessels of God which Nebuchadnezzar had plundered out of Jerusalem, and had not made use of, but had put them into his own temple, should be brought out of that temple. He also grew so haughty as to proceed to use them in the midst of his cups, drinking out of them, and

blaspheming against God. In the meantime, he saw a hand proceed out of the wall, and writing upon the wall certain syllables; (234) at which sight, being disturbed, he called the magicians and Chaldeans together, and all that sort of men that are among these barbarians, and were able to interpret signs and dreams, that they might explain the writing to him. (235) But when the magicians said they could discover nothing, nor did understand it, the king was in great disorder of mind, and under great trouble, at this surprising accident; so he promised, that to him who could explain the writing, and give the signification couched therein, he would give him a golden chain for his neck, and leave to wear a purple garment, as did the kings of Chaldea, and would bestow on him the third part of his own dominions. (236) When this proclamation was made, the magicians ran together more earnestly, and were very ambitious to find out the importance of the writing; but still hesitated about it as much as before. (237) Now when the king's grandmother saw him cast down at this accident, she began to encourage him, and to say, that there was a certain captive who came from Judea, a Jew by birth, but brought away thence by Nebuchadnezzar when he had destroyed Jerusalem, whose name was Daniel, a wise man, and one of great sagacity in finding out what was impossible for others to discover, and what was known to God alone; who brought to light and answered such questions to Nebuchadnezzar as no one else was able to answer when they were consulted. (238) She therefore desired that he would send for him, and inquire of him concerning the writing, and to condemn the unskilfulness of those that could not find their meaning, and this, although what God signified thereby should be of a melancholy nature.

(239) When Baltasar heard this, he called for Daniel: and when he had discoursed to him what he had learned concerning him and his wisdom, and how a divine spirit was with him, and that he alone was fully capable of finding out what others would never have thought of, he desired him to declare to him what this writing meant: (240) that if he did so, he would give him leave to wear purple, and to put a chain of gold about his neck, and would bestow on him the third part of his dominion, as an honorary reward for his wisdom, that thereby he might become illustrious to those who saw him, and who inquired upon what occasion he obtained such honours. (241) But Daniel desired that he would keep his gifts to himself; for what is the effect of wisdom and of divine revelation admits of no gifts, and bestows its advantages on petitioners freely; but that still he would explain the writing to him; which denoted that he should soon die, and this because he had not learnt to honour God, and not to admit things above human nature, by what punishments his progenitor had undergone for the injuries he had offered to God; (242) and because he had quite forgotten how Nebuchadnezzar was removed to feed among wild beasts for his impieties, and did not recover his former life among

men and his kingdom, but upon God's mercy to him, after many supplications and prayers; who did thereupon praise God all the days of his life, as one of almighty power, and who takes care of mankind. [He also put him in mind] how he had greatly blasphemed against God, and had made use of his vessels amongst his concubines; (243) that therefore God saw this, and was angry with him, and declared by this writing beforehand what a sad conclusion of his life he should come to. And he explained the writing thus: 'MANEH. This, if it be expounded in the Greek language, may signify a *Number*, because God hath numbered so long a time for thy life and for thy government, and that there remains but a small portion. (244) THEKEL. This signifies a *Weight*, and means that God hath weighed thy kingdom in a balance, and finds it going down already. PHARES. This also, in the Greek tongue, denotes a *Fragment*; God will therefore break thy kingdom in pieces, and divide it among the Medes and Persians.'

(245) When Daniel had told the king that the writing upon the wall signified these events, Baltasar was in great sorrow and affliction, as was to be expected, when the interpretation was so heavy upon him. (246) However, he did not refuse what he had promised Daniel, although he were become a foreteller of misfortunes to him, but bestowed it all upon him: as reasoning thus, that what he was to reward was peculiar to himself and to fate, and did not belong to the prophet, but that it was the part of a good and just man to give what he had promised, although the events were of a melancholy nature. (247) Accordingly, the king determined so to do. Now after a little while, both himself and the city were taken by Cyrus, the king of Persia, who fought against him; for it was Baltasar, under whom Babylon was taken, when he had reigned seventeen years. (248) And this is the end of the posterity of King Nebuchadnezzar, as history informs us; but when Babylon was taken by Darius, and when he, with his kinsman Cyrus, had put an end to the dominion of the Babylonians, he was sixty-two years old. He was the son of Astyages, and had another name among the Greeks. (249) Moreover, he took Daniel the prophet, and carried him with him into Media, and honoured him very greatly, and kept him with him; for he was one of the three presidents whom he set over his three hundred and sixty provinces; for into so many did Darius part them.

(250) However, while Daniel was in so great dignity, and in so great favour with Darius, and was alone entrusted with everything by him, as having somewhat divine in him, he was envied by the rest: for those that see others in greater honour than themselves with kings, envy them: (251) and when those that were grieved at the great favour Daniel was in with Darius, sought for an occasion against him, he afforded them no occasion at all, for he was above all the temptations of money, and despised bribery, and esteemed it a very base thing to take anything by way of reward, even when it might be justly given

him; he afforded those that envied him not the least handle for an accusation. (252) So when they could find nothing for which they might calumniate him to the king, nothing that was shameful or reproachful, and thereby deprive him of the honour he was in with him, they sought for some other method whereby they might destroy him. When therefore they saw that Daniel prayed to God three times a day, they thought they had gotten an occasion by which they might ruin him; (253) so they came to Darius, and told him, that 'the princes and governors had thought proper to allow the multitude a relaxation for thirty days, that no one might offer a petition or prayer either to himself or to the gods, but that he who shall transgress this decree shall be cast into a den of lions, and there perish.'

(254) Whereupon the king, not being acquainted with their wicked design, nor suspecting that it was a contrivance of theirs against Daniel, said he was pleased with this decree of theirs, and he promised to confirm what they desired; he also published an edict to promulgate to the people that decree which the princes had made. (255) Accordingly, all the rest took care not to transgress those injunctions, and rested in quiet; but Daniel had no regard to them, but, as he was wont, he stood and prayed to God in the sight of them all; (256) but the princes having met with the occasion they so earnestly sought to find against Daniel, came presently to the king, and accused him, that Daniel was the only person that transgressed the decree, while not one of the rest durst pray to their gods. This discovery they made, not because of his impiety, but because they had watched him, and observed him out of envy: (257) for supposing that Darius did thus out of a greater kindness to him than they expected, and that he was ready to grant him a pardon for this contempt of his injunctions, and envying this very pardon to Daniel, they did not become more favourable to him, but desired he might be cast into the den of lions, according to the law. (258) So Darius, hoping that God would deliver him, and that he would undergo nothing that was terrible by the wild beasts, bade him bear this accident cheerfully; and when he was cast into the den, he put his seal to the stone that lay upon the mouth of the den, and went his way, but he passed all the night without food and without sleep, being in great distress for Daniel; (259) but when it was day, he got up, and came to the den, and found the seal entire, which he had left the stone sealed withal; he also opened the seal, and cried out, and called to Daniel, and asked him if he were alive; and as soon as he heard the king's voice, and said that he had suffered no harm, the king gave order that he should be drawn up out of the den. (260) Now when his enemies saw that Daniel had suffered nothing which was terrible, they would not own that he was preserved by God, and by his providence; but they said, that the lions had been filled full with food, and on that account it was, as they supposed, that the lions would not touch Daniel, nor come to him; and

this they alleged to the king; (261) but the king, out of an abhorrence of their wickedness, gave order that they should throw in a great deal of flesh to the lions; and when they had filled themselves, he gave further order that Daniel's enemies should be cast into the den that he might learn whether the lions, now they were full, would touch them or not; (262) and it appeared plain to Darius, after the princes had been cast to the wild beasts, that it was God who preserved Daniel, for the lions spared none of them, but tore them all to pieces, as if they had been very hungry and wanted food. I suppose, therefore, it was not their hunger, which had been a little before satisfied with abundance of flesh, but the wickedness of these men that provoked them [to destroy the princes]: for if it so please God, that wickedness might, by even those irrational creatures, be esteemed a plain foundation for their punishment.

(263) When, therefore, those that had intended thus to destroy Daniel by treachery were themselves destroyed, King Darius sent [letters] over all the country, and praised that God whom Daniel worshipped, and said that he was the only true God, and had all power. He had also Daniel in very great esteem, and made him the principal of his friends. (264) Now when Daniel was become so illustrious and famous, on account of the opinion men had that he was beloved of God, he built a tower at Ecbatana, in Media: it was a most elegant building, and wonderfully made, and it is still remaining, and preserved to this day: and to such as see it, it appears to have been lately built, and to have been no older than that very day when anyone looks upon it, it is so fresh, flourishing, and beautiful, and no way grown old in so long time; (265) for buildings suffer the same as men do, they grow old as well as they, and by numbers of years their strength is dissolved, and their beauty withered. Now they bury the kings of Media, of Persia, and Parthia, in this tower to this day; and he who was entrusted with the care of it was a Jewish priest; which thing is also observed to this day. (266) But it is fit to give an account of what this man did, which is most admirable to hear; for he was so happy as to have strange revelations made to him, and those as to one of the greatest of the prophets, insomuch that while he was alive he had the esteem and applause both of the kings and of the multitude; and now he is dead, he retains a remembrance that will never fail, (267) for the several books that he wrote and left behind him are still read by us till this time; and from them we believe that Daniel conversed with God; for he did not only prophesy of future events, as did the other prophets, but he also determined the time of their accomplishment; (268) and while prophets used to foretell misfortunes, and on that account were disagreeable both to the kings and to the multitude, Daniel was to them a prophet of good things, and this to such a degree that, by the agreeable nature of his predictions, he procured the good will of all men; and by the accomplishment of them, he procured the belief of their truth, and the

opinion of [a sort of] divinity for himself, among the multitude. (269) He also wrote and left behind him what made manifest the accuracy and undeniable veracity of his predictions; for he saith, that when he was in Susa, the metropolis of Persia, and went out into the field with his companions, there was, on the sudden, a motion and concussion of the earth, and that he was left alone by himself, his friends flying away from him, and that he was disturbed, and fell on his face and on his two hands, and that a certain person touched him, and at the same time bade him rise, and see what would befall his countrymen after many generations. (270) He also related, that when he stood up, he was shown a great ram, with many horns growing out of his head, and that the last was higher than the rest: that after this he looked to the west, and saw a he-goat carried through the air from that quarter; that he rushed upon the ram with violence, and smote him twice with his horns, and overthrew him to the ground, and trampled upon him: (271) that afterward he saw a very great horn growing out of the head of the he-goat; and that when it was broken off, four horns grew up that were exposed to each of the four winds, and he wrote that out of them arose another lesser horn, which, as he said, waxed great; and that God showed to him that it should fight against his nation, and take their city by force, and bring the temple worship to confusion, and forbid the sacrifices to be offered for one thousand two hundred and ninety-six days. (272) Daniel wrote that he saw these visions in the Plain of Susa; and he hath informed us that God interpreted the appearance of this vision after the following manner: he said that the ram signified the kingdoms of the Medes and Persians, and the horns those kings that were to reign in them; and that the last horn signified the last king and that he should exceed all the kings in riches and glory; (273) that the he-goat signified that one should come and reign from the Greeks, who should twice fight with the Persian, and overcome him in battle, and should receive his entire dominion; (274) that by the great horn which sprang out of the forehead of the he-goat was meant the first king; and that the springing up of four horns upon its falling off, and the conversion of every one of them to the four quarters of the earth, signified the successors that should arise after the death of the first king, and the partition of the kingdom among them, and that they should be neither his children nor of his kindred that should reign over the habitable earth for many years; (275) and that from among them there should arise a certain king that should overcome our nation and their laws, and should take away our political government, and should spoil the temple, and forbid the sacrifices to be offered for three years' time. (276) And indeed it so came to pass, that our nation suffered these things under Antiochus Epiphanes, according to Daniel's vision, and what he wrote many years before they came to pass. In the very same manner Daniel also wrote concerning the Roman government, and that our country should be made desolate by them. (277) All these things did this man leave in writing, as God had showed them to him, insomuch that such as read his prophecies, and see how they have been fulfiled, would wonder at the honour wherewith God honoured Daniel; and may thence discover how the Epicureans are in an error, (278) who cast Providence out of human life, and do not believe that God takes care of the affairs of the world, nor that the universe is governed and continued in being by that blessed and immortal nature, but say that the world is carried along of its own accord, without a ruler and a curator; (279) which, were it destitute of a guide to conduct as they imagine, it would be like ships without pilots, which we see drowned by the winds, or like chariots without drivers, which are overturned; so would the world be dashed to pieces by its being carried without a Providence, and so perish, and come to nought. (280) So that, by the forementioned predictions of Daniel, those men seem to me very much to err from the truth, who determine that God exercises no providence over human affairs; for if that were the case, that the world went on by mechanical necessity, we should not see that all things would come to pass according to his prophecy. (281) Now, as to myself, I have so described these matters as I have found them and read them; but if anyone is inclined to another opinion about them, let him enjoy his different sentiments without any blame from me.

BOOK ELEVEN

CHAPTER I

(1) In the first year of the reign of Cyrus, which was the seventieth from the day that our people were removed out of their own land into Babylon, God commiserated the captivity and calamity of these poor people, according as he had foretold to them by Jeremiah the prophet before the destruction of the city, (2) that after they has served Nebuchadnezzar and his posterity, and after they had undergone that servitude seventy years, he would restore them again to the land of their fathers, and they should build their temple, and enjoy their ancient prosperity; and these things God did afford them; (3) for he stirred up the mind of Cyrus, and made him write this throughout all Asia: 'Thus saith Cyrus the king: since God Almighty hath appointed me to be king of the habitable earth, I believe that he is that God which the nation of the Israelites worship; (4) for indeed he foretold my name by the prophets, and that I should build him a house at Jerusalem, in the country of Judea.'

(5) This was known to Cyrus by his reading the book which Isaiah left behind him of his prophecies; for this prophet said that God had spoken thus to him in a secret vision: 'My will is that Cyrus, whom I have appointed to be king over many and great nations, send back my people to their own land, and build my temple.' (6) This was foretold by Isaiah one hundred and forty years before the temple was demolished. Accordingly, when Cyrus read this, and admired the divine power, an earnest desire and ambition seized upon him to fulfil what was so written; so he called for the most eminent Jews that were in Babylon, and said to them, that he gave them leave to go back to their own country, and to rebuild their city Jerusalem, and the temple of God, (7) for that he would be their assistant, and that he would write to the rulers and governors that were in the neighbourhood of their country of Judea, that they should contribute to them gold and silver for the building of the temple, and, besides that, beasts for their sacrifices.

(8) When Cyrus had said this to the Israelites, the rulers of the two tribes of Judah and Benjamin, with the Levites and priests, went in haste to Jerusalem, yet did many of them stay at Babylon, as not willing to leave their possessions; (9) and when they were come thither, all the king's friends assisted them, and brought in, for the building of the temple, some gold, and some silver, and some a great many cattle and horses. So they performed their vows to God, and offered the sacrifices that had been accustomed of old time; I mean this

upon the rebuilding of their city, and the revival of the ancient practices relating to their worship. (10) Cyrus also sent back to them the vessels of God which King Nebuchadnezzar had pillaged out of the temple, and carried to Babylon. (11) So he committed these things to Mithridates, the treasurer, to be sent away, with an order to give them to Sanabassar, that he might keep them till the temple was built; and when it was finished, he might deliver them to the priest and rulers of the multitude, in order to their being restored to the temple. (12) Cyrus also sent an epistle to the governors that were in Syria, the contents whereof here follow:

'I have given leave to as many of the Jews that dwell in my country as please to return to their own country, and to rebuild their city, and to build the temple of God at Jerusalem, on the same place where it was before. (13) I have also sent my treasurer, Mithridates, and Zorobabel, the governor of the Jews, that they may lay the foundations of the temple, and may build it sixty cubits high, and of the same latitude, making three edifices of polished stones, and one of the wood of the country, and the same order extends to the altar whereon they offer sacrifices to God. (14) I require also, that the expenses for these things may be given out of my revenues. Moreover, I have also sent the vessels which King Nebuchadnezzar pillaged out of the temple, and have given them to Mithridates the treasurer, and to Zorobabel the governor of the Jews, that they may have them carried to Jerusalem, and may restore them to the temple of God. (15) Now their number is as follows: fifty chargers of gold and five hundred of silver; forty Thericlean cups of gold, and five hundred of silver; fifty basins of gold, and five hundred of silver; thirty vessels for pouring [the drink offerings], and three hundred of silver, thirty vials of gold, and two thousand four hundred of silver; with a thousand other large vessels. (16) I permit them to have the same honour which they were used to have from their forefathers, as also for their small cattle, and for wine and oil, two hundred and five thousand and five hundred drachmae; and for wheat flour, twenty thousand and five hundred artabae; and I give order that these expenses shall be given them out of the tributes due from Samaria. (17) The priests shall also offer these sacrifices according to the laws of Moses in Jerusalem; and when they offer them, they shall pray to God for the preservation of the king and of his family, that the kingdom of Persia may continue. But my will is, that those who disobey these injunctions and make them void, shall be hung upon a cross, and their substance brought into the king's treasury.' (18) And such was the import of this epistle. Now the number of those that came out of captivity to Jerusalem, were forty-two thousand four hundred and sixty-two.

CHAPTER 2

(19) When the foundations of the temple were laying, and when the Jews were very zealous about the building it, the neighbouring nations, and especially the Cutheans, whom Shalmanezer, king of Assyria, had brought out of Persia and Media, and had planted in Samaria, when he carried the people of Israel captive, besought the governors, and those that had the care of such affairs, that they would interrupt the Jews, both in the rebuilding of their city and in the building of their temple. (20) Now as these men were corrupted by them with money, they sold the Cutheans their interest for rendering this building a slow and careless work, for Cyrus, who was busy about other wars, knew nothing of all this; and it so happened, that when he had led his army against the Massagetae, he ended his life. (21) But when Cambyses, the son of Cyrus, had taken the kingdom, the governors in Syria and Phoenicia, and in the countries of Ammon and Moab and Samaria, wrote an epistle to Cambyses whose contents were as follow: (22) 'To our lord Cambyses. We thy servants, Rathumus the historiographer and Semellius the scribe, and the rest that are thy judges in Syria and Phoenicia, send greeting. It is fit, O king, that thou shouldest know that those Jews who were carried to Babylon, are come into our country, and are building that rebellious and wicked city, and its market places, and setting up its walls, and raising up the temple: (23) know, therefore, that when these things are finished, they will not be willing to pay tribute, nor will they submit to thy commands, but will resist kings, and will choose rather to rule over others, than be ruled over themselves. (24) We therefore thought it proper to write to thee, O king, while the works about the temple are going on so fast, and not to overlook this matter, that thou mayest search into the books of thy fathers, for thou wilt find in them that the Jews have been rebels, and enemies to kings, as hath their city been also, which, for that reason, hath been till now laid waste. (25) We thought proper also to inform thee of this matter, because thou mayest otherwise perhaps be ignorant of it, that if this city be once inhabited, and be entirely encompassed with walls, thou wilt be excluded from the passage to Celesyria and Phoenicia.'

(26) When Cambyses had read the epistle, being naturally wicked, he was irritated at what they told him; and wrote back to them as follows: 'Cambyses the king, to Rathumus the historiographer, to Beeltethmus, to Semellius the scribe, and the rest that are in commission, and dwelling in Samaria and Phoenicia, after this manner: (27) I have read the epistle that was sent from you, and I gave order that the books of my forefathers should be searched into; and it is there found, that this city hath always been an enemy to kings, and its inhabitants have raised seditions and wars. We also are sensible that their kings

have been powerful and tyrannical, and have exacted tribute of Celesyria and Phoenicia: (28) wherefore I give order, that the Jews shall not be permitted to build that city, lest such mischief as they used to bring upon kings be greatly augmented.' (29) When this epistle was read, Rathumus, and Semellius the scribe, and their associates, got suddenly on horseback, and made haste to Jerusalem; they also brought a great company with them, and forbade the Jews to build the city and the temple. (30) Accordingly, these works were hindered from going on till the second year of the reign of Darius, for nine years more; for Cambyses reigned six years, and within that time overthrew Egypt, and when he was come back, he died at Damascus.

CHAPTER 3

(31) After the slaughter of the magi, who, upon the death of Cambyses, attained the government of the Persians for a year, those families which were called the seven families of the Persians, appointed Darius, the son of Hystaspes, to be their king. Now he, while he was a private man, had made a vow to God, that if he came to be king, he would send all the vessels of God that were in Babylon to the temple at Jerusalem. (32) Now it so fell out, that about this time Zorobabel, who had been made governor of the Jews that had been in captivity, came to Darius from Jerusalem; for there had been an old friendship between him and the king. He was also, with two others, thought worthy to be guard of the king's body; and obtained that honour which he hoped for.

(33) Now, in the first year of the king's reign, Darius feasted those that were about him, and those born in his house, with the rulers of the Medes and princes of the Persians, and the toparchs of India and Ethiopia, and the generals of the armies of his hundred and twenty-seven provinces; (34) but when they had eaten and drunken to satiety and abundantly, they every one departed to go to bed at their own houses, and Darius the king went to bed; but after he had rested a little part of the night, he awaked, and not being able to sleep any more, he fell into conversation with the three guards of his body, (35) and promised, that to him who should make an oration about points that he should inquire of, such as should be most agreeable to truth and to the dictates of wisdom, he would grant it as a reward of his victory, to put on a purple garment, and to drink in cups of gold, and to sleep upon gold, and to have a chariot with bridles of gold, and a head-tire of fine linen, and a chain of gold about his neck, and to sit next to himself, on account of his wisdom: 'And,' says he, 'he shall be called my cousin.' (36) Now when he had promised to give them these gifts, he asked the first of them, 'Whether wine was not the strongest?' – the second, 'Whether kings were not such?' – and the third, 'Whether women were not such? Or whether truth was not the strongest of

all?' When he had proposed that they should make their inquiries about these problems, he went to rest; (37) but in the morning he sent for his great men, his princes and toparchs of Persia and Media, and set himself down in the place where he used to give audience, and bid each of the guards of his body to declare what they thought proper concerning the proposed questions, in the hearing of them all.

(38) Accordingly, the first of them began to speak of the strength of wine, and demonstrated it thus: 'When,' said he, 'I am to give my opinion of wine, O you men, I find that it exceeds everything, by the following indications: (39) it deceives the mind of those that drink it, and reduces that of the king to the same state with that of the orphan, and he who stands in need of a tutor; and erects that of the slave to the boldness of him that is free; and that of the needy becomes like that of the rich man, (40) for it changes and renews the souls of men when it gets into them; and it quenches the sorrow of those that are under calamities, and makes men forget the debts they owe to others, and makes them think themselves to be of all men the richest; it makes them talk of no small things, but of talents, and such other things as become wealthy men only; (41) nay more, it makes them insensible of their commanders and of their kings, and takes away the remembrance of their friends and companions, for it arms men even against those that are dearest to them, and makes them appear the greatest strangers to them; (42) and when they are become sober, and they have slept out their wine in the night, they arise without knowing anything they have done in their cups. I take these for signs of power, and by them discover that wine is the strongest and most insuperable of all things.

(43) As soon as the first had given the forementioned demonstrations of the strength of wine, he left off; and the next to him began to speak about the strength of a king, and demonstrated that it was the strongest of all, and more powerful than anything else that appears to have any force or wisdom. He began his demonstration after the following manner, and said: (44) 'They are men who govern all things: they force the earth and the sea to become profitable to them in what they desire, and over these men do kings rule, and over them they have authority. Now those who rule over that animal which is of all the strongest and most powerful must needs deserve to be esteemed insuperable in power and force. (45) For example, when these kings command their subjects to make wars, and undergo dangers, they are hearkened to; and when they send them against their enemies, their power is so great that they are obeyed. They command men to level mountains, and to pull down walls and towers; nay, when they are commanded to be killed and to kill they submit to it, that they may not appear to transgress the king's commands; and when they have conquered, they bring what they have gained in the war to the king. (46) Those also who are not soldiers, but cultivate the ground, and

plough it, after they have endured the labour and all the inconveniences of such works of husbandry, when they have reaped and gathered in their fruits, they bring tributes to the king; (47) and whatsoever it is which the king says or commands it is done of necessity, and that without any delay, while he in the meantime is satiated with all sorts of food and pleasures, and sleeps in quiet. He is guarded by such as watch, and such as are, as it were, fixed down to the place through fear; (48) for no one dares leave him, even when he is asleep, nor does anyone go away and take care of his own affairs, but he esteems this one thing the only work of necessity, to guard the king; and accordingly to this he wholly addicts himself. How then can it be otherwise, but that it must appear that the king exceeds all in strength, while so great a multitude obeys his injunctions?'

(49) Now when this man had held his peace the third of them, who was Zorobabel, began to instruct them about women, and about truth, who said thus: 'Wine is strong, as is the king also, whom all men obey, but women are superior to them in power; (50) for it was a woman that brought the king into the world; and for those that plant the vines and make the wine, they are women who bear them, and bring them up; nor indeed is there anything which we do not receive from them; for these women weave garments for us, and our household affairs are by their means taken care of, and preserved in safety; (51) nor can we live separate from women; and when we have gotten a great deal of gold and silver, and any other thing that is of great value, and deserving regard, and see a beautiful woman, we leave all these things, and with open mouth fix our eyes upon her countenance, and are willing to forsake what we have, that we may enjoy her beauty, and procure it to ourselves. (52) We also leave father and mother, and the earth that nourishes us, and frequently forget our dearest friends, for the sake of women; nay, we are so hardy as to lay down our lives for them; but what will chiefly make you take notice of the strength of women is this that follows: (53) do not we take pains, and endure a great deal of trouble, and that both by land and sea, and when we have procured somewhat as the fruit of our labours, do not we bring them to the women, as to our mistresses, and bestow them upon them? (54) Nay, I once saw the king, who is lord of so many people, smitten on the face by Apame the daughter of Rabsaces Themasius his concubine, and his diadem taken from him, and put upon her own head, while he bore it patiently; and when she smiled he smiled, and when she was angry he was sad, and according to the change of her passions, he flattered his wife, and drew her to reconciliation by the great humiliation of himself to her, if at any time he saw her displeased at him.'

(55) And when the princes and rulers looked one upon another, he began to speak about truth; and he said, 'I have already demonstrated how powerful

women are; but both these women themselves, and the king himself, are weaker than truth: for although the earth be large, and the heaven high, and the course of the sun swift, yet are all these moved according to the will of God, who is true and righteous, for which cause we also ought to esteem truth to be the strongest of all things, and that what is unrighteous is of no force against it. (56) Moreover, all things else that have any strength are mortal and short-lived, but truth is a thing that is immortal and eternal. It affords us not indeed such a beauty as will wither away by time, nor such riches as may be taken away by fortune, but righteous rules and laws. It distinguishes them from injustice, and puts what is unrighteous to rebuke.'

(57) So when Zorobabel had left off his discourse about truth, and the multitude had cried out aloud that he had spoken the most wisely, and that it was truth alone that had immutable strength, and such as never would wax old, the king commanded that he should ask for somewhat over and above what he had promised, for that he would give it him because of his wisdom, and that prudence wherein he exceeded the rest; 'and thou shalt sit with me,' said the king, (58) 'and shalt be called my cousin.' When he had said this, Zorobabel put him in mind of the vow he had made in case he should ever have the kingdom. Now this vow was, 'to rebuild Jerusalem, and to build therein the temple of God, as also to restore the vessels which Nebuchadnezzar had pillaged, and carried to Babylon. And this,' said he, 'is that request which thou now permittest me to make, on account that I have been judged to be wise and understanding.'

(59) So the king was pleased with what he had said, and arose and kissed him; and wrote to the toparchs and governors, and enjoined them to conduct Zorobabel and those that were going with him to build the temple. (60) He also sent letters to those rulers that were in Syria and Phoenicia to cut down and carry cedar trees from Lebanon to Jerusalem, and to assist him in building the city. He also wrote to them, that all the captives who should go to Judea should be free; (61) and he prohibited his deputies and governors to lay any king's taxes upon the Jews: he also permitted that they should have all the land which they could possess themselves of without tributes. He also enjoined the Idumeans and Samaritans, and the inhabitants of Celesyria, to restore those villages which they had taken from the Jews; and that, besides all this, fifty talents should be given them for the building of the temple. (62) He also permitted them to offer their appointed sacrifices, and that whatsoever the high priests and the priests wanted, and those sacred garments wherein they used to worship God, should be made at his own charges; and that the musical instruments which the Levites used in singing hymns to God should be given them. (63) Moreover, he charged them that portions of land should be given to those that guarded the city and the temple, as also a determinate sum of money

every year for their maintenance: and withal he sent the vessels. And all that Cyrus intended to do before him relating to the restoration of Jerusalem, Darius also ordained should be done accordingly.

(64) Now when Zorobabel had obtained these grants from the king, he went out of the palace, and looking up to heaven, he began to return thanks to God for the wisdom he had given him, and the victory he had gained thereby, even in the presence of Darius himself; for, said he, 'I had not been thought worthy of these advantages, O Lord, unless thou hadst been favourable to me.' (65) When therefore he had returned these thanks to God for the present circumstances he was in and had prayed to him to afford him the like favour for the time to come, he came to Babylon, and brought the good news to his countrymen of what grants he had procured for them from the king; (66) who, when they heard the same, gave thanks also to God that he restored the land of their forefathers to them again. So they betook themselves to drinking and eating, and for seven days they continued feasting, and kept a festival, for the rebuilding and restoration of their country: (67) after this they chose themselves rulers, who should go up to Jerusalem, out of the tribes of their forefathers, with their wives and children and cattle, who travelled to Jerusalem with joy and pleasure, under the conduct of those whom Darius sent along with them, and making a noise with songs and pipes and cymbals. The rest of the Jewish multitude besides also accompanied them with rejoicing.

(68) And thus did these men go, a certain and determinate number out of every family, though I do not think it proper to recite particularly the names of those families, that I may not take off the minds of my readers from the connection of the historical facts and make it hard for them to follow the coherence of my narration; (69) but the sum of those that went up, above the age of twelve years, of the tribes of Judah and Benjamin was four hundred and sixty-two myriads and eight thousand; the Levites were seventy-four: the number of the women and children mixed together was forty thousand seven hundred and forty-two; (70) and besides these, there were singers of the Levites one hundred and twenty-eight, and porters one hundred and ten, and of the sacred ministers three hundred and ninety two; there were also others besides these, who said they were of the Israelites, but were not able to show their genealogies, six hundred and sixty-two: (71) some there were also who were expelled out of the number and honour of the priests, as having married wives whose genealogies they could not produce, nor were they found in the genealogies of the Levites and priests; they were about five hundred and twenty-five; (72) the multitude also of servants who followed those that went up to Jerusalem seven thousand three hundred and thirty-seven; the singing men and singing women were two hundred and forty-five; the camels were

four hundred and thirty-five; the beasts used to the yoke were five thousand five hundred and twenty-five; (73) and the governors of all this multitude thus numbered were Zorobabel, the son of Salathiel, of the posterity of David and of the tribe of Judah; and Jeshua, the son of Josedek the high priest; and besides these there were Mordecai and Serebeus, who were distinguished from the multitude, and were rulers, who also contributed a hundred pounds of gold and five thousand of silver. (74) By this means, therefore, the priests and the Levites, and a certain part of the entire people of the Jews that were in Babylon, came and dwelt in Jerusalem; but the rest of the multitude returned every one to their own countries.

CHAPTER 4

(75) Now in the seventh month after they were departed out of Babylon, both Jeshua the high priest, and Zorobabel the governor, sent messengers every way round about, and gathered those that were in the country together to Jerusalem universally, who came very gladly thither. (76) He then built the altar on the same place it had formerly been built, that they might offer the appointed sacrifices upon it to God, according to the laws of Moses. But while they did this they did not please the neighbouring nations, who all of them bare an ill will to them. (77) They also celebrated the feast of tabernacles at that time, as the legislator had ordained concerning it; and after that they offered sacrifices, and what were called the daily sacrifices, and the oblations proper for the Sabbaths, and for all the holy festivals. Those also that had made vows performed them, and offered their sacrifices from the first day of the seventh month. (78) They also began to build the temple, and gave a great deal of money to the masons and to the carpenters, and what was necessary for the maintenance of the workmen. The Sidonians also were very willing and ready to bring the cedar trees from Libanus, to bind them together, and to make a united float of them, and to bring them to the port of Joppa, for that was what Cyrus had commanded at first, and what was now done at the command of Darius.

(79) In the second year of their coming to Jerusalem, as the Jews were there, in the second month, the building of the temple went on apace; and when they had laid its foundations on the first day of the second month of that second year, they set, as overseers of the work, such Levites as were full twenty years old, and Jeshua and his sons and brethren, and Codmiel the brother of Judas, the son of Aminadab, with his sons; (80) and the temple, by the great diligence of those that had the care of it, was finished sooner than anyone would have expected. And when the temple was finished, the priests, adorned with their accustomed garments, stood with their trumpets, while the Levites and the

sons of Asaph stood and sung hymns to God, according as David first of all appointed them to bless God. (81) Now the priests and Levites, and the elder part of the families, recollecting with themselves how much greater and more sumptuous the old temple had been, seeing that now made how much inferior it was, on account of their poverty, to that which had been built of old, considered with themselves how much their happy state was sunk below what it had been of old, as well as their temple. Hereupon they were disconsolate, and not able to contain their grief, and proceeded so far as to lament and shed tears on those accounts; (82) but the people in general were contented with their present condition; and because they were allowed to build them a temple, they desired no more, and neither regarded nor remembered, nor indeed at all tormented themselves with the comparison of that and the former temple, as if this were below their expectations. (83) But the wailing of the old men and of the priests, on account of the deficiency of this temple, in their opinion, if compared with that which had been demolished, overcame the sounds of the trumpets and the rejoicing of the people.

(84) But when the Samaritans, who were still enemies to the tribes of Judah and Benjamin, heard the sound of the trumpets, they came running together, and desired to know what was the occasion of this tumult; and when they perceived that it was from the Jews who had been carried captive to Babylon, and were rebuilding their temple, they came to Zorobabel and to Jeshua, and to the heads of the families, and desired that they would give them leave to build the temple with them, and to be partners with them in building it; for they said, (85) 'We worship their God, and especially pray to him, and are desirous of their religious settlement, and this ever since Shalmanezer, the king of Assyria, transplanted us out of Cuthah and Media to this place.' (86) When they said thus, Zorobabel, and Jeshua the high priest, and the heads of the families of the Israelites, replied to them, that it was impossible for them to permit them to be their partners, whilst they [only] had been appointed to build that temple at first by Cyrus, and now by Darius, (87) although it was indeed lawful for them to come and worship there if they pleased, and that they could allow them nothing but that in common with them, which was common to them with all other men, to come to their temple and worship God there.

(88) When the Cetheans heard this, for the Samaritans have that appellation, they had indignation at it, and persuaded the nations of Syria to desire of the governors, in the same manner as they had done formerly in the days of Cyrus, and again in the days of Cambyses afterwards, to put a stop to the building of the temple, and to endeavour to delay and protract the Jews in their zeal about it. (89) Now at this time Sisinnes, the governor of Syria and Phoenicia, and Sathrabuzanes, with certain others, came up to Jerusalem, and asked the rulers

of the Jews, by whose grant it was that they built the temple in this manner, since it was more like to a citadel than a temple; and for what reason it was that they built cloisters and walls, and those strong ones too, about the city? (90) To which Zorobabel and Jeshua the high priest replied, that they were the servants of God Almighty; that this temple was built for him by a king of theirs that lived in great prosperity, and one that exceeded all men in virtue; and that it continued a long time, (91) but that because of their fathers' impiety towards God, Nebuchadnezzar, king of the Babylonians and of the Chaldeans, took their city by force and destroyed it, and pillaged the temple and burnt it down, and transplanted the people whom he had made captives, and removed them to Babylon; (92) that Cyrus, who after him was king of Babylonia and Persia, wrote to them to build the temple and committed the gifts and vessels, and whatsoever Nebuchadnezzar had carried out of it, to Zorobabel and Mithridates the treasurer; and gave order to have them carried to Jerusalem, and to have them restored to their own temple when it was built; (93) for he had sent to them to have it done speedily, and commanded Sanabassar to go up to Jerusalem, and to take care of the building of the temple; who upon receiving that epistle from Cyrus, came and immediately laid its foundations: 'and although it hath been in building from that time to this, it hath not yet been finished, by reason of the malignity of our enemies. (94) If therefore you have a mind, and think it proper, write this account to Darius, that when he hath consulted the records of the kings, he may find that we have told you nothing that is false about this matter.'

(95) When Zorobabel and the high priest had made this answer, Sisinnes and those that were with him, did not resolve to hinder the building, until they had informed King Darius of all this. So they immediately wrote to him about these affairs; (96) but as the Jews were now under terror, and afraid lest the king should change his resolutions as to the building of Jerusalem and of the temple, there were two prophets at that time amongst them, Haggai and Zechariah, who encouraged them, and bade them be of good cheer, and to suspect no discouragement from the Persians, for that God foretold this to them. So in dependence on those prophets, they applied themselves earnestly to building, and did not intermit one day.

(97) Now Darius, when the Samaritans had written to him, and in their epistle had accused the Jews how they fortified the city, and built the temple more like to a citadel than a temple; and said, that their doings were not expedient for the king's affairs; and besides, they showed the epistle of Cambyses, wherein he forbade them to build the temple: (98) and when Darius thereby understood that the restoration of Jerusalem was not expedient for his affairs, and when he had read the epistle that was brought him from Sisinnes and those that were with him, he gave order that what concerned

these matters should be sought for among the royal records. (99) Whereupon a book was found at Ecbatana, in the tower that was in Media, wherein was written as follows: 'Cyrus the king, in the first year of his reign commanded that the temple should be built in Jerusalem; and the altar in height threescore cubits, and its breadth of the same, with three edifices of polished stone, and one edifice of stone of their own country; (100) and he ordained that the expenses of it should be paid out of the king's revenue. He also commanded that the vessels which Nebuchadnezzar had pillaged [out of the temple], and had carried to Babylon, should be restored to the people of Jerusalem; (101) and that the care of these things should belong to Sanabassar, the governor and president of Syria and Phoenicia, and to his associates, that they may not meddle with that place, but may permit the servants of God, the Jews and their rulers, to build the temple. (102) He also ordained that they should assist them in the work; and that they should pay to the Jews, out of the tribute of the country where they were governors, on account of the sacrifices, bulls and rams and lambs and kids of the goats, and fine flour and oil and wine, and all other things that the priests should suggest to them; and that they should pray for the preservation of the king and of the Persians: (103) and that for such as transgressed any of these orders thus sent to them, he commanded that they should be caught, and hung upon a cross, and their substance confiscated to the king's use. He also prayed to God against them, that if anyone attempted to hinder the building of the temple, God would strike him dead, and thereby restrain his wickedness.'

(104) When Darius found this book among the records of Cyrus, he wrote an answer to Sisinnes and his associates, whose contents were these: 'King Darius to Sisinnes the governor, and to Sathrabuzanes, sendeth greeting. Having found a copy of this epistle among the records of Cyrus, I have sent it to you; and I will that all things be done as therein written. Farewell.' (105) So when Sisinnes, and those that were with him, understood the intention of the king, they resolved to follow his directions entirely for the time to come. So they forwarded the sacred works, and assisted the elders of the Jews, and the princes of the sanhedrin; (106) and the structure of the temple was with great diligence brought to a conclusion, by the prophecies of Haggai and Zechariah, according to God's commands and by the injunctions of Cyrus and Darius the kings. Now the temple was built in seven years' time: (107) and in the ninth year of the reign of Darius, on the twenty-third day of the twelfth month, which is by us called *Adar*, but by the Macedonians *Dystrus*, the priests and Levites, and the other multitude of the Israelites, offered sacrifices, as the renovation of their former prosperity after their captivity, and because they had now the temple rebuilt: a hundred bulls, two hundred rams, four hundred lambs, and twelve kids of the goats, according to the number of their tribes (for

so many are the tribes of the Israelites); and this last for the sins of every tribe. (108) The priests also and the Levites set the porters at every gate according to the laws of Moses. The Jews also built the cloisters of the inner temple that were round about the temple itself.

(109) And as the feast of unleavened bread was at hand, in the first month, which according to the Macedonians is called *Xanthicus*, but according to us *Nisam*, all the people ran together out of the villages to the city and celebrated the festival, having purified themselves, with their wives and children, according to the law of their country; (110) and they offered the sacrifice which was called the *passover*, on the fourteenth day of the same month, and feasted seven days, and spared for no cost, but offered whole burnt offerings to God, and performed sacrifices of thanksgiving, because God had led them again to the land of their fathers, and to the laws thereto belonging, and had rendered the mind of the king of Persia favourable to them. (111) So these men offered the largest sacrifices on these accounts, and used great magnificence in the worship of God, and dwelt in Jerusalem, and made use of a form of government that was aristocratical, but mixed with an oligarchy, for the high priests were at the head of their affairs, until the posterity of the Asamoneans set up kingly government; (112) for before their captivity, and the dissolution of their polity, they at first had kingly government from Saul and David for five hundred and thirty-two years, six months, and ten days: but before those kings, such rulers governed them as were called Judges and Monarchs. Under this form of government, they continued for more than five hundred years, after the death of Moses, and of Joshua their commander. (113) And this is the account I had to give of the Jews who had been carried into captivity, but were delivered from it in the times of Cyrus and Darius.

(114) But the Samaritans, being evil and enviously disposed to the Jews, wrought them many mischiefs, by reliance on their riches, and by their pretence that they were allied to the Persians on account that thence they came; (115) and whatsoever it was that they were enjoined to pay the Jews by the king's order out of their tributes for the sacrifices, they would not pay it. They had also the governors favourable to them, and assisting them for that purpose; nor did they spare to hurt them, either by themselves or by others, as far as they were able. (116) So the Jews determined to send an embassage to king Darius, in favour of the people of Jerusalem, and in order to accuse the Samaritans. The ambassadors were Zorobabel, and four others of the rulers; (117) and as soon as the king knew from the ambassadors the accusations and complaints they brought against the Samaritans, he gave them an epistle to be carried to the governors and council of Samaria; the contents of which epistle were these: (118) 'King Darius to Tanganas and Sambabas, the governors of the Samaritans; to Sadraces and Bobelo, and the rest of their fellow servants

that are in Samaria: Zorobabel, Ananias, and Mordecai, the ambassadors of the Jews, complain of you, that you obstruct them in the building of the temple, and do not supply them with the expenses which I commanded you to do for the offering their sacrifices. (119) My will therefore is this: that upon the reading of this epistle, you supply them with whatsoever they want for their sacrifices, and that out of the royal treasury of the tributes of Samaria, as the priests shall desire, that they may not leave off their offering daily sacrifices, nor praying to God for me and the Persians' – and these were the contents of that epistle.

CHAPTER 5

(120) Upon the death of Darius, Xerxes his son took the kingdom; who, as he inherited his father's kingdom, so did he inherit his piety towards God, and honour of him; for he did all things suitably to his father relating to divine worship, and he was exceeding friendly to the Jews. (121) Now about this time a son of Jeshua, whose name was Joacim, was the high priest. Moreover, there was now in Babylon a righteous man, and one that enjoyed a great reputation among the multitude; he was the principal priest of the people, and his name was Esdras. He was very skilful in the laws of Moses, and was well acquainted with King Xerxes. (122) He had determined to go up to Jerusalem, and to take with him some of those Jews that were in Babylon; and he desired that the king would give him an epistle to the governors of Syria, by which they might know who he was. (123) Accordingly, the king wrote the following epistle to those governors: 'Xerxes, king of kings, to Esdras the priest, and reader of the divine law, greeting. I think it agreeable to that love which I bear to mankind, to permit those of the Jewish nation who are so disposed, as well as those of the priests and Levites that are in our kingdom, to go together to Jerusalem. (124) Accordingly, I have given command for that purpose, and let everyone that hath a mind go, according as it hath seemed good to me and to my seven counsellors, and this in order to their review of the affairs of Judea, to see whether they be agreeable to the law of God. Let them also take with them those presents which I and my friends have vowed, (125) with all that silver and gold which is found in the country of the Babylonians, as dedicated to God, and let all this be carried to Jerusalem to God, for sacrifices. Let it also be lawful for thee and thy brethren to make as many vessels of silver and gold as thou pleasest. (126) Thou shalt also dedicate those holy vessels which have been given thee, and as many more as thou hast a mind to make, and shalt take the expenses out of the king's treasury. (127) I have moreover written to the treasurers of Syria and Phoenicia, that they take care of those affairs that Esdras the priest, and reader of the laws of God, is sent about; and that God may not

be at all angry with me or with my children, I grant all that is necessary for sacrifices to God according to the law, as far as a hundred cori of wheat; (128) and I enjoin you not to lay any treacherous imposition, or any tributes, upon their priests or Levites, or sacred singers, porters, or sacred servants, or scribes of the temple; (129) and do thou, O Esdras, appoint judges according to the wisdom [given thee] of God, and those such as understand the law, that they may judge in all Syria and Phoenicia; and do thou instruct those also which are ignorant of it, (130) that if anyone of thy countrymen transgress the law of God or that of the king, he may be punished, as not transgressing it out of ignorance, but as one that knows it indeed, but boldly despises and condemns it; and such may be punished by death, or by paying fines. Farewell.'

(131) When Esdras had received this epistle, he was very joyful, and began to worship God, and confessed that he had been the cause of the king's great favour to him, and that for the same reason he gave all the thanks to God. So he read the epistle at Babylon to those Jews that were there; but he kept the epistle itself, (132) and sent a copy of it to all those of his own nation that were in Media; and when these Jews had understood what piety the king had towards God, and what kindness he had for Esdras, they were all greatly pleased; nay, many of them took their effects with them, (133) and came to Babylon, as very desirous of going down to Jerusalem; but then the entire body of the people of Israel remained in that country; wherefore there are but two tribes in Asia and Europe subject to the Romans, while the ten tribes are beyond Euphrates till now, and are an immense multitude, and not to be estimated by numbers. (134) Now there came a great number of priests and Levites, and porters, and sacred singers and sacred servants, to Esdras. So he gathered those that were in the captivity together beyond Euphrates, and stayed there three days, and ordained a fast for them, that they might make their prayers to God for their preservation, that they might suffer no misfortunes by the way, either from their enemies, or from any other ill accident; (135) for Esdras had said beforehand, that he had told the king how God would preserve them, and so he had not thought fit to request that he would send horsemen to conduct them. So when they had finished their prayers, they removed from Euphrates, on the twelfth day of the first month of the seventh year of the reign of Xerxes, and they came to Jerusalem on the fifth month of the same year. (136) Now Esdras presented the sacred money to the treasurers, who were of the family of the priests, of silver six hundred and fifty talents, vessels of silver one hundred talents, vessels of gold twenty talents, vessels of brass, that was more precious than gold, twelve talents by weight; for these presents had been made by the king and his counsellors, and by all the Israelites that stayed at Babylon. (137) When Esdras had delivered these things to the priests, he gave to God, as the appointed sacrifices of whole burnt offerings, twelve bulls on account of the

common preservation of the people, ninety rams, seventy-two lambs, and twelve kids of the goats, for the remission of sins. (138) He also delivered the king's epistle to the king's officers, and to the governors of Celesyria and Phoenicia; and as they were under the necessity of doing what was enjoined by him, they honoured our nation, and were assistant to them in all their necessities.

(139) Now these things were truly done under the conduct of Esdras; and he succeeded in them, because God esteemed him worthy of the success of his conduct, on account of his goodness and righteousness. (140) But some time afterward there came some persons to him, and brought an accusation against certain of the multitude, and of the priests and Levites, who had transgressed their settlement, and dissolved the laws of their country, by marrying strange wives, and had brought the family of the priests into confusion. (141) These persons desired him to support the laws, lest God should take up a general anger against them all, and reduce them to a calamitous condition again. Hereupon he rent his garment immediately, out of grief, and pulled off the hair of his head and beard, and cast himself upon the ground, because this crime had reached the principal men among the people; (142) and considering that if he should enjoin them to cast out their wives, and the children they had by them, he should not be hearkened to, he continued lying upon the ground. However, all the better sort came running to him, who also themselves wept, and partook of the grief he was under for what had been done. (143) So Esdras rose up from the ground, and stretched out his hands towards Heaven, and said that he was ashamed to look towards it, because of the sins which the people had committed while they had cast out of their memories what their fathers had undergone on account of their wickedness; (144) and he besought God, who had saved a seed and a remnant out of the calamity and captivity they had been in, and had restored them again to Jerusalem, and to their own land, and had obliged the king of Persia to have compassion on them, that he would also forgive them their sins they had now committed, which, though they deserved death, yet was it agreeable to the mercy of God to remit even to these the punishment due to them.

(145) After Esdras had said this, he left off praying; and when all those that came to him with their wives and children were under lamentation, one, whose name was Jechonias, a principal man in Jerusalem, came to him, and said, that they had sinned in marrying strange wives; and he persuaded him to adjure them all to cast those wives out, and the children born of them; and that those should be punished who would not obey the law. (146) So Esdras hearkened to this advice, and made the heads of the priests, and of the Levites, and of the Israelites, swear that they would put away those wives and children, according to the advice of Jechonias; (147) and when he had received their

oaths, he went in haste out of the temple into the chamber of Johanan, the son of Eliasib, and as he had hitherto tasted nothing at all for grief, so he abode there that day; (148) and when proclamation was made, that all those of the captivity should gather themselves together to Jerusalem, and those that did not meet there in two or three days should be banished from the multitude, and that their substance should be appropriated to the uses of the temple, according to the sentence of the elders, those that were of the tribes of Judah and Benjamin came together in three days, viz., on the twentieth day of the ninth month, which according to the Hebrews is called *Tebeth*, and according to the Macedonians, *Apelleius*. (149) Now as they were sitting in the upper room of the temple, where the elders also were present, but were uneasy because of the cold, Esdras stood up and accused them, and told them that they had sinned in marrying wives that were not of their own nation; but that now they would do a thing both pleasing to God and advantageous to themselves, if they would put those wives away. (150) Accordingly, they all cried out that they would do so. That, however, the multitude was great, and that the season of the year was winter, and that this work would require more than one or two days; 'Let their rulers, therefore [said they], and those that have married strange wives, come hither at a proper time, while the elders of every place, that are in common, to estimate the number of those that have thus married, are to be there also.' (151) Accordingly, this was resolved on by them; and they began the inquiry after those that had married strange wives on the first day of the tenth month, and continued the inquiry to the first day of the next month, and found a great many of the posterity of Jeshua the high priest, and of the priests and Levites, and Israelites, (152) who had a greater regard to the observation of the law than to their natural affection, and immediately cast out their wives, and the children which were born of them; and in order to appease God, they offered sacrifices and slew rams, as oblations to him; but it does not seem to me to be necessary to set down the names of these men. (153) So when Esdras had reformed this sin about the marriages of the forementioned persons, he reduced that practice to purity, so that it continued in that state for the time to come.

(154) Now when they kept the feast of tabernacles in the seventh month, and almost all the people were come together to it, they went up to the open part of the temple, to the gate which looked eastward, and desired of Esdras that the laws of Moses might be read to them. (155) Accordingly, he stood in the midst of the multitude and read them; and this he did from morning to noon. Now, by hearing the laws read to them, they were instructed to be righteous men for the present and for the future; but as for their past offences, they were displeased at themselves and proceeded to shed tears on their account, as considering with themselves, that if they had kept the law, they had

endured none of these miseries which they had experienced; (156) but when Esdras saw them in that disposition, he bade them go home and not weep, for that it was a festival, and that they ought not to weep thereon, for that it was not lawful so to do. He exhorted them rather to proceed immediately to feasting, and to do what was suitable to a feast, and what was agreeable to a day of joy; but to let their repentance and sorrow for their former sins be a security and a guard to them, that they fell no more into the like offences. (157) So upon Esdras' exhortation they began to feast: and when they had so done for eight days, in their tabernacles, they departed to their own homes, singing hymns to God, and returning thanks to Esdras for his reformation of what corruptions had been introduced into their settlement. (158) So it came to pass, that after he had obtained this reputation among the people, he died an old man, and was buried in a magnificent manner at Jerusalem. About the same time it happened also that Joacim, the high priest, died; and his son Eliasib succeeded in the high priesthood.

(159) Now there was one of those Jews that had been carried captive, who was cupbearer to King Xerxes; his name was Nehemiah. As this man was walking before Susa, the metropolis of the Persians, he heard some strangers that were entering the city, after a long journey, speaking to one another in the Hebrew tongue; so he went to them and asked from whence they came; (160) and when their answer was, that they came from Judea, he began to inquire of them again in what state the multitude was, and in what condition Jerusalem was; (161) and when they replied that they were in a bad state, for that their walls were thrown down to the ground, and that the neighbouring nations did a great deal of mischief to the Jews, while in the daytime they overran the country and pillaged it, and in the night did them mischief, insomuch that not a few were led away captive out of the country, and out of Jerusalem itself, and that the roads were in the daytime found full of dead men; (162) hereupon Nehemiah shed tears, out of commiseration of the calamities of his countrymen; and, looking up to Heaven he said, 'How long, O Lord, wilt thou overlook our nation, while it suffers so great miseries, and while we are made the prey and spoil of all men?' (163) And while he stayed at the gate, and lamented thus, one told him that the king was going to sit down to supper; so he made haste, and went as he was, without washing himself, to minister to the king in his office of cupbearer: (164) but as the king was very pleasant after supper, and more cheerful than usual, he cast his eyes on Nehemiah, and seeing him look sad, he asked him why he was sad. (165) Whereupon he prayed to God to give him favour, and afford him the power of persuading by his words; and said, 'How can I, O king, appear otherwise than thus, and not be in trouble, while I hear that the walls of Jerusalem, the city where are the sepulchres of my fathers, are thrown down to the ground, and that its gates are

consumed by fire? But do thou grant me the favour to go and build its wall, and to finish the building of the temple.' (166) Accordingly the king gave him a signal that he freely granted him what he asked; and told him, that he should carry an epistle to the governors, that they might pay him due honour, and afford him whatsoever assistance he wanted, and as he pleased. 'Leave off thy sorrow then,' said the king, 'and be cheerful in the performance of thy office hereafter.' (167) So Nehemiah worshipped God, and gave the king thanks for his promise, and cleared up his sad and cloudy countenance, by the pleasure he had from the king's promises. Accordingly, the king called for him the next day, and gave him an epistle to be carried to Adeus, the governor of Syria and Phoenicia and Samaria; wherein he sent to him to pay due honour to Nehemiah, and to supply him with what he wanted for his building.

(168) Now when he was come to Babylon, and had taken with him many of his countrymen, who voluntarily followed him, he came to Jerusalem in the twenty and fifth year of the reign of Xerxes; and when he had shown the epistles to God, he gave them to Adeus and to the other governors. He also called together all the people to Jerusalem, and stood in the midst of the temple, and made the following speech to them: (169) 'You know, O Jews, that God hath kept our fathers, Abraham, Isaac, and Jacob, in mind continually; and for the sake of their righteousness hath not left off the care of you. Indeed, he hath assisted me in gaining this authority of the king to raise up our wall, and finish what is wanting of the temple. (170) I desire you, therefore, who well know the ill will our neighbouring nations bear to us, and that when once they are made sensible that we are in earnest about building, they will come upon us and contrive many ways of obstructing our works, (171) that you will, in the first place, put your trust in God, as in him that will assist us against their hatred, and to intermit building neither night nor day, but to use all diligence, and to hasten on the work, now we have this especial opportunity for it.' (172) When he had said this, he gave order that the rulers should measure the wall, and part the work of it among the people, according to their villages and cities, as everyone's ability should require. And when he had added this promise, that he himself, with his servants, would assist them, he dissolved the assembly. (173) So the Jews prepared for the work: that is the name they are called by from the day that they came up from Babylon, which is taken from the tribe of Judah, which came first to these places, and thence both they and the country gained that appellation.

(174) But now when the Ammonites, and Moabites, and Samaritans, and all that inhabited Celesyria, heard that the building went on apace, they took it heinously, and proceeded to lay snares for them, and to hinder their intentions. (175) They also slew many of the Jews, and sought how they might destroy Nehemiah himself, by hiring some of the foreigners to kill him. They also put

the Jews in fear, and disturbed them, and spread abroad rumours, as if many nations were ready to make an expedition against them, by which means they were harassed, and had almost left off the building. (176) But none of these things could deter Nehemiah from being diligent about the work; he only set a number of men about him as a guard to his body, and so unweariedly persevered therein, and was insensible of any trouble out of his desire to perfect this work. And thus did he attentively, and with great forecast, take care of his own safety; not that he feared death, but of this persuasion, that if he were dead, the walls for his citizens would never be raised. (177) He also gave orders that the builders should keep their ranks, and have their armour on while they were building. Accordingly, the mason had his sword on, as well as he that brought the materials for building. He also appointed that their shields should lie very near them; and he placed trumpeters at every five hundred feet, and charged them, that if their enemies appeared, they should give notice of it to the people, that they might fight in their armour, and their enemies might not fall upon them naked. (178) He also went about the compass of the city by night, being never discouraged, neither about the work itself, nor about his own diet and sleep, for he made no use of those things for his pleasure, but out of necessity. (179) And this trouble he underwent for two years and four months; for in so long a time was the wall built, in the twenty-eighth year of the reign of Xerxes, in the ninth month. (180) Now when the walls were finished, Nehemiah and the multitude offered sacrifices to God for the building of them; and they continued in feasting eight days. However, when the nations which dwelt in Syria heard that the building of the wall was finished, they had indignation at it; (181) but when Nehemiah saw that the city was thin of people, he exhorted the priests and the Levites that they would leave the country, and remove themselves to the city, and there continue, and he built them houses at his own expenses; (182) and he commanded that part of the people who were employed in cultivating the land to bring the tithes of their fruits to Jerusalem, that the priests and Levites having whereof they might live perpetually, might not leave the divine worship; who willing hearkened to the constitutions of Nehemiah, by which means the city Jerusalem came to be fuller of people than it was before. (183) So when Nehemiah had done many other excellent things, and things worthy of commendation, in a glorious manner, he came to a great age, and then died. He was a man of a good and righteous disposition, and very ambitious to make his own nation happy; and he hath left the walls of Jerusalem as an eternal monument for himself. Now this was done in the days of Xerxes.

CHAPTER 6

(184) After the death of Xerxes, the kingdom came to be transferred to his son Cyrus, whom the Greeks called Artaxerxes. When this man had obtained the government over the Persians, the whole nation of the Jews, with their wives and children, were in danger of perishing; (185) the occasion whereof we shall declare in a little time; for it is proper, in the first place, to explain somewhat relating to this king, and how he came to marry a Jewish wife, who was herself of the royal family also, and who is related to have saved our nation; (186) for when Artaxerxes had taken the kingdom, and had set governors over the hundred twenty and seven provinces, from India even unto Ethiopia, in the third year of his reign, he made a costly feast for his friends, and for the nations of Persia, and for their governors, such a one as was proper for a king to make, when he had a mind to make a public demonstration of his riches, and this for a hundred and fourscore days; (187) after which he made a feast for other nations, and for their ambassadors, at Shushan, for seven days. Now this feast was ordered after the manner following: he caused a tent to be pitched, which was supported by pillars of gold and silver, with curtains of linen and purple spread over them, that it might afford room for many ten thousands to sit down. (188) The cups with which the waiters ministered were of gold, and adorned with precious stones, for pleasure and for sight. He also gave order to the servants, that they should not force them to drink by bringing them wine continually, as is the practice of the Persians, but to permit every one of the guests to enjoy himself according to his own inclination. (189) Moreover, he sent messengers through the country, and gave order that they should have a remission of their labours, and should keep a festival many days, on account of his kingdom. (190) In like manner did Vashti the queen gather her guests together, and made them a feast in the palace. Now the king was desirous to show her, who exceeded all other women in beauty, to those that feasted with him, and he sent some to command her to come to his feast. (191) But she, out of regard to the laws of the Persians, which forbid the wives to be seen by strangers, did not go to the king; and though he oftentimes sent the eunuchs to her, she did nevertheless stay away, and refused to come, (192) till the king was so much irritated, that he brake up the entertainment, and rose up, and called for those seven who had the interpretation of the laws committed to them, and accused his wife, and said, that he had been affronted by her, because that when she was frequently called by him to his feast, she did not obey him once. (193) He therefore gave order that they should inform him what could be done by the law against her. So one of them, whose name was Memucan, said that this affront was offered not to him alone, but to all the Persians, who were

in danger of leading their lives very ill with their wives, if they must be thus despised by them; (194) for that none of their wives would have any reverence for their husbands, if they had 'such an example of arrogance in the queen towards thee, who rulest over all'. Accordingly, he exhorted him to punish her, who had been guilty of so great an affront to him, after a severe manner; and when he had so done, to publish to the nations what had been decreed about the queen. So the resolution was to put Vashti away, and to give her dignity to another woman.

(195) But the king having been fond of her, he did not well bear a separation, and yet by the law he could not admit of a reconciliation, so he was under trouble, as not having it in his power to do what he desired to do: but when his friends saw him so uneasy, they advised him to cast the memory of his wife, and his love for her, out of his mind, (196) but to send abroad over all the habitable earth, and to search out for comely virgins, and to take her whom he should best like for his wife, because his passion for his former wife would be quenched by the introduction of another, and the kindness he had for Vashti would be withdrawn from her, and be placed on her that was with him. (197) Accordingly, he was persuaded to follow this advice, and gave order to certain persons to choose out of the virgins that were in his kingdom those that were esteemed the most comely. (198) So when a great number of these virgins were gathered together, there was found a damsel in Babylon, whose parents were both dead, and she was brought up with her uncle Mordecai, for that was her uncle's name. This uncle was of the tribe of Benjamin, and was one of the principal persons among the Jews. (199) Now it proves that this damsel, whose name was Esther, was the most beautiful of all the rest, and that the grace of her countenance drew the eyes of the spectators principally upon her: (200) so she was committed to one of the eunuchs to take the care of her; and she was very exactly provided with sweet odours, in great plenty, and with costly ointments, such as her body required to be anointed withal; and this was used for six months by the virgins, who were in number four hundred; (201) and when the eunuch thought the virgins had been sufficiently purified, in the forementioned time, and were now fit to go to the king's bed, he sent one to be with the king every day. So when he had accompanied with her, he sent her back to the eunuch; (202) and when Esther had come to him, he was pleased with her, and fell in love with the damsel, and married her, and made her his lawful wife, and kept a wedding feast for her on the twelfth month of the seventh year of his reign which was called Adao. (203) He also sent *angari*, as they are called, or messengers, unto every nation, and gave orders that they should keep a feast for his marriage, while he himself treated the Persians and the Medes, and the principal men of the nations, for a whole month, on account of this his marriage. Accordingly, Esther came to his royal palace, and

he set a diadem on her head; and thus was Esther married, without making known to the king what nation she was derived from. (204) Her uncle also removed from Babylon to Shushan, and dwelt there, being every day about the palace, and inquiring how the damsel did, for he loved her as though she had been his own daughter.

(205) Now the king had made a law, that none of his own people should approach him unless they were called, when he sat upon his throne; and men with axes in their hands stood round about his throne, in order to punish such as approached to him without being called. (206) However, the king sat with a golden sceptre in his hand, which he held out when he had a mind to save anyone of those that approached to him without being called; and he who touched it was free from danger. But of this matter we have discoursed sufficiently.

(207) Some time after this [two eunuchs], Bigthan and Teresh, plotted against the king; and Barnabazus, the servant of one of the eunuchs, being by birth a Jew, was acquainted with their conspiracy, and discovered it to the queen's uncle; and Mordecai, by means of Esther, made the conspirators known to the king. (208) This troubled the king; but he discovered the truth, and hanged the eunuchs upon a cross, while at that time he gave no reward to Mordecai, who had been the occasion of his preservation. He only bade the scribes to set down his name in the records, and bade him stay in the palace, as an intimate friend of the king.

(209) Now there was one Haman, the son of Amedatha, by birth an Amalekite, that used to go into the king; and the foreigners and Persians worshipped him, as Artaxerxes had commanded that such honour should be paid to him; (210) but Mordecai was so wise, and so observant of his own country's laws, that he would not worship the man. When Haman observed this, he inquired whence he came; and when he understood that he was a Jew, he had indignation at him, and said within himself, that whereas the Persians, who were free men, worshipped him, this man, who was no better than a slave, does not vouchsafe to do so. (211) And when he desired to punish Mordecai, he though it too small a thing to request of the king that he alone might be punished; he rather determined to abolish the whole nation, for he was naturally an enemy to the Jews, because the nation of the Amalekites, of which he was, had been destroyed by them. (212) Accordingly he came to the king, and accused them, saying, 'There is a certain wicked nation, and it is dispersed over all the habitable earth that was under his dominion; a nation separate from others, unsociable, neither admitting the same sort of divine worship that others do, nor using laws like to the laws of others, at enmity with thy people, and with all men, both in their manners and practices. (213) Now, if thou wilt be a benefactor to thy subjects, thou wilt give order to destroy

them utterly, and not leave the least remains of them, nor preserve any of them, either for slaves or for captives.' (214) But that the king might not be damnified by the loss of the tributes which the Jews paid him, Haman promised to give him out of his own estate forty thousand talents whensoever he pleased; and he said he would pay this money very willingly, that the kingdom might be freed from such a misfortune.

(215) When Haman had made this petition, the king both forgave him the money, and granted him the men, to do what he would with them. So Haman, having gained what he desired, sent out immediately a decree, as from the king, to all nations, the contents whereof were these: (216) 'Artaxerxes, the great king, to the rulers of the hundred twenty-seven provinces, from India to Ethiopia, sends this writing. Whereas I have governed many nations and obtained the dominions of all the habitable earth, according to my desire, and have not been obliged to do anything that is insolent or cruel to my subjects by such my power, but have showed myself mild and gentle, by taking care of their peace and good order, and have sought how they might enjoy those blessings for all time to come; (217) and whereas I have been kindly informed by Haman, who, on account of his prudence and justice, is the first in my esteem and in dignity, and only second to myself, for his fidelity and constant good will to me, that there is an ill-natured nation intermixed with all mankind, that is averse to our laws and not subject to kings, and of a different conduct of life from others, that hateth monarchy, and of a disposition that is pernicious to our affairs; (218) I give order that these men, of whom Haman, our second father, hath informed us, be destroyed, with their wives and children, and that none of them be spared, and that none prefer pity to them before obedience to this decree; (219) and this I will to be executed on the fourteenth day of the twelfth month of this present year, that so when all that have enmity to us are destroyed, and this in one day, we may be allowed to lead the rest of our lives in peace hereafter.' (220) Now when this decree was brought to the cities, and to the country, all were ready for the destruction and entire abolishment of the Jews, against the day before-mentioned; and they were very hasty about it at Shushan, in particular. Accordingly, the king and Haman spent their time in feasting together with good cheer and wine; but the city was in disorder.

(221) Now when Mordecai was informed of what was done, he rent his clothes, and put on sackcloth, and sprinkled ashes upon his head, and went about the city, crying out, that 'a nation that had been injurious to no man, was to be destroyed.' And he went on saying thus as far as to the king's palace, and there he stood, for it was not lawful for him to go into it in that habit. (222) The same thing was done by all Jews that were in the several cities wherein this decree was published, with lamentation and mourning, on account of the

calamities denounced against them. But as soon as certain persons had told the queen that Mordecai stood before the court in a mourning habit, she was disturbed at this report, and sent out such as should change his garments; (223) but when he could not be induced to put off his sackcloth, because the sad occasion that forced him to put in was not yet ceased, she called the eunuch Acratheus for he was then present, and sent him to Mordecai, in order to know of him what sad accident had befallen him, for which he was in mourning, and would not put off the habit he had put on, at her desire. (224) Then did Mordecai inform the eunuch of the occasion of his mourning, and of the decree which was sent by the king into all the country, and of the promise of money whereby Haman brought the destruction of their nation. (225) He also gave him a copy of what was proclaimed at Shushan, to be carried to Esther; and he charged her to petition the king about this matter, and not to think it a dishonourable thing in her to put on a humble habit, for the safety of her nation, wherein she might deprecate the ruin of the Jews, who were in danger of it; for that Haman, whose dignity was only inferior to that of the king, had accused the Jews, and had irritated that king against them. (226) When she was informed of this, she sent to Mordecai again, and told him that she was not called by the king, and that he who goes in to him without being called, is to be slain, unless when he is willing to save anyone, he holds out his golden sceptre to him; but that to whomsoever he does so, although he go in without being called, that person is so far from being slain, that he obtains pardon, and is entirely preserved. (227) Now when the eunuch carried this message from Esther to Mordecai, he bade him also tell her that she must not only provide for her own preservation, but for the common preservation of her nation, for that if she now neglected this opportunity, there would certainly arise help to them from God some other way: but she and her father's house would be destroyed by those whom she now despised. (228) But Esther sent the very same eunuch back to Mordecai [to desire him], to go to Shushan, and to gather the Jews that were there together to a congregation, and to fast, and abstain from all sorts of food, on her account, and [to let him know that] she with her maidens would do the same; and then she promised that she would go to the king, though it were against the law, and that if she must die for it, she would not refuse it.

(229) Accordingly, Mordecai did as Esther had enjoined him, and made the people fast; and he besought God, together with them, not to overlook his nation, particularly at this time when it was going to be destroyed: but that, as he had often before provided for them, and forgiven them when they had sinned, so he would now deliver them from that destruction which was denounced against them; (230) for although it was not all the nation that had offended, yet must they so ingloriously be slain, and that he was himself the

occasion of the wrath of Haman, 'Because,' said he, 'I did not worship him, nor could I endure to pay that honour to him which I used to pay to thee, O Lord; for upon that his anger hath he contrived this present mischief against those that have not transgressed thy laws.' (231) The same supplications did the multitude put up; and entreated that God would provide for their deliverance, and free the Israelites that were in all the earth from this calamity which was now coming upon them, for they had it before their eyes, and expected its coming. Accordingly Esther made supplication to God after the manner of her country, by casting herself down upon the earth, and putting on her mourning garments, (232) and bidding farewell to meat and drink and all delicacies, for three days' time; and she entreated God to have mercy upon her, and make her words appear persuasive to the king, and render her countenance more beautiful than it was before, (233) that both by her words and beauty she might succeed, for the averting of the king's anger, in case he were at all irritated against her, and for the consolation of those of her own country, now they were in the utmost danger of perishing: as also that he would excite a hatred in the king against the enemies of the Jews, and those that had contrived their future destruction, if they proved to be condemned by him.

(234) When Esther had used this supplication for three days, she put off those garments, and changed her habit, and adorned herself as became a queen, and took two of her handmaids with her, the one of which supported her, as she gently leaned upon her, and the other followed after, and lifted up her large train (which swept along the ground) with the extremities of her fingers; and thus she came to the king, having a blushing redness in her countenance, with a pleasant agreeableness in her behaviour, yet did she go in to him with fear; (235) and as soon as she was come over against him, as he was sitting on his throne, in his royal apparel, which was a garment interwoven with gold and precious stones, (236) which made him seem to her more terrible, especially when he looked at her somewhat severely and with a countenance on fire with anger; her joints failed her immediately, out of the dread she was in, and she fell down sideways in a swoon: (237) but the king changed his mind, which happened, as I suppose, by the will of God, and was concerned for his wife, lest her fear should bring some very evil thing upon her, (238) and he leaped from his throne, and took her in his arms, and recovered her, by embracing her and speaking comfortably to her, exhorting her to be of good cheer, and not to suspect anything that was sad on account of her coming to him without being called, because that law was made for subjects, but that she, who was a queen, as well as he a king, might be entirely secure: (239) and as he said this, he put the sceptre into her hand, and laid his rod upon her neck on account of the law; and so freed her from her fear. (240) And after she had recovered herself by these encouragements, she said, 'My lord, it is not easy for me, on the

sudden, to say what hath happened, for as soon as I saw thee to be great and comely and terrible, my spirit departed from me, and I had no soul left in me.' (241) And while it was with difficulty and in a low voice that she could say thus much, the king was in a great agony and disorder, and encouraged Esther to be of good cheer, and to expect better fortune, since he was ready, if occasion should require it, to grant to her the half of his kingdom. (242) Accordingly, Esther desired that he and his friend Haman would come to her to a banquet, for she said she had prepared a supper for him. He consented to it; and when they were there, as they were drinking, he bade Esther to let him know what she desired; (243) for that she should not be disappointed, though she should desire the half of his kingdom. But she put off the discovery of her petition till the next day, if he would come again, together with Haman, to her banquet.

(244) Now when the king had promised so to do, Haman went away very glad, because he alone had the honour of supping with the king at Esther's banquet, and because no one else partook of the same honour with kings but himself; yet when he saw Mordecai in the court, he was very much displeased, for he paid him no manner of respect when he saw him. (245) So he went home and called for his wife Zeresh and his friends, and when they were come, he showed them what honour he enjoyed, not only from the king, but from the queen also, for as he alone had that day supped with her, together with the king, so he was also invited again for the next day; (246) 'Yet,' said he, 'am I not pleased to see Mordecai the Jew in the court.' Hereupon his wife Zeresh advised him to give order that a gallows should be made fifty cubits high, and that in the morning he should ask it of the king that Mordecai might be hanged thereon. So he commended her advice, and gave order to his servants to prepare the gallows, and to place it in the court, for the punishment of Mordecai thereon, (247) which was accordingly prepared. But God laughed to scorn the wicked expectations of Haman; and as he knew what the event would be, he was delighted at it, for that night he took away the king's sleep: (248) and as the king was not willing to lose the time of his lying awake, but to spend it in something that might be of advantage to his kingdom, he commanded the scribe to bring him the chronicles of the former kings and the records of his own actions; (249) and when he had brought them, and was reading them, one was found to have received a country on account of his excellent management on a certain occasion, and the name of the country was set down; another was found to have had a present made him on account of his fidelity: then the scribe came to Bigthan and Teresh, the eunuchs that had made a conspiracy against the king, which Mordecai had discovered; (250) and when the scribe said no more but that, and was going on to another history, the king stopped him, and inquired, 'whether it was not added that Mordecai

had a reward given him?' and when he said there was no such addition, he bade him leave off; and he inquired of those that were appointed for that purpose, what hour of the night it was; (251) and when he was informed that it was already day, he gave order that, if they found anyone of his friends already come, and standing before the court, they should tell him. Now it happened that Haman was found there, for he was come sooner than ordinary, to petition the king to have Mordecai put to death: (252) and when the servants said, that Haman was before the court, he bade them call him in; and when he was come in, he said, 'Because I know that thou art my only fast friend, I desire thee to give me advice how I may honour one that I greatly love, and that after a manner suitable to my magnificence.' (253) Now Haman reasoned with himself, that what opinion he should give it would be for himself, since it was he alone who was beloved by the king; so he gave that advice which he thought of all other the best; for he said, (254) 'If thou wouldst truly honour a man whom thou sayest thou does love, give order that he may ride on horseback, with the same garment which thou wearest, and with a gold chain about his neck, and let one of thy intimate friends go before him, and proclaim through the whole city, that whosoever the king honoureth, obtaineth this mark of his honour.' (255) This was the advice which Haman gave, out of a supposal that such reward would come to himself. Hereupon the king was pleased with the advice, and said, 'Go thou, therefore, for thou hast the horse, the garment, and the chain, ask for Mordecai the Jew, and give him those things, and go before his horse and proclaim accordingly; for thou art,' said he, 'my intimate friend, and hast given me good advice; be thou then the minister of what thou hast advised me to. This shall be his reward from us for preserving my life.' (256) When he heard this order, which was entirely unexpected, he was confounded in his mind, and knew not what to do. However, he went out and led the horse, and took the purple garment, and the golden chain for the neck, and finding Mordecai before the court, clothed in sackcloth, he bade him put that garment off, and put the purple garment on: (257) but Mordecai not knowing the truth of the matter, but thinking that it was done in mockery, said, 'O thou wretch, the vilest of all mankind, dost thou thus laugh at our calamities?' But when he was satisfied that the king bestowed this honour upon him, for the deliverance he had procured him when he convicted the eunuchs who had conspired against him, he put on that purple garment which the king always wore, and put the chain about his neck, (258) and got on horseback, and went round the city, while Haman went before, and proclaimed, 'This shall be the reward which the king will bestow on everyone whom he loves, and esteems worthy of honour.' (259) And when they had gone round the city, Mordecai went in to the king; but Haman went home, out of shame, and informed his wife and friends of what had happened, and this with tears: who said that he would never be able to be revenged of Mordecai, for that God was with him.

(260) Now while these men were thus talking one to another, Esther's eunuchs hastened Haman away to come to supper: (261) but one of the eunuchs named Sabuchadas, saw the gallows that was fixed in Haman's house, and inquired of one of his servants for what purpose they had prepared it. So he knew that it was for the queen's uncle, because Haman was about to petition the king that he might be punished; but at present he held his peace. (262) Now when the king, with Haman, were at the banquet, he desired the queen to tell him what gift she desired to obtain, and assured her that she should have whatsoever she had a mind to. She then lamented the danger her people were in; and said, that 'she and her nation were given up to be destroyed, and that she, on that account, made this her petition: (263) that she would not have troubled him if he had only given order that they should be sold into bitter servitude, for such a misfortune would not have been intolerable; but she desired that they might be delivered from such destruction.' (264) And when the king inquired of her who was the author of this misery to them, she then openly accused Haman, and convicted him, that he had been the wicked instrument of this, and had formed this plot against them. (265) When the king was hereupon in disorder, and was gone hastily out of the banquet into the gardens, Haman began to intercede with Esther, and to beseech her to forgive him as to what he had offended, for he perceived that he was in a very bad case. And as he had fallen upon the queen's bed, and was making supplications to her, the king came in, and being still more provoked at what he saw, 'O thou wretch,' said he, 'thou vilest of mankind, dost thou aim to force my wife?' (266) And when Haman was astonished at this, and not able to speak one word more, Sabuchadas the eunuch came in, and accused Haman, and said, 'he found a gallows at his house, prepared for Mordecai; for that the servant told him so much, upon his inquiry, when he was sent to him to call him to supper.' He said further, that the gallows was fifty cubits high: (267) which when the king heard, he determined that Haman should be punished after no other manner than that which had been devised by him against Mordecai; so he gave order immediately that he should be hung upon those gallows, and be put to death after that manner. (268) And from hence I cannot forbear to admire God, and to learn hence his wisdom and his justice, not only in punishing the wickedness of Haman, but in so disposing it, that he should undergo the very same punishment which he had contrived for another; as also, because thereby he teaches others this lesson, that what mischiefs anyone prepares against another, he, without knowing of it, first contrives it against himself.

(269) Wherefore Haman, who had immoderately abused the honour he had from the king, was destroyed after this manner; and the king granted his estate

to the queen. He also called for Mordecai (for Esther had informed him that she was akin to him), and gave that ring to Mordecai which he had before given to Haman. (270) The queen also gave Haman's estate to Mordecai; and prayed the king to deliver the nation of the Jews from the fear of death, and showed him what had been written over all the country by Haman the son of Ammedatha; for that if her country were destroyed, and her countrymen were to perish, she could not bear to live herself any longer. (271) So the king promised her that he would not do anything that should be disagreeable to her, nor contradict what she desired; but he bade her write what she pleased about the Jews in the king's name, and seal it with his seal, and send it to all his kingdom, for that those who read epistles whose authority is secured by having the king's seal to them, would no way contradict what was written therein. (272) So he commanded the king's scribes to be sent for, and to write to the nations, on the Jews' behalf, and to his lieutenants and governors that were over his hundred twenty-seven provinces, from India to Ethiopia. Now the contents of this epistle were these: (273) 'The great king Artaxerxes to our rulers, and those that are our faithful subjects, sendeth greeting. Many men there are who, on account of the greatness of the benefits bestowed on them, and because of the honour which they have obtained from the wonderful kind treatment of those that bestowed it, are not only injurious to their inferiors, (274) but do not scruple to do evil to those that have been their benefactors, as if they would take away gratitude from among men, and by their insolent abuse of such benefits as they never expected, they turn the abundance they have against those that are the authors of it, and suppose that they shall lie concealed from God in that case, and avoid that vengeance which comes from him. (275) Some of these men, when they have had the management of affairs committed to them by their friends, and bearing private malice of their own against some others, by deceiving those that have the power, persuade them to be angry at such as have done them no harm, till they are in danger of perishing, and this by laying accusations and calumnies: (276) nor is this state of things to be discovered by ancient examples, or such as we have learned by report only, but by some examples of such impudent attempts under our own eyes, so that it is not fit to attend any longer to calumnies and accusations, nor to the persuasion of others, but to determine what anyone knows of himself to have been really done, and to punish what justly deserves it, and to grant favours to such as are innocent. (277) This hath been the case of Haman, the son of Ammedatha, by birth an Amalekite, and alien from the blood of the Persians, who, when he was hospitably entertained by us, and partook of that kindness which we bear to all men to so great a degree as to be called my father, and to be all along worshipped, and to have honour paid him by all in the second rank after the royal honour due to ourselves, he could not bear his good fortune, nor govern the magnitude of his prosperity with sound reason; (278) nay, he made a conspiracy against me and my life, who gave him his authority, by endeavouring to take away Mordecai, my benefactor and my saviour, and by basely and treacherously requiring to have Esther, the partner of my life and of my dominion, brought to destruction; for he contrived by this means to deprive me of my faithful friends, and transfer the government to others: (279) but since I perceived that these Jews, that were by this pernicious fellow devoted to destruction, were not wicked men, but conducted their lives after the best manner, and were men dedicated to the worship of that God who hath preserved the kingdom to me and to my ancestors, I do not only free them from the punishment which the former epistle, which was sent by Haman, ordered to be inflicted on them – to which if you refuse obedience you shall dwell; (280) but I will that they have all honour paid them. Accordingly, I have hanged up the man that contrived such things against them, with his family, before the gates of Shushan; that punishment being sent upon him by God, who seeth all things. (281) And I give you in charge, that you publicly propose a copy of this epistle through all my kingdom, that the Jews may be permitted peaceably to use their own laws, and that you assist them, that at the same season whereto their miserable estate did belong, they may defend themselves the very same day from unjust violence, the thirteenth day of the twelfth month, which is Adar – (282) for God hath made that day a day of salvation instead of a day of destruction to them; and may it be a good day to those that wish us well, and a memorial of the punishment of the conspirators against us: (283) and I will that you take notice that every city, and every nation that shall disobey anything that is contained in this epistle, shall be destroyed by fire and sword. However, let this epistle be published through all the country that is under our obedience, and let all the Jews by all means be ready against the day before mentioned, that they may avenge themselves upon their enemies.'

(284) Accordingly, the horsemen who carried the epistles proceeded on the ways which they were to go with speed; but as for Mordecai, as soon as he had assumed the royal garment and the crown of gold, and had put the chain about his neck, he went forth in a public procession; and when the Jews who were at Shushan saw him in so great honour with the king, they thought his good fortune was common to themselves also; (285) and joy and a beam of salvation encompassed the Jews, both those that were in the cities and those that were in the countries, upon the publication of the king's letters, insomuch that many even of other nations circumcised their foreskin for fear of the Jews, that they might procure safety to themselves thereby; (286) for on the thirteenth day of the twelfth month, which according to the Hebrews is called *Adar*, but according to the Macedonians, *Dystrus*, those that carry the king's epistle gave them notice, that the same day wherein their danger was to have

been, on that very day should they destroy their enemies. (287) But now the rulers of the provinces, and the tyrants and the kings and the scribes, had the Jews in esteem; for the fear they were in of Mordecai forced them to act with discretion. (288) Now when the royal decree was come to all the country that was subject to the king, it fell out that the Jews at Shushan slew five hundred of their enemies: (289) and when the king had told Esther the number of those that were slain in that city, but did not well know what had been done in the provinces, he asked her whether she would have anything further done against them, for that it should be done accordingly: upon which she desired that the Jews might be permitted to treat their remaining enemies in the same manner the next day; and also, that they might hang the ten sons of Haman upon the gallows. (290) So the king permitted the Jews so to do, as desirous not to contradict Esther. So they gathered themselves together again on the fourteenth day of the month Dystrus, and slew about three hundred of their enemies, but touched nothing of what riches they had. (291) Now there were slain by the Jews that were in the country, and in the other cities, seventy-five thousand of their enemies, and these were slain on the thirteenth day of the month, and the next day they kept as a festival. (292) In like manner the Jews that were in Shushan gathered themselves together, and feasted on the fourteenth day and that which followed it; whence it is, that even now all the Jews that are in the habitable earth keep these days festivals, and send portions to one another. (293) Mordecai also wrote to the Jews that lived in the kingdom of Artaxerxes to observe these days, and to celebrate them as festivals, and to deliver them down to posterity, that this festival might continue for all time to come, and that it might never be buried in oblivion; (294) for since they were about to be destroyed on these days by Haman they would do a right thing, upon escaping the danger in them, and on them inflicting punishment on their enemies, to observe those days, and give thanks to God on them; (295) for which cause the Jews still keep the forementioned days, and call them days of Phurim [or Purim]. And Mordecai became a great and illustrious person with the king, and assisted him in the government of the people. He also lived with the queen; (296) so that the affairs of the Jews were, by their means, better than they could ever have hoped for. And this was the state of the Jews under the reign of Artaxerxes.

CHAPTER 7

(297) When Eliasib the high priest was dead, his son Judas succeeded in the high priesthood: and when he was dead, his son John took that dignity; on whose account it was also that Bagoses, the general of another Artaxerxes' army, polluted the temple, and imposed tributes on the Jews, that out of the public stock, before they offered the daily sacrifices, they should pay for every

lamb fifty shekels. (298) Now Jesus was the brother of John, and was a friend of Bagoses, who had promised to procure him the high priesthood. (299) In confidence of whose support, Jesus quarrelled with John in the temple, and so provoked his brother, that in his anger his brother slew him. Now it was a horrible thing for John when he was high priest, to perpetrate so great a crime, and so much the more horrible, that there never was so cruel and impious a thing done, neither by the Greeks nor barbarians. (300) However, God did not neglect its punishment; but the people were on that very account enslaved, and the temple was polluted by the Persians. Now when Bagoses the general of Artaxerxes' army, knew that John, the high priest of the Jews, had slain his own brother Jesus in the temple, he came upon the Jews immediately, and began in anger to say to them, 'Have you had the impudence to perpetrate a murder in your temple?' (301) And as he was aiming to go into the temple, they forbade him so to do; but he said to them. 'Am not I purer than he that was slain in the temple?' And when he had said these words, he went into the temple. Accordingly, Bagoses made use of this pretence, and punished the Jews seven years for the murder of Jesus.

(302) Now when John had departed this life, his son Jaddua succeeded in the high priesthood. He had a brother, whose name was Manasseh. Now there was one Sanballat who was sent by Darius, the last king [of Persia], into Samaria. He was a Cuthean by birth; of which stock were the Samaritans also. (303) This man knew that the city Jerusalem was a famous city, and that their kings had given a great deal of trouble to the Assyrians and the people of Celesyria; so that he willingly gave his daughter, whose name was Nicaso, in marriage to Manasseh, as thinking this alliance by marriage would be a pledge and security that the nation of the Jews should continue their good will to him.

CHAPTER 8

(304) About this time it was that Philip, king of Macedon was treacherously assaulted and slain at Egae by Pausanias the son of Cerastes, who was derived from the family of Orestae, (305) and his son Alexander succeeded him in the kingdom; who passing over the Hellespont, overcame the generals of Darius' army in a battle fought at Granicum. So he marched over Lydia, and subdued Ionia, and overran Caria and fell upon the places of Pamphylia, as has been related elsewhere.

(306) But the elders of Jerusalem being very uneasy that the brother of Jaddua the high priest, though married to a foreigner, should be a partner with him in the high priesthood quarrelled with him; (307) for they esteemed this man's marriage a step to such as should be desirous of transgressing about the marriage of [strange] wives, and that this would be the beginning of a mutual

society with foreigners, (308) although the offence of some about marriages, and their having married wives that were not of their own country, had been an occasion of their former captivity, and of the miseries they then underwent; so they commanded Manasseh to divorce his wife, or not to approach the altar, (309) the high priest himself joining with the people in their indignation against his brother, and driving him away from the altar. Whereupon Manasseh came to his father-in-law, Sanballat, and told him, that although he loved his daughter Nicaso, yet was he not willing to be deprived of his sacerdotal dignity on her account, which was the principal dignity in their nation, and always continued in the same family. (310) And then Sanballat promised him not only to preserve to him the honour of his priesthood, but to procure for him the power and dignity of a high priest, and would make him governor of all the places he himself now ruled, if he would keep his daughter for his wife. He also told him further, that he would build him a temple like that at Jerusalem upon Mount Gerizzim, which is the highest of all the mountains that are in Samaria; (311) and he promised that he would do this with the approbation of Darius the king. Manasseh was elevated with these promises, and stayed with Sanballat upon a supposal that he should gain a high priesthood, as bestowed on him by Darius, for it happened Sanballat was then in years. (312) But there was now a great disturbance among the people of Jerusalem, because many of those priests and Levites were entangled in such matches; for they all revolted to Manasseh, and Sanballat afforded them money, and divided among them land for tillage, and habitations also; and all this in order every way to gratify his son-in-law.

(313) About this time it was that Darius heard how Alexander had passed over the Hellespont, and had beaten his lieutenants in the battle at Granicum, and was proceeding farther; whereupon he gathered together an army of horse and foot, and determined that he would meet the Macedonians before they should assault and conquer all Asia. (314) So he passed over the river Euphrates and came over Taurus, the Cilician mountain; and at Issus of Cilicia he waited for the enemy, as ready there to give him battle. (315) Upon which Sanballat was glad that Darius was come down; and told Manasseh that he would suddenly perform his promises to him, and this as soon as ever Darius should come back, after he had beaten his enemies; for not he only, but all those that were in Asia also, were persuaded that the Macedonians would not so much as come to battle with the Persians, on account of their multitude; (316) but the event proved otherwise than they expected, for the king joined battle with the Macedonians, and was beaten, and lost a great part of his army. His mother also, and his wife and children, were taken captives, and he fled into Persia. (317) So Alexander came into Syria, and took Damascus, and when he had obtained Sidon, he besieged Tyre, when he sent an epistle to the Jewish high

priest, to send him some auxiliaries, and to supply his army with provisions; and that what presents he formerly sent to Darius he would now send to him, and choose the friendship of the Macedonians, and that he should never repent of so doing; (318) but the high priest answered the messengers, that he had given his oath to Darius not to bear arms against him and he said that he would not transgress this while Darius was in the land of the living. Upon hearing this answer, Alexander was very angry; (319) and though he determined not to leave Tyre, which was just ready to be taken, yet, as soon as he had taken it, he threatened that he would make an expedition against the Jewish high priest, and through him teach all men to whom they must keep their oaths. (320) So when he had, with a good deal of pains during the siege, taken Tyre, and had settled its affairs, he came to the city of Gaza, and besieged both the city and him that was governor of the garrison, whose name was Babemeses.

(321) But Sanballat thought he had now gotten a proper opportunity to make his attempt, so he renounced Darius, and taking with him seven thousand of his own subjects, he came to Alexander; and finding him beginning the siege of Tyre, he said to him, that he delivered up to him these men who came out of places under his dominion, and did gladly accept of him for their lord instead of Darius. (322) So when Alexander had received him kindly, Sanballat thereupon took courage, and spake to him about his present affair. He told him, that he had a son-in-law, Manasseh, who was brother to the high priest Jaddua; and that there were many others of his own nation now with him, that were desirous to have a temple in the places subject to him; (323) that it would be for the king's advantage to have the strength of the Jews divided into two parts, lest when the nation is of one mind and united, upon any attempt for innovation, it prove troublesome to kings, as it had formerly proved to the kings of Assyria. (324) Whereupon Alexander gave Sanballat leave so to do; who used the utmost diligence, and built the temple, and made Manasseh the priest, and deemed it a great reward that his daughter's children should have that dignity; (325) but when the seven months of the siege of Tyre were over, and the two months of the siege of Gaza, Sanballat died. Now Alexander, when he had taken Gaza, made haste to go up to Jerusalem; (326) and Jaddua the high priest, when he heard that, was in an agony, and under terror, as not knowing how he should meet the Macedonians, since the king was displeased at his foregoing disobedience. He therefore ordained that the people should make supplications, and should join with him in offering sacrifices to God, whom he besought to protect that nation, and to deliver them from the perils that were coming upon them; (327) whereupon God warned him in a dream, which came upon him after he had offered sacrifice, that he should take courage, and adorn the city, and open the gates; that the rest appear in white garments, but that he and the priests should meet the king

in the habits proper to their order, without the dread of any ill consequences, which the providence of God would prevent. (328) Upon which, when he rose from his sleep, he greatly rejoiced; and declared to all the warning he had received from God, according to which dream he acted entirely, and so waited for the coming of the king.

(329) And when he understood that he was not far from the city, he went out in procession, with the priests and the multitude of the citizens. The procession was venerable, and the manner of it different from that of other nations. It reached to a place called Sapha; which name, translated into Greek, signifies a *prospect*, for you have thence a prospect both of Jerusalem and of the temple; (330) and when the Phoenicians and the Chaldeans that followed him, thought they should have liberty to plunder the city, and torment the high priest to death, which the king's displeasure fairly promised them, the very reverse of it happened; (331) for Alexander, when he saw the multitude at a distance, in white garments, while the priests stood clothed with fine linen, and the high priest in purple and scarlet clothing, with his mitre on his head having the golden plate on which the name of God was engraved, he approached by himself, and adored that name, and first saluted the high priest. (332) The Jews also did all together, with one voice, salute Alexander, and encompass him about: whereupon the kings of Syria and the rest were surprised at what Alexander had done, and supposed him disordered in his mind. (333) However, Parmenio alone went up to him, and asked him how it came to pass, that when all others adored him, he should adore the high priest of the Jews? To whom he replied, 'I did not adore him, but that God who hath honoured him with that high priesthood; (334) for I saw this very person in a dream, in this very habit, when I was at Dios in Macedonia, who when I was considering with myself how I might obtain the dominion of Asia, exhorted me to make no delay, but boldly to pass over the sea thither, for that he would conduct my army, and would give me the dominion over the Persians; (335) whence it is, that having seen no other in that habit, and now seeing this person in it, and remembering that vision and the exhortation which I had in my dream, I believe that I bring this army under the divine conduct, and shall therewith conquer Darius, and destroy the power of the Persians, and that all things will succeed according to what is in my own mind.' (336) And when he had said this to Parmenio, and had given the high priest his right hand, the priests ran along by him, and he came into the city; and when he went up into the temple, he offered sacrifice to God, according to the high priest's direction, and magnificently treated both the high priest and the priests. (337) And when the book of Daniel was showed him, wherein Daniel declared that one of the Greeks should destroy the empire of the Persians, he supposed that himself was the person intended; and as he was then glad, he dismissed the multitude for

the present, but the next day he called them to him, and bid them ask what favours they pleased of him: (338) whereupon the high priest desired that they might enjoy the laws of their forefathers, and might pay no tribute on the seventh year. He granted all they desired: (339) and when they entreated him that he would permit the Jews in Babylon and Media to enjoy their own laws also, he willingly promised to do hereafter what they desired: and when he said to the multitude, that if any of them would enlist themselves in his army on this condition, that they should continue under the laws of their forefathers, and live according to them, he was willing to take them with him, many were ready to accompany him in his wars.

(340) So when Alexander had thus settled matters at Jerusalem, he led his army into the neighbouring cities; and when all the inhabitants to whom he came, received him with great kindness, the Samaritans, who had then Shechem for their metropolis (a city situate at Mount Gerizzim, and inhabited by apostates of the Jewish nation), seeing that Alexander had so greatly honoured the Jews, determined to profess themselves Jews; (341) for such is the disposition of the Samaritans, as we have already elsewhere declared, that when the Jews are in adversity they deny that they are of kin to them, and then they confess the truth; but when they perceive that some good fortune hath befallen them, they immediately pretend to have communion with them, saying that they belong to them, and derive their genealogy from the posterity of Joseph, Ephraim and Manasseh. (342) Accordingly, they made their address to the king with splendour, and showed great alacrity in meeting him at a little distance from Jerusalem; and when Alexander had commended them, the Shechemites approached to him, taking with them the troops that Sanballat had sent him, and they desired that he would come to their city, and do honour to their temple also; (343) to whom he promised, that when he returned he would come to them; and when they petitioned that he would remit the tribute of the seventh year to them, because they did not now sow thereon, he asked who they were that made such a petition; (344) and when they said that they were Hebrews, but had the name of Sidonians, living at Shechem, he asked them again whether they were Jews; and when they said they were not Jews, 'It was to the Jews,' said he, 'that I granted that privilege; however, when I return, and am thoroughly informed by you of this matter, I will do what I shall think proper.' And in this manner he took leave of the Shechemites; (345) but ordered that the troops of Sanballat should follow him into Egypt, because there he designed to give them lands, which he did a little after in Thebais, when he ordered them to guard that country.

(346) Now when Alexander was dead, the government was parted among his successors; but the temple upon Mount Gerizzim remained; and if anyone were accused by those of Jerusalem of having eaten things common, or of

having broken the Sabbath, or of any other crime of the like nature, (347) he fled away to the Shechemites, and said that he was accused unjustly. About this time it was that Jaddua the high priest died, and Onias his son took the high priesthood. This was the state of the affairs of the people of Jerusalem at this time.

BOOK TWELVE

CHAPTER I

(1) Now when Alexander, king of Macedon, had put an end to the dominion of the Persians, and had settled the affairs of Judea after the forementioned manner, he ended his life; (2) and as his government fell among many, Antigonus obtained Asia, Seleucus Babylon, and of the other nations which were there, Lysimachus governed the Hellespont, and Cassander possessed Macedonia; as did Ptolemy, the son of Lagus, seize upon Egypt: (3) and while these princes ambitiously strove one against another, every one for his own principality, it came to pass that there were continual wars, and those lasting wars too; and the cities were sufferers, and lost a great many of their inhabitants in these times of distress, insomuch that all Syria, by the means of Ptolemy, the son of Lagus, underwent the reverse of that denomination, of Saviour, which he then had. (4) He also seized upon Jerusalem, and for that end made use of deceit and treachery; for as he came into the city on a Sabbath day, as if he would offer sacrifice, he without any trouble gained the city; while the Jews did not oppose him for they did not suspect him to be their enemy; and he gained it thus, because they were free from suspicion of him, and because on that day they were at rest and quietness; and when he had gained it, he reigned over it in a cruel manner. (5) Nay, Agatharchides of Cnidus, who wrote the acts of Alexander's successors, reproaches us with superstition, as if we, by it, had lost our liberty, where he says thus: (6) 'There is a nation called the nation of the Jews, who inhabit a city strong and great, named Jerusalem. These men took no care, but let it come into the hands of Ptolemy, as not willing to take arms, and thereby they submitted to be under a hard master, by reason of their unseasonable superstition.' (7) This is what Agatharchides relates of our nation. But when Ptolemy had taken a great many captives, both from the mountainous parts of Judea and from the places about Jerusalem and Samaria, and the places near Mount Gerizzim, he led them all into Egypt, and settled them there. (8) And as he knew that the people of Jerusalem were most faithful in the observation of oaths and covenants, and this formed the answer they made to Alexander, when he sent an embassage to them, after he had beaten Darius in battle, so he distributed many of them into garrisons, and at Alexandria gave them equal privileges of citizens with the Macedonians themselves; and required of them to take their oaths that they would keep their fidelity to the posterity of those who committed these places to their care. (9) Nay, there

were not a few other Jews who, of their own accord, went into Egypt, as
invited by the goodness of the soil and by the liberality of Ptolemy. (10)
However, there were disorders among their posterity, with relation to the
Samaritans, on account of their resolution to preserve that conduct of life
which was delivered to them by their forefathers, and they thereupon contended one with another, while those of Jerusalem said that their temple was
holy, and resolved to send their sacrifices thither, but the Samaritans were
resolved that they should be sent to Mount Gerizzim.

CHAPTER 2

(11) When Alexander had reigned twelve years, and after him Ptolemy Soter
forty years, Philadelphus then took the kingdom of Egypt, and held it forty
years within one. He procured the law to be interpreted, and set free those
that were come from Jerusalem into Egypt, and were in slavery there, who
were a hundred and twenty thousand. The occasion was this: (12) Demetrius
Phalerius, who was library keeper to the king, was now endeavouring, if it were
possible, to gather together all the books that were in the habitable earth,
and buying whatsoever was anywhere valuable, or agreeable to the king's
inclination (who was very earnestly set upon collecting of books); to which
inclination of his Demetrius was zealously subservient. (13) And when once
Ptolemy asked him how many ten thousands of books he had collected, he
replied, that he had already about twenty times ten thousand; but that, in a little
time, he should have fifty times ten thousand. (14) But he said, he had been
informed that there were many books of laws among the Jews worthy of
inquiring after, and worthy of the king's library, but which, being written in
characters and in a dialect of their own, will cause no small pains in getting them
translated into the Greek tongue: (15) that the character in which they are
written seems to be like to that which is the proper character of the Syrians, and
that its sound, when pronounced, is like theirs also; and that this sound appears
to be peculiar to themselves. Wherefore he said, that nothing hindered why
they might not get those books to be translated also; for while nothing is
wanting that is necessary for that purpose, we may have their books also in this
library. (16) So the king thought that Demetrius was very zealous to procure
him abundance of books, and that he suggested what was exceeding proper for
him to do; and therefore he wrote to the Jewish high priest that he should act
accordingly.

(17) Now there was one Aristeus, who was among the king's most intimate
friends, and, on account of his modesty, very acceptable to him. This Aristeus
resolved frequently, and that before now, to petition the king that he would set
all the captive Jews in his kingdom free; (18) and he thought this to be a

convenient opportunity for the making that petition. So he discoursed, in the first place, with the captains of the king's guards, Sosibius of Tarentum, and Andreas, and persuaded them to assist him in what he was going to intercede with the king for. (19) Accordingly Aristeus embraced the same opinion with those that have been before mentioned, and went to the king and made the following speech to him: (20) 'It is not fit for us, O king, to overlook things hastily, or to deceive ourselves, but to lay the truth open: for since we have determined not only to get the laws of the Jews transcribed, but interpreted also, for thy satisfaction, by what means can we do this, while so many of the Jews are now slaves in thy kingdom? (21) Do thou then what will be agreeable to thy magnanimity and to thy good nature: free them from the miserable condition they are in, because that God, who supporteth thy kingdom, was the author of their laws, (22) as I have learned by particular inquiry; for both these people and we also worship the same God, the framer of all things. We call him, and that truly, by the name of *Zena* [or life, or Jupiter], because he breathes life into all men. Wherefore, do thou restore these men to their own country; and this do to the honour of God, because these men pay a peculiarly excellent worship to him. (23) And know this farther, that though I be not of kin to them by birth, nor one of the same country with them, yet do I desire these favours to be done them, since all men are the workmanship of God; and I am sensible that he is well pleased with those that do good. I do therefore put up this petition to thee, to do good to them.'

(24) When Aristeus was saying thus, the king looked upon him with a cheerful and joyful countenance, and said, 'How many ten thousands dost thou suppose there are of such as want to be made free?' To which Andreas replied, as he stood by, and said, 'A few more than ten times ten thousand.' The king made answer, 'And is this a small gift that thou askest, Aristeus?' (25) But Sosibius, and the rest that stood by, said that he ought to offer such a thank offering as was worthy of his greatness of soul, to that God who had given him his kingdom. With this answer he was much pleased; and gave order, that when they paid the soldiers their wages, they should lay down [a hundred and] twenty drachmae for every one of the slaves. (26) And he promised to publish a magnificent decree, about what they requested, which should confirm what Aristeus had proposed, and especially what God willed should be done; whereby, he said, he would not only set those free who had been led away captive by his father and his army, but those who were in this kingdom before, and those also, if any such there were, who had been brought away since. (27) And when they said that their redemption money would amount to above four hundred talents, he granted it. A copy of which decree I have determined to preserve, that the magnanimity of this king may be known. (28) Its contents were as follows: 'Let all those who were soldiers under our father, and who,

when they overran Syria and Phoenicia, and laid waste Judea, took the Jews captives and made them slaves, and brought them into our cities and into this country, and then sold them; as also all those that were in my kingdom before them, and if there be any that have lately been brought thither, be made free by those that possess them; and let them accept of [a hundred and] twenty drachmae for every slave. And let the soldiers receive this redemption money with their pay, but the rest out of the king's treasury; (29) for I suppose that they were made captives without our father's consent, and against equity; and that their country was harassed by the insolence of the soldiers, and that, by removing them into Egypt, the soldiers have made a great profit by them. (30) Out of regard, therefore, to justice, and out of pity to those that have been tyrannised over, contrary to equity, I enjoin those that have such Jews in their service to set them at liberty, upon the receipt of the before-mentioned sum; and that no one use any deceit about them, but obey what is here commanded. (31) And I will, that they give in their names within three days after the publication of this edict, to such as are appointed to execute the same, and to produce the same slaves before them also, for I think it will be for the advantage of my affairs; and let everyone that will, inform against those that do not obey this decree; and I will, that their estates be confiscated into the king's treasury.' (32) When this decree was read to the king, it at first contained the rest that is here inserted, and only omitted those Jews that had formerly been brought, and those brought afterwards, which had not been distinctly mentioned; so he added these clauses out of his humanity, and with great generosity. He also gave order that the payment, which was likely to be done in a hurry, should be divided among the king's ministers, and among the officers of his treasury. (33) When this was over, what the king had decreed was quickly brought to a conclusion; and this in no more than seven day's time, the number of the talents paid for the captives being above four hundred and sixty, and this, because their masters required the [hundred and] twenty drachmae for the children also, the king having, in effect, commanded that these should be paid for, when he said, in his decree, that they should receive the forementioned sum for every slave.

(34) Now when this had been done after so magnificent a manner, according to the king's inclinations, he gave order to Demetrius to give him in writing his sentiments concerning the transcribing of the Jewish books; for no part of the administration is done rashly by these kings, but all things are managed with great circumspection. (35) On which account I have subjoined a copy of these epistles, and set down the multitude of the vessels sent as gifts [to Jerusalem], and the construction of every one, that the exactness of the artificers' workmanship, as it appeared to those that saw them, and which workmen made every vessel, may be made manifest, and this on account of the

excellency of the vessels themselves. Now the copy of the epistle was to this purpose: (36) 'Demetrius to the great king. When thou, O king, gavest me a charge concerning the collection of books that were wanting to fill your library, and concerning the care that ought to be taken about such as are imperfect, I have used the utmost diligence about those matters. And I let you know, that we want the books of Jewish legislation, with some others; for they are written in the Hebrew characters, and being in the language of that nation, are to us unknown. (37) It hath also happened to them, that they have been transcribed more carelessly than they should have been, because they have not had hitherto royal care taken about them. Now it is necessary that thou shouldst have accurate copies of them. And indeed this legislation is full of hidden wisdom, and entirely blameless, as being the legislation of God; (38) for which cause it is, as Hecateus of Abdera says, that the poets and historians make no mention of it, nor of those men who lead their lives according to it, since it is a holy law, and ought not to be published by profane mouths. (39) If then it please thee, O king, thou mayest write to the high priest of the Jews, to send six of the elders out of every tribe, and those such as are most skilful of the laws, that by their means we may learn the clear and agreeing sense of these books, and may obtain an accurate interpretation of their contents, and so may have such a collection of these as may be suitable to thy desire.'

(40) When this epistle was sent to the king, he commanded that an epistle should be drawn up for Eleazar, the Jewish high priest, concerning these matters; and that they should inform him of the release of the Jews that had been in slavery among them. He also sent fifty talents of gold for the making of large basins, and vials, and cups, and an immense quantity of precious stones. (41) He also gave order to those who had the custody of the chests that contained those stones, to give the artificers leave to choose out what sorts of them they pleased. He withal appointed, that a hundred talents in money should be sent to the temple for sacrifices and for other uses. (42) Now I will give a description of these vessels and the manner of their construction, but not till after I have set down a copy of the epistle which was written to Eleazar the high priest, who had obtained that dignity on the occasion following: (43) when Onias the high priest was dead, his son Simon became his successor. He was called Simon the Just, because of both his piety towards God, and his kind disposition to those of his own nation. (44) When he was dead, and had left a young son, who was called Onias, Simon's brother Eleazar, of whom we are speaking, took the high priesthood; and he it was to whom Ptolemy wrote, and that in the manner following: (45) 'King Ptolemy to Eleazar the high priest, sendeth greeting. There are many Jews who now dwell in my kingdom, whom the Persians, when they were in power, carried captives. These were honoured by my father; some of whom he placed in the army, and gave them

greater pay than ordinary, to others of them, when they came with him into
Egypt, he committed his garrisons and the guarding of them, that they might
be a terror to the Egyptians; (46) and when I had taken the government, I
treated all men with humanity, and especially those that are thy fellow citizens,
of whom I have set free above a hundred thousand that were slaves, and paid
the price of their redemption to their masters out of my own revenues; (47)
and those that are of a fit age, I have admitted into the number of my soldiers;
and for such as are capable of being faithful to me, and proper for my court, I
have put them in such a post, as thinking this [kindness done to them] to be a
very great and an acceptable gift, which I devote to God for his providence
over me; (48) and as I am desirous to do what will be grateful to these, and to
all the other Jews in the habitable earth, I have determined to procure an
interpretation of your law, and to have it translated out of Hebrew into Greek,
and to be deposited in my library. (49) Thou wilt therefore do well to choose
out and send to me men of a good character, who are now elders in age, and
six in number out of every tribe. These, by their age, must be skilful in the
laws, and of abilities to make an accurate interpretation of them; and when this
shall be finished, I shall think that I have done a work glorious to myself; (50)
and I have sent to thee Andreas, the captain of my guard, and Aristeus, men
whom I have in very great esteem; by whom I have sent those first fruits which
I have dedicated to the temple, and to the sacrifices, and to other uses, to the
value of a hundred talents; and if thou wilt send to us, to let us know what thou
wouldst have further, thou wilt do a thing acceptable to me.'

(51) When this epistle of the king was brought to Eleazar, he wrote an
answer to it with all the respect possible: 'Eleazar the high priest to King
Ptolemy, sendeth greeting. If thou and thy queen Arsinoë, and thy children, be
well, we are entirely satisfied. (52) When we received thy epistle, we greatly
rejoiced at thy intentions; and when the multitude were gathered together, we
read it to them, and thereby made them sensible of the piety thou hast towards
God. (53) We also showed them the twenty vials of gold, and thirty of silver,
and the five large basins, and the table for the shewbread; and also the hundred
talents for the sacrifices, and for the making what shall be needful at the temple:
which things Andreas and Aristeus, those most honoured friends of thine, have
brought us; and truly they are persons of an excellent character, and of great
learning, and worthy of thy virtue. (54) Know then that we will gratify thee in
what is for thy advantage, though we do what we used not to do before; for we
ought to make a return for the numerous acts of kindness which thou hast
done to our countrymen. (55) We immediately, therefore, offered sacrifices for
thee and thy sister, with thy children and friends; and the multitude made
prayers, that thy affairs may be to thy mind; and that thy kingdom may be
preserved in peace, and that the translation of our law may come to the

conclusion thou desirest, and be for thy advantage. (56) We have also chosen six elders out of every tribe, whom we have sent, and the law with them. It will be thy part, out of thy piety and justice to send back the law when it hath been translated, and to return those to us that bring it in safety. Farewell.'

(57) This was the reply which the high priest made; but it does not seem to me to be necessary to set down the names of the seventy [two] elders who were sent by Eleazar, and carried the law, which yet were subjoined at the end of the epistle. (58) However, I thought it not improper to give an account of those very valuable and artificially contrived vessels which the king sent to God, that all may see how great a regard the king had for God; for the king allowed a vast deal of expenses for these vessels, and came often to the workmen, and viewed their works, and suffered nothing of carelessness or negligence to be any damage to their operations; (59) and I will relate how rich they were as well as I am able, although, perhaps, the nature of this history may not require such a description; but I imagine I shall thereby recommend the elegant taste and magnanimity of this king to those that read this history.

(60) And first I will describe what belongs to the table. It was indeed in the king's mind to make this table vastly large in its dimensions; but then he gave orders that they should learn what was the magnitude of the table which was already at Jerusalem, and how large it was, and whether there were a possibility of making one larger than it; (61) and when he was informed how large that was which was already there, and that nothing hindered but a larger might be made, he said that he was willing to have one made that should be five times as large as the present table; but his fear was that it might be then useless in their sacred ministrations by its too great largeness; for he desired that the gifts he presented them should not only be there for show, but should be useful also in their sacred ministrations. (62) According to which reasoning, that the former table was made of so moderate a size for use, and not for want of gold, he resolved that he would not exceed the former table in largeness, but would make it exceed it in the variety and elegancy of its materials; (63) and as he was sagacious in observing the nature of all things, and in having a just notion of what was new and surprising, and where there were no sculptures, he would invent such as were proper by his own skill, and would show them to the workmen, he commanded that such sculptures would now be made; and that those which were delineated should be most accurately formed by a constant regard to their delineation.

(64) When therefore the workmen had undertaken to make the table, they framed it in length two cubits [and a half], in breadth one cubit, and in height one cubit and a half; and the entire structure of the work was of gold. They withal made a crown of a handbreadth round it, with wave-work wreathed about it, and with an engraving which imitated a cord, and was admirably

turned on its three parts; (65) for as they were of a triangular figure, every angle had the same disposition of its sculptures, that when you turned them about, the very same form of them was turned about without any variation. Now that part of the crown-work that was enclosed under the table had its sculptures very beautiful; but that part which went round on the outside was more elaborately adorned with most beautiful ornaments, because it was exposed to sight, and to the view of the spectators; (66) for which reason it was that both those sides which were extant above the rest were acute, and none of the angles, which we before told you were three, appeared less than another when the table was turned about. Now into the cord-work thus turned were precious stones inserted, in rows parallel one to the other enclosed in golden buttons, which had buckles in them; (67) but the parts which were on the side of the crown and were exposed to the sight, were adorned with a row of oval figures obliquely placed, of the most excellent sort of precious stones, which imitated rods laid close, and encompassed the table round about; (68) but under these oval figures thus engraven, the workmen had put a crown all round it, where the nature of all sorts of fruit was represented, insomuch that the bunches of grapes hung up; and when they had made the stones to represent all the kinds of fruit before mentioned, and that each in its proper colour, they made them fast with gold round the whole table. (69) The like disposition of the oval figures, and of the engraved rods, was framed under the crown, that the table might on each side show the same appearance of variety and elegancy of its ornaments, so that neither the position of the wave-work nor of the crown might be different, although the table were turned on the other side, but that the prospect of the same artificial contrivances might be extended as far as the feet; (70) for there was made a plate of gold four fingers broad, through the entire breadth of the table, into which they inserted the feet, and then fastened them to the table by buttons and buttonholes, at the place where the crown was situate, that so on what side soever of the table one should stand, it might exhibit the very same view of the exquisite workmanship, and of the vast expenses bestowed upon it; (71) but upon the table itself they engraved a meander, inserting into it very valuable stones in the middle, like stars, of various colours: the carbuncle and the emerald, each of which sent out agreeable rays of light to the spectators, with such stones of other sorts also as were most curious and best esteemed as being most precious in their kind. (72) Hard by this meander a texture of network ran round it, the middle which appeared like a rhombus, into which were inserted rock-crystal and amber, which, by the great resemblance of the appearance they made, gave wonderful delight to those that saw them. (73) The chapiters of the feet imitated the first budding of lilies, while their leaves were bent and laid under the table but so that the chives were seen standing upright within them. (74) Their bases were made of a carbuncle; and one palm deep, and eight fingers in breadth. (75) Now they had engraven upon it, with a very fine tool, and with a great deal of pains, a branch of ivy and tendrils of the vine sending forth clusters of grapes, that you would guess they were nowise different from real tendrils; for they were so very thin, and so very far extended at their extremities, that they were moved with the wind, and made one believe that they were the product of nature, and not the representation of art. (76) They also made the entire workmanship of the table appear to be threefold, while the joints of the several parts were so united together as to be invisible, and the places where they joined could not be distinguished. Now the thickness of the table was not less than half a cubit. (77) So that this gift, by the king's great generosity, by the great value of the materials and the variety of its exquisite structure, and the artificer's skill in imitating nature with graving tools, was at length brought to perfection, while the king was very desirous that though in largeness it were not to be different from that which was already dedicated to God, yet that in exquisite workmanship and the novelty of the contrivances, and in the splendour of its construction, it should far exceed it, and be more illustrious than that was.

(78) Now of the cisterns of gold there were two, whose sculpture was of scale-work, from its basis to its belt-like circle, with various sorts of stones enchased in the spiral circles. (79) Next to which there was upon it a meander of a cubit in height; it was composed of stones of all sorts of colours; and next to this was the rod-work engraven; and next to that was a rhombus in a texture of network, drawn out to the brim of the basin, (80) while small shields, made of stones, beautiful in their kind and of four fingers' depth, filled up the middle parts. About the top of the basin were wreathed the leaves of lilies and of the convolvulus, and the tendrils of vines in a circular manner; (81) and this was the construction of the two cisterns of gold, each containing two firkins: but those which were of silver were much more bright and splendid than looking glasses; and you might in them see images that fell upon them more plainly than in the other. (82) The king also ordered thirty vials; those of which the parts that were of gold, and filled up with precious stones, were shadowed over with the leaves of ivy and vines, artificially engraven; (83) and these were the vessels that were, after an extraordinary manner, brought to this perfection, partly by the skill of the workmen, who were admirable in such fine work, but much more by the diligence and generosity of the king, (84) who not only supplied the artificers abundantly and with great generosity, with what they wanted, but he forbade public audiences for the time, and came and stood by the workmen, and saw the whole operation; and this was the cause why the workmen were so accurate in their performance, because they had regard to the king, and to his great concern about the vessels, and so the more indefatigably kept close to the work.

(85) And these were what gifts were sent by Ptolemy to Jerusalem, and dedicated to God there. But when Eleazar the high priest had devoted them to God, and had paid due respect to those that brought them, and had given them presents to be carried to the king, he dismissed them. (86) And when they were come to Alexandria, and Ptolemy heard that they were come, and that the seventy elders were come also, he presently sent for Andreas and Aristeus, his ambassadors, who came to him, and delivered him the epistle which they brought him from the high priest, and made answer to all the questions he put to them by word of mouth. (87) He then made haste to meet the elders that came from Jerusalem for the interpretation of the laws; and he gave command, that everybody who came on other occasions would be sent away, which was a thing surprising, and what he did not use to do; (88) for those that were drawn thither upon such occasions used to come to him on the fifth day, but ambassadors at the month's end. But when he had sent those away, he waited for these that were sent by Eleazar; (89) but as the old men came in with presents, which the high priest had given them to bring to the king and with the membranes, upon which they had their laws written in golden letters, he put questions to them concerning those books; (90) and when they had taken off the covers wherein they were wrapped up, they showed him the membranes. So the king stood admiring the thinness of those membranes, and the exactness of the junctures, which could not be perceived (so exactly were they connected one with another); and this he did for a considerable time. He then said that he returned them thanks for coming to him, and still greater thanks to him that sent them; and, above all, to that God whose laws they appeared to be. (91) Then did the elders, and those that were present with them, cry out with one voice, and wished all happiness to the king. Upon which he fell into tears by the violence of the pleasure he had, it being natural to men to afford the same indications in great joy that they do under sorrow. (92) And when he had bidden them deliver the books to those that were appointed to receive them, he saluted the men, and said that it was but just to discourse, in the first place, of the errand they were sent about, and then to address himself to themselves. He promised, however, that he would make this day on which they came to him remarkable and eminent every year through the whole course of his life; (93) for their coming to him, and the victory which he gained over Antigonus by sea, proved to be on the very same day. He also gave orders that they should sup with him; and gave it in charge that they should have excellent lodgings provided for them in the upper part of the city.

(94) Now he that was appointed to take care of the reception of strangers, Nicanor by name, called for Dorotheus, whose duty it was to make provision for them, and bade him prepare for every one of them what should be requisite

for their diet and way of living: which thing was ordered by the king after this manner; (95) he took care that those that belonged to every city which did not use the same way of living, that all things should be prepared for them according to the custom of those that came to him, that, being feasted according to the usual method of their own way of living, they might be the better pleased, and might not be uneasy at anything done to them from which they were naturally averse. And this was now done in the case of these men by Dorotheus, who was put into this office because of his great skill in such matters belonging to common life: (96) for he took care of all such matters as concerned the reception of strangers, and appointed them double seats for them to sit on, according as the king had commanded him to do; for he had commanded that half of their seats should be set at his right hand, and the other half behind his table, and took care that no respect should be omitted that could be shown them. (97) And when they were thus set down, he bid Dorotheus to minister to all those that were come to him from Judea, after the manner they used to be ministered to: for which cause he sent away their sacred heralds, and those that slew the sacrifices, and the rest that used to say grace, but called to one of those that were come to him, whose name was Eleazar, who was a priest, and desired him to say grace: (98) who then stood in the midst of them, and prayed that all prosperity might attend the king and those that were his subjects. Upon which an acclamation was made by the whole company, with joy and a great noise; and when that was over, they fell to eating their supper, and to the enjoyment of what was set before them. (99) And at a little interval afterward, when the king thought a sufficient time had been interposed, he began to talk philosophically to them, and he asked every one of them a philosophical question, and such a one as might give light in those inquiries; and when they had explained all the problems that had been proposed by the king about every point, he was well pleased with their answers. This took up the twelve days in which they were treated; (100) and he that pleases may learn the particular questions in that book of Aristeus, which he wrote on this very occasion.

(101) And while not the king only, but the philosopher Menedemus also, admired them, and said, that all things were governed by Providence, and that it was probable that thence it was that such force or beauty was discovered in these men's words — they then left off asking any more questions. (102) But the king said that he had gained very great advantages by their coming, for that he had received this profit from them, that he had learned how he ought to rule his subjects. And he gave order that they should have every one three talents given them; and that those that were to conduct them to their lodging should do it. (103) Accordingly, when three days were over Demetrius took them, and went over the causeway seven furlongs long: it was a bank in the sea

to an island. And when they had gone over the bridge, he proceeded to the northern parts, and showed them where they should meet, which was in a house that was built near the shore, and was a quiet place, and fit for their discoursing together about their work. (104) When he had brought them thither, he entreated them (now they had all things about them which they wanted for the interpretation of their law), that they would suffer nothing to interrupt them in their work. Accordingly, they made an accurate interpretation, with great zeal and great pains; and this they continued to do till the ninth hour of the day; (105) after which time they relaxed and took care of their body, while their food was provided for them in great plenty: besides, Dorotheus, at the king's command, brought them a great deal of what was provided for the king himself. (106) But in the morning they came to the court, and saluted Ptolemy, and then went away to their former place, where, when they had washed their hands and purified themselves, they betook themselves to the interpretation of the laws. (107) Now when the law was transcribed, and the labour of interpretation was over, which came to its conclusion in seventy-two days, Demetrius gathered all the Jews together to the place where the laws were translated, and where the interpreters were, and read them over. (108) The multitude did also approve of those elders that were the interpreters of the law. They withal commended Demetrius for his proposal, as the inventor of what was greatly for their happiness; and they desired that he would give leave to their rulers also to read the law. Moreover they all, both the priests and the ancientest of the elders, and the principal men of their commonwealth, made it their request, that since the interpretation was happily finished, it might continue in the state it now was, and might not be altered. (109) And when they all commended that determination of theirs, they enjoined, that if anyone observed either anything superfluous, or anything omitted, that he would take a view of it again, and have it laid before them and corrected; which was a wise action of theirs, that when the thing was judged to have been well done, it might continue forever.

(110) So the king rejoiced when he saw that his design of this nature was brought to perfection, to so great advantage: and he was chiefly delighted with hearing the laws read to him; and was astonished at the deep meaning and wisdom of the legislator. And he began to discourse with Demetrius, 'how it came to pass that, when this legislation was so wonderful, no one, either of the poets or of the historians, had made mention of it.' (111) Demetrius made answer, 'that no one durst be so bold as to touch upon the description of these laws, because they were divine and venerable, and because some that had attempted it were afflicted by God.' (112) He also told him, that 'Theopompus was desirous of writing somewhat about them, but was thereupon disturbed in his mind for above thirty days' time; and upon some intermission of his

distemper, he appeased God [by prayer], as suspecting that his madness proceeded from that cause.' Nay, indeed he further saw in a dream, that his distemper befell him while he indulged too great a curiosity about divine matters, and was desirous of publishing them among common men; but when he left off that attempt he recovered his understanding again. (113) Moreover, he informed him of Theodectes, the tragic poet, concerning whom it was reported, that when in a certain dramatic representation he was desirous to make mention of things that were contained in the sacred books, he was afflicted with a darkness in his eyes; and that upon his being conscious of the occasion of his distemper, and appeasing God (by prayer), he was freed from that affliction.

(114) And when the king had received these books from Demetrius, as we have said already, he adored them; and gave order, that great care should be taken of them, that they might remain uncorrupted. He also desired that the interpreters would come often to him out of Judea, (115) and that both on account of the respects that he would pay them, and on account of the presents he would make them; for he said, it was now but just to send them away, although if, of their own accord, they would come to him hereafter, they should obtain all that their own wisdom might justly require, and what his generosity was able to give them. (116) So he sent them away, and gave to every one of them three garments of the best sort, and two talents of gold, and a cup of the value of one talent, and the furniture of the room wherein they were feasted. And these were the things he presented to them. (117) But by them he sent to Eleazar the high priest ten beds, with feet of silver, and the furniture to them belonging, and a cup of the value of thirty talents; and besides these, ten garments, and purple, and a very beautiful crown, and a hundred pieces of the finest woven linen; and also vials and dishes, and vessels for pouring, and two golden cisterns, to be dedicated to God. (118) He also desired him, by an epistle, that he would give these interpreters leave, if any of them were desirous, of coming to him; because he highly valued a conversation with men of such learning, and should be very willing to lay out his wealth upon such men. And this was what came to the Jews, and was much to their glory and honour, from Ptolemy Philadelphus.

CHAPTER 3

(119) The Jews also obtained honours from the kings of Asia when they became their auxiliaries; for Seleucus Nicator made them citizens in those cities which he built in Asia, and in the Lower Syria, and in the metropolis itself, Antioch; and gave them privileges equal to those of the Macedonians and Greeks, who were the inhabitants, insomuch that these privileges continue

to this very day; (120) an argument for which you have in this, that whereas the Jews do make use of oil prepared by foreigners, they receive a certain sum of money from the proper officers belonging to their exercises as the value of that oil; which money, when the people of Antioch would have deprived them of, in the last war, Mucianus, who was then president of Syria, preserved it to them. (121) And when the people of Alexandria and of Antioch did after that, at the time that Vespasian and Titus his son governed the habitable earth, pray that these privileges of citizens might be taken away, they did not obtain their request. (122) In which behaviour anyone may discern the equity and generosity of the Romans, especially of Vespasian and Titus, who, although they had been at a great deal of pains in the war against the Jews, and were exasperated against them, because they did not deliver up their weapons to them, but continued the war to the very last, (123) yet did not they take away any of their forementioned privileges belonging to them as citizens, but restrained their anger, and overcame the prayers of the Alexandrians and Antiochians, who were a very powerful people, (124) insomuch that they did not yield to them, neither out of their favour to these people, nor out of their old grudge at those whose wicked opposition they had subdued in the war; nor would they alter any of the ancient favours granted to the Jews, but said, that those who had borne arms against them, and fought them, had suffered punishment already, and that it was not just to deprive those that had not offended of the privileges they enjoyed.

(125) We also know that Marcus Agrippa was of the like disposition towards the Jews: for when the people of Ionia were very angry at them, and besought Agrippa that they, and they only, might have those privileges of citizens which Antiochus, the grandson of Seleucus (who by the Greeks was called *the God*), had bestowed on them; and desired that, if the Jews were to be joint partakers with them, (126) they might be obliged to worship the gods they themselves worshipped: but when these matters were brought to trial, the Jews prevailed, and obtained leave to make use of their own customs, and this under the patronage of Nicolas of Damascus; for Agrippa gave sentence, that he could not innovate. (127) And if anyone hath a mind to know this matter accurately, let him peruse the hundred and twenty-third and hundred and twenty-fourth books of the history of this Nicolas. Now, as to this determination of Agrippa, it is not so much to be admired; for at that time our nation had not made war against the Romans. (128) But one may well be astonished at the generosity of Vespasian and Titus, that after so great wars and contests which they had from us, they should use such moderation. But I will now return to that part of my history whence I made the present digression.

(129) Now it happened that in the reign of Antiochus the Great, who ruled over all Asia, that the Jews, as well as the inhabitants of Celesyria, suffered

greatly, and their land was sorely harassed; (130) for while he was at war with Ptolemy Philopater, and with his son, who was called Epiphanes, it fell out that these nations were equally sufferers, both when he was beaten and when he beat the others; so that they were very like to a ship in a storm, which is tossed by the waves on both sides; and just thus were they in their situation in the middle between Antiochus's prosperity and its change to adversity. (131) But at length, when Antiochus had beaten Ptolemy, he seized upon Judea: and when Philopater was dead, his son sent out a great army under Scopas the general of his forces, against the inhabitants of Celesyria, who took many of their cities, and in particular our nation; (132) which, when he fell upon them, went over to him. Yet was it not long afterward when Antiochus overcame Scopas, in a battle fought at the fountains of Jordan, and destroyed a great part of his army. (133) But afterward, when Antiochus subdued those cities of Celesyria which Scopas had gotten into his possession, and Samaria with them, the Jews, of their own accord, went over to him, and received him into the city [Jerusalem], and gave plentiful provision to all his army, and to his elephants, and readily assisted him when he besieged the garrison which was in the citadel of Jerusalem. (134) Wherefore Antiochus thought it but just to requite the Jews' diligence and zeal in his service: so he wrote to the generals of his armies, and to his friends, and gave testimony to the good behaviour of the Jews towards him, and informed them what rewards he had resolved to bestow on them for that their behaviour. (135) I will set down presently the epistles themselves which he wrote to the generals concerning them, but will first produce the testimony of Polybius of Megalopolis; for thus does he speak, in the sixteenth book of his history: 'Now Scopas, the general of Ptolemy's army, went in haste to the superior parts of the country, and in the winter time overthrew the nation of the Jews.' (136) He also saith, in the same book, that 'when Scopas was conquered by Antiochus, Antiochus received Batanea and Samaria, and Abila and Gadara; and that, awhile afterwards, there came in to him those Jews that inhabited near that temple which was called Jerusalem; concerning which, although I have more to say, and particularly concerning the presence of God about that temple, yet do I put off that history till another opportunity.' (137) This it is which Polybius relates; but we will return to the series of the history, when we have first produced the epistles of King Antiochus.

KING ANTIOCHUS TO PTOLEMY, SENDETH GREETING.

(138) 'Since the Jews upon our first entrance on their country demonstrated their friendship towards us, and when we came to their city [Jerusalem], received us in a splendid manner, and came to meet us with their senate, and gave abundance of provisions to our soldiers, and to the elephants, and joined with us in ejecting the garrison of the Egyptians that were in the citadel, (139)

we have thought fit to reward them, and to retrieve the condition of their city, which hath been greatly depopulated by such accidents as have befallen its inhabitants, and to bring those that have been scattered abroad back to the city; (140) and, in the first place, we have determined, on account of their piety towards God, to bestow on them, as a pension, for their sacrifices of animals that are fit for sacrifice, for wine and oil and frankincense, the value of twenty thousand pieces of silver, and [six] sacred artabrae of fine flour, with one thousand four hundred and sixty medimni of wheat, and three hundred and seventy-five medimni of salt; (141) and these payments I would have fully paid them, as I have sent orders to you. I would also have the work about the temple finished, and the cloisters, and if there be anything else that ought to be rebuilt; and for the materials of wood, let it be brought them out of Judea itself, and out of the other countries, and out of Libanus, tax free, and the same I would have observed as to those other materials which will be necessary, in order to render the temple more glorious; (142) and let all of that nation live according to the laws of their own country; and let the senate and the priests, and the scribes of the temple, and the sacred singers, be discharged from poll money and the crown tax, and other taxes also; (143) and that the city may the sooner recover its inhabitants, I grant a discharge from taxes for three years to its present inhabitants, and to such as shall come to it, until the month Hyperberetus. (144) We also discharge them for the future from a third part of their taxes, that the losses they have sustained may be repaired; and all those citizens that have been carried away, and are become slaves, we grant them and their children their freedom; and give order that their substance be restored to them.'

(145) And these were the contents of this epistle. He also published a decree, through all his kingdom, in honour of the temple, which contained what follows: 'It shall be lawful for no foreigner to come within the limits of the temple round about; which thing is forbidden also to the Jews, unless to those who, according to their own custom, have purified themselves. (146) Nor let any flesh of horses or of mules or of asses, be brought into the city, whether they be wild or tame, nor that of leopards or foxes or hares; and in general that of any animal which is forbidden for the Jews to eat. Nor let their skins be brought into it; nor let any such animal be bred up in this city. Let them only be permitted to use the sacrifices derived from their forefathers, with which they have been obliged to make acceptable atonements to God. And he that transgresseth any of these orders, let him pay to the priests three thousand drachmae of silver.' (147) Moreover, this Antiochus bare testimony to our piety and fidelity in an epistle of his, written when he was informed of a sedition in Phrygia and Lydia at which time he was in the superior provinces, wherein he commanded Zeuxis, the general of his forces, and his most intimate friend, to send some of our nation out of Babylon into Phrygia. The epistle was this:

(148) KING ANTIOCHUS TO ZEUXIS HIS FATHER,
SENDETH GREETING.

'If you are in health, it is well. I also am in health. (149) Having been informed
that a sedition is arisen in Lydia and Phrygia, I thought that matter required
great care; and upon advising with my friends what was fit to be done, it hath
been thought proper to remove two thousand families of Jews, with their
effects, out of Mesopotamia and Babylon, unto the castles and places that lie
most convenient; (150) for I am persuaded that they will be well disposed
guardians of our possessions, because of their piety towards God, and because
I know that my predecessors have borne witness to them that they are faithful,
and with alacrity do what they are desired to do. I will, therefore, though it be
a laborious work, that thou remove these Jews; under a promise, that they shall
be permitted to use their own laws; (151) and when thou shalt give every one
of their families a place for building their houses, and a portion of land for their
husbandry, and for the plantation of their vines; and thou shalt discharge them
from paying taxes of the fruits of the earth for ten years, (152) and let them have
a proper quantity of wheat for the maintenance of their servants, until they
receive bread-corn out of the earth; also let a sufficient share be given to such
as minister to them in the necessaries of life, that by enjoying the effects of our
humanity, they may show themselves the more willing and ready about our
affairs. (153) Take care likewise of that nation, as far as thou art able, that they
may not have any disturbance given them by anyone.' Now these testimonials
which I have produced, are sufficient to declare the friendship that Antiochus
the Great bare to the Jews.

CHAPTER 4

(154) After this Antiochus made a friendship and a league with Ptolemy, and
gave him his daughter Cleopatra to wife, and yielded up to him Celesyria and
Samaria and Judea and Phoenicia, by way of dowry; (155) and upon the
division of the taxes between the two kings, all the principal men farmed the
taxes of their several countries, and collecting the sum that was settled for them
paid the same to the [two] kings. (156) Now at this time the Samaritans were in
a flourishing condition, and much distressed the Jews, cutting off parts of their
land, and carrying off slaves. This happened when Onias was high priest; (157)
for after Eleazar's death, his uncle Manasseh took the priesthood, and after he
had ended his life, Onias received that dignity. He was the son of Simon, who
was called *the Just;* (158) which Simon was the brother of Eleazar, as I said
before. This Onias was one of a little soul, and a great lover of money; and for
that reason, because he did not pay that tax of twenty talents of silver, which

his forefathers paid to these kings, out of their own estates, he provoked King Ptolemy Euergetes to anger, who was the father of Philopater. (159) Euergetes sent an ambassador to Jerusalem, and complained that Onias did not pay his taxes, and threatened that if he did not receive them, he would seize upon their land, and send soldiers to live upon it. When the Jews heard this message of the king, they were confounded; but so sordidly covetous was Onias, that nothing of this nature made him ashamed.

(160) There was now one Joseph, young in age, but of great reputation among the people of Jerusalem for gravity, prudence, and justice. His father's name was Tobias; and his mother was the sister of Onias the high priest, who informed him of the coming of the ambassador; for he was then sojourning at a village named Phicol, where he was born. (161) Hereupon he came to the city [Jerusalem], and reproved Onias for not taking care of the preservation of his countrymen, but bringing the nation into dangers, by not paying this money. For which preservation of them, he told him he had received the authority over them, and had been made high priest; (162) but that, in case he was so great a lover of money as to endure to see his country in danger on that account, and his countrymen suffer the greatest damages, he advised him to go to the king, and petition him to remit either the whole or a part of the sum demanded. (163) Onias' answer was this: that he did not care for his authority, and that he was ready, if the thing were practicable, to lay down his high priesthood; and that he would not go to the king, because he troubled not himself at all about such matters. Joseph then asked him if he would not give him leave to go ambassador on behalf of the nation; (164) he replied, that he would give him leave. Upon which Joseph went up into the temple, and called the multitude together to a congregation, and exhorted them not to be disturbed nor affrighted because of his uncle Onias' carelessness, but desired them to be at rest, and not terrify themselves with fear about it; for he promised them that he would be their ambassador to the king, and persuade him that they had done him no wrong; (165) and when the multitude heard this, they returned thanks to Joseph. So he went down from the temple, and treated Ptolemy's ambassador in an hospitable manner. He also presented him with rich gifts, and feasted him magnificently for many days, and then sent him to the king before him, and told him that he would soon follow him; (166) for he was now more willing to go to the king, by the encouragement of the ambassador, who earnestly persuaded him to come into Egypt, and promised him that he would take care that he should obtain everything that he desired of Ptolemy; for he was highly pleased with his frank and liberal temper, and with the gravity of his deportment.

(167) When Ptolemy's ambassador was come into Egypt, he told the king of the thoughtless temper of Onias; and informed him of the goodness of the disposition of Joseph; and that he was coming to him, to excuse the multitude,

as not having done him any harm, for that he was their patron. In short, he was so very large in his encomiums upon the young man, that he disposed both the king and his wife Cleopatra to have a kindness for him before he came. (168) So Joseph sent to his friends at Samaria, and borrowed money of them; and got ready what was necessary for his journey, garments and cups, and beasts for burden, which amounted to about twenty thousand drachmae, and went to Alexandria. (169) Now it happened that at this time all the principal men and rulers went up out of the cities of Syria and Phoenicia, to bid for their taxes; for every year the king sold them to the men of the greatest power in every city. (170) So these men saw Joseph journeying on the way, and laughed at him for his poverty and meanness; but when he came to Alexandria, and heard that King Ptolemy was at Memphis, he went up thither to meet with him; (171) which happened as the king was sitting in his chariot with his wife, and with his friend Athenion, who was the very person who had been ambassador at Jerusalem, and had been entertained by Joseph. As soon therefore as Athenion saw him, he presently made him known to the king, how good and generous a young man he was. (172) So Ptolemy saluted him first, and desired him to come up into his chariot; and as Joseph sat there, he began to complain of the management of Onias: to which he answered, 'Forgive him, on account of his age; for thou canst not certainly be unacquainted with this, that old men and infants have their minds exactly alike; but thou shalt have from us, who are young men, everything thou desirest, and shalt have no cause to complain.' (173) With this good humour and pleasantry of the young man, the king was so delighted, that he began already, as though he had had long experience of him, to have a still greater affection for him, insomuch that he bade him take his diet in the king's palace, and be a guest at his own table every day; (174) but when the king was come to Alexandria, the principal men of Syria saw him sitting with the king, and were much offended at it.

(175) And when the day came on which the king was to let the taxes of the cities to farm, and those that were the principal men of dignity in their several countries were to bid for them, the sum of the taxes together, of Celesyria and Phoenicia and Judea, with Samaria [as they were bidden for], came to eight thousand talents. (176) Hereupon Joseph accused the bidders, as having agreed together to estimate the value of the taxes at too low a rate; and he promised that he would himself give twice as much for them; but for those who did not pay, he would send the king home their whole substance; for this privilege was sold together with the taxes themselves. (177) The king was pleased to hear that offer; and, because it augmented his revenues, he said he would confirm the sale of the taxes to him; but when he asked him this question whether he had any sureties that would be bound for the payment of the money, he answered very pleasantly, 'I will give such security, and those of persons good and responsible,

and which you shall have no reason to distrust:' (178) and when he bade him name them, who they were he replied, 'I give thee no other persons, O king, for my sureties, than thyself and this thy wife; and you shall be security for both parties.' So Ptolemy laughed at the proposal, and granted him the farming of the taxes without any sureties. (179) This procedure was a sore grief to those that came from the cities into Egypt, who were utterly disappointed; and they returned every one to their own country with shame.

(180) But Joseph took with him two thousand foot soldiers from the king, for he desired he might have some assistance, in order to force such as were refractory in the cities to pay. And borrowing of the king's friends at Alexandria five hundred talents, he made haste back into Syria. (181) And when he was at Askelon, and demanded the taxes of the people of Askelon, they refused to pay anything, and affronted him also: upon which he seized upon about twenty of the principal men, and slew them, and gathered what they had together, and sent it all to the king; and informed him what he had done. (182) Ptolemy admired the prudent conduct of the man, and commended him for what he had done; and gave him leave to do as he pleased. When the Syrians heard of this, they were astonished: and having before them a sad example in the men of Askelon that were slain, they opened their gates, and willingly admitted Joseph, and paid their taxes. (183) And when the inhabitants of Scythopolis attempted to affront him, and would not pay him those taxes which they formerly used to pay, without disputing about him, he slew also the principal men of that city, and sent their effects to the king. (184) By this means he gathered great wealth together, and made vast gains by this farming of the taxes; and he made use of what estate he had thus gotten, in order to support his authority, as thinking it a piece of prudence to keep what had been the occasion and foundation of his present good fortune; and this he did by the assistance of what he was already possessed of, (185) for he privately sent many presents to the king, and to Cleopatra, and to their friends, and to all that were powerful about the court, and thereby purchased their good will to himself.

(186) This good fortune he enjoyed for twenty-two years; and was become the father of seven sons, by one wife; he had also another son, whose name was Hyrcanus, by his brother Solymius's daughter, (187) whom he married on the following occasion. He once came to Alexandria with his brother, who had along with him a daughter already marriageable, in order to give her in wedlock to some of the Jews of chief dignity there. He then supped with the king, and falling in love with an actress that was of great beauty, and came into the room where they feasted, he told his brother of it, and entreated him, because a Jew is forbidden by their law to come near to a foreigner, to conceal his offence, and to be kind and subservient to him, and to give him an opportunity of fulfilling his desires. (188) Upon which his brother willingly

entertained the proposal of serving him, and adorned his own daughter, and brought her to him by night, and put her into his bed. And Joseph being disordered with drink, knew not who she was, and so lay with his brother's daughter; and this did he many times, and loved her exceedingly; and said to his brother that he loved this actress so well, that he should run the hazard of his life [if he must part with her], and yet probably the king would not give him leave [to take her with him]. (189) But his brother bade him be in no concern about that matter, and told him he might enjoy her whom he loved without any danger, and might have her for his wife; and opened the truth of the matter to him, and assured him that he chose rather to have his own daughter abused, than to overlook him, and see him come to [public] disgrace. So Joseph commended him for this his brotherly love, and married his daughter; and by her begot a son whose name was Hyrcanus, as we said before. (190) And when this his youngest son showed, at thirteen years old, a mind that was both courageous and wise, and was greatly envied by his brethren, as being of a genius much above them, and such a one as they might well envy, (191) Joseph had once a mind to know which of his sons had the best disposition to virtue; and when he sent them severally to those that had then the best reputation for instructing youth, the rest of his children, by reason of their sloth and unwillingness to take pains, returned to him foolish and unlearned. (192) After them he sent out the youngest, Hyrcanus, and gave him three hundred yoke of oxen, and bid him go two days' journey into the wilderness, and sow the land there, and yet kept back privately the yokes of the oxen that coupled them together. (193) When Hyrcanus came to the place, and found he had no yokes with him, he condemned the drivers of the oxen, who advised him to send some to his father, to bring them some yokes; but he thinking that he ought not to lose his time while they should be sent to bring him the yokes, he invented a kind of stratagem, and what suited an age elder than his own; (194) for he slew ten yoke of the oxen, and distributed their flesh among the labourers, and cut their hides into several pieces, and made him yokes, and yoked the oxen together with them; by which means he sowed as much land as his father had appointed him to sow, and returned to him. (195) And when he was come back, his father was mightily pleased with his sagacity, and commended the sharpness of his understanding, and his boldness in what he did. And he still loved him the more, as if he were his only genuine son, while his brethren were much troubled at it.

(196) But when one told him that Ptolemy had a son just born, and that all the principal men of Syria, and the other countries subject to him, were to keep a festival on account of the child's birthday, and went away in haste with great retinues to Alexandria, he was himself indeed hindered from going by old age; but he made trial of his sons, whether any of them would be willing to

go to the king. (197) And when the elder sons excused themselves for going, and said they were not courtiers good enough for such conversation, and advised him to send their brother Hyrcanus, he gladly hearkened to that advice, and called Hyrcanus, and asked him, whether he would go to the king; and whether it was agreeable to him to go or not. (198) And upon his promise that he would go, and his saying that he should not want much money for his journey, because he would live moderately, and that ten thousand drachmae would be sufficient, he was pleased with his son's prudence. (199) After a little while, the son advised his father not to sent his presents to the king from thence, but to give him a letter to his steward at Alexandria, that he might furnish him with money, for purchasing what should be most excellent and most precious. (200) So he thinking that the expense of ten talents would be enough for presents to be made the king, and commending his son as giving him good advice, wrote to Arion his steward, that managed all his money matters at Alexandria; which money was not less than three thousand talents on his account, (201) for Joseph sent the money he received in Syria to Alexandria. And when the day appointed for payment of the taxes to the king came, he wrote to Arion to pay them. (202) So when the son had asked his father for a letter to the steward, and had received it, he made haste to Alexandria. And when he was gone, his brethren wrote to all the king's friends, that they should destroy him.

(203) But when he was come to Alexandria, he delivered his letter to Arion, who asked him how many talents he would have (hoping he would ask for no more than ten, or a little more); he said he wanted a thousand talents. At which the steward was angry, and rebuked him, as one that intended to live extravagantly; and he let him know how his father had gathered together his estate by painstaking and resisting his inclinations, and wished him to imitate the example of his father: he assured him, withal, that he would give him but ten talents, and that for a present to the king also. (204) The son was irritated at this, and threw Arion into prison. But when Arion's wife had informed Cleopatra of this, with her entreaty that she would rebuke the child for what he had done (for Arion was in great esteem with her), Cleopatra informed the king of it. (205) And Ptolemy sent for Hyrcanus, and told him that he wondered, when he was sent to him by his father, that he had not yet come into his presence, but had laid the steward in prison. And he gave order, therefore, that he should come to him, and give an account of the reason of what he had done. (206) And they report that the answer he made to the king's messenger was this: that 'there was a law of his that forbade a child that was born to taste of the sacrifice, before he had been at the temple and sacrificed to God. According to which way of reasoning, he did not himself come to him in expectation of the present he was to make to him, as to one who had been his

father's benefactor; (207) and that he had punished the slave for disobeying his commands, for that it mattered not whether a master was little or great: so that unless we punish such as these, thou thyself mayst also expect to be despised by thy subjects.' Upon hearing this his answer, he fell a-laughing, and wondered at the great soul of the child.

(208) When Arion was apprised that this was the king's disposition, and that he had no way to help himself, he gave the child a thousand talents, and was let out of prison. So after three days were over Hyrcanus came and saluted the king and queen. (209) They saw him with pleasure, and feasted him in an obliging manner, out of the respect they bare to his father. So he came to the merchants privately, and bought a hundred boys that had learning, and were in the flower of their ages, each at a talent apiece; as also he bought a hundred maidens, each at the same price as the other. (210) And when he was invited to feast with the king among the principal men in the country, he sat down the lowest of them all, because he was little regarded, as a child in age still; and this by those who placed every one according to their dignity. (211) Now when all those that sat with him had laid the bones of the several parts on a heap before Hyrcanus (for they had themselves taken away the flesh belonging to them), till the table where he sat was filled full with them, (212) Trypho, who was the king's jester, and was appointed for jokes and laughter at festivals, was now asked by the guests that sat at the table [to expose him to laughter]. So he stood by the king, and said, 'Dost thou not see, my lord, the bones that lie by Hyrcanus? By this similitude thou mayst conjecture that his father made all Syria as bare as he hath made these bones.' (213) And the king laughing at what Trypho said, and asking of Hyrcanus, how he came to have so many bones before him, he replied, 'Very rightfully, my lord; for they are dogs that eat flesh and the bones together, as these thy guests have done (looking in the meantime at those guests), for there is nothing before them; but they are men that eat the flesh and cast away the bones as I who am also a man have now done.' (214) Upon which the king admired at his answer, which was so wisely made; and bade them all make an acclamation, as a mark of their approbation of his jest, which was truly a facetious one. (215) On the next day Hyrcanus went to every one of the king's friends, and of the men powerful at court, and saluted them; but still inquired of the servants what present they would make the king on his son's birthday; (216) and when some said that they would give twelve talents, and that others of greater dignity would everyone give according to the quantity of their riches, he pretended to every one of them to be grieved that he was not able to bring so large a present; for that he had no more than five talents. And when the servants heard what he said, they told their masters; (217) and they rejoiced in the prospect that Joseph would be disapproved, and would make the king angry, by the smallness of his present. When the day

came, the others, even those that brought the most, offered the king not above twenty talents; but Hyrcanus gave to every one of the hundred boys and hundred maidens that he had bought a talent apiece, for them to carry, and introduced them, the boys to the king and the maidens to Cleopatra; (218) everybody wondering at the unexpected richness of the presents, even the King and queen themselves. He also presented those that attended about the king with gifts to the value of a great number of talents, that he might escape the danger he was in from them; for to these it was that Hyrcanus's brethren had written to destroy him. (219) Now Ptolemy admired at the young man's magnanimity, and commanded him to ask what gift he pleased. But he desired nothing else to be done for him by the king than to write to his father and brethren about him. (220) So when the king had paid him very great respects, and had given him very large gifts, and had written to his father and his brethren, and all his commanders and officers, about him, he sent him away. (221) But when his brethren heard that Hyrcanus had received such favours from the king, and was returning home with great honour, they went out to meet him, and to destroy him, and that with the privity of their father: for he was angry at him for the [large] sum of money that he bestowed for presents, and so had no concern for his preservation. However, Joseph concealed the anger he had at his son, out of fear of the king. (222) And when Hyrcanus's brethren came to fight him, he slew many others of those that were with them, and also two of his brethren themselves; but the rest of them escaped to Jerusalem to their father. But when Hyrcanus came to the city, where nobody would receive him, he was afraid for himself, and retired beyond the river Jordan, and there abode; but obliging the barbarians to pay their taxes.

(223) At this time Seleucus, who was called Soter, reigned over Asia, being the son of Antiochus the Great. (224) And [now] Hyrcanus's father, Joseph, died. He was a good man, and of great magnanimity; and brought the Jews out of a state of poverty and meanness to one that was more splendid. He retained the farm of the taxes of Syria and Phoenicia and Samaria, twenty-two years. His uncle also, Onias, died [about this time], and left the high priesthood to his son Simon. (225) And when he was dead, Onias his son succeeded him in that dignity. To him it was that Areus, king of the Lacedemonians, sent an embassage, with an epistle; the copy whereof here follows: (226)

AREUS, KING OF THE LACEDEMONIANS, TO ONIAS, SENDETH GREETING.

'We have met with a certain writing, whereby we have discovered that both the Jews and the Lacedemonians are of one stock, and are derived from the kindred of Abraham. It is but just, therefore, that you, who are our brethren, should send to us about any of your concern as you please. (227) We will also do the same thing, and esteem your concerns as our own, and will look upon our concerns as in common with yours. Demotoles, who brings you this letter, will bring your answer back to us. This letter is foursquare; and the seal is an eagle, with a dragon in his claws.'

(228) And these were the contents of the epistle which was sent from the king of the Lacedemonians. But upon the death of Joseph, the people grew seditious, on account of his sons; (229) for whereas the elders made war against Hyrcanus, who was the youngest of Joseph's sons, the multitude was divided, but the greater part joined with the elders in this war; as did Simon the high priest, by reason he was of kin to them. However, Hyrcanus determined not to return to Jerusalem any more, but seated himself beyond Jordan, and was at perpetual war with the Arabians, and slew many of them, and took many of them captives. (230) He also erected a strong castle, and built it entirely of white stone to the very roof, and had animals of a prodigious magnitude engraven upon it. He also drew round it a great and deep canal of water. (231) He also made caves of many furlongs in length, by hollowing a rock that was over against him; and then he made large rooms in it, some for feasting, and some for sleeping and living in. He introduced also a vast quantity of waters which ran along it, and which were very delightful and ornamental in the court. (232) But still he made the entrances at the mouth of the caves so narrow, that no more than one person could enter by them at once. And the reason why he built them after that manner was a good one; it was for his own preservation, lest he should be besieged by his brethren, and run the hazard of being caught by them. (233) Moreover, he built courts of greater magnitude than ordinary, which he adorned with vastly large gardens. And when he had brought the place to this state, he named it Tyre. This place is between Arabia and Judea, beyond Jordan, not far from the country of Heshbon. (234) And he ruled over those parts for seven years, even all the time that Seleucus was king of Syria. But when he was dead, his brother Antiochus, who was called Epiphanes, took the kingdom. (235) Ptolemy also, the king of Egypt died, who was besides called Epiphanes. He left two sons, and both young in age; the elder of whom was called Philometer, and the younger Physcon. (236) As for Hyrcanus, when he saw that Antiochus had a great army, and feared lest he should be caught by him, and brought to punishment for what he had done to the Arabians, he ended his life, and slew himself with his own hand; while Antiochus seized upon all his substance.

CHAPTER 5

(237) About this time, upon the death of Onias the high priest, they gave the high priesthood to Jesus his brother; for that son which Onias left [or Onias 4] was yet but an infant; and, in its proper place, we will inform the reader of all the circumstances that befell this child. (238) But this Jesus, who was the brother of Onias, was deprived of the high priesthood by the king, who was angry with him and gave it to his younger brother, whose name also was Onias; for Simon had these three sons, to each of whom the priesthood came, as we have already informed the reader. (239) This Jesus changed his name to Jason; but Onias was called Menelaus. Now as the former high priest, Jesus, raised a sedition against Menelaus, who was ordained after him, the multitude were divided between them both. And the sons of Tobias took the part of Menelaus, (240) but the greater part of the people assisted Jason; and by that means Menelaus and the sons of Tobias were distressed, and retired to Antiochus and informed him, that they were desirous to leave the laws of their country, and the Jewish way of living according to them, and to follow the king's laws, and the Grecian way of living: (241) wherefore they desired his permission to build them a gymnasium at Jerusalem. And when he had given them leave they also hid the circumcision of their genitals, that even when they were naked they might appear to be Greeks. Accordingly, they left off all the customs that belonged to their own country, and imitated the practices of the other nations.

(242) Now Antiochus, upon the agreeable situation of the affairs of his kingdom, resolved to make an expedition against Egypt both because he had a desire to gain it, and because he condemned the son of Ptolemy, as now weak, and not yet of abilities to manage affairs of such consequence; (243) so he came with great forces to Pelusium, and circumvented Ptolemy Philometer by treachery, and seized upon Egypt. He then came to the places about Memphis; and when he had taken them, he made haste to Alexandria, in hopes of taking it by siege, and of subduing Ptolemy, who reigned there. (244) But he was driven not only from Alexandria, but out of all Egypt, by the declaration of the Romans, who charged him to let that country alone. Accordingly, as I have elsewhere formerly declared,, (245) I will now give a particular account of what concerns this king – how he subdued Judea and the temple; for in my former work I mentioned those things very briefly, and have therefore now thought it necessary to go over that history again, and that with great accuracy.

(246) King Antiochus returning out of Egypt, for fear of the Romans, made an expedition against the city Jerusalem; and when he was there, in the hundred and forty-third year of the kingdom of the Seleucidae, he took the

city without fighting, those of his own party opening the gates to him. (247) And when he had gotten possession of Jerusalem, he slew many of the opposite party; and when he had plundered it of a great deal of money, he returned to Antioch.

(248) Now it came to pass after two years in the hundred and forty-fifth year, on the twenty-fifth day of that month which is by us called Chasleu, and by the Macedonians Apelleus, in the hundred and fifty-third Olympiad, that the king came up to Jerusalem, and, pretending peace, he got possession of the city by treachery: (249) at which time he spared not so much as those that admitted him into it, on account of the riches that lay in the temple; but, led by his covetous inclination (for he saw there was in it a great deal of gold, and many ornaments that had been dedicated to it of very great value), and in order to plunder its wealth, he ventured to break the league he had made. (250) So he left the temple bare, and took away the golden candlesticks and the golden altar [of incense] and table [of shewbread] and the altar [of burnt offering]; and did not abstain from even the veils, which were made of fine linen and scarlet. He also emptied it of its secret treasures, and left nothing at all remaining; and by this means cast the Jews into great lamentation, (251) for he forbade them to offer those daily sacrifices which they used to offer to God, according to the law. And when he had pillaged the whole city, some of the inhabitants he slew, and some he carried captive, together with their wives and children, so that the multitude of those captives that were taken alive amounted to about ten thousand. (252) He also burnt down the finest building; and when he had overthrown the city walls, he built a citadel in the lower part of the city, for the place was high, and overlooked the temple, on which account he fortified it with high walls and towers and put into it a garrison of Macedonians. However, in that citadel dwelt the impious and wicked part of the [Jewish] multitude, from whom it proved that the citizens suffered many and sore calamities. (253) And when the king had built an idol altar upon God's altar, he slew swine upon it, and so offered a sacrifice neither according to the law, nor the Jewish religious worship in that country. He also compelled them to forsake the worship which they paid their own God, and to adore those whom he took to be gods; and made them build temples, and raise idol altars, in every city and village, and offer swine upon them every day. (254) He also commanded them not to circumcise their sons, and threatened to punish any that should be found to have transgressed his injunction. He also appointed overseers, who should compel them to do what he commanded. (255) And indeed many Jews there were who complied with the king's commands, either voluntarily, or out of fear of the penalty that was denounced; but the best men, and those of the noblest souls, did not regard him, but did pay a greater respect to the customs of their country than concern as to the punishment which he

threatened to the disobedient; on which account they every day underwent great miseries and bitter torments; (256) for they were whipped with rods and their bodies were torn to pieces, and were crucified while they were still alive and breathed: they also strangled those women and their sons whom they had circumcised, as the king had appointed, hanging their sons about their necks as they were upon the crosses. And if there were any sacred book of the law found, it was destroyed and those with whom they were found miserably perished also.

(257) When the Samaritans saw the Jews under these sufferings, they no longer confessed that they were of their kindred; nor that the temple on Mount Gerizzim belonged to Almighty God. This was according to their nature, as we have already shown. And they now said that they were a colony of Medes and Persians; and indeed they were a colony of theirs. (258) So they sent ambassadors to Antiochus, and an epistle, whose contents are these: 'To King Antiochus the god, Epiphanes, a memorial from the Sidonians, who live at Shechem. (259) Our forefathers, upon certain frequent plagues, and as following a certain ancient superstition, had a custom of observing that day which by the Jews is called the Sabbath. And when they had erected a temple at the mountain called Gerizzim, though without a name, they offered upon it the proper sacrifices. (260) Now, upon the just treatment of these wicked Jews those that manage their affairs, supposing that we were of kin to them, and practised as they do, make us liable to the same accusations, although we are originally Sidonians, as is evident from the public records. (261) We therefore beseech thee, our benefactor and saviour, to give order to Apollonius, the governor of this part of the country, and to Nicanor, the procurator of thy affairs, to give us no disturbance, nor to lay to our charge what the Jews are accused for, since we are aliens from their nation and from their customs; but let our temple which at present hath no name at all, be named the Temple of Jupiter Hellenius. If this were once done, we should be no longer disturbed, but should be more intent on our own occupation with quietness, and so bring in a greater revenue to thee.' (262) When the Samaritans had petitioned for this, the king sent them back the following answer in an epistle: 'King Antiochus to Nicanor. The Sidonians, who live at Shechem, have sent me the memorial enclosed. (263) When, therefore, we were advising with our friends about it, the messengers sent by them represented to us that they are no way concerned with accusations which belong to the Jews, but choose to live after the customs of the Greeks. Accordingly, we declare them free from such accusations, and order that, agreeable to their petition, their temple be named the Temple of Jupiter Hellenius.' (264) He also sent the like epistle to Apollonius, the governor of that part of the country, in the forty-sixth year, and the eighteenth day of the month Hecatombeon.

CHAPTER 6

(265) Now at this time there was one whose name was Mattathias, who dwelt at Modin, the son of John, the son of Simeon, the son of Asamoneus, a priest of the order of Joarib, and a citizen of Jerusalem. (266) He had five sons: John, who was called Gaddis, and Simon, who was called Matthes, and Judas, who was called Maccabeus, and Eleazar, who was called Auran, and Jonathan, who was called Apphus. (267) Now this Mattathias lamented to his children the sad state of their affairs, and the ravage made in the city and the plundering of the temple, and the calamities the multitude were under; and he told them that it was better for them to die for the laws of their country than to live so ingloriously as they then did.

(268) But when those that were appointed by the king were come to Modin, that they might compel the Jews to do what they were commanded, and to enjoin those that were there to offer sacrifice, as the king had commanded, they desired that Mattathias, a person of the greatest character among them, both on other accounts, and particularly on account of such a numerous and so deserving a family of children, would begin the sacrifice, (269) because his fellow citizens would follow his example, and because such a procedure would make him honoured by the king. But Mattathias said that he would not do it; and that if all the other nations would obey the commands of Antiochus, either out of fear or to please him, yet would not he nor his sons leave the religious worship of their country; (270) but as soon as he had ended his speech, there came one of the Jews into the midst of them, and sacrificed as Antiochus had commanded. At which Mattathias had great indignation, and ran upon him violently with his sons, who had swords with them, and slew both the man himself that sacrificed, and Apelles the king's general, who compelled them to sacrifice, with a few of his soldiers. He also overthrew the idol altar, and cried out, (271) 'If,' said he, 'anyone be zealous for the laws of his country, and for the worship of God, let him follow me;' and when he had said this, he made haste into the desert with his sons, and left all his substance in the village. (272) Many others did the same also, and fled with their children and wives into the desert and dwelt in caves; but when the king's generals heard this, they took all the forces they then had in the citadel at Jerusalem, and pursued the Jews into the desert; (273) and when they had overtaken them, they in the first place endeavoured to persuade them to repent, and to choose what was most for their advantage, and not put them to the necessity of using them according to the law of war; (274) but when they would not comply with their persuasions, but continued to be of a different mind, they fought against them on the Sabbath day, and they burnt them as they were in the caves, without resistance, and

without so much as stopping up the entrances of the caves. And they avoided to defend themselves on that day, because they were not willing to break in upon the honour they owed the Sabbath, even in such distresses; for our law required that we rest upon that day. (275) There were about a thousand, with their wives and children, who were smothered and died in these caves; but many of those that escaped joined themselves to Mattathias, and appointed him to be their ruler, (276) who taught them to fight even on the Sabbath day; and told them that unless they would do so, they would become their own enemies, by observing the law [so rigorously], while their adversaries would still assault them on this day, and they would not then defend themselves; and that nothing could then hinder but they must all perish without fighting. (277) This speech persuaded them; and this rule continues among us to this day, that if there be a necessity, we may fight on Sabbath days. (278) So Mattathias got a great army about him, and overthrew their idol altars, and slew those that broke the laws, even all that he could get under his power; for many of them were dispersed among the nations round about them for fear of him. He also commanded that those boys which were not yet circumcised should be circumcised now; and he drove those away that were appointed to hinder such their circumcision.

(279) But when he had ruled one year, and was fallen into a distemper, he called for his sons, and set them round about him, and said, 'O my sons, I am going the way of all the earth; and I recommend to you my resolution, and beseech you not to be negligent in keeping it, (280) but to be mindful of the desires of him who begat you, and brought you up, and to preserve the customs of your country, and to recover your ancient form of government, which is in danger of being overturned, and not to be carried away with those that, either by their own inclination or out of necessity, betray it, (281) but to become such sons as are worthy of me; to be above all force and necessity, and so to dispose your souls, as to be ready, when it shall be necessary, to die for your laws, as sensible of this, by just reasoning: that if God see that you are so disposed he will not overlook you, but will have a great value for your virtue, and will restore to you again what you have lost, and will return to you that freedom in which you shall live quietly, and enjoy your own customs. (282) Your bodies are mortal, and subject to fate; but they receive a sort of immortality, by the remembrance of what actions they have done; and I would have you so in love with this immortality, that you may pursue after glory, and that, when you have undergone the greatest difficulties, you may not scruple, for such things, to lose your lives. (283) I exhort you especially to agree one with another; and in what excellency any one of you exceeds another, to yield to him so far, and by that means to reap the advantage of everyone's own virtues. Do you then esteem Simon as your father, because he is a man of

extraordinary prudence, and be governed by him in what counsels he gives you. (284) Take Maccabeus for the general of your army, because of his courage and strength, for he will avenge your nation, and will bring vengeance on your enemies. Admit among you the righteous and religious, and augment their power.'

(285) When Mattathias had thus discoursed to his sons, and had prayed to God to be their assistant, and to recover to the people their former constitution, he died a little afterward, and was buried at Modin, all the people making great lamentation for him. Whereupon his son Judas took upon him the administration of public affairs, in the hundred and forty-sixth year; (286) and thus, by the ready assistance of his brethren, and of others, Judas cast their enemies out of the country, and put those of their own country to death who had transgressed its laws, and purified the land of all the pollutions that were in it.

CHAPTER 7

(287) When Apollonius, the general of the Samaritan forces, heard this, he took his army, and made haste to go against Judas, who met him, and joined battle with him, and beat him, and slew many of his men, and among them Apollonius himself, their general, whose sword, being that which he happened then to wear, he seized upon and kept for himself; but he wounded more than he slew, and took a great deal of prey from the enemy's camp, and went his way; (288) but when Seron, who was general of the army of Celesyria, heard that many had joined themselves to Judas, and that he had about him an army sufficient for fighting and for making war, he determined to make an expedition against him, as thinking it became him to endeavour to punish those that transgressed the king's injunctions. (289) He then got together an army, as large as he was able, and joined to it the runagate and wicked Jews, and came against Judas. He then came as far as Bethoron, a village of Judea, and there pitched his camp; (290) upon which Judas met him, and when he intended to give him battle, he saw that his soldiers were backward to fight, because their number was small, and because they wanted food, for they were fasting; he encouraged them, and said to them, that victory and conquest of enemies are not derived from the multitude in armies, but in the exercise of piety towards God; (291) and that they had the plainest instances in their forefathers, who, by their righteousness, and exerting themselves on behalf of their own laws and their own children, had frequently conquered many ten thousands − for innocence is the strongest army. (292) By this speech he induced his men to condemn the multitude of the enemy, and to fall upon Seron; and upon joining battle with him, he beat the Syrians; and when their general fell among the rest, they all ran away with speed, as thinking that to be

their best way of escaping. So he pursued them unto the plain, and slew about eight hundred of the enemy; but the rest escaped to the region which lay near to the sea.

(293) When King Antiochus heard of these things, he was very angry at what had happened; so he got together all his own army with many mercenaries, whom he had hired from the islands, and took them with him, and prepared to break into Judea about the beginning of the spring; (294) but when, upon his mustering his soldiers, he perceived that his treasures were deficient, and there was a want of money in them, for all the taxes were not paid, by reason of the seditions there had been among the nations, he having been so magnanimous and so liberal that what he had was not sufficient for him, he therefore resolved first to go into Persia, and collect the taxes of that country. (295) Hereupon he left one whose name was Lysias, who was in great repute with him, governor of the kingdom as far as the bounds of Egypt and of the Lower Asia, and reaching from the river Euphrates, and committed to him a certain part of his forces, and of his elephants, (296) and charged him to bring up his son Antiochus with all possible care, until he came back; and that he should conquer Judea, and take its inhabitants for slaves, and utterly destroy Jerusalem, and abolish the whole nation; (297) and when King Antiochus had given these things in charge to Lysias, he went into Persia; and in the hundred and forty-seventh year, he passed over Euphrates, and went to the superior provinces.

(298) Upon this Lysias chose Ptolemy, the son of Dorymenes, and Nicanor and Gorgias, very potent men among the king's friends, and delivered to them forty thousand foot soldiers and seven thousand horsemen, and sent them against Judea, who came as far as the city Emmaus, and pitched their camp in the plain country. (299) There came also to them auxiliaries out of Syria, and the country round about; as also many of the runagate Jews; and besides these came some merchants to buy those that should be carried captives (having bonds with them to bind those that should be made prisoners), with that silver and gold which they were to pay for their price; (300) and when Judas saw their camp, and how numerous their enemies were, he persuaded his own soldiers to be of good courage; and exhorted them to place their hopes of victory in God, and to make supplication to him, according to the custom of their country, clothed in sackcloth; and to show what was their usual habit of supplication in the greatest dangers, and thereby to prevail with God to grant you the victory over your enemies. (301) So he set them in their ancient order of battle used by their forefathers, under their captains of thousands and other officers, and dismissed such as were newly married, as well as those that had newly gained possessions, that they might not fight in a cowardly manner, out of an inordinate love of life, in order to enjoy those blessings. (302) When he had thus disposed his soldiers, he encouraged them to fight by the following

speech which he made to them: 'O my fellow-soldiers, no other time remains more opportune than the present for courage and contempt of dangers; for if you now fight manfully, you may recover your liberty, which, as it is a thing of itself agreeable to all men, (303) so it proves to be to us much more desirable, by its affording us the liberty of worshipping God. Since, therefore, you are in such circumstances at present, you must either recover that liberty, and so regain a happy and blessed way of living, which is that according to our laws and the customs of our country, or to submit to the most opprobrious sufferings; (304) nor will any seed of your nation remain if you be beat in this battle. Fight therefore manfully; and suppose that you must die, though you do not fight; but believe that, besides such glorious rewards as those of the liberty of your country, of your laws, of your religion, you shall then obtain ever-lasting glory. Prepare yourselves, therefore, and put yourselves into such an agreeable posture, that you may be ready to fight with the enemy as soon as it is day tomorrow morning.'

(305) And this was the speech which Judas made to encourage them. But when the enemy sent Gorgias, with five thousand foot and one thousand horse, that he might fall upon Judas by night, and had for that purpose certain of the runagate Jews as guides, the son of Mattathias perceived it, and resolved to fall upon those enemies that were in their camp, now their forces were divided. (306) When they had therefore supped in good time, and had left many fires in their camp, he marched all night to those enemies that were at Emmaus; so that when Gorgias found no enemy in their camp, but suspected that they were retired and had hidden themselves among the mountains, he resolved to go and seek them wheresoever they were. (307) But, about break of day, Judas appeared to those enemies that were at Emmaus, with only three thousand men, and those ill armed, by reason of their poverty, and when he saw the enemy very well and skilfully fortified in their camp, he encouraged the Jews, and told them, that they ought to fight, though it were with their naked bodies, for that God had sometimes of old given such men strength and that against such as were more in number, and were armed also, out of regard to their great courage. So he commanded the trumpeters to sound for the battle: (308) and by thus falling upon the enemy when they did not expect it, and thereby astonishing and disturbing their minds, he slew many of those that resisted him, and went on pursuing the rest as far as Gadara and the plains of Idumea, and Ashdod and Jamnia; and of these there fell about three thousand. (309) Yet did Judas exhort his soldiers not to be too desirous of the spoils, for that still they must have a contest and battle with Gorgias and the forces that were with him: but that when they had once overcome them, then they might securely plunder the camp, because they were the only enemies remaining, and they expected no others. (310) And just as he was speaking to his soldiers,

Gorgias's men looked down into that army which they left in their camp, and saw that it was overthrown, and the camp burnt; for the smoke that arose from it showed them, even when they were a great way off, what had happened. (311) When, therefore, those that were with Gorgias understood that things were in this posture, and perceived that those that were with Judas were ready to fight them, they also were affrighted, and put to flight; (312) but then Judas, as though he had already beaten Gorgias's soldiers without fighting, returned and seized on the spoils. He took a great quantity of gold and silver, and purple and blue, and then returned home with joy, and singing hymns to God for their good success; for this victory greatly contributed to the recovery of their liberty.

(313) Hereupon Lysias was confounded at the defeat of the army which he had sent, and the next year he got together sixty thousand chosen men. He also took five thousand horsemen, and fell upon Judea; and he went up to the hill country of Bethsur, a village of Judea, and pitched his camp there, (314) where Judas met him with ten thousand men; and when he saw the great number of his enemies, he prayed to God that he would assist him, and joined battle with the first of the enemy that appeared, and beat them, and slew about five thousand of them, and thereby became terrible to the rest of them. (315) Nay, indeed, Lysias observing the great spirit of the Jews, how they were prepared to die rather than lose their liberty, and being afraid of their desperate way of fighting, as if it were real strength, he took the rest of the army back with him, and returned to Antioch, where he listed foreigners into the service, and prepared to fall upon Judea with a greater army.

(316) When, therefore, the generals of Antiochus' armies had been beaten so often, Judas assembled the people together, and told them, that after these many victories which God had given them, they ought to go up to Jerusalem, and purify the temple and offer the appointed sacrifices. (317) But as soon as he, with the whole multitude, was come to Jerusalem, and found the temple deserted, and its gates burnt down, and plants growing in the temple of their own accord, on account of its desertion, he and those that were with him began to lament, and were quite confounded at the sight of the temple; (318) so he chose out some of his soldiers, and gave them order to fight against those guards that were in the citadel, until he should have purified the temple. When therefore he had carefully purged it, and had brought in new vessels, the candlestick, the table [of shewbread], and the altar [of incense], which were made of gold, he hung up the veils at the gates, and added doors to them. He also took down the altar [of burnt offering], and built a new one of stones that he gathered together, and not of such as were hewn with iron tools. (319) So on the five and twentieth day of the month Casleu, which the Macedonians call Apelleus, they lighted the lamps that were on the candlestick, and offered incense upon the altar [of incense], and laid the loaves upon the table [of

shewbread], and offered burnt offerings upon the new altar [of burnt offering]. (320) Now it so fell out, that these things were done on the very same day on which their divine worship had fallen off, and was reduced to a profane and common use, after three years' time; for so it was, that the temple was made desolate by Antiochus, and so continued for three years. (321) This desolation happened to the temple in the hundred forty and fifth year, on the twenty-fifth day of the month Apelleus, and on the hundred and fifty-third Olympiad: (322) but it was dedicated anew, on the same day, the twenty-fifth of the month Apelleus, on the hundred and forty-eighth year, and on the hundred and fifty-fourth Olympiad. (322) And this desolation came to pass according to the prophecy of Daniel, which was given four hundred and eight years before; for he declared that the Macedonians would dissolve that worship [for some time].

(323) Now Judas celebrated the festival of the restoration of the sacrifices of the temple for eight days; and omitted no sort of pleasures thereon: but he feasted them upon very rich and splendid sacrifices; and he honoured God, and delighted them by hymns and psalms. (324) Nay, they were so very glad at the revival of their customs, when after a long time of intermission, they unexpectedly had regained the freedom of their worship, that they made it a law for their posterity, that they should keep a festival, on account of the restoration of their temple worship, for eight days. (325) And from that time to this we celebrate this festival, and call it Lights. I suppose the reason was, because this liberty beyond our hopes appeared to us; and that thence was the name given to that festival. (326) Judas also rebuilt the walls round about the city, and reared towers of great height against the incursions of enemies, and set guards therein. He also fortified the city Bethsura, that it might serve as a citadel against any distresses that might come from our enemies.

CHAPTER 8

(327) When these things were over, the nations round about the Jews were very uneasy at the revival of their power, and rose up together, and destroyed many of them, as gaining advantage over them by laying snares for them, and making secret conspiracies against them. Judas made perpetual expeditions against these men, and endeavoured to restrain them from those incursions, and to prevent the mischiefs they did to the Jews. (328) So he fell upon the Idumeans, the posterity of Esau, at Acrabattene, and slew a great many of them, and took their spoils. He also shut up the sons of Bean, that laid wait for the Jews; and he sat down about them, and besieged them, and burnt their towers, and destroyed the men [that were in them]. (329) After this he went thence in haste against the Ammonites, who had a great and a numerous army, of which Timotheus was the commander. And when he had subdued them,

he seized on the city Jazer, and took their wives and their children captives, and burnt the city, and then returned into Judea. (330) But when the neighbouring nations understood that he was returned, they got together in great numbers in the land of Gilead, and came against those Jews that were at their borders, who then fled to the garrison of Dathema; and sent to Judas, to inform him that Timotheus was endeavouring to take the place whither they were fled. (331) And as these epistles were reading, there came other messengers out of Galilee, who informed him that the inhabitants of Ptolemais, and of Tyre and Sidon, and strangers of Galilee, were gotten together.

(332) Accordingly Judas, upon considering what was fit to be done with relation to the necessity both these cases required, gave order that Simon his brother should take three thousand chosen men, and go to the assistance of the Jews in Galilee, (333) while he and another of his brothers, Jonathan, made haste into the land of Gilead with eight thousand soldiers. And he left Joseph the son of Zacharias, and Azarias, to be over the rest of the forces; and charged them to keep Judea very carefully, and to fight no battles with any persons whomsoever until his return. (334) Accordingly, Simon went into Galilee, and fought the enemy, and put them to flight, and pursued them to the very gates of Ptolemais, and slew about three thousand of them, and took the spoils of those that were slain, and those Jews whom they had made captives, with their baggage, and then returned home.

(335) Now as for Judas Maccabeus and his brother Jonathan, they passed over the river Jordan; and when they had gone three days' journey, they lighted upon the Nabateans, who came to meet them peaceably, (336) and who told them how the affairs of those in the land of Galilee stood, and how many of them were in distress, and driven into garrisons, and into the cities of Galilee; and exhorted him to make haste to go against the foreigners, and to endeavour to save his own countrymen out of their hands. To this exhortation Judas hearkened, and returned in to the wilderness; and in the first place fell upon the inhabitants of Bosor, and took the city, and beat the inhabitants, and destroyed all the males, and all that were able to fight, and burnt the city. (337) Nor did he stop even when night came on but he journeyed in it to the garrison where the Jews happened to be then shut up, and where Timotheus lay round the place with his army; and Judas came upon the city in the morning; (338) and when he found that the enemy were making an assault upon the walls, and that some of them brought ladders, on which they might get upon those walls, and that others brought engines [to batter them], he bid the trumpeter to sound his trumpet, and he encouraged his soldiers cheerfully to undergo dangers for the sake of their brethren and kindred; he also parted his army into three bodies, and fell upon the backs of their enemies. (339) But when Timotheus' men perceived that it was Maccabeus that was upon them,

of both whose courage and good success in war they had formerly had sufficient experience, they were put to flight; but Judas followed them with his army, and slew about eight thousand of them. (340) He then turned aside to a city of the foreigners called Malle, and took it, and slew all the males, and burnt the city itself. He then removed from thence, and overthrew Casphom and Bosor, and many other cities of the land of Gilead.

(341) But not long after this, Timotheus prepared a great army, and took many others as auxiliaries, and induced some of the Arabians, by the promise of rewards, to go with him in this expedition, and came with his army beyond the brook, (342) over against the city Raphon; and he encouraged his soldiers, if it came to a battle with the Jews, to fight courageously, and to hinder their passing over the brook; for he said to them beforehand, that, 'if they come over it, we shall be beaten.' (343) And when Judas heard that Timotheus prepared himself to fight, he took all his own army, and went in haste against Timotheus his enemy; and when he had passed over the brook, he fell upon his enemies, and some of them met him, whom he slew, and others of them he so terrified, that he compelled them to throw down their arms and fly; and some of them escaped, (344) but some of them fled to what was called the Temple of Carnaim, and hoped thereby to preserve themselves, but Judas took the city, and slew them, and burnt the temple, and so used several ways of destroying his enemies.

(345) When he had done this, he gathered the Jews together, with their children and wives, and the substance that belonged to them, and was going to bring them back into Judea. (346) But as soon as he was come to a certain city, the name of which was Ephron, that lay upon the road (and as it was not possible for him to go any other way, so he was not willing to go back again), he then sent to the inhabitants, and desired that they would open their gates, and permit them to go on their way through the city; for they had stopped up the gates with stones, and cut off their passage through it. (347) And when the inhabitants of Ephron would not agree to this proposal, he encouraged those that were with him, and encompassed the city round, and besieged it, and, lying round it, by day and night, took the city, and slew every male in it, and burnt it all down, and so obtained a way through it; and the multitude of those that were slain was so great, that they went over the dead bodies. (348) So they came over Jordan, and arrived at the great plain, over against which is situate the city Bethshan, which is called by the Greeks Scythopolis. (349) And going away hastily from thence, they came into Judea, singing psalms and hymns as they went, and indulging such tokens of mirth as are usual in triumphs upon victory. They also offered thank offerings, both for their good success, and for the preservation of their army, for not one of the Jews was slain in these battles.

(350) But as to Joseph the son of Zacharias, and Azarias, whom Judas left

generals [of the rest of his forces] at the same time when Simon was in Galilee fighting against the people of Ptolemais, and Judas himself and his brother Jonathan were in the land of Gilead, did these men also affect the glory of being courageous generals in war, in order whereto they took the army that was under their command, and came to Jamnia. (351) There Gorgias, the general of the forces of Jamnia, met them; and upon joining battle with him, they lost two thousand of their army, and fled away, and were pursued to the very borders of Judea. (352) And this misfortune befell them by their disobedience to what injunctions Judas had given them, not to fight with anyone before his return. For besides the rest of Judas's sagacious counsels, one may well wonder at this concerning the misfortune that befell the forces commanded by Joseph and Azarias, which he understood would happen if they broke any of the injunctions he had given them. (353) But Judas and his brethren did not leave off fighting with the Idumeans, but pressed upon them on all sides, and took from them the city of Hebron, and demolished all its fortifications, and set all its towers on fire, and burnt the country of the foreigners, and the city Marissa. They came also to Ashdod, and took it, and laid it waste, and took away a great deal of the spoils and prey that were in it, and returned to Judea.

CHAPTER 9

(354) About this time it was that King Antiochus, as he was going over the upper countries heard that there was a very rich city in Persia, called Elymais; and therein a very rich temple of Diana, and that it was full of all sorts of donations dedicated to it; as also weapons and breastplates, which, upon inquiry, he found had been left there by Alexander, the son of Philip, king of Macedonia; (355) and being incited by these motives, he went in haste to Elymais, and assaulted it, and besieged it. But as those that were in it were not terrified at his assault, nor at his siege, but opposed him very courageously, he was beaten off his hopes; for they drove him away from the city, and went out and pursued after him, insomuch that he fled away as far as Babylon, and lost a great many of his army; (356) and when he was grieving for this disappointment, some persons told him of the defeat of his commanders, whom he had left behind him to fight against Judea, and what strength the Jews had already gotten. (357) When this concern about these affairs was added to the former, he was confounded, and by the anxiety he was in, fell into a distemper, which, as it lasted a great while, and as his pains increased upon him, so he at length perceived he should die in a little time; so he called his friends to him, and told them that his distemper was severe upon him, and confessed withal, that this calamity was sent upon him for the miseries he had

brought upon the Jewish nation, while he plundered their temple and condemned their God; and when he had said this, he gave up the ghost. (358) Whence one may wonder at Polybius of Megalopolis, who, though otherwise a good man, yet saith that 'Antiochus died, because he had a purpose to plunder the temple of Diana in Persia'; for the purposing to do a thing, but not actually doing it, is not worthy of punishment. (359) But if Polybius could think that Antiochus thus lost his life on that account, it is much more probable that this king died on account of his sacrilegious plundering of the temple at Jerusalem. But we will not contend about this matter with those who may think that the cause assigned by this Polybius of Megalopolis is nearer the truth than that assigned by us.

(360) However, Antiochus, before he died, called for Philip, who was one of his companions, and made him the guardian of his kingdom; and gave him his diadem and his garment and his ring, and charged him to carry them, and deliver them to his son Antiochus; and desired him to take care of his education, and to preserve the kingdom for him. (361) This Antiochus died in the hundred forty and ninth year: but it was Lysias that declared his death to the multitude, and appointed his son Antiochus to be king (of whom at present he had the care), and called him Eupator.

(362) At this time it was that the garrison in the citadel of Jerusalem, with the Jewish runagates, did a great deal of harm to the Jews: for the soldiers that were in that garrison rushed out upon the sudden, and destroyed such as were going up to the temple in order to offer their sacrifices, for this citadel adjoined to and overlooked the temple. (363) When these misfortunes had often happened to them, Judas resolved to destroy that garrison; whereupon he got all the people together, and vigorously besieged those that were in the citadel. This was in the hundred and fiftieth year of the dominion of the Seleucidae. So he made engines of war, and erected bulwarks, and very zealously pressed on to take the citadel. (364) But there were not a few of the runagates who were in the place, that went out by night into the country, and got together some other wicked men like themselves, and went to Antiochus the king, and desired of them that he would not suffer them to be neglected, under the great hardships that lay upon them from those of their own nation; and this because their sufferings were occasioned on his father's account, while they left the religious worship of their fathers and preferred that which he had commanded them to follow: (365) that there was danger lest the citadel, and those appointed to garrison it by the king, should be taken by Judas and those that were with him, unless he would send them succours. (366) When Antiochus, who was but a child, heard this, he was angry, and sent for his captains and his friends, and gave order that they should get an army of mercenaries together, with such men also of his own kingdom as were of an age fit for war. Accordingly an army was collected

of about a hundred thousand footmen, and twenty thousand horsemen, and thirty-two elephants.

(367) So the king took this army, and marched hastily out of Antioch, with Lysias, who had the command of the whole, and came to Idumea, and thence went up to the city Bethsura, a city that was strong, and not to be taken without great difficulty. He set about this city, and besieged it; (368) and while the inhabitants of Bethsura courageously opposed him, and sallied out upon him, and burnt his engines of war, a great deal of time was spent in the siege; (369) but when Judas heard of the king's coming, he raised the siege of the citadel, and met the king, and pitched his camp in certain straits, at a place called Bethzachariah, at the distance of seventy furlongs from the enemy; (370) but the king soon drew his forces from Bethsura, and brought them to those straits; and as soon as it was day he put his men in battle array, (371) and made his elephants follow one another through the narrow passes, because they could not be set sideways by one another. Now round about every elephant there were a thousand footmen and five hundred horsemen. The elephants also had high towers [upon their backs], and archers [in them]; and he also made the rest of his army to go up the mountains, and put his friends before the rest; (372) and gave orders for the army to shout aloud, and so he attacked the enemy. He also exposed to sight their golden and brazen shields, so that a glorious splendour was sent from them; and when they shouted, the mountains echoed again. When Judas saw this, he was not terrified, but received the enemy with great courage, and slew about six hundred of the first ranks. (373) But when his brother Eleazar, whom they called Auran, saw the tallest of all the elephants armed with royal breastplates, and supposed that the king was upon him, he attacked him with great quickness and bravery. He also slew many of those that were about the elephant, and scattered the rest, and then went under the belly of the elephant, and smote him, and slew him; (374) so the elephant fell upon Eleazar, and by his weight crushed him to death. And thus did this man come to his end, when he had first courageously destroyed many of his enemies.

(375) But Judas, seeing the strength of the enemy, retired to Jerusalem, and prepared to endure a siege. As for Antiochus, he sent part of his army to Bethsura, to besiege it, and with the rest of his army he came against Jerusalem; (376) but the inhabitants of Bethsura were terrified at his strength; and seeing that their provisions grew scarce, they delivered themselves up on the security of oaths that they should suffer no hard treatment from the king. And when Antiochus had thus taken the city, he did them no other harm than sending them out naked. He also placed a garrison of his own in the city: (377) but as for the temple of Jerusalem, he lay at its siege a long time, while they within bravely defended it; for what engines soever the king set against them, they set other engines again to oppose them. (378) But then their provisions failed

them; what fruits of the ground they had laid up were spent, and the land being not ploughed that year, continued unsowed, because it was the seventh year, on which, by our laws, we are obliged to let it lie uncultivated. And withal, so many of the besieged ran away for want of necessaries, that but a few only were left in the temple.

(379) And these happened to be the circumstances of such as were besieged in the temple. But then, because Lysias the general of the army, and Antiochus the king, were informed that Philip was coming upon them out of Persia, and was endeavouring to get the management of public affairs to himself, they came into these sentiments, to leave the siege, and to make haste to go against Philip; yet did they resolve not to let this be known to the soldiers or the officers; (380) but the king commanded Lysias to speak openly to the soldiers and the officers, without saying a word about the business of Philip; and to intimate to them that a siege would be very long; that the place was very strong; that they were already in want of provisions; that many affairs of the kingdom wanted regulation; (381) and that it was much better to make a league with the besieged, and to become friends to their whole nation, by permitting them to observe the laws of their fathers, while they broke out into this war only because they were deprived of them, and so to depart home. When Lysias had discoursed thus with them, both the army and the officers were pleased with this resolution.

(382) Accordingly the king sent to Judas and to those that were with him, and promised to give them peace, and to permit them to make use of and live according to the laws of their fathers; and they gladly received his proposals; and when they had gained security upon oath for their performance, they went out of the temple: (383) but when Antiochus came into it, and saw how strong the place was, he broke his oaths, and ordered his army that was there to pluck down the walls to the ground; and when he had so done, he returned to Antioch. He also carried with him Anias the high priest, who was also called Menelaus; (384) for Lysias advised the king to slay Menelaus, if he would have the Jews be quiet, and cause him no further disturbance, for that this man was the origin of all the mischief the Jews had done them, by persuading his father to compel the Jews to leave the religion of their fathers; (385) so the king sent Menelaus to Berea, a city of Syria, and there had him put to death, when he had been high priest ten years. He had been a wicked and an impious man; and in order to get the government to himself, had compelled his nation to transgress their own laws. After the death of Menelaus, Alcimus, who was also called Jacimus, was made high priest. (386) But when King Antiochus found that Philip had already possessed himself of the government, he made war against him, and subdued him, and took him and slew him. (387) Now as to Onias, the son of the high priest, who, as we before informed you, was left a child when his father died, when he saw that the king had slain his uncle Menelaus, and given the high

priesthood to Alcimus, who was not of the high priest stock, but was induced by Lysias to translate that dignity from his family to another house, he fled to Ptolemy, king of Egypt; (388) and when he found he was in great esteem with him and with his wife Cleopatra, he desired and obtained a place in the Nomus of Heliopolis, wherein he built a temple like to that at Jerusalem; of which, therefore, we shall hereafter give an account, in a place more proper for it.

CHAPTER 10

(389) About the same time Demetrius, the son of Seleucus, fled away from Rome, and took Tripoli, a city of Syria, and set the diadem on his own head. He also gathered certain mercenary soldiers together, and entered into his kingdom, and was joyfully received by all, who delivered themselves up to him; (390) and when they had taken Antiochus the king, and Lysias, they brought them to him alive; both which were immediately put to death by the command of Demetrius, when Antiochus had reigned two years, as we have already elsewhere related; (391) but there were now many of the wicked Jewish runagates that came together to him, and with them Alcimus the high priest, who accused the whole nation, and particularly Judas and his brethren; (392) and said that they had slain all his friends; and that those in his kingdom that were of his party, and waited for his return, were by them put to death; that these men had ejected them out of their own country, and caused them to be sojourners in a foreign land; and they desired that he would send some one of his own friends, and know from him what mischief Judas's part had done.

(393) At this Demetrius was very angry, and sent Bacchides, a friend of Antiochus Epiphanes, a good man, and one that had been entrusted with all Mesopotamia, and gave him an army, and committed Alcimus the high priest to his care; and gave him charge to slay Judas and those that were with him. (394) So Bacchides made haste, and went out of Antioch with his army; and when he was come into Judea, he sent to Judas and his brethren, to discourse with him about a league of friendship and peace, for he had a mind to take him by treachery; (395) but Judas did not give credit to him, for he saw that he came with so great an army as men do not bring when they come to make peace, but to make war. However, some of the people acquiesced in what Bacchides caused to be proclaimed; and supposing they should undergo no considerable harm from Alcimus, who was their countryman, they went over to them; (396) and when they had received oaths from both of them, that neither they themselves nor those of the same sentiments should come to any harm, they entrusted themselves with them; but Bacchides troubled not himself about the oaths he had taken, but slew threescore of them, although, by not keeping his faith with those that first went over, he deterred all the rest

who had intentions to go over to him, from doing it; (397) but as he was gone out of Jerusalem, and was at the village called Bethzetho, he sent out and caught many of the deserters, and some of the people also, and slew them all: and enjoined all that lived in the country to submit to Alcimus. So he left him there, with some part of the army, that he might have wherewith to keep the country in obedience, and returned to Antioch to King Demetrius.

(398) But Alcimus was desirous to have the dominion more firmly assured to him; and understanding that, if he could bring it about that the multitude should be his friends, he should govern with greater security, he spake kind words to them all, and discoursed to each of them after an agreeable and pleasant manner; by which means he quickly had a great body of men and an army about him, (399) although the greater part of them were of the wicked, and the deserters. With these, whom he used as his servants and soldiers, he went all over the country, and slew all that he could find of Judas's party; (400) but when Judas saw that Alcimus was already become great, and had destroyed many of the good and holy men of the country, he also went all over the country and destroyed those that were of the other party; but when Alcimus saw that he was not able to oppose Judas, nor was equal to him in strength, he resolved to apply himself to King Demetrius for his assistance; (401) so he came to Antioch, and irritated him against Judas, and accused him, alleging that he had undergone a great many miseries by his means, and that he would do more mischief unless he was prevented, and brought to punishment, which must be done by sending a powerful force against him.

(402) So Demetrius, being already of opinion that it would be a thing pernicious to his own affairs to overlook Judas, now he was becoming so great, sent against him Nicanor, the most kind and most faithful of all his friends; for he it was who fled away with him from the city of Rome. He also gave him as many forces as he thought sufficient for him to conquer Judas withal, and bade him not to spare the nation at all. (403) When Nicanor was come to Jerusalem, he did not resolve to fight Judas immediately, but judged it better to get him into his power by treachery; so he sent him a message of peace, and said there was no manner of necessity for them to fight and hazard themselves; and that he would give him his oath that he would do him no harm, for that he only came with some friends, in order to let him know what King Demetrius' intentions were, and what opinion he had of their nation. (404) When Nicanor had delivered this message, Judas and his brethren complied with him, and suspecting no deceit, they gave him assurances of friendship, and received Nicanor and his army; but while he was saluting Judas, and they were talking together, he gave a certain signal to his own soldiers, upon which they were to seize upon Judas; (405) but he perceived the treachery, and ran back to his own soldiers, and fled away with them. So upon this discovery of his purpose, and

of the snares laid for Judas, Nicanor determined to make open war with him, and gathered his army together, and prepared for fighting him; and upon joining battle with him at a certain village called Capharsalama, he beat Judas, and forced him to fly to that citadel which was at Jerusalem.

(406) And when Nicanor came down from the citadel unto the temple, some of the priests and elders met him, and saluted him; and showed him the sacrifices which they said they offered to God for the king: upon which he blasphemed, and threatened them, that unless the people would deliver up Judas to him, upon his return he would pull down their temple. (407) And when he had thus threatened them, he departed from Jerusalem: but the priests fell into tears out of grief at what he had said, and besought God to deliver them from their enemies. (408) But now Nicanor, when he was gone out of Jerusalem, and was at a certain village called Bethoron, he there pitched his camp – another army out of Syria having joined him. And Judas pitched his camp at Adasa, another village, which was thirty furlongs distant from Bethoron, having no more than one thousand soldiers. (409) And when he had encouraged them not to be dismayed at the multitude of their enemies, nor to regard how many they were against whom they were going to fight, but to consider who they themselves were, and for what great rewards they hazarded themselves, and to attack the enemy courageously, he led them out to fight, and joining battle with Nicanor, which proved to be a severe one, he overcame the enemy, and slew many of them; and at last Nicanor himself, as he was fighting gloriously, fell: (410) upon whose fall the army did not stay; but when they had lost their general, they were put to flight, and threw down their arms. Judas also pursued them and slew them; and gave notice by the sound of his trumpets to the neighbouring villages that he had conquered the enemy; (411) which when the inhabitants heard, they put on their armour hastily, and met their enemies in the face as they were running away, and slew them, insomuch that not one of them escaped out of this battle; who were in number nine thousand. (412) This victory happened to fall on the thirteenth day of that month which by the Jews is called Adar, and by the Macedonians Dystrus: and the Jews therein celebrate this victory every year, and esteem it as a festival day. After which the Jewish nation were, for a while, free from wars, and enjoyed peace; but afterward they returned into their former state of wars and hazards.

(413) But now as the high priest Alcimus was resolving to pull down the wall of the sanctuary, which had been there of old time, and had been built by the holy prophets, he was smitten suddenly by God, and fell down. This stroke made him fall down speechless upon the ground; and undergoing torments for many days, he at length died, when he had been high priest four years. (414) And when he was dead, the people bestowed the high priesthood on Judas; who, hearing of the power of the Romans, and that they had conquered in war

Galatia, and Iberia, and Carthage, and Lybia; and that, besides these, they had subdued Greece and their kings, Perseus and Philip, and Antiochus the Great also, he resolved to enter into a league of friendship with them. (415) He therefore sent to Rome some of his friends, Eupolemus the son of John, and Jason the son of Eleazar, and by them desired the Romans that they would assist them, and be their friends, and would write to Demetrius that he would not fight against the Jews. (416) So the senate received the ambassadors that came from Judas to Rome, and discoursed with them about the errand on which they came, and then granted them a league of assistance. They also made a decree concerning it, and sent a copy of it into Judea. It was also laid up in the capital, and engraven in brass. (417) The decree itself was this: 'The decree of the senate concerning a league of assistance and friendship with the nation of the Jews. It shall not be lawful for any that are subject to the Romans to make war with the nation of the Jews, nor to assist those that do so, either by sending them corn, or ships, or money. (418) And if any attack be made upon the Jews, the Romans shall assist them, as far as they are able; and, again, if any attack be made upon the Romans, the Jews shall assist them. And if the Jews have a mind to add to, or to take away anything from, this league of assistance, that shall be done with the common consent of the Romans. And whatsoever addition shall thus be made, it shall be of force.' (419) This decree was written by Eupolemus the son of John, and by Jason the son of Eleazar, when Judas was high priest of the nation, and Simon his brother was general of the army. And this was the first league that the Romans made with the Jews, and was managed after this manner.

CHAPTER II

(420) But when Demetrius was informed of the death of Nicanor, and of the destruction of the army that was with him, he sent Bacchides again with an army into Judea; (421) who marched out of Antioch, and came into Judea, and pitched his camp at Arbela, a city of Galilee; and having besieged and taken those that were in caves (for many of the people fled into such places), he removed, and made all the haste he could to Jerusalem. (422) And when he had learned that Judas had pitched his camp at a certain village whose name was Bethzetho, he led his army against him: they were twenty thousand footmen, and two thousand horsemen. (423) Now Judas had no more soldiers than one thousand. When these saw the multitude of Bacchides's men, they were afraid, and left their camp, and fled all away, excepting eight hundred. Now when Judas was deserted by his own soldiers, and the enemy pressed upon him, and gave him no time to gather his army together, he was disposed to fight with Bacchides' army, though he had but eight hundred men with him; so he exhorted these men to undergo the danger courageously, (424) and

encouraged them to attack the enemy. And when they said they were not a body sufficient to fight so great an army, and advised that they should retire now and save themselves, and that when he had gathered his own men together, then he fall upon the enemy afterwards, his answer was this: 'Let not the sun ever see such a thing, that I should show my back to the enemy; (425) and although this be the time that will bring me to my end, and I must die in this battle, I will rather stand to it courageously, and bear whatsoever comes upon me, than by now running away, bring reproach upon my former great actions, or tarnish their glory.' This was the speech he made to those that remained with him, whereby he encouraged them to attack the enemy.

(426) But Bacchides drew his army out of their camp, and put them in array for the battle. He set the horsemen on both the wings, and the light soldiers and the archers he placed before the whole army, but was himself on the right wing. (427) And when he had thus put his army in order of battle, and was going to join battle with the enemy, he commanded the trumpeter to give a signal of battle, and the army to make a shout, and to fall on the enemy. (428) And when Judas had done the same, he joined battle with them; and as both sides fought valiantly, and the battle continued till sunset, Judas saw that Bacchides and the strongest part of the army was in the right wing, and thereupon took the most courageous men with him, and ran upon that part of the army, and fell upon those that were there, and broke their ranks, (429) and drove them into the middle, and forced them to run away, and pursued them as far as to a mountain called Aza; but when those of the left wing saw that the right wing was put to flight, they encompassed Judas, and pursued him, and came behind him, and took him into the middle of their army; (430) so not being able to fly, but he and those that were with him fought; and when he had slain a great many of those that came against him, he at last was himself wounded, and fell, and gave up the ghost, and died in a way like to his former famous actions. (431) When Judas was dead, those that were with him had no one whom they could regard [as their commander]; but when they saw themselves deprived of such a general, they fled. (432) But Simon and Jonathan, Judas's brethren, received his dead body by a treaty from the enemy, and carried it to the village Modin, where their father had been buried, and there buried him; while the multitude lamented him many days, and performed the usual solemn rites of a funeral to him. (433) And this was the end that Judas came to. He had been a man of valour and a great warrior, and mindful of all the commands of their father Mattathias; and had undergone all difficulties, both in doing and suffering, for the liberty of his countrymen. (434) And when his character was so excellent [while he was alive], he left behind him a glorious reputation and memorial, by gaining freedom for his nation, and delivering them from slavery under the Macedonians. And when he had retained the high priesthood three years, he died.

BOOK THIRTEEN

CHAPTER I

(1) By what means the nation of the Jews recovered their freedom when they had been brought into slavery by the Macedonians, and what struggles and how great battles Judas, the general of their army, ran through till he was slain as he was fighting for them, hath been related in the foregoing book; (2) but after he was dead, all the wicked, and those that transgressed the laws of their forefathers, sprang up again in Judea, and grew upon them, and distressed them on every side. (3) A famine also assisted their wickedness, and afflicted the country, till not a few, who by reason of their want of necessaries, and because they were not able to bear up against the miseries that both the famine and their enemies brought upon them, deserted their country, and went to the Macedonians. (4) And now Bacchides gathered those Jews together who had given up their ancestral customs and chosen the common life; to these he entrusted the government of the country. They arrested the friends of Judas, and those of the same views, and delivered them up to Bacchides, who, when he had, in the first place, tortured and tormented them at his pleasure, he, by that means, at length killed them. (5) And when this calamity of the Jews was become so great, as they had never had experience of the like since their return out of Babylon, those that remained of the companions of Judas, seeing that the nation was about to be destroyed after a miserable manner, came to his brother Jonathan, and desired him that he would imitate his brother, and that care which he took of his countrymen, for whose liberty in general he died also; and that he would not permit the nation to be without a governor, especially in those destructive circumstances wherein it now was. (6) And when Jonathan said that he was ready to die for them, and was indeed esteemed no way inferior to his brother, he was appointed to be the general of the Jewish army.

(7) When Bacchides heard this, and was afraid that Jonathan might be very troublesome to the king and the Macedonians, as Judas had been before him, he sought how he might slay him by treachery; (8) but this intention of his was not unknown to Jonathan, nor his brother Simon; but when these two were apprised of it, they took all their companions, and presently fled into that wilderness which was nearest to the city; and when they were come to a lake called Asphar, they abode there. (9) But when Bacchides was sensible that they were in a low state, and were in that place, he hasted to fall upon them with all his forces, and pitching his camp beyond Jordan, he recruited his army; (10)

but when Jonathan knew that Bacchides was coming upon him, he sent his brother John, who was also called Gaddis, to the Nabatean Arabs, that he might lodge his baggage with them until the battle with Bacchides should be over, for they were the Jews' friends. (11) And the sons of Ambri laid an ambush for John, from the city Medaba, and seized upon him, and upon those that were with him, and plundered all that they had with them; they also slew John and all his companions. However, they were sufficiently punished for what they now did by John's brethren, as we shall relate presently.

(12) But when Bacchides knew that Jonathan had pitched his camp among the lakes of Jordan, he observed when their Sabbath day came, and then assaulted him, as supposing that he would not fight because of the law for resting on that day; (13) but he exhorted his companions [to fight], and told them that their lives were at stake, since they were encompassed by the river and by their enemies, and had no way to escape, for that their enemies pressed upon them before, and the river was behind them. So after he had prayed to God to give them victory, he joined battle with the enemy, (14) of whom he overthrew many: and as he saw Bacchides coming up boldly to him, he stretched out his right hand to smite him; but the other foreseeing and avoiding the stroke, Jonathan with his companions leaped into the river, and swam over it, and by that means escaped beyond Jordan, while the enemy did not pass over that river; but Bacchides returned presently to the citadel at Jerusalem, having lost about two thousand of his army. (15) He also fortified many cities of Judea whose walls had been demolished: Jericho, and Emmaus, and Bethoron, and Bethel, and Timna, and Pharatho, and Tecoa, and Gazara, (16) and built towers in every one of these cities, and encompassed them with strong walls, that were very large also, and put garrisons into them that they might issue out of them, and do mischief to the Jews. (17) He also fortified the citadel at Jerusalem more than all the rest. Moreover, he took the sons of the principal Jews as pledges, and shut them up in the citadel, and in that manner guarded it.

(18) About the same time, one came to Jonathan and to his brother Simon, and told them that the sons of Ambri were celebrating a marriage, and bringing the bride from the city Gabatha, who was the daughter of one of the illustrious men among the Arabians, and that the damsel was to be conducted with pomp and splendour, and much riches: (19) so Jonathan and Simon thinking this appeared to be the fittest time for them to avenge the death of their brother, and that they had forces sufficient for receiving satisfaction from them for his death, they made haste to Medaba, and lay in wait among the mountains for the coming of their enemies; (20) and as soon as they saw them conducting the virgin and her bridegroom, and such a great company of their friends with them as was to be expected at this wedding, they sallied out of their ambush

and slew them all – and took their ornaments and all the prey that then followed them, and so returned, (21) and received this satisfaction for their brother John from the sons of Ambri; for as well these sons themselves as their friends and wives and children that followed them perished, being in number about four hundred.

(22) However, Simon and Jonathan returned to the lakes of the river, and abode there; but Bacchides, when he had secured all Judea with his garrisons, returned to the king; and then it was that the affairs of Judea were quiet for two years; (23) but when the deserters and the wicked saw that Jonathan and those that were with him lived in the country very quietly, by reason of the peace, they sent to King Demetrius, and excited him to send Bacchides to seize upon Jonathan, which they said was to be done without any trouble, and in one night's time; and that if they fell upon them before they were aware, they might slay them all. (24) So the king sent Bacchides, who, when he was come into Judea, wrote to all his friends, both Jews and auxiliaries, that they should seize upon Jonathan, and bring him to him; (25) and when, upon all their endeavours, they were not able to seize upon Jonathan, for he was sensible of the snares they laid for him, and very carefully guarded against them, Bacchides was angry at these deserters, as having imposed upon him and upon the king, and slew fifty of their leaders; (26) whereupon Jonathan, with his brother and those that were with him, retired to Bethagla, a village that lay in the wilderness, out of his fear of Bacchides. He also built towers in it, and encompassed it with walls, and took care that it should be safely guarded. (27) Upon the hearing of which Bacchides led his own army along with him, and besides took his Jewish auxiliaries, and came against Jonathan, and made an assault upon his fortifications, and besieged him many days; (28) but Jonathan did not abate of his courage at the zeal Bacchides used in the siege, but courageously opposed him; and while he left his brother Simon in the city to fight with Bacchides, he went privately out himself into the country, and got a great body of men together of his own party, and fell upon Bacchides's camp in the night-time, and destroyed a great many of them. His brother Simon knew also of this his falling upon them, because he perceived that the enemies were slain by him, (29) so he sallied out upon them, and burnt the engines which the Macedonians used, and made a great slaughter of them; (30) and when Bacchides saw himself encompassed with enemies, and some of them before, and some behind him, he fell into despair and trouble of mind, as confounded at the unexpected ill success of this siege. (31) However he vented his displeasure at these misfortunes upon those deserters who sent for him from the king, as having deluded him. So he had a mind to put an end to this siege after a decent manner, if it were possible for him so to do, and then to return home.

(32) When Jonathan understood these his intentions, he sent ambassadors to him about a league of friendship and mutual assistance, and that they might restore those they had taken captive on both sides. (33) So Bacchides thought this a pretty decent way of retiring home, and made a league of friendship with Jonathan, when they sware that they would not any more make war against one another. Accordingly, he restored the captives, and took his own men with him, and returned to the king at Antioch; and after this his departure, he never came into Judea again. (34) Then did Jonathan take the opportunity of this quiet state of things, and went and lived in the city Michmash; and there governed the multitude, and punished the wicked and ungodly, and by that means purged the nation of them.

CHAPTER 2

(35) Now in the hundred and sixtieth year, it fell out that Alexander, the son of Antiochus Epiphanes, came up into Syria and took Ptolemais, the soldiers having betrayed it to him, for they were at enmity with Demetrius on account of his insolence and difficulty of access: (36) for he shut himself up in a palace of his that had four towers, which he had built himself, not far from Antioch, and admitted nobody. He was withal slothful and negligent about the public affairs, whereby the hatred of his subjects was the more kindled against him, as we have elsewhere already related. (37) When, therefore, Demetrius heard that Alexander was in Ptolemais, he took his whole army, and led it against him; he also sent ambassadors to Jonathan, about a league of mutual assistance and friendship, for he resolved to be beforehand with Alexander, lest the other should treat with him first, and gain assistance from him; (38) and this he did out of the fear he had lest Jonathan should remember how ill Demetrius had formerly treated him, and should join with him in this war against him. He therefore gave orders that Jonathan should be allowed to raise an army, and should get armour made, and should receive back those hostages of the Jewish nation whom Bacchides had shut up in the citadel of Jerusalem. (39) When this good fortune had befallen Jonathan, by the concession of Demetrius, he came to Jerusalem, and read the king's letter in the audience of the people, and of those that kept the citadel. (40) When these were read, these wicked men and deserters, who were in the citadel, were greatly afraid, upon the king's permission to Jonathan to raise an army, and to receive back the hostages: so he delivered every one of them to his own parents; (41) and thus did Jonathan make his abode at Jerusalem, renewing the city to a better state, and reforming the buildings as he pleased; for he gave orders that the walls of the city should be rebuilt with square stones, that it might be more secure from their enemies; (42) and when those that kept the garrisons that were in Judea saw this, they all

left them, and fled to Antioch, excepting those that were in the city Bethsura, and those that were in the citadel of Jerusalem, for the greater part of these was of the wicked Jews and deserters, and on that account these did not deliver up their garrisons.

(43) When Alexander knew what promises Demetrius had made Jonathan, and withal knew his courage, and what great things he had done when he fought the Macedonians, and besides what hardships he had undergone by the means of Demetrius and of Bacchides, the general of Demetrius' army, he told his friends that he could not at present find anyone else that might afford him better assistance than Jonathan, who was both courageous against his enemies, and had a particular hatred against Demetrius, as having both suffered many hard things from him, and acted many hard things against him. (44) If, therefore, they were of opinion that they should make him their friend against Demetrius, it was more for their advantage to invite him to assist them now than at another time. It being therefore determined by him and his friends to send to Jonathan, he wrote to him this epistle: (45) 'King Alexander to his brother Jonathan, sendeth greeting. We have long ago heard of thy courage and thy fidelity, and for that reason have sent to thee, to make with thee a league of friendship and mutual assistance. We therefore do ordain thee this day the high priest of the Jews, and that thou beest called my friend. I have also sent thee, as presents, a purple robe and a golden crown, and desire that, now thou art by us honoured, thou wilt in like manner respect us also.'

(46) When Jonathan had received this letter, he put on the pontifical robe at the time of the feast of tabernacles, four years after the death of his brother Judas, for at that time no high priest had been made. So he raised great forces, and had abundance of armour got ready. (47) This greatly grieved Demetrius when he heard of it, and made him blame himself for his slowness, that he had not prevented Alexander, and got the good will of Jonathan, but had given him time so to do. However, he also himself wrote a letter to Jonathan, and to the people, the contents whereof are these: (48) 'King Demetrius to Jonathan, and to the nation of the Jews, sendeth greeting. Since you have preserved your friendship for us, and when you have been tempted by our enemies, you have not joined yourselves to them, I both commend you for this your fidelity, and exhort you to continue in the same disposition; for which you shall be repaid, and receive rewards from us; (49) for I will free you from the greatest part of the tributes and taxes which you formerly paid to the kings my predecessors, and to myself; and I do now set you free from those tributes which you have ever paid; and besides, I forgive you the tax upon salt, and the value of the crowns which you used to offer to me: and instead of the third part of the fruits [of the field], and the half of the fruits of the trees, I relinquish my part of them from this day: (50) and as to the poll money, which

ought to be given me for every head of the inhabitants of Judea, and of the three toparchies that adjoin to Judea, Samaria and Galilee and Perea, that I relinquish to you for this time, and for all time to come. (51) I will also, that the city of Jerusalem be holy and inviolable, and free from the tithe, and from the taxes, unto its utmost bonds: and I so far recede from my title to the citadel, as to permit Jonathan your high priest to possess it, that he may place such a garrison in it as he approves of for fidelity and good will to himself that they may keep it for us. (52) I also make free all those Jews who have been made captives and slaves in my kingdom. I also give order that the beasts of the Jews be not pressed for our service: and let their Sabbaths, and all their festivals and three days before each of them, be free from any imposition. (53) In the same manner, I set free the Jews that are inhabitants in my kingdom, and order that no injury be done them. I also give leave to such of them as are willing to list themselves in my army, that they may do it, and those as far as thirty thousand; which Jewish soldiers, wheresoever they go, shall have the same pay that my own army hath; and some of them I will place in my garrisons, and some as guards about mine own body, and as rulers over those that are in my court. (54) I give them leave also to use the laws of their forefathers, and to observe them; and I will that they have power over the three toparchies that are added to Judea; and it shall be in the power of the high priest to take care that no one Jew shall have any other temple for worship but only that at Jerusalem. (55) I bequeath also, out of my own revenues, yearly, for the expenses about the sacrifices, one hundred and fifty thousand [drachmae]; and what money is to spare, I will that it shall be your own. I also release to you those ten thousand drachmae which the kings received from the temple, because they appertain to the priests that minister in that temple. (56) And whosoever shall fly to the temple at Jerusalem, or to the places thereto belonging, or who owe the king money, or are there on any other account, let them be set free, and let their goods be in safety. (57) I also give you leave to repair and rebuild your temple, and that all be done at my expenses. I also allow you to build the walls of your city, and to erect high towers, and that they be erected at my charge. And if there be any fortified town that would be convenient for the Jewish country to have very strong, let it be so built at my expenses.'

(58) This was what Demetrius promised and granted to the Jews, by this letter. But King Alexander raised a great army of mercenary soldiers, and of those that deserted to him out of Syria, and made an expedition against Demetrius. (59) And when it was come to a battle, the left wing of Demetrius put those who opposed them to flight, and pursued them a great way, and slew many of them, and spoiled their camp; but the right wing, where Demetrius happened to be, was beaten; (60) and as for all the rest, they ran away. But Demetrius fought courageously, and slew a great many of the enemy; but as he

was in the pursuit of the rest, his horse carried him into a deep bog, where it was hard to get out, and there it happened that, upon his horse's falling down, he could not escape being killed; (61) for when his enemies saw what had befallen him, they returned back, and encompassed Demetrius round, and they all threw their darts at him; but he, being now on foot, fought bravely. But at length he received so many wounds, that he was not able to bear up any longer, but fell. And this is the end that Demetrius came to, when he had reigned eleven years, as we have elsewhere related.

CHAPTER 3

(62) But then the son of Onias the high priest, who was of the same name with his father, and who fled to King Ptolemy, who was called Philometor, lived now at Alexandria, as we have said already. When this Onias saw that Judea was oppressed by the Macedonians and their kings, (63) out of a desire to purchase to himself a memorial and eternal fame, he resolved to send to King Ptolemy and Queen Cleopatra, to ask leave of them that he might build a temple in Egypt like to that at Jerusalem, and might ordain Levites and priests out of their own stock. (64) The chief reason why he was desirous so to do, was, that he relied upon the prophet Isaiah, who lived above six hundred years before, and foretold that there certainly was to be a temple built to Almighty God in Egypt by a man that was a Jew. Onias was elevated with this prediction, and wrote the following epistle to Ptolemy and Cleopatra: (65) 'Having done many and great things for you in the affairs of the war, by the assistance of God, and that in Celesyria and Phoenicia, I came at length with the Jews to Leontopolis, and to other places of your nation, (66) where I found that the greatest part of your people had temples in an improper manner, and that on this account they bore ill will one against another, which happens to the Egyptians by reason of the multitude of their temples and the difference of opinions about divine worship. Now I found a very fit place in a castle that hath its name from the country Diana; this place is full of materials of several sorts, and replenished with sacred animals: (67) I desire, therefore, that you will grant me leave to purge this holy place, which belongs to no master and is fallen down, and to build there a temple to Almighty God, after the pattern of that in Jerusalem, and of the same dimensions, that may be for the benefit of thyself, and thy wife and children, that those Jews who dwell in Egypt may have a place whither they may come and meet together in mutual harmony one with another, and be subservient to thy advantages; (68) for the prophet Isaiah foretold, that "there should be an altar in Egypt to the Lord God:" and many other such things did he prophesy relating to that place.'

(69) And this was what Onias wrote to King Ptolemy. Now anyone may

observe his piety, and that of his sister and wife Cleopatra, by that epistle which they wrote in answer to it; for they laid the blame and the transgression of the law upon the head of Onias. And this was their reply: (70) 'King Ptolemy and Queen Cleopatra to Onias, send greeting. We have read thy petition, wherein thou desirest leave to be given to thee to purge that temple which is fallen down, at Leontopolis in the Nomus of Heliopolis, and which is named from the country Bubastis; on which account we cannot but wonder that it should be pleasing to God to have a temple erected in a place so unclean, and so full of sacred animals. (71) But since thou sayest that Isaiah the prophet foretold this long ago, we give thee leave to do it, if it may be done according to your law, and so that we may not appear to have at all offended God herein.'

(72) So Onias took the place, and built a temple and an altar to God, like indeed to that in Jerusalem, but smaller and poorer. I do not think it proper for me now to describe its dimensions, or its vessels, which have been already described in my seventh book of the *Wars of the Jews*. (73) However, Onias found other Jews like to himself, together with priests and Levites, that there performed divine service. But we have said enough about this temple.

(74) Now it came to pass that the Alexandrian Jews, and those Samaritans who paid their worship to the temple that was built in the days of Alexander at Mount Gerizzim, did now make a sedition one against another, and disputed about their temples before Ptolemy himself, the Jews saying that, according to the laws of Moses, the temple was to be built at Jerusalem; and the Samaritans saying that it was to be built at Gerizzim. (75) They desired therefore the king to sit with his friends and hear the debates about these matters, and punish those with death who were baffled. Now Sabbeus and Theodosius managed the argument for the Samaritans, and Andronicus, the son of Messalamus, for the people of Jerusalem; (76) and they took an oath by God and the king, to make their demonstrations according to the law; and they desired of Ptolemy, that whomsoever he should find that transgressed what they had sworn to, he would put him to death. Accordingly, the king took several of his friends into the council, and sat down, in order to hear what the pleaders said. (77) Now the Jews that were at Alexandria were in great concern for those men whose lot it was to contend for the temple at Jerusalem: for they took it very ill that any should take away the reputation of that temple, which was so ancient and so celebrated all over the habitable earth. (78) Now when Sabbeus and Theodosius had given leave to Andronicus to speak first, he began to demonstrate out of the law, and out of the successions of the high priests, how they every one in succession from his father had received that dignity, and ruled over the temple; and how all the kings of Asia had honoured that temple with their donations, and with the most splendid gifts dedicated thereto: but as for that at Gerizzm, he made no account of it, and regarded it as if it had never

had a being. (79) By this speech, and other arguments, Andronicus persuaded the king to determine that the temple at Jerusalem was built according to the laws of Moses, and to put Sabbeus and Theodosius to death. And these were the events that befell the Jews at Alexandria in the days of Ptolemy Philometor.

CHAPTER 4

(80) Demetrius being thus slain in battle, as we have above related, Alexander took the kingdom of Syria; and wrote to Ptolemy Philometor, and desired his daughter in marriage; and said it was but just that he should be joined in affinity to one that had now received the principality of his forefathers, and had been promoted to it by God's providence, and had conquered Demetrius; and that was on other accounts not unworthy of being related to him. (81) Ptolemy received this proposal of marriage gladly; and wrote him an answer, saluting him on account of his having received the principality of his forefathers: and promising him that he would give him his daughter in marriage; and assured him that he would there meet him, for that he would accompany her from Egypt so far, and would there marry his child to him. (82) When Ptolemy had written thus, he came suddenly to Ptolemais, and brought his daughter Cleopatra along with him; and as he found Alexander there before him, as he desired him to come, he gave him his child in marriage, and for her portion gave her as much silver and gold as became such a king to give.

(83) When the wedding was over, Alexander wrote to Jonathan, the high priest, and desired him to come to Ptolemais. So when he came to these kings, and had made them magnificent presents, he was honoured by them both. (84) Alexander compelled him also to put off his own garment, and to take a purple garment, and made him sit with him on his throne; and commanded his captains that they should go with him into the middle of the city, and proclaim that it was not permitted to anyone to speak against him, or to give him any disturbance. (85) And when the captains had thus done, those that were prepared to accuse Jonathan, and who bore him ill will, when they saw the honour that was done him by proclamation, and that by the king's order, ran away, and were afraid lest some mischief should befall them. Nay, King Alexander was so very kind to Jonathan, that he set him down as the principal of his friends.

(86) But then, upon the hundred and sixty-fifth year, Demetrius, the son of Demetrius, came from Crete with a great number of mercenary soldiers, which Leosthenes the Cretan brought him, and sailed to Cilicia. (87) This thing cast Alexander into great concern and disorder when he heard it; so he made haste immediately out of Phoenicia and came to Antioch, that he might put matters in a safe posture there before Demetrius should come. (88) He also left

Apollonius Daus governor of Celesyria, who, coming to Jamnia with a great army, sent to Jonathan, the high priest, and told him that it was not right that he alone should live at rest, and with authority, and not be subject to the king; that this thing had made him a reproach among all men, that he had not yet made him subject to the king. (89) 'Do not thou, therefore, deceive thyself, and sit still among the mountains, and pretend to have forces with thee; but if thou hast any dependence on thy strength, come down into the plain, and let our armies be compared together, and the event of the battle will demonstrate which of us is the most courageous. (90) However, take notice, that the most valiant men of every city are in my army, and that these are the very men who have always beaten thy progenitors; but let us have the battle in such a place of the country where we may fight with weapons, and not with stones, and where there may be no place whither those that are beaten may fly.

(91) With this Jonathan was irritated; and choosing himself out ten thousand of his soldiers, he went out of Jerusalem in haste, with his brother Simon, and came to Joppa, and pitched his camp on the outside of the city, because the people of Joppa had shut their gates against him, for they had a garrison in the city put there by Apollonius. (92) But when Jonathan was preparing to besiege them, they were afraid he would take them by force, and so they opened the gates to him. But Apollonius, when he heard that Joppa was taken by Jonathan, took three thousand horsemen, and eight thousand footmen, and came to Ashdod; and removing thence, he made his journey silently and slowly, and going up to Joppa, he made as if he was retiring from the place, and so drew Jonathan into the plain, as valuing himself highly upon his horsemen, and having his hopes of victory principally in them. (93) However Jonathan sallied out, and pursued Apollonius to Ashdod; but as soon as Apollonius perceived that his enemy was in the plain, he came back and gave him battle. (94) But Apollonius had laid a thousand horsemen in ambush in a valley that they might be seen by their enemies as behind them; which when Jonathan perceived, he was under no consternation, but, ordering his army to stand in a square battle array, he gave them a charge to fall on the enemy on both sides, and set them to face those that attacked them, both before and behind; (95) and while the fight lasted till the evening, he gave part of his forces to his brother Simon, and ordered him to attack the enemies; but for himself he charged those that were with him to cover themselves with their armour and receive the darts of the horsemen, who did as they were commanded; so that the enemy's horsemen, (96) while they threw their darts till they had no more left, did them no harm, for the darts that were thrown did not enter into their bodies, being thrown upon the shields that were united and conjoined together, the closeness of which easily overcame the force of the darts, and they flew about without any effect. (97) But when the enemy grew remiss in throwing their darts from

morning till late at night, Simon perceived their weariness, and fell upon the body of men before him; and because his soldiers showed great alacrity, he put the enemy to flight: (98) and when the horsemen saw that the footmen ran away, neither did they stay themselves; but they being very weary, by the duration of the fight till the evening, and their hope from the footmen being quite gone, they basely ran away, and in great confusion also, till they were separated one from another, and scattered over all the plain. (99) Upon which Jonathan pursued them as far as Ashdod, and slew a great many of them, and compelled the rest, in despair of escaping, to fly to the temple of Dagon, which was at Ashdod, but Jonathan took the city on the first onset, and burnt it and the villages about it: (100) nor did he abstain from the temple of Dagon itself, but burnt it also, and destroyed those that had fled to it. Now the entire multitude of the enemies that fell in the battle and were consumed in the temple were eight thousand. (101) When Jonathan therefore had overcome so great an army, he removed from Ashdod, and came to Askelon; and when he had pitched his camp without the city, the people of Askelon came out and met him, bringing him hospitable presents, and honouring him; so he accepted of their kind intentions, and returned thence to Jerusalem with a great deal of prey, which he brought thence when he conquered his enemies. (102) But when Alexander heard that Apollonius, the general of his army, was beaten, he pretended to be glad of it, because he had fought with Jonathan his friend and ally against his directions. Accordingly, he sent to Jonathan, and gave testimony to his worth; and gave him honorary rewards, as a golden button, which it is the custom to give the king's kinsmen, and allowed him Ekron and its toparchy for his own inheritance.

(103) About this time it was that King Ptolemy, who was called Philometor, led an army, part by sea and part by land, and came to Syria, to the assistance of Alexander, who was his son-in-law; (104) and accordingly all the cities received him willingly, as Alexander had commanded them to do, and conducted him as far as Ashdod; where they all made loud complaints about the temple of Dagon, which was burnt, and accused Jonathan of having laid it waste, and destroyed the country adjoining with fire, and slain a great number of them. (105) Ptolemy heard these accusations, but said nothing. Jonathan also went to meet Ptolemy as far as Joppa, and obtained from him hospitable presents, and those glorious in their kinds, with all the marks of honour; and when he had conducted him as far as the river called Eleutherus, he returned again to Jerusalem.

(106) But as Ptolemy was at Ptolemais, he was very near to a most unexpected destruction; for a treacherous design was laid for his life by Alexander, by the means of Ammonius, who was his friend: (107) and as the treachery was very plain, Ptolemy wrote to Alexander, and required of him that he should bring

Ammonius to condign punishment, informing him what snares had been laid for him by Ammonius, and desired that he might be accordingly punished for it; but when Alexander did not comply with his demands, he perceived that it was he himself who laid the design, and was very angry at him. (108) Alexander had also formerly been on very ill terms with the people of Antioch, for they had suffered very much by his means; yet did Ammonius at length undergo the punishment his insolent crimes had deserved, for he was killed in an opprobrious manner, like a woman, while he endeavoured to conceal himself in a feminine habit, as we have elsewhere related.

(109) Hereupon Ptolemy blamed himself for having given his daughter in marriage to Alexander, and for the league he had made with him to assist him against Demetrius; so he dissolved his relation to him, (110) and took his daughter away from him, and immediately sent to Demetrius, and offered to make a league of mutual assistance and friendship with him, and agreed with him to give him his daughter in marriage, and to restore him to the principality of his fathers. Demetrius was well pleased with this embassage, and accepted of his assistance, and of the marriage of his daughter; (111) but Ptolemy had still one more hard task to do, and that was to persuade the people of Antioch to receive Demetrius, because they were greatly displeased at him, on account of the injuries his father Demetrius had done them; (112) yet did he bring this about, for as the people of Antioch hated Alexander on Ammonius's account, as we have shown already, they were easily prevailed with to cast him out of Antioch; who, thus expelled out of Antioch, came into Cilicia. (113) Ptolemy came then to Antioch, was make king by its inhabitants and by the army; so that he was forced to put on his own two diadems, the one of Asia, the other of Egypt; (114) but being naturally a good and a righteous man, and not desirous of what belonged to others, and besides these dispositions, being also a wise man in reasoning about futurities, he determined to avoid the envy of the Romans, so he called the people of Antioch together to an assembly, and persuaded them to receive Demetrius; (115) and assured them that he would not be mindful of what they did to his father in case he should be now obliged by them; and he undertook that he would himself be a good monitor and governor to him; and promised that he would not permit him to attempt any bad actions; but that, for his own part, he was contented with the kingdom of Egypt. By which discourse he persuaded the people of Antioch to receive Demetrius.

(116) But now Alexander made haste, with a numerous and great army, and came out of Cilicia into Syria, and burnt the country belonging to Antioch, and pillaged it; whereupon Ptolemy and his son-in-law Demetrius brought their army against him (for he had already given him his daughter in marriage), and beat Alexander, and put him to flight; (117) and accordingly he fled into Arabia. Now, it happened in the time of the battle that Ptolemy's horse, upon

hearing the noise of an elephant, cast him off his back, and threw him on the ground; upon the sight of which accident his enemies fell upon him, and gave him many wounds upon his head, and brought him into danger of death, for when his guards caught him up he was so very ill, that for four days' time he was not able either to understand or to speak. (118) However, Zabdiel, a prince among the Arabians, cut off Alexander's head and sent it to Ptolemy, who recovering of his wounds, and returning to his understanding, on the fifth day, heard at once a most agreeable hearing, and saw a most agreeable sight, which were the death and the head of Alexander; (119) yet a little after this his joy for the death of Alexander, with which he was so greatly satisfied, he also departed this life. Now Alexander, who was called Balas, reigned over Asia five years, as we have elsewhere related.

(120) But when Demetrius, who was styled Nicator, had taken the kingdom, he was so wicked as to treat Ptolemy's soldiers very hardly, neither remembering the league of mutual assistance that was between them, nor that he was his son-in-law and kinsman, by Cleopatra's marriage to him; so the soldiers fled from his wicked treatment to Alexandria; but Demetrius kept his elephants. (121) But Jonathan the high priest levied an army out of all Judea, and attacked the citadel at Jerusalem, and besieged it. It was held by a garrison of Macedonians, and by some of those men who had deserted the customs of their forefathers. (122) These men at first despised the attention of Jonathan for taking the place, as depending on its strength; but some of those wicked men went out by night, and came to Demetrius, and informed him that the citadel was besieged; (123) who was irritated with what he heard, and took his army, and came from Antioch, against Jonathan. And when he was at Antioch, he wrote to him, and commanded him to come to him quickly to Ptolemais: (124) upon which Jonathan did not intermit the siege of the citadel, but took with him the elders of the people, and priests, and carried with him gold and silver and garments, and a great number of presents of friendship, and came to Demetrius, and presented him with them, and thereby pacified the king's anger. So he was honoured by him, and received from him the confirmation of his high priesthood, as he had possessed it by the grants of the kings his predecessors. (125) And when the Jewish deserters accused him, Demetrius was so far from giving credit to them, that when he petitioned him that he would demand no more than three hundred talents for the tribute of all Judea, and the three toparchies of Samaria and Perea and Galilee, he complied with the proposal, and gave him a letter confirming those grants; the contents of which were as follows: (126) 'King Demetrius to Jonathan his brother, and to the nation of the Jews, sendeth greeting. We have sent you a copy of that epistle which we have written to Lasthenes our kinsman, that you may know its contents – (127) "King Demetrius to Lasthenes our father, sendeth greeting. I have determined to

return thanks, and to show favour to the nation of the Jews, who hath observed the rules of justice in our concerns. Accordingly, I remit to them the three prefectures, Apherima and Lydda and Ramatha, which have been added to Judea out of Samaria, with their appurtenances; (128) as also what the kings my predecessors received from those that offered sacrifices in Jerusalem, and what are due from the fruits of the earth, and of the trees, and what else belongs to us; with the salt pits and the crowns that used to be presented to us. Nor shall they be compelled to pay any of those taxes from this time to all futurity. Take care, therefore, that a copy of this epistle be taken and given to Jonathan, and be set up in an eminent place of their holy temple." ' (129) And these were the contents of this writing. And now when Demetrius saw that there was peace everywhere, and that there was no danger nor fear of war, he disbanded the greatest part of his army, and diminished their pay, and even retained in pay no others than such foreigners as came up with him from Crete and from the other islands. (130) However, this procured him ill will and hatred from the soldiers, on whom he bestowed nothing from this time, while the kings before him used to pay them in time of peace, as they did before, that they might have their good will, and that they might be very ready to undergo the difficulties of war, if any occasion should require it.

CHAPTER 5

(131) Now there was a certain commander of Alexander's forces, an Apanemian by birth, whose name was Diodotus, and was also called Trypho, took notice of the ill will the soldiers bare to Demetrius, and went to Malchus the Arabian, who brought up Antiochus, the son of Alexander, and told him what ill will the army bare Demetrius, and persuaded him to give him Antiochus, because he would make him king, and recover to him the kingdom of his father. (132) Malchus at first opposed him in this attempt, because he could not believe him; but when Trypho lay hard at him for a long time, he over-persuaded him to comply with Trypho's intentions and entreaties. And this was the state Trypho was now in.

(133) But Jonathan the high priest, being desirous to get clear of those that were in the citadel of Jerusalem, and of the Jewish deserters and wicked men, as well as those in all the garrisons in the country, sent presents and ambassadors to Demetrius, and entreated him to take away his soldiers out of the strongholds of Judea. (134) Demetrius made answer, that after the war, which he was now deeply engaged in, was over, he would not only grant him that but greater things than that also: and he desired he would send him some assistance; and informed him that his army had deserted him. So Jonathan chose out three thousand of his soldiers, and sent them to Demetrius.

(135) Now the people of Antioch hated Demetrius, both on account of what mischief he had himself done them, and because they were his enemies also on account of his father Demetrius, who had greatly abused them: so they watched some opportunity which they might lay hold on, to fall upon him. (136) And when they were informed of the assistance that was coming to Demetrius from Jonathan, and considered at the same time that he would raise a numerous army, unless they prevented him and seized upon him, they took their weapons immediately, and encompassed his palace in the way of a siege, and seizing upon all the ways of getting out, they sought to subdue their king. (137) And when he saw that the people of Antioch were become his bitter enemies, and that they were thus in arms, he took the mercenary soldiers which he had with him, and those Jews who were sent by Jonathan, and assaulted the Antiochians; but he was overpowered by them, for they were many ten thousands, and was beaten. (138) But when the Jews saw that the Antiochians were superior, they went up to the top of the palace, and shot at them from thence; and because they were so remote from them by their height, that they suffered nothing on their side, but did great execution on the others, as fighting from such an elevation, they drove them out of the adjoining houses, (139) and immediately set them on fire, whereupon the flame spread itself over the whole city, and burnt it all down. This happened by reason of the closeness of the houses, and because they were generally built of wood; (140) so the Antiochians, when they were not able to help themselves, nor to stop the fire, were put to flight. And as the Jews leaped from the top of one house to the top of another, and pursued them after that manner, it thence happened that the pursuit was very surprising. (141) But when the king saw that the Antiochians were very busy in saving their children and their wives, and so did not fight any longer, he fell upon them in the narrow passages, and fought them, and slew a great many of them, till at last they were forced to throw down their arms, and to deliver themselves up to Demetrius. (142) So he forgave them this their insolent behaviour, and put an end to the sedition: and when he had given rewards to the Jews out of the rich spoils he had gotten, and had returned them thanks, as the cause of his victory, he sent them away to Jerusalem to Jonathan, with an ample testimony of the assistance they had afforded him. (143) Yet did he prove an ill man to Jonathan afterwards, and broke the promises he had made: and he threatened that he would make war upon him, unless he would pay all that tribute which the Jewish nation owed to the first kings [of Syria]. And this he had done if Trypho had not hindered him, and diverted his preparations against Jonathan to a concern for his own preservation; (144) for he now returned out of Arabia into Syria, with the child Antiochus, for he was yet in age but a youth, and put the diadem on his head; and as the whole forces that had left Demetrius, because they had no pay, came to his assistance, he made war upon Demetrius,

and joining battle with him, overcame him in the fight, and took from him both his elephants and the city Antioch.

(145) Demetrius, upon this defeat, returned into Cilicia; but the child Antiochus sent ambassadors and an epistle to Jonathan, and made him his friend and confederate, and confirmed to him the high priesthood, and yielded up to him the four prefectures which had been added to Judea. (146) Moreover, he sent him vessels and cups of gold, and a purple garment, and gave him leave to use them. He also presented him with a golden button, and styled him one of his principal friends, and appointed his brother Simon to be the general over the forces from the Ladder of Tyre unto Egypt. (147) So Jonathan was so pleased with these grants made him by Antiochus, that he sent ambassadors to him and to Trypho, and professed himself to be their friend and confederate, and said he would join with him in a war against Demetrius, informing him that he had made no proper returns for the kindness he had done him; for that when he had received many marks of kindness from him, when he stood in great need of them, he, for such good turns, had requited him with further injuries.

(148) So Antiochus gave Jonathan leave to raise himself a numerous army out of Syria and Phoenicia, and to make war against Demetrius' generals; whereupon he went in haste to the several cities, which received him splendidly indeed, but put no forces into his hands. (149) And when he was come from thence to Askelon, the inhabitants of Askelon came and brought him presents, and met him in a splendid manner. He exhorted them, and everyone of the cities of Celesyria, to forsake Demetrius, and to join with Antiochus, and in assisting him, to endeavour to punish Demetrius for what offences he had been guilty of against themselves; and told them there were many reasons for that their procedure, if they had a mind so to do. (150) And when he had persuaded those cities to promise their assistance to Antiochus, he came to Gaza, in order to induce them also to be friends to Antiochus; but he found the inhabitants of Gaza much more alienated from him than he expected, for they had shut their gates against him; and although they had deserted Demetrius, they had not resolved to join themselves to Antiochus. (151) This provoked Jonathan to besiege them, and to harass their country; for as he set a part of his army round about Gaza itself, so with the rest he overran their land, and spoiled it, and burned what was in it. When the inhabitants of Gaza saw themselves in this state of affliction, and that no assistance came to them from Demetrius; that what distressed them was at hand, but what should profit them was still at a great distance, and it was uncertain whether it would come at all or not, they thought it would be prudent conduct to leave off any longer continuance with him, and to cultivate friendship with the other; (152) so they sent to Jonathan, and professed they would be his friends, and afford

him assistance; for such is the temper of men, that before they have had the trial of great afflictions, they do not understand what is for their advantage; but when they find themselves under such afflictions, they then change their minds, and what it had been better for them to have done before they had been at all damaged, they choose to do, but not till after they have suffered such damages. (153) However, he made a league of friendship with them, and took from them hostages for their performance of it, and sent these hostages to Jerusalem, while he went himself over all the country, as far as Damascus.

(154) But when he heard that the generals of Demetrius' forces were come to the city Cadesh with a numerous army (the place lies between the land of the Tyrians and Galilee), for they supposed they should hereby draw him out of Syria, in order to preserve Galilee, and that he would not overlook the Galileans, who were his own people, when war was made upon them, he went to meet them, (155) having left Simon in Judea, who raised as great an army as he was able out of the country, and then sat down before Bethsura, and besieged it, that being the strongest place in all Judea; and a garrison of Demetrius' kept it, as we have already related. (156) But as Simon was raising banks, and bringing his engines of war against Bethsura, and was very earnest about the siege of it, the garrison was afraid lest the place should be taken of Simon by force, and they put to the sword; so they sent to Simon, and desired the security of his oath, that they should come to no harm from him, and that they would leave the place, and go away to Demetrius. (157) Accordingly, he gave them his oath, and ejected them out of the city, and he put therein a garrison of his own.

(158) But Jonathan removed out of Galilee, and from the waters which are called Gennesar, for there he was before encamped, and came into the plain that is called Asor, without knowing that the enemy was there. (159) When therefore Demetrius' men knew a day beforehand that Jonathan was coming against them, they laid an ambush in the mountain, who were to assault him on the sudden, while they themselves met him with an army in the plain; which army, when Jonathan saw ready to engage him, he also got ready his own soldiers for the battle as well as he was able. (160) But those that were laid in ambush by Demetrius' generals being behind them, the Jews were afraid lest they should be caught in the midst between two bodies, and perish; so they ran away in haste, (161) and indeed all the rest left Jonathan, but a few that were in number about fifty, who stayed with him, and with them Mattathias, the son of Absalom, and Judas, the son of Chapseus, who were commanders of the whole army. These marched boldly, and like men desperate, against the enemy, and so pushed them, that by their courage they daunted them, and with their weapons in their hands, they put them to flight. (162) And when those soldiers of Jonathan that had retired, saw the enemy giving way, they got

together after their flight, and pursued them with great violence; and this did they as far as Cadesh, where the camp of the enemy lay.

(163) Jonathan having thus gotten a glorious victory, and slain two thousand of the enemy, returned to Jerusalem. So when he saw that all his affairs prospered according to his mind, by the providence of God, he sent ambassadors to the Romans, being desirous of renewing that friendship which their nation had with them formerly. (164) He enjoined the same ambassadors, that, as they came back they should go to the Spartans, and put them in mind of their friendship and kindred. So when the ambassadors came to Rome they went in to their senate, and said what they were commanded by Jonathan their high priest to say, how he had sent them to confirm their friendship. (165) The senate then confirmed what had been formerly decreed concerning their friendship with the Jews, and gave them letters to carry to all the kings of Asia and Europe, and to the governors of the cities that they might safely conduct them to their own country. Accordingly, as they returned, they came to Sparta, and delivered the epistle which they had received of Jonathan to them; (166) a copy of which here follows: 'Jonathan the high priest of the Jewish nation, and the senate and body of the people of the Jews, to the ephori and senate and body of the people of the Lacedemonians, send greeting. If you be well, and both your public and private affairs be agreeable to your mind, it is according to our wishes. We are well also. (167) When in former times an epistle was brought to Onias, who was then our high priest, from Areus, who at that time was your king, by Demoteles, concerning the kindred that was between us and you, a copy of which is here subjoined, we both joyfully received the epistle, and were well pleased with Demoteles and Areus, although we did not need such a demonstration, because we were well satisfied about it from the sacred writings; (168) yet did not we think fit first to begin the claim of this relation to you, lest we should seem too early in taking to ourselves the glory which is now given us by you. It is a long time since this relation of ours to you hath been renewed; and when we, upon holy and festival days, offer sacrifices to God, we pray to him for your preservation and victory. (169) As to ourselves, although we have had many wars that have compassed us around, by reason of the covetousness of our neighbours, yet did not we determine to be troublesome either to you or to others that were related to us, but since we have now overcome our enemies, and have occasion to send Numenius, the son of Antiochus, and Antipater, the son of Jason, who are both honourable men belonging to our senate, to the Romans, we gave them this epistle to you also, that they might renew that friendship which is between us. (170) You will therefore do well yourselves to write to us, and send us an account of what you stand in need of from us, since we are in all things disposed to act according to your desires.' So the

Lacedemonians received the ambassadors kindly, and made a decree for friendship and mutual assistance, and sent it to them.

(171) At this time there were three sects among the Jews, who had different opinions concerning human actions; the one was called the sect of the Pharisees, another the sect of the Sadducees, and the other the sect of the Essenes. (172) Now for the Pharisees, they say that some actions, but not all, are the work of fate, and some of them are in our own power, and that they are liable to fate, but are not caused by fate. But the sect of the Essenes affirm, that fate governs all things, and that nothing befalls men but what is according to its determination. (173) And for the Sadducees, they take away fate, and say there is no such thing, and that the events of human affairs are not at its disposal; but they suppose that all our actions are in our own power, so that we are ourselves the cause of what is good, and receive what is evil from our own folly. However, I have given a more exact account of these opinions in the second book of the Jewish War.

(174) But now the generals of Demetrius being willing to recover the defeat they had had, gathered a greater army together than they had before, and came against Jonathan; but as soon as he was informed of their coming, he went suddenly to meet them, to the country of Hamath, for he resolved to give them no opportunity of coming into Judea; (175) so he pitched his camp at fifty furlongs' distance from the enemy, and sent out spies to take a view of their camp, and after what manner they were encamped. When his spies had given him full information, and had seized upon some of them by night, who told him the enemy would soon attack him, he, thus apprised beforehand, (176) provided for his security and placed watchmen beyond his camp, and kept all his forces armed all night; and he gave them a charge to be of good courage, and to have their minds prepared to fight in the night-time, if they should be obliged so to do, lest their enemy's designs should seem concealed from them. (177) But when Demetrius's commanders were informed that Jonathan knew what they intended, their counsels were disordered, and it alarmed them to find that the enemy had discovered those their intentions; nor did they expect to overcome them any other way, now they had failed in the snares they had laid for them; for should they hazard an open battle, they did not think they should be a match for Jonathan's army; (178) so they resolved to fly, and having lighted many fires, that when the enemy saw them they might suppose they were there still, they retired. But when Jonathan came to give them battle in the morning in their camp, and found it deserted, and understood they were fled, he pursued them; (179) yet he could not overtake them, for they had already passed over the river Eleutherus, and were out of danger. So when Jonathan was returned thence, he went into Arabia, and fought against the Nabateans, and drove away a great deal of their prey, and took

[many] captives, and came to Damascus, and there sold off what he had taken. (180) About the same time it was that Simon his brother went over all Judea and Palestine, as far as Askelon, and fortified the strongholds: and when he had made them very strong, both in the edifices erected and in the garrisons placed in them, he came to Joppa; and when he had taken it, he brought a great garrison into it, for he heard that the people of Joppa were disposed to deliver up the city to Demetrius's generals.

(181) When Simon and Jonathan had finished these affairs, they returned to Jerusalem, where Jonathan gathered all the people together, and took counsel to restore the walls of Jerusalem, and to rebuild the wall that encompassed the temple, which had been thrown down, and to make the places adjoining stronger by very high towers; (182) and besides that, to build another wall in the midst of the city, in order to exclude the market place from the garrison, which was in the citadel, and by that means to hinder them from any plenty of provisions; and moreover, to make the fortresses that were in the country much stronger and more defensible than they were before. (183) And when these things were approved of by the multitude as rightly proposed, Jonathan himself took care of the building that belonged to the city, and sent Simon away to make the fortresses in the country more secure than formerly. (184) But Demetrius passed over [Euphrates], and came into Mesopotamia, as desirous to retain that country still, as well as Babylon; (185) and when he should have obtained the dominion of the upper provinces, to lay a foundation for recovering his entire kingdom; for these Greeks and Macedonians dwelt there, frequently sent ambassadors to him, and promised that if he would come to them, they would deliver themselves up to him, and assist him in fighting against Arsaces, the king of the Parthians. (186) So he was elevated with these hopes, and came hastily to them, as having resolved that, if he had once overthrown the Parthians, and gotten an army of his own, he would make war against Trypho, and eject him out of Syria; and the people of that country received him with great alacrity. So he raised forces with which he fought against Arsaces, and lost all his army; and was himself taken alive, as we have elsewhere related.

CHAPTER 6

(187) Now when Trypho knew what had befallen Demetrius, he was no longer firm to Antiochus, but contrived by subtlety to kill him, and then to take possession of his kingdom; but the fear that he was in of Jonathan was an obstacle to this his design, for Jonathan was a friend to Antiochus, for which cause he resolved first to take Jonathan out of the way, and then to set about his design relating to Antiochus; (188) but he, judging it best to take him off by deceit and treachery, came from Antioch to Bethshan, which by the Greeks is

called Scythopolis, at which place Jonathan met him with forty thousand chosen men, for he thought that he came to fight him; (189) but when he perceived that Jonathan was ready to fight, he attempted to gain him by presents and kind treatment, and gave order to his captains to obey him, and by these means was desirous to give assurance of his good will, and to take away all suspicions out of his mind, that so he might make him careless and inconsiderate, and might take him when he was unguarded. (190) He also advised him to dismiss his army, because there was no occasion for bringing it with him, when there was no war, but all was in peace. However, he desired him to retain a few about him, and go with him to Ptolemais, for that he would deliver the city up to him, and would bring all the fortresses that were in the country under his dominion; and he told him that he came with those very designs.

(191) Yet did not Jonathan suspect anything at all by this his management, but believed that Trypho gave this advice out of kindness, and with a sincere design. Accordingly, he dismissed his army, and retained no more than three thousand of them with him, and left two thousand in Galilee; and he himself, with one thousand, came with Trypho to Ptolemais; (192) but when the people of Ptolemais had shut their gates, as it had been commanded by Trypho to do, he took Jonathan alive, and slew all that were with him. He also sent soldiers against those two thousand that were left in Galilee, in order to destroy them: (193) but those men having heard the report of what had happened to Jonathan, they prevented the execution, and before those that were sent by Trypho came, they covered themselves with their armour, and went away out of the country. Now when those that were sent against them saw that they were ready to fight for their lives, they gave them no disturbance, but returned back to Trypho.

(194) But when the people of Jerusalem heard that Jonathan was taken, and that the soldiers who were with him were destroyed, they deplored his sad fate; and there was earnest inquiry made about him by everybody, (195) and a great and just fear fell upon them, and made them sad, lest now they were deprived of the courage and conduct of Jonathan, the nations about them should bear them ill will; and as they were before quiet on account of Jonathan they should now rise up against them, and by making war with them, should force them into the utmost dangers. (196) And indeed what they suspected really befell them; for when those nations heard of the death of Jonathan, they began to make war with the Jews as now destitute of a governor: Trypho himself got an army together and had an intention to go up to Judea, and make war against its inhabitants. (197) But when Simon saw that the people of Jerusalem were terrified at the circumstances they were in, he desired to make a speech to them, and thereby to render them more resolute in opposing Trypho when he should

come against them. He then called the people together into the temple, and thence began thus to encourage them: (198) 'O my countrymen, you are not ignorant that our father, myself, and my brethren, have ventured to hazard our lives, and that willingly, for the recovery of your liberty; since I have therefore, such plenty of examples before me, and we of our family have determined with ourselves to die for our laws and our divine worship, there shall no terror be so great as to banish this resolution from our souls, nor to introduce in its place a love of life and a contempt of glory. (199) Do you therefore follow me with alacrity whithersoever I shall lead you, as not destitute of such a captain as is willing to suffer and to do the greatest things for you; for neither am I better than my brethren that I should be sparing of my own life, nor so far worse than they as to avoid and refuse what they thought the most honourable of all things – I mean to undergo death for your laws, and for that worship of God which is peculiar to you; (200) I will therefore give such proper demonstrations as will show that I am their own brother; and I am so bold as to expect that I shall avenge their blood upon our enemies, and deliver you all, with your wives and children, from the injuries they intend against you, and with God's assistance, to preserve your temple from destruction by them; for I see that these nations have you in contempt, as being without a governor, and that they thence are encouraged to make war against you.'

(201) By this speech of Simon he inspired the multitude with courage; and as they had before been dispirited through fear, they were now raised to a good hope of better things, insomuch that the whole multitude of the people cried out all at once, that Simon should be leader; and that instead of Judas and Jonathan his brethren, he should have the government over them; and they promised that they would readily obey him in whatsoever he should command them. (202) So he got together immediately all his own soldiers that were fit for war, and made haste in rebuilding the walls of the city, and strengthening them by very high and strong towers, and sent a friend of his, one Jonathan, the son of Absalom, to Joppa, and gave him order to eject the inhabitants out of the city, for he was afraid lest they should deliver up the city to Trypho; but he himself stayed to secure Jerusalem.

(203) But Trypho removed from Ptolemais with a great army, and came into Judea, and brought Jonathan with him in bonds. Simon also met him with his army at the city Adida, which is upon a hill, and beneath it lie the plains of Judea. (204) And when Trypho knew that Simon was by the Jews made their governor, he sent to him, and would have imposed upon him by deceit and treachery, and desired, if he would have his brother Jonathan released, that he would send him a hundred talents of silver, and two of Jonathan's sons as hostages, that when he shall be released, he may not make Judea revolt from the king; for that at present he was kept in bonds on account of the money he

had borrowed of the king, and now owed it to him. (205) But Simon was aware of the craft of Trypho; and although he knew that if he gave him the money he should lose it, and that Trypho would not set his brother free, and withal should deliver the sons of Jonathan to the enemy, yet because he was afraid that he should have a calumny raised against him among the multitude as the cause of his brother's death, if he neither gave the money nor sent Jonathan's sons, he gathered his army together, and told them what offers Trypho had made, (206) and added this, that the offers were ensnaring and treacherous, and yet that it was more eligible to send the money and Jonathan's sons, than to be liable to the imputation of not complying with Trypho's offers, and thereby refusing to save his brother. Accordingly, Simon sent the sons of Jonathan and the money; (207) but when Trypho had received them, he did not keep his promise, nor set Jonathan free, but took his army and went about all the country, and resolved to go afterward to Jerusalem, by the way of Idumea, while Simon went over against him with his army, and all along pitched his camp over against his.

(208) But when those that were in the citadel had sent to Trypho, and besought him to make haste and come to them, and to send them provisions, he prepared his cavalry as though he would be at Jerusalem that very night; but so great a quantity of snow fell in the night, that it covered the roads, and made them so deep, that there was no passing, especially for the cavalry. This hindered him from coming to Jerusalem; (209) whereupon Trypho removed thence, and came into Celesyria, and falling vehemently upon the land of Gilead, he slew Jonathan there; and when he had given order for his burial, he returned himself to Antioch. (210) However, Simon sent some to the city Basca to bring away his brother's bones, and buried them in their own city Modin; and all the people made great lamentation over him. (211) Simon also erected a very large monument for his father and his brethren, of white and polished stone, and raised it a great height, and so as to be seen a long way off, and made cloisters about it, and set up pillars, which were of one stone apiece, a work it was wonderful to see. Moreover, he built seven pyramids also for his parents and brethren, one for each of them, which were made very surprising, both for their largeness and beauty, (212) and which have been preserved to this day; and we know that it was Simon who bestowed so much zeal about the burial of Jonathan, and the building of these monuments for his relations. Now Jonathan died when he had been high priest four years, and had been also the governor of his nation. And these were the circumstances that concerned his death.

(213) But Simon, who was made high priest by the multitude, on the very first year of his high priesthood, set his people free from their slavery under the Macedonians, and permitted them to pay tribute to them no longer; which

liberty and freedom from tribute they obtained after a hundred and seventy years of the kingdom of the Assyrians, which was after Seleucus, who was called Nicator, got the dominion over Syria. (214) Now the affection of the multitude towards Simon was so great, that in their contracts one with another, and in their public records, they wrote, 'in the first year of Simon the benefactor, and ethnarch of the Jews;' for under him they were very happy, and overcame the enemies that were round about them; (215) for Simon overthrew the city Gazara, and Joppa, and Jamnia. He also took the citadel of Jerusalem by siege, and cast it down to the ground, that it might not be any more a place of refuge to their enemies when they took it, to do them a mischief, as it had been till now. And when he had done this, he thought it their best way, and most for their advantage, to level the very mountain itself upon which the citadel happened to stand, that so the temple might be higher than it. (216) And indeed, when he had called the multitude to an assembly, he persuaded them to have it so demolished, and this by putting them in mind what miseries they had suffered by its garrison and the Jewish deserters; and what miseries they might hereafter suffer in case any foreigner should obtain the kingdom, and put a garrison into that citadel. (217) This speech induced the multitude to a compliance, because he exhorted them to do nothing but what was for their own good: so they all set themselves to the work, and levelled the mountain, and in that work spent both day and night without intermission, which cost them three whole years before it was removed, and brought to an entire level with the plain of the rest of the city. After which the temple was the highest of all the buildings, now the citadel, as well as the mountain whereon it stood, were demolished. And these actions were thus performed under Simon.

CHAPTER 7

(218) Now a little while after Demetrius had been carried into captivity, Trypho his governor destroyed Antiochus, the son of Alexander, who was also called *The God*, and this when he had reigned four years, though he gave it out that he died under the hands of the surgeons. (219) He then sent his friends, and those that were most intimate with him, to the soldiers, and promised that he would give them a great deal of money if they would make him king. He intimated to them that Demetrius was made a captive by the Parthians; and that Demetrius's brother Antiochus, if he came to be king, would do them a great deal of mischief, in way of revenge for revolting from his brother. (220) So the soldiers, in expectation of the wealth they should get by bestowing the kingdom upon Trypho, made him their ruler. However, when Trypho had gained the management of affairs, he demonstrated his disposition to be

wicked; for while he was a private person he cultivated a familiarity with the multitude, and pretended to great moderation, and so drew them on artfully to whatsoever he pleased; but when he had once taken the kingdom, he laid aside any further dissimulation, and was the true Trypho; (221) which behaviour made his enemies superior to him; for the soldiers hated him, and revolted from him to Cleopatra, the wife of Demetrius, who was then shut up in Seleucia with her children; (222) but as Antiochus, the brother of Demetrius who was called Soter, was not admitted by any of the cities, on account of Trypho, Cleopatra sent to him, and invited him to marry her, and to take the kingdom. The reasons why she made this invitation were these: that her friends persuaded her to it, and that she was afraid for herself, in case some of the people of Seleucia should deliver up the city to Trypho.

(223) As Antiochus was now come to Seleucia, and his forces increased every day, he marched to fight Trypho; and having beaten him in the battle, he ejected him out of the Upper Syria into Phoenicia, and pursued him thither, and besieged him in Dora, which was a fortress hard to be taken, whither he had fled. He also sent ambassadors to Simon the Jewish high priest, about a league of friendship and mutual assistance; (224) who readily accepted of the invitation, and sent to Antiochus great sums of money and provisions for those that besieged Dora, and thereby supplied them very plentifully, so that for a little while he was looked upon as one of his most intimate friends; but still Trypho fled from Dora to Apamia, where he was taken during the siege, and put to death, when he had reigned three years.

(225) However, Antiochus forgot the kind assistance that Simon had afforded him in his necessity, and committed an army of soldiers to his friend Cendebeus, and sent him at once to ravage Judea, and to seize Simon. (226) When Simon heard of Antiochus's breaking his league with him, although he were now in years, yet, provoked with the unjust treatment he had met with from Antiochus, and taking a resolution brisker than his age could well bear, he went like a young man to act as general of his army. (227) He also sent his sons before among the most hardy of his soldiers, and he himself marched on with his army another way, and laid many of his men in ambushes in the narrow valleys between the mountains; nor did he fail of success in any one of his attempts, but was too hard for his enemies in every one of them. So he led the rest of his life in peace, and did also himself make a league with the Romans.

(228) Now he was ruler of the Jews in all eight years; but at a feast came to his end. It was caused by the treachery of his son-in-law Ptolemy, who caught also his wife, and two of his sons, and kept them in bonds. He also sent some to kill John the third son, whose name was Hyrcanus: (229) but the young man perceiving them coming, he avoided the danger he was in from them, and made haste into the city [Jerusalem], as relying on the good will of the

multitude, because of the benefits they had received from his father, and because of the hatred the same multitude bare to Ptolemy; so that when Ptolemy was endeavouring to enter the city by another gate, they drove him away, as having already admitted Hyrcanus.

CHAPTER 8

(230) So Ptolemy retired to one of the fortresses that was above Jericho, which was called Dagon. But Hyrcanus having taken the high priesthood that had been his father's before, and in the first place propitiated God by sacrifices, he then made an expedition against Ptolemy; and when he made his attacks upon the place, in other points he was too hard for him, but was rendered weaker than he, by the commiseration he had for his mother and brethren, and by that only; (231) for Ptolemy brought them upon the wall, and tormented them in the sight of all, and threatened that he would throw them down headlong, unless Hyrcanus would leave off the siege; and as he thought that, so far as he relaxed to the siege and taking of the place, so much favour did he show to those that were dearest to him by preventing their misery, his zeal about it was cooled. (232) However, his mother spread out her hands, and begged of him that he would not grow remiss on her account, but indulge his indignation so much the more, and that he would do his utmost to take the place quickly, in order to get their enemy under his power, and then to avenge upon him what he had done to those that were dearest to himself; for that death would be to her sweet, though with torment, if that enemy of theirs might but be brought to punishment for his wicked dealings to them. (233) Now when his mother said so, he resolved to take the fortress immediately; but when he saw her beaten, and torn to pieces, his courage failed him, and he could not but sympathise with what his mother suffered, and was thereby overcome; (234) and as the siege was drawn out into length by this means, that year on which the Jews use to rest, came on; for the Jews observe this rest every seventh year, as they do every seventh day; (235) so that Ptolemy being for this cause released from the war, he slew the brethren of Hyrcanus and his mother: and when he had so done, he fled to Zeno, who was called Cotylas, who was then the tyrant of the city Philadelphia.

(236) But Antiochus, being very uneasy at the miseries that Simon had brought upon him, he invaded Judea in the fourth year of his reign, and the first year of the principality of Hyrcanus, in the hundred and sixty-second Olympiad. (237) And when he had burnt the country, he shut up Hyrcanus in the city, which he encompassed round with seven encampments; but did nothing at the first, because of the strength of the walls, and because of the valour of the besieged, although they were once in want of water, which yet

they were delivered from by a large shower of rain, which fell at the setting of the Pleiades. (238) However, about the north part of the wall, where it happened the city was upon a level with the outward ground, the king raised a hundred towers of three stories high, and placed bodies of soldiers upon them; (239) and as he made his attacks every day, he cut a double ditch, deep and broad, and confined the inhabitants with it as within a wall; but the besieged contrived to make frequent sallies out; and if the enemy were not anywhere upon their guard, they fell upon them, and did them a great deal of mischief; and if they perceived them, they then returned into the city with ease. (240) But because Hyrcanus discerned the inconvenience of so great a number of men in the city, while the provisions were the sooner spent by them, and yet, as it natural to suppose, those great numbers did nothing, he separated the useless part, and excluded them out of the city, and retained that part only who were in the flower of their age, and fit for war. (241) However, Antiochus would not let those that were excluded go away; who, therefore, wandering about between the walls, and consuming away by famine, died miserably; but when the feast of tabernacles was at hand, those that were within commiserated their condition, and received them in again. (242) And when Hyrcanus sent to Antiochus, and desired there might be a truce for seven days, because of the festival, he gave way to this piety towards God, and made that truce accordingly; and besides that, he sent in a magnificent sacrifice, bulls with their horns gilded, with all sorts of sweet spices, and with cups of gold and silver. (243) So those that were at the gates received the sacrifices from those that brought them and led them to the temple, Antiochus the meanwhile feasting his army, which was a quite different conduct from Antiochus Epiphanes, who, when he had taken the city, offered swine upon the altar, and sprinkled the temple with the broth of their flesh, in order to violate the laws of the Jews, and the religion they derived from their forefathers; for which reason our nation made war with him, and would never be reconciled to him; (244) but for this Antiochus, all men called him *Antiochus the Pious*, for the great zeal he had about religion.

(245) Accordingly, Hyrcanus took this moderation of his kindly; and when he understood how religious he was towards the Deity, he sent an embassage to him, and desired that he would restore the settlements they received from their forefathers. So he rejected the counsel of those that would have him utterly destroy the nation by reason of their way of living, which was to others unsociable, and did not regard what they said. (246) But being persuaded that all they did was out of a religious mind, he answered the ambassadors, that if the besieged would deliver up their arms, and pay tribute for Joppa, and the other cities which bordered upon Judea, and admit a garrison of his, on these terms he would make war against them no longer. (247) But the Jews, although they were content with the other conditions, did not agree to admit

the garrison, because they could not associate with other people, nor converse with them; yet were they willing, instead of the admission of the garrison, to give him hostages, and five hundred talents of silver; of which they paid down three hundred, and lent the hostages immediately, which King Antiochus accepted. One of those hostages was Hyrcanus' brother. But still he broke down the fortifications that encompassed the city. (248) And upon these conditions Antiochus broke up the siege, and departed.

(249) But Hyrcanus opened the sepulchre of David, who excelled all other kings in riches, and took out of it three thousand talents. He was also the first of the Jews that, relying on this wealth, maintained foreign troops. There was also a league of friendship and mutual assistance made between them; upon which Hyrcanus admitted him into the city, and furnished him with whatsoever his army wanted in great plenty, and with great generosity, (250) and marched along with him when he made an expedition against the Parthians, of which Nicolaus of Damascus is a witness for us; who, in his history writes thus: (251) 'When Antiochus had erected a trophy at the river Lycus, upon his conquest of Indates, the general of the Parthians, he stayed there two days. It was at the desire of Hyrcanus the Jew, because it was such a festival, derived to them from their forefathers, whereupon the law of the Jews did not allow them to travel.' (252) And truly he did not speak falsely in saying so; for that festival, which we call *Pentecost*, did then fall out to be the next day to the Sabbath: nor is it lawful for us to journey either on the Sabbath day or on a festival day. (253) But when Antiochus joined battle with Arsaces, the king of Parthia, he lost a great part of his army, and was himself slain; and his brother Demetrius succeeded in the kingdom of Syria, by the permission of Arsaces, who freed him from his captivity at the same time that Antiochus attacked Parthia, as we have formerly related elsewhere.

CHAPTER 9

(254) But when Hyrcanus heard of the death of Antiochus he presently made an expedition against the cities of Syria, hoping to find them destitute of fighting men, and of such as were able to defend them. (255) However, it was not till the sixth month that he took Medaba, and that not without the greatest distress of his army. After this he took Samega, and the neighbouring places; and, besides these, Shechem and Gerizzim, and the nation of the Cutheans, (256) who dwelt at the temple which resembled that temple which was at Jerusalem, and which Alexander permitted Sanballat, the general of his army, to build for the sake of Manasseh, who was son-in-law to Jadua the high priest, as we have formerly related; which temple was now deserted two hundred years after it was built. (257) Hyrcanus took also Dora and Marissa, cities of

Idumea, and subdued all the Idumeans; and permitted them to stay in that country, if they would circumcise their genitals, and make use of the laws of the Jews; (258) and they were so desirous of living in the country of their forefathers, that they submitted to the use of circumcision, and the rest of the Jewish ways of living; at which time therefore this befell them, that they were hereafter no other than Jews.

(259) But Hyrcanus the high priest was desirous to renew that league of friendship they had with the Romans: accordingly he sent an embassage to them; and when the senate had received their epistle, they made a league of friendship with them, after the manner following: (260) 'Fanius, the son of Marcus, the praetor, gathered the senate together on the eighth day before the Ides of February, in the senate house, when Lucius Manlius, the son of Lucius, of the Mentine tribe, and Caius Sempronius, the son of Caius, of the Falernian tribe, were present. The occasion was, that the ambassadors sent by the people of the Jews, Simon the son of Dositheus, and Apollonius the son of Alexander, and Diodorus the son of Jason, who were good and virtuous men, (261) had somewhat to propose about that league of friendship and mutual assistance which subsisted between them and the Romans, and about other public affairs; who desired that Joppa, and the havens, and Gazara, and the springs [of Jordan] and the several other cities and countries of theirs, which Antiochus had taken from them in the war, contrary to the decree of the senate, might be restored to them; (262) and that it might not be lawful for the king's troops to pass through their country, and the countries of those that are subject to them; and that what attempts Antiochus had made during that war, without the decree of the senate, might be made void: (263) and that they would send ambassadors, who should take care that restitution be made them of what Antiochus had taken from them, and that they should make an estimate of the country that had been laid waste in the war: and that they would grant them letters of protection to the kings and free people, in order to their quiet return home. (264) It was therefore decreed as to these points, to renew their league of friendship and mutual assistance with these good men, and who were sent by a good and friendly people.' (265) But as to the letters desired, their answer was, that the senate would consult about that matter when their own affairs would give them leave, and that they would endeavour, for the time to come, that no like injury should be done to them: and that their praetor Fanius should give them money out of the public treasury to bear their expenses home. (266) And thus did Fanius dismiss the Jewish ambassadors, and gave them money out of the public treasury; and gave the decree of the senate to those that were to conduct them, and to take care that they should return home in safety.

(267) And thus stood the affairs of Hyrcanus the high priest. But as for King Demetrius, who had a mind to make war against Hyrcanus, there was no

opportunity nor room for it, while both the Syrians and soldiers bare ill will to him, because he was an ill man. But when they had sent ambassadors to Ptolemy, who was called Physcon, that he would send them one of the family of Seleucus, in order to take the kingdom, (268) and he sent them Alexander, who was called Zebina, with an army, and there had been a battle between them, Demetrius was beaten in the fight, and fled to Cleopatra his wife, to Ptolemais; but his wife would not receive him. He went thence to Tyre, and was there caught; and when he had suffered much from his enemies before his death, he was slain by them. (269) So Alexander took the kingdom, and made a league with Hyrcanus. Yet, when he afterward fought with Antiochus the son of Demetrius, who was called Grypus, he was also beaten in the fight, and slain.

CHAPTER 10

(270) When Antiochus had taken the kingdom, he was afraid to make war against Judea, because he heard that his brother by the same mother, who was called Antiochus, was raising an army against him out of Cyzicum; (271) so he stayed in his own land, and resolved to prepare himself for the attack he expected from his brother, who was called Cyzicenus, because he had been brought up in that city. He was the son of Antiochus that was called Soter, who died in Parthia. He was the brother of Demetrius, the father of Grypus; for it had so happened, that one and the same Cleopatra was married to two who were brethren, as we have related elsewhere. (272) But Antiochus Cyzicenus coming into Syria, continued many years at war with his brother. Now Hyrcanus lived all this while in peace; (273) for after the death of Antiochus, he revolted from the Macedonians, nor did he any longer pay them the least regard, either as their subject or their friend, but his affairs were in a very improving and flourishing condition in the times of Alexander Zebina, and especially under these brethren, for the war which they had with one another gave Hyrcanus the opportunity of enjoying himself in Judea quietly, insomuch that he got an immense quantity of money. (274) However, when Antiochus Cyzicenus distressed his land, he then openly showed what he meant. And when he saw that Antiochus was destitute of Egyptian auxiliaries, and that both he and his brother were in an ill condition in the struggles they had one with another, he despised them both.

(275) So he made an expedition against Samaria, which was a very strong city; of whose present name Sebaste, and its rebuilding by Herod, we shall speak at a proper time; but he made his attack against it, and besieged it with a great deal of pains; for he was greatly displeased with the Samaritans for the injuries they had done to the people of Marissa, a colony of the Jews, and confederate with them, and this in compliance to the kings of Syria. (276)

When he had therefore drawn a ditch, and built a double wall round the city which was fourscore furlongs long, he set his sons Antigonus and Aristobulus over the siege; which brought the Samaritans to that great distress by famine that they were forced to eat what used not to be eaten, and to call for Antiochus Cyzicenus to help them, (277) who came readily to their assistance, but was beaten by Aristobulus; and when he was pursued as far as Scythopolis by the two brethren, he got away; so they returned to Samaria, and shut them again within the wall, till they were forced to send for the same Antiochus a second time to help them, (278) who procured about six thousand men from Ptolemy Lathyrus, which were sent them without his mother's consent, who had then in a manner turned him out of his government. With these Egyptians Antiochus did at first overrun and ravage the country of Hyrcanus after the manner of a robber, for he durst not meet him in the face to fight with him, as not having an army sufficient for that purpose, but only from this supposal, that by thus harassing his land he should force Hyrcanus to raise the siege of Samaria; (279) but because he fell into snares, and lost many of his soldiers therein, he went away to Tripoli, and committed the prosecution of the war against the Jews to Callimander and Epicrates.

(280) But as to Callimander, he attacked the enemy too rashly, and was put to flight and destroyed immediately; and as to Epicrates, he was such a lover of money, that he openly betrayed Scythopolis, and other places near it, to the Jews; but was not able to make them raise the siege of Samaria. (281) And when Hyrcanus had taken that city, which was not done till after a year's siege, he was not contented with doing that only, but he demolished it entirely, and brought rivulets to it to drown it, for he dug such hollows as might let the waters run under it; nay he took away the very marks that there had ever been such a city there. (282) Now a very surprising thing is related of this high priest Hyrcanus, how God came to discourse with him; for they say that on the very same day on which his sons fought with Antiochus Cyzicenus, he was alone in the temple as high priest offering incense, and heard a voice, that his sons had just then overcome Antiochus. (283) And this he openly declared before all the multitude on his coming out of the temple; and it accordingly proved true; and, in this posture were the affairs of Hyrcanus.

(284) Now it happened at this time, that not only those Jews who were at Jerusalem and in Judea were in prosperity, but also those of them that were at Alexandria, and in Egypt and Cyprus, (285) for Cleopatra the queen was at variance with her son Ptolemy, who was called Lathyrus, and appointed for her generals Chelcias and Ananias, the sons of that Onias who built the temple in the prefecture of Heliopolis, like that at Jerusalem, as we have elsewhere related. (286) Cleopatra entrusted these men with her army; and did nothing without their advice, as Strabo of Cappadocia attests, when he saith thus: (287)

'Now the greater part, both those that came to Cyprus with us, and those that were sent afterward thither, revolted to Ptolemy immediately; only those that were called Onias' party, being Jews, continued faithful, because their countrymen Chelcias and Ananias were in chief favour with the queen.' These are the words of Strabo.

(288) However, this prosperous state of affairs moved the Jews to envy Hyrcanus; but they that were the worst disposed to him were the Pharisees, who were one of the sects of the Jews, as we have informed you already. These have so great a power over the multitude, that when they say anything against the king or against the high priest, they are presently believed. (289) Now Hyrcanus was a disciple of theirs, and greatly beloved by them. And when he once invited them to a feast, and entertained them very kindly, when he saw them in a good humour, he began to say to them, that they knew he was desirous to be a righteous man, and to do all things whereby he might please God, which was the profession of the Pharisees also. (290) However, he desired, that if they observed him offending in any point, and going out of the right way, they would call him back and correct him. On which occasion they attested to his being entirely virtuous, with which commendation he was well pleased; but still there was one of his guests there, whose name was Eleazar, (291) a man of an ill temper, and delighting in seditious practices. This man said, 'Since thou desirest to know the truth, if thou wilt be righteous in earnest, lay down the high priesthood, and content thyself with the civil government of the people.' (292) And when he desired to know for what cause he ought to lay down the high priesthood, the other replied, 'We have heard it from old men, that thy mother had been a captive under the reign of Antiochus Epiphanes.' This story was false, and Hyrcanus was provoked against him; and all the Pharisees had a very great indignation against him.

(293) Now there was one Jonathan, a very great friend of Hyrcanus, but of the sect of the Sadducees, whose notions are quite contrary to those of the Pharisees. He told Hyrcanus that Eleazar had cast such a reproach upon him, according to the common sentiments of all the Pharisees, and that this would be made manifest if he would but ask him the question, What punishment they thought this man deserved? (294) For that he might depend upon it, that the reproach was now laid on him with their approbation, if they were for punishing him as his crime deserved. So the Pharisees made answer, that he deserved stripes and bonds; but that it did not seem right to punish reproaches with death; and indeed the Pharisees, even upon other occasions, are not apt to be severe in punishments. (295) At this gentle sentence Hyrcanus was very angry, and thought that this man reproached him by their approbation. It was this Jonathan who chiefly irritated him, and influenced him so far, (296) that he made him leave the party of the Pharisees, and abolish the decrees they had

imposed on the people, and punish those that observed them. From this source arose that hatred which he and his sons met with from the multitude; (297) but of these matters we shall speak hereafter. What I would now explain is this, that the Pharisees have delivered to the people a great many observances by succession from their fathers, which are not written in the laws of Moses; and for that reason it is that the Sadducees reject them and say that we are to esteem those observances to be obligatory which are in the written word, but are not to observe what are derived from the tradition of our forefathers; (298) and concerning these things it is that great disputes and differences have arisen among them, while the Sadducees are able to persuade none but the rich, and have not the populace obsequious to them, but the Pharisees have the multitude on their side; but about these two sects, and that of the Essenes, I have treated accurately in the second book of Jewish affairs.

(299) But when Hyrcanus had put an end to this sedition, he after that lived happily, and administered the government in the best manner for thirty-one years, and then died, leaving behind him five sons. He was esteemed by God worthy of the three privileges – the government of his nation, the dignity of the high priesthood, and prophecy; (300) for God was with him, and enabled him to know futurities and to foretell this in particular, that as to his two eldest sons, he foretold that they would not long continue in the government of public affairs; whose unhappy catastrophe will be worth our description, that we may thence learn how very much they were inferior to their father's happiness.

CHAPTER II

(301) Now when their father Hyrcanus was dead, the eldest son Aristobulus, intending to change the government into a kingdom, for so he resolved to do, first of all put a diadem on his head, four hundred and eighty-one years and three months after the people had been delivered from the Babylonish slavery, and were returned to their own country again. (302) This Aristobulus loved his next brother Antigonus, and treated him as his equal; but the others he held in bonds. He also cast his mother into prison, because she disputed the government with him; for Hyrcanus had left her to be mistress of all. He also proceeded to that degree of barbarity, as to kill her in prison with hunger; (303) nay he was alienated from his brother Antigonus by calumnies, and added him to the rest whom he slew; yet he seemed to have an affection for him, and made him above the rest a partner with him in the kingdom. Those calumnies he at first did not give credit to, partly because he loved him, and so did not give heed to what was said against him, and partly because he thought the reproaches were derived from the envy of the relaters. (304) But when

Antigonus was once returned from the army, and that feast was then at hand when they make tabernacles [to the honour of] God, it happened that Aristobulus was fallen sick, and that Antigonus went up most splendidly adorned, and with his soldiers about him in their armour, to the temple to celebrate the feast, and to put up many prayers for the recovery of his brother; (305) when some wicked persons, who had a great mind to raise a difference between the brethren, made use of this opportunity of the pompous appearance of Antigonus, and of the great actions which he had done, and went to the king, and spitefully aggravated the pompous show of his at the feast, (306) and pretended that all these circumstances were not like those of a private person; that these actions were indications of an affectation of royal authority; and that his coming with a strong body of men must be with an intention to kill him; and that his way of reasoning was this: that it was a silly thing in him, while it was in his power to reign himself, to look upon it as a great favour that he was honoured with a lower dignity by his brother.

(307) Aristobulus yielded to these imputations, but took care both that his brother should not suspect him, and that he himself might not run the hazard of his own safety; so he ordered his guards to lie in a certain place that was under ground, and dark (he himself then lying sick in the tower which was called Antonia); and he commanded them, that in case Antigonus came in to him unarmed, they should not touch anybody, but if armed, they should kill him; (308) yet did he send to Antigonus, and desired that he would come unarmed: but the queen, and those that joined with her in the plot against Antigonus, persuaded the messenger to tell him the direct contrary: how his brother had heard that he had made himself a fine suit of armour for war and desired him to come to him in that armour, that he might see how fine it was. (309) So Antigonus, suspecting no treachery, but depending on the good will of his brother, came to Aristobulus armed, as he used to be, with his entire armour, in order to show it to him; but when he was come to a place which was called Strato's Tower, where the passage happened to be exceeding dark, the guards slew him; (310) which death demonstrates that nothing is stronger than envy and calumny, and that nothing does more certainly divide the good will and natural affection of men than those passions. (311) But here one may take occasion to wonder at one Judas, who was of the sect of the Essenes, and who never missed the truth in his predictions; for this man, when he saw Antigonus passing by the temple, cried to his companions and friends, who abode with him as his scholars, in order to learn the art of foretelling things to come. (312) 'That it was good for him to die now, since he had spoken falsely about Antigonus, who is still alive, and I see him passing by, although he had foretold he should die at the place called Strato's Tower that very day, while yet the place is six hundred furlongs off where he had foretold he should be

slain; and still this day is a great part of it already past, so that he was in danger of proving a false prophet.' (313) As he was saying this, and that in a melancholy mood, the news came that Antigonus was slain in a place under ground, which itself was called also Strato's Tower or of the same name with that Caesarea which is seated at the sea. This event put the prophet into a great disorder.

(314) But Aristobulus repented immediately of this slaughter of his brother; on which account his disease increased upon him, and he was disturbed in his mind, upon the guilt of such wickedness, insomuch that his entrails were corrupted by his intolerable pain, and he vomited blood; at which time one of the servants that attended upon him, and was carrying his blood away, did, by divine providence, as I cannot but suppose, slip down, and shed part of his blood at the very place where there were spots of Antigonus's blood there slain, still remaining; (315) and when there was a cry made by the spectators, as if the servant had on purpose shed the blood on that place, Aristobulus heard it, and inquired what the matter was; and as they did not answer him, he was the more earnest to know what it was, it being natural to men to suspect that what is thus concealed is very bad: (316) so upon his threatening, and forcing them by terrors to speak, they at length told him the truth; whereupon he shed many tears, in that disorder of mind which arose from his consciousness of what he had done, and gave a deep groan, and said, 'I am not therefore, I perceive, to be concealed from God, in the impious and horrid crimes I have been guilty of; but a sudden punishment is coming upon me for the shedding the blood of my relations. (317) And now, O thou most impudent body of mine, how long wilt thou retain a soul that ought to die, in order to appease the ghost of my brother and my mother? Why dost thou not give it all up at once? And why do I deliver up my blood, drop by drop, to those whom I have so wickedly murdered.' In saying which last words he died, having reigned a year. (318) He was called a lover of the Grecians; and had conferred many benefits on his own country, and made war against Iturea, and added a great part of it to Judea, and compelled the inhabitants, if they would continue in that country, to be circumcised, and to live according to the Jewish laws. (319) He was naturally a man of candour, and of great modesty, as Strabo bears witness in the name of Timagenes: who says thus: 'This man was a person of candour, and very serviceable to the Jews, for he added a country to them, and obtained a part of the nation of the Itureans for them and bound them to them by the bond of the circumcision of their genitals.'

CHAPTER 12

(320) When Aristobulus was dead, his wife Salome, who by the Greeks was called Alexandra, let his brethren out of prison (for Aristobulus had kept them in bonds, as we have said already), and made Alexander Janneus king, who was the superior in age and in moderation. (321) This child happened to be hated by his father as soon as he was born, and could never be permitted to come into his father's sight till he died. The occasion of which hatred is thus reported: (322) when Hyrcanus chiefly loved the two eldest of his sons, Antigonus and Aristobulus, God appeared to him in his sleep, of whom he inquired which of his sons should be his successor. Upon God's representing to him the countenance of Alexander, he was grieved that he was to be the heir of all his goods, and suffered him to be brought up in Galilee. However, God did not deceive Hyrcanus, (323) for after the death of Aristobulus, he certainly took the kingdom; and one of his brethren who affected the kingdom he slew; and the other, who chose to live a private and quiet life, he had in esteem.

(324) When Alexander Janneus had settled the government in the manner that he judged best, he made an expedition against Ptolemais; and having overcome the men in battle, he shut them up in the city, and sat round about it, and besieged it; for of the maritime cities there remained only Ptolemais and Gaza to be conquered, besides Strato's Tower and Dora, which were held by the tyrant Zoilus. (325) Now while Antiochus Philometor, and Antiochus who was called Cyzicenus, were making war against one another, and destroying one another's armies, the people of Ptolemais could have no assistance from them; (326) but when they were distressed with this siege, Zoilus, who possessed Strato's Tower and Dora, and maintained a legion of soldiers, and on occasion of the contest between the kings affected tyranny himself, came and brought some small assistance to the people of Ptolemais; (327) nor indeed had the kings such a friendship for them as that they should hope for any advantage from them. Both those kings were in the case of wrestlers, who finding themselves deficient in strength, and yet being ashamed to yield, put off the fight by laziness, and by lying still as long as they can. (328) The only hope they had remaining was from the kings of Egypt, and from Ptolemy Lathyrus, who now held Cyprus, and who came to Cyprus when he was driven from the government of Egypt by Cleopatra his mother: so the people of Ptolemais sent to this Ptolemy Lathyrus and desired him to come as a confederate, to deliver them, now they were in such danger, out of the hands of Alexander. (329) And as the ambassadors gave him hopes, that if he would pass over into Syria, he would have the people of Gaza on the side of those of Ptolemais; as they also said that Zoilus, and besides these the

Sidonians and many others would assist them, so he was elevated at this, and got his fleet ready as soon as possible.

(330) But in this interval Demenetus, one that was of abilities to persuade men to do as he would have them, and a leader of the populace, made those of Ptolemais change their opinions; and said to them, that it was better to run the hazard of being subject to the Jews than to admit of evident slavery by delivering themselves up to a master; and besides that, to have not only a war at present, but to expect a much greater war from Egypt; (331) for that Cleopatra would not overlook an army raised by Ptolemy for himself out of the neighbourhood, but would come against them with a great army of her own, and this because she was labouring to eject her son out of Cyprus also; that as for Ptolemy, if he fail of his hopes, he can still retire to Cyprus; but that they will be left in the greatest danger possible. (332) Now Ptolemy, although he had heard of the change that was made in the people of Ptolemais, yet did he still go on with his voyage, and came to the country called Sycamine, and there set his army on shore. (333) This army of his, in the whole horse and foot together, were about thirty thousand, with which he marched near to Ptolemais, and there pitched his camp: but when the people of Ptolemais neither received his ambassadors, nor would hear what they had to say, he was under a very great concern.

(334) But when Zoilus and the people of Gaza came to him, and desired his assistance, because their country was laid waste by the Jews, and by Alexander, Alexander raised the siege, for fear of Ptolemy: and when he had drawn off his army into his own country, he used a stratagem afterwards, by privately inviting Cleopatra to come against Ptolemy, but publicly pretending to desire a league of friendship and mutual assistance with him; (335) and promising to give him four hundred talents of silver, he desired that, by way of requital, he would take off Zoilus the tyrant, and give his country to the Jews. And then indeed Ptolemy, with pleasure, made such a league of friendship with Alexander, and subdued Zoilus: (336) but when he afterwards heard that he had privily sent to Cleopatra his mother, he broke the league with him, which yet he had confirmed with an oath, and fell upon him, and besieged Ptolemais, because it would not receive him. However, leaving his generals, with some part of his forces, to go on with the siege, he went himself immediately with the rest to lay Judea waste: (337) and when Alexander understood this to be Ptolemy's intention, he also got together about fifty thousand soldiers out of his own country; nay, as some writers have said, eighty thousand. He then took his army, and went to meet Ptolemy; but Ptolemy fell upon Asochis, a city of Galilee, and took it by force on the Sabbath day, and there he took about ten thousand slaves, and a great deal of other prey.

(338) He then tried to take Sepphoris, which was a city not far from that which was destroyed, but lost many of his men; yet did he then go to fight

with Alexander. Alexander met him at the river Jordan, near a certain place called Saphoth [not far from the river Jordan] and pitched his camp near to the enemy. (339) He had however eight thousand in the first rank, which he styled Hecatontomachi, having shields of brass. – Those in the first rank of Ptolemy's soldiers also had shields covered with brass: but Ptolemy's soldiers in other respects were inferior to those of Alexander, and therefore were more fearful of running hazards; (340) but Philostephanus, the camp master, put great courage into them, and ordered them to pass the river, which was between their camps: nor did Alexander think fit to hinder their passage over it: for he thought, that if the enemy had once gotten the river on their back, that he should the easier take them prisoners, when they could not flee out of the battle: (341) in the beginning of which, the acts on both sides, with their hands, and with their alacrity, were alike, and a great slaughter was made by both the armies; but Alexander was superior, till Philostephanus opportunely brought up the auxiliaries, to help those that were giving way; (342) but as there were no auxiliaries to afford help to that part of the Jews that gave way, it fell out that they fled, and those near them did not assist them, but fled along with them. However, Ptolemy's soldiers acted quite otherwise; (343) for they followed the Jews, and killed them, till at length those that slew them pursued after them when they had made them all run away, and slew them so long, that their weapons of iron were blunted, and their hands quite tired with the slaughter; (344) for the report was, that thirty thousand men were then slain. Timagenes says they were fifty thousand. As for the rest, they were part of them taken captives; and the other part ran away to their own country.

(345) After this victory, Ptolemy overran all the country; and when night came on, he abode in certain villages of Judea, which when he found full of women and children, he commanded his soldiers to strangle them, and to cut them in pieces, and then to cast them into boiling caldrons, and then to devour their limbs as sacrifices. (346) This commandment was given, that such as fled from the battle, and came to them, might suppose their enemies were cannibals, and eat men's flesh, and might on that account be still more terrified at them upon such a sight. (347) And both Strabo and Nicholaus [of Damascus] affirm, that they used these people after this manner, as I have already related. Ptolemy also took Ptolemais by force, as we have declared elsewhere.

CHAPTER 13

(348) When Cleopatra saw that her son was grown great, and laid Judea waste without disturbance, and had gotten the city of Gaza under his power, she resolved no longer to overlook what he did, when he was almost at her gates; and she concluded, that, now he was so much stronger than before, he would

be very desirous of the dominion over the Egyptians; (349) but she immediately marched against him, with a fleet at sea and an army of foot on land, and made Chelcias and Ananias, the Jews, generals of her whole army, while she sent the greatest part of her riches, her grandchildren, and her testament, to the people of Cos. (350) Cleopatra also ordered her son Alexander to sail with a great fleet to Phoenicia; and when that country had revolted, she came to Ptolemais; and because the people of Ptolemais did not receive her, she besieged the city; (351) but Ptolemy went out of Syria, and made haste unto Egypt, supposing that he should find it destitute of an army, and soon take it, though he failed of his hopes. At this time Chelcias, one of Cleopatra's generals, happened to die in Celesyria, as he was in pursuit of Ptolemy.

(352) When Cleopatra heard of her son's attempt, and that his Egyptian expedition did not succeed according to his expectations, she sent thither part of her army, and drove him out of that country; so when he was returned out of Egypt again, he abode during the winter at Gaza, (353) in which time Cleopatra took the garrison that was in Ptolemais by siege, as well as the city; and when Alexander came to her, he gave her presents, and such marks of respect as were but proper, since, under the miseries he endured by Ptolemy, he had no other refuge but her. Now there were some of her friends who persuaded her to seize Alexander, and to overrun and take possession of the country, and not to sit still and see such a multitude of brave Jews subject to one man; (354) but Ananias' counsel was contrary to theirs, who said that she would do an unjust action if she deprived a man that was her ally of that authority which belonged to him, and this a man who is related to us; 'for (said he) I would not have thee ignorant of this, that what injustice thou dost to him will make all us that are Jews to be thy enemies.' (355) This desire of Ananias, Cleopatra complied with; and did no injury to Alexander, but made a league of mutual assistance with him at Scythopolis, a city of Celesyria.

(356) So when Alexander was delivered from the fear he was in of Ptolemy, he presently made an expedition against Celesyria. He also took Gadara, after a siege of ten months. He took also Amathus, a very strong fortress belonging to the inhabitants above Jordan, where Theodorus, the son of Zeno, had his chief treasure, and what he esteemed most precious. This Zeno fell unexpectedly upon the Jews, and slew ten thousand of them, and seized upon Alexander's baggage: (357) yet did not this misfortune terrify Alexander; but he made an expedition upon the maritime parts of the country, Raphia and Anthedon (the name of which King Herod afterwards changed to Agrippas), and took even that by force. (358) But when Alexander saw that Ptolemy was retired from Gaza to Cyprus, and his mother Cleopatra was returned to Egypt, he grew angry at the people of Gaza, because they had invited Ptolemy to assist them, and besieged their city, and ravaged their country. (359) But as Apollodorus,

the general of the army of Gaza, fell upon the camp of the Jews by night, with two thousand foreign, and ten thousand of his own forces, while the night lasted those of Gaza prevailed, because the enemy was made to believe that it was Ptolemy who attacked them; but when day was come on, and that mistake was corrected, and the Jews knew the truth of the matter, they came back again and fell upon those of Gaza and slew of them about a thousand. (360) But as those of Gaza stoutly resisted them, and would not yield for either their want of anything, nor for the great multitude that were slain (for they would rather suffer any hardship whatever than come under the power of their enemies), Aretas, king of the Arabians, a person then very illustrious, encouraged them to go on with alacrity, and promised them that he would come to their assistance; (361) but it happened that before he came Apollodotus was slain; for his brother Lysimachus, envying him for the great reputation he had gained among the citizens, slew him, and got the army together, and delivered up the city to Alexander; (362) who when he came in at first lay quiet, but afterwards set his army upon the inhabitants of Gaza, and gave them leave to punish them; so some went one way, and some went another, and slew the inhabitants of Gaza; yet were not they of cowardly hearts, but opposed those that came to slay them, and slew as many of the Jews; (363) and some of them, when they saw themselves deserted, burnt their own houses, that the enemy might get none of their spoils: nay, some of them, with their own hands, slew their children and their wives, having no other way but this of avoiding slavery for them; (364) but the senators, who were in all five hundred, fled to Apollo's temple (for this attack happened to be made as they were sitting), whom Alexander slew; and when he had utterly overthrown their city, he returned to Jerusalem, having spent a year in that siege.

(365) About this very time Antiochus, who was called Grypus, died. His death was caused by Heracleon's treachery, when he had lived forty-five years, and had reigned twenty-nine. (366) His son Seleucus succeeded him in the kingdom, and made war with Antiochus, his father's brother, who was called Antiochus Cyzicenus, and beat him, and took him prisoner, and slew him; (367) but after a while Antiochus, the son of Cyzicenus, who was called Pius, came to Aradus, and put the diadem on his own head, and made war with Seleucus, and beat him, and drove him out of all Syria. (368) But when he fled out of Syria, he came to Mopsuestia again, and levied money upon them; but the people of Mopsuestia had indignation at what he did, and burnt down his palace, and slew him, together with his friends. (369) But when Antiochus the son of Cyzicenus was king of Syria, Antiochus the brother of Seleucus made war upon him, and was overcome and destroyed, he and his army. After him, his brother Philip put on the diadem, and reigned over some part of Syria; (370) but Ptolemy Lathyrus sent for his fourth brother Demetrius, who was

called Eucerus, from Cnidus, and made him king of Damascus. (371) Both these brothers did Antiochus vehemently oppose, but presently died; for when he was come as an auxiliary to Laodice, queen of the Gileadites, when she was making war against the Parthians, and he was fighting courageously, he fell, while Demetrius and Philip governed Syria, as hath been elsewhere related.

(372) As to Alexander, his own people were seditious against him; for at a festival which was then celebrated, when he stood upon the altar, and was going to sacrifice, the nation rose upon him and pelted with citrons [which they then had in their hands, because] the laws of the Jews required that at the feast of tabernacles everyone should have branches of the palm tree and citron tree; which thing we have elsewhere related. They also reviled him, as derived from a captive, and so unworthy of his dignity and of sacrificing. (373) At this he was in a rage, and slew of them about six thousand. He also built a partition wall of wood round the altar and the temple, as far as that partition within which it was only lawful for the priest to enter; and by this means he obstructed the multitude from coming at him. (374) He also maintained foreigners of Pisidiae and Cilicia; for as to the Syrians, he was at war with them, and so made no use of them. He also overcame the Arabians, such as the Moabites and Gileadites, and made them bring tribute. Moreover, he demolished Amathus, while Theodorus durst not fight with him: (375) but as he had joined battle with Obedas, king of the Arabians, and fell into an ambush in the places that were rugged and difficult to be travelled over, he was thrown down into a deep valley by the multitude of the camels at Gadara, a village of Gilead, and hardly escaped with his life. From thence he fled to Jerusalem, (376) where, besides his other ill success, the nation insulted him, and he fought against them for six years, and slew no fewer than fifty thousand of them; and when he desired that they would desist from their ill will to him, they hated him so much the more, on account of what had already happened; and when he had asked them what he ought to do, they all cried out, that he ought to kill himself. They also sent to Demetrius Eucerus, and desired him to make a league of mutual defence with them.

CHAPTER 14

(377) So Demetrius came with an army, and took those that invited him, and pitched his camp near the city Shechem; upon which Alexander, with his six thousand two hundred mercenaries, and about twenty thousand Jews, who were of his party, went against Demetrius, who had three thousand horsemen, and forty thousand footmen. (378) Now there were great endeavours used on both sides – Demetrius trying to bring off the mercenaries that were with Alexander, because they were Greeks; and Alexander trying to bring off the

Jews that were with Demetrius. However, when neither of them could persuade them so to do, they came to a battle, and Demetrius was the conqueror; in which all Alexander's mercenaries were killed, when they had given demonstration of their fidelity and courage. A great number of Demetrius' soldiers were slain also.

(379) Now as Alexander fled to the mountains, six thousand of the Jews hereupon came together [from Demetrius] to him out of pity at the change of his fortune; upon which Demetrius was afraid, and retired out of the country; after which the Jews fought against Alexander, and being beaten were slain in great numbers in the several battles which they had, (380) and when he had shut up the most powerful of them in the city Bethome, he besieged them therein; and when he had taken the city, and gotten the men into his power, he brought them to Jerusalem, and did one of the most barbarous actions in the world to them; for as he was feasting with his concubines, in the sight of all the city, he ordered about eight hundred of them to be crucified; and while they were living, he ordered the throats of their children and wives to be cut before their eyes. (381) This was indeed by way of revenge for the injuries they had done him; which punishment yet was of an inhuman nature, though we suppose that he had been ever so much distressed, as indeed he had been, by his wars with them, for he had by their means come to the last degree of hazard, both of his life and of his kingdom, while they were not satisfied by themselves only to fight against him, but introduced foreigners also for the same purpose; (382) nay, at length they reduced him to that degree of necessity, that he was forced to deliver back to the king of Arabia the land of Moab and Gilead, which he had subdued, and the places that were in them, that they might not join with them in the war against him, as they had done ten thousand other things that tended to affront and reproach him. (383) However, this barbarity seems to have been without any necessity, on which account he bare the name of a Thracian among the Jews; whereupon the soldiers that had fought against him, being about eight thousand in number, ran away by night, and continued fugitives all the time that Alexander lived; who being now freed from any further disturbance from them, reigned the rest of his time in the utmost tranquility.

(384) But when Demetrius was departed out of Judea, he went to Berea and besieged his brother Philip, having with him ten thousand footmen and a thousand horsemen. However, Strato the tyrant of Berea, the confederate of Philip, called in Zizon the ruler of the Arabian tribes, and Mithridates Sinax, the ruler of the Parthians, (385) who coming with a great number of forces, and besieging Demetrius in his encampment, into which they had driven him with their arrows, they compelled those that were with him, by thirst, to deliver up themselves. So they took a great many spoils out of that country,

and Demetrius himself, whom they sent to Mithridates, who was then king of Parthia; but as to those whom they took captives of the people of Antioch, they restored them to the Antiochians without any reward. (386) Now Mithridates, the king of Parthia, had Demetrius in great honour, till Demetrius ended his life by sickness. So Philip presently after the fight was over came to Antioch, and took it, and reigned over Syria.

CHAPTER 15

(387) After this, Antiochus, who was called Dionysius, and was Philip's brother, aspired to the dominion, and came to Damascus, and got the power into his hands, and there he reigned; but as he was making war against the Arabians, his brother Philip heard of it, and came to Damascus, (388) where Milesius, who had been left governor of the citadel, and the Damascens themselves delivered up the city to him; yet because Philip was become ungrateful to him, and had bestowed upon him nothing of that in hopes whereof he had received him into the city, but had a mind to have it believed that it was rather delivered up out of fear than by the kindness of Milesius, and because he had not rewarded him as he ought to have done, he became suspected by him, and so he was obliged to leave Damascus again; for (389) Milesius caught him marching out of the Hippodrome, and shut him up in it, and kept Damascus for Antiochus [Eucerus], who, hearing how Philip's affairs stood, came back out of Arabia. He also came immediately, and made an expedition against Judea, with eight thousand armed footmen and eight hundred horsemen. (390) So Alexander, out of fear of his coming, dug a deep ditch, beginning at Chabarzaba, which is now called Antipatris, to the Sea of Joppa, on which part only his army could be brought against him. He also raised a wall, and erected wooden towers and intermediate redoubts, for one hundred and fifty furlongs in length, and there expected the coming of Antiochus; (391) but he soon burnt them all, and made his army pass by that way into Arabia. The Arabian king [Aretas] at first retreated, but afterward appeared on the sudden with ten thousand horsemen. Antiochus gave them the meeting, and fought desperately; and indeed when he had gotten the victory, and was bringing some auxiliaries to that part of his army that was in distress, he was slain. When Antiochus was fallen, his army fled to the village Cana, where the greatest part of them perished by famine.

(392) After him Aretas reigned over Celesyria, being called to the government by those that held Damascus, by reason of the hatred they bare to Ptolemy Menneus. He also made thence an expedition against Judea, and beat Alexander in battle, near a place called Adida; yet did he, upon certain conditions agreed on between them, retire out of Judea.

(393) But Alexander marched again to the city Dios, and took it, and then

made an expedition against Essa, where was the best part of Zeno's treasures, and there he encompassed the place with three walls; and when he had taken the city by fighting, he marched to Golan and Seleucia; (394) and when he had taken these cities, he, besides them, took that valley which is called *The Valley of Antiochus*, as also the fortress of Gamala. He also accused Demetrius, who was governor of those places, of many crimes, and turned him out; and after he had spent three years in this war, he returned to his own country, when the Jews joyfully received him upon this his good success.

(395) Now at this time the Jews were in possession of the following cities that had belonged to the Syrians and Idumeans and Phoenicians: At the seaside, Strato's Tower, Apollonia, Joppa, Jamnia, Ashdod, Gaza, Anthedon, Raphia, and Rhinocolura; (396) in the middle of the country, near to Idumea, Adora and Marissa; near the country of Samaria, Mount Carmel and Mount Tabor, Scythopolis, and Gadara; of the country of the Gaulonites, Seleucia and Gabala; (397) in the country of Moab, Heshbon and Medaba, Lemba and Oronas, Gelithon, Zorn, the valley of the Cilices, and Pella; which last they utterly destroyed, because its inhabitants would not bear to change their religious rites for those peculiar to the Jews. The Jews also possessed others of the principal cities of Syria, which had been destroyed.

(398) After this, King Alexander, although he fell into a distemper by hard drinking, and had a quartan ague which held him three years, yet would not leave off going out with his army, till he was quite spent with the labours he had undergone, and died in the bounds of Ragaba, a fortress beyond Jordan. (399) But when his queen saw that he was ready to die, and had no longer any hopes of surviving, she came to him weeping and lamenting, and bewailed herself and her sons on the desolate condition they should be left in; and said to him, 'To whom dost thou thus leave me and my children, who are destitute of all other supports, and this when thou knowest how much ill will thy nation bears thee?' (400) But he gave her the following advice: that she need but follow what he would suggest to her in order to retain the kingdom securely, with her children: that she should conceal his death from the soldiers till she should have taken that place; (401) after this, she should go in triumph, as upon a victory, to Jerusalem, and put some of her authority into the hands of the Pharisees; for that they would commend her for the honour she had done them, and would reconcile the nation to her; for he told her they had great authority among the Jews, both to do hurt to such as they hated, and to bring advantages to those to whom they were friendly disposed; (402) for that they are then believed best of all by the multitude when they speak any severe thing against others, though it be only out of envy at them. And he said, that it was by their means that he had incurred the displeasure of the nation, whom indeed he had injured. (403) 'Do thou therefore,' said he, 'when thou art

come to Jerusalem send for the leading men among them, and show them my body, and with great appearance of sincerity give them leave to use it as they themselves please, whether they will dishonour the dead body by refusing it burial, as having severely suffered by my means, or whether in their anger they will offer any other injury to that body. Promise them also, that thou wilt do nothing without them in the affairs of the kingdom. (404) If thou dost but say this to them, I shall have the honour of a more glorious funeral from them than thou couldst have made for me: and when it is in their power to abuse my dead body, they will do it no injury at all, and thou wilt rule in safety.' So when he had given his wife this advice, he died – after he had reigned twenty-seven years, and lived fifty years, within one.

CHAPTER 16

(405) So Alexandra, when she had taken the fortress, acted as her husband had suggested to her, and spake to the Pharisees, and put all things into their power, both as to the dead body and as to the affairs of the kingdom, and thereby pacified their anger against Alexander, and made them bear good will and friendship to him; (406) who then came among the multitude, and made speeches to them, and laid before them the actions of Alexander, and told them that they had lost a righteous king; and by the commendation they gave him, they brought them to grieve, and to be in heaviness for him, so that he had a funeral more splendid than had any of the kings before him. (407) Alexander left behind him two sons, Hyrcanus and Aristobulus, but committed the kingdom to Alexandra. Now, as to these two sons, Hyrcanus was indeed unable to manage public affairs, and delighted rather in a quiet life; but the younger, Aristobulus, was an active and a bold man; and for this woman herself, Alexandra, she was loved by the multitude, because she seemed displeased at the offences her husband had been guilty of.

(408) So she made Hyrcanus high priest because he was the elder, but much more because he cared not to meddle with politics, and permitted the Pharisees to do everything; to whom also she ordered the multitude to be obedient. She also restored again those practices which the Pharisees had introduced, according to the traditions of their forefathers, and which her father-in-law, Hyrcanus, had abrogated. (409) So she had indeed the name of the regent, but the Pharisees had the authority; for it was they who restored such as had been banished, and set such as were prisoners at liberty, and to say all at once, they differed in nothing from lords. However, the queen also took care of the affairs of the kingdom, and got together a great body of mercenary soldiers, and increased her own army to such a degree, that she became terrible to the neighbouring tyrants, and took hostages of them: (410) and the country

was entirely at peace, excepting the Pharisees; for they disturbed the queen, and desired that she would kill those who persuaded Alexander to slay the eight hundred men; after which they cut the throat of one of them, Diogenes: and after him they did the same to several, one after another, (411) till the men that were the most potent came into the palace, and Aristobulus with them, for he seemed to be displeased at what was done; and it appeared openly that, if he had an opportunity, he would not permit his mother to go on so. These put the queen in mind what great dangers they had gone through, and great things they had done, whereby they had demonstrated the firmness of their fidelity to their master, insomuch that they had received the greatest marks of favour from him: (412) and they begged of her, that she would not utterly blast their hopes, as it now happened, that when they had escaped the hazards that arose from their [open] enemies, they were to be cut off at home by their [private] enemies, like brute beasts, without any help whatsoever. (413) They said also, that if their adversaries would be satisfied with those that had been slain already, they would take what had been done patiently, on account of their natural love to their governors; but if they must expect the same for the future also, they implored of her a dismission from her service; for they could not bear to think of attempting any method for their deliverance without her, but would rather die willingly before the palace gate, in case she would not forgive them. (414) And that it was a great shame, both for themselves and for the queen, that when they were neglected by her, they should come under the lash of her husband's enemies; for that Aretas, the Arabian king, and the monarchs, would give any reward if they could get such men as foreign auxiliaries, to whom their very names, before their voices be heard, may perhaps be terrible; (415) but if they could not obtain this their second request, and if she had determined to prefer the Pharisees before them, they still insisted that she would place them every one in her fortresses; for if some fatal demon hath a constant spite against Alexander's house, they would be willing to bear their part, and to live in a private station there.

(416) As these men said thus, and called upon Alexander's ghost for commiseration of those already slain, and those in danger of it, all the bystanders brake out into tears: but Aristobulus chiefly made manifest what were his sentiments, and used many reproachful expressions to his mother [saying], (417) 'Nay, indeed, the case is this, that they have been themselves the authors of their own calamities, who have permitted a woman who, against reason, was mad with ambition, to reign over them, when there were some in the flower of their age fitter for it.' So Alexandra, not knowing what to do with any decency, committed the fortresses to them, all but Hyrcania and Alexandrium, and Macherus, where her principal treasures were. (418) After a little while also, she sent her son Aristobulus with an army to Damascus

against Ptolemy, who was called Menneus, who was such a bad neighbour to the city; but he did nothing considerable there, and so returned home.

(419) About this time news was brought that Tigranes, the king of Armenia, had made an irruption into Syria with five hundred thousand soldiers, and was coming against Judea. This news, as may well be supposed, terrified the queen and the nation. Accordingly they sent him many and very valuable presents, as also ambassadors, and that as he was besieging Ptolemais; (420) for Selene the queen, the same that was also called Cleopatra, ruled then over Syria, who had persuaded the inhabitants to exclude Tigranes. So the Jewish ambassadors interceded with him, and entreated him that he would determine nothing that was severe about their queen or nation. (421) He commended them for the respects they paid him at so great a distance: and gave them good hopes of his favour. But as soon as Ptolemais was taken, news came to Tigranes that Lucullus, in his pursuit of Mithridates, could not light upon him, who was fled into Iberia, but was laying waste Armenia and besieging its cities. Now, when Tigranes knew this, he returned home.

(422) After this, when the queen was fallen into a dangerous distemper, Aristobulus resolved to attempt the seizing of the government; so he stole away secretly by night, with only one of his servants, and went to the fortresses, wherein his friends, that were such from the days of his father, were settled; (423) for as he had been a great while displeased at his mother's conduct, so he was now much more afraid, lest, upon her death, their whole family should be under the power of the Pharisees; for he saw the inability of his brother, who was to succeed in the government: (424) nor was anyone conscious of what he was doing but only his wife, whom he left at Jerusalem with their children. He first of all came to Agaba, where was Galestes, one of the potent men before mentioned, and was received by him. (425) When it was day the queen perceived that Aristobulus was fled, and for some time she supposed that his departure was not in order to make any innovation; but when messengers came one after another with the news that he had secured the first place, the second place, and all the places, for as soon as one had begun, they all submitted to his disposal, then it was that the queen and the nation were in the greatest disorder, (426) for they were aware that it would not be long ere Aristobulus would be able to settle himself firmly in the government. What they were principally afraid of was this, that he would inflict punishment upon them for the mad treatment his house had had from them: so they resolved to take his wife and children into custody, and keep them in the fortress that was over the temple. (427) Now there was a mighty conflux of people that came to Aristobulus from all parts, insomuch that he had a kind of royal attendants about him; for in a little more than fifteen days, he got twenty-two strong places, which gave him the opportunity of raising an army from Libanus and

Trachonitis, and the monarchs; for men are easily led by the greater number, and easily submit to them. And, besides this, that by affording him their assistance, when he could not expect it, they, as well as he, should have the advantages that would come by his being king, because they had been the occasion of his gaining the kingdom. (428) Now the elders of the Jews, and Hyrcanus with them, went in unto the queen, and desired that she would give them her sentiments about the present posture of affairs, for that Aristobulus was in effect lord of almost all the kingdom, by possessing of so many strongholds, and that it was absurd for them to take any counsel by themselves, how ill soever she were, whilst she was alive, and that the danger would be upon them in no long time. (429) But she bade them do what they thought proper to be done: that they had many circumstances in their favour still remaining; a nation in good heart, an army, and money in their several treasuries: for that she had small concern about public affairs now, when the strength of her body already failed her.

(430) Now a little while after she had said this to them, she died, when she had reigned nine years, and had in all lived seventy-three. A woman she was who showed no signs of the weakness of her sex, for she was sagacious to the greatest degree in her ambition of governing, and demonstrated by her doings at once that her mind was fit for action, and that sometimes men themselves show the little understanding they have by the frequent mistakes they make in point of government; (431) for she always preferred the present to futurity, and preferred the power of an imperious dominion above all things, and in comparison of that, had no regard to what was good or what was right. However, she brought the affairs of her house to such an unfortunate condition, that she was the occasion of the taking away that authority from it, and that in no long time afterward, which she had obtained by a vast number of hazards and misfortunes, and this out of a desire of what does not belong to a woman, and all by a compliance in her sentiments with those that bare ill will to their family, and by leaving the administration destitute of a proper support of great men; (432) and indeed, her management during her administration, while she was alive, was such as filled the palace after her death with calamities and disturbance. However, although this had been her way of governing, she preserved the nation in peace: and this is the conclusion of the affairs of Alexandra.

BOOK FOURTEEN

CHAPTER I

(1) We have related the affairs of Queen Alexandra, and her death, in the foregoing book, and will now speak of what followed, and was connected with those histories; declaring, before we proceed, that we have nothing so much at heart as this, that we may omit no facts either through ignorance or laziness; (2) for we are upon the history and explication of such things as the greatest part are unacquainted withal, because of their distance from our times; and we aim to do it with a proper beauty of style, so far as that is derived from proper words harmonically disposed, and from such ornaments of speech also as may contribute to the pleasure of our readers, (3) that they may entertain the knowledge of what we write with some agreeable satisfaction and pleasure. But the principal scope that authors ought to aim at, above all the rest, is to speak accurately, and to speak truly for the satisfaction of those that are otherwise unacquainted with such transactions, and obliged to believe what these writers inform them of.

(4) Hyrcanus then began his high priesthood on the third year of the hundred and seventy-seventh Olympiad, when Quintus Hortensius and Quintus Metellus, who was called Metellus of Crete, were consuls at Rome; when presently Aristobulus began to make war against him, and as it came to a battle with Hyrcanus at Jericho, many of his soldiers deserted him, and went over to his brother; (5) upon which Hyrcanus fled into the citadel, where Aristobulus's wife and children were imprisoned by his mother, as we have said already, and attacked and overcame those his adversaries that had fled thither, and lay within the walls of the temple. (6) So when he had sent a message to his brother about agreeing the matters between them, he laid aside his enmity to him on these conditions, that Aristobulus should be king, that he should live without intermeddling with public affairs, and quietly enjoy the estate he had acquired. (7) When they had agreed upon these terms in the temple, and had confirmed the agreement with oaths, and the giving one another their right hands, and embracing one another in the sight of the whole multitude, they departed – the one, Aristobulus, to the palace, and Hyrcanus, as a private man, to the former house of Aristobulus.

(8) But there was a certain friend of Hyrcanus, an Idumean, called Antipater, who was very rich, and in his nature an active and a seditious man; who was at enmity with Aristobulus, and had differences with him on account of his good

will to Hyrcanus. (9) It is true, that Nicolaus of Damascus says, that Antipater was of the stock of the principal Jews who came out of Babylon into Judea; but that assertion of his was to gratify Herod, who was his son, and who, by certain revolutions of fortune, came afterwards to be king of the Jews, whose history we shall give you in its proper place hereafter. (10) However, this Antipater was at first called Antipas, and that was his father's name also; of whom they relate this: that King Alexander and his wife made him general of all Idumea, and that he made a league of friendship with those Arabians, and Gazites, and Ascalonites, that were of his own party, and had, by many and large presents, made them his fast friends; (11) but now this young Antipater was suspicious of the power of Aristobulus, and was afraid of some mischief he might do him, because of his hatred to him; so he stirred up the most powerful of the Jews, and talked against him to them privately; and said, that it was unjust to overlook the conduct of Aristobulus, who had gotten the government unrighteously, and ejected his brother out of it, who was the elder, and ought to retain what belonged to him by prerogative of his birth; (12) and the same speeches he perpetually made to Hyrcanus, and told him that his own life would be in danger unless he guarded himself, and got quit of Aristobulus; for he said that the friends of Aristobulus omitted no opportunity of advising him to kill him, as being then, and not before, sure to retain his principality. (13) Hyrcanus gave no credit to these words of his, as being of a gentle disposition, and one that did not easily admit of calumnies against other men. This temper of his not disposing him to meddle with public affairs, and want of spirit, occasioned him to appear to spectators to be degenerate and unmanly, while Aristobulus was of a contrary temper, an active man, and one of a great and generous soul.

(14) Since therefore Antipater saw that Hyrcanus did not attend to what he said, he never ceased, day by day, to charge feigned crimes upon Aristobulus, and to calumniate him before him, as if he had a mind to kill him; and so, by urging him perpetually, he advised him and persuaded him to fly to Aretas, the king of Arabia; and promised, that if he would comply with his advice, he would also himself assist him, [and go with him]. (15) When Hyrcanus heard this, he said that it was for his advantage to fly away to Aretas. Now Arabia is a country that borders upon Judea. However, Hyrcanus sent Antipater first to the king of Arabia, in order to receive assurances from him, that when he should come in the manner of a supplicant to him, he would not deliver him up to his enemies. (16) So Antipater having received such assurances, returned to Hyrcanus to Jerusalem. A while afterward he took Hyrcanus, and stole out of the city by night, and went a great journey, and came and brought him to the city called Petra, where the palace of Aretas was; (17) and as he was a very familiar friend of that king, he persuaded him to bring back Hyrcanus into Judea; and this persuasion he continued every day without any intermission.

He also proposed to make him presents on that account. At length he prevailed with Aretas in his suit. (18) Moreover, Hyrcanus promised him, that when he had been brought thither, and had received his kingdom, he would restore that country, and those twelve cities which his father Alexander had taken from the Arabians, which were these: Medaba, Naballo, Libyas, Tharabasa, Agala, Athone, Zoar, Orone, Marissa, Rudda, Lussa, and Oruba.

CHAPTER 2

(19) After these promises had been given to Aretas he made an expedition against Aristobulus, with an army of fifty thousand horse and foot, and beat him in the battle. And when after that victory many went over to Hyrcanus as deserters, Aristobulus was left desolate, and fled to Jerusalem; (20) upon which the king of Arabia took all his army and made an assault upon the temple, and besieged Aristobulus therein, the people still supporting Hyrcanus, and assisting him in the siege, while none but the priests continued with Aristobulus. (21) So Aretas united the forces of the Arabians and of the Jews together, and pressed on the siege vigorously. As this happened at the time when the feast of unleavened bread was celebrated, which we call the Passover, the principal men among the Jews left the country, and fled into Egypt. (22) Now there was one, whose name was Onias, a righteous man he was, and beloved of God, who, in a certain drought, had prayed to God to put an end to the intense heat, and whose prayers God had heard, and had sent them rain. This man had hid himself, because he saw that this sedition would last a great while. However, they brought him to the Jewish camp, and desired, that as by his prayers he had once put an end to the drought, so he would in like manner make imprecations on Aristobulus and those of his faction. (23) And when, upon his refusal, and the excuses that he made, he was still by the multitude compelled to speak, he stood up in the midst of them, and said, (24) 'O God, the king of the whole world! since those that stand now with me are thy people, and those that are besieged are also thy priests, I beseech thee, that thou wilt neither hearken to the prayers of those against these, nor bring to effect what these pray against those.' Whereupon such wicked Jews as stood about him, as soon as he had made this prayer, stoned him to death.

(25) But God punished them immediately for this their barbarity, and took vengeance of them for the murder of Onias, in the manner following: while the priests and Aristobulus were besieged, it happened that the feast called the Passover was come, at which it is our custom to offer a great number of sacrifices to God; (26) but those that were with Aristobulus wanted sacrifices, and desired that their countrymen without would furnish them with such sacrifices, and assured them they should have as much money for them as they

should desire; and when they required them to pay a thousand drachmae for each head of cattle, Aristobulus and the priests willingly undertook to pay for them accordingly; and those within let down the money over the walls, and gave it them. (27) But when the others had received it they did not deliver the sacrifices, but arrived at the height of wickedness as to break the assurances they had given, and to be guilty of impiety towards God, by not furnishing those that wanted them with sacrifices. (28) And when the priests found they had been cheated, and that the agreements they had made were violated, they prayed to God that he would avenge them on their countrymen. Nor did he delay that their punishment, but sent a strong and vehement storm of wind, that destroyed the fruits of the whole country, till a modius of wheat was then bought for eleven drachmae.

(29) In the meantime Pompey sent Scaurus into Syria, while he was himself in Armenia, and making war with Tigranes; but when Scaurus was come to Damascus, and found that Lollius and Metellus had newly taken the city, he came himself hastily into Judea. (30) And when he was come thither ambassadors came to him, both from Aristobulus and Hyrcanus, and both desired he would assist them; and when both of them promised to give him money, Aristobulus four hundred talents, and Hyrcanus no less, he accepted of Aristobulus' promise, (31) for he was rich, and had a great soul, and desired to obtain nothing but what was moderate; whereas the other was poor and tenacious, and made incredible promises in hope of greater advantages; for it was not the same thing to take a city that was exceeding strong and powerful, as it was to eject out of the country some fugitives, with a greater number of Nabateans, who were no very warlike people. (32) He therefore made an agreement with Aristobulus for the reason before mentioned, and took his money, and raised the siege, and ordered Aretas to depart, or else he should be declared an enemy to the Romans. (33) So Scaurus returned to Damascus again; and Aristobulus, with a great army, made war with Aretas and Hyrcanus, and fought them at a place called Papyron, and beat them in the battle, and slew about six thousand of the enemy, with whom fell Phalion also, the brother of Antipater.

CHAPTER 3

(34) A little afterward Pompey came to Damascus, and marched over Celesyria; at which time there came ambassadors to him from all Syria, and Egypt, and out of Judea also, for Aristobulus had sent him a great present, which was a golden vine, of the value of five hundred talents. (35) Now Strabo of Cappadocia mentions this present in these words: 'There came also an embassage out of Egypt, and a crown of the value of four thousand pieces of gold; and out of

Judea there came another, whether you call it a *vine* or a *garden;* they call the thing Terpole, *the Delight*. (36) However, we ourselves saw that present reposited at Rome, in the temple of Jupiter Capitolinus with this inscription: "The Gift of Alexander, the King of the Jews". It was valued at five hundred talents; and the report is, that Aristobulus, the governor of the Jews, sent it.'

(37) In a little time afterward came ambassadors again to him: Antipater from Hyrcanus, and Nicodemus from Aristobulus; which last also accused such as had taken bribes; first Gabinius, and then Scaurus – the one three hundred talents, and the other four hundred; by which procedure he made these two his enemies, besides those he had before; (38) and when Pompey had ordered those that had controversies one with another to come to him in the beginning of the spring, he brought his army out of their winter quarters, and marched into the country of Damascus; and as he went along he demolished the citadel that was at Apamea, which Antiochus Cyzicenus had built, (39) and took cognisance of the country of Ptolemy Menneus, a wicked man, and not less so than Dionysius of Tripoli, who had been beheaded, who was also his relation by marriage: yet did he buy off the punishment of his crimes for a thousand talents, with which money Pompey paid the soldiers their wages. (40) He also conquered the place called Lysias, of which Silas a Jew was tyrant; and when he had passed over the cities of Heliopolis and Chalcis, and got over the mountain which is on the limit of Celesyria, he came from Pella to Damascus; (41) and there it was that he heard the causes of the Jews, and of their governors Hyrcanus and Aristobulus, who were at difference one with another, as also of the nation against them both, which did not desire to be under kingly government, because the form of government they received from their forefathers was that of subjection to the priests of that God whom they worshipped; and [they complained] that though these two were the posterity of priests, yet did they seek to change the government of their nation to another form, in order to enslave them. (42) Hyrcanus complained, that although he were the elder brother, he was deprived of the prerogative of his birth by Aristobulus, and that he had but a small part of the country under him, Aristobulus having taken away the rest from him by force. (43) He also accused him, that the incursions which had been made into their neighbours' countries, and the piracies that had been at sea, were owing to him; and that the nation would not have revolted, unless Aristobulus had been a man given to violence and disorder; and there were no fewer than a thousand Jews, of the best esteem among them, who confirmed this accusation; which confirmation was procured by Antipater; (44) but Aristobulus alleged against him, that it was Hyrcanus's own temper, which was inactive, and on that account contemptible, which caused him to be deprived of the government; and that for himself he was necessitated to take it upon him, for fear lest it should be transferred to others; and that as to his title [of king], it was no other than

what his father had taken [before him]. (45) He also called for witnesses of what he said, some persons who were both young and insolent; whose purple garments, fine heads of hair, and other ornaments, were detested [by the court], and which they appeared in, not as though they were to plead their cause in a court of justice, but as if they were marching in a pompous procession.

(46) When Pompey had heard the causes of these two, and had condemned Aristobulus for his violent procedure, he then spake civilly to them, and sent them away; and told them, that when he came again into their country he would settle all their affairs, after he had first taken a view of the affairs of the Nabateans. In the meantime, he ordered them to be quiet, and treated Aristobulus civilly, lest he should make the nation revolt, and hinder his return; (47) which yet Aristobulus did, for without expecting any further determination, which Pompey had promised them, he went to the city Delius, and thence marched into Judea.

(48) At this behaviour Pompey was angry and taking with him that army which he was leading against the Nabateans, and the auxiliaries that came from Damascus, and the other parts of Syria, with the other Roman legions which he had with him, he made an expedition against Aristobulus; (49) but as he passed by Pella and Scythopolis, he came to Coreae, which is the first entrance into Judea when one passes over the midland countries, where he came to a most beautiful fortress that was built on the top of a mountain called Alexandrium, whither Aristobulus had fled; and thence Pompey sent his commands to him, that he should come to him. (50) Accordingly, at the persuasions of many that he would not make war with the Romans, he came down; and when he had disputed with his brother about the right to the government, he went up again to the citadel, as Pompey gave him leave to do; (51) and this he did two or three times, as flattering himself with the hopes of having the kingdom granted him; so that he still pretended he would obey Pompey in whatsoever he commanded, although at the same time he retired to his fortress, that he might not depress himself too low, and that he might be prepared for a war, in case it should prove as he feared, that Pompey would transfer the government to Hyrcanus; (52) but when Pompey enjoined Aristobulus to deliver up the fortresses he held, and to send an injunction to their governors under his own hand for that purpose, for they had been forbidden to deliver them up upon any other commands, he submitted indeed to do so; but still he retired in displeasure to Jerusalem, and made preparation for war. (53) A little after this, certain persons came out of Pontus, and informed Pompey, as he was on the way, and conducting his army against Aristobulus, that Mithridates was dead, and was slain by his son Pharnaces.

CHAPTER 4

(54) Now when Pompey had pitched his camp at Jericho (where the palm tree grows, and that balsam which is an ointment of all the most precious, which, upon any incision made in the wood with a sharp stone, distils out thence like a juice), he marched in the morning to Jerusalem. (55) Hereupon Aristobulus repented of what he was doing, and came to Pompey, and [promised to] give him money, and received him into Jerusalem, and desired that he would leave off the war, and do what he pleased peaceably. So Pompey, upon his entreaty, forgave him, and sent Gabinius, and soldiers with him, to receive the money and the city: (56) yet was no part of this performed; but Gabinius came back, being both excluded out of the city, and receiving none of the money promised, because Aristobulus' soldiers would not permit the agreements to be executed. (57) At this Pompey was very angry, and put Aristobulus into the prison, and came himself to the city, which was strong on every side, excepting the north, which was not so well fortified, for there was a broad and deep ditch, that encompassed the city, and included within it the temple, which was itself encompassed about with a very strong stone wall.

(58) Now there was a sedition of the men that were within the city, who did not agree what was to be done in their present circumstances, while some thought it best to deliver up the city to Pompey; but Aristobulus' party exhorted them to shut the gates, because he was kept in prison. Now these prevented the others, and seized upon the temple, and cut off the bridge which reached from it to the city, and prepared themselves to abide a siege; (59) but the others admitted Pompey's army in, and delivered up both the city and the king's palace to him. So Pompey sent his lieutenant Piso with an army, and placed garrisons both in the city and in the palace, to secure them, and fortified the houses that joined to the temple, and all those which were more distant and without it. (60) And in the first place, he offered terms of accommodation to those that were within; but when they would not comply with what was desired, he encompassed all the places thereabout with a wall, wherein Hyrcanus did gladly assist him on all occasions; but Pompey pitched his camp within [the wall], on the north part of the temple, where it was most practicable; (61) but even on that side there were great towers, and a ditch had been dug, and a deep valley begirt it round about, for on the parts towards the city were precipices, and the bridge on which Pompey had gotten in was broken down. However, a bank was raised day by day, with a great deal of labour, while the Romans cut down materials for it from the places round about; (62) and when this bank was sufficiently raised, and the ditch filled up, though but poorly, by reason of its immense depth, he brought his mechanical

engines, and battering-rams from Tyre, and placing them on the bank, he battered the temple with the stones that were thrown against it; (63) and had it not been our practice, from the days of our forefathers, to rest on the seventh day, this bank could never have been perfected, by reason of the opposition the Jews would have made; for though our law gives us leave then to defend ourselves against those that begin to fight with us and assault us, yet does it not permit us to meddle with our enemies while they do anything else.

(64) Which thing when the Romans understood, on those days which we call Sabbaths, they threw nothing at the Jews, nor came to any pitched battle with them, but raised up their earthen banks, and brought their engines into such forwardness, that they might do execution the next days; (65) and anyone may hence learn how very great piety we exercise towards God, and the observance of his laws, since the priests were not at all hindered from their sacred ministrations, by their fear during this siege, but did still twice each day, in the morning and about the ninth hour, offer their sacrifices on the altar; nor did they omit those sacrifices, if any melancholy accident happened, by the stones that were thrown among them; (66) for although the city was taken on the third month, on the day of the fast, upon the hundred and seventy-ninth Olympiad, when Caius Antonius and Marcus Tullius Cicero were consuls, and the enemy then fell upon them, and cut the throats of those that were in the temple, (67) yet could not those that offered the sacrifices be compelled to run away, neither by the fear they were in of their own lives, nor by the number that were already slain, as thinking it better to suffer whatever came upon them, at their very altars, than to omit anything that their laws required of them; (68) and that this is not a mere brag, or an encomium to manifest a degree of our piety that was false, but is the real truth, I appeal to those that have written of the acts of Pompey; and among them, to Strabo and Nicolaus [of Damascus]; and besides these, to Titus Livius, the writer of the *Roman History*, who will bear witness to this thing.

(69) But when the battering-engine was brought near, the greatest of the towers was shaken by it, and fell down, and broke down a part of the fortifications, so the enemy poured in apace; and Cornelius Faustus, the son of Sylla, with his soldiers, first of all ascended the wall, and next to him Furius the centurion, with those that followed, on the other part; while Fabius, who was also a centurion, ascended it in the middle, with a great body of men after him; but now all was full of slaughter, (70) some of the Jews being slain by the Romans, and some by one another; nay, some there were who threw themselves down the precipices, or put fire to their houses, and burnt them, as not able to bear the miseries they were under. (71) Of the Jews there fell twelve thousand, but of the Romans very few. Absalom, who was at once both uncle and father-in-law to Aristobulus, was taken captive; and no small enormities were

committed about the temple itself, which, in former ages, had been inaccessible, and seen by none; (72) for Pompey went into it, and not a few of those that were with him also, and saw all that which it was unlawful for any other men to see, but only for the high priests. There were in that temple the golden table, the holy candlestick, and the pouring vessels, and a great quantity of spices; and besides these there were among the treasures two thousand talents of sacred money; yet did Pompey touch nothing of all this, on account of his regard to religion; and in this point also he acted in a manner that was worthy of his virtue:(73) the next day he gave order to those that had the charge of the temple to cleanse it, and to bring what offerings the law required to God; and restored the high priesthood to Hyrcanus, both because he had been useful to him in other respects, and because he hindered the Jews in the country from giving Aristobulus any assistance in his war against him. He also cut off those that had been the authors of that war, and bestowed proper rewards on Faustus and those others that mounted the wall with such alacrity; (74) and he made Jerusalem tributary to the Romans, and took away those cities of Celesyria which the inhabitants of Judea had subdued, and put them under the government of the Roman president, and confined the whole nation, which had elevated itself so high before, within its own bounds. (75) Moreover, he rebuilt Gadara, which had been demolished a little before, to gratify Demetrius of Gadara, who was his freedman, and restored the rest of the cities, Hippos and Scythopolis, and Pella, and Dios, and Samaria, as also Marissa, and Ashdod, and Jamnia, and Arethusa, to their own inhabitants; (76) these were in the inland parts., besides those that had been demolished, and also of the maritime cities, Gaza, and Joppa, and Dora, and Strato's Tower: which last Herod rebuilt after a glorious manner, and adorned with havens and temples, and changed its name to Caesarea. All these Pompey left in a state of freedom, and joined them to the province of Syria.

(77) Now the occasions of this misery which came upon Jerusalem were Hyrcanus and Aristobulus, by raising a sedition one against the other; for now we lost our liberty, and became subject to the Romans, and were deprived of that country which we had gained by our arms from the Syrians, and were compelled to restore it to the Syrians. (78) Moreover, the Romans exacted of us, in a little time, above ten thousand talents; and the royal authority, which was a dignity formerly bestowed on those that were high priests, by the right of their family, became the property of private men; but of these matters we shall treat in their proper places. (79) Now Pompey committed Celesyria, as far as the river Euphrates and Egypt, to Scaurus, with two Roman legions, and then went away to Cilicia, and made haste to Rome. He also carried bound along with him Aristobulus and his children; for he had two daughters, and as many sons; the one of whom ran away, but the younger, Antigonus, was carried to Rome, together with his sisters.

CHAPTER 5

(80) Scaurus made now an expedition against Petrea, in Arabia, and set on fire all the places round about it, because of the great difficulty of access to it; and as his army was pinched by famine, Antipater furnished him with corn out of Judea, and with whatever else he wanted, and this at the command of Hyrcanus; (81) and when he was sent to Aretas as an ambassador, by Scaurus, because he had lived with him formerly, he persuaded Aretas to give Scaurus a sum of money, to prevent the burning of his country; and undertook to be his surety for three hundred talents. So Scaurus, upon these terms, ceased to make war any longer; which was done as much at Scaurus's desire as at the desire of Aretas.

(82) Some time after this, when Alexander, the son of Aristobulus, made an incursion into Judea, Gabinius came from Rome to Syria, as commander of the Roman forces. He did many considerable actions; and particularly made war with Alexander, since Hyrcanus was not yet able to oppose his power, but was already attempting to rebuild the wall of Jerusalem, which Pompey had overthrown, (83) although the Romans who were there restrained him from that his design. However, Alexander went over all the country round about and armed many of the Jews, and suddenly got together ten thousand armed footmen and fifteen hundred horsemen, and fortified Alexandrium, a fortress near to Coreae, and Macherus, near the mountains of Arabia. (84) Gabinius therefore came upon him, having sent Marcus Antonius, with other commanders, before. These armed such Romans as followed them, and together with them, such Jews as were subject to them, whose leaders were Pitholaus and Malichus; and they took with them also their friends that were with Antipater, and met Alexander, while Gabinius himself followed with his legion. (85) Hereupon Alexander retired to the neighbourhood of Jerusalem, where they fell upon one another, and it came to a pitched battle; in which the Romans slew of their enemies about three thousand, and took a like number alive.

(86) At which time Gabinius came to Alexandrium, and invited those that were in it to deliver it up on certain conditions, and promised that then their former offences should be forgiven: but as a great number of the enemy had pitched their camp before the fortress, whom the Romans attacked, Marcus Antonius fought bravely, and slew a great number and seemed to come off with the greatest honour. (87) So Gabinius left part of his army there, in order to take the place, and he himself sent into other parts of Judea, and gave order to rebuild all the cities that he met with that had been demolished; (88) at which time were rebuilt Samaria, Ashdod, Scythopolis, Anthedon, Raphia, and Dora; Marissa also, and Gaza, and not a few others besides; and as the men

acted according to Gabinius's command, it came to pass, that at this time these cities were securely inhabited, which had been desolate for a long time.

(89) When Gabinius had done thus in the country he returned to Alexandrium; and when he urged on the siege of the place, Alexander sent an embassage to him, desiring that he would pardon his former offences; he also delivered up the fortresses, Hyrcania and Macherus, and at the last Alexandrium itself, (90) which fortresses Gabinius demolished; but when Alexander's mother, who was on the side of the Romans, as having her husband and other children at Rome, came to him, he granted her whatsoever she asked; (91) and when he had settled matters with her, he brought Hyrcanus to Jerusalem, and committed the care of the temple to him; and when he had ordained five councils, he distributed the nation into the same number of parts: so these councils governed the people; the first was at Jerusalem, the second at Gadara, the third at Amathus, the fourth at Jericho, and the fifth at Sepphoris, in Galilee. So the Jews were now freed from monarchic authority, and were governed by an aristocracy.

CHAPTER 6

(92) Now Aristobulus ran away from Rome to Judea, and set about the rebuilding of Alexandrium, which had been newly demolished: hereupon Gabinius sent soldiers against him, and for their commanders Sisenna and Antonius and Servilius, in order to hinder him from getting possession of the country, and to take him again; (93) and indeed many of the Jews ran to Aristobulus on account of his former glory, as also because they should be glad of an innovation. Now, there was one Pitholaus, a lieutenant at Jerusalem, who deserted to him with a thousand men, although a great number of those that came to him were unarmed; (94) and when Aristobulus had resolved to go to Macherus, he dismissed those people, because they were unarmed; for they could not be useful to him in what actions he was going about; but he took with him eight thousand that were armed, and marched on; (95) and as the Romans fell upon them severely, the Jews fought valiantly, but were beaten in the battle; and when they had fought with alacrity, but were overborne by the enemy, they were put to flight; of whom were slain about five thousand, and the rest being dispersed, tried, as well as they were able, to save themselves. (96) However, Aristobulus had with him still above a thousand, and with them he fled to Macherus, and fortified the place; and though he had had ill success, he still had good hope of his affairs; but when he had struggled against the siege for two days' time, and had received many wounds, he was brought as a captive to Gabinius, with his son Antigonus, who also fled with him from Rome; (97) and this was the fortune of Aristobulus, who was sent back again to Rome, and

was there retained in bonds, having been both king and high priest for three years and six months; and was indeed an eminent person, and one of a great soul. However, the senate let his children go, upon Gabinius' writing to them that he had promised their mother so much when she delivered up the fortresses to him; and accordingly they then returned into Judea.

(98) Now when Gabinius was making an expedition against the Parthians, and had already passed over Euphrates, he changed his mind, and resolved to return into Egypt, in order to restore Ptolemy to his kingdom. This hath also been related elsewhere. (99) However, Antipater supplied his army, which he sent against Archelaus, with corn and weapons and money. He also made those Jews who were above Pelusium his friends and confederates, and had been the guardians of the passes that led into Egypt. (100) But when he came back out of Egypt, he found Syria in disorder with seditions and troubles; for Alexander, the son of Aristobulus, having seized on the government a second time by force, made many of the Jews revolt to him; and so he marched over the country with a great army, and slew all the Romans he could light upon, and proceeded to besiege the mountain called Gerizzim, whither they had retreated.

(101) But when Gabinius found Syria in such a state, he sent Antipater, who was a prudent man, to those that were seditious, to try whether he could cure them of their madness, and persuade them to return to a better mind; (102) and when he came to them, he brought many of them to a sound mind, and induced them to do what they ought to do. But he could not restrain Alexander, for he had an army of thirty thousand Jews, and met Gabinius, and, joining battle with him, was beaten, and lost ten thousand of his men about Mount Tabor.

(103) So Gabinius settled the affairs which belonged to the city Jerusalem, as was agreeable to Antipater's inclination, and went against the Nabateans, and overcame them in battle. He also sent away in a friendly manner, Mithridates and Orsanes, who were Parthian deserters, and came to him, though the report went abroad that they had run away from him. (104) And when Gabinius had performed great and glorious actions in his management of the affairs of war, he returned to Rome, and delivered the government to Crassus. Now, Nicolaus of Damascus, and Strabo of Cappadocia, both describe the expeditions of Pompey and Gabinius against the Jews, while neither of them say anything new which is not in the other.

CHAPTER 7

(105) Now Crassus, as he was going upon his expedition against the Parthians, came into Judea, and carried off the money that was in the temple, which Pompey had left, being two thousand talents, and was disposed to spoil it of all the gold belonging to it, which was eight thousand talents. (106) He also took

a beam, which was made of solid beaten gold, of the weight of three hundred minae, each of which weighed two pounds and a half. It was the priest who was guardian of the sacred treasures, and whose name was Eleazar, that gave him this beam, not out of a wicked design, (107) for he was a good and a righteous man; but being entrusted with the custody of the veils belonging to the temple, which were of admirable beauty, and of very costly workmanship, and hung down from this beam, when he saw that Crassus was busy in gathering money, and was in fear for the entire ornaments of the temple, he gave him this beam of gold as a ransom for the whole, (108) but this not till he had given his oath that he would remove nothing else out of the temple, but be satisfied with this only, which he should give him, being worth many ten thousand [shekels]. Now, this beam was contained in a wooden beam that was hollow, but was known to no others; but Eleazar alone knew it; (109) yet did Crassus take away this beam, upon the condition of touching nothing else that belonged to the temple – and then brake his oath, and carried away all the gold that was in the temple.

(110) And let no one wonder that there was so much wealth in our temple, since all the Jews throughout the habitable earth, and those that worshipped God, nay, even those of Asia and Europe, sent their contributions to it, and this from very ancient times. (111) Nor is the largeness of these sums without its attestation; nor is that greatness owing to our vanity, as raising it without ground to so great a height: but there are many witnesses to it, and particularly Strabo of Cappadocia, who says thus: (112) 'Mithridates sent to Cos, and took the money which Queen Cleopatra had deposited there; as also eight hundred talents belonging to the Jews.' (113) Now we have no public money but only what appertains to God; and it is evident that the Asian Jews removed this money, out of fear of Mithridates; for it is not probable that those of Judea, who had a strong city and temple, should send their money to Cos; nor is it likely that the Jews who are inhabitants of Alexandria, should do so neither, since they were in no fear of Mithridates. (114) And Strabo himself bears witness to the same thing in another place; that at the same time that Sylla passed over into Greece, in order to fight against Mithridates, he sent Lucullus to put an end to a sedition that our nation, of whom the habitable earth is full, had raised in Cyrene; where he speaks thus: (115) 'There were four classes of men among those of Cyrene; that of citizens, that of husbandmen, the third of strangers, and the fourth of Jews. Now these Jews are already gotten into all cities; and it is hard to find a place in the habitable earth that hath not admitted this tribe of men, and is not possessed by them: (116) and it hath come to pass that Egypt and Cyrene, as having the same governors, and great number of other nations, imitate their way of living and maintain great bodies of these Jews in a peculiar manner, and grow up to greater prosperity with them, and

make use of the same laws with that nation also. (117) Accordingly, the Jews have places assigned them in Egypt, wherein they inhabit, besides what is peculiarly allotted to this nation at Alexandria, which is a large part of that city. There is also an ethnarch allowed them, who governs the nation, and distributes justice to them, and takes care of their contracts, and of the laws to them belonging, as if he were the ruler of a free republic. (118) In Egypt, therefore, this nation is powerful, because the Jews were originally Egyptians, and because the land wherein they inhabit, since they went thence, is near to Egypt. They also removed into Cyrene, because that this land adjoined to the government of Egypt, as well as does Judea, or rather was formerly under the same government.' And this is what Strabo says.

(119) So when Crassus had settled all things as he himself pleased, he marched into Parthia, where both he himself and all his army perished, as hath been related elsewhere. But Cassius, as he fled from Rome to Syria, took possession of it, and was an impediment to the Parthians, who, by reason of their victory over Crassus, made incursions upon it: (120) and as he came back to Tyre, he went up into Judea also, and fell upon Taricheae, and presently took it, and carried about thirty thousand Jews captives; and slew Pitholaus, who succeeded Aristobulus in his seditious practices, and that by the persuasion of Antipater, (121) who proved to have great interest in him, and was at that time in great repute with the Idumeans also: out of which nation he married a wife, who was the daughter of one of their eminent men, and her name was Cypros, by whom he had four sons, Phasael and Herod, who was afterwards made king, and Joseph and Pheroras; and a daughter, named Salome. (122) This Antipater cultivated also a friendship and mutual kindness with other potentates, but especially with the king of Arabia, to whom he committed his children while he fought against Aristobulus. So Cassius removed his camp, and marched to Euphrates, to meet those that were coming to attack him, as hath been related by others.

(123) But sometime afterwards Caesar, when he had taken Rome, and after Pompey and the senate were fled beyond the Ionian Sea, freed Aristobulus from his bonds, and resolved to send him into Syria, and delivered two legions to him, that he might set matters right, as being a potent man in that country: (124) but Aristobulus had no enjoyment of what he hoped for from the power that was given him by Caesar; for those of Pompey's party prevented it, and destroyed him by poison; and those of Caesar's party buried him. His dead body also lay, for a good while, embalmed in honey, till Antony afterwards sent it to Judea, and caused him to be buried in the royal sepulchre. (125) But Scipio, upon Pompey's sending to him to slay Alexander, the son of Aristobulus, because the young man was accused of what offences he had been guilty of at first against the Romans, cut off his head; and thus did he die at Antioch. (126)

But Ptolemy, the son of Menneus, who was the ruler of Chalcis, under Mount Libanus, took his brethren to him, and sent his son Philippion to Askelon to Aristobulus' wife, and desired her to send back with him her son Antigonus and her daughters: the one of whom, whose name was Alexandra, Philippion fell in love with, and married her; though afterwards his father Ptolemy slew him, and married Alexandra, and continued to take care of her brethren.

CHAPTER 8

(127) Now after Pompey was dead, and after that victory Caesar had gained over him, Antipater, who managed the Jewish affairs, became very useful to Caesar when he made war against Egypt, and that by the order of Hyrcanus; (128) for when Mithridates of Pergamus was bringing his auxiliaries, and was not able to continue his march through Pelusium, but obliged to stay at Askelon, Antipater came to him, conducting three thousand of the Jews, armed men: he had also taken care the principal men of the Arabians should come to his assistance; (129) and on his account it was that all the Syrians assisted him also, as not willing to appear behindhand in their alacrity for Caesar, viz. Jamblicus the ruler, and Ptolemy his son, and Tholomy the son of Sohemus, who dwelt at Mount Libanus, and almost all the cities. (130) So Mithridates marched out of Syria, and came to Pelusium; and when its inhabitants would not admit him, he besieged the city. Now Antipater signalised himself here, and was the first who plucked down a part of the wall, and so opened a way to the rest, whereby they might enter the city, and by this means Pelusium was taken. (131) But it happened that the Egyptian Jews, who dwelt in the country called Onion, would not let Antipater and Mithridates, with their soldiers, pass to Caesar; but Antipater persuaded them to come over to their party because he was of the same people with them, and that chiefly by showing them the epistles of Hyrcanus the high priest, wherein he exhorted them to cultivate friendship with Caesar, and to supply his army with money, and all sorts of provisions which they wanted; (132) and accordingly, when they saw Antipater and the high priest of the same sentiments, they did as they were desired. And when the Jews about Memphis heard that these Jews were come over to Caesar, they also invited Mithridates to come to them; so he came and received them also into his army.

(133) And when Mithridates had gone over all Delta, as the place is called, he came to a pitched battle with the enemy, near the place called the Jewish Camp. Now Mithridates had the right wing, and Antipater the left, (134) and when it came to a fight, that wing where Mithridates was gave way, and was likely to suffer extremely, unless Antipater had come running to him with his own soldiers along the shore, when he had already beaten the enemy that

opposed him; so he delivered Mithridates and put those Egyptians who had been too hard for him to flight. (135) He also took their camp, and continued in the pursuit of them. He also recalled Mithridates, who had been worsted, and was retired a great way off, of whose soldiers eight hundred fell; but of Antipater's fifty. (136) So Mithridates sent an account of this battle to Caesar, and openly declared that Antipater was the author of this victory, and of his own preservation; insomuch that Caesar commended Antipater then, and made use of him all the rest of that war in the most hazardous undertakings; he happened also to be wounded in one of those engagements.

(137) However, when Caesar, after some time, had finished that war, and was sailed away for Syria, he honoured Antipater greatly, and confirmed Hyrcanus in the high priesthood; and bestowed on Antipater the privilege of a citizen of Rome, and a freedom from taxes everywhere; (138) and it is reported by many, that Hyrcanus went along with Antipater in this expedition, and came himself into Egypt. And Strabo of Cappadocia bears witness to this, when he says thus, in the name of Asinius: 'After Mithridates had invaded Egypt, and with him Hyrcanus the high priest of the Jews'. (139) Nay, the same Strabo says thus again, in another place, in the name of Hypsicrates, that 'Mithridates at first went out alone, but that Antipater, who had the care of the Jewish affairs, was called by him to Askelon, and that he had gotten ready three thousand soldiers to go along with him, and encouraged other governors of the country to go along with him also; and that Hyrcanus the high priest was also present in this expedition.' This is what Strabo says.

(140) But Antigonus the son of Aristobulus came at this time to Caesar, and lamented his father's fate; and complained, that it was by Antipater's means that Aristobulus was taken off by poison, and his brother was beheaded by Scipio, and desired that he would take pity of him who had been ejected out of that principality which was due to him. He also accused Hyrcanus and Antipater as governing the nation by violence, and offering injuries to himself. (141) Antipater was present, and made his defence as to the accusations that were laid against him. He demonstrated that Antigonus and his party were given to innovation, and were seditious persons. He also put Caesar in mind what difficult services he had undergone when he assisted him in his wars, and discoursed about what he was a witness of himself. (142) He added, that Aristobulus was justly carried away to Rome, as one that was an enemy to the Romans, and could never be brought to be a friend to them, and that his brother had no more than he deserved from Scipio, as being seized in committing robberies, and that this punishment was not inflicted on him in a way of violence or injustice by him that did it.

(143) When Antipater had made this speech, Caesar appointed Hyrcanus to be high priest, and gave Antipater what principality he himself should choose,

leaving the determination to himself; so he made him procurator of Judea. (144)
He also gave Hyrcanus leave to raise up the walls of his own city, upon his
asking that favour of him, for they had been demolished by Pompey. And this
grant he sent to the consuls to Rome, to be engraven in the capitol. The decree
of the senate was this that follows: (145) 'Lucius Valerius, the son of Lucius the
praetor, referred this to the senate, upon the Ides of December, in the temple of
Concord. There were present at the writing of this decree Lucius Coponius,
the son of Lucius of the Colline tribe, and Papirius of the Quirine tribe, (146)
concerning the affairs which Alexander the son of Jason, and Numenius the son
of Antiochus, and Alexander the son of Dositheus, ambassadors of the Jews,
good and worthy men, proposed, who came to renew that league of good will
and friendship with the Romans which was in being before. (147) They also
brought a shield of gold, as a mark of confederacy, valued at fifty thousand
pieces of gold; and desired that letters might be given them, directed both to the
free cities and to the kings, that their country and their havens might be at
peace, and that no one among them might receive any injury. (148) It therefore
pleased [the senate] to make a league of friendship and good will with them, and
to bestow on them whatsoever they stood in need of, and to accept of the shield
which was brought by them. This was done in the ninth year of Hyrcanus the
high priest and ethnarch, in the month Panemus.' (149) Hyrcanus also received
honours from the people of Athens, as having been useful to them on many
occasions; and when they wrote to him, they sent him this decree, as it
here follows: 'Under the prytaneia and priesthood of Dionysius, the son of
Esculapius, on the fifth day of the latter part of the month Panemus, this decree
of the Athenians was given to their commanders, (150) when Agathocles was
archon, and Eucles the son of Menander of Alimusia, was the scribe. In the
month Munychion, on the eleventh day of the prytaneia, a council of the
presidents was held in the theatre. Dorotheus the high priest, and the fellow-
presidents with him, put it to the vote of the people. Dionysius, the son of
Dionysius, gave the sentence. (151) Since Hyrcanus, the son of Alexander, the
high priest and ethnarch of the Jews, continues to bear good will to our people
in general, and to every one of our citizens in particular, and treats them with all
sorts of kindness; and when any of the Athenians come to him, either as
ambassadors or on any occasion of their own, he receives them in an obliging
manner, and sees that they are conducted back in safety, (152) of which we
have had several former testimonies; it is now also decreed, at the report of
Theodosius the son of Theodorus, and upon his putting the people in mind of
the virtue of this man, and that his purpose is to do us all the good that is in his
power, (153) to honour him with a crown of gold, the usual reward according
to the law, and to erect his statue in brass in the temple of Demus and of the
Graces; and that this present of a crown shall be proclaimed publicly in the

theatre, in the Dionysian shows, while the new tragedies are acting; and in the Panathenean, and Eleusinian, and Gymnical shows also; (154) and that the commanders shall take care, while he continues in his friendship and preserves his good will to us, to return all possible honour and favour to the man for his affection and generosity; that by this treatment it may appear how our people receive the good kindly, and repay them a suitable reward; and he may be induced to proceed in his affection towards us, by the honours we have already paid him. (155) That ambassadors be also chosen out of all the Athenians, who shall carry this decree to him, and desire him to accept of the honours we do him, and to endeavour always to be doing some good to our city.' And this shall suffice us to have spoken as to the honours that were paid by the Romans and the people of Athens to Hyrcanus.

CHAPTER 9

(156) Now when Caesar had settled the affairs of Syria, he sailed away; and as soon as Antipater had conducted Caesar out of Syria, he returned to Judea. He then immediately raised up the wall which had been thrown down by Pompey; and by coming thither, he pacified that tumult which had been in the country, and this by both threatening and advising them to be quiet; (157) for that, if they would be of Hyrcanus' side, they would live happily, and lead their lives without disturbance, in the enjoyment of their own possessions; but if they were addicted to the hopes of what might come by innovation, and aimed to get wealth thereby, they should have him a severe master, instead of a gentle governor, and Hyrcanus a tyrant instead of a king, and the Romans, together with Caesar, their bitter enemies, instead of rulers, for that they would never bear him to be set aside whom they had appointed to govern. And when Antipater had said this to them, he himself settled the affairs of this country.

(158) And seeing that Hyrcanus was of a slow and slothful temper, he made Phasaelus, his eldest son, governor of Jerusalem, and of the places that were about it, but committed Galilee to Herod, his next son, who was then a very young man, for he was but fifteen years of age; (159) but that youth of his was no impediment to him, but as he was a youth of great mind, he presently met with an opportunity of signalising his courage; for, finding that there was one Hezekias, a captain of a band of robbers, who overran the neighbouring parts of Syria with a great troop of them, he seized him and slew him, as well as a great number of the other robbers that were with him; (160) for which action he was greatly beloved by the Syrians, for when they were very desirous to have their country freed from this nest of robbers, he purged it of them; so they sung songs in his commendation in their villages and cities, as having procured them peace and the secure enjoyment of their possessions; and on this account

it was that he became known to Sextus Caesar, who was a relation of the great Caesar, and was now president of Syria. (161) Now Phasaelus, Herod's brother, was moved with emulation at his actions, and envied the fame he had thereby gotten, and became ambitious not to be behindhand with him in deserving it: so he made the inhabitants of Jerusalem bear him the greatest good will while he held the city himself, but did neither manage its affairs improperly, nor abuse his authority therein. (162) This conduct procured from the nation to Antipater such respect as is due to kings, and such honours as he might partake of if he were an absolute lord of the country. Yet did not this splendour of his, as frequently happens, in the least diminish in him that kindness and fidelity which he owed to Hyrcanus.

(163) But now the principal men among the Jews, when they saw Antipater and his sons to grow so much in the good will the nation bare to them, and in the revenues which they received out of Judea, and out of Hyrcanus' own wealth, they became ill-disposed to him; (164) for indeed Antipater had contracted a friendship with the Roman emperors, and when he had prevailed with Hyrcanus to send them money, he took it to himself, and purloined the present intended, and sent it as if it were his own, and not Hyrcanus' gift to them. (165) Hyrcanus heard of this his management, but took no care about it, nay he rather was very glad of it; but the chief men of the Jews were therefore in fear, because they saw that Herod was a violent and bold man, and very desirous of acting tyrannically; so they came to Hyrcanus, and now accused Antipater openly, and said to him, 'How long wilt thou be quiet under such actions as are now done? Or dost thou not see that Antipater and his sons have already seized upon the government, and that it is only the name of a king which is given thee? (166) But do not thou suffer these things to be hidden from thee; nor do thou think to escape danger by being so careless of thyself and of thy kingdom, for Antipater and his sons are not now stewards of thine affairs; do not thou deceive thyself with such a notion; they are evidently absolute lords, (167) for Herod, Antipater's son, hath slain Hezekiah and those that were with him, and hath thereby transgressed our law, which hath forbidden to slay any man, even though he were a wicked man, unless he had been first condemned to suffer death by the sanhedrin; yet hath he been so insolent as to do this, and that without any authority from thee.'

(168) Upon Hyrcanus hearing this he complied with them. The mothers also of those that had been slain by Herod raised his indignation; for those women continued every day in the temple, persuading the king and the people that Herod might undergo a trial before the sanhedrin for what he had done. (169) Hyrcanus was so moved by these complaints, that he summoned Herod to come to his trial for what was charged upon him. Accordingly he came, but his father had persuaded him to come not like a private man, but with a guard,

for the security of his person; and that when he had settled the affairs of Galilee
in the best manner he could for his own advantage, he should come to his trial,
but still with a body of men sufficient for his security on his journey, yet so that
he should not come with so great a force as might look like terrifying
Hyrcanus, but still such a one as might not expose him naked and unguarded
[to his enemies]. (170) However, Sextus Caesar, president of Syria, wrote to
Hyrcanus, and desired him to clear Herod, and dismiss him at his trial, and
threatened him beforehand if he did not do it. Which epistle of his was the
occasion of Hyrcanus delivering Herod from suffering any harm from the
sanhedrin, for he loved him as his own son; (171) but when Herod stood
before the sanhedrin, with his body of men about him, he affrighted them all,
and no one of his former accusers durst after that bring any charge against him,
but there was a deep silence, and nobody knew what was to be done. (172)
When affairs stood thus, one whose name was Sameas, a righteous man he was,
and for that reason above all fear, rose up and said, 'O you that are assessors
with me, and O thou that art our king, I neither have ever myself known such
a case, nor do I suppose that any one of you can name its parallel, that one who
is called to take his trial by us ever stood in such a manner before us; but
everyone, whosoever he be, that comes to be tried by this sanhedrin, presents
himself in a submissive manner, and like one that is in fear of himself, and that
endeavours to move us to compassion, with his hair dishevelled, and in a black
and mourning garment: (173) but this admirable man Herod, who is accused
of murder, and called to answer so heavy an accusation, stands here clothed in
purple, and with the hair of his head finely trimmed, and with his armed men
about him, that if we shall condemn him by our law, he may slay us, and by
overbearing justice may himself escape death; (174) yet do not I make this
complaint against Herod himself: he is, to be sure, more concerned for himself
than for the laws; but my complaint is against yourselves and your king, who
give him a licence so to do. However, take you notice, that God is great, and
that this very man, whom you are going to absolve and dismiss, for the sake of
Hyrcanus, will one day punish both you and your king himself also.' (175) Nor
did Sameas mistake in any part of this prediction; for when Herod had received
the kingdom, he slew all the members of this sanhedrin, and Hyrcanus himself
also, excepting Sameas, (176) for he had a great honour for him on account of
his righteousness, and because, when the city was afterwards besieged by
Herod and Sosius, he persuaded the people to admit Herod into it; and told
them that for their sins they would not be able to escape his hands; which
things will be related by us in their proper places.

(177) But when Hyrcanus saw that the members of the sanhedrin were ready
to pronounce the sentence of death upon Herod, he put off the trial to another
day, and sent privately to Herod, and advised him to fly out of the city; for that

by this means he might escape. (178) So he retired to Damascus, as though he fled from the king; and when he had been with Sextus Caesar, and had put his own affairs in a sure posture, he resolved to do thus: that in case he were again summoned before the sanhedrin to take his trial, he would not obey that summons. (179) Hereupon the members of the sanhedrin had great indignation at this posture of affairs, and endeavoured to persuade Hyrcanus that all these things were against him; which state of matters he was not ignorant of; but his temper was so unmanly and so foolish, that he was able to do nothing at all; (180) but when Sextus had made Herod general of the army of Celesyria, for he sold him that post for money, Hyrcanus was in fear lest Herod should make war upon him; nor was the effect of what he feared long in coming upon him, for Herod came, and brought an army along with him to fight with Hyrcanus, as being angry at the trial he bad been summoned to undergo before the sanhedrin; (181) but his father Antipater, and his brother [Phasaelus] met him, and hindered him from assaulting Jerusalem. They also pacified his vehement temper, and persuaded him to do no overt action, but only to affright them with threatenings, and to proceed no farther against one who had given him the dignity he had: (182) they also desired him not only to be angry that he was summoned, and obliged to come to his trial, but to remember withal how he was dismissed without condemnation, and how he ought to give Hyrcanus thanks for the same; and that he was not to regard only what was disagreeable to him, and be unthankful for his deliverance. (183) So they desired him to consider, that since it is God that turns the scales of war, there is great uncertainty in the issue of battles, and that therefore he ought not to expect the victory when he should fight with his king, and him that had supported him, and bestowed many benefits upon him, and had done nothing itself very severe to him; for that his accusation, which was derived from evil counsellors, and not from himself, had rather the suspicion of some severity, than anything really severe in it. (184) Herod was persuaded by these arguments, and believed that it was sufficient for his future hopes to have made a show of his strength before the nation, and done no more to it – and in this state were the affairs of Judea at this time.

CHAPTER 10

(185) Now when Caesar was come to Rome, he was ready to sail into Africa to fight against Scipio and Cato, when Hyrcanus sent ambassadors to him, and by them desired that he would ratify that league of friendship and mutual alliance which was between them; (186) and it seems to me to be necessary here to give an account of all the honours that the Romans and their emperors paid to our nation, and of the leagues of mutual assistance they have made with it, that all

the rest of mankind may know what regard the kings of Asia and Europe have had to us, and that they have been abundantly satisfied of our courage and fidelity; (187) for whereas many will not believe what hath been written about us by the Persians and Macedonians, because those writings are not everywhere to be met with, nor do lie in public places, but among us ourselves and certain other barbarous nations, (188) while there is no contradiction to be made against the decrees of the Romans, for they are laid up in the public places of the cities and are extant still in the capitol, and engraven upon pillars of brass; nay, besides this, Julius Caesar made a pillar of brass for the Jews at Alexandria, and declared publicly that they were citizens of Alexandria. (189) Out of these evidences will I demonstrate what I say, and will now set down the decrees made both by the senate and by Julius Caesar, which relate to Hyrcanus and to our nation.

(190) 'Caius Julius Caesar, imperator and high priest, and dictator the second time, to the magistrates, senate and people of Sidon, sendeth greeting. If you be in health, it is well. I also and the army are well, (191) I have sent you a copy of that decree, registered on the tables, which concerns Hyrcanus, the son of Alexander, the high priest and ethnarch of the Jews, that it may be laid up among the public records; and I will that it be openly proposed in a table of brass, both in Greek and in Latin. (192) It is as follows: I, Julius Caesar, imperator the second time and high priest, have made this decree, with the approbation of the senate: Whereas Hyrcanus, the son of Alexander the Jew, hath demonstrated his fidelity and diligence about our affairs, and this both now and in former times, both in peace and in war, as many of our generals have borne witness, (193) and came to our assistance in the last Alexandrian war, with fifteen hundred soldiers; and when he was sent by me to Mithridates, showed himself superior in valour to all the rest of that army – (194) for these reasons I will that Hyrcanus, the son of Alexander, and his children, be ethnarchs of the Jews, and have the high priesthood of the Jews forever, according to the customs of their forefathers, and that he and his son be our confederates; and that besides this, every one of them be reckoned among our particular friends. (195) I also ordain, that he and his children retain whatsoever privileges belong to the office of high priest, or whatsoever favours have been hitherto granted them; and if at any time hereafter there arise any questions about the Jewish customs, I will that he determine the same; and I think it not proper that they should be obliged to find us winter quarters, or that any money should be required of them.'

(196) 'The decrees of Caius Caesar, consul, containing what hath been granted and determined, are as follow: that Hyrcanus and his children bear rule over the nation of the Jews, and have the profits of the places to them bequeathed; and that he, as himself the high priest and ethnarch of the Jews,

defend those that are injured; (197) and that ambassadors be sent to Hyrcanus, the son of Alexander the high priest of the Jews, that may discourse with him about a league of friendship and mutual assistance; and that a table of brass, containing the premises, be openly proposed in the capitol, and at Sidon, and at Tyre, and Askelon, and in the temple, engraven in Roman and Greek letters; (198) that this decree may also be communicated to the questors and praetors of the several cities, and to the friends of the Jews: and that the ambassadors may have presents made them, and that these decrees be sent everywhere.'

(199) 'Caius Caesar, imperator, dictator, consul, hath granted, That out of regard to the honour, and virtue, and kindness of the man, and for the advantage of the senate, and of the people of Rome, Hyrcanus, the son of Alexander, both he and his children, be high priests and priests of Jerusalem, and of the Jewish nation, by the same right, and according to the same laws, by which their progenitors have held the priesthood.'

(200) 'Caius Caesar, consul the fifth time, hath decreed, That the Jews shall possess Jerusalem, and may encompass that city with walls; and that Hyrcanus, the son of Alexander, the high priest and ethnarch of the Jews, retain it in the manner he himself pleases; (201) and the Jews be allowed to deduct out of their tribute, every second year the land is let [in the Sabbatic period], a corus of that tribute; and that the tribute they pay be not let to farm, nor that they pay always the same tribute.'

(202) 'Caius Caesar, imperator the second time, hath ordained, That all the country of the Jews, excepting Joppa, do pay a tribute yearly for the city Jerusalem, excepting the seventh, which they call the Sabbatical Year, because thereon they neither receive the fruits of their trees, nor do they sow their land; (203) and that they pay their tribute in Sidon on the second year [of that Sabbatic period], the fourth part of what was sown: and besides this, they are to pay the same tithes to Hyrcanus and his sons which they paid to their forefathers. (204) And that no one, neither president, nor lieutenant, nor ambassador, raise auxiliaries within the bounds of Judea, nor may soldiers exact money of them for winter quarters, or under any other pretence, but that they be free from all sorts of injuries: (205) and that whatsoever they shall hereafter have, and are in possession of, or have bought, they shall retain them all. It is also our pleasure that the city Joppa, which the Jews had originally, when they made a league of friendship with the Romans, shall belong to them, as it formerly did; (206) and that Hyrcanus, the son of Alexander, and his sons, have as tribute of that city, from those that occupy the land, for the country and for what they export every year to Sidon, twenty thousand six hundred and seventy-five modii every year, the seventh year, which they call the Sabbatic Year, excepted, whereon they neither plough, nor receive the product of their trees. (207) It is also the pleasure of the senate, that as to the villages which are

in the great plain, which Hyrcanus and his forefathers formerly possessed, Hyrcanus and the Jews have them, with the same privileges with which they formerly had them also; (208) and that the same original ordinances remain still in force which concern the Jews with regard to their high priests; and that they enjoy the same benefits which they have had formerly by the concession of the people, and of the senate; and let them enjoy the like privileges in Lydda. (209) It is the pleasure also of the senate, that Hyrcanus the ethnarch, and the Jews, retain those places, countries, and villages which belonged to the kings of Syria and Phoenicia, the confederates of the Romans, and which they had bestowed on them as their free gifts. (210) It is also granted to Hyrcanus, and to his sons, and to the ambassadors by them sent to us, that in the fights between single gladiators, and in those with beasts, they shall sit among the senators to see those shows; and that when they desire an audience, they shall be introduced into the senate by the dictator, or by the general of the horse; and when they have introduced them, their answers shall be returned them in ten days at the farthest, after the decree of the senate is made about their affairs.'

(211) 'Caius Caesar, imperator, dictator the fourth time, and consul the fifth time, declared to be perpetual dictator, made this speech concerning the rights and privileges of Hyrcanus, the son of Alexander, the high priest and ethnarch of the Jews. (212) Since those imperators that have been in the provinces before me have borne witness to Hyrcanus, the high priest of the Jews, and to the Jews themselves, and this before the senate and people of Rome, when the people and senate returned their thanks to them, it is good that we now also remember the same, and provide that a requital be made to Hyrcanus, to the nation of the Jews, and to the sons of Hyrcanus, by the senate and people of Rome, and that suitable to what good will they have shown us, and to the benefits they have bestowed upon us.'

(213) 'Julius Caius, praetor [consul] of Rome, to the magistrates, senate, and people of the Parians, sendeth greeting. The Jews of Delos, and some other Jews that sojourn there in the presence of your ambassadors, signified to us, that, by a decree of yours, you forbid them to make use of the customs of their forefathers, and their way of sacred worship. (214) Now it does not please me that such decrees should be made against our friends and confederates, whereby they are forbidden to live according to their own customs, or to bring in contributions for common suppers and holy festivals, while they are not forbidden so to do even at Rome itself; (215) for even Caius Caesar, our imperator and consul, in that decree wherein he forbade the Bacchanal rioters to meet in the city, did yet permit these Jews and these only, both to bring in their contributions, and to make their common suppers. (216) Accordingly, when I forbid other Bacchanal rioters, I permit these Jews to gather themselves together, according to the customs and laws of their forefathers, and to persist

therein. It will be therefore good for you, that if you have made any decree against these our friends and confederates, to abrogate the same, by reason of their virtue, and kind disposition towards us.'

(217) Now after Caius was slain, when Marcus Antonius and Publius Dolabella were consuls, they both assembled the senate, and introduced Hyrcanus' ambassadors into it and discoursed of what they desired and made a league of friendship with them. The Senate also decreed, to grant them all they desired. (218) I add the decree itself, that those who read the present work, may have ready by them a demonstration of the truth of what we say. The decree was this:

(219) The decree of the senate, copied out of the treasury, from the public tables belonging to the quaestors, when Quintus Rutilius and Caius Cornelius were quaestors, and taken out of the second table of the first class, on the third day before the Ides of April, in the temple of Concord. (220) There were present at the writing of this decree, Lucius Calpurnius Piso, of the Menenian tribe, Servius Papinius Potitus of the Lemonian tribe, Caius Caninius Rebilius of the Terentine tribe, Publius Tidetius, Lucius Apulinus the son of Lucius, of the Sergian tribe, Flavius the son of Lucius, of the Lemonian tribe, Publius Platius the son of Publius, of the Papyrian tribe, Marcus Acilius the son of Marcus, of the Mecian tribe, Lucius Erucius the son of Lucius, of the Stellatine tribe, Marcus Quintus Plancillus the son of Marcus, of the Pollian tribe, and Publius Serius. (221) Publius Dolabella and Marcus Antonius, the consuls, made this reference to the senate, that as to those things which, by the decree of the senate, Caius Caesar had adjudged about the Jews, and yet had not hitherto that decree been brought into the treasury, it is our will, as it is also the desire of Publius Dolabella and Marcus Antonius, our consuls, to have these decrees put into the public tables, and brought to the city quaestors, that they may take care to have them put upon the double tables. (222) This was done before the fifth of the Ides of February, in the temple of Concord. Now the ambassadors from Hyrcanus the high priest were these: Lysimachus the son of Pausanius, Alexander the son of Theodorus, Patroclus the son of Chereas, and Jonathan the son of Onias.'

(223) Hyrcanus sent also one of these ambassadors to Dolabella, who was then the prefect of Asia, and desired him to dismiss the Jews from military services, and to preserve to them the customs of their forefathers, and to permit them to live according to them. (224) And when Dolabella had received Hyrcanus' letter, without any farther deliberation, he sent an epistle to all the Asiatics, and particularly to the city of the Ephesians, the metropolis of Asia, about the Jews; a copy of which epistle here follows:

(225) 'When Artermon was prytanis, on the first day of the month Leneon, Dolabella, imperator, to the senate and magistrates and people of the Ephesians,

sendeth greeting. (226) Alexander, the son of Theodorus, the ambassador of Hyrcanus, the son of Alexander, the high priest and ethnarch of the Jews, appeared before me, to show that his countrymen could not go into their armies, because they are not allowed to bear arms or to travel on the Sabbath days, nor there to procure themselves those sorts of food which they have been used to eat from the times of their forefathers – (227) I do therefore grant them a freedom from going into the army, as the former prefects have done, and permit them to use the customs of their forefathers in assembling together for sacred and religious purposes, as their law requires, and for collecting oblations necessary for sacrifices; and my will is, that you write this to the several cities under your jurisdiction.'

(228) And these were the concessions that Dolabella made to our nation when Hyrcanus sent an embassage to him; but Lucius the consul's decree ran thus: 'I have at my tribunal set these Jews, who are citizens of Rome, and follow the Jewish religious rites, and yet live at Ephesus, free from going into the army, on account of the superstition they are under. This was done before the twelfth of the Calends of October, when Lucius Lentulus and Caius Marcellus were consuls, (229) in the presence of Titus Appius Balbus, the son of Titus, and lieutenant of the Horatian tribe; of Titus Tongius, the son of Titus, of the Crustumine tribe; of Quintus Resius, the son of Quintus; of Titus Pompeius Longinus, the son of Titus; of Caius Servilius, the son of Caius, of the Terentine tribe; of Bracchus the military tribune; of Publius Lucius Gallus, the son of Publius, of Veturian tribe; of Caius Sentius, the son of Caius, of the Sabbatine tribe; (230) of Titus Atilius Bulbus, the son of Titus, lieutenant and vice-praetor to the magistrates, senate, and people of the Ephesians, sendeth greeting. Lucius Lentulus the consul freed the Jews that are in Asia from going into the armies, at my intercession for them; and when I had made the same petition some time afterward to Phanius the imperator, and to Lucius Antonius the vice-quaestor, I obtained the privilege of them also; and my will is, that you take care that no one give them any disturbance.'

(231) The decree of the Delians: 'The answer of the praetors, when Beotus was archon, on the twentieth day of the month Thargeleon. While Marcus Piso the lieutenant lived in our city, who was also appointed over the choice of the soldiers, he called us, and many other of the citizens, and gave order, (232) that if there be here any Jews who are Roman citizens, no one is to give them any disturbance about going into the army, because Cornelius Lentulus, the consul, freed the Jews from going into the army, on account of the superstition they are under – you are therefore obliged to submit to the praetor:' and the like decree was made by the Sardians about us also.

(233) 'Caius Phanius, the son of Caius, imperator and consul, to the magistrates of Cos, sendeth greeting. I would have you know that the

ambassadors of the Jews have been with me, and desired they might have those decrees which the senate had made about them: which decrees are here subjoined. My will is, that you have a regard to and take care of these men, according to the senate's decree, that they may be safely conveyed home through your country.'

(234) The declaration of Lucius Lentulus the consul: 'I have dismissed those Jews who are Roman citizens, and who appear to me to have their religious rites, and to observe the laws of the Jews at Ephesus, on account of the superstition they are under. This act was done before the thirteenth of the Calends of October.'

(235) 'Lucius Antonius, the son of Marcus, vice-quaestor, and vice-praetor, to the magistrates, senate, and people of the Sardians, sendeth greeting. Those Jews that are our fellow-citizens of Rome, came to me, and demonstrated that they had an assembly of their own, according to the laws of their forefathers, and this from the beginning, as also a place of their own, wherein they determined their suits and controversies with one another. Upon their petition therefore to me, that these might be lawful for them, I gave order that these their privileges be preserved, and they be permitted to do accordingly.'

(236) The declaration of Marcus Publius, the son of Spurius, and of Marcus, the son of Marcus, and of Lucius, the son of Publius: 'We went to the proconsul, and informed him of what Dositheus, the son of Cleopatrida of Alexandria, desired, that if he thought good, (237) he would dismiss those Jews who were Roman citizens, and were wont to observe the rites of the Jewish religion, on account of the superstition they were under. Accordingly, he did dismiss them. This was done before the thirteenth of the Calends of October.'

'In the month Quintilis, when Lucius Lentulus and Caius Marcellus were consuls (238) and there were present Titus Appius Balbus, the son of Titus, lieutenant of the Horatian tribe, Titus Tongius of the Crustumine tribe, Quintus Resius, the son of Quintus, Titus Pompeius, the son of Titus, Cornelius Longinus, Caius Servilius Bracchus, the son of Caius, a military tribune, of the Terentine tribe, Publius Clusius Gallus, the son of Publius, of the Veturian tribe, Caius Teutius, the son of Caius, a military tribune, of the Emilian tribe, Sextus Atilius Serranus, the son of Sextus, of the Esquiline tribe, (239) Caius Pompeius, the son of Caius, of the Sabbatine tribe, Titus Appius Menander, the son of Titus, Publius Servilius Strabo, the son of Publius, Lucius Paccius Capito, the son of Lucius, of the Colline tribe, Aulus Furius Tertius, the son of Aulus, and Appius Menas. (240) In the presence of these it was that Lentulus pronounced this decree: I have before the tribunal dismissed those Jews that are Roman citizens, and are accustomed to observe the sacred rites of the Jews at Ephesus, on account of the superstition they are under.'

(241) 'The magistrates of the Laodiceans to Caius Rubilius, the son of Caius

the consul, sendeth greeting. Sopater, the ambassador of Hyrcanus the high priest, hath delivered us an epistle from thee, whereby he lets us know that certain ambassadors were come from Hyrcanus, the high priest of the Jews, and brought an epistle written concerning their nation, (242) wherein they desire that the Jews may be allowed to observe their Sabbaths and other sacred rites, according to the laws of their forefathers, and that they may be under no command, because they are our friends and confederates: and that nobody may injure them in our provinces. Now although the Trallians there present contradicted them, and were not pleased with these decrees, yet didst thou give order that they should be observed, and informed us that thou hadst been desired to write this to us about them. (243) We therefore, in obedience to the injunctions we have received from thee, have received the epistle which thou sentest us, and have laid it up by itself among our public records; and as to the other things about which thou didst send to us, we will take care that no complaint be made against us.'

(244) 'Publius Servilius, the son of Publius, of the Galban tribe, the proconsul, to the magistrates, senate and people of the Milesians, sendeth greeting. (245) Prytanes, the son of Hermes, a citizen of yours, came to me when I was at Tralles, and held a court there, and informed me that you used the Jews in a way different from my opinion, and forbade them to celebrate their Sabbaths, and to perform the sacred rites received from their forefathers, and to manage the fruits of the earth according to their ancient custom; and that he had himself been the promulger of your decree, according as your laws require; (246) I would therefore have you know, that upon hearing the pleading on both sides, I gave sentence that the Jews should not be prohibited to make use of their own customs.'

(247) The decree of those of Pergamus: 'When Cratippus was prytanis, on the first day of the month Desius, the decree of the praetors was this: Since the Romans, following the conduct of their ancestors, undertake dangers for the common safety of all mankind, and are ambitious to settle their confederates and friends in happiness, and in firm peace, (248) and since the nation of the Jews, and their high priest Hyrcanus, sent as ambassadors to them, Strato the son of Theodotus, and Apollonius the son of Alexander, and Enaus the son of Antipater, (249) and Aristobulus the son of Amyntas, and Sosipater the son of Philip, worthy and good men, who gave a particular account of their affairs, the senate thereupon made a decree about what they had desired of them, that Antiochus the king, the son of Antiochus, should do no injury to the Jews, the confederates of the Romans; and that the fortresses and the havens, and the country, and whatsoever else he had taken from them, should be restored to them; and that it may be lawful for them to export their goods out of their own havens; (250) and that no king nor people may have leave to export any

goods either out of the country of Judea, or out of their havens, without paying customs, but only Ptolemy, the king of Alexandria, because he is our confederate and friend: and that, according to their desire, the garrison that is in Joppa may be ejected. (251) Now Lucius Pettius, one of our senators, a worthy and good man, gave order that we should take care that these things should be done according to the senate's decree; and that we should take care also that their ambassadors might return home in safety. (252) Accordingly we admitted Theodorus into our senate and assembly, and took the epistle out of his hands, as well as the decree of the senate: and as he discoursed with great zeal about the Jews, and described Hyrcanus' virtue and generosity, (253) and how he was a benefactor to all men in common, and particularly to everybody that comes to him, we laid up the epistle in our public records; and made a decree ourselves, that since we also are in confederacy with the Romans, we would do everything we could for the Jews, according to the senate's decree. (254) Theodorus also, who brought the epistle, desired of our praetors, that they would send Hyrcanus a copy of that decree, as also ambassadors to signify to him the affection of our people to him, and to exhort them to preserve and augment their friendship for us, and be ready to bestow other benefits upon us, (255) as justly expecting to receive proper requitals from us; and desiring them to remember that our ancestors were friendly to the Jews, even in the days of Abraham, who was the father of all the Hebrews, as we have [also] found it set down in our public records.'

(256) The decree of those of Halicarnassus. 'When Memnon, the son of Orestidas by descent, but by adoption of Euonymus, was priest on the [. . .] day of the month Aristerion, the decree of the people, upon the representation of Marcus Alexander, was this: (257) Since we have ever a great regard to piety towards God, and to holiness; and since we aim to follow the people of the Romans, who are the benefactors of all men, and what they have written to us about a league of friendship and mutual assistance between the Jews and our city, and that their sacred offices and accustomed festivals and assemblies may be observed by them; (258) we have decreed, that as many men and women of the Jews as are willing so to do, may celebrate their Sabbaths, and perform their holy offices, according to the Jewish laws; and may make their proseuchae at the seaside, according to the customs of their forefathers; and if anyone whether he be a magistrate or a private person, hindereth them from so doing, he shall be liable to a fine, to be applied to the uses of the city.'

(259) The decree of the Sardians. 'This decree was made by the senate and people upon the representation of the praetors: whereas those Jews who are fellow-citizens, and live with us in this city, have ever had great benefits heaped upon them by the people, and have come now into the senate, (260) and desired of the people, that upon the restitution of their law and their

liberty, by senate and people of Rome, they may assemble together according to their ancient legal custom, and that we will not bring any suit against them about it; and that a place may be given them where they may have their congregations, with their wives and children, and may offer, as did their forefathers, their prayers and sacrifices to God – (261) now the senate and people have decreed to permit them to assemble together on the days formerly appointed, and to act according to their own laws; and that such a place be set apart for them by the praetors, for the building and inhabiting the same, as they shall esteem fit for that purpose: and that those that take care of the provisions for the city, shall take care that such sorts of food as they esteem fit for their eating, may be imported into the city.'

(262) The decree of the Ephesians: 'When Menophilus was prytanis, on the first day of the month Artemisius, this decree was made by the people: Nicanor, the son of Euphemus, pronounced it, upon the representation of the praetors. (263) Since the Jews that dwell in this city have petitioned Marcus Junius Brutus, son of Pontius, the proconsul, that they might be allowed to observe their Sabbaths, and to act in all things according to the customs of their forefathers, without impediment from anybody, the praetor hath granted their petition. (264) Accordingly, it was decreed by the senate and people, that in this affair that concerned the Romans, no one of them should be hindered from keeping the Sabbath day, nor be fined for so doing; but that they may be allowed to do all things according to their own laws.'

(265) Now there are many such decrees of the senate and imperators of the Romans, and those different from these before us, which have been made in favour of Hyrcanus, and of our nation; as also, there have been more decrees of the cities, and rescripts of the praetors to such epistles as concerned our rights and privileges: and certainly such as are not ill-disposed to what we write, may believe that they are all to this purpose, and that by the specimens which we have inserted: (266) for since we have produced evident marks that may still be seen, of the friendship we have had with the Romans, and demonstrated that those marks are engraven upon columns and tables of brass in the capitol, that are still in being, and preserved to this day, we have omitted to set them all down, as needless and disagreeable; (267) for I cannot suppose anyone so perverse as not to believe the friendship we have had with the Romans, while they have demonstrated the same by such a great number of their decrees relating to us; nor will they doubt of our fidelity as to the rest of these decrees, since we have shown the same in those we have produced. And thus have we sufficiently explained that friendship and confederacy we at those times had with the Romans.

CHAPTER 11

(268) Now it so fell out, that about this very time the affairs of Syria were in great disorder, and this on the occasion following: Caecilius Bassus, one of Pompey's party, laid a treacherous design against Sextus Caesar, and slew him, and then took his army, and got the management of public affairs into his own hand; so there arose a great war about Apamea, while Caesar's generals came against him with an army of horsemen and footmen; (269) to these Antipater sent also succours, and his sons with them, as calling to mind the kindnesses they had received from Caesar, and on that account he thought it but just to require punishment for him, and to take vengeance on the man that had murdered him. (270) And as the war was drawn out into a great length, Marcus came from Rome to take Sextus' government upon him; but Caesar was slain by Cassius and Brutus in the senate-house, after he had retained the government three years and six months. This fact, however, is related elsewhere.

(271) As the war that arose upon the death of Caesar was now begun, and the principal men were all gone, some one way and some another, to raise armies, Cassius came from Rome into Syria, in order to receive the [army that lay in the] camp at Apamea; (272) and having raised the siege, he brought over both Bassus and Marcus to his party. He then went over the cities, and got together weapons and soldiers, and laid great taxes upon those cities: and he chiefly oppressed Judea, and exacted of it seven hundred talents: (273) but Antipater, when he saw the state to be in so great consternation and disorder, he divided the collection of that sum and appointed his sons to gather it; and so that part of it was to be exacted by Malichus, who was ill-disposed to him, and by others. (274) And because Herod did exact what is required of him from Galilee before others, he was in the greatest favour with Cassius; for he thought it a part of prudence to cultivate a friendship with the Romans, and to gain their good will at the expense of others; (275) whereas the curators of the other cities, with their citizens, were sold for slaves; and Cassius reduced four cities into a state of slavery, the two most potent of which were Gophna and Emmaus; and, besides these, Lydia and Thamna. (276) Nay, Cassius was so very angry at Malichus, that he had killed him (for he assaulted him) had not Hyrcanus, by the means of Antipater, sent him an hundred talents of his own, and thereby pacified his anger against him.

(277) But after Cassius was gone out of Judea, Malichus laid snares for Antipater, as thinking that his death would be the preservation of Hyrcanus' government; but his design was not unknown to Antipater, which, when he perceived, he retired beyond Jordan, and got together an army, partly of Arabs, and partly of his own countrymen. (278) However, Malichus being one of

great cunning, denied that he had laid any snare for him, and made his defence with an oath, both to himself and his sons; and said that while Phasaelus had a garrison in Jerusalem, and Herod had the weapons of war in his custody, he could never have a thought of any such thing. So Antipater, perceiving the distress that Malichus was in, was reconciled to him, (279) and made an agreement with him: this was when Marcus was president of Syria; who yet perceiving that this Malichus was making a disturbance in Judea, proceeded so far that he had almost killed him; but still, at the intercession of Antipater, he saved him.

(280) However, Antipater little thought that by saving Malichus, that he had saved his own murderer: for now Cassius and Marcus had got together an army, and entrusted the entire care of it with Herod, and made him general of the forces of Celesyria, and gave him a fleet of ships, and an army of horsemen and footmen; and promised him that after the war was over they would make him king of Judea; for a war was already begun between Antony and the younger Caesar; (281) but as Malichus was most afraid of Antipater, he took him out of the way; and by the offer of money, persuaded the butler of Hyrcanus with whom they were both to feast, to kill him by poison. This being done, and he having armed men with him, settled the affairs of the city. (282) But when Antipater's sons, Herod and Phasaelus, were acquainted with this conspiracy against their father, and had indignation at it, Malichus denied all, and utterly renounced any knowledge of the murder. (283) And thus died Antipater, a man that had distinguished himself for piety and justice, and love to his country. And whereas one of his sons, Herod, resolved immediately to revenge their father's death, and was coming upon Malichus with an army for that purpose, the elder of his sons, Phasaelus, thought it best rather to get this man into their hands by policy, lest they should appear to begin a civil war in the country; (284) so he accepted of Malichus's defence for himself, and pretended to believe him, that he had had no hand in the violent death of Antipater his father, but erected a fine monument for him. Herod also went to Samaria: and when he found them in great distress, he revived their spirits, and composed their difficulties.

(285) However, a little after this, Herod, upon the approach of a festival, came with his soldiers into the city; whereupon Malichus was affrighted, and persuaded Hyrcanus not to permit him to come into the city. Hyrcanus complied; and for a pretence of excluding him, alleged, that a rout of strangers ought not to be admitted while the multitude were purifying themselves. (286) But Herod had little regard to the messengers that were sent to him, and entered the city in the night-time, and affrighted Malichus, yet did he remit nothing of his former dissimulation, but wept for Antipater, and bewailed him as a friend of his with a loud voice; (287) but Herod and his friends thought it

proper not openly to contradict Malichus's hypocrisy, but to give him tokens of mutual friendship, in order to prevent his suspicion of them.

(288) However, Herod sent to Cassius, and informed him of the murder of his father; who, knowing what sort of man Malichus was as to his morals, sent him back word, that he should revenge his father's death; and also sent privately to the commanders of his army at Tyre, with orders to assist Herod in the execution of a very just design of his. (289) Now when Cassius had taken Laodicea, they all went together to him, and carried him garlands and money: and Herod thought that Malichus might be punished while he was there; (290) but he was somewhat apprehensive of the thing, and designed to make some great attempt, and because his son was then a hostage at Tyre, he went to that city and resolved to steal him away privately, and to march thence into Judea; and as Cassius was in haste to march against Antony, he thought to bring the country to revolt, and to procure the government for himself. (291) But Providence opposed his counsels; and Herod being a shrewd man, and perceiving what his intention was, he sent thither beforehand a servant, in appearance indeed to get a supper ready, for he had said before, that he would feast them all there, but in reality to the commanders of the army, whom he persuaded to go out against Malichus with their daggers. (292) So they went out and met the man near the city, upon the seashore, and there stabbed him. Whereupon Hyrcanus was so astonished at what had happened, that his speech failed him; and when after some difficulty, he had recovered himself, he asked Herod what the matter could be, and who it was that slew Malichus: (293) and when he said that it was done by the command of Cassius, he commended the action, for that Malichus was a very wicked man, and one that conspired against his own country. And this was the punishment that was inflicted on Malichus for what he wickedly did to Antipater.

(294) But when Cassius was marched out of Syria, disturbances arose in Judea: for Felix, who was left at Jerusalem with an army, made a sudden attempt against Phasaelus, and the people themselves rose in arms: (295) but Herod went to Fabius, the prefect of Damascus, and was desirous to run to his brother's assistance, but was hindered by a distemper that seized upon him, till Phasaelus by himself had been too hard for Felix, and had shut him up in the tower, and there on certain conditions, dismissed him. Phasaelus also complained of Hyrcanus, that although he had received a great many benefits from them, yet did he support their enemies; (296) for Malichus' brother had made many places to revolt, and kept garrisons in them, and particularly Masada, the strongest fortress of them all. In the meantime Herod was recovered of his disease, and came and took from Felix all the places he bad gotten; and, upon certain conditions, dismissed him also.

CHAPTER 12

(297) Now Ptolemy, the son of Menneus, brought back into Judea Antigonus, the son of Aristobulus, who had already raised an army, and had, by money, made Fabius to be his friend, and this because he was of kin to him. Marion also gave him assistance. He had been left by Cassius to tyrannise over Tyre; for this Cassius was a man that seized on Syria, and then kept it under, in the way of a tyrant. (298) Marion also marched into Galilee, which lay in his neighbourhood, and took three of its fortresses, and put garrisons into them to keep them. But when Herod came, he took all from him; but the Tyrian garrison he dismissed in a very civil manner; nay, to some of the soldiers he made presents out of the good will he bare to that city. (299) When he had despatched these affairs, and was gone to meet Antigonus, he joined battle with him and beat him, and drove him out of Judea, presently, when he was just come into its border; but when he was come to Jerusalem, Hyrcanus and the people put garlands about his head; (300) for he had already contracted an affinity with the family of Hyrcanus by having espoused a descendant of his, and for that reason Herod took the greater care of him, as being to marry the daughter of Alexander the son of Aristobulus, and the granddaughter of Hyrcanus; by which wife he became the father of three male and two female children. He had also married before this another wife, out of a lower family of his own nation, whose name was Doris, by whom he had his eldest son, Antipater.

(301) Now Antonius and Caesar had beaten Cassius near Philippi, as others have related; but after the victory, Caesar went into Gaul [Italy], and Antony marched for Asia, who when he was arrived at Bithynia, he had ambassadors that met him from all parts. (302) The principal men also of the Jews came thither, to accuse Phasaelus and Herod, and they said that Hyrcanus had indeed the appearance of reigning, but that these men had all the power; (303) but Antony paid great respect to Herod, who was come to him to make his defence against his accusers, on which account his adversaries could not so much as obtain a hearing; which favour Herod had gained of Antony by money; (304) but still, when Antony was come to Ephesus, Hyrcanus the high priest, and our nation, sent an embassage to him, which carried a crown of gold with them, and desired that he would write to the governors of the provinces, to set those Jews free who had been carried captive by Cassius, and this without their having fought against him, and to restore them that country which, in the days of Cassius, had been taken from them. (305) Antony thought the Jews' desires were just, and wrote immediately to Hyrcanus and to the Jews. He also sent, at the same time, a decree to the Tyrians, the contents of which were to the same purpose.

(306) 'Marcus Antonius, imperator, to Hyrcanus the high priest and ethnarch of the Jews, sendeth greeting. It you be in health it is well; I am also in health, with the army. (307) Lysimachus the son of Pausanias, and Josephus the son of Menneus, and Alexander the son of Theodorus, your ambassadors, met me at Ephesus, and have renewed the embassage which they had formerly been upon at Rome, and have diligently acquitted themselves of the present embassage, which thou and thy nation have entrusted to them, and have fully declared the good will thou hast for us. (308) I am therefore satisfied, both by your actions and your words, that you are well-disposed to us; and I understand that your conduct of life is constant and religious; so I reckon you as our own; (309) but when those that were adversaries to you and to the Roman people, abstained neither from cities nor temples, and did not observe the agreement they had confirmed by oath, it was not only on account of our contest with them, but on account of all mankind in common, that we have taken vengeance on those who have been the authors of great injustice towards men, and of great wickedness towards the gods; for the sake of which we suppose that it was that the sun turned away his light from us, as unwilling to view the horrid crime they were guilty of in the case of Caesar. (310) We have also overcome their conspiracies, which threatened the gods themselves, which Macedonia received, as it is a climate peculiarly proper for impious and insolent attempts; and we have overcome that confused rout of men, half mad with spite against us, which they got together at Philippi, in Macedonia, when they seized on the places that were proper for their purpose, and, as it were, walled them round with mountains to the very sea, and where the passage was open only through a single gate. This victory we gained, because the gods had condemned those men for their wicked enterprises. (311) Now Brutus, when he had fled as far as Philippi, was shut up by us, and became a partaker of the same perdition with Cassius; and now these have received their punishment, we suppose that we may enjoy peace for the time to come, and that Asia may be at rest from war. (312) We therefore make that peace which God hath given us common to our confederates also, insomuch that the body of Asia is not recovered out of that distemper it was under by means of our victory. I, therefore, bearing in mind both thee and your nation, shall take care of what may be for your advantage. (313) I have also sent epistles in writing to the several cities, that if any persons, whether freemen or bondmen, have been sold under the spear by Caius Cassius or his subordinate officers, they may be set free; and I will that you kindly make use of the favours which I and Dolabella have granted you. I also forbid the Tyrians to use any violence with you; and for what places of the Jews they now possess, I order them to restore them. I have withal accepted of the crown which thou sentest me.'

(314) 'Marcus Antonius, imperator, to the magistrates, senate, and people of Tyre, sendeth greeting. The ambassadors of Hyrcanus, the high priest and ethnarch [of the Jews], appeared before me at Ephesus, and told me that you are in possession of part of their country, which you entered upon under the government of our adversaries. (315) Since, therefore, we have undertaken a war for the obtaining the government, and have taken care to do what was agreeable to piety and justice, and have brought to punishment those that had neither any remembrance of the kindness they had received, nor have kept their oaths, I will that you be at peace with those that are our confederates; as also, that what you have taken by the means of our adversaries shall not be reckoned your own, but be returned to those from whom you took them; (316) for none of them took their provinces or their armies by the gift of the senate, but they seized them by force, and bestowed them by violence upon such as became useful to them in their unjust proceedings. (317) Since, therefore, those men have received the punishment due to them, we desire that our confederates may retain whatsoever it was that they formerly possessed without disturbance, and that you restore all the places which belong to Hyrcanus, the ethnarch of the Jews, which you have had, though it were but one day before Caius Cassius began an unjustifiable war against us, and entered into our province; nor do you use any force against him, in order to weaken him, that he may not be able to dispose of that which is his own; (318) but if you have any contest with him about your respective rights, it shall be lawful for you to plead your cause when we come upon the places concerned, for we shall alike preserve the rights, and hear all the causes, of our confederates.'

(319) 'Marcus Antonius, imperator, to the magistrates, senate, and people of Tyre, sendeth greeting. I have sent you my decree, of which I will that ye take care that it be engraven on the public tables, in Roman and Greek letters, and that it stand engraven in the most illustrious places, and that it may be read by all. (320) Marcus Antonius, imperator, one of the triumvirate over the public affairs, made this declaration: since Caius Cassius in this revolt he hath made, hath pillaged that province which belonged not to him, and was held by garrisons there encamped, while they were our confederates, and hath spoiled that nation of the Jews which was in friendship with the Roman people, as in war; (321) and since we have overcome his madness by arms, we now correct, by our decrees and judicial determinations, what he hath laid waste, that those things may be restored to our confederates; and as for what hath been sold of the Jewish possessions, whether they be bodies or possessions, let them be released – the bodies into that state of freedom they were originally in, and the possessions to their former owners. (322) I also will, that he who shall not comply with this decree of mine, shall be punished for his disobedience; and if such a one be caught, I will take care that the offenders suffer condign punishment.'

(323) The same thing did Antony write to the Sidonians, and the Antioch-ians, and the Aradians. We have produced these decrees, therefore, as marks for futurity of the truth of what we have said, that the Romans had a great concern about our nation.

CHAPTER 13

(324) When after this Antony came into Syria, Cleopatra met him in Cilicia, and brought him to fall in love with her. And there came now also a hundred of the most potent of the Jews to accuse Herod and those about him, and set the men of the greatest eloquence among them to speak. (325) But Messala contradicted them, on behalf of the young men, and all this in the presence of Hyrcanus, who was Herod's father-in-law already. When Antony had heard both sides at Daphne, he asked Hyrcanus who they were that governed the nation best? He replied, Herod and his friends. (326) Hereupon Antony, by reason of the old hospitable friendship he had made with his father [Antipater], at that time when he was with Gabinius, he made both Herod and Phasaelus tetrarchs, and committed the public affairs of the Jews to them, and wrote letters to that purpose. He also bound fifteen of their adversaries, and was going to kill them, but that Herod obtained their pardon.

(327) Yet did not these men continue quiet when they were come back, but a thousand of the Jews came to Tyre to meet him there, whither the report was that he would come. But Antony was corrupted by the money which Herod and his brother had given him; and so he gave order to the governor of the place to punish the Jewish ambassadors, who were for making innovations, and to settle the government upon Herod: (328) but Herod went out hastily to them, and Hyrcanus was with him (for they stood upon the shore before the city): and he charged them to go their ways, because great mischief would befall them if they went on with their accusation. (329) But they did not acquiesce: whereupon the Romans ran upon them with their daggers, and slew some, and wounded more of them, and the rest fled away, and went home, and lay still in great consternation: and when the people made a clamour against Herod, Antony was so provoked at it, that he slew the prisoners.

(330) Now, in the second year, Pacorus, the king of Parthia's son, and Barzapharnes, a commander of the Parthians, possessed themselves of Syria. Ptolemy, the son of Menneus, also was now dead, and Lysanias his son took his government, and made a league of friendship with Antigonus, the son of Aristobulus: and, in order to obtain it, made use of that commander, who had a great interest in him. (331) Now Antigonus had promised to give the Parthians a thousand talents, and five hundred women, upon condition they would take the government away from Hyrcanus, and bestow it upon him,

and withal kill Herod. (332) And although he did not give them what he had promised, yet did the Parthians make an expedition into Judea on that account, and carried Antigonus with them. Pacorus went along the maritime parts, but the commander Barzapharnes through the midland. (333) Now the Tyrians excluded Pacorus; but the Sidonians, and those of Ptolemais, received him. However, Pacorus sent a troop of horsemen into Judea, to take a view of the state of the country, and to assist Antigonus; and sent also the king's butler, of the same name with himself. (334) So when the Jews that dwelt about Mount Carmel came to Antigonus, and were ready to march with him into Judea, Antigonus hoped to get some part of the country by their assistance. The place is called Drymi; and when some others came and met them, the men privately fell upon Jerusalem; and when some more were come to them, they got together in great numbers and came against the king's palace, and besieged it. (335) But as Phasaelus' and Herod's party came to the other's assistance, and a battle happened between them in the marketplace, the young men beat their enemies, and pursued them into the temple, and sent some armed men into the adjoining houses, to keep them in, who yet being destitute of such as should support them, were burnt, and the houses with them, by the people who rose up against them. (336) But Herod was revenged on these seditious adversaries of his a little afterward for this injury they had offered him, when he fought with them, and slew a great number of them.

(337) But while there were daily skirmishes, the enemy waited for the coming of the multitude out of the country to Pentecost, a feast of ours so called; (338) and when that day was come, many ten thousands of the people were gathered together about the temple, some in armour and some without. Now those that came, guarded both the temple and the city, excepting what belonged to the palace, which Herod guarded with a few of his soldiers; (339) and Phasaelus had the charge of the wall, while Herod with a body of his men sallied out upon the enemy, who lay in the suburbs, and fought courageously, and put many ten thousands to flight, some flying into the city, and some into the temple, and some into the outer fortifications, for some such fortifications there were in that place. Phasaelus came also to his assistance; (340) yet was Pacorus, the general of the Parthians, at the desire of Antigonus, admitted into the city, with a few of his horsemen, under pretence indeed as if he would still the sedition, but in reality to assist Antigonus in obtaining the government. (341) And when Phasaelus met him, and received him kindly, Pacorus persuaded him to go himself as ambassador to Barzapharnes, which was done fraudulently. Accordingly Phasaelus, suspecting no harm, complied with his proposal, while Herod did not give his consent to what was done, because of the perfidiousness of these barbarians, but desired Phasaelus rather to fight those that were come into the city.

(342) So both Hyrcanus and Phasaelus went on the embassage; but Pacorus left with Herod two hundred horsemen, and ten men who were called the *freemen;* and conducted the others on their journey; and when they were in Galilee, the governors of the cities there met them in their arms. (343) Barzapharnes also received them at the first with cheerfulness, and made them presents, though he afterward conspired against them; and Phasaelus with his horsemen were conducted to the seaside; but when they heard that Antigonus had promised to give the Parthians a thousand talents, and five hundred women, to assist him against them, they soon had a suspicion of the barbarians. (344) Moreover, there was one who informed them that snares were laid for them by night, while a guard came about them secretly; and they had then been seized upon, had they not waited for the seizure of Herod by the Parthians that were about Jerusalem, lest upon the slaughter of Hyrcanus and Phasaelus, he should have an intimation of it, and escape out of their hands. And these were the circumstances they were now in; and they saw who they were that guarded them. (345) Some persons indeed would have persuaded Phasaelus to fly away immediately on horseback, and not to stay any longer; and there was one Ophellius, who, above all the rest, was earnest with him to do so, for he had heard of this treachery from Saramalla, the richest of all the Syrians at that time, who also promised to provide him ships to carry him off, for the sea was just by them; (346) but he had no mind to desert Hyrcanus, nor bring his brother into danger; but he went to Barzapharnes, and told him he did not act justly when he made such a contrivance against them, for that if he wanted money, he would give him more than Antigonus; and besides, that it was a horrible thing to slay those that came to him upon the security of their oaths, and that when they had done them no injury. (347) But the barbarian swore to him that there was no truth in any of his suspicions, but that he was troubled with nothing but false proposals, and then went away to Pacorus.

(348) But as soon as he was gone away, some men came and bound Hyrcanus and Phasaelus, while Phasaelus greatly reproached the Parthians for their perjury. However, that butler who was sent against Herod had it in command to get him without the walls of the city, and seize upon him; (349) but messengers had been sent by Phasaelus to inform Herod of the perfidiousness of the Parthians; and when he knew that the enemy had seized upon them, he went to Pacorus, and to the most potent of the Parthians, as to the lords of the rest, (350) who, although they knew the whole matter, dissembled with him in a deceitful way; and said that he ought to go out with them before the walls, and meet those who were bringing him his letters, for that they were not taken by his adversaries, but were coming to give him an account of the good success Phasaelus had had. (351) Herod did not give credit to what they said; for he had heard that his brother was seized upon by others

also; and the daughter of Hyrcanus, whose daughter he had espoused, was his monitor also [not to credit them], which made him still more suspicious of the Parthians; for although other people did not give heed to her, yet did he believe her, as a woman of very great wisdom.

(352) Now while the Parthians were in consultation what was fit to be done, for they did not think it proper to make an open attempt upon a person of his character, and while they put off the determination to the next day, Herod was under great disturbance of mind; and rather inclining to believe the reports he heard about his brother and the Parthians than to give heed to what was said on the other side, he determined that when the evening came on, he would make use of it for his flight, and not make any longer delay, as if the dangers from the enemy were not yet certain. (353) He therefore removed with the armed men whom he had with him, and set his wives upon the beasts, as also his mother and sister, and her whom he was about to marry [Mariamne], the daughter of Alexander the son of Aristobulus, with her mother, the daughter of Hyrcanus, and his youngest brother, and all their servants, and the rest of the multitude that was with him, and without the enemy's privity pursued his way to Idumea: (354) nor could any enemy of his who then saw him in this case, be so hardhearted, but would have commiserated his fortune, while the women drew along their infant children, and left their own country, and their friends in prison, with tears in their eyes and sad lamentations, and in expectation of nothing but what was of a melancholy nature.

(355) But for Herod himself, he raised his mind above the miserable state he was in, and was of good courage in the midst of his misfortunes; and as he passed along, he bade them every one to be of good cheer, and not to give themselves up to sorrow, because that would hinder them in their flight, which was now the only hope of safety that they had. (356) Accordingly, they tried to bear with patience the calamity they were under, as he exhorted them to do; yet was he once almost going to kill himself, upon the overthrow of a wagon, and the danger his mother was then in of being killed, and this on two accounts: because of his great concern for her, and because he was afraid lest by this delay, the enemy should overtake him in the pursuit; (357) but as he was drawing his sword, and going to kill himself therewith, those that were present restrained him, and being so many in number, were too hard for him; and told him that he ought not to desert them, and leave them a prey to their enemies, for that it was not the part of a brave man to free himself from the distresses he was in, and to overlook his friends that were in the same distresses also. (358) So he was compelled to let that horrid attempt alone, partly out of shame at what they said to him, and partly out of regard to the great number of those that would not permit him to do what he intended. So he encouraged his mother, and took all the care of her the time would allow, and proceeded on

the way he proposed to go with the utmost haste, and that was to the fortress of Masada. As he had many skirmishes with such of the Parthians as attacked him and pursued him, he was conqueror in them all.

(359) Nor indeed was he free from the Jews all along as he was in his flight: for by that time he was gotten sixty furlongs out of the city, and was upon the road, they fell upon him, and fought hand to hand with him, (360) whom he also put to flight, and overcame, not like one that was in distress and in necessity, but like one that was excellently prepared for war, and had what he wanted in great plenty. And in this very place where he overcame the Jews, it was that he some time afterwards built a most excellent palace, and a city round about it, and called it Herodium. (361) And when he was come to Idumea, at a place called Thressa, his brother Joseph met him, and he then held a council to take advice about all his affairs, and what was fit to be done in his circumstances, since he had a great multitude that followed him, besides his mercenary soldiers, and the place Masada, whither he proposed to fly, was too small to contain so great a multitude; (362) so he sent away the greater part of his company, being above nine thousand, and bade them go, some one way and some another and so save themselves in Idumea, and gave them what would buy them provisions in their journey. But he took with him those that were the least encumbered, and were most intimate with him, and came to the fortress, and placed there his wives and his followers, being eight hundred in number, there being in the place a sufficient quantity of corn and water, and other necessaries, and went directly for Petra, in Arabia. (363) But when it was day, the Parthians plundered all Jerusalem, and the palace, and abstained from nothing but Hyrcanus' money, which was three hundred talents. (364) A great deal of Herod's money escaped, and principally all that the man had been so provident as to send into Idumea beforehand: nor indeed did what was in the city suffice the Parthians; but they went out into the country, and plundered it, and demolished the city Marissa.

(365) And thus was Antigonus brought back into Judea by the king of the Parthians, and received Hyrcanus and Phasaelus for his prisoners; but he was greatly cast down because the women had escaped, whom he intended to have given the enemy, as having promised they should have them, with the money, for their reward; (366) but being afraid that Hyrcanus, who was under the guard of the Parthians, might have his kingdom restored to him by the multitude, he cut off his ears, and thereby took care that the high priesthood should never come to him any more, because he was maimed, while the law required that this dignity should belong to none but such as had all their members entire. (367) But now one cannot but here admire the fortitude of Phasaelus, who, perceiving that he was to be put to death, did not think death any terrible thing at all; but to die thus by the means of his enemy, this he

thought a most pitiable and dishonourable thing, and therefore, since he had not his hands at liberty, for the bonds he was in prevented him from killing himself thereby, he dashed his head against a great stone, and thereby took away his own life, which he thought to be the best thing he could do in such a distress as he was in, and thereby put it out of the power of the enemy to bring him to any death he pleased. (368) It is also reported, that when he had made a great wound in his head, Antigonus sent physicians to cure it, and, by ordering them to infuse poison into the wound, killed him. (369) However, Phasaelus hearing, before he was quite dead, by a certain woman, that his brother Herod had escaped the enemy, underwent his death cheerfully, since he now left behind him one who would revenge his death, and who was able to inflict punishment on his enemies.

CHAPTER 14

(370) As for Herod, the great miseries he was in did not discourage him, but made him sharp in discovering surprising undertakings; for he went to Malchus, king of Arabia, whom he had formerly been very kind to, in order to receive somewhat by way of requital, now he was in more than ordinary want of it, and desired he would let him have some money, either by way of loan, or as his free gift, on account of the many benefits he had received from him; (371) for not knowing what was become of his brother, he was in haste to redeem him out of the hand of his enemies, as willing to give three hundred talents for the price of his redemption. He also took with him the son of Phasaelus, who was a child of but seven years of age; for this very reason, that he might be an hostage for the repayment of the money. (372) But there came messengers from Malchus to meet him, by whom he was desired to be gone, for that the Parthians had laid a charge upon him, not to entertain Herod. This was only a pretence which he made use of, that he might not be obliged to repay him what he owed him; and this he was further induced to by the principal men among the Arabians, that they might cheat him of what sums they had received from [his father] Antipater, and which he had committed to their fidelity. (373) He made answer, that he did not intend to be troublesome to them by his coming thither, but that he desired only to discourse with them about certain affairs that were to him of the greatest importance.

(374) Hereupon he resolved to go away, and did go very prudently the road to Egypt; and then it was that he lodged in a certain temple, for he had left a great many of his followers there. On the next day he came to Rhinocolura, and there it was that he heard what had befallen his brother, (375) though Malchus soon repented of what he had done, and came running after Herod; but with no manner of success, for he was gotten a very great way off, and

made haste into the road to Palusium; and when the stationary ships that lay there hindered him from sailing to Alexandria, he went to their captains, by whose assistance, and that out of much reverence of, and great regard to him, he was conducted into the city [Alexandria], and was retained here by Cleopatra, (376) yet was she not able to prevail with him to stay there, because he was making haste to Rome, even though the weather was stormy, and he was informed that the affairs of Italy were very tumultuous, and in great disorder.

(377) So he set sail from thence to Pamphylia, and falling into a violent storm, he had much ado to escape to Rhodes, with the loss of the ship's burden; and there it was that two of his friends, Sappinas and Ptolemeus, met with him; (378) and as he found that city very much damaged in the war against Cassius, though he were in necessity himself, he neglected not to do it a kindness, but did what he could to recover it to its former state. He also built there a three-decked ship and set sail thence, with his friends, for Italy, and came to the port of Brundusium: (379) and when he was come from thence to Rome, he first related to Antony what had befallen him in Judea, and how Phasaelus his brother was seized on by the Parthians, and put to death by them; and how Hyrcanus was detained captive by them, and how they had made Antigonus king, who had promised them a sum of money, no less than a thousand talents, with five hundred women, who were to be of the principal families, and of the Jewish stock; and that he had carried off the women by night; and that, by undergoing a great many hardships, he had escaped the hands of his enemies; (380) as also, that his own relations were in danger of being besieged and taken, and that he had sailed through a storm, and contemned all these terrible dangers, in order to come, as soon as possible, to him who was his hope and only succour at this time.

(381) This account made Antony commiserate the change that had happened in Herod's condition; and reasoning with himself that this was a common case among those that are placed in such great dignities, and that they are liable to the mutations that come from fortune, he was very ready to give him the assistance he desired; and this because he called to mind the friendship he had had with Antipater, (382) because Herod offered him money to make him king, as he had formerly given it him to make him tetrarch, and chiefly because of his hatred to Antigonus, for he took him to be a seditious person, and an enemy to the Romans. Caesar was also the forwarder to raise Herod's dignity, and to give him his assistance in what he desired, (383) on account of the toils of war which he had himself undergone with Antipater his father in Egypt, and of the hospitality he had treated him withal, and the kindness he had always showed him; as also to gratify Antony, who was very zealous for Herod. (384) So a senate was convocated; and Messala first, and then Atratinus, introduced

Herod into it, and enlarged upon the benefits they had received from his father, and put them in mind of the good will he had borne to the Romans. At the same time, they accused Antigonus, and declared him an enemy, not only because of his former opposition to them, but that he had now overlooked the Romans, and taken the government from the Parthians. (385) Upon this the senate was irritated; and Antony informed them farther, that it was for their advantage in the Parthian war that Herod should be king. This seemed good to all the senators; and so they made a decree accordingly.

(386) And this was the principal instance of Antony's affection for Herod, that he not only procured him a kingdom which he did not expect (for he did not come with an intention to ask the kingdom for himself, which he did not suppose the Romans would grant him, who used to bestow it on some of the royal family, (387) but intended to desire it for his wife's brother, who was grandson by his father to Aristobulus, and to Hyrcanus by his mother), but that he procured it for him so suddenly, that he obtained what he did not expect, and departed out of Italy in so few days as seven in all. (388) This young man [the grandson] Herod afterward took care to have slain, as we shall show in its proper place. But when the senate was dissolved, Antony and Caesar went out of the senate house, with Herod between them, and with the consuls and other magistrates before them, in order to offer sacrifices, and to lay up their decrees in the capitol. (389) Antony also feasted Herod the first day of his reign. And thus did this man receive the kingdom, having obtained it on the hundred and eighty-fourth Olympiad, when Caius Domitius Calvinus was consul the second time, and Caius Asinius Pollio [the first time].

(390) All this while Antigonus besieged those that were in Masada, who had plenty of all other necessaries, but were only in want of water, insomuch that on this occasion Joseph, Herod's brother, was contriving to run away from it, with two hundred of his dependents, to the Arabians; for he had heard that Malchus repented of the offences he had been guilty of with regard to Herod; (391) but God, by sending rain in the night-time, prevented his going away, for their cisterns were thereby filled; and as he was under no necessity of running away on that account, but they were now of good courage, and the more so, because the sending that plenty of water which they had been in want of seemed a mark of divine providence, so they made a sally, and fought hand to hand with Antigonus' soldiers (with some openly, with some privately), and destroyed a great number of them. (392) At the same time Ventidius, the general of the Romans, was sent out of Syria, to drive the Parthians out of it, and marched after them into Judea, on pretence indeed to succour Joseph, but in reality the whole affair was no more than a stratagem, in order to get money of Antigonus; so they pitched their camp very near to Jerusalem, and stripped Antigonus of a great deal of money, (393) and then he retired himself with the

greater part of the army; but, that the wickedness he had been guilty of might not be found out, he left Silo there, with a certain part of his soldiers, with whom also Antigonus cultivated an acquaintance, that they might cause him no disturbance, and was still in hopes that the Parthians would come again and defend him.

CHAPTER 15

(394) By this time Herod had sailed out of Italy to Ptolemais, and had gotten together no small army, both of strangers and of his own countrymen, and marched through Galilee against Antigonus. Silo also, and Ventidius, came and assisted him, being persuaded by Dellius, who was sent by Antony to assist in bringing back Herod. (395) Now, for Ventidius, he was employed in composing the disturbances that had been made in the cities by the means of the Parthians; and for Silo, he was indeed in Judea, but corrupted by Antigonus. However, as Herod went along, his army increased every day, and all Galilee, with some small exception, joined him; (396) but as he was marching to those that were in Masada (for he was obliged to endeavour to save those that were in that fortress, now they were besieged, because they were his relations), Joppa was a hindrance to him, for it was necessary for him to take that place first, it being a city at variance with him, that no stronghold might be left in his enemies' hands behind him when he should go to Jerusalem. (397) And when Silo made this a pretence for rising up from Jerusalem, and was thereupon pursued by the Jews, Herod fell upon them with a small body of men, and both put the Jews to flight and saved Silo, when he was very poorly able to defend himself; but when Herod had taken Joppa, he made haste to set free those of his family that were in Masada. (398) Now of the people of the country, some joined him because of the friendship they had had with his father, and some because of the splendid appearance he made, and others by way of requital for the benefits they had received from both of them; but the greatest number came to him in hopes of getting somewhat from him afterwards, if he were once firmly settled in the kingdom.

(399) Herod had now a strong army; and as he marched on, Antigonus laid snares and ambushes in the passes and places most proper for them, but in truth he thereby did little or no damage to the enemy; (400) so Herod received those of his family out of Masada, and the fortress Ressa, and then went on for Jerusalem. The soldiery also that was with Silo accompanied him all along, as did many of the citizens, being afraid of his power; (401) and as soon as he had pitched his camp on the west side of the city, the soldiers that were set to guard that part shot their arrows, and threw their darts at him; (402) and when some sallied out in a crowd, and came to fight hand to hand with the first ranks

of Herod's army, he gave orders that they should, in the first place, make proclamation about the wall, that he came for the good of the people, and for the preservation of the city, and not to bear any old grudge at even his most open enemies, but ready to forget the offences which his greatest adversaries had done him; (403) but Antigonus, by way of reply to what Herod had caused to be proclaimed, and this before the Romans, and before Silo also, said that they would not do justly if they gave the kingdom to Herod, who was no more than a private man, and an Idumean, i.e., a half Jew, whereas they ought to bestow it on one of the royal family, as their custom was; (404) for, that in case they at present bear an ill will to him, and had resolved to deprive him of the kingdom, as having received it from the Parthians, yet were there many others of his family that might by their law take it, and these such as had no way offended the Romans; and being of the sacerdotal family, it would be an unworthy thing to put them by. (405) Now while they said thus one to another, and fell to reproaching one another on both sides, Antigonus permitted his own men that were upon the wall to defend themselves; who, using their bows, and showing great alacrity against their enemies, easily drove them away from the towers.

(406) And now it was that Silo discovered that he had taken bribes: for he set a good number of his soldiers to complain aloud of the want of provisions they were in, and to require money to buy them food; and that it was fit to let them go into places proper for winter quarters, since the places near the city were a desert, by reason that Antigonus's soldiers had carried all away; so he set his army upon removing, and endeavoured to march away; (407) but Herod pressed Silo not to depart, and exhorted Silo's captains and soldiers not to desert him, when Caesar and Antony and the senate had sent him thither, for that he would provide them plenty of all the things they wanted, and easily procure them a great abundance of what they required; (408) after which entreaty, he immediately went out into the country, and left not the least pretence to Silo for his departure, for he brought an unexpected quantity of provisions, and sent to those friends of his who inhabited about Samaria, to bring down corn, and wine, and oil, and cattle, and all other provisions, to Jericho, that there might be no want of a supply for the soldiers for the time to come. (409) Antigonus was sensible of this, and sent presently over the country such as might restrain and lie in ambush for those that went out for provisions. So these men obeyed the orders of Antigonus, and got together a great number of armed men about Jericho, and sat up on the mountains, and watched those that brought the provisions. (410) However, Herod was not idle in the meantime, for he took ten bands of soldiers, of whom five were of the Romans, and five of the Jews, with some mercenaries among them, and with some few horsemen, and came to Jericho; and as they found the city deserted, but that five hundred of them had settled themselves on the tops of the hills,

with their wives and children, those he took and sent away; but the Romans fell upon the city, and plundered it, and found the houses full of all sorts of good things. (411) So the king left a garrison at Jericho, and came back again, and sent the Roman army to take their winter quarters in the countries that were come over to him, Judea and Galilee and Samaria. (412) And so much did Antigonus gain of Silo for the bribes he gave him, that part of the army should be quartered at Lydda, in order to please Antony. So the Romans laid their weapons aside, and lived in plenty of all things.

(413) But Herod was not pleased with lying still, but sent out his brother Joseph against Idumea with two thousand armed footmen and four hundred horsemen, while he himself came to Samaria, and left his mother and his other relations there, for they were already gone out of Masada, and went into Galilee, and took certain places which were held by the garrisons of Antigonus; (414) and he passed on to Sepphoris, and God sent a snow, while Antigonus' garrisons withdrew themselves, and had great plenty of provisions. (415) He also went thence, and resolved to destroy those robbers that dwelt in the caves, and did much mischief in the country; so he sent a troop of horsemen and three companies of armed footmen, against them. They were very near to a village called Arbela; (416) and on the fortieth day after, he came himself with his whole army; and as the enemy sallied out boldly upon him, the left wing of his army gave way, but he appearing with a body of men, put those to flight who were already conquerors, and recalled his men that ran away. (417) He also pressed upon his enemies, and pursued them as far as the river Jordan, though they ran away by different roads. So he brought over to him all Galilee, excepting those that dwelt in the caves, and distributed money to every one of his soldiers, giving them a hundred and fifty drachmae apiece, and much more to their captains, and sent them into winter quarters; (418) at which time Silo came to him, and his commanders with him, because Antigonus would not give them provisions any longer; for he supplied them for no more than one month; nay, he had sent to all the country about, and ordered them to carry off the provisions that were there, and retired to the mountains, that the Romans might have no provisions to live upon, and so might perish by famine; (419) but Herod committed the care of that matter to Pheroras, his youngest brother, and ordered him to repair Alexandrium also. Accordingly, he quickly made the soldiers abound with great plenty of provisions, and rebuilt Alexandrium, which had been before desolate.

(420) About this time it was that Antony continued some time at Athens, and that Ventidius, who was now in Syria, sent for Silo, and commanded him to assist Herod, in the first place to finish the present war, and then to send for their confederates for the war they were themselves engaged in; (421) but as for Herod, he went in haste against the robbers that were in the caves, and sent

Silo away to Ventidius, while he marched against them. (422) These caves were in mountains that were exceeding abrupt, and in their middle were no other than precipices, with certain entrances into the caves, and those caves were encompassed with sharp rocks, and in these did the robbers lie concealed, with all their families about them; (423) but the king caused certain chests to be made, in order to destroy them, and to be hung down, bound about with iron chains, by an engine, from the top of the mountains, it being not possible to get up to them, by reason of the sharp ascent of the mountains, nor to creep down to them from above. (424) Now these chests were filled with armed men, who had long hooks in their hands, by which they might pull out such as resisted them, and then tumble them down, and kill them by so doing; (425) but the letting the chests down proved to be a matter of great danger because of the vast depth they were to be let down, although they had their provisions in the chests themselves; but when the chests were let down, and not one of those in the mouths of the caves durst come near them, but lay still out of fear, some of the armed men girt on their armour, and by both their hands took hold of the chain by which the chests were let down, and went into the mouths of the caves, because they fretted that such delay was made by the robbers not daring to come out of the caves; (426) and when they were at any of those mouths, they first killed many of those that were in the mouths with their darts, and afterwards pulled those to them that resisted them with their hooks, and tumbled them down the precipices, and afterwards went into the caves, and killed many more, and then went into their chests again, and lay still there; (427) but, upon this, terror seized the rest, when they heard the lamentations that were made, and they despaired of escaping; however, when the night came on, that put an end to the whole work; and as the king proclaimed pardon by any herald to such as delivered themselves up to him, many accepted of the offer. (428) The same method of assault was made use of the next day; and they went farther, and got out in baskets to fight them, and fought them at their doors, and sent fire among them, and set their caves on fire, for there was a great deal of combustible matter within them. (429) Now there was one old man who was caught within one of these caves, with seven children and a wife; these prayed him to give them leave to go out, and yield themselves up to the enemy; but he stood at the cave's mouth, and always slew that child of his who went out, till he had destroyed them every one, and after that he slew his wife, and cast their dead bodies down the precipice, and himself after them, and so underwent death rather than slavery; (430) but before he did this he greatly reproached Herod with the meanness of his family, although he was then king. Herod also saw what he was doing, and stretched out his hand, and offered him all manner of security for his life; by which means all these caves were at length subdued entirely.

(431) And when the king had set Ptolemy over these parts of the country as his general, he went to Samaria with six hundred horsemen and three thousand armed footmen, as intending to fight Antigonus; (432) but still this command of the army did not succeed well with Ptolemy, but those that had been troublesome to Galilee before attacked him, and slew him; and when they had done this, they fled among the lakes and places almost inaccessible, laying waste and plundering whatsoever they could come at in those places; (433) but Herod soon returned, and punished them for what they had done; for some of those rebels he slew, and others of them, who had fled to the strongholds he besieged, and both slew them and demolished their strongholds; and when he had thus put an end to their rebellion, he laid a fine upon the cities of a hundred talents.

(434) In the meantime Pacorus was fallen in a battle, and the Parthians were defeated, when Ventidius sent Macheras to the assistance of Herod, with two legions and a thousand horsemen, while Antony encouraged him to make haste; (435) but Macheras, at the instigation of Antigonus, without the approbation of Herod, as being corrupted by money, went about to take a view of his affairs; but Antigonus, suspecting this intention of his coming, did not admit him into the city, but kept him at a distance, with throwing stones at him, and plainly showed what he himself meant; (436) but when Macheras was sensible that Herod had given him good advice, and that he had made a mistake himself in not hearkening to that advice, he retired to the city Emmaus; and what Jews he met with he slew them, whether they were enemies or friends, out of the rage he was in at what hardships he had undergone. (437) The king was provoked at this conduct of his, and went to Samaria, and resolved to go to Antony about these affairs, and to inform him that he stood in no need of such helpers, who did him more mischief that they did his enemies; and that he was able of himself to beat Antigonus. (438) But Macheras followed him, and desired that he would not go to Antony; or, if he was resolved to go, that he would join his brother Joseph with them, and let them fight against Antigonus. So he was reconciled to Macheras, upon his earnest entreaties. Accordingly he left Joseph there with his army, but charged him to run no hazards, nor to quarrel with Macheras.

(439) But for his own part, he made haste to Antony (who was then at the siege of Samosata, a place upon Euphrates) with his troops, both horsemen and footmen, to be auxiliaries to him; (440) and when he came to Antioch, and met there a great number of men gotten together that were very desirous to go to Antony, but durst not venture to go, out of fear, because the barbarians fell upon men on the road, and slew many, so he encouraged them, and became their conductor upon the road. (441) Now when they were within two days' march of Samosata, the barbarians had laid an ambush there to disturb those that came to Antony, and where the woods made the passes narrow, as they led

to the plains, there they laid not a few of their horsemen, who were to lie still until those passengers were gone by into the wide place. (442) Now as soon as the first ranks were gone by (for Herod brought on the rear), those that lay in ambush, who were about five hundred, fell upon them on the sudden, and when they had put the foremost to flight, the king came riding hard, with the forces that were about him, and immediately drove back the enemy; by which means he made the minds of his own men courageous, and emboldened them to go on, insomuch that those who ran away before, now returned back, and the barbarians were slain on all sides. (443) The king also went on killing them, and recovered all the baggage, among which were a great number of beasts for burden, and of slaves, and proceeded on in his march; (444) and whereas there were a great number of those in the woods that attacked them, and were near the passage that led into the plain, he made a sally upon these also with a strong body of men; and put them to flight, and slew many of them, and thereby rendered the way safe for those that came after; and these called Herod their saviour and protector.

(445) And when he was near to Samosata, Antony sent out his army in all their proper habiliments to meet him, in order to pay Herod this respect, and because of the assistance he had given him; for he had heard what attacks the barbarians had made upon him [in Judea]. (446) He also was very glad to see him there, as having been made acquainted with the great actions he had performed upon the road; so he entertained him very kindly, and could not but admire his courage. Antony also embraced him as soon as he saw him, and saluted him after a most affectionate manner, and gave him the upper hand, as having himself lately made him a king; (447) and in a little time Antiochus delivered up the fortress, and on that account this war was at an end; then Antony committed the rest to Sosius, and gave him orders to assist Herod, and went himself to Egypt. Accordingly, Sosius sent two legions before into Judea to the assistance of Herod, and he followed himself with the body of the army.

(448) Now Joseph was already slain in Judea, in the manner following: he forgot what charge his brother Herod had given him when he went to Antony; and when he had pitched his camp among the mountains, for Macheras had lent him five regiments, with these he went hastily to Jericho, in order to reap the corn thereto belonging; (449) and as the Roman regiments were but newly raised, and were unskilful in war, for they were in great part collected out of Syria, he was attacked by the enemy, and caught in those places of difficulty, and was himself slain, as he was fighting bravely, and the whole army was lost, for there were six regiments slain. (450) So when Antigonus had got possession of the dead bodies, he cut off Joseph's head, although Pheroras his brother would have redeemed it at the price of fifty talents. After which defeat, the Galileans revolted from their commanders,

and took those of Herod's party, and drowned them in the lake; and a great part of Judea was become seditious; but Macheras fortified the place Gitta [in Samaria].

(451) At this time messengers came to Herod, and informed him of what had been done; and when he was come to Daphne by Antioch, they told him of the ill fortune that had befallen his brother; which yet he expected, from certain visions that appeared to him in his dreams, which clearly foreshowed his brother's death. (452) So he hastened his march; and when he came to Mount Libanus, he received about eight hundred of the men of that place, having already with him also one Roman legion, and with these he came to Ptolemais. He also marched thence by night with his army, and proceeded along Galilee. (453) Here it was that the enemy met him, and fought him, and were beaten, and shut up in the same place of strength whence they had sallied out the day before. So he attacked the place in the morning; but, by reason of a great storm that was then very violent, he was able to do nothing, but drew off his army into the neighbouring villages; yet as soon as the other legion that Antony sent him was come to his assistance, those that were in garrison in the place were afraid, and deserted it in the night-time. (454) Then did the king march hastily to Jericho, intending to avenge himself on the enemy for the slaughter of his brother; and when he had pitched his tents, he made a feast for the principal commanders, and after this collation was over, and he had dismissed his guests, he retired to his own chamber; (455) and here may one see what kindness God had for the king, for the upper part of the house fell down when nobody was in it, and so killed none, insomuch that all the people believed that Herod was beloved of God, since he had escaped such a great and surprising danger.

(456) But the next day six thousand of the enemy came down from the tops of the mountains to fight the Romans, which greatly terrified them; and the soldiers that were in light armour came near, and pelted the king's guards that were come out with darts and stones, and one of them hit him on the side with a dart. (457) Antigonus also sent a commander against Samaria, whose name was Pappus, with some forces, being desirous to show the enemy how potent he was, and that he had men to spare in his war with them: he sat down to oppose Macheras; but Herod, when he had taken five cities, took such as were left in them, being about two thousand, and slew them, and burnt the cities themselves, and then returned to go against Pappus, (458) who was encamped at a village called Isanas; and there ran in to him many out of Jericho and Judea, near to which places he was, and the enemy fell upon his men, so stout were they at this time, and joined battle with them, but he beat them in the fight; and in order to be revenged on them for the slaughter of his brother, he pursued them sharply, and killed them as they ran away; (459) and as the

houses were full of armed men, and many of them ran as far as the tops of the houses, he got them under his power, and pulled down the roofs of the houses, and saw the lower rooms full of soldiers that were caught, and lay all on a heap; (460) so they threw stones down upon them as they lay piled one upon another, and thereby killed them; nor was there a more frightful spectacle in all the war then this, where, beyond the walls, an immense multitude of dead men lay heaped one upon another. (461) This action it was which chiefly brake the spirits of the enemy, who expected now what would come; for there appeared a mighty number of people that came from places far distant, that were now about the village, but then ran away; and had it not been for the depth of winter, which then restrained them, the king's army had presently gone to Jerusalem, as being very courageous at this good success, and the whole work had been done immediately; for Antigonus was already looking about how he might fly away and leave the city.

(462) At this time the king gave order that the soldiers should go to supper, for it was late at night, while he went into a chamber to use the bath, for he was very weary: and here it was that he was in the greatest danger, which yet, by God's providence, he escaped, (463) for, as he was naked, and had but one servant that followed him, to be with him while he was bathing in an inner room, certain of the enemy, who were in their armour, and had fled thither out of fear, were then in the place; and as he was bathing, the first of them came out with his naked sword drawn, and went out at the doors, and after him a second, and a third, armed in like manner, and were under such a consternation, that they did no hurt to the king, and thought themselves to have come off very well in suffering no harm themselves in their getting out of the house. (464) However, on the next day, he cut off the head of Pappus, for he was already slain, and sent it to Pheroras, as a punishment of what their brother had suffered by his means, for he was the man that slew him with his own hand.

(465) When the rigour of winter was over, Herod removed his army, and came near to Jerusalem, and pitched his camp hard by the city. Now this was the third year since he had been made king at Rome; (466) and as he removed his camp, and came near that part of the wall where it could be most easily assaulted, he pitched that camp before the temple, intending to make his attacks in the same manner as did Pompey. So he encompassed the place with three bulwarks, and erected towers, and employed a great many hands about the work, and cut down the trees that were round about the city; (467) and when he had appointed proper persons to oversee the works, even while the army lay before the city, he himself went to Samaria, to complete his marriage, and to take to wife the daughter of Alexander, the son of Aristobulus; for he had betrothed her already, as I have before related.

CHAPTER 16

(468) After the wedding was over, came Sosius through Phoenicia, having sent out his army before him over the midland parts. He also, who was their commander, came himself, with a great number of horsemen and footmen. The king also came himself from Samaria, and brought with him no small army, besides that which was there before, for they were about thirty thousand; (469) and they all met together at the walls of Jerusalem, and encamped at the north wall of the city, being now an army of eleven legions, armed men on foot, and six thousand horsemen, with other auxiliaries out of Syria. The generals were two: Sosius, sent by Antony to assist Herod, and Herod on his own account, in order to take the government from Antigonus, who was declared an enemy at Rome, and that he might himself be king, according to the decree of the senate.

(470) Now the Jews that were enclosed within the walls of the city fought against Herod with great alacrity and zeal (for the whole nation was gathered together); they also gave out many prophecies about the temple, and many things agreeable to the people, as if God would deliver them out of the dangers they were in; (471) they had also carried off what was out of the city, that they might not leave anything to afford sustenance either for men or for beasts; and by private robberies, they made the want of necessaries greater. (472) When Herod understood this, he opposed ambushes in the fittest places against their private robberies, and he sent legions of armed men to bring in provisions, and that from remote places, to that in a little time they had great plenty of provisions. (473) Now the three bulwarks were easily erected, because so many hands were continually at work upon it; for it was summertime, and there was nothing to hinder them in raising their works, neither from the air nor from the workmen; so they brought their engines to bear, and shook the walls of the city, and tried all manner of ways to get in; (474) yet did not those within discover any fear, but they also contrived not a few engines to oppose their engines withal. They also sallied out, and burnt not only those engines that were not yet perfected, but those that were; and when they came hand to hand, their attempts were not less bold than those of the Romans, though they were behind them in skill. (475) They also erected new works when the former were ruined, and making mines under ground, they met each other, and fought there; and making use of brutish courage rather than a prudent valour, they persisted in this war to the very last; and this they did while a mighty army lay round about them, and while they were distressed by famine and the want of necessaries, for this happened to be a Sabbatic Year. (476) The first that scaled the walls were twenty chosen men; the next were Sosius'

centurions; for the first wall was taken in forty days, and the second in fifteen more, when some of the cloisters that were about the temple were burnt, which Herod gave out to have been burnt by Antigonus, in order to expose him to the hatred of the Jews. (477) And when the outer court of the temple, and the lower city, were taken, the Jews fled into the inner court of the temple, and into the upper city; but now fearing lest the Romans should hinder them from offering their daily sacrifices to God, they sent an embassage, and desired that they would only permit them to bring in beasts for sacrifices, which Herod granted, hoping they were going to yield; (478) but when he saw that they did nothing of what he supposed, but bitterly opposed him, in order to preserve the kingdom to Antigonus, he made an assault upon the city, and took it by storm; (479) and now all parts were full of those that were slain, by the rage of the Romans at the long duration of the siege, and by the zeal of the Jews that were on Herod's side, who were not willing to leave one of their adversaries alive; (480) so they were murdered continually in the narrow streets and in the houses by crowds, and as they were flying to the temple for shelter, and there was no pity taken of either infants or the aged, nor did they spare so much as the weaker sex; nay, although the king sent about, and besought them to spare the people, yet nobody restrained their hand from slaughter, but as if they were a company of madmen, they fell upon persons of all ages, without distinction; (481) and then Antigonus, without regard to either his past or present circumstances, came down from the citadel, and fell down at the feet of Sosius, who took no pity of him, in the change of his fortune, but insulted him beyond measure, and called him Antigone [i.e., a woman, and not a man]: yet did he not treat him as if he were a woman, by letting him go at liberty, but put him into bonds, and kept him in close custody.

(482) And now Herod having overcome his enemies, his care was to govern those foreigners who had been his assistants, for the crowd of strangers rushed to see the temple, and the sacred things in the temple; (483) but the king thinking a victory to be a more severe affliction than a defeat, if any of those things which it was not lawful to see should be seen by them, used entreaties and threatenings, and even sometimes force itself, to restrain them. (484) He also prohibited the ravage that was made in the city, and many times asked Sosius, whether the Romans would empty the city both of money and men, and leave him king of a desert; and told him, that he esteemed the dominion over the whole habitable earth as by no means an equivalent satisfaction for such a murder of his citizens: (485) and when he said that this plunder was justly to be permitted the soldiers for the siege they had undergone, he replied, that he would give everyone his reward out of his own money; (486) and by this means be redeemed what remained of the city from destruction; and he performed what he had promised him, for he gave a noble present to every

soldier, and a proportionable present to their commander; but a most royal present to Sosius himself, till they all went away full of money.

(487) This destruction befell the city of Jerusalem when Marcus Agrippa and Caninius Gallus were consuls at Rome, on the hundred and eighty-fifth Olympiad, on the third month, on the solemnity of the fast, as if a periodical revolution of calamities had returned since that which befell the Jews under Pompey; (488) for the Jews were taken by him on the same day, and this was after twenty-seven years' time. So when Sosius had dedicated a crown of gold to God, he marched away from Jerusalem, and carried Antigonus with him in bonds to Antony; (489) but Herod was afraid lest Antigonus should be kept in prison [only] by Antony, and that when he was carried to Rome by him, he might get his cause to be heard by the senate, and might demonstrate, as he was himself of the royal blood, and Herod but a private man, that therefore it belonged to his sons, however, to have the kingdom, on account of the family they were of, (490) in case he had himself offended the Romans by what he had done. Out of Herod's fear of this it was that he, by giving Antony a great deal of money, endeavoured to persuade him to have Antigonus slain, which, if it were once done, he should be free from that fear. And thus did the government of the Asamoneans cease, a hundred and twenty-six years after it was first set up. This family was a splendid and an illustrious one, both on account of the nobility of their stock, and of the dignity of the high priesthood, as also for the glorious actions their ancestors had performed for our nation: (491) but these men lost the government by their dissensions one with another, and it came to Herod, the son of Antipater, who was of no more than a vulgar family, and of no eminent extraction, but one that was subject to other kings. And this is what history tells us was the end of the Asamonean family.

BOOK FIFTEEN

CHAPTER I

(1) How Sosius and Herod took Jerusalem by force; and besides that, how they took Antigonus captive, has been related by us in the foregoing book. (2) We will now proceed in the narration. And since Herod had now the government of all Judea put into his hands, he promoted such of the private men of the city as had been of his party, but never left off avenging and punishing every day those that had chosen to be of the party of his enemies; (3) but Pollio the Pharisee, and Sameas, a disciple of his, were honoured by him above all the rest; for when Jerusalem was besieged, they advised the citizens to receive Herod; for which advice they were well requited. (4) But this Pollio, at the time when Herod was once upon his trial of life and death, foretold, in way of reproach, to Hyrcanus and the other judges, how this Herod, whom they suffered now to escape, would afterward inflict punishment on them all; which had its completion in time, while God fulfilled the words he had spoken.

(5) At this time Herod, now he had got Jerusalem under his power, carried off all the royal ornaments, and spoiled the wealthy men of what they had gotten; and when, by these means, he had heaped together a great quantity of silver and gold, he gave it all to Antony, and his friends that were about him. (6) He also slew forty-five of the principal men of Antigonus' party, and set guards at the gates of the city, that nothing might be carried out together with their dead bodies. They also searched the dead, and whatsoever was found, either of silver or gold or other treasure, it was carried to the king; nor was there any end of the miseries he brought upon them; (7) and this distress was in part occasioned by the covetousness of the prince regent, who was still in want of more, and in part by the Sabbatic Year, which was still going on, and forced the country to lie still uncultivated, since we are forbidden to sow our land in that year. (8) Now when Antony had received Antigonus as his captive, he determined to keep him against his triumph; but when he heard that the nation grew seditious, and that, out of their hatred to Herod, they continued to bear good will to Antigonus, he resolved to behead him at Antioch, (9) for otherwise the Jews could no way be brought to be quiet. And Strabo of Cappadocia attests to what I have said, when he thus speaks: 'Antony ordered Antigonus the Jew to be brought to Antioch, and there to be beheaded; and this Antony seems to me to have been the very first man who beheaded a king, as supposing he could no other way bend the minds of the Jews so as to receive

Herod, whom he had made king in his stead; for by no torments could they be forced to call him king, (10) so great a fondness they had for their former king; so he thought that this dishonourable death would diminish the value they had for Antigonus' memory, and at the same time would diminish the hatred they bare to Herod.' Thus far Strabo.

CHAPTER 2

(11) Now after Herod was in possession of the kingdom, Hyrcanus the high priest, who was then a captive among the Parthians, came to him again, and was set free from his captivity in the manner following: (12) Barzapharnes and Pacorus, the generals of the Parthians, took Hyrcanus, who was first made high priest and afterwards king, and Herod's brother Phasaelus, captives, and were carrying them away into Parthia. (13) Phasaelus indeed could not bear the reproach of being in bonds, and thinking that death with glory was better than any life whatsoever, he became his own executioner, as I have formerly related.

(14) But when Hyrcanus was brought in Parthia, the king Phraates treated him after a very gentle manner, as having already learned of what an illustrious family he was; on which account he set him free from his bonds, and gave him a habitation at Babylon, where there were Jews in great numbers. (15) These Jews honoured Hyrcanus as their high priest and king, as did all the Jewish nation that dwelt as far as Euphrates, which respect was very much to his satisfaction. (16) But when he was informed that Herod had received the kingdom, new hopes came upon him, as having been himself still of a kind disposition towards him; and expecting that Herod would bear in mind what favour he had received from him, and when he was upon his trial, and when he was in danger that a capital sentence would be pronounced against him, he delivered him from that danger, and from all punishment. Accordingly, he talked of that matter with the Jews that came often to him with great affection; (17) but they endeavoured to retain him among them, and desired that he would stay with them, putting him in mind of the kind offices and honours they did him, and that those honours they paid him were not at all inferior to what they could pay to either their high priests or their kings: and what was a greater motive to determine him, they said, was this, that he could not have those dignities [in Judea] because of that maim in his body, which had been inflicted on him by Antigonus; and that kings do not use to requite men for those kindnesses which they received when they were private persons, the height of their fortune making usually no small changes in them.

(18) Now, although they suggested these arguments to him for his own advantage, yet did Hyrcanus still desire to depart. Herod also wrote to him, and

persuaded him to desire of Phraates, and the Jews that were there, that they should not grudge him the royal authority, which he should have jointly with himself, for that now was the proper time for himself to make him amends for the favours he had received from him, as having been brought up by him, and saved by him also, as well as for Hyrcanus to receive it. (19) And as he wrote thus to Hyrcanus, so did he send also Saramallas his ambassador to Phraates, and many presents with him, and desired him in the most obliging way, that he would be no hindrance to his gratitude towards his benefactor. (20) But this zeal of Herod's did not flow from that principle, but because he had been made governor of that country without having any just claim to it, he was afraid, and that upon reasons good enough, of a change in his condition, and so made what haste he could to get Hyrcanus into his power, or indeed to put him quite out of the way; which last thing he effected afterwards.

(21) Accordingly, when Hyrcanus came, full of assurance, by the permission of the king of Parthia and at the expense of the Jews, who supplied him with money, Herod received him with all possible respect, and gave him the upper place at public meetings, and set him above all the rest at feasts, and thereby deceived him. He called him his father, and endeavoured, by all the ways possible, that he might have no suspicion of any treacherous design against him. (22) He also did other things in order to secure his government, which yet occasioned a sedition in his own family; for being cautious how he made any illustrious person the high priest of God, he sent for an obscure priest out of Babylon, whose name was Ananelus, and bestowed the high priesthood upon him.

(23) However, Alexandra, the daughter of Hyrcanus, and wife of Alexander the son of Aristobulus the king, who had also brought Alexander [two] children, could not bear this indignity. Now this son was one of the greatest comeliness, and was called Aristobulus; and the daughter, Mariamne, was married to Herod, and eminent for her beauty also. (24) This Alexandra was much disturbed, and took this indignity offered to her son exceeding ill, that while he was alive, anyone else should be sent to have the dignity of the high priesthood conferred upon him. Accordingly she wrote to Cleopatra (a musician assisting her in taking care to have her letters carried) to desire her intercession with Antony, in order to gain the high priesthood for her son.

(25) But as Antony was slow in granting this request, his friend Dellius came into Judea upon some affairs, and when he saw Aristobulus, he stood in admiration at the tallness and handsomeness of the child, and no less at Mariamne, the king's wife, and was open in his commendations of Alexandra, as the mother of most beautiful children: (26) and when she came to discourse with him, he persuaded her to get pictures drawn of them both, and to send them to Antony, for that when he saw them, he would deny her nothing that

she should ask. (27) Accordingly, Alexandra was elevated with these words of his, and sent the pictures to Antony. Dellius also talked extravagantly, and said that these children seemed not derived from men but from some god or other. His design in doing so was to entice Antony into lewd pleasures with them, (28) who was ashamed to send for the damsel, as being the wife of Herod, and avoided it because of the reproaches he should have from Cleopatra on that account; but he sent in the most decent manner he could, for the young man; but added this withal, unless he thought it hard upon him so to do. (29) When this letter was brought to Herod, he did not think it safe for him to send one so handsome as was Aristobulus, in the prime of his life, for he was sixteen years of age and of so noble a family, and particularly not to Antony, the principal man among the Romans, and one that would abuse him in his amours, and besides, one that openly indulged himself in such pleasures as his power allowed him, without control. (30) He therefore wrote back to him that if this boy should only go out of the country, all would be in a state of war and uproar, because the Jews were in hopes of a change in the government, and to have another king over them.

(31) When Herod had thus excused himself to Antony, he resolved that he would not entirely permit the child or Alexandra to be treated dishonourably; but his wife Mariamne lay vehemently at him to restore the high priesthood to her brother: and he judged it was for his advantage so to do, because if he once had that dignity he could not go out of the country. So he called all his friends together and told them that Alexandra (32) privately conspired against his royal authority, and endeavoured, by the means of Cleopatra, so to bring it about, that he might be deprived of the government and that by Antony's means this youth might have the management of public affairs in his stead; (33) and that this procedure of her was unjust, since she would at the same time deprive her daughter of the dignity she now had, and would bring disturbances upon the kingdom, for which he had taken a great deal of pains, and had gotten it with extraordinary hazards: (34) that yet, while he well remembered her wicked practices, he would not leave off doing what was right himself, but would even now give the youth the high priesthood; and that he formerly set up Ananelus, because Aristobulus was then so very young a child. (35) Now when he had said this, not at random, but as he thought with the best discretion he had, in order to deceive the women, and those friends whom he had taken to consult withal, Alexandra, out of the great joy she had at this unexpected promise, and out of fear from the suspicions she lay under, fell a weeping, and made the following apology for herself, (36) and said, that as to the [high] priesthood, she was very much concerned for the disgrace her son was under and so did her utmost endeavours to procure it for him, but that as to the kingdom, she had made no attempts, and that if it were offered her [for her son], she would not

accept it; and that now she would be satisfied with her son's dignity, while he himself held the civil government, and she had thereby the security that arose from his peculiar ability in governing, to all the remainder of her family: (37) that she was now overcome by his benefits, and thankfully accepted of this honour shown by him to her son, and that she would hereafter be entirely obedient; and she desired him to excuse her, if the nobility of her family and that freedom of acting which she thought that allowed her, and made her act too precipitately and imprudently in this matter. (38) So when they had spoken thus to one another, they came to an agreement; and all suspicions so far as appeared, were vanished away.

CHAPTER 3

(39) So King Herod immediately took the high priesthood away from Ananelus, who as we said before was not of this country, but one of those Jews that had been carried captive beyond Euphrates; for there were not a few ten thousands of this people that had been carried captives, and dwelt about Babylonia, (40) whence Ananelus came. He was one of the stock of the high priests, and had been of old a particular friend of Herod; and when he was first made king, he conferred that dignity upon him, and now put him out of it again in order to quiet the troubles in his family, though what he did was plainly unlawful, for at no other time [of old] was anyone that had once been in that dignity deprived of it. (41) It was Antiochus Epiphanes who first broke that law, and deprived Jesus, and made his brother Onias high priest in his stead. Aristobulus was the second that did so, and took that dignity from his brother [Hyrcanus]; and this Herod was the third who took that high office away [from Ananelus], and gave it to this young man, Aristobulus, in his stead.

(42) And now Herod seemed to have healed the divisions in his family; yet was he not without suspicion, as is frequently the case of people seeming to be reconciled to one another, but thought that, as Alexandra had already made attempts tending to innovations, so did he fear that she would go on therein, if she found a fit opportunity for so doing; (43) so he gave a command that she should dwell in the palace and meddle with no public affairs; her guards also were so careful, that nothing she did in private life every day was concealed. (44) All these hardships put her out of patience, by little and little, and she began to hate Herod; for as she had the pride of a woman to the utmost degree, she had great indignation at this suspicious guard that was about her, as desirous rather to undergo anything that could befall her than to be deprived of her liberty of speech, and, under the notion of an honorary guard to live in a state of slavery and terror. (45) She therefore sent to Cleopatra, and made a long complaint of the circumstances she was in, and entreated her to do her utmost

for her assistance. Cleopatra hereupon advised her to take her son with her, and come away immediately to her into Egypt. (46) This advice pleased her; and she had this contrivance for getting away: she got two coffins made, as if they were to carry away two dead bodies, and put herself into one and her son into the other, and gave orders to such of her servants as knew of her intentions, to carry them away in the night-time. Now their road was to be thence to the seaside; and there was a ship ready to carry them into Egypt. (47) Now Aesop, one of her servants, happened to fall upon Sabion, one of her friends, and spake of this matter to him, as thinking he had known of it before. When Sabion knew this (who had formerly been an enemy of Herod, and been esteemed one of those that laid snares for and gave the poison to [his father] Antipater), he expected that this discovery would change Herod's hatred into kindness; so he told the king of this private stratagem of Alexandra: (48) whereupon he suffered her to proceed to the execution of her project, and caught her in the very fact; but still he passed by her offence; and though he had a great mind to do it he durst not inflict anything that was severe upon her, for he knew that Cleopatra would not bear that he should have her accused, on account of her hatred to him; but made a show as if it were rather the generosity of his soul and his great moderation that made him forgive them. (49) However he fully proposed to himself to put this young man out of the way, by one means or other: but he thought he might in all probability be better concealed in doing it, if he did it not presently nor immediately after what had lately happened.

(50) And now, upon the approach of the feast of tabernacles, which is a festival very much observed among us, he let those days pass over, and both he and the rest of the people were therein very merry; yet did the envy which at this time arose in him, cause him to make haste to do what he was about, and provoke him to it; (51) for when this youth, Aristobulus, who was now in the seventeenth year of his age, went up to the altar, according to the law, to offer the sacrifices, and this with the ornaments of his high priesthood, and when he performed the sacred offices, he seemed to be exceeding comely, and taller than men usually were at that age, and to exhibit in his countenance a great deal of that high family he was sprung from − (52) a warm zeal and affection towards him appeared among the people; and the memory of the actions of his grandfather Aristobulus was fresh in their minds; and their affections got so far the mastery of them, that they could not forbear to show their inclinations to him. They at once rejoiced and were confounded, and mingled with good wishes their joyful acclamations which they made to him, till the good will of the multitude was made too evident; and they more rashly proclaimed the happiness they had received from his family than was fit under a monarchy to have done. (53) Upon all this Herod resolved to

complete what he had intended against the young man. When therefore the festival was over, and he was feasting at Jericho with Alexandra, who entertained him there, he was then very pleasant with the young man, and drew him into a lonely place, and at the same time played with him in a juvenile and ludicrous manner. (54) Now the nature of that place was hotter than ordinary, so they went out in a body, and of a sudden, and in a vein of madness; and as they stood by the fish ponds, of which there were large ones about the house, they went to cool themselves [by bathing], because it was in the midst of a hot day. (55) At first they were only spectators of Herod's servants and acquaintances as they were swimming; but after a while, the young man, at the instigation of Herod, went into the water among them, while such of Herod's acquaintance as he had appointed to do it, dipped him as he was swimming, and plunged him under water, in the dark of the evening, as if it had been done in sport only; nor did they desist till he was entirely suffocated. (56) And thus was Aristobulus murdered, having lived no more in all than eighteen years, and kept the high priesthood one year only; which high priesthood Ananelus now recovered again.

(57) When this sad accident was told the women, their joy was soon changed into lamentation, at the sight of the dead body that lay before them, and their sorrow was immoderate. The city also [of Jerusalem], upon the spreading of this news, was in very great grief, every family looking on this calamity as if it had not belonged to another, but that one of themselves was slain; (58) but Alexandra was more deeply affected, upon her knowledge that he had been destroyed [on purpose]. Her sorrow was greater than that of others, by her knowing how the murder was committed; but she was under the necessity of bearing up under it, out of her prospect of a greater mischief that might otherwise follow; (59) and she sometimes came to an inclination to destroy herself with her own hand, but still she restrained herself, in hopes she might live long enough to revenge the unjust murder thus privately committed; nay, she further resolved to endeavour to live longer, and to give no occasion to think she suspected that her son was slain on purpose, and supposed that she might thereby be in a capacity of revenging it at a proper opportunity. (60) Thus did she restrain herself, that she might not be noted for entertaining any such suspicion. However, Herod endeavoured that none abroad should believe that the child's death was caused by any design of his; and for this purpose he did not only use the ordinary signs of sorrow, but fell into tears also, and exhibited a real confusion of soul; and perhaps his affections were overcome on this occasion, when he saw the child's countenance so young and so beautiful, although his death was supposed to tend to his own security. (61) So far at least this grief served as to make some apology for him; and as for his funeral, that he took care should be very magnificent, by making

great preparation for a sepulchre to lay his body in, and providing a great quantity of spices, and burying many ornaments together with him, till the very women, who were in such deep sorrow, were astonished at it, and received in this way some consolation.

(62) However, no such things could overcome Alexandra's grief; but the remembrance of this miserable case made her sorrow both deep and obstinate. Accordingly she wrote an account of this treacherous scene to Cleopatra, and how her son was murdered; (63) but Cleopatra, as she had formerly been desirous to give her what satisfaction she could, and commiserating Alexandra's misfortunes, made the case her own, and would not let Antony be quiet, but excited him to punish the child's murder; for that it was an unworthy thing that Herod, who had by him been made a king of a kingdom that no way belonged to him, should be guilty of such horrid crimes against those that were of the royal blood in reality. (64) Antony was persuaded by these arguments; and when he came to Laodicea, he sent and commanded Herod to come and make his defence as to what he had done to Aristobulus, for that such a treacherous design was not well done, if he had any hand in it. (65) Herod was now in fear, both of the accusation and of Cleopatra's ill will to him, which was such that she was ever endeavouring to make Antony hate him. He therefore determined to obey his summons, for he had no possible way to avoid it; so he left his uncle, Joseph, procurator for his government and for the public affairs, and gave him a private charge, that if Antony should kill him, he also should kill Mariamne immediately; (66) for that he had a tender affection for this his wife, and was afraid of the injury that should be offered him if, after his death, she, for her beauty, should be engaged to some other man: (67) but his intimation was nothing but this at the bottom, that Antony had fallen in love with her, when he had formerly heard somewhat of her beauty. So when Herod had given Joseph this charge, and had indeed no sure hopes of escaping with his life, he went away to Antony.

(68) But as Joseph was administering the public affairs of the kingdom, and for that reason was very frequently with Mariamne, both because his business required it, and because of the respects he ought to pay to the queen, he frequently let himself into discourses about Herod's kindness and great affection towards her; (69) and when the women, especially Alexandra, used to turn his discourses into feminine raillery, Joseph was so over-desirous to demonstrate the king's inclinations, that he proceeded so far as to mention the charge he had received, and thence drew his demonstration, that Herod was not able to live without her; and that if he should come to any ill end, he could not endure a separation from her, even after he was dead. Thus spake Joseph. (70) But the women, as was natural, did not take this to be an instance of Herod's strong affection for them, but of his severe usage of them, that they

could not escape destruction, nor a tyrannical death, even when he was dead himself; and this saying [of Joseph] was a foundation for the women's severe suspicions about him afterwards.

(71) At this time a report went about the city Jerusalem, among Herod's enemies, that Antony had tortured Herod, and put him to death. This report, as is natural, disturbed those that were about the palace, but chiefly the women: (72) upon which Alexandra endeavoured to persuade Joseph to go out of the palace, and fly away with them to the ensigns of the Roman legion, which then lay encamped about the city, as a guard to the kingdom, under the command of Julius; (73) for that by this means, if any disturbance should happen about the palace, they should be in greater security, as having the Romans favourable to them; and that besides, they hoped to obtain the highest authority, if Antony did but once see Mariamne, by whose means they should recover the kingdom, and want nothing which was reasonable for them to hope for, because of their royal extraction.

(74) But as they were in the midst of these deliberations, letters were brought from Herod about all his affairs, and proved contrary to the report, and of what they before expected; (75) for when he was come to Antony, he soon recovered his interest with him, by the presents he made him, which he had brought with him from Jerusalem; and he soon induced him, upon discoursing with him, to leave off his indignation at him, so that Cleopatra's persuasions had less force than the arguments and presents he brought to regain his friendship: (76) for Antony said, that it was not good to require an account of a king as to the affairs of his government, for at this rate he could be no king at all, but that those who had given him that authority ought to permit him to make use of it. He also said the same things to Cleopatra, that it would be best for her not busily to meddle with the acts of the king's government. (77) Herod wrote an account of these things; and enlarged upon the other honours which he had received from Antony: how he sat by him at his hearing causes, and took his diet with him every day, and that he enjoyed those favours from him, notwithstanding the reproaches that Cleopatra so severely laid against him, who having a great desire of his country, and earnestly entreating Antony that the kingdom might be given to her, laboured with her utmost diligence to have him out of the way; (78) but that he still found Antony just to him, and had no longer any apprehensions of hard treatment from him; and that he was soon upon his return, with a firmer additional assurance of his favour to him, in his reigning and managing public affairs; (79) and that there was no longer any hope for Cleopatra's covetous temper, since Antony had given her Celesyria instead of what she desired; by which means he had at once pacified her, and got clear of the entreaties which she made him to have Judea bestowed upon her.

(80) When these letters were brought, the women left off their attempt for flying to the Romans, which they thought of while Herod was supposed to be dead; yet was not that purpose of theirs a secret; but when the king had conducted Antony on his way against the Parthians, he returned to Judea, when both his sister Salome and his mother informed him of Alexandra's intentions. (81) Salome also added somewhat farther against Joseph, though it was no more than a calumny, that he had often had criminal intercourse with Mariamne. The reason of her saying so was this, that she for a long time bare her ill will; for when they had differences with one another, Mariamne took great freedoms, and reproached the rest for the meanness of their birth. (82) But Herod, whose affection to Mariamne was always very warm, was presently disturbed at this, and could not bear the torments of jealousy, but was still restrained from doing any rash thing to her by the love he had for her; yet did his vehement affection and jealousy together make him ask Mariamne by herself about this matter of Joseph; (83) but she denied it upon her oath, and said all that an innocent woman could possibly say in her own defence; so that by little and little the king was prevailed upon to drop the suspicion, and left off his anger at her; and being overcome with his passion for his wife, he made an apology to her for having seemed to believe what he had heard about her, and returned her a great many acknowledgments of her modest behaviour, (84) and professed the extraordinary affection and kindness he had for her, till at last as is usual between lovers, they both fell into tears, and embraced one another with a most tender affection. (85) But as the king gave more and more assurances of his belief of her fidelity, and endeavoured to draw her to a like confidence in him, Mariamne said, 'Yet was not that command thou gavest, that if any harm came to thee from Antony, I, who had been no occasion of it, should perish with thee, a sign of thy love to me?' (86) When these words were fallen from her, the king was shocked at them, and presently let her go out of his arms, and cried out, and tore his hair with his own hands, and said, that now he had an evident demonstration that Joseph had had criminal intercourse with his wife; (87) for that he would never have uttered what he had told him alone by himself, unless there had been such a great familiarity and firm confidence between them. And while he was in this passion he had liked to have killed his wife; but being overborne by his love to her, he restrained this his passion, though not without a lasting grief and disquietness of mind. However, he gave order to slay Joseph, without permitting him to come into his sight; and as for Alexandra, he bound her, and kept her in custody, as the cause of all this mischief.

CHAPTER 4

(88) Now at this time the affairs of Syria were in confusion by Cleopatra's constant persuasions to Antony to make an attempt upon everybody's dominions; for she persuaded him to take those dominions away from their several princes, and bestow them upon her; and she had a mighty influence upon him, by reason of his being enslaved to her by his affections. (89) She was also by nature very covetous, and stuck at no wickedness. She had already poisoned her brother, because she knew that he was to be king of Egypt, and this when he was but fifteen years old; and she got her sister Arsinoë to be slain, by the means of Antony, when she was a supplicant at Diana's temple at Ephesus; (90) for if there were but any hopes of getting money, she would violate both temples and sepulchres. Nor was there any holy place that was esteemed the most inviolable, from which she would not fetch the ornaments it had in it; nor any place so profane, but was to suffer the most flagitious treatment possible from him, if it could but contribute somewhat to the covetous humour of this wicked creature; (91) yet did not all this suffice so extravagant a woman, who was a slave to her lusts, but she still imagined that she wanted everything she could think of, and did her utmost to gain it; for which reason she hurried Antony on perpetually to deprive others of their dominions, and give them to her; and as she went over Syria with him, she contrived to get it into her possession; (92) so he slew Lysanias, the son of Ptolemy, accusing him of his bringing the Parthians upon those countries. She also petitioned Antony to give her Judea and Arabia, and in order thereto desired him to take these countries away from their present governors. (93) As for Antony, he was so entirely overcome by this woman, that one would not think her intercourse only could do it, but that he was some way or other bewitched to do whatsoever she would have him; yet did the grossest parts of her injustice make him so ashamed, that he would not always hearken to her to do those flagrant enormities she would have persuaded him to. (94) That therefore he might not totally deny her, nor by doing everything which she enjoined him, appear openly to be an ill man, he took some parts of each of those countries away from their former governors, and gave them to her. (95) Thus he gave her the cities that were within the river Eleutherus, as far as Egypt, excepting Tyre and Sidon, which he knew to have been free cities from their ancestors, although she pressed him very often to bestow those on her also.

(96) When Cleopatra had obtained thus much, and had accompanied Antony in his expedition to Armenia, as far as Euphrates, she returned back, and came to Apamea and Damascus, and passed on to Judea; where Herod met her, and farmed of her her parts of Arabia, and those revenues that came to her

from the region about Jericho. This country bears that balsam, which is the most precious drug that is there, and grows there alone. The place bears also palm trees, both many in number, and those excellent in their kind. (97) When she was there, and was very often with Herod, she endeavoured to have criminal intercourse with the king; nor did she affect secrecy in the indulgence of such sort of pleasures; and perhaps she had in some measure a passion of love to him, or rather, what is most probable, she laid a treacherous snare for him by aiming to obtain such adulterous intercourse from him; however, upon the whole, she seemed overcome with love to him. (98) Now Herod had a great while borne no good will to Cleopatra, as knowing that she was a woman irksome to all: and at that time he thought her particularly worthy of his hatred, if this attempt proceeded out of lust; he had also thought of preventing her intrigues, by putting her to death, if such were her endeavours. However, he refused to comply with her proposals, and called a council of his friends to consult with them whether he should not kill her, now he had her in his power: (99) for that he should thereby deliver all those from a multitude of evils to whom she was already become irksome and was expected to be still so for the time to come; and that this very thing would be much for the advantage of Antony himself, since she would certainly not be faithful to him, in case any such season or necessity should come upon him as that he should stand in need of her fidelity. (100) But when he thought to follow this advice, his friends would not let him; and told him, that, in the first place, it was not right to attempt so great a thing, and run himself thereby into the utmost danger; and they laid hard at him, and begged of him to undertake nothing rashly, (101) for that Antony would never bear it, no, not though anyone should evidently lay before his eyes that it was for his own advantage; and that the appearance of depriving him of her intercourse, by this violent and treacherous method, would probably set his affections more on a flame than before. Nor did it appear that he could offer anything of tolerable weight in his defence, this attempt being against such a woman as was of the highest dignity of any of her sex at that time in the world; and as to any advantage to be expected from such an undertaking, if any such could be supposed in this case, it would appear to deserve condemnation on account of the insolence he must take upon him in doing it; (102) which considerations made it very plain, that in so doing he would find his government filled with mischiefs, both great and lasting, both to himself and his posterity, whereas it was still in his power to reject that wickedness she would persuade him to, and to come off honourably at the same time. (103) So by thus affrighting Herod, and representing to him the hazards he must, in all probability, run by this undertaking, they restrained him from it. So he treated Cleopatra kindly, and made her presents and conducted her on her way to Egypt.

(104) But Antony subdued Armenia, and sent Artabazes, the son of Tigranes, in bonds, with his children and procurators to Egypt, and made a present of them, and of all the royal ornaments which he had taken out of that kingdom, to Cleopatra; (105) and Artaxias, the eldest of his sons, who had escaped at that time, took the kingdom of Armenia; who yet was ejected by Archelaus and Nero Caesar, when they restored Tigranes, his younger brother, to that kingdom; but this happened a good while afterward.

(106) But then, as to the tributes which Herod was to pay Cleopatra for that country which Antony had given her, he acted fairly with her, as deeming it not safe for him to afford any cause for Cleopatra to hate him. (107) As for the king of Arabia, whose tribute Herod had undertaken to pay her, for some time indeed he paid him as much as came to two hundred talents; but he afterward became very niggardly and slow in his payments, and could hardly be brought to pay some parts of it, and was not willing to pay even them without some deductions.

CHAPTER 5

(108) Hereupon Herod held himself ready to go against the king of Arabia, because of his ingratitude to him, and because, after all, he would do nothing that was just to him, although Herod made the Roman war an occasion of delaying his own; (109) for the battle at Actium was now expected, which fell into the hundred and eighty-seventh Olympiad, where Caesar and Antony were to fight for the supreme power of the world; but Herod having enjoyed a country that was very fruitful, and that now for a long time, and having received great taxes, and raised great armies therewith, got together a body of men, and carefully furnished them with all necessaries, and designed them as auxiliaries for Antony; (110) but Antony said he had no want of his assistance, but he commanded him to punish the king of Arabia, for he had heard, both from him and from Cleopatra, how perfidious he was; for this was what Cleopatra desired, who thought it for her own advantage that these two kings should do one another as great mischief as possible. (111) Upon this message from Antony, Herod returned back, but kept his army with him, in order to invade Arabia immediately. So when his army of horsemen and footmen was ready, he marched to Diospolis, whither the Arabians came also to meet them, for they were not unapprised of this war that was coming upon them; and after a great battle had been fought, the Jews had the victory; (112) but afterward there were gotten together another numerous army of the Arabians, at Cana, which is a place of Celesyria. Herod was informed of this beforehand, so he marched against them with the greatest part of the forces he had; and when he was come near to Cana, he resolved to encamp himself; and he cast up a

bulwark, that he might take a proper season for attacking the enemy; (113) but as he was giving those orders the multitude of the Jews cried out that he should make no delay, but lead them against the Arabians. They went with great spirit, as believing they were in very good order; and those especially were so that had been in the former battle, and had been conquerors, and had not permitted their enemies so much as to come to a close fight with them; (114) and when they were so tumultuous, and showed such great alacrity, the king resolved to make use of that zeal the multitude then exhibited; and when he had assured them he would not be behindhand with them in courage, he led them on, and stood before them all in his armour, all the regiments following him in their several ranks; (115) whereupon a consternation fell upon the Arabians; for when they perceived that the Jews were not to be conquered, and were full of spirit, the greater part of them ran away, and avoided fighting; and they had been quite destroyed, had not Athenion fallen upon the Jews, and distressed them; (116) for this man was Cleopatra's general over the soldiers she had there, and was at enmity with Herod, and very wistfully looked on to see what the event of the battle would be. He had also resolved, that in case the Arabians did anything that was brave and successful, he would lie still; but in case they were beaten, as it really happened, he would attack the Jews with those forces he had of his own, and with those that the country had gotten together for him; (117) so he fell upon the Jews unexpectedly, when they were fatigued, and thought they had already vanquished the enemy, and made a great slaughter of them; for as the Jews had spent their courage upon their known enemies, and were about to enjoy themselves in quietness after their victory, they were easily beaten by these that attacked them afresh, and in particular received a great loss in places where the horses could not be of service and which were very stony, and where those that attacked them were better acquainted with the places than themselves; (118) and when the Jews had suffered this loss, the Arabians raised their spirits after their defeat, and returning back again, slew those that were already put to flight; and indeed all sorts of slaughter were now frequent, and of those that escaped, a few only returned into the camp. (119) So King Herod, when he despaired of the battle, rode up to them to bring them assistance, yet did he not come in time enough to do them any service, though he laboured hard to do it; but the Jewish camp was taken, so that the Arabians had unexpectedly a most glorious success, having gained that victory which of themselves they were no way likely to have gained, and slaying a great part of the enemy's army; (120) whence afterward Herod could only act like a private robber, and make excursions upon many parts of Arabia, and distress them by sudden incursions, while he encamped among the mountains, and avoided by any means to come to a pitched battle; yet did he greatly harass the enemy by his assiduity, and the hard labour he took in this matter. He also took great care of his own forces, and used all the means he could to restore his affairs to their old state.

(121) At this time it was that the fight happened at Actium, between Octavius Caesar and Antony, in the seventh year of the reign of Herod, and then it was also that there was an earthquake in Judea, such a one as had not happened at any other time, and which earthquake brought a great destruction upon the cattle in that country. (122) About ten thousand men also perished by the fall of houses; but the army, which lodged in the field, received no damage by this sad accident. (123) When the Arabians were informed of this, and when those that hated the Jews, and pleased themselves with aggravating the reports, told them of it, they raised their spirits, as if their enemy's country was quite overthrown, and the men were utterly destroyed, and thought there now remained nothing that could oppose them. (124) Accordingly, they took the Jewish ambassadors, who came to them after all this had happened to make peace with them, and slew them, and came with great alacrity against their army; (125) but the Jews durst not withstand them, and were so cast down by the calamities they were under, that they took no care of their affairs, but gave up themselves to despair, for they had no hope that they should be upon a level again with them in battles, nor obtain any assistance elsewhere, while their affairs at home were in such great distress also. (126) When matters were in this condition, the king persuaded the commanders by his words, and tried to raise their spirits, which were quite sunk: and first he endeavoured to encourage and embolden some of the better sort beforehand, and then ventured to make a speech to the multitude, which he had before avoided to do, lest he should find them uneasy thereat, because of the misfortunes which had happened; so he made a consolatory speech to the multitude, in the manner following:

(127) 'You are not unacquainted, my fellow soldiers, that we have had, not long since, many accidents that have put a stop to what we are about; and it is probable, that even those that are most distinguished above others for their courage, can hardly keep up their spirits in such circumstances; (128) but since we cannot avoid fighting, and nothing that hath happened is of such a nature but it may by ourselves be recovered into a good state, and this by one brave action only well performed, I have proposed to myself both to give you some encouragement, and, at the same time, some information; both which parts of my design will tend to this point, that you may still continue in your own proper fortitude. (129) I will then, in the first place, demonstrate to you, that this war is a just one on our side, and that on this account it is a war of necessity, and occasioned by the injustice of our adversaries; for, if you be once satisfied of this, it will be a real cause of alacrity to you; after which I will further demonstrate, that the misfortunes we are under are of no great consequence, and that we have the greatest reason to hope for victory. (130) I shall begin

with the first, and appeal to yourselves as witnesses to what I shall say. You are not ignorant certainly of the wickedness of the Arabians, which is to that degree as to appear incredible to all other men, and to include somewhat that shows the grossest barbarity and ignorance of God. The chief things wherein they have affronted us have arisen from covetousness and envy; and they have attacked us in an insidious manner, and on the sudden. (131) And what occasion is there for me to mention many instances of such their procedure? When they were in danger of losing their own government of themselves, and of being slaves to Cleopatra, what others were they that freed them from that fear? For it was the friendship I had with Antony, and the kind disposition he was in towards us, that hath been the occasion that even these Arabians have not been utterly undone, Antony being unwilling to undertake anything which might be suspected by us of unkindness: (132) but when he had a mind to bestow some parts of each of our dominions on Cleopatra, I also managed that matter so, that by giving him presents of my own, I might obtain a security to both nations, while I undertook myself to answer for the money, and gave him two hundred talents, and became surety for those two hundred more which were imposed upon the land that was subject to this tribute: and this they have defrauded us of, (133) although it was not reasonable that Jews should pay tribute to any man living, or allow part of their land to be taxable; but although that was to be, yet ought we not to pay tribute for these Arabians, whom we have ourselves preserved; nor is it fit that they who have professed (and that with great integrity and sense of our kindness) that it is by our means that they keep their principality, should injure us, and deprive us of what is our due, and this while we have been still not their enemies but their friends. (134) And whereas observation of covenants takes place among the bitterest enemies, but among friends is absolutely necessary, this is not observed among these men, who think gain to be the best of all things, let it be by any means whatsoever, and that injustice is no harm, if they may but get money by it: (135) is it therefore a question with you, whether the unjust are to be punished or not, when God himself hath declared his mind that so it ought to be, and hath commanded that we ever should hate injuries and injustice, which is not only just but necessary in wars between several nations; (136) for these Arabians have done what both the Greeks and barbarians own to be an instance of the grossest wickedness, with regard to our ambassadors, whom they have beheaded, while the Greeks declare that such ambassadors are sacred and inviolable. And for ourselves, we have learned from God the most excellent of our doctrines, and the most holy part of our law, by angels or ambassadors; for this name brings God to the knowledge of mankind, and is sufficient to reconcile enemies one to another. (137) What wickedness then can be greater than the slaughter of ambassadors, who come to treat about doing what is right? And when such have been their actions, how is it possible they can either live securely in common life, or be successful in war? In my opinion, this is impossible. (138) But perhaps some will say that what is holy and what is righteous is indeed on our side, but that the Arabians are either more courageous or more numerous than we are. Now, as to this, in the first place, it is not fit for us to say so, for with whom is what is righteous, with them is God himself; now, where God is, there is both multitude and courage. (139) But to examine our own circumstances a little, we were conquerors in the first battle; and when we fought again, they were not able to oppose us, but ran away, and could not endure our attacks or our courage; but when we had conquered them, then came Athenion, and made war against us without declaring it; (140) and pray, is this an instance of their manhood, or is it not a second instance of their wickedness and treachery? Why are we therefore of less courage, on account of that which ought to inspire us with stronger hopes? And why are we terrified at these, who when they fight upon the level, are continually beaten, and when they seem to be conquerors they gain it by wickedness? (141) And if we suppose that anyone should deem them to be men of real courage, will not he be excited by that very consideration to do his utmost against them? For true valour is not shown by fighting against weak persons, but in being able to overcome the most hardy. (142) But then, if the distresses we are ourselves under, and the miseries that have come by the earthquake, have affrighted anyone, let him consider in the first place, that this very thing will deceive the Arabians, by their supposal that what hath befallen us is greater than it really is. Moreover, it is not right that the same thing that emboldens them should discourage us; (143) for these men, you see, do not derive their alacrity from any advantageous virtue of their own, but from their hope, as to us, that we are quite cast down by our misfortunes; but when we boldly march against them, we shall soon pull down their insolent conceit of themselves, and shall gain this by attacking them, that they will not be so insolent when we come to the battle; (144) for our distresses are not so great, nor is what hath happened all indication of the anger of God against us, as some imagine; for such things are accidental, and adversities that come in the usual course of things; and if we allow that this was done by the will of God, we must allow that it is now over by his will also, and that he is satisfied with what hath already happened; for had he been willing to afflict us still more thereby, he had not changed his mind so soon. (145) And as for the war we are engaged in, he hath himself demonstrated that he is willing it should go on, and that he knows it to be a just war; for while some of the people in the country have perished, all you who were in arms have suffered nothing, but are all preserved alive; whereby God makes it plain to us, that if you had universally, with your children and wives, been in the army, it had come to pass that you had not undergone anything that would have much hurt you. (146) Consider these things, and, what is more than all the rest, that you have God at all times for your protector; and prosecute these men with a just bravery, who in point of friendship are unjust, in their battles perfidious, towards ambassadors impious, and always inferior to you in valour.'

(147) When the Jews heard this speech, they were much raised in their minds, and more disposed to fight than before. So Herod, when he had offered the sacrifices appointed by law, made haste, and took them, and led them against the Arabians; and in order to that, passed over Jordan, (148) and pitched his camp near to that of the enemy. He also thought fit to seize upon a certain castle that lay in the midst of them, as hoping it would be for his advantage, and would the sooner produce a battle; and that if there were occasion for delay, he should by it have his camp fortified; (149) and as the Arabians had the same intentions upon that place, a contest arose about it; at first they were but skirmishes, after which there came more soldiers, and it proved a sort of fight, and some fell on both sides, till those of the Arabian side were beaten, and retreated. (150) This was no small encouragement to the Jews immediately; and when Herod observed that the enemy's army were disposed to anything rather than to come to an engagement, he ventured boldly to attempt the bulwark itself, and to pull it to pieces, and so to get nearer to their camp, in order to fight them; for when they were forced out of their trenches, they went out in disorder, and had not the least alacrity, or hope of victory; (151) yet did they fight hand to hand, because they were more in number than the Jews, and because they were in such a disposition of war that they were under a necessity of coming on boldly; so they came to a terrible battle, while not a few fell on each side. However, at length the Arabians fled; (152) and so great a slaughter was made upon their being routed, that they were not only killed by their enemies, but became the authors of their own deaths also, and were trodden down by the multitude, and the great current of people in disorder, and were destroyed by their own armour; so five thousand men lay dead upon the spot, (153) while the rest of the multitude soon ran within the bulwark [for safety], but had no firm hope of safety by reason of their want of necessaries, and especially of water. (154) The Jews pursued them, but could not get in with them, but sat round about the bulwark, and watched any assistance that would get into them, and prevented any there that had a mind to it, from running away.

(155) When the Arabians were in these circumstances, they sent ambassadors to Herod, in the first place to propose terms of accommodation, and after that to offer him, so pressing was their thirst upon them, to undergo whatsoever he pleased, if he would free them from their present distress; (156) but he would admit of no ambassadors, of no price of redemption, nor of any other moderate

terms whatever, being very desirous to revenge those unjust actions which they had been guilty of towards his nation. So they were necessitated by other motives, and particularly by their thirst, to come out, and deliver themselves up to him, to be carried away captives; (157) and in five days' time, the number of four thousand were taken prisoners, while all the rest resolved to make a sally upon their enemies, and to fight it out with them, choosing rather, if so it must be, to die therein, than to perish gradually and ingloriously. (158) When they had taken this resolution, they came out of their trenches, but could no way sustain the fight, being too much disabled, both in mind and body, and having not room to exert themselves, and thought it an advantage to be killed, and a misery to survive; so at the first onset there fell about seven thousand of them, (159) after which stroke they let all the courage they had put on before fall, and stood amazed at Herod's warlike spirit under his own calamities; so for the future they yielded, and made him ruler of their nation; (160) whereupon he was greatly elevated at so seasonable a success, and returned home, taking great authority upon him, on account of so bold and glorious an expedition as he had made.

CHAPTER 6

(161) Herod's other affairs were now very prosperous, and he was not to be easily assaulted on any side. Yet did there come upon him a danger that would hazard his entire dominions, after Antony had been beaten at the battle of Actium by Caesar [Octavian]; (162) for at that time both Herod's enemies and friends despaired of his affairs, for it was not probable that he would remain without punishment, who had shown so much friendship for Antony. (163) So it happened that his friends despaired, and had no hopes of his escape; but for his enemies, they all outwardly appeared to be troubled at his case, but were privately very glad of it, as hoping to obtain a change for the better. (164) As for Herod himself, he saw that there was no one of royal dignity left but Hyrcanus, and therefore he thought it would be for his advantage not to suffer him to be an obstacle in his way any longer: for that in case he himself survived, and escaped the danger he was in, he thought it was the safest way to put it out of the power of such a man to make any attempt against him at such junctures of affairs, as was more worthy of the kingdom than himself; and in case he should be slain by Caesar, his envy prompted him to desire to slay him that would otherwise be king after him.

(165) While Herod had these things in his mind, there was a certain occasion afforded him; for Hyrcanus was of so mild a temper, both then and at other times, that he desired not to meddle with public affairs, nor to concern himself with innovations, but left all to fortune, and contented himself with what that

afforded him: (166) but Alexandra [his daughter] was a lover of strife, and was exceeding desirous of a change of the government; and spoke to her father not to bear forever Herod's injurious treatment of their family, but to anticipate their future hopes, as she safely might; (167) and desired him to write about these matters to Malchus, who was then governor of Arabia, to receive them, and to secure them [from Herod], for that if they went away, and Herod's affairs proved to be as it was likely they would be by reason of Caesar's enmity to him, they should then be the only persons that could take the government; and this, both on account of the royal family they were of, and on account of the good disposition of the multitude to them. (168) While she used these persuasions, Hyrcanus put off her suit; but as she showed that she was a woman, and a contentious woman too, and would not desist either night or day, but would always be speaking to him about these matters, and about Herod's treacherous designs, she at last prevailed with him to entrust Dositheus, one of his friends, with a letter, wherein his resolution was declared; and he desired the Arabian governor to send him some horsemen, who should receive him, and conduct him to the lake Asphaltitis, which is from the bounds of Jerusalem three hundred furlongs: (169) and he did therefore trust Dositheus with this letter, because he was a careful attendant on him, and on Alexandra, and had no small occasion to bear ill will to Herod; for he was a kinsman of one Joseph, whom he had slain, and a brother of those that were formerly slain at Tyre by Antony: (170) yet could not these motives induce Dositheus to serve Hyrcanus in this affair; for, preferring the hopes he had from the present king to those he had from him, he gave Herod the letter. (171) So he took his kindness in good part, and bade him besides do what he had already done, that is, go again, and delivering it to Malchus, and then to bring back the letter in answer to it; for it would be much better if he could know Malchus' intentions also. (172) And when Dositheus was very ready to serve him in this point also, the Arabian governor returned back for answer, that he would receive Hyrcanus, and all that should come with him, and even all the Jews that were of his party: that he would, moreover, send forces sufficient to secure them in their journey; and that he should be in no want of anything he should desire. (173) Now as soon as Herod had received this letter, he immediately sent for Hyrcanus and questioned him about the league he had made with Malchus; and when he denied it, he showed his letter to the sanhedrin, and put the man to death immediately.

(174) And this account we give the reader, as it is contained in the commentaries of King Herod: but other historians do not agree with them, for they suppose that Herod did not find, but rather make, this an occasion for thus putting him to death, and that by treacherously laying a snare for him; (175) for thus do they write: that Herod and he were once at a treat, and that

Herod had given no occasion to suspect [that he was displeased at him], but put this question to Hyrcanus, whether he had received any letters from Malchus? And when he answered that he had received letters, but those of salutation only; (176) and when he asked further, whether he had not received any presents from him; and when he had replied, that he had received no more than four horses to ride on, which Malchus had sent him, they pretended that Herod charged these upon him as the crimes of bribery and treason, and gave order that he should be led away and slain. (177) And in order to demonstrate that he had been guilty of no offence, when he was thus brought to his end, they allege how mild his temper had been: and that even in his youth he had never given any demonstration of boldness or rashness, and that the case was the same when he came to be king, but that he even then committed the management of the greatest part of public affairs to Antipater: (178) and that he was now above fourscore years old, and knew that Herod's government was in a secure state. He also came over Euphrates, and left those who greatly honoured him beyond that river, though he were to be entirely under Herod's government; and that it was a most incredible thing that he should enterprise anything by way of innovation, and not at all agreeable to his temper, but that this was a plot of Herod's own contrivance.

(179) And this was the fate of Hyrcanus; and thus did he end his life, after he had endured various and manifold turns of fortune in his lifetime; for he was made high priest of the Jewish nation in the beginning of his mother Alexandra's reign, who held the government nine years; (180) and when after his mother's death he took the kingdom himself, and held it three months, he lost it, by the means of his brother Aristobulus. He was then restored by Pompey, and received all sorts of honours from him, and enjoyed them forty years; (181) but when he was again deprived by Antigonus, and was maimed in his body, he was made a captive by the Parthians, and thence returned home again after some time, on account of the hopes that Herod had given him; none of which came to pass according to his expectation, but he still conflicted with many misfortunes through the whole course of his life; and what was the heaviest calamity of all, as we have related already, he came to an end which was undeserved by him. (182) His character appeared to be that of a man of a mild and moderate disposition, who suffered the administration of affairs to be generally done by others under him. He was averse to much meddling with the public, nor had shrewdness enough to govern a kingdom: both Antipater and Herod came to their greatness by reason of his mildness; and at last he met with such an end from them as was not agreeable either to justice or piety.

(183) Now Herod, as soon as he had put Hyrcanus out of the way, made haste to Caesar; and because he could not have any hopes of kindness from

him, on account of the friendship he had for Antony, he had a suspicion of Alexandra, lest she should take this opportunity to bring the multitude to a revolt, and introduce a sedition into the affairs of the kingdom; (184) so he committed the care of everything to his brother Pheroras, and placed his mother Cyprus, and his sister [Salome], and the whole family, at Masada, and gave him a charge, that if he should hear any sad news about him, he should take care of the government; (185) but as to Mariamne his wife, because of the misunderstanding between him and his sister, and his sister's mother, which made it impossible for them to live together, he placed her at Alexandrium, with Alexandra her mother, and left his treasurer Joseph and Sohemus of Iturea, to take care of that fortress. These two had been very faithful to him from the beginning, and were now left as a guard to the women. (186) They also had it in charge, that if they should hear any mischief had befallen him, they should kill them both; and, as far as they were able, to preserve the kingdom for his sons, and for his brother Pheroras.

(187) When he had given them this charge, he made haste to Rhodes, to meet Caesar; and when he had sailed to that city, he took off his diadem, but remitted nothing else of his usual dignity: and when, upon his meeting him, he desired that he would let him speak to him, he therein exhibited a much more noble specimen of a great soul, (188) for he did not betake himself to supplications, as men usually do upon such occasions, nor offered him any petition, as if he were an offender, but after an undaunted manner, gave an account of what he had done; (189) for he spake thus to Caesar: that he had the greatest friendship for Antony, and did everything he could that he might attain the government: that he was not indeed in the army with him, because the Arabians had diverted him, but that he had sent him both money and corn, (190) which was but too little in comparison of what he ought to have done for him; 'for, if a man owns himself to be another's friend and knows him to be a benefactor, he is obliged to hazard everything, to use every faculty of his soul, every member of his body, and all the wealth he hath, for him in which I confess I have been too deficient. However, I am conscious to myself, that so far I have done right, that I have not deserted him upon his defeat at Actium; (191) nor upon the evident change of his fortune have I transferred my hopes from him to another, but have preserved myself, though not as a valuable fellow-soldier, yet certainly as a faithful counsellor, to Antony, when I demonstrated to him that the only way he had to save himself, and not to lose all his authority, was to slay Cleopatra; (192) for when she was once dead, there would be room for him to retain his authority, and rather to bring thee to make a composition with him, than to continue at enmity any longer. None of which advices would he attend to, but preferred his own rash resolutions before them, which have happened unprofitably for

him, but profitably for thee. (193) Now, therefore, in case thou determinest about me, and my alacrity in serving Antony, according to thy anger at him, I own there is no room for me to deny what I have done, nor will I be ashamed to own, and that publicly too, that I had a great kindness for him: but if thou wilt put him out of the case, and only examine how I behave myself to my benefactors in general, and what sort of friend I am, thou wilt find by experience that we shall do and be the same to thyself, for it is but changing the names, and the firmness of friendship that we shall bear to thee, will not be disapproved by thee.'

(194) By this speech, and by his behaviour, which showed Caesar the frankness of his mind, he greatly gained upon him, who was himself of a generous and magnificent temper, insomuch that those very actions which were the foundation of the accusation against him, procured him Caesar's good will. (195) Accordingly, he restored him his diadem again; and encouraged him to exhibit himself as great a friend to himself as he had been to Antony, and then had him in great esteem. Moreover, he added this, that Quintus Didius had written to him that Herod had very readily assisted him in the affair of the gladiators. (196) So when he had obtained such a kind reception, and had, beyond all his hopes, procured his crown to be more entirely and firmly settled upon him than ever, by Caesar's donation as well as by that decree of the Romans, which Caesar took care to procure for his greater security, he conducted Caesar on his way to Egypt, and made presents, even beyond his ability, to both him and his friends; and in general behaved himself with great magnanimity. (197) He also desired that Caesar would not put to death one Alexander, who had been a companion of Antony; but Caesar had sworn to put him to death, and so he could not obtain that his petition; (198) and now he returned to Judea again with greater honour and assurance than ever, and affrighted those that had expectations to the contrary, as still acquiring from his very dangers greater splendour that before, by the favour of God to him. So he prepared for the reception of Caesar as he was going out of Syria to invade Egypt; (199) and when he came, he entertained him at Ptolemais with all royal magnificence. He also bestowed presents on the army, and brought them provisions in abundance. He also proved to be one of Caesar's most cordial friends, and put the army in array, and rode along with Caesar, and had a hundred and fifty men, well appointed in all respects, after a rich and sumptuous manner, for the better reception of him and his friends. (200) He also provided them with what they should want as they passed over the dry desert, insomuch that they lacked neither wine nor water, which last the soldiers stood in the greatest need of; and besides, he presented Caesar with eight hundred talents, and procured to himself the good will of them all, because he was assisting to them in a much greater and more splendid degree than the kingdom he had

obtained could afford; (201) by which he more and more demonstrated to Caesar the firmness of his friendship, and his readiness to assist him: and what was of the greatest advantage to him was this, that his liberality came at a seasonable time also; and when they returned again out of Egypt, his assistances were no way inferior to the good offices he had formerly done them.

CHAPTER 7

(202) However, when he came into his kingdom again, he found his house all in disorder, and his wife Mariamne and her mother Alexandra very uneasy; (203) for, as they supposed (what was easy to be supposed) that they were not put into that fortress [Alexandrium] for the security of their persons, but as into a garrison for their imprisonment, and that they had no power over anything, either of others or of their own affairs, they were very uneasy; and (204) Mariamne, supposing that the king's love to her was but hypocritical, and rather pretended (as advantageous to himself) than real, she looked upon it as fallacious. She also was grieved that he would not allow her any hopes of surviving him, if he should come to any harm himself. She also recollected what commands he had formerly given to Joseph, insomuch that she endeavoured to please her keepers, and especially Sohemus, as well apprised how all was in his power; (205) and at the first Sohemus was faithful to Herod, and neglected none of the things he had given him in charge. But when the women, by kind words and liberal presents, had gained his affections over to them, he was by degrees overcome, and at length discovered to them all the king's injunctions, and this on that account principally, that he did not so much as hope he would come back with the same authority he had before, (206) so that he thought he should both escape any danger from him, and supposed that he did hereby much gratify the women, who were likely not to be overlooked in the settling of the government, nay, that they would be able to make him abundant recompense, since they must either reign themselves, or be very near to him that should reign. (207) He had a farther ground of hope also, that though Herod should have all the success he could wish for, and should return again, he knew that the king's fondness for his wife was inexpressible. These were the motives that drew Sohemus to discover what injunctions had been given him. (208) So Mariamne was greatly displeased to hear that there was no end of the dangers she was under from Herod, and was greatly uneasy at it, and wished that he might obtain no favours [from Caesar], and esteemed it almost an insupportable task to live with him any longer; and this she afterwards openly declared, without concealing her resentment.

(209) And now Herod sailed home with joy at the unexpected good success he had had and went first of all, as was proper, to this his wife, and told her, and her only, the good news, as preferring her before the rest, on account of his

fondness for her, and the intimacy there had been between them, and saluted her; (210) but so it happened, that as he told her of the good success he had had, she was so far from rejoicing at it, that she rather was sorry for it; nor was she able to conceal her resentments, but, depending on her dignity and the nobility of her birth, in return for his salutations she gave a groan, and declared evidently that she rather grieved than rejoiced at his success – and this till Herod was disturbed at her, as affording him, not only marks of her suspicion, but evident signs of her dissatisfaction. (211) This much troubled him, to see that this surprising hatred of his wife to him was not concealed, but open: and he took this so ill, and yet was so unable to bear it, on account of the fondness he had for her, that he could not continue long in any one mind, but sometimes was angry at her, and sometimes reconciled himself to her; but by always changing one passion for another he was still in great uncertainty, (212) and thus was entangled between hatred and love, and was frequently disposed to inflict punishment on her for her insolence towards him; but being deeply in love with her in his soul, he was not able to get quit of this woman. In short, as he would gladly have her punished, so was he afraid lest, ere he were aware, he should, by putting her to death, bring a heavier punishment upon himself at the same time.

(213) When Herod's sister and mother perceived that he was in this temper with regard to Mariamne, they thought they had now got an excellent opportunity to exercise their hatred against her, and provoked Herod to wrath by telling him such long stories and calumnies about her, as might at once excite his hatred and jealousy. (214) Now, though he willingly enough heard their words, yet had not he courage enough to do anything to her as if he believed them, but still he became worse and worse disposed to her, and these ill passions were more and more inflamed on both sides, while she did not hide her disposition towards him, and he turned his love to her into wrath against her; (215) but when he was just going to put this matter past all remedy, he heard the news that Caesar was the victor in the war, and that Antony and Cleopatra were both dead, and that he had conquered Egypt; whereupon he made haste to go to meet Caesar, and left the affairs of his family in their present state. (216) However, Mariamne recommended Sohemus to him, as he was setting out on his journey, and professed that she owed him thanks for the care he had taken of her, and asked of the king for him a place in the government: (217) upon which an honourable employment was bestowed upon him accordingly. Now, when Herod was come into Egypt, he was introduced to Caesar with great freedom, as already a friend of his, and received very great favours from him; for he made him a present of those four hundred Galatians, who had been Cleopatra's guards, and restored that country to him again, which by her means had been taken away from him. He

also added to his kingdom Gadara, Hippos, and Samaria; and besides those, the maritime cities, Gaza, Anthedon, Joppa, Strato's Tower.

(218) Upon these new acquisitions, he grew more magnificent, and conducted Caesar as far as Antioch; but upon his return, as much as his prosperity was augmented by the foreign additions that had been made him, so much the greater were the distresses that came upon him in his own family, and chiefly in the affair of his wife, wherein he formerly appeared to have been most of all fortunate; for the affection he had for Mariamne was in no way inferior to the affections of such as are on that account celebrated in history, and this very justly. (219) As for her, she was in other respects a chaste woman, and faithful to him; yet had she somewhat of a woman rough by nature, and treated her husband imperiously enough, because she saw he was so fond of her as to be enslaved to her. She did not also consider seasonably with herself that she lived under a monarchy, and that she was at another's disposal, and accordingly would behave herself after a saucy manner to him, which yet he usually put off in a jesting way, and bore with moderation and good temper. (220) She would also expose his mother and his sister openly on account of the meanness of their birth, and would speak unkindly of them, insomuch that there was before this a disagreement of unpardonable hatred among the women, and it was now come to greater reproaches of one another than formerly, (221) which suspicions increased, and lasted a whole year after Herod returned from Caesar. However, these misfortunes, which had been kept under some decency for a great while, burst out all at once upon such an occasion as was now offered; (222) for as the king was one day about noon lain down on his bed to rest him, he called for Mariamne, out of the great affection he had always for her. She came in accordingly, but would not lie down by him; and when he was very desirous of her company, she showed her contempt of him; and added by way of reproach, that he had caused her father and her brother to be slain; (223) and when he took this injury very unkindly, and was ready to use violence to her in a precipitate manner, the king's sister, Salome, observing that he was more than ordinarily disturbed, sent in to the king his cupbearer who had been prepared long beforehand for such a design, and bade him tell the king how Mariamne had persuaded him to give his assistance in preparing a love potion for him; (224) and if he appeared to be greatly concerned, and to ask what that love potion was, to tell him that she had the potion, and that he was desired only to give it him; but in case he did not appear to be much concerned at this potion, to let the thing drop; and that if he did so no harm should thereby come to him. When she had given him these instructions, she sent him in at this time to make such a speech. (225) So he went in after a composed manner, to gain credit to what he should say, and yet somewhat hastily; and said, that Mariamne had given him presents, and persuaded him to

give him a love potion; and when this moved the king, he said that this love potion was a composition that she had given him, whose effects he did not know, which was the reason of his resolving to give him this information, as the safest course he could take, both for himself and for the king. (226) When Herod heard what he said, and was in an ill disposition before, his indignation grew more violent; and he ordered that eunuch of Mariamne who was most faithful to her, to be brought to torture about this potion, as well knowing it was not possible that anything small or great could be done without him; (227) and when the man was under the utmost agonies, he could say nothing concerning the thing he was tortured about, but so far he knew, that Mariamne's hatred against him was occasioned by somewhat that Sohemus had said to her. (228) Now, as he was saying this, Herod cried out aloud, and said, that Sohemus, who had been at all other times the most faithful to him, and to his government, would not have betrayed what injunctions he had given him unless he had had a nearer intercourse than ordinary, with Mariamne. (229) So he gave order that Sohemus should be seized on and slain immediately; but he allowed his wife to take her trial; and got together those that were most faithful to him, and laid an elaborate accusation against her for this love potion and composition, which had been charged upon her by way of calumny only. However, he kept no temper in what he said, and was in too great a passion for judging well about this matter. Accordingly, when this court was at length satisfied that he was so resolved, they passed the sentence of death upon her; (230) but when the sentence was passed upon her, this temper was suggested by himself, and by some others of the court, that she should not be thus hastily put to death, but be laid in prison in one of the fortresses belonging to the kingdom; (231) but Salome and her party laboured hard to have the woman put to death; and they prevailed with the king to do so, and advised this out of caution, lest the multitude should be tumultuous if she were suffered to live; and thus was Mariamne led to execution.

(232) When Alexandra observed how things went, and that there were small hopes that she herself should escape the like treatment from Herod, she changed her behaviour to quite the reverse of what might have been expected from her former boldness, and this after a very indecent manner; (233) for out of her desire to show how entirely ignorant she was of the crimes laid against Mariamne, she leaped out of her place, and reproached her daughter in the hearing of all the people; and cried out that she had been an ill woman, and ungrateful to her husband, and that her punishment came justly upon her for such her insolent behaviour, for that she had not made proper returns to him who had been their common benefactor. (234) And when she had for some time acted after this hypocritical manner, and had been so outrageous as to tear her hair, this indecent and dissembling behaviour, as was to be expected, was

greatly condemned by the rest of the spectators, as it was principally by the poor woman who was to suffer; (235) for at the first she gave her not a word, nor was discomposed at her peevishness, and only looked at her, yet did she, out of a greatness of soul, discover her concern for her mother's offence, and especially for her exposing herself in a manner so unbecoming her: (236) but as for herself, she went to her death with an unshaken firmness of mind, and without changing the colour of her face, and thereby evidently discovered the nobility of her descent to the spectators, even in the last moments of her life.

(237) And thus died Mariamne, a woman of an excellent character, both for chastity and greatness of soul; but she wanted moderation, and had too much of contention in her nature, yet had she all that can be said in the beauty of her body, and her majestic appearance in conversation; (238) and thence arose the greatest part of the occasions why she did not prove so agreeable to the king, nor live so pleasantly with him as she might otherwise have done; for while she was most indulgently used by the king, out of his fondness for her, and did not expect that he could do anything hard to her, she took too unbounded a liberty. (239) Moreover, that which most afflicted her, was what he had done to her relations, and she ventured to speak of all they had suffered by him, and at last greatly provoked both the king's mother and sister, till they became enemies to her; and even he himself also did the same, on whom alone she depended for her expectations of escaping the last of punishments.

(240) But when she was once dead, the king's affections for her were kindled in a more outrageous manner than before, whose old passion for her we have already described; for his love to her was not of a calm nature, nor such as we usually meet with among other husbands; for at its commencement it was of an enthusiastic kind; nor was it, by their long cohabitation and free conversation together brought under his power to manage; (241) but at this time his love to Mariamne seemed to seize him in such a peculiar manner, as looked like divine vengeance upon him for the taking away her life; for he would frequently call for her, and frequently lament for her, in a most indecent manner. Moreover, he bethought him of everything he could make use of to divert his mind from thinking of her, and contrived feasts and assemblies for that purpose, but nothing would suffice: (242) he therefore laid aside the administration of public affairs, and was so far conquered by his passion, that he would order his servants to call for Mariamne, as if she were still alive, and could still hear them; (243) and when he was in this way, there arose a pestilential disease, and carried off the greatest part of the multitude, and of his best and most esteemed friends, and made all men suspect that this was brought upon them by the anger of God, for the injustice that had been done to Mariamne. (244) The circumstance affected the king still more, till at length he forced himself to go into desert places, and there, under pretence of going a hunting, bitterly afflicted

himself; yet had he not borne his grief there many days before he fell into a most dangerous distemper himself: (245) he had an inflammation upon him, and a pain in the hinder part of his head, joined with madness; and for the remedies that were used, they did him no good at all, but proved contrary to his case, and so at length brought him to despair. (246) All the physicians also that were about him, partly because the medicines they brought for his recovery could not at all conquer the disease, and partly because his diet could be no other than what his disease inclined him to, desired him to eat whatever he had a mind to, and so left the small hopes they had of his recovery in the power of that diet, and committed him to fortune. And thus did his distemper go on, while he was at Samaria, now called Sebaste.

(247) Now Alexandra abode at this time at Jerusalem; and being informed what condition Herod was in, she endeavoured to get possession of the fortified places that were about the city, (248) which were two, the one belonging to the city itself, the other belonging to the temple; and those that could get them into their hands had the whole nation under their power, for without the command of them it was not possible to offer their sacrifices; and to think of leaving off those sacrifices, is to every Jew plainly impossible, who are still more ready to lose their lives than to leave off that divine worship which they have been wont to pay unto God. (249) Alexandra, therefore, discoursed with those that had the keeping of these strongholds, that it was proper for them to deliver the same to her and to Herod's sons, lest, upon his death, any other person should seize upon the government; and that upon his recovery none could keep them more safely for him than those of his own family. (250) These words were not by them at all taken in good part; and, as they had been in former times faithful [to Herod], they resolved to continue so more than ever, both because they hated Alexandra, and because they thought it a sort of impiety to despair of Herod's recovery while he was yet alive, for they had been his old friends; and one of them, whose name was Achiabas, was his cousin-german. (251) They sent messengers, therefore, to acquaint him with Alexandra's design; so he made no longer delay, but gave orders to have her slain; yet was it still with difficulty, and after he had endured great pain, that he got clear of his distemper. He was still sorely afflicted, both in mind and body, and made very uneasy, and readier than ever upon all occasions to inflict punishment upon those that fell under his hand. (252) He also slew the most intimate of his friends, Costobarus and Lysimachus and Gadias, who was also called Antipater; as also Dositheus, and that upon the following occasion.

(253) Costobarus was an Idumean by birth, and one of principal dignity among them, and one whose ancestors had been priests to the Koze, whom the Idumeans had [formerly] esteemed as a god; (254) but after Hyrcanus had made a change in their political government, and made them receive the

Jewish customs and law, Herod made Costobarus governor of Idumea and Gaza, and gave him his sister Salome to wife; and this was upon his slaughter of [his uncle] Joseph, who had that government before, as we have related already. (255) When Costobarus had gotten to be so highly advanced, it pleased him, and was more than he hoped for, and he was more and more puffed up by his good success, and in a little while he exceeded all bounds, and did not think fit to obey what Herod, as their ruler, commanded him, or that the Idumeans should make use of the Jewish customs, or be subject to them. (256) He therefore sent to Cleopatra, and informed her that the Idumeans had been always under his progenitors, and that for the same reason it was but just that she should desire that country for him of Antony, for that he was ready to transfer his friendship to her: (257) and this he did, not because he was better pleased to be under Cleopatra's government, but because he thought that, upon the diminution of Herod's power, it would not be difficult for him to obtain himself the entire government over the Idumeans, and somewhat more also; for he raised his hopes still higher, as having no small pretences, both by his birth and by these riches which he had gotten by his constant attention to filthy lucre; and accordingly it was not a small matter that he aimed at. (258) So Cleopatra desired this country of Antony, but failed of her purpose. An account of this was brought to Herod, who was thereupon ready to kill Costobarus; yet, upon the entreaties of his sister and mother, he forgave him, and vouchsafed to pardon him entirely, though he still had a suspicion of him afterward for this his attempt.

(259) But some time afterward, when Salome happened to quarrel with Costobarus, she sent him a bill of divorce, and dissolved her marriage with him, though this was not according to the Jewish laws; for with us it is lawful for a husband to do so; but a wife, if she departs from her husband, cannot of herself be married to another, unless her former husband put her away. (260) However, Salome chose not to follow the law of her country, but the law of her authority, and so renounced her wedlock; and told her brother Herod, that she left her husband out of her good will to him, because she perceived that he, with Antipater, and Lysimachus, and Dositheus, were raising a sedition against him: as an evidence whereof, she alleged the case of the sons of Babas, that they had been by him preserved alive already for the interval of twelve years, (261) which proved to be true. But when Herod thus unexpectedly heard of it, he was greatly surprised at it, and was the more surprised, because the relation appeared incredible to him. As for the fact relating to these sons of Babas, Herod had formerly taken great pains to bring them to punishment, as being enemies to his government; but they were now forgotten by him, on account of the length of time [since he had ordered them to be slain]. (262) Now the cause of his ill will and hatred to them arose

hence: that while Antigonus was king, Herod, with his army, besieged the city of Jerusalem, where the distress and miseries which the besieged endured were so pressing, that the greater number of them invited Herod into the city, and already placed their hopes on him. (263) Now, the sons of Babas were of great dignity, and had power among the multitude, and were faithful to Antigonus, and were always raising calumnies against Herod, and encouraged the people to preserve the government to that royal family which held it by inheritance. So these men acted thus politically, and, as they thought, for their own advantage; (264) but when the city was taken, and Herod had gotten the government into his hands, and Costobarus was appointed to hinder men from passing out at the gates, and to guard the city, that those citizens that were guilty, and of the party opposite to the king, might not get out of it – Costobarus being sensible that the sons of Babas were had in respect and honour by the whole multitude, and supposing that their preservation might be of great advantage to him in the changes of government afterward, he set them by themselves, and concealed them in his own farms, (265) and when the thing was suspected, he assured Herod upon oath that he really knew nothing of that matter, and so overcame the suspicions that lay upon him; nay, after that, when the king had publicly proposed a reward for the discovery, and had put in practice all sorts of methods for searching out this matter, he would not confess it; but being persuaded that when he had at first denied it, if the men were found, he should not escape unpunished, he was forced to keep them secret, not only out of his good will to them, but out of a necessary regard to his own preservation also. (266) But when the king knew the thing, by his sister's information, he sent men to the places where he had the intimation they were concealed, and ordered both them and those that were accused as guilty with them, to be slain, insomuch that there were now none at all left to the kindred of Hyrcanus; and the kingdom was entirely in Herod's own power, and there was nobody remaining of such dignity as could put a stop to what he did against the Jewish laws.

CHAPTER 8

(267) On this account it was that Herod revolted from the laws of his country, and corrupted their ancient constitution, by the introduction of foreign practices, which constitution yet ought to have been preserved inviolable; by which means we became guilty of great wickedness afterward while those religious observances which used to lead the multitude to piety, were now neglected; (268) for, in the first place, he appointed solemn games to be celebrated every fifth year, in honour of Caesar, and built a theatre at Jerusalem, as also a very great amphitheatre in the plain. Both of them were

indeed costly works, but opposite to the Jewish customs; for we have had no such shows delivered down to us as fit to be used or exhibited by us, (269) yet did he celebrate these games every five years, in the most solemn and splendid manner. He also made proclamation to the neighbouring countries, and called men together out of every nation. The wrestlers, and the rest of those that strove for the prizes in such games, were invited out of every land, both by the hopes of the rewards there to be bestowed, and by the glory of victory to be there gained. So the principal persons that were the most eminent in these sorts of exercises, were gotten together, (270) for there were very great rewards for victory proposed, not only to those that performed their exercises naked, but to those that played the musicians also, and were called *Thymelici*; and he spared no pains to induce all persons, the most famous for such exercises, to come to this contest for victory. (271) He also proposed no small rewards to those who ran for the prizes in chariot races, when they were drawn by two, or three, or four pair of horses. He also imitated everything, though ever so costly or magnificent, in other nations, out of an ambition that he might give most public demonstration of his grandeur. (272) Inscriptions also of the great actions of Caesar, and trophies of those nations which he had conquered in his wars, and all made of the purest gold and silver, encompassed the theatre itself; (273) nor was there anything that could be subservient to his design, whether it were precious garments, or precious stones set in order, which was not also exposed to sight in these games. He had also made a great preparation of wild beasts, and of lions themselves in great abundance, and of such other beasts as were either of uncommon strength, or of such a sort as were rarely seen. (274) These were prepared either to fight with one another, or that men who were condemned to death were to fight with them. And truly foreigners were greatly surprised and delighted at the vastness of the expenses here exhibited, and at the great dangers that were here seen; but to natural Jews, this was no better than a dissolution of those customs for which they had so great a veneration. (275) It appeared also no better than an instance of barefaced impiety, to throw men to wild beasts, for the affording delight to the spectators; and it appeared an instance of no less impiety, to change their own laws for such foreign exercises: (276) but, above all the rest, the trophies gave most distaste to the Jews; for as they imagined them to be images, included within the armour that hung round about them, they were sorely displeased at them, because it was not the custom of their country to pay honours to such images.

(277) Nor was Herod unacquainted with the disturbance they were under; and, as he thought it unseasonable to use violence with them, so he spake to some of them by way of consolation, and in order to free them from that superstitious fear they were under; yet could not he satisfy them, but they cried

out with one accord, out of their great uneasiness at the offences they thought he had been guilty of, that although they should think of bearing all the rest, yet would they never bear images of men in their city, meaning the trophies, because this was disagreeable to the laws of their country. (278) Now when Herod saw them in such a disorder, and that they would not easily change their resolution unless they received satisfaction in this point, he called to him the most eminent men among them, and brought them upon the theatre, and showed them the trophies, and asked them, what sort of things they took these trophies to be; (279) and when they cried out that they were the images of men, he gave order that they should be stripped of these outward ornaments which were about them, and showed them the naked pieces of wood; which pieces of wood, now without any ornament, became matter of great sport and laughter to them, because they had before always had the ornaments of images themselves in derision.

(280) When therefore Herod had thus got clear of the multitude, and had dissipated the vehemency of passion under which they had been, the greatest part of the people were disposed to change their conduct, and not to be displeased at him any longer; (281) but still some of them continued in their displeasure against him for his introduction of new customs, and esteemed the violation of the laws of their country as likely to be the origin of very great mischiefs to them, so that they deemed it an instance of piety rather to hazard themselves [to be put to death], than to seem as if they took no notice of Herod, who, upon the change he had made in their government, introduced such customs, and that in a violent manner, which they had never been used to before, as indeed in pretence a king, but in reality one that showed himself an enemy to their whole nation; (282) on which account ten men that were citizens [of Jerusalem], conspired together against him, and sware to one another to undergo any dangers in the attempt, and took daggers with them under their garments for the purpose of killing Herod. (283) Now there was a certain blind man among those conspirators who had thus sworn to one another, on account of the indignation he had against what he heard to have been done; he was not indeed able to afford the rest any assistance in the undertaking, but was ready to undergo any suffering with them, if so be they should come to any harm, insomuch that he became a very great encourager of the rest of the undertakers.

(284) When they had taken this resolution, and that by common consent, they went into the theatre, hoping that, in the first place, Herod himself could not escape them, as they should fall upon him so unexpectedly; and supposing, however, that if they missed him, they should kill a great many of those that were about him; and this resolution they took, though they should die for it, in order to suggest to the king what injuries he had done to the multitude. These

conspirators, therefore, standing thus prepared beforehand, went about their design with great alacrity; (285) but there was one of those spies of Herod that were appointed for such purposes, to fish out and inform him of any conspiracies that should be made against him, who found out the whole affair, and told the king of it, as he was about to go into the theatre. (286) So when he reflected on the hatred which he knew the greatest part of the people bore him, and on the disturbances that arose upon every occasion, he thought this plot against him not to be improbable. Accordingly, he retired into his palace, and called those that were accused of this conspiracy before him by their several names; (287) and as, upon the guards falling upon them, they were caught in the very fact, and knew they could not escape, they prepared themselves for their ends with all the decency they could, and so as not at all to recede from their resolute behaviour, (288) for they showed no shame for what they were about, nor denied it; but when they were seized, they showed their daggers, and professed, that the conspiracy they had sworn to was a holy and a pious action; that what they intended to do was not for gain, or out of any indulgence to their passions, but principally for those common customs of their country, which all the Jews were obliged to observe, or to die for them. (289) This was what these men said, out of their undaunted courage in this conspiracy. So they were led away to execution by the king's guards that stood about them, and patiently underwent all the torments inflicted on them till they died. Nor was it long before that spy who had discovered them, was seized on by some of the people, out of the hatred they bore to him; and was not only slain by them, but pulled to pieces, limb from limb, and given to the dogs. (290) This execution was seen by many of the citizens, yet would not one of them discover the doers of it, till upon Herod's making a strict scrutiny after them, by bitter and severe tortures, certain women that were tortured confessed what they had seen done; the authors of which fact were so terribly punished by the king, that their entire families were destroyed for this their rash attempt; (291) yet did not the obstinacy of the people, and the undaunted constancy they showed in the defence of their laws, make Herod any easier to them, but he still strengthened himself after a more secure manner, and resolved to encompass the multitude every way, lest such innovations should end in an open rebellion.

(292) Since, therefore, he had now the city fortified by the palace in which he lived, and by the temple which had a strong fortress by it, called Antonia, and was rebuilt by himself, he contrived to make Samaria a fortress for himself also against all the people, and called it Sebaste, (293) supposing that this place would be a stronghold against the country, not inferior to the former. So he fortified that place, which was a day's journey distant from Jerusalem, and which would be useful to him in common, to keep both the country and the

city in awe. He also built another fortress for the whole nation; it was of old called Strato's Tower; but it was by him named Caesarea. (294) Moreover, he chose out some select horsemen, and placed them in the great plain; and built [for them] a place in Galilee, called Gaba, with Hesebonitis, in Perea; (295) and these were the places which he particularly built, while he always was inventing somewhat further for his own security and encompassing the whole nation with guards, that they might by no means get from under his power, nor fall into tumults, which they did continually upon any small commotion; and that if they did make any commotions, he might know of it, while some of his spies might be upon them from the neighbourhood, and might both be able to know what they were attempting, and to prevent it (296); and when he went about building the wall of Samaria, he contrived to bring thither many of those that had been assisting to him in his wars, and many of the people in that neighbourhood also, whom he made fellow-citizens with the rest. This he did, out of an ambitious desire of building a temple, and out of a desire to make the city more eminent than it had been before, but principally because he contrived that it might at once be for his own security, and a monument of his magnificence. He also changed its name and called it Sebaste. Moreover, he parted the adjoining country, which was excellent in its kind, among the inhabitants of Samaria, that they might be in a happy condition, upon their first coming to inhabit. (297) Besides all which, he encompassed the city with a wall of great strength, and made use of the acclivity of the place for making its fortifications stronger; nor was the compass of the place made now so small as it had been before, but was such as rendered it not inferior to the most famous cities, for it was twenty furlongs in circumference. (298) Now within, and about the middle of it, he built a sacred place, of a furlong and a half [in circuit], and adorned it with all sorts of decorations, and therein erected a temple, which was illustrious on account of both its largeness and beauty: and as to the several parts of the city, he adorned them with decorations of all sorts also; and as to what was necessary to provide for his own security, he made the walls very strong for that purpose, and made it for the greatest part a citadel; and as to the elegance of the buildings, it was taken care of also, that he might leave monuments of the fineness of his taste, and of his beneficence, to future ages.

CHAPTER 9

(299) Now on this very year, which was the thirteenth year of the reign of Herod, very great calamities came upon the country, whether they were derived from the anger of God, or whether this misery returns again naturally in certain periods of time; (300) for, in the first place, there were perpetual droughts, and for that reason the ground was barren, and did not bring forth

the same quantity of fruits that it used to produce; and after this barrenness of the soil, that change of food which the want of corn occasioned, produced distempers in the bodies of men, and a pestilential disease prevailed, one misery following upon the back of another; (301) and these circumstances, that they were destitute both of methods of cure and of food, made the pestilential distemper, which began after a violent manner, the more lasting. The destruction of men also, after such a manner, deprived those that survived of all their courage, because they had no way to provide remedies sufficient for the distresses they were in. (302) When therefore the fruits of that year were spoiled, and whatsoever they had laid up beforehand was spent, there was no foundation of hope for relief remaining, but the misery, contrary to what they expected, still increased upon them; and this, not only on that year, while they had nothing for themselves left [at the end of it], but what seed they had sown perished also, by reason of the ground not yielding its fruits on the second year. (303) This distress they were in made them also out of necessity, to eat many things that did not use to be eaten; nor was the king himself free from this distress any more than other men, as being deprived of that tribute he used to have from the fruits of the ground; and having already expended what money he had, in his liberality to those whose cities he had built; (304) nor had he any people that were worthy of his assistance, since this miserable state of things had procured him the hatred of his subjects; for it is a constant rule, that misfortunes are still laid to the account of those that govern.

(305) In these circumstances, he considered with himself how to procure some seasonable help; but this was a hard thing to be done, while their neighbours had no food to sell them; and their money also was gone, had it been possible to purchase a little food at a great price. (306) However, he thought it his best way, by all means, not to leave off his endeavours to assist his people; so he cut off the rich furniture that was in his palace, both of silver and gold, insomuch that he did not spare the finest vessels he had, or those that were made with the most elaborate skill of the artificers, (307) but sent the money to Petronius, who had been made prefect of Egypt by Caesar; and as not a few had already fled to him under their necessities, and as he was particularly a friend to Herod, and desirous to have his subjects preserved, he gave leave to them, in the first place, to export corn, and assisted them every way, both in purchasing and exporting the same; so that he was the principal, if not the only person, who afforded them what help they had. (308) And Herod, taking care the people should understand that this help came from himself, did thereby not only remove the ill opinion of those that formerly hated him, but gave them the greatest demonstration possible of his good will to them, and care of them; (309) for, in the first place, as for those who were able to provide their own food, he distributed to them their proportion of

corn in the exactest manner; but for those many that were not able, either by reason of their old age or any other infirmity, to provide food for themselves, he made this provision for them, that the bakers should make their bread ready for them. (310) He also took care that they might not be hurt by the dangers of winter, since they were in great want of clothing also, by reason of the utter destruction and consumption of their sheep and goats, till they had no wool to make use of, nor anything else to cover themselves withal. (311) And when he had procured these things for his own subjects he went further, in order to provide necessaries for their neighbours; and gave seed to the Syrians; which things turned greatly to his own advantage also, this charitable assistance being afforded most seasonable to their fruitful soil, so that everyone had now a plentiful provision of food. (312) Upon the whole, when the harvest of the land was approaching, he sent no fewer than fifty thousand men, whom he had sustained, into the country; by which means he both repaired the afflicted condition of his own kingdom with great generosity and diligence, and lightened the afflictions of his neighbours, who were under the same calamities; (313) for there was nobody who had been in want that was left destitute of a suitable assistance by him; nay, further, there were neither any people, nor any cities, nor any private men, who were to make provision for the multitudes, and on that account were in want of support, and had recourse to him, but received what they stood in need of, (314) insomuch that it appeared, upon a computation, that the number of cori of wheat, of ten Attic medimni apiece, that were given to foreigners, amounted to ten thousand: and the number that was given in his own kingdom was fourscore thousand. (315) Now it happened that this care of his, and this seasonable benefaction, had such influence on the Jews, and was so cried up among other nations, as to wipe off that old hatred which his violation of some of their customs, during his reign, had procured him among all the nation, and that this liberality of his assistance in this their greatest necessity was full satisfaction for all that he had done of that nature, (316) as it also procured him great fame among foreigners; and it looked as if these calamities that afflicted his land to a degree plainly incredible, came in order to raise his glory, and to be to his great advantage; for the greatness of his liberality in these distresses, which he now demonstrated beyond all expectation, did so change the disposition of the multitude towards him, that they were ready to suppose he had been from the beginning not such a one as they had found him to be by experience, but such a one as the care he had taken of them in supplying their necessities proved him now to be.

(317) About this time it was that he sent five hundred chosen men out of the guards of his body as auxiliaries to Caesar, whom Aelius Gallus led to the Red Sea, and who were of great service to him there. (318) When therefore his

affairs were thus improved, and were again in a flourishing condition, he built himself a palace in the upper city, raising the rooms to a very great height, and adorning them with the most costly furniture of gold, and marble seats, and beds; and these were so large that they could contain very many companies of men. These apartments were also of distinct magnitudes, and had particular names given them; (319) for one apartment was called Caesar's, another Agrippa's. He also fell in love again, and married another wife, not suffering his reason to hinder him from living as he pleased. The occasion of this his marriage was as follows: (320) there was one Simon, a citizen of Jerusalem, the son of one Boethus, a citizen of Alexandria, and a priest of great note there: this man had a daughter, who was esteemed the most beautiful woman of that time; (321) and when the people of Jerusalem began to speak much in her commendation, it happened that Herod was much affected with what was said of her; and when he saw the damsel, he was smitten with her beauty, yet did he entirely reject the thoughts of using his authority to abuse her, as believing, what was the truth, that by so doing he should be stigmatised for violence and tyranny; so he thought it best to take the damsel to wife. (322) And while Simon was of a dignity too inferior to be allied to him, but still too considerable to be despised, he governed his inclinations after the most prudent manner, by augmenting the dignity of the family, and making them more honourable; so he immediately deprived Jesus the son of Phabet of the high priesthood, and conferred that dignity on Simon, and so joined in affinity with him [by marrying his daughter].

(323) When this wedding was over, he built another citadel in that place where he had conquered the Jews, when he was driven out of his government, and Antigonus enjoyed it. (324) This citadel is distant from Jerusalem about threescore furlongs. It was strong by nature, and fit for such a building. It is a sort of a moderate hill, raised to a farther height by the hand of man, till it was of the shape of a woman's breast. It is encompassed with circular towers, and hath a strait ascent up to it, which ascent is composed of steps of polished stones, in number two hundred. Within it are royal and very rich apartments, of a structure that provided both for security and for beauty. (325) About the bottom there are habitations of such a structure as are well worth seeing, both on other accounts, and also on account of the water which is brought thither from a great way off, and at vast expenses; for the place itself is destitute of water. The plain that is about this citadel is full of edifices, not inferior to any city in largeness, and having the hill above it in the nature of a castle.

(326) And now, when all Herod's designs had succeeded according to his hopes, he had not the least suspicion that any troubles could arise in his kingdom, because he kept his people obedient, as well by the fear they stood in of him, for he was implacable in the infliction of his punishments, as by the

provident care he had showed towards them, after the most magnanimous manner, when they were under their distresses: (327) but still he took care to have external security for his government, as a fortress against his subjects; for the orations he made to the cities were very fine, and full of kindness; and he cultivated a seasonable good understanding with their governors, and bestowed presents on every one of them, inducing them thereby to be more friendly to him, and using his magnificent dispositions so as his kingdom might be the better secured to him, and this till all his affairs were every way more and more augmented. (328) But then, this magnificent temper of his, and that submissive behaviour and liberality which he exercised towards Caesar and the most powerful men of Rome, obliged him to transgress the customs of his nation, and to set aside many of their laws, by building cities after an extravagant manner, and erecting temples – (329) not in Judea indeed, for that would not have been borne, it being forbidden for us to pay any honour to images, or representations of animals, after the manner of the Greeks; but still he did this in the country [properly] out of our bounds, and in the cities thereof. (330) The apology which he made to the Jews for these things was this: that all was done, not out of his own inclinations, but by the commands and injunctions of others, in order to please Caesar and the Romans; as though he had not the Jewish customs so much in his eye as he had the honour of those Romans, while yet he had himself entirely in view all the while, and indeed was very ambitious to leave great monuments of his government to posterity; whence it was that he was so zealous in building such fine cities, and spent such vast sums of money upon them.

(331) Now upon his observation of a place near the sea, which was very proper for containing a city, and was before called Strato's Tower, he set about getting a plan for a magnificent city there, and erected many edifices with great diligence all over it, and this of white stone. He also adorned it with most sumptuous palaces, and large edifices for containing the people; (332) and, what was the greatest and most laborious work of all, he adorned it with a haven, that was always free from the waves of the sea. Its largeness was not less than the Piraeum [at Athens]; and had towards the city a double station for the ships. It was of excellent workmanship; and this was the more remarkable for its being built in a place that of itself was not suitable to such noble structures, but was to be brought to perfection by materials from other places, and at very great expenses. (333) This city is situate in Phoenicia, in the passage by sea to Egypt, between Joppa and Dora, which are lesser maritime cities, and not fit for havens, on account of the impetuous south winds that beat upon them, which, rolling the sands that come from the sea against the shores, do not admit of ships lying in their station; but the merchants are generally there forced to ride at their anchors in the sea itself. (334) So Herod endeavoured to rectify this

inconvenience, and laid out such a compass towards the land as might be sufficient for a haven, wherein the great ships might lie in safety; and this he effected by letting down vast stones of above fifty feet in length, not less than eighteen in breadth, and nine in depth, into twenty fathoms deep; and as some were lesser, so were others bigger, than those dimensions. (335) This mole which he built by the seaside was two hundred feed wide, the half of which was opposed to the current of the waves, so as to keep off those waves which were to break upon them, and so was called Procymatia, or the first breaker of the waves; (336) but the other half had upon it a wall, with several towers, the largest of which was named Drusus, and was a work of very great excellence, and had its name from Drusus, the son-in-law of Caesar, who died young. (337) There were also a great number of arches, where the mariners dwelt: there was also before them a quay [or landing place], which ran round the entire haven, and was a most agreeable walk to such as had a mind to that exercise; but the entrance or mouth of the port was made on the north quarter, on which side was the stillest of the winds of all in this place: (338) and the basis of the whole circuit on the left hand, as you enter the port, supported a round turret, which was made very strong, in order to resist the greatest waves; while, on the right hand, as you enter, stood two vast stones, and those each of them larger than the turret, which was over against them: these stood upright, and were joined together. (339) Now there were edifices all along the circular haven, made of the most polished stone, with a certain elevation, whereon was erected a temple, that was seen a great way off by those that were sailing for that haven, and had in it two statues, the one of Rome, the other of Caesar. The city itself was called Caesarea, which was also itself built of fine materials, and was of a fine structure; (340) nay, the very subterranean vaults and cellars had no less of architecture bestowed on them than had the buildings above ground. Some of these vaults carried things at even distances to the haven and to the sea; but one of them ran obliquely, and bound all the rest together, that both the rain and the filth of the citizens were together carried off with ease, and the sea itself, upon the flux of the tide from without, came into the city, and washed it all clean. (341) Herod also built therein a theatre of stone; and on the south quarter, behind the port, an amphitheatre also, capable of holding a vast number of men, and conveniently situated for a prospect to the sea. So this city was thus finished in twelve years; during which time the king did not fail to go on both with the work, and to pay the charges that were necessary.

CHAPTER 10

(342) When Herod was engaged in such matters, and when he had already re-edified Sebaste [Samaria], he resolved to send his sons Alexander and Aristobulus to Rome, to enjoy the company of Caesar; (343) who, when they came thither, lodged at the house of Pollio, who was very fond of Herod's friendship: and they had leave to lodge in Caesar's own palace, for he received these sons of Herod with all humanity, and gave Herod leave to give his kingdom to which of his sons he pleased; and, besides all this, he bestowed on him Trachon, and Batanea, and Auranitis, which he gave him on the occasion following: (344) one Zenodorus had hired what was called the house of Lysanias, who, as he was not satisfied with its revenues, became a partner with the robbers that inhabited the Trachonites, and so procured him a larger income; for the inhabitants of those places lived in a mad way, and pillaged the country of the Damascenes, while Zenodorus did not restrain them, but partook of the prey they acquired. (345) Now as the neighbouring people were hereby great sufferers, they complained to Varro, who was then president [of Syria], and entreated him to write to Caesar about this injustice of Zenodorus. When these matters were laid before Caesar, he wrote back to Varro to destroy those nests of robbers, and to give the land to Herod, that by his care the neighbouring countries might be no longer disturbed with these doings of the Trachonites, (346) for it was not an easy thing to restrain them, since this way of robbery had been their usual practice, and they had no other way to get their living, because they had neither any city of their own, nor lands in their possession, but only some receptacles and dens in the earth, and there they and their cattle lived in common together: however, they had made contrivances to get pools of water, and laid up corn in granaries for themselves, and were able to make great resistance, by issuing out on the sudden against any that attacked them; (347) for the entrances of their caves were narrow, in which but one could come in at a time, and the places within incredibly large, and made very wide; but the ground over their habitations was not very high, but rather on a plain, while the rocks are altogether hard and difficult to be entered upon, unless anyone gets into the plain road by the guidance of another, for these roads are not straight, but have several revolutions. (348) But when these men are hindered from their wicked preying upon their neighbours, their custom is to prey one upon another, insomuch that no sort of injustice comes amiss to them. But when Herod had received this grant from Caesar, and was come into this country, he procured skilful guides, and put a stop to their wicked robberies, and procured peace and quietness to the neighbouring people.

(349) Hereupon Zenodorus was grieved, in the first place because his

principality was taken away from him, and still more so, because he envied Herod, who had gotten it; so he went up to Rome to accuse him, but returned back again without success. (350) Now Agrippa was [about this time] sent to succeed Caesar in the government of the countries beyond the Ionian Sea, upon whom Herod lighted when he was wintering about Mitylene, for he had been his particular friend and companion, and then returned into Judea again. (351) However, some of the Gadarenes came to Agrippa, and accused Herod, whom he sent back bound to the king, without giving them the hearing: but still the Arabians, who of old bare ill will to Herod's government, were nettled, and at that time attempted to raise a sedition in his dominions, and, as they thought, upon a more justifiable occasion; (352) for Zenodorus, despairing already of success as to his own affairs, prevented [his enemies] by selling to those Arabians a part of his principality, called Auranitis, for the value of fifty talents; but as this was included in the donations of Caesar, they contested the point with Herod, as unjustly deprived of what they had bought. Sometimes they did this by making incursions upon him, and sometimes by attempting force against him, and sometimes by going to law with him. (353) Moreover, they persuaded the poorer soldiers to help them, and were troublesome to him, out of a constant hope that they should reduce the people to raise a sedition; in which designs those that are in the most miserable circumstances of life are still the most earnest; and although Herod had been a great while apprised of these attempts, yet did not he indulge any severity to them, but by rational methods aimed to mitigate things, as not willing to give any handle for tumults.

(354) Now when Herod had already reigned seventeen years, Caesar came into Syria; at which time the greatest part of the inhabitants of Gadara clamoured against Herod, as one that was heavy in his injunctions, and tyrannical. (355) These reproaches they mainly ventured upon by the encouragement of Zenodorus, who took his oath that he would never leave Herod till he had procured that they should be severed from Herod's kingdom, and joined to Caesar's province. (356) The Gadarenes were induced hereby, and made no small cry against him; and that the more boldly, because those that had been delivered up by Agrippa were not punished by Herod, who let them go, and did them no harm; for indeed he was the principal man in the world who appeared almost inexorable in punishing crimes in his own family, but very generous in remitting the offences that were committed elsewhere. (357) And while they accused Herod of injuries and plunderings, and subversion of temples, he stood unconcerned, and was ready to make his defence. However, Caesar gave him his right hand, and remitted nothing of his kindness to him, upon this disturbance by the multitude; (358) and indeed these things were alleged the first day, but the hearing proceeded no further; for as the Gadarens

saw the inclination of Caesar and of his assessors, and expected, as they had reason to do, that they should be delivered up to the king, some of them, out of a dread of the torments they might undergo, cut their own throats in the night-time, and some of them threw themselves down precipices, and others of them cast themselves into the river, and destroyed themselves of their own accord; (359) which accidents seemed a sufficient condemnation of the rashness and crimes they had been guilty of; whereupon Caesar made no longer delay, but cleared Herod from the crimes he was accused of. Another happy accident there was, which was a further great advantage to Herod at this time; for Zenodorus's belly burst, and a great quantity of blood issued from him in his sickness, and he thereby departed this life at Antioch in Syria; (360) so Caesar bestowed his country, which was no small one, upon Herod; it lay between Trachon and Galilee, and contained Ulatha, and Paneas, and the country round about. He also made him one of the procurators of Syria, and commanded that they should do everything with his approbation; (361) and, in short, he arrived at that pitch of felicity, that whereas there were but two men that governed the vast Roman empire, first Caesar and then Agrippa, who was his principal favourite, Caesar preferred no one to Herod besides Agrippa; and Agrippa made no one his greater friend than Herod besides Caesar; (362) and when he had acquired such freedom, he begged of Caesar a tetrarchy for his brother Pheroras, while he did himself bestow upon him a revenue of a hundred talents out of his own kingdom, that in case he came to any harm himself, his brother might be in safety, and that his sons might not have dominion over him. (363) So when he had conducted Caesar to the sea, and was returned home, he built him a most beautiful temple, of the whitest stone of Zenodorus' country, near the place called Panium. (364) This is a very fine cave in a mountain, under which there is a great cavity in the earth, and the cavern is abrupt, and prodigiously deep, and full of a still water; over it hangs a vast mountain; and under the caverns arise the springs of the river Jordan. Herod adorned this place, which was already a very remarkable one, still further by the erection of this temple, which he dedicated to Caesar.

(365) At which time Herod released to his subjects the third part of their taxes, under pretence indeed of relieving them, after the dearth they had had; but the main reason was, to recover their good will, which he now wanted; for they were uneasy at him because of the innovations he had introduced in their practices of the dissolution of their religion, and of the disuse of their own customs; and the people everywhere talked against him, like those that were still more provoked and disturbed at his procedure; (366) against which discontents he greatly guarded himself, and took away the opportunities they might have to disturb him, and enjoined them to be always at work; nor did he permit the citizens either to meet together, or to walk or eat together, but

watched everything they did, and when any were caught, they were severely punished; and many there were who were brought to the citadel Hyrcania, both openly and secretly, and were there put to death; and there were spies set everywhere, both in the city and in the roads, who watched those that met together; (367) nay, it is reported that he did not himself neglect this part of caution, but that he would oftentimes himself take the habit of a private man, and mix among the multitude, in the night-time, and make trial what opinion they had of his government; (368) and as for those that could no way be reduced to acquiesce under his scheme of government, he persecuted them all manner of ways; but for the rest of the multitude, he required that they should be obliged to take an oath of fidelity to him, and at the same time compelled them to swear that they would bear him good will, and continue certainly so to do, in his management of the government; (369) and indeed a great part of them, either to please him or out of fear of him, yielded to what he required of them; but for such as were of a more open and generous disposition, and had indignation at the force he used to them, he by one means or another made away with them. (370) He endeavoured also to persuade Pollio the Pharisee, and Sameas, and the greatest part of their scholars to take the oath; but these would neither submit so to do, nor were they punished together with the rest, out of the reverence he bore to Pollio. (371) The Essenes also, as we call a sect of ours, were excused from this imposition. These men live the same kind of life as do those whom the Greeks call Pythagoreans; concerning whom I shall discourse more fully elsewhere. (372) However, it is but fit to set down here the reasons wherefore Herod had these Essenes in such honour, and thought higher of them than their mortal nature required: nor will this account be unsuitable to the nature of this history, as it will show the opinion men had of these Essenes.

(373) Now there was one of these Essenes, whose name was Manahem, who had this testimony, that he not only conducted his life after an excellent manner, but had the foreknowledge of future events given him by God also. This man once saw Herod when he was a child, and going to school, and saluted him as king of the Jews; (374) but he, thinking that either he did not know him, or that he was in jest, put him in mind that he was but a private man; but Manahem smiled to himself, and clapped him on his backside with his hand, and said, 'However that be, thou wilt be king, and wilt begin thy reign happily, for God finds thee worthy of it; and do thou remember the blows that Manahem hath given thee, as being a signal of the change of thy fortune; (375) and truly this will be the best reasoning for thee, that thou love justice [towards men], and piety towards God, and clemency towards thy citizens; yet do I know how thy whole conduct will be, that thou wilt not be such a one, (376) for thou wilt excel all men in happiness, and obtain an

everlasting reputation, but wilt forget piety and righteousness; and these crimes will not be concealed from God at the conclusion of thy life, when thou wilt find that he will be mindful of them, and punish thee for them.' (377) Now at that time Herod did not at all attend to what Manahem said, as having no hopes of such advancement; but a little afterward, when he was so fortunate as to be advanced to the dignity of king, and was in the height of his dominion, he sent for Manahem, and asked him how long he should reign. (378) Manahem did not tell him the full length of his reign; wherefore, upon that silence of his, he asked him further, whether he should reign ten years or not? He replied, 'Yes, twenty, nay, thirty years;' but did not assign the just determinate limit of his reign. Herod was satisfied with these replies, and gave Manahem his hand, and dismissed him; and from that time he continued to honour all the Essenes. (379) We have thought it proper to relate these facts to our readers, how strange soever they be, and to declare what hath happened among us, because many of these Essenes have by their excellent virtue, been thought worthy of this knowledge of divine revelations.

CHAPTER II

(380) And now Herod, in the eighteenth year of his reign, and after the acts already mentioned, undertook a very great work, that is, to build of himself the temple of God, and make it larger in compass, and to raise it to a most magnificent altitude, as esteeming it to be the most glorious of all his actions, as it really was, to bring it to perfection, and that this would be sufficient for an everlasting memorial of him; (381) but as he knew the multitude were not ready nor willing to assist him in so vast a design, he thought to prepare them first by making a speech to them, and then set about the work itself; so he called them together, and spake thus to them: (382) 'I think I need not speak to you, my countrymen, about such other works as I have done since I came to the kingdom, although I may say they have been performed in such a manner as to bring more security to you than glory to myself; (383) for I have neither been negligent in the most difficult times about what tended to ease your necessities, nor have the buildings I have made been so proper to preserve me as yourselves from injuries; and I imagine that, with God's assistance, I have advanced the nation of the Jews to a degree of happiness which they never had before; (384) and for the particular edifices belonging to your own country, and your own cities, as also to those cities that we have lately acquired, which we have erected and greatly adorned, and thereby augmented the dignity of your nation, it seems to me a needless task to enumerate them to you, since you well know them yourselves; but as to that undertaking which I have a mind to set about at present, and which will be a work of the greatest piety and

excellence that can possibly be undertaken by us, I will now declare it to you. (385) Our fathers, indeed, when they were returned from Babylon, built this temple to God Almighty, yet does it want sixty cubits of its largeness in altitude; for so much did that first temple which Solomon built exceed this temple: (386) nor let anyone condemn our fathers for their negligence or want of piety herein, for it was not their fault that the temple was no higher; for they were Cyrus, and Darius the son of Hystaspes, who determined the measures for its rebuilding; and it hath been by reason of the subjection of those fathers of ours to them and to their posterity, and after them to the Macedonians, that they had not the opportunity to follow the original model of this pious edifice, nor could raise it to its ancient altitude; (387) but since I am now, by God's will, your governor, and I have had peace a long time, and have gained great riches and large revenues, and, what is the principal thing of all, I am at amity with and well regarded by the Romans, who, if I may so say, are the rulers of the whole world, I will do my endeavour to correct that imperfection, which hath arisen from the necessity of our affairs, and the slavery we have been under formerly, and to make a thankful return after the most pious manner to God, for what blessings I have received from him, by giving me this kingdom, and that by rendering his temple as complete as I am able.'

(388) And this was the speech which Herod made to them: but still this speech affrighted many of the people, as being unexpected by them, and because it seemed incredible, it did not encourage them, but put a damp upon them, for they were afraid that he would pull down the whole edifice, and not be able to bring his intentions to perfection for its rebuilding; and this danger appeared to them to be very great, and the vastness of the undertaking to be such as could hardly be accomplished. (389) But while they were in this disposition, the king encouraged them, and told them he would not pull down their temple till all things were gotten ready for building it up entirely again. And as he promised them this beforehand, so he did not break his word with them, (390) but got ready a thousand waggons, that were to bring stones for the building, and chose out ten thousand of the most skilful workmen, and bought a thousand sacerdotal garments for as many of the priests, and had some of them taught the arts of stone cutters, and others of carpenters, and then began to build; but this not till everything was well prepared for the work.

(391) So Herod took away the old foundations, and laid others, and erected the temple upon them, being in length a hundred cubits, and in height twenty additional cubits, which [twenty], upon the sinking of their foundations, fell down: and this part it was that we resolved to raise again in the days of Nero. (392) Now the temple was built of stones that were white and strong, and each of their length was twenty-five cubits, their height was eight, and their breadth about twelve; (393) and the whole structure, as also the structure of the royal

cloister, was on each side much lower, but the middle was much higher, till they were visible to those that dwelt in the country for a great many furlongs, but chiefly to such as lived over against them and those that approached to them. (394) The temple had doors also at the entrance, and lintels over them, of the same height with the temple itself. They were adorned with embroidered veils, with their flowers of purple, and pillars interwoven: (395) and over these, but under the crown-work, was spread out a golden vine, with its branches hanging down from a great height, the largeness and fine workmanship of which was a surprising sight to the spectators, to see what vast materials there were, and with what great skill the workmanship was done. (396) He also encompassed the entire temple with very large cloisters, contriving them to be in a due proportion thereto; and he laid out larger sums of money upon them than had been done before him, till it seemed that no one else had so greatly adorned the temple as he had done. There was a large wall to both the cloisters; which wall was itself the most prodigious work that was ever heard of by man. (397) The hill was a rocky ascent, that declined by degrees towards the east parts of the city, till it came to an elevated level. (398) This hill it was which Solomon, who was the first of our kings, by divine revelation, encompassed with a wall; it was of excellent workmanship upwards, and round the top of it. He also built a wall below, beginning at the bottom, which was encompassed by a deep valley; and at the south side he laid rocks together and bound them one to another with lead, and included some of the inner parts, till it proceeded to a great height, (399) and till both the largeness of the square edifice and its altitude were immense, and till the vastness of the stones in the front were plainly visible on the outside, yet so that the inward parts were fastened together with iron, and preserved the joints immovable for all future times. (400) When this work [for the foundation] was done in this manner, and joined together as part of the hill itself to the very top of it, he wrought it all into one outward surface, and filled up the hollow places which were about the wall, and made it a level on the external upper surface, and a smooth level also. This hill was walled all round, and in compass four furlongs, [the distance of] each angle containing in length a furlong: (401) but within this wall, and on the very top of all, there ran another wall of stone also, having, on the east quarter, a double cloister, of the same length with the wall; in the midst of which was the temple itself. This cloister looked to the gates of the temple; and it had been adorned by many kings in former times; (402) and round about the entire temple were fixed the spoils taken from barbarous nations; all these had been dedicated to the temple by Herod, with the addition of these he had taken from the Arabians.

(403) Now on the north side [of the temple] was built a citadel, whose walls were square and strong, and of extraordinary firmness. This citadel was built by

the kings of the Asamonean race, who were also high priests before Herod, and they called it the Tower, in which were reposited the vestments of the high priest, which the high priest only put on at the time when he was to offer sacrifice. (404) These vestments King Herod kept in that place; and after his death they were under the power of the Romans, until the time of Tiberius Caesar; (405) under whose reign Vitellius, the president of Syria, when he once came to Jerusalem, and had been most magnificently received by the multitude, he had a mind to make them some requital for the kindness they had shown him; so, upon their petition to have those holy vestments in their own power, he wrote about them to Tiberius Caesar, who granted his request: and this their power over the sacerdotal vestments continued with the Jews till the death of King Agrippa; (406) but after that, Cassius Longinus, who was president of Syria, and Cuspius Fadus, who was procurator of Judea, enjoined the Jews to reposit those vestments in the tower of Antonia, (407) for that they ought to have them in their power, as they formerly had. However, the Jews sent ambassadors to Claudius Caesar, to intercede with him for them; upon whose coming, King Agrippa junior, being then at Rome, asked for and obtained the power over them from the emperor; who gave command to Vitellius, who was then commander in Syria, to give them it accordingly. (408) Before that time they were kept under the seal of the high priest, and of the treasurers, of the temple; which treasurers, the day before a festival, went up to the Roman captain of the temple guards, and viewed their own seal, and received the vestments; and again when the festival was over, they brought it to the same place, and showed the captain of the temple guards their seal, which corresponded with his seal, and reposited them there. (409) And that these things were so, the afflictions that happened to us afterwards [about them] are sufficient evidence: but for the tower itself, when Herod the king of the Jews had fortified it more firmly than before, in order to secure and guard the temple, he gratified Antonius, who was his friend, and the Roman ruler, and then gave it the name of the Tower of Antonia.

(410) Now, in the western quarter of the enclosures of the temple there were four gates; the first led to the king's palace, and went to a passage over the intermediate valley; two more led to the suburbs of the city; and the last led to the other city, where the road descended down into the valley by a great number of steps, and thence up again by the ascent; for the city lay over against the temple in the manner of a theatre, and was encompassed with a deep valley along the entire south quarter; (411) but the fourth front of the temple, which was southward, had indeed itself gates in its middle, as also it had the royal cloisters, with three walks, which reached in length from the east valley unto that on the west, for it was impossible it should reach any farther; (412) and this cloister deserves to be mentioned better than any other under the sun; for

while the valley was very deep, and its bottom could not be seen, if you looked from above into the depth, this farther vastly high elevation of the cloister stood upon that height, insomuch that if anyone looked down from the top of the battlements, or down both those altitudes, he would be giddy, while his sight could not reach to such an immense depth. (413) This cloister had pillars that stood in four rows one over against the other all along, for the fourth row was interwoven into the wall, which [also was built of stone]; and the thickness of each pillar was such, that three men might, with their arms extended, fathom it round, and join their hands again, while its length was twenty-seven feet, with a double spiral at its basis; (414) and the number of all the pillars [in that court] was an hundred and sixty-two. Their chapiters were made with sculptures after the Corinthian order, and caused an amazement [to the spectators], by reason of the grandeur of the whole. (415) These four rows of pillars included three intervals for walking in the middle of this cloister; two of which walks were made parallel to each other, and were contrived after the same manner; the breadth of each of them was thirty feet, the length was a furlong, and the height fifty feet; but the breadth of the middle part of the cloister was one and a half of the other, and the height was double, for it was much higher than those on each side; (416) but the roofs were adorned with deep sculptures in wood, representing many sorts of figures: the middle was much higher than the rest, and the wall of the front was adorned with beams, resting upon pillars that were interwoven into it, and that front was all of polished stone, insomuch that its fineness, to such as had not seen it, was incredible, and to such as had seen it, was greatly amazing. (417) Thus was the first enclosure. In the midst of which, and not far from it, was the second, to be gone up to by a few steps; this was encompassed by a stone wall for a partition, with an inscription, which forbade any foreigner to go in, under pain of death. (418) Now this inner enclosure had on its southern and northern quarters three gates [equally] distant from one another, but on the east quarter, towards the sunrising, there was one large gate through which such as were pure came in, together with their wives; (419) but the temple farther inward in that gate was not allowed to the women; but still more inward was there a third [court of the] temple, whereinto it was not lawful for any but the priests alone to enter. The temple itself was within this; and before that temple was the altar, upon which we offer our sacrifices and burnt offerings to God. (420) Into none of these three did King Herod enter, for he was forbidden, because he was not a priest. However, he took care of the cloisters and the outer enclosures; and these he built in eight years.

(421) But the temple itself was built by the priests in a year and six months, upon which all the people were full of joy; and presently they returned thanks, in the first place to God; and in the next place for the alacrity the king had

shown. They feasted and celebrated this rebuilding of the temple: (422) and for the king, he sacrificed three hundred oxen to God; as did the rest, everyone according to his ability: the number of which sacrifices is not possible to set down, for it cannot be that we should truly relate it; (423) for at the same time with this celebration for the work about the temple, fell also the day of the king's inauguration, which he kept of an old custom as a festival, and it now coincided with the other; which coincidence of them both made the festival most illustrious.

(424) There was also an occult passage built for the king; it led from Antonia to the inner temple, at its eastern gate; over which he also erected for himself a tower, that he might have the opportunity of a subterraneous ascent to the temple, in order to guard against any sedition which might be made by the people against their kings. (425) It is also reported, that during the time that the temple was building, it did not rain in the daytime, but that the showers fell in the nights, so that the work was not hindered. And this our fathers have delivered to us; nor is it incredible, if any have regard to the manifestations of God. And thus was performed the work of the rebuilding of the temple.

BOOK SIXTEEN

CHAPTER I

(1) As King Herod was very zealous in the administration of his entire government, and desirous to put a stop to particular acts of injustice which were done by criminals about the city and country, he made a law, no way like our original laws, and which he enacted of himself, to expose housebreakers to be ejected out of his kingdom; which punishment was not only grievous to be borne by the offenders, but contained in it a dissolution of the customs of our forefathers; (2) for this slavery to foreigners, and such as did not live after the manner of Jews, and this necessity that they were under to do whatsoever such men should command, was an offence against our religious settlement, rather than a punishment to such as were found to have offended, such a punishment being avoided in our original laws; (3) for those laws ordain, that the thief shall restore fourfold: and that if he have not so much, he shall be sold indeed, but not to foreigners, nor so that he be under perpetual slavery, for he must have been released after six years. (4) But this law, thus enacted in order to introduce a severe and illegal punishment, seemed to be a piece of insolence of Herod, when he did not act as a king but as a tyrant, and thus contemptuously, and without any regard to his subjects, did he venture to introduce such a punishment. (5) Now this penalty thus brought into practice, was like Herod's other actions, and became a part of his accusation, and an occasion of the hatred he lay under.

(6) Now at this time it was that he sailed to Italy, as very desirous to meet with Caesar, and to see his sons who lived at Rome; and Caesar was not only very obliging to him in other respects but delivered him his sons again, that he might take them home with him, as having already completed themselves in the sciences; (7) but as soon as the young men were come from Italy, the multitude were very desirous to see them, and they became conspicuous among them all, as adorned with great blessing of fortune, and having the countenances of persons of royal dignity. (8) So they soon appeared to be the objects of envy to Salome, the king's sister, and to such as had raised calumnies against Mariamne; for they were suspicious, that when these came to the government, they should be punished for the wickedness they had been guilty of against their mother; (9) so they made this very fear of theirs a motive to raise calumnies against them also. They gave it out that they were not pleased with their father's company, because he had put their mother to death, as if it were not agreeable to piety to appear to converse with their mother's murderer. (10) Now, by carrying these

stories, that had indeed a true foundation [in the fact], but were only built on probabilities as to the present accusation, they were able to do them mischief, and to make Herod take away that kindness from his sons which he had before borne to them; for they did not say these things to him openly, but scattered abroad such words among the rest of the multitude; from which words, when carried to Herod, he was induced [at last] to hate them, and which natural affection itself, even in length of time, was not able to overcome; (11) yet was the king at that time in a condition to prefer the natural affection of a father before all the suspicions and calumnies his sons lay under: so he respected them as he ought to do, and married them to wives, now they were of an age suitable thereto. To Aristobulus he gave for a wife Berenice, Salome's daughter; and to Alexander, Glaphyra, the daughter of Archelaus, king of Cappadocia.

CHAPTER 2

(12) When Herod had dispatched these affairs, and he understood that Marcus Agrippa had sailed again out of Italy into Asia, he made haste to him, and besought him to come to him into his kingdom, and to partake of what he might justly expect from one that had been his guest, and was his friend. (13) This request he greatly pressed, and to it Agrippa agreed, and came into Judea: whereupon Herod omitted nothing that might please him. He entertained him in his new-built cities, and showed him the edifices he had built, and provided all sorts of the best and most costly dainties for him and his friends, and that at Sebaste and Caesarea, about that port that he had built, and at the fortresses which he had erected at great expenses, Alexandrium, and Herodium, and Hyrcania. (14) He also conducted him to the city Jerusalem, where all the people met him in their festival garments, and received him with acclamations. Agrippa also offered a hecatomb of sacrifices to God, and feasted the people, without omitting any of the greatest dainties that could be gotten. (15) He also took so much pleasure there, that he abode many days with them, and would willingly have stayed longer, but that the season of the year made him make haste away; for as winter was coming on, he thought it not safe to go to sea later, and yet he was of necessity to return again to Ionia.

(16) So Agrippa went away, when Herod had bestowed on him, and on the principal of those that were with him, many presents: but King Herod, when he had passed the winter in his own dominions, made haste to get to him again in the spring, when he knew he designed to go to a campaign at the Bosphorus. (17) So when he had sailed by Rhodes and by Cos, he touched at Lesbos, as thinking he should have overtaken Agrippa there; but he was taken short here by a north wind, which hindered his ship from going to the shore; (18) so he continued many days at Chius, and there he kindly treated a great

many that came to him, and obliged them by giving them royal gifts. And when he saw that the portico of the city was fallen down, which as it was overthrown in the Mithridatic war, and was a very large and fine building, so was it not so easy to rebuild that as it was the rest, (19) yet did he furnish a sum not only large enough for that purpose, but what was more than sufficient to finish the building; and ordered them not to overlook that portico, but to rebuild it quickly, that so the city might recover its proper ornaments. (20) And when the high winds were laid, he sailed to Mitylene, and thence to Byzantium; and when he heard that Agrippa was sailed beyond the Cyanean rocks, he made all the haste possible to overtake him (21) and came up with him about Sinope, in Pontus. He was seen sailing by the shipmen most unexpectedly, but appeared to their great joy; and many friendly salutations there were between them, insomuch that Agrippa thought he had received the greatest marks of the king's kindness and humanity towards him possible, since the king had come so long a voyage, and at a very proper season, for his assistance, and had left the government of his own dominions, and thought it more worth his while to come to him. (22) Accordingly, Herod was all in all to Agrippa in the management of the war, and a great assistant in civil affairs, and in giving him counsel as to particular matters. He was also a pleasant companion for him when he relaxed himself, and a joint partaker with him in all things: in troubles because of his kindness; and in prosperity because of the respect Agrippa had for him. (23) Now as soon as those affairs of Pontus were finished, for whose sake Agrippa was sent thither, they did not think fit to return by sea, but passed through Paphlagonia and Cappadocia; they then travelled thence over great Phrygia, and came to Ephesus, and then they sailed from Ephesus to Samos. (24) And indeed the king bestowed a great many benefits on every city that he came to according as they stood in need of them; for as for those that wanted either money or kind treatment, he was not wanting to them, but he supplied the former himself out of his own expenses; he also became an intercessor with Agrippa for all such as sought after his favour, and he brought things so about, that the petitioners failed in none of their suits to him, (25) Agrippa being himself of a good disposition, and of great generosity, and ready to grant all such requests as might be advantageous to the petitioners, provided they were not to the detriment of others. The inclination of the king was of great weight also, and still excited Agrippa, who was himself ready to do good; (26) for he made a reconciliation between the people of Ilium, at whom he was angry, and paid what money the people of Chius owed Caesar's procurators, and discharged them of their tributes; and helped all others, according as their several necessities required.

(27) But now, when Agrippa and Herod were in Ionia, a great multitude of Jews, who dwelt in their cities, came to them, and laying hold of the

opportunity and the liberty now given them, laid before them the injuries which they suffered, while they were not permitted to use their own laws, but were compelled to prosecute their lawsuits, by the ill usage of the judges, upon their holy days, (28) and were deprived of the money they used to lay up at Jerusalem, and were forced into the army, and upon such other offices as obliged them to spend their sacred money; from which burdens they always used to be freed by the Romans, who had still permitted them to live according to their own laws. (29) When this clamour was made, the king desired of Agrippa that he would hear their cause, and assigned Nicolaus, one of his friends, to plead for those their privileges. (30) Accordingly, when Agrippa had called the principal of the Romans, and such of the kings and rulers as were there, to be his assessors, Nicolaus stood up, and pleaded for the Jews, as follows: (31) 'It is of necessity incumbent on such as are in distress to have recourse to those that have it in their power to free them from those injuries they lie under; and for those that now are complainants, they approach you with great assurance; (32) for as they have formerly often obtained your favour, so far as they have even wished to have it, they now only entreat that you, who have been the donors, will take care that those favours you have already granted them may not be taken away from them. We have received these favours from you, who alone have power to grant them, but have them taken from us by such as are no greater than ourselves, and by such as we know are as much subjects as we are; (33) and certainly, if we have been vouchsafed great favours, it is to our commendation who have obtained them, as having been found deserving of such great favours; and if those favours be but small ones, it would be barbarous for the donors not to confirm them to us; (34) and for those that are the hindrance of the Jews, and use them reproachfully, it is evident that they affront both the receivers, while they will not allow those to be worthy men to whom their excellent rulers themselves have borne their testimony, and the donors while they desire those favours already granted may be abrogated. (35) Now if anyone should ask these Gentiles themselves which of the two things they would choose to part with – their lives, or the customs of their forefathers, their solemnities, their sacrifices, their festivals, which they celebrate in honour of those they suppose to be gods – I know very well that they would choose to suffer anything whatsoever rather than a dissolution of any of the customs of their forefathers; (36) for a great many of them have rather chosen to go to war on that account, as very solicitous not to transgress in those matters: and indeed we take an estimate of that happiness which all mankind do now enjoy by your means from this very thing, that we are allowed every one to worship as our own institutions require, and yet to live [in peace]; (37) and although they would not be thus treated themselves, yet do they endeavour to compel others to comply with them, as if it were not as great an instance of impiety, profanely to dissolve the religious solemnities of any others, as to be negligent in the observation of their own towards their gods. (38) And let us now consider the one of these practices: is there any people, or city, or community of men, to whom your government and the Roman power does not appear to be the greatest blessing? Is there anyone that can desire to make void the favours they have granted? (39) No one is certainly so mad; for there are no men but such as have been partakers of their favours, both public and private; and indeed those that take away what you have granted, can have no assurance, but every one of their own grants made them by you may be taken from them also; (40) which grants of yours can yet never be sufficiently valued; for if they consider the old governments under kings, together with your present government, besides the great number of benefits which this government hath bestowed on them, in order to their happiness, this is instead of all the rest, that they appear to be no longer in a state of slavery, but of freedom. (41) Now the privileges we desire, even when we are in the best circumstances, are not such as deserve to be envied, for we are indeed in a prosperous state by your means, but this is only in common with others; and it is no more than this which we desire, to preserve our religion without any prohibition, which as it appears not in itself a privilege to be envied us, so it is for the advantage of those that grant it to us: (42) for if the Divinity delights in being honoured, it must delight in those that permit him to be honoured. And there are none of our customs which are inhuman, but all tending to piety, and devoted to the preservation of justice; (43) nor do we conceal those injunctions of ours by which we govern our lives, they being memorials of piety, and of a friendly conversation among men. And the seventh day we set apart from labour; it is dedicated to the learning of our customs and laws, we thinking it proper to reflect on them as well as on any [good] thing else, in order to our avoiding of sin. (44) If anyone therefore examine into our observances, he will find they are good in themselves, and that they are ancient also, though some think otherwise, insomuch that those who have received them cannot easily be brought to depart from them, out of that honour they pay to the length of time they have religiously enjoyed them and observed them. (45) Now our adversaries take these our privileges away in the way of injustice; they violently seize upon that money of ours which is offered to God, and called sacred money, and this openly, after a sacrilegious manner; and they impose tributes upon us, and bring us before tribunals on holy days, and then require other like debts of us, not because the contracts require it, and for their own advantage, but because they would put an affront on our religion, of which they are conscious as well as we, and have indulged themselves in an unjust, and to them involuntary hatred; (46) for your government over all is one, tending to the establishing of benevolence, and abolishing of ill will among such as are disposed to it. (47) This is therefore what we implore from thee, most excellent Agrippa, that we may not be ill treated; that we may not be abused; that we may not be hindered from making use of our own customs, nor be despoiled of our goods; nor be forced by these men to do what we ourselves force nobody to do: for these privileges of ours are not only according to justice, but have formerly been granted us by you; (48) and we are able to read to you many decrees of the senate, and the tables that contain them, which are still extant in the capitol concerning these things, which it is evident were granted after you had experience of our fidelity towards you, which ought to be valued, though no such fidelity had been; (49) for you have hitherto preserved what people were in possession of, not to us only, but almost to all men, and have added greater advantages than they could have hoped for, and thereby your government is become a great advantage to them. And if anyone were able to enumerate the prosperity you have conferred on every nation, which they possess by your means, he could never put an end to his discourse; (50) but that we may demonstrate that we are not unworthy of all those advantages we have obtained, it will be sufficient for us to say nothing of other things, but to speak freely of this king who now governs us, and is now one of thy assessors; (51) and indeed in what instance of good will, as to your house, hath he been deficient? What mark of fidelity to it hath he omitted? What token of honour hath he not devised? What occasion for his assistance of you hath he not regarded at the very first? What hindereth, therefore, but that your kindness may be as numerous as his so great benefits to you have been? (52) It may also perhaps be fit not here to pass over in silence the valour of his father Antipater, who when Caesar made an expedition into Egypt, assisted him with two thousand armed men, and proved inferior to none, neither in the battles on land, nor in the management of the navy; (53) and what need I say anything of how great weight those soldiers were at that juncture? Or how many and how great presents they were vouchsafed by Caesar? And truly I ought before now to have mentioned the epistles which Caesar wrote to the senate; and how Antipater had honours, and the freedom of the city of Rome, bestowed upon him; (54) for these are demonstrations both that we have received these favours by our own deserts, and do on that account petition thee for thy confirmation of them, from whom we had reason to hope for them, though they had not been given us before, both out of regard to our king's disposition towards you, and your disposition towards him; (55) and further, we have been informed by those Jews that were there, with what kindness thou camest into our country, and how thou offeredst the most perfect sacrifices to God, and honoredst him with remarkable vows, and how thou gavest the people a feast, and acceptedst of their own hospitable presents to thee. (56) We ought to esteem all these kind entertainments made both by our nation and to our city, to a man who is the ruler and manager of so much of the public affairs, as indications of that friendship which thou hast returned to the Jewish nation, and which hath been procured them by the family of Herod. (57) So we put thee in mind of these things in the presence of the king now sitting by thee, and make our request for no more but this, that what you have given us yourselves, you will not see taken away by others from us.'

(58) When Nicolaus had made this speech, there was no opposition made to it by the Greeks, for this was not an inquiry made, as in a court of justice, but an intercession to prevent violence to be offered to the Jews any longer; (59) nor did the Greeks make any defence of themselves, or deny what it was supposed they had done. Their pretence was no more than this, that while the Jews inhabited in their country, they were entirely unjust to them [in not joining in their worship]; but they demonstrated their generosity in this own that though they worshipped according to their own institutions, they did nothing that ought to grieve them. (60) So when Agrippa perceived that they had been oppressed by violence, he made this answer: that, on account of Herod's good will and friendship, he was ready to grant the Jews whatsoever they should ask him, and that their requests seemed to him in themselves just; and that if they requested anything further, he should not scruple to grant it them, provided they were no way to the detriment of the Roman government; but that, while their request was not more than this, that what privileges they had already given them might not be abrogated, he confirmed this to them, that they might continue in the observation of their own customs, without anyone offering them the least injury; and when he had said thus, he dissolved the assembly: (61) upon which Herod stood up and saluted him, and gave him thanks for the kind disposition he showed to them. Agrippa also took this in a very obliging manner, and saluted him again, and embraced him in his arms; (62) after which he went away from Lesbos; but the king determined to sail from Samos to his own country; and when he had taken his leave of Agrippa, he pursued his voyage, and landed at Caesarea in a few days' time, as having favourable winds; from whence he went to Jerusalem, and there gathered all the people together to an assembly, not a few being there out of the country also. (63) So he came to them, and gave them a particular account of all his journey, and of the affairs of all the Jews in Asia, how by his means they would live without injurious treatment for the time to come. (64) He also told them of the entire good fortune he had met with, and how he had administered the government, and had not neglected anything which was for their advantage; and as he was very joyful, he now remitted to them the fourth part of their taxes for the last year. (65) Accordingly, they were so pleased with his favour and speech to them, that they went their ways with great gladness, and wished the king all manner of happiness.

CHAPTER 3

(66) But now the affairs in Herod's family were in more and more disorder, and became more severe upon him, by the hatred of Salome to the young men [Alexander and Aristobulus], which descended as it were by inheritance [from their mother Mariamne]: and as she had fully succeeded against their mother, so she proceeded to that degree of madness and insolence, as to endeavour that none of her posterity might be left alive, who might have it in their power to revenge her death. (67) The young men had also somewhat of a bold and uneasy disposition towards their father, occasioned by the remembrance of what their mother had unjustly suffered, and by their own affectation of dominion. (68) The old grudge was also renewed, and they cast reproaches on Salome and Pheroras, who requited the young men with malicious designs, and actually laid treacherous snares for them. (69) Now, as for this hatred, it was equal on both sides, but the manner of exerting that hatred was different; for as for the young men, they were rash, reproaching and affronting the others openly, and were inexperienced enough to think it the most generous to declare their minds in that undaunted manner; but the others did not take that method, but made use of calumnies after a subtle and a spiteful manner, still provoking the young men, and imagining that their boldness might in time turn to the offering violence to their father, (70) for inasmuch as they were not ashamed of the pretended crimes of their mother, nor thought she suffered justly, these supposed that might at length exceed all bounds, and induce them to think they ought to be avenged on their father, though it were by dispatching him with their own hands. (71) At length it came to this, that the whole city was full of their discourses, and as is usual in such contests, the unskilfulness of the young men was pitied; but the contrivance of Salome was too hard for them, and what imputations she laid upon them came to be believed by means of their own conduct; (72) for they were so deeply affected with the death of their mother, that while they said both she and themselves were in a miserable case, they vehemently complained of her pitiable end; which indeed was truly such, and said that they were themselves in a pitiable case also, because they were forced to live with those that had been her murderers, and to be partakers with them.

(73) These disorders increased greatly, and the king's absence abroad had afforded a fit opportunity for that increase; but as soon as Herod was returned, and had made the forementioned speech to the multitude, Pheroras and Salome let fall words immediately as if he were in great danger, and as if the young men openly threatened that they would not spare him any longer, but revenge their mother's death upon him. (74) They also added another circumstance, that their hopes were fixed on Archelaus, the king of Cap-

padocia, that they should be able by his means to come to Caesar, and accuse their father. (75) Upon hearing such things, Herod was immediately disturbed; and indeed was the more astonished, because the same things were related to him by some others also. He then called to mind his former calamity, and considered that the disorders in his family had hindered him from enjoying any comfort from those that were dearest to him, or from his wife whom he loved so well; and suspecting that his future troubles would soon be heavier and greater than those that were past, he was in great confusion of mind, (76) for divine providence had in reality conferred upon him a great many outward advantages for his happiness, even beyond his hopes, but the troubles he had at home were such as he never expected to have met with, and rendered him unfortunate; nay, both sorts came upon him to such a degree as no one could imagine, and made it a doubtful question (77) whether, upon the comparison of both, he ought to have exchanged so great a success of outward good things for so great misfortunes at home, or whether he ought not to have chosen to avoid the calamities relating to his family, though he had, for a compensation, never been possessed of the admired grandeur of a kingdom.

(78) As he was thus disturbed and afflicted, in order to depress these young men, he brought to court another of his sons, that was born to him when he was a private man; his name was Antipater: yet did he not then indulge him as he did afterwards, and when he was quite overcome by him, and let him do everything as he pleased, (79) but rather with a design of depressing the insolence of the sons of Mariamne, and managing this elevation of his son, that it might be for a warning to them; for this bold behaviour of theirs [he thought] would not be so great, if they were once persuaded that the succession to the kingdom did not appertain to them alone, or must of necessity come to them. (80) So he introduced Antipater as their antagonist, and imagined that he made a good provision for discouraging their pride, and that after this was done to the young men, there might be a proper season for expecting these to be of a better disposition: (81) but the event proved otherwise than he intended, for the young men thought he did them a very great injury; and as Antipater was a shrewd man, when he had once obtained this degree of freedom, and began to expect greater things than he had before hoped for, he had but one single design in his head, and that was to distress his brethren, and not at all to yield to them the pre-eminence, but to keep close to his father, who was already alienated from them by the calumnies he had heard about them, and ready to be brought upon in any way his zeal against them should advise him to pursue, that he might be continually more and more severe against them. (82) Accordingly all the reports that were spread abroad came from him, while he avoided himself the suspicion, as if those discoveries proceeded from him; but he rather chose to make use of those persons for his assistants that were unsuspected, and such as

might be believed to speak truth by reason of the good will they bore to the king; (83) and indeed there were already not a few who cultivated a friendship with Antipater, in hopes of gaining somewhat by him, and these were the men who most of all persuaded Herod, because they appeared to speak thus out of their good will to him: and while these joint accusations, which, from various foundations, supported one another's veracity, the young men themselves afforded further occasions to Antipater also; (84) for they were observed to shed tears often, on account of the injury that was offered them, and had their mother in their mouths: and among their friends they ventured to reproach their father as not acting justly by them; all which things were with an evil intention reserved in memory by Antipater against a proper opportunity; and when they were told to Herod, with aggravations, increased the disorder so much, that it brought a great tumult into the family; (85) for, while the king was very angry at imputations that were laid upon the sons of Mariamne, and was desirous to humble them, he still increased the honour that he had bestowed on Antipater, and was at last so overcome by his persuasions, that he brought his mother to court also. He also wrote frequently to Caesar in favour of him, and more earnestly recommended him to his care particularly. (86) And when Agrippa was returned to Rome, after he had finished his ten years' government in Asia, Herod sailed from Judea; and when he met with him, he had none with him but Antipater, whom he delivered to Agrippa, that he might take him along with him, together with many presents, that so he might become Caesar's friend, insomuch that things already looked as if he had all his father's favour, and that the young men were already entirely rejected from any hopes of the kingdom.

CHAPTER 4

(87) And now what happened during Antipater's absence augmented the honour to which he had been promoted, and his apparent eminence above his brethren; for he had made a great figure in Rome, because Herod had sent recommendations of him to all his friends there: (88) only he was grieved that he was not at home, nor had proper opportunities of perpetually calumniating his brethren; and his chief fear was, lest his father should alter his mind and entertain a more favourable opinion of the sons of Mariamne; (89) and as he had this in his mind, he did not desist from his purpose, but continually sent from Rome any such stories as he hoped might grieve and irritate his father against his brethren, under pretence indeed of a deep concern for his preservation, but in truth, such as his malicious mind dictated, in order to purchase a greater hope of the succession, which yet was already great in itself: (90) and thus he did till he had excited such a degree of anger in Herod, that he was already become very

ill disposed towards the young men; but still while he delayed to exercise so violent a disgust against them, and that he might not either be too remiss or too rash, and so offend, he thought it best to sail to Rome, and there accuse his sons before Caesar, and not indulge himself in any such crime as might be heinous enough to be suspected of impiety. (91) But as he was going up to Rome, it happened that he made such haste as to meet with Caesar at the city Aquileia: so when he came to the speech of Caesar, he asked for a time for hearing this great cause, wherein he thought himself very miserable, and presented his sons there, and accused them of their mad actions, and of their attempts against him: (92) that they were enemies to him; and by all the means they were able, did their endeavours to show their hatred to their own father, and would take away his life, and so obtain his kingdom, after the most barbarous manner: that he had power from Caesar to dispose of it, not by necessity but by choice, to him who shall exercise the greatest piety towards him; (93) while these my sons are not so desirous of ruling, as they are upon a disappointment thereof, to expose their own life, if so be they may but deprive their father of his life; so wild and polluted is their mind by time become, out of their hatred to him; that whereas he had a long time borne this his misfortune, he was now compelled to lay it before Caesar and to pollute his ears with such language, (94) while he himself wants to know what severity they have ever suffered from him, or what hardships he had ever laid upon them to make them complain of him; and how they can think it just that he should not be lord of that kingdom which he in a long time, and with great danger, had gained and not allow him to keep it and dispose of it to him who should deserve best; (95) and this, with other advantages, he proposes as a reward for the piety of such a one as will hereafter imitate the care he hath taken of it, and that such a one may gain so great a requital as that is: (96) and that it is an impious thing for them to pretend to meddle with it beforehand, for he who hath ever the kingdom in his view, at the same time reckons upon procuring the death of his father, because otherwise he cannot come at the government: (97) that, as for himself, he had hitherto given them all that he was able, and what was agreeable to such as are subject to the royal authority, and the sons of a king; what ornaments they wanted, with servants and delicate fare, and had married them into the most illustrious families, the one [Aristobulus] to his sister's daughter, but Alexander to the daughter of King Archelaus; (98) and, what was the greatest favour of all, when their crimes were so very bad, and he had authority to punish them, yet had he not made use of it against them, but had brought them before Caesar, their common benefactor, and had not used the severity which either as a father who had been impiously abused, or as a king who had been assaulted treacherously, he might have done, but made them stand upon level with him in judgment; (99) that however, it was necessary that all this should not be passed over without punishment, nor himself live in the greatest fears; nay, that it was not for their own advantage to see the light of the sun after what they had done, although they should escape at this time, since they had done the vilest things, and would certainly suffer the greatest punishments that ever were known among mankind.

(100) These were the accusations which Herod laid with great vehemency against his sons before Caesar. Now the young men, both while he was speaking, and chiefly at his concluding, wept, and were in confusion. Now, as to themselves, they knew in their own conscience they were innocent, (101) but because they were accused by their father, they were sensible, as the truth was, that it was hard for them to make their apology, since though they were at liberty to speak their minds freely as the occasion required, and might with force and earnestness refute the accusation, yet was it not now decent so to do. (102) There was therefore a difficulty how they should be able to speak; and tears, and at length a deep groan followed, while they were afraid that if they said nothing, they should seem to be in this difficulty from a consciousness of guilt – nor had they any defence ready, by reason of their youth and the disorder they were under; (103) yet was not Caesar unapprised, when he looked upon them in the confusion they were in, that their delay to make their defence did not arise from any consciousness of great enormities, but from their unskilfulness and modesty. They were also commiserated by those that were there in particular; and they moved their father's affections in earnest till he had much ado to conceal them.

(104) But when they saw there was a kind disposition arisen both in him and in Caesar, and that every one of the rest did either shed tears, or at least did all grieve with them, the one of them whose name was Alexander, called to his father, and attempted to answer his accusation, and said, (105) 'O father, the benevolence thou hast showed to us is evident, even in this very judicial procedure, for hadst thou any pernicious intentions about us, thou hadst not produced us here before the common saviour of all, (106) for it was in thy power, both as a king and as a father, to punish the guilty; but by thus bringing us to Rome, and making Caesar himself a witness to what is done, thou intimatest that thou intendest to save us; for no one that hath a design to slay a man will bring him to the temples, and to the altars; (107) yet are our circumstances still worse, for we cannot endure to live ourselves any longer, if it be believed that we have injured such a father; nay, perhaps it would be worse for us to live with this suspicion upon us, that we have injured him, than to die without such guilt; (108) and if our open defence may be taken to be true, we shall be happy, both in pacifying thee, and in escaping the danger we are in; but if this calumny so prevails, it is more than enough for us that we have seen the sun this day; which why should we see, if this suspicion be fixed upon us? (109) Now it is easy to say of young men, that they desired to reign;

and to say further, that this evil proceeds from the case of our unhappy mother. This is abundantly sufficient to produce our present misfortune out of the former; (110) but consider well, whether such an accusation does not suit all such young men, and may not be said of them all promiscuously; for nothing can hinder him that reigns, if he have children, and their mother be dead, but the father may have a suspicion upon all his sons, as intending some treachery to him; but a suspicion is not sufficient to prove such an impious practice. (111) Now let any man say, whether we have actually and insolently attempted any such thing, whereby actions otherwise incredible used to be made credible? Can anybody prove that poison hath been prepared? Or prove a conspiracy of our equals, or the corruption of servants, or letters written against thee? (112) Though indeed there are none of those things but have sometimes been pretended by way of calumny, when they were never done; for a royal family that is at variance with itself is a terrible thing; and that which thou callest a reward of piety, often becomes among very wicked men, such a foundation of hope, as makes them leave no sort of mischief untried. (113) Nor does anyone lay any wicked practices to our charge; but as to calumnies by hearsay, how can he put an end to them, who will not hear what we have to say? Have we talked with too great freedom? Yes; but not against thee, for that would be unjust, but against those that never conceal anything that is spoken to them. (114) Hath either of us lamented our mother? Yes; but not because she is dead, but because she was evil spoken of by those that had no reason so to do. Are we desirous of that dominion which we know our father is possessed of? For what reason can we do so? If we already have royal honours, as we have, should not we labour in vain? And if we have them not, yet are not we in hopes of them? (115) Or supposing that we had killed thee, could we expect to obtain thy kingdom while neither the earth would let us tread upon it, nor the sea let us sail upon it, after such an action as that? Nay, the religion of all your subjects, and the piety of the whole nation, would have prohibited parricides from assuming the government, and from entering into that most holy temple which was built by thee. (116) But suppose we had made light of other dangers, can any murderer go off unpunished while Caesar is alive? We are thy sons, and not so impious, or so thoughtless as that comes to, though perhaps more unfortunate than is convenient for thee. (117) But in case thou neither findest any causes of complaint, nor any treacherous designs, what sufficient evidence hast thou to make such a wickedness of ours credible? Our mother is dead indeed, but then what befell her might be an instruction to us to caution, and not an incitement to wickedness. (118) We are willing to make a larger apology for ourselves; but actions never done do not admit of discourse: nay, we will make this agreement with thee, and that before Caesar, the lord of all, who is now a mediator between us: (119) if thou, O father, canst bring thyself by the evidence of truth, to have a mind free from suspicion concerning us, let us live, though even then we shall live in an unhappy way, for to be accused of great acts of wickedness, though falsely, is a terrible thing; (120) but if thou hast any fear remaining, continue thou on in thy pious life, we will give this reason for our own conduct; our life is not so desirable to us as to desire to have it, if it tend to the harm of our father who gave it us.'

(121) When Alexander had thus spoken, Caesar, who did not before believe so gross a calumny, was still more moved by it, and looked intently upon Herod, and perceived he was a little confounded: the persons there present were under an anxiety about the young men, and the fame that was spread abroad made the king hated, (122) for the very incredibility of the calumny, and the commiseration of the flower of youth, the beauty of body, which were in the young men, pleaded strongly for assistance, and the more so on this account, that Alexander had made their defence with dexterity and prudence; nay, they did not themselves any longer continue in their former countenances, which had been bedewed with tears, and cast downwards to the ground, (123) but now there arose in them hope of the best: and the king himself appeared not to have had foundation enough to build such an accusation upon, he having no real evidence wherewith to convict them. Indeed he wanted some apology for making the accusation; (124) but Caesar, after some delay, said that although the young men were thoroughly innocent of that for which they were calumniated yet had they been so far to blame, that they had not demeaned themselves towards their father so as to prevent that suspicion which was spread abroad concerning them. (125) He also exhorted Herod to lay all such suspicions aside, and to be reconciled to his sons; for that it was not just to give any credit to such reports concerning his own children; and that this repentance on both sides might heal those breaches that had happened between them, and might improve that their good will to one another, whereby those on both sides, excusing the rashness of their suspicions, might resolve to bear a greater degree of affection towards each other than they had before. (126) After Caesar had given them this admonition, he beckoned to the young men. When, therefore, they were disposed to fall down to make intercession to their father, he took them up, and embraced them, as they were in tears, and took each of them distinctly in his arms, till not one of those that were present, whether freeman or slave, but was deeply affected with what they saw.

(127) Then did they return thanks to Caesar, and went away together; and with them went Antipater, with an hypocritical pretence that he rejoiced at this reconciliation. (128) And in the last days they were with Caesar, Herod made him a present of three hundred talents, as he was then exhibiting shows and largesses to the people of Rome: and Caesar made him a present of half the revenue of the copper mines in Cyprus, and committed the care of the other

half to him, and honoured him with other gifts and incomes; (129) and as to his own kingdom, he left it in his power to appoint which of his sons he pleased for his successor, or to distribute it in parts to everyone, that the dignity might thereby come to them all; and when Herod was disposed to make such a settlement immediately, Caesar said he would not give him leave to deprive himself, while he was alive, of the power over his kingdom, or over his sons.

(130) After this, Herod returned to Judea again; but during his absence, no small part of his dominions about Trachon had revolted, whom yet the commanders he left there had vanquished, and compelled to a submission again. (131) Now, as Herod was sailing with his sons, and was come over against Cilicia, to [the island] Eleusa, which hath now changed its name for Sebaste, he met with Archelaus, king of Cappadocia, who received him kindly, as rejoicing that he was reconciled to his sons, and that the accusation against Alexander, who had married his daughter, was at an end. They also made one another such presents as it became kings to make. (132) From thence Herod came to Judea and to the temple, where he made a speech to the people concerning what had been done in this his journey: he also discoursed to them about Caesar's kindness to him, and about as many of the particulars he had done as he thought it for his advantage other people should be acquainted with. (133) At last he turned his speech to the admonition of his sons; and exhorted those that lived at court, and the multitude, to concord, and informed them that his sons were to reign after him; Antipater first, and then Alexander and Aristobulus, the sons of Mariamne; (134) but he desired that at present they should all have regard to himself, and esteem him king and lord of all, since he was not yet hindered by old age, but was in that period of life when he must be the most skilful in governing; and that he was not deficient in other arts of management that might enable him to govern the kingdom well, and to rule over his children also. He further told the rulers under him, and the soldiery, that in case they would look upon him alone, their life would be led in a peaceable manner, and they would make one another happy; and when he had said this, he dismissed the assembly. (135) Which speech was acceptable to the greatest part of the audience, but not so to them all; for the contention among his sons, and the hopes he had given them, occasioned thoughts and desires of innovations among them.

CHAPTER 5

(136) About this time it was that Caesarea Sebaste which he had built, was finished. The entire building being accomplished in the tenth year, the solemnity of it fell into the twenty-eighth year of Herod's reign, and into the hundred and ninety-second Olympiad; (137) there was accordingly a great

festival, and most sumptuous preparations made presently, in order to its dedication; for he had appointed a contention in music, and games to be performed naked; he had also gotten ready a great number of those that fight single combats, and of beasts for the like purpose; horse races also, and the most chargeable of such sports and shows as used to be exhibited at Rome, and in other places. (138) He consecrated this combat to Caesar, and ordered it to be celebrated every fifth year. He also sent all sorts of ornaments for it out of his own furniture, that it might want nothing to make it decent; (139) nay, Julia, Caesar's wife, sent a great part of her most valuable furniture [from Rome], insomuch that he had no want of anything; the sum of them all was estimated at five hundred talents. (140) Now when a great multitude was come to that city to see the shows, as well as the ambassadors whom other people sent, on account of the benefits they had received [from Herod], he entertained them all in the public inns, and at public tables, and with perpetual feasts; this solemnity having in the daytime the diversions of the fights, and in the night-time such merry meetings as cost vast sums of money, and publicly demonstrated the generosity of his soul; (141) for in all his undertakings he was ambitious to exhibit what exceeded whatsoever had been done before of the same kind; and it is related that Caesar and Agrippa often said, that the dominion of Herod were too little for the greatness of his soul; for that he deserved to have both all the kingdom of Syria, and that of Egypt also.

(142) After this solemnity and these festivals were over, Herod erected another city in the plain called Capharsaba, where he chose out a fit place, both for plenty of water and goodness of soil, and proper for the production of what was there planted, where a river encompassed the city itself, and a grove of the best trees for magnitude was round about it; (143) this he named Antipatris, from his father Antipater. He also built upon another spot of ground above Jericho, of the same name with his mother, a place of great security, and very pleasant for habitation, and called it Cyprus. (144) He also dedicated the finest monuments to his brother Phasaelus, on account of the great natural affection there had been between them, by erecting a tower in the city itself, not less than the tower of Pharos, which he named Phasaelus, which was at once a part of the strong defences of the city, and a memorial for him that was deceased, because it bare his name. (145) He also built a city of the same name in the valley of Jericho, as you go from it northward, whereby he rendered the neighbouring country more fruitful, by the cultivation its inhabitants introduced, and this also he called Phasaelus.

(146) But as for his other benefits, it is impossible to reckon them up, those which he bestowed on cities, both in Syria and in Greece, and in all the places he came to in his voyages; for he seems to have conferred, and that after a most plentiful manner, what would minister to many necessities, and the building of

public works, and gave them the money that was necessary to such works as wanted it, to support them upon the failure of their other revenues; (147) but what was the greatest and most illustrious of all his works, he erected Apollo's temple at Rhodes, at his own expenses, and gave them a great number of talents of silver for the repair of their fleet. He also built the greatest part of the public edifices for the inhabitants of Nicopolis, at Actium; (148) and for Antiochians, the inhabitants of the principal city of Syria, where a broad street cuts through the place lengthways, he built cloisters along it on both sides, and laid the open road with polished stone, and was of very great advantage to the inhabitants: (149) and as to the Olympic games, which were in a very low condition by reason of the failure of the revenues, he recovered their reputation, and appointed revenues for their maintenance, and made that solemn meeting more venerable as to the sacrifices and other ornaments; and by reason of this vast liberality, he was generally declared in their inscriptions to be one of the perpetual managers of those games.

(150) Now some there are who stand amazed at the diversity of Herod's nature and purposes; for when we have respect to his magnificence, and the benefits which he bestowed on all mankind, there is no possibility for even those that had the least respect for him to deny, or not openly to confess, that he had a nature vastly beneficent: (151) but when anyone looks upon the punishments he inflicted, and the injuries he did not only to his subjects, but to his nearest relations, and takes notice of his severe and unrelenting disposition there, he will be forced to allow that he was brutish, and a stranger to all humanity; (152) insomuch that these men suppose his nature to be different, and sometimes at contradiction with itself; but I am myself of another opinion, and imagine that the occasion of both these sorts of actions was one and the same; (153) for being a man ambitious of honour, and quite overcome by that passion, he was induced to be magnificent, wherever there appeared any hopes of a future memorial, or of reputation at present; (154) and as his expenses were beyond his abilities, he was necessitated to be harsh to his subjects, for the persons on whom he expended his money were so many, that they made him a very bad procurer of it; (155) and because he was conscious that he was hated by those under him or the injuries he did them, he thought it not an easy thing to amend his offences, for that was inconvenient for his revenues; he therefore strove on the other side to make their ill will an occasion of his gains. (156) As to his own court, therefore, if anyone was not very obsequious to him in his language, and would not confess himself to be his slave, or but seem to think of any innovation in his government, he was not able to contain himself, but prosecuted his very kindred and friends, and punished them as if they were enemies; and this wickedness he undertook out of a desire that he might be himself alone honoured. (157) Now for this my assertion about that passion of

his, we have the greatest evidence, by what he did to honour Caesar and Agrippa, and his other friends; for with what honours he paid his respects to them who were his superiors, the same did he desire to be paid to himself; and which he thought the most excellent present he could make another, he discovered an inclination to have the like presented to himself; (158) but now the Jewish nation is by their law a stranger to all such things, and accustomed to prefer righteousness to glory; for which reason that nation was not agreeable to him, because it was out of their power to flatter the king's ambition with statues or temples, or any other such performances; (159) and this seems to me to have been at once the occasion of Herod's crimes as to his own courtiers and counsellors, and of his benefactions as to foreigners and those that had no relation to him.

CHAPTER 6

(160) Now the cities ill-treated the Jews in Asia, and all those also of the same nation which lived in Libya, which joins to Cyrene; while the former kings had given them equal privileges with the other citizens, but the Greeks affronted them at this time, and that so far as to take away their sacred money, and to do them mischief on other particular occasions. (161) When, therefore, they were thus afflicted, and found no end of the barbarous treatment they met with among the Greeks, they sent ambassadors to Caesar on those accounts; who gave them the same privileges as they had before, and sent letters to the same purpose to the governors of the provinces, copies of which I subjoin here, as testimonials of the ancient favourable disposition the Roman emperors had towards us.

(162) 'Caesar Augustus, high priest and tribune of the people, ordains thus: since the nation of the Jews have been found grateful to the Roman people, not only at this time but in times past also, and chiefly Hyrcanus the high priest, under my father, Caesar the emperor, (163) it seemed good to me and my counsellors, according to the sentence and oath of the people of Rome, that the Jews have liberty to make use of their own customs, according to the law of their forefathers, as they made use of them under Hyrcanus, the high priest of Almighty God; and that their sacred money be not touched, but be sent to Jerusalem, and that it be committed to the care of the receivers at Jerusalem; and that they be not obliged to go before any judge on the Sabbath day, nor on the day of the preparation to it, after the ninth hour; (164) but if any be caught stealing their holy books, or their sacred money, whether it be out of the synagogue or public school, he shall be deemed a sacrilegious person, and his goods shall be brought into the public treasury of the Romans. (165) And I give order that the testimonial which they have given me, on

account of my regard to that piety which I exercise toward all mankind, and out of regard to Caius Marcus Censorinus, together with the present decree, be proposed in that most eminent place which hath been consecrated to me by the community of Asia at Ancyra. And if anyone transgress any part of what is above decreed, he shall be severely punished.' This was inscribed upon a pillar in the temple of Caesar.

(166) 'Caesar to Norbanus Flaccus, sendeth greeting. Let those Jews, how many soever they may be, who have been used, according to their ancient custom, to send their sacred money to Jerusalem, do the same freely.' These were the decrees of Caesar.

(167) Agrippa also did himself write, after the manner following, on behalf of the Jews: 'Agrippa, to the magistrates, senate and people of the Ephesians, sendeth greeting. I will that the care and custody of the sacred money that is carried to the temple at Jerusalem be left to the Jews of Asia, to do with it according to their ancient custom; (168) and that such as steal that sacred money of the Jews, and fly to a sanctuary, shall be taken thence and delivered to the Jews, by the same law that sacrilegious persons are taken thence. I have also written to Sylvanus the praetor, that no one compel the Jews to come before a judge on the Sabbath day.'

(169) 'Marcus Agrippa to the magistrates, senate and people of Cyrene, sendeth greeting. The Jews of Cyrene have interceded with me for the performance of what Augustus sent orders about to Flavius, the then praetor of Libya, and to the other procurators of that province, that the sacred money may be sent to Jerusalem freely, as hath been their custom from their forefathers, (170) they complaining that they are abused by certain informers, and, under pretence of taxes which were not due, are hindered from sending them; which I command to be restored without any diminution or disturbance given to them; and if any of that sacred money in the cities be taken from their proper receivers, I farther enjoin, that the same be exactly returned to the Jews in that place.'

(171) 'Caius Norbanus Flaccus, proconsul, to the magistrates of the Sardians, sendeth greeting. Caesar hath written to me, and commanded me not to forbid the Jews, how many soever they be, from assembling together according to the custom of their forefathers, nor from sending their money to Jerusalem: I have therefore written to you, that you may know that both Caesar and I would have you act accordingly.'

(172) Nor did Julius Antonius, the proconsul, write otherwise: 'To the magistrates, senate and people of the Ephesians, sendeth greeting. As I was dispensing justice at Ephesus, on the Ides of February, the Jews that dwell in Asia demonstrated to me that Augustus and Agrippa had permitted them to use their own laws and customs, and to offer those their first fruits, which every

one of them freely offers to the Deity on account of piety, and to carry them in a company together to Jerusalem without disturbance. (173) They also petitioned me, that I would confirm what had been granted by Augustus and Agrippa by my own sanction. I would therefore have you take notice, that according to the will of Augustus and Agrippa, I permit them to use and do according to the customs of their forefathers without disturbance.'

(174) I have been obliged to set down these decrees, because the present history of our own acts will go generally among the Greeks; and I have hereby demonstrated to them, that we have formerly been in great esteem, and have not been prohibited by those governors we were under from keeping any of the laws of our forefathers; nay, that we have been supported by them, while we followed our own religion and the worship we paid to God: (175) and I frequently make mention of these decrees, in order to reconcile other people to us, and to take away the causes of that hatred which unreasonable men bear to us. (176) As for our customs, there is no nation which always makes use of the same, and in every city almost we meet with them different from one another; (177) but natural justice is most agreeable to the advantage of all men equally, both Greeks and barbarians, to which our laws have the greatest regard, and thereby render us, if we abide in them after a pure manner, benevolent and friendly to all men: (178) on which account we have reason to expect the like return from others, and to inform them that they ought not to esteem difference of positive institutions a sufficient cause of alienation, but [join with us in] the pursuit of virtue and probity, for this belongs to all men in common, and of itself alone is sufficient for the preservation of human life. I now return to the thread of my history.

CHAPTER 7

(179) As for Herod, he had spent vast sums about the cities, both without and within his own kingdom: and as he had before heard that Hyrcanus, who had been king before him, had opened David's sepulchre, and taken out of it three thousand talents of silver, and that there was a much greater number left behind, and indeed enough to suffice all his wants, he had a great while an intention to make the attempt; (180) and at this time he opened that sepulchre by night, and went into it, and endeavoured that it should not be at all known in the city, but took only his most faithful friends with him. (181) As for any money, he found none, as Hyrcanus had done, but that furniture of gold and those precious goods that were laid up there; all which he took away. However, he had a great desire to make a more diligent search, and to go farther in, even as far as the very bodies of David and Solomon; (182) where two of his guards were slain by a flame that burst out upon those that went in,

as the report was. So he was terribly affrighted, and went out, and built a propitiatory monument of that fright he had been in; and this of white stone, at the mouth of the sepulchre, and that at great expense also. (183) And even Nicolaus his historiographer makes mention of this monument built by Herod, though he does not mention his going down into the sepulchre, as knowing that action to be of ill repute; and many other things he treats of in the same manner in his book; (184) for he wrote in Herod's lifetime, and under his reign, and so as to please him, and as a servant to him, touching upon nothing but what tended to his glory, and openly excusing many of his notorious crimes, and very diligently concealing them. (185) And as he was desirous to put handsome colours on the death of Mariamne and her sons, which were barbarous actions in the king, he tells falsehoods about the incontinence of Mariamne, and the treacherous designs of his sons upon him; and thus he proceeded in his whole work, making a pompous encomium upon what just actions he had done, but earnestly apologising for his unjust ones. (186) Indeed a man, as I said, may have a great deal to say by way of excuse for Nicolaus, for he did not so properly write this as a history for others, as somewhat that might be subservient to the king himself. (187) As for ourselves, who come of a family nearly allied to the Asamonean kings, and on that account have an honourable place, which is the priesthood, we think it indecent to say anything that is false about them, and accordingly we have described their actions after an unblemished and upright manner. And although we reverence many of Herod's posterity, who still reign, yet do we pay a greater regard to truth than to them, and this though it sometimes happens that we incur their displeasure by so doing.

(188) And indeed Herod's troubles in his family seemed to be augmented, by reason of this attempt he made upon David's sepulchre; whether divine vengeance increased the calamities he lay under, in order to render them incurable, or whether fortune made an assault upon him in those cases wherein the seasonableness of the cause made it strongly believed that the calamities came upon him for his impiety; (189) for the tumult was like a civil war in his palace; and their hatred towards one another was like that where each one strove to exceed another in calumnies. (190) However, Antipater used stratagems perpetually against his brethren, and that very cunningly; while abroad he loaded them with accusations, but still took upon him frequently to apologise for them, that this apparent benevolence to them might make him be believed, and forward his attempts against them; by which means he, after various manners, circumvented his father, who believed that all he did was for his preservation. (191) Herod also recommended Ptolemy, who was a great director of the affairs of his kingdom, to Antipater; and consulted with his mother about the public affairs also. And indeed these were all in all, and did

what they pleased, and made the king angry against any other persons, as they thought it might be to their own advantage: (192) but still the sons of Mariamne were in a worse and worse condition perpetually; and while they were thrust out, and set in a more dishonourable rank, who yet by birth were the most noble, they could not bear the dishonour. (193) And for the women, Glaphyra, Alexander's wife, the daughter of Archelaus, hated Salome, both because of her love to her husband, and because Glaphyra seemed to behave herself somewhat insolently towards Salome's daughter, who was the wife of Aristobulus, which equality of hers to herself Glaphyra took very impatiently.

(194) Now, besides this second contention that had fallen among them, neither did the king's brother Pheroras keep himself out of trouble, but had a particular foundation for suspicion and hatred; for he was overcome with the charms of his wife, to such a degree of madness, that he despised the king's daughter, to whom he had been betrothed, and wholly bent his mind to the other, who had been but a servant. (195) Herod also was grieved by the dishonour that was done him, because he had bestowed many favours upon him, and had advanced him to that height of power that he was almost a partner with him in the kingdom; and saw that he had not made him a due return for his favours, and esteemed himself unhappy on that account. (196) So upon Pheroras's unworthy refusal, he gave the damsel to Phasaelus' son; but after some time, when he thought the heat of his brother's affections was over, he blamed him for his former conduct, and desired him to take his second daughter, whose name was Cypros. (197) Ptolemy also advised him to leave off affronting his brother, and to forsake her whom he had loved, for that it was a base thing to be so enamoured of a servant, as to deprive himself of the king's good will to him and become an occasion of his trouble and make himself hated by him. (198) Pheroras knew that this advice would be for his own advantage, particularly because he had been accused before, and forgiven; so he put his wife away, although he already had a son by her, and engaged to the king that he would take his second daughter, and agreed that the thirtieth day after should be the day of marriage; and sware he would have no farther conversation with her whom he had put away; (199) but when the thirty days were over, he was such a slave to his affections, that he no longer performed anything he had promised, but continued still with his former wife. This occasioned Herod to grieve openly, and made him angry, (200) while the king dropped one word or other against Pheroras perpetually; and many made the king's anger an opportunity for raising calumnies against him. Nor had the king any longer a single quiet day or hour, but occasions of one fresh quarrel or another arose among his relations, and those that were dearest to him; (201) for Salome was of a harsh temper, and ill-natured to Mariamne's sons; nor would she suffer her own daughter, who was the wife of Aristobulus, one of those

young men, to bear a good will to her husband, but persuaded her to tell her if he said anything to her in private, and when any misunderstandings happened, as is common, she raised a great many suspicions out of it: (202) by which means she learned all their concerns, and made the damsel ill-natured to the young man. (203) And in order to gratify her mother, she often said that the young men used to mention Mariamne when they were by themselves; and that they hated their father, and were continually threatening, that if they had once got the kingdom, they would make Herod's sons by his other wives country-schoolmasters, for that the present education which was given them, and their diligence in learning, fitted them for such an employment. (204) And as for the women, whenever they saw them adorned with their mother's clothes, they threatened, that instead of their present gaudy apparel, they should be clothed in sackcloth, and confined so closely that they should not see the light of the sun. (205) These stories were presently carried by Salome to the king, who was troubled to hear them, and endeavoured to make up matters: but these suspicions afflicted him, and becoming more and more uneasy, be believed everybody against everybody. However, upon his rebuking his sons, and hearing the defence they made for themselves, he was easier for a while, though a little afterwards much worse accidents came upon him.

(206) For Pheroras came to Alexander, the husband of Glaphyra, who was the daughter of Archelaus, as we have already told you, and said that he had heard from Salome, that Herod was enamoured on Glaphyra, and that his passion for her was incurable. (207) When Alexander heard that, he was all on fire, from his youth and jealousy; and he interpreted the instances of Herod's obliging behaviour to her, which were very frequent, for the worse, which came from those suspicions he had on account of that word which fell from Pheroras; (208) nor could he conceal his grief at the thing, but informed him what words Pheroras had said. Upon which Herod was in a greater disorder than ever; and not bearing such a false calumny, which was to his shame, was much disturbed at it: (209) and often did he lament the wickedness of his domestics, and how good he had been to them, and how ill requitals they had made him. So he sent for Pheroras, and reproached him, and said, 'Thou vilest of all men! Art thou come to that unmeasurable and extravagant degree of ingratitude, and not only to suppose such things of me, but to speak of them? (210) I now indeed perceive what thy intentions are: it is not thy only aim to reproach me, when thou usest such words to my son, but thereby to persuade him to plot against me, and get me destroyed by poison; and who is there, if he had not a good genius at his elbow, as hath my son, that would bear such a suspicion of his father, but would revenge himself upon him? (211) Dost thou suppose that thou hast only dropped a word for him to think of, and not rather hast put a sword into his hand to slay his father? And what dost thou mean,

when thou really hatest both him and his brother, to pretend kindness to them, only in order to raise a reproach against me, and talk of such things as no one but such an impious wretch as thou art could either devise in their mind or declare in their words? (212) Begone, thou that art such a plague to thy benefactor and thy brother; and may that evil conscience of thine go along with thee, while I still overcome my relations by kindness, and am so far from avenging myself of them, as they deserve, that I bestow greater benefits upon them than they are worthy of.'

(213) Thus did the king speak. Whereupon Pheroras, who was caught in the very act of his villainy, said that, 'it was Salome who was the framer of this plot, and that the words came from her;' (214) but as soon as she heard that, for she was at hand, she cried out, like one that would be believed, that no such thing ever came out of her mouth; that they all earnestly endeavoured to make the king hate her, and to make her away, because of the good will she bore to Herod, and because she was always foreseeing the dangers that were coming upon him, (215) and that at present there were more plots against him than usual; for while she was the only person who persuaded her brother to put away the wife he now had, and to take the king's daughter, it was no wonder if she were hated by him. (216) As she said this, and often tore her hair, and often beat her breast, her countenance made her denial to be believed, but the perverseness of her manners declared at the same time her dissimulation in these proceedings; (217) but Pheroras was caught between them, and had nothing plausible to offer in his own defence, while he confessed that he had said what was charged upon him, but was not believed when he said he had heard it from Salome; so the confusion among them was increased, and their quarrelsome words one to another. (218) At last the king, out of his hatred to his brother and sister, sent them both away; and when he had commended the moderation of his son, and that he had himself told him of the report, he went in the evening to refresh himself. (219) After such a contest as this had fallen out among them, Salome's reputation suffered greatly, since she was supposed to have first raised the calumny; and the king's wives were grieved at her, as knowing she was a very ill-natured woman, and would sometimes be a friend, and sometimes an enemy, at different seasons; so they perpetually said one thing or another against her; and somewhat that now fell out made them the bolder in speaking against her.

(220) There was one Obodas, king of Arabia, an inactive and slothful man in his nature; but Sylleus managed most of his affairs for him. He was a shrewd man, although he was but young, and was handsome withal. (221) This Sylleus, upon some occasion coming to Herod, and supping with him, saw Salome, and set his heart upon her; and understanding that she was a widow, he discoursed with her. (222) Now because Salome was at this time less in

favour with her brother, she looked upon Sylleus with some passion, and was very earnest to be married to him; and on the days following there appeared many, and those very great, indications of their agreement together. (223) Now the women carried this news to the king, and laughed at the indecency of it; whereupon Herod inquired about it further of Pheroras, and desired him to observe them at supper, how their behaviour was one towards another; who told him, that by the signals which came from their heads and their eyes, they both were evidently in love. (224) After this, Sylleus the Arabian being suspected, went away, but came again in two or three months afterwards, as it were on that very design, and spake to Herod about it, and desired that Salome might be given him to wife; for that his affinity might not be disadvantageous to his affairs, by a union with Arabia, the government of which country was already in effect under his power, and more evidently would be his hereafter. (225) Accordingly, when Herod discoursed with his sister about it, and asked her whether she were disposed to this match, she immediately agreed to it; but when Sylleus was desired to come over to the Jewish religion, and then he should marry her, and that it was impossible to do it on any other terms, he could not bear that proposal, and went his way; for he said, that if he should do so, he should be stoned by the Arabs. (226) Then did Pheroras reproach Salome for her incontinency, as did the women much more; and said that Sylleus had debauched her. (227) As for that damsel which the king had betrothed to his brother Pheroras, but he had not taken her, as I have before related, because he was enamoured on his former wife, Salome desired of Herod she might be given to her son by Costobarus; (228) which match he was very willing to, but was dissuaded from it by Pheroras, who pleaded, that this young man would not be kind to her since his father had been slain by him, and that it was more just that his son, who was to be his successor in the tetrarchy, should have her; so he begged his pardon, and persuaded him to do so. Accordingly the damsel, upon this change of her espousals, was disposed of to this young man, the son of Pheroras, the king giving for her portion a hundred talents.

CHAPTER 8

(229) But still the affairs of Herod's family were no better, but perpetually more troublesome. Now this accident happened, which arose from no decent occasion, but proceeded so far as to bring great difficulties upon him. (230) There were certain eunuchs which the king had, and on account of their beauty was very fond of them; and the care of bringing him drink was entrusted to one of them; of bringing him his supper, to another; and of putting him to bed, to the third, who also managed the principal affairs of the

government; (231) and there was one told the king that these eunuchs were corrupted by Alexander the king's son, with great sums of money; and when they were asked whether Alexander had had criminal intercourse with them, they confessed it, but said they knew of no farther mischief of his against his father; (232) but when they were more severely tortured, and were in the utmost extremity, and the tormentors, out of compliance with Antipater, stretched the rack to the very utmost, they said that Alexander bare great ill will and innate hatred to his father; (233) and that he told them that Herod despaired to live much longer; and that, in order to cover his great age, he coloured his hair black, and endeavoured to conceal what would discover how old he was; but that if he would apply himself to him, when he should attain the kingdom, which in spite of his father, could come to no one else, he should quickly have the first place in that kingdom under him, (234) for that he was now ready to take the kingdom, not only as his birthright, but by the preparations he had made for obtaining it, because a great many of the rulers, and a great many of his friends, were of his side, and those no ill men neither, ready both to do and to suffer whatsoever should come on that account.

(235) When Herod heard this confession, he was all over anger and fear, some parts seeming to him reproachful, and some made him suspicious of dangers that attended him, insomuch that on both accounts he was provoked, and bitterly afraid lest some more heavy plot was laid against him than he should be then able to escape from; (236) whereupon he did not now make an open search, but sent about spies to watch such as he suspected, for he was now overrun with suspicion and hatred against all about him; and indulging abundance of those suspicions, in order to his preservation, he continued to suspect those that were guiltless; (237) nor did he set any bounds to himself, but supposing that those who stayed with him had the most power to hurt him, they were to him very frightful; and for those that did not use to come to him, it seemed enough to name them [to make them suspected], and he thought himself safer when they were destroyed; (238) and at last his domestics were come to that pass, that being no way secure of escaping themselves, they fell to accusing one another, and imagining that he who first accused another was most likely to save himself; yet, when any had overthrown others, they were hated; and they were thought to suffer justly, who unjustly accused others; and they only thereby prevented their own accusation; (239) nay, they now executed their own private enmities by this means, and when they were caught, they were punished in the same way. Thus these men contrived to make use of this opportunity as an instrument and a snare against their enemies; yet, when they tried it, were themselves caught also in the same snare which they laid for others: (240) and the king soon repented of what he had done, because he had no clear evidence of the guilt of those whom he had slain; and

yet what was still more severe in him, he did not make use of his repentance, in order to leave off doing the like again, but in order to inflict the same punishment upon their accusers.

(241) And in this state of disorder were the affairs of the palace; and he had already told many of his friends directly that they ought not to appear before him, nor come into the palace; and the reason of this injunction was, that [when they were there] he had less freedom of acting, or a greater restraint on himself on their account; (242) for at this time it was that he expelled Andromachus and Gamellus, men who had of old been his friends, and been very useful to him in the affairs of his kingdom, and been of advantage to his family by their embassages and counsels; and had been tutors to his sons, and had in a manner the first degree of freedom with him. (243) He expelled Andromachus, because his son Demetrius was a companion to Alexander: and Gamellus, because he knew that he wished him well, which arose from his having been with him in his youth when he was at school, and absent at Rome. These he expelled out of his palace, and was willing enough to have done worse by them; but that he might not seem to take such liberty against men of so great reputation, he contented himself with depriving them of their dignity, and of their power to hinder his wicked proceedings.

(244) Now it was Antipater who was the cause of all this; who when he knew what a mad and licentious way of acting his father was in, and had been a great while one of his counsellors, he hurried him on, and then thought he should bring him to do somewhat to purpose, when everyone that could oppose him was taken away. (245) When therefore Andromachus and his friends were driven away, and had no discourse nor freedom with the king any longer, the king, in the first place, examined by torture all whom he thought to be faithful to Alexander, whether they knew of any of his attempts against him; but these died without having anything to say to that matter, (246) which made the king more zealous [after discoveries], when he could not find out what evil proceedings he suspected them of. As for Antipater, he was very sagacious to raise a calumny against those that were really innocent, as if their denial was only their constancy and fidelity [to Alexander], and thereupon provoked Herod to discover by the torture of great numbers, what attempts were still concealed. (247) Now there was a certain person among the many that were tortured, who said that he knew that the young man had often said, that when he was commended as a tall man in his body, and a skilful marksman, and that in his other commendable exercises he exceeded all men, these qualifications, given him by nature, though good in themselves, were not advantageous to him, (248) because his father was grieved at them, and envied him for them; and that when he walked along with his father, he endeavoured to depress and shorten himself, that he might not appear too tall; and that when

he shot at anything as he was hunting, when his father was by, he missed his mark on purpose; for he knew how ambitious his father was of being superior in such exercises. (249) So when the man was tormented about this saying, and had ease given his body after it, he added, that he had his brother Aristobulus for his assistance, and contrived to lie in wait for their father, as they were hunting, and kill him; and when they had done so, to fly to Rome, and desire to have the kingdom given them. (250) There were also letters of the young man found written to his brother; wherein he complained that his father did not act justly in giving Antipater a country, whose [yearly] revenues amounted to ten hundred talents. (251) Upon these confessions Herod presently thought he had somewhat to depend on, in his own opinion, as to his suspicion about his sons; so he took up Alexander and bound him; yet did he still continue to be uneasy, and was not quite satisfied of the truth of what he had heard, and when he came to recollect himself, he found that they had only made juvenile complaints and contentions, and that it was an incredible thing, that when his son should have slain him, he should openly go to Rome [to beg the kingdom]; (252) so he was desirous to have some surer mark of his son's wickedness, and was very solicitous about it, that he might not appear to have condemned him to be put in prison too rashly; so he tortured the principal of Alexander's friends, and put not a few of them to death, without getting any of the things out of them which he suspected. (253) And while Herod was very busy about this matter, and the palace was full of terror and trouble, one of the younger sort, when he was in the utmost agony, confessed that Alexander had sent to his friends at Rome, and desired that he could discover a plot against him; that Mithridates, the king of Parthia, was joined in friendship with his father against the Romans, and that he had a poisonous potion ready prepared at Askelon.

(254) To these accusations Herod gave credit, and enjoyed hereby, in his miserable case, some sort of consolation, in excuse of his rashness, as flattering himself with finding things in so bad a condition; but as for the poisonous potion, which he laboured to find, he could find none. (255) As for Alexander, he was very desirous to aggravate the vast misfortunes he was under, so he pretended not to deny the accusations, but punished the rashness of his father with a greater crime of his own; and perhaps he was willing to make his father ashamed of his easy belief of such calumnies: he aimed especially, if he could gain belief to his story, to plague him and his whole kingdom; (256) for he wrote four letters and sent them to him, that 'he did not need to torture any more persons, for he had plotted against him; and that he had for his partners, Pheroras and the most faithful of his friends: and that Salome came in to him by night, and that she lay with him whether he would or not; (257) and that all men were come to be of one mind to make away with him as soon as they could, and so get clear of the continual fear they were in from

him. Among these were accused Ptolemy and Sapinnius, who were the most faithful friends to the king. (258) And what more can be said, but that those who before were the most intimate friends, were become wild beasts to one another, as if a certain madness had fallen upon them, while there was no room for defence or refutation, in order to the discovery of the truth, but all were at random doomed to destruction! So that some lamented those that were in prison, some those that were put to death, and others lamented that they were in expectation of the same miseries and a melancholy solitude rendered the kingdom deformed, and quite the reverse to that happy state it was formerly in. (259) Herod's own life also was entirely disturbed; and, because he could trust nobody, he was sorely punished by the expectation of further misery; for he often fancied in his imagination, that his son had fallen upon him, or stood by him with a sword in his hand, (260) and thus was his mind night and day intent upon this thing, and revolved it over and over, no otherwise than if he were under a distraction. And this was the sad condition Herod was now in.

(261) But when Archelaus, king of Cappadocia, heard of the state that Herod was in, and being in great distress about his daughter, and the young man [her husband], and grieving with Herod, as with a man that was his friend, on account of so great a disturbance as he was under, he came [to Jerusalem] on purpose to compose their differences; (262) and when he found Herod in such a temper, he thought it wholly unseasonable to reprove him, or to pretend that he had done anything rashly, for that he should thereby naturally bring him to dispute the point with him, and by still more and more apologising for himself to be the more irritated; (263) he went, therefore, another way to work, in order to correct the former misfortunes, and appeared angry at the young man, and said that Herod had been so very mild a man that he had not acted a rash part at all. He also said he would dissolve his daughter's marriage with Alexander, nor could in justice spare his own daughter, if she were conscious of anything, and did not inform Herod of it. (264) When Archelaus appeared to be of this temper, and otherwise than Herod expected or imagined, and for the main took Herod's part, and was angry on his account, the king abated of his harshness, and took occasion from his appearing to have acted justly hitherto, to come by degrees to put on the affection of a father, (265) and was on both sides to be pitied; for when some persons refuted the calumnies that were laid on the young man, he was thrown into a passion, but when Archelaus joined in the accusation he was dissolved into tears and sorrow after an affectionate manner. Accordingly, he desired that he would not dissolve his son's marriage, and became not so angry as before for his offences. (266) So when Archelaus had brought him to a more moderate temper, he transferred the calumnies upon his friends; and said it must be owing to them that so

young a man, and one unacquainted with malice, was corrupted; and he supposed that there was more reason to suspect the brother than the son. (267) Upon which Herod was very much displeased at Pheroras, who indeed now had no one that could make a reconciliation between him and his brother. So when he saw that Archelaus had the greatest power with Herod, he betook himself to him in the habit of a mourner, and like one that had all the signs upon him of an undone man. (268) Upon this Archelaus did not overlook the intercession he made to him, nor yet did he undertake to change the king's disposition towards him immediately; and he said that it was better for him to come himself to the king, and confess himself the occasion of all; that this would make the king's anger not to be extravagant towards him and that then he would be present to assist him. (269) When he had persuaded him to this, he gained his point with both of them; and the calumnies raised against the young man were, beyond all expectation, wiped off. And Archelaus, as soon as he had made the reconciliation, went then away to Cappadocia, having proved at this juncture of time the most acceptable person to Herod in the world; on which account he gave him the richest presents, as tokens of his respect to him, and being on other occasions magnanimous, he esteemed him one of his dearest friends. (270) He also made an agreement with him that he would go to Rome, because he had written to Caesar about these affairs; so they went together as far as Antioch, and there Herod made a reconciliation between Archelaus and Titus, the president of Syria, who had been greatly at variance; and so returned back to Judea.

CHAPTER 9

(271) When Herod had been at Rome, and was come back again, a war arose between him and the Arabians on the occasion following: the inhabitants of Trachonitis, after Caesar had taken the country away from Zenodorus, and added it to Herod, had not now power to rob, but were forced to plough the land, and to live quietly, which was a thing they did not like; (272) and when they did take that pains, the ground did not produce much fruit for them. However, at the first, the king would not permit them to rob; and so they abstained from that unjust way of living upon their neighbours, which procured Herod a great reputation for his care. (273) But when he was sailing to Rome, it was at that time when he was going to accuse his son Alexander, and to commit Antipater to Caesar's protection, the Trachonites spread a report as if he were dead, and revolted from his dominion, and betook themselves again to their accustomed way of robbing their neighbours; (274) at which time the king's commanders subdued them during his absence: but about forty of the principal robbers, being terrified by those that had been taken, left the country,

(275) and retired into Arabia, Sylleus entertaining them, after he had missed of marrying Salome, and gave them a place of strength, in which they dwelt. So they overran not only Judea, but all Celesyria also, and carried off the prey, while Sylleus afforded them places of protection and quietness during their wicked practices. (276) But when Herod came back from Rome, he perceived that his dominions had greatly suffered by them, and since he could not reach the robbers themselves, because of the secure retreat they had in that country, and which the Arabian government afforded them, and yet being very uneasy at the injuries they had done him, he went all over Trachonitis, and slew their relations; (277) whereupon these robbers were more angry than before, it being a law among them to be avenged on the murderers of their relations by all possible means; so they continued to tear and rend everything under Herod's dominion with impunity; then did he discourse about these robberies to Saturninus and Volumnius, and required that they should be punished; (278) upon which occasion they still the more confirmed themselves in their robberies, and became more numerous and made very great disturbances, laying waste the countries and villages that belonged to Herod's kingdom, and killing those men whom they caught, till these unjust proceedings came to be like a real war, for the robbers were now become about a thousand; (279) at which Herod was sore displeased, and required the robbers as well as the money which he had lent Obodas, by Sylleus, which was sixty talents, and since the time of payment was now past, he desired to have it paid him: (280) but Sylleus, who had laid Obodas aside, and managed all by himself, denied that the robbers were in Arabia, and put off the payment of the money; about which there was a hearing before Saturninus and Volumnius, who were then the presidents of Syria. (281) At last he, by their means, agreed that within thirty days time Herod should be paid his money, and that each of them should deliver up the other's subjects reciprocally. Now, as to Herod, there was not one of the other's subjects found in his kingdom either as doing any injustice or on any other account; but it was proved that the Arabians had the robbers amongst them.

(282) When the day appointed for payment of the money was past, without Sylleus' performing any part of his agreement, and he was gone to Rome, Herod demanded the payment of the money, and that the robbers that were in Arabia should be delivered up; (283) and, by the permission of Saturninus and Volumnius, executed the judgment himself upon those that were refractory. He took an army that he had, and led it into Arabia, and in three days time marched seven mansions; and when he came to the garrison wherein the robbers were, he made an assault upon them, and took them all, and demolished the place, which was called Raepta, but did no harm to any others. (284) But as the Arabians came to their assistance, under Naceb, their captain, there ensued a battle, wherein a few of Herod's soldiers, and Naceb

the captain of the Arabians, and about twenty of his soldiers fell, while the rest betook themselves to flight. (285) So when he had brought these to punishment, he placed three thousand Idumeans in Trachonitis, and thereby restrained the robbers that were there. He also sent an account to the captains that were about Phoenicia, and demonstrated that he had done nothing but what he ought to do in punishing the refractory Arabians, which, upon an exact inquiry, they found to be no more than what was true.

(286) However, messengers were hasted away to Sylleus to Rome, and informed him what had been done, and, as is usual, aggravated everything. (287) Now Sylleus had already insinuated himself into the knowledge of Caesar, and was then about the palace; and as soon as he heard of these things, he changed his habit into black, and went in and told Caesar that Arabia was afflicted with war, and that all his kingdom was in great confusion, upon Herod's laying it waste with his army; (288) and he said, with tears in his eyes, that two thousand five hundred of the principal men among the Arabians had been destroyed, and that their captain Nacebus, his familiar friend and kinsman, was slain; and that the riches that were at Raepta were carried off, and that Obodas was despised, whose infirm state of body rendered him unfit for war; on which account neither he nor the Arabian army were present. (289) When Sylleus said so, and added invidiously, that he would not himself have come out of the country, unless he had believed that Caesar would have provided that they should all have peace, one with another, and that had he been there he would have taken care that the war should not have been to Herod's advantage. Caesar was provoked when this was said; and asked no more than this one question, both of Herod's friends that were there, and of his own friends who were come from Syria, whether Herod had led an army thither? (290) And when they were forced to confess so much, Caesar, without staying to hear for what reason he did it, and how it was done, grew very angry, and wrote to Herod sharply. The sum of his epistle was this, that whereas of old he had used him as his friend, he should now use him as his subject. (291) Sylleus also wrote an account of this to the Arabians; who were so elevated with it, that they neither delivered up the robbers that had fled to them, nor paid the money that was due: they retained those pastures also which they had hired, and kept them without paying their rent, and all this because the king of the Jews was now in a low condition by reason of Caesar's anger at him. (292) Those of Trachonitis also made use of this opportunity, and rose up against the Idumean garrison, and followed the same way of robbing with the Arabians, who had pillaged their country, and were more rigid in their unjust proceedings, not only in order to get by it, but by way of revenge also.

(293) Now Herod was forced to bear all this, that confidence of his being

quite gone with which Caesar's favour used to inspire him; for Caesar would not admit so much as an embassage from him, to make an apology for him; and when they came again, he sent them away without success: (294) so he was cast into sadness and fear, and Sylleus' circumstances grieved him exceedingly; he was now believed by Caesar, and was present at Rome, nay, sometimes aspiring higher. Now it came to pass that Obodas was dead: and Aeneas, whose name was afterwards changed to Aretas, (295) took the government, for Sylleus endeavoured by calumnies to get him turned out of his principality that he might himself take it; with which design he gave much money to the courtiers, and promised much money to Caesar, who indeed was angry that Aretas had not sent to him first before he took the kingdom, (296) yet did Aeneas send an epistle and presents to Caesar, and a crown of gold, of the weight of many talents. Now that epistle accused Sylleus as having been a wicked servant, and having killed Obodas by poison; and that while he was alive he had governed him as he pleased; and had also debauched the wives of the Arabians; and had borrowed money in order to obtain the dominion for himself: (297) yet did not Caesar give heed to these accusations, but sent his ambassadors back, without receiving any of his presents. But in the meantime the affairs of Judea and Arabia became worse and worse, partly because of the anarchy they were under, and partly because, bad as they were, nobody had power to govern them; (298) for of the two kings, the one was not yet confirmed in his kingdom, and so had not authority sufficient to restrain the evildoers; and as for Herod, Caesar was immediately angry at him for having avenged himself, and so he was compelled to bear all the injuries that were offered him. (299) At length, when he saw no end of the mischief which surrounded him, he resolved to send ambassadors to Rome again, to see whether his friends had prevailed to mitigate Caesar, and to address themselves to Caesar himself; and the ambassador he sent thither was Nicolaus of Damascus.

CHAPTER 10

(300) The disorders about Herod's family and children about this time grew much worse; for it now appeared certain, nor was it unforeseen beforehand, that fortune threatened the greatest and most insupportable misfortunes possible to his kingdom. Its progress and augmentation at this time arose on the occasion following: (301) One Eurycles, a Lacedemonian (a person of note there, but a man of a perverse mind, and so cunning in his ways of voluptuousness and flattery, as to indulge both, and yet seem to indulge neither of them), came in his travels to Herod, and made him presents, but so that he received more presents from him. He also took such proper seasons for insinuating himself into his friendship, that he became one of the most intimate of the king's friends.

(302) He had his lodging in Antipater's house; but he had not only access, but free conversation, with Alexander, as pretending to him that he was in great favour with Archelaus, the king of Cappadocia, (303) whence he pretended much respect to Glaphyra, and in an occult manner, cultivated a friendship with them all but always attending to what was said and done, that he might be furnished with calumnies to please them all. (304) In short, he behaved so to everybody in his conversation, as to appear to be his particular friend, and he made others believe that his being anywhere was for that person's advantage. So he won upon Alexander, who was but young; and persuaded him that he might open his grievances to him with assurance, and with nobody else. (305) So he declared his grief to him, how his father was alienated from him. He related to him also the affairs of his mother, and of Antipater; that he had driven them from their proper dignity, and had the power over everything himself; that no part of this was tolerable, since his father was already come to hate them; and he added, that he would neither admit them to his table nor to his conversation. (306) Such were the complaints as was but natural, of Alexander about the things that troubled him: and these discourses Eurycles carried to Antipater, and told him he did not inform him of this on his own account, but that being overcome by his kindness, the great importance of the thing obliged him to do it: and he warned him to have a care of Alexander, for that what he said was spoken with vehemency, and that, in consequence of what he said, he would certainly kill him with his own hand. (307) Whereupon Antipater, thinking him to be his friend by this advice, gave him presents upon all occasions, and at length persuaded him to inform Herod of what he had heard. (308) So when he related to the king Alexander's ill temper, as discovered by the words he had heard him speak, he was easily believed by him; and he thereby brought the king to that pass, turning him about by his words, and irritating him, till he increased his hatred to him, and made him implacable, (309) which he showed at that very time, for he immediately gave Eurycles a present of fifty talents; who, when he had gotten them, went to Archelaus, king of Cappadocia, and commended Alexander before him, and told him that he had been many ways of advantage to him, in making a reconciliation between him and his father. (310) So he got money from him also, and went away, before his pernicious practices were found out; but when Eurycles was returned to Lacedemon, he did not leave off doing mischief; and so, for his many acts of injustice, he was banished from his own country.

(311) But as for the king of the Jews, he was not now in the temper he was in formerly towards Alexander and Aristobulus, when he had been content with the hearing their calumnies when others told him of them, but he was now come to that pass as to hate them himself, and to urge men to speak against them, though they did not do it of themselves. (312) He also observed

all that was said, and put questions, and gave ear to everyone that would but speak, if they could but say anything against them, till at length he heard that Euaratus of Cos was a conspirator with Alexander; which thing to Herod was the most agreeable and sweetest news imaginable.

(313) But still a greater misfortune came upon the young men, while the calumnies against them were continually increased, and, as a man may say, one would think it was everyone's endeavour to lay some grievous thing to their charge, which might appear to be for the king's preservation. (314) There were two guards of Herod's body, who were in great esteem for their great strength and tallness, Jucundus and Tyrannus; these men had been cast off by Herod, who was displeased at them; these now used to ride along with Alexander, and for their skill in their exercises were in great esteem with him, and had some gold and other gifts bestowed on them. (315) Now the king, having an immediate suspicion of these men, had them tortured; who endured the torture courageously for a long time; but at last confessed that Alexander would have persuaded them to kill Herod when he was in pursuit of the wild beasts that it might be said he fell from his horse and was run through with his own spear, for that he had once such a misfortune formerly. (316) They also showed where there was money hidden in the stable, underground, and these convicted the king's chief hunter, that he had given the young men the royal hunting spears, and weapons to Alexander's dependants, and at Alexander's command.

(317) After these, the commander of the garrison of Alexandria was caught and tortured; for he was accused to have promised to receive the young men into his fortress, and to supply them with that money of the king's which was laid up in that fortress, (318) yet did not he acknowledge anything of it himself; but his son came in, and said it was so, and delivered up the writing, which, so far as could be guessed, was in Alexander's hand. Its contents were these: 'When we have finished, by God's help, all that we have proposed to do, we will come to you; but do you endeavour, as you have promised, to receive us into your fortress.' (319) After this writing was produced, Herod had no doubt about the treacherous designs of his sons against him; but Alexander said that Diophantus, the scribe, had imitated his hand, and that the paper was maliciously drawn up by Antipater; for Diophantus appeared to be very cunning in such practices, and as he was afterward convicted of forging other papers, he was put to death for it.

(320) So the king produced those that had been tortured before the multitude at Jericho, in order to have them accuse the young men, which accusers many of the people stoned to death; (321) and when they were going to kill Alexander and Aristobulus likewise, the king would not permit them to do so, but restrained the multitude, by means of Ptolemy and Pheroras. However,

the young men were put under a guard, and kept in custody, that nobody might come at them: and all that they did or said was watched, and the reproach and fear they were in was little or nothing different from those of condemned criminals; (322) and one of them, who was Aristobulus, was so deeply affected, that he brought Salome, who was his aunt and his mother-in-law, to lament with him for his calamities, and to hate him who had suffered things to come to that pass; when he said to her, 'Art thou not in danger of destruction also, while the report goes that thou hadst disclosed beforehand all our affairs to Sylleus, when thou wast in hopes of being married to him?' (323) But she immediately carried those words to her brother: upon this he was out of patience, and gave command to bind him; and enjoined them both, now they were kept separate one from the other, to write down all the ill things they had done against their father, and bring the writings to him. (324) So when this was enjoined them, they wrote this: that they had laid no treacherous designs, nor made any preparations against their father, but that they had intended to fly away, and that by the distress they were in, their lives being now uncertain and tedious to them.

(325) About this time there came an ambassador out of Cappadocia from Archelaus, whose name was Melas; he was one of the principal rulers under him. So Herod being desirous to show Archelaus' ill will to him, called for Alexander, as he was in his bonds, and asked him again concerning his flight, whether and how they had resolved to retire; (326) Alexander replied – To Archelaus, who had promised to send them away to Rome; but that they had no wicked or mischievous designs against their father, and that nothing of that nature which their adversaries had charged upon them was true; (327) and that their desire was, that he might have examined Tyrannus and Jucundus more strictly, but that they had been suddenly slain by the means of Antipater, who put his own friends among the multitude [for that purpose.]

(328) When this was said, Herod commanded that both Alexander and Melas should be carried to Glaphyra, Archelaus' daughter, and that she should be asked, whether she did not know somewhat of Alexander's treacherous designs against Herod? (329) Now as soon as they were come to her, and she saw Alexander in bonds, she beat her head, and in a great consternation, gave a deep and moving groan. The young man also fell into tears. This was so miserable a spectacle to those present that, for a great while, they were not able to say or to do anything; (330) but at length Ptolemy, who was ordered to bring Alexander, bade him say whether his wife was conscious of his actions. He replied, 'How is it possible that she, whom I love better than my own soul, and by whom I have had children, should not know what I do?' (331) Upon which she cried out, that she knew of no wicked designs of his; but that yet, if her accusing herself falsely would tend to his preservation, she would confess it

all. Alexander replied, 'There is no such wickedness as those (who ought the least of all so to do) suspect, which either I have imagined or thou knowest of, but this only, that we had resolved to retire to Archelaus, and from thence to Rome.' (332) Which she also confessed. Upon which Herod, supposing that Archelaus' ill will to him was fully proved, sent a letter by Olympus and Volumnius; and bade them, as they sailed by, to touch at Eleusa of Cilicia, and give Archelaus the letter. And that when they had expostulated with him, that he had a hand in his son's treacherous design against him, they should from thence sail to Rome; (333) and that, in case they found Nicolaus had gained any ground, and that Caesar was no longer displeased at him, he should give him his letters, and the proof which he had ready to show against the young men. (334) As to Archelaus, he made his defence for himself, that he had promised to receive the young men, because it was both for their own and their father's advantage so to do, lest some too severe procedure should be gone upon in that anger and disorder they were in on occasion of the present suspicions; but that still he had not promised to send them to Caesar; and that he had not promised anything else to the young men that could show any ill will to him.

(335) When these ambassadors were come to Rome, they had a fit opportunity of delivering their letters to Caesar, because they found him reconciled to Herod; for the circumstances of Nicolaus' embassage had been as follows: (336) as soon as he was come to Rome, and was about the court, he did not first of all set about what he was come for only, but he thought fit also to accuse Sylleus. (337) Now, the Arabians, even before he came to talk with them, were quarrelling one with another; and some of them left Sylleus' party, and joining themselves to Nicolaus, informed him of all the wicked things that had been done; and produced to him evident demonstrations of the slaughter of a great number of Obodas' friends by Sylleus; for when these men left Sylleus, they had carried off with them those letters whereby they could convict him. (338) When Nicolaus saw such an opportunity afforded him, he made use of it in order to gain his own point afterward, and endeavoured immediately to make a reconciliation between Caesar and Herod; for he was fully satisfied, that if he should desire to make a defence for Herod directly, he should not be allowed that liberty; but that if he desired to accuse Sylleus, there would an occasion present itself of speaking on Herod's behalf. (339) So when the cause was ready for a hearing, and the day was appointed, Nicolaus, while Aretas' ambassadors were present, accused Sylleus, and said that he imputed to him the destruction of the king [Obodas], and of many others of the Arabians: (340) that he had borrowed money for no good design; and he proved that he had been guilty of adultery, not only with the Arabian, but Roman women also. And he added, that above all the rest he had alienated Caesar from

Herod; and that all that he had said about the actions of Herod were falsities. (341) When Nicolaus was come to this topic, Caesar stopped him from going on, and desired him only to speak to this affair of Herod, and to show that he had not led an army into Arabia, nor slain two thousand five hundred men there, nor taken prisoners, nor pillaged the country. (342) To which Nicolaus made this answer: 'I shall principally demonstrate, that either nothing at all, or but a very little, of those imputations are true, of which thou hast been informed; for had they been true, thou mightest justly have been still more angry at Herod.' (343) At this strange assertion, Caesar was very attentive; and Nicolaus said, that there was a debt due to Herod of five hundred talents, and a bond, wherein it was written, that if the time appointed be elapsed, it should be lawful to make a seizure out of any part of his country. 'As for the pretended army,' he said, 'it was no army, but a party sent out to require the just payment of the money: (344) that this was not sent immediately, nor so soon as the bond allowed, but that Sylleus had frequently come before Saturninus and Volumnius, the presidents of Syria: and that at last he had sworn at Berytus, by thy fortune, that he would certainly pay the money within thirty days, and deliver up the fugitives that were under his dominion. (345) And that when Sylleus had performed nothing of this, Herod came again before the presidents; and upon their permission to make a seizure for his money, he with difficulty went out of his country with a party of soldiers for that purpose. (346) And this is all the war which these men so tragically describe; and this is the affair of the expedition into Arabia. And how can this be called a war, when thy presidents permitted it, the covenants allowed it, and it was not executed till thy name, O Caesar, as well as that of the other gods, had been profaned? (347) And now I must speak in order about the captives. There were robbers that dwelt in Trachonitis: at first their number was no more than forty, but they became more afterwards, and they escaped the punishment Herod would have inflicted on them, by making Arabia their refuge. Sylleus received them, and supported them with food, that they might be mischievous to all mankind; and gave them a country to inhabit, and himself received the gains they made by robbery; (348) yet did he promise that he would deliver up these men, and that by the same oaths and same time that he swore and fixed for payment of his debt: nor can he by any means show that any other persons have at this time been taken out of Arabia besides these, and indeed not all these neither, but only so many as could not conceal themselves. (349) And thus does the calumny of the captives, which hath been so odiously represented, appear to be no better than a fiction and a lie, made on purpose to provoke thy indignation; (350) for I venture to affirm, that when the forces of the Arabians came upon us, and one or two of Herod's party fell, he then only defended himself, and there fell Nacebus their general, and in all about twenty-five others, and no more; whence Sylleus, by multiplying every single soldier to a hundred, he reckons the slain to have been two thousand five hundred.'

(351) This provoked Caesar more than ever: so he turned to Sylleus full of rage, and asked him how many of the Arabians were slain. Hereupon he hesitated, and said he had been imposed upon. The covenants were also read about the money he had borrowed, and the letters of the presidents of Syria, and the complaints of the several cities, so many as had been injured by the robbers. (352) The conclusion was this, that Sylleus was condemned to die, and that Caesar was reconciled to Herod, and owned his repentance for what severe things he had written to him, occasioned by calumny, insomuch that he told Sylleus that he had compelled him, by his lying account of things, to be guilty of ingratitude against a man that was his friend. (353) At the last all came to this – Sylleus was sent away to answer Herod's suit, and to repay the debt that he owed, and after that to be punished [with death]; but still Caesar was offended with Aretas, that he had taken upon himself the government, without his consent first obtained, for he had determined to bestow Arabia upon Herod; but that the letters he had sent hindered him from so doing; (354) for Olympus and Volumnius, perceiving that Caesar was now become favourable to Herod, thought fit immediately to deliver him the letters they were commanded by Herod to give him concerning his sons. (355) When Caesar had read them, he thought it would not be proper to add another government to him, now he was old, and in an ill state with relation to his sons, so he admitted Aretas' ambassadors; and after he had just reproved him for his rashness, in not tarrying till he received the kingdom from him, he accepted of his presents, and confirmed him in his government.

CHAPTER II

(356) So Caesar was now reconciled to Herod, and wrote thus to him: that he was grieved for him on account of his sons; and that in case they had been guilty of any profane and insolent crimes against him, it would behoove him to punish them as parricides, for which he gave him power accordingly; but if they had only contrived to fly away, he would have him give them an admonition, and not proceed to extremity with them. (357) He also advised him to get an assembly together, and to appoint some place near Berytus, which is a city belonging to the Romans, and to take the presidents of Syria, and Archelaus, king of Cappadocia, and as many more as he thought to be illustrious for their friendship to him, and the dignities they were in, and determine what should be done by their approbation. (358) These were the directions that Caesar gave him. Accordingly Herod, when the letter was

brought to him, was immediately very glad of Caesar's reconciliation to him, and very glad also that he had a complete authority given him over his sons. (359) And it strangely came about, that whereas before, in his adversity, though he had indeed shown himself severe, yet had he not been very rash, nor hasty, in procuring the destruction of his sons; he now in his prosperity took advantage of this change for the better, and the freedom he now had, to exercise his hatred against them after an unheard-of manner; (360) he therefore sent and called as many as he thought fit to this assembly, excepting Archelaus; for as for him, he either hated him, so that he would not invite him, or he thought he would be an obstacle to his designs.

(361) When the presidents, and the rest that belonged to the cities were come to Berytus, he kept his sons in a certain village belonging to Sidon, called Platana, but near to the city, that if they were called he might produce them, (362) for he did not think fit to bring them before the assembly: and when there were one hundred and fifty assessors present, Herod came by himself alone, and accused his sons, and that in such a way as if it were not a melancholy accusation, and not made but out of necessity, and upon the misfortunes he was under; indeed, in such a way as was very indecent for a father to accuse his sons, (363) for he was very vehement and disordered when he came to the demonstration of the crime they were accused of, and gave the greatest signs of passion and barbarity: nor would he suffer the assessors to consider the weight of the evidence, but asserted them to be true by his own authority, after a manner most indecent in a father against his sons, and read himself what they themselves had written, wherein there was no confession of any plots or contrivances against him, but only how they had contrived to fly away, and containing withal certain reproaches against him, on account of the ill will he bore them; (364) and when he came to those reproaches, he cried out most of all, and exaggerated what they said, as if they had confessed the design against him – and took his oath that he had rather lose his life than hear such reproachful words. (365) At last he said that he had sufficient authority, both by nature and by Caesar's grant to him, [to do what he thought fit]. He also added an allegation of a law of their country, which enjoined this: that if parents laid their hands on the head of him that was accused, the standers-by were obliged to cast stones at him, and thereby to slay him; (366) which though he were ready to do in his own country and kingdom, yet did he wait for their determination, and yet they came thither not so much as judges to condemn them for such manifest designs against him, whereby he had almost perished by his sons' means, but as persons that had an opportunity of showing their detestation of such practices, and declaring how unworthy a thing it must be in any, even the most remote, to pass over such treacherous designs [without punishment].

(367) When the king had said this, and the young men had not been

produced to make any defence for themselves, the assessors perceived there was no room for equity and reconciliation, so they confirmed his authority. (368) And in the first place, Saturninus, a person that had been consul, and one of great dignity, pronounced his sentence, but with great moderation and trouble; and said, that he condemned Herod's sons, but did not think they should be put to death. He had sons of his own; and to put one's son to death is a greater misfortune than any other that could befall him by their means. (369) After him Saturninus' sons, for he had three sons that followed him, and were his legates, pronounced the same sentence with their father. On the contrary, Volumnius' sentence was to inflict death on such as had been so impiously undutiful to their father; and the greatest part of the rest said the same, insomuch that the conclusion seemed to be, that the young men were condemned to die. (370) Immediately after this Herod came away from thence, and took his sons to Tyre, where Nicolaus met him in his voyage from Rome; of whom he inquired after he had related to him what had passed at Berytus, what his sentiments were about his sons, and what his friends at Rome thought of that matter. (371) His answer was, 'That what they had determined to do to thee was impious, and that thou oughtest to keep them in prison: (372) and if thou thinkest anything further necessary, thou mayest indeed so punish them, that thou mayest not appear to indulge thy anger more than to govern thyself by judgment; but if thou inclinest to the milder side, thou mayest absolve them, lest perhaps thy misfortunes be rendered incurable: and this is the opinion of the greatest part of thy friends at Rome also.' Whereupon Herod was silent, and in great thoughtfulness, and bade Nicolaus sail along with him.

(373) Now as they came to Caesarea, everybody was there talking of Herod's sons, and the kingdom was in suspense, and the people in great expectation of what would become of them; (374) for a terrible fear seized upon all men, lest the ancient disorders of the family should come to a sad conclusion, and they were in great trouble about their sufferings; nor was it without danger to say any rash thing about this matter, nor even to hear another saying it, but men's pity was forced to be shut up in themselves, which rendered the excess of their sorrow very irksome, but very silent; (375) yet was there an old soldier of Herod's, whose name was Tero, who had a son of the same age as Alexander, and his friend, who was so very free as openly to speak out what others silently thought about that matter; and was forced to cry out often among the multitude, (376) and said, in the most unguarded manner, that truth was perished, and justice taken away from men, while lies and ill will prevailed, and brought such a mist before public affairs, that the offenders were not able to see the greatest mischiefs that can befall men. (377) And as he was so bold, he seemed not to have kept himself out of danger, by speaking so freely; but the reasonableness of what he said moved men to regard him as having behaved

himself with great manhood, and this at a proper time also, (378) for which reason everyone heard what he said with pleasure: and although they first took care of their own safety by keeping silent themselves, yet did they kindly receive the great freedom he took; for the expectation they were in of so great an affliction, put a force upon them to speak of Tero whatsoever they pleased.

(379) This man had thrust himself into the king's presence with the greatest freedom, and desired to speak with him by himself alone, which the king permitted him to do; where he said thus: 'Since I am not able, O king, to bear up under so great a concern as I am under, I have preferred the use of this bold liberty that I now take, which may be for thy advantage, if thou mind to get any profit by it, before my own safety. (380) Whither is thy understanding gone, and left thy soul empty? Whither is that extraordinary sagacity of thine gone, whereby thou hast performed so many and such glorious actions? (381) Whence comes this solitude, and desertion of thy friends and relations? Of which I cannot but determine that they are neither thy friends nor relations, while they overlook such horrid wickedness in thy once happy kingdom. Dost not thou perceive what is doing? (382) Wilt thou slay these two young men, born of thy queen, who are accomplished with every virtue in the highest degree, and leave thyself destitute in thy old age, but exposed to one son, who hath very ill managed the hopes thou hast given him, and to relations, whose death thou hast so often resolved on thyself? (383) Dost not thou take notice, that the very silence of the multitude at once sees the crime, and abhors the fact? The whole army and the officers have commiseration on the poor unhappy youths, and hatred to those that are the actors in this matter.' (384) These words the king heard, and for some time with good temper. But what can one say? When Tero plainly touched upon the bad behaviour and perfidiousness of his domestics, he was moved at it; (385) but Tero went on further, and by degrees used an unbounded military freedom of speech, nor was he so well disciplined as to accommodate himself to the time: so Herod was greatly disturbed, (386) and seemed to be rather reproached by this speech, than to be hearing what was for his advantage, while he learned thereby that both the soldiers abhorred the thing he was about, and the officers had indignation at it, he gave order that all whom Tero had named, and Tero himself, should be bound and kept in prison.

(387) When this was over, one Trypho, who was the king's barber, took the opportunity, and came and told the king that Tero would often have persuaded him, when he trimmed him with a razor, to cut his throat, for that by this means he should be among the chief of Alexander's friends, and receive great rewards from him. (388) When he had said this, the king gave order that Tero and his son and the barber should be tortured, which was done accordingly; (389) but while Tero bore up himself, his son, seeing his father

already in a sad case, and with no hope of deliverance, and perceiving what would be the consequence of his terrible sufferings, said that if the king would free him and his father from these torments for what he should say, he would tell the truth. (390) And when the king had given his word to do so, he said that there was an agreement made, that Tero should lay violent hands on the king, because it was easy for him to come when he was alone; and that if, when he had done the thing, he should suffer death for it, as was not unlikely, it would be an act of generosity done in favour of Alexander. (391) This was what Tero's son said, and thereby freed his father from the distress he was in; but uncertain it is whether he had been thus forced to speak what was true, or whether it were a contrivance of his, in order to procure his own and his father's deliverance from their miseries.

(392) As for Herod, if he had before any doubt about the slaughter of his sons, there was now no longer any room left in his soul for it; but he had banished away whatsoever might afford him the least suggestion of reasoning better about this matter, so he already made haste to bring his purpose to a conclusion. (393) He also brought out three hundred of the officers that were under an accusation, as also Tero and his son, and the barber that accused them, before an assembly, and brought an accusation against them all; (394) whom the multitude stoned with whatsoever came to hand, and thereby slew them. Alexander also and Aristobulus were brought to Sebaste, by their father's command, and there strangled; but their dead bodies were, in the night-time, carried to Alexandrium, where their uncle, by the mother's side, and the greatest part of their ancestors, had been deposited.

(395) And now perhaps it may not seem unreasonable to some, that such an inveterate hatred might increase so much [on both sides] as to proceed farther, and overcome nature; but it may justly deserve consideration, whether it be to be laid to the charge of the young men, that they gave such an occasion to their father's anger, and led him to do what he did, and by going on long in the same way, put things past remedy, and brought him to use them so unmercifully; (396) or whether it be to be laid to the father's charge, that he was so hard-hearted, and so very tender in the desire of government, and of other things that would tend to his glory, that he would take no one into a partnership with him, that so whatsoever he would have done himself might continue immovable; (397) or indeed, whether fortune have not greater power than all prudent reasonings: whence we are persuaded that human actions are thereby determined beforehand by an inevitable necessity, and we call her Fate, because there is nothing which is not done by her; (398) wherefore I suppose it will be sufficient to compare this notion with that other, which attributes somewhat to ourselves, and renders men not accountable for the different conducts of their lives, which notion is no other than the philosophical

determination of our ancient law. (399) Accordingly, of the two other causes of this sad event, anybody may lay the blame on the young men, who acted by youthful vanity, and pride of their royal birth, that they should bear to hear the calumnies that were raised against their father, while certainly they were not equitable judges of the actions of his life, but ill-natured in suspecting, and intemperate in speaking of it, and on both accounts easily caught by those that observed them, and revealed them to gain favour; (400) yet cannot their father be thought worthy of excuse, as to that horrid impiety which he was guilty of about them, while he ventured, without any certain evidence of their treacherous designs against him, and without any proofs that they had made preparations for such attempt, to kill his own sons, who were of very comely bodies, and the great darlings of other men, and no way deficient in their conduct, whether it were in hunting, or in warlike exercises, or in speaking upon occasional topics of discourse; (401) for in all these they were skilful, and especially Alexander, who was the eldest; for certainly it had been sufficient, even though he had condemned them, to have kept them alive in bonds, or to let them live at a distance from his dominions in banishment, while he was surrounded by the Roman forces, which were a strong security to him, whose help would prevent his suffering anything by a sudden onset, or by open force; (402) but for him to kill them on the sudden, in order to gratify a passion that governed him, was a demonstration of insufferable impiety. He also was guilty of so great a crime in his older age; (403) nor will the delays that he made, and the length of time in which the thing was done, plead at all for his excuse; for when a man is on a sudden amazed, and in commotion of mind, and then commits a wicked action, although this be a heavy crime, yet is it a thing that frequently happens; but to do it upon deliberation, and after frequent attempts, and as frequent puttings-off to undertake it at last, and accomplish it, was the action of a murderous mind, and such as was not easily moved from that which is evil: (404) and this temper he showed in what he did afterwards when he did not spare those that seemed to be the best beloved of his friends that were left, wherein, though the justice of the punishment caused those that perished to be the less pitied, yet was the barbarity of the man here equal, in that he did not abstain from their slaughter also. But of those persons we shall have occasion to discourse more hereafter.

BOOK SEVENTEEN

CHAPTER I

(1) When Antipater had thus taken off his brethren, and had brought his father into the highest degree of impiety, till he was haunted with furies for what he had done, his hopes did not succeed to his mind, as to the rest of his life; for although he was delivered from the fear of his brethren being his rivals as to the government, yet did he find it a very hard thing, and almost impracticable, to come at the kingdom, because the hatred of the nation against him on that account was become very great; (2) and, besides this very disagreeable circumstance, the affairs of the soldiery grieved him still more, who were alienated from him, from which yet these kings derived all the safety which they had, whenever they found the nation desirous of innovation; and all this danger was drawn upon him by his destruction of his brethren. (3) However, he governed the nation jointly with his father, being indeed no other than a king already; and he was for that very reason trusted, and the more firmly depended on, for the which he ought himself to have been put to death, as appearing to have betrayed his brethren out of his concern for the preservation of Herod, and not rather out of his ill will to them, and before them to his father himself: and this was the accursed state he was in. (4) Now, all Antipater's contrivances tended to make his way to take off Herod, that he might have nobody to accuse him in the vile practices he was devising; and that Herod might have no refuge, nor any to afford him their assistance, since they must thereby have Antipater for their open enemy; (5) insomuch that the very plots he had laid against his brethren, were occasioned by the hatred he bore his father. But at this time he was more than ever set upon the execution of his attempts against Herod, because, if he were once dead, the government would now be firmly secured to him: but if he were suffered to live any longer, he should be in danger upon a discovery of that wickedness of which he had been the contriver, and his father would then of necessity become his enemy. (6) And on this account it was that he became very bountiful to his father's friends, and bestowed great sums on several of them, in order to surprise men with his good deeds, and take off their hatred against them. And he sent great presents to his friends at Rome particularly, to gain their good will; and above all, to Saturninus, the president of Syria. (7) He also hoped to gain the favour of Saturninus' brother with the large presents he bestowed on him; as also he used the same art to [Salome] the king's sister, who had married one of Herod's chief friends. And,

when he counterfeited friendship to those with whom he conversed, he was very subtle in gaining their belief, and very cunning to hide his hatred against any that he really did hate. (8) But he could not impose upon his aunt, who understood him of a long time, and was a woman not easily to be deluded, especially while she had already used all possible caution in preventing his pernicious designs. (9) Although Antipater's uncle by the mother's side was married to her daughter, and this by his own connivance and management, while she had before been married to Aristobulus, and while Salome's other daughter by that husband was married to the son of Calleas, yet that marriage was no obstacle to her, who knew how wicked he was, in her discovering his designs, as her former kindred to him could not prevent her hatred of him. (10) Now Herod had compelled Salome, while she was in love with Sylleus the Arabian, and had taken a fondness to him, to marry Alexas; which match was by her submitted to at the instance of Julia, who persuaded Salome not to refuse it, lest she should herself be their open enemy, since Herod had sworn that he would never be friends with Salome if she would not accept of Alexas for her husband; so she submitted to Julia, as being Caesar's wife; and besides that, she advised her to nothing but what was very much for her own advantage. (11) At this time also it was that Herod sent back King Archelaus' daughter, who had been Alexander's wife, to her father, returning the portion he had with her out of his own estate, that there might be no dispute between them about it.

(12) Now Herod brought up his sons' children with great care; for Alexander had two sons by Glaphyra; and Aristobulus had three sons by Berenice, Salome's daughter, and two daughters; (13) and as his friends were once with him, he presented the children before them; and deploring the hard fortune of his own sons, he prayed that no such ill fortune should befall these who were their children, but that they might improve in virtue, and obtain what they justly deserved and might make him amends for his care of their education. (14) He also caused them to be betrothed against they should come to the proper age of marriage; the elder of Alexander's sons to Pheroras' daughter, and Antipater's daughter to Aristobulus' eldest son. He also allotted one of Aristobulus' daughters to Antipater's son, and Aristobulus' other daughter to Herod, a son of his own, who was born to him by the high priest's daughter; for it is the ancient practice among us to have many wives at the same time. (15) Now, the king made those espousals for the children, out of commiseration of them now they were fatherless, as endeavouring to render Antipater kind to them by these intermarriages. (16) But Antipater did not fail to bear the same temper of mind to his brother's children which he had borne to his brothers themselves; and his father's concern about them provoked his indignation against them upon his supposal that they would become greater than ever his brothers had been: while Archelaus, a king, would support his daughter's sons, and Pheroras, a tetrarch,

would accept of one of the daughters as a wife to his son. (17) What provoked him also was this, that all the multitude would so commiserate these fatherless children, and so hate him [for making them fatherless], that all would come out, since they were no strangers to his vile disposition towards his brethren. He contrived, therefore, to overturn his father's settlements, as thinking it a terrible thing that they should be so related to him and be so powerful withal. (18) So Herod yielded to him, and changed his resolution at his entreaty; and the determination now was, that Antipater himself should marry Aristobulus' daughter, and Antipater's son should marry Pheroras' daughter. So the espousals for the marriages were changed after this manner, even without the king's real approbation.

(19) Now Herod the king had at this time nine wives; one of them, Antipater's mother, and another the high priest's daughter, by whom he had a son of his own name. He had also one who was his brother's daughter, and another his sister's daughter; which two had no children. (20) One of his wives also was of the Samaritan nation, whose sons were Antipas and Archelaus, and whose daughter was Olympias; which daughter was afterward married to Joseph, the king's brother's son; but Archelaus and Antipas were brought up with a certain private man at Rome. (21) Herod had also to wife Cleopatra of Jerusalem, and by her he had his sons Herod and Philip: which last was also brought up at Rome; Pallas also was one of his wives, who bare him his son Phasaelus; and besides these, he had for his wives Phedra and Elpis, by whom he had his daughters Roxana and Salome. (22) As for his elder daughters by the same mother with Alexander and Aristobulus, and whom Pheroras was neglected to marry, he gave the one in marriage to Antipater, the king's sister's son, and the other to Phasaelus, his brother's son; and this was the posterity of Herod.

CHAPTER 2

(23) And now it was that Herod, being desirous of securing himself on the side of the Trachonites, resolved to build a village as large as a city for the Jews, in the middle of that country, which might make his own country difficult to be assaulted, and whence he might be at hand to make sallies upon them, and do them a mischief. (24) Accordingly, when he understood that there was a man that was a Jew come out of Babylon, with five hundred horsemen, all of whom could shoot their arrows as they rode on horseback, and, with a hundred of his relations, had passed over Euphrates, and now abode at Antioch by Daphne of Syria, where Saturninus, who was then president, had given them a place for habitation, called Valatha, (25) he sent for this man, with the multitude that followed him, and promised to give him land in the toparchy called Batanea,

which country is bounded with Trachonitis, as desirous to make that his habitation a guard to himself. He also engaged to let him hold the country free from tribute, and that they should dwell entirely without paying such customs as used to be paid, and gave it him tax free.

(26) The Babylonian was induced by these offers to come hither; so he took possession of the land, and built in it fortresses and a village, and named it Bathyra. Whereby this man became a safeguard to the inhabitants against the Trachonites, and preserved those Jews who came out of Babylon to offer their sacrifices at Jerusalem, from being hurt by the Trachonite robbers: so that a great number came to him from all those parts where the ancient Jewish laws were observed, (27) and the country became full of people, by reason of their universal freedom from taxes. This continued during the life of Herod; but when Philip, who was [tetrarch] after him, took the government, he made them pay some small taxes, and that for a little while only; (28) and Agrippa the Great, and his son of the same name, although they harassed them greatly, yet would they not take their liberty away. From whom, when the Romans have now taken the government into their own hands, they still gave them the privilege of their freedom, but oppress them entirely with the imposition of taxes. Of which matter I shall treat more accurately in the progress of this history.

(29) At length Zamaris the Babylonian, to whom Herod had given that country for a possession, died; having lived virtuously, and left children of a good character behind him; one of whom was Jacim, who was famous for his valour, and taught his Babylonians how to ride their horses; and a troop of them were guards to the forementioned kings; (30) and when Jacim was dead in his old age, he left a son, whose name was Philip, one of great strength in his hands, and in other respects also more eminent for his valour than any of his contemporaries; (31) on which account there was a confidence and firm friendship between him and King Agrippa. He had also an army which he maintained, as great as that of a king; which he exercised and led wheresoever he had occasion to march.

(32) When the affairs of Herod were in the condition I have described, all the public affairs depended upon Antipater; and his power was such, that he could do good turns to as many as he pleased, and this by his father's concession, in hopes of his good will and fidelity to him; and this till he ventured to use his power still further, because his wicked designs were concealed from his father, and he made him believe everything he said. (33) He was also formidable to all, not so much on account of the power of authority he had, as for the shrewdness of his vile attempts beforehand; but he who principally cultivated a friendship with him was Pheroras, who received the like marks of his friendship; while Antipater had cunningly encompassed him about by a company of women, whom he placed as guards about him;

(34) for Pheroras was greatly enslaved to his wife, and to her mother, and to her sister; and this notwithstanding the hatred he bare them, for the indignities they had offered to his virgin daughters. Yet did he bear them; and nothing was to he done without the women, who had got this man into their circle, and continued still to assist each other in all things, (35) in so much that Antipater was entirely addicted to them, both by himself and by his mother; for these four women said all one and the same thing; but the opinions of Pheroras and Antipater were different in some points of no consequence. (36) But the king's sister [Salome] was their antagonist, who for a good while had looked about all their affairs, and was apprised that this their friendship was made in order to do Herod some mischief, and was disposed to inform the king of it; (37) and since these people knew that their friendship was very disagreeable to Herod, as tending to do him a mischief, they contrived that their meetings should not be discovered; so they pretended to hate one another, and abuse one another when time served, and especially when Herod was present, or when anyone was there that would tell him; but still their intimacy was firmer than ever when they were private; and this was the course they took. (38) But they could not conceal from Salome neither their first contrivance, when they set about these their intentions, nor when they had made some progress in them; but she searched out everything, and, aggravating the relations to her brother, declared to him, as well their secret assemblies and compotations, as their counsels taken in a clandestine manner, which, if they were not in order to destroy him, they might well enough have been open and public; (39) but to appearance they are at variance, and speak about one another as if they intended one another a mischief, but agree so well together when they are out of the sight of the multitude; for when they are alone by themselves they act in concert, and profess that they will never leave off their friendship, but will fight against those from whom they conceal their designs: (40) and thus did she search out these things, and get a perfect knowledge of them, and then told her brother of them, who understood also of himself a great deal of what she said, but still durst not depend upon it, because of the suspicions he had of his sister's calumnies; (41) for there was a certain sect of men that were Jews, who valued themselves highly upon the exact skill they had in the law of their fathers, and made men believe they were highly favoured by God, by whom this set of women were inveigled. These are those that are called the sect of the Pharisees, who were in a capacity of greatly opposing kings. A cunning sect they were, and soon elevated to a pitch of open fighting and doing mischief. (42) Accordingly, when all the people of the Jews gave assurance of their good will to Caesar, and to the king's government, these very men did not swear, being above six thousand; and when the king imposed a fine upon them, Pheroras' wife paid their fine for

them. (43) In order to requite which kindness of hers, since they were believed to have the foreknowledge of things to come by Divine inspiration, they foretold how God had decreed that Herod's government should cease, and his posterity should be deprived of it; but that the kingdom should come to her and Pheroras, and to their children. (44) These predictions were not concealed from Salome, but were told the king; as also how they had perverted some persons about the palace itself. So the king slew such of the Pharisees as were principally accused, and Bagoas the eunuch, and one Carus, who exceeded all men of that time in comeliness, and one that was his catamite. He slew also all those of his own family who had consented to what the Pharisees foretold; (45) and for Bagoas, he had been puffed up by them, as though he should be named the father and the benefactor of him who by the prediction, was foretold to be their appointed king; for that this king would have all things in his power, and would enable Bagoas to marry, and to have children of his own body begotten.

CHAPTER 3

(46) When Herod had punished those Pharisees who had been convicted of the foregoing crimes, he gathered an assembly together of his friends, and accused Pheroras' wife; and ascribing the abuses of the virgins to the imprudence of that woman, brought an accusation against her for the dishonour she had brought upon them: (47) that she had studiously introduced a quarrel between him and his brother; and, by her ill temper, had brought them into a state of war, both by her words and actions; that the fines which he had laid had not been paid, and the offenders had escaped punishment by her means; and that nothing which had of late been done, had been done without her; (48) 'for which reason Pheroras would do well, if he would of his own accord, and by his own command, and not at my entreaty, or as following my opinion, put this his wife away, as one that will still be the occasion of war between thee and me. And now, Pheroras, if thou valuest thy relation to me, put this wife of thine away; for by this means thou wilt continue to be a brother to me, and wilt abide in thy love to me.' (49) Then said Pheroras (although he was pressed hard by the former words), that as he would not do so unjust a thing as to renounce his brotherly relation to him, so would he not leave off his affection for his wife; that he would rather choose to die, than to live and be deprived of a wife that was so dear unto him. (50) Hereupon Herod put off his anger against Pheroras on these accounts, although he himself thereby underwent a very uneasy punishment. However, he forbade Antipater and his mother to have any conversation with Pheroras, and bade them to take care to avoid the assemblies of the women: (51) which they promised to do, but still got together when occasion served; and both Pheroras and Antipater had their own merry

meetings. The report went also, that Antipater had criminal intercourse with Pheroras' wife, and that they were brought together by Antipater's mother.

(52) But Antipater had now a suspicion of his father and was afraid that the effects of his hatred to him might increase; so he wrote to his friends at Rome, and bade them to send to Herod, that he would immediately send Antipater to Caesar; (53) which when it was done, Herod sent Antipater thither, and sent most noble presents along with him; as also his testament, wherein Antipater was appointed to be his successor; and that if Antipater should die first, his son [Herod Philip,] by the high priest's daughter, should succeed. (54) And, together with Antipater, there went to Rome Sylleus the Arabian, although he had done nothing of all that Caesar had enjoined him. Antipater also accused him of the same crimes of which he had been formerly accused by Herod. Sylleus was also accused by Aretas, that without his consent he had slain many of the chief of the Arabians at Petra, and particularly Soemus, a man that deserved to be honoured by all men; and that he had slain Fabatus, a servant of Caesar. (55) These were the things of which Sylleus was accused, and that on the occasion following: there was one Corinthus, belonging to Herod, of the guards of the king's body, and one who was greatly trusted by him. Sylleus had persuaded this man with the offer of a great sum of money to kill Herod; and he had promised to do it. When Fabatus had been made acquainted with this, for Sylleus had himself told him of it, he informed the king of it: (56) who caught Corinthus, and put him to the torture, and thereby got out of him the whole conspiracy. He also caught two other Arabians, who were discovered by Corinthus; the one the head of a tribe, and the other a friend to Sylleus, (57) who both were by the king brought to the torture, and confessed that they were come to encourage Corinthus not to fail of doing what he had undertaken to do; and to assist him with their own hands in the murder, if need should require their assistance. So Saturninus, upon Herod's discovering the whole to him, sent them to Rome.

(58) At this time Herod commanded Pheroras, that since he was so obstinate in his affection for his wife, he should retire into his own tetrarchy; which he did very willingly, and sware many oaths that he would not come again till he heard that Herod was dead. And indeed when, upon a sickness of the king, he was desired to come to him before he died, that he might entrust him with some of his injunctions, he had such a regard to his oath, that he would not come to him; (59) yet did not Herod so retain his hatred to Pheroras, but remitted of his purpose [not to see him] which he before had, and that for such great causes as have been already mentioned; but as soon as he began to be ill he came to him, and this without being sent for; and when he was dead he took care of his funeral, and had his body brought to Jerusalem, and buried there, and appointed a solemn mourning for him. (60) This [death of Pheroras]

became the origin of Antipater's misfortunes, although he had already sailed for Rome, God now being about to punish him for the murder of his brethren. I will explain the history of this matter very distinctly, that it may be for a warning to mankind, that they take care of conducting their whole lives by the rules of virtue.

CHAPTER 4

(61) As soon as Pheroras was dead, and his funeral was over, two of Pheroras' freedmen, who were much esteemed by him, came to Herod, and entreated him not to leave the murder of his brother without avenging it, but to examine into such an unreasonable and unhappy death. (62) When he was moved with these words, for they seemed to him to be true, they said that Pheroras supped with his wife the day before he fell sick, and that a certain potion was brought him in such a sort of food as he was not used to eat; but that when he had eaten he died of it; that this potion was brought out of Arabia by a woman, under a pretence indeed as a love potion, for that was its name, but in reality to kill Pheroras, (63) for that the Arabian women are skilful in making such poisons; and the woman to whom they ascribe this, was confessedly a most intimate friend of one of Sylleus' mistresses; and that both the mother and the sister of Pheroras' wife had been at the place where she lived, and had persuaded her to sell them this potion, and had come back and brought it with them the day before that of his supper. (64) Hereupon the king was provoked, and put the women-slaves to the torture, and some that were free with them; and as the fact did not yet appear, because none of them would confess it, at length one of them under the utmost agonies, said no more but this, that she prayed that God would send the like agonies upon Antipater's mother, who had been the occasion of these miseries to all of them. (65) This prayer induced Herod to increase the women's tortures, till thereby all was discovered: their merry meetings, their sacred assemblies, and the disclosing of what he had said to his son alone unto Pheroras' women. (Now what Herod had charged Antipater to conceal, was the gift of a hundred talents to him, not to have any conversation with Pheroras.) (66) And what hatred he bore to his father; and that he complained to his mother how very long his father lived; and that he was himself almost an old man, insomuch that if the kingdom should come to him, it would not afford him any great pleasure; and that there were a great many of his brothers, or brother's children, bringing up, that might have hopes of the kingdom as well as himself; all which made his own hopes of it uncertain; (67) for that even now, if he should himself not live, Herod had ordained that the government should be conferred, not on his son, but rather on a brother. He also had accused the king of great barbarity, and of the slaughter of his sons; and

that it was out of the fear he was under, lest he should do the like to him, that made him contrive this his journey to Rome, and Pheroras contrived to go to his own tetrarchy.

(68) These confessions agreed with what his sister had told him, and tended greatly to corroborate her testimony, and to free her from the suspicion of her unfaithfulness to him. So the king having satisfied himself of the spite which Doris, Antipater's mother, as well as himself, bore to him, took away from her all her fine ornaments, which were worth many talents, and then sent her away, and entered into friendship with Pheroras' women. (69) But he who most of all irritated the king against his son, was one Antipater, the procurator of Antipater the king's son, who, when he was tortured, among other things, said that Antipater had prepared a deadly potion, and given it to Pheroras, with his desire that he would give it to his father during his absence, and when he was too remote to have the least suspicion cast upon him thereto relating; (70) that Antiphilus, one of Antipater's friends, brought that potion out of Egypt; and that it was sent to Pheroras by Theudion, the brother of the mother of Antipater, the king's son, and by that means came to Pheroras' wife, her husband having given it her to keep. (71) And when the king asked her about it, she confessed it; and as she was running to fetch it, she threw herself down from the house-top, yet did she not kill herself, because she fell upon her feet: (72) by which means, when the king had comforted her, and had promised her and her domestics pardon, upon condition of their concealing nothing of the truth from him, but had threatened her with the utmost miseries if she proved ungrateful [and concealed anything]; so she promised him, and swore that she would speak out everything, and tell after what manner everything was done; and said, what many took to be entirely true, (73) that the potion was brought out of Egypt by Antiphilus, and that his brother, who was a physician, had procured it; and that, 'when Theudion brought it us, she kept it upon Pheroras' committing it to her; and that it was prepared by Antipater for thee. (74) When, therefore, Pheroras was fallen sick, and thou camest to him and tookest care of him, and when he saw the kindness thou hadst for him, his mind was overborne thereby. So he called me to him, and said to me, "O woman! Antipater hath circumvented me in this affair of his father and my brother, by persuading me to have a murderous intention to him, and procuring a potion to be subservient thereto; do thou, therefore, go and fetch my potion (75) (since my brother appears to have still the came virtuous disposition towards me which he had formerly, and I do not expect to live long myself, and that I may not defile my forefathers by the murder of a brother) and burn it before my face;" that accordingly she immediately brought it and did as her husband bade her; (76) and that she burnt the greatest part of the potion; but that a little of it was left, that if the king, after Pheroras's death, should treat her ill, she

might poison herself, and thereby get clear of her miseries.' (77) Upon her saying thus, she brought out the potion, and the box in which it was, before them all. Nay, there was another brother of Antiphilus, and his mother also, who, by the extremity of pain and torture, confessed the same things, and owned the box [to be that which had been brought out of Egypt]. (78) The high priest's daughter also, who was the king's wife, was accused to have been conscious of all this, and had resolved to conceal it; for which reason Herod divorced her, and blotted her son out of his testament, wherein he had been mentioned as one that was to reign after him; and he took the high priesthood away from his father-in-law, Simeon the son of Boethus, and appointed Matthias the son of Theophilus, who was born at Jerusalem, to be high priest in his room.

(79) While this was doing, Bathyllus also, Antipater's freedman, came from Rome, and upon the torture was found to have brought another potion, to give it into the hands of Antipater's mother, and of Pheroras, that if the former potion did not operate upon the king, this at least might carry him off. (80) There came also letters from Herod's friends at Rome, by the approbation and at the suggestion of Antipater, to accuse Archelaus and Philip, as if they calumniated their father on account of the slaughter of Alexander and Aristobulus, and as if they commiserated their deaths, and as if, because they were sent for home (for their father had already recalled them), they concluded they were themselves also to be destroyed. (81) These letters had been procured by great rewards, by Antipater's friends: but Antipater himself wrote to his father about them, and laid the heaviest things to their charge; yet did he entirely excuse them of any guilt, and said they were but young men, and so imputed their words to their youth. But he said, that he had himself been very busy in the affair relating to Sylleus, and in getting interest among the great men: and on that account had bought splendid ornaments to present them withal, which cost him two hundred talents. (82) Now, one may wonder how it came about, that while so many accusations were laid against him in Judea during seven months before this time, he was not made acquainted with any of them. The causes of which were, that the roads were exactly guarded, and that men hated Antipater; for there was nobody who would run any hazard himself, to gain him any advantages.

CHAPTER 5

(83) Now Herod, upon Antipater's writing to him, that having done all that he was to do, and this in the manner he was to do it, he would suddenly come to him, concealed his anger against him, and wrote back to him, and bade him not delay his journey, lest any harm should befall himself in his absence. At the

same time also he made some little complaint about his mother, but promised that he would lay those complaints aside when he should return. (84) He withal expressed his entire affection for him, as fearing lest he should have some suspicion of him, and defer his journey to him; and lest, while he lived at Rome, he should lay plots for the kingdom, and, moreover, do somewhat against himself. (85) This letter Antipater met with in Cilicia; but had received an account of Pheroras' death before at Tarentum. This last news affected him deeply; not out of any affection for Pheroras, but because he was dead without having murdered his father, which he had promised him to do. (86) And when he was at Celendris in Cilicia, he began to deliberate with himself about his sailing home, as being much grieved with the ejection of his mother. Now, some of his friends advised him that he should tarry a while somewhere, in expectation of farther information. But others advised him to sail home without delay; for that if he were once come thither, he would soon put an end to all accusations, and that nothing afforded any weight to his accusers at present but his absence. (87) He was persuaded by these last, and sailed on, and landed at the haven called Sebastus, which Herod had built at vast expenses in honour of Caesar, and called Sebastus. (88) And now was Antipater evidently in a miserable condition, while nobody came to him nor saluted him, as they did at his going away, with good wishes of joyful acclamations; nor was there now anything to hinder them from entertaining him, on the contrary, with bitter curses, while they supposed he was come to receive his punishment for the murder of his brethren.

(89) Now Quintilius Varus was at this time at Jerusalem, being sent to succeed Saturninus as president of Syria, and was come as an assessor to Herod, who had desired his advice in his present affairs; (90) and as they were sitting together, Antipater came upon them, without knowing anything of the matter; so he came into the palace clothed in purple. The porters indeed received him in, but excluded his friends. (91) And now he was in great disorder, and presently understood the condition he was in, while, upon his going to salute his father, he was repulsed by him, who called him a murderer of his brethren, and a plotter of destruction against himself, and told him that Varus should be his auditor and his judge the very next day; (92) so he found, that what misfortunes he now heard of as already upon him, with the greatness of which he went away in confusion; upon which his mother and his wife met him (which wife was the daughter of Antigonus, who was king of the Jews before Herod), from whom he learned all circumstances which concerned him, and then prepared himself for his trial.

(93) On the next day Varus and the king sat together in judgment, and both their friends were also called in, as also the king's relations, with his sister Salome, and as many as could discover anything, and such as had been

tortured; and besides these, some slaves of Antipater's mother, who were taken up a little before Antipater's coming, and brought with them a written letter, the sum of which was this: That he should not come back, because all was come to his father's knowledge, and that Caesar was the only refuge he had left to prevent both his and her delivery into his father's hands. (94) Then did Antipater fall down at his father's feet, and besought him not to prejudge his cause, but that he might be first heard by his father, and that his father would keep himself still unprejudiced. So Herod ordered him to be brought into the midst, and then lamented himself about his children, from whom he had suffered such great misfortunes; and because Antipater fell upon him in his old age. He also reckoned up what maintenance, and what education he had given them; and what seasonable supplies of wealth he had afforded them, according to their own desire; (95) none of which favours had hindered them from contriving against him, and from bringing his very life into danger in order to gain his kingdom, after an impious manner, by taking away his life before the course of nature, their father's wishes, or justice, required that that kingdom should come to them; (96) and that he wondered what hopes could elevate Antipater to such a pass as to be hardy enough to attempt such things; that he had by his testament in writing declared him his successor in the government; and while he was alive, he was in no respect inferior to him either in his illustrious dignity, or in power or authority, he having no less than fifty talents for his yearly income, and had received for his journey to Rome no fewer than thirty talents. (97) He also objected to him the case of his brethren whom he had accused; and if they were guilty, he had imitated their example; and if not, he had brought him groundless accusations against his near relations; (98) for that he had been acquainted with all those things by him, and by nobody else, and had done what was done by his approbation, and whom he now absolved from all that was criminal, by becoming the inheritor of the guilt of such their parricide.

(99) When Herod had thus spoken, he fell a weeping, and was not able to say any more; but at his desire Nicolaus of Damascus, being the king's friend, and always conversant with him, and acquainted with whatsoever he did and with the circumstances of his affairs, proceeded to what remained, and explained all that concerned the demonstrations and evidences of the facts. (100) Upon which Antipater, in order to make his legal defence, turned himself to his father, and enlarged upon the many indications he had given of his good will to him; and instanced in the honours that had been done him, which yet had not been done, had he not deserved them by his virtuous concern about him; (101) for that he had made provisions for everything that was fit to be foreseen beforehand, as to giving him his wisest advice; and whenever there was occasion for the labour of his own hands, he had not

grudged any such pains for him. And that it was almost impossible that he, who had delivered his father from so many treacherous contrivances laid against him, should be himself in a plot against him, and so lose all the reputation he had gained for his virtue, by his wickedness which succeeded it; (102) and this while he had nothing to prohibit him, who was already appointed his successor, to enjoy the royal honour with his father also at present; and that there was no likelihood that a person who had the one half of that authority without any danger, and with a good character, should hunt after the whole with infamy and danger, and this when it was doubtful whether he could obtain it or not; and when he saw the sad example of his brethren before him, and was both the informer and the accuser against them, at a time when they might not otherwise have been discovered; nay, was the author of the punishment inflicted upon them when it appeared evidently that they were guilty of a wicked attempt against their father; (103) and that even the contentions that were in the king's family were indications that he had ever managed affairs out of the sincerest affection to his father. And as to what he had done at Rome, Caesar was a witness thereto, who was yet no more to be imposed upon than God himself; (104) of whose opinions his letters sent hither are sufficient evidence: and that it was not reasonable to prefer the calumnies of such as proposed to raise disturbances, before those letters; the greatest part of which calumnies had been raised during his absence, which gave scope to his enemies to forge them, which they had not been able to do if he had been there. (105) Moreover he showed the weakness of the evidence obtained by torture, which was commonly false, because the distress men are in under such tortures, naturally obliges them to say many things in order to please those that govern them. He also offered himself to the torture.

(106) Hereupon there was a change observed in the assembly, while they greatly pitied Antipater, who by weeping and putting on a countenance suitable to his sad case, made them commiserate the same; insomuch that his very enemies were moved to compassion; and it appeared plainly that Herod himself was affected in his own mind, although he was not willing it should be taken notice of. Then did Nicolaus begin to prosecute what the king had begun, and that with great bitterness; and summed up all the evidence which arose from the tortures, or from the testimonies. (107) He principally and largely cried up the king's virtues, which he had exhibited in the maintenance and education of his sons; while he never could gain any advantage thereby, but still fell from one misfortune to another. (108) Although he owned that he was not so much surprised with that thoughtless behaviour of his former sons, who were but young, and were besides corrupted by wicked counsellors, who were the occasion of their wiping out of their minds all the righteous dictates of nature, and this out of a desire of coming to the government sooner than

they ought to do; (109) yet that he could not but justly stand amazed at the horrid wickedness of Antipater, who, although he had not only had great benefits bestowed on him by his father, enough to tame his reason, yet could not be more tamed than the most envenomed serpents; whereas even those creatures admit of some mitigation, and will not bite their benefactors, while Antipater hath not let the misfortunes of his brethren be any hindrance to him, but he hath gone on to imitate their barbarity notwithstanding. (110) 'Yet wast thou, O Antipater! (as thou hast thyself confessed) the informer as to what wicked actions they had done, and the searcher out of the evidence against them, and the author of the punishment they underwent upon their detection. Nor do we say this as accusing thee for being so zealous in thy anger against them, but are astonished at thy endeavours to imitate their profligate behaviour; and we discover thereby, that thou didst not act thus for the safety of thy father, but for the destruction of thy brethren, that by such outside hatred of their impiety thou mightest be believed a lover of thy father, and mightest thereby get thee power enough to do mischief with the greatest impunity; which design thy actions indeed demonstrate. (111) It is true, thou tookest thy brethren off, because thou didst convict them of their wicked designs; but thou didst not yield up to justice those who were their partners; and thereby didst make it evident to all men that thou madest a covenant with them against thy father, when thou chosest to be the accuser of thy brethren, (112) as desirous to gain to thyself alone this advantage of laying plots to kill thy father, and so to enjoy double pleasure, which is truly worthy of thy evil disposition – which thou hast openly shown against thy brethren; on which account thou didst rejoice, as having done a most famous exploit, nor was that behaviour unworthy of thee; but if thy intention were otherwise, thou art worse then they: (113) while thou didst contrive to hide thy treachery against thy father, thou didst hate them, not as plotters against thy father, for in that case thou hadst not thyself fallen upon the like crime, but as successors of his dominions, and more worthy of that succession than thyself. (114) Thou wouldest kill thy father after thy brethren, lest thy lies raised against them might be detected; and lest thou shouldest suffer what punishment thou hadst deserved, thou hadst a mind to exact that punishment of thy unhappy father, and didst devise such a sort of uncommon parricide as the world never yet saw; (115) for thou who art his son didst not only lay a treacherous design against thy father, and didst it while he loved thee, and had been thy benefactor – had made thee in reality his partner in the kingdom, and had openly declared thee his successor, while thou wast not forbidden to taste the sweetness of authority already, and hadst the firm hope of what was future by thy father's determination, and the security of a written testament; (116) but for certain, thou didst not measure these things according to thy father's various disposition, but according to thy own thoughts and inclinations; and wast desirous to take the part that remained away from thy too indulgent father, and soughtest to destroy him with thy deeds, whom thou in words pretendedst to preserve. (117) Nor wast thou content to be wicked thyself, but thou filledst thy mother's head with thy devices, and raisedst disturbance among thy brethren, and hadst the boldness to call thy father a wild beast; while thou hadst thyself a mind more cruel than any serpent, whence thou sentest out that poison among thy nearest kindred and greatest bene-factors, and invitedst them to assist thee and guard thee, and didst hedge thyself in on all sides by the artifices of both men and women, against an old man – as though that mind of thine was not sufficient of itself to support so great a hatred as thou barest to him; (118) and here thou appearest, after the tortures of freemen, of domestics, of men and women, which have been examined on thy account, and after the informations of thy fellow-conspirators, as making haste to contradict the truth; and hast thought on ways not only how to take thy father out of the world, but to disannul that written law which is against thee, and the virtue of Varus, and the nature of justice; (119) nay, such is that impudence of thine on which thou confidest, that thou desirest to be put to the torture thyself, while thou allegest that the tortures of those already examined thereby have made them tell lies; that those that have been the deliverers of thy father may not be allowed to have spoken the truth; but that thy tortures may be esteemed the discoverers of truth. Wilt not thou, O Varus! deliver the king from the injuries of his kindred? (120) Wilt not thou destroy this wicked wild beast, which hath pretended kindness to his father, in order to destroy his brethren; while yet he is himself alone ready to carry off the kingdom immediately, and appears to be the most bloody butcher to him of them all? For thou art sensible that parricide is a general injury both to nature and to common life, and that the intention of parricide is not inferior to its preparation; and he who does not punish it, is injurious to nature itself.'

(121) Nicolaus added further what belonged to Antipater's mother, and whatsoever she had prattled like a woman; as also about the predictions and the sacrifices relating to the king; and whatsoever Antipater had done lasciviously in his cups and his amours among Pheroras' women; the examination upon torture; and whatsoever concerned the testimonies of the witnesses, which were many, and of various kinds; some prepared beforehand, and others were sudden answers, which further declared and confirmed the foregoing evidence. (122) For those men who were not acquainted with Antipater's practices, but had concealed them out of fear, when they saw that he was exposed to the accusations of the former witnesses, and that his great good fortune, which had supported him hitherto, had now evidently betrayed him into the hands of his enemies, who were now insatiable in their hatred to him, told all they knew of him; (123) and his ruin was now hastened, not so much

by the enmity of those that were his accusers, as by his gross, impudent, and wicked contrivances, and by his ill will to his father and his brethren; while he had filled their house with disturbance, and caused them to murder one another; and was neither fair in his hatred nor kind in his friendship, but just so far as served his own turn. (124) Now, there were a great number who for a long time beforehand had seen all this, and especially such as were naturally disposed to judge of matters by the rules of virtue, because they were used to determine about affairs without passion, but had been restrained from making any open complaints before; these, upon the leave now given them, produced all that they knew before the public. (125) The demonstrations also of these wicked facts could no way be disproved, because the many witnesses there were did neither speak out of favour to Herod, nor were they obliged to keep what they had to say silent, out of suspicion of any danger they were in; but they spake what they knew, because they thought such actions very wicked, and that Antipater deserved the greatest punishment; and indeed not so much for Herod's safety, as on account of the man's own wickedness. (126) Many things were also said, and those by a great number of persons, who were no way obliged to say them: insomuch that Antipater, who used generally to be very shrewd in his lies and impudence, was not able to say one word to the contrary. (127) When Nicolaus had left off speaking, and had produced the evidence, Varus bade Antipater to betake himself to the making his defence, if he had prepared anything whereby it might appear that he was not guilty of the crimes he was accused of; for that, as he was himself desirous, so did he know that his father was in like manner desirous also to have him found entirely innocent; (128) but Antipater fell down on his face, and appealed to God and to all men, for testimonials of his innocency, desiring that God would declare, by some evident signals, that he had not laid any plot against his father. (129) This being the usual method of all men destitute of virtue, that, when they set about any wicked undertakings, they fall to work according to their own inclinations, as if they believed that God was unconcerned in human affairs; but when once they are found out, and are in danger of undergoing the punishment due to their crimes, they endeavoured to overthrow all the evidence against them, by appealing to God; (130) which was the very thing which Antipater now did; for whereas he had done everything as if there were no God in the world, when he was on all sides distressed by justice, and when he had no other advantage to expect from any legal proofs, by which he might disprove the accusations laid against him, he impudently abused the majesty of God, and ascribed it to his power, that he had been preserved hitherto; and produced before them all what difficulties he had ever undergone in his bold acting for his father's preservation.

(131) So when Varus, upon asking Antipater what he had to say for himself, found that he had nothing to say besides his appeal to God, and saw that there

was no end of that, he bade them bring the potion before the court, that he might see what virtue still remained in it; (132) and when it was brought, and one that was condemned to die had drank it by Varus' command, he died presently. Then Varus got up, and departed out of the court, and went away, the day following, to Antioch, where his usual residence was, because that was the palace of the Syrians; upon which Herod laid his son in bonds: (133) but what were Varus' discourses to Herod, was not known to the generality, and upon what words it was that he went away; though it was also generally supposed, that whatsoever Herod did afterward about his son, was done with his approbation: but when Herod had bound his son, he sent letters to Rome to Caesar about him, and such messengers withal as should, by word of mouth, inform Caesar of Antipater's wickedness. (134) Now, at this very time, there was seized a letter of Antiphilus, written to Antipater out of Egypt (for he lived there); and, when it was opened by the king, it was found to contain what follows: 'I have sent thee Acme's letter, and hazarded my own life: for thou knowest that I am in danger from two families, if I be discovered. (135) I wish thee good success in thy affair.' These were the contents of this letter; but the king made inquiry about the other letter also, for it did not appear; and Antiphilus' slave, who brought that letter which had been read, denied that he had received the other: (136) but while the king was in doubt about it, one of Herod's friends seeing a seam upon the inner coat of the slave, and a doubling of the cloth (for he had two coats on) he guessed that the letter might be within that doubling; which accordingly proved to be true. (137) So they took out the letter: and its contents were these: 'Acme to Antipater. I have written such a letter to thy father as thou desiredst me. I have also taken a copy and sent it, as if it came from Salome, to my lady [Livia]; which when thou readest, I know that Herod will punish Salome, as plotting against him.' (138) Now, this pretended letter of Salome to her lady was composed by Antipater, in the name of Salome, as to its meaning, but in the words of Acme. (139) The letter was this: 'Acme to King Herod. I have done my endeavour that nothing that is done against thee should be concealed from thee. So, upon my finding a letter of Salome written to my lady against thee, I have written out a copy and sent it to thee; with hazard to myself, but for thy advantage. The reason why she wrote it was this – that she had a mind to be married to Sylleus. Do thou therefore tear this letter in pieces, that I may not come into danger of my life.' (140) Now Acme had written to Antipater himself, and informed him, that in compliance with his command, she had both herself written to Herod, as if Salome had laid a sudden plot entirely against him, and had herself sent a copy of an epistle, as coming from Salome to her lady. (141) Now Acme was a Jew by birth, and a servant of Julia, Caesar's wife; and did this out of her friendship for Antipater, as having been corrupted by him with a large present of money, to assist in his pernicious designs against his father and his aunt.

(142) Hereupon Herod was so amazed at the prodigious wickedness of Antipater, that he was ready to have ordered him to be slain immediately, as a turbulent person in the most important concerns, and as one that had laid a plot not only against himself, but against his sister also; and even corrupted Caesar's own domestics. Salome also provoked him to it, beating her breast, and bidding him kill her, if he could produce any credible testimony that she had acted in that manner. (143) Herod also sent for his son, and asked him about this matter, and bade him contradict if he could, and not suppress anything he had to say for himself; and when he had not one word to say, he asked him, since he was everyway caught in his villainy, that he would make no further delay but discover his associates in these his wicked designs. (144) So he laid all upon Antiphilus, but discovered nobody else. Hereupon Herod was in such great grief, that he was ready to send his son to Rome to Caesar, there to give an account of these his wicked contrivances. (145) But he soon became afraid, lest he might there, by the assistance of his friends, escape the danger he was in: so he kept him bound as before, and sent more ambassadors and letter [to Rome] to accuse his son, and an account of what assistance Acme had given him in his wicked designs, with copies of the epistles before mentioned.

CHAPTER 6

(146) Now Herod's ambassadors made haste to Rome; but sent, as instructed beforehand, what answers they were to make to the questions put to them. They also carried the epistles with them. But Herod now fell into a distemper, and made his will, and bequeathed his kingdom to [Antipas], his youngest son; and this out of that hatred to Archelaus and Philip, which the calumnies of Antipater had raised against them. He also bequeathed a thousand talents to Caesar, and five hundred to Julia, Caesar's wife, to Caesar's children, and friends and freedmen. (147) He also distributed among his sons and their sons his money, his revenues, and his lands. He also made Salome, his sister, very rich, because she had continued faithful to him in all his circumstances, and was never so rash as to do him any harm. (148) And as he despaired of recovering, for he was about the seventieth year of his age, he grew fierce, and indulged the bitterest anger upon all occasions; the cause whereof was this, that he thought himself despised, and that the nation was pleased with his misfortunes; besides which, he resented a sedition which some of the lower sort of men excited against him, the occasion of which was as follows:

(149) There was one Judas, the son of Saripheus, and Matthias, the son of Margalothus, two of the most eloquent men among the Jews, and the most celebrated interpreters of the Jewish laws, and men well-beloved by the

people, because of their education of their youth; for all those that were studious of virtue frequented their lectures every day. (150) These men, when they found that the king's distemper was incurable, excited the young men that they would pull down all those works which the king had erected contrary to the law of their fathers, and thereby obtain the rewards which the law will confer on them for such actions of piety; for that it was truly on account of Herod's rashness in making such things as the law had forbidden, that his other misfortunes, and this distemper also, which was so unusual among mankind, and with which he was now afflicted, came upon him: (151) for Herod had caused such things to be made, which were contrary to the law, of which he was accused by Judas and Matthias; for the king had erected over the great gate of the temple a large golden eagle, of great value, and had dedicated it to the temple. Now, the law forbids those that propose to live according to it, to erect images, or representations of any living creature. (152) So these wise men persuaded [their scholars] to pull down the golden eagle; alleging, that although they should incur any danger which might bring them to their deaths, the virtue of the action now proposed to them would appear much more advantageous to them than the pleasures of life, since they would die for the preservation and observation of the law of their fathers; since they would also acquire an everlasting fame and commendation; since they would be both commended by the present generation, and leave an example of life that would never be forgotten to posterity; (153) since that common calamity of dying cannot be avoided by our living so as to escape any such dangers: that therefore it is a right thing for those who are in love with a virtuous conduct, to wait for that fatal hour by such behaviour as may carry them out of the world with praise and honour; (154) and that this will alleviate death to such a degree, thus to come at it by the performance of brave actions, which bring us into danger of it; and at the same time to leave that reputation behind them to their children, and to all their relations, whether they be men or women, which will be of great advantage to them afterward.

(155) And with such discourses as this did these men excite the young men to this action; and a report being come to them that the king was dead, this was an addition to the wise men's persuasions; so, in the very middle of the day they got upon the place, they pulled down the eagle, and cut it into pieces with axes, while a great number of the people were in the temple. (156) And now the king's captain, upon hearing what the undertaking was, and supposing it was a thing of a higher nature than it proved to be, came up thither, having a great band of soldiers with him, such as was sufficient to put a stop to the multitude of those who pulled down what was dedicated to God: so he fell upon them unexpectedly, and as they were upon this bold attempt, in a foolish presumption rather than a cautious circumspection, as is usual with the multitude, and while

they were in disorder, and incautious of what was for their advantage – (157) so he caught no fewer than forty of the young men, who had the courage to stay behind when the rest ran away, together with the authors of this bold attempt, Judas and Matthias, who thought it an ignominious thing to retire upon his approach, and led them to the king. (158) And when they were come to the king, and he asked them if they had been so bold as to pull down what he had dedicated to God, 'Yes (said they), what was contrived we contrived, and what hath been performed, we performed it; and that with such a virtuous courage as becomes men; for we have given our assistance to those things which were dedicated to the majesty of God, (159) and we have provided for what we have learned by hearing the law: and it ought not to be wondered at, if we esteem those laws which Moses had suggested to him, and were taught him by God, and which he wrote and left behind him, more worthy of observation than thy commands. Accordingly we will undergo death, and all sorts of punishments which thou canst inflict upon us, with pleasure, since we are conscious to ourselves that we shall die, not for any unrighteous actions, but for our love to religion.' (160) And thus they all said, and their courage was still equal to their profession, and equal to that with which they readily set about this undertaking. And when the king had ordered them to be bound, he sent them to Jericho, and called together the principal men among the Jews; (161) and when they were come, he made them assemble in the theatre, and because he could not himself stand, he lay upon a couch, and enumerated the many labours that he had long endured on their account, (162) and his building of the temple, and what a vast charge that was to him; while the Asamoneans, during the hundred and twenty-five years of their government, had not been able to perform any so great a work for the honour of God as that was: (163) that he had also adorned it with very valuable donations; on which account he hoped that he had left himself a memorial, and procured himself a reputation after his death. He then cried out, that these men had not abstained from affronting him, even in his lifetime, but that, in the very daytime, and in the sight of the multitude, they had abused him to that degree, as to fall upon what he had dedicated, and in that way of abuse, had pulled it down to the ground. They pretended, indeed, that they did it to affront him; but if anyone consider the thing truly, they will find that they were guilty of sacrilege against God therein.

(164) But the people, on account of Herod's barbarous temper, and for fear he should be so cruel as to inflict punishment on them, said what was done, was done without approbation, and that it seemed to them that the actors might well be punished for what they had done. But as for Herod, he dealt more mildly with others [of the assembly]; but he deprived Matthias of the high priesthood, as in part an occasion of this action, and made Joazar, who was Matthias's wife's brother, high priest in his stead. (165) Now it happened, that

during the time of the high priesthood of this Matthias, there was another person made high priest for a single day, that very day which the Jews observed as a fast. (166) The occasion was this: this Matthias the high priest, on the night before that day when the fast was to be celebrated, seemed, in a dream, to have intercourse with his wife; and because he could not officiate himself on that account, Joseph, the son of Ellemus, his kinsman, assisted him in that sacred office. (167) But Herod deprived this Matthias of the high priesthood, and burnt the other Matthias, who had raised the sedition, with his companions, alive. And that very night there was an eclipse of the moon.

(168) But now Herod's distemper greatly increased upon him after a severe manner, and this by God's judgment upon him for his sins: for a fire glowed in him slowly, which did not so much appear to the touch outwardly as it augmented his pains inwardly; (169) for it brought upon him a vehement appetite to eating, which he could not avoid to supply with one sort of food or other. His entrails were also exulcerated, and the chief violence of his pain lay on his colon; an aqueous and transparent liquor also settled itself about his feet, and a like matter afflicted him at the bottom of his belly. Nay, farther, his privy member was putrified, and produced worms; and when he sat upright he had a difficulty of breathing, which was very loathsome, on account of the stench of his breath, and the quickness of its returns; he had also convulsions in all parts of his body, which increased his strength to an insufferable degree. (170) It was said by those who pretended to divine, and who were endowed with wisdom to foretell such things, that God inflicted this punishment on the king on account of his great impiety; (171) yet was he still in hopes of recovering, though his afflictions seemed greater than anyone could bear. He also sent for physicians, and did not refuse to follow what they prescribed for his assistance; and went beyond the river Jordan, and bathed himself in warm baths that were at Calirrhoe, which, besides their other general virtues, were also fit to drink; which water runs into the lake called Asphaltitis. (172) And when the physicians once thought fit to have him bathed in a vessel full of oil, it was supposed that he was just dying; but, upon the lamentable cries of his domestics, he revived; and having no longer the least hopes of recovering, he gave order that every soldier should be paid fifty drachmae; (173) and he also gave a great deal to their commanders, and to his friends, and came again to Jericho, where he grew so choleric, that it brought him to do all things like a madman; and though he were near his death, he contrived the following wicked designs. (174) He commanded that all the principal men of the entire Jewish nation wheresoever they lived, should be called to him. Accordingly, they were a great number that came, because the whole nation was called, and all men heard of this call, and death was the penalty of such as should despise the epistles that were sent to call them. And now the king was in a wild rage against them all, the innocent as

well as those that had afforded ground for accusations; (175) and when they were come, he ordered them all to be shut up in the hippodrome, and sent for his sister Salome, and her husband Alexas, and spoke thus to them: 'I shall die in a little time, so great are my pains; which death ought to be cheerfully borne, and to be welcomed by all men; but what principally troubles me is this, that I shall die without being lamented, and without such mourning as men usually expect at a king's death.' (176) For that he was not unacquainted with the temper of the Jews, that his death would be a thing very desirable, and exceedingly acceptable to them; because during his lifetime they were ready to revolt from him, and to abuse the donations he had dedicated to God: (177) that it therefore was their business to resolve to afford him some alleviation of his great sorrows on this occasion; for that, if they do not refuse him their consent in what he desires, he shall have a great mourning at his funeral, and such as never any king had before him; for then the whole nation would mourn from their very soul, which otherwise would be done in sport and mockery only. (178) He desired therefore that as soon as they see he hath given up the ghost, they shall place soldiers round the hippodrome, while they do not know that he is dead; and that they shall not declare his death to the multitude till this is done, but that they shall give orders to have those that are in custody shot with their darts; and that this slaughter of them all will cause that he shall not miss to rejoice on a double account; that as he is dying, they will make him secure that his will shall be executed in what he charges them to do; and that he shall have the honour of a memorable mourning at his funeral. (179) So he deplored his condition, with tears in his eyes, and obtested them by the kindness due from them, as of his kindred, and by the faith they owed to God, and begged of them that they would not hinder him of this honourable mourning at his funeral. So they promised him not to transgress his commands.

(180) Now anyone may easily discover the temper of this man's mind, which not only took pleasure in doing what he had done formerly against his relations, out of the love of life, but by those commands of his which savoured of no humanity, (181) since he took care, when he was departing out of this life, that the whole nation should be put into mourning, and indeed made desolate of their dearest kindred, when he gave order that one out of every family should be slain, although they had done nothing that was unjust, or against him, nor were they accused of any other crimes; while it is usual for those who have any regard to virtue to lay aside their hatred at such a time, even with respect to those they justly esteemed their enemies.

CHAPTER 7

(182) As he was giving these commands to his relations, there came letters from his ambassadors, who had been sent to Rome unto Caesar, which when they were read, their purport was this: that Acme was slain by Caesar, out of his indignation at what hand she had in Antipater's wicked practices; and that as to Antipater himself, Caesar left it to Herod to act as became a father and a king, and either to banish him or to take away his life, which he pleased. (183) When Herod heard this, he was somewhat better, out of the pleasure he had from the contents of the letters, and was elevated at the death of Acme, and at the power that was given him over his son; but, as his pains were become very great, he was now ready to faint for want of something to eat; so he called for an apple and a knife; for it was his custom formerly to pare the apple himself, and soon afterward to cut it, and eat it. (184) When he had got the knife, he looked about, and had a mind to stab himself with it; and he had done it, had not his first cousin, Achiabus, prevented him, and held his hand, and cried out loudly. Whereupon a woeful lamentation echoed through the palace, and a great tumult was made, as if the king were dead. (185) Upon which Antipater, who verily believed his father was deceased, grew bold in his discourse, as hoping to be immediately and entirely released from his bonds, and to take the kingdom into his hands, without any more ado; so he discoursed with the jailer about letting him go, and in that case promised him great things, both now and hereafter, as if that were the only thing now in question; (186) but the jailer did not only refuse to do what Antipater would have him, but informed the king of his intentions, and how many solicitations he had had from him [of that nature]. (187) Hereupon Herod, who had formerly no affection nor good will towards his son to restrain him, when he heard what the jailer said, he cried out, and beat his head, although he was at death's door, and raised himself upon his elbow, and sent for some of his guards, and commanded them to kill Antipater without tiny further delay, and to do it presently, and to bury him in an ignoble manner at Hyrcania.

CHAPTER 8

(188) And now Herod altered his testament upon the alteration of his mind; for he appointed Antipas, to whom he had before left the kingdom, to be tetrarch of Galilee and Berea, and granted the kingdom to Archelaus. (189) He also gave Gaulonitis and Trachonitis and Paneas to Philip, who was his son, but own brother to Archelaus, by the name of a tetrarchy; and bequeathed Jamnia and Ashdod and Phasaelis to Salome his sister, with five hundred

thousand [drachmae] of silver that was coined. (190) He also made provision for all the rest of his kindred, by giving them sums of money and annual revenues, and so left them all in a wealthy condition. He bequeathed also to Caesar ten millions [of drachmae] of coined money; besides both vessels of gold and silver, and garments exceeding costly, to Julia, Caesar's wife, and to certain others, five millions. (191) When he had done those things, he died, the fifth day after he had caused Antipater to be slain; having reigned, since he had procured Antigonus to be slain, thirty-four years; but since he had been declared king by the Romans, thirty-seven. A man he was of great barbarity towards all men equally, and a slave to his passions, but above the consideration of what was right; (192) yet was he favoured by fortune as much as any man ever was, for from a private man he became a king; and though he were encompassed with ten thousand dangers, he got clear of them all, and continued his life till a very old age; but then, as to the affairs of his family and children, in which indeed, according to his own opinion, he was also very fortunate, because he was able to conquer his enemies, yet in my opinion, he was herein very unfortunate.

(193) But then Salome and Alexas, before the king's death was made known, dismissed those that were shut up in the hippodrome, and told them that the king ordered them to go away to their own lands, and take care of their own affairs, which was esteemed by the nation a great benefit; (194) and now the king's death was made public, when Salome and Alexas gathered the soldiery together in the amphitheatre at Jericho; and the first thing they did was, they read Herod's letter written to the soldiery, thanking them for their fidelity and good will to him, and exhorting them to afford his son Archelaus, whom he had appointed for their king, like fidelity and good will. (195) After which Ptolemy, who had the king's seal entrusted to him, read the king's testament, which was to be of force no otherwise than as it should stand when Caesar had inspected it; so there was presently an acclamation made to Archelaus, as king, and the soldiers came by bands, and their commanders with them, and promised the same good will to him, and readiness to serve him, which they had exhibited to Herod; and they prayed God to be assistant to him.

(196) After this was over, they prepared for his funeral, it being Archelaus's care that the procession to his father's sepulchre should be very sumptuous. Accordingly he brought out all his ornaments to adorn the pomp of the funeral. (197) The body was carried upon a golden bier, embroidered with very precious stones of great variety, and it was covered over with purple, as well as the body itself; he had a diadem upon his head, and above it a crown of gold; he also had a sceptre in his right hand. (198) About the bier were his sons and his numerous relations; next to these was the soldiery distinguished

according to their several countries and denominations; and they were put into the following order: first of all went his guards, then the band of Thracians; and after them the Germans; and next the band of Galatians, everyone in their habiliments of war; and behind these marched the whole army in the same manner as they used to go out to war, (199) and as they used to be put in array by their muster-masters and centurions; these were followed by five hundred of his domestics, carrying spices. So they went eight furlongs, to Herodium; for there, by his own command, he was to be buried – and thus did Herod end his life.

(200) Now Archelaus paid him so much respect, as to continue his mourning till the seventh day; for so many days are appointed for it by the law of our fathers; and when he had given a treat to the multitude, and left off his mourning, he went up into the temple; he had also acclamations and praises given him, which way soever he went, everyone striving with the rest who should appear to use the loudest acclamations. (201) So he ascended a high elevation made for him, and took his seat, in a throne made of gold, and spake kindly to the multitude, and declared with what joy he received their acclamations and the marks of the good will they showed to him: and returned them thanks that they did not remember the injuries his father had done them, to his disadvantage; and promised them he would endeavour not to be behind hand with them in rewarding their alacrity in his service, after a suitable manner; (202) but that he should abstain at present from the name of King; and that he should have the honour of that dignity, if Caesar should confirm and settle that testament which his father had made; and that it was on this account, that when the army would have put the diadem on him at Jericho, he would not accept of that honour, which is usually so much desired, because it was not yet evident that he who was to be principally concerned in bestowing it, would give it him; (203) although, by his acceptance of the government, he should not want the ability of rewarding their kindness to him; and that it should be his endeavour, as to all things wherein they were concerned, to prove in every respect better than his father. (204) Whereupon the multitude, as it is usual with them, supposed that the first days of those that enter upon such governments, declare the intentions of those that accept them; and so by how much Archelaus spake the more gently and civilly to them, by so much did they more highly commend him, and made application to him for the grant of what they desired. Some made a clamour that he would ease them of some of their annual payments; but others desired him to release those that were put into prison by Herod, who were many and had been put there at several times; (205) others of them required that he would take away those taxes which had been severely laid upon what was publicly sold and bought. So Archelaus contradicted them in nothing, since he pretended to do all things so as to get the good will of the

multitude to him, as looking upon that good will to be a great step towards his preservation of the government. Hereupon he went and offered sacrifice to God, and then betook himself to feast with his friends.

CHAPTER 9

(206) At this time also it was that some of the Jews got together, out of a desire of innovation. They lamented Matthias, and those that were slain with him by Herod, who had not any respect paid them by a funeral mourning, out of the fear men were in of that man; they were those who had been condemned for pulling down the golden eagle. The people made a great clamour and lamentation hereupon, and cast out some reproaches against the king also, as if that tended to alleviate the miseries of the deceased. (207) The people assembled together, and desired of Archelaus that, in way of revenge on their account, he would inflict punishment on those who had been honoured by Herod; and that, in the first and principal place, he would deprive that high priest whom Herod had made, and would choose one more agreeable to the law, and of greater purity, to officiate as high priest. (208) This was granted by Archelaus, although he was mightily offended at their importunity, because he proposed to himself to go to Rome immediately, to look after Caesar's determination about him. (209) However, he sent the general of his forces to use persuasions, and to tell them that the death which was inflicted on their friends, was according to the law; and to represent to them, that their petitions about these things were carried to a great height of injury to him; that the time was not now proper for such petitions, but required their unanimity until such time as he should be established in the government by the consent of Caesar, and should then be come back to them; for that he would then consult with them in common concerning the purport of their petitions; but that they ought at present to be quiet, lest they should seem seditious persons.

(210) So when the king had suggested these things, and instructed his general in what he was to say, be sent him away to the people; but they made a clamour, and would not give him leave to speak, and put him in danger of his life, and as many more as were desirous to venture upon saying openly anything which might reduce them to a sober mind, and prevent their going on in their present courses – because they had more concern to have all their own wills performed than to yield obedience to their governors, (211) thinking it to be a thing insufferable that, while Herod was alive, they should lose those that were the most dear to them, and that when he was dead, they could not get the actors to be punished. So they went on with their designs after a violent manner, and thought all to be lawful and right which tended to please them, and being unskilful in foreseeing what dangers they incurred; and when they had suspicion

of such a thing, yet did the present pleasure they took in the punishment of those they deemed their enemies overweigh all such considerations; (212) and although Archelaus sent many to speak to them, yet they treated them not as messengers sent by him, but as persons that came of their own accord to mitigate their anger, and would not let one of them speak. The sedition, also, was made by such as were in a great passion; and it was evident that they were proceeding farther in seditious practices, by the multitude running so fast upon them.

(213) Now, upon the approach of that feast of unleavened bread which the law of their fathers had appointed for the Jews at this time, which feast is called the Passover, and is a memorial of their deliverance out of Egypt (when they offer sacrifices with great alacrity; and when they are required to slay more sacrifices in number than at any other festival; (214) and when an innumerable multitude came thither out of the country, nay, from beyond its limits also, in order to worship God), the seditious lamented Judas and Matthias, those teachers of the laws, and kept together in the temple, and had plenty of food, because these seditious persons were not ashamed to get it. (215) And as Archelaus was afraid lest some terrible thing should spring up by means of these men's madness, he sent a regiment of armed men, and with them a captain of a thousand, to suppress the violent efforts of the seditious, before the whole multitude should be infected with the like madness; and gave them this charge, that if they found any much more openly seditious than others, and more busy in tumultuous practices, they should bring them to him. (216) But those that were seditious on account of those teachers of the law, irritated the people by the noise and clamours they used to encourage the people in their designs; so they made an assault upon the soldiers, and came up to them, and stoned the greatest part of them, although some of them ran away wounded, and their captain among them; and when they had thus done, they returned to the sacrifices which were already in their hands. (217) Now Archelaus thought there was no way to preserve the entire government, but by cutting off those who made this attempt upon it; so he sent out the whole army upon them, and sent the horsemen to prevent those that had their tents without the temple, from assisting those that were within the temple, and to kill such as ran away from the footmen when they thought themselves out of danger; (218) which horsemen slew three thousand men, while the rest went to the neighbouring mountains. Then did Archelaus order proclamation to be made to them all, that they should retire to their own homes; so they went away, and left the festival, out of fear of somewhat worse which would follow, although they had been so bold by reason of their want of instruction. (219) So Archelaus went down to the sea with his mother, and took with him Nicolaus and Ptolemy, and many others of his friends, and left Philip his brother as governor of all things belonging both to his own family and to the public. (220) There went

out also with him Salome, Herod's sister, who took with her her children, and many of her kindred were with her; which kindred of hers went, as they pretended, to assist Archelaus in gaining the kingdom, but in reality to oppose him, and chiefly to make loud complaints of what he had done in the temple. (221) But Sabinus, Caesar's steward for Syrian affairs, as he was making haste into Judea, to preserve Herod's effects, met with Archelaus at Caesarea; but Varus (president of Syria) came at that time, and restrained him from meddling with them, for he was there as sent for by Archelaus, by the means of Ptolemy. (222) And Sabinus, out of regard to Varus, did neither seize upon any of the castles that were among the Jews, nor did he seal up the treasures in them, but permitted Archelaus to have them, until Caesar should declare his resolution about them; so that, upon this his promise, he tarried still at Caesarea. But after Archelaus was sailed for Rome, and Varus was removed to Antioch, Sabinus went to Jerusalem, and seized on the king's palace. (223) He also sent for the keepers of the garrisons, and for all those that had the charge of Herod's effects, and declared publicly that he should require them to give an account of what they had; and he disposed of the castles in the manner he pleased; but those who kept them did not neglect what Archelaus had given them in command, but continued to keep all things in the manner that had been enjoined them; and their pretence was, that they kept them all for Caesar.

(224) At the same time also did Antipas, another of Herod's sons, sail to Rome, in order to gain the government; being buoyed up by Salome with promises that he should take that government; and that he was a much honester and fitter man than Archelaus for that authority, since Herod had, in his former testament, deemed him the worthiest to be made king; which ought to be esteemed more valid than his latter testament. (225) Antipas also brought with him his mother, and Ptolemy the brother of Nicolaus, one that had been Herod's most honoured friend, and was now zealous for Antipas; (226) but it was Ireneus the orator, and one who, on account of his reputation for sagacity, was entrusted with the affairs of the kingdom, who most of all encouraged him to attempt to gain the kingdom; by whose means it was that, when some advised him to yield to Archelaus, as to his elder brother, and who had been declared king by their father's last will, he would not submit so to do. (227) And when he was come to Rome, all his relations revolted to him; not out of their good will to him, but out of their hatred to Archelaus; though indeed they were most of all desirous of gaining their liberty, and to be put under a Roman governor; but, if there were too great an opposition made to that, they thought Antipas preferable to Archelaus, and so joined with him, in order to procure the kingdom for him. Sabinus also, by letters, accused Archelaus to Caesar.

(228) Now when Archelaus had sent in his papers to Caesar, wherein he

pleaded his right to the kingdom and his father's testament, with the account of Herod's money, and with Ptolemy, who brought Herod's seal, he so expected the event; (229) but when Caesar had read these papers, and Varus' and Sabinus' letters, with the accounts of the money, and what were the annual incomes of the kingdom, and understood that Antipas had also sent letters to lay claim to the kingdom, he summoned his friends together, to know their opinions, and with them Caius, the son of Agrippa and of Julia his daughter, whom he had adopted, and took him, and made him sit first of all, and desired such as pleased to speak their minds about the affairs now before them. (230) Now, Antipater, Salome's son, a very subtle orator, and a bitter enemy to Archelaus, spake first to this purpose: that it was ridiculous in Archelaus to plead now to have the kingdom given him, since he had, in reality, taken already the power over it to himself, before Caesar had granted it to him; and appealed to those bold actions of his, in destroying so many at the Jewish festival; (231) and, if the men had acted unjustly, it was but fit the punishing of them should have been reserved to those that were out of the country, but had the power to punish them, and not been executed by a man that, if he pretended to be a king, he did an injury to Caesar, by usurping that authority before it was determined for him by Caesar; but if he owned himself to be a private person, his case was much worse, since he who was putting in for the kingdom, could by no means expect to have that power granted him, of which he had already deprived Caesar [by taking it to himself]. (232) He also touched sharply upon him, and appealed to his changing the commanders in the army, and his sitting in the royal throne beforehand, and his determination of lawsuits; all done as if he were no other than a king. He appealed also to his concessions to those that petitioned him on a public account, and indeed doing such things, than which he could devise no greater if he had been already settled in the kingdom by Caesar. (233) He also ascribed to him the releasing of the prisoners that were in the Hippodrome, and many other things that either had been certainly done by him, or were believed to be done, and easily might be believed to have been done, because they were of such a nature as to be usually done by young men, and by such as, out of a desire of ruling, seize upon the government too soon. He also charged him with his neglect of the funeral mourning for his father and with having merry meetings the very night in which he died; (234) and that it was thence the multitude took the handle of raising a tumult; and if Archelaus could thus requite his dead father, who had bestowed such benefits upon him and bequeathed such great things to him, by pretending to shed tears for him in the daytime, like an actor on the stage, but every night making mirth for having gotten the government, (235) he would appear to be the same Archelaus with regard to Caesar, if he granted him the kingdom, which he hath been to his father; since he had then dancing and singing, as though an enemy of his were fallen, and not as though a man were carried to his funeral that was so nearly related, and had been so great a benefactor to him. (236) But he said that the greatest crime of all was this, that he came now before Caesar to obtain the government by his grant, while he had before acted in all things as he could have acted if Caesar himself, who ruled all, had fixed him firmly in the government. (237) And what he most aggravated in his pleading, was the slaughter of those about the temple, and the impiety of it, as done at the festival; and how they were slain like sacrifices themselves, some of whom were foreigners, and others of their own country, till the temple was full of dead bodies: and all this was done, not by an alien, but by one who pretended to the lawful title of a king, that he might complete the wicked tyranny which his nature prompted him to, and which is hated by all men. (238) On which account his father never so much as dreamed of making him his successor in the kingdom, when he was of a sound mind, because he knew his disposition; and, in his former and more authentic testament, he appointed his antagonist Antipas to succeed; but that Archelaus was called by his father to that dignity, when he was in a dying condition, both of body and mind; while Antipas was called when he was ripest in his judgment, and of such strength of body as made him capable of managing his own affairs: (239) and if his father had the like notion of him formerly that he hath now shown, yet hath he given a sufficient specimen what a king he is likely to be when he hath [in effect] deprived Caesar of that power of disposing of the kingdom, which he justly hath, and hath not abstained from making a terrible slaughter of his fellow citizens in the temple, while he was but a private person.

(240) So when Antipater had made this speech, and had confirmed what he had said by producing many witnesses from among Archelaus's own relations, he made an end of his pleading. Upon which Nicolaus arose up to plead for Archelaus, and said, 'That what had been done at the temple was rather to be attributed to the mind of those that had been killed, than to the authority of Archelaus; for that those who were the authors of such things, are not only wicked in the injuries they do of themselves, but in forcing sober persons to avenge themselves upon them. (241) Now, it is evident that what these did in way of opposition was done under pretence, indeed against Archelaus, but in reality against Caesar himself, for they, after an injurious manner, attacked and slew those who were sent by Archelaus, and who came only to put a stop to their doings. They had no regard either to God or to the festival, (242) whom Antipater yet is not ashamed to patronise, whether it be out of his indulgence of an enmity to Archelaus, or out of his hatred of virtue and justice. For as to those who begin such tumults, and first set about such unrighteous actions, they are the men who force those that punish them to betake themselves to arms even against their will. (243) So that Antipater in effect ascribes the rest of

what was done to all those who were of counsel to the accusers: for nothing which is here accused of injustice has been done, but what was derived from them as its authors; nor are those things evil in themselves, but so represented only, in order to do harm to Archelaus. Such is these men's inclination to do an injury to a man that is of their kindred, their father's benefactor, and familiarly acquainted with them, and that hath ever lived in friendship with them; (244) for that, as to this testament, it was made by the king when he was of a sound mind, and so ought to be of more authority than his former testament; and that for this reason, because Caesar is therein left to be the judge and disposer of all therein contained; (245) and for Caesar, he will not, to be sure, at all imitate the unjust proceedings of those men who, during Herod's whole life, had on all occasions been joint partakers of power with him, and yet do zealously endeavour to injure his determination, while they have not themselves had the same regard to their kinsman [which Archelaus had]. (246) Caesar will not therefore disannul the testament of a man whom he had entirely supported, of his friend and confederate, and that which is committed to him in trust to ratify; nor will Caesar's virtuous and upright disposition, which is known and uncontested through all the habitable world, (247) imitate the wickedness of these men in condemning a king as a madman, and as having lost his reason, while he hath bequeathed the succession to a good son of his, and to one who flies to Caesar's upright determination for refuge. Nor can Herod at any time have been mistaken in his judgment about a successor, while he showed so much prudence as to submit all to Caesar's determination.'

(248) Now when Nicolaus had laid these things before Caesar, he ended his plea; whereupon Caesar was so obliging to Archelaus, that he raised him up when he had cast himself down at his feet, and said, that he well deserved the kingdom; and he soon let them know that he was so far moved in his favour, that he would not act otherwise than his father's testament directed, and than was for the advantage of Archelaus. (249) However, while he gave this encouragement to Archelaus to depend on him securely, he made no full determination about him; and, when the assembly was broken up, he considered by himself whether he should confirm the kingdom to Archelaus, or whether he should part it among all Herod's posterity; and this because they all stood in need of such assistance to support them.

CHAPTER 10

(250) But before these things could be brought to a settlement, Malthace, Archelaus' mother, fell into a distemper, and died of it; and letters came from Varus the president of Syria, which informed Caesar of the revolt of the Jews; for after Archelaus was sailed, the whole nation was in a tumult. (251) So

Varus, since he was there himself, brought the authors of the disturbance to punishment; and when he had restrained them for the most part from this sedition, which was a great one, he took his journey to Antioch, leaving one legion of his army at Jerusalem to keep the Jews quiet, who were now very fond of innovation. (252) Yet did not this at all avail to put an end to that their sedition, for, after Varus was gone away, Sabinus, Caesar's procurator, stayed behind, and greatly distressed the Jews, relying on the forces that were left there, that they would by their multitude protect him; (253) for he made use of them, and armed them as his guard, thereby so oppressing the Jews, and giving them so great disturbance, that at length they rebelled; for he used force in seizing the citadels, and zealously pressed on the search after the king's money, in order to seize upon it by force, on account of his love of gain, and his extraordinary covetousness.

(254) But on the approach of pentecost, which is a festival of ours, so called from the days of our forefathers, a great many ten thousands of men got together; nor did they come only to celebrate the festival, but out of their indignation at the madness of Sabinus, and at the injuries he offered them. A great number there was of Galileans, and Idumeans, and many men from Jericho, and others who had passed over the river Jordan, and inhabited those parts. This whole multitude joined themselves to all the rest, and were more zealous than the others in making an assault on Sabinus, in order to be avenged on him; (255) so they parted themselves into three bands, and encamped themselves in the places following: some of them seized on the Hippodrome; and of the other two bands, one pitched themselves from the northern part of the temple to the southern, on the east quarter, but the third band held the western part of the city, where the king's palace was. Their work tended entirely to besiege the Romans, and to enclose them on all sides. (256) Now Sabinus was afraid of these men's number, and of their resolution, who had little regard to their lives, but were very desirous not to be overcome, while they thought it a point of puissance to overcome their enemies; so he sent immediately a letter to Varus, and, as he used to do, was very pressing with him, and entreated him to come quickly to his assistance, because the forces he had left were in imminent danger, and would probably, in no long time, be seized upon, and cut to pieces; (257) while he did himself get up to the highest tower of the fortress Phasaelus, which had been built in honour of Phasaelus, King Herod's brother, and called so when the Parthians had brought him to his death. So Sabinus gave thence a signal to the Romans to fall upon the Jews, although he did not himself venture so much as to come down to his friends, and thought he might expect that the others should expose themselves first to die on account of his avarice. (258) However, the Romans ventured to make a sally out of the place, and a terrible battle ensued: wherein, though it is true

the Romans beat their adversaries, yet were not the Jews daunted in their resolutions, even when they had the sight of that terrible slaughter that was made of them; (259) but they went round about, and got upon those cloisters which encompassed the outer court of the temple, where a great fight was still continued, and they cast stones at the Romans, partly with their hands, and partly with slings, as being much used to those exercises. (260) All the archers also in array did the Romans a great deal of mischief, because they used their hands dexterously from a place superior to the others, and because the others were at an utter loss what to do; for when they tried to shoot their arrows against the Jews upwards, these arrows could not reach them, insomuch that the Jews were easily too hard for their enemies. And this sort of fight lasted a great while, (261) till at last the Romans, who were greatly distressed by what was done, set fire to the cloisters so privately, that those who were gotten upon them did not perceive it. This fire, being fed by a great deal of combustible matter, caught hold immediately on the roof of the cloisters; (262) so the wood, which was full of pitch and wax, and whose gold was laid on it with wax, yielded to the flame presently, and those vast works which were of the highest value and esteem, were destroyed utterly, while those that were on the roof unexpectedly perished at the same time; for as the roof tumbled down, some of these men tumbled down with it, and others of them were killed by their enemies who encompassed them. (263) There was a great number more, who out of despair of saving their lives, and out of astonishment at the misery that surrounded them, did either cast themselves into the fire, or threw themselves upon their own swords, and so got out of their misery. But as to those that retired behind the same way by which they ascended, and thereby escaped, they were all killed by the Romans, as being unarmed men, and their courage failing them; their wild fury being now not able to help them, because they were destitute of armour, (264) insomuch that of those that went up to the top of the roof, not one escaped. The Romans also rushed through the fire, where it gave them room so to do, and seized on that treasure where the sacred money was reposited, a great part of which was stolen by the soldiers; and Sabinus got openly four hundred talents.

(265) But this calamity of the Jews' friends, who fell in this battle, grieved them, as did also this plundering of the money dedicated to God in the temple. Accordingly that body of them which continued best together, and was the most warlike, encompassed the palace, and threatened to set fire to it, and kill all that were in it. Yet still they commanded them to go out presently, and promised that if they would do so, they would not hurt them, nor Sabinus neither; (266) at which time the greatest part of the king's troops deserted to them, while Rufus and Gratus, who had three thousand of the most warlike of Herod's army with them, who were men of active bodies, went over to the

Romans. There was also a band of horsemen under the command of Rufus, which itself went over to the Romans also. (267) However, the Jews went on with the siege, and dug mines under the palace walls, and besought those that were gone over to the other side, not to be their hindrance, now they had such a proper opportunity for the recovery of their country's ancient liberty; (268) and for Sabinus, truly he was desirous of going away with his soldiers, but was not able to trust himself with the enemy, on account of what mischief he had already done them; and he took this great [pretended] lenity of theirs for an argument why he should not comply with them; and so, because he expected that Varus was coming, he still bore the siege.

(269) Now, at this time there were ten thousand other disorders in Judea, which were like tumults, because a great number put themselves into a warlike posture, either out of hopes of gain to themselves, or out of enmity to the Jews. (270) In particular, two thousand of Herod's old soldiers, who had been already disbanded, got together in Judea itself, and fought against the king's troops, although Achiabus, Herod's first cousin, opposed them; but as he was driven out of the plains into the mountainous parts by the military skill of those men, he kept himself in the fastnesses that were there, and saved what he could.

(271) There was also Judas, the son of that Ezekias who had been head of the robbers; which Ezekias was a very strong man, and had with great difficulty been caught by Herod. This Judas having gotten together a multitude of men of a profligate character about Sepphoris in Galilee, and made an assault upon the palace [there], and seized upon all the weapons that were laid up in it, and with them armed every one of those that were with him, and carried away what money was left there; (272) and he became terrible to all men, by tearing and rending those that came near him: and all this in order to raise himself, and out of an ambitious desire of the royal dignity; and he hoped to obtain that as the reward, not of his virtuous skill in war, but of his extravagance in doing injuries.

(273) There was also Simon, who had been a slave of Herod the king, but in other respects a comely person, of a tall and robust body; he was one that was much superior to others of his order, and had had great things committed to his care. This man was elevated at the disorderly state of things, and was so bold as to put a diadem on his head, (274) while a certain number of the people stood by him, and by them he was declared to be a king, and thought himself more worthy of that dignity than anyone else. He burnt down the royal palace at Jericho, and plundered what was left in it. He also set fire to many others of the king's houses in several places of the country, and utterly destroyed them, and permitted those that were with him to take what was left in them for a prey; (275) and he would have done greater things, unless care had been taken to repress him immediately; for Gratus, when he had joined himself to some

Roman soldiers, took the forces he had with him, and met Simon, (276) and after a great and a long fight, no small part of those that came from Perea, who were a disordered body of men, and fought rather in a bold than in a skilful manner, were destroyed; and although Simon had saved himself by flying away through a certain valley, yet Gratus overtook him, and cut off his head. (277) The royal palace also, at Amathus, by the river Jordan, was burnt down by a party of men that were got together, as were those belonging to Simon. And thus did a great and wild fury spread itself over the nation, because they had no king to keep the multitude in good order; and because those foreigners, who came to reduce the seditious to sobriety, did, on the contrary, set them more in aflame, because of the injuries they offered them, and the avaricious management of their affairs.

(278) But because Athronges, a person neither eminent by the dignity of progenitors, nor for any great wealth he was possessed of, but one that had in all respects been a shepherd only, and was not known by anybody; yet because he was a tall man, and excelled others in the strength of his hands, he was so bold as to set up for king. This man thought it so sweet a thing to do more than ordinary injuries to others, that although he should be killed, he did not much care if he lost his life in so great a design. (279) He had also four brethren, who were tall men themselves, and were believed to be superior to others in the strength of their hands, and thereby were encouraged to aim at great things, and thought that strength of theirs would support them in retaining the kingdom. Each of these ruled over a band of men of their own; for those that got together to them were very numerous. (280) They were every one of them also commanders; but, when they came to fight, they were subordinate to him and fought for him, while he put a diadem about his head, and assembled a counsel to debate about what things should be done; and all things were done according to his pleasure. (281) And this man retained his power a great while; he was also called king, and had nothing to hinder him from doing what he pleased. He also, as well as his brethren, slew a great many both of the Romans and of the king's forces, and managed matters with the like hatred to each of them. The king's forces they fell upon, because of the licentious conduct they had been allowed under Herod's government; and they fell upon the Romans, because of the injuries they had so lately received from them. (282) But in process of time they grew more cruel to all sorts of men; nor could anyone escape from one or other of these seditions, since they slew some out of the hopes of gain, and others from a mere custom of slaying men. They once attacked a company of Romans at Emmaus, who were bringing corn and weapons to the army, and fell upon Arius, the centurion, who commanded the company, and shot forty of the best of his foot soldiers; (283) but the rest of them were affrighted at their slaughter, and left their dead behind them, but

saved themselves by the means of Gratus, who came with the king's troops that were about him to their assistance. Now, these four brethren continued the war a long while by such sort of expeditions, and much grieved the Romans (but did their own nation also a great deal of mischief); (284) yet were they afterwards subdued; one of them in a fight with Gratus, another with Ptolemy; Archelaus also took the eldest of them prisoner; while the last of them was so dejected at the others' misfortune, and saw so plainly that he had no way now left to save himself, his army being worn away with sickness and continual labours, that he also delivered himself up to Archelaus, upon his promise and oath to God [to preserve his life]. But these things came to pass a good while afterward.

(285) And now Judea was full of robberies; and as the several companies of the seditious lighted upon anyone to head them, he was created a king immediately, in order to do mischief to the public. They were in some small measure indeed, and in small matters, hurtful to the Romans, but the murders they committed upon their own people lasted a long while.

(286) As soon as Varus was once informed of the state of Judea by Sabinus' writing to him, he was afraid for the legions he had left there; so he took the two other legions (for there were three legions in all belonging to Syria), and four troops of horsemen, with the several auxiliary forces which either the kings or certain of the tetrarchs afforded him, and made what haste he could to assist those that were then besieged in Judea. (287) He also gave order, that all that were sent out for this expedition should make haste to Ptolemais. The citizens of Berytus also gave him fifteen hundred auxiliaries, as he passed through their city. Aretas also, the king of Arabia Petrea out of his hatred to Herod, and in order to purchase the favour of the Romans, sent him no small assistance, besides their footmen and horsemen: (288) and when he had now collected all his forces together, he committed part of them to his sons, and to a friend of his, and sent them upon an expedition into Galilee, which lies in the neighbourhood of Ptolemais; (289) who made an attack upon the enemy, and put them to flight, and took Sepphoris, and made its inhabitants slaves and burnt the city. But Varus himself pursued his march for Samaria with his whole army; yet did not he meddle with the city of that name, because it had not at all joined with the seditious, but pitched his camp at a certain village that belonged to Ptolemy, whose name was Arus, (290) which the Arabians burnt, out of their hatred to Herod, and out of the enmity they bore to his friends; whence they marched to another village, whose name was Sampho, which the Arabians plundered and burnt, although it was a fortified and strong place: and all along this march nothing escaped them, but all places were full of fire and of slaughter. (291) Emmaus was also burnt by Varus' order, after its inhabitants had deserted it, that he might avenge those that had there been destroyed.

(292) From thence he now marched to Jerusalem; whereupon those Jews whose camp lay there, and who had besieged the Roman legion, not bearing the coming of this army, left the siege imperfect: (293) but as to the Jerusalem Jews, when Varus reproached them bitterly for what had been done, they cleared themselves of the accusation, and alleged that the conflux of the people was occasioned by the feast; that the war was not made with their approbation, but by the rashness of the strangers, while they were on the side of the Romans, and besieged together with them, rather than having any inclination to besiege them. (294) There also came beforehand to meet Varus, Joseph, the cousin-german of King Herod, as also Gratus and Rufus, who brought their soldiers along with them, together with those Romans who had been besieged: but Sabinus did not come into Varus' presence, but stole out of the city privately, and went to the seaside.

(295) Upon this, Varus sent a part of his army into the country, to seek out those that had been the authors of the revolt; and when they were discovered, he punished some of them that were most guilty, and some he dismissed: now the number of those that were crucified on this account were two thousand: (296) after which he disbanded his army, which he found nowise useful to him in the affairs he came about; for they behaved themselves very disorderly, and disobeyed his orders, and what Varus desired them to do; and this out of regard to that gain which they made by the mischief they did. (297) As for himself, when he was informed that ten thousand Jews had gotten together, he made haste to catch them; but they did not proceed so far as to fight him, but by the advice of Achiabus, they came together and delivered themselves up to him: hereupon Varus forgave the crime of revolting to the multitude, but sent their several commanders to Caesar, (298) many of whom Caesar dismissed; but for the several relations of Herod who had been among these men in this war, they were the only persons whom he punished, who, without the least regard to justice, fought against their own kindred.

CHAPTER 11

(299) So when Varus had settled these affairs, and had placed the former legion at Jerusalem, he returned back to Antioch; but as for Archelaus, he had new sources of trouble come upon him at Rome, on the occasions following: (300) for embassage of the Jews was come to Rome, Varus having permitted the nation to send it, that they might petition for the liberty of living by their own laws. Now, the number of the ambassadors that were sent by the authority of the nation were fifty, to which they joined above eight thousand of the Jews that were at Rome already. (301) Hereupon Caesar assembled his friends, and the chief men among the Romans, in the temple of Apollo, which he had built

at a vast charge; whither the ambassadors came, and a multitude of the Jews that were there already came with them, as did also Archelaus and his friends; (302) but as for the several kinsmen which Archelaus had, they would not join themselves with him, out of their hatred to him; and yet they thought it too gross a thing for them to assist the ambassadors [against him], as supposing it would be a disgrace to them in Caesar's opinion to think of thus acting in opposition to a man of their own kindred: (303) Philip also was come hither out of Syria, by the persuasion of Varus, with this principal intention to assist his brother [Archelaus]: for Varus was his great friend; but still so, that if there should any change happen in the form of government (which Varus suspected there would), and if any distribution should be made on account of the number that desired the liberty of living by their own laws, that he might not be disappointed, but might have his share in it.

(304) Now, upon the liberty that was given to the Jewish ambassadors to speak, they who hoped to obtain a dissolution of kingly government, betook themselves to accuse Herod of his iniquities; and they declared that he was indeed in name a king, but that he had taken to himself that uncontrollable authority which tyrants exercise over their subjects, and had made use of that authority for the destruction of the Jews, and did not abstain from making many innovations among them besides, according to his own inclinations; (305) and that whereas there were a great many who perished by that destruction he brought upon them, so many indeed as no other history relates, they that survived were far more miserable than those that suffered under him, not only by the anxiety they were in from his looks and disposition towards them, but from the danger their estates were in of being taken away by him. (306) That he did never leave off adorning these cities that lay in their neighbourhood, but were inhabited by foreigners; but so that the cities belonging to his own government were ruined, and utterly destroyed: (307) that whereas, when he took the kingdom, it was in an extraordinary flourishing condition, he had filled the nation with the utmost degree of poverty; and when upon unjust pretences, he had slain any of the nobility, he took away their estates: and when he permitted any of them to live, he condemned them to the forfeiture of what they possessed. (308) And, besides the annual impositions which he laid upon every one of them, they were to make liberal presents to himself, to his domestics and friends, and to such of his slaves as were vouchsafed the favour of being his tax gatherers, because there was no way of obtaining a freedom from unjust violence, without giving either gold or silver for it. (309) That they would say nothing of the corruption of the chastity of their virgins, and the reproach laid on their wives for incontinency, and those things acted after an insolent and inhuman manner; because it was not a smaller pleasure to the sufferers to have such things concealed, than it would have been not to have

suffered them. That Herod had put such abuses upon them as a wild beast would not have put on them, if he had power given him to rule over us: (310) and that although their nation had passed through many subversions and alterations of government, their history gave no account of any calamity they had ever been under, that could be compared with this which Herod had brought upon their nation; (311) that it was for this reason that they thought they might justly and gladly salute Archelaus as king, upon this supposition, that whosoever should be set over their kingdom, he would appear more mild to them than Herod had been; and that they had joined with him in the mourning for his father, in order to gratify him, and were ready to oblige him in other points also, if they could meet with any degree of moderation from him: (312) but that he seemed to be afraid lest he should not be deemed Herod's own son; and so, without any delay, he immediately let the nation understand his meaning and this before his dominion was well established, since the power of disposing of it belonged to Caesar, who could either give it to him or not as he pleased. (313) That he had given a specimen of his future virtue to his subjects, and with what kind of moderation and good administration he would govern them, by that his first action which concerned them, his own citizens, and God himself also, when he made the slaughter of three thousand of his own countrymen at the temple. How, then could they avoid their just hatred of him who, to the rest of his barbarity, hath added this as one of our crimes, that we have opposed and contradicted him in the exercise of his authority? (314) Now, the main thing they desired was this: that they might be delivered from kingly and the like forms of government, and might be added to Syria, and be put under the authority of such presidents of theirs as should be sent to them; for that it would thereby be made evident, whether they be really a seditious people, and generally fond of innovations, or whether they would live in an orderly manner, if they might have governors of any sort of moderation set over them.

(315) Now when the Jews had said this, Nicolaus vindicated the kings from those accusations, and said, that as for Herod, since he had never been thus accused all the time of his life, it was not fit for those that might have accused him of lesser crimes than those now mentioned, and might have procured him to be punished during his lifetime, to bring an accusation against him now he is dead. (316) He also attributed the actions of Archelaus to the Jews' injuries to him, who, affecting to govern contrary to the laws, and going about to kill those that would have hindered them from acting unjustly, when they were by him punished for what they had done, made their complaints against him; so he accused them of their attempts for innovation, and of the pleasure they took in sedition, by reason of their not having learned to submit to justice and to the laws, but still desiring to be superior in all things. This was the substance of what Nicolaus said.

(317) When Caesar had heard these pleadings, he dissolved the assembly; but a few days afterwards he appointed Archelaus, not indeed to be the king of the whole country, but ethnarch of one half of that which had been subject to Herod, and promised to give him the royal dignity hereafter, if he governed his part virtuously. (318) But as for the other half, he divided it into two parts, and gave it to two other of Herod's sons, to Philip and to Antipas, that Antipas who disputed with Archelaus for the whole kingdom. Now, to him it was that Perea and Galilee paid their tribute, which amounted annually to two hundred talents, (319) while Batanea with Trachonitis, as well as Auranitis, with a certain part of what was called the *House of Lenodorus*, paid the tribute of one hundred talents to Philip; but Idumea, and Judea, and the country of Samaria, paid tribute to Archelaus, but had now a fourth part of that tribute taken off by the order of Caesar, who decreed them that mitigation, because they did not join in this revolt with the rest of the multitude. (320) There were also certain of the cities which paid tribute to Archelaus: Strato's Tower and Sebaste, with Joppa and Jerusalem; for as to Gaza, and Gadara, and Hippos, they were Grecian cities, which Caesar separated from his government and added them to the province of Syria. Now the tribute money that came to Archelaus every year from his own dominions, amounted to six hundred talents.

(321) And so much came to Herod's sons from their father's inheritance; but Salome, besides what her brother left her by his testament, which were Jamnia, Ashdod, and Phasaelis, and five hundred thousand [drachmae] of coined silver, Caesar made her a present of a royal habitation at Askelon; in all, her revenues amounted to sixty talents by the year, and her dwelling house was within Archelaus' government. (322) The rest also of the king's relations received what his testament allotted them. Moreover, Caesar made a present to each of Herod's two virgin daughters, besides what their father left them, of two hundred and fifty thousand [drachmae] of silver and married them to Pheroras' sons; (323) he also granted all that was bequeathed to himself to the king's sons which was one thousand five hundred talents, excepting a few of the vessels, which he reserved for himself; and they were acceptable to him, not so much for the great value they were of, as because they were memorials of the king to him.

CHAPTER 12

(324) When these affairs had been thus settled by Caesar, a certain young man, by birth a Jew, but brought up by a Roman freedman in the city Sidon, ingrafted himself into the kindred of Herod, by the resemblance of his countenance, which those that saw him attested to be that of Alexander, the son of Herod, whom he had slain; (325) and this was an incitement to him to

endeavour to obtain the government; so he took to him as an assistant, a man of his own country (one that was well acquainted with the affairs of the palace, but on other accounts, an ill man, and one whose nature made him capable of causing great disturbances to the public, and one that became a teacher of such a mischievous contrivance to the other), (326) and declared himself to be Alexander, and the son of Herod, but stolen away by one of those that were sent to slay him; who, in reality, slew other men, in order to deceive the spectators, but saved both him and his brother Aristobulus. (327) Thus was this man elated, and able to impose on those that came to him; and when he was come to Crete, he made all the Jews that came to discourse with him believe him to be [Alexander]. And when he had gotten much money which had been presented to him there, he passed over to Melos, where he got much more money than he had before, out of the belief they had that he was of the royal family, and their hopes that he would recover his father's principality, and reward his benefactors; (328) so he made haste to Rome, and was conducted thither by those strangers who entertained him. He was also so fortunate as, upon his landing at Dicearchia, to bring the Jews that were there into the same delusion; and not only other people, but also all those that had been great with Herod, or had a kindness for him, joined themselves to this man as to their king. (329) The cause of it was this, that men were glad of his pretences, which were seconded by the likeness of his countenance, which made those that had been acquainted with Alexander strongly to believe that he was no other but the very same person, which they also confirmed to others by oath; (330) insomuch that when the report went about him that he was coming to Rome, the whole multitude of the Jews that were there went out to meet him, ascribing to it Divine Providence that he has so unexpectedly escaped, and being very joyful on account of his mother's family. And when he was come, he was carried in a royal litter through the streets; (331) and all the ornaments about him were such as kings are adorned withal; and this was at the expense of those that entertained him. The multitude also flocked about him greatly, and made mighty acclamations to him, and nothing was omitted which could be thought suitable to such as had been so unexpectedly preserved.

(332) When this thing was told Caesar, he did not believe it, because Herod was not easily to be imposed upon in such affairs as were of great concern to him; yet, having some suspicion it might be so, he sent one Celadus, a freedman of his, and one that had conversed with the young men themselves, and bade him bring Alexander into his presence; so he brought him, being no more accurate in judging about him than the rest of the multitude. (333) Yet did not he deceive Caesar; for although there was a resemblance between him and Alexander, yet it was not so exact as to impose on such as were prudent in

discerning; for this spurious Alexander had his hands rough, by the labours he had been put to; and instead of that softness of body which the other had, and this as derived from his delicate and generous education, this man, for the contrary reason, had a rugged body. (334) When, therefore, Caesar saw how the master and the scholar agreed in this lying story, and in a bold way of talking, he inquired about Aristobulus, and asked what became of him, who (it seems) was stolen away together with him, and for what reason it was that he did not come along with him, and endeavour to recover that dominion which was due to his high birth also. (335) And when he said that he had been left in the Isle of Crete, for fear of the dangers of the sea, that, in case any accident should come to himself, the posterity of Mariamne might not utterly perish, but that Aristobulus might survive, and punish those that laid such treacherous designs against them; (336) and when he persevered in his affirmations, and the author of the imposture agreed in supporting it, Caesar took the young man by himself, and said to him, 'If thou wilt not impose upon me, thou shalt have this for thy reward, that thou shalt escape with thy life; tell me, then, who thou art and who it was that had boldness enough to contrive such a cheat as this. For this contrivance is too considerable a piece of villainy to be undertaken by one of thy age.' (337) Accordingly, because he had no other way to take, he told Caesar the contrivance, and after what manner, and by whom, it was laid together. So Caesar, upon observing the spurious Alexander to be a strong active man, and fit to work with his hands, that he might not break his promise to him, put him among those that were to row among the mariners, but slew him that induced him to do what he had done; (338) for as for the people of Melos, he thought them sufficiently punished, in having thrown away so much of their money upon this spurious Alexander. And such was the ignominious conclusion of this bold contrivance about the spurious Alexander.

CHAPTER 13

(339) When Archelaus was entered on his ethnarchy, and was come into Judea, he accused Joazar, the son of Boethus, of assisting the seditious, and took away the high priesthood from him, and put Eleazar his brother in his place. (340) He also magnificently rebuilt the royal palace that had been at Jericho, and he diverted half the water with which the village of Neara used to be watered, and drew off that water into the plain, to water those palm trees which he had there planted: he also built a village, and put his own name upon it, and called it Archelaus. (341) Moreover, he transgressed the law of our fathers, and married Glaphyra, the daughter of Archelaus, who had been the wife of his brother Alexander, which Alexander had three children by her, while it was a thing detestable among the Jews to marry the brother's wife.

Nor did this Eleazar abide long in the high priesthood, Jesus, the son of Sie, being put in his room while he was still living.

(342) But in the tenth year of Archelaus' government, both his brethren and the principal men of Judea and Samaria, not being able to bear his barbarous and tyrannical usage of them, accused him before Caesar, and that especially because they knew he had broken the commands of Caesar, which obliged him to behave himself with moderation among them. (343) Whereupon Caesar, when he heard it, was very angry, and called for Archelaus' steward, who took care of his affairs at Rome, and whose name was Archelaus also; and thinking it beneath him to write to Archelaus, he bade him sail away, as soon as possible, and bring him to Rome; (344) so the man made haste in his voyage, and when he came into Judea he found Archelaus feasting with his friends; so he told him what Caesar had sent him about, and hastened him away. And when he was come [to Rome], Caesar, upon hearing what certain accusers of his had to say, and what reply he could make, both banished him, and appointed Vienna, a city of Gaul, to be the place of his habitation, and took his money away from him.

(345) Now, before Archelaus was gone up to Rome upon this message, he related this dream to his friends: that he saw ears of corn, in number ten, full of wheat, perfectly ripe; which ears, as it seemed to him, were devoured by oxen. (346) And when he was awake and gotten up, because the vision appeared to be of great importance to him, he sent for the diviners, whose study was employed about dreams and while some were of one opinion and some of another (for all their interpretations did not agree), Simon, a man of the sect of the Essenes, desired leave to speak his mind freely, and said, that the vision denoted a change in the affairs of Archelaus, and that not for the better; (347) that oxen, because that animal takes uneasy pains in his labours, denoted afflictions, and indeed denoted, farther, a change of affairs; because that land which is ploughed by oxen cannot remain in its former state; and that the ears of corn being ten, determined the like number of years, because an ear of corn grows in one year; and that the time of Archelaus's government was over. And thus did this man expound the dream. (348) Now, on the fifth day after this dream came first to Archelaus, the other Archelaus, that was sent to Judea by Caesar to call him away, came hither also.

(349) The like accident befell Glaphyra his wife, who was the daughter of King Archelaus, who, as I said before, was married, while she was a virgin, to Alexander, the son of Herod and brother of Archelaus; but since it fell out so that Alexander was slain by his father, she was married to Juba, the king of Libya; (350) and when he was dead, and she lived in widowhood in Cappadocia with her father, Archelaus divorced his former wife, Mariamne, and married her, so great was his affection for her; who, during her marriage

to him, saw the following dream: she thought she saw Alexander standing by her, at which she rejoiced, and embraced him with great affection; but that he complained of her, and said (351): 'O Glaphyra! Thou provest that saying to be true, which assures us that women are not to be trusted. Didst thou not pledge thy faith to me? And wast thou not married to me when thou wast a virgin? And had we not children between us? Yet hast thou forgotten the affection I bare to thee, out of a desire of a second husband. Nor hast thou been satisfied with that injury thou didst me, but thou hast been so bold as to procure thee a third husband to lie by thee, and in an indecent and imprudent manner hast entered into my house, and hast been married to Archelaus, thy husband and my brother. (352) However, I will not forget thy former kind affection for me; but will set thee free from every such reproachful action, and cause thee to be mine again, as thou once wast.' When she had related this to her female companions, in a few days' time she departed this life.

(353) Now, I did not think these histories improper for the present discourse, both because my discourse now is concerning kings, and otherwise also on account of the advantage hence to be drawn, as well for the confirmation of the immortality of the soul, as of the providence of God over human affairs, I thought them fit to be set down; but if anyone does not believe such relations, let him indeed enjoy his own opinion, but let him not hinder another that would thereby encourage himself in virtue. (354) So Archelaus' country was laid to the province of Syria; and Cyrenius, one that had been consul, was sent by Caesar to take account of people's effects in Syria, and to sell the house of Archelaus.

BOOK EIGHTEEN

CHAPTER I

(1) Now Cyrenius, a Roman senator, and one who had gone through other magistracies, and had passed through them till he had been consul, and one who on other accounts was of great dignity, came at this time into Syria, with a few others, being sent by Caesar to be a judge of that nation, and to take an account of their substance; (2) Coponius also, a man of the equestrian order, was sent together with him, to have the supreme power over the Jews. Moreover, Cyrenius came himself into Judea, which was now added to the province of Syria, to take an account of their substance, and to dispose of Archelaus' money; (3) but the Jews, although at the beginning they took the report of a taxation heinously, yet did they leave off any further opposition to it, by the persuasion of Joazar, who was the son of Boethus, and high priest. So they, being over-persuaded by Joazar's words, gave an account of their estates, without any dispute about it; (4) yet there was one Judas, a Gaulonite, of a city whose name was Gamala, who, taking with him Sadduc, a Pharisee, became zealous to draw them to a revolt, who both said that this taxation was no better than an introduction to slavery, and exhorted the nation to assert their liberty, (5) as if they could procure them happiness and security for what they possessed, and an assured enjoyment of a still greater good, which was that of the honour and glory they would thereby acquire for magnanimity. They also said that God would not otherwise be assisting to them, than upon their joining with one another in such counsels as might be successful, and for their own advantage; and this especially, if they would set about great exploits, and not grow weary in executing the same; (6) so men received what they said with pleasure, and this bold attempt proceeded to a great height. All sorts of misfortunes also sprang from these men, and the nation was infected with this doctrine to an incredible degree; (7) one violent war came upon us after another, and we lost our friends, who used to alleviate our pains; there were also very great robberies and murders of our principal men. This was done in pretence indeed for the public welfare, but in reality for the hopes of gain to themselves; (8) whence arose seditions, and from them murders of men, which sometimes fell on those of their own people (by the madness of these men towards one another, while their desire was that none of the adverse party might be left), and sometimes on their enemies; a famine also coming upon us, reduced us to the last degree of despair, as did also the taking and demolishing

of cities; nay, the sedition at last increased so high, that the very temple of God was burnt down by their enemy's fire. (9) Such were the consequences of this, that the customs of our fathers were altered and such a change was made, as added a mighty weight toward bringing all to destruction, which these men occasioned by thus conspiring together; for Judas and Sadduc, who excited a fourth philosophic sect among us, and had a great many followers therein, filled our civil government with tumults at present, and laid the foundations of our future miseries, by this system of philosophy, which we were before unacquainted withal; (10) concerning which I shall discourse a little, and this the rather, because the infection which spread thence among the younger sort, who were zealous for it, brought the public to destruction.

(11) The Jews had for a great while three sects of philosophy peculiar to themselves: the sect of the Essenes, and the sect of the Sadducees, and the third sort of opinions was that of those called Pharisees; of which sects although I have already spoken in the second book of the *Jewish War*, yet will I a little touch upon them now.

(12) Now, for the Pharisees, they live meanly, and despise delicacies in diet; and they follow the conduct of reason, and what that prescribes to them as good for them they do; and they think they ought earnestly to strive to observe reason's dictates for practice. They also pay a respect to such as are in years, nor are they so bold as to contradict them in anything which they have introduced; (13) and when they determine that all things are done by fate, they do not take away the freedom from men of acting as they think fit; since their notion is, that it hath pleased God to make a temperament, whereby what he wills is done, but so that the will of man can act virtuously or viciously. (14) They also believe that souls have an immortal rigour in them, and that under the earth there will be rewards or punishments, according as they have lived virtuously or viciously in this life; and the latter are to be detained in an everlasting prison, but that the former shall have power to revive and live again; (15) on account of which doctrines, they are able greatly to persuade the body of the people; and whatsoever they do about divine worship, prayers, and sacrifices, they perform them according to their direction, insomuch that the cities gave great attestations to them on account of their entire virtuous conduct, both in the actions of their lives and their discourses also.

(16) But the doctrine of the Sadducees is this: that souls die with the bodies; nor do they regard the observation of anything besides what the law enjoins them; for they think it an instance of virtue to dispute with those teachers of philosophy whom they frequent; (17) but this doctrine is received but by a few, yet by those still of the greatest dignity; but they are able to do almost nothing of themselves, for when they become magistrates, as they are unwillingly and by force sometimes obliged to be, they addict themselves

to the notions of the Pharisees, because the multitude would not otherwise bear them.

(18) The doctrine of the Essenes is this: that all things are best ascribed to God. They teach the immortality of souls, and esteem that the rewards of righteousness are to be earnestly striven for; (19) and when they send what they have dedicated to God into the temple, they do not offer sacrifices, because they have more pure lustrations of their own; on which account they are excluded from the common court of the temple, but offer their sacrifices themselves; yet is their course of life better than that of other men; and they entirely addict themselves to husbandry. (20) It also deserves our admiration, how much they exceed all other men that addict themselves to virtue, and this in righteousness; and indeed to such a degree, that as it hath never appeared among any other man, neither Greeks nor barbarians, no, not for a little time, so hath it endured a long while among them. This is demonstrated by that institution of theirs which will not suffer anything to hinder them from having all things in common; so that a rich man enjoys no more of his own wealth than he who hath nothing at all. There are about four thousand men that live in this way, (21) and neither marry wives, nor are desirous to keep servants; as thinking the latter tempts men to be unjust, and the former gives the handle to domestic quarrels; but as they live by themselves, they minister one to another. (22) They also appoint certain stewards to receive the incomes of their revenues, and of the fruits of the ground; such as are good men and priests, who are to get their corn and their food ready for them. They none of them differ from others of the Essenes in their way of living, but do the most resemble those Dacae who are called *Polistae* [dwellers in cities.]

(23) But of the fourth sect of Jewish philosophy, Judas the Galilean was the author. These men agree in all other things with the Pharisaic notions, but they have an inviolable attachment to liberty, and say that God is to be their only Ruler and Lord. They also do not value dying any kinds of death, nor indeed do they heed the deaths of their relations and friends, nor can any such fear make them call any man Lord; (24) and since this immovable resolution of theirs is well known to a great many, I shall speak no farther about that matter; nor am I afraid that anything I have said of them should be disbelieved, but rather fear, that what I have said is beneath the resolution they show when they undergo pain; (25) and it was in Gessius Florus' time that the nation began to grow mad with this distemper, who was our procurator, and who occasioned the Jews to go wild with it by the abuse of his authority, and to make them revolt from the Romans: and these are the sects of Jewish philosophy.

CHAPTER 2

(26) When Cyrenius had now disposed of Archelaus' money, and when the taxings were come to a conclusion, which were made in the thirty-seventh year of Caesar's victory over Antony at Actium, he deprived Joazar of the high priesthood, which dignity had been conferred on him by the multitude, and he appointed Ananus, the son of Seth, to be high priest; (27) while Herod and Philip had each of them received their own tetrarchy, and settled the affairs thereof. Herod also built a wall about Sepphoris (which is the security of all Galilee), and made it the metropolis of the country. He also built a wall round Betharanphtha, which was itself a city also, and called it Julias, from the name of the emperor's wife. (28) When Philip, also, had built Paneas, a city at the fountains of Jordan, he named it Caesarea. He also advanced the village Bethsaida, situate at the lake of Gennesareth, unto the dignity of a city, both by the number of inhabitants it contained, and its other grandeur, and called it by the name of Julias, the same name with Caesar's daughter.

(29) As Coponius, who we told you was sent along with Cyrenius, was exercising his office of procurator, and governing Judea, the following accidents happened. As the Jews were celebrating the feast of unleavened bread, which we call the Passover, it was customary for the priests to open the temple gates just after midnight. (30) When, therefore, those gates were first opened, some of the Samaritans came privately into Jerusalem, and threw about dead men's bodies in the cloisters; on which account the Jews afterward excluded them out of the temple, which they had not used to do at such festivals; and on other accounts also they watched the temple more carefully than they had formerly done. (31) A little after which accident, Coponius returned to Rome, and Marcus Ambivius came to be his successor in that government; under whom Salome, the sister of King Herod, died, and left to Julia [Caesar's wife] Jamnia, all its toparchy, and Phasaelis in the plain, and Archelaus, where is a great plantation of palm trees, and their fruit is excellent in its kind. (32) After him came Annius Rufus, under whom died Caesar, the second emperor of the Romans, the duration of whose reign was fifty-seven years, besides six months and two days (of which time Antonius ruled together with him fourteen years; but the duration of his life was seventy-seven years); (33) upon whose death Tiberius Nero, his wife Julia's son, succeeded. He was now the third emperor; and he sent Valerius Gratus to be procurator of Judea, and to succeed Annius Rufus. (34) This man deprived Ananus of the high priesthood, and appointed Ismael, the son of Phabi, to be high priest. He also deprived him in a little time, and ordained Eleazar, the son of Ananus, who had been high priest before, to be high

priest: which office, when he had held for a year, Gratus deprived him of it, and gave the high priesthood to Simon, the son of Camithus; (35) and when he had possessed that dignity no longer than a year, Joseph Caiaphas was made his successor. When Gratus had done those things, he went back to Rome, after he had tarried in Judea eleven years, when Pontius Pilate came as his successor.

(36) And now Herod the tetrarch, who was in great favour with Tiberius, built a city of the same name with him, and called it Tiberias. He built it in the best part of Galilee, at the lake of Gennesareth. There are warm baths at a little distance from it, in a village named Emmaus. (37) Strangers came and inhabited this city; a great number of the inhabitants were Galileans also; and many were necessitated by Herod to come thither out of the country belonging to him, and were by force compelled to be its inhabitants; some of them were persons of condition. He also admitted poor people, such as those that were collected from all parts, to dwell in it. Nay, some of them were not quite freemen; (38) and these he was benefactor to, and made them free in great numbers; but obliged them not to forsake the city, by building them very good houses at his own expenses, and by giving them land also; for he was sensible, that to make this place a habitation was to transgress the Jewish ancient laws, because many sepulchres were to be here taken away, in order to make room for the city Tiberias; whereas our law pronounces, that such inhabitants are unclean for seven days.

(39) About this time died Phraates, king of the Parthians, by the treachery of Phraataces his son, upon the occasion following: (40) when Phraates had had legitimate sons of his own, he had also an Italian maidservant, whose name was Thermusa, who had been formerly sent to him by Julius Caesar, among other presents. He first made her his concubine; but he being a great admirer of her beauty, in process of time having a son by her, whose name was Phraataces, he made her his legitimate wife, and had a great respect for her. (41) Now, she was able to persuade him to do anything that she said, and was earnest in procuring the government of Parthia for her son; but still she saw that her endeavours would not succeed, unless she could contrive how to remove Phraates' legitimate sons [out of the kingdom]: (42) so she persuaded him to send those his sons as pledges of his fidelity to Rome; and they were sent to Rome accordingly, because it was not easy for him to contradict her commands. Now, while Phraataces was alone brought up in order to succeed in the government, he thought it very tedious to expect that government by his father's donation [as his successor]; he therefore formed a treacherous design against his father, by his mother's assistance, with whom, as the report went, he had criminal intercourse also. (43) So he was hated for both these vices, while his subjects esteemed this [wicked] love of his mother to be no way inferior to his parricide;

and he was by them, in a sedition, expelled out of the country before he grew too great, and died. (44) But as the best sort of Parthians agreed together that it was impossible they should be governed without a king, while also it was their constant practice to choose one of the family of Arsaces [nor did their law allow of any others, and they thought this kingdom had been sufficiently injured already by the marriage with an Italian concubine, and by her issue], they sent ambassadors, and called Orodes to take the crown; for the multitude would not otherwise have borne them; and though he was accused of very great cruelty, and was of an untractable temper, and prone to wrath, yet still he was one of the family of Arsaces. (45) However, they made a conspiracy against him, and slew him, and that, as some say, at a festival, and among their sacrifices (for it is the universal custom there to carry their swords with them); but, as the more general report is, they slew him when they had drawn him out a-hunting. (46) So they sent ambassadors to Rome and desired they would send one of those that were there as pledges, to be their king. Accordingly, Vonones was preferred before the rest, and sent to them (for he seemed capable of such great fortune, which two of the greatest kingdoms under the sun now offered him, his own and a foreign one). (47) However, the barbarians soon changed their minds, they being naturally of a mutable disposition upon the supposal that this man was not worthy to be their governor; for they could not think of obeying the commands of one that had been a slave (for so they called those that had been hostages), nor could they bear the ignominy of that name: and this was the more intolerable, because then the Parthians must have such a king set over them, not by right of war, but in time of peace. (48) So they presently invited Artabanus, king of Media, to be their king, he being also of the race of Arsaces. Artabanus complied with the offer that was made him, and came to them with an army. So Vonones met him; and at first the multitude of the Parthians stood on his side, and he put his army in array; but Artabanus was beaten, and fled to the mountains of Media. (49) Yet did he a little after gather a great army together and fought with Vonones, and beat him; whereupon Vonones fled away on horseback, with a few of his attendants about him, to Selucia [upon Tigris]. So when Artabanus had slain a great number, and this after he had gotten the victory by reason of the very great dismay the barbarians were in, he retired to Ctesiphon with a great number of his people; and so he now reigned over the Parthians. (50) But Vonones fled away to Armenia; and as soon as he came thither, he had an inclination to have the government of the country given him, and sent ambassadors to Rome [for that purpose]. (51) But because Tiberius refused it him, and because he wanted courage, and because the Parthian king threatened him, and sent ambassadors to him, to denounce war against him if he proceeded, and because he had no way to take to regain any other kingdom (for the people of authority among the Armenians, about

Niphates, joined themselves to Artabanus), (52) he delivered up himself to Silanus, the president of Syria, who out of regard to his education at Rome, kept him in Syria, while Artabanus gave Armenia to Orodes, one of his own sons.

(53) At this time died Antiochus, the king of Commagene; whereupon the multitude contended with the nobility, and both sent ambassadors to [Rome]; for the men of power were desirous that their form of government might be changed into that of a [Roman] province; as were the multitude desirous to be under kings, as their fathers had been. (54) So the senate made a decree, that Germanicus should be sent to settle the affairs of the east, fortune hereby taking a proper opportunity for depriving him of his life; for when he had been in the east, and settled all affairs there, his life was taken away by the poison which Piso gave him, as hath been related elsewhere.

CHAPTER 3

(55) But now Pilate, the procurator of Judea, removed the army from Caesarea to Jerusalem, to take their winter quarters there, in order to abolish the Jewish laws. So he introduced Caesar's effigies, which were upon the ensigns, and brought them into the city, whereas our law forbids us the very making of images; (56) on which account the former procurators were wont to make their entry into the city with such ensigns as had not those ornaments. Pilate was the first who brought those images to Jerusalem, and set them up there; which was done without the knowledge of the people, because it was done in the night-time; (57) but as soon as they knew it, they came in multitudes to Caesarea, and interceded with Pilate many days, that he would remove the images; and when he would not grant their requests, because it would tend to the injury of Caesar, while yet they persevered in their request, on the sixth day he ordered his soldiers to have their weapons privately, while he came and sat upon his judgment seat, which seat was so prepared in the open place of the city, that it concealed the army that lay ready to oppress them: (58) and when the Jews petitioned him again, he gave a signal to the soldiers to encompass them round, and threatened that their punishment should be no less than immediate death, unless they would leave off disturbing him, and go their ways home. (59) But they threw themselves upon the ground, and laid their necks bare, and said they would take their death very willingly, rather than the wisdom of their laws should be transgressed; upon which Pilate was deeply affected with their firm resolution to keep their laws inviolable, and presently commanded the images to be carried back from Jerusalem to Caesarea.

(60) But Pilate undertook to bring a current of water to Jerusalem, and did it with the sacred money, and derived the origin of the stream from the distance of two hundred furlongs. However the Jews were not pleased with what had

been done about this water; and many ten thousands of the people got together, and made a clamour against him, and insisted that he should leave off that design. Some of them also used reproaches, and abused the man, as crowds of such people usually do. (61) So he habited a great number of his soldiers in their habit, who carried daggers under their garments, and sent them to a place where they might surround them. So he bade the Jews himself go away; but they boldly casting reproaches upon him, he gave the soldiers that signal which had been beforehand agreed on; (62) who laid upon them much greater blows than Pilate had commanded them, and equally punished those that were tumultuous and those that were not, nor did they spare them in the least; and since the people were unarmed, and were caught by men prepared for what they were about, there were a great number of them slain by this means, and others of them ran away wounded; and thus an end was put to this sedition.

(63) Now, there was about this time Jesus, a wise man, if it be lawful to call him a man, for he was a doer of wonderful works – a teacher of such men as receive the truth with pleasure. He drew over to him both many of the Jews, and many of the Gentiles. He was [the] Christ; (64) and when Pilate, at the suggestion of the principal men amongst us, had condemned him to the cross, those that loved him at the first did not forsake him, for he appeared to them alive again the third day, as the divine prophets had foretold these and ten thousand other wonderful things concerning him; and the tribe of Christians, so named from him, are not extinct at this day.

(65) About the same time also another sad calamity put the Jews into disorder; and certain shameful practices happened about the temple of Isis that was at Rome. I will now first take notice of the wicked attempt about the temple of Isis, and will then give an account of the Jewish affairs. (66) There was at Rome a woman whose name was Paulina; one who on account of the dignity of her ancestors, and by the regular conduct of a virtuous life, had a great reputation: she was also very rich; and although she was of a beautiful countenance, and in that flower of her age wherein women are the most gay, yet did she lead a life of great modesty. She was married to Saturninus, one that was every way answerable to her in an excellent character. (67) Decius Mundus fell in love with this woman, who was a man very high in the equestrian order; and as she was of too great dignity to be caught by presents, and had already rejected them, though they had been sent in great abundance, he was still more inflamed with love to her, insomuch that he promised to give her two hundred thousand Attic drachmae for one night's lodging; (68) and when this would not prevail upon her and he was not able to bear this misfortune in his amours, he thought it the best way to famish himself to death for want of food, on account of Paulina's sad refusal; and he determined with himself to die after such a manner, and he went on with his purpose accordingly. (69) Now, Mundus had a

freedwoman, who had been made free by his father, whose name was Ide, one skilful in all sorts of mischief. This woman was very much grieved at the young man's resolution to kill himself (for he did not conceal his intentions to destroy himself from others) and came to him, and encouraged him, by her discourse, and made him to hope, by some promises she gave him, that he might obtain a night's lodging with Paulina; (70) and when he joyfully hearkened to her entreaty, she said she wanted no more than fifty thousand drachmae for the entrapping of the woman. So when she had encouraged the young man, and gotten as much money as she required, she did not take the same methods as had been taken before, because she perceived that the woman was by no means to be tempted by money; but as she knew that she was very much given to the worship of the goddess Isis, she devised the following stratagem: (71) she went to some of Isis' priests, and upon the strongest assurances [of concealment], she persuaded them by words, but chiefly by the offer of money of twenty-five thousand drachmae in hand, and as much more when the thing had taken effect; and told them the passion of the young man, and persuaded them to use all means possible to beguile the woman. (72) So they were drawn in to promise so to do, by that large sum of gold they were to have. Accordingly, the oldest of them went immediately to Paulina; and upon his admittance, he desired to speak with that he was sent by the god Anubis, who was fallen in love with her, and enjoined her to come to him. (73) Upon this she took the message very kindly, and valued herself greatly upon this condescension of Anubis; and told her husband that she had a message sent her, and was to sup and lie with Anubis; so he agreed to her acceptance of the offer, as fully satisfied with the chastity of his wife. (74) Accordingly, she went to the temple; and after she had supped there, and it was the hour to go to sleep, the priest shut the doors of the temple, when in the holy part of it, the lights were also put out. Then did Mundus leap out (for he was hidden therein) and did not fail of enjoying her, who was at his service all the night long, as supposing he was the god (75); and when he was gone away, which was before those priests who knew nothing of this stratagem were stirring, Paulina came early to her husband, and told him how the god Anubis had appeared to her. Among her friends also she declared how great a value she put upon this favour, (76) who partly disbelieved the thing, when they reflected on its nature, and partly were amazed at it, as having no pretence for not believing it, when they considered the modesty and the dignity of the person; (77) but now, on the third day after what had been done, Mundus met Paulina, and said, 'Nay, Paulina, thou hast saved me two hundred thousand drachmae, which sum thou mightest have added to thy own family; yet hast thou not failed to be at my service in the manner I invited thee. As for the reproaches thou hast laid upon Mundus, I value not the business of names; but I rejoice in the pleasure I reaped by what I did, while I took to myself the name of Anubis.' (78) When he had said this, he went his way; but now she began to come to the sense of the grossness of what she had done, and rent her garments, and told her husband of the horrid nature of this wicked contrivance and prayed him not to neglect to assist her in this case. So he discovered the fact to the emperor; (79) whereupon Tiberius inquired into the matter thoroughly, by examining the priests about it, and ordered them to be crucified, as well as Ide, who was the occasion of their perdition, and who had contrived the whole matter, which was so injurious to the woman. He also demolished the temple of Isis, and gave order that her statue should be thrown into the river Tiber; (80) while he only banished Mundus, but did no more to him, because he supposed that what crime he had committed was done out of the passion of love; and these were the circumstances which concerned the temple of Isis, and the injuries occasioned by her priests – I now return to the relation of what happened about this time to the Jews at Rome, as I formerly told you I would.

(81) There was a man who was a Jew, but had been driven away from his own country by an accusation laid against him for transgressing their laws, and by the fear he was under of punishment for the same; but in all respects a wicked man. He then living at Rome, professed to instruct men in the wisdom of the laws of Moses. (82) He procured also three other men, entirely of the same character with himself, to be his partners. These men persuaded Fulvia, a woman of great dignity, and one that had embraced the Jewish religion, to send purple and gold to the temple at Jerusalem; and, when they had gotten them, they employed them for their own uses, and spent the money themselves; on which account it was that they at first required it of her. (83) Whereupon Tiberius, who had been informed of the thing by Saturninus, the husband of Fulvia, who desired inquiry might be made about it, ordered all the Jews to be banished out of Rome; (84) at which time the consuls listed four thousand men out of them, and sent them to the island Sardinia; but punished a greater number of them, who were unwilling to become soldiers on account of keeping the laws of their forefathers. Thus were these Jews banished out of the city by the wickedness of four men.

CHAPTER 4

(85) But the nation of the Samaritans did not escape without tumults. The man who excited them to it, was one who thought lying a thing of little consequence, and who contrived everything so, that the multitude might be pleased; so he bade them to get together upon Mount Gerizzim, which is by them looked upon as the most holy of all mountains, and assured them that, when they were come thither, he would show them those sacred vessels which were laid under that place, because Moses put them there. (86) So they came

thither armed, and thought the discourse of the man probable; and as they abode at a certain village, which was called Tirathaba, they got the rest together to them, and desired to go up the mountain in a great multitude together. (87) But Pilate prevented their going up, by seizing upon roads with a great band of horsemen and footmen, who fell upon those that were gotten together in the village; and when it came to an action, some of them they slew, and others of them they put to flight, and took a great many alive, the principal of whom, and also the most potent of those that fled away, Pilate ordered to be slain.

(88) But when this tumult was appeased, the Samaritan senate sent an embassy to Vitellius, a man that had been consul, and who was now president of Syria, and accused Pilate of the murder of those that were killed; for that they did not go to Tirathaba in order to revolt from the Romans, but to escape the violence of Pilate. (89) So Vitellius sent Marcellus, a friend of his, to take care of the affairs of Judea, and ordered Pilate to go to Rome, to answer before the emperor to the accusation of the Jews. So Pilate, when he had tarried ten years in Judea, made haste to Rome, and this in obedience to the orders of Vitellius, which he durst not contradict; but before he could get to Rome, Tiberius was dead.

(90) But Vitellius came into Judea, and went up to Jerusalem; it was at the time of that festival which is called the Passover. Vitellius was there magnificently received, and released the inhabitants of Jerusalem from all the taxes upon the fruits that were bought and sold, and gave them leave to have the care of the high priest's vestments, with all their ornaments, and to have them under the custody of the priests in the temple; which power they used to have formerly, (91) although at this time they were laid up in the tower of Antonia, the citadel so called, and that on the occasion following: there was one of the [high] priests, named Hyrcanus, and as there were many of that name, he was the first of them; this man built a tower near the temple, and when he had so done, he generally dwelt in it, and had these vestments with him, because it was lawful for him alone to put them on; and he had them there reposited when he went down into the city, and took his ordinary garments; (92) the same things were continued to be done by his sons, and by their sons after them; but when Herod came to be king, he rebuilt this tower, which was very conveniently situated, in a magnificent manner; and because he was a friend to Antonius, he called it by the name of Antonia; and as he found these vestments lying there, he retained them in the same place, as believing that, while he had them in his custody, the people would make no innovations against him. (93) The like to what Herod did was done by his son Archelaus, who was made king after him; after whom the Romans, when they entered on the government, took possession of these vestments of the high priest, and had them reposited in a stone chamber, under the seal of the priests,

and of the keepers of the temple, the captain of the guard lighting a lamp there every day; (94) and seven days before a festival they were delivered to them by the captain of the guard, when the high priest having purified them, and made use of them, laid them up again in the same chamber where they had been laid up before, and this the very next day after the feast was over. This was the practice at the three yearly festivals, and on the fast day; (95) but Vitellius put those garments into our own power, as in the days of our forefathers, and ordered the captain of the guard not to trouble himself to inquire where they were laid, or when they were to be used; and this he did as an act of kindness, to oblige the nation to him. Besides which, he also deprived Joseph, who was called Caiaphas, of the high priesthood, and appointed Jonathan, the son of Ananus, the former high priest, to succeed him. After which he took his journey back to Antioch.

(96) Moreover, Tiberius sent a letter to Vitellius, and commanded him to make a league of friendship with Artabanus, the king of Parthia; for while he was his enemy, he terrified him, because he had taken Armenia away from him, lest he should proceed farther, and told him he should no otherwise trust him than upon his giving him hostages, and especially his son Artabanus. (97) Upon Tiberius' writing thus to Vitellius, by the offer of great presents of money, he persuaded both the king of Iberia and the king of Albania to make no delay, but to fight against Artabanus; and although they would not do it themselves, yet did they give the Scythians a passage through their country, and opened the Caspian gates to them, and brought them upon Artabanus. (98) So Armenia was again taken from the Parthians, and the country of Parthis was filled with war, and the principal of their men were slain, and all things were in disorder among them: the king's son also himself fell in these wars together with many ten thousands of his army. (99) Vitellius had also sent such great sums of money to Artabanus' father's kinsmen and friends, that he had almost procured him to be slain by the means of those bribes which they had taken. And when Artabanus perceived that the plot laid against him was not to be avoided, because it was laid by the principal men, and those a great many in number, and that it would certainly take effect, (100) when he had estimated the number of those that were truly faithful to him, as also of those who were already corrupted, but were deceitful in the kindness they professed to him, and were likely, upon trial, to go over to his enemies, he made his escape to the upper provinces where he afterwards raised a great army out of the Dahae and Sacae, and fought with his enemies, and retained his principality.

(101) When Tiberius had heard of these things, he desired to have a league of friendship made between him and Artabanus; and when, upon this invitation, he received the proposal kindly, Artabanus and Vitellius went to Euphrates, (102) and as a bridge was laid over the river, they each of them

came with their guards about them, and met one another on the midst of the bridge. And when they had agreed upon the terms of peace, Herod the tetrarch erected a rich tent on the midst of the passage, and made them a feast there. (103) Artabanus also, not long afterwards, sent his son Darius as an hostage, with many presents, among which there was a man seven cubits tall, a Jew he was by birth, and his name was Eleazar, who, for his tallness, was called a giant. (104) After which Vitellius went to Antioch, and Artabanus to Babylon: but Herod [the tetrarch], being desirous to give Caesar the first information that they had obtained hostages, sent posts with letters, wherein he had accurately described all the particulars, and had left nothing for the consular Vitellius to inform him of. (105) But when Vitellius' letters were sent, and Caesar had let him know that he was acquainted with the affairs already, because Herod had given him an account of them before, Vitellius was very much troubled at it; and supposing that he had been thereby a greater sufferer than he really was, he kept up a secret anger upon this occasion, till he could be revenged on him; which he was after Caius had taken the government.

(106) About this time it was that Philip, Herod's brother, departed this life, in the twentieth year of the reign of Tiberius, after he had been tetrarch of Trachonitis, and Gaulonitis, and of the nation of the Bataneans also, thirty-seven years. He had shown himself a person of moderation and quietness in the conduct of his life and government; (107) he constantly lived in that country which was subject to him; he used to make his progress with a few chosen friends; his tribunal also, on which he sat in judgment, followed him in his progress; and when anyone met him who wanted his assistance, he made no delay but had his tribunal set down immediately, wheresoever he happened to be, and sat down upon it, and heard his complaint: he there ordered the guilty that were convicted to be punished, and absolved those that had been accused unjustly. (108) He died at Julias; and when he was carried to that monument which he had already erected for himself beforehand, he was buried with great pomp. His principality Tiberius took (for he left no sons behind him) and added it to the province of Syria, but gave order that the tributes which arose from it should be collected, and laid up in his tetrarchy.

CHAPTER 5

(109) About this time Aretas (the king of Arabia Petrea) and Herod had a quarrel, on the account following: Herod the tetrarch had married the daughter of Aretas, and had lived with her a great while; but when he was once at Rome, he lodged with Herod, who was his brother indeed, but not by the same mother; for this Herod was the son of the high priest Simon's daughter.

(110) However, he fell in love with Herodias, this last Herod's wife, who was the daughter of Aristobulus their brother, and the sister of Agrippa the Great. This man ventured to talk to her about a marriage between them; which address when she admitted, an agreement was made for her to change her habitation, and come to him as soon as he should return from Rome; one article of this marriage also was this, that he should divorce Aretas' daughter. (111) So Antipas, when he had made this agreement, sailed to Rome; but when he had done there the business he went about, and was returned again, his wife having discovered the agreement he had made with Herodias, and having learned it before he had notice of her knowledge of the whole design, she desired him to send her to Macherus, which is a place in the borders of the dominions of Aretas and Herod, without informing him of any of her intentions. (112) Accordingly Herod sent her thither, as thinking his wife had not perceived anything; now she had sent a good while before to Macherus, which was subject to her father, and so all things necessary for her journey were made ready for her by the general of Aretas' army and by that means she soon came into Arabia, under the conduct of the several generals, who carried her from one to another successively; and she soon came to her father, and told him of Herod's intentions. (113) So Aretas made this the first occasion of his enmity between him and Herod, who had also some quarrel with him about their limits at the country of Gamalitis. So they raised armies on both sides, and prepared for war, and sent their generals to fight instead of themselves; (114) and, when they had joined battle, all Herod's army was destroyed by the treachery of some fugitives, who, though they were of the tetrarchy of Philip, joined with Aretas' army. (115) So Herod wrote about these affairs to Tiberius, who, being very angry at the attempt made by Aretas, wrote to Vitellius to make war upon him, and either to take him alive, and bring him to him in bonds, or to kill him, and send him his head. This was the charge that Tiberius gave to the president of Syria.

(116) Now, some of the Jews thought that the destruction of Herod's army came from God, and that very justly, as a punishment of what he did against John, that was called the *Baptist*; (117) for Herod slew him, who was a good man and commanded the Jews to exercise virtue, both as to righteousness towards one another, and piety towards God, and so to come to baptism; for that the washing [with water] would be acceptable to him, if they made use of it, not in order to the putting away [or the remission] of some sins [only], but for the purification of the body; supposing still that the soul was thoroughly purified beforehand by righteousness. (118) Now, when [many] others came in crowds about him, for they were very greatly moved [or pleased] by hearing his words, Herod, who feared lest the great influence John had over the people might put it into his power and inclination to raise a rebellion (for they seemed

ready to do anything he should advise), thought it best, by putting him to death, to prevent any mischief he might cause, and not bring himself into difficulties, by sparing a man who might make him repent of it when it would be too late. (119) Accordingly he was sent a prisoner, out of Herod's suspicious temper, to Macherus, the castle I before mentioned, and was there put to death. Now the Jews had an opinion that the destruction of this army was sent as a punishment upon Herod, and a mark of God's displeasure to him.

(120) So Vitellius prepared to make war with Aretas, having with him two legions of armed men; he also took with him all those of light armature, and of the horsemen which belonged to them, and were drawn out of those kingdoms which were under the Romans, and made haste for Petra, and came to Ptolemais. (121) But as he was marching very busily, and leading his army through Judea, the principal men met him, and desired that he would not thus march through their land; for that the laws of their country would not permit them to overlook those images which were brought into it, of which there were a great many in their ensigns; (122) so he was persuaded by what they said, and changed that resolution of his, which he had before taken in this matter. Whereupon he ordered the army to march along the Great Plain, while he himself, with Herod the tetrarch and his friends, went up to Jerusalem to offer sacrifice to God, an ancient festival of the Jews being then just approaching; (123) and when he had been there and been honourably entertained by the multitude of the Jews, he made a stay there for three days, within which time he deprived Jonathan of the high priesthood, and gave it to his brother Theophilus; (124) but when on the fourth day letters came to him, which informed him of the death of Tiberius, he obliged the multitude to take an oath of fidelity to Caius; he also recalled his army, and made them every one go home, and take their winter quarters there, since, upon the devolution of the empire upon Caius, he had not the like authority of making this war which he had before. (125) It was also reported, that when Aretas heard of the coming of Vitellius to fight him, he said upon his consulting the diviners, that it was impossible that this army of Vitellius's could enter Petra; for that one of the rulers would die, either he that gave orders for the war, or he that was marching at the other's desire, in order to be subservient to his will, or else he against whom this army is prepared. (126) So Vitellius truly retired to Antioch, but Agrippa, the son of Aristobulus, went up to Rome, a year before the death of Tiberius, in order to treat of some affairs with the emperor, if he might be permitted so to do. (127) I have now a mind to describe Herod and his family, how it fared with them, partly because it is suitable to this history to speak of that matter, and partly because this thing is a demonstration of the interposition of Providence; how a multitude of children is of no advantage, no more than any other strength that mankind set their hearts upon, besides those acts of piety

which are done towards God; (128) for it happened, that, within the revolution of a hundred years, the posterity of Herod, who were a great many in number, were, excepting a few, utterly destroyed. One may well apply this for the instruction of mankind, and learn thence how unhappy they were: (129) it will also show us the history of Agrippa, who, as he was a person most worthy of admiration, so was he from a private man, beyond all the expectation of those that knew him, advanced to great power and authority. I have said something of them formerly; but I shall now also speak accurately about them.

(130) Herod the Great had two daughters by Mariamne, the [grand] daughter of Hyrcanus; the one was Salampsio, who was married to Phasaelus – her first cousin, who was himself the son of Phasaelus, Herod's brother, her father making the match: the other was Cypros, who was herself married also to her first cousin Antipater, the son of Salome, Herod's sister. (131) Phasaelus had five children by Salampsio: Antipater, Herod, and Alexander, and two daughters, Alexandra and Cypros; which last Agrippa, the son of Aristobulus, married; and Timius of Cyprus married Alexandra; he was a man of note, but had by her no children. (132) Agrippa had by Cypros two sons and three daughters, which daughters were named Berenice, Mariamne, and Drusilla; but the names of the sons were Agrippa and Drusus, of which Drusus died before he came to the years of puberty; (133) but their father, Agrippa, was brought up with his other brethren, Herod and Aristobulus, for these were also the sons of Herod the Great by Berenice; but Berenice was the daughter of Costobarus and of Salome, who was Herod's sister. (134) Aristobulus left these infants when he was slain by his father, together with his brother Alexander, as we have related, but when they were arrived at years of puberty, this Herod, the brother of Agrippa, married Mariamne, the daughter of Olympias (who was the daughter of Herod the king) and of Joseph, the son of Joseph, who was brother to Herod the king; and had by her a son, Aristobulus; (135) but Aristobulus, the third brother of Agrippa, married Jotape, the daughter of Sampsigeramus, king of Emesa; they had a daughter who was deaf, whose name also was Jotape; and these hitherto were the children of the male line; (136) but Herodias, their sister, was married to Herod [Philip], the son of Herod the Great, who was born of Mariamne, the daughter of Simon the high priest, who had a daughter, Salome; after whose birth Herodias took upon her to confound the laws of our country, and divorce herself from her husband while he was alive, and was married to Herod [Antipas], her husband's brother by the father's side; he was tetrarch of Galilee; (137) but her daughter Salome was married to Philip, the son of Herod, and tetrarch of Trachonitis; and, as he died childless, Aristobulus, the son of Herod, the brother of Agrippa, married her; they had three sons, Herod, Agrippa, and Aristobulus; (138) and this was the posterity of Phasaelus and Salampsio; but the daughter of Antipater by Cypros, was Cypros, whom Alexas Selcias, the son of

Alexas, married; they had a daughter, Cypros; but Herod and Alexander, who, as we told you, were the brothers of Antipater, died childless. (139) As to Alexander, the son of Herod the king, who was slain by his father, he had two sons, Alexander and Tigranes, by the daughter of Archelaus, king of Cappadocia. Tigranes, who was king of Armenia, was accused at Rome, and died childless; (140) Alexander had a son of the same name with his brother Tigranes, and was sent to take possession of the kingdom of Armenia by Nero; he had a son, Alexander, who married Jotape, the daughter of Antiochus, the king of Commagene; Vespasian made him king of an island in Cilicia. (141) But these descendants of Alexander, soon after their birth, deserted the Jewish religion, and went over to that of the Greeks; but for the rest of the daughters of Herod the king, it happened that they died childless. (142) and as these descendants of Herod, whom we have enumerated, were in being at the same time that Agrippa the Great took the kingdom, and I have now given an account of them, it now remains that I relate the several hard fortunes which befell Agrippa, and how he got clear of them, and was advanced to the greatest height of dignity and power.

CHAPTER 6

(143) A little before the death of Herod the king, Agrippa lived at Rome, and was generally brought up and conversed with Drusus the emperor Tiberius' son, and contracted a friendship with Antonia, the wife of Drusus the Great, who had his mother Berenice in great esteem, and was very desirous of advancing her son. (144) Now, as Agrippa was by nature magnanimous and generous in the presents he made while his mother was alive, this inclination of his mind did not appear, that he might be able to avoid her anger for such his extravagance; (145) but when Berenice was dead, and he was left to his own conduct, he spent a great deal extravagantly in his daily way of living, and a great deal in the immoderate presents he made, and those chiefly among Caesar's freedmen, in order to gain their assistance, insomuch that he was in a little time reduced to poverty, (146) and could not live at Rome any longer. Tiberius also forbade the friends of his deceased son to come into his sight, because on seeing them he should be put in mind of his son, and his grief would thereby be revived.

(147) For these reasons he went away from Rome and sailed to Judea, but in evil circumstances, being dejected with the loss of that money which he once had, and because he had not wherewithal to pay his creditors, who were many in number, and such as gave no room for escaping them. Whereupon he knew not what to do; so for shame of his present condition, he retired to a certain tower at Malatha, in Idumea, and had thoughts of killing himself; (148) but his

wife Cypros perceived his intentions, and tried all sorts of methods to divert him from his taking such a course; so she sent a letter to his sister Herodias, who was now the wife of Herod the tetrarch, and let her know Agrippa's present design, and what necessity it was which drove him thereto, (149) and desired her, as a kinswoman of his, to give him her help, and to engage her husband to do the same, since she saw how she alleviated these her husband's troubles all she could, although she had not the like wealth to do it withal. So they sent for him, and allotted him Tiberias for his habitation, and appointed him some income of money for his maintenance, and made him a magistrate of that city, by way of honour to him. (150) Yet did not Herod long continue in that resolution of supporting him, though even that support was not sufficient for him; for, as once they were at a feast at Tyre, and in their cups, and reproaches were cast upon one another, Agrippa thought that was not to be borne, while Herod hit him in the teeth with his poverty, and with his owing his necessary food to him. So he went to Flaccus, one that had been consul, and had been a very great friend to him at Rome formerly, and was now president of Syria.

(151) Hereupon Flaccus received him kindly; and he lived with him. Flaccus had also with him there Aristobulus, who was indeed Agrippa's brother, but was at variance with him; yet did not their enmity to one another hinder the friendship of Flaccus to them both; but still they were honourably treated by him. (152) However, Aristobulus did not abate of his ill will to Agrippa, till at length he brought him into ill terms with Flaccus; the occasion of bringing on which estrangement was this: (153) the Damascens were at difference with the Sidonians about their limits, and when Flaccus was about to hear the cause between them, they understood that Agrippa had a mighty influence upon him; so they desired that he would be of their side, and for that favour promised him a great deal of money; (154) so he was zealous in assisting the Damascens as far as he was able. Now, Aristobulus had gotten intelligence of this promise of money to him, and accused him to Flaccus of the same; and when, upon a thorough examination of the matter, it appeared plainly so to be, he rejected Agrippa out of the number of his friends. (155) So he was reduced to the utmost necessity, and came to Ptolemais; and because he knew not where else to get a livelihood, he thought to sail to Italy; but as he was restrained from so doing by want of money he desired Marsyas, who was his freedman, to find some method for procuring him so much as he wanted for that purpose, by borrowing such a sum of some person or other. (156) So Marsyas desired of Peter, who was the freedman of Berenice, Agrippa's mother, and by the right of her testament was bequeathed to Antonia, to lend so much upon Agrippa's own bond and security; (157) but he accused Agrippa of having defrauded him of certain sums of money, and so obliged Marsyas, when

he made the bond of twenty thousand Attic drachmae, to accept of twenty-five hundred drachmae less than what he desired; which the other allowed of, because he could not help it. (158) Upon the receipt of this money, Agrippa came to Anthedon, and took shipping, and was going to set sail; but Herennius Capito, who was the procurator of Jamnia, sent a band of soldiers to demand of him three hundred thousand drachmae of silver, which were by him owing to Caesar's treasury while he was at Rome, and so forced him to stay. (159) He then pretended that he would do as he bade him; but when night came on, he cut his cables, and went off, and sailed to Alexandria, where he desired Alexander the alabarch to lend him two hundred thousand drachmae; but he said he would not lend it to him, but would not refuse it to Cypros, as greatly astonished at her affection to her husband, and at the other instances of her virtue; (160) so she undertook to repay it. Accordingly, Alexander paid them five talents at Alexandria, and promised to pay them the rest of that sum at Dicearchia [Puteoli]; and this he did out of the fear he was in that Agrippa would soon spend it. So this Cypros set her husband free, and dismissed him to go on with his navigation to Italy, while she and children departed for Judea.

(161) And now Agrippa was come to Puteoli, whence he wrote a letter to Tiberius Caesar, who then lived at Capreae, and told him that he was come so far, in order to wait on him, and to pay him a visit; and desired that he would give him leave to come over to Capreae; (162) so Tiberius made no difficulty, but wrote to him in an obliging way in other respects; and withal told him he was glad of his safe return, and desired him to come to Capreae; and, when he was come, he did not fail to treat him as kindly as he had promised him in his letter to do. (163) But the next day came a letter to Caesar from Herennius Capito, to inform him that Agrippa had borrowed three hundred thousand drachmae, and not paid it at the time appointed; but, when it was demanded of him, he ran away like a fugitive, out of the places under his government, and put it out of his power to get the money of him. (164) When Caesar had read this letter, he was much troubled at it, and gave order that Agrippa should be excluded from his presence until he had paid that debt; upon which he was no way daunted at Caesar's anger but entreated Antonia, the mother of Germanicus and of Claudius, who was afterwards Caesar himself, to lend him those three hundred thousand drachmae, that he might not be deprived of Tiberius's friendship; (165) so, out of regard to the memory of Berenice, his mother (for those two women were very familiar with one another), and out of regard to his and Claudius' education together, she lent him the money; and, upon the payment of this debt, there was nothing to hinder Tiberius' friendship to him. (166) After this, Tiberius Caesar recommended to him his grandson, and ordered that he should always accompany him when he went abroad. But, upon Agrippa's kind reception by Antonia, he betook him to pay

his respects to Caius, who was her grandson, and in very high reputation by reason of the good will they bare his father. (167) Now there was one Thallus, a freedman of Caesar, of whom he borrowed a million of drachmae, and thence repaid Antonia the debt he owed her; and by sending the overplus in paying his court to Caius, became a person of great authority with him.

(168) Now as the friendship which Agrippa had for Caius was come to a great height, there happened some words to pass between them, as they once were in a chariot together, concerning Tiberius; Agrippa praying [to God] (for they two sat by themselves) that Tiberius might soon go off the stage, and leave the government to Caius, who was in every respect more worthy of it. Now, Eutychus, who was Agrippa's freedman, and drove his chariot, heard these words, and at that time said nothing of them; (169) but when Agrippa accused him of stealing some garments of his (which was certainly true), he ran away from him; but when he was caught and brought before Piso, who was governor of the city, and the man was asked why he ran away, be replied that he had somewhat to say to Caesar, that tended to his security and preservation: so Piso bound him and sent him to Capreae. But Tiberius, according to his usual custom, kept him still in bonds, being a delayer of affairs, if ever there was any other king or tyrant that was so; (170) for he did not admit ambassadors quickly, and no successors were despatched away to governors or procurators of the provinces that had formerly been sent, unless they were dead; whence it was that he was so negligent in hearing the causes of prisoners; (171) insomuch that when he was asked by his friends what was the reason of his delay in such cases, he said that he delayed to hear ambassadors, lest upon their quick dismission, other ambassadors should be appointed, and return upon him; and so he should bring trouble upon himself in their public reception and dismission; (172) that he permitted those governors who had been sent once to their government [to stay there a long while], out of regard to the subjects that were under them; for that all governors are naturally disposed to get as much as they can; and that those who are not to fix there but to stay a short time, and that at an uncertainty when they shall be turned out, do the more severely hurry themselves on to fleece the people; (173) but that, if their government be long continued to them, they are at last satiated with the spoils, as having gotten a vast deal, and so become at length less sharp in their pillaging; but that, if successors are sent quickly, the poor subjects, who are exposed to them as a prey, will not be able to bear the new ones, while they shall not have the same time allowed them wherein their predecessors have filled themselves, and so grew more unconcerned about getting more; and this because they are removed before they have had time [for their oppressions]. (174) He gave them an example to show his meaning: a great number of flies came about the sore places of a man that had been wounded; upon which one of the standers-

by pitied the man's misfortune, and thinking he was not able to drive away those flies himself, was going to drive them away for him; (175) but he prayed him to let them alone: the other, by way of reply, asked him the reason of such a preposterous proceeding, in preventing relief from his present misery, to which he answered, 'If thou drivest these flies away, thou wilt hurt me worse; for as these are already full of my blood, they do not crowd about me, nor pain me so much as before, but are somewhat more remiss, while the fresh ones that come, almost famished, and find me quite tired down already, will be my destruction. (176) For this cause, therefore, it is that I am myself careful not to send such new governors perpetually to those my subjects, who are already sufficiently harassed by many oppressions, as may, like these flies, farther distress them; and so, besides their natural desire of gain, may have this additional incitement to it, that they expect to be suddenly deprived of that pleasure which they take in it.' (177) And, as a farther attestation to what I say of the dilatory nature of Tiberius, I appeal to this his practice itself; for although he was emperor twenty-two years, he sent in all but two procurators to govern the nation of the Jews – Gratus, and his successor in the government, Pilate. (178) Nor was he in one way of acting with respect to the Jews, and in another with respect to the rest of his subjects. He further informed them, that even in the hearing of the causes of prisoners, he made such delays, because immediate death to those that must be condemned to die, would be an alleviation of their present miseries, while those wicked wretches have not deserved any favour: 'but I do it, that by being harassed with the present calamity, they may undergo greater misery.'

(179) On this account it was that Eutychus could not obtain a hearing, but was kept still in prison. However, some time afterwards, Tiberius came from Capreae to Tusculanum, which is about a hundred furlongs from Rome. Agrippa then desired of Antonia that she would procure a hearing for Eutychus, let the matter whereof he accused him prove what it would. (180) Now, Antonia was greatly esteemed by Tiberius on all accounts, from the dignity of her relation to him, who had been his brother Drusus' wife, and from her eminent charity; for though she was still a young woman, she continued in her widowhood, and refused all other matches, although Augustus had enjoined her to be married to somebody else; yet did she all along preserve her reputation free from reproach. (181) She had also been the greatest benefactress to Tiberius, when there was a very dangerous plot laid against him by Sejanus, a man who had been her husband's friend, and who had the greatest authority, because he was general of the army, and when many members of the senate, and many of the freedmen joined with him, and the soldiery was corrupted, and the plot was come to a great height. Now Sejanus had certainly gained his point, had not Antonia's boldness been more wisely conducted than Sejanus'

malice; (182) for, when she had discovered his designs against Tiberius, she wrote him an exact account of the whole, and gave the letter to Pallas, the most faithful of her servants, and sent him to Capreae to Tiberius, who, when he understood it, slew Sejanus and his confederates; so that Tiberius, who had her in great esteem before, now looked upon her with still greater respect, and depended upon her in all things. (183) So, when Tiberius was desired by this Antonia to examine Eutychus, he answered, 'If indeed Eutychus hath falsely accused Agrippa in what he hath said of him, he hath had sufficient punishment by what I have done to him already; but if, upon examination, the accusation appears to be true, let Agrippa have a care, lest, out of desire of punishing his freedman, he do not rather bring a punishment upon himself.' (184) Now when Antonia told Agrippa of this, he was still much more pressing that the matter might be examined into; so Antonia, upon Agrippa's lying hard at her continually to beg this favour, took the following opportunity: (185) as Tiberius lay once at his ease upon his sedan, and was carried about, and Caius, her grandson, and Agrippa, were before him after dinner, she walked by the sedan, and desired him to call Eutychus, and have him examined; (186) to which he replied, 'O Antonia! The gods are my witnesses that I am induced to do what I am going to do, not by my own inclination, but because I am forced to it by thy prayers.' When he had said this, he ordered Macro, who succeeded Sejanus, to bring Eutychus to him; accordingly, without any delay, he was brought. Then Tiberius asked him what he had to say against a man who had given him his liberty. (187) Upon which he said, 'O my lord! This Caius, and Agrippa with him, were once riding in a chariot, when I sat at their feet, and, among other discourses that passed, Agrippa said to Caius, O that the day would once come when this old fellow will die, and name thee for the governor of the habitable earth! For then this Tiberius, his grandson, would be no hindrance, but would be taken off by thee, and that earth would be happy, and I happy, also.' (188) Now, Tiberius took these to be truly Agrippa's words, and bearing a grudge withal at Agrippa, because, when he had commanded him to pay his respects to Tiberius, his grandson and the son of Drusus, Agrippa had not paid him that respect, but had disobeyed his commands, and transferred all his regard to Caius; (189) he said to Macro, 'Bind this man.' But Macro, not distinctly knowing which of them it was whom he bade him bind, and not expecting that he would have any such thing done to Agrippa, he forbore, and came to ask more distinctly what it was that he said. (190) But when Caesar had gone round the hippodrome, he found Agrippa standing: 'For certain,' said he, 'Macro, this is the man I meant to have bound;' and when he still asked, which of these is to be bound? he said, Agrippa. (191) Upon which Agrippa betook himself to make supplication for himself, putting him in mind of his son, with whom he was brought up, and of Tiberius [his grandson] whom he had educated, but all to no purpose, for they led him about bound even in his purple garments. (192) It was also very hot weather, and they had but little wine to their meal, so that he was very thirsty; he was also in a sort of agony, and took this treatment of him heinously: as he therefore saw one of Caius' slaves, whose name was Thaumastus, carrying some water in a vessel, (193) he desired that he would let him drink; so the servant gave him some water to drink; and he drank heartily, and said, 'O thou boy! This service of thine to me will be for thy advantage; for if I once get clear of these my bonds, I will soon procure thee thy freedom from Caius, who has not been wanting to minister to me now I am in bonds, in the same manner as when I was in my former state and dignity.' (194) Nor did he deceive him in what he promised him, but made him amends for what he had now done; for, when afterward Agrippa was come to the kingdom, he took particular care of Thaumastus, and got him his liberty from Caius, and made him the steward over his own estate; and when he died, he left him to Agrippa his son, and to Berenice his daughter, to minister to them in the same capacity. The man also grew old in that honourable post and therein died. But all this happened a good while later.

(195) Now Agrippa stood in his bonds before the royal palace, and leaned on a certain tree for grief, with many others, who were in bonds also; and as a certain bird sat upon the tree on which Agrippa leaned (the Romans called this bird bubo [an owl]), one of those that were bound, a German by nation, saw him, and asked a soldier who that man in purple was; (196) and when he was informed that his name was Agrippa, and that he was by nation a Jew, and one of the principal men of that nation, he asked leave of the soldier to whom he was bound, to let him come near to him, to speak with him; for that he had a mind to inquire of him about some things relating to his country; (197) which liberty, when he had obtained, as he stood near him, he said thus to him by an interpreter – 'This sudden change of thy condition, O young man, is grievous to thee, as bringing on thee a manifold and very great adversity; nor wilt thou believe me, when I foretell how thou wilt get clear of this misery which thou art now under, and how Divine Providence will provide for thee. (198) Know therefore (and I appeal to my own country gods, as well as to the gods of this place, who have awarded these bonds to us), that all I am going to say about thy concerns, shall neither be said for favour nor bribery, nor out of an endeavour to make thee cheerful without cause; (199) for such predictions, when they come to fail, make the grief at last, and in earnest, more bitter then if the party had never heard of any such thing. However, though I run the hazard of my own self, I think it fit to declare to thee the prediction of the gods. (200) It cannot be that thou shouldst long continue in these bonds; but thou wilt soon be delivered from them, and wilt be promoted to the highest dignity and power, and thou wilt be envied by all those who now pity thy hard

fortune; and thou wilt be happy till thy death, and wilt leave thine happiness to the children whom thou shalt have. But do thou remember, when thou seest this bird again, that thou wilt then live but five days longer. (201) This event will be brought to pass by that God who hath sent this bird hither to be a sign unto thee. And I cannot but think it unjust to conceal from thee what I foreknow concerning thee, that, by thy knowing beforehand what happiness is coming upon thee, thou mayst not regard thy present misfortunes. But, when this happiness shall actually befall thee, do not forget what misery I am in myself, but endeavour to deliver me.' (202) So when the German had said this, he made Agrippa laugh at him as much as he afterwards appeared worthy of admiration. But now Antonia took Agrippa's misfortune to heart: however, to speak to Tiberius on his behalf, she took to be a very difficult thing, and indeed quite impracticable as to any hope of success; (203) yet did she procure of Macro that the soldiers that kept him should be of a gentle nature, and that the centurion who was over them, and was to diet with him, should be of the same disposition, and that he might have leave to bathe himself every day, and that his freedmen and friends might come to him, and that other things that tended to ease him might be indulged him. (204) So his friend Silas came in to him, and two of his freedmen, Marsyas and Stechus, brought him such sorts of food as he was fond of, and indeed took great care of him; they also brought him garments, under pretence of selling them, and when night came on, they laid them under him; and the soldiers assisted them, as Macro had given them order to do beforehand. And this was Agrippa's condition for six months' time; and in this case were his affairs.

(205) But, as for Tiberius, upon his return to Capreae he fell sick. At first his distemper was but gentle; but as that distemper increased upon him, he had small or no hopes of recovery. Hereupon he bade Euodus, who was that freedman whom he most of all respected, to bring the children to him, for that he wanted to talk to them before he died. (206) Now he had at present no sons of his own alive; for Drusus, who was his only son, was dead; but Drusus' son Tiberius was still living, whose additional name was Gemellus: there was also living Caius, the son of Germanicus, who was the son of his brother [Drusus]. He was now grown up, and had had a liberal education, and was well improved by it, and was in esteem and favour with the people, on account of the excellent character of his father Germanicus, (207) who had attained the highest honour among the multitude, by the firmness of his virtuous behaviour, by the easiness and agreeableness of his conversing with the multitude, and because the dignity he was in did not hinder his familiarity with them all, as if they were his equals; (208) by which behaviour he was not only greatly esteemed by the people and the senate, but by every one of those nations that were subject to the Romans; some of whom were affected when they came to him, with the gracefulness of

their reception by him; and others were affected in the same manner by the report of the others that had been with him: and, upon his death there was a lamentation made by all men; (209) not such a one as was to be made in way of flattery to their rulers, while they did but counterfeit sorrow, but such as was real, while everybody grieved at his death, as if they had lost one that was near to them. And truly such had been his easy conversation with men, (210) that it turned greatly to the advantage of his son among all; and, among others, the soldiery were so peculiarly affected to him, that they reckoned it an eligible thing, if need were, to die themselves, if he might but attain to the government.

(211) But when Tiberius had given order to Euodus to bring the children to him the next day in the morning, he prayed to his country gods to show him a manifest signal, which of those children should come to the government; being very desirous to leave it to his son's son, but still depending upon what God would foreshow concerning them, more than upon his own opinion and inclination (212); so he made this to be the omen, that the government should be left to him who should come to him first the next day. When he had thus resolved within himself, he sent to his grandson's tutor, and ordered him to bring the child to him early in the morning, as supposing that God would permit him to be made emperor. But God proved opposite to his designation; (213) for, while Tiberius was thus contriving matters, and as soon as it was at all day, he bid Euodus to call in that child which should be there ready. So he went out, and found Caius before the door, for Tiberius was not yet come, but stayed waiting for his breakfast; for Euodus knew nothing of what his lord intended, so he said to Caius, 'Thy father calls thee,' and then brought him in. (214) As soon as Tiberius saw Caius, and not before, he reflected on the power of God, and how the ability of bestowing the government on whom he would was entirely taken from him; and thence he was not able to establish what he had intended. So he greatly lamented that his power of establishing what he had before contrived was taken from him, (215) and that his grandson Tiberius was not only to lose the Roman empire by his fatality, but his own safety also; because his preservation would now depend upon such as would be more potent than himself, who would think it a thing not to be borne, that a kinsman should live with them, and so his relation would not be able to protect him; but he would be feared and hated by him who had the supreme authority, partly on account of his being next to the empire, and partly on account of his perpetually contriving to get the government, both in order to preserve himself, and to be at the head of affairs also. (216) Now Tiberius had been very much given to astrology, and the calculation of nativities; and had spent his life in the esteem of what predictions had proved true, more than those whose profession it was. Accordingly, when he once saw Galba coming in to him, he said to his most intimate friends, that there came in a man that

would one day have the dignity of the Roman empire. (217) So that this Tiberius was more addicted to all such sorts of diviners than any other of the Roman emperors, because he had found them to have told him truth in his own affairs; (218) and indeed he was now in great distress upon this accident that had befallen him, and was very much grieved at the destruction of his son's son, which he foresaw, and complained of himself, that he should have made use of such a method of divination beforehand, while it was in his power to have died without grief by this knowledge of futurity; whereas he was not tormented by his foreknowledge of the misfortune of such as were dearest to him, and must die under that torment. (219) Now, although he was disordered at this unexpected revolution of the government to those for whom he did not intend it, he spake thus to Caius, though unwillingly, and against his own inclination: 'O child, although Tiberius be nearer related to me than thou art, I, by my own determination, and the conspiring suffrage of the gods, do give, and put into thy hand, the Roman empire; (220) and I desire thee never to be unmindful when thou comest to it, either of my kindness to thee, who set thee in so high a dignity, (221) or of thy relation to Tiberius: but as thou knowest that I am, together with and after the gods, the procurer of so great happiness to thee, so I desire that thou wilt make me a return for my readiness to assist thee, and wilt take care of Tiberius because of his near relation to thee. Besides which, thou art to know, that, while Tiberius is alive, he will be a security to thee, both as to empire and as to thy own preservation; but, if he die, that will be but a prelude to thy own misfortunes; (222) for to be alone under the weight of such vast affairs, is very dangerous; nor will the gods suffer those actions which are unjustly done, contrary to that law which directs men to do otherwise, to go off unpunished.' (223) This was the speech which Tiberius made; which did not persuade Caius to act accordingly, although he promised so to do; but, when he was settled in the government, he took off this Tiberius, as was predicted by the other Tiberius; as he was also himself, in no long time afterward, slain by a secret plot laid against him.

(224) So when Tiberius had at this time appointed Caius to be his successor, he outlived but a few days, and then died, after he had held the government twenty-two years five months and three days. Now Caius was the fourth emperor: (225) but when the Romans understood that Tiberius was dead, they rejoiced at the good news, but had not courage to believe it; not because they were unwilling it should be true, for they would have given large sums of money that it might be so, but because they were afraid that, if they had shown their joy when the news proved false, their joy should be openly known, and they should be accused for it, and be thereby undone; (226) for this Tiberius had brought a vast number of miseries on the best families of the Romans, since he was easily inflamed with passion in all cases, and was of such a temper as

rendered his anger irrevocable, till he had executed the same, although he had taken a hatred against men without reason: for he was by nature fierce in all the sentences he gave and made death the penalty for the slightest offences; (227) insomuch that when the Romans heard the rumour about his death gladly, they were restrained from the enjoyment of that pleasure by the dread of such miseries as they foresaw would follow, if their hopes proved ill-grounded. (228) Now Marsyas, Agrippa's freedman, as soon as he heard of Tiberius' death, came running to tell Agrippa the news; and finding him going out to the bath, he gave him a nod, and said, in the Hebrew tongue, 'The lion is dead'; (229) who, understanding his meaning, and being overjoyed at the news, 'Nay,' said he, 'but all sorts of thanks and happiness attend thee for this news of thine; only I wish that what thou sayest may prove true.' (230) Now the centurion who was set to keep Agrippa, when he saw with what haste Marsyas came, and what joy Agrippa had from what he said, he had a suspicion that his words implied some great innovation of affairs, and he asked them about what was said. (231) They at first diverted the discourse; but upon his further pressing, Agrippa, without more ado, told him, for he was already become his friend; so he joined with him in that pleasure which this news occasioned, because it would be fortunate to Agrippa, and made him a supper: but, as they were feasting, and the cups went about, there came one who said, that Tiberius was still alive, and would return to the city in a few days. (232) At which news the centurion was exceedingly troubled, because he had done what might cost him his life, to have treated so joyfully a prisoner, and this upon the news of the death of Caesar; so he thrust Agrippa from the couch whereon he lay, and said, 'Dost thou think to cheat me by a lie about the emperor without punishment? and shalt not thou pay for this thy malicious report at the price of thine head?' (233) When he had so said, he ordered Agrippa to be bound again (for he had loosed him before), and kept a severer guard over him than formerly, and in that evil condition was Agrippa that night; (234) but the next day the rumour increased in the city, and confirmed the news that Tiberius was certainly dead; insomuch that men durst now openly and freely talk about it; nay, some offered sacrifices on that account. Several letters also came from Caius; one of them to the senate, which informed them of the death of Tiberius, and of his own entrance on the government, (235) another to Piso, the governor of the city, which told him the same thing. He also gave order that Agrippa should be removed out of the camp, and go to that house where he lived before he was put in prison; so that he was now out of fear as to his own affairs: for, although he was still in custody, yet it was now with ease to his own affairs. (236) Now, as soon as Caius was come to Rome, and had brought Tiberius' dead body with him, and had made a sumptuous funeral for him, according to the laws of his country, he was much disposed to set Agrippa at liberty that very day; but

Antonia hindered him, not out of any ill will to the prisoner, but out of regard to decency in Caius, lest that should make men believe that he received the death of Tiberius with pleasure, when he loosed one whom he had bound immediately. (237) However, there did not many days pass ere he sent for him to his house, and had him shaved, and made him change his raiment; after which he put a diadem upon his head, and appointed him to be king of the tetrarchy of Philip. He also gave him the tetrarchy of Lysanias, and changed his iron chain for a golden one of equal weight. He also sent Marullus to be procurator of Judea.

(238) Now, in the second year of the reign of Caius Caesar, Agrippa desired leave to be given him to sail home, and settle the affairs of his government; and he promised to return again when he had put the rest in order, as it ought to be put. (239) So upon the emperor's permission, he came into his own country, and appeared to them all unexpectedly as a king, and thereby demonstrated to the men that saw him, the power of fortune, when they compared his former poverty with his present happy affluence; so some called him a happy man; and others could not well believe that things were so much changed with him for the better.

CHAPTER 7

(240) But Herodias, Agrippa's sister, who now lived as wife to that Herod who was tetrarch of Galilee and Perea, took this authority of her brother in an envious manner, particularly when she saw that he had a greater dignity bestowed on him than her husband had; since, when he ran away, he was not able to pay his debts; and now he was come back, it was because he was in a way of dignity and of great fortune. (241) She was therefore grieved and much displeased at so great a mutation of his affairs; and chiefly when she saw him marching among the multitude with the usual ensigns of royal authority, she was not able to conceal how miserable she was, by reason of the envy she had towards him; but she excited her husband, and desired him that he would sail to Rome, to court honours equal to his; (242) for she said, that she could not bear to live any longer, while Agrippa, the son of that Aristobulus who was condemned to die by his father, one that came to her husband in such extreme poverty, that the necessaries of life were forced to be entirely supplied him day by day; and when he fled away from his creditors by sea, he now returned a king: while he was himself the son of a king, and while the near relation he bare to royal authority, called upon him to gain the like dignity, he sat still, and was contented with a privater life. (243) 'But then, Herod, although thou wast formerly not concerned to be in a lower condition than thy father, from whom thou wast derived, had been, yet do thou now seek after the dignity

which thy kinsman hath attained to; and do not thou bear this contempt, that a man who admired thy riches should be in greater honour than thyself, nor suffer his poverty to show itself able to purchase greater things than our abundance; nor do thou esteem it other than a shameful thing to be inferior to one who, the other day, lived upon thy charity. (244) But let us go to Rome, and let us spare no pains nor expenses, either of silver or gold, since they cannot be kept for any better use than for the obtaining of a kingdom.'

(245) But for Herod, he opposed her request at this time, out of the love of ease, and having a suspicion of the trouble he should have at Rome; so he tried to instruct her better. But the more she saw him draw back, the more she pressed him to it, and desired him to leave no stone unturned in order to be king; (246) and at last she left not off till she engaged him, whether he would or not, to be of her sentiments, because he could no otherwise avoid her importunity. So he got all things ready, after as sumptuous a manner as he was able, and spared for nothing, and went up to Rome, and took Herodias along with him. (247) But Agrippa, when he was made sensible of their intentions and preparations, he also prepared to go thither; and as soon as he heard they set sail, he sent Fortunatus, one of his freedmen, to Rome, to carry presents to the emperor, and letters against Herod, and to give Caius a particular account of those matters, if he should have any opportunity. (248) This man followed Herod so quick, and had so prosperous a voyage, and came so little after Herod, that while Herod was with Caius, he came himself, and delivered his letters; for they both sailed to Dicearchia, and found Caius at Baiae, (249) which is itself a little city of Campania, at the distance of about five furlongs from Dicearchia. There are in that place royal palaces, with sumptuous apartments, every emperor still endeavouring to outdo his predecessor's magnificence; the place also affords warm baths, that spring out of the ground of their own accord, which are of advantage for the recovery of the health of those that make use of them; and, besides, they minister to men's luxury also. (250) Now Caius saluted Herod, for he first met with him, and then looked upon the letters which Agrippa had sent him, and which were written in order to accuse Herod; wherein he accused him, that he had been in confederacy with Sejanus, against Tiberius' government, and that he was now confederate with Artabanus, the king of Parthia, in opposition to the government of Caius; (251) as a demonstration of which, he alleged that he had armour sufficient for seventy thousand men ready in his armoury. Caius was moved at this information, and asked Herod, whether what was said about the armour was true; (252) and when he confessed there was such armour there, for he could not deny the same, the truth of it being too notorious, Caius took that to be a sufficient proof of the accusation, that he intended to revolt. So he took away from him his tetrarchy, and gave it by

way of addition to Agrippa's kingdom; he also gave Herod's money to Agrippa, and, by way of punishment, awarded him a perpetual banishment, and appointed Lyons a city of Gaul, to be his place of habitation. (253) But when he was informed that Herodias was Agrippa's sister, he made her a present of what money was her own, and told her that it was her brother who prevented her being put under the same calamity with her husband. (254) But she made this reply: 'Thou, indeed, O emperor, actest after a magnificent manner, and as becomes thyself, in what thou offerest me; but the kindness which I have for my husband hinders me from partaking of the favour of thy gift: for it is not just that I who have been made a partner in his prosperity, should forsake him in his misfortunes.' (255) Hereupon Caius was angry at her, and sent her with Herod into banishment, and gave her estate to Agrippa. And thus did God punish Herodias for her envy at her brother, and Herod also for giving ear to the vain discourses of a woman. (256) Now Caius managed public affairs with great magnanimity during the first and second year of his reign, and behaved himself with such moderation, that he gained the good will of the Romans themselves, and of his other subjects. But, in process of time, he went beyond the bounds of human nature in his conceit of himself, and, by reason of the vastness of his dominions, made himself a god, and took upon himself to act in all things to the reproach of the Deity itself.

CHAPTER 8

(257) There was now a tumult arisen at Alexandria, between the Jewish inhabitants and the Greeks; and three ambassadors were chosen out of each party that were at variance, who came to Caius. Now, one of these ambassadors from the people of Alexandria was Apion, who uttered many blasphemies against the Jews; and, among other things, that he said he charged them with neglecting the honours that belonged to Caesar; (258) for that while all who were subject to the Roman empire built altars and temples to Caius, and in other regards universally received him as they received the gods, these Jews alone thought it a dishonourable thing for them to erect statues in honour of him, as well as to swear by his name. (259) Many of these severe things were said by Apion, by which he hoped to provoke Caius to anger at the Jews, as he was likely to be. But Philo, the principal of the Jewish embassage, a man eminent on all accounts, brother to Alexander the alabarch, and one not unskilful in philosophy, was ready to betake himself to make his defence against those accusations; (260) but Caius prohibited him, and bid him be gone: he was also in such a rage, that it openly appeared he was about to do them some very great mischief; So Philo, being thus affronted, went out, and said to those Jews who were about him, that they should be of good courage, since Caius' words

indeed showed anger at them, but in reality had already set God against himself.

(261) Hereupon Caius, taking it very heinously that he should be thus despised by the Jews alone, sent Petronius to be president of Syria, and successor in the government to Vitellius, and gave him order to make an invasion into Judea, with a great body of troops, and if they would admit of his statue willingly, to erect it in the temple of God; but if they were obstinate, to conquer them by war, and then to do it. (262) Accordingly Petronius took the government of Syria, and made haste to obey Caesar's epistle. He got together as great a number of auxiliaries as he possibly could, and took with him two legions of the Roman army, and came to Ptolemais, and there wintered, as intending to set about the war in the spring. He also wrote word to Caius what he had resolved to do; who commended him for his alacrity, and ordered him to go on, and to make war with them, in case they would not obey his commands. (263) But there came many ten thousands of the Jews to Petronius, to Ptolemais, to offer their petitions to him, that he would not compel them to transgress and violate the law of their forefathers; (264) 'but if,' said they, 'thou art entirely resolved to bring this statue, and erect it, do thou first kill us, and then do what thou hast resolved on, for, while we are alive, we cannot permit such things as are forbidden us to be done by the authority of our legislator, and by our forefathers' determination that such prohibitions are instances of virtue.' (265) But Petronius was angry at them, and said, 'If indeed I were myself emperor, and were at liberty to follow my own inclination, and then had designed to act thus, these your words would be justly spoken to me; but now Caesar hath sent to me, I am under the necessity of being subservient to his decrees, because a disobedience to them will bring upon me inevitable destruction.' (266) Then the Jews replied, 'Since therefore thou art so disposed, O Petronius, that thou wilt not disobey Caius' epistles, neither will we transgress the commands of our law; and as we depend upon the excellency of our laws, and, by the labours of our ancestors, have continued hitherto without suffering them to be transgressed, we dare not by any means suffer ourselves to be so timorous as to transgress those laws out of the fear of death, (267) which God hath determined are for our advantage; and if we fall into misfortunes we will bear them, in order to preserve our laws, as knowing that those who expose themselves to dangers, have good hope of escaping them; because God will stand on our side when out of regard to him, we undergo afflictions, and sustain the uncertain turns of fortune. (268) But, if we should submit to thee, we should be greatly reproached for our cowardice, as thereby showing ourselves ready to transgress our law; and we should incur the great anger of God also, who, even thyself being judge, is superior to Caius.

(269) When Petronius saw by their words that their determination was hard to be removed, and that, without a war, he should not be able to be subservient

to Caius in the dedication of his statue, and that there must be a great deal of bloodshed, he took his friends, and the servants that were about him, and hasted to Tiberias, as wanting to know in what posture the affairs of the Jews were; (270) and many ten thousands of the Jews met Petronius again, when he was come to Tiberias. These thought they must run a mighty hazard if they should have a war with the Romans, but judged that the transgression of the law was of much greater consequence, (271) and made supplication to him, that he would by no means reduce them to such distresses, nor defile their city with the dedication of the statue. Then Petronius said to them, 'Will you then make war with Caesar, without considering his great preparations for war and your own weakness?' They replied, 'We will not by any means make war with him; but still we will die before we see our laws transgressed.' So they threw themselves down upon their faces, and stretched out their throats, and said they were ready to be slain; (272) and this they did for forty days together, and in the meantime left off the tilling of their ground, and that while the season of the year required them to sow it. Thus they continued firm in their resolution, and proposed to themselves to die willingly rather than to see the dedication of the statue.

(273) When matters were in this state, Aristobulus, king Agrippa's brother, and Helcias the Great, and the other principal men of that family with them, went in unto Petronius, and besought him, (274) that, since he saw the resolution of the multitude, he would not make any alteration, and thereby drive them to despair; but would write to Caius, that the Jews had an insuperable aversion to the reception of the statue, and how they continued with him, and left of the tillage of their ground: that they were not willing to go to war with him, because they were not able to do it, but were ready to die with pleasure, rather than suffer their laws to be transgressed: and how, upon the land's continuing unsown, robberies would grow up, on the inability they would be under of paying their tributes; (275) and that perhaps Caius might be thereby moved to pity, and not order any barbarous action to be done to them, nor think of destroying the nation: that if he continues inflexible in his former opinion to bring a war upon them, he may then set about it himself. (276) And thus did Aristobulus, and the rest with him, supplicate Petronius. So Petronius, partly on account of the pressing instances which Aristobulus and the rest with him made, and because of the great consequence of what they desired, and the earnestness wherewith they made their supplication – (277) partly on account of the firmness of the opposition made by the Jews, which he saw, while he thought it a horrible thing for him to be such a slave to the madness of Caius, as to slay so many ten thousand men only because of their religious disposition towards God, and after that to pass his life in expectation of punishment – Petronius, I say, thought it much better to send to Caius, and to let him know how intolerable it was to him to bear the anger

he might have against him for not serving him sooner, in obedience to his epistle, (278) for that perhaps he might persuade him; and that if this mad resolution continued, he might then begin the war against them; nay, that in case he should turn his hatred against himself, it was fit for virtuous persons even to die for the sake of such vast multitudes of men. Accordingly he determined to hearken to the petitions in this matter.

(279) He then called the Jews together to Tiberias, who came many ten thousands in number; he also placed that army he now had with him opposite to them: but did not discover his own meaning, but the commands of the emperor and told them that his wrath would, without delay, be executed on such as had the courage to disobey what he had commanded, and this immediately; and that it was fit for him who had received so great a dignity by his grant, not to contradict him in anything: (280) 'yet (said he) I do not think it just to have such a regard to my own safety and honour as to refuse to sacrifice them for your preservation, who are so many in number, and endeavour to preserve the regard that is due to your law; which as it hath come down to you from your forefathers, so do you esteem it worthy of your utmost contention to preserve it: nor, with the supreme assistance and power of God, will I be so hardy as to suffer your temple to fall into contempt by the means of the imperial authority. (281) I will, therefore, send to Caius, and let him know what your resolutions are, and will assist your suit as far as I am able, that you may not be exposed to suffer on account of the honest designs you have proposed to yourselves; and may God be your assistant, for his authority is beyond all the contrivance and power of men; and may he procure you the preservation of your ancient laws, and may not he be deprived, though without your consent, of his accustomed honours. (282) But if Caius be irritated, and turn the violence of his rage upon me, I will rather undergo all that danger and that affliction that may come either on my body or my soul, than see so many of you to perish, while you are acting in so excellent a manner. (283) Do you, therefore, every one of you go your way about your own occupations, and fall to the cultivation of your ground; I will myself send to Rome, and will not refuse to serve you in all things, both by myself and by my friends.'

(284) When Petronius had said this, and had dismissed the assembly of the Jews, he desired the principal of them to take care of their husbandry, and to speak kindly to the people, and encourage them to have good hope of their affairs. Thus did he readily bring the multitude to be cheerful again. And now did God show his presence to Petronius, and signify to him, that he would afford him his assistance in his whole design; (285) for he had no sooner finished the speech that he made to the Jews, but God sent down great showers of rain, contrary to human expectation; for that day was a clear day, and gave

no sign, by the appearance of the sky, of any rain; nay, the whole year had been subject to a great drought, and made men despair of any water from above, even when at any time they saw the heavens overcast with clouds; (286) insomuch, that when such a great quantity of rain came, and that in an unusual manner and without any other expectation of it, the Jews hoped that Petronius would by no means fail in his petition for them. But as to Petronius, he was mightily surprised when he perceived that God evidently took care of the Jews, and gave very plain signs of his appearance, and this to such a degree, that those that were in earnest much inclined to the contrary, had no power left to contradict it. (287) This was also among those other particulars which he wrote to Caius, which all tended to dissuade him, and by all means to entreat him not to make so many ten thousands of these men go distracted; whom, if he should slay (for without war they would by no means suffer the laws of their worship to be set aside) he would lose the revenue they paid him, and would be publicly cursed by them for all future ages. (288) Moreover, that God who was their governor, had shown his power most evidently on their account, and that such a power of his as left no room for doubt about it. And this was the business that Petronius was now engaged in.

(289) But King Agrippa, who now lived at Rome, was more and more in the favour of Caius; and when he had once made him a supper, and was careful to exceed all others, both in expenses and in such preparations as might contribute most to his pleasure; (290) nay, it was so far from the ability of others, that Caius himself could never equal, much less exceed it (such care had he taken beforehand to exceed all men, and particularly to make all agreeable to Caesar); (291) hereupon Caius admired his understanding and magnificence that he should force himself to do all to please him, even beyond such expenses as he could bear, and was desirous not to be behind Agrippa in that generosity which he exerted, in order to please him. So Caius, when he had drank wine plentifully, and was merrier than ordinary, said thus during the feast, when Agrippa had drank to him: (292) 'I knew before now how great a respect thou hast had for me, and how great kindness thou hast shown me, though with those hazards to thyself, which thou underwentest under Tiberius on that account; nor hast thou omitted anything to show thy good will towards us, even beyond thy ability; whence it would be a base thing for me to be conquered by thy affection. I am therefore desirous to make thee amends for everything in which I have been formerly deficient; (293) for all that I have bestowed on thee, that may be called *my gifts*, is but little. Everything that may contribute to thy happiness shall be at thy service, and that cheerfully, and so far as my ability will reach' – and this was what Caius said to Agrippa, thinking be would ask for some large country, or the revenues of certain cities; (294) but, although he had prepared beforehand what he would ask, yet had he not

discovered his intentions, but made this answer to Caius immediately, that it was not out of any expectation of gain that he formerly paid his respects to him, contrary to the commands of Tiberius, nor did he now do anything relating to him out of regard to his own advantage, and in order to receive anything from him: (295) that the gifts he had already bestowed upon him were great, and beyond the hopes of even a craving man; for, although they may be beneath thy power [who art the donor] yet are they greater than my inclination and dignity, who am the receiver – (296) and, as Caius was astonished at Agrippa's inclinations, and still the more pressed him to make his request for somewhat which he might gratify him with, Agrippa replied, 'Since thou, O my lord, declarest such is thy readiness to grant, that I am worthy of thy gifts, I will ask nothing relating to my own felicity; for what thou hast already bestowed on me has made me excel therein; (297) but I desire somewhat which may make thee glorious for piety, and render the Divinity assistant to thy designs, and may be for an honour to me among those that inquire about it, as showing that I never once fail of obtaining what I desire of thee; for my petition is this, that thou wilt no longer think of the dedication of that statue which thou hast ordered to be set up in the Jewish temple by Petronius.'

(298) And thus did Agrippa venture to cast the die upon this occasion, so great was the affair in his opinion, and in reality, though he knew how dangerous a thing it was so to speak; for, had not Caius approved it, it had tended to no less than the loss of his life. (299) So Caius, who was mightily taken with Agrippa's obliging behaviour, and on other accounts thinking it a dishonourable thing to be guilty of falsehood before so many witnesses, in points wherein he had with such alacrity forced Agrippa to become a petitioner, and that it would look as if he had already repented of what he had said, (300) and because he greatly admired Agrippa's virtue, in not desiring him at all to augment his own dominions, either with larger revenues or other authority, but took care of the public tranquillity, of the laws, and of the Divinity itself, he granted him what he had requested. He also wrote thus to Petronius, commending him for his assembling his army, and then consulting him about these affairs. (301) 'If, therefore,' said he, 'thou hast already erected my statue, let it stand; but if thou hast not yet dedicated it, do not trouble thyself further about it, but dismiss thy army, go back, and take care of those affairs which I sent thee about at first, for I have now no occasion for the erection of that statue. This I have granted as a favour to Agrippa, a man whom I honour so very greatly, that I am not able to contradict what he would have, or what he desired me to do for him.' (302) And this was what Caius wrote to Petronius, which was before he received his letter, informing him that the Jews were very ready to revolt about this statue, and that they seemed resolved to threaten war against the Romans, and nothing else.

(303) When therefore Caius was much displeased that any attempt should be made against his government, as he was a slave to base and vicious actions on all occasions, and had no regard to what was virtuous and honourable, and against whomsoever he resolved to show his anger, and that for any cause whatsoever, he suffered not himself to be restrained by any admonition, but thought the indulging his anger to be a real pleasure, he wrote thus to Petronius: (304) 'Seeing thou esteemest the presents made thee by the Jews to be of greater value than my commands, and art grown insolent enough to be subservient to their pleasure, I charge thee to become thy own judge, and to consider what thou art to do, now thou art under my displeasure; for I will make thee an example to the present and to all future ages, that they may not dare to contradict the commands of their emperor.'

(305) This was the epistle which Caius wrote to Petronius; but Petronius did not receive it while Caius was alive, that ship which carried it sailing so slow, that other letters came to Petronius before this, by which he understood that Caius was dead; (306) for God would not forget the dangers Petronius had undertaken on account of the Jews, and of his own honour. But when he had taken Caius away, out of his indignation of what he had so insolently attempted, in assuming to himself divine worship, both Rome and all that dominion conspired with Petronius, especially those that were of the senatorian order, to give Caius his due reward, because he had been unmercifully severe to them; (307) for he died not long after he had written to Petronius that epistle which threatened him with death. But as for the occasion of his death, and the nature of the plot against him, I shall relate them in the progress of this narration. (308) Now, that epistle which informed Petronius of Caius' death came first; and a little afterward came that which commanded him to kill himself with his own hands. Whereupon he rejoiced at this coincidence as to the death of Caius, (309) and admired God's providence, who, without the least delay, and immediately, gave him a reward for the regard he had to the temple, and the assistance he afforded the Jews for avoiding the dangers they were in. And by this means Petronius escaped that danger of death which he could not foresee.

CHAPTER 9

(310) A very sad calamity now befell the Jews that were in Mesopotamia, and especially those that dwelt in Babylonia. Inferior it was to none of the calamities which had gone before, and came together with a great slaughter of them, and that greater than any upon record before; concerning all which I shall speak accurately, and shall explain the occasions whence these miseries came upon them. (311) There was a city of Babylonia called Neerda; not only a very populous one, but one that had a good and large territory about it; and,

besides its other advantages, full of men also. It was, besides, not easily to be assaulted by enemies, from the river Euphrates encompassing it all round, and from the walls that were built about it. (312) There was also the city Nisibis, situate on the same current of the river. For which reason the Jews, depending on the natural strength of these places, deposited in them that half shekel which everyone, by the custom of our country, offers unto God, as well as they did other things devoted to him; for they made use of these cities as a treasury, (313) whence at a proper time, they were transmitted to Jerusalem; and many ten thousand men undertook the carriage of those donations, out of fear of the ravages of the Parthians, to whom the Babylonians were then subject. (314) Now, there were two men, Asineus and Anileus, of the city Neerda by birth, and brethren to one another. They were destitute of a father; and their mother put them to learn the art of weaving curtains, it not being esteemed a disgrace among them for men to be weavers of cloth. Now, he that taught them that art, and was set over them, complained that they came too late to their work, and punished them with stripes: (315) but they took this just punishment as an affront, and carried off all the weapons which were kept in that house, which were not a few, and went into a certain place where was a partition of the rivers, and was a place naturally very fit for the feeding of cattle, and for preserving such fruits as were usually laid up against winter. The poorest sort of the young men also resorted to them, whom they armed with the weapons they had gotten, and became their captains; and nothing hindered them from being their leaders into mischief; (316) for, as soon as they were become invincible, and had built them a citadel, they sent to such as fed cattle, and ordered them to pay them so much tribute out of them as might be sufficient for their maintenance, proposing also that they would be their friends, if they would submit to them, and that they would defend them from all their other enemies on every side; but that they would kill the cattle of those that refused to obey them. (317) So they hearkened to their proposals (for they could do nothing else), and sent them as many sheep as were required of them; whereby their forces grew greater, and they became lords over all they pleased because they marched suddenly, and did them a mischief, insomuch that everybody who had to do with them chose to pay them respect; and they became formidable to such as came to assault them, till the report about them came to the ears of the king of Parthia himself.

(318) But when the governor of Babylonia understood this, and had a mind to put a stop to them before they grew greater, and before greater mischiefs should arise from them, he got together as great an army as he could, both of Parthians and Babylonians, and marched against them, thinking to attack them and destroy them before anyone should carry them the news that he had got an army together. (319) He then encamped at a lake, and lay still; but on the next

day (it was the Sabbath, which is among the Jews a day of rest from all sorts of work) he supposed that the enemy would not dare to fight him thereon, but that he would take them and carry them away prisoners, without fighting. He therefore proceeded gradually, and thought to fall upon them on the sudden. (320) Now Asineus was sitting with the rest, and their weapons lay by them; upon which he said, 'Sirs, I hear a neighing of horses; not of such as are feeding, but such as have men on their backs; I also hear such a noise of their bridles, that I am afraid that some enemies are coming upon us to encompass us round. However, let somebody go to look about, and make report of what reality there is in the present state of things; and may what I have said prove a false alarm!' (321) And when he had said this, some of them went out to spy out what was the matter; and they came again immediately, and said to him, that 'neither hast thou been mistaken in telling us what our enemies were doing, nor will those enemies permit us to be injurious to people any longer. (322) We are caught by their intrigues like brute beasts, and there is a large body of cavalry marching upon us, while we are destitute of hands, to defend ourselves withal, because we are restrained from doing it by the prohibition of our law, which obliges us to rest [on this day].' (323) But Asineus did not by any means agree with the opinion of his spy as to what was to be done, but thought it more agreeable to the law to pluck up their spirits in this necessity they were fallen into, and break their law by avenging themselves, although they should die in the action, than by doing nothing to please their enemies in submitting to be slain by them. Accordingly, he took up his weapons, and infused courage into those that were with him, to act as courageously as himself. (324) So they fell upon their enemies, and slew a great many of them, because they despised them, and came as to a certain victory, and put the rest to flight.

(325) But when the news of this fight came to the king of Parthia, he was surprised at the boldness of these brethren, and was desirous to see them, and speak with them. He therefore sent the most trusty of all his guards to say thus to them: (326) 'That King Artabanus, although he had been unjustly treated by you, who have made an attempt against his government, yet hath he more regard to your courageous behaviour than to the anger he bears to you, and hath sent me to give you his right hand and security: and he permits you to come to him safely, and without any violence upon the road, and he wants to have you address yourselves to him as friends, without meaning any guile or deceit to you. He also promises to make you presents, and to pay you those respects which will make an addition of his power to your courage, and thereby be of advantage to you.' (327) Yet did Asineus himself put off his journey thither, but sent his brother Anileus with all such presents as he could procure. So he went, and was admitted to the king's presence; and when Artabanus saw Anileus coming alone he inquired into the reason why Asineus

avoided to come alone with him; (328) and when he understood that he was afraid, and stayed by the lake, he took an oath, by the gods of his country, that he would do them no harm, if they came to him upon the assurances he gave them, and gave him his right hand. This is of the greatest force there with all these barbarians, and affords a firm security to those who converse with them; (329) for none of them will deceive you when once they have given you their right hands, nor will anyone doubt of their fidelity, when that is once given, even though they were before suspected of injustice. When Artabanus had done this, he sent away Anileus to persuade his brother to come to him. (330) Now this the king did, because he wanted to curb his own governors of provinces by the courage of these Jewish brethren, lest they should make a league with them; for they were ready for a revolt, and were disposed to rebel, had they been sent on an expedition against them. (331) He was also afraid, lest when he was engaged in a war, in order to subdue those governors of provinces that had revolted, the party of Asineus and those in Babylonia should be augmented, and either make war upon him when they should hear of that revolt, or if they should be disappointed in that case, they would not fail of doing further mischief to him.

(332) When the king had these intentions, he sent away Anileus; and Anileus prevailed on his brother [to come to the king], when he had related to him the king's good will, and the oath that he had taken. Accordingly they made haste to go to Artabanus, (333) who received them, when they were come, with pleasure, and admired Asineus' courage in the actions he had done, and this because he was a little man to see to, and at first sight appeared contemptible also, and such as one might deem a person of no value at all. He also said to his friends, how, upon the comparison, he showed his soul to be, in all respects, superior to his body; and when as they were drinking together, he once showed Asineus to Abdagases, one of the generals of his army, and told him his name, and described the great courage he was of in war, (334) and Abdagases had desired leave to kill him, and thereby to inflict on him a punishment for those injuries he had done to the Parthian government, the king replied, 'I will never give thee leave to kill a man who hath depended on my faith, especially not after I have set him my right hand, and endeavoured to gain his belief by oaths made by the gods. (335) But, if thou beest a truly warlike man, thou standest not in need of my perjury. Go thou, then, and avenge the Parthian government, attack this man, when he is returned back, and conquer him by the forces that are under thy command, without my privity.' (336) Hereupon the king called for Asineus, and said to him, 'It is time for thee, O thou young man! to return home, and not provoke the indignation of my generals in this place any further, lest they attempt to murder thee, and that without my approbation. (337) I commit to thee the country of Babylonia

in trust, that it may, by thy care, be preserved free from robbers, and from other mischiefs. I have kept my faith inviolable to thee, and that not in trifling affairs, but in those that concerned thy safety, and do therefore deserve thou shouldst be kind to me.' (338) When he had said this, and given Asineus some presents, he sent him away immediately, who, when he was come home, built fortresses, and became great in a little time, and managed things with such courage and success, as no other person, that had no higher a beginning, ever did before him. (339) Those Parthian governors also, who were sent that way, paid him great respect; and the honour that was paid him by the Babylonians seemed to them too small, and beneath his deserts, although he were in no small dignity and power there; nay, indeed, all the affairs of Mesopotamia depended upon him; and he more and more flourished in this happy condition of his for fifteen years.

(340) But as their affairs were in so flourishing a state, there sprang up a calamity among them on the following occasion. When once they had deviated from that course of virtue whereby they had gained so great power, they affronted and transgressed the laws of their forefathers, and fell under the dominion of their lusts and pleasures. A certain Parthian, who came as general of an army into those parts, (341) had a wife following him, who had a vast reputation for other accomplishments, and particularly was admired above all other women for her beauty. (342) Anileus, the brother of Asineus, either heard of that her beauty from others, or perhaps saw her himself also, and so became at once her lover and her enemy; partly because he could not hope to enjoy this woman but by obtaining power over her as a captive, and partly because he thought he could not conquer his inclinations for her. (343) As soon, therefore, as her husband had been declared an enemy to them, and was fallen in the battle, the widow of the deceased was married to this her lover. However, this woman did not come into their house without producing great misfortunes, both to Anileus himself, and to Asineus also; but brought great mischiefs upon them on the occasion following. (344) Since she was led away captive, on the death of her husband, she concealed the images of those gods which were their country gods, common to her husband and herself: now it is the custom of that country for all to have the idols they worship in their own houses, and to carry them along with them when they go into a foreign land; agreeable to which custom of theirs she carried her idols with her. Now, at first she performed her worship to them privately, but when she was become Anileus' married wife, she worshipped them in her accustomed manner, and with the same appointed ceremonies which she used in her former husband's days: (345) upon which their most esteemed friends blamed him at first, that he did not act after the manner of the Hebrews, nor perform what was agreeable to their laws, in marrying a foreign wife, and one that transgressed the accurate

appointments of their sacrifices and religious ceremonies; that he ought to consider, lest by allowing himself in many pleasures of the body he might lose his principality, on account of the beauty of a wife, and that high authority which, by God's blessing, he had arrived at. (346) But when they prevailed not at all upon him, he slew one of them for whom he had greatest respect, because of the liberty he took with him; who, when he was dying, out of regard to the laws, imprecated a punishment upon his murderer Anileus and upon Asineus also, and that all their companions might come to a like end from their enemies; (347) upon the two first as the principal actors of this wickedness, and upon the rest as those that would not assist him when he suffered in the defence of their laws. Now these latter were sorely grieved, yet did they tolerate these doings, because they remembered that they had arrived at their present happy state by no other means than their fortitude. (348) But when they also heard of the worship of those gods whom the Parthians adore, they thought the injury that Anileus offered to their laws was to be borne no longer; and a greater number of them came to Asineus, and loudly complained of Anileus, (349) and told him, that it had been well that he had of himself seen what was advantageous to them; but that, however, it was now high time to correct what had been done amiss, before the crime that had been committed proved the ruin of himself and all the rest of them. They added, that the marriage of this woman was made without their consent, and without a regard to their old laws; and that the worship which this woman paid [to her gods] was a reproach to the God whom they worshipped. (350) Now Asineus was sensible of his brother's offence, that it had been already the cause of great mischiefs, and would be so for the time to come; yet did he tolerate the same from the good will he had to so near a relation, and forgiving it to him, on account that his brother was quite overborne by his wicked inclinations. (351) But as more and more still came about him every day, and the clamours about it became greater, he at length spake to Anileus about these clamours, reproving him for his former actions, and desiring him for the future to leave them off, and send the woman back to her relations. (352) But nothing was gained by these reproofs; for as the woman perceived what a tumult was made among the people on her account, and was afraid for Anileus, lest he should come to any harm for his love to her, she infused poison into Asineus's food, and hereby took him off, and was now secure of prevailing, when her lover was to be judge of what should be done about her.

(353) So Anileus took the government upon himself alone, and led his army against the villages of Mithridates, who was a man of principal authority in Parthia, and had married King Artabanus' daughter; he also plundered them, and among that prey was found much money, and many slaves, as also a great

number of sheep, and many other things, which, when gained, make men's condition happy. (354) Now, when Mithridates, who was there at this time, heard that his villages were taken, he was very much displeased to find that Anileus had first begun to injure him, and to affront him in his present dignity, when he had not offered any injury to him beforehand; and he got together the greatest body of horsemen he was able, and those out of that number which were of an age fit for war, and came to fight Anileus: and when he was arrived at a certain village of his own, he lay still there, as intending to fight him on the day following, because it was the Sabbath, the day on which the Jews rest. (355) And when Anileus was informed of this by a Syrian stranger of another village, who not only gave him an exact account of other circumstances, but told him where Mithridates would have a feast, he took his supper at a proper time, and marched by night, with an intent of falling upon the Parthians while they were unapprised what they should do; (356) so he fell upon them about the fourth watch of the night; and some of them he slew while they were asleep, and others he put to flight, and took Mithridates alive, and set him naked upon an ass, which among the Parthians, is esteemed the greatest reproach possible. (357) And when he had brought him into a wood with such a resolution, and his friends desired him to kill Mithridates, he soon told them his own mind to the contrary, and said, that it was not right to kill a man who was of one of the principal families among the Parthians, and greatly honoured with matching into the royal family; (358) that so far as they had hitherto gone was tolerable; for although they had injured Mithridates, yet if they preserved his life, this benefit would be remembered by him to the advantage of those that gave it him; (359) but that if he were once put to death, the king would not be at rest till he had made a great slaughter of the Jews that dwelt at Babylon: 'to whose safety we ought to have a regard, both on account of our relation to them, and because, if any misfortune befall us, we have no other place to retire to, since he hath gotten the flower of their youth under him.' (360) By this thought, and this speech of his made in council, he persuaded them to act accordingly; so Mithridates was let go. But, when he was got away, his wife reproached him, that although he was son-in-law to the king, he neglected to avenge himself on those that had injured him, while he took no care about it, (361) but was contented to have been made a captive by the Jews, and to have escaped them; and she bade him either to go back like a man of courage, or else she sware by the gods of their royal family, that she would certainly dissolve her marriage with him. (362) Upon which, partly because he could not bear the daily trouble of her taunts, and partly because he was afraid of her insolence, lest she should in earnest dissolve their marriage, he unwillingly, and against his inclinations, got together again as great an army as he could, and marched along with them, as himself thinking it a thing not to be borne any longer, that he, a Parthian, should owe his preservation to the Jews, when they had been too hard for him in the war.

(363) But as soon as Anileus understood that Mithridates was marching with a great army against him, he thought it too ignominious a thing to tarry about the lakes, and not to take the first opportunity of meeting his enemies, and he hoped to have the same success, and to beat their enemies as they did before; as also he ventured boldly upon the like attempts. Accordingly he led out his army; (364) and a great many more joined themselves to that army, in order to betake themselves to plunder the people, and in order to terrify the enemy again by their numbers. (365) But when they had marched ninety furlongs, while the road had been through dry [and sandy] places, and about the midst of the day, they were become very thirsty; and Mithridates appeared, and fell upon them, as they were in distress for want of water, on which account, and on account of the time of the day, they were not able to bear their weapons. (366) So Anileus and his men were put to an ignominious rout, while men in despair were to attack those that were fresh, and in good plight; so a great slaughter was made, and many ten thousand men fell. Now Anileus, and all that stood firm about him, ran away, as fast as they were able, into a wood, and afforded Mithridates the pleasure of having gained a great victory over them. (367) But there now came in to Anileus a conflux of bad men, who regarded their own lives very little if they might but gain some present ease, insomuch that they, by thus coming to him, compensated the multitude of those that perished in the fight. Yet were not these men like to those that fell, because they were rash, and unexercised in war; (368) however, with these he came upon the villages of the Babylonians, and a mighty devastation of all things was made there by the injuries that Anileus did them. (369) So the Babylonians, and those that had already been in the war, sent to Neerda to the Jews there, and demanded Anileus. But, although they did not agree to their demands (for if they had been willing to deliver him up, it was not in their power so to do); yet did they desire to make peace with them. To which the other replied, that they also wanted to settle conditions of peace with them, and sent men together with the Babylonians, who discoursed with Anileus about them. (370) But the Babylonians, upon taking a view of his situation, and having learned where Anileus and his men lay, fell secretly upon them as they were drunk and fallen asleep, and slew all that they caught of them, without any fear, and killed Anileus himself also.

(371) The Babylonians were now freed from Anileus's heavy incursions, which had been a great restraint to the effects of that hatred they bore to the Jews: for they were almost always at variance, by reason of the contrariety of their laws; and which party soever grew boldest before the other, they assaulted the other: and at this time in particular it was, that upon the ruin of

Anileus' party, the Babylonians attacked the Jews, (372) which made those Jews so vehemently to resent the injuries they received from the Babylonians, that, being neither able to fight them, nor bearing to live with them, they went to Seleucia, the principal city of those parts, which was built by Seleucus Nicator. It was inhabited by many of the Macedonians, but by more of the Grecians; not a few of the Syrians also dwelt there; (373) and thither did the Jews fly and lived there five years, without any misfortunes. But, on the sixth year, a pestilence came upon these at Babylon, which occasioned new removals of men's habitations out of that city; and because they came to Seleucia, it happened that a still heavier calamity came upon them on that account – which I am going to relate immediately.

(374) Now the way of living of the people of Seleucia, who were Greeks and Syrians, was commonly quarrelsome, and full of discords, though the Greeks were too hard for the Syrians. When, therefore, the Jews were come thither, and dwelt among them, there arose a sedition; and the Syrians were too hard for the other, by the assistance of the Jews, who are men that despise dangers, and very ready to fight upon any occasion. (375) Now, when the Greeks had the worst in this sedition, and saw that they had but one way of recovering their former authority, and that was, if they could prevent the agreement between the Jews and the Syrians, they every one discoursed with such of the Syrians as were formerly their acquaintance, and promised they would be at peace and friendship with them. (376) Accordingly, they gladly agreed so to do; and when this was done by the principal men of both nations, they soon agreed to a reconciliation; and when they were so agreed, they both knew that the great design of such their union would be their common hatred to the Jews. Accordingly they fell upon them, and slew about fifty thousand of them; nay, the Jews were all destroyed, excepting a few who escaped, either by the compassion which their friends or neighbours afforded them in order to let them fly away. (377) These retired to Ctesiphon, a Grecian city, and situated near to Seleucia, where the king [of Parthia] lives in winter every year, and where the greatest part of his riches are reposited; but the Jews had here no certain settlement, those of Seleucia having little concern for the king's honour. (378) Now the whole nation of the Jews were in fear both of the Babylonians and of the Seleucians, because all the Syrians that live in those places agreed with the Seleucians in the war against the Jews; (379) so the most of them gathered themselves together, and went to Neerda and Nisibis, and obtained security there by the strength of those cities; besides which, their inhabitants, who were a great many, were all warlike men. And this was the state of the Jews at this time in Babylonia.

BOOK NINETEEN

(1) Now this Caius did not demonstrate his madness in offering injuries only to the Jews at Jerusalem, or to those that dwelt in the neighbourhood, but suffered it to extend itself through all the earth and sea, so far as was in subjection to the Romans, and filled it with ten thousand mischiefs; so many indeed in number as no former history relates. (2) But Rome itself felt the most dismal effects of what he did, while he deemed that not to be any way more honourable than the rest of the cities; but he pulled and hauled its other citizens, but especially the senate, and particularly the nobility, and such as had been dignified by illustrious ancestors; (3) he also had ten thousand devices against such of the equestrian order, as it was styled, who were esteemed by the citizens equal in dignity and wealth with the senators, because out of them the senators were themselves chosen; these he treated after an ignominious manner, and removed them out of his way while they were at once slain, and their wealth plundered; because he slew men generally, in order to seize on their riches. (4) He also asserted his own divinity, and insisted on greater honours to be paid him by his subjects than are due to mankind. He also frequented that temple of Jupiter which they style the Capitol, which is with them the most holy of all temples, and had boldness enough to call himself the brother of Jupiter. (5) And other pranks he did like a madman; as when he laid a bridge from the city Dicearchia, which belongs to Campania, to Misenum, another city upon the seaside, (6) from one promontory to another, of the length of thirty furlongs, as measured over the sea. And this was done, because he esteemed it to be a most tedious thing to row over it in a small ship, and thought withal that it became him to make that bridge, as he was lord of the sea, and might oblige it to give marks of obedience as well as the earth; so he enclosed the whole bay within his bridge, and drove his chariot over it; and thought, that as he was a god, it was fit for him to travel over such roads as this was. (7) Nor did he abstain from the plunder of any of the Grecian temples, and gave order that all the engravings and sculptures, and the rest of the ornaments of the statues and donations therein dedicated, should be brought to him, saying that the best things ought to be set nowhere but in the best place, and that the city of Rome was that best place. (8) He also adorned his own house and his gardens with the curiosities brought from those temples, together with the houses he lay at when he travelled all over Italy; whence he did not

scruple to give a command, that the statue of Jupiter Olympius, so called because he was honoured at the Olympian games by the Greeks, which was the work of Phidias the Athenian, should be brought to Rome. (9) Yet did not he compass his end, because the architects told Memmius Regulus, who was commanded to remove that statue of Jupiter, that the workmanship was such as would be spoiled, and would not bear the removal. It was also reported that Memmius, both on that account, and on account of some such mighty prodigies as are of an incredible nature, put off the taking it down, (10) and wrote to Caius those accounts, as his apology for not having done what his epistle required of him; and that when he was thence in danger of perishing, he was saved by Caius being dead himself, before he had put him to death.

(11) Nay, Caius' madness came to this height, that when he had a daughter born, he carried her into the capitol, and put her upon the knees of the statue, and said that the child was common to him and to Jupiter, and determined that she had two fathers – but which of these fathers were the greatest, he left undetermined; (12) and yet mankind bore him in such his pranks. He also gave leave to slaves to accuse their masters of any crimes whatsoever they pleased; for all such accusations were terrible, because they were in great part made to please him, and at his suggestion, (13) insomuch that Pollux, Claudius' slave, had the boldness to lay an accusation against Claudius himself; and Caius was not ashamed to be present at his trial of life and death, to hear that trial of his own uncle, in hopes of being able to take him off, although he did not succeed to his mind; (14) but when he had filled the whole habitable world which he governed with false accusations and miseries, and had occasioned the greatest insults of slaves against their masters, who indeed, in a great measure ruled them, there were many secret plots now laid against him; some in anger, and in order for men to revenge themselves on account of the miseries they had already undergone from him; and others made attempts upon him, in order to take him off before they should fall into such great miseries, (15) while his death came very fortunately for the preservation of the laws of all men, and had a great influence upon the public welfare; and this happened most happily for our nation in particular, which had almost utterly perished if he had not been suddenly slain; and I confess I have a mind to give a full account of this matter particularly, (16) because it will afford great assurance of the power of God, and great comfort to those that are under afflictions, and wise caution to those who think their happiness will never end, nor bring them at length to the most lasting miseries, if they do not conduct their lives by the principles of virtue.

(17) Now there were three several conspiracies made, in order to take off Caius, and each of these three were conducted by excellent persons. Emilius Regulus, born at Corduba in Spain, got some men together, and was desirous to take Caius off, either by them or by himself. (18) Another conspiracy there

was laid by them, under the conduct of Cherea Cassius, the tribune [of the pretorian band]; Minucianus Annius was also one of great consequence among those that were prepared to oppose his tyranny. (19) Now the several occasions of these men's several hatred and conspiracy against Caius were these: Regulus had indignation and hatred against all injustice, for he had a mind naturally angry, and bold, and free, which made him not conceal his counsels; so he communicated them to many of his friends, and to others who seemed to him persons of activity and vigour; (20) Minucianus entered into this conspiracy, because of the injustice done to Lepidus, his particular friend, and one of the best character of all the citizens, whom Caius had slain, as also because he was afraid for himself, since Caius' wrath tended to the slaughter of all alike; (21) and for Cherea, he came in because he thought it a deed worthy of a free, ingenuous man to kill Caius, and was ashamed of the reproaches he lay under from Caius, as though he were a coward; as also because he was himself in danger every day from his friendship with him, and the observance he paid him. (22) These men proposed this attempt to all the rest that were concerned, who saw the injuries that were offered them, and were desirous that Caius' slaughter might succeed by their mutual assistance of one another, that they might themselves escape being killed by the taking off Caius; that perhaps they should gain their point, and that it would be a happy thing if they should gain it, to approve themselves to so many excellent persons as earnestly wished to be partakers with them in their design, for the delivery of the city and of the government, even at the hazard of their own lives; (23) but still Cherea was the most zealous of them all, both out of a desire of getting himself the greatest name, and also by reason of his access to Caius' presence with less danger, because he was tribune, and could therefore the more easily kill him.

(24) Now, at this time came on the horse races [Circensian games]; the view of which games was eagerly desired by the people of Rome, for they come with great alacrity into the hippodrome [circus] at such times, and petition their emperors, in great multitudes, for what they stand in need of; who usually did not think fit to deny them their requests, but readily and gratefully granted them. (25) Accordingly they most importunately desired that Caius would now ease them in their tributes, and abate somewhat of the rigour of the taxes imposed upon them; but he would not hear their petition, and when their clamours increased, he sent soldiers, some one way and some another, and gave order that they should lay hold on those that made the clamours, and without any more ado, bring them out and put them to death. (26) These were Caius' commands, and those who were commanded executed the same; and the number of those who were slain on this occasion was very great. Now the people saw this, and bore it so far, that they left off clamouring, because they saw with their own eyes, that this petition to be relieved, as to the payment of

their money, brought immediate death upon them. (27) These things made Cherea more resolute to go on with his plot, in order to put an end to this barbarity of Caius against men. He then, at several times, thought to fall upon Caius as he was feasting, yet did he restrain himself by some considerations; not that he had any doubt on him about killing him, but as watching for a proper season, that the attempt might not be frustrated, but that he might give the blow so as might certainly gain his purpose.

(28) Cherea had been in the army a long time, yet was he not pleased with conversing so much with Caius: but Caius had set him to require the tributes and other dues, which, when not paid in due time, were forfeited to Caesar's treasury; and he had made some delays in requiring them, because those burdens had been doubled: and had rather indulged his own mild disposition than performed Caius' command; (29) nay, indeed, be provoked Caius to anger by his sparing men, and pitying the hard fortunes of those from whom he demanded the taxes; and Caius upbraided him with his sloth and effeminacy in being so long about collecting the taxes: and indeed he did not only affront him in other respects, but when he gave him the watchword of the day, to whom it was to be given by his place, he gave him feminine words, (30) and those of a nature very reproachful; and these watchwords he gave out, as having been initiated in the secrets of certain mysteries, which he had been himself the author of. Now, although he had sometimes put on women's clothes, and had been wrapped in some embroidered garments to them belonging, and done a great many other things in order to make the company mistake him for a woman, yet did he, by way of reproach, object the like womanish behaviour to Cherea. (31) But when Cherea received the watchword from him, he had indignation at it, but had greater indignation at the delivery of it to others, as being laughed at by those that received it; insomuch that his fellow tribunes made him the subject of their drollery; for they would foretell that he would bring them some of his usual watchwords when he was about to take the watchword from Caesar, and would thereby make him ridiculous; (32) on which account he took the courage of assuming certain partners to him, as having just reasons for his indignation against Caius. Now there was one Pompedius, a senator, and one who had gone through almost all posts in the government, but otherwise an Epicurean, and for that reason loved to lead an inactive life. (33) Now Timidius, an enemy of his, had informed Caius that he had used indecent reproaches against him, and he made use of Quintilia for a witness to them: a woman she was much beloved by many that frequented the theatre, and particularly by Pompedius, on account of her great beauty. (34) Now this woman thought it a horrible thing to attest to an accusation that touched the life of her lover, which was also a lie. Timidius, however, wanted to have her brought to the torture. Caius was irritated at this

reproach upon him, and commanded Cherea, without any delay, to torture Quintilia, as he used to employ Cherea in such bloody matters, and those that required the torture, because he thought he would do it the more barbarously, in order to avoid that imputation of effeminacy which he had laid upon him. (35) But Quintilia, when she was brought to the rack, trod upon the foot of one of her associates, and let him know that he might be of good courage, and not be afraid of the consequence of her tortures, for that she would bear them with magnanimity. Cherea tortured this woman after a cruel manner; unwillingly indeed, but because he could not help it. He then brought her, without being in the least moved at what she had suffered, into the presence of Caius, and that in such a state as was sad to behold; (36) and Caius, being somewhat affected with the sight of Quintilia, who had her body miserably disordered by the pains she had undergone, freed both her and Pompedius of the crime laid to their charge. He also gave her money to make her an honourable amends, and comfort her for that maiming of her body which she had suffered, and for her glorious patience under such unsufferable torments.

(37) This matter sorely grieved Cherea, as having been the cause, as far as he could, or the instrument, of those miseries to men, which seemed worthy of consolation to Caius himself; on which account he said to Clement and to Papinius (of whom Clement was general of the army, and Papinius was a tribune): (38) 'To be sure, O Clement, we have no way failed in our guarding the emperor; for as to those that have made conspiracies against his government, some have been slain by our care and pains, and some have been by us tortured, and this to such a degree, that he hath himself pitied them. How great then is our virtue in submitting to conduct his armies!' (39) Clement held his peace, but showed the shame he was under in obeying Caius' orders, both by his eyes and his blushing countenance, while he thought it by no means right to accuse the emperor in express words, lest their own safety should be endangered thereby. (40) Upon which Cherea took courage, and spake to him without fear of the danger that were before him, and discoursed largely of the sore calamities under which the city and the government then laboured, and said, 'We may indeed pretend in words that Caius is the person unto whom the cause of such miseries ought to be imputed; (41) but, in the opinion of such as are able to judge uprightly, it is I, O Clement! and this Papinius, and before us thou thyself, who bring these tortures upon the Romans, and upon all mankind. It is not done by our being subservient to the commands of Caius, but it is done by our own consent; (42) for whereas it is in our power to put an end to the life of this man, who hath so terribly injured the citizens and his subjects, we are his guard in mischief and his executioners, instead of his soldiers, and are the instruments of his cruelty. We bear these weapons, not for our liberty, not for the Roman

government, but only for his preservation, who hath enslaved both their bodies and their minds; and we are every day polluted with the blood that we shed and the torments we inflict upon others; and this we do, till somebody becomes Caius' instrument in bringing the like miseries upon ourselves. (43) Nor does he thus employ us, because he hath a kindness for us, but rather because he hath a suspicion of us as also because, when abundance more have been killed (for Caius will set no bounds to his wrath, since he aims to do all, not out of regard to justice, but to his own pleasure) we shall also ourselves be exposed to his cruelty; whereas we ought to be the means of confirming the security and liberty of all, and at the same time to resolve to free ourselves from dangers.

(44) Hereupon Clement openly commended Cherea's intentions, but bade him hold his tongue; for that in case his words should get out among many, and such things should be spread abroad as were fit to be concealed, the plot would come to be discovered before it was executed, and they should be brought to punishment; but that they should leave all to futurity, and the hopes which thence arose, that some fortunate event would come to their assistance: (45) that, as for himself, his age would not permit him to make any attempt in that case. 'However, although perhaps I could not suggest what may be safer than what thou, Cherea, hast contrived and said, yet how is it possible for anyone to suggest what is more for thy reputation?' (46) So Clement went his way home, with deep reflections on what he had heard, and what he had himself said. Cherea also was under a concern, and went quickly to Cornelius Sabinus, who was himself one of the tribunes, and whom he otherwise knew to be a worthy man and a lover of liberty, and on that account very uneasy at the present management of public affairs, (47) he being desirous to come immediately to the execution of what had been determined, and thinking it right for him to propose it to the other, and afraid lest Clement should discover them, and besides looking upon delays and puttings-off to be the next to desisting from the enterprise.

(48) But as all was agreeable to Sabinus who had himself, equally with Cherea, the same design, but had been silent for want of a person to whom he could safely communicate that design; so having now met with one, who not only promised to conceal what he heard, but who had already opened his mind to him, he was much more encouraged, and desired of Cherea that no delay might be made therein. (49) Accordingly they went to Minucianus, who was as virtuous a man and as zealous to do glorious actions as themselves, and suspected by Caius on occasion of the slaughter of Lepidus; for Minucianus and Lepidus were intimate friends and both in the fear of the danger that they were under; (50) for Caius was terrible to all the great men, as appearing ready to act a mad part towards each of them in particular, and towards all of them in

general; (51) and these men were afraid of one another, while they were yet uneasy at the posture of affairs, but avoided to declare their mind and their hatred against Caius to one another, out of fear of the dangers they might be in thereby, although they perceived by other means their mutual hatred against Caius, and on that account were not averse to a mutual kindness one towards another.

(52) When Minucianus and Cherea had met together, and saluted one another (as they had been used in former conversations to give the upper hand to Minucianus, both on account of his eminent dignity, for he was the noblest of all the citizens, and highly commended by all men, (53) especially when he made speeches to them), Minucianus began first, and asked Cherea, What was the watchword he had received that day from Caius? For the affront which was offered Cherea in giving the watchwords, was famous over the city. (54) But Cherea made no delay so long as to reply to that question, out of the joy he had that Minucianus would have such confidence in him as to discourse with him. 'But do thou,' said he, 'give me the watchword of Liberty. And I return thee my thanks, that thou hast so greatly encouraged me to exert myself after an extraordinary manner; (55) nor do I stand in need of many words to encourage me, since both thou and I are of the same mind, and partakers of the same resolutions, and this before we have conferred together. I have indeed but one sword girt on, but this one will serve us both. (56) Come on, therefore, let us set about the work. Do thou go first if thou hast a mind, and bid me follow thee; or else I will go first, and thou shalt assist me, and we will assist one another, and trust one another. Nor is there a necessity for even one sword to such as have a mind disposed to such works, by which mind the sword uses to be successful. (57) I am zealous about this action, nor am I solicitous what I may myself undergo; for I am not at leisure to consider the danger that may come upon myself, so deeply am I troubled at the slavery our once free country is now under, and at the contempt cast upon our excellent laws, and at the destruction which hangs over all men, by the means of Caius. (58) I wish that I may be judged by thee, and that thou mayst esteem me worthy of credit in these matters, seeing we are both of the same opinion, and there is herein no difference between us.'

(59) When Minucianus saw the vehemency with which Cherea delivered himself, he gladly embraced him, and encouraged him in his bold attempt, commending him and embracing him; so he let him go with his good wishes; (60) and some affirm, that he thereby confirmed Minucianus in the prosecution of what had been agreed among them; for as Cherea entered into the court, the report runs that a voice came from among the multitude to encourage him, which bade him finish what he was about, and take the opportunity that Providence afforded; (61) and that Cherea at first suspected that some one of the

conspirators had betrayed him, and he was caught, but at length perceived that it was by way of exhortation. Whether somebody that was conscious of what he was about, gave a signal for his encouragement, or whether it was God himself, who looks upon the actions of men, that encouraged him to go on boldly in his design is uncertain. (62) The plot was now communicated to a great many, and they were all in their armour, some of the conspirators being senators, and some of the equestrian order, and as many of the soldiery as were made acquainted with it; for there was not one of them who would not reckon it a part of his happiness to kill Caius; (63) and on that account they were all very zealous in the affair, by what means soever anyone could come at it, that he might not be behindhand in these virtuous designs, but might be ready with all his alacrity or power, both by words and actions, to complete this slaughter of a tyrant. (64) And besides these, Callistus also, who was a freedman of Caius, and was the only man that had arrived at the greatest degree of power under him – such a power, indeed, as was in a manner equal to the power of the tyrant himself by the dread that all men had of him, and by the great riches he had acquired; (65) for he took bribes most plenteously, and committed injuries without bounds; and was more extravagant in the use of his power in unjust proceedings than any other. He also knew the disposition of Caius to be implacable, and never to be turned from what he had resolved on. He had withal many other reasons why he thought himself in danger, and the vastness of his wealth was not one of the least of them: (66) on which account he privately ingratiated himself with Claudius, and transferred his courtship to him, out of this hope, that in case, upon the removal of Caius, the government should come to him, his interest in such changes should lay a foundation for his preserving his dignity under him, since he laid in beforehand a stock of merit, and did Claudius good offices in his promotion. (67) He also had the boldness to pretend that he had been persuaded to make away with Claudius, by poisoning him, but had still invented ten thousand excuses for delaying to do it. (68) But it seems probable to me that Callistus only counterfeited this, in order to ingratiate himself with Claudius; for if Caius had been in earnest resolved to take off Claudius, he would not have admitted of Callistus' excuses, nor would Callistus, if he had been enjoined to do such an act as was desired by Caius, have put it off, nor, if he had disobeyed those injunctions of his master, had he escaped immediate punishment; (69) while Claudius was preserved from the madness of Caius by a certain divine providence, and Callistus pretended to such a piece of merit as he no way deserved.

(70) However, the execution of Cherea's designs was put off from day to day, by the sloth of many therein concerned; for as to Cherea himself, he would not willingly make any delay in that execution, thinking every time a fit time for it, for frequent opportunities offered themselves; (71) as when

Caius went up to the capitol to sacrifice for his daughter, or when he stood upon his royal palace, and threw gold and silver pieces of money among the people, he might be pushed down headlong, because the top of the palace, that looks toward the market place, was very high; and also when he celebrated the mysteries, which he had appointed at that time; (72) for he was then no way secluded from the people, but solicitous to do everything carefully and decently; and was free from all suspicion that he should be then assaulted by anybody; and although the gods should afford him no divine assistance to enable him to take away his life, (73) yet had he strength himself sufficient to despatch Caius, even without a sword. Thus was Cherea angry at his fellow-conspirators, for fear they should suffer a proper opportunity to pass by; (74) and they were themselves sensible that he had just cause to be angry at them, and that his eagerness was for their advantage; yet did they desire he would have a little longer patience, lest, upon any disappointment they might meet with, they should put the city into disorder, and an inquisition should be made after the conspiracy, and should render the courage of those that were to attack Caius, without success, while he would then secure himself more carefully than ever against them; (75) that it would therefore be the best to set about the work when the shows were exhibited in the palace. These shows were acted in honour of that Caesar who first of all changed the popular government, and transferred it to himself; galleries being fixed before the palace, where the Romans that were patricians became spectators, together with their children and their wives, and Caesar himself was to be also a spectator; (76) and they reckoned, among those many ten thousands who would there be crowded into a narrow compass, they should have a favourable opportunity to make their attempt upon him as he came in; because his guards that should protect him, if any of them should have a mind to do it, would not here be able to give him any assistance.

(77) Cherea consented to this delay; and when the shows were exhibited, it was resolved to do the work the first day. But fortune, which allowed a further delay to his slaughter, was too hard for their foregoing resolution: and, as the days of the regular time for these shows were now over, they had much ado to get the business done on the last day. (78) Then Cherea called the conspirators together, and spake thus to them: 'So much time passed away with effect is a reproach to us, as delaying to go through such a virtuous design as we are engaged in; but more fatal will this delay prove if we be discovered, and the design be frustrated; for Caius will then become more cruel in his unjust proceedings. (79) Do not we see how long we deprive all our friends of their liberty, and give Caius leave still to tyrannise over them? While we ought to have procured them security for the future, and, by laying a foundation for the happiness of others, gain to ourselves great admiration and honour for all time

to come.' (80) Now, while the conspirators had nothing tolerable to say by way of contradiction, and yet did not quite relish what they were doing, but stood silent and astonished, he said further, 'O, my brave comrades! Why do we make such delays? Do not you see that this is the last day of these shows, and that Caius is about to go to sea? (81) For he is preparing to sail to Alexandria, in order to see Egypt. Is it therefore for your honour to let a man go out of your hands who is a reproach to mankind, and to permit him to go after a pompous manner, triumphing both at land and sea? (82) Shall not we be justly ashamed of ourselves if we give leave to some Egyptian or other, who shall think his injuries insufferable to free men, to kill him? (83) As for myself, I will no longer bear your slow proceedings, but will expose myself to the dangers of the enterprise this very day, and bear cheerfully whatsoever shall be the consequence of the attempt; nor, let them be ever so great, will I put them off any longer; for, to a wise and courageous man, what can be more miserable than that, while I am alive, anyone else should kill Caius, and deprive me of the honour of so virtuous an action?'

(84) When Cherea had spoken thus, he zealously set about the work and inspired courage into the rest to go on with it; and they were all eager to fall to it without further delay. So he was at the palace in the morning, with his equestrian sword girt on him; (85) for it was the custom that the tribunes should ask for the watchword with their swords on, and this was the day on which Cherea was by custom to receive the watchword; (86) and the multitude were already come to the palace, to be soon enough for seeing the shows, and that in great crowds, and one tumultuously crushing another, while Caius was delighted with this eagerness of the multitude; for which reason there was no order observed in the seating men, nor was any peculiar place appointed for the senators, or for the equestrian order; but they sat at random, men and women together, and freemen were mixed with the slaves. (87) So Caius came out in a solemn manner, and offered sacrifice to Augustus Caesar, in whose honour indeed these shows were celebrated. Now it happened, upon the fall of a certain priest, that the garment of Asprenas, a senator, was filled with blood, which made Caius laugh, although this was an evident omen to Asprenas, for he was slain at the same time with Caius. (88) It is also related, that Caius was that day, contrary to his usual custom, so very affable and good-natured in his conversation, that every one of those that were present were astonished at it. (89) After the sacrifice was over, Caius betook himself to see the shows, and sat down for that purpose, as did also the principal of his friends sit near him. (90) Now the parts of the theatre were so fastened together, as it used to be every year, in the manner following: it had two doors; the one door led to the open air, the other was for going into, or going out of, the cloisters, that those within the theatre might not be thereby

disturbed; but out of one gallery there went an inward passage, parted into partitions also, which led into another gallery, to give room to the combatants and to the musicians to go out as occasion served. (91) When the multitude were set down, and Cherea with the other tribunes were set down also, and the right corner of the theatre was allotted to Caesar, one Vatinius, a senator, commander of the Praetorian band, asked of Cluvius, one that sat by him, and was of consular dignity also, whether he had heard anything of news or not – but took care that nobody should hear what he said; (92) and when Cluvius replied, that he had heard no news – 'Know then, (said Vatinius) that the game of slaughter of tyrants is to be played this day.' But Cluvius replied, 'O brave comrade! Hold thy peace, lest some other of the Achaians hear thy tale.' (93) And as there was abundance of autumnal fruit thrown among the spectators, and a great number of birds, that were of great value to such as possessed them, on account of their rareness, Caius was pleased with the birds fighting for the fruits and with the violence wherewith the spectators seized upon them: (94) and here he perceived two prodigies that happened there; for an actor was introduced, by whom a leader of robbers was crucified, and the pantomime brought in a play called Cinyras, wherein he himself was to be slain, as well as his daughter Myrrha, and wherein a great deal of fictitious blood was shed, both about him that was crucified, and also about Cinyras. (95) It is also confessed, that this was the same day wherein Pausanias, a friend of Philip, the son of Amyntas, who was king of Macedonia, slew him as he was entering into the theatre. (96) And now Caius was in doubt whether he should tarry to the end of the shows, because it was the last day, or whether he should not go first to the bath, and to dinner, and then return and sit down as before. Hereupon Minucianus, who sat over Caius, and was afraid that the opportunity should fail them, got up, because he saw Cherea was already gone out, and made haste out to confirm him in his resolution: (97) but Caius took hold of his garment in an obliging way, and said to him – 'O brave man, whither art thou going?' Whereupon, out of reverence to Caesar, as it seemed, he sat down again; but his fear prevailed over him, and in a little time he got up again, (98) and then Caius did noway oppose his going out, as thinking that he went out to perform some necessities of nature. And Asprenas, who was one of the confederates, persuaded Caius to go out to the bath, and to dinner, and then to come in again, as desirous that what had been resolved on might be brought to a conclusion immediately.

(99) So Cherea's associates placed themselves in order, as the time would permit them, and they were obliged to labour hard, that the place which was appointed them should not be left by them; but they had an indignation at the tediousness of the delays, and that what they were about should be put off any longer, for it was already about the ninth hour of the day; (100) and Cherea,

upon Caius' tarrying so long, had a great mind to go in, and fall upon him in his seat, although he foresaw that this could not be done without much bloodshed, both of the senators and of those of the equestrian order that were present; and although he knew this must happen, yet had he a great mind to do so, as thinking it a right thing to procure security and freedom to all, at the expense of such as might perish at the same time. (101) And as they were just going back into the entrance to the theatre, word was brought them that Caius was arisen, whereby a tumult was made; hereupon the conspirators thrust away the crowd, under pretence as if Caius was angry at them, but in reality as desirous to have a quiet place, that should have none in it to defend him, while they set about Caius' slaughter. (102) Now Claudius, his uncle, was gone out before, and Marcus Vinicius, his sister's husband, as also Valerius of Asia; whom, though they had had such a mind to put out of their places, the reverence to their dignity hindered them so to do; then followed Caius, with Paulus Arruntius: (103) and because Caius was now gotten within the palace, he left the direct road, along which those his servants stood that were in waiting, and by which road Claudius had gone out before; (104) Caius turned aside into a private narrow passage, in order to go to the place for bathing, as also in order to take a view of the boys that came out of Asia, who were sent thence partly to sing hymns in these mysteries which were now celebrated, and partly to dance in the Pyrrhic way of dancing upon the theatres. (105) So Cherea met him, and asked him for the watchword; upon Caius' giving him one of his ridiculous words, he immediately reproached him, and drew his sword, and gave him a terrible stroke with it, yet was not this stroke mortal. (106) And although there be those that say it was so contrived on purpose by Cherea, that Caius should not be killed at one blow, but should be punished more severely by a multitude of wounds, (107) yet does this story appear to me incredible; because the fear men are under in such actions does not allow them to use their reason. And if Cherea was of that mind, I esteem him the greatest of all fools, in pleasing himself in his spite against Caius, rather than immediately procuring safety to himself and to his confederates from the dangers they were in, because there might many things still happen for helping Caius' escape, if he had not already given up the ghost; for certainly Cherea would have regard, not so much to the punishment of Caius, as to the affliction himself and his friends were in, (108) while it was in his power, after such success, to keep silent, and to escape the wrath of Caius' defenders, and not to leave it to uncertainty whether he should gain the end he aimed at or not; and after an unreasonable manner to act as if he had a mind to ruin himself, and lose the opportunity that lay before him. But everybody may guess as he pleases about this matter. (109) However, Caius was staggered with the pain that the blow gave him; for the stroke of the sword falling in the middle, between the shoulder and the neck, was hindered by the first bone of the breast from proceeding any further. Nor did he either cry out (in such astonishment was he), nor did he call out for any of his friends; whether it were that he had no confidence in them, or that his mind was otherwise disordered, but he groaned under the pain he endured, and presently went forward and fled – (110) when Cornelius Sabinus, who was already prepared in mind so to do, thrust him down upon his knee, where many of them stood round about him, and struck him with their swords, and they cried out, and encouraged one another all at once to strike him again; but all agree that Aquila gave him the finishing stroke, which directly killed him. (111) But one may justly ascribe this act to Cherea; for although many concurred in the act itself, yet was he the first contriver of it, and began long before all the rest to prepare for it; (112) and was the first man that boldly spake of it to the rest; and upon their admission of what he said about it, he got the dispersed conspirators together; he prepared everything after a prudent manner, and by suggesting good advice, showed himself far superior to the rest, and made obliging speeches to them, insomuch that he even compelled them all to go on, who otherwise had not courage enough for that purpose; (113) and when opportunity served to use his sword in hand, he appeared first of all ready so to do, and gave the first blow in this virtuous slaughter; he also brought Caius easily into the power of the rest, and almost killed him himself, insomuch that it is but just to ascribe all that the rest did to the advice and bravery and labours of the hands of Cherea.

(114) Thus did Caius come to his end, and lay dead, by the many wounds which had been given him. (115) Now Cherea and his associates, upon Caius' slaughter, saw that it was impossible for them to save themselves, if they should all go the same way, partly on account of the astonishment they were under; for it was no small danger they had incurred by killing an emperor, who was honoured and loved by the madness of the people, especially when the soldiers were likely to make a bloody inquiry after his murderers. (116) The passages also were narrow wherein the work was done, which were also crowded with a great multitude of Caius' attendants, and of such of the soldiers as were of the emperor's guard that day; (117) whence it was that they went by other ways, and came to the house of Germanicus, the father of Caius, whom they had now killed (which house adjoined to the palace; for while the edifice was one, it was built in its several parts by those particular persons who had been emperors, and those parts bare the names of those that built them, or the name of him who had begun to build any of its parts). (118) So they got away from the insults of the multitude, and then were for the present out of danger, that is, so long as the misfortune which had overtaken the emperor was not known. (119) The Germans were the first who perceived that Caius was slain. These Germans were Caius' guard, and carried the name of the country whence they

were chosen, and composed the Celtic legion. (120) The men of that country are naturally passionate, which is commonly the temper of some other of the barbarous nations also, as being not used to consider much about what they do; they are of robust bodies, and fall upon their enemies as soon as ever they are attacked by them; and which way soever they go, they perform great exploits. (121) When therefore, these German guards understood that Caius was slain, they were very sorry for it, because they did not use their reason in judging about public affairs, but measured all by the advantages themselves received, Caius being beloved by them, because of the money he gave them, by which he had purchased their kindness to him: (122) so they drew their swords, and Sabinus led them on. He was one of the tribunes, not by the means of the virtuous actions of his progenitors, for he bad been a gladiator, but he had obtained that post in the army by his having a robust body. So these Germans marched along the houses in quest of Caesar's murderers, (123) and cut Asprenas to pieces, because he was the first man they fell upon, and whose garment it was that the blood of the sacrifices stained, as I have said already, and which foretold that this his meeting the soldiers would not be for his good. Then did Norbanus meet them, who was one of the principal nobility of the city, and could show many generals of armies among his ancestors; (124) but they paid no regard to his dignity: yet was he of such great strength, that he wrested the sword of the first of those that assaulted him out of his hands, and appeared plainly not to be willing to die without a struggle for his life, until he was surrounded by a great number of assailants, and died by the multitude of the wounds which they gave him. (125) The third man was Anteius, a senator, and a few others with him. He did not meet with these Germans by chance, as the rest did before, but came to show his hatred to Caius, and because he loved to see Caius lie dead with his own eyes, and took a pleasure in that sight; for Caius had banished Anteius' father, who was of the same name with himself, and, being not satisfied with that, he sent out his soldiers, and slew him; (126) so he was come to rejoice at the sight of him, now he was dead. But as the house was now all in a tumult, when he was aiming to hide himself, he could not escape that accurate search which the Germans made, while they barbarously slew those that were guilty and those that were not guilty, and this equally also. And thus were these [three] persons slain.

(127) But when the rumour that Caius was slain reached the theatre, they were astonished at it, and could not believe it: even some that entertained his destruction with great pleasure, and were more desirous of its happening than almost any other satisfaction that could come to them, were under such a fear, that they could not believe it. (128) There were also those who greatly distrusted it, because they were unwilling that any such thing should come to

Caius, nor could believe it, though it were ever so true, because they thought no man could possibly have so much power as to kill Caius. (129) These were the women, and the children, and the slaves, and some of the soldiery. This last sort had taken his pay, and in a manner tyrannised with him, and had abused the best of the citizens, in being subservient to his unjust commands, in order to gain honours and advantages to themselves; (130) but for the women and the youth, they had been inveigled with shows, and the fightings of the gladiators, and certain distributions of flesh-meat among them, which things in pretence were designed for the pleasing of multitude, but in reality to satiate the barbarous cruelty and madness of Caius. (131) The slaves also were sorry, because they were by Caius allowed to accuse and to despise their masters, and they could have recourse to his assistance when they had unjustly affronted them; for he was very easy in believing them against their masters, even when they accused them falsely; and, if they would discover what money their masters had, they might soon obtain both riches and liberty, as the rewards of their accusations, because the reward of these informers was the eighth part of the criminal's substance. (132) As to the nobles, although the report appeared credible to some of them, either because they knew of the plot beforehand, or because they wished it might be true, however they concealed not only the joy they had at the relation of it, but that they had heard anything at all about it. (133) These last acted so, out of the fear they had that if the report proved false, they should be punished for having so soon let men know their minds. But those that knew Caius was dead, because they were partners with the conspirators, they concealed all still more cautiously, as not knowing one another's minds, and fearing lest they should speak of it to some of those to whom the continuance of tyranny was advantageous; and if Caius should prove to be alive, they might be informed against, and punished. (134) And another report went about, that although Caius had been wounded indeed, yet was not he dead, but alive still and under the physician's hands. (135) Nor was anyone looked upon by another as faithful enough to be trusted, and to whom anyone would open his mind; for he was either a friend to Caius, and therefore suspected to favour his tyranny, or he was one that hated him, who therefore might be suspected to deserve the less credit, because of his ill will to him. (136) Nay, it was said by some (and this indeed it was that deprived the nobility of their hopes, and made them sad) that Caius was in a condition to despise the dangers he had been in, and took no care of healing his wounds, but was gotten away into the market place, and, bloody as he was, was making an harangue to the people. (137) And these were the conjectural reports of those that were so unreasonable as to endeavour to raise tumults, which they turned different ways, according to the opinions of the bearers. Yet did they not leave their seats, for fear of being accused, if they should go out before the rest; for they should not be sentenced according to the real intention with which they went out, but according to the supposals of the accusers, and of the judges.

(138) But now a multitude of Germans had surrounded the theatre with their swords drawn: all the spectators looked for nothing but death; and at everyone's coming in, a fear seized upon them, as if they were to be cut in pieces immediately; and in great distress they were, as neither having courage enough to go out of the theatre, nor believing themselves safe from dangers if they tarried there. (139) And when the Germans came upon them, the cry was so great, that the theatre rang again with the entreaties of the spectators to the soldiers pleading that they were entirely ignorant of everything that related to such seditious contrivances, and that if there were any sedition raised, they knew nothing of it; (140) they therefore begged that they would spare them, and not punish those that had not the least hand in such bold crimes as belonged to other persons, while they neglected to search after such as had really done whatsoever it be that hath been done. (141) Thus did these people appeal to God, and deplore their infelicity with shedding of tears and beating their faces, and said everything that the most imminent danger, and the utmost concern for their lives, could dictate to them. (142) This brake the fury of the soldiers, and made them repent of what they minded to do to the spectators, which would have been the greatest instance of cruelty. And so it appeared to even these savages, when they had once fixed the heads of those that were slain with Asprenas upon the altar; (143) at which sight the spectators were sorely afflicted, both upon the consideration of the dignity of the persons, and out of a commiseration of their sufferings; nay, indeed, they were almost in as great disorder at the prospect of the danger themselves were in, seeing it was still uncertain whether they should entirely escape the like calamity. (144) Whence it was that such as thoroughly and justly hated Caius, could yet no way enjoy the pleasure of his death, because they were themselves in jeopardy of perishing together with him; nor had they hitherto any firm assurance of surviving.

(145) There was at this time one Euaristus Arruntius, a public crier in the market, and therefore of a strong and audible voice, who vied in wealth with the richest of the Romans, and was able to do what he pleased in the city, both then and afterward. (146) This man put himself into the most mournful habit he could, although he had a greater hatred against Caius than anyone else; his fear and his wise contrivance to gain his safety taught him so to do, and prevailed over his present pleasure; (147) so he put on such a mournful dress as he would have done, had he lost his dearest friends in the world; this man came into the theatre, and informed them of the death of Caius, and by this means put an end to that state of ignorance the men had been in. (148) Arruntius also went round about the pillars, and called out to the Germans, as did the tribunes

with him, bidding them put up their swords, and telling them that Caius was dead; (149) and this proclamation it was plainly which saved those that were collected together in the theatre, and all the rest who any way met the Germans; for while they had hopes that Caius had still any breath in him, they abstained from no sort of mischief; (150) and such an abundant kindness they still had for Caius, that they would willingly have prevented the plot against him, and procured his escape from so sad a misfortune, at the expense of their own lives; (151) but they now left off the warm zeal they had to punish his enemies, now they were fully satisfied that Caius was dead, because it was now in vain for them to show their zeal and kindness to him, when he who should reward them was perished. They were also afraid that they should be punished by the senate if they should go on in doing such injuries, that is, in case the authority of the supreme governor should revert to them; (152) and thus at length a stop was put, though not without difficulty, to that rage which possessed the Germans on account of Caius's death.

(153) But Cherea was so much afraid for Minucianus, lest he should light upon the Germans, now they were in their fury, that he went and spake to every one of the soldiers, and prayed them to take care of his preservation, and made himself great inquiry about him, lest he should have been slain; (154) and for Clement, he let Minucianus go when he was brought to him, and, with many other of the senators, affirmed the action was right, and commended the virtue of those that contrived it and had courage enough to execute it; and said, that (155) 'tyrants do indeed please themselves and look big for a while, upon having the power to act unjustly; but do not, however, go happily out of the world, because they are hated by the virtuous; (156) and that Caius, together with all his unhappiness, was become a conspirator against himself before these other men who attacked him did so; and by becoming intolerable, in setting aside the wise provision the laws had made, taught his dearest friends to treat him as an enemy; insomuch that although in common discourse these conspirators were those that slew Caius, yet that, in reality, he lies now dead as perishing by his own self.'

(157) Now by this time the people in the theatre were arisen from their seats, and those that were within made a very great disturbance; the cause of which was this, that the spectators were too hasty in getting away. There was also one Alcyon, a physician, who hurried away, as if to cure those that were wounded; and, under that pretence, he sent those that were with him to fetch what things were necessary for the healing of those wounded persons, but in reality to get them clear of the present dangers they were in. (158) Now the senate, during this interval, had met, and the people also assembled together in the accustomed form, and were both employed in searching after the murderers of Caius. The people did it very zealously, but the senate in

appearance only; (159) for there was present Valerius of Asia, one that had been consul; this man went to the people, as they were in disorder, and very uneasy that they could not yet discover who they were that had murdered the emperor; he was then earnestly asked by them all, who it was that had done it? He replied, 'I wish I had been the man.' (160) The consuls also published an edict, wherein they accused Caius, and gave order to the people then got together, and to the soldiers, to go home, and gave the people hopes of the abatement of the oppressions they lay under; and promised the soldiers, if they lay quiet as they used to do, and would not go abroad to do mischief unjustly, that they would bestow rewards upon them; for there was reason to fear lest the city might suffer harm by their wild and ungovernable behaviour, if they should once betake themselves to spoil the citizens, or plunder the temples. (161) And now the whole multitude of the senators were assembled together, and especially those that had conspired to take away the life of Caius, who put on at this time an air of great assurance, and appeared with great magnanimity, as if the administration of the public affairs were already devolved upon them.

CHAPTER 2

(162) When the public affairs were in this posture, Claudius was on the sudden hurried away out of his house; for the soldiers had a meeting together, and when they had debated about what was to be done, they saw that a democracy was incapable of managing such a vast weight of public affairs, and that if it should be set up, it would not be for their advantage; (163) and in case any one of those already in the government should obtain the supreme power, it would in all respects be to their grief, if they were not assisting to him in this advancement (164) that it would therefore be right for them, while the public affairs were unsettled, to choose Claudius emperor, who was uncle to the deceased, Caius, and of a superior dignity and worth to every one of those who were assembled together in the senate, both on account of the virtues of his ancestors, and of the learning he had acquired in his education; (165) and who, if once settled in the empire, would reward them according to their deserts, and bestow largesses upon them. These were their consultations, and they executed the same immediately. Claudius was therefore seized upon suddenly by the soldiery. (166) But Cnaeus Sentius Saturninus, although he understood that Claudius was seized, and that he intended to claim the government, unwillingly indeed in appearance, but in reality by his own free consent, stood up in the senate, and, without being dismayed, made an exhortatory oration to them, and such a one indeed as was fit for men of freedom and generosity, and spake thus:

(167) 'Although it be a thing incredible, O Romans, because of the great length of time, that so unexpected an event hath happened, yet are we now in possession of liberty. How long indeed this will last is uncertain, and lies at the disposal of the gods, whose grant it is; yet such it is as is sufficient to make us rejoice, and be happy for the present, although we may soon be deprived of it, (168) for one hour is sufficient to those that are exercised in virtue, wherein we may live with a mind accountable only to ourselves, in our own country, now free, and governed by such laws as this country once flourished under. (169) As for myself, I cannot remember our former time of liberty, as being born after it was gone; but I am beyond measure filled with joy at the thoughts of our present freedom. I also esteem those that were born and brought up in that our former liberty happy men, and that those men are worthy of no less esteem than the gods themselves, who have given us a taste of it in this age; (170) and I heartily wish that this quiet enjoyment of it, which we have at present, might continue to all ages. However, this single day may suffice for our youth, as well as for us that are in years. It will seem an age to our old men, if they might die during its happy duration: it may also be for the instruction of the younger sort, (171) what kind of virtue those men, from whose loins we are derived, were exercised in. As for ourselves, our business is, during the space of time, to live virtuously – than which nothing can be more to our advantage; which course of virtue it is alone that can preserve our liberty; (172) for, as to our ancient state, I have heard of it by the relations of others; but as to our later state, during my lifetime, I have known it by experience, and learned thereby what mischief tyrannies have brought upon this commonwealth, discouraging all virtue, and depriving persons of magnanimity of their liberty, and proving the teachers of flattery and slavish fear, because it leaves the public administration not to be governed by wise laws, but by the humour of those that govern. (173) For since Julius Caesar took it into his head to dissolve our democracy, and by overbearing the regular system of our laws, to bring disorders into our administration, and to get above right and justice, and to be a slave to his own inclinations, there is no kind of misery but what hath tended to the subversion of this city; (174) while all those that have succeeded him have striven one with another to overthrow the ancient laws of their country, and have left it destitute of such citizens as were of generous principles, because they thought it tended to their safety to have vicious men to converse withal, and not only to break the spirits of those that were best esteemed for their virtue, but to resolve upon their utter destruction. (175) Of all which emperors, who have been many in number, and who laid upon us insufferable hardships during the times of their government, this Caius, who hath been slain today, hath brought more terrible calamities upon us than did all the rest, not only by exercising his ungoverned rage upon his fellow citizens, but also upon his kindred and

friends, and alike upon all others, and by inflicting still greater miseries upon them, as punishments, which they never deserved, he being equally furious against men and against the gods; (176) for tyrants are not content to gain their sweet pleasure, and this by acting injuriously, and in the vexation they bring both upon men's estates and their wives – but they look upon that to be their principal advantage, when they can utterly overthrow the entire families of their enemies, (177) while all lovers of liberty are the enemies of tyranny. Nor can those that patiently endure what miseries they bring of them gain their friendship; for as they are conscious of the abundant mischiefs they have brought on these men, and how magnanimously they have borne their hard fortunes, they cannot but be sensible what evils they have done, and thence only depend on security from what they are suspicious of, if it may be in their power to take them quite out of the world. (178) Since, then, we are now gotten clear of such great misfortunes, and are only accountable to one another (which form of government affords us the best assurance of our present concord, and promises us the best security from all evil designs, and will be most for our own glory in settling the city in good order), you ought, every one of you in particular, to make provision for his own, and in general for the public utility; (179) or, on the contrary, they may declare their dissent to such things as have been proposed, and this without any hazard of danger to come upon them – because they have now no lord set over them, who, without fear of punishment, could do mischief to the city, and had an uncontrollable power to take off those that freely declared their opinions. (180) Nor has anything so much contributed to this increase of tyranny of late as sloth, and a timorous forbearance of contradicting the emperor's will; (181) while men had an over-great inclination to the sweetness of peace, and had learned to live like slaves, and as many of us as either heard of intolerable calamities that happened at a distance from us, or saw the miseries that were near us, out of the dread of dying virtuously, endured a death joined with the utmost infamy. (182) We ought, then, in the first place, to decree the greatest honours we are able to those that have taken off the tyrant, especially to Cherea Cassius; for this one man, with the assistance of the gods, hath, by his counsel and by his actions, been the procurer of our liberty. (183) Nor ought we to forget him now we have recovered our liberty, who, under the foregoing tyranny, took counsel beforehand, and beforehand hazarded himself for our liberties; but ought to decree him proper honours, and thereby freely declare, that he from the beginning acted with our approbation. (184) And certainly it is a very excellent thing, and what becomes freemen, to requite their benefactors, as this man hath been a benefactor to us all, though not at all like Cassius and Brutus, who slew Caius Julius [Caesar]; for those men laid the foundations of sedition and civil wars in our city, but this man, together with his slaughter of the tyrant, hath set our city free from all those sad miseries which arose from the tyranny.'

(185) And this was the purport of Sentius's oration, which was received with pleasure by the senators, and by as many of the equestrian order as were present. And now one Trebellius Maximus rose up hastily, and took from Sentius' finger a ring, which had a stone with the image of Caius engraven upon it, and which, in his zeal in speaking, and his earnestness in doing what he was about, as it was supposed, he had forgotten to take off himself. This sculpture was broken immediately. (186) But as it was now far in the night, Cherea demanded of the consuls the watchword, who gave him this word, Liberty. These facts were the subjects of admiration to themselves, and almost incredible; (187) for it was a hundred years since the democracy had been laid aside, when this giving the watchword returned to the consuls; for, before the city was subject to tyrants, they were the commanders of the soldiers. (188) But when Cherea had received that watchword, he delivered it to those who were on the senate's side, which were four regiments, who esteemed the government without emperors to be preferable to tyranny. (189) So these went away with their tribunes. The people also now departed very joyful, full of hope and of courage, as having recovered their former democracy, and no longer under an emperor; and Cherea was in very great esteem with them.

(190) And now Cherea was very uneasy that Caius' daughter and wife were still alive, and that all his family did not perish with him, since whosoever was left of them must be left for the ruin of the city and of the laws. Moreover, in order to finish this matter with the utmost zeal, and in order to satisfy his hatred of Caius, he sent Julius Lupus, one of the tribunes, to kill Caius' wife and daughter. (191) They proposed this office to Lupus as to a kinsman of Clement, that he might be so far a partaker of this murder of the tyrant, and might rejoice in the virtue of having assisted his fellow citizens, and that he might appear to have been a partaker with those that were first in their designs against him; (192) yet did this action appear to some of the conspirators to be too cruel, as to using such severity to a woman, because Caius did more indulge his own ill nature than use her advice in all that he did; from which ill nature it was that the city was in so desperate a condition with the miseries that were brought on it, and the flower of the city was destroyed: (193) but others accused her of giving her consent to these things; nay, they ascribed all that Caius had done to her as the cause of it, and said she had given a potion to Caius, which had made him obnoxious to her, and had tied him down to love her by such evil methods; insomuch that she, having rendered him distracted, was become the author of all the mischiefs that had befallen the Romans, and that habitable world which was subject to them. (194) So that at length it was determined that she must die; nor could those of the contrary opinion at all

prevail to have her saved; and Lupus was sent accordingly. Nor was there any delay made in executing what he went about, but he was subservient to those that sent him on the first opportunity, as desirous to be no way blameable in what might be done for the advantage of the people. (195) So, when he was come into the palace, he found Cesonia, who was Caius' wife, lying by her husband's dead body, which also lay down on the ground, and destitute of all such things as the law allows to the dead, and all over herself besmeared with the blood of her husband's wounds, and bewailing the great affliction she was under, her daughter lying by her also; and nothing else was heard in these her circumstances but her complaint of Caius, as if he had not regarded what she had often told him of beforehand; (196) which words of hers were taken in a different sense even at that time, and are now esteemed equally ambiguous by those that hear of them, and are still interpreted according to the different inclinations of people. Now some said that the words denoted, that she had advised him to leave off his mad behaviour and his barbarous cruelty to the citizens, and to govern the public with moderation and virtue, lest he should perish by the same way, upon their using him as he had used them. (197) But some said, that as certain words had passed concerning the conspirators, she desired Caius to make no delay, but immediately to put them all to death; and this whether they were guilty or not, and that thereby he would be out of the fear of any danger; and that this was what she reproached him for when she advised him so to do, but he was too slow and tender in the matter. (198) And this was what Cesonia said; and what the opinions of men were about it. But when she saw Lupus approach, she showed him Caius' dead body, and persuaded him to come nearer, with lamentations and tears; (199) and as she perceived that Lupus was in disorder, and approached her in order to execute some design disagreeable to himself, she was well aware for what purpose he came, and stretched out her naked throat, and that very cheerfully to him, bewailing her case, like one utterly despaired of her life, and bidding him not to boggle at finishing the tragedy they had resolved upon relating to her. (200) So she boldly received her death's wound at the hand of Lupus, as did the daughter after her. So Lupus made haste to inform Cherea of what he had done.

(201) This was the end of Caius, after he had reigned four years, within four months. He was, even before he came to be emperor, ill-natured, and one that had arrived at the utmost pitch of wickedness; a slave to his pleasures, and a lover of calumny; greatly affected by every terrible accident, and on that account of a very murderous disposition where he durst show it. He enjoyed his exorbitant power to this only purpose, to injure those who least deserved it, with unreasonable insolence, and got his wealth by murder and injustice. (202) He laboured to appear above regarding either what was divine or agreeable to the laws, but was a slave to the commendations of the populace; and

whatsoever the laws declared to be shameful, and punished, that he esteemed more honourable than what was virtuous. (203) He was unmindful of his friends, how intimate soever, and though they were persons of the highest character; and if he was once angry at any of them he would inflict punishment upon them on the smallest occasions; and esteemed every man that endeavoured to lead a virtuous life his enemy! And whatsoever he commanded, he would not admit of any contradiction to his inclinations; (204) whence it was that he had criminal intercourse with his own sister; from which occasion chiefly it was also that a bitter hatred first sprang up against him among the citizens, that sort of incest not having been known of a long time; and so this provoked men to distrust him, and to hate him that was guilty of it. (205) And for any great or royal work that he ever did, which might be for the present or future ages, nobody can name any such, but only the haven that he made about Rhegium and Sicily, for the reception of the ships that brought corn from Egypt; (206) which was indeed a work without dispute very great in itself, and of very great advantage to the navigation. Yet was not this work brought to perfection by him, but was the one-half of it left imperfect, by reason of his want of application to it; (207) the cause of which was this, that he employed his studies about useless matters, and that by spending his money upon such pleasures as concerned no one's benefit but his own, he could not exert his liberality in things that were undoubtedly of great consequence. (208) Otherwise he was an excellent orator, and thoroughly acquainted with the Greek tongue, as well as with his own country or Roman language. He was also able, offhand and readily, to give answers to compositions made by others, of considerable length and accuracy. He was also more skilful in persuading others to very great things than anyone else, and this from a natural affability of temper, which had been improved by much exercise and painstaking: (209) for as he was the grandson of the brother of Tiberius, whose successor he was, this was a strong inducement to his acquiring of learning, because Tiberius aspired after the highest pitch of that sort of reputation: and Caius aspired after the like glory for eloquence, being induced thereto by the letters of his kinsman and his emperor. He was also among the first rank of his own citizens. (210) But the advantages he received from his learning did not countervail the mischief he brought upon himself in the exercise of his authority; so difficult it is for those to obtain the virtue that is necessary for a wise man, who have the absolute power to do what they please without control. (211) At the first he got himself such friends as were in all respects the most worthy, and was greatly beloved by them, while he imitated their zealous application to the learning and to the glorious actions of the best men; but when he became insolent towards them, they laid aside the kindness they had for him, and began to hate him; from which hatred came that plot which they raised against him, and wherein he perished.

CHAPTER 3

(212) Now Claudius, as I said before, went out of that way along which Caius was gone; and as the family was in a mighty disorder upon the sad accident of the murder of Caius, he was in great distress how to save himself, and was found to have hidden himself in a certain narrow place, though he had no other occasion for suspicion of any dangers besides the dignity of his birth; (213) for while he was a private man, he behaved himself with moderation, and was contented with his present fortune, applying himself to learning, and especially to that of the Greeks, and keeping himself entirely clear from everything that might bring on any disturbance. (214) But at this time the multitude were under a consternation, and the whole palace was full of the soldiers' madness, and the very emperor's guards seemed under the like fear and disorder with private persons; the band called *pretorian*, which was the purest part of the army, was in consultation what was to be done at this juncture. Now all those that were at this consultation had little regard to the punishment Caius had suffered, because he justly deserved such his fortune: (215) but they were rather considering their own circumstances, how they might take the best care of themselves, especially while the Germans were busy in punishing the murderers of Caius; which yet was rather done to gratify their own savage temper, than for the good of the public; (216) all which things disturbed Claudius, who was afraid for his own safety, and this particularly because he saw the heads of Asprenas and his partners carried about. His station had been on a certain elevated place, whither a few steps led him, and whither he had retired in the dark by himself. (217) But when Gratus, who was one of the soldiers that belonged to the palace, saw him, but did not well know by his countenance who he was, because it was dark, though he could well judge that it was a man who was privately there on some design, he came nearer to him; and when Claudius desired that he would retire, be discovered who he was, and owned him to be Claudius. So he said to his followers, 'This is a Germanicus; come on, let us choose him for our emperor.' (218) But when Claudius saw they were making preparations for taking him away by force, and was afraid they would kill him, as they had killed Caius, he besought them to spare him, putting them in mind how quietly he had demeaned himself, and that he was unacquainted with what had been done. (219) Hereupon Gratus smiled upon him, and took him by the right hand, and said, 'Leave off, sir, these low thoughts of saving yourself, while you ought to have greater thoughts, even of obtaining the empire, which the gods, out of their concern of the habitable world, by taking Caius out of the way, commit to thy virtuous conduct. Go to, therefore, and accept the throne of thy ancestors.' (220) So

they took him up and carried him, because he was not then able to go on foot, such was his dread and his joy at what was told him.

(221) Now there was already gathered together about Gratus, a great number of the guards; and when they saw Claudius carried off, they looked with a sad countenance, as supposing that he was carried to execution for the mischiefs that had been lately done, while yet they thought him a man who never meddled with public affairs all his life long, and one that had met with no contemptible dangers under the reign of Caius; and some of them thought it reasonable that the consuls should take cognisance of these matters; (222) and, as still more and more of the soldiery got together, the crowd about him ran away, and Claudius could hardly go on, his body was then so weak; and those who carried his sedan, upon an inquiry that was made about his being carried off, ran away and saved themselves, as despairing of their lord's preservation. (223) But when they were come into the large court of the palace (which, as the report goes about it, was inhabited first of all the parts of the city of Rome), and had just reached the public treasury, many more soldiers came about him, as glad to see Claudius's face, and thought it exceedingly right to make him emperor on account of their kindness for Germanicus, who was his brother, and had left behind him a vast reputation among all that were acquainted with him. (224) They reflected also on the covetous temper of the leading men of the senate, and what great errors they had been guilty of when the senate had the government formerly; (225) they also considered the impossibility of such an undertaking, as also what dangers they should be in, if the government should come to a single person, and that such a one should possess it as they had no hand in advancing, and not to Claudius, who would take it as their grant, and as gained by their good will to him, and would remember the favours they had done him, and would make them a sufficient recompense for the same.

(226) These were the discourses the soldiers had one with another by themselves, and they communicated them to all such as came in to them. Now those that inquired about this matter, willingly embraced the invitation that was made them to join with the rest; so they carried Claudius into the camp, crowding about him as his guard, and encompassing him about, one chairman still succeeding another, that their vehement endeavours might not be hindered. (227) But as to the populace and senators, they disagreed in their opinions. The latter were very desirous to recover their former dignity, and were zealous to get clear of the slavery that had been brought on them by the injurious treatment of the tyrants, which the present opportunity afforded them; (228) but for the people, who were envious against them, and knew that the emperors were capable of curbing their covetous temper, and were a refuge from them, they were very glad that Claudius had been seized upon, and brought to them, and thought that, if Claudius were made emperor, he would prevent a civil war,

such as there was in the days of Pompey. (229) But when the senate knew that Claudius was brought into the camp by the soldiers, they sent to him those of their body which had the best character for their virtues, that they might inform him that he ought to do nothing by violence, in order to gain the government; (230) that he who was a single person, one either already, or hereafter to be a member of their body, ought to yield to the senate, which consisted of so great a number; that he ought to let the law take place in the disposal of all that related to the public order, and to remember how greatly the former tyrants had afflicted their city, and what dangers both he and they had escaped under Caius; and that he ought not to hate the heavy burden of tyranny, when the injury is done by others, while he did himself wilfully treat his country after a mad and insolent manner; (231) that if he would comply with them, and demonstrate that his firm resolution was to live quietly and virtuously, he would have the greatest honours decreed to him that a free people could bestow; and by subjecting himself to the law, would obtain this branch of commendation, that he acted like a man of virtue, both as a ruler and a subject; (232) but that if he would act foolishly, and learn no wisdom by Caius's death, they would not permit him to go on; that a great part of the army was got together for them, with plenty of weapons, and a great number of slaves, which they could make use of; (233) that good hope was a great matter in such cases, as was also good fortune; and that the gods would never assist any others but those that undertook to act with virtue and goodness, who can be no other than such as fight for the liberty of their country.

(234) Now the ambassadors, Veranius and Brocchus, who were both of them tribunes of the people, made this speech to Claudius; and falling down upon their knees, they begged of him that he would not throw the city into wars and misfortunes; but when they saw what a multitude of soldiers encompassed and guarded Claudius, and that the forces that were with the consuls were, in comparison with them, perfectly inconsiderable, (235) they added, that if he did desire the government, he should accept of it as given by the senate; that he would prosper better, and be happier if he came to it, not by the injustice, but by the good will of those that would bestow it upon him.

CHAPTER 4

(236) Now Claudius, though he was sensible after what an insolent manner the senate had sent to him, yet did he, according to their advice, behave himself for the present with moderation; but not so far that he could not recover himself out of his fright; so he was encouraged [to claim the government] partly by the boldness of the soldiers, and partly by the persuasion of King Agrippa, who exhorted him not to let such a dominion slip out of his hands, when it came

thus to him of its own accord. (237) Now this Agrippa, with relation to Caius, did what became one that had been so much honoured by him; for he embraced Caius' body after he was dead, and laid it upon a bed, and covered it as well as he could, and went out to the guards, and told them that Caius was still alive; but he said that they should call for physicians, since he was very ill of his wounds. (238) But when he had learned that Claudius was carried away violently by the soldiers, he rushed through the crowd to him, and when he found that he was in disorder, and ready to resign up the government to the senate, he encouraged him, and desired him to keep the government; (239) but when he had said this to Claudius, he retired home. And, upon the senate's sending for him, he anointed his head with ointment, as if he had lately accompanied with his wife, and had dismissed her, and then came to them; he also asked of the senators what Claudius did; (240) who told him the present state of affairs, and then asked his opinion about the settlement of the public. He told them in words, that he was ready to lose his life for the honour of the senate, but desired them to consider what was for their advantage, without any regard to what was most agreeable to them; (241) for that those who grasp at governments, will stand in need of weapons and soldiers to guard them, unless they will set up without any preparation for it, and so fall into danger. (242) And when the senate replied, that they would bring in weapons in abundance, and money, and that as to an army, a part of it was already collected together for them, and they would raise a larger one by giving the slaves their liberty, Agrippa made answer, 'O senators, may you be able to compass what you have a mind to; yet will I immediately tell you my thoughts, because they tend to your preservation. (243) Take notice, then, that the army which will fight for Claudius hath been long exercised in warlike affairs: but our army will be no better than a rude multitude of raw men, and those such as have been unexpectedly made free from slavery, and ungovernable; we must then fight against those that are skilful in war with men who know not so much as how to draw their swords. (244) So that my opinion is, that we should send some persons to Claudius, to persuade him to lay down the government; and I am ready to be one of your ambassadors.'

(245) Upon this speech of Agrippa, the senate complied with him, and he was sent among others, and privately informed Claudius of the disorder the senate was in, and gave him instructions to answer them in a somewhat commanding strain, and as one invested with dignity and authority. (246) Accordingly Claudius said to the ambassadors, that he did not wonder the senate had no mind to have an emperor over them, because they had been harassed by the barbarity of those that had formerly been at the head of their affairs; but that they should taste of an equitable government under him, and moderate times, while he should only be their ruler in name, but the authority

should be equally common to them all: and since he had passed through many and various scenes of life before their eyes, it would be good for them not to distrust him. (247) So the ambassadors, upon their hearing this his answer, were dismissed. But Claudius discoursed with the army which was there gathered together, who took oath that they would persist in their fidelity to him; upon which he gave the guards every man five thousand drachmae apiece, and a proportionable quantity to their captains, and promised to give the same to the rest of the armies wheresoever they were.

(248) And now the consuls called the senate together, into the temple of Jupiter the Conqueror, while it was still night; but some of those senators concealed themselves in the city, being uncertain what to do, upon the hearing of this summons; and some of them went out of the city to their own farms, as foreseeing whither the public affairs were going and despairing of liberty; nay, these supposed it much better for them to be slaves without danger to themselves, and to live a lazy and inactive life, than by claiming the dignity of their forefathers, to run the hazard of their own safety. (249) However, a hundred, and no more, were gotten together; and as they were in consultation about the present posture of affairs, a sudden clamour was made by the soldiers that were on their side, desiring that the senate would choose them an emperor, and not bring the government into ruin by setting up a multitude of rulers. (250) So they fully declared themselves to be for the giving the government not to all, but to one; but they gave the senate leave to look out for a person worthy to be set over them, insomuch that now the affairs of the senate were much worse than before; because they had not only failed in the recovery of their liberty, which they boasted themselves of, but were in dread of Claudius also. (251) Yet there were those that hankered after the government, both on account of the dignity of their families, and that accruing to them by their marriages; for Marcus Minucianus was illustrious, both by his own nobility and by his having married Julia, the sister of Caius, who accordingly was very ready to claim the government, although the consuls discouraged him, and made one delay after another in proposing it: (252) that Minucianus also, who was one of Caius' murderers, restrained Valerius of Asia from thinking of such things; and a prodigious slaughter there had been, if leave had been given to these men to set up for themselves, and oppose Claudius. (253) There were also a considerable number of gladiators besides, and of those soldiers who kept watch by night in the city, and rowers of ships, who all ran into the camp: insomuch that of those who put in for the government, some left off their pretensions in order to spare the city, and others out of fear for their own persons.

(254) But as soon as ever it was day, Cherea, and those that were with him, came into the senate, and attempted to make speeches to the soldiers.

However, the multitude of those soldiers, when they saw that they were making signals for silence with their hands, and were ready to begin to speak to them, grew tumultuous, and would not let them speak at all, because they were all zealous to be under a monarchy; and they demanded of the senate one for their ruler, as not enduring any longer delays. (255) But the senate hesitated about either their own governing, or how they should themselves be governed, while the soldiers would not admit them to govern, and the murderers of Caius would not permit the soldiers to dictate to them. (256) When they were in these circumstances, Cherea was not able to contain the anger he had, and promised, that if they desired an emperor, he would give them one, if anyone would bring him the watchword from Eutychus. (257) Now, this Eutychus was charioteer of the green-band faction, styled Prasine, and a great friend of Caius, who used to harass the soldiery with building stables for the horses, and spent his time in ignominious labours, (258) which occasioned Cherea to reproach them with him, and to abuse them with much other scurrilous language; and told them he would bring them the head of Claudius; and that it was an amazing thing that, after their former madness, they should commit their government to a fool. (259) Yet were not they moved with his words, but drew their swords, and took up their ensigns, and went to Claudius, to join in taking the oath of fidelity to him. So the senate were left without anybody to defend them; and the very consuls differed nothing from private persons. (260) They were also under consternation and sorrow, men not knowing what would become of them, because Claudius was very angry at them; so they fell a-reproaching one another, and repented of what they had done. (261) At which juncture Sabinus, one of Caius' murderers, threatened that he would sooner come into the midst of them and kill himself, than consent to make Claudius emperor, and see slavery returning upon them; he also abused Cherea for loving his life too well, while he who was the first in his contempt of Caius, could think it a good thing to live, when, even by all that they had done for the recovery of their liberty, they had found it impossible to do it. (262) But Cherea said he had no manner of doubt upon him about killing himself; yet he would first sound the intentions of Claudius before he did it.

(263) These were the debates [about the senate]; but in the camp everybody was crowding on all sides to pay their court to Claudius, and the other consul, Quintus Pomponius, was reproached by the soldiery as having rather exhorted the senate to recover their liberty; whereupon they drew their swords, and were going to assault him, and they had done it, if Claudius had not hindered them, (264) who snatched the consul out of the danger he was in, and set him by him. But he did not receive that part of the senate which was with Quintus in the like honourable manner; nay, some of them received blows, and were

thrust away as they came to salute Claudius; nay, Aponius went away wounded, and they were all in danger. (265) However, King Agrippa went up to Claudius, and desired he would treat the senators more gently; for if any mischief should come to the senate, he would have no others over whom to rule. (266) Claudius complied with him, and called the senate together into the palace, and was carried thither himself through the city, while the soldiery conducted him, though this was to the great vexation of the multitude; (267) for Cherea and Sabinus, two of Caius' murderers, went in the forefront of them, in an open manner, while Pollio, whom Claudius, a little before, had made captain of his guards, had sent them an epistolary edict, to forbid them to appear in public. (268) Then did Claudius, upon his coming to the palace, get his friends together, and desired their suffrages about Cherea. They said that the work he had done was a glorious one; but they accused him that he did it of perfidiousness, and thought it just to inflict the punishment [of death] upon him, to discountenance such actions for the time to come. (269) So Cherea was led to his execution, and Lupus and many other Romans with him. Now it is reported that Cherea bore this calamity courageously; and this not only by the firmness of his own behaviour under it, but by the reproaches he laid upon Lupus, who fell into tears; (270) for when Lupus laid his garment aside and complained of the cold, he said, that cold was never hurtful to Lupus [i.e., a wolf]. And as a great many men went along with them to see the sight, when Cherea came to the place, he asked the soldier who was to be their executioner, whether this office was what he was used to, or whether this was the first time of his using his sword in that manner; and desired him to bring him that very sword with which he himself slew Caius. So he was happily killed at one stroke. (271) But Lupus did not meet with such good fortune in going out of the world, since he was timorous, and had many blows levelled at his neck, because he did not stretch it out boldly [as he ought to have done].

(272) Now a few days after this, as the Parental solemnities were just at hand, the Roman multitude made their usual oblations to their several ghosts, and put portions into the fire in honour of Cherea, and besought him to be merciful to them, and not continue his anger against them for their ingratitude. And this was the end of the life that Cherea came to. (273) But for Sabinus, although Claudius not only set him at liberty, but gave him leave to retain his former command in the army, yet did he think it would be unjust in him to fail of performing his obligations to his fellow confederates; so he fell upon his sword, and killed himself, the wound reaching up to the very hilt of the sword.

CHAPTER 5

(274) Now, when Claudius had taken out of the way all those soldiers whom he suspected, which he did immediately, he published an edict, and therein confirmed that kingdom to Agrippa which Caius had given him, and therein commended the king highly. He also made an addition to it of all that country over which Herod, who was his grandfather, had reigned, that is, Judea and Samaria; (275) and this he restored to him as due to his family. But for Abila of Lysanias, and all that lay at Mount Libanus, he bestowed them upon him, as out of his own territories. He also made a league with this Agrippa, confirmed by oaths, in the middle of the forum, in the city of Rome: (276) he also took away from Antiochus that kingdom which he was possessed of, but gave him a certain part of Cilicia and Commagena: he also set Alexander Lysimachus, the alabarch, at liberty, who had been his old friend, and steward to his mother Antonia, but had been imprisoned by Caius, whose son [Marcus] married Berenice, the daughter of Agrippa. (277) But when Marcus, Alexander's son, was dead, who had married her when she was a virgin, Agrippa gave her in marriage to his brother Herod, and begged for him of Claudius the kingdom of Chalcis.

(278) Now, about this time there was a sedition between the Jews and the Greeks, at the city of Alexandria; for, when Caius was dead, the nation of the Jews, which had been very much mortified under the reign of Caius, and reduced to very great distress by the people of Alexandria, recovered itself, and immediately took up their arms to fight for themselves. (279) So Claudius sent an order to the president of Egypt, to quiet that tumult; he also sent an edict, at the requests of King Agrippa and King Herod, both to Alexandria and to Syria, whose contents were as follows: (280) 'Tiberius Claudius Caesar Augustus Germanicus, high priest, and tribune of the people, ordains thus: (281) since I am assured that the Jews of Alexandria, called Alexandrians, have been joint inhabitants in the earliest times with the Alexandrians, and have obtained from their kings equal privileges with them, as is evident by the public records that are in their possession, and the edicts themselves; (282) and that after Alexandria had been subjected to our empire by Augustus, their rights and privileges have been preserved by those presidents who have at diverse times been sent thither; and that no dispute had been raised about those rights and privileges, (283) even when Aquila was governor of Alexandria; and that when the Jewish ethnarch was dead, Augustus did not prohibit the making such ethnarchs, as willing that all men should be so subject [to the Romans] as to continue in the observation of their own customs, and not be forced to transgress the ancient rules of their own country religion; (284) but that, in the

time of Caius, the Alexandrians became insolent toward the Jews that were among them, which Caius, out of his great madness, and want of understanding, reduced the nation of the Jews very low, because they would not transgress the religious worship of their country, and call him a god: (285) I will, therefore, that the nation of the Jews be not deprived of their rights and privileges, on account of the madness of Caius; but that those rights and privileges, which they formerly enjoyed, be preserved to them, and that they may continue in their own customs. And I charge both parties to take very great care that no troubles may arise after the promulgation of this edict.'

(286) And such were the contents of this edict on behalf of the Jews, that was sent to Alexandria. But the edict that was sent into the other parts of the habitable earth was this which follows – (287) 'Tiberius Claudius Caesar Augustus Germanicus, high priest, tribune of the people, chosen consul the second time, ordains thus: (288) upon the petition of King Agrippa and King Herod, who are persons very dear to me, that I would grant the same rights and privileges should be preserved to the Jews which are in all the Roman empire, which I have granted to those of Alexandria, I very willingly comply therewith; and this grant I make not only for the sake of the petitioners, (289) but as judging those Jews for whom I have been petitioned worthy of such a favour, on account of their fidelity and friendship to the Romans. I think it also very just that no Grecian city should be deprived of such rights and privileges, since they were preserved to them under the great Augustus. (290) It will therefore be fit to permit the Jews, who are in all the world under us, to keep their ancient customs without being hindered so to do. And I do charge them also to use this my kindness to them with moderation, and not to show a contempt of the superstitious observances of other nations, but to keep their own laws only. (291) And I will that this decree of mine be engraven on tables by the magistrates of the cities and colonies, and municipal places, both those within Italy and those without it, both kings and governors, by the means of the ambassadors, and to have them exposed to the public for full thirty days, in such a place whence it may plainly be read from the ground.'

CHAPTER 6

(292) Now Claudius Caesar, by these decrees of his which were sent to Alexandria and to all the habitable earth, made known what opinion he had of the Jews. So he soon sent Agrippa away to take his kingdom, now he was advanced to a more illustrious dignity than before, and sent letters to the presidents and procurators of the provinces, that they should treat him very kindly. (293) Accordingly he returned in haste, as was likely he would, now he returned in much greater prosperity than he had before. He also came to

Jerusalem and offered all the sacrifices that belonged to him, and omitted nothing which the law required; (294) on which account he ordained that many of the Nazirites should have their heads shorn. And for the golden chain which had been given him by Caius, of equal weight with that iron chain wherewith his royal hands had been bound, he hung it up within the limits of the temple, over the treasury, that it might be a memorial of the severe fate he had lain under, and a testimony of his change for the better; that it might be a demonstration how the greatest prosperity may have a fall, and that God sometimes raises what is fallen down; (295) for this chain thus dedicated, afforded a document, to all men, that King Agrippa had been once bound in a chain for a small cause, but recovered his former dignity again; and a little while afterwards got out of his bonds, and was advanced to be a more illustrious king than he was before. (296) Whence men may understand, that all that partake of human nature, how great soever they are, may fall; and that those that fall may gain their former illustrious dignity again.

(297) And when Agrippa had entirely finished all the duties of the divine worship, he removed Theophilus, the son of Ananus, from the high priesthood, and bestowed that honour of his on Simon the son of Boethus, whose name was also Cantheras, whose daughter King Herod had married, as I have related above. (298) Simon, therefore, had the [high] priesthood with his brethren, and with his father, in like manner as the sons of Simon, the son of Onias, who were three, had it formerly under the government of the Macedonians, as we have related in a former book.

(299) When the king had settled the high priesthood after this manner, he returned the kindness which the inhabitants of Jerusalem had shown him; for he released them from the tax upon houses, every one of whom paid it before, thinking it a good thing to requite the tender affection of those that loved him. He also made Silas the general of his forces, as a man who had partaken with him in many of his troubles. (300) But after a very little while the young men of Doris, preferring a rash attempt before piety and being naturally bold and insolent, carried a statue of Caesar into a synagogue of the Jews, and erected it there. (301) This procedure of theirs greatly provoked Agrippa; for it plainly tended to the dissolution of the laws of his country. So he came without delay to Publius Petronius, who was then president of Syria, and accused the people of Doris. (302) Nor did he less resent what was done than did Agrippa; for he judged it a piece of impiety to transgress the laws that regulate the actions of men. So he wrote the following letter to the people of Doris in an angry strain: (303) 'Publius Petronius, the president under Tiberius Claudius Caesar Augustus Germanicus, to the magistrates of Doris, ordains as follows: (304) Since some of you have had the boldness, or madness rather, after the edict of Claudius Caesar Augustus Germanicus was published, for

permitting the Jews to observe the laws of their country, not to obey the same, (305) but have acted in entire opposition thereto, as forbidding the Jews to assemble together in the synagogue, by removing Caesar's statue, and setting it up therein, and thereby offended not only the Jews, but the emperor himself, whose statue is more commodiously placed in his own temple than in a foreign one, where is the place of assembling together; while it is but a part of natural justice, that everyone should have the power over the place belonging peculiarly to themselves, according to the determination of Caesar — (306) to say nothing of my own determination, which it would be ridiculous to mention after the emperor's edict, which gives the Jews leave to make use of their own customs, as also gives order that they enjoy equally the rights of citizens with the Greeks themselves — (307) I therefore ordain that Proculus Vitellius, the centurion, bring those men to me, who, contrary to Augustus's edict, have been so insolent as to do this thing, at which those very men who appear to be of principal reputation among them, have an indignation also, and allege for themselves, that it was not done with their consent, but by the violence of the multitude, that they may give an account of what hath been done. (308) I also exhort the principal magistrates among them, unless they have a mind to have this action esteemed to be done with their consent, to inform the centurion of those that were guilty of it, and take care that no handle be hence taken for raising a sedition or quarrel among them; which those seem to me to hunt after, who encourage such doings; (309) while both I myself, and King Agrippa, for whom I have the highest honour, have nothing more under our care than that the nation of the Jews may have no occasion given them of getting together, under the pretence of avenging themselves, and become tumultuous. (310) And that it may be more publicly known what Augustus hath resolved about this whole matter, I have subjoined those edicts which he hath lately caused to be published at Alexandria, and which, although they may be well known to all, yet did King Agrippa, for whom I have the highest honour, read them at that time before my tribunal, and pleaded that the Jews ought not to be deprived of those rights which Augustus hath granted them. (311) I therefore charge you, that you do not, for the time to come, seek for any occasion of sedition or disturbance, but that everyone be allowed to follow their own religious customs.'

(312) Thus did Petronius take care of this matter, that such a breach of the law might be corrected, and that no such thing might be attempted afterwards against the Jews. (313) And now King Agrippa took the [high] priesthood away from Simon Cantheras, and put Jonathan, the son of Ananus, into it again, and owned that he was more worthy of that dignity than the other. But this was not a thing acceptable to him, to recover that his former dignity. So he

refused it, and said, (314) 'O king, I rejoice in the honour that thou hast for me, and take it kindly that thou wouldst give me such a dignity of thy own inclinations, although God hath judged that I am not at all worthy of the high priesthood. I am satisfied with having once put on the sacred garments; for I then put them on after a more holy manner than I should now receive them again. (315) But, if thou desirest that a person more worthy than myself should have this honourable employment, give me leave to name thee such a one. I have a brother that is pure from all sin against God, and of all offences against thyself; I recommend him to thee, as one that is fit for this dignity.' (316) So the king was pleased with these words of his, and passed by Jonathan, and, according to his brother's desire, bestowed the high priesthood upon Matthias. Nor was it long before Marcus succeeded Petronius, as president of Syria.

CHAPTER 7

(317) Now Silas, the general of the king's horse, because he had been faithful to him under all his misfortunes, and had never refused to be a partaker with him in any of his dangers, but had oftentimes undergone the most hazardous dangers for him, was full of assurance, and thought he might expect a sort of equality with the king, on account of the firmness of the friendship he had shown to him. (318) Accordingly, he would nowhere let the king sit as his superior, and took the like liberty in speaking to him upon all occasions, till he became troublesome to the king, when they were merry together, extolling himself beyond measure, and oft putting the king in mind of the severity of fortune he had undergone, that he might, by way of ostentation, demonstrate what zeal he had shown in his service; and was continually harping upon this string, what pains he had taken for him, and much enlarged still upon that subject. (319) The repetition of this so frequently seemed to reproach the king, insomuch that he took this ungovernable liberty of talking very ill at his hands. For the commemoration of times when men have been under ignominy, is by no means agreeable to them; and he is a very silly man, who is perpetually relating to a person what kindness he has done him. (320) At last, therefore, Silas had so thoroughly provoked the king's indignation, that he acted rather out of passion than good consideration, and did not only turn Silas out of his place, as general of his horse, but sent him in bonds into his own country. (321) But the edge of his anger wore off by length of time, and made room for more just reasonings as to his judgment about this man; and he considered how many labours he had undergone for his sake. So when Agrippa was solemnising his birthday, and he gave festival entertainments to all his subjects, he sent for Silas on the sudden to be his guest. (322) But, as he was a very frank man, he thought he had now a just handle given him to be

angry; which he could not conceal from those that came for him, but said to them, (323) 'What honour is this the king invites me to, which I conclude will soon be over? For the king hath not let me keep those original marks of the good will I bore him which I once had from him, but hath plundered me, and that unjustly also. (324) Does he think that I can leave off that liberty of speech, which, upon the consciousness of my deserts, I shall use more loudly than before, and shall relate how many misfortunes I have delivered him from? How many labours I have undergone for him, whereby I procured him deliverance and respect? As a reward for which I have borne the hardships of bonds and a dark prison! (325) I shall never forget this usage. Nay, perhaps my very soul, when it is departed out of the body, will not forget the glorious actions I did on his account.' This was the clamour he made: and he ordered the messengers to tell it to the king. So he perceived that Silas was incurable in his folly, and still suffered him to lie in prison.

(326) As for the walls of Jerusalem, that were adjoining to the new city [Bezetha], he repaired them at the expense of the public, and built them wider in breadth and higher in altitude; and he had made them too strong for all human power to demolish, unless Marcus, the then president of Syria, had by letter informed Claudius Caesar of what he was doing. (327) And when Claudius had some suspicion of attempts for innovation, he sent to Agrippa to leave off the building of those walls presently. So he obeyed, as not thinking it proper to contradict Claudius.

(328) Now, this king was by nature very beneficent, and liberal in his gifts, and very ambitious to oblige people with such large donations; and he made himself very illustrious by the many chargeable presents he made them. He took delight in giving, and rejoiced in living with good reputation. He was not at all like that Herod who reigned before him; (329) for that Herod was ill-natured, and severe in his punishments, and had no mercy on them that he hated; and everyone perceived that he was more friendly to the Greeks than to the Jews; for he adorned foreign cities with large presents in money; with building them baths and theatres besides: nay, in some of those places he erected temples, and porticoes in others; but he did not vouchsafe to raise one of the least edifices in any Jewish city, or make them any donation that was worth mentioning. (330) But Agrippa's temper was mild, and equally liberal to all men. He was humane to foreigners, and made them sensible of his liberality. He was in like manner rather of a gentle and compassionate temper. (331) Accordingly, he loved to live continually at Jerusalem, and was exactly careful in the observance of the laws of his country. He therefore kept himself entirely pure: nor did any day pass over his head without its appointed sacrifice.

(332) However, there was a certain man of the Jewish nation at Jerusalem, who appeared to be very accurate in the knowledge of the law. His name was

Simon. This man got together an assembly, while the king was absent at Caesarea, and had the insolence to accuse him as not living holily, and that he might justly be excluded out of the temple, since it belonged only to native Jews. (333) But the general of Agrippa's army informed him, that Simon had made such a speech to the people. So the king sent for him; and, as he was then sitting in the theatre, he bade him sit down by him, and said to him with a low and gentle voice, 'What is there done in this place that is contrary to the law?' (334) But he had nothing to say for himself, but begged his pardon. So the king was more easily reconciled to him than one could have imagined, as esteeming mildness a better quality in a king than anger; and knowing that moderation is more becoming in great men than passion. So he made Simon a small present, and dismissed him.

(335) Now, as Agrippa was a great builder in many places, he paid a peculiar regard to the people of Berytus; for he erected a theatre for them, superior to many others of that sort, both in sumptuousness and elegance, as also an amphitheatre, built at vast expenses; and besides these, he built them baths and porticoes, and spared for no costs in any of his edifices, to render them both handsome and large. (336) He also spent a great deal upon their dedication, and exhibited shows upon them, and brought thither musicians of all sorts, and such as made the most delightful music of the greatest variety. He also showed his magnificence upon the theatre, in his great number of gladiators; (337) and there it was that he exhibited the several antagonists, in order to please the spectators; no fewer indeed than seven hundred men to fight with seven hundred other men; and allotted all the malefactors he had for this exercise, that both the malefactors might receive their punishment, and that this operation of war might be a recreation in peace. And thus were these criminals all destroyed at once.

CHAPTER 8

(338) When Agrippa had finished what I have above related at Berytus, he removed to Tiberias, a city of Galilee. Now he was in great esteem among other kings. Accordingly there came to him Antiochus, king of Commagene, Sampsigeramus, king of Emesa, and Cotys, who was king of the Lesser Armenia, and Polemo, who was king of Pontus, as also Herod his brother, who was king of Chalcis. (339) All these he treated with agreeable entertainments, and after an obliging manner, and so as to exhibit the greatness of his mind – and so as to appear worthy of those respects which the kings paid to him, by coming thus to see him. (340) However, while these kings stayed with him, Marcus, the president of Syria, came thither. So the king, in order to preserve the respect that was due to the Romans, went out of

the city to meet him, as far as seven furlongs. (341) But this proved to be the beginning of a difference between him and Marcus; for he took with him in his chariot those other kings as his assessors. But Marcus had a suspicion what the meaning could be of so great a friendship of these kings one with another, and did not think so close an agreement of so many potentates to be for the interest of the Romans. He therefore sent some of his domestics to every one of them, and enjoined them to go their ways home without further delay. (342) This was very ill taken by Agrippa, who after that became his enemy. And now he took the high priesthood away from Matthias, and made Elioneus, the son of Cantheras, high priest in his stead.

(343) Now, when Agrippa had reigned three years over all Judea, he came to the city Caesarea, which was formerly called Strato's Tower; and there he exhibited shows in honour of Caesar, upon his being informed that there was a certain festival celebrated to make vows for his safety. At which festival, a great multitude was gotten together of the principal persons, and such as were of dignity through his province. (344) On the second day of which shows he put on a garment made wholly of silver, and of a contexture truly wonderful, and came into the theatre early in the morning; at which time the silver of his garment being illuminated by the fresh reflection of the sun's rays upon it, shone out after a surprising manner, and was so resplendent as to spread a horror over those that looked intently upon him; (345) and presently his flatterers cried out, one from one place, and another from another (though not for his good), that he was a god; and they added, 'Be thou merciful to us; for although we have hitherto reverenced thee only as a man, yet shall we henceforth own thee as superior to mortal nature.' (346) Upon this the king did neither rebuke them, nor reject their impious flattery. But, as he presently afterwards looked up, he saw an owl sitting on a certain rope over his head, and immediately understood that this bird was the messenger of ill tidings, as it had once been the messenger of good tidings to him; and fell into the deepest sorrow. A severe pain also arose in his belly, and began in a most violent manner. (347) He therefore looked upon his friends, and said, 'I whom you call a god, am commanded presently to depart this life; while Providence thus reproves the lying words you just now said to me, and I, who was by you called immortal, am immediately to be hurried away by death. But I am bound to accept of what Providence allots as it pleases God; for we have by no means lived ill, but in a splendid and happy manner.' (348) When he said this, his pain was become violent. Accordingly he was carried into the palace; and the rumour went abroad everywhere, that he would certainly die in a little time. (349) But the multitude presently sat in sackcloth, with their wives and children, after the law of their country, and besought God for the king's recovery. All places were also full of mourning and lamentation. Now the king

rested in a high chamber, and as he saw them below lying prostrate on the ground, he could not himself forbear weeping. (350) And when he had been quite worn out by the pain in his belly for five days, he departed this life, being in the fifty-fourth year of his age, and in the seventh year of his reign; (351) for he reigned four years under Caius Caesar, three of them were over Philip's tetrarchy only, and on the fourth he had that of Herod added to it; and he reigned besides those, three years under the reign of Claudius Caesar: in which time he reigned over the forementioned countries, and also had Judea added to them, as also Samaria and Caesarea. (352) The revenues that he received out of them were very great, no less than twelve millions of drachmae. Yet did he borrow great sums from others; for he was so very liberal, that his expenses exceeded his incomes; and his generosity was boundless.

(353) But before the multitude were made acquainted with Agrippa's being expired, Herod the king of Chalcis, and Helcias the master of his horse, and the king's friend, sent Aristo, one of the king's most faithful servants, and slew Silas, who had been their enemy, as if it had been done by the king's own command.

CHAPTER 9

(354) And thus did King Agrippa depart this life. But he left behind him a son, Agrippa by name, a youth in the seventeenth year of his age, and three daughters, one of whom, Berenice, was married to Herod, his father's brother, and was sixteen years old; the other two, Mariamne and Drusilla, were still virgins; the former was ten years old, and Drusilla six. (355) Now these his daughters were thus espoused by their father: Mariamne to Julius Archelaus Epiphanes, the son of Antiochus, the son of Chalcias: and Drusilla to the king of Commagene. (356) But when it was known that Agrippa was departed this life, the inhabitants of Caesarea and of Sebaste forgot the kindnesses he had bestowed on them, and acted the part of the bitterest enemies; (357) for they cast such reproaches upon the deceased as are not fit to be spoken of: and so many of them as were then soldiers, which were a great number, went to his house, and hastily carried off the statues of this king's daughters, and all at once carried them into the brothel houses, and when they had set them on the tops of those houses, they abused them to the utmost of their power, and did such things to them as are too indecent to be related. (358) They also laid themselves down in public places, and celebrated general feastings, with garlands on their heads, and with ointments and libations to Charon, and drinking to one another for joy that the king was expired. (359) Nay, they were not only unmindful of Agrippa, who had extended his liberality to them in abundance, but of his grandfather, Herod also, who had himself rebuilt their cities, and had raised them havens and temples at vast expenses.

(360) Now Agrippa, the son of the deceased, was at Rome, and brought up with Claudius Caesar. (361) And when Caesar was informed that Agrippa was dead, and that the inhabitants of Sebaste and Caesarea had abused him, he was sorry for the fist news, and was displeased with the ingratitude of those cities. (362) He was therefore disposed to send Agrippa junior, away presently to succeed his father in the kingdom, and was willing to confirm him in it by his oath. But those freemen and friends of his who had the greatest authority with him, dissuaded him from it, and said that it was a dangerous experiment to permit so large a kingdom to come under the government of so very young a man, and one hardly yet arrived at the years of discretion, who would not be able to take sufficient care of its administration; while the weight of a kingdom is heavy enough to a grown man. So Caesar thought what they said to be reasonable. (363) Accordingly he sent Cuspius Fadus to be procurator of Judea, and of the entire kingdom, and paid that respect to the deceased as not to introduce Marcus, who had been at variance with him, into his kingdom. But he determined, in the first place, to send orders to Fadus, that he should chastise the inhabitants of Caesarea and Sebaste for those abuses they had offered to him that was deceased, and their madness towards his daughters that were still alive; (364) and that he should remove that body of soldiers that were at Caesarea and Sebaste, with the five regiments, into Pontus, that they might do their military duty there, and that he should choose an equal number of soldiers out of the Roman legions that were in Syria, to supply their place. (365) Yet were not those that had such orders actually removed; for by sending ambassadors to Claudius, they mollified him, and got leave to abide in Judea still; and these were the very men that became the source of very great calamities to the Jews in after-times, and sowed the seeds of that war which began under Florus; whence it was that, when Vespasian had subdued the country, he removed them out of his province, as we shall relate hereafter.

BOOK TWENTY

(1) Upon the death of King Agrippa, which we have related in the foregoing book, Claudius Caesar sent Cassius Longinus as successor to Marcus, out of regard to the memory of King Agrippa, who had often desired of him by letters, while he was alive, that he would not suffer Marcus to be any longer president of Syria. (2) But Fadus, as soon as he was come procurator into Judea, found quarrelsome doings between the Jews that dwelt in Perea and the people of Philadelphia, about their borders, at a village called Mia, that was filled with men of a warlike temper; for the Jews of Perea had taken up arms without the consent of their principal men, and had destroyed many of the Philadelphians. (3) When Fadus was informed of this procedure, it provoked him very much that they had not left the determination of the matter to him, if they thought that the Philadelphians had done them any wrong, but had rashly taken up arms against them. (4) So he seized upon three of their principal men, who were also the causes of this sedition, and ordered them to be bound, and afterward had one of them slain, whose name was Hannibal; and he banished the other two, Amram and Eleazar; (5) Tholomy also, the arch robber, was, after some time, brought to him bound, and slain, but not till he had done a world of mischief to Idumea and the Arabians. And indeed, from that time, Judea was cleared of robberies by the care and providence of Fadus. (6) He also at this time sent for the high priests and the principal citizens of Jerusalem, and this at the command of the emperor, and admonished them that they should lay up the long garment and the sacred vestment, which it is customary for nobody but the high priest to wear, in the tower of Antonia, that it might be under the power of the Romans, as it had been formerly. (7) Now the Jews durst not contradict what he had said, but desired Fabius, however, and Longinus (which last was come to Jerusalem, and had brought a great army with him, out of a fear that the [rigid] injunctions of Fadus should force the Jews to rebel), that they might, in the first place, have leave to send ambassadors to Caesar, to petition him that they might have the holy vestments under their own power; and that, in the next place, they would tarry till they knew what answer Claudius would give to that their request. (8) So they replied, that they would give them leave to send their ambassadors, provided they would give them their sons as pledges [for their peaceable behaviour]. And when they had agreed so to do, and had given them the pledges they

desired, the ambassadors were sent accordingly. (9) But when, upon their coming to Rome, Agrippa junior, the son of the deceased, understood the reason why they came (for he dwelt with Claudius Caesar, as we said before), he besought Caesar to grant the Jews their request about the holy vestments, and to send a message to Fadus accordingly.

(10) Hereupon, Claudius called for the ambassadors, and told them that he granted their request; and bade them to return their thanks to Agrippa for this favour, which had been bestowed on them upon his entreaty. And besides these answers of his, he sent the following letter by them: (11) 'Claudius Caesar Germanicus, tribune of the people the fifth time, and designed consul the fourth time, and imperator the tenth time, the father of his country, to the magistrates, senate and people, and the whole nation of the Jews, sendeth greeting. (12) Upon the representation of your ambassadors to me by Agrippa my friend, whom I have brought up, and have now with me, and who is a person of very great piety, who are come to give me thanks for the care I have taken of your nation, and to entreat me, in an earnest and obliging manner, that they may have the holy vestments, with the crown belonging to them, under their power – I grant their request, as that excellent person Vitellius, who is very dear to me, had done before me. (13) And I have complied with your desire, in the first place out of regard to that piety which I profess, and because I would have everyone worship God according to the laws of their own country; and this I do also, because I shall hereby highly gratify King Herod and Agrippa junior, whose sacred regards to me, and earnest good will to you, I am well acquainted with, and with whom I have the greatest friendship, and whom I highly esteem, and look on as persons of the best character. (14) Now I have written about these affairs to Cuspius Fadus, my procurator. The names of those that brought me your letter are Cornelius the son of Cero, Trypho the son of Theudio, Dorotheus the son of Nathaniel, and John the son of John. This is dated before the fourth of the Calends of July, when Rufus and Pompeius Sylvanus are consuls.'

(15) Herod, also, the brother of the deceased Agrippa, who was then possessed of the royal authority over Chalcis, petitioned Claudius Caesar for the authority over the temple, and the money of the sacred treasure, and the choice of the high priests, and obtained all that he petitioned for. (16) So that after that time this authority continued among all his descendants till the end of the war. Accordingly Herod removed the last high priest, called Cantheras, and bestowed that dignity on his successor, Joseph the son of Camus.

CHAPTER 2

(17) About this time it was that Helena, queen of Adiabene, and her son Izates, changed their course of life, and embraced the Jewish customs, and this on the occasion following: (18) Monobazus, the king of Adiabene, who had also the name of Bazeus, fell in love with his sister Helena, and took her to be his wife, and begat her with child. But as he was in bed with her one night, he laid his hands upon his wife's belly, and fell asleep, and seemed to hear a voice which bade him take his hands off his wife's belly, and not to hurt the infant that was therein, which, by God's providence, would be safely born, and have a happy end. (19) This voice put him into disorder; so he awaked immediately, and told the story to his wife; and when his son was born, he called him Izates. (20) He had indeed Monobazus, his elder brother, by Helena also, as he had other sons by other wives besides. Yet did he openly place all his affections on this his only begotten son Izates, (21) which was the origin of that envy which his other brethren, by the same father, bare to him; while on this account they hated him more and more, and were all under great affliction that their father should prefer Izates before them all. (22) Now although their father was very sensible of these their passions, yet did he forgive them, as not indulging those passions out of an ill disposition, but out of a desire each of them had to be beloved by their father. However, he sent Izates, with many presents, to Abennerig, the king of Charax-Spasini, and that out of the great dread he was in about him, lest he should come to some misfortune by the hatred his brethren bore him; and he committed his son's preservation to him. (23) Upon which Abennerig gladly received the young man, and had a great affection for him, and married him to his own daughter, whose name was Samacha; he also bestowed a country upon him, from which he received large revenues.

(24) But when Monobazus was grown old, and saw that he had but a little time to live, he had a mind to come to the sight of his son before he died. So he sent for him and embraced him after the most affectionate manner, and bestowed on him the country called Carrae; (25) it was a soil that bare amomum in great plenty: there are also in it the remains of that ark, wherein it is related that Noah escaped the deluge, and where they are still shown to such as are desirous to see them. (26) Accordingly Izates abode in that country until his father's death. But the very day that Monobazus died, Queen Helena sent for all the grandees and governors of the kingdom, and for those that had the armies committed to their command; (27) and when they were come, she made the following speech to them: 'I believe you are not unacquainted that my husband was desirous Izates should succeed him in the government, and thought him worthy so to do. However, I wait your determination; for happy

is he who receives a kingdom, not from a single person only, but from the willing suffrages of a great many.' (28) This she said, in order to try those that were invited, and to discover their sentiments. Upon the hearing of which they first of all paid their homage to the queen, as their custom was, and then they said that they confirmed the king's determination, and would submit to it; and they rejoiced that Izates' father had preferred him before the rest of his brethren, as being agreeable to all their wishes: (29) but that they were desirous first of all to slay his brethren and kinsmen, that so the government might come securely to Izates; because if they were once destroyed, all that fear would be over which might arise from their hatred and envy to him. (30) Helena replied to this, that she returned them her thanks for their kindness to herself and to Izates; but desired that they would however defer the execution of this slaughter of Izates' brethren till he should be there himself, and give his approbation to it. (31) So since these men had not prevailed with her when they advised her to slay them, they exhorted her at least to keep them in bonds till he should come, and that for their own security; they also gave her counsel to set up someone whom she could put the greatest trust in, as governor of the kingdom in the meantime. (32) So Queen Helena complied with this counsel of theirs, and set up Monobazus, the eldest son, to be king, and put the diadem upon his head, and gave him his father's ring, with its signet; as also the ornament which they call Sampser, and exhorted him to administer the affairs of the kingdom till his brother should come; (33) who came suddenly upon hearing that his father was dead, and succeeded his brother Monobazus, who resigned up the government to him.

(34) Now, during the time Izates abode at Charax-Spasini, a certain Jewish merchant, whose name was Ananias, got among the women that belonged to the king, and taught them to worship God according to the Jewish religion. (35) He, moreover, by their means became known to Izates: and persuaded him, in like manner, to embrace that religion; he also, at the earnest entreaty of Izates, accompanied him when he was sent for by his father to come to Adiabene; it also happened that Helena, about the same time, was instructed by a certain other Jew, and went over to them. (36) But, when Izates had taken the kingdom, and was come to Adiabene, and there saw his brethren and other kinsmen in bonds, he was displeased at it; (37) and as he thought it an instance of impiety either to slay or imprison them, but still thought it a hazardous thing for to let them have their liberty, with the remembrance of the injuries that had been offered them, he sent some of them and their children for hostages to Rome, to Claudius Caesar, and sent the others to Artabanus, the king of Parthia, with the like intentions.

(38) And when he perceived that his mother was highly pleased with the Jewish customs, he made haste to change, and to embrace them entirely; and

as he supposed that he could not he thoroughly a Jew unless he were circumcised, he was ready to have it done. (39) But when his mother understood what he was about, she endeavoured to hinder him from doing it, and said to him that this thing would bring him into danger; and that as he were a king he would thereby bring himself into great odium among his subjects, when they would understand that he was so fond of rites that were to them strange and foreign; and that they would never bear to be ruled over by a Jew. (40) This it was that she said to him, and for the present persuaded him to forbear. And when he had related what she had said to Ananias, he confirmed what his mother had said; and when he had also threatened to leave him, unless he complied with him, he went away from him; (41) and said that he was afraid lest such an action being once become public to all, he should himself be in danger of punishment for having been the occasion of it, and having been the king's instructor in actions that were of ill reputation; and he said, that he might worship God without being circumcised, even though he did resolve to follow the Jewish law entirely; which worship of God was of a superior nature to circumcision. (42) He added, that God would forgive him, though he did not perform the operation, while it was omitted out of necessity, and for fear of his subjects. So the king at that time complied with these persuasions of Ananias. (43) But afterwards, as he had not quite left off his desire of doing this thing, a certain other Jew that came out of Galilee, whose name was Eleazer, and who was esteemed very skilful in the learning of his country, persuaded him to do the thing; (44) for as he entered into his palace to salute him, and found him reading the law of Moses, he said to him, 'Thou dost not consider, O king, that thou unjustly breakest the principal of those laws, and art injurious to God himself, [by omitting to be circumcised]; for thou oughtest not only to read them, but chiefly to practise what they enjoin thee. (45) How long wilt thou continue uncircumcised? But, if thou hast not yet read the law about circumcision, and dost not know how great impiety thou art guilty of by neglecting it, read it now.' (46) When the king had heard what he said, he delayed the thing no longer, but retired to another room, and sent for a surgeon, and did what he was commanded to do. He then sent for his mother, and Ananias his tutor, and informed them that he had done the thing; (47) upon which they were presently struck with astonishment and fear, and that to a great degree, lest the thing should be openly discovered and censured, and the king should hazard the loss of his kingdom, while his subjects would not bear to be governed by a man who was so zealous in another religion; and lest they should themselves run some hazard, because they would be supposed the occasion of his so doing. (48) But it was God himself who hindered what they feared from taking effect; for he preserved both Izates himself and his sons when they fell into many dangers, and procured their deliverance when it seemed to be impossible, and demonstrated thereby, that the fruit of piety does not perish as to those that have regard to him, and fix their faith upon him only: but these events we shall relate hereafter.

(49) But as to Helena, the king's mother, when she saw that the affairs of Izates' kingdom were in peace, and that her son was a happy man, and admired among all men and even among foreigners, by the means of God's providence over him, she had a mind to go to the city of Jerusalem, in order to worship at that temple of God which was so very famous among all men, and to offer her thank offerings there. So she desired her son to give her leave to go thither: (50) upon which he gave his consent to what she desired very willingly, and made great preparations for her dismission, and gave her a great deal of money, and she went down to the city of Jerusalem, her son conducting her on her journey a great way. (51) Now her coming was of very great advantage to the people of Jerusalem; for whereas a famine did oppress them at that time, and many people died for want of what was necessary to procure food withal, Queen Helena sent some of her servants to Alexandria with money to buy a great quantity of corn, and others of them to Cyprus, to bring a cargo of dried figs; (52) and as soon as they were come back, and brought those provisions, which was done very quickly, she distributed food to those that were in want of it, and left a most excellent memorial behind her of this benefaction, which she bestowed on our whole nation; (53) and when her son Izates was informed of this famine, he sent great sums of money to the principal men in Jerusalem. However, what favours this queen and king conferred upon our city Jerusalem, shall be further related hereafter.

CHAPTER 3

(54) But now Artabanus, king of the Parthians, perceiving that the governors of the provinces had framed a plot against him, did not think it safe for him to continue among them; but resolved to go to Izates, in hopes of finding some way for his preservation by his means, and, if possible, for his return to his own dominions. (55) So he came to Izates, and brought a thousand of his kindred and servants with him, and met him upon the road, (56) while he well knew Izates, but Izates did not know him. When Artabanus stood near him, and in the first place, worshipped him according to the custom, he then said to him, 'O king, do not thou overlook me thy servant, nor do thou proudly reject the suit I make thee; for as I am reduced to a low estate, by the change of fortune, and of a king am become a private man, I stand in need of thy assistance. (57) Have regard, therefore, unto the uncertainty of my fortune, and esteem the care thou shalt take of me to be taken of thyself also; for if I be neglected, and my subjects go off unpunished, many other subjects will become more insolent

towards other kings also.' (58) And this speech Artabanus made with tears in his eyes, and with a dejected countenance. Now, as soon as Izates heard Artabanus' name, and saw him stand as a supplicant before him, he leaped down from his horse immediately, (59) and said to him, 'Take courage, O king! Nor be disturbed at thy present calamity, as if it were incurable; for the change of thy sad condition shall be sudden; for thou shalt find me to be more thy friend and thy assistant than thy hopes can promise thee; for I will either re-establish thee in the kingdom of Parthia, or lose my own.'

(60) When he had said this, he set Artabanus upon his horse, and followed him on foot, in honour of a king whom he owned as greater than himself – which when Artabanus saw, he was very uneasy at it, and sware by his present fortune and honour, that he would get down from his horse, unless Izates would get upon his horse again and go before him. (61) So he complied with his desire, and leaped upon his horse; and, when he had brought him to his royal palace, he showed him all sorts of respect when they sat together, and he gave him the upper place at festivals also, as regarding not his present fortune, but his former dignity; and that upon this consideration also, that the changes of fortune are common to all men. (62) He also wrote to the Parthians, to persuade them to receive Artabanus again; and gave them his right hand and his faith, that he should forget what was past and done, and that he would undertake for this as a mediator between them. (63) Now the Parthians did not themselves refuse to receive him again, but pleaded that it was not now in their power so to do, because they had committed the government to another person, who had accepted of it, and whose name was Cinnamus; and that they were afraid lest a civil war should arise on this account. (64) When Cinnamus understood their intentions, he wrote to Artabanus himself, for he had been brought up by him, and was of a nature good and gentle also, and desired him to put confidence in him, and to come and take his own dominions again. (65) Accordingly Artabanus trusted him, and returned home; when Cinnamus met him, worshipped him, and saluted him as a king, and took the diadem off his own head, and put it on the head of Artabanus.

(66) And thus was Artabanus restored to his kingdom again by the means of Izates, when he had lost it by the means of the grandees of the kingdom. Nor was he unmindful of the benefits he had conferred upon him, but rewarded him with such honours as were of the greatest esteem among them; (67) for he gave him leave to wear his tiara upright, and to sleep upon a golden bed, which are privileges and marks of honour peculiar to the kings of Parthia. (68) He also cut off a large and fruitful country from the king of Armenia, and bestowed it upon him. The name of the country is Nisibis, wherein the Macedonians had formerly built that city which they called Antioch of Mygodonia. And these were the honours that were paid Izates by the king of the Parthians.

(69) But in no long time Artabanus died, and left his kingdom to his son Bardanes. Now this Bardanes came to Izates, and would have persuaded him to join him with his army, and to assist him in the war he was preparing to make with the Romans; (70) but he could not prevail with him. For Izates so well knew the strength and good fortune of the Romans, that he took Bardanes to attempt what was impossible to be done; (71) and having, besides, sent his sons, five in number, and they but young also, to learn accurately the language of our nation, together with our learning, as well as he had sent his mother to worship at our temple, as I have said already, was the more backward to a compliance; and restrained Bardanes, telling him perpetually of the great armies and famous actions of the Romans, and thought thereby to terrify him, and desired thereby to hinder him from that expedition. (72) But the Parthian king was provoked at this his behaviour, and denounced war immediately against Izates. Yet did he gain no advantage by this war, because God cut off all his hopes therein; (73) for the Parthians, perceiving Bardanes' intention, and how he had determined to make war with the Romans, slew him, and gave his kingdom to his brother Gotarzes. (74) He also, in no long time, perished by a plot made against him, and Vologases, his brother, succeeded him, who committed two of his provinces to two of his brothers by the same father – that of the Medes to the elder, Pacorus; and Armenia to the younger, Tiridates.

CHAPTER 4

(75) Now when the king's brother, Monobazus, and his other kindred, saw how Izates, by his piety to God, was become greatly esteemed by all men, they also had a desire to leave the religion of their country, and to embrace the customs of the Jews; (76) but that act of theirs was discovered by Izates' subjects. Whereupon the grandees were much displeased, and could not contain their anger at them, but had an intention, when they should find a proper opportunity, to inflict a punishment upon them. (77) Accordingly, they wrote to Abia, king of the Arabians, and promised him great sums of money, if he would make an expedition against their king: and they further promised him that, on the first onset, they would desert their king, because they were desirous to punish him, by reason of the hatred he had to their religious worship; then they obliged themselves, by oaths, to be faithful to each other, and desired that he would make haste in this design. (78) The king of Arabia complied with their desires, and brought a great army into the field, and marched against Izates; and, in the beginning of the first onset, and before they came to a close fight, those grandees, as if they had a panic terror upon them, all deserted Izates, as they had agreed to do, and, turning their backs upon their enemies, ran away. (79) Yet was not Izates dismayed at this; but when he

understood that the grandees had betrayed him, he also retired into his camp, and made inquiry into the matter; and as soon as he knew who they were that had made this conspiracy with the king of Arabia, he cut off those that were found guilty; and renewing the fight on the next day, he slew the greatest part of his enemies, (80) and forced all the rest to betake themselves to flight. He also pursued their king, and drove him into a fortress called Arsamus, and, following on the siege vigorously, he took that fortress. And, when he had plundered it of all the prey that was in it, which was not small, he returned to Adiabene; yet did not he take Abia alive; because, when he found himself encompassed on every side, he slew himself.

(81) But although the grandees of Adiabene had failed in their first attempt, as being delivered up by God into their king's hands, yet would they not even then be quiet, but wrote again to Vologases, who was then king of Parthia, and desired that he would kill Izates, and set over them some other potentate, who should be of a Parthian family; for they said that they hated their own king for abrogating the laws of their forefathers, and embracing foreign customs. (82) When the king of Parthia heard this, he boldly made war upon Izates; and, as he had no just pretence for this war, he sent to him, and demanded back those honourable privileges which had been bestowed on him by his father, and threatened, on his refusal, to make war upon him. (83) Upon hearing of this, Izates was under no small trouble of mind, as thinking it would be a reproach upon him to appear to resign those privileges that had been bestowed upon him out of cowardice; (84) yet, because he knew, that though the king of Parthia should receive back those honours, yet would he not be quiet, he resolved to commit himself to God, his protector, in the present danger he was in of his life; (85) and as he esteemed him to be his principal assistant, he entrusted his children and his wives to a very strong fortress, and laid up his corn in his citadels, and set the hay and the grass on fire. And when he had thus put things in order, as well as he could, he awaited the coming of the enemy. (86) And when the king of Parthia was come, with a great army of footmen and horsemen, which he did sooner than was expected (for he marched in great haste), and had cast up a bank at the river that parted Adiabene from Media – Izates also pitched his camp not far off, having with him six thousand horsemen. (87) But there came a messenger to Izates, sent by the king of Parthia, who told him how large his dominions were, as reaching from the river Euphrates to Bactria, and enumerated that king's subjects: (88) he also threatened him that he should be punished, as a person ungrateful to his lords; and said that the God whom he worshipped could not deliver him out of the king's hands. (89) When the messenger had delivered this his message, Izates replied, that he knew the king of Parthia's power was much greater than his own; but that he knew also that God was much more powerful than all men.

And when he had returned him this answer, he betook himself to make supplication to God, and threw himself on the ground, and put ashes upon his head, in testimony of his confusion, and fasted, together with his wives and children. Then he called upon God, and said, (90) 'O Lord and Governor, if I have not in vain committed myself to thy goodness, but have justly determined that thou only art the Lord and principal of all beings, come to my assistance, and defend me from my enemies, not only on my own account, but on account of their insolent behaviour with regard to thy power, while they have not feared to lift up their proud and arrogant tongue against thee.' (91) Thus did he lament and bemoan himself, with tears in his eyes; whereupon God heard his prayer. And immediately that very night Vologases received letters, the contents of which were these, that a great band of Dahae and Sacae, despising him, now he was gone so long a journey from home, had made an expedition, and laid Parthia waste; so that he [was forced to] retire back, without doing anything. And thus it was that Izates escaped the threatenings of the Parthians, by the providence of God.

(92) It was not long ere Izates died, when he had completed fifty-five years of his life, and had ruled his kingdom twenty-four years. He left behind him twenty-four sons and twenty-four daughters. (93) However, he gave order that his brother Monobazus should succeed in the government, thereby requiting him, because, while he was himself absent, after the father's death, he had faithfully preserved the government for him. (94) But when Helena, his mother, heard of her son's death, she was in great heaviness, as was but natural, upon her loss of such a most dutiful son; yet was it a comfort to her that she heard the succession came to her eldest son. Accordingly she went to him in haste; and when she was come into Adiabene, she did not long outlive her son Izates. (95) But Monobazus sent her bones, as well as those of Izates, his brother, to Jerusalem, and gave order that they should be buried at the pyramids which their mother had erected; they were three in number, and distant no more than three furlongs from the city of Jerusalem. (96) But for the actions of Monobazus the king, which he did during the rest of his life, we will relate them hereafter.

CHAPTER 5

(97) Now it came to pass, while Fadus was procurator of Judea, that a certain magician, whose name was Theudas, persuaded a great part of the people to take their effects with them, and follow him to the river Jordan; for he told them he was a prophet, and that he would, by his own command, divide the river, and afford them an easy passage over it; (98) and many were deluded by his words. However, Fadus did not permit them to make any advantage of his

wild attempt, but sent a troop of horsemen out against them; who, falling upon them unexpectedly, slew many of them and took many of them alive. They also took Theudas alive, and cut off his head, and carried it to Jerusalem. (99) This was what befell the Jews in the time of Cuspius Fadus' government.

(100) Then came Tiberius Alexander as successor to Fadus; he was the son of Alexander the alabarch of Alexandria; which Alexander was a principal person among all his contemporaries, both for his family and wealth: he was also more eminent for his piety than this his son Alexander, for he did not continue in the religion of his country. (101) Under these procurators that great famine happened in Judea, in which Queen Helena bought corn in Egypt at a great expense, and distributed it to those that were in want, as I have related already; (102) and besides this, the sons of Judas of Galilee were now slain; I mean of that Judas who caused the people to revolt, when Cyrenius came to take an account of the estates of the Jews, as we have shown in a foregoing book. The names of those sons were James and Simon, whom Alexander commanded to be crucified; (103) but now Herod, king of Chalcis, removed Joseph, the son of Camydus, from the high priesthood, and made Ananias, the son of Nebedeus, his successor; and now it was that Cumanus came as successor to Tiberius Alexander; (104) as also that Herod, brother of Agrippa the great king, departed this life, in the eighth year of the reign of Claudius Caesar. He left behind him three sons: Aristobulus, whom he had by his first wife, with Bernicianus and Hyrcanus, both whom he had by Berenice his brother's daughter; but Claudius Caesar bestowed his dominions on Agrippa junior.

(105) Now, while the Jewish affairs were under the administration of Cumanus, there happened a great tumult at the city of Jerusalem, and many of the Jews perished therein; but I shall first explain the occasion whence it was derived. (106) When that feast which is called the Passover was at hand, at which time our custom is to use unleavened bread, and a great multitude was gathered together from all parts to that feast, Cumanus was afraid lest some attempt of innovation should then be made by them; so he ordered that one regiment of the army should take their arms, and stand in the temple cloisters, to repress any attempts of innovation, if perchance any such should begin; (107) and this was no more than what the former procurators of Judea did at such festivals; (108) but on the fourth day of the feast, a certain soldier let down his breeches, and exposed his privy members to the multitude, which put those that saw him into a furious rage, and made them cry out that this impious action was not done to reproach them, but God himself; nay, some of them reproached Cumanus, and pretended that the soldier was set on by him; (109) which when Cumanus heard, he was also himself not a little provoked at such reproaches laid upon him; yet did he exhort them to leave off such seditious attempts, and not to raise a tumult at the festival; (110) but when he could not

induce them to be quiet, for they still went on in their reproaches to him, he gave order that the whole army should take their entire armour, and come to Antonia, which was a fortress, as we have said already, which overlooked the temple; (111) but when the multitude saw the soldiers there, they were affrighted at them, and ran away hastily; but as the passages out were but narrow, and as they thought their enemies followed them, they were crowded together in their flight, and a great number were pressed to death in those narrow passages; (112) nor indeed was the number fewer than twenty thousand that perished in this tumult. So, instead of a festival they had at last a mournful day of it; and they all of them forgot their prayers and sacrifices, and betook themselves to lamentation and weeping; so great an affliction did the impudent obsceneness of a single soldier bring upon them.

(113) Now before this their first mourning was over, another mischief befell them also; for some of those that raised the foregoing tumult, when they were travelling along the public road, about a hundred furlongs from the city, robbed Stephanus, a servant of Caesar, as he was journeying, and plundered him of all that he had with him; (114) which things when Cumanus heard of, he sent soldiers immediately, and ordered them to plunder the neighbouring villages, and to bring the most eminent persons among them in bonds to him. (115) Now, as this devastation was making, one of the soldiers seized the Laws of Moses, that lay in one of those villages, and brought them out before the eyes of all present, and tore them to pieces; and this was done with reproachful language, and much scurrility; (116) which things when the Jews heard of, they ran together, and that in great numbers, and came down to Caesarea, where Cumanus then was, and besought him that he would avenge, not themselves, but God himself, whose laws had been affronted; for that they could not bear to live any longer, if the laws of their forefathers must be affronted after this manner. (117) Accordingly Cumanus, out of fear lest the multitude should go into a sedition, and by the advice of his friends also, took care that the soldier who had offered the affront to the laws should be beheaded; and thereby put a stop to the sedition which was ready to be kindled a second time.

CHAPTER 6

(118) Now there arose a quarrel between the Samaritans and the Jews on the occasion following: it was the custom of the Galileans, when they came to the holy city at the festivals, to take their journeys through the country of the Samaritans; and at this time there lay, in the road they took, a village that was called Ginea, which was situated in the limits of Samaria and the great plain, where certain persons thereto belonging fought with the Galileans, and killed

a great many of them; (119) but when the principal of the Galileans were informed of what had been done, they came to Cumanus, and desired him to avenge the murder of those that were killed; but he was induced by the Samaritans, with money, to do nothing in the matter; (120) upon which the Galileans were much displeased, and persuaded the multitude of the Jews to betake themselves to arms, and to regain their liberty, saying that slavery was in itself a bitter thing, but that when it was joined with direct injuries, it was perfectly intolerable. (121) And when their principal men endeavoured to pacify them, and promised to endeavour to persuade Cumanus to avenge those that were killed, they would not hearken to them, but took their weapons, and entreated the assistance of Eleazar, the son of Dineus, a robber, who had many years made his abode in the mountains, with which assistance they plundered many villages of the Samaritans. (122) When Cumanus heard of this action of theirs, he took the band of Sebaste, with four regiments of footmen, and armed the Samaritans, and marched out against the Jews, and caught them, and slew many of them, and took a great number of them alive; (123) whereupon those that were the most eminent persons at Jerusalem, and that both in regard to the respect that was paid them, and the families they were of, as soon as they saw to what a height things were gone, put on sackcloth, and heaped ashes upon their heads, and by all possible means besought the seditious, and persuaded them that they would set before their eyes the utter subversion of their country, the conflagration of their temple, and the slavery of themselves, their wives, and children, which would be the consequences of what they were doing, and would alter their minds, would cast away their weapons, and for the future be quiet, and return to their own homes. These persuasions of theirs prevailed upon them. (124) So the people dispersed themselves, and the robbers went away again to their places of strength; and after this time all Judea was overrun with robberies.

(125) But the principal of the Samaritans went to Ummidius Quadratus, the president of Syria, who at that time was at Tyre, and accused the Jews of setting their villages on fire, and plundering them; (126) and said withal, that they were not so much displeased at what they had suffered, as they were at the contempt thereby shown to the Romans; while if they had received any injury, they ought to have made them the judges of what had been done, and not presently to make such devastation, as if they had not the Romans for their governors; (127) on which account they came to him, in order to obtain that vengeance they wanted. This was the accusation which the Samaritans brought against the Jews. But the Jews affirmed, that the Samaritans were the authors of this tumult and fighting, and that, in the first place, Cumanus had been corrupted by their gifts, and passed over the murder of those that were slain in silence — (128) which allegations when Quadratus heard, he put off the hearing of the cause,

and promised that he would give sentence when he should come into Judea, and should have a more exact knowledge of the truth of that matter. (129) So these men went away without success. Yet was it not long ere Quadratus came to Samaria; where, upon hearing the cause, he supposed that the Samaritans were the authors of that disturbance. But when he was informed that certain of the Jews were making innovations, he ordered those to be crucified whom Cumanus had taken captives. (130) From whence he came to a certain village called Lydda, which was not less than a city in largeness, and there heard the Samaritan cause a second time before his tribunal, and there learned from a certain Samaritan, that one of the chief of the Jews, whose name was Dortus, and some other innovators with him, four in number, persuaded the multitude to a revolt from the Romans; (131) whom Quadratus ordered to be put to death: but still he sent away Ananias the high priest, and Ananus the commander [of the temple], in bonds to Rome, to give an account of what they had done to Claudius Caesar. (132) He also ordered the principal men, both of the Samaritans and of the Jews, as also Cumanus the procurator, and Celer the tribune, to go to Italy to the emperor, that he might hear their cause, and determine their differences one with another. (133) But he came again to the city of Jerusalem, out of his fear that the multitude of the Jews should attempt some innovations; but he found the city in a peaceable state, and celebrating one of the usual festivals of their country to God. So he believed that they would not attempt any innovations, and left them at the celebration of the festival, and returned to Antioch.

(134) Now Cumanus and the principal of the Samaritans, who were sent to Rome, had a day appointed them by the emperor, whereon they were to have pleaded their cause about the quarrels they had one with another. (135) But now Caesar's freedmen and his friends were very zealous on the behalf of Cumanus and the Samaritans; and they had prevailed over the Jews, unless Agrippa junior, who was then at Rome, had seen the principal of the Jews hard set, and had earnestly entreated Agrippina, the emperor's wife, to persuade her husband to hear the cause, so as was agreeable to his justice, and to condemn those to be punished who were really the authors of this revolt from the Roman government: (136) whereupon Claudius was so well disposed beforehand, that when he had heard the cause, and found that the Samaritans had been the ringleaders in those mischievous doings, he gave order that those who came up to him should be slain, and that Cumanus should be banished. He also gave order that Celer the tribune should be carried back to Jerusalem, and should be drawn through the city in the sight of all the people, and then should be slain.

CHAPTER 7

(137) So Claudius sent Felix, the brother of Pallas, to take care of the affairs of Judea; (138) and, when he had already completed the twelfth year of his reign, he bestowed upon Agrippa the tetrarchy of Philip, and Batanea, and added thereto Trachonitis, with Abila; which last had been the tetrarchy of Lysanius; but he took from him Chalcis, when he had been governor thereof four years. (139) And when Agrippa had received these countries as the gift of Caesar, he gave his sister Drusilla in marriage to Azizus, king of Emesa, upon his consent to be circumcised; for Epiphanes, the son of King Antiochus, had refused to marry her, because after he had promised her father formerly to come over to the Jewish religion, he would not now perform that promise. (140) He also gave Mariamne in marriage to Archelaus, the son of Helcias, to whom she had formerly been betrothed by Agrippa her father; from which marriage was derived a daughter, whose name was Berenice.

(141) But for the marriage of Drusilla with Azizus, it was in no long time afterward dissolved, upon the following occasion: (142) while Felix was procurator of Judea, he saw this Drusilla, and fell in love with her; for she did indeed exceed all other women in beauty, and he sent to her a person whose name was Simon, one of his friends; a Jew he was, and by birth a Cypriot, and one who pretended to be a magician, and endeavoured to persuade her to forsake her present husband, and marry him; and promised, that if she would not refuse him, he would make her a happy woman. (143) Accordingly she acted ill, and because she was desirous to avoid her sister Berenice's envy, for she was very ill treated by her on account of her beauty, was prevailed upon to transgress the laws of her forefathers, and to marry Felix; and when he had had a son by her, he named him Agrippa. (144) But after what manner that young man, with his wife, perished at the conflagration of the mountain Vesuvius, in the days of Titus Caesar, shall be related hereafter.

(145) But as for Berenice, she lived a widow a long while after the death of Herod [king of Chalcis], who was both her husband and her uncle. But, when the report went that she had criminal intercourse with her brother [Agrippa junior], she persuaded Polemo, who was king of Cilicia, to be circumcised, and to marry her, as supposing that by this means she should prove those calumnies upon her to be false; (146) and Polemo was prevailed upon, and that chiefly on account of her riches. Yet did not this matrimony endure long; but Berenice left Polemo, and, as was said, with impure intentions. So he forsook at once this matrimony and the Jewish religion: (147) and, at the same time, Mariamne put away Archelaus, and was married to Demetrius, the principal man among the Alexandrian Jews both for his family and his wealth; and

indeed he was then their alabarch. So she named her son whom she had by him Agrippinus. But of all these particulars we shall hereafter treat more exactly.

CHAPTER 8

(148) Now Claudius Caesar died when he had reigned thirteen years, eight months, and twenty days; and a report went about that he was poisoned by his wife Agrippina. Her father was Germanicus, the brother of Caesar. Her husband was Domitius Aenobarbus, one of the most illustrious persons that was in the city of Rome; (149) after whose death, and her long continuance in widowhood, Claudius took her to wife. She brought along with her a son, Domitius, of the same name with his father. He had before this slain his wife Messalina, out of jealousy, by whom he had his children Britannicus and Octavia; (150) their eldest sister was Antonia, whom he had by Pelina his first wife. He also married Octavia to Nero; for that was the name that Caesar gave him afterward, upon his adopting him for his son.

(151) But now Agrippina was afraid, lest when Britannicus should come to man's estate, he should succeed his father in the government, and desired to seize upon the principality beforehand for her own son [Nero]; upon which the report went, that she thence compassed the death of Claudius. (152) Accordingly she sent Burrus, the general of the army, immediately, and with him the tribunes, and such also of the freedmen as were of the greatest authority, to bring Nero away into the camp, and to salute him emperor. (153) And when Nero had thus obtained the government, he got Britannicus to be so poisoned, that the multitude should not perceive it; although he publicly put his own mother to death not long afterward, making her this requital, not only for being born of her, but for bringing it so about by her contrivances, that he obtained the Roman empire. He also slew Octavia his own wife, and many other illustrious persons, under this pretence, that they plotted against him.

(154) But I omit any farther discourse about these affairs; for there have been a great many who have composed the history of Nero; some of whom have departed from the truth of facts, out of favour, as having received benefits from him; while others, out of hatred to him, and the great ill will which they bare him, have so impudently raved against him with their lies, that they justly deserved to be condemned. (155) Nor do I wonder at such as have told lies of Nero, since they have not in their writings preserved the truth of history as to those facts that were earlier than his time, even when the actors could have no way incurred their hatred, since those writers lived a long time after them; (156) but as to those that have no regard to truth, they may write as they please,

for in that they take delight, (157) but as to ourselves, who have made truth our direct aim, we shall briefly touch upon what only belongs remotely to this undertaking, but shall relate what hath happened to us Jews with great accuracy, and shall not grudge our pains in giving an account both of the calamities we have suffered and of the crimes we have been guilty of. – I will now therefore return to the relation of our own affairs.

(158) For in the first year of the reign of Nero, upon the death of Azizus, king of Emesa, Soemus, his brother, succeeded in his kingdom, and Aristobulus, the son of Herod, king of Chalcis, was entrusted by Nero with the government of the Lesser Armenia. (159) Caesar also bestowed on Agrippa a certain part of Galilee, Tiberias and Taricheae, and ordered them to submit to his jurisdiction. He gave him also Julias, a city of Perea, with fourteen villages that lay about it.

(160) Now, as for the affairs of the Jews, they grew worse and worse continually; for the country was again filled with robbers and impostors, who deluded the multitude. (161) Yet did Felix catch and put to death many of those impostors every day, together with the robbers. He also caught Eleazar, the son of Dineus, who had gotten together a company of robbers; and this he did by treachery; for he gave him assurance that he should suffer no harm, and thereby persuaded him to come to him; but when he came, he bound him and sent him to Rome. (162) Felix also bore an ill will to Jonathan, the high priest, because he frequently gave him admonitions about governing the Jewish affairs better than he did, lest he should himself have complaints made of him by the multitude, since he it was who had desired Caesar to send him as procurator of Judea. So Felix contrived a method whereby he might get rid of him, now he was become so continually troublesome to him; for such continual admonitions are grievous to those who are disposed to act unjustly. (163) Wherefore Felix persuaded one of Jonathan's most faithful friends, a citizen of Jerusalem whose name was Doras, to bring the robbers upon Jonathan, in order to kill him; and this he did by promising to give him a great deal of money for so doing. Doras complied with the proposal, and contrived matters so, that the robbers might murder him after the following manner: (164) certain of those robbers went up to the city, as if they were going to worship God, while they had daggers under their garments; and, by thus mingling themselves among the multitude, they slew Jonathan; (165) and as this murder was never avenged, the robbers went up with the greatest security at the festivals after this time; and having weapons concealed in like manner as before, and mingling themselves among the multitude, they slew certain of their own enemies, and were subservient to other men for money; and slew others not only in remote parts of the city, but in the temple itself also; for they had the boldness to murder men there, without thinking of the impiety of

which they were guilty. (166) And this seems to me to have been the reason why God, out of his hatred to these men's wickedness, rejected our city; and as for the temple, he no longer esteemed it sufficiently pure for him to inhabit therein, but brought the Romans upon us, and threw a fire upon the city to purge it; and brought upon us, our wives, and children, slavery – as desirous to make us wiser by our calamities.

(167) These works that were done by the robbers, filled the city with all sorts of impiety. And now these impostors and deceivers persuaded the multitude to follow them into the wilderness, (168) and pretended that they would exhibit manifest wonders and signs, that should be performed by the providence of God. And many that were prevailed on by them suffered the punishments of their folly; for Felix brought them back, and then punished them. (169) Moreover, there came out of Egypt about this time to Jerusalem, one that said he was a prophet, and advised the multitude of the common people to go along with him to the Mount of Olives, as it was called, which lay over against the city, and at the distance of five furlongs. (170) He said farther, that he would show them from hence how, at his command, the walls of Jerusalem would fall down; and he promised that he would procure them an entrance into the city through those walls, when they were fallen down. (171) Now when Felix was informed of these things, he ordered his soldiers to take their weapons, and came against them with a great number of horsemen and footmen, from Jerusalem, and attacked the Egyptian and the people that were with him. He also slew four hundred of them, and took two hundred alive. (172) But the Egyptian himself escaped out of the fight, but did not appear any more. And again the robbers stirred up the people to make war with the Romans, and said they ought not to obey them at all; and when any persons would not comply with them, they set fire to their villages, and plundered them.

(173) And now it was that a great sedition arose between the Jews that inhabited Caesarea, and the Syrians who dwelt there also, concerning their equal right to the privileges belonging to citizens; for the Jews claimed the pre-eminence, because Herod their king was the builder of Caesarea, and because he was by birth a Jew. Now the Syrians did not deny what was alleged about Herod; but they said that Caesarea was formerly called Strato's Tower, and that then there was not one Jewish inhabitant. (174) When the presidents of that country heard of these disorders, they caught the authors of them on both sides, and tormented them with stripes and by that means put a stop to the disturbance for a time. (175) But the Jewish citizens depending on their wealth, and on that account despising the Syrians, reproached them again, and hoped to provoke them by such reproaches. (176) However, the Syrians, though they were inferior in wealth, yet valuing themselves highly on this account, that the greatest part of the Roman soldiers that were there, were either of Caesarea or

Sebaste, they also for some time used reproachful language to the Jews also; and thus it was, till at length they came to throwing stones at one another; and several were wounded, and fell on both sides, though still the Jews were the conquerors. (177) But when Felix saw that this quarrel was become a kind of war, he came upon them on the sudden, and desired the Jews to desist; and when they refused so to do, he armed his soldiers, and sent them out upon them, and slew many of them, and took more of them alive, and permitted his soldiers to plunder some of the houses of the citizens, which were full of riches. (178) Now those Jews that were more moderate, and of principal dignity among them, were afraid for themselves, and desired of Felix that he would sound a retreat to his soldiers, and spare them for the future, and afford them room for repentance for what they had done; and Felix was prevailed upon to do so.

(179) About this time King Agrippa gave the high priesthood to Ismael, who was the son of Fabi. (180) And now arose a sedition between the high priests and the principal men of the multitude of Jerusalem; each of whom got them a company of the boldest sort of men, and of those that loved innovations, about them, and became leaders to them; and when they struggled together, they did it by casting reproachful words against one another, and by throwing stones also. And there was nobody to reprove them; but these disorders were done after a licentious manner in the city, as if it had no government over it. (181) And such was the impudence and boldness that had seized on the high priests, that they had the hardness to send their servants into the threshing floors, to take away those tithes that were due to the priests, insomuch that it so fell out that the poorer sort of the priests died for want. To this degree did the violence of the seditious prevail over all right and justice.

(182) Now, when Porcius Festus was sent as successor to Felix by Nero, the principal of the Jewish inhabitants of Caesarea went up to Rome to accuse Felix; and he had certainly been brought to punishment, unless Nero had yielded to the importunate solicitations of his brother Pallas, who was at that time had in the greatest honour by him. (183) Two of the principal Syrians in Caesarea persuaded Burrus, who was Nero's tutor, and secretary for his Greek epistles, by giving him a great sum of money, to disannul that equality of the Jewish privileges of citizens which they hitherto enjoyed. (184) So Burrus, by his solicitations, obtained leave of the emperor, that an epistle should be written to that purpose. This epistle became the occasion of the following miseries that befell our nation; for, when the Jews of Caesarea were informed of the contents of this epistle to the Syrians, they were more disorderly than before, till a war was kindled.

(185) Upon Festus' coming into Judea, it happened that Judea was afflicted by the robbers, while all the villages were set on fire, and plundered by them.

(186) And then it was that the *sicarii*, as they were called, who were robbers, grew numerous. They made use of small swords, not much different in length from the Persian *acinacae*, but somewhat crooked, and like the Roman *sicae* [or sickles] as they were called; and from these weapons these robbers got their denomination; and with these weapons they slew a great many; (187) for they mingled themselves among the multitude at their festivals, when they were come up in crowds from all parts to the city to worship God, as we said before, and easily slew those that they had a mind to slay. They also came frequently upon the villages belonging to their enemies, with their weapons, and plundered them and set them on fire. (188) So Festus sent forces, both horsemen and footmen, to fall upon those that had been seduced by a certain impostor, who promised them deliverance and freedom from the miseries they were under, if they would but follow him as far as the wilderness. Accordingly those forces that were sent destroyed both him that had deluded them, and those that were his followers also.

(189) About the same time King Agrippa built himself a very large dining room in the royal place at Jerusalem, near to the portico. (190) Now this palace had been erected of old by the children of Asamoneus, and was situated upon an elevation, and afforded a most delightful prospect to those that had a mind to take a view of the city, which prospect was desired by the king; and there he could lie down, and eat, and thence observe what was done in the temple; (191) which thing, when the chief men of Jerusalem saw, they were very much displeased at it; for it was not agreeable to the institutions of our country or law that what was done in the temple should be viewed by others, especially what belonged to the sacrifices. They therefore erected a wall upon the uppermost building which belonged to the inner court of the temple towards the west; (192) which wall, when it was built, did not only intercept the prospect of the dining room in the palace, but also of the western cloisters that belonged to the outer court of the temple also, where it was that the Romans kept guards for the temple at the festivals. (193) At these doings both King Agrippa, and principally Festus the procurator, were much displeased; and Festus ordered them to pull the wall down again; but the Jews petitioned him to give them leave to send an embassage about this matter to Nero; for they said they could not endure to live if any part of the temple should be demolished; (194) and when Festus had given them leave so to do, they sent ten of their principal men to Nero, as also Ismael the high priest, and Helcias the keeper of the sacred treasure. (195) And when Nero had heard what they had to say, he not only forgave them what they had already done, but also gave them leave to let the wall they had built stand. This was granted them in order to gratify Poppea, Nero's wife, who was a religious woman, and had requested these favours of Nero, and who gave order to the ten ambassadors to go their way home; but

retained Helcias and Ismael as hostages with herself. (196) As soon as the king heard this news, he gave the high priesthood to Joseph, who was called Cabi, the son of Simon, formerly high priest.

CHAPTER 9

(197) And now Caesar, upon hearing the death of Festus, sent Albinus into Judea, as procurator; but the king deprived Joseph of the high priesthood, and bestowed the succession to that dignity on the son of Ananus, who was also himself called Ananus. (198) Now the report goes, that this elder Ananus proved a most fortunate man; for he had five sons, who had all performed the office of a high priest to God, and he had himself enjoyed that dignity a long time formerly, which had never happened to any other of our high priests: (199) but this younger Ananus, who, as we have told you already, took the high priesthood, was a bold man in his temper, and very insolent; he was also of the sect of the Sadducees, who are very rigid in judging offenders, above all the rest of the Jews, as we have already observed; (200) when, therefore, Ananus was of this disposition, he thought he had now a proper opportunity [to exercise his authority]. Festus was now dead, and Albinus was but upon the road; so he assembled the sanhedrin of judges, and brought before them the brother of Jesus, who was called Christ, whose name was James, and some others, [or, some of his companions]; and when he had formed an accusation against them as breakers of the law, he delivered them to be stoned; (201) but as for those who seemed the most equitable of the citizens, and such as were the most uneasy at the breach of the laws, they disliked what was done; they also sent to the king [Agrippa], desiring him to send to Ananus that he should act so no more, for that what he had already done was not to be justified; (202) nay, some of them went also to meet Albinus, as he was upon his journey from Alexandria, and informed him that it was not lawful for Ananus to assemble a sanhedrin without his consent; (203) whereupon Albinus complied with what they said, and wrote in anger to Ananus, and threatened that he would bring him to punishment for what he had done; on which King Agrippa took the high priesthood from him, when he had ruled but three months, and made Jesus, the son of Damneus, high priest.

(204) Now, as soon as Albinus was come to the city of Jerusalem, he used all his endeavours and care that the country might be kept in peace, and this by destroying many of the *sicarii*; (205) but as for the high priest Ananias, he increased in glory every day, and this to a great degree, and had obtained the favour and esteem of the citizens in a signal manner; for he was a great hoarder up of money; he therefore cultivated the friendship of Albinus, and of the high priest [Jesus], by making them presents; (206) he also had servants who were

very wicked, who joined themselves to the boldest sort of the people, and went to the thrashing floors, and took away the tithes that belonged to the priests by violence, and did not refrain from beating such as would not give these tithes to them. (207) So the other high priests acted in the like manner, as did those his servants without anyone being able to prohibit them; so that [some of the] priests, that of old were wont to be supported with those tithes, died for want of food.

(208) But now the *sicarii* went into the city by night, just before the festival, which was now at hand, and took the scribe belonging to the governor of the temple, whose name was Eleazar, who was the son of Ananus (Ananias) the high priest, and bound him, and carried him away with them; (209) after which they sent to Ananias, and said that they would send the scribe to him, if he would persuade Albinus to release ten of those prisoners which he had caught of their party; so Ananias was plainly forced to persuade Albinus, and gained his request of him. (210) This was the beginning of greater calamities; for the robbers perpetually contrived to catch some of Ananias' servants; and when they had taken them alive, they would not let them go till they thereby recovered some of their own *sicarii*; and as they were again become no small number, they grew bold, and were a great affliction to the whole country.

(211) About this time it was that Agrippa built Caesarea Philippi larger than it was before, and, in honour of Nero, named it Neronias; and when he had built a theatre at Berytus, with vast expenses, he bestowed on them shows, to be exhibited every year, and spent therein many ten thousand [drachmae]; (212) he also gave the people a largesse of corn, and distributed oil among them, and adorned the entire city with statues of his own donation, and with original images made by ancient hands; nay, he almost transferred all that was most ornamental in his own kingdom thither. This made him more than ordinarily hated by his subjects; because he took those things away that belonged to them, to adorn a foreign city; (213) and now Jesus, the son of Gamaliel, became the successor of Jesus, the son of Damneus, in the high priesthood, which the king had taken from the other; on which account a sedition arose between the high priests, with regard to one another; for they got together bodies of the boldest sort of the people, and frequently came, from reproaches, to throwing of stones at each other; but Ananias was too hard for the rest, by his riches – which enabled him to gain those that were most ready to receive. (214) Costobarus also, and Saulus, did themselves get together a multitude of wicked wretches, and this because they were of the royal family; and so they obtained favour among them, because of their kindred to Agrippa: but still they used violence with the people, and were very ready to plunder those that were weaker than themselves. And from that time it principally came to pass, that our city was greatly disordered, and that all things grew worse and worse among us.

(215) But when Albinus heard that Gessius Florus was coming to succeed him, he was desirous to appear to do somewhat that might be grateful to the people of Jerusalem; so he brought out all those prisoners who seemed to him to be most plainly worthy of death, and ordered them to be put to death accordingly. But as to those who had been put into prison on some trifling occasion, he took money of them, and dismissed them; by which means the prisons were indeed emptied, but the country was filled with robbers.

(216) Now, as many of the Levites, which is a tribe of ours, as were singers of hymns, persuaded the king to assemble a sanhedrin, and to give them leave to wear linen garments, as well as the priests: for they said that this would be a work worthy the times of his government, that he might have a memorial of such a novelty, as being his doing. (217) Nor did they fail of obtaining their desire; for the king, with the suffrages of those that came into the sanhedrin, granted the singers of hymns this privilege, that they might lay aside their former garments, and wear such a linen one as they desired; (218) and as a part of this tribe ministered in the temple, he also permitted them to learn those hymns as they had besought him for. Now all this was contrary to the laws of our country, which whenever they have been transgressed, we have never been able to avoid the punishment of such transgressions.

(219) And now it was that the temple was finished. So, when the people saw that the workmen were employed who were above eighteen thousand, and that they, receiving no wages, were in want, because they had earned their bread by their labours about the temple; (220) and while they were unwilling to keep them by their treasuries that were there deposited, out of fear of [their being carried away by] the Romans; and while they had a regard to the making provision for the workmen, they had a mind to expend those treasures upon them; for if any one of them did but labour for a single hour, he received his pay immediately; so they persuaded him to rebuild the eastern cloisters. (221) These cloisters belonged to the outer court, and were situated in a deep valley, and had walls that reached four hundred cubits [in length], and were built of square and very white stones, the length of each of which stones was twenty cubits, and their height six cubits. This was the work of King Solomon, who first of all built the entire temple. (222) But King Agrippa, who had the care of the temple committed to him by Claudius Caesar, considering that it is easy to demolish any building, but hard to build it up again, and that it was particularly hard to do it to those cloisters, which would require a considerable time, and great sums of money, he denied the petitioners their request about that matter; but he did not obstruct them when they desired the city might be paved with white stone. (223) He also deprived Jesus, the son of Gamaliel, of the high priesthood, and gave it to Matthias, the son of Theophilus, under whom the Jews' war with the Romans took its beginning.

(224) And now I think it proper, and agreeable to this history, to give an account of our high priests; how they began, who those are which are capable of that dignity, and how many of them there had been at the end of the war. (225) In the first place, therefore, history informs us that Aaron, the brother of Moses, officiated to God as a high priest; and that after his death, his sons succeeded him immediately; and that this dignity hath been continued down from them all to their posterity. (226) Whence it is a custom of our country, that no one should take the high priesthood of God, but he who is of the blood of Aaron, while everyone that is of another stock, though he were a king, can never obtain that high priesthood. (227) Accordingly, the number of all the high priests from Aaron, of whom we have spoken already as of the first of them, until Phanas, who was made high priest during the war by the seditious, was eighty-three; (228) of whom thirteen officiated as high priests in the wilderness, from the days of Moses, while the tabernacle was standing, until the people came into Judea, when King Solomon erected the temple to God; (229) for at the first they held the high priesthood till the end of their life, although afterward they had successors while they were alive. Now these thirteen, who were the descendants of two of the sons of Aaron, received this dignity by succession, one after another; for their form of government was an aristocracy, and after that a monarchy, and in the third place the government was regal. (230) Now, the number of years during the rule of these thirteen, from the day when our fathers departed out of Egypt under Moses their leader, until the building of that temple which King Solomon erected at Jerusalem, were six hundred and twelve. (231) After those thirteen high priests, eighteen took the high priesthood at Jerusalem, one in succession to another, from the days of King Solomon until Nebuchadnezzar, king of Babylon, made an expedition against that city, and burnt the temple, and removed our nation into Babylon, and then took Josadek the high priest captive; (232) the times of these high priests were four hundred and sixty-six years, six months, and ten days, while the Jews were still under the regal government. (233) But after the term of seventy years' captivity under the Babylonians, Cyrus, king of Persia, sent the Jews from Babylon to their own land again, and gave them leave to rebuild their temple; (234) at which time Jesus, the son of Josadek, took the high priesthood over the captives when they returned home. Now he and his posterity, who were in all fifteen, unto King Antiochus Eupator, were under a democratical government for four hundred and fourteen years; (235) and then the forementioned Antiochus and Lysias the general of his army, deprived Onias, who was also called Menelaus, of the high priesthood, and slew him at

Berea; and, driving away the son [of Onias the third], put Jacimus into the high priest's place, one that was indeed of the stock of Aaron, but not of the family of Onias. (236) On which account Onias, who was the nephew of Onias that was dead, and bore the same name with his father, came into Egypt, and got into the friendship of Ptolemy Philometor, and Cleopatra his wife, and persuaded them to make him the high priest of that temple which he built to God in the prefecture of Heliopolis, and this in imitation of that at Jerusalem; (237) but as for that temple which was built in Egypt, we have spoken of it frequently already. Now, when Jacimus had retained the priesthood three years, he died, and there was no one that succeeded him, but the city continued seven years without a high priest. (238) But then the posterity of the sons of Asamoneus, who had the government of the nation conferred upon them, when they had beaten the Macedonians in war, appointed Jonathan to be their high priest, who ruled over them seven years. (239) And when he had been slain by the treacherous contrivance of Trypho, as we have related somewhere, Simon his brother took the high priesthood; (240) and when he was destroyed at a feast by the treachery of his son-in-law, his own son, whose name was Hyrcanus, succeeded him, after he had held the high priesthood one year longer than his brother. This Hyrcanus enjoyed that dignity thirty years, and died an old man, leaving the succession to Judas, who was also called Aristobulus, (241) whose brother Alexander was his heir; which Judas died of a sore distemper, after he had kept the priesthood, together with the royal authority, for this Judas was the first that put on his head a diadem, for one year. (242) And when Alexander had been both king and high priest twenty-seven years, he departed this life, and permitted his wife Alexandra to appoint him that should be high priest; so she gave the high priesthood to Hyrcanus, but retained the kingdom herself nine years, and then departed this life. The like duration [and no longer] did her son Hyrcanus enjoy the high priesthood; (243) for after her death his brother Aristobulus fought against him, and beat him, and deprived him of his principality; and he did himself both reign and perform the office of high priest to God. (244) But when he had reigned three years, and as many months, Pompey came upon him, and not only took the city of Jerusalem by force, but put him and his children in bonds, and sent them to Rome. He also restored the high priesthood to Hyrcanus, and made him governor of the nation, but forbade him to wear a diadem. (245) This Hyrcanus ruled, besides his first nine years, twenty-four years more, when Barzapharnes and Pacorus, the generals of the Parthians, passed over Euphrates, and fought with Hyrcanus, and took him alive, and made Antigonus, the son of Aristobulus, king; (246) and when he had reigned three years and three months, Sosius and Herod besieged him, and took him, when Antony had him brought to Antioch, and slain there. (247) Herod was then made king by the Romans, but did no longer appoint high priests out of the family of Asamoneus; but made certain men to be so that were of no eminent families, but barely of those that were priests, excepting that he gave that dignity to Aristobulus; (248) for when he had made this Aristobulus, the grandson of that Hyrcanus who was then taken by the Parthians, and had taken his sister Mariamne to wife, he thereby aimed to win the good will of the people, who had a kind remembrance of Hyrcanus [his grandfather]. Yet did he afterward, out of his fear lest they should all bend their inclinations to Aristobulus, put him to death, and that by contriving how to have him suffocated, as he was swimming at Jericho, as we have already related that matter; (249) but after this man, he never entrusted the high priesthood to the posterity of the sons of Asamoneus. Archelaus also, Herod's son, did like his father in the appointment of the high priests as did the Romans also, who took the government over the Jews into their hands afterward. (250) Accordingly the number of the high priests, from the days of Herod until the day when Titus took the temple and the city, and burnt them, were in all twenty-eight; the time also that belonged to them was a hundred and seven years. (251) Some of these were the political governors of the people under the reign of Herod, and under the reign of Archelaus his son, although, after their death, the government became an aristocracy, and the high priests were entrusted with a dominion over the nation. And thus much may suffice to be said concerning our high priests.

CHAPTER 11

(252) Now Gessius Florus, who was sent as successor to Albinus by Nero, filled Judea with abundance of miseries. He was by birth of the city of Clazomenae, and brought along with him his wife Cleopatra (by whose friendship with Poppea, Nero's wife, he obtained this government), who was no way different from him in wickedness. (253) This Florus was so wicked, and so violent in the use of his authority, that the Jews took Albinus to have been [comparatively] their benefactor; so excessive were the mischiefs that he brought upon them. (254) For Albinus concealed his wickedness, and was careful that it might not be discovered to all men; but Gessius Florus, as though he had been sent on purpose to show his crimes to everybody, made a pompous ostentation of them to our nation, as never omitting any sort of violence, nor any unjust sort of punishment; (255) for he was not to be moved by pity, and never was satisfied with any degree of gain that came in his way; nor had he any more regard to great than to small acquisitions, but became a partner with the robbers themselves; for a great many fell then into that practice without fear, as having him for their security, and depending on him, that he would save them harmless in their particular robberies; so that there were no bounds set to the

nation's miseries; (256) but the unhappy Jews, when they were not able to bear the devastations which the robbers made among them, were all under a necessity of leaving their own habitations, and of flying away, as hoping to dwell more easily anywhere else in the world among foreigners [than in their own country.] And what need I say any more upon this head, (257) since it was this Florus who necessitated us to take up arms against the Romans, while we thought it better to be destroyed at once, than by little and little? Now this war began in the second year of the government of Florus, and the twelfth year of the reign of Nero. (258) But then what actions we were forced to do, or what miseries we were enabled to suffer, may be accurately known by such as will peruse those books which I have written about the Jewish war.

(259) I shall now, therefore, make an end here of my *Antiquities*; after the conclusion of which events, I began to write that account of the war; and these *Antiquities* contain what hath been delivered down to us from the original creation of man until the twelfth year of the reign of Nero, as to what hath befallen the Jews, as well in Egypt as in Syria, and in Palestine, (260) and what we have suffered from the Assyrians and Babylonians, and what afflictions the Persians and Macedonians, and after them the Romans, have brought upon us; for I think I may say that I have composed this history with sufficient accuracy in all things. (261) I have attempted to enumerate those high priests that we have had during the interval of two thousand years; I have also carried down the succession of our kings, and related their actions and political administration, without [considerable] errors, as also the power of our monarchs; and all according to what is written in our sacred books; for this it was that I promised to do in the beginning of this history. (262) And I am so bold as to say, now I have so completely perfected the work I proposed to myself to do, that no other person, whether he were a Jew or a foreigner, had he ever so great an inclination to it, could so accurately deliver these accounts to the Greeks as is done in these books. (263) For those of my own nation freely acknowledge that I far exceed them in the learning belonging to Jews. I have also taken a great deal of pains to obtain the learning of the Greeks, and understand the elements of the Greek language, although I have so long accustomed myself to speak our own tongue, that I cannot pronounce Greek with sufficient exactness: (264) for our nation does not encourage those that learn the languages of many nations, and so adorn their discourses with the smoothness of their periods, because they look upon this sort of accomplishment as common, not only to all sorts of freemen, but to as many of the servants as please to learn them. But they give him the testimony of being a wise man who is fully acquainted with our laws, and is able to interpret their meaning; (265) on which account, as there have been many who have done their endeavours with great patience to obtain this learning,

there have yet hardly been so many as two or three that have succeeded therein, who were immediately well rewarded for their pains.

(266) And now it will not be perhaps an invidious thing, if I treat briefly of my own family, and of the actions of my own life, while there are still living such as can either prove what I say to be false, or can attest that it is true; (267) with which accounts I shall put an end to these *Antiquities* which are contained in twenty books, and sixty thousand verses. And if God permit me, I will briefly run over this war again, with what befell us therein to this very day, which is the thirteenth year of the reign of Caesar Domitian, and the fifty-sixth of my own life. (268) I have also an intention to write three books concerning our Jewish opinions about God and his essence, and about our laws; why, according to them, some things are permitted us to do, and others are prohibited.

INDEX

Araunah, 278, 311, 312

Archelaus, son of Herod the Great, 590, 647, 695, 706, 707, 713, 714, 720, 721, 724, 730, 731, 738, 746, 751–9, 764–8, 770, 771–3, 776, 783, 882

Archelaus, king of Cappadocia, 686, 692, 699, 713, 718, 720, 723, 789

Archelaus, Julius Epiphanes, 855, 871

Aretas, king of the Arabians, 570, 573, 576, 580–2, 588, 717, 721, 723, 735

Aretas, king of Celesyria, 573

Aretas, king of Arabia Petrea, 764, 785–787

Arioch, 23, 435, 436, 437

Arion, 506, 507

Aristobulus, also called Judas, son of Hyrcanus, 881

Aristobulus, king of Chalcis, son of Herod the tetrarch and Mariamne, 788, 867, 873

Aristobulus, son of the above, 788

Aristobulus, son of Alexander Janneus, 575–94, 612, 615, 618, 622, 630, 637–40, 655, 881, 882

Aristobulus, grandson of the above, and brother to Herod's wife Mariamne, 637–42

Aristobulus, son of Amyntas, in a decree from Pergamum, 606

Aristobulus, son of Herod the Great, 675, 686, 692, 695, 699, 706, 712, 718–20, 727, 730, 731, 738, 786–8, 800

Aristobulus, son of Herod the Great ('third brother of Agrippa'), 788, 790, 804

Aristobulus, son of Hyrcanus, 561–6

Arsaces, 550, 558, 778

Artabanus, 778, 779, 784, 785, 801, 810–3, 860–4

Artabazes, 647

Artaxerxes, 467–70, 476–9

Artaxias, 647

Arucas, 19

Arudeus, 19

Arruntius, Euaristus, 832

Arruntius, Paulus, 828

Artabanus, king of Media and the Parthians, 778, 779, 784, 785, 801, 810, 811, 813, 860–4

Artabanus, son of the above, 784

Asa, 358–62

Asamoneans, 459, 633, 748

Asermoth, 20

Ashdod, 188, 217, 218, 517, 522, 540, 541, 574, 587, 588, 751, 768

Ashpenaz, 435

Ashur, 20

Asineus, 809–13

Asprenas, 826, 827, 830, 832, 840

Assyrians, 20, 23, 24, 194, 229, 404–7, 415, 416, 421, 434, 479, 554, 883

Athronges, 763

Atratinus, 621

Augustus Caesar, Roman emperor, 610, 612, 621, 622, 624, 647, 649, 653–60, 665, 666, 670–7, 685, 687, 693–703, 714, 716, 717, 721–4, 730, 733, 735, 739–41, 745, 746, 751–4, 756–60, 765–73, 776, 793, 826, 847, 848, 850

Axioramus, 431

Azariah, 359, 403 *see* also Uzziah

Azarias, second high priest after Zadok, 430

Azarias, another high priest, 431

Azarias, later Abednego, 435

Azarias, a commander under Judas Maccabaeus, 520–2